The Firebird Book:
A Reference for
Database Developers

HELEN BORRIE

APress Media, LLC

ISBN 978-1-59059-279-3   ISBN 978-1-4302-0743-6 (eBook)
DOI 10.1007/978-1-4302-0743-6

Trademarked names may appear in this book. Rather than use a trademark symbol with every occurrence of a trademarked name, we use the names only in an editorial fashion and to the benefit of the trademark owner, with no intention of infringement of the trademark.

Lead Editor: Chris Mills

Technical Reviewer: Geoff Worboys

Editorial Board: Steve Anglin, Dan Appleman, Ewan Buckingham, Gary Cornell, Tony Davis, Jason Gilmore, Jonathan Hassell, Chris Mills, Dominic Shakeshaft, Jim Sumser

Project Manager: Kylie Johnston

Production Manager: Kari Brooks

Production Editor: Janet Vail

Compositor: Molly Sharp, Content Works

Proofreaders: Patrick Vincent and Katie Stence

Indexer: Valerie Perry

Cover Designer: Kurt Krames

Manufacturing Manager: Tom Debolski

In the United States: phone 1-800-SPRINGER, email orders@springer-ny.com, or visit http://www.springer-ny.com. Outside the United States: fax +49 6221 345229, email orders@springer.de, or visit http://www.springer.de.

For information on translations, please contact Apress directly at 2560 Ninth Street, Suite 219, Berkeley, CA 94710. Phone 510-549-5930, fax 510-549-5939, email info@apress.com, or visit http://www.apress.com.

The information in this book is distributed on an "as is" basis, without warranty. Although every precaution has been taken in the preparation of this work, neither the author(s) nor Apress shall have any liability to any person or entity with respect to any loss or damage caused or alleged to be caused directly or indirectly by the information contained in this work.

Contents at a Glance

Contents

Part Three Firebird Data Types

Appendices

About the Author

Helen Borrie is a contracting software engineer who doubles as a writer and technical editor. She has been involved in database development for more than 20 years and with Firebird and its ancestors since 1996.

Helen is an active member of the Firebird online support community and a founding member of the FirebirdSQL Foundation Inc.

Helen is a New Zealander resident in Australia. She telecommutes via the Internet, from a home studio located among eucalyptus trees on the picturesque central coast of rural New South Wales.

About the Technical Reviewer

Geoff Worboys has been involved with database-related application design and development for around 15 years. He has spent much of the last 10 years using Firebird, and before that its ancestor InterBase, as his RDBMS for applications, management tools, and components developed with Delphi, C, or C++, as demanded by the situation.

He now works from a secluded office in the country in New South Wales, Australia, on developments for clients both in Australia and internationally. He watches kangaroos and other wildlife out his window while pondering the problems of database and application design—the Internet is a wonderful thing.

Acknowledgments

HERE WE ARE, WITH *THE FIREBIRD BOOK* in front of us, at last! Writing it has kept me away from *other* dangerous pursuits for nearly a year. I've been such a constant bother to my good friends in the Firebird community that I must start by thanking you all, even if I don't mention everyone by name. We have our book, thanks to you.

Pavel Cisar, my longtime friend in the online Kingdom of Geek, shared his time and expertise above and beyond the call of duty. Pavel was the linchpin in the review team, but he also passed on several invaluable ideas and perspectives from the experience of writing his own book about Firebird and InterBase last year (in Czech), and from his research on the inner workings of the query optimizer. Ann Harrison, "the Mother of InterBase," has been the transcendent sage in the most abstruse areas of wisdom about the Firebird engine. Ivan Prenosil shared generously from his accumulated store of practical experience, and Dmitry Sibiryakov's X-ray vision saved me from several gaffes. Claudio Valderrama Cortès shared his insights into the mysteries of the RDB$DB_KEY. Thanks, too, to David Brookestone Schnepper for his helpful comments about character sets and to Gregory Deatz for allowing me to document the FreeUDFLib external functions in Appendix I.

To my friend Geoff Worboys goes a special acknowledgment for the enormous care and patience he devoted, as technical reviewer, to the book's content and detail. We didn't always agree, but *The Firebird Book* got better because of Geoff. Thanks, too, to Doug Chamberlin and Ioana Pirtea for their "reader's eye view."

I have also to thank the directors of the IBPhoenix company, Paul Beach and Ann Harrison, and my fellow staffers, for seeing me through the financial challenges of committing to the book and weathering the unforeseen delays.

Proposals for a book in English about Firebird bounced around publishers' "out" trays for more than 3 years before Apress took the risk and brought *The Firebird Book* into the light. Apress, the Firebird community thanks you for hearing us.

Finally, I owe a heartfelt "thank you" on behalf of us all to the Firebird core developers, whose passion, skill, and dedication have given us Firebird.

Kia ora! Kia manawa!
Helen Borrie
April 2004

Introduction to Firebird

What Is Firebird?

Firebird is a powerful, compact client/server SQL relational database management system (RDBMS) that can run on a variety of server and client operating system platforms, including Windows, Linux, and several other UNIX platforms, including FreeBSD and Mac OS X. It is an industrial-strength RDBMS that features a high level of compliance with SQL standards, while implementing some powerful language features in the vendor-specific sphere of procedure programming.

Who Needs This Book?

Developers with some database experience, who may be moving to client/server for the first time, will discover all of the basics they need to become productive with Firebird in this book. Although not a primary tutorial on SQL or database design, this guide emphasizes good client/server RDBMS design practice and documents Firebird's SQL definition, manipulation, and programming language sets with plenty of detail, insider tips, and examples.

Firebird is serious software designed for deployment on networks small and large, and it has some useful capabilities for stand-alone configurations. Its small footprint makes it easy for sole developers to do large enterprise development from a home office. For the database administrator or system designer, the book is a basic installation, configuration, tuning, security, and tools resource. Firebird's strengths and high compliance with standards make it an attractive medium for university-level IT study. The book will serve amply as a resource for second- and third-year computer science students using Firebird for assignment work.

For those who have been using Firebird 1.0.x or InterBase until now, *The Firebird Book* introduces the security, language, and optimizer enhancements that were added with the v.1.5 release.

Where to Find What You Need

Part One is a "boot camp" for those who are new to Firebird. There, you will find the basics for installing the software, for getting a network client up and running, and for configuring some useful settings. The part ends with a chapter about the absolute basics of operation: connecting to a sample database and creating your own, first database using Firebird's **isql** utility. It introduces the various command-line administration tools and tells you how to start and stop the server.

Part Two provides an overview of client/server concepts and models, and how Firebird's implementation fits in with them. The final chapter in this part provides some general and practical instructions for using the Firebird client libraries.

In Part Three, you will find a detailed reference to each of the SQL data types supported in Firebird. There is a chapter for each class of data type—numbers, date/time types, character types, and so on—with plenty of tips for using them.

Part Four examines database objects in detail, beginning with the database itself and moving on to tables, indexes, and other types of objects. The data definition language (DDL) statement syntaxes and usages are covered in this section.

Part Five contains the documentation for the data manipulation language (DML) of Firebird SQL.

Part Six covers transactions: how they work, how to configure them, and tips for using them in your application programs.

Part Seven covers server-side programming with Firebird: writing triggers and stored procedures, creating and using database events, and working error handling into your server code.

Part Eight addresses the issues of security, architecture, and configuration.

Finally, Part Nine documents the command-line administration tools and their shells.

Appendixes and Glossary

Details of materials available in the appendixes and glossary are as follows:

Appendix I: External Function Summary contains names, descriptions and examples for the external functions (UDFs) in the shipped *fb_udf* and *ib_udf* libraries for POSIX platforms and in the freeware *FreeUDFLib.dll* for Windows, by Gregory Deatz.

Appendix II: Solving Network Problems is a collection of troubleshooting tips you can refer to if you encounter problems connecting to a Firebird server from a remote client.

Appendix III: Application Interfaces summarizes some of the main driver and programming interface layers available for Firebird. It includes links to download and support sites for these materials.

Appendix IV: Database Repair How-to is a step-by-step walk-through of the procedure to follow if you ever encounter logical corruption in a Firebird database.

Appendix V: Administration Tools enumerates a selection of the many graphical tools available for working with your Firebird databases. It includes links to downloads.

Appendix VI: The Sample Database provides some notes about the database *employee.fdb* (*employee.gdb* in v.1.0.x) that the Firebird installers install in the /examples subdirectory beneath your Firebird root directory.

Appendix VII: Firebird Limits enumerates the various physical limits applicable to Firebird 1.0.*x* and 1.5 databases.

Appendix VIII: Character Sets and Collations is a full reference to the international character sets and language-specific collation sequences distributed with Firebird 1.5.

Appendix IX: System Tables and Views provides the data description specifications for the schema tables maintained by the Firebird server inside every database. It includes source code listings for some useful views you can create to interrogate the system tables.

Appendix X: Error Codes is a full, tabulated listing of the exception codes (SQLCODE and GDSCODE) defined in Firebird 1.5, along with the associated symbolic constants and the message texts in English.

Appendix XI: Reserved Words lists all of the SQL keywords that Firebird 1.0.*x* and 1.5 treat as reserved words.

Appendix XII: Readings and Resources is a compilation of resources available to Firebird users. It includes book and other documentary recommendations, descriptions, and links to support forums.

The **Glossary** provides detailed descriptions of terminology and concepts you are likely to encounter on your journey into Firebird. It was compiled from a survey of experienced and not-so-experienced Firebird community members who were asked to provide a "wish list" for a glossary.

Firebird's Origins

Developed as an ongoing open source project, Firebird is the first new-generation descendant of Borland's InterBase 6.0 Open Edition code, which was released for open source development in July 2000 under the InterBase Public License (IPL).

The Firebird source code tree is maintained and developed on the international open source code foundry, SourceForge.net (`http://sourceforge.net`), by a large team of professional developers, comprising both volunteers and others in specialist roles that are partly funded from community and commercial sources.

 TIP   The Firebird RDBMS products and several associated modules are distributed completely free of registration or deployment fees under a variety of open source licenses. The Firebird project, its developers, and its software are not associated with Borland Software Corporation in any way.

The Firebird Project

Development

The developers, designers, and testers who gave you Firebird and several of the drivers are members of the Firebird open source project at SourceForge, an amazing virtual community that is home to thousands of open source software teams. The Firebird project's address there is http://sourceforge.net/projects/firebird. At that site are the CVS source code tree, the bug tracker, and a number of technical files that can be downloaded for various purposes related to the development and testing of the codebases.

The Firebird Project developers and testers use an e-mail list forum, firebird-devel@lists.sourceforge.net, as their "virtual laboratory" for communicating with one another about their work on enhancements, bug fixing, and producing new versions of Firebird.

Anyone who is interested in watching the progress and feedback on beta development can join this forum.

Support for Application Developers and DBAs

Firebird has a powerful community of willing helpers, including a large body of active developers with many years of experience developing with and deploying Firebird and its InterBase ancestors. The esprit de corps among this large group is such that, having acquired the skills and learned the "inside tricks" from the advice of others, its members stay around the lists as mentors to new users. The mainstream free support channel is the Firebird support forum.

More specialized groups within the project's arena conduct specific forums—Java, Delphi and C++Builder, tools, Visual Basic, .NET, PHP, and more. The groups run as e-mail lists, and many are mirrored to a news server. The latest links to these forums can always be found at the main community website, http://firebirdsql.org, and at the affiliated IBPhoenix commercial site, http://www.ibphoenix.com.

The IBPhoenix site also hosts an enormous volume of searchable technical and user documentation, links to third-party tools, and a running news board of events happening throughout the Firebird community.

Refer to Appendix XII for a comprehensive compilation of support resources in the community.

The FirebirdSQL Foundation

The FirebirdSQL Foundation (Inc.) is a non-profit foundation incorporated in New South Wales, Australia, that raises funds around the world for grants to developers working on general and special projects for extending, testing, and enhancing Firebird. Funds come in through private and corporate sponsorships, donations, and membership subscriptions. It provides a way for appreciative Firebird users to return a contribution for the free use of software and community support. Look it up at http://firebirdsql.org/ff/foundation.

Sparky

Sparky, a young, scarlet phoenix with a beaky grin, is Firebird's mascot. Sparky has been around the Firebird project in various guises since the beginning, but he emerged "in person" for the first time at the first international Firebird Conference in Fulda, Germany, in May 2003.

Overview of Features

Firebird is a true client/server software, designed especially for use in local and wide-area networks. Accordingly, its core consists of two main software programs: the database server, which runs on a network host computer, and the client library, through which users on remote workstations connect to and communicate with databases managed by the server.

NOTE Administering and developing with a full-blooded SQL client/server RDBMS may be new territory for you. It can present a steep learning curve if this is your first venture into data management software that is purpose-built for multiple concurrent writers. Part Two of this guide provides an introduction to client/server concepts. If you find yourself getting lost in the following descriptions, you might like to visit Part Two first to acquire some context.

Firebird Versions

Firebird version 1.0.*x* binaries were developed by correcting and enhancing the modules, written in the C language, that the open source community inherited from InterBase 6.0. For Firebird 1.5, the modules were completely rewritten in C++, with a high degree of standardization across compilers.

The step from version 1 to version 1.5 is a major one "under the hood," but the application programming interface (API) is unchanged. Application software written for version 1 requires little or no modification to work with version 1.5.

While it is recommended that you install and use the highest version available, operating system incompatibilities—especially with respect to Linux—mean that the highest 1.0.*x* version remains the only option for some sites. Many enhancements in v.1.5 have been backported to v.1.0.*x*, with regular sub-releases.

Network Access

A Firebird server running on any platform accepts TCP/IP client attachments from any client platform that can implement the Firebird API.

Clients cannot attach to a Firebird server through any medium of filesystem sharing (NFS shares, Samba client connections, Windows shares or mapped drives, etc.).

A client must attach through an absolute physical path. However, from Firebird 1.5 onward, a database aliasing feature allows applications to "soft-connect" through named aliases, whose absolute paths are configured specifically on each deployed server.

A Firebird server running on a services-capable Windows host can accept attachments from Windows clients through the Named Pipes network protocol.

Multi-generational Architecture

Firebird's model for isolating and controlling the work of multiple users revolves around an architecture that is able to store more than one version of a record in the database concurrently. Multiple generations of a record can exist simultaneously—hence the term "multi-generational." Each user task holds its own contextual view of database state (see the next section) and, when ready, writes its own versions of records on the server's disk. At that point, the new version (or a deletion) cannot be accessed by other user tasks.

The most recently committed record version is the only one visible outside the user task that successfully posted a new version, and it continues to be the version seen by other tasks. Others will be aware that something has happened to the record because they will be blocked from updating or deleting the same record until the new version becomes "official" by being committed.

Because of its multi-generational architecture (known as MGA), Firebird has no need for the two-phase locking used by other DBMSs to control multi-user concurrency.

Transactions

All user tasks in Firebird are enclosed within transactions. A task begins with a START TRANSACTION statement and ends when work posted by the user task is committed or rolled back. A user task can make multiple requests for operations to be performed within a single transaction, including operations in more than one database.

Work is saved to the database in two stages. In the first stage, changes are stored to disk, without changing database state. In the second stage, changes are committed or rolled back by the client process. In v.1.5 and higher, clients can "unpost" parts of work by tagging stages in a process as *savepoints* and rolling back to a savepoint without rolling back an entire transaction.

Firebird transactions are *atomic*, which means that all work posted in a transaction will succeed or all will fail.

Every transaction is configurable, with three levels of isolation and a variety of strategies for fine-tuning concurrency and read-write conditions.

Stored Procedures and Triggers

Firebird has a rich language of procedural extensions, PSQL, for writing stored procedures and triggers. It is a structured language with support for FOR looping through sets, conditional branching, exception handling, and event triggering. PSQL code is compiled at creation and stored in binary form.

Trigger support is strong, with a Before and After phase for each DML event. Multiple triggers may be stored for each phase/event and optionally numbered in an execution sequence. Firebird 1.5 and higher support Before or After triggers that comprise behaviors for all three DML events, with conditional branching per event.

Referential Integrity

Firebird has full support for formal, SQL-standard referential integrity—sometimes known as *declarative referential integrity*—including optional cascading updates and deletes with a number of RI trigger action options.

Database Shadowing

Firebird servers can optionally maintain database shadows. A *shadow* is a real-time copy of the database with some extra attributes that make it unavailable for reading until it is made available by the server. Shadows can be "kicked in" if required, either manually or automatically. The purpose of shadowing is to enable the database to become available very quickly if a disk crash occurs.

Shadowing is *not* replication.

Security

Host Security

Firebird provides user access security to the server by means of user IDs and encrypted passwords. Like any database server, it relies on adequate physical, network access, and filesystem security being in place. Firebird can store encrypted data but, except for password encryption, it provides no capability to encrypt data itself.

 CAUTION   While an embedded server application (see the "Embedded Server" section) has its uses for single-user, stand-alone applications, it bypasses the host's security gateway altogether. SQL privileges defined at database level still apply, but an embedded application can get password-free access to any database on the server. For the implications, refer to Chapter 34.

SQL Privileges

Although a user must be authorized to access a Firebird server, no user except the SYSDBA and the database owner has automatic rights to anything within an individual database. Database-level security is supported on an "opt-in" basis, by means of SQL privileges. Users must be granted privileges to any object explicitly.

SQL Roles allow sets of privileges to be aggregated and granted as a "package" to individual users. A single user may have privileges under several roles, although only one may be selected when logging into the database.

Operating Modes

Firebird server can be installed to run in one of three modes: Superserver, Classic server, or Embedded Server. The distinction is largely a question of architecture. Any client application written to attach to the Superserver can attach in exactly the same way to the Classic server and perform exactly the same tasks. The reverse is also true, except that Superserver has more exacting thread-safety requirements for external function modules (user-defined functions, character set libraries, and BLOB filters).

The Embedded Server is a variant of Superserver.

Classic Server

The Classic server preceded Superserver historically. It was designed late in the 1980s, when machine resources on servers were scarce and programs used them with great economy. The Classic server model continued for operating systems whose threading capabilities were non-existent or too limited to support the Superserver. Classic server remains the best option for environments where high performance is important and system resources are adequate to accommodate linear growth of usage as each new connection is added.

Because Classic server processes can utilize multiple CPUs, it is very suitable for sites needing to run a number of continuous, online, automated data collection applications with little or no interactive input.

NOTE   Classic server for Windows is not available in pre-1.5 versions of Firebird.

Superserver

In 1996, Firebird's ancestor, InterBase 4.1, introduced the multi-threaded Superserver for the then-new Windows 32-bit platforms. It promised to make better use of the advancing capabilities of servers and networks. Superserver's abilities to spin off process threads and to allocate cache memory dynamically make it more capable than Classic server where the number of interactive read/write users is high and system resources are limited.

With the explosion of the GNU/Linux operating system on Intel toward the end of the 1990s, a Superserver became a realizable goal for some POSIX platforms. A Superserver skeleton for Linux was released with the InterBase 6.0 beta open source code and was fully realized in Firebird 1.0. Superserver builds eventually became available for the Sun Solaris platforms.

Embedded Server

Firebird 1.5 introduced an embedded variant of Superserver for Windows platforms. In this model, a fully functional Superserver is compiled with an embedded client that connects directly and exclusively to its database. This single dynamic library (fbembed.dll) uses the Windows inter-process communication space to transport client requests and server responses. The API is identical to that presented by a regular Superserver or by Classic server. Nothing special is required in application code to implement an Embedded Server application.

An embedded application can use only the local access method (see Chapter 2) and supports *one and only one* client process. You can deploy as many embedded applications as you like on a machine, but a single database can have only one such application attached to it at a time. An Embedded Server application can run concurrently on the same machine as a regular Firebird server. However, a database cannot be accessed by the server and an Embedded Server at the same time.

Embedded Server caters to the extreme "low end" of scalability requirements for a Firebird server, enabling a stand-alone, fast-performing, single-machine database application to be packaged and deployed with a small footprint. Since the database can be accessed by a regular server performing a replication service when the embedded application is offline, Embedded Server is particularly suitable for "briefcase" deployment—for example, on a notebook computer, or even on a flash disk.

For a comparison of the Superserver and Classic server models, refer to Chapter 36. In the same chapter, you will find full details about working with the Embedded Server on Windows, in the section "Working with Embedded Server."

The Sample Database

Throughout this guide, the language examples use the sample database that can be found in the examples directory beneath the Firebird installation root. In the Firebird 1.0.*x* distribution, its name is *employee.gdb*. In Firebird 1.5, it is *employee.fdb*.

For a brief description of the sample database, refer to Appendix VI.

Document Conventions

General body text is in this font.

```
Passages in this font are code, scripts, or command-line examples.
```

NOTE Passages highlighted like this are to draw your attention to something important that might affect your decision to use the feature under discussion.

TIP   Passages highlighted like this contain tips, bright ideas, or special recommendations.

CAUTION   Pay special attention to passages like this.

Syntax Patterns

Some code passages present *syntax patterns*—that is, code models that demonstrate the optional and mandatory elements of statement and command-line syntax. Certain symbol conventions apply to syntax patterns. To illustrate the conventions, the following extract from Chapter 20, for example, shows a syntax pattern for the SQL SELECT statement:

```
SELECT
 [FIRST (m)] [SKIP (n)] [[ALL] | DISTINCT]
  <list of columns> [, [column-name] | expression |constant ] AS alias-name]
FROM <table-or-procedure-or-view>
[{[[INNER] | [{LEFT | RIGHT | FULL} [OUTER]] JOIN}] <table-or-procedure-or-view>
  ON <join-conditions [{JOIN..]]
[WHERE <search-conditions>]
[GROUP BY <grouped-column-list>]
[HAVING <search-condition>]
[UNION <select-expression> [ALL]]
[PLAN <plan-expression>]
[ORDER BY <column-list>]
[FOR UPDATE [OF col1 [,col2..]] [WITH LOCK]]
```

Special Symbols

Elements (keywords, parameters) that are mandatory in all cases appear without any markings. In the preceding example, the keywords SELECT and FROM are mandatory for every SELECT statement.

Certain characters that never occur in SQL statements or command-line commands are used in syntax patterns to indicate specific rules about usage. These symbols are [ ], { }, |, **<string>**, and **...** . They are used in the patterns, as follows:

Square brackets [ ] indicate that the element(s) within the brackets are *optional*. When square brackets are nested, it means that the nesting, or the nested element, is optional.

Curly braces { } indicate that the elements within the braces are *mandatory*. The usual usage of curly braces is seen within an optional (square-bracketed) element, meaning "If the optional element is used, the curly-braced portion is mandatory." In the preceding example, if the optional explicit JOIN clause is used

```
[{[[INNER] | [{LEFT | RIGHT | FULL} [OUTER]] JOIN}]
```

the outer pair of curly braces indicates that the keyword JOIN is mandatory. The inner pair of curly braces indicates that, if an OUTER join is specified, it must be qualified as either LEFT, RIGHT, or FULL, with optional use of the keyword OUTER.

The *pipe symbol* | is used to separate mutually exclusive elements. In the preceding example, LEFT, RIGHT, and FULL are mutually exclusive, and inner join and any outer join are mutually exclusive.

Parameters are indicated with a string representing the parameter, enclosed *angle brackets* <>. For example, [WHERE *<search-conditions>*] indicates that one or more search conditions are required as parameters to the optional WHERE clause in the SELECT syntax.

In some cases, the <string> convention may be a shorthand for more complex options, that subsequent lines in the syntax pattern would "explode," level by level, to provide finer details. For example, you might see an expansion line like this:

```
<search-conditions> = <column-expression> = <constant> | <expression>
```

Pairs or triplets of dots ... may be used in some syntax patterns to indicate that the current element is repeatable.

NOTE None of these symbols is valid in either SQL statements or command line commands.

Enough of the introductions! The first four chapters are intended to get you started with Firebird—downloading and installing your server and client software, tweaking some basic network settings (should it be needed), configuring a few settings if the defaults don't quite fit your environment, and, finally, in Chapter 4, beginning to work with the server and a database using a basic client tool.

Part One

Boot Camp

CHAPTER 1

Installation

THIS CHAPTER DESCRIBES HOW TO OBTAIN an installation kit for the platform and version of Firebird server that you want to install on your server machine. The full installers install both the server and the client on a single machine.

Remote clients do not require the server at all. The procedure for installing the Firebird client varies somewhat, according to platform. For instructions, refer to the "Installing Clients" section in Chapter 7 for information about client-only installs. If you are new to Firebird, do not attempt a client-only install until you have worked out how all the pieces fit together in the default installation.

System Requirements

Server Memory (All Platforms)

Estimating server memory involves a number of factors:

- **Firebird server process**: The Firebird server process makes efficient use of the server's resources. The Superserver utilizes around 2MB of memory. On POSIX, the Classic server uses no memory until a client connection is made. On Windows, a small utility service is listening for connection requests.

- **Client connections**: Each connection to the Superserver adds approximately 115K, more or less, according to the style and characteristics of client applications and the design of the database schema. Each connection to the Classic server uses about 2MB.

- **Database cache**: The default is configurable, in database pages. The Superserver shares a single cache (with a default size of 2,048 pages) among all connections and increases cache automatically when required. The Classic server creates an individual cache (with a default of 75 pages) per connection.

As an estimate, allow 64MB of available RAM for a server and 16MB for a local client. The more clients you add, the more RAM will be used. Databases with large page sizes consume resources in larger chunks than do those with smaller page sizes. Resource usage on the Classic server grows by a fixed amount per client attachment; on Superserver, resources are shared and will grow dynamically as needed. Firebird 1.5

will use extra available RAM for sorting if it is available. Memory usage is discussed in more detail in Chapter 6.

Installation Drives

Firebird server—and any databases you create or connect to—must reside on a hard drive that is physically connected to the host machine. You cannot locate components of the server, or any database, on a mapped drive, a filesystem share, or a network filesystem.

CD-ROM

You cannot run a Firebird server from a CD-ROM. However, you can attach to a read-only database on a CD-ROM drive that is physically attached to the server.[1]

Disk Space

When estimating the disk space required for an installation, consider the sizes of the following executables. Disk space, over and above these minimum estimates, must also be available for database files, shadows (if used), sort files, logs, and backups.

- **Server**: A minimal server installation requires disk space ranging from 9MB to 12MB, depending on platform and architecture.

- **Client library**: Allow 350K (embedded: 1.4MB–2MB).

- **Command-line tools**: Allow ~900K.

- **DB administration utility**: Allow 1MB–6MB, depending on the utility selected. For a list of free and commercial utilities available, refer to Appendix V.

Minimum Machine Specifications

Minimum specifications depend on how you plan to use the system. You can run a server and develop database schemas on a minimally configured PC—even a "fast" 486 or a Pentium II with 64MB RAM will run Firebird 1.0.*x*—but such a configuration

---

1. Do not assume that copying a database file to a CD makes it a read-only database. The database must be made read-only, using the **gbak** or **gfix** utilities, *before* being written to the CD. See the relevant Tools chapters in Part Nine.

would not provide much capability if deployed into a network. For v.1.5 and later, a 586 with 128MB RAM should be regarded as minimum. Windows is more demanding on CPU and memory than a Linux server running at the console level. Operating system versions will influence the requirements: some UNIX platforms are expected to demand more resources at both server and client, and the requirements of some Windows versions push the baseline out, independent of any software requirements.

SMP and Hyperthreading Support

Firebird Superserver and Classic server can use shared memory multi-processors on Linux. On Windows, SMP support is available only for Classic server.

Hyperthreading is uncertain and seems to depend on several variables, including operating system platform, hardware vendor, and server version. Some users have reported success; others have had problems. If you have a machine with this feature, try your selected server with it enabled initially, and be prepared to disable it at the BIOS level if performance appears slow.

Processor affinity can be configured at the server level in firebird.conf (v.1.5) or ibconfig/isc_config (v.1.0.*x*). On Windows, for v.1.0.*x* and for v.1.5 Superserver, the CPU affinity mask should be set to a single CPU on an SMP machine. For instructions, refer to the section "The Firebird Configuration File" in Chapter 36.

Operating System

Table 1-1 shows the minimum operating system requirements for running Firebird servers. However, always check the README files in the /doc directory of your kit for late-breaking information about operating system issues.

Table 1-1. Firebird Minimum Operating System Requirements

OPERATING SYSTEM	VERSION	COMMENTS
Microsoft	Windows NT 4.0	Requires Service Pack 6a.
	Windows 95/98/ME	Possible upgrades needed: Microsoft C runtime library (msvcrt.dll) v.6 or higher. For Firebird.1.5, C++ runtime (msvcp60.dll or higher) is required. In Firebird 1.5, copies are located in Firebird's \bin directory. Winsock 2 is required for all servers; it may need to be installed on Windows 95.
	Windows 2000 with Service Pack 2	
	Windows XP	Databases should not have the .gdb file extension.
	Server2003	Databases should be on partitions that have the VSS (volume shadowing) feature disabled.

continued

Table 1-1. Firebird Minimum Operating System Requirements (continued)

OPERATING SYSTEM	VERSION	COMMENTS
Linux	Red Hat	v.7.1 or higher for Firebird 1.0.*x*, v.8.0 or higher for Firebird 1.5. For Red Hat 9 and higher, refer to the following Linux installation notes regarding the NPTL implementation.
	SuSE	v.7.2 or higher for Firebird 1.0.*x*, v.8.10 or higher for Firebird 1.5.
	Mandrake	v.8.0 or higher for Firebird 1.0.*x*, v.9.0 or higher for Firebird 1.5.
	All Linuxen	Firebird 1.5 (server and client) requires glibc-2.2.5 or higher and a libstdc++.so linked from libstdc++-5.0 or higher.
Other OS	Solaris (Intel, SPARC), Mac OS X, FreeBSD, HP-UX 10 +	Refer to Firebird distribution kits for details.

How to Get an Installation Kit

The main download area for Firebird release kits can be linked from the main Firebird website, http://firebirdsql.org, or at the SourceForge site, http://firebird.sourceforge.net. Links on either of those pages will take you to http://sourceforge.net/project/showfiles.php?group_id=9028.

The main page of the Firebird site usually displays a list of links to the latest releases for Linux and Windows. Other links will point you to distributions for other platforms. If a file has "src" in its name, it is buildable source code, not an installable kit.

Kit Contents

All of the kits contain all of the components needed to install the Firebird server:

- The Firebird server executable

- A number of other executables needed during installation and/or runtime

- Shell scripts or batch files needed during installation, which may also be available as server utilities

- The security database (isc4.gdb for v.1.0.*x*; security.fdb for v.1.5+)

- One or more versions of the client library for installing on both the server and the client workstations

- The command-line tools

- The standard external function libraries and their declaration scripts (*.sql)

- A sample database

- The C header files (not needed by beginners!)

- Text files containing up-to-the-minute notes for use during installation and configuration

- Release notes and various README files (these are essential reading)

Kit Naming Conventions

File naming of kits across platforms is not consistent. Alas, it is not even "consistently inconsistent," with builders often needing to conform to platform-specific conventions or simply making their own rules. However, certain elements in the file names will help you to identify the kit you want.

Classic or Superserver?

In general, the first part of the name string is "Firebird."

- If a Windows release supports the Classic server, it will be included in the same installer as the Superserver.

- For POSIX platforms that support both architectures, separate installers are provided for the Classic server and Superserver. The kit name will begin with "FirebirdCS" (for Classic server) or "FirebirdSS" (for Superserver).

- For minor platforms, the architecture might be less obvious and the first part of the name might be that of the OS or hardware platform.

Version Numbers

All release kit names should contain a dot-separated string of numbers in the following order: version number, release number, sub-release number. For example, "1.0.3" is the third sub-release of the initial (C code) release of Firebird version 1, while "1.5.0" is the initial sub-release of the release 5 (C++ code) of version 1. Most kits also include the absolute build number (e.g., 1.0.3.972 or 1.5.0.4306). For some minor platforms, especially those that impose their own naming rules and build on different compilers, version numbers may be less obvious.

64-Bit I/O

For platforms that require a special build to support 64-bit I/O, you should look for the infix "64IO" somewhere in the name string. It will not be present in the names of kits for operating systems that provide 64-bit I/O support automatically, if it is available.

Do not try to install a kit marked "64IO" on a version of that OS or hardware that does not support 64-bit I/O.

CPU Architecture

CPU architecture is usually included in the name string of the kit. For example, RPM installers for Linux generally include a chipset designator (e.g., i686). The showfiles display in the download list is generally a more useful indicator of the *minimum* chipset supported by the distribution. Assume Solaris kits are for Intel unless the "SPARC" tag is present in the kit name.

Mirror Sites

Once you find the required kit, click its hyperlinked file name. You will be directed to a list of mirror sites around the world, as shown in Figure 1-1.

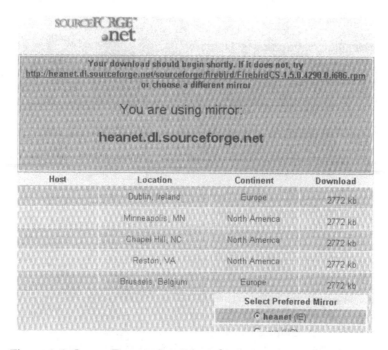

Figure 1-1. SourceForge mirror site selector

It does not matter which mirror site you choose—the download kits are identical at all sites.

Linux Kits

Scroll down the SourceForge showfiles display until you find the files shown in Figure 1-2.

Package	Release & Notes	Filename	Size	D/L	Date Arch.	Type
firebird [show only this package]						

...
...

firebird-linux-i386 [show only this package]

1.5.0-Release [show only this release]					2004-02-19 21:00	
FirebirdCS-1.5.0.4290-0.i686.rpm			2837886	0 i386		.rpm
FirebirdCS-1.5.0.4290-0.i686.tar.gz			2802184	0 i386		.gz
FirebirdCS-debuginfo-1.5.0.4290-0.i686.tar.gz			13512406	0 i386		.gz
FirebirdSS-1.5.0.4290-0.i686.rpm			3003269	0 i386		.rpm
FirebirdSS-1.5.0.4290-0.i686.tar.gz			2990059	0 i386		.gz
FirebirdSS-debuginfo-1.5.0.4290-0.i686.tar.gz			13512109	0 i386		.gz
1.0.3-Release [show only this release]					2003-06-02 22:00	
FirebirdCS-1.0.3.972-0.64IO.i386.rpm			2649789	1329 i386		.rpm
FirebirdCS-1.0.3.972-0.64IO.tar.gz			2618305	582 i386		.gz
FirebirdCS-1.0.3.972-0.i386.rpm			2649105	3160 i386		.rpm
FirebirdCS-1.0.3.972-0.tar.gz			2618227	1406 i386		.gz
FirebirdSS-1.0.3.972-0.64IO.i386.rpm			2676106	1260 i386		.rpm
FirebirdSS-1.0.3.972-0.64IO.tar.gz			2660131	637 i386		.gz
FirebirdSS-1.0.3.972-0.i386.rpm			2675525	5367 i386		.rpm
FirebirdSS-1.0.3.972-0.tar.gz			2659575	1879 i386		.gz

Figure 1-2. Linux kits on SourceForge

Where practicable, executable installers are provided. Both RPM installers and tarballs are available. If your Linux distribution supports RPM installers, make that your choice. It will create the directories and install everything required, set a password for the SYSDBA user, and start your chosen server. Release names of the installers are as follows:

- **Firebird 1.5**: FirebirdCS-1.5.0.4290.i686.rpm (Classic) and FirebirdSS-1.5.0.4290.i686.rpm (Superserver)

- **Firebird 1.03**: FirebirdCS-1.0.0.972-0.i386.rpm (Classic) and FirebirdSS-1.0.0.972-0.i386.rpm (Superserver)

Consult the appropriate platform documentation for instructions about using Red Hat Package Manager. In most distributions you will have the choice of running the RPM installer from a command shell or through a GUI interface.

Compressed Files (Tarballs)

For Linux distributions that cannot process **rpm** packages, and for the various UNIX flavors, use the tarball kit (usually .tar.gz or .bz2), as it will give the experienced Linux hand more control over the installation process. The appropriate decompression utility will be needed on your server for decompressing and "untarring" the kit into the filesystem. You will find detailed instructions in the release notes, README files, and distribution notes. Skilled users can also study and adjust the installation scripts to make it work on the less common Linuxen.

> **TIP**   Shell scripts have been provided. In some cases, the distribution notes may instruct you to modify the scripts and make some manual adjustments. The scripts are described later in this chapter.

In all cases, read any distributed text files, along with any specific topics in the official release notes that pertain to the version of Firebird that you are going to install. There may be significant variations between POSIX-compliant OS distributions and releases, especially the open source ones. Where possible, the build engineers for each Firebird version attempt to document in release notes any known issues with various kernel versions and distributions.

> **TIP**   If you do not find a copy of the release notes in your kit, go to the Main Downloads page at the IBPhoenix website at `http://www.ibphoenix.com` and download a copy from there.

NPTL Implementation on Higher Linuxen

The new Native POSIX Thread Library (NPTL) in Red Hat 9 (and possibly more recent Linux distributions) will cause problems for Superserver and locally compiled programs, including the utilities. **gbak** is reported to throw a "broken pipe" error. To fix this, follow these steps:

1.   Take care of the server instance. In /etc/init.d/firebird,

```
LD_ASSUME_KERNEL=2.2.5
export LD_ASSUME_KERNEL
```

2. You need to have the environment variable set up within the local environment as well, so add the following to /etc/profile, to ensure every user picks it
   up for the command line utilities. After

   ```
   HISTSIZE=1000
   ```

   add

   ```
   LD_ASSUME_KERNEL=2.2.5
   ```

   On the following line, export it:

   ```
   export PATH USER LOGNAME MAIL HOSTNAME HISTSIZE INPUT_RC LD_ASSUME_KERNEL
   ```

Windows Kits

The official kits for Windows (see Figure 1-3) are distributed as executable installers. It
is strongly recommended that you use the installer in preference to any .zip or .rar version that might appear.

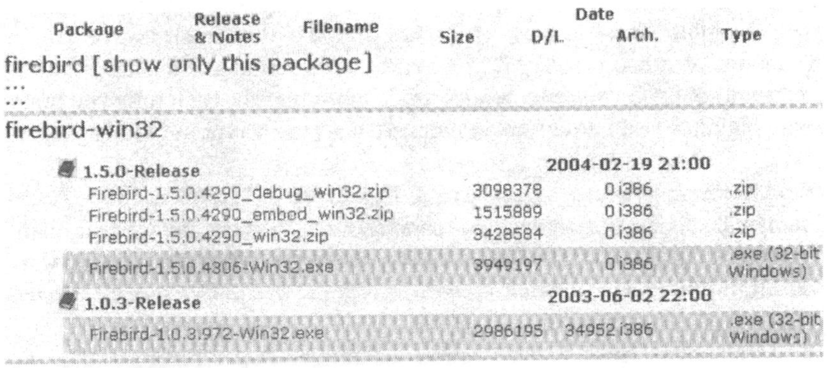

Package	Release & Notes	Filename	Size	D/L.	Date Arch.	Type
firebird [show only this package]						
...						
...						
firebird-win32						
1.5.0-Release					2004-02-19 21:00	
		Firebird-1.5.0.4290_debug_win32.zip	3098378	0 i386		.zip
		Firebird-1.5.0.4290_embed_win32.zip	1515889	0 i386		.zip
		Firebird-1.5.0.4290_win32.zip	3428584	0 i386		.zip
		Firebird-1.5.0.4306-Win32.exe	3949197	0 i386		.exe (32-bit Windows)
1.0.3-Release					2003-06-02 22:00	
		Firebird-1.0.3.972-Win32.exe	2986195	34952 i386		.exe (32-bit Windows)

Figure 1-3. Windows kits on SourceForge

The Firebird 1.5 install kits include executables and associated files for both
server models: Superserver and Classic. Dialog boxes in the installer will prompt you
for the model you want to install, and the other one will not be copied to your disk.
For Firebird 1.0.x, the only model supported is Superserver.

Release names of the installers are as follows:

- **Firebird 1.5**: Firebird-1.5.0.4306_Win32.exe

- **Firebird 1.03**: Firebird-1.0.3.972-Win32.exe

Compressed Files

If a Windows kit appears as a .zip file, you will require a utility, such as WinZip, PKZip, or WinRAR, to inspect and/or extract the contents before you begin. These kits (not intended for beginners) are as follows:

- The v.1.5 .zip full client/server kit, Firebird-1.5.0.4290_ win32.zip. It can be decompressed to a standard directory tree structure without being installed into the system. Some installation programs must be run after unzipping. Instructions are included in various text files in the /doc subdirectory.

- A separate kit for the v.1.5 Windows Embedded Server. The release file name of the kit is Firebird-1.5.0.4290_embed_win32.zip.

NOTE   There is no embedded server version for v.1.0.x.

Servers

On service-capable platforms—Windows NT, 2000, and XP—the Firebird server is installed, by default, to run as a service. The service will be installed and started automatically at the end of the installation process and, subsequently, each time you boot up your server machine. To find out how to stop and start the server manually, see Chapter 4.

Low-end Windows platforms—Windows 95, 98, and ME—do not support services. The installation will start Firebird server as an application, protected by the Guardian program. If the server application should terminate abnormally for some reason, the Guardian will attempt to restart it. For a server that is going to run as a service, it is recommended that you accept the Guardian option.

Do not try to install a Classic server if you already have a Superserver installed, or vice versa.

The Client Libraries

Copies of the client libraries are installed as follows:

- For Firebird 1.0.x, the name of the client library is gds32.dll, and it is installed into your system directory: C:\WINNT\system32 on service-capable Windows versions, or C:\Windows on non-service-capable Windows versions.

- For Firebird 1.5 and onward, the client is named fbclient.dll, and it is installed by default into the ..\bin directory beneath the Firebird root directory. By default, v.1.5+ utilities load the client from there, not the System directory.

NOTE   For legacy client applications—including many database components and admin tools, placement and naming of the client library is not so straightforward. Refer to Chapter 7 for details about the alternatives available for installing the client library—on the server and on client-only workstations—for compatibility with many GUI tools and other legacy application software.

Testing Your Installation

If everything works as designed, the Firebird server process will be running on your server when the installation finishes. You can run some tests to verify the installation and work out any adjustments you might need in your configuration.

Network Protocol

At this point, it is assumed that you will use the recommended TCP/IP protocol for your Firebird client/server network, to take advantage of the benefits of platform-independent networking.

TIP   For information about using the Named Pipes (NetBEUI) protocol in an all-Windows environment, refer to the "Network Protocols" section in Chapter 2.

CAUTION   IPX/SX networks, such as Novell Netware 3 and 4, are not supported by Firebird at all.

Pinging the Server

Usually, the first thing you will want to do once installation is complete is ping the server. This just gives you a reality check, to ensure that your client machine is able to see the host machine in your network. For example, if your server's IP address in the domain that is visible to your client is 192.13.14.1, go to a command shell and type the following command:

```
ping 192.13.14.1
```

Substitute this example IP address for the IP address that your server is broadcasting.

 TIP   If you get a timeout message, refer to Chapter 2 and Appendix II for further instructions. If you need more information about how to set up or find out your server's IP address, see the section "A Network Address for the Server" in Chapter 2.

If you are connecting to the server from a local client—that is, a client running on the same machine as the server—you can ping the virtual TCP/IP loopback server:

```
ping localhost [or] ping 127.0.0.1
```

Checking That the Firebird Server Is Running

POSIX Classic Server

Use the **ps** command in a command shell to inspect the running processes. If any clients are connected to a Firebird Classic process, you should see one process named fb_inet_server (or gds_inet_server for Firebird 1.0.x) for each connected client. The **ps** command has several switches, but the following will provide a satisfactory list. The **grep** command will filter the output so you only see the Firebird processes:

```
[xxx]$  ps -aux | grep fb
```

In Figure 1-4, three client processes are running.

```
USER       PID #CPU #MEM   VSZ  RSS TTY      STAT START   TIME COMMAND
root      1046  0.0  0.7  6920 3552 ?        S    00:07   0:00 fb_inet_server
root      1052  0.1  0.6  6608 2916 ?        S    00:10   0:00 fb_inet_server
root      1056  1.0  0.7  6920 3548 ?        S    00:12   0:00 fb_inet_server
```

Figure 1-4. Listing Classic processes with ps

POSIX Superserver

Because Superserver forks off a thread for each connection, it is interesting to throw the –f[ork] switch into the mix for examining its processes and threads. You get a formatted display of the forking processes, similar to Figure 1-5:

```
[xxx]$ ps -auxf | grep fb
```

```
USER      PID %CPU %MEM    VSZ  RSS TTY      STAT START   TIME COMMAND
root     1215  0.0  0.2   3608 1348 ?         S   18:43   0:00 /opt/firebird/bin/fbguard -f
root     1216  0.0  1.0  65664 5068 ?         S   18:43   0:00  \_ /opt/firebird/bin/fbserver
root     1217  0.0  1.0  65664 5068 ?         S   18:43   0:00      \_ /opt/firebird/bin/fbserver
root     1220  0.0  1.0  65664 5068 ?         S   18:43   0:00          \_ /opt/firebird/bin/fbserver
root     1978  0.0  1.0  65664 5068 ?         S   18:48   0:00          \_ /opt/firebird/bin/fbserver
root     1979  0.0  1.0  65664 5068 ?         S   18:48   0:00          \_ /opt/firebird/bin/fbserver
root     1980  0.0  1.0  65664 5068 ?         S   18:48   0:00          \_ /opt/firebird/bin/fbserver
root     1981  0.0  1.0  65664 5068 ?         S   18:48   0:00          \_ /opt/firebird/bin/fbserver
```

Figure 1-5. Listing Superserver process and threads with ps

The same **ps** command should show one process named fbguard (or ibguard) if the server was started with the –f[orever] switch, and one main process named fbserver (or ibserver). There will be at least one child process thread named fbserver (or ibserver) forking off one more such process thread. This first group is "the running server," sans any client connections except those that the server uses for listening on ports and for garbage collection. Beyond that will be a group of threads for each connection.

> **NOTE** The "fb" prefix belongs to Firebird 1.5, and "gds" and "ib" belong to Firebird 1.0.x. Use ps -aux | grep gds if you are running v.1.0.x.

Windows NT 4, 2000, and XP

For the Windows server platforms, start the Firebird Server Control applet from the Control Panel.

Server Control Applet

Figure 1-6 shows the Firebird Server Control applet display on Windows 2000 Server. If you used the installer, this applet will have been installed to your Control Panel. Its appearance may vary from one Windows server edition to another.

Figure 1-6. Server Control applet

You can use the applet to start and stop the service and to modify the start and run options. It is not recommended to change to "Run as an application" for multi-user use, for security reasons—you have to leave the server logged in to keep the server running.

Services Applet

If you have no Control Panel applet, you can inspect the Services applet (see Figure 1-7) in the Administration Tools display. On NT 4, you can access this applet directly from the Control Panel.

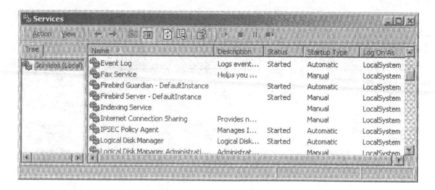

Figure 1-7. Services applet on Windows server platforms

Figure 1-7 shows the service names for Firebird 1.5 for the Guardian and the server. They may have different service names because of version changes; the Guardian may not appear at all. A user with Administrator privileges can right-click the service name to stop or restart the service. If you are using the Guardian, stop that service to stop both Guardian and server.

On Windows 2000 and Windows Server 2003, the Guardian is a convenience rather than a necessity, since these two operating systems have the facility to watch and restart services. It is recommended that you keep the Guardian active for other platforms if a SYSDBA is not available to restart the server manually in the event that it is stopped for some reason.

Other Control Panel Applets

If you want a Firebird Manager applet and you do not find one installed in the Control Panel of your Windows server, or if you need an applet in a language other than English, download one from the Firebird website or from http://www.ibphoenix.com. Simply close the Control Panel window and copy the .cpl file directly to your Windows system directory.

Windows 9x, ME, and XP Home

Windows 9x, ME, and XP Home do not support services. Firebird server should be running as an application, monitored by the Guardian. If you used an installation kit that installed but did not automatically start the Guardian and the Firebird server, you can set it up manually, as follows:

1. Locate the executable file for the Guardian program (ibguard.exe) and create a shortcut for it in the Startup area of your machine's Start menu.

2. Open the Properties dialog box of the shortcut and go to the field where the command line is.

3. Edit the command line so it reads as follows:

   ```
   fbguard.exe -a
   ```

4. Save and close the Properties dialog box.

5. Double-click the shortcut to start the Guardian. The Guardian will proceed to start fbserver.exe.

The Guardian should start up automatically the next time you boot your machine.

Server Control Applet

Some versions of the Server Control applet can be installed on a non-services-capable Windows platform. If the installer installs one for you, then it can be used in a similar manner as previously described for the services-capable versions. It will not be possible to choose a "Run as a service" option, if it is displayed. On the Home versions of Windows, to avoid confusion, the better applets hide or gray-out the option.

Installing an Embedded Server

 CAUTION   If you have not used Firebird before, it is strongly recommended that you bypass this option until you have gained some experience of working with one of the server versions and the "regular" client. You will not lose anything by attempting your first applications under the normal client/server model; they will work just fine with the embedded server.

The merged server and client are in the dynamic link library fbembed.dll, which you will find in the /bin directory of your regular Firebird server installation. You can install an embedded server if you already have a full server or other embedded servers installed.

For each embedded server application, the home directory of your application executable becomes the root directory for that embedded server application. To set up an embedded installation with your application, do as follows:

- Copy fbembed.dll to the home directory and rename it to either fbclient.dll or gds32.dll, according to the client file name your database connectivity software expects.

- Copy the files firebird.msg, firebird.conf, and aliases.conf to the home directory.

- If you want to use the database aliasing feature (recommended), copy aliases.conf to the home directory and configure it for this particular application.

- If external libraries are required for your application, such as international language support (fbintl.dll), UDF libraries, or blob filter libraries, create folders for them (../intl, ../UDF) directly beneath your application home directory and copy them to these locations.

Example of an Embedded Installation Structure

The following is an example of the directory structure and configuration for an installed embedded server application:

```
D:\my_app\MyApp.exe
D:\my_app\gds32.dll
D:\my_app\fb\firebird.conf
D:\my_app\fb\aliases.conf
D:\my_app\fb\firebird.msg
D:\my_app\fb\intl\fbintl.dll
D:\my_app\fb\UDF\fbudf.dll
```

firebird.conf:

```
RootDirectory = D:\my_app\fb
```

aliases.conf:

```
MyApplication = D:\databases\MyDB.fdb
```

Other Things You Need to Know

Users

Default User Name and Password

The SYSDBA user has all privileges on the server. The installation program will install the SYSDBA user into the security database (security.fdb).

On Windows and in the v.1.0.*x* Linux versions, the password is *masterkey*.

> **TIP** The password is actually masterke, since all characters after the eighth one are ignored.

On the v.1.5 and higher Linux versions, the installer generates a random password during installation, sets it in the security database, and stores it in-clear in the text file SYSDBA.password. Either memorize it or use it to get access to the security database and change it to something easier to remember.

> **CAUTION** If your server is exposed to the Internet at all, you should change this password immediately.

How to Change the SYSDBA Password

If you are on a Linux or another system that can run a bash script, cd to the ../bin directory of your installation and find the script named changeDBAPassword.sh. All you need to do is run this script and respond to the prompts. The first time you run the script, you will need to enter the password that the installer wrote in SYSDBA.password—it is in the Firebird root directory:

```
[bin]# sh changeDBAPassword.sh
```

or

```
[bin]# ./changeDBAPassword.sh
```

Using gsec Directly

The following procedure will work on both Windows and Linux. On Linux, you need to be logged into the operating system as Superuser (root) to run **gsec**. Let's say you decide to change the SYSDBA password from *masterkey* to *icuryy4me* (although, on Firebird 1.5 for Linux, the installed password will not be *masterkey*, but something much more obscure!). You would need to follow these steps to do so:

1. Go to a command shell on your server and change to the directory where the command-line utilities are located. Refer to Tables 1-2 through 1-5 to find this location.

2. Type the following on Windows, treating it as case-sensitive:

    ```
    gsec -user sysdba -password masterkey
    ```

    Type the following on POSIX platforms:

    ```
    ./gsec -user sysdba -password masterkey
    ```

    You should now see the shell prompt for the **gsec** utility:

    ```
    GSEC>
    ```

3. Type this command:

    ```
    GSEC> modify sysdba -pw icuryy4me
    ```

4. Press Enter. The new password *icuryy4me* is now encrypted and saved, and *masterkey* is no longer valid.

5. Now quit the **gsec** shell:

    ```
    GSEC> quit
    ```

Because Firebird ignores all characters in a password past the eighth character, *icuryy4m* will work, as will *icuryy4monkeys*.

> **TIP**   Full instructions for using *gsec* are in Chapter 34.

Linux/UNIX Users and Groups

From Firebird 1.5, the root user is no longer the default user that runs the server software. This means you need to put non-root users into the firebird group to enable them to access databases.

To add a user (for example, "sparky") to the firebird group, the root user needs to enter:

```
$ usermod -G firebird sparky
```

The next time sparky logs on, he or she can start working with Firebird databases.

To list the groups that a user belongs to, type the following at the command line:

```
$ groups
```

> **TIP**   The firebird user will also need read-write privileges to all databases and read-write-execute privileges to all directories where databases are located.

An Admin Tool

The Firebird kit does not come with a GUI admin tool. It does have a set of command-line tools, executable programs that are located in the ./bin directory of your Firebird installation. Their use is described in detail in Part Nine.

The excellent GUI tools available for use with a Windows client machine are too numerous to describe here. A few GUI tools written in Borland Kylix, for use on Linux client machines, are also in various stages of completion.

A list of the better-known admin tools for Firebird appears in Appendix V. For up-to-date listings, visit http://www.ibphoenix.com, select the Contributed link from the Downloads area, and then choose the Administration Tools link.

> **TIP** You can use a Windows admin client to access a Linux server and vice versa.

Default Disk Locations

The tables in this section describe the default disk locations for the components on Windows and Linux. Information is provided in two version contexts:

- Versions prior to Firebird 1.5

- Versions from Firebird 1.5 onward

These differences are important. Versions prior to Firebird 1.5 use many of the same locations, component names, and resource links as InterBase 6.*x* and prior versions of InterBase. Hence, it is not possible to run both a Firebird server and an InterBase server on the same machine with these versions.

In the major codebase revision starting at v.1.5, the old hard links to InterBase artifacts were removed and many of the major components were renamed. Firebird 1.5 may permit a running InterBase server to be present. It is a certain objective for Firebird 2.

Tables 1-2 through 1-5 show where to look for the components of the standard installation after running an installer. The exact locations may change from release to release.

Table 1-2. Firebird 1.5 Installation on Linux and Some UNIX Platforms

COMPONENT	FILE NAME	DEFAULT LOCATION
Classic server	fb_inet_server	/opt/firebird/bin
Lock Manager program (Classic server only)	fb_lock_mgr	/opt/firebird/bin
Embedded client for Classic server	libfbembed.so.1.5.0	/opt/lib
Firebird Guardian (Superserver only)	fbguard	/opt/firebird/bin
Superserver	fbserver.exe	/opt/firebird/bin
Thread-safe client for Superserver and Classic server	libfbclient.so	/usr/lib
Configuration file	firebird.conf	/opt/firebird
Database alias file	aliases.conf	/opt/firebird
Message file	firebird.msg	/opt/firebird

Table 1-2. Firebird 1.5 Installation on Linux and Some UNIX Platforms (continued)

COMPONENT	FILE NAME	DEFAULT LOCATION
Generated password file	SYSDBA.password	/opt/firebird
Security database	security.fdb	/opt/firebird
Backup of security database	security.fbk	/opt/firebird
Command-line tools	isql, gbak, gfix, gstat, gsec, gdef, gpre, qli	/opt/firebird/bin
Server tool (Superserver only)	fbmgr	/opt/firebird/bin
Shell scripts	Various; refer to the README files and release notes	/opt/firebird/bin
Template init script for Firebird (Classic server only)	firebird.xinetd	/opt/firebird/misc
External function libraries (UDF libraries)	ib_udf.so, fbudf.so	/opt/firebird/UDF
Memory utility library (used by ib_udf)	libib_util.so	/opt/firebird/lib
DDL scripts for external function libraries	ib_udf.sql, fbudf.sql	/opt/firebird/UDF
International language support library	fbintl	/opt/firebird/intl
Release notes	Firebird_v15.nnn_ReleaseNotes.pdf	/opt/firebird
Other documentation	README files on various topics	/opt/firebird/doc
Sample database	employee.fdb	/opt/firebird/sample
C header files	ibase.h, iberror.h, and others	opt/firebird/include

Table 1-3. Firebird 1.5 Installation on Windows 32-Bit Platforms

COMPONENT	FILE NAME	DEFAULT LOCATION
Classic server	fb_inet_server.exe	C:\Program Files\Firebird\ Firebird_1_5\bin
Lock Manager program (Classic server only)	fb_lock_mgr.exe	C:\Program Files\Firebird\ Firebird_1_5\bin
Firebird Guardian (Superserver only)	fbguard.exe	C:\Program Files\Firebird\ Firebird_1_5\bin
Superserver	fbserver.exe	C:\Program Files\Firebird\ Firebird_1_5\bin

continued

Table 1-3. Firebird 1.5 Installation on Windows 32-Bit Platforms (continued)

COMPONENT	FILE NAME	DEFAULT LOCATION
Embedded Superserver	fbembed.dll	C:\Program Files\Firebird\ Firebird_1_5\bin (install to application root and rename to fbclient.dll)
Client library for Superserver and Classic server	gds32.dll (stub) and fbclient.dll	C:\Program Files\Firebird\ Firebird_1_5
Configuration file	firebird.conf	C:\Program Files\Firebird\ Firebird_1_5
Database alias file	aliases.conf	C:\Program Files\Firebird\ Firebird_1_5
Message file	firebird.msg	C:\Program Files\Firebird\ Firebird_1_5
Security database	security.fdb	C:\Program Files\Firebird\ Firebird_1_5
Backup of security database	security.fbk	C:\Program Files\Firebird\ Firebird_1_5
Command-line tools	isql, gbak, gfix, gstat, gsec, gpre, gdef, qli, fb_lock_print	C:\Program Files\Firebird\ Firebird_1_5\bin
Services and registration tools	instsvc.exe, instreg.exe	C:\Program Files\Firebird\ Firebird_1_5\bin
External function libraries (UDF libraries)	ib_udf.dll, fbudf.dll	C:\Program Files\Firebird\ Firebird_1_5\UDF
Memory utility library (used by ib_udf.dll)	ib_util.dll	C:\Program Files\Firebird\ Firebird_1_5\bin
DDL scripts for external function libraries	ib_udf.sql, fbudf.sql	C:\Program Files\Firebird\ Firebird_1_5\UDF
International language support library	fbintl.dll	C:\Program Files\Firebird\ Firebird_1_5\intl
Release notes	Firebird_v15.nnn_ ReleaseNotes.pdf	C:\Program Files\Firebird\ Firebird_1_5

Table 1-3. Firebird 1.5 Installation on Windows 32-Bit Platforms (continued)

COMPONENT	FILE NAME	DEFAULT LOCATION
Other documentation	README files on various topics	C:\Program Files\Firebird\ Firebird_1_5\doc
Sample database	employee.fdb	C:\Program Files\Firebird\ Firebird_1_5\sample
C header files	ibase.h, iberror.h, and others	C:\Program Files\Firebird\ Firebird_1_5\include

Table 1-4. Firebird 1.0.3 Installation on Linux and Some UNIX Platforms

COMPONENT	FILE NAME	DEFAULT LOCATION
Classic server	gds_inet_server	/opt/interbase/bin
Lock Manager program (Classic server only)	ib_lock_mgr	/opt/interbase/bin
Embedded client for Classic server	gdslib.so	/usr/lib
Superserver	ibserver.exe	/opt/interbase/bin
Thread-safe client for Superserver and Classic server	gdslib.so	/usr/lib
Configuration file	isc_config	/opt/interbase
Message file	interbase.msg	/opt/interbase
Security database	isc4.gdb	/opt/interbase
Backup of security database	isc4.gbk	/opt/interbase
Command-line tools	isql, gbak, gfix, gstat, gsec, gdef, gpre, qli	/opt/interbase/bin
Server tool (Superserver only)	ibmgr	/opt/interbase/bin
Shell scripts	Various; refer to README files and release notes	/opt/interbase/bin or /opt/interbase/sample
Template init script for Firebird (Classic server only)	firebird.xinetd	/opt/interbase/bin or /opt/interbase/sample
External function libraries (UDF libraries)	ib_udf.so, fbudf.so	/opt/interbase/udf
Memory utility library (used by ib_udf)~TSROr	libib_util.so~TSR ib_util	/opt/interbase/lib/udf ~TSR/opt/ interbase
DDL scripts for external function libraries	ib_udf.sql	/opt/interbase/udf
International language support library	intl or intl.so	/opt/interbase/intl
Sample database	employee.gdb	/opt/interbase/sample
C header files	ibase.h, iberror.h, and others	/opt/interbase/ include

Table 1-5. Firebird 1.0.3 Installation on Windows 32-Bit Platforms

COMPONENT	FILE NAME	DEFAULT LOCATION
Firebird Guardian	ibguard.exe	C:\Program Files\Firebird\bin
Superserver	ibserver.exe	C:\Program Files\Firebird\bin
Client library	gds32.dll	C:\WINNT\system32 (services-capable platforms) or C:\Windows (others)
Configuration file	ibconfig	C:\Program Files\Firebird
Message file	interbase.msg	C:\Program Files\Firebird
Security database	isc4.gdb	C:\Program Files\Firebird
Backup of security database	isc4.gbk	C:\Program Files\Firebird
Command-line tools	isql, gbak, gfix, gstat, gsec, gpre, gdef, qli, iblockpr	C:\Program Files\Firebird\bin
Services and registration tools	instsvc.exe, instreg.exe	C:\Program Files\Firebird\ bin
External function libraries (UDF libraries)	ib_udf.dll, fbudf.dll	C:\Program Files\Firebird\Firebird_1_5\UDF
Memory utility library (used by ib_udf.dll)	ib_util.dll	C:\Program Files\Firebird\bin
DDL scripts for external function libraries	ib_udf.sql, fbudf.sql	C:\Program Files\Firebird\Firebird_1_5\UDF
International language support library	gdsintl.dll	C:\Program Files\Firebird\intl
Documentation	README files on various topics	C:\Program Files\Firebird
Sample database	employee.gdb	C:\Program Files\Firebird\ sample
C header files	ibase.h, iberror.h, and others	C:\Program Files\Firebird\ include

Up Next

Firebird consists of a server program and client applications, with a network protocol layer between the server and each client. If you used the appropriate installer for your platform and took the defaults, you probably have nothing further to do before getting started. You might like to skip the next two chapters and move straight to the operating "basics" described in Chapter 4. If you are curious about the network protocols, or you seem to have a network-related problem, read the next chapter and perhaps look into some of the configuration tips in Chapter 3.

Network Setup

AS A RELATIONAL DATABASE MANAGEMENT SYSTEM (RDBMS) purposely built for client/ server deployment, Firebird is designed to allow remote and local clients to connect concurrently to the server using a variety of network protocols.

The installers will set up a default configuration for connecting the server-based client to your server and for receiving connections from clients using the default port settings. Unless there is some external reason to use a custom network configuration, it should not be necessary to configure anything in order to get your first installation of Firebird up and running.

Network Protocols

Firebird supports TCP/IP for all combinations of client and server platforms.

Named Pipes

Firebird supports the Microsoft WNet Named Pipes protocol for Windows NT/2000, XP servers, and Windows clients. The default pipe name is *interbas*. Windows 9*x* and ME do not have the capability to be WNet servers.

 NOTE The Windows Named Pipes protocol is often referred to as NetBEUI. Strictly speaking, NetBEUI is a transport layer used by WNet.

Local Access

Although Firebird is designed to be a database server for remote clients, it offers a number of options for local access.

Client/Server

Local access options include

- **TCP/IP local loopback**: For *n*-tier server application layers and other clients accessing a local server on any supported platform using TCP/IP, even without a network card, connection can be made through the special *localhost* server at IP address 127.0.0.1.

 CAUTION   The localhost connection is not possible for embedded server applications.

- **Windows local connection mode**: For Windows clients running the Firebird Superserver on the same physical machine, Firebird supports a *local connection mode*, involving interprocess communication to simulate a network connection without a physical network interface or wire protocol. It is useful for access to a database during development, for embedded server applications, and for console-tool clients, but it does not support Firebird's event mechanism.

  Local connection's client/server capabilities are thus limited and must be avoided for deployment. Deploy stand-alone client/server applications, and web and other server tiers using TCP/IP local loopback for connection.

- **Direct local connect on POSIX:** Whether a local client can connect to a database on Linux and some other POSIX systems depends primarily on the server mode you have installed (Classic server or Superserver) and, secondarily, on the type of client connection.

  Superserver does not accept local connections through the normal API clients at all. The connection path must always include the TCP/IP host name. However, it does accept local connections from "embedded applications" (i.e., applications written using embedded SQL [ESQL]). The command-line tools **gsec**, **gfix**, **gbak**, and **gstat**, which are embedded applications, can make local connections to a Superserver.

  If you are running the Classic server, direct connection is possible from a local client.

Embedded Server

From Firebird 1.5 onward, the Firebird Windows packages include a fully functional embedded server (client and server merged as a dynamic library). Its features are identical to those of the normal client/server model except that there is no network protocol support: connection must be via the "Windows local" style of emulated network connection.

 CAUTION The embedded server does not support Firebird's password security access feature.

Mixed Platforms

Firebird's design enables clients running one operating system to access a Firebird server that is running on a different platform and operating system to the client. A common arrangement, for example, is to run several inexpensive Windows 98 PCs concurrently as client workstations accessing a departmental server running on Windows NT/2000/XP, Linux, or any of several brands of UNIX.

A database that was built for access by one server model can be served by any of them. For example, when an embedded server application is offline, its database can be under the control of a different embedded server application or a full Firebird server serving remote clients. The same database can be ported from platform to platform without modification.[1]

Besides the Windows and Linux platforms, server implementations of Firebird (Classic, Superserver, or both) are available also for Mac OS X (Darwin), FreeBSD, Sun Solaris (Intel and SPARC), HP-UX, and potentially AIX, and can be built for a number of additional UNIX platforms.

Firebird does not currently have platform support for any version of NetWare by Novell, nor for any other species of networking that accords to the largely obsolete IPX/SPX protocol. With the demise of Novell support for this protocol, sites often operate Firebird servers on a Linux system, with network clients connecting to this subsystem via TCP/IP.

---

1. Note, however, that custom external function libraries are not cross-platform capable. It is necessary to build versions of these libraries for each platform where the database is to be served. All supported Windows platforms can use the same Windows libraries; shared object libraries for POSIX platforms will not necessarily run on all POSIX platforms.

A Network Address for the Server

For TCP/IP communications, you must connect to a host that has a known IP address. Determining what that IP address is (or should be, if it is missing) depends on the kind of network environment your host machine is running in:

- If you are on a managed network, get the server's IP address from your system administrator.

- If you have a simple network of two machines linked by a crossover cable, or a small, switched network, you can set up your server with any suitable unique IP address you like except 127.0.0.1 (which is reserved for a local loopback server).

- If you know the "native" IP addresses of your network cards, and they are different, you can simply use those.

- If you are intending to try out a single-machine installation of both client and server, you should use the local loopback server address—localhost, or its IP address 127.0.0.1.

 CAUTION   On Windows, it is possible for a single user to connect locally to the server, without using a local TCP/IP loopback, as either an external or embedded client. A server address is neither required nor valid for such a connection and cannot be used to verify that TCP/IP is working properly in your setup.

HOSTS File

If your TCP/IP network is not running a domain name service, it will be necessary to inform each node individually of the mappings of IP addresses to host names in your network. To enable this, update the HOSTS file of *each* node (server *and* client).

When you are setting up Firebird nodes for TCP/IP networking, it is recommended that you configure the host name files on clients and use these, rather than the IP addresses directly, for attaching to the server. Although most up-to-date operating systems can use the host's IP address in your client connection string in lieu of the host name, connection through a host name ensures that the server's address remains static, regardless of dynamic address changes in the network.

CAUTION For Windows 95 and early Windows 98 workstations, on client stations running older 32-bit Windows versions, network support does not recognize an IP address in the connection string at all because those versions are installed with Winsock 1. In any case, installing Winsock 2 is effectively a requirement for current Firebird versions. Free upgrade packs can be downloaded from Microsoft customer support sites.

Locating the HOSTS File

Here is where to find the HOSTS file:

- On Linux and many UNIX versions, the HOSTS file is normally located in /etc/. Note that file names are case-sensitive on the UNIX family of platforms.

- On Windows NT/2000, the HOSTS file is located in C:\WINNT\system32\ drivers\etc\.

- On Windows XP/Server2003, the HOSTS file is located in C:\Windows\system32. On Windows 95/98/ME, look in C:\Windows.

 TIP If HOSTS is not present, you will find a file named Hosts.SAM in the same location. Copy this file and rename it as HOSTS.

Examples of hosts file entries are as follows:

```
10.12.13.2 db_server # Firebird server (in your LAN)
65.215.221.149 apress.com # (server on a WAN)
127.0.0.1 localhost # local loopback server (on Windows)
127.0.0.1 localhost.localdomain # local loopback server (on Linux)
```

Open and edit the HOSTS file with a plain text editor.
Writing the entry is simple. However, ensure that

- The IP address, if not 127.0.01 (localhost), must be the valid one configured for the host in your network.

- Server_name can be any unique name in your network.

TIP   A Windows server machine that has been set up with a Windows Networking (Named Pipes) host name of //Server_name will broadcast the same name as its TCP/IP host name.

- The comments following the hash symbol (#) are optional, but recommended.

- The format is identical, regardless of whether the host is running on Windows or Linux/UNIX.

CAUTION   After you edit the HOSTS file, check that your editor saved HOSTS with no file extension. If necessary, remove any extension by renaming the file.

Server Name and Path

When you create or move a database, ensure that it is on a hard disk that is physically attached to your server machine. Database files located on shares, mapped drives, or (on UNIX) mounted as SMB (Samba) filesystems cannot be seen by the server.

From Firebird 1.5 onward, you have the option of storing the paths to databases on your server as *database path aliases*. This not only simplifies the business of setting up portable connection strings in your applications, but also adds an extra layer of security to your remote connections. Database path aliasing prevents sniffer programs from determining where your databases are located and using that information to compromise your files.

Refer to Chapter 4 for information about database aliasing.

Connection String Syntax

These are the "in-clear" connection strings for each platform, which you need for configuring aliases and for attaching clients to databases running on Firebird server versions that do not support database aliasing.

TCP/IP

A TCP/IP connection string has two elements: the *server name* and the *absolute disk/filesystem path* as seen from the server. Its format is as follows.

For connecting to a Linux server:

```
servername:/filesystem-path/database-file
```

Here's an example on a Linux or other UNIX-family server named hotchicken:

```
hotchicken:/opt/firebird15/examples/LeisureStore.fdb
```

 CAUTION Remember, all file names are case-sensitive on these platforms.

For connecting to a Windows server:

```
servername:Drive:\filesystem-path\database-file
```

Here's an example:

```
hotchicken:C:\Program Files\Firebird15\examples\LeisureStore.fdb
```

Forward slashes are also valid on Windows:

```
hotchicken:C:/Program Files/Firebird15/examples/LeisureStore.fdb
```

Windows Local Connection

For connecting an embedded client or a local external client in Windows local mode:

```
C:\Program Files\Firebird15\examples\LeisureStore.fdb
```

Windows Networking (Named Pipes/WNet)

For connecting a remote client to a Windows server using the Named Pipes protocol:

```
\\servername\filesystem-path\database-file
```

where \\servername must be the properly identified node name of the server machine on the Windows network, *not* a share or a mapped drive. For example,

```
\\hotchicken\c:\databases\LeisureStore.fdb
```

Inconsistent Connection Strings for Windows Connections

Superserver on Windows establishes an exclusive lock on the database file when the first client connection is activated to protect databases from a long-standing bug.

The Connection Path Bug

Windows will accept two forms of the absolute local path to a file, one (correct according to the DOS standard) being *Drive:\path-to-database* and the other being *Drive:path-to-database* (optionally omitting the backslash following the drive designator).

If the server were to receive two client connection requests, the first using the standard path form and the subsequent one using the optional form, it would treat the two attachments as though they were connected to two different databases. The effects of any concurrent DML operations would cause destructive corruption to the database.

For connections to Superserver, the exclusive lock pre-empts the problem by requiring all connections to use the same path format as was used by the first connection. The same solution cannot be applied to the Classic server process because each connection works with its own instance of the server. Take care to ensure that your application always passes consistent path strings.

TIP   It is highly recommended that you use the database aliasing feature (see the section "Database Aliasing" in Chapter 4) for all connections and also ensure that aliases.conf contains one and only one alias for each database.

Configuring the TCP/IP Port Service

By default, a Firebird server listens on port 3050 for TCP/IP connection requests from clients. Its registered port service name is **gds_db**. The good news is that, if you can go with these defaults, you have to do nothing on either server or clients to configure the port service.

You can use a different port, a different port service name, or both. You might need to do this if port 3050 is required for another service, for example, a concurrently running **gds_db** configured for a different version of Firebird or for an InterBase server. There are several ways to override the defaults. Both the server and the clients must be configured to override the port service name or number, or both, in at least one of these ways:

- In the client connection string

- In the command used to start the server executable

- By activating the RemoteServicePort or RemoteServiceName parameters in firebird.conf (v.1.5 onward)

- In the daemon configuration (for Classic server on POSIX)

- By an entry in the *services* file

Before examining each of these techniques, it will be helpful to look at the logic used by the server to set the listening port and by the client to set the port that it should poll for requests.

How the Server Sets the Listening Port

The server executable has an optional command-line switch (–p) by which it can signify either the port number it will be listening on or the name of the port service that will be listening. At this point, if the switch is present, either port number 3050 or the port service name (**gds_db**) is replaced by the argument supplied with the –p switch.

Next—or first, if there is no –p switch—a v.1.5 server checks firebird.conf to look at the parameters RemoteServiceName and RemoteServicePort:

- If both are commented with #, then the defaults are assumed and no further change occurs. Any –p argument stands and the "missing" argument remains as the default.

- If RemoteServiceName has been uncommented, but not RemoteServicePort, then the port service name is substituted *only* if it has not been overridden already by the –p switch.

- If RemoteServicePort has been uncommented, but not RemoteServiceName, then the port number is substituted *only* if it has not been overridden already by the –p switch.

- If both RemoteServicePort and RemoteServiceName are uncommented, then RemoteServiceName takes precedence if it has not already been overridden by a –p argument. If there is already a port service name override, the RemoteServiceName value is ignored and the RemoteServicePort value overrides 3050.

- At this point, if an override of either the port number or the service name has been signaled, both v.1.0 and v.1.5 servers proceed to check the *services* file for an entry with the correct combination of service name and port number. If a match is found, all is well. If not, and the port service name is not **gds_db**, the server will throw an exception and fail to start. If **gds_db** is the port service name and it cannot be resolved to any other port, it will map to port 3050 automatically.

If the default port number or service name is to be overridden, then you may need to make an entry in the *services* file. To understand whether it will be necessary with your override choices, follow through the steps outlined later in the chapter in the "Configuring the services File" section.

Using the -p Switch Override

Starting the server with the optional –p switch enables you to override either the default port number (3050) or the default port service name (**gds_db**) that the server uses to listen for connection requests. The switch can override one, but not both. From Firebird 1.5 onward, you can use the –p switch in combination with a configuration in firebird.conf to enable an override to both the port number and the port service name.

Syntax for TCP/IP

The syntax pattern for commands is

```
server-command <other switches> -p port-number | service-name
```

For example, to start the Superserver as an application and override the service name "gds_db" with "fb_db", use this:

```
fbserver -a -p fb_db
```

Or, to override port 3050 to 3051, use this:

```
fbserver -a -p 3051
```

Syntax for WNet Redirection

On a WNet network, replace the preceding –p switch argument syntax with the following "backslash-backslash-dot-at" syntax:

```
fbserver -a -p \\.@fb_db
```

or

```
fbserver -a -p \\.@3051
```

Classic on POSIX: The inetd or xinetd Daemon

With Firebird Classic server on Linux or UNIX, the inetd or xinetd daemon is configured to listen on the default port and broadcast the default service name. The installation script will write the appropriate entry in the configuration file /etc/inetd.conf or /etc/xinetd.conf.

Problems attaching to a Classic server are often due to missing or bad port service entries in this file. You can check the current entry by opening it in a plain text editor (e.g., vim), and editing it if necessary. The following is an example of what you should see in xinetd.conf or inetd.conf after installing Firebird Classic on Linux:

```
# default: on
# description: FirebirdSQL server
```

```
#
service gds_db
{
    flags =             REUSE KEEPALIVE
    socket_type =       stream
    wait =              no
    user =              root
    # user =            @FBRunUser@
    log_on_success += USERID
    log_on_failure += USERid
    server =            /opt/firebird/bin/fb_inet_server
    disable =           no
}
```

If you configured the port service to be different to the defaults, you will need to alter xinetd.conf or inetd.conf accordingly. Restart xinetd (or inetd) with `kill -HUP` to make sure the daemon will use the new configuration.

 CAUTION   Connection requests will fail if both xinetd (or inetd) and fbserver (or ibserver) attempt to listen on the same port. If your host machine has this double configuration, it will be necessary to set things up so that each server version has its own service port.

Using a Configuration File Parameter

From Firebird 1.5 onward, you can configure either RemoteServiceName or RemoteServicePort in firebird.conf to override either the default port number (3050) or the default port service name (**gds_db**) that the server uses to listen for connection requests.

The engine will use one RemoteService* parameter, but not both. If you configure both, it will ignore RemoteServicePort in all cases, except where the server start command was invoked with the –p switch supplying an override to the port service name. Thus, you can use the –p switch and a RemoteService* parameter, in combination, to override both port number and service name.

If the default port number or service name is to be overridden, then you need to make an entry in the *services* file.

 CAUTION   Gotcha! If you uncomment RemoteServiceName or RemoteServicePort, but leave the default values intact, they will be treated as overrides. It will then be necessary to make an explicit entry in the services file for the default port service settings.

Setting Up a Client to Find the Service Port

If you set up your server with the installation defaults (service **gds_db** listening on port 3050), then no configuration is required. If the server is listening on a different port or is using a different port service name, the client application and/or its host machine need some enabling configuration to help the Firebird client library find the listening port.

The connection string used by a client can include information for polling the server's listening port in various ways. Firebird 1.5 clients can optionally use a local copy of firebird.conf. Changes may also be needed in the client's *services* file.

Using the Connection String

If only the port name or the service name has been reconfigured, then include the alternative port number or service name in the connection string. This works for all versions of Firebird.

Syntax for TCP/IP Connections

To connect to a database named server named hotchicken that is broadcasting on port 3050 with the service name **fb_db**, the connection string would be this for POSIX:

```
hotchicken/fb_db:/data/leisurestore.fdb
```

Or, if the service name is **gds_db** and the port number is 3051, this would be the connection string:

```
hotchicken/3051:/data/leisurestore.fdb
```

For Windows, the connection string would be this:

```
hotchicken/3051:D:\data\leisurestore.fdb
hotchicken/fb_db:D:\data\leisurestore.fdb
```

Notice that the separator between the server name and the port is a slash, not a colon. The colon before the physical path string is still required.

Syntax for WNet Connections

On a WNet network, use UNC-style notation:

```
\\hotchicken@3051\d:\leisurestore.fdb
```

or

```
\\hotchicken@fb_db\d:\leisurestore.fdb
```

If the server's port number or service name is an override, then you need to make an entry in the *services* file.

Using Port Syntax with Database Aliases

To connect through a non-default port with a database alias, affix the port number or service name to the server name, not to the alias. For example, suppose the database alias is stored in aliases.conf as

```
hotstuff = /data/leisurestore.fdb
```

Your application's connection string for server hotchicken would be this:

```
hotchicken/fb_db:hotstuff
```

or this:

```
hotchicken/3051:hotstuff
```

Using a Copy of firebird.conf

From Firebird 1.5 onward, you can optionally include a client-side copy of firebird.conf in the firebird root directory and configure RemoteServiceName or RemoteServicePort to help the client locate the server port.

You can configure *one* of these two parameters to extend the override provided for the other one through the connection string (shown previously), or to override only RemoteServiceName or RemoteServicePort without using the connection string to do it.

If you need to avoid passing the port service name or the port number in the connection string, and the server is using non-defaults for both, you can configure both RemoteServiceName and RemoteServicePort. You would use this technique if your client application needed to retain the capability to connect to InterBase or Firebird 1.0 servers.

Location of Firebird Artifacts on Clients

When you rely on firebird.conf on client machines, it is important that the client library knows where to find it. You will need to set up a Firebird root directory and inform the system of its location. Use the FIREBIRD environment variable to do this, in a manner similar to that described in Chapter 3 for servers. Windows clients can alternatively use a Registry key. With a correct client setup, you can also make use of a local version of the message file. For more information, refer to the section "Installing Clients" in Chapter 7.

Configuring the services File

You do not need to configure a service port entry for your Firebird server or clients if the server uses the installation defaults, **gds_db** on port 3050. If **gds_db** is the port service name and it cannot be resolved to any other port, it will map to port 3050 automatically.

If you are configuring the service port for a different port or service name, both the server and the client must be explicitly updated to reflect the reconfiguration. On both Linux and Windows, this information is stored in the *services* file.

Locating the services File

Here are the locations of the *services* file on the different platforms:

- On Windows NT/2000/XP, this file is located at C:\ winnt\system32\drivers\ etc\services.

- On Windows 95/98/ME, this file is located at C:\windows\services.

- On Linux/UNIX, this file is located at /etc/services.

A *services* entry looks like this:

```
gds_db 3050/tcp # Firebird Server 1.5
```

Open the file using a text editor and either add a line or edit the existing **gds_db** entry, as follows:

- For a Firebird 1.0.*x* server or client, alter either the service name or the port number to reflect how your server will start up.

- For a Firebird 1.5 or higher server, edit or add a line, as required. If you have a Firebird 1.0 or InterBase server installed on the same host, retain the entries they require and add a new entry reflecting how the Firebird 1.5 server will start up.

Testing the Connection with ping

All things being equal, the last reality check is to make sure your client machine is communicating with the server host. You can quickly test whether a TCP/IP client can reach the server, using the **ping** command in the command shell, as follows:

```
ping server_name  // substituting the name you entered in the hosts file
```

If the connection is good and everything is properly configured, you should see something like this:

```
Pinging hotchicken [10.10.0.2] with 32 bytes of data
reply from 10.10.0.2: bytes=32 time<10ms TTL=128
reply from 10.10.0.2: bytes=32 time<10ms TTL=128
reply from 10.10.0.2: bytes=32 time<10ms TTL=128
reply from 10.10.0.2: bytes=32 time<10ms TTL=128
```

Press Ctrl+C to stop the ping responses.

If ping Fails

If you get something like this:

```
Bad IP address hotchicken
```

then your host name file entry for the server_name (in this example, hotchicken) may be missing or spelled incorrectly. For example, all identifiers on Linux/UNIX are case-sensitive. Another cause might be simply that your server machine's host name has not been configured.

If you see this:

```
Request timed out
```

it means that the IP address referred to in your host name file cannot be found in the subnet. Check that

- There are no typos in the host name file entry.

- The network cable is plugged in and the wires and contacts are free from damage and corrosion.

- The network configuration allows you to route network traffic between the client and server in question. Subnet or firewall restrictions may be preventing the host server from receiving the ping from the client.

  - **Subnet restrictions**: TCP/IP can be configured to restrict traffic between subnets. If your client machine is part of a complex network of subnets, check with the network administrator that it has unrestricted access to the host server.

 CAUTION   WNet cannot route network traffic between subnets.

- **Firewalls**: Your connection test might fail if the database server is behind a software or hardware firewall that blocks port 3050 or your reconfigured port.

Problems with Events

Although each client connects with the server through a single pipe, Firebird *events*—a callback mechanism that can channel event notifications back to clients from triggers and stored procedures—uses random available ports. On static, self-contained networks without internal firewalls, this usually causes no problems. On networks where there are multiple subnets, dynamic IP addressing, and tightly configured firewalls, the event channels can fail.

In Firebird 1.0.*x*, your network administrator needs to configure some way to ensure that a port is available that is always free, open, and static. It can be solved in one way or another on most networks.

Firebird 1.5 simplified matters and made it possible to configure an IP address in the network explicitly for events traffic. Use the firebird.conf parameter RemoteAuxPort to set statically the IP address of an interface (card, router, gateway, etc.) that is available for event routing.

For more information about Firebird events, refer to Chapter 32.

Other Network Problems

If things just will not go right, you will find more tips and techniques in Appendix II.

Up Next

Where to next? If you are happy with your network setup and are rarin' to go, head straight to Chapter 4 for some "basics" that will get you connected to a database. If you have installed Firebird on a multiprocessor system, or you suspect that something in your machine configuration might be causing a problem, read on. Although it is rarely necessary to alter Firebird's configuration for basic operations, Chapter 3 introduces a few configuration options that could help you past any teething problems.

CHAPTER 3

Configuring Firebird

AFTER INSTALLATION, FIREBIRD IS USUALLY READY to go, with little or no configuration required. If your installation and network setup went according to plan, there will be nothing for the new user to do but proceed to discover the ways and means of Firebird and experiment with the software. You can simply skip this chapter and move on to the next chapter.

However, this statement might not quite hold true for some of the minor platforms or where operating system conditions might have blocked one or two aspects of automatic configuration by the installer script or program. This chapter will be of immediate interest to the new user for solving some of these problems.

The first section of this chapter describes how to configure some environment variables and filesystem resources for Firebird use. It goes on to examine the server configuration parameters and how to modify them for specific performance and compatibility requirements.

Database-Level Configuration

The topics in this chapter refer to server-level configuration. A single Firebird server can manage several databases simultaneously. Accordingly, databases can be configured individually to meet their varying requirements. For information about database-level configuration, refer to Chapters 15 and 39.

Environment Variables

Environment variables are global system settings that take effect when the operating system is booted. On Windows, Linux, and most UNIX systems, the Firebird server will recognize and use certain environment variables if they are configured. The **fbserver** process (Superserver architecture) or the **fb_inet_server** process (Classic server architecture) will not recognize settings that point to networked resources (disks and filesystems) not physically controlled by the server machine.

Where to Set Environment Variables

Windows

The type of environment variable to set and the method of setting it varies from one version of Windows to another. Table 3-1 shows which types to set (if applicable), and where and how to set them.

Table 3-1. Setting Environment Variables on Windows

WINDOWS VERSION	VARIABLE TYPE	DESCRIPTION	IN REGISTRY
Windows 95/98	Not applicable	Use Notepad and set environment variables in autoexec.bat or config.sys. The format is SET <*variable_name*>= <*variable_value*>. For example, SET FIREBIRD=C:\PROGRA~1\ FIREBIRD. To view all current environment variables, type **SET** in a command window.	No
Windows NT/2000/XP	User Variables for <user>. Makes variables available to applications being run by <user>, only if <user> is logged on.	Use to restrict visibility of variables to the appointed user. System Properties dialog box, accessed from the System applet on the Control Panel or by right-clicking the My Computer icon on the desktop and selecting Properties.	Yes
Windows NT		Select Advanced ➤ Environment ➤ New.	
Windows 2000/XP		Select Advanced ➤ Environment Variables ➤ New.	
Windows NT/2000/XP	System Variables. Available to the entire system (all services, all users).	Use if running Firebird as a service. Select Advanced ➤ Environment Variables ➤ New (or Edit, if applicable).	Yes
	SET commands written from a command window. Variables can be accessed only by processes started from the command line.	Useful to set an environment variable in a very temporary fashion (e.g., ISC_USER and ISC_PASSWORD for simplifying access with command-line tools during an admin task). Use SET <*variable_name*>= <*variable_value*> to set the variable; use SET <*variable_name*>=, leaving value blank, to unset.	No

POSIX

On Linux and UNIX, the easiest way to define environment variables is to add their definitions to the systemwide default shell profile.

The root user can also choose to either

- Issue **setenv()** commands from a shell *or* shell script.

- For temporary use, set and export a variable from a shell (e.g., export ISC_USER=SYSDBA)

ISC_USER and ISC_PASSWORD

The effect of this dangerous pair of environment variables is to give SYSDBA access to the Firebird server and its databases, via the command-line tools or other client applications, to anyone who can log into the host machine. They are a convenience for developers.

If you do not provide a user name and password when you connect locally to a database or when you run the command-line utilities such as **gbak**, **gstat**, and **gfix**, Firebird looks to see if the ISC_USER and ISC_PASSWORD environment variables are set; if they are, Firebird lets you log in without entering a password. Never allow these variables to remain configured on a server that has production databases running unless your server room is physically very secure!

FIREBIRD (or INTERBASE) Variable

The FIREBIRD environment variable (INTERBASE in version 1.0.*x*), if configured, is used during both installation and runtime, on all platforms, to locate the root directory of the Firebird server installation. If present, it overrides all other settings—installation kit defaults, Windows Registry settings, firebird.conf configuration, operating system global paths defaults, etc.

During installation, it points to the root directory where Firebird is (to be) installed. The value must point to a fully qualified path that exists within the host machine's own physical filesystem. At startup, the server reads non-default settings from a configuration file named firebird.conf (or ibconfig/isc_config in version 1.0.*x*), which must be located in the directory assigned to the FIREBIRD (or INTERBASE) variable. This directory must be the parent of the /bin directory where the Firebird binaries reside. It is also the default location of the message and lock files, firebird.msg (interbase.msg) and the *hostname*.lck file(s).

NOTE   You can specifically configure different locations for firebird.msg (interbase.msg) and firebird.lck (interbase.lck) by setting the environment variables FIREBIRD_MSG (INTERBASE_MSG) and FIREBIRD_LOCK (INTERBASE_LOCK). See the following topics.

If the FIREBIRD variable is not configured, the defaults are used: /opt/firebird (on Linux/UNIX platforms), or C:\Program Files\Firebird (v. 1.0.*x*) or C:\Program Files\ Firebird\Firebird_1_5 (v. 1.5) (on Windows platforms). Refer to Tables 1-2 through 1-5 in Chapter 1 for exact locations. If Firebird is installed in a path that is different from the default and the FIREBIRD variable is configured, the client library can read the variable to find the installation path.

On Windows, client applications can also find the installation path by reading the field DefaultInstance under the Registry key that is installed in a client-only installation.

```
HKEY_LOCAL_MACHINE\SOFTWARE\Firebird Project\Firebird Server\Instances
```

For more discussion of the trail followed by the server to locate its files, refer to the "The Firebird Root Directory" section later in this chapter. Look up the section "Installing Clients" in Chapter 7 for information about client-only installs.

FIREBIRD_TMP

By default, Firebird will use the global temporary file space, usually configured as a system default by the environment variable TMP (discussed below). The FIREBIRD_TMP (v.1.0.*x* INTERBASE_TMP) environment variable is one means by which a custom location for Firebird's sort files can be configured. The value must point to a fully qualified path that exists within the host machine's own physical filesystem.

Other options are available for defining the location of these files. Configuration of the parameter TempDirectories (tmp_directory in Firebird 1.0.*x*) is described in Chapter 36, in the section "The Firebird Configuration File" under "Parameters for Configuring Temporary Sort Space."

*_LOCK and *_MSG

FIREBIRD_LOCK (INTERBASE_LOCK in v.1.0.*x*) sets the location of the lock file. FIREBIRD_MSG (INTERBASE_MSG in v.1.0.*x*) sets the location of the Firebird message file.

These two variables are independent of each other and can be set to different locations. The value must point to a fully qualified path that exists within the host machine's own physical filesystem.

TMP

Sort Space on the Server Machine

Sort space is space on disk where the engine stores the intermediate output sets, in runtime temporary files, for queries that have to be sorted or aggregated. Firebird 1.0.*x* uses only disk files for such storage. Firebird 1.5 stores these files in RAM, if it can, and pages them out to disk sort space only if resources become exhausted.

The global environment variable TMP (or TEMP on some systems) points to a directory path on the server where applications should store temporary files. Firebird will attempt to store temporary sort files here if the FIREBIRD_TMP environment variable (see the previous section titled "FIREBIRD_TMP") is not defined and no other sort space has been configured in the Firebird configuration file (see TempDirectories and tmp_directory in Chapter 36).

isq*l Script Files on a Client*

The interactive command-line SQL utility **isql** provides the capability to "record" sequences of interactive SQL commands to a script file, using the OUTPUT switch. On a client machine, the TMP setting is the only place to control the space where these script files will be stored if an absolute path specification is not supplied. If the TMP location is not set, a Firebird client uses any temporary directory it finds defined for the local system, usually the /tmp filesystem on a Linux/UNIX client, or C:\Temp on a Windows client.

The Firebird Configuration File

Firebird does not require the intense and constant reconfiguration that many other heavy-duty RDBMSs do. However, a range of configuration options is available for customizing a Firebird server and the host system on which it runs for your special needs.

The Firebird configuration file is named firebird.conf in all Firebird versions from 1.5 onward. In prior versions, its name depends on the operating system:

- On Linux/UNIX, the name is isc_config.

- On Windows, the name is ibconfig.

Several new parameters were added to version 1.5.

When a Firebird server process starts up, it reads the configuration file and adjusts its runtime flags to any non-default values contained in the configuration file. The file will not be read again until the next time the server is restarted. The default configuration parameters and their values are listed in the configuration file, commented out by # comment markers. It is not necessary to uncomment the defaults in order to make them visible to the server's startup procedure.

Changing Configuration Parameters

It should be unnecessary to change any defaults until and unless you need to customize something. This procedure is not recommended if you lack a clear understanding of the effects.

A handful of default configuration settings that may be showstoppers for some legacy applications or non-default installations are discussed briefly here. A complete reference to all configuration parameters can be found in Chapter 36. The configuration file can be edited with any plain text editor (e.g., vim in Linux or Notepad in Windows). Do not copy the file from a Windows machine to a Linux one, or vice versa, because the two systems store line breaks differently.

Parameter entries in firebird.conf are in the form

```
parameter_name = value
```

where parameter_name is a string that contains no white space and names a property of the server being configured, and value is a number, Boolean (1=True, 0=False), or string that specifies the value for the parameter.

To set any parameter to a non-default setting, delete the comment (#) marker and edit the value.

The Firebird 1.0.*x* ibconfig/isc_config parameter names and syntaxes are not interchangeable with those in firebird.conf. The format, size, and number of parameters are more restrictive.

The ibconfig/isc_config format is

```
parameter_name    value
```

where the white space between the name and the value can be tabs or spaces, as desired, to please the eye. Each line of the file is limited to 80 characters. Unused parameters and installation defaults are commented with #.

On Linux, you should assume that parameter names are case-sensitive.

NOTE   You can edit the configuration file while the server is running. To activate configuration changes, it is necessary to stop and restart the service.

The Firebird Root Directory

The root directory of your Firebird installation is used in many ways, both during installation and as an attribute that server routines, configuration parameters, and clients depend on. Because several ways exist to tell the server where to find a value for this attribute, developers and system administrators should be aware of the precedence trail that the server follows at startup, to determine it correctly.

1. On any platform, the first place the server looks is the (optional) global environment variable FIREBIRD. If it finds this variable, its value is used unconditionally.

2. If the FIREBIRD environment variable is not present, the next signpost on the trail applies to Windows platforms only. It seeks the Registry key

```
HKEY_LOCAL_MACHINE\SOFTWARE\Firebird Project\Firebird Server\Instances
```

and looks for the field DefaultInstance. If it finds a valid directory path in this field, this is the value used. Other platforms do not have an equivalent signpost.

3. If the root directory is still not detected, then the interim root directory is assumed to be the level above the running process (..\ on Windows, ../ or the link to /proc/self/exe on POSIX, as applicable).

4. The startup procedure now looks in this location for the firebird.conf file. If it finds firebird.conf, it looks for the RootDirectory parameter. If this parameter is present, its value becomes the final root directory; otherwise, the interim value in step 3 becomes final.

 CAUTION If firebird.conf is not found in the level above the running process, it may mean that the root directory has been incorrectly detected because of a non-standard installation. The engine must find the root directory files. If you encounter security or filesystem errors when logging in or during runtime, you should review your installation paths to ensure that the steps in this section will correctly resolve the location of the root files and subdirectories.

Parameters Relating to File Access

Firebird has several parameters for protecting its files and databases from accidents and unauthorized access. If you are porting an existing database application or admin tool to Firebird 1.5, it may be important for you to refer to the section "The Firebird Configuration File" in Chapter 36 for detailed information about these parameters:

- **RootDirectory**: This parameter can be used to configure the absolute path to a directory root on the local filesystem. It should remain commented unless you want to force the startup procedure to override the path to the root directory of the Firebird server installation, which it would otherwise detect for itself (see step 3 in the preceding section).

- **DatabaseAccess**: In Firebird 1.0.*x*, the server can attach to any database in its local filesystem and is always accessed by applications passing the file's absolute filesystem path. This parameter was introduced in v.1.5 to provide tighter security controls on access to database files and to support the database-aliasing feature.

  The default installation configures this to Full, mimicking v.1.0.*x* behavior. Alternative options can restrict the server's access to aliased databases only, or to databases located in specified filesystem trees.

CAUTION It is strongly recommended that you set this option and make use of the database-aliasing feature. For information about database aliasing, refer to Chapter 4.

- **ExternalFileAccess**: This parameter replaces the external_file_directory parameter introduced in release 1.0. This parameter provides three levels of security regarding EXTERNAL FILES (fixed format text files that are to be accessed as database tables). If you are porting a database that defines any EXTERNAL FILE tables, you will need to configure this parameter in v.1.5 because it is disabled by default. Configuration is optional, although recommended, in v.1.0.*x*.

- **UDFAccess**: This parameter is for protecting the locations where external code modules reside. It replaces not just the name of the optional v.1.0.*x* parameter, external_function_directory, but also the form in which the values are presented. Firebird 1.5 installs with access to external function libraries disabled by default, affecting many servers that previously allowed full access.

- **TempDirectories (tmp_directory in v.1.0.*x*)**: This parameter can be configured as one of the ways to allocate temporary sort space for the server in a specific disk location. Firebird 1.5 syntax is different from that of Firebird 1.0.*x*.

Other Parameters of Interest

The following parameters might be of interest in some hardware configurations:

- **CPUAffinityMask (cpu_affinity in v.1.0.*x*)**: This parameter can be used to assign the processors that a Windows Superserver is to use on an SMP machine. There is a problem, known as the "see-saw effect," where the operating system continually swaps the entire Superserver process back and forth between processors on some SMP machines. The CPU affinity must be set to a single CPU if you encounter this problem.

  By default, the affinity mask is set to use the first CPU in the array.

- **LockMemSize**: This parameter is specific to Classic servers and represents the number of bytes of shared memory allocated to the memory table used by the lock manager. You may need to adjust this if you encounter the error "Lock manager is out of room" on Classic. Refer also to the LockHashSlots parameter in relation to this problem.

- **SortMemBlockSize and SortMemUpperLimit**: These two parameters were added in v.1.5 to enable you to set and limit the amount of RAM the server uses for in-memory sorting. For Classic server, the default is too large to sustain more than a few connections.

- **DummyPacketInterval (dummy_packet_interval on v.1.0.*x*)**: This parameter is a relic from 16-bit systems that causes problems on 32-bit Windows. It was an old InterBase timeout parameter that was supposed to set the number of seconds (integer) the server should wait on a silent client connection before sending dummy packets to request acknowledgment. It is set by default to 0 on Firebird 1.5 (disabled) and to 60 on Firebird 1.0.*x*. It should be disabled (set to 0) on all Windows systems. Disabling it on other operating systems is also strongly recommended.[1]

- **RemoteBindAddress**: By default, clients may connect from any network interface through which the host server accepts traffic. This parameter allows you to bind the Firebird service to incoming requests through a single IP address (e.g., network card) and to reject connection requests from any other network interfaces. This helps to solve problems in some networks when the server is hosting multiple subnets. It is not supported on v.1.0.*x*.

- **CompleteBooleanEvaluation**: This parameter can be used to revert the short Boolean evaluation logic used in Firebird 1.5 and higher to the full evaluation logic used in Firebird 1.0.*x*.

- **OldParameterOrdering**: This parameter will be of interest to users of the IB Objects (IBO) data access components who are upgrading to Firebird 1.5 from v.1.0.*x* or InterBase. If your IBO version is lower than v.4.2, you should set this parameter to true as a temporary measure for compatibility until you upgrade IBO. It effectively "restores" an InterBase bug that scrambles stored procedure parameters in some conditions.

---

1. Due to a Windows bug, enabling DummyPacketInterval may hang or crash Windows on the client side. For an explanation, refer to this Microsoft Support article: http://support.microsoft.com/default.aspx?kbid=296265. It is not recommended that you enable it for non-Windows systems, either, as it may actually interfere with the eventual disconnection of an inactive client.

Up Next

There should be nothing left to do now but to connect to a database and begin doing some serious experimentation. Chapter 4, the last in our "boot camp" section, will get you connected to the sample database or any other Firebird-compatible database you might have on your server.

CHAPTER 4

Operating Basics

ONCE YOU HAVE FIREBIRD SERVER INSTALLED on your host server machine, what then?
This chapter should get you up to speed on the basics.

Running Firebird on Linux/UNIX

Superserver

The default installation directory is /opt/firebird. In the /bin directory is the Firebird server binary fbserver (ibserver for Firebird 1.0.*x*), which runs as a daemon process on Linux/UNIX. It is started automatically at the end of an RPM or script installation and whenever the host server is rebooted, by running the daemon script **firebird** residing in /etc/rc.d/init.d (or /etc/init.d on SuSE), which calls the command-line Firebird Manager utility, fbmgr.bin. Firebird Manager can be used from a shell to start and stop the process manually.

Starting the Server

If you have to start the Firebird server manually for some reason, log in as root or as the firebird user. Take care about which account you use when starting fbserver because, once it has been started, all of the objects created belong to that account. If another user later starts the process using one of the other special user accounts, those objects will be inaccessible.

It is strongly recommended that you create a system user named "firebird" and run the Firebird server process under that account.

To start the process, execute the following command from a shell:

```
./fbmgr.bin -start -forever
```

For Firebird versions before 1.5, use this command:

```
./ibmgr -start -forever
```

The **–forever** switch causes the Guardian monitor process to start. Under the Guardian, the fbserver process will be restarted, should it terminate abnormally for some reason.

To start the server without the Guardian, enter

```
./fbmgr.bin -start -once
```

For Firebird versions before 1.5, use this:

```
./ibmgr -start -once
```

The **–once** switch makes it so that, if the server crashes, it stays down until manually restarted.

Stopping the Server

For safety, if possible, ensure that all attachments to databases have been disconnected before you stop the server.

The **–shut** switch rolls back all current transactions and shuts down the server immediately.

You do not need to be logged in as root to stop the Firebird server with fbmgr, but you do need SYSDBA authority. Execute the following command:

```
./fbmgr.bin -shut -password <SYSDBA password
```

Use this command for pre-1.5 versions:

```
./ibmgr.bin -shut -password <SYSDBA password>
```

Controlled Shutdown

On this platform, Firebird does not provide a utility for counting users connected to a database on the Superserver. If you need to allow clients an interval to complete work and detach gracefully, shut down individual databases using the **gfix** tool with –shut and one of a range of available arguments to control detachment. See the section "Shutting Down a Database" in Chapter 39.

Other fbmgr Commands

Syntax

From the command shell:

```
./fbmgr.bin -command [-option [parameter] ...]
```

Alternatively, you can start an interactive fbmgr or ibmgr shell session (i.e., go into *prompt mode*). Type

```
./fbmgr <press Return/Enter>
```

to bring up the following prompt:

```
FBMGR>
```

In prompt mode, the syntax for commands is

```
FBMGR> command [-option [parameter] ...]
```

For example, you can start the server in either of the following ways. From the command shell:

```
./fbmgr -start -password password
```

In prompt mode:

```
FBMGR> start -password password
```

fbmgr Switches

Table 4-1 presents a summary of the switches available for fbmgr and ibmgr in either shell or prompt mode.

Table 4-1. Switches for fbmgr/ibmgr

SWITCH	ARGUMENT	OTHER SWITCHES	DESCRIPTION
–start	–forever | –once	–user, –password	Starts the fbserver process if it is not already running
–shut		–user, –password	Stops the fbserver process
–show			Shows host and user
–user	user_name		SYSDBA; used with –start and –stop switches if system user is not root or equivalent
–password	SYSDBA password		Used with –start and –stop switches if system user is not root or equivalent
–help			Prints brief help text for fbmgr
–quit			Use to quit prompt mode

Classic Server

Firebird Classic server uses the xinetd or inetd process to handle incoming requests. (The process it uses depends on which one is in your Linux version.) There is no need to start the server explicitly. The xinetd or inetd process runs automatically and, when it accepts a request from a Firebird client to attach, it forks off a process named fb_inet_server for that client.

How the Server Listens for Connection Requests

If Firebird Classic server was installed using a scripted or RPM installer, a startup configuration file for fb_inet_server, named firebird, should have been added to the services that [x]inetd knows about. On most Linux distributions, the location of this file is the directory /etc/xinetd.d. To have [x]inetd "listen" for connection requests from clients to your Firebird Classic server, the firebird script must be in this directory when the [x]inetd process starts.

TIP   If [x]inetd is running and no client connection requests succeed at all, check whether the firebird script is actually where it is supposed to be. If not, the script firebird.xinetd may be extracted from the compressed install kit, copied to the correct location, and renamed as firebird. To make [x]inetd "see" the Firebird service, stop and restart [x]inetd.

Stopping and Starting [x]inetd and Its Services

The [x]inetd daemon is itself a service that manages on-demand services like the Firebird Classic daemon. Stopping [x]inetd will cause each of the processes it manages to stop also. Starting or restarting it will cause it to resume listening for requests to start any of its managed processes.

If all of the services in the ../rc.d root are safe to shut down, log in as root and stop x[inetd] with the following shell command:

```
#  service xinetd stop
```

or this command, as appropriate:

```
#  service inetd stop
```

If x[inetd] has not been configured to restart automatically when shut down, restart it with this:

```
#  service xinetd restart
```

Stopping a Firebird Process

If you need stop a runaway Firebird process, in Classic server you can do it. Find the offending process by running the **top** command from a shell. This utility displays a list of the most CPU-intensive running processes and updates it constantly. Any fb_inet_server instances with extraordinary resource usage should appear in this list.

Get the process ID (PID) of the offending fb_inet_server process from the leftmost column of the display. You can use this PID with the **kill** command to send a signal to an errant process. For example, for a PID of 12345, you can attempt a controlled shutdown with

```
#  kill 12345
```

If the process remains visible in the top display, you can attempt a forced shutdown with

```
#  kill -9 12345
```

CAUTION   Exercise great care with the **kill** command, especially if you are logged in as root.

Running Firebird Server on Windows

Superserver

The Firebird Superserver executable is fbserver.exe. Although it can run as a stand-alone program, it can be monitored by the Guardian program, fbguard.exe. The Guardian provides a capability that emulates the auto-restart capabilities of Windows services and POSIX services running with the –forever switch. If the fbserver.exe application should terminate abnormally, the Guardian will attempt to restart it. It is recommended that you use the Guardian option on hosts running Windows 95/98 and ME and on the NT/XP platforms when running the server as an application.

On Windows NT and Windows 2000, the Firebird server program can run as a service or as an application. The default installation installs the Firebird server—and the Guardian, if selected—to run automatically as services. Both can be changed to run instead as applications.

On Windows 95/98, ME, and XP Home Edition, Firebird can run only as an application. When Firebird runs as an application, an icon appears in the system tray. Certain administration tasks can be done manually by right-clicking the tray icon.

Running Firebird As a Service on Windows NT, 2000, and XP

Unless you have a special contrary requirement, it is *strongly recommended* that you keep Firebird server running as a service.

> **NOTE** Users migrating from InterBase 6.0 or lower should note that it is not required that Firebird be run as an application on SMP host machines in order to be set for single-CPU affinity. The Firebird service CPU affinity configuration is done in the configuration file. For more information, see the section "The Firebird Configuration File" in Chapter36.

Stopping and Starting the Service Manually

To stop the service manually, open a command shell window and enter the following command:

```
NET STOP FirebirdServer
```

To start or restart the server manually, enter this command:

```
NET START FirebirdServer
```

> **CAUTION** Because the **NET** commands return messages to the command shell, do not try to run them using the Run window directly on the Start menu.

Using the instsvc Utility

The alternative, "native Firebird" way to start and stop the Firebird and Guardian services is to use the instsvc.exe utility, which is located in the /bin folder beneath the Firebird root directory. instsvc.exe is used by the system to install the Firebird service—and Guardian, if selected—when the host server is booted up. Because it was not originally intended for general use by humans, it is a DOS-style command with switches.

NOTE Firebird 1.5 introduced an additional, optional login switch to allow installer scripts to include the capability to make a "real user" the logged-in user for installing the service at boot-up. It is recommended that, for this purpose, the scripts create a "Firebird" user with restricted privileges and set up the service install accordingly. For more information, refer to the section "Platform-Based Protection" in Chapter 33.

Stopping and Restarting the Service Using instsvc

Open a command shell and navigate to the rootdirectory/bin folder. To stop the Firebird service, enter this:

```
C:\Program Files\Firebird\Firebird_1_5\bin> instsvc stop
```

To (re)start the Firebird service, optionally with altered process priority, use this in a single command-line:

```
C:\Program Files\Firebird\Firebird_1_5\bin> instsvc start
    [-boostpriority | -regularpriority]
```

NOTE These commands do not respectively unload and install the service.

Firebird Manager Applets

When Firebird runs as a service, a small degree of administration, including stopping and restarting, can be done through the Firebird Manager Control Panel applet. A bare-bones applet is installed with Firebird. Richer-featured applets, including international language versions, can be downloaded from the Firebird CVS tree on SourceForge or from several Firebird-related websites.

Running Firebird As an Application on Any Windows Platform

If Firebird server is running as an application, you should see an icon in the system tray of the server machine, as shown in Figure 4-1. The appearance of the tray icon depends on whether you are running the server stand-alone or you have the Guardian control-ling its running. It is recommended that you use the Guardian when running Superserver as an application and to *avoid* it when running Classic server.

Figure 4-1. Application tray icon

You will not see a tray icon if the server has not been *started* (in the case of the Superserver) or *initialized* (in the case of the Classic server). Unless you checked the installation option to start the server automatically, you will need to start or initialize it manually.

Starting the Server As an Application Manually

If the Superserver is not running, or the Classic server is not initialized, it can be started or restarted manually by selecting it from the Start ➤ Programs ➤ Firebird menu.

Alternatively, the Guardian or the server can be started from the command prompt. Invoke the command shell window and change to the \bin folder of your Firebird instal-lation. Proceed as follows, according to whether you want to have Guardian protection or to run the server without the capability to restart automatically.

Superserver

The Guardian program is called fbguard.exe on Firebird 1.5 and ibguard.exe on lower versions. Use the following command to start the Guardian:

```
fbguard.exe -a
ibguard.exe -a  /* for v.1.0.x */
```

The Guardian places its icon in the tray and automatically starts the Superserver.

The name of the server program for Superserver is fbserver.exe (ibserver.exe on Firebird 1.0.*x*). To start the Superserver directly yourself, without no Guardian protec-tion, use this command instead:

```
fbserver.exe -a
ibserver.exe -a  /* for v.1.0.x */
```

The server starts and places its own icon in the tray.

Classic Server

NOTE   These notes apply to Firebird 1.5 and later. The Classic server on Windows is not supported in older versions.

An appreciable benefit of running a Classic server on Windows is its ability to use multiple processors, a feature not available to the Superserver with many SMP systems. However, because memory usage on the Classic server is directly related to the number of concurrent attachments, it may be impracticable to deploy at sites where server resource capacity is not adequate to support large numbers of users on the system.

The process that is the "ears" for clients requesting attachment to a Classic server is an initial instance of a program named fb_inet_server.exe. If this initial instance of fb_inet_server is not running, it will not be possible for a client/server connection to be made and you will get the error "Unable to connect to server. Database cannot be found."

When clients attach to the database, one instance of this 1.2MB executable and, if configured, one instance of the Guardian (72KB) runs for each client attachment. One allocation of database cache memory is made to each attachment.

Classic Server and the Guardian

By accident or by design, the Firebird 1.5.0 installer is capable of causing a minor but confusing anomaly. If you don't check the option Use Guardian during installation, the installer will write the Superserver version of the Guardian into your Firebird \bin directory and it will never work with the Classic server. If you do check this option, you will encounter an error message during installation, but the Guardian version that is installed will work with the Classic server. You can test whether you have the right version by attempting to start it. If you see an error dialog box containing the word "fbserver," you will know you did not select Guardian support during installation.

The Guardian is redundant for the Classic server, in any case. You will lose nothing if it turns out that you didn't install it. I recommend ignoring the Guardian for the Classic server.

To start the initializing instance of the Classic server manually as an application, go to a command window, cd to your Firebird\bin directory, and type

```
fb_inet_server.exe -a
```

The server icon should appear in the tray, and your server is ready to start receiving connections.

Alternatively, if you selected the Use Guardian option during installation, you may start the Guardian instead, from the same location:

```
fbguard.exe -c -a
```

In this case, the Guardian's icon appears in the tray, but it cannot be used to deinitialize the server (see the note about the Classic server in the upcoming section titled "Classic Server").

Stopping the Server

Stopping the server is an operation that affects the Superserver and the Classic server differently.

Superserver

Right-click the Firebird Guardian or server icon and choose Shutdown from the context menu. If the Guardian is running, it first stops the server and then shuts down itself. Users currently logged on will lose any uncommitted work.

Classic Server

Under most conditions, it should be unnecessary to "stop" the Classic server. Taking the Shutdown option from the server tray icon will prevent any further connections to the server, but it does not affect any processes that are currently connected.

NOTE   Using the Shutdown option from the Guardian tray icon does nothing.

It is rarely, if ever, necessary to shut down Classic processes manually, since closing a client connection terminates its process instance cleanly and correctly. The only way to stop a Classic process that is running as an application is by applying brute force, via the Task List.

Database Aliasing

Firebird release 1.5 introduced the concept of database aliasing, not just to relieve keyboard-weary developers, but also to improve the portability of applications and to tighten up control of both internal and external database file access.

aliases.conf

With database aliasing came the configuration file aliases.conf. It is located in the root directory of your Firebird server installation and should not be moved from there.

Portability

Before release 1.5, all client applications had to connect to the server using a connection string that included the absolute path to the server. The format of the absolute path varies according to whether the server is running on Windows or a POSIX-compliant platform (Linux, UNIX, etc.) and, with a Windows server, whether the clients are using TCP/IP or NetBEUI for network connectivity.

For example, suppose you have a server named "hotchicken." With the server running on a POSIX-compliant platform, TCP/IP clients would connect to databases using a string of this format:

```
hotchicken:/opt/databases/Employee.fdb
```

With the server running on Windows, TCP/IP clients would connect with a different path format:

```
hotchicken:D:\databases\Employee.fdb
```

Database aliasing makes it so that, for TCP/IP clients, these differences become transparent. The absolute path portion of the connection string goes into the alias file, associated with a simple alias name. For example, in aliases.conf on a Linux server, the example could be stored as

```
db1 = /opt/databases/Employee.fdb
```

On a Windows server installation with TCP/IP clients, it could be

```
db1 = D:\databases\Employee.fdb
```

Regardless of whether the server is POSIX or Windows, the connection string becomes

```
hotchicken:db1
```

It is not quite so neat if you want to make it so your application's connection string to a Windows host is transparent across either a TCP/IP or a NetBEUI connection, however. The UNC notation for a Windows host server to NetBEUI clients means that, although the database alias would be identical, the server portion is not portable:

```
\\hotchicken\db1
```

versus

```
hotchicken:db1
```

Access Control

The principal benefit of the aliasing option is that it can be used, in combination with the firebird.conf parameter DatabaseAccess = NONE, to restrict the server to opening only a specific set of named database files, namely those identified in aliases.conf.

Database aliasing was introduced in Firebird 1.5. To implement it, edit the file aliases.conf in the root directory of your Firebird installation, using a plain text editor such as Notepad (on Windows) or vi (on Linux).

The aliases.conf File Layout

The installed aliases.conf looks similar to this:

```
#
# List of known database aliases
# -----------------------------
#
# Examples:
#
#   dummy = c:\data\dummy.fdb
#
```

As in all of Firebird's configuration files, the # symbols are comment markers. To configure an alias, simply delete the # and change the dummy line to the appropriate database path:

```
# fbdb1 is on a Windows server:
fbdb1 = c:\Firebird15\sample\Employee.fdb
# fbdb2 is on a Linux server
fbdb2 = /opt/databases/killergames.fdb
#
```

Each connection request containing a path using the alias format causes the server to read aliases.conf. You can edit aliases.conf while the server is running. The change will not affect current connections, but future connections will use the new or modified alias.

Connecting Using an Aliased Database Path

For TCP/IP connections, using the previous aliases.conf examples, the modified connection string in your application looks like this:

```
Server_name:aliasname
```

For example:

```
hotchicken:fbdb2
```

For Windows Named Pipes connections, it looks like this:

```
\\hotchicken\fbdb2
```

For a local connection, simply use the alias on its own.

Administering Databases

Many excellent graphical tools—both free and commercial—are available for Firebird database administration. For further information about these offerings, refer to Appendix V. An updated catalog is maintained on the Contributed Downloads pages at http://www.ibphoenix.com.

Firebird comes with a range of command-line tools for server and database administration. In general, they work the same way in both the Linux/UNIX and MS-DOS shells. On Linux/UNIX, case-sensitivity of commands, parameters, and switches is a consideration. On Windows, it is not an issue.

The interactive query tool **isql** is introduced in this chapter and is fully documented in Chapter 37. The other command-line tools are summarized in the following sections.

fbmgr/ibmgr

fbmgr/ibmgr is the command and shell interface to the Superserver daemon process on Linux, for starting and stopping the Firebird Superserver on Linux. The shell script fbmgr (ibmgr in Firebird 1.0.*x*) provides an interface to the server executable, fbmgr.bin (ibmgr.bin in v.1.0.*x*). Details are provided in this chapter.

instsvc.exe

This is the command-line interface to the Superserver service on Windows NT platforms for installing, starting, and stopping the Firebird Superserver on Windows. Details are provided in this chapter.

gbak

This utility is for backing up and restoring databases. Because it operates at the structural and data format levels, **gbak** is the only correct utility to use for safe backups. It also detects corruption, frees disk space left tied up by deletions, resolves uncompleted transactions, and enables you to split databases into multiple files. It is also used to make a transportable backup for restoring your database to a different platform or for upgrading the on-disk structure of databases.

 CAUTION Never use file-copy backup utilities like tar/gzip, WinZip, Microsoft Backup, filesystem copying, or third-party utilities for backing up or transporting a database unless the server is completely shut down and you are certain the database is free of corruption. Databases that are transported as file copies will contain uncollected garbage.

For details about using **gbak**, refer to Chapter 38.

gsec

This user and password maintenance tool is the command-line interface to the security.fdb database, for managing user accounts on the Firebird server. For details about using **gsec**, refer to Chapter 34.

gfix

This is a set of general housekeeping utilities for reconfiguring database properties, doing minor repairs, performing various cleanup tasks, etc. It also provides the means for the administrator to shut down individual databases before a server shutdown. It can be used in conjunction with **gbak** for recovering from some types of database corruption—see the section "Database Repair How-To" in Appendix IV.

For details about using **gfix**, refer to Chapter 39.

gstat

This statistics reporting tool extracts and displays index and data statistics for a database. For details about using **gstat**, refer to the "Optimization Topic" at the end of Chapter 18.

fb_lock_print

This utility retrieves statistics from the lock file that Firebird maintains to control the consistency of database changes by multiple transactions. It can be a useful analysis tool when deadlocks are a problem.

For details about using **fb_lock_print,** refer to Chapter 40.

Introducing isql

The command-line utility **isql** ("isql" stands for Interactive SQL) incorporates tools and techniques for using SQL to maintain database objects, manage transactions, display metadata, and manage database definition scripts. A shell interface is available that is consistent across all platforms. This brief introduction will get you started on the basics of connecting (attaching) to a database and creating your first database.

Starting isql

There are several different ways to connect to a database using **isql**. One way is to start its interactive shell. To begin, in a command shell, go to the /bin directory of your Firebird installation where the **isql** program is installed, and start **isql** as follows. For a POSIX server:

```
[chick@hotchicken]# ./isql <press Return/Enter]
```

For a Windows server:

```
C:\Program Files\Firebird\Firebird_1_5\bin>isql <press Return/Enter]
```

The **isql** shell should now open, displaying this message:

```
Use CONNECT or CREATE DATABASE to specify a database
```

Using isql

Once connected to a database, you can query its data and metadata by entering regular dynamic SQL statements as well as a special subset of statements that work only in the **isql** environment.

The CONNECT Statement

The CONNECT statement is a standard SQL command statement for connecting to a database. Here it is assumed you have not changed the *sysdba* password yet. If you have (this is recommended), then use your own *sysdba* password.

Each of the command-line statements in the following examples is a single statement. For connecting to a Linux/UNIX server:

```
SQL> CONNECT 'hotchicken:/opt/firebird/examples/employee.fdb'
    user 'sysdba' password 'masterkey';
```

For connecting to a Windows server:

```
SQL> CONNECT
    'WINSERVER:C:\Program Files\Firebird\Firebird_1_5\examples\employee.fdb'
    user 'SYSDBA' password 'masterkey';
```

> **NOTE**   On Linux Classic and Windows Superserver it is possible to connect to a
> database locally (e.g., CONNECT '/opt/firebird/examples/employee.fdb' on
> Linux Classic or CONNECT 'c:\Program Files\Firebird\Firebird_1_5\examples\
> employee.fdb' on Windows Superserver).

Make sure you terminate each SQL command with a semicolon (;) character. If you
forget to do so, the next thing you will see is **isql**'s continuation prompt:

```
CON>
```

Whenever you see the continuation prompt, simply type a semicolon and press
Enter/Return. At this point, **isql** will inform you that you are connected:

```
DATABASE 'hotchicken:/opt/firebird/examples/employee.fdb', User: sysdba
SQL>
```

If the server is on Windows, you will see this:

```
DATABASE "WINSERVER:C:\Program
Files\Firebird\Firebird_1_5\examples\employee.fdb", User: sysdba
SQL>
```

Continue to play about with the employee.fdb database. You can use **isql** for
querying data, getting information about the metadata, creating database objects,
running data definition scripts, and much more.

To get back to the command prompt, type

```
SQL> QUIT;
```

Creating a Database Using isql

There is more than one way to create a database using **isql**. Here, you will look at one
simple way to create a database interactively—although, for your serious database

definition work, you should create and maintain your metadata objects using data definition scripts (also known as DDL scripts, SQL scripts, metadata scripts, and schema scripts). This topic is covered in detail in Chapter 14, in the "Schema Scripts" section.

If you are currently logged into a database through the **isql** shell, leave it now with the following command:

```
SQL> QUIT;
```

Next, restart it, without connecting to a database. For a Linux server:

```
[chick@hotchicken]# ./isql
Use CONNECT or CREATE DATABASE to specify a database
```

For a Windows server:

```
C:\Program Files\Firebird\Firebird_1_5\bin>isql
Use CONNECT or CREATE DATABASE to specify a database
```

The CREATE DATABASE Statement

Now, you can create your new database interactively. Let's suppose that you want to create a database named test.fdb on your Windows server and store it in a directory named "data" on your D drive:

```
SQL> CREATE DATABASE 'D:\data\test.fdb' user 'SYSDBA' password 'masterkey';
```

The database will be created and, after a few moments, the SQL prompt will reappear. You are now connected to the new database and can proceed to create some test objects in it.

To verify that there really is a database there, type in this query:

```
SQL> SELECT * FROM RDB$RELATIONS; <press Enter>
```

The screen will fill up with a large amount of data! This query selects all of the rows in the system table where Firebird stores the metadata for tables. An "empty" database is not empty—it contains a database that will become populated with metadata as you begin creating objects in your database.

 TIP   Almost all metadata objects in Firebird databases have identifiers prefixed with "RDB$".

To get back to the command prompt, type

```
SQL> QUIT;
```

For full information about using **isql**, refer to Chapter 37.

Up Next

Part Two deals with client/server architecture. First, Chapter 5 examines the terminology and the variety of models in which client/server networks are implemented. Chapters 6 and 7 take a closer look at Firebird servers and clients, respectively.

Part Two

Client/Server

CHAPTER 5

Introduction to Client/Server Architecture

IN GENERAL, A CLIENT/SERVER SYSTEM IS a pair of software modules designed to communicate with each other across a network using an agreed protocol. The client module makes requests across the network to a listening server program and the server responds to the requests.

For example, an e-mail client dispatches a message across a network to an e-mail server, with a request directing the server to send the message to an address on a server somewhere. If the request complies with the agreed protocol and the destination address is valid, the server responds by repackaging the message and dispatching it, returning an acknowledgment to the client.

The key principle is that the task is split—or *distributed*—between two separate software components that are running independently on two physically separate computers. The model does not even require that the components be running on compatible operating or file systems. The e-mail client could be any e-mail client program that runs on a Windows, Mac, or any other system, and the e-mail server is usually running on a UNIX or Linux system. The client and the server programs are able to cooperate successfully because they have been designed to be *interoperable*.

In a client/server database system, the model is identical. On a host machine in a network, a program is running that manages databases and client connections—a *database server*. It occupies a node that is known to client programs running on machines at other nodes in the network. It listens for requests from the network, from clients that want to attach to a database, and from other clients that are already attached to databases.

As with the e-mail example, the protocol for communication is at two levels. Like the e-mail system, the client/server database system uses a standard network protocol and overlays it with other, purpose-specific protocols. For e-mail, the overlay will be POP3, IMAP, and SMTP; for the database system, it is protocols for database connection, security, database transfer, and language.

Client/Server vs. File-Served Databases

File-sharing systems are another example of client/server systems. File servers and filesystem servers serve client requests for access to files and filesystems, sometimes in very sophisticated ways. NFS and the Windows Named Pipes and NetBEUI services are examples. The file server gives clients access to files that the client machine can read into its own memory and write to, as though it were performing I/O on its own local storage system.

A desktop-based data management system, lacking its own internal provisions to manage I/O requests from a network, is itself a client of the file server. When it receives I/O requests from its own clients, it depends on operating system controls to provide the central locking and queuing system necessary to manage conflicting requests.

These file-served DBMSs are not client/server database systems. Both the client and the DBMS software are clients to a file-sharing server. Although the flow of input and, often, output are to some extent managed by the DBMS program, physical data integrity is under the control of the filesystem services.

In a client/server database relationship, clients—even if located on the same machine as the server—never get closer to the physical data than sending messages to the server about what they want to do. The server processes the messages and executes the requests using its own code and, in advanced systems like Firebird, its own disk management and accounting system. The server program performs all of the physical changes to metadata and data storage structures within a physical on-disk structure that is independent of the host's filesystem-level I/O layer and inaccessible to it.

Characteristics of a Client/Server DBMS

Scalability

The advent of comparatively inexpensive PC networks throughout the 1980s and '90s provoked an increased demand for *scalable* information systems with user-friendly human interfaces. Spreadsheet and desktop database software and graphical interfaces gave non-technical users a taste for the power of desktop computing. Once the sharing of files across networks and among different types of software became standard practice in large enterprises, the customers demanded more. Desktop and LAN-based data management also came within reach of the smallest businesses. Today, it is almost unthinkable to design an enterprise information system under the monolithic model of the mainframe and the text terminal.

Scalability is judged in two dimensions: horizontal and vertical. Horizontal scalability is the capacity of the system to accommodate additional users without impact on the capability of the software or resources. Vertical scalability corresponds with what it takes to reproduce the system on simpler or more complex platforms and hardware configurations in response to variations in load and access requirements. It ranges from the low end—making the system available to users of mobile devices, for example—to a high end that has no conceptual limit.

Interoperability

Client/server architecture for database systems evolved as a response to the fragility, low load capacity, and speed limitations of the file-sharing database model in PC networks as multi-user demand increased. Its emergence coincided with the parallel development of the SQL language. Both were, in part, strategies to neutralize the dependency on mainframe hardware and software that prevailed in the 1980s. True client/server architecture for databases is *heterogeneous* and *interoperable*—it is not restricted to a single hardware platform or a single operating system. This model allows clients and servers to be placed independently on nodes in a network, on hardware and operating systems appropriate to their function. Client applications can communicate simultaneously with multiple servers running on disparate operating systems.

Data Protection

The great flaw with file-served database systems is the vulnerability of data to error, damage, and corruption when it is physically accessible to file-sharing clients and placed under the direct control of humans. In the client/server database model, client applications never touch the physical data. When clients request changes to data state, the server subjects the requests to rigorous validation. It rejects requests that fail to comply with internal rules or metadata rules. When a write request is successful, the actual change of database state is executed entirely by code resident in the server module and within disk structures that are under the server's control.

Distribution of Function

The client/server model allows the areas of work in the system to be distributed appropriately and effectively among hardware and software components. The database server takes care of storing, managing, and retrieving data and, through stored procedures, triggers, or other callable processes, it provides the bulk of data processing capacity for the system. The client process manages the "sharp end" for applications by translating their requests into the communication structures that form the protocols for database and data access.

Applications are the dynamic layer in the model. They provide a potentially infinite variety of interfaces through which humans, machines, and external software processes interact with the client process. For its part, the client module exposes itself to applications via a comprehensive, preferably standardized, language-neutral application programming interface (API).

In some systems, it is possible for applications to act almost entirely as deliverers of information and receptors of input, delegating virtually all data manipulation to the server's processing engine. This is an ideal for client/server systems because it locates CPU-intensive tasks in which processing power is concentrated and leaves applications to utilize the capacity of the workstation to deliver the best-performing user interfaces.

At the other end of the scale are systems in which, through poor design or an impractical concern for interoperability, virtually all data processing is performed on client workstations. Such systems are often characterized by poorly performing user interfaces, delays in synchronizing database state, and unresponsive networks.

Between heaven and hell are well-performing client/server database systems that make good use of processing capacity on servers while retaining some data processing functions on workstations where it is justified to reduce network traffic or improve the flexibility of task implementations.

The Two-Tier Model

Figure 5-1 illustrates the classic two-tier client/server model. The middleware layer, which may or may not be present, represents a driver, such as ODBC, JDBC, or PHP, or a data access component layer that is integrated with the application program code. Other layerings at the client side are possible. Applications may also be written to access the API directly, with no middleware.

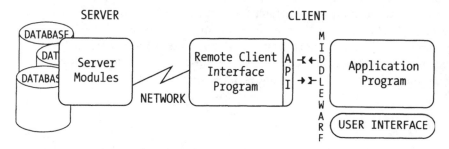

Figure 5-1. The two-tier client/server model

The N-Tier Model

Upscaling and requirements for greater interoperability give rise to a model with more layers, as shown in Figure 5-2. The client interface moves to the center of the model and is joined by one or more application server layers. In this central complex will be located middleware and network modules. The application layer becomes a kind of database superclient—being served by multiple database servers sometimes—and itself becomes a proxy server for database requests from applications. It may be located on the same hardware as the database server, but it could just as well be running on its own hardware.

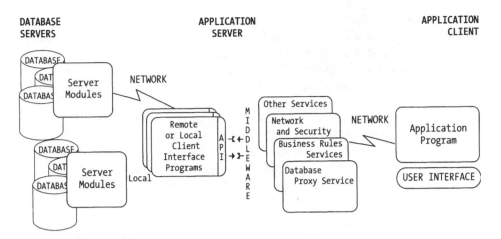

Figure 5-2. The n-tier client/server model

Standardization

Acknowledged standards for hardware and software interoperability and, especially, for metadata and query language are characteristic of client/server database systems. The rise of the relational database systems and the consolidation of SQL standards over two decades have been and remain inseparable. The abstract nature of well-designed relational database systems, along with their relative neutrality with respect to choice of application language for "front-ends," ensure that the RDBMS continues to hold its place as the preferred database architecture for client/server back-ends.

That is not to dismiss other architectures, however. Although, for the time being, object database systems continue to be closely bound to application languages, object-relational (OR) architectures are making significant inroads into the relational tradition. The most recent SQL standards make several provisions for standardizing OR methods and syntaxes. When people start demanding standards for technologies, it is generally a good indication that the technology is expected to be around for a while.

Designing for Client/Server Systems

It is a "given" that client/server systems need to be designed to be used across networks. It often comes as a shock to newcomers to discover that the "lightning-fast" task they used to run through a Paradox or Access application on a desktop takes all day after they convert the database to a client/server RDBMS.

"It's gotta be something wrong with Firebird," they say. "It can't be my application code—because I didn't change a thing! It can't be my database design—because the same design has been perfect for years!" Famous last words.

The focus of application design for clients with desktop-based back-ends is vastly different from that for remote clients and client/servers. The obligatory desktop browsing interface that displays "200,000 records at a glance" has generated a major industry in RAD data-aware grid components. The developer never needed to ponder how many human beings might be capable of browsing 200,000 records in a day, let alone at a glance!

Those RAD grid components that did such a perfect job of presenting unlimited volumes of desktop data in small containers for random browsing are not a friendly interface for remote clients. Behind the screen, the characteristic client looping operation ("start at record 1 and for every record DO repeat") that seemed so perfect for processing data that were memory images of local tables has the remote client users now demanding the developer's head on a plate.

It is very common, indeed, for the design of the database itself to have been influenced more strongly by the perception of the client interface—"I want a table just like this spreadsheet!"—than by the elegant wisdom of a sound abstract data model.

When the interface is physically separated from the data by transaction isolation and a network of busy wire, much pondering is required. There is much more to migrating from the desktop than mere data conversion. The ultimate benefits from a critical design review to users, database integrity, and performance will amply justify the effort.

Abstraction of Stored Data

Even in established client/server environments, all too many poorly performing, corruption-prone systems are found to have been "designed" using reports and spreadsheets as the blueprint for both database and user interface design. In summary, it is all too common for desktop database conversions to come through to Firebird with many of the following client/server-unfriendly "features":

- Widespread redundancy from structures that graduated from spreadsheets to databases with the same data items repeated across many tables

- Hierarchical primary key structures (needed in many desktop database systems to implement dependencies) that interfere with the refined model of foreign key constraints in mature relational database systems

- Large, composite character keys composed of meaningful data

- Lack of normalization, resulting in very large row structures containing many repeating groups and infrequently accessed information

- Large numbers of unnecessary and often overlapping indexes

That is not to say that the old desktop system was no good. If it worked well in its environment, it was good for its purpose. Client/server is simply a very different technology from desktop "databasing." It changes the scale of information management from "file and retrieve" to "store, manage, and manipulate." It shifts the client application away from its desktop role as principal actor to that of message bearer. Effective client interfaces are lightweight and very elegant in the ways they capture what users want and deliver what users need.

Shedding the Spreadsheet Mind-set

A common characteristic of desktop database applications is that they provide an interface of grids: data arranged in rows and columns, with scrollbars and other navigation devices for browsing from the first row in a table to the last. Often, the grids deliver a visual structure that exactly mimics the metadata structure of the source tables. It is a common trap to import such tables into a client/server system and consider that the migration task is done.

Moving these legacy databases to client/servers usually takes more than a data conversion program. Do your conversion and be prepared to treat your new database objects as holding places. Plan to reanalyze and reengineer to abstract this style of database into structures that work well in the new environment. In Firebird it is very easy to create new tables and move data into them. For storage, think thin—using simple keys; abstracting large table structures into families of linked, normalized relations; massaging calendar-style groups of repeating columns into separate tables; eliminating key structures that compound down dependency levels; eliminating duplicated data; and so on.

If you are all at sea about normalization and abstraction, study some of the excellent literature available in books and websites. Get yourself started using a small data model—a subset of five or six of your primary tables is ideal—rather than hitting a 200-table database as if it were a single problem that you have to solve in a day. This way, the conversion becomes a proactive exercise in self-instruction and solving the tough bits quickly becomes more intuitive. For example, learn about stored procedures and triggers and test what you know by writing a data conversion module.

Output-Driven Tables

It is essential to part with the notion that your starting point in designing a relational database is to represent everybody's favorite reports, spreadsheets, and most-used reference displays as tables in the database. These things are output, and output is retrieved by queries and stored procedures.

The Human Interface

Client applications in a system where enterprise information services have a back-end that is a full-blooded DBMS with powerful data-processing capabilities do not transform user input, beyond parsing it at the source and packaging it into prepared containers— the structures for the API transport functions. FOR loops through hundreds or thousands of rows in a client dataset buffer do not have a place in the front-ends of client/server systems.

The application designer needs to think constantly about the cost of redundant throughput. Pulling huge sets across the wire for browsing bottles up the network and makes the user's experience frustrating. The human face of the system has to concentrate on efficient ways to show users what they need to see and to collect input from them—their instructions and any new data that humans want to add. User interface design should focus on quick and intuitive techniques to capture inputs raw and pass them quickly to the server for any cooking that is required.

Client/server developers can learn a lot from studying successful web form interfaces, even if the applications are not being designed for the Internet, because a web browser is the extreme thin client.

Short, quick queries keep users in touch with the state of the database and dilute the load on the network. Effective database clients present drill-down, searching interfaces, rather than table browsers, and limit sets to no more than 200 rows.

The Relational Data Storage Model

Relational databases depend on robust, highly abstract structures to perform effectively and produce predictable, correct results from operations. Complete analysis of the entities and processes in your system is essential, so that you arrive at a logical model that is free of redundancy and represents every relationship.

The Primary Key

During logical analysis, a *primary key* is established for each grouping of data. The logical primary key helps to determine which item or items are capable of identifying a group of related data uniquely. The physical design of tables will reflect the logical groupings and uniqueness characteristics of the data model, although the table structures and key columns actually drafted are often not exactly like the model. For example, in an Employee table, the unique key involves first and last name fields, along with others. Because the composite unique key of the data model involves several large items that are vulnerable to human error, a special column would be added to the table to act as a *surrogate primary key*.

RDBMSs rely on each row having a unique column in each table, in order to target and locate a specific row unambiguously, for matching search conditions and for linking data items or streams.

Relationships

Relationships in the model map to keys in the tables. Theoretically, every relationship in the model would be realized as a pair of linked keys. When keys are linked to one another by *foreign key constraints*, the tables become bound into a network of *dependencies* that reflect how groups of data should interact, regardless of context. Underlying rules in server logic refer to these dependencies in order to protect the referential integrity of the database. The SQL standards formulate rules describing how referential dependencies should work. It is up to the vendor of an individual RDBMS to decide how to implement and enforce the dependencies internally.

In individual server engine implementations, there can be technical reasons for certain key constraints to be left without a formal declaration and implemented in an alternative way. For example, most RDBMSs require mandatory, non-unique indexes on the column elements of foreign keys. Under some data distribution conditions, it may be undesirable to index such columns, if another way can be used to protect the integrity of the relationship concerned.

An RDBMS can also realize relationships that do not involve keys. For example, it can extract sets of data on the basis of comparing values, or expressions involving values, in different columns of a single table or between columns in different tables.

The SQL query language, the structures of stored datasets, and the logical skills of the application developer interact to ensure that client/server traffic is kept down and user requests return results that are precise and appropriate.

"Hands-Off" Data Access

RDBMSs that are designed for client/server use do not make data directly accessible to users. When a user application wants an operation performed on a set of data, it tells the client module what it wants and the client negotiates with the server to satisfy the request. If the request is denied for some reason, it is the client that bears the bad news back to the application.

If the application requests to read a set of data, it is the client that fetches the output from the server's operation and carries it back to the application. The data seen by the application are images of the state of the original data in the database at the moment the conversation between the client and the server began. The images that users see are disconnected—or *isolated*—from the database. The "moment of isolation" may not be the same moment that the request was received by the server. In a client/server environment, where it is assumed that more than one user is reading and writing data, every request has a *context*.

Multiple Users and Concurrency

A DBMS that is designed to allow multiple users to work with images of stored data and to request changes that may impact the work that others are doing needs some way to manage *concurrency*. Concurrency is the set of conditions that is anticipated when two or more users request to change the same row in a table at the same time (i.e., *concurrently*). Mature DBMSs like Firebird implement some kind of scheme whereby each request is made in a concurrency context. The standard SQL term for this concurrency context is *transaction*—not to be confused with the "business transactions" that database applications frequently implement!

Transactions

For the ex-user of desktop databases, the transaction is one of the most confusing abstractions in the client/server and RDBMS environment. With desktop databases and spreadsheet programs, it is taken for granted that, once the user clicks the Save button and the drive light goes out, the operation is done, for better or for worse. It is also a fact that, once the penny drops about transactions, developers tend to spiral rapidly away from the "spreadsheet mind-set" that has preoccupied them during those years when the old database model seemed perfect.

In Firebird, all communications between the client and the server occur during transactions. Even reading a few rows from a table cannot occur if a transaction has not started. A transaction starts when the application asks the client to start it. From the point when the transaction begins until it ends—again, at the request of the application—the client/server conversation is open and the application can ask the client to make requests. During this period, operations to change database state are executed and written to disk. However, they do not change database state and they are reversible.

Transactions end when the application asks the client to request the server to commit all of the work since the transaction began (even if the work was nothing but reads) or, in the event of errors, to roll back the work. The rules of *atomicity* apply: If one pending change of database state fails, requiring it to be rolled back because it cannot be committed, then all pending changes in that transaction are rolled back too. The rollback includes any work that was executed by triggers and stored procedures during the course of the transaction.

 TIP　For the application designer, it is very useful to visualize each unit of database "work" as a task or group of tasks that are accomplished within a transaction context. Transactions are configured in various ways to condition behavior. For example, one isolation level will return a different kind of conflict message than another. The most effective application programs are aware of these variations and are responsive to them, to the extent that the scope of each transaction's context spreads to the application workspace surrounding the actual physical transaction.

Transactions matter so much in a client/server system that this guide devotes three chapters to them, Chapters 25, 26, and 27.

Up Next

Next, in Chapter 6, we examine how the various Firebird server models work and manage systems scaling from the single-user, stand-alone system up to hybrid networks of hundreds of concurrent users.

CHAPTER 6

Firebird Server

THE FIREBIRD SERVER is a program that runs on a host node in a network and listens for clients on a communication port. It serves requests from multiple clients to multiple databases simultaneously. Superserver is a multi-threaded process that starts a new thread for each attached client. In the Classic server model, a new process is started for each connection.

Firebird servers can run on almost any PC hardware and accept client connections from applications running on incompatible systems. Small-footprint server installations can be done on outdated equipment, even old Pentiums running Windows 95 or a minimal Linux. At the other end of the scale, Firebird servers are running in distributed environments, managing databases in the terabyte range.[1]

Of course, it is not realistic to plan an enterprise information system to run on a Windows 95 box. However, it is a simple matter to start with a minimally configured server and scale both vertically and horizontally as need arises. Firebird servers come in two flavors, Superserver and Classic server, to cater to differing user demand. Either can be scaled up or down to handle the simplest to the most complex configurations.

Firebird server software makes efficient use of system resources on the host computer. The Superserver process uses approximately 2MB of memory. Each Superserver client connection is likely to add about 115K to server memory consumption, more or less, according to the characteristics of the client applications and the database design. Each Classic server connection starts its own server process, consuming about 2MB.

Server cache memory consumed depends on configuration and the process model chosen. A common cache configuration for a network of 20 to 40 concurrent users is likely to be 16MB, 32MB, or 64MB for a Superserver, shared as a pool by all connections. Each Classic server is assigned a static cache, with the default being 75K per user. The 1.5 servers will also use RAM to speed up sorting, if it is available. Disk space for a minimal Firebird installation ranges from 9MB to 12MB, depending on platform. Additional disk space is required for temporary storage during operation, and additional memory is needed for database page caching. Both are configurable according to performance demands and the likely volume and type of data to be handled.

---

1 It is difficult to discover what the largest Firebird database running is. Users have reported databases of 900GB "and still growing."

The Role of the Server

The server's jobs include

- Managing database storage and disk space allocation

- Regulating all transactions started by clients, ensuring that each gets and keeps a consistent view of the permanently stored data that it has requested through the client

- Managing commits, data, and housekeeping

- Maintaining locks and statistics for each database

- Handling requests to insert, modify, or delete rows and maintain the currency and obsolescence of record versions

- Maintaining the metadata for each database and servicing client requests to create new databases and database objects, alter structures, and validate and compile stored procedures and triggers

- Servicing client requests for result sets and procedure execution

- Routing messages to clients

- Maintaining cached data to keep frequently used datasets and indexes in the foreground

- Maintaining a separate security database for verifying user access

Operating System Platforms

Firebird server platforms include, but are not limited to,

- Linux, FreeBSD, and several UNIX operating systems.

- Microsoft Windows service-capable platforms NT 4 and Windows 2000 (Server or Workstation editions), XP Professional, and Server 2003. Windows 9*x*, ME, and XP Home can support servers listening on TCP ports but not Named Pipes protocols such as NetBEUI.

- Mac OS X (Darwin).

- Sun Solaris SPARC and Intel.

- HP-UX.

Examples of Topologies

The Firebird server comes in several "models" that provide a variety of scaling options, ranging from the single-user, stand-alone desktop to the server farm.

Two-Tier Client/Server

Figure 6-1 depicts a flexible system, where multiple Firebird servers are running on different operating and filesystem platforms. There is a mix of workstations, each running remote clients appropriate to its local platform. There are gateways to other networks. The Windows server here happens to be serving the day-to-day data processing of the business and is commanding a lot of disk capacity. It is possible for the Windows clients to be conversing with the Windows server using the Named Pipes protocol—commonly called NetBEUI—although it should be avoided in favor of TCP/IP, if possible.

The Linux server may be serving firewalls, gateways, ancillary databases, and other client/server systems, including company e-mail, Internet, and file services, such as NFS and Samba.

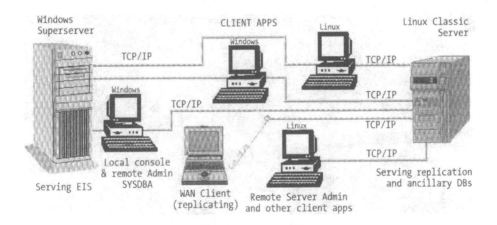

Figure 6-1. Two-tier Firebird client/server topology

Heterogeneous database-serving networks are a common environment for Firebird. In small, single-server networks where an on-site administrator may not be part of the permanent staff, the trend is moving away from running the database server on a single, high-specification, multi-purpose Windows host, toward low-cost, dedicated Linux machines, well-supplied with RAM and fast storage. Maintenance is low, making it realistic to outsource most of the administrative functions. Systems like this have capacity for growth without major upheaval.

The Single-User Model

All Firebird servers can accept local clients. The connection protocols and options vary according to the server model you choose. Single-user installations fall into two categories:

- **Stand-alone server**: In this model, the server is installed and running on the machine. Local attachments are made via network-style protocols, using the normal client libraries.

- **Embedded server**: No server is installed. The client and server programs are rolled into a single dynamic library or shared object that is invoked by the application and starts a single, exclusive server process on attachment. When the application program terminates, the server process is unloaded.

Client/Server

In the stand-alone client/server model, the localized client attaches to the running server using a local protocol. The server can listen for connections from remote clients while a local client is attached. Figure 6-2 illustrates the options.

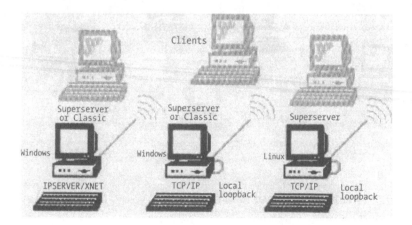

Figure 6-2. Stand-alone servers

The first example shows the *local connect* model. Up to and including Firebird 1.5, the IPSERVER subsystem simulates a network connection within the same block of interprocess communication space. Beyond v.1.5, IPSERVER is deprecated in favor of a local protocol using the faster, more robust, native XNET subsystem. A functionally equivalent local connect is supported for Classic server on POSIX.

In the other two examples, on Windows, Linux, or any other supported platform, the TCP/IP local loopback protocol is used with the Superserver. It is a regular TCP/IP attachment to the special IP address 127.0.0.1, which most TCP/IP subsystems install by default as the named host *localhost*. On Linux, the v.1.5 Classic server can be used in this mode, provided the client library libfbclient.so is used.

Embedded Server

Embedded servers are supported on both Windows and Linux/UNIX platforms, although the implementation models are different. The embedded server library on Windows, which runs an exclusive Superserver process, is called fbembed.dll. On Linux/UNIX, it is the standard mode for a local connection to the Classic server. The library libfbembed.so starts a single Classic server process (fb_inet_server or ib_inet_server) and attaches directly to a database. It is not exclusive—remote clients can connect concurrently, using fbclient.so, another libfbembed.so, or fbclient.dll.

Embedded servers are discussed in more detail in the next chapter.

Firebird Servers in DTP Environments

A detailed discussion of distributed transaction processing (DTP) environments is beyond the scope of this guide. However, suffice it to say that Firebird Superserver or Classic server sits well in a variety of DTP scenarios.

The Open Group defined the X/Open standard for DTP, envisioning three software components in a DTP system. The XA specification defines the interface between two of them: the transaction manager and the resource manager (RM). The system has one RM module for each server, and each RM is required to register with the transaction manager.

Figure 6-3 illustrates how a Firebird server could be slotted into an XA-compliant DTP environment. The database application server module provides a bridge between high-level user applications and the RM, encapsulating the XA connection. The RM performs a clientlike role to negotiate with the database server for access to data storage.

The encapsulation of the XA connection enables the application developer to build and execute SQL statements against the RM. Transaction demarcation—which requires two-phase commit capability on the part of all servers—is moderated by the global transaction processing monitor (TPM). Cross-database transactions under the management of a transaction manager are made through a two-phase commit process. In the first phase, transactions are prepared to commit; in the second, the transaction is either fully committed or rolled back.[2] The TPM will alert the calling module when a transaction does not complete for some reason.

---

2 For information about the two-phase commit, refer to Chapter 25.

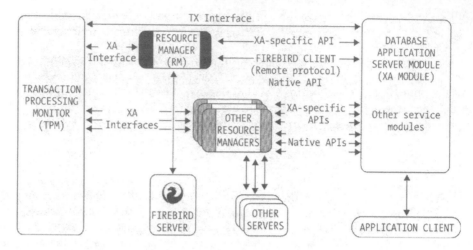

Figure 6-3. Firebird in distributed transaction processing environments

The TPM coordinates distributed transactions in multiple database systems so that, for example, one transaction can involve one or more processes and update one or more databases. It keeps account of which RMs are available and involved in transactions.

The framework supports multiple databases per server and multiple servers, which need not all be Firebird. Up to and including v.1.5, Firebird does not support spanning a single database across multiple servers or serving a database that is not controlled by its host machine.

Transaction Server Frameworks

Microsoft Transaction Server (MTS) with COM+ is one such scenario. MTS/COM+ provides a process-pooling environment that encompasses the deployment and management of business logic components, including auditing control, security, and performance monitoring. One of its most significant features is declarative transaction management. Transactions initiated by MTS/COM+ are controlled by the Microsoft Distributed Transactions Coordinator (DTC), an XA resource manager. The native Firebird interface requires an ODBC or OLE DB provider that supports both Firebird's two-phase commit capability and the MTS/COM+ call context.[3]

Terminal Servers

Firebird is successfully deployed in MTS and IBM Citrix frameworks. The protocol is TCP/IP with attachments connecting to network IP addresses in all cases.

---

3 The shareware IBProvider driver by Dmitry Kovalenko is recommended. For more information, visit http://www.lcpi.lipetsk.ru/prog/eng/.

CAUTION   It is strongly inadvisable to install the terminal server and the database server on the same node. However, in any situation where the application server is running on the same physical node as the database server, the connection must be to the IP address of the node. *TCP/IP local loopback (localhost as server) is not possible.*

Databases

Each database exists in one or more files, which grow dynamically as the need arises. Database files must be stored on disk storage that is under the physical control of the machine on which the server is hosted. Only a server process can perform direct I/O on the database files.

A Firebird database file consists of blocks of storage known as *pages*. The size of one database page can be 1K, 2K, 4K, 8K, or 16K, and it is set at database creation time. It can be changed only by restoring a backed-up database and specifying a new size. Different databases on the same server can have different page sizes.

The server maintains a number of different page types in each database—data pages, several levels of index pages, BLOB pages, inventory pages for various accounting purposes, and so on. It lays out pages in a geography known only to itself and a handful of gifted wizards. Unlike file-served DBMSs, Firebird does not store tables in physical rows and columns but in a continuous stream, on pages. When a page is nearing full capacity and more rows are to be written, the server allocates a new page. Pages from a single table are not stored in any contiguous sequence. In fact, pages belonging to a single table could be distributed across several files on several disks.

Server-Side Programming

Among Firebird's powerful features for dynamic client/server application programming is its capability to compile source code on the server into a binary form for runtime interpretation. Such procedures and functions are executed completely on the server, optionally returning values or datasets to the client application. Firebird provides two styles of server-side programming capability: stored procedures and triggers. In addition, external functions, also known as *user-defined functions*, can be written in a high-level language and made available to the server for use in SQL expressions.

Stored Procedures

Firebird's procedure language (PSQL) implements extensions to its SQL language, providing conditional logic, flow control structures, exception handling (both built-in and user-defined), local variables, an event mechanism, and the capability to accept input arguments of almost any type supported by Firebird. It implements a powerful flow control structure for processing cursors that can output a dataset directly to client memory without the need to create temporary tables. Such procedures are called from the client with a SELECT statement and are known to developers as *selectable stored procedures.*

Stored procedures can embed other stored procedures and can be recursive. All stored procedure execution, including selection of datasets from procedures and embedded calls to other procedures, is under the control of the single transaction that calls it. Accordingly, the work of a stored procedure call will be canceled totally if the client rolls back the transaction.

Triggers

Triggers are special procedures created for specific tables, for automatic execution during the process of posting insertions, updates, and deletions to the server. Any table can have any number of triggers to be executed before or after insertions, updates, and deletions. Execution order is determined by a position parameter in the trigger's declaration. Triggers have some language extensions not available to regular stored procedures or to dynamic SQL, notably the context variables OLD and NEW, which, when prefixed to a column identifier, provide references to the existing and requested new values of the column. Triggers can call stored procedures but not other triggers.

Work performed by triggers will be rolled back if the transaction that prompted them is rolled back.

User-Defined Functions

By design, in order to preserve its small footprint, Firebird comes with a modest arsenal of internally defined (native) data transformation functions. Developers can write their own precise functions in familiar host-language code such as C/C++, Pascal, or Object Pascal to accept arguments and return a single result. Once an external function—UDF—is declared to a database, it becomes available as a valid SQL function to applications, stored procedures, and triggers.

Firebird supplies two libraries of ready-to-use UDFs: ib_udf, available for both Windows and Linux, and fbudf, currently available for Windows and Linux in v.1.5 and Windows only in v.1.0.*x*. Firebird looks for UDFs in libraries stored in the /udf directory of its installation or in other directories configured by the UdfAccess (1.5) or external_function_directory (1.0.*x*) parameter in the Firebird configuration file.

Multi-database Applications

Unlike many relational databases, Firebird applications can be connected to more than one database simultaneously. The Firebird client can open and access any number of databases at the same time. Tables from separate databases cannot be joined to return linked sets, but cursors can be used to combine information.

If consistency across database boundaries is required, Firebird can manage output sets from querying multiple databases inside a single transaction. Firebird implements automatic two-phase commit when data changes occur, to ensure that changes cannot be committed in one database if changes in another database, within the same transaction context, are rolled back or lost through a network failure.

Server Security

For controlling user access to the server, the Firebird server creates and maintains the security database security.fdb (isc4.gdb in v.1.0.*x*). At installation time, this database contains one user: SYSDBA.

- In Windows installations, the SYSDBA password is *masterkey*. It is strongly recommended that you run the program gsec.exe (in the installation /bin directory) immediately after installation and change this password. This is one of the best-known passwords in the database world!

- The version 1.5 Linux RPM installers generate a random password for SYSDBA and update the database to replace *masterkey*. This password is stored in the installation root in a text file named firebird.PASSWORD. If you want to keep using the password, delete this file.

The SYSDBA user has full privileges to every database on the server and, in the current security model, this cannot be changed. The root user on Linux/UNIX gets SYSDBA privileges automatically. The database Owner (the user who created the database) has full privileges to that database. For all other users, access to objects in a database is by "opt-in" SQL privileges *only*.

Database Security

All users except those with full privileges must be granted rights to each object to which they are to be allowed access. The SQL GRANT statement is used for assigning privileges.

Firebird supports the SQL *role*. A role must first be created using a CREATE ROLE statement and committing it. Groups of privileges can be granted to a role, and then the role can be granted to a user. In order to use those privileges, the user must log into the database using *both* the user name and role name.

For more information on database security, refer to Chapter 35.

Up Next

In the next chapter, we take a closer look at the client side of the Firebird client/server relationship: the library of functions that exposes the communication and SQL language layers of the system to applications. If you need some help installing a remote client, turn to the section at the end of the chapter.

CHAPTER 7

Firebird Clients

A CLIENT ON A REMOTE WORKSTATION REQUIRES a client library and an application program that can interact with the application programming interface (API) published in the library.

A client library provides the wire protocol and the transport layer that your client application uses to communicate with the server. The standard shared library for Windows clients is a Windows DLL. For POSIX clients, it is a shared object (.so library). The size of the standard client library is approximately 350K.

Some access layers, such as the Firebird .NET provider and the JayBird Java drivers, replace the standard client library and implement the Firebird wire protocol directly. Another option is an embedded server—a library that merges both a client and a server instance—for single-user use.

A client workstation can also, optionally, have a copy of the current firebird.msg file, or a localized version, to ensure that correct server messages are displayed.

Generally, you would install a copy of the client library on the host server, for use with several of the Firebird command-line utilities and/or any server-based management programs you might use. Many of these utilities can be run remotely, however. A remote system administrator can manage some of the essential services provided by these utilities by accessing them through a host service controller interface.

What Is a Firebird Client?

A *Firebird client* is an application, usually written in a high-level language, that provides end-user access to the features and tools of the Firebird database management system and to data stored in databases. The **isql** interactive SQL utility and the other command-line utilities in your Firebird /bin directory are examples of client applications.

Firebird clients typically reside on remote workstations and connect to a Firebird server running on a host node in a network. Firebird also supports a stand-alone model allowing client applications, the Firebird client library, and the Firebird server to execute on the same physical box.

Client applications need not involve end-users at all. Daemons, scripts, and services can be clients.

Firebird is designed for heterogeneous networks. Clients running under one operating system can access a server on a different operating system platform. A common arrangement is to have Windows 98 or ME and Linux workstations concurrently accessing a departmental server running Windows NT or Windows 2000, or any of several flavors of UNIX or Linux.

In the client/server model, applications never touch the database directly. Any application process converses with the server through the Firebird client library, a copy of which must be installed on each client workstation. The Firebird client library provides the API through which programs make function calls to retrieve, store, and manipulate data and metadata. Generally, other layers are also involved in the interface between the application program and the Firebird client that surface generic or application language–specific mechanisms for populating and calling the API functions.

For Java development, Firebird's stable of supported drivers includes the JayBird JDBC/JCA-compliant Java driver for flexible, platform-independent application interfacing between many open source and commercial Java development systems and Firebird databases. Open source and third-party interfacing components and drivers are available for many other development platforms, including Borland Delphi, Kylix, and C++Builder, commercial and open source C++ variants, Python, PHP, and DBI::Perl. For .NET development, a Firebird .NET provider is under constant development. Contact and other information can be found in Appendix III.

The Firebird Client Library

The Firebird client library comes in a number of variants, all of which surface an identical API to applications, for the server release version to which they apply. Table 7-1 at the end of this chapter shows the names and locations of these libraries.

The client library uses—in most cases—the operating system's client network protocols to communicate with one or more Firebird servers, implementing a special Firebird client/server application-layer interface on top of the network protocol.

Don't Mix and Match Client and Server Versions

It is important not to mismatch the client library release version with the release version of the server. Use a v.1.0 client with a v.1.0 server and a v.1.5 client with a v.1.5 server.

Realize too that the v.1.5 client may or may not be installed to the same location as the 1.0 client. When redeploying with a new version, be sure to study the README and installation documents (located in the Firebird root directory and /doc subdirectory of the server) for items that may outdate the information in this guide.

All client applications and middleware must use the API in some way to access Firebird databases. The Firebird API is backward compatible with the InterBase API. The *InterBase API Guide* (available from Borland) provides reference documentation and guidelines for using the API to develop high-performance applications. More recent enhancements are documented in the Firebird release notes and, to a limited extent, in the header files distributed with Firebird.[1]

Application Development

Once you create and populate a database, its content can be accessed through a client application. Some client applications—such as the Firebird **isql** tool and a range of excellent commercial and open source database administration tools—provide the capability to query data interactively and to create new metadata.

Any application developed as a user interface to one or more Firebird databases will use the SQL query language, both to define the sets of data that can be stored and to pass SQL statements to the server requesting operations on data and metadata.

Firebird implements a set of SQL syntaxes that have a high degree of compliance with the recognized SQL-92 standards. The Firebird API provides complete structures for packaging SQL statements and the associated parameters, and for receiving the results back into applications.

Dynamic Client/Server Applications

Applications often need to cater for runtime SQL statements that are created and modified by applications, or entered by users on an ad hoc basis. Applications typically provide user selection lists, retrieved from database tables, from which users choose search criteria for the data they wish to retrieve and the operations they wish to perform. The program constructs queries from the users' choices and manages the data retrieved.

Client applications use dynamic SQL (DSQL) for submitting queries in runtime. The Firebird client exposes the API as a library of functions that pass the complex record structures that form the data-level protocol for communication between the application and the server.

 NOTE API programming is a big topic, and it is beyond the scope of this guide. However, because dynamic SQL does not surface certain functions in the language, this guide does refer to some API functions to help you understand how driver and component interfaces make them visible to their design environments.

---

1 For a list of links to documentation resources, refer to Appendix XII.

The Firebird Core API

Programming directly with the API is necessary when writing drivers for scripting languages such as PHP and Python and for developing object-oriented data access classes for object-oriented languages like Java, C++, and ObjectPascal. Applications may also be written to call the API functions directly, without the mediation of a driver. These "direct-to-API" applications can be powerful and flexible, with benefits in execution speed, small footprint, and fine control over memory allocation.

Core API Function Categories

API functions, all having names starting with isc_, fall into eight categories:

- Database attach and detach (e.g., isc_attach_database())

- Transaction start, prepare, commit, and rollback (e.g., isc_start_transaction())

- Statement execution calls (e.g., isc_dsql_describe())

- BLOB calls (e.g., isc_blob_info())

- Array calls (e.g., isc_array_get_slice())

- Database security (e.g., isc_add_user())

- Information calls (e.g., isc_database_info())

- Date and integer conversions (e.g., isc_encode_date())

For more information about direct-to-API programming, look for the *API Guide* volume of the InterBase 6 documentation set, published by Borland.

Application Interfaces Using the API

Applications that use drivers for generic interfaces like ODBC or JDBC rely on DSQL statements beneath user interfaces such as query builders and other tools.

With the rise of rapid application development (RAD) tools in the past decade, the encapsulation of the API functions in suites of classes and components presents a variety of attractive application development options for Firebird developers.

Object-Oriented Classes

Object-oriented data access classes and components encapsulate the function calls and structures of the API. All have properties and methods that analyze and parse request statements and manage the results passed back. The richer classes include methods and properties that support Firebird's special capabilities, such as multi-database transactions, array handling, and parameterized statements. Most component suites implement at least one class of container component for buffering one or more rows returned to the client as a result set. Some implement advanced techniques such as scrolling cursors, "live datasets," callbacks, and transaction management.

The JayBird Type 4 ("native") JDBC driver provides a dedicated interface for platform-independent development with Firebird in Java. Several component suites have become established as the interface of choice for developers using Delphi, Kylix, and C++Builder to write front-ends for Firebird databases. The two best-developed are IB Objects and FIBPlus. Several other component suites are available with lighter support for Firebird features. For more details, refer to Appendix III.

Embedded Firebird Applications

Firebird provides for two distinct embedding models: embedded SQL applications and embedded servers.

Embedded SQL Applications

In this model, the application program incorporates both the client/server interface and the end-user application layers in a single executable. SQL statements are entered directly in the source code of a program written in C, C++, or another programming language. The application source code is then passed through **gpre**, the pre-processor, which searches the code for blocks of SQL statements. It substitutes them with source code macro function calls that are functionally equivalent to the dynamic API library functions. When this pre-processed source code is compiled, all of the plumbing for the SQL conversations is compiled directly into the application. These pre-compiled statements are known as *static SQL*.

A special, extra subset of SQL-like source commands is available for this style of application. Known as Embedded SQL (ESQL), it provides a simpler, high-level language "black box" for the programmer, while **gpre** does the grunt work of packaging the more complex language structures of the equivalent API calls. These pre-compiled statements give a slight speed advantage over dynamic SQL, because they avoid the overhead of parsing and interpreting the SQL syntax at runtime.

ESQL language and techniques are not discussed in detail in this guide. The *InterBase Embedded SQL Guide* (available from Borland) provides reference documentation and guidelines for writing embedded Firebird applications.

Embedded Server Applications

In the embedded server model, there is no pre-compilation of SQL conversations. The client and the server are merged into one compact dynamic library for deployment with a stand-alone application. The application loads the library when it starts up, just as a regular Firebird application would load the client library, and the API functions are called directly at runtime. However, no external server need be installed because this client communicates internally with its own instance of a Firebird server process. When the application terminates, it unloads the embedded server along with the client and no server process remains.

Although it does not use or emulate a network connection, the merged client/server accesses the database in the same way as any other dynamic Firebird client application does. Existing application code written for use on a normal client server network works unmodified with the embedded server.

Embedded Server on Windows

The embedded server library fbembed.dll, included in the installer for Firebird 1.5 for Windows, is a variant of Firebird Superserver. If you plan to install it and give it a try, take care to read the special instructions for placement of Firebird's libraries and executables. Updated README files and other notes are usually located in the \doc directory of a regular server installation.

You can install and run embedded server applications on a Windows machine that is also hosting a Firebird Superserver or Classic server, although remote clients cannot attach to a database while it is being accessed by an embedded server application. At release 1.5, when the deprecated IPSERVER protocol was still in use for the client/server communication, it was possible to use the embedded server library as a client to other host servers. In later versions, where the XNET communication protocol replaces IPSERVER, it is not possible.

Firebird 1.0.*x* does not have an embedded server option on Windows.

Embedded Server on Linux/UNIX

Embedded server is the "native" mode of access for a local client to the Firebird Classic server on Linux/UNIX, including Firebird 1.0.*x*. The embedded server library for local access is libfbembed.so in Firebird 1.5 and higher, and libgds.so in Firebird 1.0.*x*.

Like the Windows IPSERVER version, the Linux/UNIX embedded client can do double duty as a remote client to another Firebird Classic server. However, this client is not certain to be thread-safe. For mult-ithreaded applications it should be avoided in favor of the thread-capable remote client, libfbclient.so. In Firebird 1.0.*x*, the full remote client is distributed in the Linux Superserver kit and is confusingly named libgds.so, like the embedded Classic client.

 CAUTION   The Superserver client for Linux is thread-safe for multi-threaded applications, but does not support running multiple threads using the same connection. A separate connection instance must be created for each thread.

The Services API

The opened InterBase 6.0 code—from which Firebird was developed—surfaced for the first time as an API providing a function call interface to certain server activities such as backup/restore, statistics, and user management. Many of these calls provide programming interfaces to the code in the command-line tools. A few lower-level server functions are included as well, some of which overlap functions already available in the core API.

Several shops have developed and distributed *service components*, encapsulating access to the Services API function calls from Delphi, Kylix, and C++Builder development environments. Most are free to download from authors' or Firebird community websites. For more information, refer to Appendix III.

In Firebird 1.0.*x*, the Services API and service components work only with Superserver servers. In Firebird 1.5, some functions—those that call the **gbak** (backup/ restore) and **gfix** (database housekeeping) modules—work with Classic server on Linux as well.

Installing Clients

Installing remote clients is an essential part of deploying your database applications in a client/server network. If you are new to Firebird and client/server networking, it is recommended that you bypass this section until you have had a chance to experiment with clients running locally on the same machine as the server.

Each remote client machine needs to have the client library that matches the release version of the Firebird server. In general, it will be safe to use a client library from a different *build* of a release, as long as the version numbers match. However, when upgrading the server, do read any README documents that come with a point release, to determine whether any "gotchas" exist regarding lower client versions.

Search carefully in the system path of any client workstation on which you want to deploy a Firebird client, to find and, if necessary, disable existing client installations for InterBase or Firebird.

- In Firebird 1.0.*x*, the client libraries share names and default locations with their InterBase counterparts. Although it is possible to set up applications to use a renamed client library, it is strongly recommended to avoid housing Firebird 1.0.*x* and InterBase applications on the same workstation unless you are confident that your applications are positioned to find and load the right library.

- Firebird 1.5 and later versions on Windows can coexist with InterBase or Firebird 1.0.*x* on both the server and client. In Firebird 1.5, it is still a matter of setting things up manually, although with less trouble than 1.0.*x*. In versions later than 1.5, multiple servers and versions can be installed automatically on Windows.

Installing a Linux/UNIX Client

POSIX operating system layouts are famously idiosyncratic. The suggestions presented in this section should be helpful as a guide to installing clients on many common Linux and UNIX flavors, but this is an area where uncertainty is the only certainty!

Log into the client machine as root and look for the client library in the server installation.

- For Firebird 1.0.*x*, its name is libgds.so.0 and its default location is /usr/lib.

- For Firebird 1.5, the binary for remote clients is libfbclient.so.1.5.0, installed by default in /opt/firebird/lib.

CAUTION In the same location, Classic server has another client library named libfbembed.so.1.5 that can be used for embedded applications. Don't use it for remote clients.

Copy the library to /usr/lib on the client and create symbolic links for it, using the following commands:

- For v.1.0.*x*:

```
ln -s /usr/lib/libgds.so.0 /usr/lib/libgds.so
```

- For v.1.5 (two linkings):

```
ln -s /usr/lib/libfbclient.so.1.5 /usr/lib/libfbclient.so.0
ln -s /usr/lib/libfbclient.so.0 /usr/lib/libfbclient.so
```

Create a directory /opt/firebird (/opt/interbase for v.1.0.*x*) on the client for the message file and copy the file from the firebird root on server to the client:

- For v.1.0.*x*, copy interbase.msg to /opt/interbase/.

- For v.1.5 and higher, copy firebird.msg to /opt/firebird/.

In a systemwide default shell profile, or using setenv() from a shell, create the environment variable that will enable the API routines to find the messages:

- For v.1.0.*x*, create the variable INTERBASE and point it to /opt/interbase/.

- For v.1.5 and higher, create the variable FIREBIRD and point it to /opt/firebird/.

Installing a Windows Client

Firebird 1.0.x

On Windows, the InterBase client library was always installed by default in the system directory. By default, it is C:\WINNT\system32 on Windows NT 4 and 2000, C:\Windows\system32 on Windows XP and Server 2003, and C:\Windows or C:\Windows\system[2] on Windows 9*x* and ME. Firebird 1.0.*x* followed suit as a temporary measure, retaining the old names and locations. The library is gds32.dll.

Using the Firebird Installer

The simplest way to install a Firebird 1.0.*x* client is to copy the Firebird installer to a CD-ROM or flash drive and run it on the client machine, selecting a client-only install option when prompted by the installer dialog box. You can choose whether to install the client with or without the command-line tools. Most clients will not need the tools and it is not recommended to install them on client workstations that do not need admin access to the server.

The installer will create the default root directory in C:\Program Files\Firebird, which you can vary when it prompts for a location. Here, it will write the message file, interbase.msg, and, if you selected to install the tools, it will create a \bin directory beneath the root and install the tools there.

It writes gds32.dll to the system directory and, if the Microsoft C runtime library is old or absent, it will write msvcrt.dll there also.

Finally, it runs a program named instreg.exe to install the Registry key. If you chose the default installation directory, the key is HKLM\Software\Borland\InterBase. If any running DLLs were overwritten during the installation, you will be prompted to reboot the machine.

Installing a Client Manually

Installing a client manually requires all of the preceding steps. You will need to copy the files gds32.dll, interbase.msg, and instreg.exe to a diskette or flash drive. Also copy msvcrt.dll from the system directory if you have clients where it is not installed.

---

2 On these non-service-capable platforms, the location seems to vary. If a previous Firebird or InterBase client has been installed, you should check both.

Once you have created your Firebird root directory, copy interbase.msg there. Next, run instreg.exe from the diskette, in a command window:

```
A:\> instreg.exe 'C:\Program Files\Firebird'
```

If you placed your Firebird root directory somewhere different, use that path as the root directory argument.

Copy gds32.dll and, if needed, msvcrt.dll to the system directory.

NOTE msvcrt.dll is the runtime library for many programs compiled with the Windows C compiler. gds32.dll is the name of the client library for InterBase servers as well as Firebird 1.0.x. In the event that you cannot copy one or both of the libraries because another program has loaded them, it will be necessary to stop those programs and try again. If it is still not possible to overwrite them because the applications failed to unload them, restart the computer in "safe" mode in order to do this step.

Firebird 1.5 and Higher

In Firebird versions from 1.5 onward, client installations come with a number of options aimed at avoiding "DLL hell" in the Windows system directory. Until existing third-party tools, drivers, and component sets catch up with the changes, Firebird 1.5 on Windows creates its own special brand of DLL hell. The default client install, using the installer, will almost certainly be incompatible with software built using Borland RAD products such as Delphi or C++Builder.

Read through this section carefully before you start, to work out what you need for the particular client environment for which you are doing the installation. You can go back later and adapt the installation manually.

Using the Firebird Installer

Although there are other options, the recommended way to install a client is to use the Firebird 1.5 installer program.

If you use the installer, the first choice you need to make is where to locate the root of the client installation (see Figure 7-1). It is recommended that you take the default (C:\Program Files\Firebird\Firebird_1_5), since it will simplify future upgrades. However, you can specify a custom location if necessary.

Although you are not going to install the server, allowing the installer to install to a root location will ensure that optional pieces, including the Registry key, that are needed by some software products are available on the client machine. If you are installing the command-line tools, a properly installed root location is essential. Later, you can customize the setup manually, if necessary.

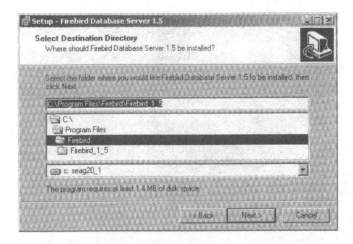

Figure 7-1. Choosing a location for the installation root

The next decision is to choose your install option. You can choose whether to install the client with or without the command-line tools, as shown in Figure 7-2.

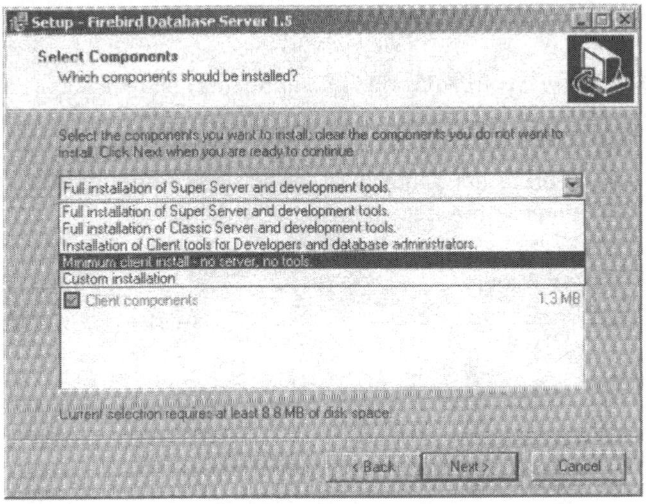

Figure 7-2. Selecting a client-only install

Most clients will not need the tools and it is not recommended to install them on client workstations that do not need admin access to the server. For a minimal installation, select the option "Minimum client install - no server, no tools" and click Next.

The selection you make on the next dialog box (see Figure 7-3) is especially important if you are using third-party software on the client.

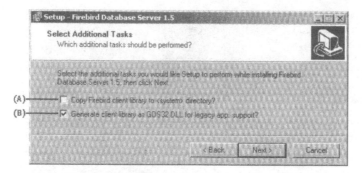

Figure 7-3. Selecting client "version" and location

Previously, installers would install the old client library, gds32.dll, in the system directory, along with the C language runtime, msvcrt.dll, if it was not present.

For version 1.5, by default the installer installs all DLLs—the new client, fbclient.dll, and (if required) the C runtime and the C++ runtime, msvcp60.dll—into the /bin directory beneath the Firebird root.

- **(A) Relocation of the client library**: If you need compatibility with software that expects to find the client library in the system directory, check this box. The library will be copied to the system directory as fbclient.dll.

- **(B) Name of the client library**: If your software or components need the client library to be named gds32.dll, check this box. The installer will generate a special copy of fbclient.dll named gds32.dll and set an internal version string that is compatible with the Borland proprietary InterBase drivers and components. The location of this file depends on the state of the first check box (A).

Click Next to complete the installation.

Installing a Client Manually

Installing a client manually requires all of the steps that would be performed by the installer. You will need to copy the following files from your server installation to a diskette or flash drive:

- %system%\gds32.dll (C:\WINNT\system32 or C:\Windows)

- firebird.msg

- bin\fbclient.dll

- bin\msvcrt.dll (if needed)

- bin\msvcp60.dll (if needed)

- bin\instreg.exe

- bin\instclient.exe

- bin\fbclient.local

- bin\msvcrt.local

- bin\msvcp60.local

On the client, follow these steps:

1. Create a Firebird root directory and copy firebird.msg there.

2. Beneath the new directory, create a directory named **bin**.

3. Copy the files from the bin directory on the diskette to this new bin directory.

4. Run instreg.exe from the new \bin directory, in a command window. It is essential that you run this program from the \bin directory of the Firebird root, where instreg.exe is located. For example, if your Firebird root directory is C:\Firebird_Client:

   ```
   C:\Firebird_Client\bin> instreg.exe
   ```

5. If you have an application that needs a client library named gds32.dll, you will need to run the program instclient.exe. Instructions are in the next section.

Running instclient.exe

The program instclient.exe can be run when you need a client version that can be accessed and used by existing software, drivers, or components that expect the client to be named gds32.dll and/or to be located in the Windows system path. It is a command-line program, located in the \bin directory beneath the Firebird root of your server installation. If necessary, copy this file to the equivalent location on the client machine.

Installing the Client in the System Directory

Open a command window and cd to the root\bin location. The syntax for installing the client is

```
instclient.exe {i[nstall]} [-f[orce]] {fbclient | gds32}
```

The parameters **i** (or **install**) and either **fbclient** or **gds32** are required.

If the program finds there is already a file in the system directory with the name of the file you are trying to install (fbclient.dll or gds32.dll), it will not proceed. To have the program write the file even if it finds a pre-existing copy, use the **–f** (or **–force**) switch.

Your operating system may require you to reboot the machine to complete the installation.

 CAUTION If you choose to force the installation, you risk breaking a client that is already installed for use with other software that is designed to connect to a Firebird 1.0 or InterBase server.

Querying the Installed Client

The instclient.exe program can be used for querying about Firebird 1.5 clients running on the machine. The syntax for querying about the client is

```
instclient.exe {q[uery] fbclient | gds32}
```

Figure 7-4 shows the information that is returned.

Figure 7-4. Querying with instclient.exe

Using instclient.exe to Uninstall a v.1.5 Client

To remove a Firebird 1.5 client that is installed in the system directory, use the following syntax:

```
instclient.exe {r[emove] fbclient | gds32}
```

Summary of Client Library Names and Locations

Table 7-1 presents a summary of client library names and default locations of Firebird clients.

Table 7-1. Names and Default Locations of Firebird Clients

VERSION AND PACKAGE	CLIENT OS	LIBRARY NAME	DEFAULT LOCATION OF CLIENT	CONNECT TO
Firebird 1.0.*x* Classic server	Linux/UNIX	libgds.so.0, symlinked as libgds.so	/usr/lib	Classic server 1.0 only
Firebird 1.0 Superserver for Windows	Windows NT/2000	gds32.dll	C:\WINNT\ system32	Any 1.0 server
	Windows XP/Server 2003	gds32.dll	C:\Windows\ system32	Ditto
	Windows 9*x*/ME	gds32.dll	C:\Windows	Ditto
Firebird 1.0.*x* Superserver for Linux	Linux/UNIX	libgds.so.0, symlinked as libgds.so. Note that this library is different from the libgds.so client in Classic server.	/usr/lib	Any 1.0 server except Classic
Firebird 1.5 Classic server for Linux	Linux/UNIX	libfbembed.so.0 or libfbclient.so.0, symlinked as libfbembed.so or libfbclient.so, respectively[3]	/usr/lib	Classic server 1.5 for Linux only, non-threaded applications only; local connect possible
Firebird 1.5 Superserver for Linux	Linux/UNIX	libfbclient.so.0 symlinked as libfbclient.so	/usr/lib	Any 1.5 server
Firebird 1.5 Classic and Superserver for Windows	Windows NT/2000	Native: fbclient.dll	Firebird root\bin	Any 1.5 server
		Compatibility: fbclient.dll or gds32.dll built by instclient.exe	C:\WINNT\ system32	Ditto

3   The embedded model on Linux is not parallel to that on Windows. Like the Windows model, the libfbembed.so client incorporates a "direct-connect" server instance. On Linux, the same library can instantiate an embedded server instance on a network server. Nevertheless, libfbclient.so is strongly recommended as the client to use if the application involves threading.

continued

Table 7-1. Names and Default Locations of Firebird Clients (continued)

VERSION AND PACKAGE	CLIENT OS	LIBRARY NAME	DEFAULT LOCATION OF CLIENT	CONNECT TO
	Windows XP/Server 2003	Native: As above Compatibility:	C:\Windows\ system32	Any 1.5 server
	Windows 9x/ME	Native: fbclient.dll	Firebird root\bin	Ditto
		Compatibility: fbclient.dll or gds32.dll built by instclient.exe	C:\Windows or C:\Windows\ system[4]	Ditto
Firebird 1.5 Embedded Server	All Windows embedded clients	fbembed.dll	Root directory of application executable	Ditto

4   The official installer and instclient.exe treat C:\Windows\system as the "system directory" on these platforms. Some "unofficial" installers follow the convention established by Borland for InterBase, which was followed for some Firebird 1.0 installers, of treating C:\Windows as the system directory. Both locations should be checked if you need to search for an installed client.

Up Next

In Part Three, we move on to a detailed examination of the data types supported by the Firebird SQL language. The next chapter introduces the data types and some of the special issues and behaviors that you need to understand when preparing to define, store, and work with SQL data. It ends with a special discussion that will be of interest if you are preparing for the migration of a legacy database to Firebird.

Part Three

Firebird Data Types and Domains

About Firebird Data Types

DATA TYPE **IS THE PRIMARY ATTRIBUTE** that must be defined for each column in a Firebird table. It establishes and constrains the characteristics of the set of data that the column can store and the operations that can be performed on the data. It also determines how much space each data item occupies on the disk. Choosing an optimum size for data values is an important consideration for network traffic, disk economy, and index size.

Firebird supports most SQL data types. In addition, it supports dynamically sizeable typed and untyped binary large objects (BLOBs) and multi-dimensional, homogeneous arrays of most data types.

Where to Specify Data Types

A data type is defined for data items in the following situations:

- Specifying column definitions in a CREATE TABLE specification

- Creating a reusable global column template using CREATE DOMAIN

- Modifying a global column template using ALTER DOMAIN

- Adding a new column to a table or altering a column using ALTER TABLE

- Declaring arguments and local variables in stored procedures and triggers

- Declaring arguments and return values for external (user-defined) functions

Supported Data Types

Number types (discussed further in Chapter 9) are

- BIGINT, INTEGER, and SMALLINT

- NUMERIC and DECIMAL

- FLOAT and DOUBLE PRECISION

Date and time types (discussed further in Chapter 10) are

• DATE, TIME, and TIMESTAMP

Character types (discussed further in Chapter 11) are

• CHARACTER, VARYING CHARACTER, and NATIONAL CHARACTER

BLOB and ARRAY types (discussed further in Chapter 12) are

• BLOB, typed and untyped

• ARRAY

Booleans

Up to and including release 1.5, Firebird does not provide a Boolean ("logical") type. The usual practice is to define a one-character or SMALLINT *domain* for generic use whenever the design calls for a Boolean.

For tips about defining Boolean domains, refer to Chapter 13.

SQL "Dialects"

Firebird supports three SQL "dialects" that have no practical use except to facilitate conversion of an InterBase v.5 database to Firebird. Firebird's "native" dialect is currently known as *dialect 3*. By default, a Firebird server creates databases in this native dialect. If your Firebird experience brings with it no cargo of existing assumptions nor any legacy databases that you want to upgrade to Firebird, you can safely "go native" and ignore all of the notes and warnings about dialect 1.

If you are an ex-InterBase user, or you have used outdated migration tools to convert another RDBMS to InterBase, then SQL dialects will be an issue for you in one or several respects.

As you work your way through this book, issues that are affected by SQL dialect are annotated appropriately for your attention. However, some of the more serious effects arise from the dialectal differences between data types. For this reason, the question of dialects gets space at the end of this chapter as a special Migration Topic titled "SQL Dialects."

Optional SQL-92 Delimited Identifiers

In dialect 3 databases, Firebird supports the ANSI SQL convention for optionally delimiting identifiers. To use reserved words, case-sensitive strings, or embedded spaces in an object name, enclose the name in double quotes. It is then a *delimited identifier*. Delimited identifiers must always be referenced in double quotes.

For more details, follow up this topic in Chapter 14, in the section "Database Object Naming Conventions and Constraints." For more information about naming database objects with CREATE or DECLARE statements, refer to Part Four of this book. Refer to Appendix XI for the list of keywords that are reserved for SQL.

Context Variables

Firebird makes available a number of system-maintained variable values in the context of the current client connection and its activity. These *context variables* are available for use in SQL, including the trigger and stored procedure language, PSQL. Some are available only in PSQL and most are available only in dialect 3 databases. Table 8-1 outlines Firebird's context variables.

Table 8-1. List of Context Variables

CONTEXT VARIABLE	DATA TYPE	DESCRIPTION	AVAILABILITY
CURRENT_CONNECTION	INTEGER	System ID of the connection that is making this query.	Firebird 1.5 onward, DSQL and PSQL
CURRENT_DATE	DATE	Current date on the server's clock.	Firebird 1.0 onward, all SQL environments
CURRENT_ROLE	VARCHAR(31)	The ROLE name under which the CURRENT_USER is logged in. Returns an empty string if the current login isn't using a role.	Firebird 1.0 onward, all SQL environments
CURRENT_TIME	TIME	Current time on the server's clock, expressed as seconds since midnight.	Firebird 1.0 onward, all SQL environments
CURRENT_TIMESTAMP	TIMESTAMP	Current date and time on the server's clock to the nearest second.	Firebird 1.0 onward, all SQL environments
CURRENT_TRANSACTION	INTEGER	System ID of the transaction in which this query is being requested.	Firebird 1.5 onward, DSQL and PSQL
CURRENT_USER	VARCHAR(128)	User name that is communicating through this instance of the client library.	Firebird 1.0 onward, all SQL environments
ROW_COUNT	INTEGER	Count of rows changed/deleted/added by a DML statement, available when the operation is complete.	Firebird 1.5 onward, stored procedure language (PSQL) only

continued

Table 8-1. List of Context Variables (continued)

CONTEXT VARIABLE	DATA TYPE	DESCRIPTION	AVAILABILITY
UPDATING	BOOLEAN	Returns true if an update statement is executing.	Firebird 1.5 onward, trigger dialect of PSQL only
INSERTING	BOOLEAN	Returns true if an insert statement is executing.	Firebird 1.5 onward, trigger dialect of PSQL only
DELETING	BOOLEAN	Returns true if a delete statement is executing.	Firebird 1.5 onward, trigger dialect of PSQL only
SQLCODE	INTEGER	Returns the SQLCODE inside a WHEN exception block. For usage, see Chapter 32.	Firebird 1.5 onward, procedure language (PSQL) only
GDSCODE	INTEGER	Returns the GDSCODE inside a WHEN exception block. For usage, see Chapter 32.	Firebird 1.5 onward, procedure language (PSQL) only
USER	VARCHAR(128)	User name that is communicating through this instance of the client library.	InterBase ancestors, all Firebird versions, all SQL environments, available in dialect 1

Points to Note

Remember that these are transient values.

- CURRENT_CONNECTION and CURRENT_TRANSACTION have no meaning outside the current connection and transaction contexts, respectively. Do not treat them as perpetually unique, since the Firebird engine stores these identifiers on the database header page. After a restore, their series will be reinitialized to zero.

- CURRENT_TIMESTAMP records the server time at the start of the operation and should not be relied upon as the sole sequencer of a batch of rows inserted or updated by a single statement.

- Even though CURRENT_TIME is stored as the time elapsed since midnight on the server's clock, it is a TIME value, not an interval of time. To achieve a time interval, use timestamps for start and finish times and subtract the start time from the finish time. The result will be a *time interval in days*.

- The date/time context variables are based on server time, which may be different from the internal clock time on clients.

Examples Using Context Variables

This statement returns the server time at the moment the server serves the request of the Firebird client:

```
SELECT CURRENT_TIME AS TIME_FINISHED FROM RDB$DATABASE;
```

In this insert statement, the current transaction ID, the current server timestamp, and the system user name will be written to a table:

```
INSERT INTO TRANSACTIONLOG (TRANS_ID, USERNAME, DATESTAMP)
VALUES (
CURRENT_TRANSACTION,
CURRENT_USER,
CURRENT_TIMESTAMP);
```

Pre-Defined Date Literals

A number of *date literals*, single-quoted strings that Firebird SQL will accept in lieu of certain special dates, are available to both dialect 1 and dialect 3 databases. In Legacy SQL, the strings could be used directly; in both dialects of Firebird, they must cast to type in most situations. Table 8-2 shows the usage in each dialect.

Table 8-2. List of Predefined Date Literals

DATE LITERAL	DATE SUBSTITUTED	DATA TYPE DIALECT 1	DATA TYPE DIALECT 3
'NOW'	Current date and time	DATE (equivalent to dialect 3 TIMESTAMP)	TIMESTAMP
'TODAY'	Current date	DATE with zero time part	DATE (date-only type)
'YESTERDAY'	Current date – 1	DATE with zero time part	DATE
'TOMORROW'	Current date + 1	DATE with zero time part	DATE

NOTE   The dialect 1 DATE type is equivalent to a dialect 3 TIMESTAMP. In dialect 3, the DATE type is date only. Dialect 1 has no equivalent type. Any attempt to use date literal in an expression without casting will cause an exeption.

Examples Using Pre-Defined Date Literals

In Legacy SQL, this statement returns exact server time:

```
SELECT 'NOW' AS TIME_FINISHED FROM RDB$DATABASE;
```

In Firebird, the date literal must be cast as a TIMESTAMP type:

```
SELECT CAST('NOW' AS TIMESTAMP) AS TIME_FINISHED FROM RDB$DATABASE;
```

Firebird still allows date literals to be used alone as the argument in UPDATE and INSERT statements and search criteria. This UPDATE statement sets a date column to server date plus one day:

```
UPDATE TABLE_A
SET UPDATE_DATE = 'TOMORROW'
WHERE KEY_ID = 144;
```

In Firebird, using date literals in expressions will cause an exeption. A clause such as <inline code> SET UPDATE_DATE = 'TODAY' + 1</inline code> will not work. Such expressions must be explicitly cast:

```
UPDATE TABLE_A
SET UPDATE_DATE = CAST('TODAY' AS DATE) + 1
WHERE KEY_ID = 144;
```

Columns

Data in a relational database system such as Firebird is arranged logically in sets consisting of rows and columns. A column holds one piece of data with defining attributes that are identical for every row in the set. A column definition has two required attributes: an identifier (or column name) and a data type. Certain other attributes can be included in a column definition, such as a CHARACTER SET and constraints like NOT NULL and UNIQUE.

Sets that are defined for storing data are known as *tables*. The row structure of a table is defined by declaring a table identifier and listing the column identifiers, their data types, and any other attributes needed, on a column-by-column basis.

A simple example of a table definition is

```
CREATE TABLE SIMPLE (
  COLUMN1 INTEGER,
  COLUMN2 CHAR(3),
  COLUMN3 DATE);
```

For full details about defining tables and columns, refer to Chapter 16.

Domains

In Firebird you can pre-package a column definition, with a data type and a "template set" of attributes, as a *domain*. Once a domain is defined and committed, it is available for use in any table in your database, just as if it were a data type in its own right.

> **NOTE**   Some restrictions do exist on where domains can be used. Notably, a domain cannot be used in the declarations of local variables and input and output arguments in PSQL (procedure language) modules.

Columns based on a domain definition inherit all attributes of the domain: its data type, along with any number of optional, extra attributes, including a default value for inserts, validation constraints, character set, and collation order.

Any attribute except the data type can be overridden when the domain is used to define a column in a table definition, by replacing an attribute with a different, compatible attribute or by adding an attribute. Thus, for example, it is possible to define a domain with a complex set of attributes, not including NOT NULL, which can be made nullable in some usages and NOT NULL in others.

For full details about defining, maintaining, and using domains, refer to Chapter 13.

Converting Data Types

Normally, you must use compatible data types to perform arithmetic operations or to compare data in search conditions. If you need to perform operations on mixed data types, or if your programming language uses a data type that is not supported by Firebird, then data type conversions must be performed before the database operation can proceed.

Implicit Type Conversion

Dialects 1 and 3 behave differently with regard to implicit type conversion. This will be an issue if you wish to convert an existing database to dialect 3 and update its supporting applications.

- In dialect 1, for some expressions, Firebird automatically converts the data to an equivalent data type (an implicit type conversion). The CAST() function can also be used, although it is optional in most cases.

- In dialect 3, the CAST() function is required in search conditions to explicitly translate one data type into another for comparison purposes.

For example, comparing a DATE or TIMESTAMP column to '12/31/2003' in dialect 1 causes the string literal '12/31/2003' to be converted implicitly to a DATE entity.

```
SELECT * FROM TABLE_A
WHERE START_DATE < '12/31/2003';
```

In dialect 3, using the explicit cast:

```
SELECT * FROM TABLE_A
WHERE START_DATE < CAST('12/31/2003' AS DATE);
```

An expression mixing integers with string digits in dialect 1 implicitly converts the string to an integer if it can. In the following operation

```
3 + '1'
```

Dialect 1 automatically converts the character "1" to a SmallInt for the addition, whereas Firebird dialect 3 returns an error. It requires an explicit type conversion:

```
3 + CAST('1' AS SMALLINT)
```

Both dialects will return an error on the next statement, because Firebird cannot convert the character "a" to an integer:

```
3 + 'a'
```

Explicit Type Conversion: CAST()

When Firebird cannot do an implicit type conversion, you must perform an explicit type conversion using the CAST() function. Use CAST() to convert one data type to another inside a SELECT statement, typically in the WHERE clause, to compare different data types. The syntax is

```
CAST (value | NULL AS data type)
```

You can use CAST() to compare columns with different data types in the same table or across tables. For example, you can cast between properly formed strings and date/time types, and between various number types. For detailed information about casting between specific types, refer to the chapter in this part of the guide that deals with the data types in question.

Changing Column and Domain Definitions

In both dialects, you can change the data type of a column in tables and domains. If you are migrating a database from another RDBMS, this can be useful. Certain restrictions apply when altering the data type:

- Firebird does not allow the data type of a column or domain to be altered in a way that might result in data loss. For example, the number of characters in a column is not allowed to be smaller than the largest value in the column.

- Converting a numeric data type to a character type requires a minimum length for the character type, as listed in Table 8-3.

Table 8-3. Minimum Character Lengths for Numeric Conversions

DATA TYPE	MINIMUM LENGTH FOR CHARACTER TYPE
BigInt	19 (or 20 for signed numbers)
Decimal	20
Double	22
Float	13
Integer	10 (11 for signed numbers)
Numeric	20 (or 21 for signed numbers)
SmallInt	6

Altering the Data Type of a Column

Use the ALTER COLUMN clause of the ALTER TABLE statement, for example:

```
ALTER TABLE table1 ALTER COLUMN field1 TYPE char(20);
```

For more information about altering columns in a table, refer to the section "Altering Tables" in Chapter 16.

Altering the Data Type of a Domain

Use the TYPE clauselet of the ALTER DOMAIN statement to change the data type of a domain, for example:

```
ALTER DOMAIN MyDomain TYPE VARCHAR(40);
```

Figure 8-1 shows the data type conversions that are allowed. For more information about altering the attributes of a domain, refer to Chapter 13.

Convert FROM / TO →	Array	BigInt	Blob	Char	Date	Decimal	Double	Float	Integer	Numeric	Timestamp	Time	Smallint	Varchar
Array														
BigInt		●		●		●	●							●
Blob														
Char				●										●
Date				●	●									
Decimal				●		●				●				●
Double				●			●	●						●
Float				●			●	●						●
Integer	●			●		●				●				●
Numeric				●						●				●
Timestamp				●	●						●	●		
Time				●										
Smallint			●	●		●	●	●	●	●			●	●
Varchar				●										●

Figure 8-1. Allowed data type conversions using ALTER COLUMN and ALTER DOMAIN

Keywords Used for Specifying Data Type

The keywords for specifying the data type in DDL statements are provided here for quick reference. For exact syntax, refer to the relevant chapter in this part of the guide for the data type in question and to Chapters 13 and 16.

```
{SMALLINT | INTEGER | FLOAT | DOUBLE PRECISION} [<array_dim>]
| {DATE | TIME | TIMESTAMP} [<array_dim>]
|{DECIMAL |NUMERIC} [ (precision [, scale])] [<array_dim>]
| {CHAR | CHARACTER | CHARACTER VARYING | VARCHAR} [(int)]
[<array_dim>] [CHARACTER SET charname]
| {NCHAR | NATIONAL CHARACTER | NATIONAL CHAR}
[VARYING] [(int)] [<array_dim>]
| BLOB [SUB_TYPE int | subtype_name} ] [SEGMENT SIZE int]
[CHARACTER SET charname]
| BLOB [(seglen [, subtype])]
```

Special Migration Topic: SQL Dialects

If you are an ex-InterBase user, or you have used outdated migration tools to convert another RDBMS to InterBase, then SQL dialects are likely to affect several aspects of the new life of your databases and applications under a Firebird server.

On-Disk Structure and Dialect

On-disk structure (*ODS*) identifies a database with respect to the major release version of a Firebird or an InterBase server that created or restored it. The ODS of a database affects its compatibility with server versions. A file suitable for upgrading the ODS can be created by backing up the database under the server version that created it, using the **gbak** utility for that old version, with the *–t[ransportable]* switch. When that backup file is restored, using the **gbak** version distributed with the target server, the restored database will have the new ODS. It is not possible to "downgrade" the ODS of any database.

Usage of **gbak** is discussed in detail in Chapter 38.

ODS Upgrade Does Not Change the Dialect

Upgrading the ODS does not make any difference to the SQL dialect of the database: a dialect 1 database will remain a dialect 1 database.

Firebird Databases

Firebird 1.0.*x* has an ODS identified as ODS-10. Firebird 1.5 has ODS-10.1. To make an ODS-10 database created in Firebird 1.0.*x* into ODS-10.1, you merely have to back it up and restore it using the Firebird 1.5 **gbak**. By default, Firebird servers 1.0.3+ and 1.5 create dialect 3 databases. To check your databases, see the section "How to Determine Dialect" later in this chapter.

InterBase 6.0.x Databases

The "open source" InterBase 6.0.*x* versions have ODS-10. However, to upgrade IB 6.0.*x* to any Firebird version, it is advisable to use the InterBase 6.0 version of **gbak**, using the –t[ransportable] switch. The backup file should then be restored using the **gbak** appropriate to the target Firebird server version.

If the IB 6.0 database was created under default settings, it is probably dialect 1. See the section "How to Determine Dialect" later in this chapter.

InterBase 5.x Databases

InterBase 5 databases have ODS-9 or "9-point-something." Firebird servers can open them, read them as dialect 1 databases, and update them without altering their on-disk structure, enabling them to be returned to an IB 5.*x* server environment at any time.

NOTE A Firebird server cannot create ODS-9 databases. Dialect 1 databases created by a Firebird server cannot be read by an InterBase 5.x server.

There is no such thing as an ODS-9 dialect 1 or dialect 3 database. To upgrade an ODS-9 database to Firebird, use the IB 5.*x* **gbak** program, running under the IB 5.6 server with the –t[ransportable] switch. Upgrading an IB 5.*x* database to Firebird does not convert it to a dialect 3 database. Its SQL dialect will be 1 and the upgrade is irreversible.

Where Dialect Counts

The dialect concept distinguishes the data type support and language features available to ODS-9 databases (dialect 1), and ODS-10 and higher (dialect 3). The server itself has no "dialect"—the dialect of the database is stored as a database attribute. It is the *client interface* that determines which set of features to request on behalf of the database. Under some conditions, if you as application developer or admin tool user get it wrong, you will cause erroneous data to be posted and corrupt the database.

It is convenient to refer here to an instance of a client connection, whether it be through the API library itself or through a customized language driver such as JayBird (Java), ODBC, or a .NET provider, as "a dialect 1 client" or "a dialect 3 client." What it means is that the client interface has been set up to request dialect 1 or dialect 3 features.

What Can Break

The following items illustrate some of the ways in which dialect 1 and dialect 3 differ:

- Dialects 1 and 3 store large scaled numbers differently. All dialect 3 fixed decimal types—NUMERIC and DECIMAL—having precision higher than 10 are 64-bit integers with field descriptions that include some attributes to determine precision and scale. Dialect 1 fixed numeric types are stored as 8-, 16-, or 32-bit integers, and those with precision exceeding 10 are converted to a 64-bit floating-point DOUBLE PRECISION type for storage. Your data is likely to throw overflow errors if a dialect 3 client submits requests to store number data in a dialect 1 database, or generate wrong results when a dialect 1 client submits requests for number operations to a dialect 3 database.

- Dialect 3 generators are 64-bit integers, whereas dialect 1 generators are 32-bit.

- Dialect 3 arithmetic operations were brought up to SQL-92 standard, whereas dialect 1 uses non-standard rules. For example, integer-by-integer division in dialect 3 returns a truncated integer, whereas in dialect 1 it returns a double-precision floating-point number. If your application stores the result of an expression involving this arithmetic operation, "wrong" results will be stored without throwing an exception.

- Both dialects have a date/time type named DATE, but they are different types. The dialect 1 DATE is equivalent to the dialect 3 TIMESTAMP, and the dialect 3 DATE is a date-only type not supported in dialect 1.

- Dialect 3 supports a TIME (time-of-day) type, which is unsupported in dialect 1.

- In dialect 3 databases, Firebird supports the ANSI SQL convention for optionally delimiting identifiers by enclosing them in double quotes, enabling the use of identifier strings that are illegal in dialect 1. Mismatching the client and database dialects will cause exceptions and breakages.

- The SQL string delimiter is the single quote (apostrophe). Dialect 1 permits the alternative use of double quotes for delimiting strings. Dialect 3 forbids it, for obvious reasons. Again, connecting with the wrong client dialect will cause exceptions and breakages.

- Dialect 3 has more reserved keywords than dialect 1. Existing dialect 1 databases that use the new keywords as identifiers will not work with a dialect 3 client.

- Dialects 1 and 3 behave differently with regard to implicit type conversion. This will be an issue if you wish to convert an existing database to dialect 3 and update its supporting applications.

Dialect 2

There is no such thing as "a dialect 2 database." Dialect 2 is a client setting that you can use for performing the data type transitions required to convert a dialect 1 database to dialect 3. Inprise Corporation (now Borland) released a *Migration Guide* document with IB 6.0 in 2000 that describes the full sequence of tasks involved in converting a dialect 1 database to dialect 3. It is available from several Firebird community websites as a PDF document.

How to Determine Dialect

Go to a console (command window) and get to the /bin directory where the Firebird command-line tools are located. Start the **isql** utility. Now, connect to your database:

```
SQL> CONNECT '/opt/firebird/examples/employee.fdb'
CON> user 'SYSDBA' password 'icur2yy4m';
SQL>
```

Then enter this ISQL command:

```
SQL> SHOW SQL DIALECT;
        Client SQL dialect is set to: 3 and database dialect is: 3
```

This is good. If you find there is a mismatch, it will not do harm as long as you do not try to insert or alter data. You must take steps to ensure that the client will use the correct dialect.

Changing the Client Dialect in isql

Suppose that, now in **isql**, you want to close down your connection to this database and connect to another one, which you know is dialect 1. This is what you do:

```
SQL> COMMIT;
SQL> SET SQL DIALECT 1;
WARNING: client SQL dialect has been set to 1 when connecting to Database
SQL dialect 3 database.
SQL>
```

That is OK, because you are just going to connect to a dialect 1 database:

```
SQL> CONNECT 'RSERVER:D:\DATA\SAMPLE\legacy.gdb'
CON> user 'SYSDBA' password 'icur2yy4m';
SQL> SHOW SQL DIALECT;
Client SQL dialect is set to: 1 and database dialect is: 1
```

Many of the free and commercial GUI admin tools provide the ability to set the client dialect interactively. Database access components and drivers provide properties or other mechanisms to pass the dialect in the API connection structure.

Up Next

The next four chapters describe the data types supported for each main data category—number, date/time, character, and binary large object (BLOB)—in detail. Chapter 13, the final chapter in this part, describes Firebird's implementation of the SQL *domain*, for clustering a data type with a group of attributes into a single, reproducible definition.

CHAPTER 9

Number Types

FIREBIRD SUPPORTS BOTH FIXED (EXACT PRECISION) decimal and floating-point (approximate precision) number types. Fixed decimal types are the zero-scaled integer types SMALLINT, INTEGER and, in dialect 3, BIGINT, and two nearly identical scaled numeric types, NUMERIC and DECIMAL. The two floating-point types are FLOAT (single precision) and DOUBLE PRECISION.[1]

Firebird does not support an unsigned integer type.

Table 9-1 shows the numerical limits of each of the number types in Firebird.

Table 9-1. Limits of Firebird Number Types

NUMBER TYPE	MINIMUM	MAXIMUM
SMALLINT	−32,768	32,767
INTEGER	−2,147,483,648	2,147,483,647
BIGINT	-2^{63}	$2^{63}-1$
(For masochists)	−9223372036854775808	9223372036854775807
NUMERIC †	Varies	Varies
DECIMAL †	Varies	Varies
FLOAT		
Positive	1.175×10^{-38}	3.402×10^{38}
Negative	-3.402×10^{38}	
DOUBLE PRECISION		
Positive	2.225×10^{-308}	1.797×10^{308}
Negative	-1.797×10^{308}	

† Limits for NUMERIC and DECIMAL types vary according to storage type and scale. The limits will always fall within the range for the internal type in which they are stored.[2]

---

1 *Precision* describes the number of significant digits, ignoring trailing or leading zeros, that can be stored in the data type without overflow or loss of information.

2 Stored type is SMALLINT, INTEGER, or BIGINT, depending on the declared precision.

Operations on Number Types

Operations supported include

- **Comparisons**: Use the standard relational operators (=, <, >, >=, <=, <>, or !=).[3]

  String comparisons using SQL operators such as CONTAINING, STARTING WITH, and LIKE are possible. In these operations, the numbers are treated as strings. For more information about these operators, refer to Chapter 21.

- **Arithmetic operations**: The standard dyadic arithmetic operators (+, -, *, and /) can be applied.

- **Conversions**: Firebird automatically converts between fixed numeric, floating-point, and character types when performing operations on mixed data types. When an operation involves a comparison or arithmetical operation between numeric data and non-numeric data types, data is first converted to a numeric type and then operated on.

- **Sorts**: By default, a query retrieves rows in the exact order that it finds them in the table, which is likely to be unordered. You can sort rows on integer columns using the ORDER BY clause of a SELECT statement in descending or ascending order. If numbers are stored or cast as character types, the sort order will be alphanumeric, not numeric, for example, 1 – 10 – 11 . . . 19 – 2.

Integer Types

All integer types are *signed exact numerics* having a scale of zero. Firebird supports three named ranges of *precision* as integer data types: SMALLINT, INTEGER, and BIGINT.

- SMALLINT is a signed short integer with a range from –32,768 to 32,767.

- INTEGER is a signed long integer with a range from –2,147,483,648 to 2,147,483,647.

- BIGINT is a signed 64-bit integer with a range from 2^{-63} to $2^{63} - 1$. Not available in dialect 1.

---

3 The use of "!=" as a substitute for "<>" is legal in Firebird but not according to the standard. Those with good ESP will stick to "<>", if just to assist code readability.

NOTE For Firebird 1.0.x, dialect 3, declare a 64-bit integer as NUMERIC(18,0) or DECIMAL(18,0). It is always valid to use this syntax for the integer types, optionally omitting the second (scale) argument.

For more information about scale, precision, and the operations that can be performed on fixed types, refer to the upcoming section "Fixed-Decimal (Scaled) Types."

The next two statements create a domain and a column with the SMALLINT and INTEGER data types respectively:

```
CREATE DOMAIN RGB_RED_VALUE AS SMALLINT;
/**/
CREATE TABLE STUDENT_ROLL (
 STUDENT_ID INTEGER,

 ...);
```

Each of these statements creates a domain that is a 64-bit integer:

```
CREATE DOMAIN IDENTITY BIGINT CHECK (VALUE >=0); /* Firebird 1.5 and higher */
CREATE DOMAIN IDENTITY NUMERIC(18,0) CHECK (VALUE >=0);
```

SMALLINT

SMALLINT is a 2-byte integer providing compact storage for whole numbers with a limited range. For example, SMALLINT would be suitable for storing the value of colors in the RGB scale, as in the previous domain example.

SMALLINT is often used to define a two-state Boolean, usually 0=False, 1=True. An example of this usage can be found in the section "Defining a BOOLEAN Domain" in Chapter 13.

INTEGER

INTEGER is a 4-byte integer. In dialect 1, generators (see the "Generators" section) generate integers. You can store integers in BIGINT columns without casting.

BIGINT, NUMERIC(18,0)

Available in dialect 3 only, this is an 8-byte integer, useful for storing whole numbers with very low and high ranges. In dialect 3, generators (see the "Generators" section) generate BIGINT numbers.

CAUTION In a dialect 1 database, Firebird rejects any attempt to define a domain or column as BIGINT. It will not raise an exception if you try to define a NUMERIC(18,0) domain or column, but it will silently define a DOUBLE PRECISION column instead. Because of precision problems with matching floating-point numbers, be careful to avoid accidentally using NUMERIC(18,0) in a dialect 1 database to define a column that is going to be used as a key for searches or joins.

Autoincrement or Identity Type

Firebird has no *autoincrement* or *identity* type such as you find in some other database management systems. What it does have is a number-generator engine and the ability to maintain independent, named series of BIGINT numbers. Each series is known as a *generator*. A technique for using them to implement and maintain primary keys and other automatically incrementing series is described in Chapter 31.

Generators

Generators are ideal for using to populate an automatically incrementing unique key or a stepping serial number column or other series. Generators are declared in a database using a CREATE statement, just like any other database object:

```
CREATE GENERATOR AGenerator;
```

Generators can be set to any starting value:

```
SET GENERATOR AGenerator TO 1;
```

 CAUTION There are strong caveats against resetting generators once a series is in use—see the "Caveats About Resetting Generators" section later in this chapter.

Calling for the Next Value

To call for the next value, invoke the SQL function GEN_ID(*GeneratorName*, n), where GeneratorName is the name of the generator and n is an integer (dialect 1) or NUMERIC(18,0) (dialect 3) specifying the size of the step. The query

```
SELECT GEN_ID(AGenerator, 2) from RDB$DATABASE;
```

returns a number that is 2 greater than the last generated number and increments the current value of the generator to the value it just generated.

Current Value of a Generator

This line:

```
SELECT GEN_ID(AGenerator, 0) from RDB$DATABASE;
```

returns the current value of the generator, without incrementing it.[4]

PSQL, Firebird's programming language, allows a value to be generated directly into a variable:

```
...
DECLARE VARIABLE MyVar BIGINT;
...
MyVar = GEN_ID(AGenerator, 1);
```

For more details about using generators in PSQL modules—especially triggers— see Chapter 29.

Using Negative Stepping

The *step* argument of GEN_ID(..) can be negative. Thus, it is possible to set or reset a generator's current value by passing a negative argument as either an integer constant or an integer expression. This capability is sometimes used as a "trick" for meddling with generator values in PSQL, since PSQL does not allow DDL commands such as SET GENERATOR.

For example, the statement

```
SELECT GEN_ID(AGenerator,
((SELECT GEN_ID(AGenerator, 0) from RDB$DATABASE) * -1))
from RDB$DATABASE;
```

causes the generator to be reset to zero.

Caveats About Resetting Generator Values

The general rule of thumb about resetting generator values in production databases— whether through SQL, PSQL, or some admin interface—is *don't*.

---

4 The table RDB$DATABASE is often used for "dummy" queries that return a single calculated value or a context variable. It is a real system table of one and only one row. It is used much as DUAL is used in Oracle.

The benefit of generator values is that they are guaranteed to be unique. Unlike any other user-accessible operation in Firebird, generators operate *outside transaction control*. Once generated, a number is "gone" and cannot be reverted by transaction rollback. This absolutely assures the integrity of number sequences, provided the generators are not tampered with.

Reserve the resetting of generators in a production database for the rare circumstances where a design requirement calls for it. For example, some older-style accounting systems pass journals into history tables with new primary keys, empty the journal table, and reset the primary key sequence to zero or, in multi-site organizations, separated ranges of key values are allocated to each site in "chunks" to ensure key integrity on replication.

Never reset generators in an attempt to correct bugs or input errors or to "fill gaps" in a sequence.[5,6]

Fixed-Decimal (Scaled) Types

Fixed-decimal types allow the management of numbers that need to be expressed with a fractional portion that is exact to a specific number of decimal places, or *scale*. Typically, you need scaled types for monetary values and any other numbers that result from counting or performing arithmetic on whole units and parts of units.

The predictability of results from multiplying and dividing fixed-point numbers favors choosing them for storing money values. However, because fixed-point types have a finite "window" in which numbers may be accommodated, they become prone to overflow/underflow exceptions near their upper and lower limits. In countries where the unit of currency represents a small value, number limits should be considered carefully.

For example, the following statement applies a tax rate (DECIMAL(5,4)) to a net profit (NUMERIC(18,2):

```
UPDATE ATABLE
SET INCOME_AFTER_TAX = NET_PROFIT  - (NET_PROFIT * TAX_RATE);
```

Let the tax rate be 0.3333
Let the net profit be 1234567890123456.78
Result:

```
ISC ERROR CODE:335544779
Integer overflow.  The result of an integer operation caused the most
significant bit of the result to carry.
```

---

5 There are techniques for maintaining an unbroken sequence using generators that can be implemented if there is an absolute requirement to recycle unused gaps in a series that is not a key. The Tech Info sheet "An Auditable Series of Numbers" at http://www.ibobjects.com/ TechInfo.html describes such a technique.

6 Anyone who can access the database through an interface that provides the ability to execute ad hoc SQL statements can break your generators.

Firebird provides two fixed-decimal or scaled data types: NUMERIC and DECIMAL. Broadly, either scaled type is declared as TYPE(P, S), with P indicating precision (number of significant digits) and S indicating scale (number of decimal places—that is, digits to the right of the decimal-point symbol).

According to the SQL-92 standard, both NUMERIC and DECIMAL constrain the stored number to be within the declared scale. The difference between the two types is in the way the precision is constrained. Precision is exactly "as declared" for a column of type NUMERIC, whereas a DECIMAL column can accept a number whose precision *is at least equal* to that which was declared, up to the implementation limit.

NUMERIC and DECIMAL types, as implemented in Firebird, are *identical except when precision is less than 5*. Both types effectively conform to the standard DECIMAL type. NUMERIC is thus not compliant with SQL-92.

Internally, Firebird stores the scaled number as a SMALLINT (16 bits), INTEGER (32 bits), or BIGINT (64 bits) type, according to the size of precision declared. Its declared precision[7] is stored, along with the declared scale negated to a sub-zero *scale-factor*,[8] representing an exponent of 10. When the number is referred to for output or a calculation, it is produced by multiplying the stored integer by 10^{scale_factor}.

For example, for a column defined as NUMERIC(4,3), Firebird stores the number internally as a SMALLINT. If you insert the number 7.2345, Firebird silently rounds the rightmost digit (4) and stores a 16-bit integer 7235 and a scale_factor of –3. The number is retrieved as 7. 235 ($7235 * 10^{-3}$).

NUMERIC Data Type

The format of the NUMERIC data type is

```
NUMERIC(p,s)
```

For example, NUMERIC(4,2) formally defines a number consisting of up to four digits, including two digits to the right of the decimal point. Thus, the numbers 89.12 and 4.321 will be stored in a NUMERIC(4,2) column as 89.12 and 4.32, respectively. In the second example, the final 1^{-3} is out of scale and is simply dropped.

However, it is possible to store in this column a number of greater precision than that declared. The maximum here would be 327.67—that is, a number with a precision of 5. Because the database stores the actual number as a SMALLINT, numbers will not begin to cause overflow errors until the internally stored number is more than 32,767 or less than –32,768.

---

7 This is stored in the system table RDB$FIELDS as RDB$FIELD_PRECISION.

8 This is stored in the system table RDB$FIELDS as RDB$FIELD_SCALE.

DECIMAL Data Type

The format of the DECIMAL data type is

```
DECIMAL(p,s)
```

Similar to NUMERIC, DECIMAL(4,2) formally defines a number consisting of at least four digits, including two digits to the right of the decimal point. However, because Firebird stores a DECIMAL of precision 4 and below as INTEGER, this type could, in a DECIMAL(4,1) column, potentially store a number as high as 214,748,364.7 or as low as –214,748,364.8 without causing an overflow error.

Exact numerics can be confusing, not just because of the slightness of difference between the two types but also because the *dialect* of the database affects the range of precision available. Table 9-2 can assist as a summary guide for the precision and scale you need to specify for your various exact numeric requirements.

Table 9-2. Range and Storage Type of Firebird NUMERIC and DECIMAL Types

PRECISION	TYPE	DIALECT 3	DIALECT 1
1 to 4	NUMERIC	SMALLINT	SMALLINT
--	DECIMAL	INTEGER	INTEGER
5 to 9	NUMERIC and DECIMAL	INTEGER	INTEGER
10 to 18	NUMERIC and DECIMAL	BIGINT	DOUBLE PRECISION[†]

[†] Exact numerics with precision higher than 9 can be declared in a dialect 1 database without an exception occurring. However, numbers will be stored as DOUBLE PRECISION and be subject to the same precision restrictions as any floating-point numbers. During conversion of a dialect 1 database to dialect 3, a dialect 2 client opening a table containing a DECIMAL or NUMERIC column with precision > 9 will encounter an exception (by design). For more information about this and other dialect 1 to dialect 3 conversions, see the section titled "Special Migration Topic" at the end of Chapter 8.

Converted Databases

If a dialect 1 database is upgraded to dialect 3 using a **gbak** backup and then restored, numeric fields defined with precision higher than 9 will remain implemented as DOUBLE PRECISION. Although they will still appear as they were originally defined (e.g., NUMERIC(15,2)), they will continue to be stored and used in calculations as DOUBLE PRECISION.

For more information about converting dialect 1 databases to dialect 3, refer to the section titled "Special Migration Topic" at the end of Chapter 8.

Special Restrictions in Static SQL

The host languages of embedded applications cannot use or recognize small precision NUMERIC or DECIMAL data types with fractional portions when they are stored internally as SMALLINT or INTEGER types. To avoid this problem, in any database that is going to be accessed via embedded applications (ESQL)

- Do not define NUMERIC or DECIMAL columns or domains of small precision in a dialect 1 database. Either store an integer and have your application code deal with scale, or use DOUBLE PRECISION and apply a suitable rounding algorithm for calculations.

- In a dialect 3 database, define NUMERIC and DECIMAL columns or domains of any size using a precision of at least 10, to force them to be stored internally as BIGINT. Specify a scale if you want to control the precision and scale. Apply CHECK constraints if you need to control the ranges.

Behavior of Fixed Types in Operations

Division

When performing division on fixed types, dialects 1 and 3 behave differently.

In dialect 3, where both operands are of a fixed numeric type, Firebird adds together the scales of both operands to determine the scale of the result (quotient). The quotient has a precision of 18. When designing queries with division expressions, be aware that quotients will always have more precision than either of the operands, and take precautions where precision could potentially overflow the maximum of 18.

In dialect 1, division always produces a quotient of DOUBLE PRECISION type.

Examples

In dialect 3, the quotient of dividing a DECIMAL(12,3) by a DECIMAL(9,2) is a DECIMAL(18,5). The scales are added together:

```
SELECT 11223344.556/1234567.89 FROM RDB$DATABASE
```

This yields 9.09090.

Compare the difference in the quotient when the same query is run in dialect 1. The first operand is treated as a DOUBLE PRECISION number because its precision (12) is higher than the maximum for a dialect 1 scaled type. The quotient is also a DOUBLE PRECISION number. The result is 9.09090917308727 because of the errors inherent in floating-point types.

From the following table defined in dialect 3, division operations produce a variety of results:

```
CREATE TABLE t1 (
  i1 INTEGER,
  i2 INTEGER,
  n1 NUMERIC(16,2),
  n2 NUMERIC(16,2));
COMMIT;
INSERT INTO t1 VALUES (1, 3, 1.00, 3.00);
COMMIT;
```

The following query returns the NUMERIC(18,2) value 0.33, since the sum of the scales 0 (operand 1) and 2 (operand 2) is 2:

```
SELECT i1/n2 from t1
```

The following query returns the NUMERIC(18,4) value 0.3333, since the sum of the two operand scales is 4:

```
SELECT n1/n2 FROM t1
```

Integer/Integer Division

Using the preceding example, the following query in dialect 3 returns the integer 0 because each operand has a scale of 0, so the sum of the scales is 0:

```
SELECT i1/i2 FROM t1
```

In dialect 1, in line with many other DBMS software, dividing one integer by another produces a floating-point result of DOUBLE PRECISION type:

```
SELECT 1/3 AS RESULT FROM RDB$DATABASE
```

This yields .333333333333333.

Although this dialect 1 rule is intuitive for language programmers, it does not conform to the SQL-92 standard. Integer types have a scale of 0, which, for consistency, requires that the result (quotient) of any integer/integer operation conform with the scaling rules for fixed numerics and produce an integer.

Dialect 3 conforms to the standard and truncates the quotient of integer/integer division operations to integer. Hence, it can trap the unwary:

```
SELECT 1/3 AS RESULT FROM RDB$DATABASE
```

This yields 0.

When you need to preserve sub-integer parts in the result (quotient) of integer/integer divisions in dialect 3, be sure that you either scale one of the operands or include a "factor" in the expression that will guarantee a scaled result.

Examples:

```
SELECT (1 + 0.00)/3 AS RESULT FROM RDB$DATABASE
```

This yields .33.

```
SELECT (5 * 1.00)/2 AS RESULT FROM RDB$DATABASE
```

This yields 2.50.

Dialect 1 Database with Dialect 3 Client

A dialect 1 database that is opened with a dialect 3 client may cause some surprises with respect to integer division. When an operation does something that causes a CHECK condition to be checked, or a stored procedure to be executed, or a trigger to fire, the processing that takes place is based on the dialect under which the CHECK, stored procedure, or trigger was *defined*, not the dialect in effect when the application causes the check, stored procedure, or trigger to be *executed*.

For example, suppose that a dialect 1 database has a table MYCOL1 INTEGER, and MYCOL2 INTEGER with a table definition includes the following CHECK condition that was defined when the database was dialect 1:

```
CHECK(MYCOL1 / MYCOL2 > 0.5)
```

Now suppose that a user starts **isql**, or an application, and sets the dialect to 3. It tries to insert a row into the converted database:

```
INSERT INTO MYTABLE (COL1, COL2)
VALUES (2,3);
```

Because the CHECK constraint was defined in dialect 1, it returns a quotient of 0.666666666666667, and the row passes the CHECK condition.

The reverse is also true. If the same CHECK constraint were added to the dialect 1 database through a dialect 3 client, dialect 3 arithmetic is stored for the constraint. The preceding INSERT statement would fail because the check would return a quotient of 0, violating the constraint.

TIP There's a moral to this: Use dialect 3 databases and always connect as dialect 3. If you intend to use FB, then upgrade any existing databases to dialect 3—preferably scripting a brand-new database and pumping your old data into it—so that you can rest easy and avoid a raft of nasty surprises.

Multiplication and Division

If both operands are exact numeric, multiplying the operands produces an exact numeric with a scale equal to the sum of the scales of the operands, for example:

```
CREATE TABLE t1 (
  n1 NUMERIC(9,2),
  n2 NUMERIC(9,3));
COMMIT;
INSERT INTO t1 VALUES (12.12, 123.123);
COMMIT;
```

The following query returns the number 1492.25076 because n1 has a scale of 2 and n2 has a scale of 3. The sum of the scales is 5.

```
SELECT n1*n2 FROM t1
```

In dialect 3, the precision of the result of multiplying a fixed numeric by a fixed numeric is 18. Precautions must be taken to ensure that potential overflows will not result from the propagation of scale in multiplication.

In dialect 1, if the propagation of scale caused by the calculation would produce a result with precision higher than 9, the result will be DOUBLE PRECISION.

Addition and Subtraction

If all operands are exact numeric, adding or subtracting the operands produces an exact numeric with a scale equal to that of the largest operand, for example:

```
CREATE TABLE t1 (
  n1 NUMERIC(9,2),
  n2 NUMERIC(9,3));
COMMIT;
INSERT INTO t1 VALUES (12.12, 123.123);
COMMIT;
SELECT n1 + n2 FROM t1;
```

The query returns 135.243, taking the scale of the operand with the larger scale. Similarly, the following query returns the numeric –111.003:

```
SELECT n1 - n2 FROM t1;
```

In dialect 3, the result of any addition or subtraction is a NUMERIC(18,n). In dialect 1, it is a NUMERIC(9,n), where *n* is the scale of the larger operand.

Numeric Input and Exponents

Any numeric string in DSQL that can be stored as a DECIMAL(18,S) is evaluated exactly, without the loss of precision that might result from intermediate storage as a DOUBLE. The DSQL parser can be forced to recognize a numeric string as floating-point by the use of scientific notation—that is, appending the character "e" or "E" followed by an exponent, which can be zero.

For example, DSQL will recognize 16.92 as a scaled exact numeric and passes it to the engine in that form. On the other hand, it will treat 16.92E0 as a floating-point value.

Floating-Point Data Types

Floating-point types employ a sort of "sliding window" of precision appropriate to the scale of the number. By the nature of "float" types, the placement of the decimal point is not a restriction—it is valid to store, in the same column, one value as 25.33333 and another as 25.333. The values are different and both are acceptable.

Define a floating-point column when you need to store numbers of varying scale. The general rule of thumb for choosing a floating-point, rather than a fixed-decimal type, is "use them for values you measure, not for values you count." If a floating-point column or variable must be used to store money, you should pay careful attention both to rounding issues and to testing the results of calculations.

Floating-point numbers can be used to represent a value over a much larger range than is possible with plain or scaled integers. For example, the FLOAT type can carry values with a magnitude as large as 3.4E38 (that's 34 followed by 37 zeros) and as small as 1.1E-38 (that's 11 preceded by 37 zeros and then a decimal point).

The breadth of range is achieved by a loss in exactness. A floating-point number carries an approximate representation of its value that is accurate for a specific number of digits (its precision), according to the current magnitude (scale). It cannot carry a value close to either extreme of its range.

The floating-point value carries more information than the stated number digits of precision. The FLOAT type, for example, is said to have a precision of 7 digits but its *accurate* precision is 6 digits. The last part is an approximation providing additional information about the number, such as an indicator for rounding and some more things that are important when arithmetic is performed on the number.

For example, a FLOAT can carry the value 1000000000 (1,000,000,000, or 10^9). The FLOAT "container" sees this value as (effectively) 100000*E4. (This is illustrative only—an authoritative exposition of floating-point implementation is beyond the scope of this book and seriously beyond the author's reach!) If you add 1 to the value of the FLOAT, it will ignore the additional information carried in the seventh digit, because it is not significant in terms of the number's current magnitude and the precision available. If you add 10,000—a value that is significant to the magnitude of the number currently stored in the FLOAT—it can represent the result as 100001*E4.

Even values within the available precision of the floating-point number may not always store an exact representation. A value such as 1.93 or even 123 may be represented in storage as a value that is very *close* to the specific number. It is close enough that, when the floating-point number is rounded for output, it will display the value expected and, when it is used in calculations, the result is a very close approximation to the expected result.

The effect is that, when you perform some calculation that should result in the value 123, it may only be a very close approximation to 123. Exact comparisons (equality, greater than, less than, and so on) between two floating-point numbers, or between a floating-point number and zero, or a floating-point number and a fixed type, thus cannot be depended on to produce the expected results.

For this reason, do not consider using floating-point columns in keys or applying uniqueness constraints to them. They will not work predictably for foreign key relationships or joins.

For comparisons, test floating-point values as being BETWEEN some acceptable range rather than testing for an exact match. The same advice applies when testing for 0—choose a range appropriate to the magnitude and signing of your data that is between zero and a near-zero value, or between two suitable near-zero values.[9]

In a dialect 1 database, the need to store numeric data values having a wider range than the limits of a 32-bit integer may force the choice of a DOUBLE PRECISION type. Dialect 1 limitations also require the use of floating-point numbers for all reals if the database is going to be accessed by an embedded (ESQL) application.

Firebird provides two floating-point or *approximate numeric* data types, FLOAT and DOUBLE PRECISION, differing only in the limit of precision.

FLOAT

FLOAT is a 32-bit floating-point data type with a limit of approximately 7 digits of precision—assume 6 digits for reliability. A 10-digit number 25.33333312 inserted into a FLOAT column is stored as 25.33333. The range is from -3.402×10^{38} to 3.402×10^{38}. The smallest positive number it can store is 1.175×10^{-38}.

DOUBLE PRECISION

DOUBLE PRECISION is a 64-bit floating-point data type with a limit of approximately 15 digits of precision. The range is from $^{308} -1.797 \times 10^{308}$ to 1.797×10^{308}. The smallest positive number it can store is 2.225×10^{-308}.

Arithmetic Mixing Fixed and Floating-Point Types

When a dyadic operation (addition, subtraction, multiplication, division) involves an exact numeric operand and a floating-point operand, the result will be a DOUBLE PRECISION type.

---

9 Thanks to Geoff Worboys for his insightful contribution to this vexed topic.

The next statement creates a column, PERCENT_CHANGE, using a DOUBLE PRECISION type:

```
CREATE TABLE SALARY_HISTORY
(
  ...
  PERCENT_CHANGE DOUBLE PRECISION
  DEFAULT 0
  NOT NULL
  CHECK (PERCENT_CHANGE BETWEEN -50 AND 50),
  ...
);
```

The following CREATE TABLE statement provides an example of how the different numeric types can be used: an INTEGER for the total number of orders, a fixed DECIMAL for the dollar value of total sales, and a FLOAT for a discount rate applied to the sale.

```
CREATE TABLE SALES
  (...
  QTY_ORDERED INTEGER
    DEFAULT 1
    CHECK (QTY_ORDERED >= 1),
  TOTAL_VALUE DECIMAL (9,2)
    CHECK (TOTAL_VALUE >= 0),
  DISCOUNT FLOAT
    DEFAULT 0
    CHECK (DISCOUNT >= 0 AND DISCOUNT <= 1));
```

Up Next

In the next chapter, we look at the data types for storing and expressing dates and times in Firebird.

Date and Time Types

FIREBIRD SUPPORTS **DATE, TIME, AND TIMESTAMP** data types in dialect 3. In dialect 1, only one date type is supported, a timestamp-like implementation that, although named DATE, is not interchangeable with the dialect 3 DATE type.

DATE

In dialect 3, DATE stores the date alone, with no time portion: "date-only." Storage is a 32-bit signed integer. Storable dates range from January 1, 0001, to December 31, 9999.

In dialect 1, the DATE type is equivalent to a dialect 3 TIMESTAMP. Indeed, when you create a new date column in a dialect 1 database, using **isql**, a warning will appear informing you that the type has been renamed! SQLTYPE is *isc_timestamp*.

There is no "date-only" type in dialect 1. To store a dialect 1 type and make it date-only, pass a valid date and time literal with ' 00:00:00.0000' in the time portion. Date and time literals are discussed in greater detail in the following sections.

 TIP If you are using **isql** to examine dialect 1 dates, you can toggle on/off the display of the time part of date output using the **isql** command SET TIME. Off is the default.

TIMESTAMP

The dialect 3 TIMESTAMP data type is made of two 32-bit longword portions, storing a date and a time. It is stored as two 32-bit integers, equivalent to the DATE type in dialect 1.

Fractions of Seconds

Fractions of seconds, if stored, are in ten-thousandths of a second for all date and time types.

TIME

In dialect 3, TIME stores the *time of day*, with no date portion: "time-only." Storage is a 32-bit unsigned integer. Storable times range from 00:00 to 23:59:59.9999.

Dialect 1 has no equivalent to the dialect 3 TIME type. If time of day needs to be stored, extract the hours, minutes, and seconds elements from the DATE data and convert it to a string. A suggested technique follows later in this chapter—refer to the section "Combining EXTRACT( ) with Other Functions."

Interval of Time (Time Elapsed)

It is a common mistake to assume that TIME can store an interval of time (time elapsed). *It cannot.* To calculate an interval of time, subtract the later of two date or time types from the earlier. The result will be a NUMERIC(18,9) number expressing the interval (time elapsed) in days. Because of precision loss, sub-seconds should be considered accurate to milliseconds, rather than ten-thousandths of seconds. Use regular arithmetic operations to convert days to hours, minutes, or seconds, as required.

Suppose, for example, that the columns STARTED and FINISHED are both TIME-STAMP (or DATE in dialect 1). To calculate and store the time elapsed in minutes into a DOUBLE PRECISION column TIME_ELAPSED, you would use the following:

```
UPDATE ATABLE
SET TIME_ELAPSED = (FINISHED - STARTED) * 24 * 60
WHERE ((FINISHED IS NOT NULL) AND (STARTED IS NOT NULL));
```

Date Literals

Date literals are "human-readable" strings, enclosed in single quotation marks, that Firebird server recognizes as date or date-and-time constants for EXTRACT and other expressions, INSERT and UPDATE operations, and in the WHERE clause of a SELECT statement.

Specifically, date literals are used when supplying date constants to

- SELECT, UPDATE, and DELETE statements, in the search condition of a WHERE clause

- INSERT and UPDATE statements, to enter date and time constants

- The FROM argument of the EXTRACT( ) function

Recognized Date/Time Literal Formats

The formats of the strings recognized as date literals are restricted. These formats use placeholders for the elements of the strings. Table 10-1 provides a key to the conventions used.

Table 10-1. Elements of Date Literals

ELEMENT	REPRESENTING
CC	Century. First two digits of a year segment (e.g., 20 for the twenty-first century).
YY	Year in century. Firebird always stores the full year value if the year is entered without the CC segment, using a "sliding window" algorithm to determine which century to store.
MM	Month, evaluating to an integer in the range 1 to 12. In some formats, two digits are required.
MMM	Month, one of [JAN, FEB, MAR, APR, MAY, JUN, JUL, AUG, SEP, OCT, NOV, DEC]. English month names fully spelled out (correctly) are also valid.
DD	Day of the month, evaluating to an integer in the range 1 to 31. In some formats, two digits are required. An invalid day-of-month number for the given month will cause an error.
HH	Hours, evaluating to an integer in the range 00 to 23. Two digits are required when storing a time portion.
NN	Minutes, evaluating to an integer in the range 00 to 59. Two digits are required when storing a time portion.
SS	Whole seconds, evaluating to an integer in the range 00 to 59. Two digits are required when storing a time portion.
nnnn	Ten-thousandths of a second in the range 0 to 9999. Optional for time portions; defaults to 0000. If used, four digits are required.

The recognized formats are described in Table 10-2.

Table 10-2. Recognized Date and Time Literal Formats

FORMAT	DIALECT 3 DATE	DIALECT 3 TIMESTAMP	DIALECT 1 DATE
'CCYY-MM-DD' or 'YY-MM-DD'	Stores date only	Stores the date and a time portion of 00:00:00	Stores the date and a time portion of 00:00:00
'MM/DD/CCYY' or 'MM/DD/YY'	As above	As above	As above
'DD.MM.CCYY' or 'DD.MM.YY'	As above	As above	As above
'DD-MMM-CCYY' or 'DD-MMM-YY'	As above	As above	As above
'DD,MMM,CCYY' or 'DD,MMM,YY'	As above	As above	As above
'DD MMM CCYY' or 'DD MMM YY'	As above	As above	As above
'DDMMMCCYY' or 'DDMMMYY'	As above	As above	As above

Case-insensitive English month names fully spelled out are also valid in the MMM element. Correct spelling is shown in Table 10-3.

'CCYY-MM-DD HH:NN:SS.nnnn' or 'YY-MM-DD HH:NN:SS.nnnn' (".nnnn" element is optional)	Stores date only; may need to be CAST as date. Time portion is not stored.	Stores date and time	

continued

Table 10-2. Recognized Date and Time Literal Formats (continued)

FORMAT	DIALECT 3 DATE	DIALECT 3 TIMESTAMP	DIALECT 1 DATE
'MM/DD/CCYYHH:NN:SS.nnnn' or 'MM/DD/YY HH:NN:SS.nnnn'	As above	As above	As above
'DD.MM.CCYYHH:NN:SS.nnnn' or 'DD.MM.YY HH:NN:SS.nnnn'	As above	As above	As above
'DD-MMM-CCYY HH:NN:SS.nnnn' or 'DD-MMM-YY HH:NN:SS.nnnn'	As above	As above	As above

The dialect 3 TIMESTAMP type and the dialect 1 DATE type accept both date and time parts in a date literal. A date literal submitted without a time part will be stored with a time part equivalent to '00:00:00'.

The dialect 3 DATE type accepts only the date part. The TIME data type accepts only the time part.

Firebird's "Sliding Century Window"

Whether the year part of a DATE or TIMESTAMP literal is submitted in SQL as CCYY or YY, Firebird always stores the full year value. It applies an algorithm in order to deduce the CC (century) part, and it always includes the century part when it retrieves date types. Client applications are responsible for displaying the year as two or four digits.

To deduce the century, Firebird uses a *sliding window* algorithm. Its effect is to interpret a two-digit year value as the nearest year to the current year, in a range spanning the preceding 50 years and the succeeding 50 years.

For example, if the current year were 2004, two-digit year values would be interpreted as shown in Table 10-3.

Table 10-3. Deduction of Year from Two-Digit Year if Current Year is 2004

TWO-DIGIT YEAR	BECOMES YEAR	DEDUCED FROM
98	1998	(2004 – 1998 = 6) < (2998 – 2004 = 94)
00	2000	(2004 – 2000 = 4) < (2100 – 2004 = 96)
45	2045	(2004 – 1945 = 55) > (2045 – 2004 = 41)
50	2050	(2004 – 1950 = 54) > (2050 – 2004 = 46)
54	1954	(2004 – 1954 = 50) = (2054 – 2004 = 50) ‡
55	1955	(2004 – 1955 = 49) < (2055 – 2004 = 51)

‡ The apparent equivalence of this comparison could be misleading. However, 1954 is closer to 2004 than is 2054 because all dates between 1954 and 1955 are closer to 2004 than all dates between 2054 and 2055.

Separators in Non-U.S. Dates

Nothing causes more confusion for international users than Firebird's restricting the use of the forward slash character (/) to only the U.S. 'MM/DD/CCYY' format. Although almost all other countries use 'DD/MM/CCYY', Firebird will either record the wrong date or throw an exception with the date literal using the 'DD/MM/CCYY' convention.

For example, the date literal '12/01/2004' will always be stored with meaning "December 1, 2004" and '14/01/2004' will cause an out-of-range exception because there is no month 14. However, 'CCYY/MM/DD' is accepted: '2004/12/31' will be interpreted as "31 December 2004".

Note that Firebird does not honor the Windows or Linux date locale format when interpreting date literals. Its interpretation of all-number date formats is decided by the separator character. When dot (.) is used as separator, Firebird interprets it as the non-U.S. notation DD.MM, whereas with any other separator it assumes the U.S. MM/DD notation. Outside the U.S. date locale, your applications should enforce or convert locale-specific DD/MM/CCYY date input to a literal that replaces the forward slash with a period (dot) as the separator. 'DD.MM.CCYY' is valid. Other date literal formats may be substituted.

White Space in Date Literals

Spaces or tabs can appear between elements. A date part must be separated from a time part by at least one space.

Quoting of Date Literals

Date literals must be enclosed in single quotes (ASCII 39). Only single quotes are valid.

Month Literals

Table 10-4 shows the month literals.

Table 10-4. Month Literals with Correct English Spellings

CARDINAL NUMBER	ABBREVIATION	FULL MONTH NAME
	Case-Insensitive	*Case-Insensitive*
01	JAN	January
02	FEB	February
03	MAR	March
04	APR	April
05	MAY	May
06	JUN	June
07	JUL	July
08	AUG	August

continued

Table 10-4. Month Literals with Correct English Spellings (continued)

CARDINAL NUMBER	ABBREVIATION	FULL MONTH NAME
09	SEP	September
10	OCT	October
11	NOV	November
12	DEC	December

Examples of Date Literals

The twenty-fifth (25) day of the sixth month (June) in the year 2004 can be represented in all of the following ways:

```
'25.6.2004'   '06/25/2004'  'June 25, 2004'
'25.jun.2004' '6,25,2004'   '25,jun,2004'
'25jun2004'   '6-25-04'     'Jun 25 04'
'25 jun 2004' '2004 June 25' '20040625'
'25-jun-2004' '2004-jun-25' '20040625'
'25 JUN 04'   '2004-06-25'  '2004,25,06'
```

Pre-Defined Date Literals

Firebird supports a group of "pre-defined" date literals—single-quoted English words that Firebird captures or calculates and interprets in the context of an appropriate date/time type. The words 'TODAY', 'NOW', 'YESTERDAY', and 'TOMORROW' are interpreted as shown in Table 10-5.

Table 10-5. Pre-Defined Date Literals

DATE LITERAL	DIALECT 3 TYPE	DIALECT 1 TYPE	MEANING
'NOW'	TIMESTAMP	DATE	Server date and time that was current at the start of the DML operation. 'NOW' will be cast and stored correctly in dialect 3 DATE, TIME, and TIMESTAMP fields and in dialect 1 DATE fields. Like the equivalent context variable CURRENT_TIMESTAMP, it always stores the sub-second portion as '.0000'. [†]
'TODAY'	DATE	DATE stored with a time part equivalent to '00:00:00'	Server date that was current at the start of the operation. If midnight is passed during the operation, the date does not change. Equivalent to the dialect 3 CURRENT_DATE context variable. Not valid in fields of TIME type.

Table 10-5. Pre-Defined Date Literals (continued)

DATE LITERAL	DIALECT 3 TYPE	DIALECT 1 TYPE	MEANING
'TOMORROW'	DATE	DATE stored with a time part equivalent to '00:00:00'	Server date that was current at start of the operation, plus 1 day. If midnight is passed during the operation, the date from which the 'TOMORROW' date is calculated does not change. Not valid in fields of TIME type.
'YESTERDAY'	DATE	DATE stored with a time part equivalent to '00:00:00'	Server date that was current at start of the operation, minus 1 day. If midnight is passed during the operation, the date from which the 'YESTERDAY' date is calculated does not change. Not valid in fields of TIME type.

† All is not lost, however. You can get the server timestamp to one ten-thousandth of a second by using instead the UDF GetExactTimestamp(..) from the Firebird UDF library, fbudf. For more information, refer to Appendix I.

Implicit Type-Casting of Date/Time Literals

Whenever date literals—whether regular or pre-defined—are used in SQL in the context of corresponding date/time type columns or variables, the SQL parser can interpret them correctly without casting. However, in a small number of cases, where there is no typed value to which the parser can map the date literal, it treats any date literal as a string.

For example, it is perfectly valid to ask a SELECT query to return a constant that is unrelated to any database column. A common "hack" in Firebird is to use the system table RDB$DATABASE for just such a query—since this table has one and only one row and thus can always be relied upon to return a scalar set—to pick up a single context value from the server. The next two examples illustrate a typical use of this hack:

```
SELECT 'NOW' FROM RDB$DATABASE;
```

Because the query returns a constant, not a column value, its data type is interpreted as a CHAR(3), 'NOW'. This example:

```
SELECT '2.09.2004' FROM RDB$DATABASE;
```

returns a CHAR(9), '2.09.2004'.

To have the parser correctly interpret a date literal in conditions where the parser cannot determine the data type, use the CAST(..) function.

For dialect 3:

```
SELECT CAST('NOW' AS TIMESTAMP) FROM RDB$DATABASE;
SELECT CAST('2.09.2004' AS TIMESTAMP) FROM RDB$DATABASE;
```

For dialect 1:

```
SELECT CAST('NOW' AS DATE) FROM RDB$DATABASE;
SELECT CAST('2.09.2004' AS DATE) FROM RDB$DATABASE;
```

Date and Time Context Variables

The date and time context variables CURRENT_DATE, CURRENT_TIME, and CURRENT_TIMESTAMP return date and time values capturing the server time at the moment execution of the containing SQL statement begins. Table 10-6 describes these variables.

Table 10-6. Date and Time Context Variables

VARIABLE	DIALECT 3 TYPE	DIALECT 1 TYPE	MEANING
CURRENT_TIMESTAMP	TIMESTAMP	DATE	Current date and time to the nearest second. Fractions of seconds are always returned as equivalent to '.0000'.
CURRENT_DATE	DATE	Not supported	Current date.
CURRENT_TIME	TIME	Not supported	Current time, expressed as hours, minutes, and seconds since midnight. Fractions of seconds are always returned as equivalent to '.0000'.

Operations Using Date and Time Values

The use of an arithmetic operation to manipulate, calculate, set, or condition the relationships between two dates has already been visited in the section "Interval of Time (Time Elapsed)" earlier in this chapter. The capability to subtract an earlier date, time, or timestamp value from a later one is possible because of the way Firebird stores date/time types. It uses one or two 32-bit integers to store timestamps, date-only dates, or time of day, respectively. The units represented by these numbers are *days* in the date-part longword and fractions of days in the time-part integer. The date part represents the number of days since "date zero," November 17, 1898.[1] The time part represents the ten-thousandths of a second elapsed since midnight.

---

1 It is probably no accident that this date gives an integer value called the *Modified Julian Day Number*, a formal term and reference point in calendar studies. See `http://hermetic.nofadz.com/cal_stud/jdn.htm` for details.

Dialect 3 DATE stores only the date part. Dialect 3 TIME stores only the time part. TIMESTAMP and dialect 1 DATE store both parts.

Quite simply, these number structures can be operated on, using simple addition and subtraction expressions, to calculate time differences (intervals), increment or decrement dates, and set date and time ranges. Table 10-7 explains which operations are valid and the results to be achieved.

Table 10-7. Arithmetic Involving Date/Time Data Types

OPERAND 1	OPERATOR	OPERAND 2	RESULT
DATE	+	TIME	TIMESTAMP (arithmetic concatenation)
DATE	+	Numeric value n‡	Advances DATE by n whole days (ignoring fraction of n if present)
TIME	+	DATE	TIMESTAMP (arithmetic concatenation)
TIME	+	Numeric value n‡	Advances TIME by n seconds †
TIMESTAMP	+	Numeric value n‡	Advances TIMESTAMP by the whole-number part of n days plus the fraction part of n (if present) as a fraction of the number of thousandths of seconds in a day (8.64×10^8)
DATE	–	DATE	DECIMAL(9,0) days of interval
DATE	–	Numeric value n‡	Reduces DATE by n days (ignoring fraction of n if present)
TIME	–	TIME	DECIMAL(9,4) seconds of interval
TIME	–	Numeric value n‡	Reduces TIME by n seconds †
TIMESTAMP	–	TIMESTAMP	DECIMAL(18,9) days and part-day of interval
TIMESTAMP	–	Numeric value n‡	Reduces TIMESTAMP by the whole-number part of n days plus the fraction part of n (if present) as a fraction of the number of thousandths of seconds in a day (8.64×10^8)

† If necessary, repeats (result=modulo(result, (24 * 60 * 60))) until resultant day-part is eliminated.

‡ For the dialect 3 DATE type, n is an integer representing days. For TIMESTAMP and dialect 1 DATE types, n can be a numeric representing days to the left of the decimal point and a part day to the right. For the TIME type, n is an integer representing seconds.

General Rules for Operations

One date/time value can be subtracted from another, provided

- Both values are of the *same* date/time type.

- The first operand is *later* than the second.

A valid subtraction involving date/time types produces a scaled DECIMAL result in dialect 3 and a DOUBLE PRECISION result in dialect 1.

Date/time types cannot be added together. However, a date part can be *concatenated* to a time part using

- Dyadic addition syntax to concatenate a pair of fields or variables

- String concatenation to concatenate a date/time literal with another date/time literal or with a date/time field or variable

Multiplication and division operations involving date/time types are not valid.

Expressions As Operands

The operand to advance or reduce a TIMESTAMP, TIME, DATE, or dialect 1 DATE value can be a constant or an expression. An expression may be especially useful in your applications when you want to advance or reduce the value specifically in seconds, minutes, or hours, or, for example, half days rather than directly by days.

Dialect 3 uses the SQL-92 rule for integer/integer division: The result is always an integer, rounded down if necessary. When using expressions in dialect 3, ensure that one of the operands is a real number with enough decimal places to avoid the possibility of arithmetic errors or imprecision resulting from SQL-92 integer division.

Table 10-8 shows some examples.

Table 10-8. Examples of Operands Using Expressions

OPERAND INPUT N	ADD OR SUBTRACT	ALTERNATIVE
In seconds	n/86400.0	(n * 1.0)/(60 * 60 * 24)
In minutes	n/1440.0	(n * 1.0)/(60 * 24)
In hours	n/24.0	Depends on the result you want. For example, if n is 3 and the divisor for half days is 2, the result will be 1, not 1.5.
In half days	n/2	Ditto

Because years, months, and quarters are not constant, more complex algorithms are needed for handling them in date/time operations. It may be worth your while to seek out user-defined functions (UDFs) that you can use in operand expressions to suit these requirements.

Using CAST(..) with Date/Time Types

At several points in this chapter, we have encountered the CAST(..) function in expressions involving date literals and date parts. This section explores the various aspects of date and time casting in more depth and breadth.

Casting Between Date/Time Types

Generally, casting from one date/time type to another is possible wherever the source date/time type provides the right kind of data to reconstruct as the destination date/time type. For example, a TIMESTAMP can provide the date part to cast on to a date-only DATE type or a time-only TIME type, whereas a TIME type cannot provide enough data to cast on to a DATE type. Firebird allows a DATE type to be cast to TIMESTAMP by casting on a time part of midnight, and it allows a TIME type to be cast to TIMESTAMP by casting it on to CURRENT_DATE (the server date). Table 10-9 summarizes the casting rules.

Table 10-9. Dialect 3 Casting Between Date/Time Types

CAST SOURCE TYPE	AS TIMESTAMP	AS DATE	AS TIME
TIMESTAMP	N/A	Yes: Casts on date part, ignores time part	Yes: Casts on time part, ignores date part
DATE	Yes: Time part is set to midnight	N/A	No
TIME	Yes: Date part is set to CURRENT_DATE	No	N/A
DATE + TIME	Yes: CAST((DATEFIELD + TIMEFIELD AS TIMESTAMP)	No	No

Casting from Date Types to CHAR(n) and VARCHAR(n)

Use the SQL CAST() function in statements to translate between date and time data types and character-based data types.

Firebird casts date/time types to formatted strings where the date (if present) is in a set format—dependent on dialect—and the time part (if present) is in the standard Firebird HH:NN:SS.nnnn time format. It is necessary to prepare a CHAR or VARCHAR column or variable of a suitable size to accommodate the output you want.

Both fixed length CHAR and variable-length VARCHAR types can be cast to from date/time types. Because the size of a cast date/time string is known and predictable, CHAR has a slight advantage over VARCHAR where date and time castings are concerned: Using CHAR will save you transmitting over the wire the 2 bytes that are added to VARCHARs to store their length. The "right size" depends on dialect, so care is needed here. VARCHAR may be more suitable to use in application code that may need to handle both dialects.

If the character field is too small for the output, an overflow exception will occur. Suppose you want a cast string to contain only the date part of a TIMESTAMP. Preparing a character container of smaller size will not work: CAST(..) does not truncate the output string to fit. It is necessary to perform a double cast, first casting the timestamp as DATE and then casting that date to the correctly sized character type—refer to the examples in the following sections.

Dialect 3

Casting DATE or TIMESTAMP outputs the date part in ISO format (CCYY-MM-DD). To get the full length of the output, allow 10 characters for DATE and 11 for TIMESTAMP (the date part plus 1 for the blank preceding the time part). Allow 13 characters for TIME or the time part of TIMESTAMP. For example, the following:

```
SELECT CAST(timestamp_col as CHAR(24)) AS TstampTxt
FROM RDB$DATABASE ;
```

produces a string like this:

```
2004-06-25 12:15:45.2345
```

This produces an overflow exception:

```
SELECT CAST(timestamp_col as CHAR(20)) AS TstampTxt
FROM RDB$DATABASE ;
```

A double-cast will produce the right string:

```
SELECT FIRST 1 CAST (
  CAST (timestamp_col AS DATE) AS CHAR(10)) FROM table1;
```

The result is

```
2004-06-25
```

Unfortunately, it is not possible by direct casting to return a cast date plus time string without the sub-second portion. It can be done using a complex expression involving both CAST(..) and EXTRACT( ). For an example, refer to the upcoming section "The EXTRACT( ) Function."

Dialect 1

The date part of a dialect 1 DATE type is converted to the format DD-MMM-CCYY, not the ISO format as in dialect 3. So, for example, this:

```
SELECT CAST(d1date_col as CHAR(25)) AS DateTimeTxt
FROM RDB$DATABASE;
```

produces

```
26-JUN-2004 12:15:45.2345
```

Consequently, casting dialect 1 dates requires 11 characters instead of 10 for the date part, plus 1 for the blank space, plus 13 for the time part—25 in all.

More Complex Expressions

Casting can be used more complex expressions, in combination with other expression operators, for example:

```
select cast (10 + cast(('today') as date) as char(25)) texttime from rdb$database;
```

or

```
select cast (10 + current_timestamp) as date) as char(25)) texttime
  from rdb$database;
```

produces a text string showing a date 10 days advanced from today's date.

Casting Between Date/Time Types and Other Types

Any character type or expression whose content can be evaluated to a valid date literal can be cast to the appropriate date/time type.

Date and time types cannot be cast to or from SMALLINT, INTEGER, FLOAT, DOUBLE PRECISION, NUMERIC, DECIMAL, or BLOB types.

Uses for Casting

Exchanging Date/Time Data with Other Applications

Importing date/time data created elsewhere—by another database system, host language, or data-capture device, for example—usually involves some degree of "massaging" before it can become valid date/time data for storage in a Firebird database.

Most host languages do not support the DATE, TIME, and TIMESTAMP types, representing them internally as strings or structures. Data capture devices usually store dates and times in a variety of string formats and styles. Date/time types are often incompatible between different database hosts.

Conversion generally requires evaluating and decoding the date-element content of the source data. The second part of the process is to reconstruct the decoded elements and pass them in Firebird SQL by some means. For a host language that has no means to pass native Firebird date/time types, use of CAST(..) in combination with valid text strings for Firebird to process as date literals can be invaluable.[2]

In some cases, external data stored into text files in date literal formats may be the best solution. Firebird can open such files as input tables in a server-side code module—stored procedure or trigger—and use CAST(..) and other functions to process data into date/time columns in native tables. Refer to the section "Using External Files As Tables" in Chapter 16 for more information.

CAST(..) can equally be used to prepare internal data for export.

In Search Condition Expressions

Situations arise where using CAST(..) in the WHERE clause with a date/time type will solve logical problems inherent in comparing a column of one type with a column of a different type.

Suppose, for example, we want to join a customer account table, which contains a DATE column BALANCE_DATE, with a customer transaction table, which has a TIMESTAMP column TRANS_DATE. We want to make a WHERE clause that returns a set containing all of the unbilled transactions for this customer that occurred on or before the BALANCE_DATE. We might try this:

```
SELECT...
WHERE CUST_TRANS.TRANSDATE <= CUSTOMER.BALANCE_DATE;
```

This criterion does not give us what we want! It will find all of the transaction rows up to midnight of the BALANCE_DATE, because it evaluates BALANCE_DATE with a time part of 00:00:00. Any transactions after midnight on that date will fail the search criterion.

What we really want is to include all of the transactions where the date part of TRANS_DATE matches BALANCE_DATE. Casting TRANS_DATE to a DATE type saves the day:

```
SELECT...
WHERE CAST(CUST_TRANS.TRANSDATE AS DATE) <= CUSTOMER.BALANCE_DATE;
```

---

2 For API programmers, the API provides two utility functions for binary manipulation of client-language date/time structure to and from Firebird formats, respectively. Refer to the Borland *API Guide* for the functions isc_encode_date() and isc_decode_date().

In a Dialect Conversion

Dialect 3 provides richer date/time support than dialect 1. One task that is likely to catch your attention if you do such a conversion is to replace or enhance existing dialect 1 DATE type columns (which are equivalent to TIMESTAMP in dialect 3) by converting them to the dialect 3 DATE (date-only) or TIME types. CAST(..) makes this job a no-brainer.

For an example of one style of conversion using CAST( ), refer to the sample at the end of this chapter.

The EXTRACT( ) Function

EXTRACT( ) returns a variety of elements extracted by decoding fields of date/time types. It can operate on all dialect 3 and dialect 1 date/time fields.

Syntax

Here's the syntax for EXTRACT( ):

EXTRACT (*element* FROM *field*)

element must be a defined element that is valid for the data type of field. Not all elements are valid for all date/time types. The data type of element varies according to the element extracted. Table 10-10 enumerates the elements available for each date/time type.

field can be a column, a variable, or an expression that evaluates to a date/time field.

Table 10-10 shows the restrictions on the arguments and types when using EXTRACT( ).

Table 10-10. EXTRACT( ) Arguments, Types, and Restrictions

ELEMENT	DATA TYPE	LIMITS	TIMESTAMP/ DIALECT 1 DATE	DATE	TIME
YEAR	SMALLINT	0–5400	Valid	Valid	Not valid
MONTH	SMALLINT	1–12	Valid	Valid	Not valid
DAY	SMALLINT	1–31	Valid	Valid	Not valid
HOUR	SMALLINT	0–23	Valid	Not valid	Valid
MINUTE	SMALLINT	0–59	Valid	Not valid	Valid
SECOND	DECIMAL(6,4)	0–59.9999	Valid	Not valid	Valid
WEEKDAY	SMALLINT	0–6 [†]	Valid	Valid	Not valid
YEARDAY	SMALLINT	1–366	Valid	Valid	Not valid

[†] (0 = Sunday...6 = Saturday)

Combining EXTRACT( ) with Other Functions

Following are two examples where EXTRACT( ) is used with CAST( ) to obtain date representations not available with either function on its own.

To Cast Date Plus Time Without Sub-Seconds

Although it is not possible by direct casting to return a cast date plus time string without the sub-second portion, it can be done using a complex expression involving both CAST( ) and EXTRACT( ).

To Extract a TIME String

This technique has more meaning for dialect 1 than for dialect 3. However, it can be extrapolated to any dialect 3 date or time type if you need to store time of day as a string.

The EXTRACT( ) function makes it possible to extract the individual elements of date and time types to SMALLINT values. The following trigger extracts the time elements from a dialect 1 DATE column named CAPTURE_DATE and converts them into a CHAR(13), mimicking the Firebird standard time literal 'HH:NN:SS.nnnn':

```
SET TERM ^;
CREATE TRIGGER BI_ATABLE FOR ATABLE
ACTIVE BEFORE INSERT POSITION 1
AS
BEGIN
  IF (NEW.CAPTURE_DATE IS NOT NULL) THEN
  BEGIN
    NEW.CAPTURE_TIME =
      CAST(EXTRACT (HOUR FROM NEW.CAPTURE_DATE) AS CHAR(2))|| ':' ||
      CAST(EXTRACT (MINUTE FROM NEW.CAPTURE_DATE) AS CHAR(2))|| ':' ||
      CAST(EXTRACT (SECOND FROM NEW.CAPTURE_DATE) AS CHAR(7));
  END
END ^
SET TERM ;^
```

A Sample Date/Time Type Conversion Task

The CHAR(13) string stored by the trigger in the preceding example does not behave like a dialect 3 TIME type. However, by simple casting, it can be converted directly, in a later upgrade to dialect 3, to a dialect 3 TIME type.

First, we add a temporary new column to the table to store the converted time string:

```
ALTER TABLE ATABLE
  ADD TIME_CAPTURE TIME;
COMMIT;
```

Next, populate the temporary column by casting the dialect 1 time string:

```
UPDATE ATABLE
  SET TIME_CAPTURE = CAST(CAPTURE_TIME AS TIME)
  WHERE CAPTURE_TIME IS NOT NULL;
COMMIT;
```

The next thing we need to do is temporarily alter our trigger to remove the reference to the dialect 1 time string. This is needed to prevent dependency problems when we want to change and alter the old time string:

```
SET TERM ^;
RECREATE TRIGGER BI_ATABLE FOR ATABLE
ACTIVE BEFORE INSERT POSITION 1
AS
BEGIN
  /* do nothing */
END ^
SET TERM ;^
COMMIT;
```

Now, we can drop the old CAPTURE_TIME column:

```
ALTER TABLE ATABLE DROP CAPTURE_TIME;
COMMIT;
```

Create it again, this time as a TIME type:

```
ALTER TABLE ATABLE
  ADD CAPTURE_TIME TIME;
COMMIT;
```

Move the data from the temporary column into the newly added CAPTURE_TIME:

```
UPDATE ATABLE
  SET CAPTURE_TIME = TIME_CAPTURE
  WHERE TIME_CAPTURE IS NOT NULL;
COMMIT;
```

Drop the temporary column:

```
ALTER TABLE ATABLE DROP TIME_CAPTURE;
COMMIT;
```

Finally, fix up the trigger so that it now writes the CAPTURE_TIME value as a TIME type:

```
SET TERM ^;
RECREATE TRIGGER BI_ATABLE FOR ATABLE
ACTIVE BEFORE INSERT POSITION 1
AS
BEGIN
  IF (NEW.CAPTURE_DATE IS NOT NULL) THEN
  BEGIN
    NEW.CAPTURE_TIME = CAST(NEW.CAPTURE.DATE AS TIME);
  END
END ^
SET TERM ;^
COMMIT;
```

All of these steps can be written as an SQL script. For details about SQL scripting, refer to the topic "Schema Scripts" in Chapter 14.

A "Gotcha" with EXTRACT( )

EXTRACT() throws an exception if it receives a null argument. It may be possible to work around this in simple queries, by enforcing NOT NULL or using sub-query expressions for date/time fields that are subject to decoding. However, in outer joins, it is not so straightforward, since the outer-joined streams that don't match join conditions return null in the unfillable fields.

A suggested workaround is to use a subquery (see Chapters 21 and 22) that restricts the function call to non-null values. In dialect 3, another solution is to apply a CASE expression (see Chapter 21) to avoid calling EXTRACT( ) on null dates.

Up Next

The next chapter covers the large topic of using character (string) types in Firebird, including the important issues of defining and working with international character sets and collation sequences for databases and columns.

Character Types

FIREBIRD SUPPORTS BOTH FIXED-LENGTH and variable-length character (string) data types. They can be defined for local usage in any one of a large collection of character sets. Fixed-length character types cannot exceed 32,767 bytes in absolute length; for variable-length types, the limit is reduced by 2 bytes to accommodate a character count with each string stored.

Firebird stores strings very economically, using a simple run-length encoding algorithm to compress the data, even if it is a fixed-length CHAR or NCHAR type. In case that tempts you to define very large string columns, be aware that there are compelling reasons to avoid long strings—client memory limitations, index size limits and, in Firebird 1.0.*x*, decompression of the strings, both full- and variable-length types, with padding to full declared length, *before* they leave the server.

String Essentials

The CHARACTER SET attribute of character types is important not only for compatibility with localized application interfaces but also, in some cases, for deciding the size of the column. Certain character sets use multiple bytes—typically 2 or 3 bytes in Firebird—to store a single character. When such character sets are used, the maximum size is reduced by a factor of the byte size.

NOTE The CHARACTER SET attribute is optional in a declaration. If no character set is defined at the column level, the CHARACTER SET attribute is taken to be the default character set of the database. The mechanism for determining the character set of columns and variables is discussed in more detail later in this chapter.

Over-length input for Firebird character columns incurs an overflow error.

String Delimiter

Firebird's string delimiter is ASCII 39, the single-quote or apostrophe character, for example:

```
StringVar = 'This is a string.';
```

Double-quotes are not permitted at all for delimiting strings. You should remember this if you are connecting to Firebird using application code written for InterBase 5 databases, which permitted double-quoted strings. Strings should also be corrected in the source code of stored procedures and triggers in an InterBase 5 database if you plan to recompile them in Firebird.

Concatenation

Firebird uses the SQL standard symbol for concatenating strings: a doublet of ASCII characters, code 124, known as *double-pipe* (||). It can be used to concatenate string constants, string expressions, and/or column values, for example:

```
MyBiggerString = 'You are my sunshine,' || FirstName || ' my only sunshine.';
```

Character items can be concatenated to numbers and number expressions to produce an alphanumeric string result. For example, to concatenate the character '#' to an integer:

```
NEW.TICKET_NUMBER = '#' || NEW.PK_INTEGER;
```

 CAUTION Avoid using concatenation expressions where one of the elements might be null. The result of any concatenation containing a null will be null.

Escape Characters

As a rule, Firebird does not support escape characters as a means to include non-printable codes or sequences in character fields. The single exception is the "doubling" of the apostrophe character (ASCII 39) to enable it to be included as a stored character and prevent its being interpreted as the end-delimiter of the string:

```
...
SET HOSTELRY = 'O''Flaherty''s Pub'
...
```

It is possible to store non-printable characters in strings. The UDF AsciiChar(asciivalue) in the ib_udf library can be declared to enable these characters or sequences to be passed in strings. The following statement outputs a set of text fields—to an external file, for example—with a carriage return and line feed in the last one:

```
INSERT INTO EXTFILE(DATA1, DATA1, DATA3, CRLF)
VALUES ('String1', 'String2', 'String3', Ascii_Char(13)||Ascii_Char(10));
```

For the declaration of Ascii_Char(..) and other functions in the ib_udf library, look in the ../UDF subdirectory beneath the root of your Firebird installation for the script named *ib_udf.sql*. For details about the external functions, refer to Appendix I.

Limitations with Character Types

Multi-Byte Character Set Limitations

It is important to be aware of the impact of multi-byte character sets on the sizes of text items, especially those with variable length. In UNICODE_FSS, for example, even a 256-character column will be relatively large—potentially 770 bytes—both to store and to retrieve. More is said later in this chapter regarding the caution you need to observe when considering text storage for multi-byte character data.

Index Restrictions

When deciding on the length, character set, and collation sequence for a character column, you need to be aware that indexing columns of these types is somewhat limited. Currently (at v.1.5) the total width of any index cannot exceed 253 bytes—note *bytes*, not characters. Multi-byte and many of the more complex 1-byte character sets use up many more bytes than the simpler character sets. Multi-segment indexes consume extra bytes, as do collation sequences. Do the byte calculations at design time!

For more details, see Chapter 18, and note the topics later in this chapter about character sets and collation sequences.

Client Memory Consumption

Client programs will allocate memory to store copies of rows that they read from the database. Many interface layers allocate sufficient resources to accommodate the *maximum* (i.e., defined) size of a fixed- or variable-length column value, even if none of the actual data stored is that large. Buffering large numbers of rows at a time may consume a large amount of memory, and users will complain about slow screen refreshes and lost connections.

Consider, for example, the impact on the workstation if a query returns 1024 rows consisting of just one column declared as VARCHAR(1024). Even with the "leanest" character set, this column would cost at least 1MB of client memory. For a Unicode column, multiply that cost by three.

Fixed-Length Character Data

Firebird's fixed-length string data types are provided for storing strings whose length is consistently the same or very similar, or where the format or relative positions of characters might convey semantic content. Typical uses are for items such as identification codes, telecom numbers, and character-based numbering systems, and for defining fields to store pre-formatted fixed-length strings for conversion to other data types—Firebird date literals, for example.

Leading spaces characters (ASCII character 32) in fixed-length string input are significant, whereas trailing spaces are not. When storing fixed-length strings, Firebird strips trailing space characters. The strings are retrieved with right-padding out to the full declared length.

Using fixed-length types is not recommended for data that might contain significant trailing space characters or items whose actual lengths are expected to vary widely.

CHAR(n), Alias CHARACTER(n)

CHAR(n), alias CHARACTER(n), is the base fixed-length character type. *n* represents the exact number of characters stored. It will store strings in any of the supported character sets.

NOTE If the length argument, n, is omitted from the declaration, a CHAR(1) is assumed. It is acceptable to declare single-character CHAR fields simply as CHAR.

NCHAR(n), Alias NATIONAL CHARACTER(n)

NCHAR(n), alias NATIONAL CHAR(n) is a specialized implementation of CHAR(n) that is pre-defined with ISO8859_1 as its character set attribute. Of course, it is not valid to define a character set attribute for an NCHAR column, although a collation sequence—the sequence in which the sorting of characters is arranged for searches and ordered output—can be defined for a column or domain that uses this type.

A detailed section about character sets and collation sequences follows later in this chapter.

Variable-Length Character Data

Firebird's variable-length string data types are provided for storing strings that may vary in length. The mandatory size argument *n* limits the number of discrete characters that may be stored in the column to a maximum of *n* characters. The size of a VARCHAR cannot exceed 32,765 bytes because Firebird adds a 2-byte size element to each VARCHAR item.

Choosing, Storing, and Retrieving Variable-Length Text

A variable-length character type is the workhorse for storing text because the size of the stored structure is the size of the actual data plus 2 bytes. All characters submitted as input to a field of a variable-length type are treated as significant, including both leading and trailing space characters ("blanks").

Transport Across the Network

Until Firebird 1.5, retrieved variable-length text data items were padded at the server to the full, declared size before being returned to the client. From Firebird 1.5 forward, the data are not padded. At the time of this writing, the unpadded variable-length text output feature had not been backported to Firebird 1.0.*x*, which may influence your choice of column size and type if you are writing applications for remote clients connecting to a 1.0.*x* server on a slow network.

Although variable-length types can store strings of almost 32K, in practice it is not recommended to use them for defining data items longer than about 250 bytes, especially if their tables will become large or will be subject to frequent SELECT queries. BLOBs of SUB_TYPE 1 (text) are usually more suitable for storing large string data. Text BLOBs are discussed in detail in the next chapter.

VARCHAR(n), Alias CHARACTER VARYING(n)

VARCHAR(n), alias CHARACTER VARYING(n), is the base variable-length character type. *n* represents the *maximum* number of characters that can be stored in the column. It will store strings in any of the supported character sets. If no character set is defined, the character set attribute defaults to the one defined during CREATE DATABASE as DEFAULT CHARACTER SET. If there is no default character set, the column default is CHARACTER SET NONE.

NCHAR VARYING(n), Alias NATIONAL CHAR VARYING(n)

NCHAR VARYING(n), alias NATIONAL CHAR VARYING(n), alias NATIONAL CHARACTER VARYING(n), is a specialized implementation of VARCHAR(n) that is pre-defined with ISO8859_1 as its character set attribute. It is not valid to define a character set attribute for an NVARCHAR column, although a *collation sequence*—the sequence in which the sorting of characters is arranged for searches and ordered output—can be defined for a column or domain that uses this type.

Character Sets and Collation Sequences

The character set chosen for storing text data determines

- The characters that can be used in CHAR, VARCHAR, and BLOB SUB_TYPE 1 (text) columns.

- The number of bytes allocated to each character.

- The default collation sequence ("alphabetical order") to be used when sorting CHAR and VARCHAR columns. (BLOBs cannot be sorted—hence collation sequence does not apply to them.)

The default character set of the database will be used if you don't specify one. If no default character set is defined for the database, columns default to CHARACTER SET NONE. If your database is for use in an English-only language environment, you can be tempted to ignore character sets. Don't be tempted! Character set NONE will accept any single-byte characters without complaining. The problems start when—in a non-U.S.-English or mixed-language environment—you find that you are getting *transliteration errors* when you SELECT your text data. What comes out isn't always what goes in!

Text input from keyboards and other input devices such as bar-code readers—potentially for all characters—is encoded specifically according to a certain standard code page that may be linked to the *locale* that the input device is set up for. It is fairly typical for input devices to be fitted with adapter software to allow users to switch code pages at will.

In one code page, the numeric code that maps to a certain character image may be quite different from its mapping in another. Broadly, each Firebird character set reflects a certain code page or group of related code pages. Some character sets work with more than one code page; in some cases, a code page will work with more than one character set. Different languages may share one overall character set but map different uppercase/lowercase pairs, currency symbols, and so on.

Beyond character sets, different country, language, or even cultural groups using the same character mappings use different sequences to determine "alphabetical order" for sorting and comparisons. Hence, for most character sets, Firebird provides a variety of *collation sequences*. Some collation sequences also take in uppercase/lowercase pairings to resolve case-insensitive orderings. The COLLATE clause is used in several contexts where collation sequence is important, although it is not declared at the database level.

The server needs to know what character set is to be stored, in order to compute the storage space and to assess the collation characteristics for proper ordering, comparison, uppercasing, and so on. Beyond that, it is unconcerned about the character of text input.

Client Character Set

What really matters with regard to character set is the interaction between the server and client. The Firebird client library must be passed a character set attribute as part of the structure of a connection request.

If the engine detects a difference between the client's character set setting and the character set of the target storage destination, translation—"transliteration"—is performed automatically, on the assumption that the incoming codes are correct for the client's code page. The incoming codes are exchanged for codes that are correct for the corresponding characters in the character set of the storage target.

That makes it possible to store text in different targets with character sets that are not the same as the default character set of the database.

If the client and target character sets are the same, the engine assumes that the input it is receiving really is codes for the defined character set and stores the input unmodified. Troubles ensue if the input was not what the client said it was. When the data is selected, searched, or restored after a backup, it causes transliteration errors.

For more information about transliteration errors and how to fix them, refer to the section "Transliteration" later in this chapter.

Connecting applications must pass the character set of the database to the API via the database parameter block (DPB) in the parameter *isc_dpb_lc_ctype*. An ESQL application—including the **isql** utility—must execute a SET NAMES statement immediately before the CONNECT statement. SET NAMES <character-set> is also the command you use to set the character set in the **isql** utility. GUI admin tools usually provide an input field of some sort for selecting the client character set.

If you need to cater for a non-English language, spend some time studying the character sets available and choose the one which is *most appropriate* for most of your text input storage and output requirements. Remember to include that character set in the database attributes when you create the database. Refer to the section "Mandatory and Optional Attributes" in Chapter 15 for syntax. For a list of character sets recognized by Firebird, refer to Appendix VIII.

Character Set Overrides

Having set the global default for the database, you can override it further down the food chain, if required. You can include a character set attribute when you create a domain. You can override either the database default or a domain setting in an individual column definition.

 CAUTION   When columns use the database default, changing the database's default character set propagates the change only to columns and domains added subsequently. Existing columns retain the original character set attribute.

Firebird Character Sets

Firebird supports an increasingly broad variety of international character sets, including a number of 2-byte sets and a 3-byte Unicode set. In many cases, choices of collation (sorting) sequence are available. In this section, we look at

- Some background about character sets

- The global default character set for a database

- Alternative character set and collation sequence for character domains and columns

- Collation sequence for

  - A text value in a comparison operation

  - An ORDER BY or GROUP BY clause

- How to ask the server to translate input data to a particular character set

A character set is a collection of symbols that includes at least one *character reper-toire*. A character repertoire is a set of characters used by a particular culture for its publications, written communication, and—in the context of a database—for computer input and output. For example, ISO Latin_1 is a character set that encompasses the English repertoire (A, B, C . . . Z) and the French repertoire (A, Á, À, B, C, Ç, D . . . Z), making it useful for systems that span both cultural communities.

Naming of Character Sets

Most Firebird character sets are defined by standards, and their names closely reflect the standards that define them. For example, Microsoft defines Windows 1252 and Firebird implements it as WIN1252. Character set ISO8859_1 is "the set of characters defined by ISO Standard 8859-1, encoded by the values defined in ISO standard 8859-1, having each value represented by a single 8-bit byte."

Aliases

Character-set alias names support naming standard differences from one platform to another. For example, if you find yourself on an operating system that uses the identifier WIN_1252 for the WIN1252 character set, you can use an alias that is defined in the system table RDB$TYPES, as described in the next section.

Storage of Character Sets and Aliases

Characters sets, currently, are "hard-wired" in a database at creation time. One of the system tables built automatically is RDB$CHARACTER_SETS. For a listing by character set name, including the name of the default collate sequence in each case, execute this query:

```
SELECT
  RDB$CHARACTER_SET_NAME,
  RDB$DEFAULT_COLLATE_NAME,
  RDB$BYTES_PER_CHARACTER
FROM RDB$CHARACTER_SETS
  ORDER BY 1 ;
```

Aliases are added as required to RDB$TYPES, another system table that stores enumerated sets of various kinds used by the database engine. To see all of the aliases that are set up at database-creation time, run this query, filtering RDB$TYPES to see just the enumerated set of character set names:

```
SELECT
  C.RDB$CHARACTER_SET_NAME,
  T.RDB$TYPE_NAME
FROM RDB$TYPES T
JOIN RDB$CHARACTER_SETS C
ON C.RDB$CHARACTER_SET_ID = T.RDB$TYPE
  WHERE T.RDB$FIELD_NAME = 'RDB$CHARACTER_SET_NAME'
  ORDER BY 1 ;
```

NOTE   In order to use any character set other than NONE, ASCII, OCTETS, and UNICODE_FSS, it is necessary to have the fbintl library present in the /intl directory beneath the root directory. (For Windows Embedded Server, it should be in the application directory itself, where the client library fbembed.dll is located).

Storage Restrictions

It is important to understand how your choice of character set affects the storage restrictions for the data you plan to accommodate. In the case of the CHAR and VAR-CHAR columns, Firebird restricts the maximum amount of storage in any field in the column to 32,767 bytes and 32,765 bytes, respectively. The actual number required may be very limited indeed, according to a number of factors regarding its usage.

Non-indexed columns using the default collation sequence can store (number of characters) * (number of bytes per character) up to the byte limit for the data type. For example, a VARCHAR(32765) in character set ISO_8859_1 can store up to 32,765 characters, while in character set UNICODE_FSS (which uses 3 bytes per character) the upper limit is 10,291 characters.

If a column is to be indexed and/or modified with a COLLATE clause, a significant number of "spare" bytes must be allowed. Even the least demanding index—on a single VARCHAR column using a single-byte character set and the default collation sequence—is limited to 252 bytes in Firebird versions up to and including 1.5. For multi-byte character set columns, the character limit is less than (252/(number of bytes per character). Multi-column indexes consume more bytes than do single-column indexes; those using a non-default collation sequence consume still more. For more details about these effects, refer to the section "Collation Sequence and Index Size" later in this chapter.

TIP When designing columns, always consider likely needs with regard to character set, indexing, and key usage. Keep a special "scratch" table in your development database just for testing the limits of indexes and keys.

Storage for BLOB columns, which are non-indexable, is not restricted according to the storage character set.

Default Character Set for the Database

If you do not specify a default character set in the CREATE DATABASE declaration, the character set defaults to NONE. Character set NONE makes no character set assumptions for text columns, storing data exactly as entered. If the client connection specified no character set, then data will also be retrieved exactly as entered. Alphabetical ordering is in strict ASCII code order and uppercase/lowercase mapping is supported only in U.S. ASCII codes 65–90 and 97–102, respectively.

Specify a valid character set code in the DEFAULT CHARACTER SET clause:

```
CREATE DATABASE '/data/adatabase.fdb'
...
DEFAULT CHARACTER SET WIN1251;
```

Refer to Chapter 15 for more information about CREATE DATABASE.

Field-Level Character Set Overrides

A character set attribute can be added to the individual definition of a domain, table column, or PSQL variable of type CHAR, VARCHAR, or BLOB SUB_TYPE 1 to override the default character set of the database.

For example, the following script fragment creates a database with a default character set of ISO8859_1 and a table containing different language versions of similar data in separate columns:

```
CREATE DATABASE '/data/authors.fdb' DEFAULT CHARACTER SET ISO8859_1;
CREATE TABLE COUNTRY_INTL(
  CNTRYCODE BIGINT NOT NULL,
  NOM_FR VARCHAR(30) NOT NULL,  /* uses default charset */
  NOM_EN VARCHAR(30), /* uses default charset */
  NOM_RU VARCHAR(30) CHARACTER SET CYRL,
  NOM_JP VARCHAR(30) CHARACTER SET SJIS_0208
);
```

Another fragment from the same script creates a domain for storing BLOB data in the Cyrillic character set:

```
CREATE DOMAIN MEMO_RU AS BLOB SUB_TYPE 1
  CHARACTER SET CYRL;
```

Later in the script, we define a table that stores some text in Cyrillic:

```
CREATE TABLE NOTES_RU (
    DOC_ID BIGINT NOT NULL,
    NOTES MEMO_RU
);
```

This fragment defines a stored procedure that converts string input to a different character set before storing it in a table:

```
CREATE PROCEDURE CONVERT_NOTES (
  INPUT_TEXT VARCHAR(300)) AS
DECLARE VARIABLE CONV_STRING VARCHAR(300)
  CHARACTER SET CYRL;
BEGIN
  IF (INPUT_TEXT IS NOT NULL) THEN
  BEGIN
    CONV_STRING = _CYRL ''||:INPUT_TEXT; /* uses an INTRODUCER */
    INSERT INTO NOTES_RU (DOC_ID, NOTES)
    VALUES(GEN_ID(ANYGEN, 1),:CONV_STRING);
  END
END ^
```

Creating domains is explained in Chapter 13. Complete syntax for CREATE TABLE is in Chapter 15. For more information about declaring variables in PSQL, refer to Chapter 30.

Statement-Level Character Set Overrides

The character set for text values in a statement is interpreted according to the connection's character set *at runtime* (not according to the character set defined for the column when it was created) unless you specify a *character set marker* (or "introducer") to indicate a different character set.

Character Set Marker: INTRODUCER

A character set marker—also known as an INTRODUCER—consists of the character set name prefixed by an underscore character. It is required to "introduce" an input string when the client application is connected to the database using a character set that is different from that of the destination column in the database.

Position the marker directly to the left of the text value being marked. For example, the introducer for input to a UNICODE_FSS field is _UNICODE_FSS:

```
INSERT INTO EMPLOYEE(Emp_ID, Emp_Name)
values(1234, _UNICODE_FSS 'Smith, John Joseph');
```

TIP For clarity, you may leave white space between the introducer and the string without affecting the way the input is parsed.

String Literal

A string literal in a test or search condition, for example, in a WHERE clause, is interpreted according to the character set of the client's connection *at the time the condition is tested*. An introducer will be required if the database column being searched has a character set which is different from that of the client connection:

```
... WHERE name = _ISO8859_1 'joe';
```

TIP When you are developing with mixed character sets, it is good practice to use introducers as a matter of form, especially if your application will cross the boundaries of multiple databases and/or it will be deployed internationally.

Transliteration

Converting characters from one Firebird character set to another—for example, converting from DOS437 to ISO8859_1—is *transliteration*. Firebird's transliterations preserve character fidelity: by design, they will not substitute any kind of "placeholder" character for an input character that is not represented in the output character set. The purpose of this restriction is to guarantee that it will be possible to transliterate the same passage of text from one character set to another, in either direction, without losing any characters in the process.

Transliteration Errors

Firebird reports a transliteration error if a character in the input set does not have an exact representation in the output set.

An example of where a transliteration error may occur is when an application passes input of some unspecified character set into a column defined with NONE and later tries to select that data for input to another column that has been defined with a different character set. Even though you thought it should work because the character *images* looked as though they belonged to the character set of the destination column, the entire transliteration fails because a character is encountered which is not represented in the destination character set.

Fixing Transliteration Errors

How can you deal with a bunch of character data that you have stored using the wrong character set? The "trick" is to use character set OCTETS as a "staging post" between the wrong and the right encoding. Because OCTETS is a special character set that blindly stores only what you poke into it—without transliteration—it is ideal for making the character codes *neutral* with respect to code page.

For example, suppose your problem table has a column COL_ORIGINAL that you accidentally created in character set NONE, when you meant it to be CHARACTER SET ISO8859_2. You have been loading this column with Hungarian data, but every time you try to select from it, you get that darned transliteration error.

Here's what you can do:

```
ALTER TABLE TABLEA
ADD COL_ISO8859_2 VARCHAR(30) CHARACTER SET ISO8859_2;
COMMIT;
UPDATE TABLEA
SET COL_ISO8859_2 = CAST(COL_ORIGINAL AS CHAR(30) CHARACTER SET OCTETS);
```

Now you have a temporary column designed to store Hungarian text—and it is storing all of your "lost" text from the unusable COL_ORIGINAL. You can proceed to drop COL_ORIGINAL, and then add a new COL_ORIGINAL having the correct character set. Simply copy the data from the temporary column and, after committing, drop the temporary column:

```
ALTER TABLE TABLEA
DROP COL_ORIGINAL;
COMMIT;
ALTER TABLE TABLEA
ADD COL_ORIGINAL VARCHAR(30) CHARACTER SET ISO8859_2;
COMMIT;
UPDATE TABLEA
SET COL_ORIGINAL = COL_ISO8859_2;
COMMIT;
/* It would be wise to view your data now! */
ALTER TABLE TABLEA
DROP COL_ISO8859_2;
COMMIT;
```

Character Set for the Client Connection

When a client application, such as **isql**, connects to a database, it is part of its connection protocol to inform the server of its character set requirements. The character set for a connection is the character set–neutral NONE, unless specified otherwise using

- SET NAMES in embedded applications or in **isql**.

- The *isc_dpb_lc_ctype* parameter of the database parameter block (DPB) for the *isc_attach_database()* function of the API. RAD database connection classes for Delphi, Java, et al. generally surface this parameter as a property.

The client application specifies its character set *before* it connects to the database. For example, the following ISQL command specifies that **isql** is using the ISO8859_1 character set. The next command connects to the authors.fdb database of our earlier example:

```
SET NAMES ISO8859_1;
CONNECT 'lserver:/data/authors.fdb' USER 'ALICE' PASSWORD 'XINEOHP';
```

Special Character Sets

The general rule for character sets is that every byte (or pair or trio, in the case of multi-byte sets) is specifically defined by the standard it implements. There are four special exceptions—NONE, OCTETS, ASCII, and UNICODE_FSS. Table 11-1 explains the special qualities of these sets.

Table 11-1. Special Character Sets

NAME	QUALITIES
NONE	Each byte is part of a string, but no assumption is made about which character set it belongs to. Client-side or user-defined server code is responsible for character fidelity.
OCTETS	Bytes that will not be interpreted as characters. Useful for storing binary data.
ASCII	Values 0…127 are defined by ASCII; values outside that range are not characters, but are preserved. Firebird is fairly liberal about transliterating bytes in the 0…127 range of ASCII characters.
UNICODE_FSS	Developers need to know that it is effectively a UTF8 implementation. Users need to know that it can be used to store UCS16 but not UCS32 characters (that would take up to 6 bytes per character). No collation sequence other than the default binary one is available.

ISO8859_1 (LATIN_1) and WIN1252

The Firebird ISO8859_1 character set is often specified to support European languages. ISO8859_1, also known as LATIN_1, is a proper subset of WIN1252: Microsoft added characters in positions that ISO specifically defines as *Not a character* (not "undefined," but specifically "not a character"). Firebird supports both WIN1252 and ISO8859_1. You can always transliterate ISO8859_1 to WIN1252, but transliterating WIN1252 to ISO8859_1 can result in errors.

Character Sets for Microsoft Windows

Five character sets support Windows client applications, such as Paradox for Windows. These character sets are WIN1250, WIN1251, WIN1252, WIN1253, and WIN1254.

Due to Borland's historical association with Paradox and dBase, the names of collation sequences for these character sets that are specific to Paradox for Windows begin "PXW" and correspond to the Paradox/dBase language drivers supplied in the now-obsolete Borland Database Engine (BDE).

....

A "Gotcha" Regarding the WINnnn Character Sets

The PXW collation sequences really implement collations from Paradox and dBase, including *all bugs*. One exception: PXW_CSY was fixed in Firebird 1.0. Thus, legacy InterBase databases that use it, for example in indexes, are not binary-compatible with Firebird.

....

For more information about Windows character sets and Paradox for Windows collations, see the appropriate BDE documentation and driver books.

For a list of the international character sets and collation sequences that Firebird supports out of the box, see Appendix VIII.

Collation Sequence

Each character set has a default *collation sequence* that specifies how its symbols are sorted and ordered. Collation sequence determines the rules of precedence that Firebird uses to sort, compare, and transliterate character data.

Because each character set has its own subset of possible collation sequences, the character set that you choose when you define the column limits your choice. You must choose a collation sequence that is supported for the column's character set.

Collation sequence for a column is specified when the column is created or altered. When set at the column level, it overrides any collation sequence set at the domain level.

Listing Available Collation Sequences

The following query yields a list of character sets with the available collation sequences:

```
SELECT
  C.RDB$CHARACTER_SET_NAME,
  CO.RDB$COLLATION_NAME,
  CO.RDB$COLLATION_ID,
  CO.RDB$CHARACTER_SET_ID,
  CO.RDB$COLLATION_ID * 256 + CO.RDB$CHARACTER_SET_ID AS TEXTTYPEID
FROM RDB$COLLATIONS CO
JOIN RDB$CHARACTER_SETS C
  ON CO.RDB$CHARACTER_SET_ID = C.RDB$CHARACTER_SET_ID;
```

Naming of Collation Sequences

Many Firebird collation names use the naming convention XX_YY, where XX is a two-letter language code and YY is a two-letter country code. For example, DE_DE is the collation name for German as used in Germany; FR_FR is for French as used in France; and FR_CA is for French as used in Canada.

Where a character set offers a choice of collations, the one with the name matching the character set is the default collation sequence, which implements *binary collation* for the character set. Binary collation sorts a character set by the numeric codes used to represent the characters. Some character sets support alternative collation sequences using different rules for determining precedence.

This section explains how to specify collation sequence for character sets in domains and table columns, in string comparisons, and in ORDER BY and GROUP BY clauses.

Collation Sequence for a Column

When a CHAR or VARCHAR column is created for a table, either with CREATE TABLE or ALTER TABLE, the collation sequence for the column can be specified using the COLLATE clause. COLLATE is especially useful for character sets such as ISO8859_1 or DOS437 that support many different collation sequences.

For example, the following dynamic ALTER TABLE statement adds a new column to a table, and specifies both a character set and a collation sequence:

```
ALTER TABLE 'EMP_CANADIEN'
ADD ADDRESS VARCHAR(40) CHARACTER SET ISO8859_1 NOT NULL
COLLATE FR_CA;
```

Refer to Chapter 16 for complete syntax for ALTER TABLE.

Collation Sequence for String Comparisons

It can be necessary to specify a collation sequence when CHAR or VARCHAR values are compared in a WHERE clause, if the values being compared use different collation sequences and it matters to the result.

To specify the collation sequence to use for a value during a comparison, include a COLLATE clause after the value. For example, the following WHERE clause fragment forces the column value to the left of the equivalence operator to be compared with the input parameter using a specific collation sequence:

```
WHERE SURNAME COLLATE FR_CA >= :surname;
```

In this case, without matching collation sequences, the candidates for "greater than" might be different for each collation sequence.

Collation Sequence in Sort Criteria

When CHAR or VARCHAR columns are ordered in a SELECT statement, it can be necessary to specify a collation order for the ordering, especially if columns used for ordering use different collation sequences.

To specify the collation sequence to use for ordering a column in the ORDER BY clause, include a COLLATE clause after the column name. For example, in the following ORDER BY clause, the collation sequences for two columns are specified:

```
...
ORDER BY SURNAME COLLATE FR_CA, FIRST_NAME COLLATE FR_CA;
```

For the complete syntax of the ORDER BY clause, see Chapter 23.

Collation Sequence in a GROUP BY Clause

When CHAR or VARCHAR columns are grouped in a SELECT statement, it can be necessary to specify a collation order for the grouping, especially if columns used for grouping use different collation sequences.

To specify the collation sequence to use for grouping columns in the GROUP BY clause, include a COLLATE clause after the column name. For example, in the following GROUP BY clause, the collation sequences for multiple columns are specified:

```
...
GROUP BY ADDR_3 COLLATE CA_CA, SURNAME COLLATE FR_CA, FIRST_NAME COLLATE FR_CA;
```

For the complete syntax of the GROUP BY clause, see Chapter 23.

Collation Sequence and Index Size

If you specify a non-binary collation (one other than the default collation) for a character set, the index key can become larger than the stored string if the collation includes precedence rules of second, third, or fourth order.

Non-binary collations for ISO8859_1, for example, use full dictionary sorts, with spaces and punctuation of fourth-order importance:

First order: A is different from B.

Second order: A is different from À.

Third order: A is different from a.

Fourth order: The type of punctuation symbol (hyphen, space, apostrophe) is important.

For example:

```
Greenfly
Green fly
Green-fly
Greensleeves
Green sleeves
Green spot
```

If spaces and punctuation marks are treated instead as a *first-order* difference, the same list would be sorted as follows:

```
Greenfly
Greensleeves
Green fly
Green sleeves
Green spot
Green-fly
```

How Non-Binary Collations Can Limit Index Size

When an index is created, it uses the collation sequence defined for each text segment in the index. Using ISO8859_1, a single-byte character set, with the default collation, the index structure can hold about 252 characters (fewer if it is a multi-segment index). However, if you choose a non-binary collation for ISO8859_1, the index structure can hold only 84 characters, despite the fact that the characters in the column being indexed occupy only 1 byte each.

CAUTION Some ISO8859_1 collations, DE_DE for example, require an average of 3 bytes per character for an indexed column.

Custom Character Sets and Collations

It is possible to write your own character sets and collations and have the Firebird engine load them from a shared library, which should be named *fbintl2* in order to be recognized and linked.

It is also possible to implement custom character sets or collations using user-defined functions (UDFs) to transliterate input. The Firebird 1.5 engine automatically uses UDFs with names specially formatted to be recognized as character sets and collations. The name "USER_CHARSET_nnn" indicates a character set, while "USER_TRANSLATE_nnn_nnn" and "USER_TEXTTYPE_nnn" indicate a character set plus collation sequence. (*nnn* represents three-digit numbers, usually in the range 128 to 254.)

It is an advanced topic, beyond the scope of this guide. The developer of the fbintl2 plug-in for custom character sets, David Brookestone Schnepper, makes a do-it-yourself kit freely available that contains sample C code, mappings, and instructions at http://www.ibcollate.com. Because the kit includes lucid instructions for creating character sets, it is also a useful reference if you plan to use the UDF approach to implement a custom character set.

Adding Your Own Alias

In an extreme situation—where you are using a non-standard operating system that requires a character set name that Firebird does not already support as an alias—you can add one. It is not very straightforward and requires updating the system tables directly—a practice that, as a general rule, should be avoided at all costs. Before you decide to add a custom alias, be certain that Firebird does not already support the alias you need—check the lists of aliases in Appendix VIII, beside each character set name.

Installing a custom alias involves inserting a row directly into the RDB$TYPES table. Get the character set ID of the character set that you want to alias—in RDB$CHARACTER_SETS it is the value in the RDB$CHARACTER_SET_ID column—and make sure you have the exact literal string that your operating system recognizes for the character set you want supported.

Suppose you want to add an alias for the character set ISO8859_1 that your OS recognizes by the literal "LC_ISO88591". First, get the character set ID by querying RDB$CHARACTER_SETS using **isql** or another interactive query tool:

```
SELECT RDB$CHARACTER_SET_ID
  FROM RDB$CHARACTER_SETS
  WHERE RDB$CHARACTER_SET_NAME = 'ISO8859_1';
```

The example returns the character set ID "21". Next, prepare and run an INSERT statement to add your alias to RDB$TYPES:

```
INSERT INTO RDB$TYPES (
  RDB$FIELD_NAME, RDB$TYPE, RDB$TYPE_NAME )
VALUES ('RDB$CHARACTER_SET_NAME', 21, 'LC_ISO88591');
```

The technique is relatively painless if your custom alias represents a character set needed for a specific column or domain, but is not required as the *default* character set of the database. Just make sure that the alias definition exists before you create any column or domain that needs to use it.

There is a catch-22 problem if your operating system genuinely cannot support an existing character set or alias for the character set you need to use as the default. Your database cannot "know" about your custom alias until *after* the database is created and an RDB$TYPES table actually exists. The default character set of the database is defined in CREATE DATABASE, at which point only the system-defined aliases are available. By the time RDB$TYPES exists, it is too late to assign the default character set.

Because Firebird SQL currently provides no way to update the default character set attribute—it is not supported in the ALTER DATABASE syntax—the only workaround is to create the database first and then, before doing anything else, install your alias as described, commit it, and proceed to update the database header record directly:

```
UPDATE RDB$DATABASE
  SET RDB$CHARACTER_SET_NAME = 'LC_ISO88591';
COMMIT;
```

 CAUTION   Never try to perform this workaround on any database that is not "empty" of any user-defined objects.

Up Next

Next, we move on to the types that Firebird implements using binary large objects (BLOBs), including text, untyped binary and custom formats, and the specialized BLOB implementation that Firebird surfaces as typed ARRAY types.

BLOBs and Arrays

BLOB TYPES (**BINARY LARGE OBJECTS**) are complex structures used for storing discrete data objects of variable size, which may be very large. They are "complex" in the sense that Firebird stores these types in two parts: a kind of hyperlink (referred to as a *BLOB_ID*) is stored with the owning row, while the actual data is stored apart from the row, often on one or many different database pages, keyed to the BLOB_ID.

Firebird uses these BLOB structures for a number of purposes internally. It also surfaces two main categories of user types using this type of storage structure: BLOB and ARRAY. ARRAY types can be used to represent homogeneous arrays of most data types.

BLOB Types

Almost any sort of storable data can be stored in a BLOB: bitmapped graphics images, vector drawings, sound files, video segments, chapter- or book-length documents, or any other kind of multimedia information. Because a BLOB can hold different kinds of information, it requires special processing at the client for reading and writing.

BLOB types can, where practicable,[1] store data files generated by other applications such as word processors, CAD software, or XML editors. The gains can be the benefit of transaction control for dynamic data, protection from external interference, control of versions, and the ability to access externally created data through the medium of SQL statements.

BLOB types cannot be indexed.

Supported BLOB Types

Out of the box, Firebird makes two pre-defined BLOB types available, distinguished by the *sub-type attribute* (SQL keyword SUB_TYPE), as described in Table 12-1.

---

1 BLOB storage is not a magic bullet for storing and retrieving large volumes of huge binary file data. Sometimes, under production conditions, the overhead and unwieldiness of storing non-dynamic data objects like movies or sound recordings inside the database overwhelm the benefits you perceived in the lab. Storing filesystem links to objects can be a valid approach.

Table 12-1. Pre-Defined BLOB Sub-Types

DEFINITION	SQL ALIAS	PURPOSE
BLOB SUB_TYPE 0	Not applicable	Generic BLOB type for storing any sort of data, including text. Commonly referred to as "an untyped binary BLOB," but Firebird is unaware of the contents.
BLOB SUB_TYPE 1	BLOB SUB_TYPE TEXT	More specialized sub-type for storing plain text. Equivalent to CLOB and MEMO types implemented by some other DBMSs. Recommended for use with application interfaces such as RAD components or search engines that provide special treatment for such types.

More About Sub-Types

A BLOB sub-type is a positive or negative integer that identifies the nature of the data contained in the column. Besides the two sub-types pre-defined for general use, Firebird has a number of sub-types that it uses internally. All of these internal sub-types have positive numbers.

Custom sub-types can be added to distinguish and identify special types of data objects, such as HTML, XML, or word-processor documents, JPEG and PNG images, etc.—the choice is up to you. Negative sub-type numbers—from –1 to –32,768—are reserved for assigning to custom sub-types.

BLOB subtyping also allows specific conversion from one sub-type to another. Firebird has extensible support for automatic conversion between a given pair of BLOB sub-types in the form of *BLOB filters*. Blob filters are a special kind of external function with a single purpose: to take a BLOB object in one format and convert it to a BLOB object in another format. It is possible to create a BLOB filter that converts between a custom (negative) sub-type and a pre-defined sub-type, commonly the TEXT one.

The object code for BLOB filters is placed in shared object libraries. The filter, which is invoked dynamically when required, is recognized at the database (not server) level by way of a declaration in metadata:

```
DECLARE FILTER <filter-name>
  INPUT_TYPE <sub-type> /* identifies type of object to be converted */
  OUTPUT_TYPE <sub-type> /* identifies type of object to be created */
  ENTRY_POINT '<entry-point-name>' /* name of exported function */
  MODULE_NAME '<external-library-name>'; /* name of BLOB filter library */
```

NOTE   The writing and use of BLOB filters are beyond the scope of this guide. More information on the topic can be found by searching the Firebird knowledge bases.

Firebird does not check the type or format of BLOB data. When planning to store it, you must make your application code responsible for ensuring that the format of the data agrees with its sub-type, whether pre-defined or custom.

BLOB Segments

BLOB data is stored in a different format from regular column data and apart from it. It is stored as *segments* in one or more database pages, in a distinct row version that is unlike the format of a row of regular data. *Segments* are discrete chunks of unformatted data that are usually streamed by the application and passed to the API to be packaged for transmission across the network, one chunk at a time, in contiguous order.

In the regular row structure of the parent row, the BLOB is linked through a BLOB ID that is stored with the regular row data. A BLOB ID is a unique hexadecimal pair that provides a cross-reference between a BLOB and the table it belongs to. On arrival at the server, segments are laid down in the same order as they are received, although not necessarily in chunks of the same size in which they were transported.

Where possible, the BLOB row versions are stored on the same page as parent row. However, large BLOBs can extend across many pages, and this initial "BLOB row" may not contain actual data but an array of pointers to BLOB pages.

Declaration Syntax Examples

The following statement defines two BLOB columns: BLOB1 with sub-type 0 (the default) and BLOB2 with Firebird sub-type 1 (TEXT):

```
CREATE TABLE TABLE2
(BLOB1 BLOB, /* SUB_TYPE 0 */
BLOB2 BLOB SUB_TYPE 1);
```

The next statement defines a domain that is a text BLOB to store text in character set ISO_8859_1:

```
CREATE DOMAIN MEMO
  BLOB SUB_TYPE TEXT /*BLOB SUB_TYPE 1 */
  CHARACTER  SET ISO_8859_1;
```

This SQL snippet shows how a local BLOB variable is declared in a PSQL module:

```
CREATE PROCEDURE ...
...
DECLARE VARIABLE AMEMO BLOB SUB_TYPE 1;
...
```

Segment Size

When a BLOB column is defined in a table, the definition can optionally include the expected size of segments that are written to the column. The default—80 bytes—is really quite arbitrary. Mythology says it was chosen because it was exactly the length of one line on a text terminal display!

The segment size setting does not affect Firebird's performance in processing BLOBs on the server: The server does not use it at all. For DSQL applications—which are what most people write—you can simply ignore it or, if relevant, set it to some size that suits the buffer in which your application stores BLOB data.

For DML operations—SELECT, INSERT, and UPDATE— the length of the segment is specified in an API structure when it is written and can be any size, up to a maximum of 32,767 bytes. Reusable classes for development environments such as Delphi, C++, and Java usually take care of BLOB segmentation in their internal functions and procedures. If you are programming directly to the API, you will need to develop your own routines for constructing segments.

Embedded Applications

In databases for use with embedded applications—here, we're talking about ESQL apps written for preprocessing by the **gpre** preprocessor—the segment size must be declared to indicate the *maximum* number of bytes that an application is expected to write to any segment in the column. Normally, an ESQL application should not attempt to write segments larger than the segment length defined in the table; doing so overflows the internal segment buffer, corrupting memory in the process. It may be advantageous to specify a relatively large segment, to reduce the number of calls to retrieve BLOB data.

The following statement creates two BLOB columns: BLOB1, with a default segment size of 80, and BLOB2, with a specified segment length of 1024.

```
CREATE TABLE TABLE2
(BLOB1 BLOB SUB_TYPE 0,
BLOB2 BLOB SEGMENT SUB_TYPE TEXT SEGMENT SIZE 1024);
```

In this ESQL code fragment, an application inserts a BLOB segment. The segment length is specified in a host variable, *segment_length*:

```
INSERT CURSOR BCINS VALUES (:write_segment_buffer :segment_length);
```

Operations on BLOBs

A BLOB is never updated. Every update that "changes" a BLOB causes a new BLOB to be constructed, complete with a new BLOB ID. The original BLOB becomes obsolete once the update is committed.

A BLOB column can be tested for NULL/NOT NULL, but no internal function exists to compare one BLOB with another or to compare a BLOB to a string. Several BLOB UDFs are available from community download sites, including some that compare two BLOBs for equality.

It is not possible to concatenate two BLOBs or to concatenate a string to a BLOB.

String Input to BLOB Columns

When accepting data for input to BLOB columns by way of an INSERT or UPDATE operation, Firebird can take a string as input and transform it into a BLOB, for example:

```
INSERT INTO ATABLE (PK, ABLOB)
VALUES (99, 'This is some text.');
```

Note that passing a string to a stored procedure for an input argument that was defined as a BLOB will cause an exception. The following, for example, will fail:

```
CREATE PROCEDURE DEMO (INPUTARG BLOB SUB_TYPE 1)
AS
BEGIN
...
END ^
COMMIT ^
EXECUTE PROCEDURE DEMO('Show us what you can do with this!') ^
```

Instead, do one of the following:

- Define the input argument as a VARCHAR and have your procedure submit the string to the INSERT or UPDATE statement itself.

- Have your client program take care of converting the string to a text BLOB. This will be the preferred solution if the length of the string is unknown.

When to Use BLOB Types

The BLOB is preferred to character types for storing text data of infinitely variable length. Because it is transported in "mindless chunks," it is not subject to the 32K length limit of strings, as long as the client application implements the appropriate techniques to pass it in the format required by the server for segmenting it.[2]

---

2 It is possible to pass a string type as input to a BLOB and leave the server to convert it. Under these conditions, it is not possible to store a BLOB that exceeds the 32K limit for strings.

Because the BLOB is stored apart from regular row data, it is not fetched automatically when row data is selected. Rather, the client requests the data on demand, by way of the BLOB_ID. Consequently, there is big "win" in the time taken to begin fetching rows from a SELECT, compared to the traffic involved when character types are used for storing large text items. On the other hand, some developers may consider it a disadvantage to have to implement "fetch on demand."

When considering whether to use BLOB for non-text data, other issues arise. The convenience of being able to store images, sound files, and compiled documents has to be balanced against the overhead it adds to backups. It may be an unreasonable design objective to store large numbers of huge objects that are never going to change.

Security

The idea that large binary and text objects are more secure when stored in BLOBs than when stored in filesystem files is, to some extent, an illusion. Certainly, they are more difficult to access from end-user tools. However, database privileges currently do not apply to BLOB and ARRAY types beyond the context of the tables to which they are linked by indirection. It is not absurd to suppose that a malicious hacker who gained access to open the database file could write application code that scanned the file for BLOB_IDs and read the data directly from storage, as external BLOB functions do.

Array Types

Firebird allows you to create homogeneous arrays of most data types. Using an array enables multiple data items to be stored as discrete, multi-dimensional *elements* in a single column. Firebird can perform operations on an entire array, effectively treating it as a single element, or it can operate on an *array slice*, a subset of array elements. An array slice can consist of a single element or a set of many contiguous elements.

ARRAY Types and SQL

Because Firebird does not implement any dynamic SQL syntax for operating on ARRAY types, performing DML and searches on them from a dynamic SQL (DSQL) interface is not simple. The Firebird API surfaces structures and functions to enable dynamic applications to work with them directly. Some RAD data access components—for example, IB Objects for use with Borland's Delphi and Kylix products—provide classes encapsulating this API functionality as client-side properties and methods.

ESQL, which does not use the API structures and function calls, supports several static SQL syntaxes for operating on ARRAY types and integrating them with arrays declared in the host language.

For both dynamic and static applications, it is feasible, albeit not very practicable, to read array data into a stored procedure and return values that the client application can use. An example appears later in the section "Limited Dynamic SQL Access."

When to Use an Array Type

Using an array is appropriate when

- The data items naturally form a set of the same data type.

- The entire set of data items in a single database column must be represented and controlled as a unit, as opposed to storing each item in a separate column.

- Each item must also be identified and accessed individually.

- There is no requirement to access the values individually in triggers or stored procedures, or you have external functions that enable such access.

Eligible Element Types

An ARRAY can contain elements of any Firebird data type except BLOB. Arrays of ARRAY are not supported. All of the elements of a particular array are of the same data type.

Defining Arrays

An array can be defined as a domain (using CREATE DOMAIN) or as a column, in a CREATE TABLE or ALTER TABLE statement. Defining an array domain or column is similar to defining any other, with the additional inclusion of the array dimensions. Array dimensions are enclosed in square brackets following data type specification.

For example, the following statement defines both a regular character column and a one-dimensional character ARRAY column containing eight elements:

```
CREATE TABLE ATABLE
(ID BIGINT,
ARR_CHAR(14)[8] CHARACTER SET OCTETS); /* stores 1 row * 8 elements */
```

Multi-Dimensional Arrays

Firebird supports *multi-dimensional arrays*, which are arrays with 1 to 16 dimensions. For example, the following statement defines three INTEGER ARRAY columns with two, three, and four dimensions, respectively:

```
CREATE TABLE BTABLE (
/* stores 4 rows X 5 elements = 20 elements */
  ARR_INT2 INTEGER[4,5],
/* 6 layers, each 4 rows X 5 elements = 120 elements */
  ARR_INT3 INTEGER[4,5,6],
```

```
/* 7 storeys, each 6 layers of 4 rows * 5 elements = 840 elements */
  ARR_INT6 INTEGER[4,5,6,7]
);
```

Firebird stores multi-dimensional arrays in *row-major order*. Some host languages, such as FORTRAN, expect arrays to be in *column-major order*. In these cases, care must be taken to translate element ordering correctly between Firebird and the host language.

Specifying Subscript Ranges for Dimensions

Firebird's array dimensions have a specific range of upper and lower boundaries, called *subscripts*. Dimensions are 1-based by default—that is, the first element of the dimension array of n elements has subscript 1, the second element has subscript 2, and the last element has subscript n. For example, the following statement creates a table with a column that is an array of four integers:

```
CREATE TABLE TABLEC
(ARR_INT INTEGER[4]);
```

The subscripts for this array are 1, 2, 3, and 4.

Custom (Explicit) Subscript Boundaries

A custom set of upper and lower boundaries can be defined explicitly for each array dimension when an ARRAY column is created. For example, C and Pascal programmers, familiar with zero-based arrays, might want to create ARRAY columns with a lower boundary of zero to map transparently to array structures in application code.

Both the lower and upper boundaries of the dimension are required when defining custom boundaries, using the following syntax:

```
[lower:upper]
```

The following example creates a table with a single-dimension, zero-based ARRAY column:

```
CREATE TABLE TABLED
(ARR_INT INTEGER[0:3]);  /* subscripts are 0, 1, 2, and 3. */
```

Each dimension's set of subscripts is separated from the next with commas. For example, the following statement creates a table with a two-dimensional ARRAY column where both dimensions are zero-based:

```
CREATE TABLE TABLEE
(ARR_INT INTEGER[0:3, 0:3]);
```

Storage of ARRAY Columns

As with other types implemented as BLOB, Firebird stores an *array ID* with the non-BLOB column data of the database table, that points to the page(s) containing the actual data.

Updates

As with other BLOB types, the Firebird engine cannot course through the data seeking successive individual target elements for conditional or selective update. However, in a single DML operation, it is possible to isolate one element or a set of contiguous elements, known as a *slice*, and target that slice for update.

Inserts

INSERT cannot operate on a slice. When a row is inserted in a table containing ARRAY columns, it is necessary to construct and populate the array entirely, before passing it in the INSERT statement.

Accessing Array Data

Some application interfaces do provide encapsulation of the API functions and descriptors, and limited read access is possible from stored procedures.

The Array Descriptor

The API exposes the array descriptor structure for describing to the server the array or array slice to be read from or written to the database. It is presented to programmers in ibase.h, as follows (comments added):

```
typedef struct
{
    short array_bound_lower;  /* lower bound of array or slice */
    short array_bound_upper;  /* upper bound of array or slice */
} ISC_ARRAY_BOUND;

typedef struct
{
    unsigned char   array_desc_dtype;   /* data type of elements */
    char            array_desc_scale;   /* scale, for number types */
    unsigned short  array_desc_length;  /* length of array element (bytes) */
    char            array_desc_field_name[32]; /* column identifier */
    char            array_desc_relation_name[32];  /* table identifier */
    short           array_desc_dimensions; /* number of dimensions */
    short           array_desc_flags; /* 0=row-major order, 1=column-major */
    ISC_ARRAY_BOUND array_desc_bounds[16]; /* lower & upper bounds for up to 16
                                              dimensions */
} ISC_ARRAY_DESC;
```

The InterBase 6 *API Guide,* published by Borland Software Corporation, provides detailed instructions for manipulating arrays through the API structures.

More information about using arrays in embedded applications can be obtained from the *Embedded SQL Guide,* a companion volume in the Borland set.

Limited Dynamic SQL Access

The following example is a simple demonstration of how a DSQL application can get limited read access to an array slice through a stored procedure:

```
create procedure getcharslice(
  low_elem smallint, high_elem smallint)
returns (id integer, list varchar(50))
as
declare variable i smallint;
declare variable string varchar(10);
begin
  for select a1.ID from ARRAYS a1 into :id do
  begin
    i= low_elem;
    list = '';
    while (i <= high_elem) do
    begin
      select a2.CHARARRAY[:i] from arrays a2
      where  a2.ID = :id
      into :string;
      list = list||string;
      if (i < high_elem) then
        list = list||',';
      i = i + 1;
    end
    suspend;
  end
end
```

Up Next

The last chapter in this part of the book describes how to cluster a data type and a package of attributes into a *domain* that you can use to generalize a single data definition across an indefinite number of columns in many tables.

Domains

DOMAINS IN FIREBIRD ARE AKIN TO THE CONCEPT of "user-defined data types." Although it is not possible to create a new data type, with a domain you can package a set of attributes with those of an existing data type, give it an identifier and, thereafter, use it in place of the data type parameter to define columns for any table.

Domain definitions are global to the database—all columns in any table that are defined with a particular domain will have completely identical attributes unless modified by local overrides.

As is noted elsewhere, domains cannot be substituted for native data types when defining arguments and variables in stored procedures and triggers.

> **NOTE** Column-level overrides to domain attributes are discussed later in this chapter.

Columns based on a domain definition inherit all attributes of the domain, which can be

- Data type (required)

- A default value for inserts

- NULL status

- CHECK constraints

- Character set (for character and BLOB columns only)

- Collation order (for character columns only)

> **NOTE** You cannot apply referential integrity constraints to a domain.

The benefits for encapsulating a data definition are obvious. For a simple but common example, suppose your design calls for a number of small tables where you want to store the text descriptions of enumerated sets—"type" tables—account types, product types, subscriptions types, etc. You have decided that each member of each of these sets will be keyed on a three-character uppercase identifier that points to a character description or title field having a maximum of 25 characters.

All that is required is to create two domains:

- The domain for the pointer will be a CHAR(3) with two attributes added: a NOT NULL constraint because you are going to use it for primary and lookup keys and a CHECK constraint to enforce uppercase. For example:

```
CREATE DOMAIN Type_Key AS CHAR(3) NOT NULL
CHECK (VALUE = UPPER(VALUE));
```

- The description domain will be a VARCHAR(25). You want it to be non-nullable because the tables you want to use it in are control tables:

```
CREATE DOMAIN Type_Description AS VARCHAR(25) NOT NULL
```

Once you have these domains defined, all of your type-lookup tables can have similar definitions, and all tables that store lookup keys to these tables will use the matching domain for the key column.

Creating a Domain

The data definition language (DDL) syntax for creating a domain is

```
CREATE DOMAIN domain [AS] <datatype>
[DEFAULT literal |NULL |USER}]
[NOT NULL] [CHECK (<dom_search_condition>)]
[CHARSET charset | NONE}]
[COLLATE collation];
```

Domain Identifier

When you create a domain in the database, you must specify an identifier for the domain that is globally unique in the database. Developers often use a special prefix or suffix in domain identifiers, to facilitate self-documentation. For example:

```
CREATE DOMAIN D_TYPE_IDENTIFIER...
CREATE DOMAIN DESCRIPTION_D...
```

Data Type for the Domain

The *data type* is the only required attribute that must be set for the domain—all other attributes are optional. It specifies the SQL data type that will apply to a column defined using the domain. Any native Firebird data type can be used. It is not possible to use a domain as the type for another domain.

The following statement creates a domain that defines an array of CHARACTER type:

```
CREATE DOMAIN DEPTARRAY AS CHAR(31) [4:5];
```

The next statement creates a BLOB domain with a text subtype that has an assigned character set: overriding the default character set of the database. It effectively creates a specialized memo type for storing Japanese text:

```
CREATE DOMAIN DESCRIPT_JP AS BLOB SUB_TYPE TEXT
CHARACTER SET SJIS;
```

The DEFAULT Attribute

A domain can define a default value that the server will use when inserting a new row if the INSERT statement *does not include the column in its specification list*. Defaults can save time and error during data entry. For example, a possible default for a DATE column could be today's date, or to write the CURRENT_USER context variable into a UserName column.

Default values can be

- A constant. The default value is a user-specified string, numeric value, or date value—often used for placing a "zero value" into a non-nullable column.

- CURRENT_TIMESTAMP, CURRENT_DATE, CURRENT_TIME, or a Firebird predefined date literal—see Chapter 10.

- USER, CURRENT_USER, or CURRENT_ROLE (if roles are applicable).

- CURRENT_CONNECTION or CURRENT_TRANSACTION.

NOTE It is possible to specify NULL as a default. However, it is redundant, since nullable columns are initialized as NULL by default anyway. Furthermore, an explicit NULL default can cause conflicts when a column using the domain needs to be defined with a NOT NULL constraint (see "The NOT NULL Attribute" section later in this chapter).

The following statement creates a domain that must have a positive value greater than 1,000. If the INSERT statement does not present a VALUE, the column will be assigned the default value of 9,999:

```
CREATE DOMAIN CUSTNO
AS INTEGER
DEFAULT 9999
CHECK (VALUE > 1000);
```

If your operating system supports the use of multi-byte characters in user names, or you have used a multi-byte character set when defining roles, then any column into which these defaults will be stored must be defined using a compatible character set.

When Defaults Won't Work

It is a common mistake to assume that a default value will be used whenever Firebird receives NULL in a defaulted column. When relying on defaults, it must be understood that a default will be applied

- Only upon insertion of a new row

AND

- Only if the INSERT statement does not include the defaulted column in its column list

If your application includes the defaulted column in the INSERT statement and sends NULL in the values list, then NULL will be stored—or cause an exception in a non-nullable column—regardless of any default defined.

The NOT NULL Attribute

Include this attribute in the domain if you want to force all columns created with this domain to contain a value.

NULL—which is not a value, but a *state*—will always be disallowed on any column bearing the NOT NULL attribute. For a detailed discussion of NULL, see the topic "Considering NULL" in Chapter 21.

CAUTION You cannot override the NOT NULL attribute on a domain. Consider the benefit of not including it in the domain's attributes, thereby leaving it as an option to add the attribute when columns are defined.

CHECK Data Conditions

The CHECK constraint provides a wide scope for providing domain attributes that restrict the content of data that can be stored in columns using the domain. The CHECK constraint sets a search condition *(dom_search_condition)* that must be true before data can be accepted into these columns.

Here's the syntax for CHECK constraints:

```
<dom_search_condition> =
VALUE <operator> <val>
| VALUE [NOT] BETWEEN <val> AND <val>
| VALUE [NOT] LIKE <val> [ESCAPE <val>]
| VALUE [NOT] IN (<val> [, <val> ...])
| VALUE IS [NOT] NULL
| VALUE [NOT] CONTAINING <val>
| VALUE [NOT] STARTING [WITH] <val>
|(<dom_search_condition>)
|NOT<dom_search_condition>
| <dom_search_condition> OR <dom_search_condition>
| <dom_search_condition> AND <dom_search_condition>
<operator> ={=|<|>|<=|>=|!<|!>|<>|!=}
```

The VALUE Keyword

VALUE is a placeholder for any constant or variable value or expression result that would be submitted through SQL for storing in a column defined using the domain. The CHECK constraint causes VALUE to be validated against the restrictions defined in the conditions. If validation fails, an exception is raised.

If NULL is to be permitted in lieu of a value, the rule must be accommodated in the CHECK constraint, for example:

```
CHECK ((VALUE IS NULL) OR (VALUE > 1000));
```

The next statement creates a domain that disallows any input value of 1000 or less, but it also implicitly disallows NULL by presuming a value:

```
CREATE DOMAIN CUSTNO
AS INTEGER
CHECK (VALUE > 1000);
```

The next statement restricts VALUE to being one of four specific values:

```
CREATE DOMAIN PRODTYPE
AS VARCHAR(8) NOT NULL
CHECK (VALUE IN ('software', 'hardware', 'other', 'N/A'));
```

A validation condition can be made to search for a specific pattern in a string input. For example, the next validation check enforces a rule that requires a bracketed area code to precede telecom numbers (e.g., (09)438894749):

```
CREATE DOMAIN TEL_NUMBER
AS VARCHAR(18)
CHECK (VALUE LIKE '(0%)%');
```

For details of the pattern strings you can use in expressions, refer to the notes on the LIKE operator in Chapter 21, in the section "SQL Operators."

Multiple CHECK Conditions

A domain can have only one CHECK clause but multiple conditions can be ANDed or ORed within this single clause. Care is needed with bracketing the condition expressions to avoid getting logical exceptions when the DDL statement is prepared.

For example, this statement fails:

```
create domain rhubarb as varchar(20)
check (value is not null) and (value starting with 'J');
```

It excepts with a "token unknown" error upon the word "and." The corrected statement encloses the entire list of conditions within outer brackets and succeeds:

```
create domain rhubarb as varchar(20)
check ((value is not null) and (value starting with 'J'));
```

NOTE   The preceding example checks that the incoming value is not null. This is fine, but using the NOT NULL constraint directly is more powerful for application interfaces. The API can inform the client application at Prepare time of a NOT NULL constraint, whereas CHECK validation triggers do not fire until a DML request is actually posted to the server.

For details of STARTING WITH and other SQL operators used in expressions, refer to Chapter 21.

A domain's CHECK constraint cannot be overridden by one declared during column definition. However, a column can *extend* its use of the domain's CHECK constraint by adding its own CHECK conditions.

Dependencies in CHECK Constraints

In tables, CHECK constraints can be defined legally with expressions referring to other columns in the same table or, less desirably, referring to columns in other database objects (tables, stored procedures).

Domains, of course, cannot refer to other domains. It is possible, although almost always unwise, to define a domain that refers to a column in an existing table. For example:

```
create domain rather_silly as char(3)
  check (value in (select substring(registration from 1 for 3)
    from aircraft));
```

Conceptually, it's not such a wild concept to use select expressions in domains. Firebird allows it but it really does not follow through and implement it as an integrated design. It is an accidental by-product, not a feature.

As a database design approach, it integrates poorly with the referential integrity features that are purposefully implemented. Foreign key relationships enforce existence rules in all areas, whereas the scope of a CHECK constraint is limited to data entry.

CHECK constraints with inter-table dependencies would be disabled on restoring the database from a backup. They would silently fail to compile because the dependent tables had not yet been re-created. To put them back into effect, they would have to be reinstated manually, by some means. Implementing such checks at domain level has mind-boggling implications.

In some situations, where the dependency applies to a highly static table whose name is low in alphabetical sequence (**gbak** restores tables in alphabetical order), such a CHECK condition *might* be faintly arguable. The problem remains that the domain has no control over what happens to data stored in tables beyond the event of checking the data coming into columns that use it.

 TIP Another "gotcha" with this technique is that it makes it difficult (or impossible) for utility programs to extract bombproof SQL schema scripts from the system tables. There will come a time in your life when your job depends on a reliable schema extract!

If you absolutely *need* to use this kind of check condition, apply it as an extra condition when you declare the column. Preferably, evaluate all of the alternatives—including the hand-coding of referential triggers in cases where foreign keys on lookup fields would cause recognized problems with index selectivity.[1]

---

1. For more about this particular "gotcha," refer to the "Optimization Topic" section at the end of Chapter 18.

The CHARSET/CHARACTER SET Attribute

For systems that need to be concerned about multiple character sets inside a single database, declaring character set–specific domains for all of your text columns (CHAR, VARCHAR, BLOB SUB_TYPE 1, and arrays of character types) can be a very elegant way to deal with it. Refer to the previous chapter for character set definition syntax.

The COLLATE Attribute

A COLLATE clause in a domain creation statement specifies an explicit collation sequence for CHAR or VARCHAR domains. You must choose a collation that is supported for the domain's declared, inherited, or implied character set.

Refer to Chapter 11 for COLLATE definition syntax. For a list of the collation sequences available for each character set, see Appendix VIII.

Using a Domain in a Column Definition

Example

In a certain database, SYSUSER is a domain of up to 31 characters, having a DEFAULT value that is to be obtained by reading the context variable CURRENT_USER:

```
CREATE DOMAIN SYSUSER AS VARCHAR(31) DEFAULT CURRENT_USER;
```

A table is defined, having a column UPDATED_BY that uses this SYSUSER domain:

```
CREATE TABLE LOANS (
  LOAN_DATE DATE,
  UPDATED_BY SYSUSER,
  LOAN_FEE DECIMAL(15,2));
```

A client submits an INSERT statement for the LOANS table:

```
INSERT INTO ORDERS (LOAN_DATE, LOAN_FEE)
  VALUES ('16-MAY-2004', 10.75);
```

Because the statement does not name the UPDATED_BY column in its column list, Firebird automatically inserts the user name of the current user, ALICEFBIRD:

```
SELECT * FROM LOANS;
```

returns

```
16-MAY-2004 ALICEFBIRD    10.75
```

NOTE It is timely here to remember that domain and column defaults kick in only on inserts and only if the defaulted column is not named in the input list of the INSERT statement. Triggers are a much more robust way to implement defaults. Techniques are discussed in Chapter 31.

Domain Overrides

Columns defined using a domain can override some attributes inherited from the domain, by replacing an inherited attribute with an equivalent attribute clause. The column definition can also be extended by adding further attributes. In Table 13-1, you can see which attributes can and cannot be overridden.

Table 13-1. Domain Attributes and Column Overrides

ATTRIBUTE	OVERRIDE?	NOTES
Data type	No	
DEFAULT	Yes	
CHARACTER SET	Yes	Can also be used to revert a column to database default.
COLLATE	Yes	
CHECK	No override	Use a regular CHECK clause in CREATE or ALTER TABLE statement to extend CHECK clause with more conditions.
NOT NULL	No	A domain-level NOT NULL cannot be overridden at the column level. Often it is better to leave a domain as nullable and add the NOT NULL constraint to columns, where required, during CREATE or ALTER TABLE.

The following statement shows how to extend the attributes of a column that is being defined to use a domain, using an earlier domain definition example:

```
CREATE DOMAIN TEL_NUMBER
AS VARCHAR(18)
CHECK (VALUE LIKE '(0%)%');
```

Let's say we want to define a table having a telecom number column in it. We want the domain's attributes, but we also want to ensure that any non-numeral characters are input in uppercase:

```
CREATE TABLE LIBRARY_USER (
  USER_ID INTEGER NOT NULL.
  ... <other columns>,
  PHONE_NO TEL_NUMBER,
```

```
    CONSTRAINT CHK_TELNUM_UPPER
      CHECK (PHONE_NO = UPPER(PHONE_NO))
);
```

Now, we have an extra CHECK validation on this particular column. This statement:

```
INSERT INTO LIBRARY_USER VALUES(USER_ID, PHONE_NO)
VALUES (99, '(09) 43889 wish');
```

fails, because the extra CHECK constraint requires the phone number to be '(09) 43889 WISH'.

Where Domains Won't Work

A domain cannot be used

- With the `CAST (aValue AS <another type>)` function.

- In lieu of a data type when defining input or output arguments for a stored procedure.

- To declare the type of a variable in a trigger or stored procedure.

- To define the data type of the elements of an ARRAY. A domain can itself be an ARRAY type, however.

Defining a BOOLEAN Domain

Up to and including release 1.5, Firebird does not provide a Boolean type. A Boolean-styled domain is ideal, because you can define attributes that will be consistent across all tables. It is recommended that you use the smallest possible data type: a CHAR for T[rue]/F[alse] or Y[es]/N[o] switches or a SMALLINT 1/0 pairing. The following examples suggest ways you might implement your Booleans.

Example 13-1. A Two-Phase Switch That Defaults to 'F' (False)

```
CREATE DOMAIN D_BOOLEAN AS CHAR
  DEFAULT 'F' NOT NULL
  CHECK(VALUE IN ('T', 'F'));
```

Example 13-2. A Three-Phase Switch That Allows UNKNOWN (i.e., NULL)

```
CREATE DOMAIN D_LOGICAL AS SMALLINT
  CHECK (VALUE IS NULL OR VALUE IN (1,0));
```

Example 13-3. A Three-Phase Switch That Represents UNKNOWN As a Value

```
CREATE DOMAIN D_GENDER AS CHAR(4)
  DEFAULT 'N/K' NOT NULL
  CHECK (VALUE IN ('FEM', 'MASC', 'N/K'));
```

CAUTION Don't use BOOLEAN, UNKNOWN, TRUE, or FALSE as names for your Boolean domains. They are reserved words in Firebird. True logical types are planned for Firebird 2 and may appear in sub-releases between 1.5 and 2.

Changing Domain Definitions

The DDL statement ALTER DOMAIN can be used to change any aspect of an existing domain except its NOT NULL setting. Changes that you make to a domain definition affect all column definitions based on the domain that have not been overridden at the table level.

A domain can be altered by its creator, the SYSDBA user, or (on Linux/UNIX) any user with operating system root privileges.

Using ALTER DOMAIN you can

- Rename the domain

- Modify the data type

- Drop an existing default value

- Set a new default value

- Drop an existing CHECK constraint

- Add a new CHECK constraint

NOTE The only way to "change" the NOT NULL setting of a domain is to drop the domain and re-create it with the desired combination of features.

Here's the syntax:

```
ALTER DOMAIN { name | old_name TO new_name }{
[SET DEFAULT {literal | NULL | USER | etc.}]
| [DROP DEFAULT]
| [ADD [CONSTRAINT] CHECK (<match_conditions>)]
| [DROP CONSTRAINT]
|TYPE data_type
};
```

Examples

This statement sets a new default value for the BOOK_GROUP domain:

```
ALTER DOMAIN BOOK_GROUP SET DEFAULT -1;
```

In this statement, the name of the BOOK_GROUP domain is changed to PUBL_GROUP:

```
ALTER DOMAIN BOOK_GROUP TO PUBL_GROUP;
```

Constraints on Altering Data Types

The TYPE clause of ALTER DOMAIN allows the data type to be changed to another, permitted data type. For permitted type conversions, refer to Figure 8-1 in Chapter 8.

Any type conversion that could result in data loss is disallowed. For example, the number of characters in a domain could not be made smaller than the size of the largest value in any column that uses it.

Converting a numeric data type to a character type requires a minimum length for the character type as listed in Table 8-3 of Chapter 8.

The following statement changes the data type of a CHAR(80) domain, BOOK_TITLE, to VARCHAR(100):

```
ALTER DOMAIN BOOK_TITLE TYPE VARCHAR(100);
```

Dropping a Domain

DROP DOMAIN removes an existing domain definition from a database, provided the domain is not currently used for any column definition in the database.

To avoid exceptions, use ALTER TABLE to drop any table columns using the domain before executing DROP DOMAIN. The best way to do this in a single task is with a DDL script. Refer to the section "Schema Scripts" in the next chapter for instructions.

A domain can be dropped by its creator, the SYSDBA user, or (on Linux/UNIX) any user with operating system root privileges.

Here's the syntax:

```
DROP DOMAIN name;
```

The following statement deletes an unwanted domain:

```
DROP DOMAIN rather_silly;
```

Up Next

With the definition of data taken care of, it is now time to move on to the "fun stuff": designing and defining databases. The next group of chapters takes you through the concepts of the database, the objects it comprises, and the SQL language subset known as *data definition language*, or DDL, that you use to define the objects and the rules governing their behavior.

We begin, in Chapter 14, with some guidelines for designing relational databases. The chapter ends with a section about schema scripting.

Part Four

A Database and
Its Objects

CHAPTER 14

From Drawing Board to Database

A DATABASE, OF COURSE, STORES DATA. However, data alone has no use unless it is stored according to some rules that first capture its meaning and value, and secondly allow it to be retrieved consistently. A database having an existence within the context of a database management system (DBMS), such as Firebird, comprises a lot of "things" besides data.

Firebird is a *relational* database management system. As such, it is designed to support the creation and maintenance of abstract data structures, not just to store data but also to maintain relationships and to optimize the speed and consistency with which requested data can be returned to SQL client applications.

The SYSDBA User and Password

Up to and including Firebird 1.5, the SYSDBA user has full destructive rights to all databases on the server. Installation scripts install the security database with a default password, *masterkey*.

- Some Release 1.5 Linux installations run a script that generates a new password and changes the SYSDBA password. You can inspect the generated password in the file SYSDBA.password, located in the Firebird root directory.

CAUTION The masterkey password is widely known to the public. Ensure that you change it to some obscure eight-character string. Refer to Chapter 34 for instructions.

Metadata

Collectively, objects defined within a database are known as its *metadata* or, more traditionally, its *schema*. The process of creating and modifying metadata is referred to as *data definition*. The term "data definition" is often also applied to the description of a single object and its attributes.

This section covers the concepts, terminology, and language of data definition in detail.

Data Definition Language

The underlying structures of a database—its tables, views, and indexes—are created using a subset of the Firebird SQL language known as Data Definition Language (DDL). A DDL statement begins with one of the keywords CREATE, ALTER, RECREATE, or DROP, causing a single object to be created, modified, reconstructed, or destroyed, respectively. The database and, thereafter, its objects, rules, and relationships interlock to form the structure of a relational database.

The System Tables

Firebird stores metadata in a set of tables that it creates right inside the database—the *system tables*. All system tables have identifiers beginning with "RDB$". For example, the table that stores the definitions and other information about all of the table structures in your database is called RDB$RELATIONS. A related table, RDB$RELATION_FIELDS, stores information and definitions for the columns of each table.

This "database within a database" is highly normalized. DDL statements are designed to perform operations on the metadata tables safely and in full cognizance of the cascading effects.

It is possible to alter the data in the system tables by performing regular SQL operations on them. Some admin tools, such as **isql** and **gfix**, do internally change data in the system tables. However, as a sophisticated database management system, Firebird was not designed with raw end-user manipulation of the system tables in mind.

 CAUTION   It is not recommended that you attempt to bypass DDL by altering the system tables yourself, either through application code or by way of an interactive query tool. The system tables are the "meta-metadata" of any database. Any human intervention is likely to cause unpredictable types of damage.

SELECT queries on the system tables are fine and can be very useful for listing out things like character sets, dependencies, and so on. For a full schema of the system tables, refer to Appendix IX.

Designing a Database

Although relational databases are very flexible, the only way to guarantee data integrity and satisfactory database performance is a solid database design—there is no built-in protection against poor design decisions. A good database design

- **Satisfies the users' content requirements for the database**. Before you can design the database, you must do extensive research on the requirements of the users and how the database will be used. The most flexible database designs today evolve during a well-managed process of analysis, prototyping, and testing that involves all of the people who will use it.

- **Ensures the consistency and integrity of the data**. When you design a table, you define certain attributes and constraints that restrict what a user or an application can enter into the table and its columns. By validating the data before it is stored in the table, the database enforces the rules of the data model and preserves data integrity.

- **Provides a natural, easy-to-understand structuring of information**. Good design makes queries easier to understand, so users are less likely to introduce inconsistencies into the data or to be forced to enter redundant data.

- **Satisfies the users' performance requirements**. Good database design ensures better performance. If tables are allowed to be too large (wide), or if there are too many (or too few) indexes, long waits can result. If the database is very large with a high volume of transactions, performance problems resulting from poor design are magnified.

- **Insulates the system from design mistakes in subsequent development cycles.**

Description and Analysis

A database abstractly represents a world of organization, relationships, rules, and processes. Before reaching the point of being capable of designing the structures and rules for the database, the analyst/designer has much to do, working with the people involved to identify the real-life structures, rules, and requirements from which the database design will be rendered. The importance of scrupulous description and analysis cannot be emphasized too strongly.

Logical data analysis is an iterative process of refining and distilling the world of inputs, tasks, and outputs whose scope is to be encompassed by the database. Large, haphazard structures of information are reduced progressively to smaller, more specialized data objects and are gradually mapped to a data model.

An important part of this reduction process involves *normalization*—splitting out groups of data items with the goal of establishing essential relationships, eliminating redundancies, and associating connected items of data in structures that can be manipulated efficiently.

This phase can be one of the most challenging tasks for the database designer, especially in environments where the business has been attuned to operating with spreadsheets and desktop databases. Regrettably, even in established client/server environments, too many poorly performing, corruption-prone databases are found to have been "designed" using reports and spreadsheets as the basis.[1]

Data Model <> Database

The "world" that evolves during description and analysis provides a logical blueprint for your data structures. It is a given that the logical model should discover every relationship and set. It is usually a mistake—and a trap inherent in many CASE tools—to translate the data model blindly into a database schema. In sophisticated data management systems like Firebird, a table structure does not always represent the optimal object from which data should be retrieved. Queries, views, arrays, calculated columns, and "selectable" stored procedures are just a few of the retrieval and storage mechanisms available that will influence how you implement the model in the physical design.

Even an excellent data model will lack flexibility and will underperform if it does not take into account the power and economy of the server's dynamic capabilities. Dynamic structures for the selection and manipulation of data are the arteries of a client/server database.

One Database or Many?

A single Firebird server—with the exception of the local Embedded Server on Windows—can control multiple databases within its own physical filesystem. It is not unusual in large enterprises to run multiple databases to serve separated divisional subsystems. Because one database is not aware of the objects and dependencies in another, it takes careful design, planning, and balancing of system resources and network services to integrate these independent systems. Typically, such databases are synchronized periodically by a replication system.

When designing, bear in mind that Firebird does not support queries that join or union tables across database boundaries. However, it does support simultaneous queries across multiple databases within one single transaction, with two-phase commit. It is thus possible for applications to accomplish tasks that work with data images from two or more databases and perform DML on one database using data read from another. For more details about cross-database transactions and two-phase commit, refer to Chapter 27.

---

1. A wealth of literature is available that provides techniques for effective business problem analysis for relational database designers, a reflection of the maturity of our trade. The author especially recommends *Data Modeling Essentials: Analysis, Design and Innovation, 2nd Edition* by Graeme C. Simsion (Coriolis, 2000).

The Physical Objects

Tables

A database table is usually visualized as a two-dimensional block consisting of columns (the vertical dimension) and rows (the horizontal dimension). The storage attributes of individual items of data are specified in columns (usually related to or dependent upon one another in some way) and rows. A table can have any number of rows (up to a limit of 2^{32}) or even no rows at all. Although every row in one table shares the specification of its columns with every other row, rows do not depend on other rows in the same table.

TIP Firebird does support techniques for implementing self-referencing tables—row structures that enforce dependencies between rows within the same table. For details, refer to the section "Self-Referencing Relationships" in Chapter 17.

Files and Pages

If you are moving to Firebird from a database system that implements tables by physically tabulating columns and rows in the filesystem, Firebird may bring some surprises. In Firebird, all data belonging to a single database is stored in one file or a set of linked files. In multi-file databases, there is no correlation between any specific database object and a particular member of the database file-set.

Within the boundaries of the file, the Firebird server engine manages evenly sized blocks of disk known as *database pages*. It manages several different page "types," according to the type of data it needs to store—regular columns for tables, BLOBs, and indexes, for example. The engine allocates fresh blocks to itself from the host filesystem as required. All pages are the same size, regardless of type. Page size must be specified in the CREATE DATABASE statement. It cannot be altered except by backing up the database and reconstructing it with a new page size, using the **gbak** utility.

Unlike the file-based data management systems, Firebird does not maintain table data in a tabulated format at all. Rows from one table may not be stored contiguously with other rows from the same table. Indeed, row data for a single table may be distributed among several files and several disks. The engine uses various types of inventory pages to store information about the physical locations of rows belonging to each table.

Columns and Fields

Abstractly, a column is a constellation of attributes, defining the data item that can be stored in one specific cell location in the left-to-right structure of a table's row.

However, columns don't just exist in tables in the database. Each time a query is submitted to the database engine for processing, that query specifies a set of columns and one or more operations to be carried out on those columns. The columns do not have to be in the same left-to-right order as is defined for them in the table. For example, the statement

```
SELECT FIELD3, FIELD1, FIELD2 FROM ATABLE;
```

will output a set in the column order specified in the query. The query may specify columns from multiple tables, through joins, subqueries, and unions. It may define columns that do not exist in the database at all, by computing them or even just by specifying them as named constants.

Some people use the term "field" when referring to a column, for example, "I have a table TABLE1 that has three fields." Relational database textbooks often discourage the use of "field" as a substitute for "column," with some preferring to use "field" to mean "the value in the column" or "the reference to a column."

In this guide, "field" is used only as a term to generalize the concepts of column, argument, and local variable, and to refer to output items that are constructed at runtime. "Column" is used to refer to the physical columns defined for tables.

Keys

The Primary Key

An essential part of the database design process is to abstract the logical model of the database to the point where, for each table, there is a single, unique column or composite column structure that distinguishes each row from every other row in the table. This unique column or column combination is the logical *primary key*. When you implement your physical model, you use the PRIMARY KEY constraint to tell the DBMS which column or columns form this unique identifying structure. You may define only one PRIMARY KEY constraint per table. Syntax is discussed in Chapter 16, in the section "Constraints."

Other Unique Keys

It can happen in your data modeling process that, for various reasons, you end up with more than one unique column or structure in a table. For enforcing the required uniqueness on such columns or structures, Firebird provides the optional UNIQUE key constraint. It is effectively an alternative primary key and can be used in lieu of the primary key at times, if required.

Foreign Keys

The "cables" that make a relational database "relational" are foreign keys. This is the column or column structure that shows up in your data model on the "many" side of a one-to-many relationship. In the physical design, it matches up with the column or column structure of the primary key of the table on the "one" side of the relationship.

For example, in the following simple model, the detail lines of an order are linked to the order header by the ORDER NUMBER key.

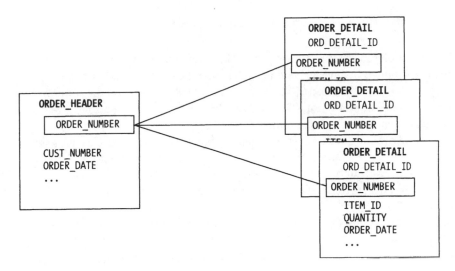

Figure 14-1. Simple relational link

This model requires that each header row have a unique ORDER_NUMBER and that at least one order detail row exists for each order header row. Other rules may apply to the existence and linking. Firebird provides powerful trigger procedure capabilities for setting, conditioning, and applying rules to relationships. Additionally, it can automate many of the typical rules governing relationships, using the FOREIGN KEY constraint with its optional action arguments. Underlying this constraint are system-generated *referential integrity triggers*. Firebird's referential integrity support is discussed briefly below under "Referential Integrity" and in detail in Chapter 17.

Surrogate Keys

The column that your analysis determines to be the primary key, or an element of the primary key, almost always stores a data item that has some meaning. Take, for example, a table storing personal details:

```
CREATE TABLE PERSON (
  FIRST_NAME VARCHAR(30) NOT NULL,
  LAST_NAME VARCHAR(50) NOT NULL,
```

```
PHONE_NUMBER VARCHAR(18) NOT NULL,
ADDRESS_1 VARCHAR(50),
...);
```

The designer decides that the combination (FIRST_NAME, LAST_NAME, PHONE_NUMBER) is a good candidate for the primary key. People do share phone numbers, but it is extremely unlikely that two people with identical first and last names would share the same number, right? So, the designer does this:

```
ALTER TABLE PERSON
  ADD CONSTRAINT PK_PERSON(LAST_NAME, FIRST_NAME, PHONE_NUMBER);
```

The first problem with this primary key is that every element has meaning. Every element is maintained by humans and may change or be misspelled. The two keys ('Smith', 'Mary', '43889474') and ('SMITH', 'Mary', '43889474') are not the same and will both be capable of being stored in this table. Which record gets changed if Mary gets married or changes her phone number?

The second problem is that this complex key has to be propagated, as a foreign key, to any tables that are dependent on PERSON. Not only is the integrity of the relationship at risk through alterations or errors in the data, but also it is a broad channel—potentially 98 characters—across which to implement the foreign key relationship.

The real showstopper may occur if these columns use multi-byte character sets or non-binary collations. Index widths are limited to 253 bytes. Mandatory indexes are created to enforce keys. Such a key will be impossible because it is simply too wide.

Making Keys Atomic

An important tenet of good relational database design is *atomicity*. In the context of primary and foreign keys, atomicity means that no key should have any meaning as data; it should have no other role or function except to be a key.

The solution is to add an extra column to tables to accommodate an artificial or *surrogate primary key*: a unique, narrow column, preferably system-generated, that replaces (surrogates) the function of the theoretical primary key. Firebird provides GENERATOR objects, which can be implemented to maintain the required unique series of BIGINT numbers, a primary key of a mere 8 bytes or less.

Refer to the section "Generators" in Chapter 9 and to Chapter 31 for a common technique to implement an autoincrementing primary key, untouched by human hands.

 CAUTION The atomicity of keys should be enforced in applications by hiding them from users or, at least, making them read-only.

Summary of Surrogate Keys vs. Natural Keys

Database developers tend to take strong positions in the arguments for and against using artificial keys. The author's position in favor of atomicity is probably evident. However, in the interest of fairness, the arguments for and against are summarized in Table 14-1.

Table 14-1. Surrogate (Artificial) Keys vs. Natural Keys

FEATURE	PRO	CON
Atomicity	**Surrogate keys** carry no meaning as data and never change.	**Natural keys** are inherently unstable because they are subject to human error and externally imposed changes.
Convenience	**Natural keys** carry information, reducing the necessity to perform joins or follow-up reads to retrieve data in context. **Natural keys** are easier to use with interactive query tools.	**Surrogate** keys carry no information beyond their linking function, necessitating joins or subqueries to retrieve the associated "meaningful" data.
Key size	**Surrogate keys** are compact.	**Natural keys** are characteristically large and often escalate into compound keys that complicate querying and schema.
Navigation	**Surrogate keys** provide clean, fast-tracking "navigation by code."	**Natural keys** are generally unsuitable for code-style navigation because of case, collation, denormalization, and size issues.
Normalization	**Surrogate keys** can be normalized throughout the database.	**Natural keys** tend toward complexity, propagating denormalized data to foreign keys.

Should you design databases with a mix of natural and artificial keys? The extreme view is to advise a consistent design approach—choose natural or artificial and apply the rule without exception. Yet a more moderate approach may offer the best of both worlds. It may be realistic to use a natural key for stable lookup or "control" tables that rarely change, are never required to participate in compound key structures, and appear often in output.

 CAUTION When designing keys for a Firebird database, be mindful that keys are enforced by indexes, and indexes in Firebird have a size limit of 253 bytes. Compounding, collation sequences and multi-byte international character sets reduce the number of characters of actual data that can be accommodated in an index.

Keys Are Not Indexes

Indexes are not keys. Keys are *table-level constraints*. The database engine responds to constraint declarations by creating a number of metadata objects for enforcing them. For primary keys and unique constraints, it creates a unique index on the column(s) assigned to the constraint. For foreign keys, it creates a non-unique index on the assigned columns, stores records for the dependency, and creates triggers to implement the actions.

- The keys are the constraints.

- The indexes are required to enforce the constraints.

CAUTION   You should not create indexes of your own that duplicate the indexes created by the system to enforce constraints. This is such an important precaution from the performance perspective that it is reiterated in several places in this guide. The "Optimization Topic" in Chapter 18 explains why duplicating these indexes can wreck the performance of queries.

Referential Integrity

Accidental altering or deletion of rows that have dependencies will corrupt the integrity of your data. Referential integrity, generally, is a qualitative expression that describes the degree to which dependencies in a database are protected from corruption. However, in the context of this guide, it refers to the in-built mechanisms for enforcing foreign key relationships and performing the desired actions when the primary key of a master row is changed or the row is deleted.

The syntax and implications of Firebird's formal referential integrity constraints are discussed in detail in Chapter 17.

Indexes and Query Plans

If foreign keys are the "cables" that make a database relational, then indexes can be seen as the suppliers of "bandwidth." Good indexing speeds things up; missing or bad indexes will slow down searches, joins, and sorting.

As a relational database management engine, Firebird can link almost any column object to almost any other column object (the exceptions being the various BLOB types, including ARRAYS) by reference to their identifiers. However, as the numbers of rows, linking columns, and tables in a query increase, performance goes down.

When columns that are searched, joined, or sorted are indexed in useful ways, performance in terms of execution time and resource usage can be dramatically improved. It must also be said that poor indexing can hurt performance!

Firebird uses optimization algorithms that are largely cost-based. In preparing a submitted query, the optimizer calculates the relative costs of choosing or ignoring available indexes and returns a *query plan* to the client, reporting its choices. Although it is possible to design and submit your own plan to the optimizer—an important feature in RDBMS engines that use rule-based optimization—as a general rule the Firebird optimizer knows best. Firebird plans tend to be most useful in detecting and eliminating problem indexes.

Index design and creation are discussed in Chapter 18.

Views

Firebird provides the capability to create and store pre-defined query specifications, known as *views*, which can be treated in most ways just as though they were tables. A view is a class of derived table that stores no data. For many tasks—especially those where access to certain columns in the underlying tables needs to be denied or where a single query specification cannot deliver the required degree of abstraction—views solve difficult problems.

Views and other derived tables are discussed in Chapter 24 and should be studied in association with the other chapters in Part Five.

Stored Procedures and Triggers

Stored procedures and triggers are modules of compiled, executable code that are executed on the server. The source code is a set of SQL language extensions known as *Procedural SQL*, or PSQL.

Stored procedures can be *executable* or *selectable*. They can take input arguments and return output sets. Executable procedures execute completely on the server and optionally return a single-row set (a *singleton*) of constants on completion. Selectable procedures generate multiple-row sets of zero or more rows, which can be used by client applications in most ways like any other output set.

Triggers are a specialized form of PSQL module that can be declared to execute at one or more of six stage/operation phases (before and after inserting, updating, and deleting) during a data manipulation (DML) operation on the table that owns them. Clusters of triggers can be defined for each phase, to execute in a defined sequence. From release 1.5 onward, the behavior for any or all DML operations can be combined, with conditions, in a single "before" or "after" trigger module. Triggers do not accept input arguments nor return output sets.

Stored procedures can call other stored procedures. Triggers can call stored procedures that, in turn, can call other stored procedures. Triggers can be called from neither a client application nor a stored procedure.

PSQL provides mechanisms for exception handling and callback events. Any number of exception messages can be defined as objects in the database using CREATE EXCEPTION statements. Callback events are created inside the PSQL module and applications can set up structures to "listen" for them.

For detailed discussion of writing and using PSQL modules, exceptions, and events, refer to Part Seven.

Database Object Naming Conventions and Constraints

The following limitations on naming database objects must be observed:

- Start each name with an alphabetic character (A–Z or a–z).

- Restrict object names to 31 characters. Some objects, such as constraint names, are restricted to 27 bytes in length.

- Allowable characters for database file names—as with all metadata objects in Firebird—include dollar signs ($), underscores (_), 0 to 9, A to Z, and a to z.

- Observe uniqueness requirements within a database:

  - In all cases, objects of the same type—all tables, for example—*must* be unique.

  - Column identifiers must be unique within a table. All other object identifiers must be unique within the database.

- Avoid the use of reserved words, spaces, diacritic characters, and any ASCII characters having codes higher than 127:

  - In dialect 1, they cannot be used at all.

  - In dialect 3, you can delimit "illegal" identifiers using pairs of double-quote symbols. Details follow.

Optional SQL-92 Delimited Identifiers

In dialect 3 databases, Firebird supports the ANSI SQL convention for optionally delimiting identifiers. To use reserved words, diacritic characters, case-sensitive strings, or embedded spaces in an object name, enclose the name in double quotes. It is then a *delimited identifier*. Delimited identifiers must always be referenced in double quotes.

 NOTE In dialect 1, reserved words, diacritic characters, and embedded spaces in an object name are not permitted and case-sensitive identifiers are not supported.

Names enclosed in double quotes are case sensitive, for example:

```
SELECT "CodAR" FROM "MyTable"
```

is different from

```
SELECT "CODAR" FROM "MYTABLE"
```

To Quote or Not to Quote

The double-quoting convention for object identifiers was introduced for compliance with standards. To those who have been used to the global case-insensitivity of InterBase in the past, the new "feature" is at best confusing and at worst exasperating.

If you define objects with double quotes, you must use them everywhere and every time with double-quotes and perfect case-matching. Most experienced Firebird developers recommend avoiding them, except in the occasional cases where you are stuck with using an "illegal" identifier. The choice is yours.

The Case-Matching Exception

If you have double-quoted identifiers in all uppercase, you can use them in SQL without the quotes and treat them as case insensitive. The ability to do this comes from the way identifiers are stored in the internal schema tables and the sequence that the engine follows to resolve them during retrieval.

TIP Most GUI database administration tools for Firebird provide the option to apply quoted identifiers automatically. One or two of these tools actually apply quoted identifiers by default to all database objects. Unless you have a strong reason to do this, it is recommended that you look for the "off switch" and avoid quoted identifiers.

Database File-Naming Conventions

The established convention for naming Firebird database files on any platform is to apply the three-character suffix .fdb to the primary file and to name secondary files .f01, .f02, etc. This is only a convention—a Firebird database file can have any extension or no extension at all.

Because of known problems on XP servers involving the SystemRestore feature actively targeting files with the suffix .gdb, developers are advised to change the traditional InterBase file suffix on databases migrating to Firebird.

The name of the security database—security.fdb in release 1.5 and higher, isc4.gdb in release 1.0.*x*—must not be changed. Unfortunately, Firebird 1.0.*x* has no workaround for its required .gdb suffix.

Schema Scripts

With Firebird, as with all true SQL database management systems, you build your database and its objects, the *metadata* or *schema* of a database, using statements from a specialized subset of SQL statements known as Data Definition Language, or DDL. A batch of DDL statements in a text file is known as a *script*. A script, or a set of scripts, can be processed by **isql** directly at the command line or through a tool that provides a user-friendly interface for **isql**'s script-processing capability.

For an overview list of such tools, refer to Appendix V.

About Firebird Scripts

A script for creating and altering database objects is sometimes referred to as a *data definition file* or, more commonly, a *DDL script*. A DDL script can contain certain **isql** statements, specifically some of the SET *<parameter>* commands. COMMIT is also a valid statement in a script.

 NOTE The **isql** (Interactive SQL) utility is a command-line program available on all platforms and is part of the Firebird distribution kits. In all cases except the Windows Embedded Server, it is installed beneath the Firebird root directory in ../bin. Full instructions can be found in Chapter 37.

Other scripts can be written for inserting basic or "control" data into tables, updating columns, performing data conversions, and doing other maintenance tasks involving data manipulation. These are known as DML scripts (for Data Manipulation Language).

DDL and DML commands can be mixed in a script. However, to avoid data integrity problems, it is strongly recommended that DDL and DML should be split into separate scripts. Script processing allows "chaining" of scripts, linking one script file to another by means of the **isql** INPUT *<filespec>* statement.

Script statements are executed in strict order. Use of the SET AUTODDL command enables you to control where statements or blocks of statements will be committed. It is also an option to defer committing the contents of a script until the entire script has been processed.

Why Use Scripts?

It is very good practice to use DDL scripts to create your database and its objects. Some of the reasons include the following:

- **Self-documentation**. A script is a plain text file, easily handled in any development system, both for updating and reference. Scripts can—and should—include detailed comment text. Alterations to metadata can be signed and dated manually.

- **Control of database development**. Scripting all database definitions allows schema creation to be integrated closely with design tasks and code review cycles.

- **Repeatable and traceable creation of metadata**. A completely reconstructable schema is a requirement in the quality assurance and disaster recovery systems of many organizations.

- **Orderly construction and reconstruction of database metadata**. Experienced Firebird programmers often create a set of DDL scripts, designed to run and commit in a specific order, to make debugging easy and ensure that objects will exist when later, dependent objects refer to them.

What Is in a DDL Script?

SQL Statements

A DDL script consists of one or more SQL statements to CREATE, ALTER, or DROP a database or any other object. It can include DML statements, although it is recommended to keep DDL and DML statements in separate scripts.

 TIP It is quite common to include (INPUT) one or more scripts among a chain of DDL scripts, containing INSERT statements to populate some tables with static control data. You might, for example, post statements to insert the initial rows in a table of account types. Ensure that all DDL statements are committed before introducing any DML.

Procedure language (PSQL) statements defining stored procedures and triggers can also be included. PSQL blocks get special treatment in scripts with regard to statement terminator symbols (see the upcoming section "Terminator Symbols").

Comments

A script can also contain comments, in two varieties.

Block Comments

Block comments in DDL scripts use the C convention:

```
/* This comment can span multiple
lines in a script */
```

A block comment can occur on the same line as a SQL statement or **isql** command and can be of any length, as long as it is preceded by /* and followed by */.

Inline Comments

The /* .... */ comment style can also be embedded inside a statement as an inline comment:

```
CREATE TABLE USERS1 (
USER_NAME VARCHAR( 128 ) /* security user name */
, GROUP_NAME VARCHAR( 128 ) /* not used on Windows */
, PASSWD VARCHAR( 32 ) /* will be stored encrypted */
, FIRST_NAME VARCHAR( 96 ) /* Defaulted */
, MIDDLE_NAME VARCHAR( 96 ) /* Defaulted */
, LAST_NAME VARCHAR( 96 ) /* Defaulted */
, FULL_NAME VARCHAR( 290 ) /* Computed */
) ;
```

One-Line Comments

In Firebird scripts you can use an alternative convention for commenting a single line: the double hyphen.

```
-- comment
```

In release 1.0.*x*, this double-hyphen style of comment *cannot* be used for inline comments or for "commenting out" part of a line.

From release 1.5 forward, the -- commenting convention can be used anywhere on a line to "comment out" everything from the marker to the end of the current line, for example:

```
CREATE TABLE MET_REPORT (ID BIGINT NOT NULL, -- COMMENT VARCHAR(40), invisible
WEATHER_CONDITIONS BLOB SUB_TYPE TEXT, LAST_REPORT TIMESTAMP);
```

isql Statements

The **isql** commands SET AUTODDL, SET SQL DIALECT, SET TERM, and INPUT are valid statements in a Firebird script—see Chapter 37 for details of these commands.

Terminator Symbols

All statements that are to be executed in the script must end with a terminator symbol. The default symbol is the semicolon (;).

The default terminator can be overridden for all statements *except procedure language statements* (PSQL) by issuing a SET TERM command in the script.

Terminators and Procedure Language (PSQL)

PSQL does not permit any terminator other than the default semicolon (;). This restriction is necessary because CREATE PROCEDURE, RECREATE PROCEDURE, ALTER PROCEDURE, CREATE TRIGGER, and ALTER TRIGGER, together with their subsequent PSQL statements, are complex statements in their own right—statements within a statement. The compiler needs to see semicolons in order to recognize each distinct PSQL statement.

Thus, in scripts, it is necessary to override the terminator being used for script commands before commencing to issue the PSQL statements for a stored procedure or a trigger. After the last END statement of the procedure source has been terminated, the terminator should be reset to the default using another SET TERM statement. For example:

```
...
CREATE GENERATOR GEN_MY_GEN ;
SET TERM ^^;
CREATE TRIGGER BI_TABLEA_0 FOR TABLEA
ACTIVE BEFORE INSERT POSITION 0
AS
BEGIN
IF (NEW.PK IS NOT NULL) THEN
NEW.PK = GEN_ID(GEN_MY_GEN, 1);
END ^^
SET TERM ;^^
...
```

Any string may be used as an alternative terminator, for example:

```
...
SET TERM @!#;
CREATE PROCEDURE...
AS
BEGIN
... ;
```

```
... ;
END @!#
SET TERM ;@!#
/**/
COMMIT;
/**/
SET TERM +;
CREATE PROCEDURE...
AS
BEGIN
... ;
... ;
END +
SET TERM ;+
/**/
COMMIT;
```

The SQL statement silently fails if significant text follows the terminator character on the same line. White space and comments can safely follow the terminator, but other statements cannot.

For example, in the following sequence, the COMMIT statement will not be executed:

```
ALTER TABLE ATABLE ADD F2 INTEGER; COMMIT;
```

whereas this one is fine:

```
ALTER TABLE ATABLE ADD F2 INTEGER;         /* counter for beans */
COMMIT;
```

Basic Steps

The basic steps for using script files are outlined in the following sections.

Step 1: Create the Script File

Use any suitable text editor. At the learning stage, you might wish to follow each DDL statement with a COMMIT statement, to ensure that an object will be visible to subsequent statements. As you become more practiced, you will learn to commit statements in blocks, employing SET AUTODDL ON and SET AUTODDL OFF as a means of controlling interdependencies and testing/debugging scripts.

 CAUTION Ensure that every script ends with a carriage return and at least one blank line.

Step 2: Execute the Script

Use the INPUT command in an **isql** session or the Execute button (or equivalent) in your database management tool.

    isql on POSIX:

```
SQL> INPUT /data/scripts/myscript.sql;
```

    isql on Win32:

```
SQL> INPUT d:\data\scripts\myscript.sql;
```

Step 3: View Output and Confirm Database Changes

Tools and Firebird **isql** versions vary in the information they return when a script trips up on a bad command. A feature added after Firebird 1.0 provides better script error reporting than previous versions.

How to Create Scripts

You can create DDL scripts in several ways, including the following:

- In an interactive **isql** session using the OUTPUT command to pass a series of DDL statements to a file.

- In a plain ASCII text editor that formats line breaks according to the rules of the operating system shell in which the DDL script will be executed.

- Using one of the many specialized script editor tools that are available in third-party admin tools for Firebird. Refer to Appendix V for a list.

- Using a CASE tool that can output DDL scripts according to the Firebird (InterBase) conventions.

You can use any text editor to create a SQL script file, as long as the final file format is plain text (ASCII) and has lines terminated according to the rules of your operating system shell:

- On Windows the line terminator is a carriage return plus a line feed (ASCII 13 followed by ASCII 10).

- On Linux/UNIX the line terminator is a line feed or a "newline" (ASCII 10).

- On Mac OS X the line terminator is a newline (ASCII 10) and on native Macintosh it is a carriage return (ASCII 13).

TIP See also the metadata extract tool in **isql**, which can be useful for extracting existing schemata in script format.

Some editing tools provide the capability to save in different text formats. It may prove useful to be able to save Linux-compatible scripts on a Windows machine, for example. However, take care that you use an editor that saves only plain ASCII text.

A complete schema script file must begin with either a CREATE DATABASE statement or, if the database already exists, a CONNECT statement (including the user name and password in single quotes) that specifies the database on which the script file is to operate. The CONNECT or CREATE keyword must be followed by a complete, absolute database file name and directory path in single quotes.

NOTE Do not use database aliases in scripts that create a database.

For example:

```
SET SQL DIALECT 3 ;
CREATE DATABASE 'd:\databases\MyDatabase.fdb'
  PAGE_SIZE 8192
  DEFAULT CHARACTER SET ISO8859_1
  USER 'SYSDBA' PASSWORD 'masterkey';
```

or

```
CONNECT 'd:\databases\MyDatabase.gdb' USER 'SYSDBA' PASSWORD 'masterkey' ;
```

Committing Statements in Scripts

DDL Statements

Statements in DDL scripts can be committed in one or more of the following ways:

- By including COMMIT statements at appropriate points in the script to ensure that new database objects are available to all subsequent statements that depend on them

- By including this statement at the beginning of the script:

```
SET AUTODDL ON ;
```

To turn off automatic commit of DDL in an **isql** script, use this:

```
SET AUTODDL OFF ;
```

The ON and OFF keywords are optional. The abbreviation SET AUTO can be used as a two-way switch. For clarity of self-documentation, it is recommended that you use SET AUTODDL with the explicit ON and OFF keywords.

Autocommit in isql

If you are running your script in **isql**, changes to the database from data definition (DDL) statements—for example, CREATE and ALTER statements—are automatically committed by default. This means that other users of the database see changes as soon as each DDL statement is executed.

Some scripting tools deliberately turn off this autocommitting behavior when running scripts, since it can make debugging difficult. Make sure you understand the behavior of any third-party tool you use for scripts.

DML Statements

Changes made to the database by data manipulation (DML) statements—INSERT, UPDATE, and DELETE—are not permanent until they are committed. *Explicitly* include COMMIT statements in your script to commit DML changes.

To undo all database changes since the last COMMIT, use ROLLBACK. Committed changes cannot be rolled back.

Executing Scripts

DDL scripts can be executed in an interactive **isql** session using the INPUT command, as described in the previous summary. Many of the third-party tools have the ability to execute and even to intelligently debug scripts in a GUI environment.

Managing Your Schema Scripts

Keeping a well-organized suite of scripts that precisely reflects the up-to-date state of your metadata is a valuable practice that admirably satisfies the most rigorous quality assurance system. The use of ample commentary within scripts is highly recommended, as is archiving all script versions in a version control system.

Disaster Recovery

The most obvious purpose of such a practice is to provide a "fallback of last resort" for disaster recovery. If worse comes to worst—a database is ruined and backups are lost—metadata can be reconstructed from scripts. Surviving data from an otherwise unrecoverable database can be reconstituted by experts and pumped back.

Development Control

It is usually likely that more than one developer will work on the development of a database during its life cycle. Developers notoriously abhor writing system documentation! Keeping an annotated script record of every database change—including those applied interactively using **isql** or a third-party tool—is a painless and secure solution that works for everybody.

Metadata Extraction

Several admin tools for Firebird, including **isql**, are capable of extracting metadata from a database for saving as a script file. For **isql** instructions, refer to the section "Extracting Metadata" in Chapter 37. While metadata extraction is a handy adjunct to your scripting, there are good reasons to treat these tools as "helpers" and make a point of maintaining your main schema scripts manually:

- Firebird does not preserve comments when it stores metadata definitions. Many of the system tables do have a BLOB column, usually named RDB$DESCRIPTION, in which a single, contiguous piece of user-provided description can be stored. The metadata extract tool in **isql** does not output it, although some third-party tools do provide support for maintaining it.

- All metadata extraction tools generate only the current metadata. There is no history of changes—dates, reasons, or authors.

- Some tools, including **isql**, are known to generate metadata in the wrong sequence for dependency, making the scripts useless for regenerating the database without editing. Such a task is between tedious and impossible, depending on how well the repairer knows the metadata.

- Even moderately sized databases may have an enormous number of objects, especially where the system design makes intensive use of embedded code modules. Very large scripts are prone to failure due to various execution or resource limits. Large, poorly organized scripts are also confusing and annoying to work with as documentation.

Manual Scripting

The author strongly advocates maintaining fully annotated schema scripts manually and splitting the mass into separate files. The sample suite of scripts in Table 14-2 records and regenerates a database named leisurestore.fdb.

Table 14-2. Sample Suite of Schema Scripts

FILE	CONTENTS
leisurestore_01.sql	CREATE DATABASE statement; CREATE DOMAIN, CREATE GENERATOR, and CREATE EXCEPTION definitions
leisturestore_02.sql	All CREATE TABLE statements, including UNIQUE constraints; ALTER TABLE statements adding all primary keys as named PRIMARY KEY constraints
leisurestore_03.sql	ALTER TABLE statements adding FOREIGN KEY constraints
leisurestore_04.sql	CREATE INDEX statements
leisurestore_05.sql	CREATE TRIGGER statements
leisurestore_06.sql	CREATE PROCEDURE statements
leisurestore_07.sql	DML script that inserts rows into static (control) tables
leisurestore_08.sql	GRANT statements (security script)
leisurestore_09.sql	Recent changes, in correct sequence for dependency
leisurestore_10.sql	QA scripts (test data)

Chaining Scripts

A stable suite of scripts can be "chained" together using the **isql** INPUT statement as the last statement in the preceding script. For example, to chain leisurestore_02.sql to the end of leisurestore_01.sql, end the script this way:

```
...
COMMIT;
    -- chain to CREATE TABLE statements
INPUT 'd:\scripts\leisurestore_02.sql' ;
    -- don't forget the carriage return!
```

The Master Script Approach

The INPUT statement is not restricted to being the last in a script. Hence, another useful approach to maintaining script suites is to have one "master" script that inputs each of the subsidiary scripts in order. It has the benefit of making it easy to maintain large suites, and you can include comments to indicate to others the contents of each input script.

Up Next

Now, to make databases! In the next chapter you will learn not just about creating databases, but also about keeping them clean, safe, and performing well. There are not many ways to corrupt Firebird databases, but a section at the end of this chapter describes five ways it can be done. Forewarned is forearmed!

Creating and Maintaining a Database

A FIREBIRD DATABASE IS, FIRST AND FOREMOST, a filesystem file under the control of the I/O subsystem of the host machine on which the Firebird server runs. Once the server has created this file, its management system takes control of managing the space, using a low-level protocol to communicate with the I/O subsystem.

Because of this protocol, a Firebird database must exist on the same physical machine as the Firebird server. It cannot be located on any sort of storage device whose physical I/O system is not directly controlled by the server's host.

A new, "empty" database occupies about 540–600K of disk. The database file is not empty at all, in fact, because the "act of creation"—the CREATE DATABASE statement—causes more than 30 *system tables* to be created. These tables will store every detail of the metadata as database objects are added and altered. Because the system tables are regular Firebird database objects, they already contain the metadata records for themselves. The server has already allocated database pages from disk for this data and has set up inventory pages for various types of objects.

Refer to the previous chapter for some discussion about database pages. The schemata of the system tables can be found in Appendix IX.

Physical Storage for a Database

Location

Before creating the database, you should know where you are going to create it. This is not as silly as it sounds. The CREATE DATABASE (alias CREATE SCHEMA) statement will create the file or files you name, but it cannot create directories and it cannot change filesystem permissions. These details must be attended to first.

Additionally, a Firebird 1.5 server may be configured to restrict the locations where databases may be accessed. Check the DatabaseAccess parameter in the firebird.conf file (see Chapter 3) to discover whether your server is restricting access. If the setting is the default, Full, then you can create the database anywhere. Otherwise,

- A Restrict setting indicates the filesystem tree-roots under which database access is permitted. Ensure that the user that starts your server has sufficient permissions to create a file there (or, in the case of the Windows Embedded Server, the user under which you are logged in).

- A None setting permits the server to attach only databases that are listed in aliases.conf. You can create a database anywhere but, except at creation, no client will be able to attach to it unless its alias and its absolute path are present in aliases.conf.

 CAUTION   It is strongly recommend that you set the DatabaseAccess option to NONE and make use of the database-aliasing feature. For more information about database aliasing, refer to the section "Database Aliasing" in Chapter 4.

About Security Access

It is not always obvious to newcomers that there is a distinction between *server access* and *database security*. When you "log into" a Firebird database using **isql** or your favorite admin tool, you always supply a user name and password, along with server, port (sometimes), and path parameters. Whenever you do this, you are *logging into the server* and *opening an attachment to a database*.

If the database does not exist yet and you have started **isql** from the command line with no parameters, then two things are "givens":

- You *are* logged into the server.

- Until you submit a CONNECT or CREATE DATABASE request to the server, the program is not attached to a database.

Password access is always required to log into the server. Once in, you can attach to any database. What you can do, once attached, depends on SQL privileges, which are stored within the database. The SYSDBA user has full destructive rights to every database and every object within it. The owner (the user that created the database) has automatic rights to the database, although not to any objects within it that were created by other users. SQL privileges are *opt-in*. That means that, although any user with server access can attach to any database, the user will have no rights to do anything to anything, other than what has been explicitly or implicitly granted to it by the owner, using GRANT statements.

The issues of server access and database security are discussed in detail in Part Eight.

ISC_USER and ISC_PASSWORD

It is possible to set up the two environment variables ISC_USER and ISC_PASSWORD on the server, to avoid the need to write and store scripts that contain passwords "in clear." You will be able do everything that the named user is allowed to do, without needing to supply credentials. This feature is handy for administrative tasks, but it must be used with a high level of caution because it leaves your database access open to any local user who happens upon your command shell.

If you want to play with fire, set these two variables permanently. If you want to have that extra level of convenience and script security, set them temporarily each time you want them and be certain to reset them whenever you leave your console.

On Linux, in the same shell from which you will launch the application, type

```
]# setenv ISC_USER=SYSDBA
]# setenv ISC_PASSWORD=masterkey
```

To unset, either use this:

```
]# setenv ISC_USER=
]# setenv ISC_PASSWORD=
```

or simply close the shell.

On Windows, go to the command prompt and type

```
set ISC_USER=SYSDBA
set ISC_PASSWORD=masterkey
```

To unset, type

```
set ISC_USER=
set ISC_PASSWORD=
```

Creating a Database

You can create a database interactively in **isql**. Some other database administration tools can meet the API requirements enumerated in this section and let you create databases interactively, while others require a script.

In any case, it is preferable to use a data definition file (DDL script) because it provides an easy way to "replay" your statements if a statement fails. It is easier to start over from a source file than to retype interactive SQL statements.

Dialect

Firebird creates a dialect 3 database by default. If you wish to create a dialect 1 database, the first statement in the script (or the prior action in your admin tool) should be

```
SET SQL DIALECT 1;
```

CAUTION   If **isql** is currently attached to a database, it will prompt you to commit the current transaction. Answer Yes to proceed with creating the new database. Some third-party tools may require that you disconnect from any existing attachment first.

The next statement—or the first, for a dialect 3 database—must be the CREATE DATABASE or CREATE SCHEMA statement, using the following syntax:[1]

```
CREATE {DATABASE | SCHEMA} 'file-specification'
[USER 'username' [PASSWORD 'password']]
[PAGE_SIZE [=] int]
[LENGTH [=] int [PAGE[S]]]
[DEFAULT CHARACTER SET charset]
[<secondary_file>];
<fileinfo> = LENGTH [=] int [PAGE[S]]
| STARTING [AT [PAGE]] int [<fileinfo>]
<secondary_file> = FILE 'filespec' [<fileinfo>][<secondary_file>]
```

TIP   Use single quotes to delimit strings such as file names, user names, and passwords.

"DATABASE" or "SCHEMA"?

CREATE DATABASE and CREATE SCHEMA are the same statement. It is merely a question of preference which you use.

Mandatory and Optional Attributes

The only mandatory attribute for the CREATE statement is the file specification—the name of the primary database file and the filesystem path to its location.

---

1. Note for API programmers: In dynamic SQL (DSQL), the CREATE DATABASE or CREATE SCHEMA statement can be executed only with EXECUTE IMMEDIATE. The database handle and transaction name, if present, must be initialized to zero before use.

Database Path and Name

The *file specification* must be a fully qualified, absolute path to the file. The path must be in a valid format for the operating system platform.

For POSIX:

```
CREATE DATABASE '/opt/databases/mydatabase.fdb'
```

For Win32:

```
CREATE SCHEMA 'd:\databases\mydatabase.fdb'
```

You can use either forward slashes (/) or backslashes (\) as directory separators. Firebird automatically converts either type of slash to the appropriate type for the server operating system.

The enclosing single quotes for *file_specification* are not optional. All elements of the file specification are case sensitive on POSIX platforms.

Creating a Database Remotely

When creating a database from a client workstation, or locally on Linux Superserver, either interactively or using a script, you must include the host name:

For POSIX:

```
CREATE DATABASE 'myserver:/opt/databases/mydatabase.fdb'
```

For Linux SS Local, as previously, or

```
CREATE DATABASE 'localhost:/opt/databases/mydatabase.fdb'
```

For Win32:

```
CREATE SCHEMA 'NTServer:d:\databases\mydatabase.fdb'
```

Ownership

If you are logged in as SYSDBA, then SYSDBA will own the new database unless you include the clause specifying the USER and PASSWORD. Although it is optional to designate an owner, it is highly desirable to do so. However, for security reasons, you will probably wish to remove the user's password from the script before archiving it with other system documentation.

```
CREATE DATABASE '/opt/databases/mydatabase.fdb'
 USER 'ADMINUSR' PASSWORD 'yyuryyub';
```

Page size

The optional PAGE_SIZE attribute is expressed in bytes. If you omit it, it will default to 4096 bytes with **isql**. Some other tools apply their own defaults, so there is a strong argument for specifying it explicitly in the script. The page size can be 1024, 2048, 4096, 8192, or 16384. Any other numbers will be resolved back to the next lowest number in this range. For example, if you specify 3072, Firebird will create a database with a page size of 2048.

```
CREATE DATABASE '/opt/databases/mydatabase.fdb'
  USER 'ADMINUSR' PASSWORD 'yyuryyub'
  PAGE_SIZE 8192
```

Factors Influencing Choice of Page Size

Choosing a page size is not a question of applying some "rule." It will do no harm to begin with the default size of 4K. When the time comes to tune the database for performance improvements, you can experiment by backing up the database and restoring it with different page sizes. For instructions, refer to Chapter 38.

The page size you choose can benefit performance or affect it adversely, according to a number of factors having mostly to do with the structures and usage of the most frequently accessed tables. Each database page will be filled to about 80 percent of its capacity, so think in terms of an actual page size that is around 125 percent of the size you determine to be the minimum.

The *row size* of the most frequently accessed tables may have an effect. A record structure that is too large to fit on a single page requires more than one page fetch to read or write to it, so access can be optimized by choosing a page size that can comfortably accommodate one row or simple row multiples of these high-volume tables.

The *number of rows* that your main tables can be predicted to accommodate over time may have an influence. If multiple rows can be accommodated in a single page, a larger page size may reduce the overall tally of data and index pages that need to be read for an operation.

Default Character Set

This is strongly recommended unless all—or nearly all—of your text data will be in U.S. ASCII.

```
CREATE DATABASE '/opt/databases/mydatabase.fdb'
  USER 'ADMINUSR' PASSWORD 'yyuryyub'
  PAGE_SIZE 8192
  DEFAULT CHARACTER SET ISO8859_1;
```

For details regarding character sets, refer to Chapter 11. Available character sets are listed in Appendix VIII.

Getting Information About the Database

Once you have created and committed the database, you can display its details in **isql** using the SHOW DATABASE command:

```
SQL> SHOW DATABASE;
Database: /opt/databases/mydatabase.fdb
        Owner: ADMINUSR
PAGE_SIZE 8192
Number of DB pages allocated = 176
Sweep interval = 20000
Forced Writes are ON
Transaction - oldest = 5
Transaction - oldest active = 6
Transaction - oldest snapshot = 6
Transaction - Next = 9
Default character set: ISO8859_1
SQL>
```

Sweep Interval and Transactions

For information about sweeping and sweep interval, refer to the section "Database 'Hygiene'" later in this chapter.

The values of the oldest ("oldest interesting"), oldest active, and next transactions are important for performance and server behavior. For details, refer to Part Six.

Forced Writes

Forced writes is synonymous with *synchronous writes*. On platforms that support asynchronous writes, Firebird databases are created with forced writes enabled by default. The phrase "disabling forced writes" means switching the write behavior from synchronous to asynchronous.

- With forced writes enabled, new records, new record versions, and deletions are physically written to disk immediately upon posting or, at the latest, upon committing.

- Asynchronous writes cause new and changed data to be withheld in the file-system cache, relying on the flushing behavior of the operating system to make them permanent on disk.

NOTE   The Windows 95 platform does not support asynchronous writes.

For discussion of the implications of disabling forced writes and instructions for setting it using **gfix**, see Chapter 39.

Single and Multi-File Databases

Any Firebird database can be multi-file. You do not have to decide between single and multiple at the beginning. A single file database can be converted to multi-file at any time, using ALTER DATABASE (discussed in this chapter) or the **gbak** tool (refer to Chapter 38).

Specifying File Size for a Single-File Database

You can optionally specify a file length, in pages, for the primary file, following the PAGE_SIZE attribute. For example, the following statement creates a database that is stored in one 10,000-page-long file:

```
CREATE DATABASE '/opt/databases/mydatabase.fdb'
  USER 'ADMINUSR' PASSWORD 'yyuryyub'
  PAGE_SIZE 8192
  LENGTH 10000 PAGES   /* the PAGES keyword is optional */
  DEFAULT CHARACTER SET ISO8859_1;
```

If the database grows larger than the specified file length, Firebird extends the primary file beyond the LENGTH limit until the filesystem size limit for shared access file is reached or disk space runs out. To avoid this, you can store a database in more than one file, called *secondary files*. The files can be on separate disks.

Creating a Multi-File Database

Multi-file databases are more of an issue on older filesystems where the absolute limit for a shared-write file is 2GB (FAT32, ext2) or 4GB (NTFS systems with 32-bit I/O). It used to be a common support problem for users to corrupt InterBase databases by "blowing the limit" and the server would start overwriting the file from the beginning. A similar problem occurred if a database exhausted its secondary file capacity. Firebird simply denies all writes when the last file hits the limit. Corruption of existing data is thus prevented, although any outstanding writes will be lost.

In the following example, a database is created consisting of three files, each potentially 2GB. If the filesystem supports a larger shared-access file, the last file will continue to grow until the filesystem limit (if any) is reached.

```
CREATE DATABASE 'LOCALHOST:/data/sample.fdb'
  PAGE_SIZE 8192
  DEFAULT CHARACTER SET ISO8859_1
  LENGTH 250000 PAGES
  FILE '/data/sample.fd1'
```

```
FILE '/data/sample.fd2'
STARTING AT 250001;
```

You must specify a range of pages for each file either by providing the *number of pages* in each file or by providing the *starting page number* for the file. For the last file, you do not need a length, because Firebird always dynamically sizes the last file and will increase the file size as necessary until all the available space is used or until it reaches the filesystem limit.

In the example, the first secondary file will "kick in" when the first primary file is nearing the 2GB limit. The "next file in the chain" comes into use when a requested operation is likely to need more pages allocated than the previous files could satisfy without exceeding their specified limits.

It is the responsibility of the database administrator to monitor database growth and ensure that a database always has ample capacity for extension. Deciding if and when to split a database file depends on how large you expect the database to grow and how quickly. More files can be added at any time using the ALTER DATABASE statement (see the next section).

With multi-file databases, you can avoid confining databases to the size of a single disk if the system does not support spanning a single, huge file across multiple disks. There will be no problems installing a RAID array and distributing a multi-file Firebird database across several disks on any supported platform.

NOTE   All files must be located on disks that are under the direct physical control of the Firebird server's host machine.

Altering the Database

The ALTER DATABASE statement is used to add one or more secondary files to an existing database. It requires exclusive access to the database—see the section "Exclusive Access" in Chapter 39.

A database can be altered by its creator (owner), the SYSDBA user or, on Linux/UNIX, any user with operating system root privileges.

Syntax

The syntax for ALTER DATABASE is

```
ALTER {DATABASE | SCHEMA}
ADD <add_clause>;
<add_clause> = FILE 'filespec' <fileinfo> [<add_clause>]
<fileinfo> = {LENGTH [=] int [PAGE[S]] | STARTING [AT [PAGE]] int }
[<fileinfo>]
```

The first example adds two secondary files to the currently connected database by specifying the starting page numbers:

```
ALTER DATABASE
ADD FILE 'mydatabase.fd2' STARTING AT PAGE 10001
ADD FILE ' mydatabase.fd3' STARTING AT PAGE 20001 ;
```

The first secondary file will grow until it nears 10,000 pages. When it, too, is determined to have insufficient capacity left to satisfy new page requests, Firebird will begin storing new pages in the second secondary file.

The next example specifies the secondary file length rather than the starting page number:

```
ALTER DATABASE
ADD FILE 'mydatabase.fd2' LENGTH 10000
ADD FILE ' mydatabase.fd3' ;
```

The effect is slightly different from the first example. In this case, Firebird will begin using the second file when the primary file reaches the point where one more page would be larger than the filesystem limit.

The difference has no effect on performance or overall database size.

The Database Cache

Database cache is a chunk of memory reserved for each database running on the server. Its purpose is to cache all of the database pages (also called *buffers*) that have been most recently used. It is configured as a default for new databases and for all databases that are not individually configured. This default setting, which constitutes a number of blocks of memory, or *page buffers*, each the size of one database page, is set in the server's configuration file:

- For v.1.5 onward, the parameter is *DefaultDbCachePages* in firebird.conf for all platforms.

- For v.1.0.*x*, the parameter is *database_cache_pages* in isc_config (POSIX) or ibconfig (Win32).

It should be emphasized that configuring the cache is not a "must-do." The default configuration for Superserver fits most normal needs and server-level reconfiguration might never be necessary. On Classic server, the default is worthy of more attention, since it may be too high for a system with more than a few concurrent users.

A newly created database has a database-level cache size of zero pages. If the cache setting is left at zero, connections to that database will use the server-level configuration setting. Thus, databases with large page sizes will use more cache memory than those with smaller page sizes.

Cache size can be configured individually and permanently, per database. It can be changed again, if required. Other databases that retain (or are changed to) zero-cache will use the server default.

The number of cache buffers required is approximate. It needs to be large enough to cater for the page requirements of databases but not so large as to consume memory that is needed for other operations. Up to a point, the more activity that can be handled in the cache, the better the overall performance. The axiom "Database servers love RAM" is true for Firebird. But Firebird uses RAM for other activities that are at least as important as caching. Transaction inventory and index bitmaps are maintained in RAM and, from v.1.5, sorting and merging are done in memory, if it is available.

It is important to realize that every system has a critical point where a too-large cache configuration will consume more memory resources than the system can "spare." Beyond this point, enlarging the cache will cause performance to degrade.

Limits and Defaults

The minimum cache size is 50 pages. There is no maximum, as long as the allocation in total does not exceed the RAM available.

Default cache allocation is

- **Superserver**: For each running database, 2048 pages. All users share this common cache pool.

  As an indication of how resources can be consumed, a single database running at the default settings for PAGE_SIZE (4K) and DefaultDbCachePages (2K) requires 8MB of memory. Two databases running with the same settings require 16MB, and so on. Default cache usage is calculated by

  ```
  PAGE_SIZE * DefaultDbCachePages * number of databases
  ```

- **Classic Server**: Per client attachment, 75 cache pages. Each attachment is allocated its own cache. The amount of memory required is the total of the cache requirements of *all client attachments to each database*. Cache usage is calculated by

  ```
  PAGE_SIZE * DefaultDbCachePages * number of attachments
  ```

Calculating the Cache Size

When Firebird reads a page from the database from disk, it stores that page in the cache. Ordinarily, the default cache size is adequate. If your application includes joins of five or more tables, Firebird Superserver automatically increases the size of the cache. If your application is well localized (i.e., it uses the same small part of the database repeatedly), you might want to consider increasing the cache size so that you never have to release one page from cache to make room for another.

Because the DbCache is configured in pages, obviously a database with a larger page size consumes more memory than one with a smaller page size. When there are multiple databases running on the same server, it may be desirable to override the serverwide cache size at the database level or, in some cases, at the application level.

An application that performs intensive indexed retrievals requires more buffers than one that performs mainly inserts.

Where many clients are accessing different tables or different parts of a single table, the demand for cache memory is higher than where most clients are working with the same, or overlapping, sets of data.

It can happen that too many cache buffers are allocated for available RAM to accommodate. With many databases running simultaneously, a request could demand more RAM than was available on the system. The cache would be swapped back and forth between RAM and disk, defeating the benefits of caching. Other applications (including the server) could be starved of memory if the cache were too large.

It is important, therefore, to ensure that adequate RAM is installed on the system to accommodate the database server's memory requirements. If database performance is important for your users, then avoid creating competition for resources by running other applications on the server.

Estimating the Size Requirement

Estimating the size of the cache is not a simple or precise science, especially if you have multiple databases that have to run concurrently. The likely server cache usage is driven by the database with the largest page size. Classic server allocates a cache for each attachment, whereas Superserver pools cache for all attachments to a particular database. As a starting point, it will be useful to work with the numbers and needs for the database with the biggest page size. Actual usage conditions will determine whether any adjustments are needed.

It is not necessary to have a cache that will accommodate an entire database. Arrive at a reduction factor for each database by estimating the proportion that is likely to be accessed during normal usage. The estimation suggested here is just that—there is no "rule." Assume when we talk about "DbCachePages" here, we are talking about the size of the cache but not necessarily the default server setting for new and unconfigured databases.

The reduction factor, r, should be a value between 0 and 1.

The size of the database, in pages, (*size*) can be established as follows:

- For a **single-file database**, take the maximum file size allowed by the filesystem, minus 1 byte, and divide it by the page size.

  On operating systems that support huge files, use the database file size instead of the maximum file size.

- For a **multi-file database**, take the STARTING AT value of the first secondary file and add the LENGTH values of all of the secondary files.

Let DbCachePages equal the number of cache pages (buffers) required by this database.

For each database, calculate

DbCachePages = *r * size*

Calculate and record this figure for each individual database.

> **TIP** Keep these records with other database documentation for use when you need to tune the cache for an individual database.

Calculating RAM Requirements

To calculate the amount of RAM required for database caching on your server, take the PAGE_SIZE of each database and multiply it by the DefaultDbCachePages value. These results for all databases, when added together, will approximate the minimum RAM required for database caching.

Setting Cache Size at the Database Level

There are several ways to configure the cache size for a specified database. Changes do not take effect until the next time a first connection is made to Firebird Superserver or the next client connects to the Classic server.

Use gfix

The recommended way to set a database-level override to DefaultDbCachePages is to use the **gfix** command-line utility with the following switches:

```
gfix -buffers n database_name
```

where *n* is the required number of database pages. This approach permits fine-tuning to reduce the risk of under-using memory or working with a cache that is too small. The override will remain in place until the next time it is changed.

> **NOTE** To run **gfix**, you must be either SYSDBA or the owner of the database. For more information about using **gfix**, see Chapter 39.

Use the isql Command-Line Query Tool

To increase the number of cache pages for the duration of one session of the command-line utility **isql**, you have two options.

The first option is to include the number of pages (*n*) as a switch when starting **isql**:

```
isql -c n database_name
```

where n is the number of cache pages to be used for the session and temporarily over-rides any value set by the DefaultDbCachePages (database_cache_pages) configuration or **gfix**. It must be greater than 9.

Alternatively, you can include CACHE *n* as an argument to the CONNECT statement once **isql** is running:

```
isql > connect database_name CACHE n
```

The value *n* can be any positive integer number of database pages. If a database cache already exists because of another attachment to the database, the cache size is increased only if *n* is greater than the current cache size.

Use the Database Parameter Buffer

In an application, the cache size can be set in a database parameter buffer (DPB) using either the *isc_dpb_num_buffers* or the *isc_dpb_set_page_buffers* parameter, according to your server's requirements.

- *isc_dpb_num_buffers* sets the number of buffers (pages of cache memory) to be used for the current connection. It makes the most sense in a Classic server architecture, where each connection gets a static allocation of cache memory. In Superserver, it will set the number of buffers to be used for the specific database, if that database is not already open, but it will not persist after the server closes the database.

- *isc_dpb_set_page_buffers* is useful in both Classic server and Superserver. It has the same effect as using **gfix** to perform a persistent override of DefaultDbCachePages.

CAUTION   Be cautious about providing end-user applications with the ability to modify the cache. Although any request to change the cache size will be ignored on all connection requests except the first, allowing non-technical users to change server settings is likely to have unpredictable effects on performance, affecting the entire server.

Changing the Server Default

Setting the value for the server-level DefaultDbCachePages to be the largest of the DbCachePages values you have recorded may be overkill. When you change the server-level default setting in the configuration file, it becomes the default for every new and zero-configured database on the server.

To change it, open the configuration file in a text editor and find the parameter:

- For v.1.5, uncomment DefaultDbCachePages and change the number.

- For v.1.0.*x*, in the v.1.0.*x* config files, it is default_cache_pages. Uncomment the line if necessary and make the entry database_cache_pages=nnnn, where nnnn is the new cache size.

For Superserver, the change will take effect the next time a first connection is made to the affected databases. For Classic server, it will affect all connections made after the reconfiguration.

A Pragmatic Approach

Do not overrate the importance of the database cache. Any cache imposes its own overhead on the overall memory resources and the filesystem cache plays its own role in optimizing the system's read-write performance. There is always a point at which the real gain in overall server performance does not justify the cost of tying up resources for the worst-case demand scenario.

The best advice is this: Do not rush into cache size optimization as a "must-do" for Firebird. Work with the default settings during development and, for deployment, just verify that the amount of RAM available can accommodate the defaults.

Once into production conditions, use a monitoring tool to observe and record how reads and writes are satisfied from the cache for typical and extreme situations. If the statistics are not satisfactory, then begin considering optimization.

The first broad-brush optimization you can try is to increase the default cache to a size that will occupy approximately two-thirds of available *free* RAM. If there is not enough RAM installed, install more.

At that point, start monitoring again. If the procedure just described fails to improve things, repeat the exercise.

Verifying Cache Size

To verify the size of the database cache currently in use, execute the following commands in **isql**:

```
ISQL> CONNECT database_name;
ISQL> SET STATS ON;
ISQL> COMMIT;
Current memory = 415768
Delta memory = 2048
```

```
Max memory = 419840
Elapsed time = 0.03 sec
Buffers = 2048
Reads = 0
Writes 2
Fetches = 2
ISQL> QUIT;
```

After SET STATS ON, the empty COMMIT command prompts **isql** to display information about memory and buffer usage. Read the **Buffers=** line to determine the current size of the cache, in pages.

Read-Only Databases

By default, databases are in read-write mode when created. Read-write databases cannot be on a read-only filesystem, even if they are used only for SELECT, because Firebird writes information about transaction states to a data structure in the database file.

A Firebird database can be deployed as a read-only file, providing the ability to distribute catalogs, albums of files, and other non-maintained types of database on CDs and other read-only filesystems. Read-only databases can, of course, be accessed on read-write systems as well.

NOTE A read-only database is not the same thing as a database file that has its read-only attribute set on. File-copying a read-write database to a CD-ROM does not make it into a read-only database.

The application will need to be written so as to avoid requests that involve writing to the database or to trap the exceptions raised when they are attempted. The following will throw the error "Attempt to write to a read-only database":

- UPDATE, INSERT, or DELETE operations

- Metadata changes

- Operations that try to increment generators

External Files

Any accompanying files linked to the database by having been declared with CREATE TABLE tablename EXTERNAL FILE 'filename' will also be opened read-only, even if the file itself is not carrying the filesystem read-only attribute.

Making a Database Read-Only

Exclusive access is required to switch a database between read-write and read-only modes—see the section "Exclusive Access" in Chapter 39 for instructions. The mode switch can be performed by the database owner or the SYSDBA.

Either **gfix** or **gbak** can be used:[2]

- Using **gbak**, back up the database and restore it in read-only mode using the –c[reate] option, for example:

```
gbak -create -mode read_only db1.fbk db1.fdb
```

- Using **gfix**, issue a –m[ode] read_only command, for example:

```
gfix -mode read_only db1.fdb
```

TIP   Restore read-only databases with full-page usage—use the –use switch to specify "use all space." In a read-write database, pages are filled by default to 80 percent of page capacity because it can help to optimize the reuse of pages. Space reservation makes no sense in a read-only database, and fully filled pages are denser and faster.

TIP   Although a Firebird server can manage InterBase 5.x databases directly, these databases cannot be made read-only. You can upgrade an InterBase 5 database to a Firebird read-only database by making an InterBase 5 transportable **gbak** backup and restoring it using Firebird's **gbak** with the –c[reate] and –mode read_only switches.

Database Shadows

Firebird has a capability that can enable immediate recovery of a database in case of disk failure, network failure, or accidental filesystem deletion of the database.[3] Called

---

2. The Services API provides access to both of these methods for making a database read-only. For more information, study the available documentation for the various groups (clusters) of *isc_action_svc_xxx* service action parameters that can be passed to the *isc_service_start()* function. A number of database access component classes implement these functions for use in various development language environments.

3. Shadowing doesn't provide a fallback in the case where a database is accidentally DROPped, unfortunately. When you DROP a database, its shadow is dropped too.

shadowing, it is an internal process that maintains a real-time, physical copy of a database. Whenever changes are written to the database, the shadow receives the same changes simultaneously.

An active shadow always reflects the current state of the database. However, although shadowing has obvious benefits as a hedge against hardware failure, it is not an online replication system.

Benefits and Limitations of Shadowing

The main benefit of shadowing is that it provides a quick way to recover from a hardware disaster. Activating a shadow makes it available immediately. It runs invisibly to users as an extra loop in the data-writing process, with minimal attention from the DBA.

Creating a shadow does not require exclusive access to the database, and the shadow can be maintained in one or many files, in controlled spaces of the server's storage system.

However, shadowing is not a protection against corruption. Data written to the shadow is an exact copy of what is written to the database, warts and all. If user errors, intermittent disk faults, or software failures have corrupted data, then the same corrupt data will show up in the shadow.

Shadowing is an all-or-nothing recovery method. It has no provision to recover some pieces and ignore others or to revert to a specific point in time. It must live in the same filesystem as the server; a shadow must be written to fixed hard drives local to the server. It cannot be written to shares, non-local filesystems, or removable media.

NOTE   On systems that support NFS, it is possible to maintain the shadow on an NFS filesystem. However, it is not recommended because the shadow will become detached—and thus, useless—if the network connection is lost.

Important Caveats

Shadowing is not a substitute for backup. Do not be lulled into the belief that shadowing is in any way a substitute for regular backup and periodic restores.

- A shadow file is no less vulnerable to the "slings and arrows of outrageous fortune" than is any other file in your system.

- One lost or damaged shadow file makes the whole shadow useless.

- A dying disk or a flaky memory module is capable of great mischief before it brings your database down totally. Every piece of mischief will be faithfully written to the shadow.

In addition, a shadow cannot accept connections. Never try to connect to a shadow or interfere with it using system or database tools. The server "knows" what it has to do to a shadow to convert it to an active database.

> **TIP**   It is not a serious problem if a shadow is accidentally damaged or deleted. As long as you know the accident has occurred, a shadow for a healthy database can be regenerated at any time by simply dropping the shadow and creating it again.

Implementing Shadowing

Firebird has DDL syntax for creating and dropping shadows with various optional clauses to specify location, operating mode, and file sizes. Altering a shadow requires dropping the existing one and creating a new one with new specifications.

A shadow that is a single disk file is referred to as a *shadow file*. A multiple-file shadow—which can be distributed across more than one disk—is known as a *shadow set*. Shadow sets are grouped by a *shadow set number*.[4]

Shadow File Location and Distribution

A shadow should be created in *different fixed disk spaces* from the location or locations of the active database files, since one of the main purposes of shadowing is to provide fallback in case of disk failure.

Disk space for shadowing must be physically attached to the Firebird server's host machine. Files in a shadow set can be distributed across multiple disks to improve file I/O and space allocation. Like file specifications for databases, those for shadows are platform specific.

Shadow Options

Mode (AUTO or MANUAL)

Mode settings, *automatic* (with or without the *conditional* attribute) or *manual*, determine what occurs if something happens to make the shadow unavailable.

---

4. It has been impossible for the author to find anyone who could explain the benefits (if any) of maintaining multiple shadow sets. The numbering system might be a legacy from some functionality that was never implemented. In the absence of better information, it seems reasonable to stick with one shadow set.

AUTO mode is the default. It allows the database to keep running in the event that the shadow becomes inoperable.

- There will be a window of time during which no shadowing happens and the DBA may be unaware of the loss.

- If the lost shadow was created with the CONDITIONAL attribute, Firebird creates a new shadow automatically, if it can.

- If shadowing is not conditional, it will be necessary to re-create a shadow manually.

MANUAL mode prevents further access to the database in the event that the shadow becomes unavailable. Choose it if continuous shadowing is more important than continuous operation of the database.

To allow connections to resume, the administrator must remove the old shadow file, delete references to it, and create a new shadow.

Conditional Shadowing

One of the ways a shadow could become unavailable is by taking over as the main database in the event of the hardware "death" of the existing database—that is, after all, the whole idea behind shadowing!

 CAUTION The CONDITIONAL attribute should also cause a new shadow to be created automatically if the existing shadow becomes the operational database. However, practice shows that it does not always do so. Be aware of the possibility that it won't work as expected and be prepared to subject it to an emergency drill.

Single-File vs. Multi-File Shadows

By default, a shadow is created as a "set" consisting of one file. However, a shadow set can comprise multiple files. As a database—and hence its shadow—grow in size, the shadow can be respecified and regenerated with more files to accommodate the increased space requirements.

Creating a Shadow

A shadow can be created without needing exclusive access or affecting any connected users. The DDL statement CREATE SHADOW creates a shadow for the database to which you are *currently connected*.

This is the syntax:

```
CREATE SHADOW set_num [AUTO | MANUAL] [CONDITIONAL]
'filespec'
[LENGTH [=] int [PAGE[S]]] [<secondary_file>];

<secondary_file> = FILE 'filespec' [<fileinfo>][<secondary_file>]
<fileinfo> = {LENGTH[=]int [PAGE[S]] | STARTING [AT [PAGE]] int }
[<fileinfo>]
```

TIP   As with CREATE DATABASE, the file specs for shadow files are always specific to platform.

Single-File Shadow

Let's assume we are on a Linux server, logged into the database employee.gdb, which is located in the examples directory beneath the Firebird root. We have decided to shadow the database to a partition named /shadows. To create a single-file shadow for it there, we use the statement

```
CREATE SHADOW 1 '/shadows/employee.shd';
```

The shadow set number can be any integer. A page size is not included, since the PAGE_SIZE attribute is taken from the specification of the database itself.

Use the **isql** command SHOW DATABASE to check that the shadow now exists:

```
SQL> SHOW DATABASE;
Database: /usr/local/firebird/examples/employee.gdb
Shadow 1: '/shadows/employee.shd' auto
PAGE_SIZE 4096
Number of DB pages allocated = 392
Sweep interval = 20000
...
```

Multi-File Shadow

The syntax for creating a multi-file shadow is quite similar to that for creating a multi-file database: the secondary shadow file specifications are "chained" to the primary file specification, with file specs and size limits for each file.

In this example, assume we are logging into employee.gdb in its default Win32 location. We are going to create a three-file shadow on drives F, H, and J, which are partitions on hard drives in the server's filesystem.

251

TIP File sizes allocated for secondary shadow files need not correspond to those of the database's secondary files.

The primary file, employee1.shd, is 10,000 database pages in length, and the first secondary file, employee2.shd, is 20,000 database pages long. As with the database, the shadow's final secondary file, employee3.shd, will grow as needed until space is exhausted on partition J or the filesystem limit is reached.

```
CREATE SHADOW 25 'F:\shadows\employee1.shd' LENGTH 10000
FILE 'H:\shadows\employee2.shd' LENGTH 20000
FILE 'J:\shadows\employee3.shd';
```

Alternatively, we can specify starting pages for the secondary files instead of absolute lengths for the primary and non-final secondary files:

```
CREATE SHADOW 25 'F:\shadows\employee1.shd'
FILE 'H:\shadows\employee2.shd' STARTING AT 10001
FILE 'J:\shadows\employee3.shd' STARTING AT 30001;
```

You can verify in **isql**:

```
SQL> SHOW DATABASE;
Database: C:\Progra~1\firebird\examples\employee.gdb
Owner: SYSDBA
Shadow 25: 'F:\SHADOWS\EMPLOYEE1.SHD" auto length 10000
file H:\SHADOWS\EMPLOYEE2.SHD starting 10001
file J:\SHADOWS\EMPLOYEE3.SHD starting 30001
PAGE_SIZE 1024
Number of DB pages allocated = 462
Sweep interval = 20000
...
```

Manual Mode

The preceding examples created shadows in the default AUTO *mode*. Now, suppose we have a requirement that work in the database must be stopped at all times when shadowing is disabled for any reason. In this case, we want to stipulate that the shadow is created in MANUAL *mode* (refer to notes earlier in this topic). In order to tell the Firebird engine that we want this rule enforced, we create the shadow using the reserved word MANUAL in the CREATE SHADOW statement:

```
CREATE SHADOW 9 MANUAL '/shadows/employee.shd';
```

Now, if the shadow "kicks in" because we lose the main database file, or if the shadow becomes unavailable for some other reason, the administrator must drop the old shadow file and create a new shadow before clients can resume connecting.

A Conditional Shadow

In both of the preceding examples, the CREATE SHADOW specifications leave the database unshadowed after the shadow becomes unavailable, whether by becoming detached from the database or by its having "kicked in" as the active database upon the physical death of the original database.

In the case of a MANUAL mode shadow, that is the situation we want. We choose this mode because we want database connections to stay blocked until we manually get a new shadow going.

In the case of an AUTO mode shadow, database connections can resume after the death, as soon as the shadow kicks in. No shadowing will occur from this point until the admin manually creates a new shadow. Also, if a shadow becomes detached for some reason, the admin will not know about it. Either way, we have a window where shadowing has lapsed.

As described earlier in this topic, we can improve this situation by including the CONDITIONAL keyword in the AUTO mode shadow's definition. The effect will be that, when the old shadow becomes unavailable, the Firebird engine will do the necessary housekeeping and create a new shadow automatically, for example:

```
CREATE SHADOW 33 CONDITIONAL '/shadows/employee.shd';
```

Increasing the Size of a Shadow

At some point, it may become necessary to increase the sizes or numbers of files in a shadow. Simply drop the shadow (as described in the next section) and create a new one.

Dropping a Shadow

A shadow needs to be dropped in the following situations:

- It is a manual shadow that has been detached from the system for some reason. Dropping the compromised shadow is a necessary precursor to creating a new shadow and resuming database service.

- It is an unconditional automatic shadow that has been offline because of some system event. It needs to be regenerated to restore its integrity.

- You need to resize the files in a shadow, add more files, or set up a new shadow with different attributes.

- Shadowing is no longer required. Dropping the shadow is the means to disable shadowing.

Dropping a shadow removes not just the physical files but also the references to it in the metadata of the database. To be eligible to run the command, you must be logged into the database as the user who created the shadow, the SYSDBA, or (on POSIX) a user with root privileges.

Syntax

Use this syntax pattern for DROP SHADOW:

```
DROP SHADOW shadow_set_number;
```

The shadow set number is a compulsory argument to the DROP SHADOW command. To discover the number, use the **isql** SHOW DATABASE command while logged into the database.

The following example drops all of the files associated with the shadow set number 25:

```
DROP SHADOW 25;
```

Using gfix -kill

The command-line **gfix** housekeeping utility tool (see Chapter 39) has a *–kill* switch that conveniently submits a DROP SHADOW command internally to clean up an unavailable shadow. After executing this command, it will be possible to proceed with creating a new shadow.

For example, to drop the unavailable shadow on our employee database on POSIX, type

```
[root@coolduck bin]# ./gfix -kill ../examples/employee.gdb -user SYSDBA
-password masterkey
```

On Win32, type

```
C:\Program Files\Firebird\bin> gfix -kill ..\examples\employee.gdb -user SYSDBA
-password masterkey
```

Database "Hygiene"

Firebird uses a *multi-generational architecture*. This means that multiple versions of data rows are stored directly on the data pages. When a row is updated or deleted, Firebird keeps a copy of the old state of the record and creates a new version. This proliferation of *record back versions* can increase the size of a database.

Background Garbage Collection

To limit this growth, Firebird continually performs *garbage collection* in the background of normal database activity.

The background garbage collection does nothing to obsolete row versions that are caught up in unresolved transactions—they will not be visited during normal housekeeping activity. To completely sanitize the database, Firebird can perform *database sweeping*.

Sweeping

Database sweeping is a systematic way of removing all outdated row versions and freeing the pages they occupied so that they can be reused. Periodic sweeping prevents a database from growing unnecessarily large. Not surprisingly, although sweeping occurs in an asynchronous background thread, it can impose some cost on system performance.

By default, a Firebird database performs a sweep when the *sweep interval* reaches 20,000 transactions. Sweeping behavior is configurable, however: It can be left to run automatically, the sweep interval can be altered, or automatic sweeping can be disabled, to be run manually on demand instead.

Manual sweeping can be initiated from the command-line housekeeping program, **gfix**. Details are in Chapter 39. Several other desktop tools are available that provide a GUI interface for initiating manual sweeps.

Sweep Interval

The Firebird server maintains an inventory of transactions. Any transaction that is uncommitted is known as an *interesting transaction*. The oldest of these "interesting" transactions (the *Oldest Interesting Transaction*, or OIT) marks the starting point for the sweep interval. If the sweep interval setting is greater than zero, Firebird initiates a full sweep of the database when the difference between the OIT and the newest transaction passes the threshold set by the sweep interval.

For instructions, see Chapter 39.

Garbage Collection During Backup

Sweeping a database is not the only way to perform systematic garbage collection. Backing up a database achieves the same result, because the Firebird server must read every record, an action that forces garbage collection throughout the database. As a result, regularly backing up a database can reduce the need to sweep and helps to maintain better application performance.

CAUTION Backup is not a replacement for sweep. While backup performs full database garbage collection, it does not clean up the transaction accounting as sweep does. The effects of sweeping—or neglecting to do so—are discussed in several sections throughout Chapter 25.

For more information about the benefits of backing up and restoring, see Chapter 38.

Validation and Repair

Firebird provides utilities for validating the logical structures in databases and identifying minor problems and, to a limited extent, repairing them. A variety of such errors may appear from time to time, particularly in environments where networks are unstable or noisy, or the power supply is subject to fluctuation. User behavior and application or database design deficiencies are also frequent causes of logical corruption.

Abnormal termination of client connections does not affect database integrity, since the Firebird server will eventually detect the lost connection. It preserves committed data changes and rolls back any left pending. Cleanup is more of a housekeeping issue, since data pages that were assigned for uncommitted changes are left as "orphans." Validation will detect such pages and free them for reassignment.

The validation tools are capable of detecting and removing minor anomalies caused by operating system or hardware faults. Such faults usually cause database integrity problems, due to corrupt writes to or loss of data or index pages.

Data thus lost or damaged is not recoverable, but its artifacts must be removed to restore database integrity. If a database containing these compromised structures is backed up, the database will not be capable of being restored. It is important, therefore, to follow a controlled course of action to detect errors, eliminate them if possible, and get the database back into a stable state.

When to Validate and Why

Periodic validation should be part of the database admin's regular housekeeping, to detect minor anomalies and recycle misallocated space. Additionally, it will be required when structural damage is indicated or suspected. The indicators include

- A "corrupt database" or "consistency check" error.

- A backup that ends abnormally.

- Power failure or brownout without UPS protection or with suspected UPS failure.

- Suspected or system-reported hard disk, network, or memory faults.

- A database shadow taking over from a dead database after a disk crash.

- A production database is about to be moved to another platform or storage system.

- Suspected compromise of the network or database by malicious attack.

For full details on using **gfix** to perform database validation, see Chapter 39.

What to Do About a Corrupt Database

If you suspect you have a corrupt database, it is important to follow a proper sequence of recovery steps in order to avoid further corruption. The first, most important thing to do is ask or, if necessary, force all users to cancel their work and log out.

Appendix IV provides a detailed how-to procedure for attempting to repair a corrupt or suspect database.

How to Corrupt a Firebird Database

Firebird is famously tolerant of trauma fatal to other DBMS systems. However, experience has shown up a few techniques that have proven useful if destruction of your database is among your objectives. The author wishes to share these database-killers with the reader.

Modify the System Tables

Firebird stores and maintains all of the metadata for its own and your user-defined objects in—a Firebird database! More precisely, it stores them in relations (tables) right in the database itself. The identifiers for the system tables, their columns, and several other types of system objects begin with the characters "RDB$".

Because these are ordinary database objects, they can be queried and manipulated just like your user-defined objects. However, just because you *can* does not mean you *should*.

It cannot be recommended too strongly that you use DDL—not direct SQL operations on the system tables—whenever you need to alter or remove metadata. Defer the "hot fix" stuff until your skills in SQL and your knowledge of the Firebird engine become very advanced. A wrecked database is neither pretty to behold nor cheap to repair.

Disable Forced Writes on Windows with Firebird 1.0.x

Firebird is installed with forced writes (synchronous writes) enabled by default. Changed and new data is written to disk immediately upon posting.

It is possible to configure a database to use asynchronous data writes, whereby modified or new data is held in the memory cache for periodic flushing to disk by the operating system's I/O subsystem. The common term for this configuration is *forced writes off* (or *disabled*). It is sometimes resorted to, in order to improve performance during large batch operations.

Win32 server platforms do not flush the Firebird server v.1.0.*x* write cache until the Firebird service is shut down. Apart from power interruptions, there is much that can go wrong on a Windows server. If it should hang, the I/O system goes out of reach and your users' work will be lost in the process of rebooting.

The big warning here is this: Do not disable forced writes on a Windows server unless you are using Firebird 1.5 or higher.

Firebird 1.5, by default, flushes the write cache every 5 seconds or at every 100 writes, whichever comes sooner. The frequency can be modified in firebird.conf by altering one or both of MaxUnflushedWrites and MaxUnflushedWriteTime.

Windows 95 does not support asynchronous writes to disk.

Linux servers are safer for running an operation with forced writes disabled temporarily. Do not leave it disabled once your large batch task is completed, unless you have a very robust fallback power system.

Restore a Backup to a Running Database

One of the restore options in the **gbak** utility (gbak -r[estore]) allows you to restore a **gbak** file over the top of an existing database—it overwrites it. It is possible for this style of restore to proceed without warning while users are logged into the database. Database corruption is almost certain to be the result.

Your admin tools and procedures must be designed to prevent any user (including SYSDBA) from overwriting your active database if any users are logged in.

If is practicable to do so, it is recommended to restore to spare disk space using the gbak -c[reate] option. Before making the restored database live, test it in the spare location using **isql** or your preferred admin tool.

Allow Users to Log In During a Restore

If your organization likes living on the edge, then use the –restore switch and let users log in and perform updates. Restore re-creates the database from scratch and, as soon as the tables are re-created, your users can, potentially at least, hit them with DML operations while referential integrity and other constraints are still in the pipeline. At best, they will cause exceptions and a stack of uncommitted transactions in the partly constructed database. At worst, they will thoroughly break data integrity in diverse, irrecoverable ways.

Copy Database Files While Users Are Logged In

Use any filesystem copying or archiving utility (DOS copy, xcopy, tar, gzip, WinZip, WinRAR, etc.) to copy files while any user (including SYSDBA) is logged in. The copy will be damaged but, worse, sector locking and/or caching by these programs can cause data loss and possibly corruption within the original file.

Dropping a Database

When a database is no longer required, it can be deleted (dropped) from the server. Dropping a database deletes all files pertaining to the entire database—primary and secondary files, shadow files, and log files—and all its data.

The command to delete a database is DROP DATABASE, and it takes no parameters. In order to execute the command, you need to be logged into the database as its owner, as SYSDBA, or (on Linux/UNIX) as a user with system root privileges.

Syntax

While logged into the database you want to drop, use this statement to perform the drop:

```
DROP DATABASE;
```

A dropped database cannot be recovered, so

- Be certain that you really want it to be gone forever.

- Take a backup first if there is any chance that you will need anything from it in future.

Up Next

Creating a database installs the infrastructure needed to begin creating objects. The primary object for storing data persistently in a database is the table. Unlike spreadsheets, most desktop database management systems, and even one or two "high-end" RDBMS contenders, Firebird does not store data in structures that are "tabulated" as physically ordered rows and columns that the filesystem recognizes. Firebird manages its own disk space and uses its own rules to lay down and map persistent data. It supports a number of ways to extract data in tablelike sets. We begin, in the next chapter, with creating the SQL persistent TABLE object.

CHAPTER 16

Tables

IN SQL-89 AND SQL-92 TERMS, Firebird tables are *persistent base tables*. The standards define several other types, including *viewed tables*, which Firebird implements as views (see Chapter 24) and *derived tables*, which Firebird could be said to implement as selectable stored procedures (see Chapters 28 and 30).

About Firebird Tables

Unlike desktop databases, such as Paradox and xBase databases, a Firebird database is not a series of "table files" physically organized in rows and columns. Firebird stores data, independent of its structure, in a compressed format, on *database pages*. It may store one or many records—or, correctly, *rows*—of a table's data on a single page. In cases where the data for one row is too large to fit on one page, a row may span multiple pages.

Although a page that stores table data will always contain only data belonging to one table, pages are not stored contiguously. The data for a table may be scattered all around the disk and, in multi-file databases, may be dispersed across several directories or disks. BLOB data is stored apart from the rows that own it, in another style of database page.

Structural Descriptions

Metadata—the physical descriptions of tables and their columns and attributes, as well as those of all other objects—is itself stored in ordinary Firebird tables inside the database. The Firebird engine writes to these tables when database objects are created, modified, or destroyed. It refers to them constantly when carrying out operations on rows. These tables are known as *system tables*. For more information, see the section "The System Tables" near the start of Chapter 14. Schemata for the system tables are in Appendix IX.

Creating Tables

It is assumed that, having reached the point where you are ready to create tables, you have already prepared your data analysis and model, and you have a very clear blueprint for the structures of your main tables and their relationships. In preparation for creating these tables, you need to have performed these steps:

- You have created a database to accommodate them. For instructions, refer to the previous chapter.

- You have connected to the database.

- If you plan to use domains for the data type definitions of your tables' columns, you have already created the domains (refer to Chapter 13).

Table Ownership and Privileges

When a table is created, Firebird automatically applies the default SQL security scheme to it. The person who creates the table (the owner) is assigned all SQL privileges for it, including the right to grant privileges to other users, triggers, and stored procedures. No other user, except the SYSDBA, will have any access to the table until explicitly granted privileges.

 CAUTION This security is as good (or bad) as the security of access to your server. Anyone who can log into your server can create a database. Anyone who can attach to a database can create tables in it. Firebird 1.5 improves slightly on this unfortunate situation by allowing you to limit the locations where databases can be created and accessed. See the DatabaseAccess parameter in firebird.conf.

For information about SQL privileges, refer to Chapter 35.

CREATE TABLE Statement

The DDL for creating a table is the CREATE TABLE statement. The syntax is

```
CREATE TABLE table [EXTERNAL [FILE] 'filespec']
(<col_def> [, <col_def> | <tconstraint> ...]);
```

The first essential argument to CREATE TABLE is the table identifier.[1] It is required and must be unique among all table, view, and procedure names in the database, otherwise you will be unable to create the table. You must also supply at least one column definition.

---

1. If you are coding CREATE TABLE in an Embedded SQL (ESQL) application, with the intention of also populating the data for this table from the application, the table must first be *declared* with a *preceding* DECLARE TABLE statement.

Defining Columns

When you create a table in the database, your main task is to define the various attributes and constraints for each of the columns in the table.

This is the syntax for defining a column:

```
<col_def> = col {datatype | COMPUTED [BY] (<expr>) | domain}
[DEFAULT {literal |NULL |USER}]
[NOT NULL] [<col_constraint>]
[COLLATE collation]
```

The next sections list the required and optional attributes that you can define for a column.

Required Attributes

These are the required attributes:

- A column identifier (name), unique among the columns in the table

- *One* of the following:

  - An SQL data type *(datatype)*

  - An expression *(expr)* for a computed column

  - A domain definition *(domain)* for a domain-based column

Columns are separated by commas, for example:

```
CREATE TABLE PERSON (
  PERSON_ID BIGINT NOT NULL,
  FIRST_NAME VARCHAR(35),
  LAST_NAMES VARCHAR (80),
  FULL_NAME COMPUTED BY FIRST_NAME ||' '|| LAST_NAMES,
  PHONE_NUMBER TEL_NUMBER);
```

The column FULL_NAME is a computed column calculated by concatenating two other columns in the definition, FIRST_NAME and LAST_NAMES. We will come back to computed columns a little later. A NOT NULL constraint is applied to PERSON_ID because we want to make it a primary key (details to come later).

For the PHONE_NUMBER column, we use the domain that was defined in our Chapter 13 example:

```
CREATE DOMAIN TEL_NUMBER
AS VARCHAR(18)
CHECK (VALUE LIKE '(0%)%');
```

Columns Based on Domains

If a column definition is based on a domain, it can include a new default value, additional CHECK constraints, or a COLLATE clause that overrides one already defined in the domain definition. It can also include additional attributes or column constraints. For example, you can add a NOT NULL constraint to the column if the domain does not already define one.

 CAUTION A domain that is configured as NOT NULL cannot be overridden at the column level to be nullable.

For example, the following statement creates a table, COUNTRY, referencing a domain called COUNTRYNAME, which doesn't have a NOT NULL constraint:

```
CREATE TABLE COUNTRY (
  COUNTRY COUNTRYNAME NOT NULL PRIMARY KEY,
  CURRENCY VARCHAR(10) NOT NULL);
```

We add the NOT NULL constraint to the column definition of COUNTRYNAME because we know it is going to be needed as the primary key of the COUNTRY table.

Optional Attributes

The following sections describe optional attributes for columns.

DEFAULT Value

Defining a default value can save data entry time and prevent data entry errors when new rows are inserted into a table. If the row is inserted without including the column in the column list, a default value—if defined—can be automatically written into the column. In a column based on a domain, the column can include a default value that locally overrides any default defined for the domain.

For example, a possible default for a TIMESTAMP column could be the context variable CURRENT_TIMESTAMP (server date and time). In a (True/False) Boolean-style character column, the default could be set to 'F' to ensure that a valid, non-null state was written on all new rows.

A default value must be compatible with the data type of the column and consistent with any other constraints on the column or its underlying domain. A default, as appropriate to data type, can be

- A **constant** (e.g., some string, numeric, or date value).

- A **context variable** (e.g., CURRENT_TIMESTAMP, CURRENT_USER,[2] CURRENT_CONNECTION, etc.).

- A **predefined date literal** such as 'NOW', 'TOMORROW', etc.

- **NULL** can be set as the default for any nullable column.[3] Nullable columns default to NULL automatically, but you may wish to override an unwanted domain-level default. Don't define this default on a column that has a NOT NULL constraint.

 CAUTION When relying on defaults, it must be understood that a default will be applied only upon insertion of a new row and only if the INSERT statement does not include the defaulted column in its column list. If your application includes the defaulted column in the INSERT statement and sends NULL in the values list, then NULL will be stored, regardless of any default defined. If the column is not nullable, passing NULL will always cause an exception.

The following example defines a column, CREATED_BY, that defaults to the context variable CURRENT_USER:

```
CREATE TABLE ORDER (
  ORDER_DATE DATE,
  CREATED_BY VARCHAR(31) DEFAULT CURRENT_USER,
  ORDER_AMOUNT DECIMAL(15,2));
```

A new row is inserted by user JILLIBEE, omitting CREATED_BY from the column list:

```
INSERT INTO ORDER (ORDER_DATE, ORDER_AMT)
VALUES ('15-SEP-2004', 1004.42);
```

---

2. If your operating system supports the use of multi-byte characters in user names, or you have used a multi-byte character set when defining roles, then any column into which CURRENT_USER or CURRENT_ROLE is to be stored as the default must be defined using a compatible character set.

3. Watch out for a NOT NULL constraint on the column. NULL would be a contradictory default.

The table is queried:

```
SELECT * FROM ORDER;
...
ORDER_DATE   CREATED_BY       ORDER_AMOUNT
==========   ==========       ================
...
15-SEP-2004  JILLIBEE              1004.42
...
```

CHARACTER SET

A CHARACTER SET can be specified for an individual character or text BLOB column when you define the column. If you do not specify a character set, the column assumes the character set of the domain, if applicable; otherwise, it takes the default character set of the database. For example:

```
CREATE TABLE TITLES_RUSSIAN (
  TITLE_ID BIGINT NOT NULL,
  TITLE_EN VARCHAR(100),
  TITLE VARCHAR(100) CHARACTER SET WIN1251);
```

Refer to Chapter 11 for details about character sets and to Appendix VIII for a list of available character sets.

The COLLATE Clause

A COLLATE clause can be added to a CHAR or VARCHAR column to override a collation sequence otherwise defined for the column's character set by the underlying domain, if applicable. Collation sequence is not applicable to BLOB types.

The following extends the previous example to include a COLLATE clause:

```
CREATE TABLE TITLES_RUSSIAN (
  TITLE_ID BIGINT NOT NULL,
  TITLE_EN VARCHAR(100),
  TITLE VARCHAR(100) CHARACTER SET WIN1251 COLLATE PXW_CYRL);
```

 CAUTION   Take care when applying COLLATE clauses to columns that need to be indexed. The index width limit of 253 bytes can be drastically reduced by some collation sequences. Experiment first!

Refer to Chapter 11 for details about the collation sequences available for each character set and to Appendix VIII for a list of available character sets and collations.

 TIP You can get your own list, which may include more recently added collation sequences, by creating a new database and running the query listed in Chapter 11, under the section "Listing Available Collation Sequences."

COMPUTED Columns

A *computed column* is one whose value is calculated each time the column is accessed at runtime. It can be a convenient way to access redundant data without the negative effects of actually storing it. Not surprisingly, such columns cannot perform like hard data—refer to the restrictions listed later in this section.

This is the syntax:

```
<col_name> COMPUTED [BY] (<expr>);
```

There is no need to specify the data type—Firebird calculates an appropriate one. *expr* is any scalar expression that is valid for the data types of the columns involved in the calculation. External functions are fine to use, as long as you are sure that the libraries used by the functions will be available on all platforms where the database might be installed. (For more information about external functions, aka UDFs, refer to Chapter 21. A listing of commonly used functions is in Appendix I.)

Other restrictions exist for computed columns:

- Any columns that the expression refers to must have been defined before the computed column is defined, so it is a useful practice to place computed columns last.

- A computed column cannot be defined as an ARRAY type or return an array.

- You can define a computed BLOB column by using a SELECT statement on a BLOB in another table, but it is strongly recommended that you don't do this.

- Computed columns cannot be indexed.

- Constraints placed on computed columns will be ignored.

- Computed columns are output-only and read-only. Including them in INSERT or UPDATE statements will cause exceptions.

CAUTION   As a general warning, though it is possible to create a computed column using a SELECT statement into another table, it is a practice to be avoided because of the undesirable dependencies involved. A properly normalized database model should not require it.

Examples of COMPUTED Columns

The following statement creates a computed column, FULL_NAME, by concatenating the LAST_NAMES and FIRST_NAME columns.

```
CREATE TABLE PERSON (
  PERSON_ID BIGINT NOT NULL,
  FIRST_NAME VARCHAR(35) NOT NULL,
  LAST_NAMES VARCHAR (80) NOT NULL,
  FULL_NAME COMPUTED BY FIRST_NAME ||' '|| LAST_NAMES);
/**/
SELECT FULL_NAME FROM PERSON
WHERE LAST_NAMES STARTING WITH 'Smi';
FULL_NAME
==============================
Arthur Smiley
John Smith
Mary Smits
```

NOTE   Notice the NOT NULL constraints on the two names being concatenated for this computed column. It is important to attend to such details with computed columns, because NULL as an element in a concatenation will always cause the result to be NULL.

The next statement computes two columns using context variables. This can be useful for logging the particulars of row creation:

```
CREATE TABLE SNIFFIT
(SNIFFID INTEGER NOT NULL,
SNIFF COMPUTED BY (CURRENT_USER),
SNIFFDATE COMPUTED BY (CURRENT_TIMESTAMP));
/**/
SELECT FIRST 1 FROM SNIFFIT;
SNIFFID  SNIFF      SNIFFDATE
==============================
      1  SYSDBA     2004-08-15 08:15:35.0000
```

The next example creates a table with a calculated column (NEW_PRICE) using the previously created OLD_PRICE and PERCENT_CHANGE definitions:

```
CREATE TABLE PRICE_HISTORY (
  PRODUCT_ID D_IDENTITY NOT NULL, /* uses a domain */
  CHANGE_DATE DATE DEFAULT CURRENT_TIMESTAMP NOT NULL,
  UPDATER_ID D_PERSON NOT NULL, /* uses a domain */
  OLD_PRICE DECIMAL(13,2) NOT NULL,
  PERCENT_CHANGE DECIMAL(4,2)
    DEFAULT 0
    NOT NULL
    CHECK (PERCENT_CHANGE BETWEEN -50.00 AND 50.00),
  NEW_PRICE COMPUTED BY
    (OLD_PRICE + (OLD_PRICE * PERCENT_CHANGE / 100)) );
```

Constraints

In the parlance of relational databases, any restriction imposed on the format, range, content, or dependency of a data structure is known as a *constraint*. Firebird provides several ways to implement constraints, including both formal, standards-defined *integrity* and *referential* constraints and user-defined CHECK constraints.

Constraints are visible to all transactions that access the database and are automatically enforced by the server. They vary in their scope of action. Some, such as NOT NULL, are applied directly to a single column (*column constraints*) while others, such as PRIMARY KEY and some CHECK constraints, take effect at the table level (*table constraints*). The FOREIGN KEY constraint has table-to-table scope.

Constraints exist "in their own right" as objects in a Firebird database. Each constraint is uniquely represented in the metadata, with the rules and dependencies of each being defined through regular relationships between the system tables.

Integrity Constraints

Integrity constraints impose rules that govern the state of acceptable data items or a relationship between the column and the table as a whole—often both. Examples are NOT NULL (rejects input that has unknown value), UNIQUE (requires that an incoming item has no matching value in that column anywhere in the table), and PRIMARY KEY (combines both of the other constraints and also "represents" the table for referential relationships with other tables).

Each of the integrity constraints is discussed individually in detail later in this chapter.

The Referential Constraint

The referential constraint is implemented as FOREIGN KEY. A foreign key constraint exists only in the context of another table and a unique key from that table, signaled implicitly or explicitly by the REFERENCES clause of its definition.

Tables that are linked in a foreign key relationship are said to be *bound by a referential integrity constraint*. Thus, any column or group of columns constrained by a PRIMARY KEY or UNIQUE constraint is also potentially subject to referential constraints. Referential integrity is discussed in detail in Chapter 17.

Named Constraints

When declaring a table-level or a column-level constraint, you can optionally name the constraint using the CONSTRAINT clause. If you omit the CONSTRAINT clause, Firebird generates a unique system constraint name. Constraints are stored in the system table, RDB$RELATION_CONSTRAINTS.

Although naming a constraint is optional, assigning a descriptive name with the CONSTRAINT clause can make the constraint easier to find for changing or dropping, or when its name appears in a constraint violation error message. Apart from its benefits for self-documentation, this style is particularly useful for distinguishing the key definitions from the column definitions in scripts.

PRIMARY KEY and FOREIGN KEY Names

Naming a constraint has special implications for PRIMARY KEY and FOREIGN KEY constraints, particularly from Firebird 1.5 onward. It is possible to override Firebird's "native" naming restrictions for keys.

In all versions, a supplied name will override the default name INTEG_nn and apply the supplied name to the constraint. However,

- In version 1.5 and later, the supporting index will have the same name as the constraint.

- In version 1.0.*x*, the default index name (RDB$PRIMARYnn or RDB$FOREIGNnn) is enforced.

NOTE Existing constraint names remain unchanged when a database is promoted from a version 1.0.x server to a version 1.5 server.

The constraint-naming behaviors are described in more detail in the next section and in the next chapter.

Integrity Constraints

The NOT NULL Constraint

Firebird does not support a nullable attribute, as some non-standard DBMSs do. In compliance with standards, all columns in Firebird are nullable unless explicitly constrained to be NOT NULL. The optional NOT NULL constraint is a *column-level constraint* that can be applied to force the user to enter a value. *Null is not a value*, so any attempt to input null to the column or set it to null will cause an exception.

Because of the NOT NULL constraint's role in the formation of keys, you need to be aware of certain restrictions pertaining to it:

- It must be applied to the definition of any column that will be involved in a PRIMARY KEY or UNIQUE constraint.

- In Firebird 1.0.*x*, it must be applied to the definition of any column that will be involved in a UNIQUE constraint or a unique index.

- It cannot be removed from a domain or column by an ALTER DOMAIN or ALTER TABLE ALTER COLUMN statement, or by overriding a domain at column level. Do not use a NOT NULL domain to define a column that is allowed to be NULL.

For more insight into NULL, refer to the section "Considering NULL" in Chapter 21.

The PRIMARY KEY Constraint

PRIMARY KEY is a table-level *integrity constraint*—a set of enforceable rules—which formally earmarks a column or group of columns as the unique identifier of each row in the table.

If you are coming to Firebird from a DBMS that uses the concept of "a primary index" to define a key (typically, file-based systems such as Paradox, Access, and MySQL), then Firebird and the world of SQL standards has a "gotcha" for you. A primary key is not an index, but a constraint in its own right. One of the rules of the constraint is that it must have an appointed unique index of one or more non-nullable elements associated with it.

Simply creating such an index does not create a primary key. Creating a primary key constraint does, however, create the required index using the columns enumerated in the constraint declaration.

 CAUTION   Do not import an existing "primary index" from a file-based legacy system or create such an index in anticipation of declaring a primary key constraint. Firebird cannot piggyback a primary key constraint onto an existing index—at least up to and including release 1.5—and the query optimizer does not perform properly if indexes are duplicated.

A table can have only one primary key. When you define the constraint, Firebird automatically creates the required index, using a set of naming rules. The names of primary key indexes are discussed next.

 CAUTION If you are converting a database to Firebird from any other source except InterBase or Oracle, it is essential that you pay attention to the schema with respect to the names and constraints concerning primary keys.

While the PRIMARY KEY constraint is not itself a referential constraint, it is usually a mandatory part of any referential constraint, being potentially the object of the REFERENCES clause of a FOREIGN KEY constraint. For more details, refer to the next chapter.

Choosing a Primary Key

Identifying candidate columns to be the primary key is a science in itself and beyond the scope of this guide. Many worthy tomes have been written on the subject of *normalization*, the process of eliminating redundancy and repeating groups in sets of data and arriving at a correct identification of the element that uniquely represents a single row set in the table. If you are a newcomer to relational databases, the value of investing in a good book about data modeling cannot be stressed enough.

A primary key candidate, which may be one column or a group of columns, has two unbreakable requirements:

- The NOT NULL attribute must be declared for *all* columns in the group of one or more columns that will be used. The integrity of the key can be enforced only by comparing values, and NULL is not a value.

- The column or group of columns has to be unique—that is, it cannot occur in more than one row in the table. A driver's license or Social Security number might be considered, for example, because they are generated by systems that are presumed not to issue duplicate numbers.

To these theoretical "givens" must be added a third one:

- The total size (width) of the candidate key must be 253 bytes or less. This is not simply a matter of counting characters. The implementation limit will be reduced—in some cases, drastically—if there are multiple columns, non-binary collations, or multi-byte character sets involved.

How Real Data Can Defeat You

Using the EMPLOYEE table from the employee.fdb database in the Firebird root/examples directory (employee.gdb in the v.1.0.*x* kits), let's illustrate how real data can defeat your theoretical assumptions about uniqueness. Here is a declaration that shows, initially, the meaningful data stored in this table:

```
CREATE TABLE EMPLOYEE (
FIRST_NAME VARCHAR(15) NOT NULL, /* assumption: an employee must have
                                             a first name */
LAST_NAME VARCHAR(20) NOT NULL, /* assumption:  an employee must have
                                             a last name */
PHONE_EXT VARCHAR(4),
HIRE_DATE DATE DEFAULT CURRENT_DATE NOT NULL,
DEPT_NO CHAR(3) NOT NULL,
JOB_CODE VARCHAR(5) NOT NULL,
JOB_GRADE SMALLINT NOT NULL,
JOB_COUNTRY VARCHAR(15) NOT NULL,
SALARY NUMERIC (15, 2) DEFAULT 0 NOT NULL,
FULL_NAME COMPUTED BY FIRST_NAME ||' '||LAST_NAME
) ;
```

This structure in fact has no candidate key. It is not possible to identify a single employee row by using (FIRST_NAME, LAST_NAME) as the key, since the combination of both elements has a medium-to-high probability of being duplicated in the organization. We could not store records for two employees named John Smith.

In order to get a key, it is necessary to invent something. That "something" is the mechanism known as a *surrogate key*.

Surrogate Keys

We have already visited the surrogate key in the introductory topic on keys in Chapter 14. A surrogate primary key is a value of guaranteed uniqueness and no semantic content that substitutes for the key in a table structure that cannot provide a candidate key from within its own structure. The EMPLOYEE table therefore introduces EMP_NO (declared from a domain) to take this surrogate role for it:

```
CREATE DOMAIN EMPNO SMALLINT ;
COMMIT;
ALTER TABLE EMPLOYEE
  ADD EMP_NO EMPNO NOT NULL,
  ADD CONSTRAINT PK_EMPLOYEE
    PRIMARY KEY(EMP_NO) ;
```

This database also maintains a generator named EMP_NO_GEN and a Before Insert trigger named SET_EMP_NO on the EMPLOYEE table, to produce a value for this key whenever a new row is inserted. The section "Implementing Autoincrementing Keys" in

Chapter 31 describes this technique in detail. It is the recommended way to implement surrogate keys in Firebird.

You may wish to consider the benefits of using a surrogate primary key not just in cases where the table cannot supply candidates, but also in cases where your candidate key is composite.

Composite Primary Keys

During data analysis, it sometimes happens that no single unique column can be found in the data structure. Theory suggests that the next best thing is to look for two or more columns that, when grouped together as the key, will ensure a unique row. When multiple columns are conjoined to form a key, the key is called a *composite key* or, sometimes, a *compound key*.

If you come to Firebird with a cargo of background experience working with a DBMS such as Paradox, using composite keys to implement hierarchical relationships, it can be quite hard to part with the notion that you cannot live without them. Yet, in practice, composite keys should be considered with a high degree of restraint in a DBMS such as Firebird, which does not track through disk-based physical index structures to implement relationships.

Firebird does not need composite indexes and, more to the point, composite indexes do impose some problems, both for development and, when large tables are involved, for performance:

- Composite keys are typically composed of non-atomic key elements—that is, the columns selected have semantic meaning (they are "significant as data") and are almost certainly vulnerable to external changes and typographical errors.

- Any foreign keys in other tables that reference this table will have to propagate every element of the composite key. Referential integrity is at risk from the use of non-atomic keys. A combination of non-atomic elements compounds the risk.

- Keys—foreign as well as primary—have mandatory indexes. Composite indexes have stricter size limits than single-column indexes.

- Composite indexes tend to be large. Large indexes use more database pages, causing indexed operations (sorts, joins, and comparisons) to be slower than is necessary.

Atomicity of PRIMARY KEY Columns

It is recommended practice to avoid involving in your primary and foreign keys any column that is *meaningful as data*. It violates one of the primary principles of relational database design, that of *atomicity*. The atomicity principle requires that each item of data exist completely in its own right, with a single, internal rule governing its existence.

For a primary key to be atomic, it should be beyond the reach of human decision. If a human has to spell it or type it, it is not atomic. If it is subject to any rule except the non-nullable, unique requirements, it is not atomic. Using the earlier example, even a systematic number such as a driver's license or a Social Security number does not have the atomicity required for a primary key, because it is subject to an external system.

Syntaxes for Declaring the Primary Key

Several syntaxes are available for assigning the PRIMARY KEY constraint to a column or group of columns. All columns that are elements in a PRIMARY KEY must be previously defined as NOT NULL. Since it is not possible to add a NOT NULL constraint to a column after it has been created, it is essential to take care of this constraint before applying the additional constraint.

The PRIMARY KEY constraint can be applied in any of the following phases of metadata creation:

- In the column definition, during CREATE TABLE or ALTER TABLE, as part of the column's definition set

- In the table definition, during CREATE TABLE or ALTER TABLE, as a separately defined table constraint

Defining PRIMARY KEY As Part of a Column Definition

In the following sequence, a non-nullable domain is defined and committed ahead, then the primary key column is defined using that domain and, simultaneously, the PRIMARY KEY constraint is applied to the table immediately:

```
CREATE DOMAIN D_IDENTITY AS BIGINT NOT NULL;
COMMIT;
CREATE TABLE PERSON (
  PERSON_ID D_IDENTITY PRIMARY KEY,
  ...
);
```

Firebird creates a table constraint with a name like INTEG_nn and an index with a name like RDB$PRIMARYnn. (*nn* in each case is a number spun from a generator. The two numbers are unrelated.) You cannot influence what these names will be or change them.

The effect is similar if you use the same approach when adding a column using ALTER TABLE and make it the primary key in a single clause:

```
ALTER TABLE BOOK
ADD BOOK_ID D_IDENTITY PRIMARY KEY;
```

Defining PRIMARY KEY As a Named Constraint

Another way to define the primary key in the table definition is to add the constraint declaration at the end of the column definitions. The constraint declarations are placed last because they are dependent on the existence of the columns to which they apply. This method gives you the option of naming the constraint. The following declaration names the primary key constraint as PK_ATABLE:

```
CREATE TABLE ATABLE (
  ID BIGINT NOT NULL,
  ANOTHER_COLUMN VARCHAR(20),
  CONSTRAINT PK_ATABLE PRIMARY KEY(ID) );
```

Now, instead of the system-generated name RDB$PRIMARYnnn, Firebird stores PK_TABLE as the name of the constraint. In Firebird 1.5 and higher, it also applies the user-defined constraint name to the enforcing unique index. In this example, the index will be named PK_TABLE, whereas in other versions the index name will be INTEG_nn.

Firebird 1.5 also allows you to use non-matching, user-defined names for the constraint and its enforcing index.

Using a Custom Index

Until Firebird 1.5, it was not possible to use a descending index to enforce the primary key. From version 1.5 onward, it is possible to ask Firebird to enforce the primary key with a descending index. To do this, Firebird 1.5 introduced a syntax extension in the form of the USING clause, enabling constraint indexes to be defined as either ASC [ENDING] or DESC[ENDING] and to have a name different from that of the named constraint.

ASC and DESC determine the direction of the search order—lowest or highest first. The concept is discussed in more detail in Chapter 18.

The following statement will create a primary key constraint named PK_ATEST and enforce it by creating a descending index named IDX_PK_ATEST:

```
CREATE TABLE ATEST (
  ID BIGINT NOT NULL,
  DATA VARCHAR(10));
COMMIT;

ALTER TABLE ATEST
ADD CONSTRAINT PK_ATEST PRIMARY KEY(ID)
USING DESC INDEX IDX_PK_ATEST;
COMMIT;
```

The alternative syntax will work, too:

```
CREATE TABLE ATEST (
  ID BIGINT NOT NULL,
```

```
DATA VARCHAR(10),
CONSTRAINT PK_ATEST PRIMARY KEY(ID)
USING DESC INDEX IDX_PK_ATEST;
```

 CAUTION   If you specify a DESCENDING index for a primary or unique constraint, you must be sure to specify USING DESC INDEX for any foreign keys that reference it.

Adding a Primary Key to an Existing Table

The addition of table constraints can be deferred. It is a common practice for developers to define all of their tables without any table constraints and to add them subsequently, using a separate script. The rationale behind this practice is good: Large scripts notoriously fail because the author overlooked some dependency. It simply causes fewer headaches to build databases in a sequence that eliminates the time and spleen spent on patching dependency errors and rerunning scripts.

Typically, in the first script, we declare and commit the tables:

```
CREATE TABLE ATABLE (
  ID BIGINT NOT NULL,
  ANOTHER_COLUMN VARCHAR(20),
  < more columns > );
CREATE TABLE ANOTHERTABLE (
  ... );
...
COMMIT;
ALTER TABLE ATABLE
  ADD CONSTRAINT PK_ATABLE
  PRIMARY KEY(ID);
ALTER TABLE ANOTHERTABLE...
```

and so on.

In the next chapter, when exploring FOREIGN KEY definitions, the benefits of building databases in a dependency-safe sequence will become obvious.

CHECK Constraints

A CHECK constraint is used for validating incoming data values. It enforces a match condition or requirement that a value must meet in order for an insert or update to succeed. It cannot change the incoming value; it will return a validation exception if the input fails the check.

TIP CHECK constraints are applied after "before" triggers have fired. Use a trigger when you need to perform a validation and conditionally change it to a valid one.

In a table definition, it is a *table-level* constraint. Unlike CHECK constraints applied to domain definitions, its VALUE element is expressed as a column reference. For example, on a domain, a CHECK clause might be

```
CHECK (VALUE > 10)
```

In a table definition, the same conditioning for a column named AColumn would be expressed as

```
CHECK (ACOLUMN > 10)
```

A CHECK constraint is active in both INSERT and UPDATE operations. Although it is a table-level constraint, its scope can range from column level, through row level and, although it is not recommended, to table level and even beyond the boundaries of the table. It guarantees data integrity only when the values being verified are *in the same row* as the value being checked.

CAUTION You should not use expressions that compare the value with values in different rows of the same table or in different tables, since any row other than the current one is potentially in the process of being altered or deleted by another transaction. Especially, do not rely on a CHECK constraint to enforce a referential relationship!

The search condition can

- Verify that the value entered falls within a defined range.

- Match the value with a list of allowed values.

- Compare the value with a constant, an expression, or with data values in other columns of the same row.

Restrictions

Certain restrictions apply to CHECK constraints:

- A column can have only one CHECK constraint, although its logic can be expressed as a complex search condition—one constraint, many conditions.

- A CHECK constraint on a domain-based column cannot override the inherited domain-level check. The column definition can use a regular CHECK clause to add *additional* constraint logic to the inherited constraint. It will be ANDed to the inherited conditions.

- A CHECK constraint cannot refer to a domain.

This is the syntax of the CHECK constraint:

```
CHECK (<search condition>);
<search_condition> =
<val> <operator> {<val> |(<select_one>)}
| <val> [NOT] BETWEEN <val> AND <val>
| <val> [NOT] LIKE <val> [ESCAPE <val>]
| <val> [NOT] IN (<val> [, <val> ...] | <select_list>)
| <val> IS [NOT] NULL
| <val> {[NOT]{=|<|>}|>=|<=}
{ALL |SOME |ANY}(<select_list>)
| EXISTS (<select_expr>)
|SINGULAR (<select_expr>)
| <val> [NOT] CONTAINING <val>
| <val> [NOT] STARTING [WITH] <val>
|(<search_condition>)
|NOT<search_condition>
| <search_condition> OR <search_condition>
| <search_condition> AND <search_condition>
```

The range of possibilities for defining CHECK constraints is very broad indeed—theoretically, almost any search condition will be accepted. It is important for the designer to choose conditions that are reasonable and safe, since they affect every INSERT and UPDATE operation on the table.

Consult Part Five of this guide for syntaxes for setting the various styles of search condition.

For example, this constraint tests the values of two columns to ensure that one is greater than the other. Although it also implies NOT NULL conditioning on both columns—the check will fail if either column is null—it does not *confer* NOT NULL constraint on the column:

```
CHECK (COL1 > COL2);
```

The check will fail if the arithmetic test fails or if either COL_1 or COL_2 is null. This succeeds:

```
INSERT INTO TABLE_1 (COL_1, COL_2) VALUES (6,5);
```

UNIQUE Constraints

A UNIQUE constraint, like a primary key, ensures that no two rows have the same value for a specified column or group of columns. You can have more than one UNIQUE constraint defined for a table, but it cannot be applied to the same set of columns that is used for either the PRIMARY KEY or another UNIQUE constraint.

A UNIQUE constraint, in fact, actually creates a *unique key* that has virtually the same powers as the primary key. It can be selected as the controlling key for a referential integrity constraint. This makes it useful for situations where you define a thin, surrogate primary key for atomicity and to improve performance of join and search operations, but you want to keep the option to form an alternative FOREIGN KEY link on the unique key for occasional use.

In Firebird 1.0.*x*, the NOT NULL attribute must be applied to all of the columns on which the UNIQUE constraint will operate.

Like the PRIMARY KEY constraint, UNIQUE creates its own mandatory, unique index to enforce its rules. Naming of both the constraint and the index follows the same rules of behavior applicable to other keys. The following example in **isql** illustrates the Firebird 1.5 naming behavior:

```
SQL> CREATE TABLE TEST_UQ (
CON>  ID BIGINT NOT NULL,
CON>  DATA VARCHAR(10),
CON>  DATA_ID BIGINT NOT NULL);
SQL> COMMIT;
SQL> ALTER TABLE TEST_UQ
CON>ADD CONSTRAINT PK_TEST_UQ PRIMARY KEY(ID),
CON>ADD CONSTRAINT UQ1_DATA UNIQUE(DATA_ID) ;
SQL> COMMIT;
SQL> SHOW TABLE TEST_UQ;
ID          BIGINT        NOT NULL
DATA        VARCHAR(10)   NULLABLE
DATA_ID     BIGINT        NOT NULL
CONSTRAINT PK_TEST_UQ:
   Primary key (ID)
CONSTRAINT UQ1_DATA:
   Unique key (DATA_ID)
SQL> SHOW INDICES TEST_UQ;
PK_TEST_UQ UNIQUE INDEX ON TEST_UQ(ID)
UQ1_DATA UNIQUE INDEX ON TEST_UQ(DATA_ID)
SQL>
```

NOTE   Remember this mantra: An index is not a key. You can define unique indexes (see Chapter 18 for details), but making a unique index does not create a unique key. If there is a chance that you might need to use a uniquely indexed column or structure as a key, consider defining the constraint instead.

Using External Files As Tables

In the current SQL argot, Firebird supports the *external virtual table*, or EVT. Filesystem files in ASCII text format can be read and manipulated by Firebird as if they were tables, albeit with considerable limitations arising from the fact that they are not internal database objects. Other applications can thus exchange data with a Firebird database, independent of any special transforming mechanism. External tables can be converted to internal tables.

The EXTERNAL FILE clause enables a table to be defined with its row structure mapping to fixed-length "fields" in "records" (usually delimited by line feeds) that reside in an external file. Firebird can select from and insert into such a file as if it were a regular table. It cannot, however, perform update or delete operations on external tables.

The text file containing the data must be created on or copied to a storage device that is physically under the control of the server—as usual, no NFS devices, shares, or mapped drives. Shared access by Firebird and other applications at the file level is not possible. Firebird requires exclusive access during times when it has the file open in a transaction. At other times, the file can be modified by other applications.

Syntax for CREATE TABLE...EXTERNAL FILE

The CREATE TABLE statement for an external file defines both the external file specification (local location and file name) and the typed Firebird columns represented by the structure of the contained records.

```
CREATE TABLE EXT_TBL
  EXTERNAL FILE filespec
  (columndef [,columndef,...],
  [line_delimiter_1 CHAR(1)
  [, line_delimiter_2 CHAR(1)]]);
```

filespec is the fully qualified local path and file specification for the external data file. The file need not exist at the time the table is created. However, from Firebird 1.5 onward, the CREATE statement will fail if the filespec refers to an unconfigured external file location. See the section "Securing External Files" later in this chapter and the configuration section in Chapter 36.

columndef is an ordinary Firebird column definition. Non-character data types can be specified, provided every string extracted from the column's location in the external record is capable of being cast implicitly to that type.

line_delimiter is an optional final column or pair of columns that can be defined to read the characters used by the file system to mark the end of a line of text. Although it makes reading the file easier for humans, it is not a requirement in a fixed-format record unless programs that are going to read the data require it.

- On Linux/UNIX, this is the single character ASCII 10, the line feed character.

- On Windows, it is the ordered pair ASCII 13 (carriage return) followed by ASCII 10.

- On Mac OS, it is ASCII 10 followed by ASCII 13.

- Other operating systems may use other variations or other characters.

Restrictions and Recommendations

Securing External Files

With all versions of Firebird, a list of directories can be configured to restrict the locations where Firebird will search for or create external files. See Chapter 3 for the configuration parameters ExternalFileAccess in firebird.conf (for v. 1.5 servers) or external_file_directory in ibconfig/isc_config (for v. 1.0.*x*). By default, Firebird 1.5 is installed with no access to external files, whereas 1.0.*x* gives open access to any file in the local filesystem.

NOTE   The method of configuration and the capability to protect the system from malicious attack via external file access differ between server versions.

Format of External Data

Firebird will create the external file itself if it does not find it in the location specified in the CREATE EXTERNAL TABLE '<filespec>' specification. If the file already exists, each record must be of fixed length, consisting of fixed-length fields that exactly match the byte length of the column specifications in the table definition. If the application that created the file uses hard line breaks (e.g., the 2-byte carriage return and line break sequence in Windows text files), include a column to accommodate this sequence. See the upcoming section titled "End-of-Line Characters."

BLOB and ARRAY data cannot be read from or written to an external file.

Most well-formed number data can be read directly from an external table and, in most cases, Firebird will be able to use its internal casting rules to interpret it correctly. However, it may be easier and more precise to read the numbers into character columns and, later, convert them using the CAST(..) function.

TIP   Make sure you allow enough width to accommodate your data. For some guidelines on sizes, refer to the relevant chapter in Part Three. Figure 8-1 in Chapter 8 summarizes the rules for data type conversions.

CHAR vs. VARCHAR

Using VARCHAR in the column definition of an external string field is not recommended because it is not a readily portable format:

```
<2-byte unsigned short><string of character bytes>
```

VARCHAR requires the initial 2-byte unsigned short to include the number of bytes in the actual string, and the string immediately follows.[4] This is difficult or impossible for many external applications to achieve and it simply is not worth the trouble. For this reason, favor CHAR over VARCHAR for string fields and ensure that the feeding application pads the strings to full length.

End-of-Line Characters

When you create the table that will be used to import the external data, you must define a column to contain the end-of-line (EOL) or newline character if the application that created the file included it. The size of this column must be exactly large enough to contain a particular system's EOL symbol (usually 1 or 2 bytes). For most versions of UNIX, it is 1 byte. For Windows and Macintosh, it is 2 bytes.

Tips for Inserting Non-Printable Characters

When inserting to an external file, the external function `ASCII_CHAR(decimal_ASCII_code)` from the ib_udf function library can be used to pass the non-printable characters as an expression to the line-delimiter columns in the SQL statement. For example, the following inserts a carriage return and line feed into a column:

```
INSERT INTO MY_EXT_TABLE (
  COLUMNS...,
  CRLF)
VALUES (
  column_values...,
  ASCII_CHAR(13) || ASCII_CHAR(10));
```

An alternative is to create a table to store any non-printable characters your applications might need to store. Simply create a regular text file on the same platform as the server, using an editor that "displays" non-printable characters. Open your "NPC" table using an interactive tool and copy and paste the characters directly to the table.

---

4. Here we are talking about Intel architecture. Alignment may be different on some architectures.

For statements performing inserts to the external file, the character can be subqueried from the table.[5]

Operations

Only INSERT and SELECT operations can be performed on the rows of an external table. Attempts to update or delete rows will return errors.

Because the data is outside the database, operations on an external table are not under Firebird's record version control. Inserts therefore take effect immediately and cannot be rolled back.

 TIP If you want your table to be under transaction control, create another, internal Firebird table, and insert the data from the external table into the internal one.

If you use DROP DATABASE to delete the database, you must also remove the external file—it will not be automatically deleted as a result of DROP DATABASE.

Importing External Files to Firebird Tables

To import an external file into a Firebird table, begin by making sure that you have set up the appropriate access conditions. Refer to Chapter 36 regarding the server parameter ExternalFileAccess in the section "Configuring External Locations."

1. Create a Firebird table that allows you to view the external data. Declare all columns as CHAR. The text file containing the data must be on the server. In the following example, the external file exists on a UNIX system, so the EOL character is 1 byte.

```
CREATE TABLE EXT_TBL EXTERNAL FILE 'file.txt' (
  FNAME CHAR(10),
  LNAME CHAR(20),
  HDATE CHAR(10),
  NEWLINE CHAR(1));
COMMIT;
```

---

5. Creating specifications for reading and writing external files may well involve much more detailed knowledge of the format than is discussed here. Character sets and byte lengths may well be an issue. In many cases, use of the character set–neutral OCTETS character set in the external table definition may solve some issues. Importing and exporting data is never a one-size-fits-all matter.

2. Create another Firebird table that will eventually be your working table. Include a column for the EOL character if you expect to export data from the internal table back to an external file later:

```
CREATE TABLE PERSONNEL (
  FIRST_NAME VARCHAR(10),
  LAST_NAME VARCHAR(20),
  HIRE_DATE DATE,
  NEW_LINE CHAR(1));
COMMIT;
```

3. Using a text editor, or an application that can output fixed-format text, create and populate the external file. Make each record the same length, pad the unused characters with blanks, and insert the EOL character(s) at the end of each record.

    The number of characters in the EOL string is platform-specific—refer to the previous notes.

    The following example illustrates a fixed-length record length is 41 characters. *b* represents a blank space, and *n* represents the EOL:

```
12345678901234567890123456789012345678901
fname.....lname...............hdate.....n
JamesbbbbbStarkeybbbbbbbbbbbbbb2004-12-10n
ClaudiobbbValderramabbbbbbbbbb2003-10-01n
```

4. A SELECT statement from table EXT_TBL returns the records from the external file:

```
SELECT FNAME, LNAME, HDATE FROM EXT_TBL;
FNAME LNAME HDATE

========= ==================== ===========
James     Starkey              2004-12-10
Claudio   Valderrama           2003-10-01
```

5. Insert the data into the destination table:

```
INSERT INTO PERSONNEL
SELECT FNAME, LNAME, CAST(HDATE AS DATE),
NEWLINE FROM EXT_TBL;
COMMIT;
```

> **NOTE** If you try to access the file while it is still opened by another application, the attempt will fail. The reverse is also true and more: Once your application has opened the file as a table, it will be unavailable to other applications until your application disconnects from the database.[6]

Now, when you perform a SELECT from PERSONNEL, the data from your external table will appear in converted form:

```
SELECT FIRST_NAME, LAST_NAME, HIRE_DATE
  FROM PERSONNEL;
FIRST_NAME LAST_NAME         HIRE_DATE
========== ================= ===========
James      Starkey           10-DEC-2004
Claudio    Valderrama        01-OCT-2003
```

Exporting Firebird Tables to an External File

Carrying on with the example illustrated in the previous section, the steps for exporting data to our external table are similar:

1. Open the external file in a text editor and remove everything from the file. Exit from the editor and again perform the SELECT query on EXT_TBL. It should be empty.

2. Use an INSERT statement to copy the Firebird records from PERSONNEL into the external file, file.txt:

```
INSERT INTO EXT_TBL
  SELECT FIRST_NAME, LAST_NAME,
  cast(HIRE_DATE AS VARCHAR(11),
ASCII_CHAR(10)
  FROM PERSONNEL
  WHERE FIRST_NAME LIKE 'Clau%';
```

3. Now query the external table:

```
SELECT FNAME, LNAME, HDATE FROM EXT_TBL;
FNAME      LNAME                HDATE
========== ==================== ===========
Claudio    Valderrama           01-OCT-2004
```

---

6. The external file ought to be released once operations on it are completed. It is not correct behavior for the server to retain its lock, since external data is not cached. It is a bug for which the reader might well request a fix.

TIP   The external function ASCII_CHAR( ) is in the library ib_udf, in the /UDF directory of your Firebird installation. Its declaration can be found in the script ib_udf.sql. For more on using external functions, see Chapter 21.

Converting External Tables to Internal Tables

It is possible to convert the current data in external tables to an internal table. The means to do this is to back up the database using the **gbak** utility with the *–convert* switch (abbreviation *–co*). All external tables defined in the database will be converted to internal tables by restoring the backup. Afterward, the external table definition will be lost.

For more information, refer to Chapter 38.

Altering Tables

The ALTER TABLE statement is used for changing the structure of a table: adding, changing, or dropping columns or constraints. One statement can encompass several changes, if required. To submit an ALTER TABLE query, you need to be logged in as the table's creator (owner), SYSDBA or (on POSIX) the Superuser.

Alterations to each table or to its triggers are reference-counted. Any one table can be altered at most 255 times before you must back up and restore the database. However, the reference count is not affected by switching a trigger on and off using

```
ALTER TRIGGER triggername ACTIVE | INACTIVE
```

TIP   Plan to perform a backup and restore after changes in table structures if the database contains any data. When a table or column is altered, Firebird does not convert any data format changes. To facilitate online metadata changes, it stores the new format description and delays the translation until the data is needed. It introduces a performance hit that could have an unanticipated impact on a user's work.

Preparing to Use ALTER TABLE

Before modifying or dropping columns or attributes in a table, you need to do three things:

1.   Make sure you have the proper database privileges.

2.   Save the existing data.

3.   Drop any dependency constraints on the column.

Modifying Columns in a Table

Existing columns in tables can be modified in a few respects, namely

- The name of the column can be changed to another name not already used in the table.

- The column can be "moved" to a different position in the left-to-right column order.

- Conversions from non-character to character data are allowed, with some restrictions.

Syntax

Use the following syntax pattern for ALTER TABLE:

```
ALTER TABLE table
  ALTER [COLUMN] simple_column_name alteration
    alteration = new_col_name | new_col_type | new_col_pos
      new_col_name = TO simple_column_name
      new_col_type = TYPE datatype_or_domain
      new_col_pos = POSITION integer
```

NOTE   If you attempt to rename a column, you will bump into dependency problems if the column is referred to by a constraint or is used in a view, trigger, or stored procedure.

Examples

Here we change the name of a column from EMP_NO to EMP_NUM:

```
ALTER TABLE EMPLOYEE
  ALTER COLUMN EMP_NO TO EMP_NUM; /* the keyword COLUMN is optional */
```

Next, the left-to-right position of the column—known as its *degree*—is moved:

```
ALTER TABLE EMPLOYEE
  ALTER COLUMN EMP_NUM POSITION 4;
```

This time, the data type of EMP_NUM is changed from INTEGER to VARCHAR(20):

```
ALTER TABLE EMPLOYEE
  ALTER COLUMN EMP_NUM TYPE VARCHAR(20);
```

Restrictions on Altering Data Type

Firebird does not let you alter the data type of a column or domain in a way that might result in data loss.

- The new column definition must be able to accommodate the existing data. If, for example, the new data type has too few bytes or the data type conversion is not supported, an error is returned and the change cannot proceed.

- When number types are converted to character types, each number type is subject to a minimum length in bytes, according to type. These are tabulated in Figure 8-1 in Chapter 8.

- Conversions from character data to non-character data are not allowed.

- Columns of BLOB and ARRAY types cannot be converted.

 CAUTION   Any changes to the field definitions may require the indexes to be rebuilt.

Dropping Columns

The owner of a table can use ALTER TABLE to drop (remove) a column definition and its data from a table. Dropping a column causes all data stored in it to be lost. The drop takes effect immediately unless another transaction is accessing the table. In this event, the other transaction continues uninterrupted and Firebird postpones the drop until the table is no longer in use.

Before attempting to drop a column, be aware of the dependencies that could prevent the operation from succeeding. It will fail if the column

- Is part of a UNIQUE, PRIMARY, or FOREIGN KEY constraint

- Is involved in a CHECK constraint (there may be table-level CHECK constraints on the column in addition to any imposed by its domain)

- Is used in a view, trigger, or stored procedure

Dependencies must be removed before the column drop can proceed. Columns involved in PRIMARY KEY and UNIQUE constraints cannot be dropped if they are referenced by FOREIGN KEY constraints. In this event, drop the FOREIGN KEY constraint before dropping the PRIMARY KEY or UNIQUE key constraint and column it references. Finally, you can drop the column.

This is the syntax:

```
ALTER TABLE name DROP colname [, colname ...];
```

For example, the following statement drops the column JOB_GRADE from the EMPLOYEE table:

```
ALTER TABLE EMPLOYEE DROP JOB_GRADE;
```

To drop several columns with a single statement:

```
ALTER TABLE EMPLOYEE
  DROP JOB_GRADE,
  DROP FULL_NAME;
```

Dropping Constraints

A correct sequence must be followed when dropping constraints, since both PRIMARY KEY and CHECK constraints are likely to have dependencies.

TIP   To find the names of constraints, it may be helpful to define and commit the four system views defined in the script system_views.sql provided in Appendix IX.

UNIQUE KEY and PRIMARY KEY Constraints

When a primary key or unique constraint is to be dropped, it will be necessary first to find and drop any foreign key (FK) constraint that references it. If it is a unique key, the FK declaration actually names the columns of the unique constraint, for example:

```
...
FK_DATA_ID FOREIGN KEY DATA_ID
  REFERENCES  TEST_UQ(DATA_ID);
```

If the referenced key is the primary key, the name of the primary key column is optional in FK declarations and is often omitted. For example, looking at the ../samples/ employee.gdb database:

```
...TABLE PROJECT (
...,
TEAM_CONSTRT FOREIGN KEY (TEAM_LEADER)
  REFERENCES EMPLOYEE );
```

Dropping a foreign key constraint is usually straightforward:

```
ALTER TABLE PROJECT
DROP CONSTRAINT TEAM_CONSTRT;
COMMIT;
```

After that, it becomes possible to drop the primary key (PK) constraint on the EMP_NO column of the EMPLOYEE table:

```
ALTER TABLE EMPLOYEE
DROP CONSTRAINT EMP_NO_CONSTRT;
```

CHECK Constraints

Any CHECK conditions that were added during table definition can be removed without complications. CHECK conditions inherited from a domain are more problematic. To be free of the domain's constraints, it will be necessary to perform an ALTER TABLE ALTER COLUMN...TYPE operation to change the column to another data type or domain.

Adding a Column

One or more columns can be added to a table in a single statement, using the ADD clause. Each ADD clause includes a full column definition, which follows the same syntax as column definitions in CREATE TABLE. Multiple ADD clauses are separated with commas.

This is the syntax:

```
ALTER TABLE table ADD <col_def>
<col_def> = col {<datatype> | [COMPUTED [BY] (<expr>) | domain}
[DEFAULT {literal |NULL |USER}]
[NOT NULL] [<col_constraint>]
[COLLATE collation]
<col_constraint> = [CONSTRAINT constraint] <constraint_def>
[<col_constraint>]
<constraint_def>=
```

```
PRIMARY KEY
| UNIQUE
| CHECK (<search_condition>)
| REFERENCES other_table [(other_col [, other_col ...])]
[ON DELETE {NO ACTION|CASCADE|SET DEFAULT|SET NULL}]
[ON UPDATE {NO ACTION|CASCADE|SET DEFAULT|SET NULL}]
```

The following statement adds a column, EMP_NO, to the EMPLOYEE table using the EMPNO domain:

```
ALTER TABLE EMPLOYEE ADD EMP_NO EMPNO NOT NULL;
```

Example

Here we add two columns, EMAIL_ID and LEAVE_STATUS, to the EMPLOYEE table:

```
ALTER TABLE EMPLOYEE
  ADD EMAIL_ID VARCHAR(10) NOT NULL,
  ADD LEAVE_STATUS DEFAULT 10 INTEGER NOT NULL;
```

Including Integrity Constraints

Integrity constraints can be included for columns that you add to the table. For example, a UNIQUE constraint could have been included for the EMAIL_ID column in the previous statement:

```
ALTER TABLE EMPLOYEE
  ADD EMAIL_ID VARCHAR(10) NOT NULL,
  ADD LEAVE_STATUS DEFAULT 10 INTEGER NOT NULL,
  ADD CONSTRAINT UQ_EMAIL_ID UNIQUE(EMAIL_ID);
```

or

```
ALTER TABLE EMPLOYEE
  ADD EMAIL_ID VARCHAR(10) NOT NULL UNIQUE,
  ADD LEAVE_STATUS DEFAULT 10 INTEGER NOT NULL;
```

Adding New Table Constraints

The ADD CONSTRAINT clause can be included to add table-level constraints relating to new or existing columns.

This is the syntax:

```
ALTER TABLE name ADD [CONSTRAINT constraint] <tconstraint_opt>;
```

where *tconstraint_opt* can be a PRIMARY KEY, FOREIGN KEY, UNIQUE, or CHECK constraint. The CONSTRAINT *constraint* phrase is omitted if you do not care to name the constraint yourself.

Example

For example, to add a UNIQUE constraint to the EMPLOYEE table, you might use this statement:

```
ALTER TABLE EMPLOYEE
ADD CONSTRAINT UQ_PHONE_EXT UNIQUE(PHONE_EXT);
```

When ALTER TABLE Is Not Enough

Sometimes, you need to make a change to a column that cannot be achieved with ALTER TABLE. Examples might be where a column that is storing international language items in character set NONE needs to be changed to another character set to correct your design error, or a telephone number, originally defined by someone as an integer, needs to be stored as an 18-character column instead.

In the first case, it is not possible to change the character set of a column, so you need a workaround that both preserves the data and makes it available in the correct character set. In the second case, simply changing the data type of the telephone number column will not work if we already have existing integer data in the column. We want to keep the actual numbers, but we have to convert them to strings. That cannot be done in the current structure, because an integer column cannot store a string.

The workaround entails creating a temporary column in your table, with the correct attributes, and "parking" the data there while you drop and re-create the original column.

1. Add a temporary column to the table that has a definition with the new attributes you need.

    ```
    ALTER TABLE PERSONNEL
      ADD TEMP_COL VARCHAR(18);
    COMMIT;
    ```

2. Copy the data from the column to be changed to the temporary column, "massaging" it appropriately (e.g., applying a character set "introducer" to convert the text data to the correct character set or, in our example, casting it appropriately).

    ```
    UPDATE PERSONNEL
      SET TEMP_COL = CAST(TEL_NUMBER AS VARCHAR(18))
      WHERE TEL_NUMBER IS NOT NULL;
    COMMIT;
    ```

3. After verifying that the data in the temporary column has been changed as planned, drop the old column.

```
ALTER TABLE PERSONNEL
  DROP TEL_NUMBER;
```

4. Create a "new" column with the same name as the one you just dropped that has the same attributes as the temporary column.

```
ALTER TABLE PERSONNEL
  ADD TEL_NUMBER VARCHAR(18);
```

5. Copy the massaged data to the newly re-created column.

```
UPDATE PERSONNEL
  SET TEL_NUMBER = TEMP_COL
  WHERE TEMP_COL IS NOT NULL;
COMMIT;
```

6. After verifying that the data in the re-created column is correct, drop the temporary column. If you wish, you can also move the re-created column back into its old position.

```
ALTER TABLE PERSONNEL
  DROP COLUMN TEMP_COL,
  ALTER TEL_NUMBER POSITION 6;
COMMIT;
```

Removing (Dropping) a Table

DROP TABLE

Use DROP TABLE to remove an entire table permanently from the database. This is permanent and, once committed, cannot be undone.

```
DROP TABLE name;
```

The following statement drops the table PERSONNEL:

```
DROP TABLE PERSONNEL;
```

RECREATE TABLE

Sometimes, you may want to drop a table and create it again "from scratch." For these occasions, Firebird has RECREATE TABLE, which does the following:

- Drops the existing table and all of the objects belonging to it

- Commits the change

- Creates the new table as specified in the clauses and sub-clauses

Syntax

The syntax is identical to that of CREATE TABLE. Simply substitute the CREATE keyword with RECREATE and proceed.

 CAUTION   Make sure that you save the source of any trigger, key, and index definitions that you want to keep before submitting a RECREATE TABLE request!

Restrictions and Recommendations

If the table is in use when you submit the DROP or RECREATE statement, the request will be denied, with an "Object *xxxxx* is in use" message.

Always take a backup before any activity that changes metadata.

Although it is possible to make metadata changes when users are online, it is not recommended, especially for radical changes like dropping and re-creating tables. If necessary, force users off and get exclusive access. Instructions for getting exclusive access are in Chapter 39.

Temporary Tables

Firebird does not currently provide any form of temporary table that is managed *as such* by the system. It has less need for them than many other DBMSs have. For example, Firebird has the capability to output a virtual table directly from a stored procedure that is written with a specific syntax. For more about this, see "Selectable Stored Procedures" in Chapters 29 and 30.

Permanent "Temporary" Tables

A popular model for storing temporary data for applications to access is to define a permanent structure for the data that includes a "session ID" or "batch ID" acquired from a generator or, in Firebird 1.5, the CURRENT_TRANSACTION value. Applications can insert, reprocess, and delete rows in such a table during the course of a task. Remember, Firebird does not put locks on tables in the normal course of events.

According to the conditions and needs of the application, it can itself be responsible for deleting the temporary rows when its session completes, using the session ID for a searched delete. Alternatively, the application could post a row to a housekeeping table signaling "cleanup required" to a later, deferred operation that runs after hours, before a backup.

 TIP   Temporary tables are likely to appear in a later release of Firebird.

Up Next

One of the important features of an RDBMS is its ability to enforce the relationships between groups of persistent data stored in tables. Next, we examine how Firebird implements rules for protecting the referential integrity of these intertable relationships.

CHAPTER 17

Referential Integrity

THE TERM *REFERENTIAL INTEGRITY* REFERS TO the capability of a database to protect itself from receiving input that would result in an inconsistent relationship. Specifically, the referential integrity of a database exists according to its ability to enforce and protect a relationship between two tables.

Implementing formal referential constraints adds some extra work to the database designer's task, so what is the payback? If you are new to the concept, then you are sure to find many reasons of your own to justify the additional time and attention, including the following:

- **Bombproofing**: Formal referential constraints—especially when used intelligently with other types of constraint—will bombproof the business rules of your databases against application bugs, regardless of their source. This becomes especially important when you deploy your systems to sites where unskilled or partly skilled staff have access to the database through third-party utilities.

- **Query speed**: Indexes automatically created for referential integrity constraints speed up join operations.[1]

- **Quality control**: During development and testing, potential bugs tend to show up early because the database rejects operations that break the rules. Effectively, they eliminate the grief from proceeding with application development under false assumptions about data consistency.

- **Self-documentation**: Integrity rules enforced by your database provide "free" documentation that eliminates the need for any descriptive documents apart from your schema scripts. The rules defined in the metadata correctly become the authoritative reference to the data model for new staff and future development.

---

1. There is, however, one exception. A foreign key index with very low selectivity—an extremely high level of duplication of a small number of values through the table—can have a serious effect on performance if its key columns form a join condition.

Terminology

When an RDBMS provides the ability to *declare* the relationship between two tables, it is sometimes termed *declarative referential integrity*, a fuzzy term that seems to have been propagated by writers of magazine articles. Referential integrity is a design objective, a quality. The author prefers the term *formal referential constraints* when referring to the mechanisms for implementing the rules.

In a *relational* database management system (RDBMS), relationships between two tables are created by means of the *foreign key constraint.* The foreign key constraint enforces the rules of existence for the rows it represents, protecting the table against attempts to store rows that are inconsistent with the data model. However, this constraint does not need to work alone. Other integrity constraints (described in detail in the previous chapter) can work in combination with the referential constraint to protect the consistency of relationships.

The FOREIGN KEY Constraint

A foreign key is a column or set of columns in one table that corresponds in exact order to a column or set of columns defined as a PRIMARY KEY or a UNIQUE constraint in another table. In its simplest form, it implements an optional one-to-many relationship.

NOTE   An optional relationship exists when the relationship is made possible by the formal structure but is not required. That is to say, a parent instance may exist without any referencing child but, if both exist, both are constrained. The other side of the coin is a mandatory relationship. Mandatory relationships are discussed later in this chapter.

The standard entity-relationship model depicts a simple one-to-many relationship between two entities as shown in Figure 17-1.

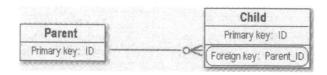

Figure 17-1. Entity-relationship model

If we implement this model as two tables, PARENT and CHILD, then rows in the CHILD table are dependent on the existence of a linking row in PARENT. Firebird's FOREIGN KEY (FK) constraint enforces this relationship in the following ways:

- It requires that the value presented in the FK column of the referencing table, CHILD (CHILD.PARENT_ID), must be able to be linked to a matching value present in the referenced unique key (in this case, the primary key) of PARENT (PARENT.ID).

- By default, it disallows a row in PARENT to be deleted, or to have its linking unique key value changed to a different value, if dependent CHILD rows exist.

- It must implement the relationship that was intended at the time the reference was created or the last time it was updated.[2]

- By default, it allows the FK column to be null. Since it is impossible to link null to anything, such child rows are *orphans*—they have no parent.

Implementing the Constraint

In order to implement the referential constraint, certain prerequisites must be attended to. In this section, we follow through a very simple example. If you are developing in an existing, complex environment, where SQL privileges are in effect, then you may need to be concerned about the REFERENCE privilege. It is introduced in a separate section later in this chapter.

The Parent Structure

It is necessary to start with the parent table and implement a controlling unique key to which the dependent table will link. This is commonly the primary key of the parent table, although it need not be. A foreign key can link to a column or group that has been constrained using the UNIQUE constraint. For present purposes, we will use the primary key:

```
CREATE TABLE PARENT (
  ID BIGINT NOT NULL,
  DATA VARCHAR(20),
  CONSTRAINT PK_PARENT PRIMARY KEY(ID));
COMMIT;
```

---

2. A thoughtful inclusion in *Data Modeling Essentials, 2nd Edition* by Graeme Simsion (Coriolis, 2000).

The Child Structure

In the child structure, we need to include a column, PARENT_ID, that exactly matches the primary key of the parent in type and size (and also column order, if the linkage involves multiple columns):

```
CREATE TABLE CHILD (
  ID BIGINT NOT NULL,
  CHILD_DATA VARCHAR(20),
  PARENT_ID BIGINT,
  CONSTRAINT PK_CHILD PRIMARY KEY(ID));
COMMIT;
```

The next thing to do is declare the relationship between the child and the parent by means of a FOREIGN KEY constraint.

Syntax for Defining a FOREIGN KEY

The syntax pattern for a referential integrity definition is as follows:

```
...
FOREIGN KEY (column [, col ...])
REFERENCES (parent-table [, col ...])
[USING [ASC | DESC] INDEX index-name] /* v.1.5 and above */
[ON DELETE {NO ACTION | CASCADE | SET NULL  | SET DEFAULT}]
[ON UPDATE {NO ACTION | CASCADE | SET NULL  | SET DEFAULT}]
```

Defining our foreign key:

```
ALTER TABLE CHILD
  ADD CONSTRAINT FK_CHILD_PARENT
  FOREIGN KEY(PARENT_ID)
  REFERENCES PARENT(ID); /* REFERENCES PARENT is also valid,
                    because ID is the primary key of PARENT */
```

Firebird stores the constraint FK_CHILD_PARENT and creates an ordinary index on the column(s) named in the FOREIGN KEY argument. In Firebird 1.5, the index will be named FK_CHILD_PARENT as well, unless you used the optional USING clause to assign a different name to the index. In Firebird 1.0.*x*, the index name will be INTEG_nn (where *nn* is a number).

 CAUTION   If you specified a DESCENDING index for the referenced primary or unique constraint, you must be sure to specify USING DESC INDEX for any foreign keys that reference it.

The two tables are now engaged in a formal referential integrity constraint. We can add new rows to PARENT without restriction:

```
INSERT INTO PARENT (ID, DATA)
VALUES (1, 'Parent No. 1');
```

However, there are restrictions on CHILD. We can do this:

```
INSERT INTO CHILD (ID, CHILD_DATA)
VALUES (1, 'Child No. 1');
```

Because the nullable column PARENT_ID was omitted from the column list, NULL is stored there. This is allowed under the default integrity rules. The row is an *orphan*.

However, we get a constraint error if we try to do this:

```
INSERT INTO CHILD(ID, CHILD_DATA, PARENT_ID)
VALUES (2, 'Child No. 2', 2);
ISC ERROR CODE:335544466
ISC ERROR MESSAGE:
violation of FOREIGN KEY constraint "FK_CHILD_PARENT" on table "CHILD"
```

There is no row in PARENT having a PK value of 2, so the constraint disallows the insert.

Both of the following are allowed:

```
UPDATE CHILD
  SET PARENT_ID = 1
  WHERE ID = 1;
COMMIT;
/**/
INSERT INTO CHILD (ID, CHILD_DATA, PARENT_ID)
VALUES (2, 'Child No.2', 1);
COMMIT;
```

Now, the PARENT row with ID=1 has two child rows. This is the classic master-detail structure—an uncomplicated implementation of the one-to-many relationship. To protect the integrity of the relationship, the default rules will disallow this:

```
DELETE FROM PARENT WHERE ID = 1;
```

Action Triggers to Vary Integrity Rules

Obviously, integrity rules take effect whenever some change in data occurs that affects the relationship. However, the default rules do not suit every requirement. We may want to override the rule that permits child rows to be created as orphans or to be made orphans by having their foreign key set to null in an operation. If it is a problem for our business rules that a parent row cannot be deleted if it has dependent child rows, we may want Firebird to take care of the problem automatically. Firebird's SQL language can oblige, through its optional automatic *action triggers*:

```
[ON DELETE {NO ACTION | CASCADE | SET NULL  | SET DEFAULT}]
[ON UPDATE {NO ACTION | CASCADE | SET NULL  | SET DEFAULT}]
```

Automatic Action Triggers

Firebird provides the optional standard DML events ON UPDATE and ON DELETE, along with a range of action options to vary the referential integrity rules. Together, the DML event and the automatic behavior specified by the action option form the action trigger—the action to be taken in this dependent table when updating or deleting the referenced key in the parent. The actions defined include *cascading* the change to associated foreign table(s).

Action Trigger Semantics

NO ACTION

Because this is the default action trigger, the keyword can be—and usually is—omitted.[3] The DML operation on the parent's PK leaves the foreign key unchanged and potentially causes the operation on the parent to fail.

ON UPDATE CASCADE

In the dependent table, the foreign key corresponding to the old value of the primary key is updated to the new value of the primary key.

ON DELETE CASCADE

In the dependent table, the row with the corresponding key is deleted.

SET NULL

The foreign key corresponding to the old parent PK is set to NULL—the dependent rows become orphans. Clearly, this action trigger cannot be applied if the foreign key column is non-nullable.

---

3. The NO ACTION action is sometimes referred to as a "restrict" action.

SET DEFAULT

The foreign key corresponding to the old parent PK is set to its default value. There are some "gotchas" about this action that are important to know about:

- The default value is the one that was in effect at the time the FOREIGN KEY constraint was defined. If the column's default changes later, the original default for the FK's SET DEFAULT action does not follow the new default—it remains as the original.

- If no default was ever declared explicitly for the column, then its default is implicitly NULL. In this case, the SET DEFAULT behavior will be the same as SET NULL.

- If the default value for the foreign key column is a value that has no corresponding PK value in the parent, then the action trigger will cause a constraint violation.

Interaction of Constraints

By combining the formal referential constraint with other integrity constraints (see the previous chapter) it is possible to implement most, if not all, of your business rules with a high degree of precision. For example, a NOT NULL column constraint will restrict the action options and prevent orphan rows, if required, whereas a foreign key column that is nullable can be used to implement special data structures such as trees (see the section "Self-Referencing Relationships").

TIP If you need to make a column of your foreign key non-nullable, then create a "dummy" parent row with an unused key value, such as 0 or –1. Use the SET DEFAULT action to emulate the SET NULL behavior by making the column default to the dummy key value.

Referential constraints can be assisted by CHECK constraints. In some cases, a CHECK constraint inherited from a domain could interfere or conflict with a referential constraint, too. It is worth spending a few minutes sketching out the effects of each constraint on paper or a whiteboard, to identify and eliminate any potential problems.

Custom Action Triggers

It is perfectly possible to write your own action triggers to customize or extend referential behavior. Although the automatic triggers are flexible enough to cover most requirements, there is one special case where custom triggers are generally called for. This is the case where creation of the mandatory enforcing index on the foreign key column is undesirable because the index would be of very *low selectivity*.

Broadly, indexes of low selectivity occur where a small number of possible values is spread over a large table, or where only a few possible values are ever used in the actual table data. The resulting massive duplication of values in the index—described as *long chains*—can impact query performance severely as the table grows.

 TIP   Index selectivity is discussed in some detail in Chapter 18. If the topic is new to you, you are urged to digest it thoroughly before deciding to implement every single one-to-many relationship in your data model using formal integrity constraints, "just because you can."

When writing custom referential triggers, you must make sure that your own triggers or your application code will preserve referential integrity when data in any key changes. Triggers are much safer than application code, since they centralize the data integrity rules in the database and enforce them for all types of access to the data, be it by program, utility tool, script, or server application layer.

Without formal cascading update and delete actions, your custom solution must take care of rows in child tables that will be affected by changes to or deletions of parent keys. For example, if a row is to be deleted from the referenced table, your solution must first delete all rows in all tables that refer to it through foreign keys.

Lookup Tables and Your Data Model

We often use lookup tables—also known as *control tables* or *definition tables*—to store static rows that can supply expanded text, conversion factors, and the like to output sets and, often, directly to applications as selector lists. Examples are "type" tables that identify entities such as account types or document types, "factor" tables used for currency conversion or tax calculation, and "code lookup" tables storing such items as color-matching codes. Dynamic tables are linked to these static tables by matching a key with the primary key of the static table.

Data modeling tools cannot distinguish a lookup relationship from a master-detail relationship since, simplistically, one lookup row can supply values to many "user" rows. Tools represent it as a parent-child dependency and may erroneously recommend a foreign key on the "child" side.

Yet, in an implemented database, this relationship is not master-detail or parent-child, because the primary key value of the lookup set commands one and only one column. It has no effect on other relationships that this "pseudo-child" participates in.

It is tempting to apply a formal foreign key constraint to columns that reference lookup tables, with the argument that a cascading referential constraint will protect data consistency. The flaw here is that properly designed lookup tables will never change their keys, so there is no potential inconsistency to protect against.

Take a look at this example of a lookup relationship, inherited by converting a very poorly designed Access camping goods application to Firebird. Access client applications can do cute things with entire tables that allow amateurs to build RAD applications. This table was used in a visual control that could display a table and "transplant" a value into another table at the click of a button.

```
CREATE TABLE COLORS (COLOR CHARACTER(20) NOT NULL PRIMARY KEY);
```

Here is a DDL fragment from one of the tables that used COLORS for a lookup:

```
CREATE TABLE STOCK_ITEM (
...
COLOR CHARACTER(20) DEFAULT 'NEUTRAL',
...,
CONSTRAINT FK_COLOR FOREIGN KEY (COLOR)
REFERENCES COLORS(COLOR)
ON UPDATE CASCADE
ON DELETE SET DEFAULT;
```

There were a lot of problems with this key. First, the COLORS table was available to the inventory buyers to edit as they saw fit. Updates cascaded all over the system whenever new items came into stock. Deletions frequently stripped the color information from the relatively few items where it mattered. Worst of all, the bulk of items in this system were one color, 'NEUTRAL', with the result that the foreign key's index was a real showstopper on inventory queries.

The "relational way" to avoid the unplanned breakage of consistency would have been to use a lookup key with no meaning as data (i.e., an *atomic* key):

```
CREATE TABLE COLORS (
  ID INTEGER NOT NULL PRIMARY KEY, /* or UNIQUE */
  COLOR CHARACTER(20));
COMMIT;
INSERT INTO COLORS (ID, COLOR)
VALUES (0, 'NEUTRAL');
COMMIT;
CREATE TABLE STOCK_ITEM (
...
COLOR INTEGER DEFAULT 0,
...);
```

Such a key need never change and it can (and should) be hidden from users entirely. Tables that use the lookup table store the stable key. Changes in available values are implemented as new lookup rows with new keys. Values already associated with keys do not change—they are preserved to ensure that history data is not compromised by subsequent changes.

In the event that, even with the higher distribution of key values, the foreign key would produce an index that was still poorly selective over a large table, the improvement to the stability of the table justifies avoiding a formal referential constraint. Existence of the referenced primary row can be easily enforced using custom triggers.

Reference Privileges

Firebird implements SQL security on all objects in the database. Every user except the owner of the database and users with SYSDBA or system root privileges must be GRANTed the necessary privileges to access an object. SQL privileges are discussed in great detail in Chapter 37.

However, one privilege may be of special significance in the design of your referential integrity infrastructure: the REFERENCES privilege. If the parent and child tables have different owners, a GRANT REFERENCES privilege may be needed to give users sufficient permission to enable referential constraint actions.

The REFERENCES privilege is granted *on the referenced table* in the relationship—that is, the table referenced by the foreign key—or, at least, on every column of the reference primary or unique key. The privilege needs to be granted *to the owner of the referencing table* (the child table) and also to any user who needs to write to the referencing table.

At runtime, REFERENCES kicks in whenever the database engine verifies that a value input to a foreign key is contained in the referenced table.

Because this privilege is also checked when a foreign key constraint is *defined*, it will be necessary for the appropriate permissions to be granted and committed beforehand. If you need to create a foreign key that refers to a table owned by someone else, that owner must first grant you REFERENCES privileges on that table. Alternatively, the owner can grant REFERENCES privileges to a role and then grant that role to you.

 TIP　Don't make this harder than it needs to be. If there is no requirement to deny read privileges on the referenced table, then have the owner grant the REFERENCES privilege on it to PUBLIC.

If you have these restrictions among your requirements, it may be necessary to maintain two separate permissions scripts: one for developers that is run following table creation and another for users that is run on an otherwise completed schema.

Handling Other Forms of Relationship

Referential constraints can be applied to other forms of relationship apart from the optional one-to-many form described so far:

- One-to-one

- Many-to-many

- Self-referencing one-to-many (nested or tree relationships)

- Mandatory variants of any form of relationship

One-to-One Relationship

Optional one-to-one structures can be valuable where an entity in your data model has a large number of distinct attributes, only some of which are accessed frequently. It can save storage and page reads dramatically to store occasional data in optional "peer" relations that share matching primary keys.

A one-to-one relationship is similar to a one-to-many relationship, insofar as it links a foreign key to a unique key. The difference here is that the linking key needs to be unique to enforce the one-to-one relationship—to allow, at most, one dependent row per parent row.

It is usual to double up the use the primary key column(s) of the "peer" table as the foreign key to the "parent."

```
CREATE TABLE PARENT_PEER (
  ID INTEGER NOT NULL,
  MORE_DATA VARCHAR(10),
  CONSTRAINT PK_PARENT_PEER PRIMARY KEY(ID),
  CONSTRAINT FK_PARENT_PEER_PARENT
  FOREIGN KEY (ID) REFERENCES PARENT);
```

The effect of this double usage is to cause two mandatory indexes to be created on the primary key column of the peer table: one for the primary key and one for the foreign key. The FK index is stored as if it were non-unique.

In versions 1.0.*x* and 1.5, the optimizer is quirky about this doubling up and ignores the peer table's primary index. For example,

```
SELECT PARENT.ID, PARENT_PEER.ID,
PARENT.DATA, PARENT_PEER.MORE_DATA
FROM PARENT JOIN PARENT_PEER
ON PARENT.ID = PARENT_PEER.ID;
```

ignores the primary key index of the peer and produces this plan:

```
PLAN JOIN (PARENT_PEER NATURAL, PARENT INDEX (PK_PARENT))
```

With a "thin" key, such as the one used in the example, the impact on performance may not be severe. With a composite key, the effect may be serious, especially if there will be multiple joins involving several parent-to-peer one-to-one relations. It should at least make you consider surrogating the primary keys of one-to-one structures.[4]

---

4. And to hope that this little optimizer quirk with one-to-one keys will get cleared up in a sub-release.

TIP It is not a bad thing if you choose to add a special column to a peer relation in order to implement distinct primary and foreign keys. It can be a useful aid to self-documentation.

Many-to-Many Relationship

In this interesting case shown in Figure 17-2, our data model shows us that each row in TableA may have relationships with multiple rows in TableB, while each row in TableB may have multiple relationships with rows in TableA.

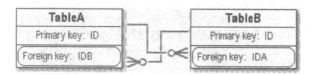

Figure 17-2. Many-to-many relationship

As modeled, this relationship gives rise to a condition known as a *circular reference.* The proposed foreign key in TableB references the primary key of TableA, which means that the TableB row cannot be created if there is no row in TableA with a matching primary key. However, for the same reason, the required row cannot be inserted into TableA if there is no matching primary key value in TableB.

Dealing with a Circular Reference

If your structural requirements dictate that such a circular reference must exist, it can be worked around. Firebird allows a foreign key value to be NULL—provided the column is not made non-nullable by another constraint—because NULL, being a "non-value," does not violate the rule that the foreign key column must have a matching value in the referenced parent column. By making the FK on one table nullable, you can insert into that table and create the primary key that the other table requires:

```
CREATE TABLE TABLEA (
  ID INTEGER NOT NULL,
  ...,
  CONSTRAINT PK_TABLEA PRIMARY KEY (ID));
COMMIT;
CREATE TABLE TABLEB (
  ID INTEGER NOT NULL,
```

```
    ...,
  CONSTRAINT PK_TABLEB PRIMARY KEY (ID));
COMMIT;
ALTER TABLE TABLEA
  ADD CONSTRAINT FK_TABLEA_TABLEB
    FOREIGN KEY(IDB) REFERENCES TABLEB(ID);
COMMIT;
ALTER TABLE TABLEB
  ADD CONSTRAINT FK_TABLEB_TABLEA
    FOREIGN KEY(IDA) REFERENCES TABLEA(ID);
COMMIT;
```

This is the workaround:

```
INSERT INTO TABLEB(ID)
VALUES(1);  /* creates a row with NULL in IDB */
COMMIT;
INSERT INTO TABLEA(ID, IDB)
VALUES(22, 1);  /* links to the TABLEB row just created */
COMMIT;
UPDATE TABLEB
  SET IDA = 22 WHERE ID = 1;
COMMIT;
```

Clearly, this model is not without potential problems. In most systems, keys are generated, not supplied by applications. To ensure consistency, it becomes a job for all client applications inserting to these tables to know the value of both keys in both tables within a single transaction context. Performing the entire operation with a stored procedure would reduce the dependence of the relationship on application code.

 CAUTION   In practice, tables with many-to-many relationships implemented circularly are very difficult to represent in GUI applications.

Using an Intersection Table

Generally, it is better practice to resolve many-to-many relationships by adding an *intersection table*. This special structure carries one foreign key for each table in the many-to-many relationship. Its own primary key (or a unique constraint) is a composite of the two foreign keys. The two related tables intersected by it do not have foreign keys relating to one another at all.

This implementation is easy to represent in applications. Before Insert and Before Update triggers on both tables take care of adding intersection rows when required. Figure 17-3 illustrates how the intersection table resolves many-to-many relationships.

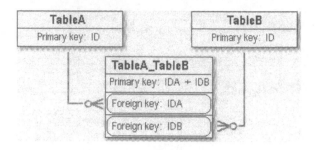

Figure 17-3. Resolution of a many-to-many relationship

This is how to implement it:

```
CREATE TABLE TABLEA (
  ID INTEGER NOT NULL,
  ...,
  CONSTRAINT PK_TABLEA PRIMARY KEY (ID));
COMMIT;
CREATE TABLE TABLEB (
  ID INTEGER NOT NULL,
  ...,
  CONSTRAINT PK_TABLEB PRIMARY KEY (ID));
COMMIT;
/**/
CREATE TABLE TABLEA_TABLEB (
  IDA INTEGER NOT NULL,
  IDB INTEGER NOT NULL,
  CONSTRAINT PK_TABLEA_TABLEB
    PRIMARY KEY (IDA, IDB));
COMMIT;
ALTER TABLE TABLEA_TABLEB
  ADD CONSTRAINT FK_TABLEA FOREIGN KEY (IDA)
    REFERENCES TABLEA,
  ADD CONSTRAINT FK_TABLEB FOREIGN KEY (IDB)
    REFERENCES TABLEB;
COMMIT;
```

Self-Referencing Relationships

If your model has an entity whose primary key refers to a foreign key located in the same entity, you have a self-referencing relationship, as shown in Figure 17-4.

Figure 17-4. Self-referencing relationship

This is the classic tree hierarchy, where any member (row) can be both parent and child—that is, it can have "child" rows dependent on it and, at the same time, it can depend on another member (row). It needs a CHECK constraint or Before Insert and Before Update triggers to ensure that a PARENT_ID never points to itself.

If your business rules require that parents must exist before children can be added, you will want to use a *value* (e.g., –1) as the root node of the tree structure. The PARENT_ID should be made NOT NULL and defaulted to your chosen root value. The alternative is to leave PARENT_ID as nullable, as in the following example, and use NULL as the root.

In general, custom triggers for Before Insert and Before Update will be required for trees that will be nested to more than two levels. For consistency in trees with a NULL root node, it is important to ensure that constraint actions do not create orphan children unintentionally.

```
CREATE TABLE PARENT_CHILD (
  ID INTEGER NOT NULL,
  PARENT_ID INTEGER
    CHECK (PARENT_ID <> ID));
COMMIT;
ALTER TABLE PARENT_CHILD
  ADD CONSTRAINT PK_PARENT
    PRIMARY KEY(ID);
COMMIT;
ALTER TABLE PARENT_CHILD
  ADD CONSTRAINT FK_CHILD_PARENT
    FOREIGN KEY(PARENT_ID)
      REFERENCES PARENT_CHILD(ID);
```

About Tree Structures

Much more can be said about designing tree structures. It is a challenging topic in relational database design that stretches standard SQL to its boundaries. Unfortunately, it is beyond the scope of this guide. For some interesting solutions, try *Joe Celko's SQL for Smarties, 2nd Edition* by Joe Celko (Morgan Kaufmann, 1999).

Mandatory Relationships

A mandatory, or *obligatory*, relationship is one that requires that a minimum of one referencing (child) row exist for each referenced (parent) row. For example, a delivery note structure (a header with customer and delivery address information) would be illogical if it were permitted to have a header row without any referencing item lines.

It is a common beginner mistake to assume that a NOT NULL constraint on the child will make a one-to-many relationship mandatory. It does not, because the FOREIGN KEY constraint operates only in the context of an *instantiated* dependency. With no referencing row, the nullability of the foreign key is irrelevant to the issue.

A mandatory relationship is one place where user-defined trigger constraints must be added to extend referential integrity. Firebird SQL does not provide a "mandatoriness" constraint. It can take some fancy logic at both the client and the server to ensure that events will occur in the right sequence to meet both the referential constraint and the mandatoriness requirements. It will involve both insert and delete triggers, since the logic must enforce the "minimum of one child" rule not only at creation time, but also when child rows are deleted.

For details about writing triggers and an example of a trigger solution for enforcing a mandatory relationship, refer to Chapter 31.

"Object Is in Use" Error

It is worth mentioning this exception in the context of applying referential integrity constraints, since it is a regular source of frustration for new users. Firebird will not allow a referential constraint to be added or dropped if a transaction is using either of the participating tables.

Sometimes it may be less than obvious to you just in *what way* the object is in use. Other dependencies—such as stored procedures or triggers that refer to your tables, or other referential constraints affecting one or both—can cause this exception to occur if they are in use by an uncommitted transaction. Metadata caches (blocks of server memory that hold metadata used to compile recent client requests and any recently used stored procedure and trigger code) keep locks on the objects in their possession. Each connection has its own metadata cache, even on a Superserver, so the server could be holding locks on objects that no connection is actually using.

It is highly recommended that you get exclusive access to the database for any metadata changes, particularly those involving dependencies.

 TIP If you have exclusive access and the exception still occurs, don't overlook the possibility that you are using it yourself. If you are working in an admin utility with a data browser focused on one of your tables, then the object is in use!

Up Next

Firebird uses indexes to enforce referential integrity. However, indexes play an equally important role in optimizing the performance of the searching and ordering operations required for queries and targeted data changes. In the next chapter, we examine the whole topic of designing, creating, and testing indexes. The chapter ends with a special optimization topic about indexing, incorporating a how-to for using Firebird's index statistics tool, **gstat**.

CHAPTER 18

Indexes

INDEXES (SOMETIMES PLURALIZED AS *INDICES*) are table attributes that can be placed on a column or a group of columns to accelerate the retrieval of rows.

An index serves as a logical pointer to the physical locations (addresses) of rows in a table, much as you search an index in a book to quickly locate the page numbers of topics that you want to read. In most cases, if the engine can fetch the requested rows directly by scanning an index instead of scanning all rows in the table, requests will complete faster. A well-designed system of indexes plays a vital role in the tuning and optimization of your entire application environment.

Limits

Firebird allows up to 256 user-created indexes per table in version 1.5 and higher, or 64 in lower releases. However, these are theoretical limits that are governed by both page size and the actual on-disk size of the index description data on the index root page. You could not store 256 indexes in a database with a page size smaller than 16KB. On the index root page, each index needs 31 bytes for its identifier, space for descriptions of each segment (column) involved in the index, and some bytes to store a pointer to the first page of the index. Even a 16KB page may not be able to accommodate 256 indexes if there are more than a few compound indexes in the database.

To create indexes, a user must be authorized to connect to the database.

An index cannot exceed 253 bytes in total width. In reality, the number of bytes may be significantly smaller. Factors that can reduce the number of actual "slots" available to store characters include

- International character sets that use multiple bytes per character

- International character sets with complex uppercase/lowercase pairings and/or dictionary sorting rules

- Use of non-binary collations

- Multiple segments (composite indexes) that require the addition of padding bytes to retain the geometry of the index

In other words, using any character set except NONE will influence your decisions about index design—particularly whether to use composite indexes. That's the bad news. The good news is that Firebird makes good use of single-column indexes in multi-column searches and sorts, reducing the need for many multi-column indexes that you might have experienced with another DBMS.

Automatic vs. User-Defined Indexes

Firebird creates indexes to enforce various integrity constraints automatically (for more information, refer to Chapters 16 and 17). To delete these indexes, it is necessary to drop the constraints that use them.

Use of the constraint indexes is not limited to their work supporting the integrity of keys and relationships. They are considered, along with all others, when queries are prepared.

When defining your own indexes, it is of utmost importance to avoid creating any index that duplicates an automatically generated one. It puts the optimizer (see the upcoming section "Query Plans") in the unhappy position of having to choose between equals. In many cases, it will solve the problem by not choosing either of them.

Importing Legacy Indexes

Do not import "primary indexes" with tables from a migrating DBMS. There are two important reasons to abandon these indexes:

- Many legacy systems use hierarchical index structures to implement referential integrity. SQL databases do not use this logic to implement referential integrity, and these indexes usually interfere with Firebird's optimizer logic.

- Firebird creates its own indexes to support primary and foreign key constraints, regardless of any existing index. As noted previously, duplicate indexes cause problems for the optimizer and should be avoided completely.

Directional Indexes

The sort direction of indexes in Firebird is important. It is a mistake to assume that the same index can be used to sort or search "both ways"—that, is lowest-to-highest and highest-to-lowest. As a rule of thumb, ASC (ascending) indexes will help searches where relatively low values are sought, whereas DESC (descending) indexes will help for maximum or high values.

If an automatic index is ASC (the default), there will be no problems if you need to define a DESC index using the same column(s). The reverse is also true: From v.1.5 onward, you can choose to have the automatic indexes for keys created in descending order. The optimizer will not be upset if you also create an ascending one on the same columns.

Query Plans

Before a query is executed, a set of preparation routines—known as the *optimizer*—begins analyzing the columns and operations in the request, to calculate the fastest way to respond. It starts by looking for indexes on the tables and columns involved. Working its way through a sequence of cost-based decision paths, it develops a *plan*—a kind of "road map" for the route it will follow when it actually executes the query. The final plan it chooses reflects the "cheapest" route it can predict according to the indexes it can use.

The optimizer's plan can be viewed in an **isql** shell session in two ways:

- By default, **isql** does not display the plan. Use SET PLAN ON to have the plan displayed at the top of the output from a SELECT query.

- Use SET PLANONLY to submit queries and view the plans without actually running the queries. This enables you to inspect the plan for any query, not just SELECT queries.

It is possible to override the optimizer's plan with one of your own, by including a PLAN clause in your query statement. Most third-party GUI tools provide the ability to view the plan, with or without running the query, and to override it.

 TIP   Do not override the optimizer's plan unless you have tested your own and found it to be consistently faster on realistic data.

For more information about query plans, refer to the "Optimization Topic" in Chapter 20. For details about using **isql**, refer to Chapter 37.

How Indexes Can Help

If the optimizer decides to use an index, it searches the pages of the index to find the key values required and follows the pointers to locate the indicated rows in the table data pages. Data retrieval is fast because the values in the index are ordered. This allows the system to locate wanted values directly, by pointer, and avoid visiting unwanted rows at all. Using an index typically requires fewer page fetches than "walking through" every row in the table. The index is small, relative to the row size of the table and, provided the index design is good, it occupies relatively fewer database pages than the row data.

Sorting and Grouping

When the columns specified in an ORDER BY or GROUP BY clause are indexed, the optimizer can sequence the output by navigating the index(es) and assemble the ordered sets more directly than it can with non-indexed reads.

A DESCENDING index on the aggregated column can speed up the query for the aggregating function MAX(..), since the row with the maximum value will be the only one it visits. For more information about using function expressions in queries, refer to Chapters 21 and 23.

Joins

For joins, the optimizer goes through a process of merging streams of data by matching the values specified in the implicit or explicit "ON" criteria. If an index is available for the column or columns on one side of the join, the optimizer builds its initial stream by using the index to match the join key with its correspondent from the table on the other side of the join. Without an index on either side, it must generate a bitmap of one side first and navigate that, in order to make the selections from the table on the other side of the join.

Comparisons

When an indexed column is evaluated to determine whether it is greater than, equal to, or less than a constant, the value of the index is used for the comparison, and non-matching rows are not fetched. Without an index, all of the candidate rows have to be fetched and compared sequentially.

What to Index

The length of time it takes to search a whole table is directly proportional to the number of rows in the table. An index on a column can mean the difference between an immediate response to a query and a long wait. So, why not index every column?

The main drawbacks are that indexes consume additional disk space, and inserting, deleting, and updating rows takes longer on indexed columns than on non-indexed columns. The index must be updated each time a data item in the indexed column changes and each time a row is added to or deleted from the table.

Nevertheless, the boost in performance for data retrieval usually outweighs the overhead of maintaining a conservative but useful collection of indexes. You should create an index on a column when

- Search conditions frequently reference the column. An index will help in date and numeric searches when direct comparisons or BETWEEN evaluations are wanted. Search indexes for character columns are useful when strings are to be evaluated for exact matches or against STARTING WITH and CONTAINING predicates. They are not useful with the LIKE predicate.[1]

---

1. In cases where the search condition specifies "LIKE 'string%'", the optimizer will usually resolve the predicate to "STARTING WITH 'string'" and use an index if one is available.

- The column does not carry an integrity constraint but is referenced frequently as a JOIN condition.

- ORDER BY clauses frequently use the column to sort data. When sets must be ordered on multiple columns, composite indexes that reflect the output order specified in ORDER BY clauses can improve retrieval speed.[2]

- You need an index with special characteristics not provided by data or existing indexes, such as a non-binary collation or an ascending or descending direction.

- Aggregations are to be performed on large sets. Single-column or suitably ordered complex indexes can improve the speed with which aggregations are formed in complex GROUP BY clauses.

You should not create indexes for columns that

- Are seldom referenced in search conditions

- Are frequently updated non-key values, such as timestampers or user signatures

- Have a small number of possible or actual values spread over a wide campus of rows

- Are styled as two- or three-phase Boolean

When to Index

Some indexes will suggest themselves to you during the initial design period—typically for requirements that you know will need particular sortings, groupings, and evaluations. It is very good practice to be conservative about creating indexes until it becomes clear that they might be beneficial. It is a rewarding strategy to defer the creation of doubtful indexes until after a point in development where you have good samplings of typical test data and an awareness of which operations are too slow.

The benefits of deferred index design include

- Reduction of "performance fogging" that can interfere with the functional integrity testing

- Faster identification of the real sources of bottlenecks

- Avoidance of unnecessary or inefficient indexing

---

2. Composite indexes are not as important in Firebird as in many other DBMSs. Often, they are unjustified, since Firebird makes intelligent use of single-column indexes.

Using CREATE INDEX

The CREATE INDEX statement creates an index on one or more columns of a table. A single-column index searches only one column in response to a query, whereas a multi-column index searches one or more columns.

This is the syntax:

```
CREATE [UNIQUE] [ASC[ENDING] | DESC[ENDING]]
INDEX index-name ON table-name (col [, col ...]);
```

Mandatory Elements

The mandatory elements of the CREATE INDEX syntax are as follows:

- **CREATE INDEX index-name** names the index. The identifier must be distinct from all other object identifiers in the database, apart from constraint and column identifiers. It is a good idea to use a systematic naming scheme, however, as an aid to self-documentation.

NOTE   From release 1.5 onward, the default automatic naming behavior for named constraints is to apply the constraint name to its enforcing index.

- **table-name** is the name of the table to which the index applies.

- **col [, col...]** is column name or a comma-separated list naming the columns that are to be the index keys. Column order is significant in indexes. For more information, see the upcoming section titled "Multi-column Indexes."

Example

The following declaration creates a non-unique, ascending index on a personal name column in the PERSON table. It may aid search conditions like WHERE LAST_NAME = 'Johnston' or WHERE LAST_NAME STARTING WITH 'Johns':

```
CREATE INDEX LAST_NAME_X ON PERSON(LAST_NAME);
```

Optional Elements

UNIQUE

The UNIQUE keyword can be used on indexes for which you want to disallow duplicate entries. The column or group is checked for duplicate values when the index is created and for existing values each time a row is inserted or updated.

Unique indexes make sense only when you need to enforce uniqueness as an intrinsic characteristic of the data item or group. For example, you would not define a unique index on a column storing a person's name, because personal names are not intrinsically unique. Conversely, a unique index is a good idea on a column containing a Social Security number, since a unique key violation on it would alert the user to an error that needed attention.

Example

In this example, a unique index is created on three columns of an inventory table to ensure that the system stores at most one row for each size and color of an item:

```
CREATE UNIQUE INDEX STK_SIZE_COLOR_UQX
  ON STOCK_ITEM (PRODUCT_ID, SIZE, COLOR);
```

Note that a unique index is not a key. If you require a unique key for referential purposes, apply a UNIQUE constraint to the column(s) instead. Refer to Chapter 16 for details on the UNIQUE constraint.

Finding Duplicates

Of course, it will not be possible to create a unique index on a column that already contains duplicate values. Before defining a unique index, use a SELECT statement to find duplicate items in the table. For example, before putting a unique index on PRODUCT_NAME in this PRODUCT table, this check would reveal any duplicates in the column:

```
SELECT PRODUCT_ID, UPPER(PRODUCT_NAME) FROM PRODUCT
GROUP BY PRODUCT_ID, UPPER(PRODUCT_NAME)
HAVING COUNT(*) > 1;
```

NOTE Uppercasing the column to make the search case-insensitive is not necessary from the point of view of data uniqueness. Still, if uniqueness has been "broken" by faulty data entry, we would want to find the offending records.

How you deal with duplicates depends on what they signify, according to your business rules, and the number of duplicates needing to be eliminated. Usually, a stored procedure will be the most efficient way to handle it. Stored procedures are discussed in detail in Chapters 28, 29, and 30.

ASC[ENDING] or DESC[ENDING]

The keywords ASC[ENDING] and DESC[ENDING] determine the vertical sort order of the index. ASC specifies an index that sorts the values from lowest to highest. It is the default and can be omitted. DESC sorts the values from highest to lowest and must be specified if a descending index is wanted. A descending index may prove useful for queries that are likely to search for high values (oldest age, most recent, biggest, etc.) and for any ordered searches or outputs that will specify a descending sort order.

Example

The following definition creates a descending index on a table in the employee database:

```
CREATE DESCENDING INDEX DESC_X ON SALARY_HISTORY (CHANGE_DATE);
```

The optimizer will use this index in a query such as the following, which returns the employee numbers and salaries of the ten employees who most recently had a raise:

```
SELECT FIRST 10 EMP_NO, NEW_SALARY
  FROM SALARY_HISTORY
  ORDER BY CHANGE_DATE DESCENDING;
```

If you intend to use both ascending and descending sort orders on a particular column, define both an ascending and a descending index for the same column. For example, it will be fine to create the following index in addition to the one in the previous example:

```
CREATE ASCENDING INDEX ASCEND_X ON SALARY_HISTORY (CHANGE_DATE);
```

Multi-Column Indexes

If your applications frequently need to search, order, or group on the same group of multiple columns in a particular table, it will be of benefit to create a multi-column index (also known as a *composite* or *complex* index).

The optimizer will use a subset of the segments of a multicolumn index to optimize a query if the *left-to-right order* in which the query accesses the columns in an ORDER BY clause matches the left-to-right order of the column list defined in the index. However, queries do not need to be constructed with the exact column list that is defined in the index in order for it to be available to the optimizer. The index can also be used if the subset of columns used in the ORDER BY clause begins with the first column in the multicolumn index.

Firebird can use a single element of composite index to optimize a search if all of the preceding elements of the index are also used. Consider a segmented index on three columns, Col_w, Col_x and Col_y, in that order, as shown in Figure 18-1.

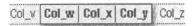

Figure 18-1. Using a segmented index

The index would be picked by the optimizer for this query:

```
SELECT <list of columns> FROM ATABLE
ORDER BY COL_w, COL_x;
```

It would not be picked for either of these queries:

```
SELECT <list of columns> FROM ATABLE
ORDER BY COL_x, COL_y;
/**/
SELECT <list of columns> FROM ATABLE
ORDER BY COL_x, COL_w;
```

OR Predicates in Queries

If you expect to issue frequent queries against a table where the queries use the OR operator, it is better to create a single-column index for *each* condition. Since multi-column indexes are sorted hierarchically, a query that is looking for any one of two or more conditions must search the whole table, losing the advantage of an index.

For example, suppose the search requested

```
...
WHERE A > 10000 OR B < 300 OR C BETWEEN 40 AND 80
...
```

An index on (A,B,C) would be used to find rows containing eligible values of A, but it could not be used for searching for B or C values. By contrast, individual indexes on A, B, and C would all be used. For A, a descending index would be more useful than an ascending one if the search value is at the high end of a range of stored values.

Search Criteria

The same rules that apply to the ORDER BY clause also apply to queries containing a WHERE clause. The next example creates a multicolumn index for the PROJECT table in employee.gdb:

```
CREATE UNIQUE INDEX PRODTYPEX ON PROJECT (PRODUCT, PROJ_NAME);
```

The optimizer will pick the PRODTYPEX index for this query, because the WHERE clause refers to the first segment of the index:

```
SELECT * FROM PROJECT
WHERE PRODUCT ='software';
```

Conversely, it will ignore the index for the next query, because PROJ_NAME is not the first segment:

```
SELECT * FROM PROJECT
WHERE PROJ_NAME STARTING WITH 'Firebird 1';
```

Inspecting Indexes

To inspect all indexes defined in the current database, use the **isql** command SHOW INDEX:

- To see all indexes defined for a specific table, use the command

```
SHOW INDEX tablename
```

- To view information about a specific index, use

```
SHOW INDEX indexname
```

Altering an Index

Activating/Deactivating

The ALTER INDEX statement is used to switch the state of an index from active to inactive and vice versa. It can be used to switch off indexing before inserting or updating a large batch of rows and avoid the overhead of maintaining the indexes during the long operation. After the operation, indexing can be reactivated and the indexes will be rebuilt.

Its other use is a housekeeping one. The distribution of values changes, gradually under normal conditions and, under some operating conditions, more frequently. The binary tree structures in which indexes are maintained can become unbalanced. Switching an index from active to inactive and back to active rebuilds and rebalances it.

The syntax is

```
ALTER INDEX index-name INACTIVE | ACTIVE ;
```

"Index Is in Use" Error

An index that is being used in a transaction cannot be altered or dropped until the transaction has finished using it. Attempts will have different results, according to the *lock setting* of the active transaction:

- In a WAIT transaction, the ALTER INDEX operation waits until the transaction completes.

- In a NOWAIT transaction, Firebird returns an error.

For more information about transaction lock settings, refer to the section "Lock Resolution" in Chapter 26.

Altering the Structure of an Index

Unlike many ALTER statements, the ALTER INDEX syntax cannot be used to alter the structure of the object. For this, it is necessary to drop the index and define it anew, using CREATE INDEX.

Dropping an Index

The DROP INDEX statement removes a *user-defined* index from the database.

Use DROP INDEX also when an index needs to have a change of structure: segments added, removed, or reordered, or the sort order altered. First use a DROP INDEX statement to delete the index, and then use a CREATE INDEX statement to re-create it, using the same name and the new characteristics.

This is the syntax:

```
DROP INDEX name;
```

The following statement deletes an index from the JOB table:

```
DROP INDEX MINSALX;
```

Restrictions

No user can drop an index except the user who created it, or SYSDBA, or (on POSIX) a user with root privileges.

System-defined indexes, created automatically on columns defined with UNIQUE, PRIMARY KEY, and FOREIGN KEY constraints, cannot be dropped. It is necessary to drop the constraints in order to drop these indexes.

OPTIMIZATION TOPIC: Optimal Indexing

Unlike many other relational database systems, Firebird never has need of a full-time DBA with an armory of algorithms for keeping databases running smoothly. For the most part, well-kept Firebird databases just "keep on keeping on."

Indexes do play an important part in the performance of a database. It is important to recognize that they are dynamic structures that, like moving parts in an engine, need to be "cleaned and lubed" from time to time.

This section provides some guidelines for keeping your indexes working at full capacity.

Housekeeping Indexes

Indexes are binary structures that may become unbalanced after many changes to the database, especially if general database housekeeping is neglected. Indexes can be rebalanced and tuned in a number of ways to restore performance to optimal levels.

- Rebuilding an index will restore the balance of its tree structure by removing entries made obsolete by deletions and redistributing branches created by successive insertions. The tool for switching the state of an index between active and inactive is the ALTER INDEX statement.

- A complete rebuild of an index from scratch, by dropping and re-creating it in a pristine state, may improve the performance of an old index on a very large or dynamic table.

- Restoring a database from a **gbak** backup also re-creates pristine indexes.

Improving Index Selectivity

Broadly, the selectivity of an index is an evaluation of the number of rows that would be selected by each index value in a search. A unique index has the highest possible selectivity, because it can never select more than one row per value, whereas an index on a Boolean has almost the lowest selectivity.

Indexing a column that, in production conditions, will store a single value predominantly, such as the Country of Birth item in the earlier election data example, is worse than not indexing the column at all. Firebird is quite efficient at building bitmaps for non-indexed sorts and searches.

Measuring Selectivity

The selectivity of a unique index is 1. All non-unique indexes have a value lower than 1. Selectivity (s) is calculated as

```
s = n / number of rows in the table
```

where n is the number of distinct occurrences of the index value in the table. The smaller the number of distinct occurrences, the lower the selectivity. Indexes with higher selectivity perform better than those with low selectivity.

The Firebird optimizer looks up a factor for calculating selectivity when a table is first accessed and stores it in memory for use in calculating plans for subsequent queries on that table. Over time, the initially calculated factors on frequently updated tables gradually become outdated, perhaps affecting the optimizer's index choices in extreme cases.

Recalculating Selectivity

Recalculating index selectivity updates a statistical factor stored in the system tables. The optimizer reads this just once when choosing a plan—it is not highly significant to its choices. Frequent, large DML operations do not necessarily spoil the distribution of distinct index key values. If the indexing is reasonable, the "demographics" of value distribution may change very little.

Knowing the most accurate selectivity of an index has its greatest value to the developer. It provides a metric to assist in determining the usefulness of the index.

If the efficacy of a plan degrades over time because of large numbers of inserts or changes to the key column(s) that change the distribution of index key values, the query may slow down gradually. Any index whose selectivity drops dramatically over time should be dropped because of its effect on performance.

Understanding and dealing with a rogue index that deteriorates with table growth, to the extent that it interferes with plans, is an important part of database tuning. However, the most crucial effect of using an index that intrinsically has very low selectivity has nothing to do with the optimizer and everything to do with index geometry.

Why Low Selectivity Is a Killer

Firebird builds binary trees for indexes. It stores these structures on index pages, which are nothing more special than pages that are allocated for storing index trees. Each distinct value in an index segment has its own node off the root of the tree. As a new entry is added to an index, it is either placed into a new node if its value does not already exist or stacked on top of any existing duplicate values.

Figure 18-2 illustrates this binary mechanism in a simplified form.

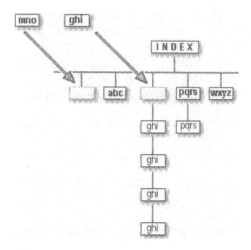

Figure 18-2. Building a binary index tree

When duplicate values arrive, they are slotted into the first node at the front of the "chain" of other duplicates—this is what is occurring with value "ghi" in the diagram. This structure is referred to as a *duplicate chain*.

Duplicate Chains[3]

A duplicate chain, per se, is fine—all non-unique indexes have them. An update of the segment value, or the deletion of a row, is very costly when the chain of duplicates is very long. One of the worst things you can do to a Firebird database is define a table with a million rows, all with the same key value for a secondary index, and then delete all those rows. The last duplicate stored appears first in the list, and the first stored is last. The deletion ordinarily takes the first row stored first, then the second, and so on. The index walking code has to run through the whole duplicate chain for each deletion, always finding the entry it wants in the very last position. To quote Ann Harrison, "It churns the cache like nothing you ever saw."

The cost of all that churning and roiling is *never* borne by the transaction that deletes or updates all the rows in a table. Updating a key value or deleting a row affects the index later, when the old back version is garbage collected. The cost goes to *the next transaction that touches the row*, following the completion of all of the transactions that were active when the update or delete occurred.

---

3. This passage speaks in the voice of Ann Harrison, "the mother of InterBase."

Index Toolkit

The standard Firebird installation provides a number of tools and tricks for querying the state of indexes and for keeping them in good shape:

- For finding out about the selectivity and other meaningful characteristics of indexes, use **gstat**, a data statistics analyzer. Later in this chapter, we look at what **gstat** can tell you about your indexes.

- The tool for recalculating index selectivity is the SET STATISTICS statement (discussed in the next section). SET STATISTICS does not rebuild indexes.

- The best tool of all for cleaning up tired indexes is **gbak**, the backup and restore utility. Restoring a database from its latest backup will both rebuild all indexes and cause their selectivity to be freshly computed.

Using SET STATISTICS

In some tables, the number of duplicate values in indexed columns can increase or decrease radically as a result of the relative "popularity" of a particular value in the index when compared with other candidate values. For example, indexes on dates in a sales system might tend to become less selective when business starts to boom.

Periodically recomputing *index selectivity* can improve the performance of indexes that are subject to significant swings in the distribution of distinct values. SET STATISTICS recomputes the selectivity of an index. It is a statement that can be run from an **isql** interactive session or, in Embedded SQL (ESQL), can be passed from an application. To run this statement, you need to be connected to the database and logged in as the user that created the index, the SYSDBA user, or (on POSIX) a user with operating system root privileges.

This is the syntax:

```
SET STATISTICS INDEX name;
```

The following statement recomputes the selectivity for an index in the employee.gdb database:

```
SET STATISTICS INDEX MINSALX;
```

On its own, SET STATISTICS will not cure current problems resulting from previous index maintenance that depended on obsolete selectivity statistics, since it does not rebuild the index.

TIP   To rebuild an index, use ALTER INDEX, or drop and re-create it, or restore the database from a **gbak** backup.

Getting Index Statistics

Firebird provides a command-line tool that displays real-time statistical reports about the state of objects in a database. The tool produces a number of reports about what is going on in a database. Our main focus for this section is the index statistics. The other reports are described after the index reports.

gstat Command-Line Tool

You need to run **gstat** on the server machine since it is a completely local program that does not access databases as a client. Its default location is the /bin directory of your Firebird installation. It reports on a specified database and can be used by the SYSDBA or the owner of the database.

gstat on POSIX

Because **gstat** accesses database files at the filesystem level, it is necessary on Linux and UNIX platforms to have system-level read access to the file. You can achieve this in one of the following two ways:

- Log in under the account that is running the server (by default, user *firebird* on v.1.5; *root* or *interbas* on v.1.0.*x*).

- Set the system-level permissions on the database file to include read permission for your group.

The gstat Interface

Unlike some of the other command-line tools, **gstat** does not have its own shell interface. Each request involves calling **gstat** with switches.

This is the syntax:

```
gstat [switches] db_name
```

db_name is the fully qualified local path to the database you want to query.

Graphical Tools

gstat is not user-friendly, and some GUI tools do a neater job of reproducing **gstat**'s output, generating the equivalent of the **gstat** switches though the Services API ("Services Manager"). Upcoming screenshots were taken using the open source IBOConsole utility.[4]

Switches

Table 18-1 lists the switches for **gstat**.

*Table 18-1. Switches for **gstat***

SWITCH	DESCRIPTION
–user *username*	Checks for user *username* before accessing database.
–pa[ssword] *password*	Checks for password *password* before accessing database.
–header	Reports the information on the header page, then stops reporting.
–log	Reports the information on the header and log pages, then stops reporting.
–index	Retrieves and displays statistics on indexes in the database.
–data	Retrieves and displays statistics on user data tables in the database.
–all	This is the default report if you do not request –index, –data, or –all. It retrieves and displays statistics from both –index and –data.
–system	As –all (above) but additionally includes statistics on the system tables.
–r	Retrieves and displays record size and version statistics (including back versions).
–t *table_list*	Used in conjunction with –data. Restricts output to the tables listed in *table_list*.
–z	Print product version of **gstat**.

It is recommended that you pipe the output to a text file and view it with a scrolling text editor.

---

4. IBOConsole is maintained by Lorenzo Mengoni. See http://www.mengoni.it.

NOTE Because **gstat** performs its analysis at the file level, it does not run in a transaction context. Consequently, index statistics include information about indexes involved in non-committed transactions. Do not be alarmed, for example, if a report shows some duplicate entries in a primary key index.

The -index Switch

This is the syntax:

```
gstat -i[ndex] db_path_and_name
```

This switch retrieves and displays statistics about indexes in the database: average key length (bytes), total duplicates, and maximum duplicates for a single key. Include the –s[ystem] switch if you would like the system indexes in the report.

Unfortunately, there is no way to get the stats for a single index, but you can restrict the output to a single table using the –t switch followed by the name of the table. You can supply a space-separated list of table names to get output for more than one table. If your table names are case sensitive—having been declared with double-quoted identifiers—then the –t switch argument[s] must be correct for case but not double-quoted. For tables with spaces in their names, **gstat** –t does not work at all.

You can add the switch –system to include the system indexes in the report.

To run it over the employee database and pipe it to a text file named *gstat.index.txt*, do the following.

On POSIX, type (all on one line)

```
./gstat -index /opt/firebird/examples/employee.fdb -t CUSTOMER
-user SYSDBA -password masterkey
   > /opt/firebird/examples/gstat.index.txt
```

On Win32, type (all on one line)

```
gstat -index
   "c:\Program Files\Firebird\Firebird_1_5\examples\employee.fdb" -t CUSTOMER
   -user SYSDBA -password masterkey
      > "c:\Program Files\Firebird\Firebird_1_5\examples\gstat.index.txt"
```

NOTE The double quotes around the database path are required on Windows if you have spaces in the path name.

Figure 18-3 shows how an index page summary is displayed.

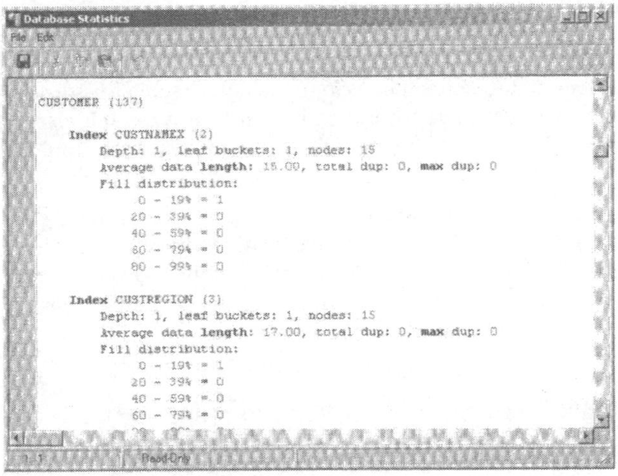

Figure 18-3. Example of index page summary output

What It All Means

A summary of the index information appears first. Table 18-2 explains the entries, line by line:

Table 18-2. **gstat** *–i[ndex] Output*

ITEM	DESCRIPTION
Index	The name of the index.
Depth	The number of levels of indirection in the index page tree. If the depth of the index page tree is greater than 3, then record access through the index will not be as efficient as possible. To reduce the depth of the index page tree, increase the page size. If increasing the page size does not reduce the depth, then increase the page size again.
Leaf buckets	The number of lowest-level (leaf node) pages in the index tree. These are the pages that contain the actual record pointers. Higher-level pages store indirection linkages.
Nodes	The total number of records indexed in the tree. This should be equivalent to the number of indexed rows in the table, although **gstat** output may include nodes that have been deleted but are not yet garbage collected. It may also include multiple entries for records that have had their index key modified.
Average data length	The average length of each key, in bytes. This is typically much shorter than the length of the declared key because of suffix and prefix compression.
Total dup	The total number of rows that share duplicate indexes.

continued

Table 18-2. **gstat** *–i[ndex] Output (continued)*

ITEM	DESCRIPTION
Max dup	The number of duplicated nodes in the "chain" having the most duplicates. This will always be zero for unique indexes. It is a sign of poor selectivity if the number is high in proportion to the Total Dup figure.
Average fill	This is a histogram with five 20-percent "bands," each showing the number of index pages whose average fill percentage falls within that range. Fill percentage is the proportion of the space on each page that actually contains data. The sum of these numbers gives the total number of pages containing index data.

Because **gstat** performs its analysis at the file level, it has no concept of transactions. Consequently, index statistics include information about indexes involved in non-committed transactions.

Index Depth

The index is a tree structure, with pages at one level pointing to pages at the next level, and so on, down to the pages that point to actual rows. The more depth, the more levels of indirection. *Leaf buckets*[5] are the bottom-level pages of the index, which point to individual rows.

In Figure 18-4, the index root page (created when the database is created) stores a pointer for each index and an offset pointing to another page of pointers that contains pointers for that index. In turn, that page points to the pages containing the leaf data—the actual data of the nodes—either directly (depth=1) or indirectly (adding one level for each level of indirection).

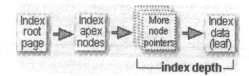

Figure 18-4. Index depth

Two factors affect depth: page size and key size. If the depth is larger than 3 and the page size is less than 8192, increasing the page size to 8192 or 16384 should reduce the levels of indirection and help the speed.

---

5. "Bucket" is an old-fashioned synonym for "page."

TIP   You can calculate the approximate size (in pages) of the max dup chain from the stats data. Divide nodes by leaf buckets to get the number of nodes per page. Multiplying that result by max dup gives the approximate number of pages.

Analyzing Some Statistics

The following excerpts are **gstat** –index output from a badly performing database.

Analysis 1

The first is the supporting index that was automatically created for a foreign key:

```
Index RDB$FOREIGN14 (3)
Depth: 2, leaf buckets: 109, nodes: 73373
Average data length: 0.00, total dup: 73372, max dup: 32351
Fill distribution:
80 - 99% = 109
```

Depth: 2, leaf buckets: 109, nodes: 73373 tells us that the bottom level of the index has 109 buckets (pages), for an index of 73373 nodes. That may not be the total row count of the table. For one thing, **gstat** is not aware of transactions, so it cannot tell whether it is looking at committed or uncommitted pages. For another, the column may have nulls, and they are not considered in the statistics.

The bottom level of the index—where leaf nodes are stored—has only 109 pages in it. That seems suspiciously few pages for so many rows. The next statistic tells us why.

In Average data length: 0.00, total dup: 73372, max dup: 32351, *max dup* is the length of the longest duplicate chain, accounting for almost half of the nodes. The *total dup* figure says that every node but one is duplicated.

This is a fairly classic case where the designer applies a foreign key without considering its distribution. It is probably a Boolean-style column, or perhaps a lookup table with either very few possible values or a practical bias toward a single value.

An example of this was an electoral register application that stored a column for country of residence. The electorate was approximately 3 million voters and registration was compulsory. The database supplied a COUNTRY table of more than 300 countries, keyed by the CCCIT country code. It was present on nearly every table in the database as a foreign key. The trouble was, nearly every elector lived in the same country.

The average data length is the average length of the key as stored. This has very little to do with the length as defined. An average length of zero only means that, by a process of suppression and compression, there is not enough "meat" left on which to calculate an average.

Fill distribution shows that all 109 pages are in the 80–99 percent range, which is well filled. The *fill distribution* is the proportion of space in each page of the index that is being used for data and pointers. Eighty to 90 percent is good. Lower fill distributions are the strongest clue that you should rebuild the index.

Analysis 2

The next example shows the statistics for the system-generated index for the primary key of the same table:

```
Index RDB$PRIMARY10 (0)
Depth: 3, leaf buckets: 298, nodes: 73373
Average data length: 10.00, total dup: 0, max dup: 0
Fill distribution:
0 - 19% = 1
80 - 99% = 297
```

The key length of 10 indicates that some compression is done. This is normal and good. That one page is underfilled is quite normal—the number of nodes did not fit evenly into the pages.

Analysis 3

This database has a smaller table that holds data temporarily for validation. It is flushed and reloaded periodically. The following statistics were generated for a foreign key on that table:

```
Index RDB$FOREIGN263 (1)
Depth: 1, leaf buckets: 10, nodes: 481
Average data length: 0.00, total dup: 480, max dup: 480
Fill distribution:
0 - 19% = 10
```

Total dup and *max dup* are identical—every row has the same value in the index key. Selectivity does not get worse than that. The fill level is very low in all pages, suggesting spotty deletions. If this were not such a small table, it would be an index from hell.

The table—a work-in-progress queue—is very dynamic, storing up to 1000 new rows per day. After validation, the rows are moved to production tables and the rows in the WIP table were being deleted, causing the system to slow down. Frequent backup and restore of the database was necessary to get things moving.

The problem was that foreign keys should have been avoided. In such cases, if referential integrity constraints are deemed essential, they can be user-defined in triggers.

However, if database design absolutely requires foreign key constraints for volatile tables on columns with low selectivity, there are recommended ways to mitigate the overhead and index page deterioration caused by constantly deleting and repopulating the table. Monitor the fill level on the problem indexes and take action whenever it drops below 40 percent. The choice of action depends on your requirements:

- First choice, if possible, is to delete all the rows at once rather than deleting them one by one, at random. Drop the foreign key constraint, delete the rows, and commit that transaction. Re-create the constraint. As long as there are no long-running transactions inhibiting garbage collection, the new index will be completely empty.

- If the deletions must be incremental, choose a time to get exclusive access and use ALTER INDEX to rebuild the index. It will be faster and more predictable than incremental garbage collection on huge duplicate chains.

Other gstat Switches

The **gstat** statistics can provide useful information about other activities in databases.

The -header Switch

This line:

```
gstat -header db_path_and_name
```

displays a database summary showing the header page information. Figure 18-5 shows an example.

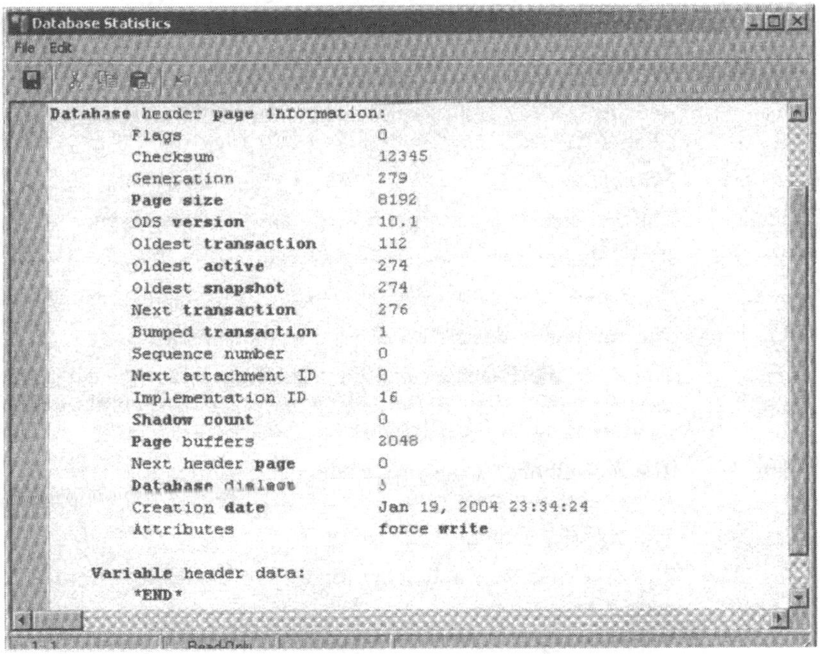

*Figure 18-5. Example of **gstat** header page summary output*

The first line displays the name and location of the primary database file. The following lines contain information from the database header page. Table 18-3 describes the output.

Table 18-3. **gstat** –h[eader] Output

ITEM	DESCRIPTION
Flags	
Checksum	The header page checksum. In ancestor versions of InterBase, it was a unique value computed from all the data in the header page. It was turned off and, in Firebird, it is always 12345. When the header page is stored to disk and later read, the checksum of the retrieved page is compared to 12345 and, if it does not match, a checksum error is raised. This catches some kinds of physical corruption.
Generation	Counter incremented each time the header page is written to.
Page size	The current database page size, in bytes.
ODS version	The version of the database's on-disk structure. It will be 10 for v.1.0.x and 10.1 for v.1.5.
Oldest transaction	The transaction ID of the oldest "interesting" transaction. For information about these, refer to Chapter 25.
Oldest active	The transaction ID of the oldest active transaction.
Oldest snapshot	The ID of the oldest transaction that is not currently eligible for garbage collection (i.e., it and any newer transactions are not eligible).
Next transaction	The ID that Firebird will assign to the next transaction. The difference between the oldest active transaction and the oldest snapshot transaction determines when database sweeping occurs. The default value is 20,000. See the section "Database 'Hygiene'" in Chapter 15.
Bumped transaction	Now obsolete.
Sequence number	The sequence number of the header page. It is always zero.
Next connection ID	ID number of the next database connection.
Implementation ID	The architecture of the hardware on which the database was created.
Shadow count	The number of shadow sets defined for the database.
Number of cache buffers	The size of the database cache, in pages. Zero means the database uses the server's default (DefaultDbCachePages in firebird.config, default_cache_pages in ibconfig/isc_config v.1.0.x).
Next header page	The page number of the next header page—although it appears not to be maintained.
Database dialect	The SQL dialect of the database.
Creation date	The date when the database was created or last restored from a **gbak** backup.
Attributes	*force write* indicates that forced database writes are enabled. *no_reserve* indicates that space is not reserved on each page for old generations of data. This enables data to be packed more closely on each page and therefore makes the database occupy less disk space. It is ideal for read-only databases. *shutdown* indicates the database is shut down (i.e., no users are connected).
Variable header data	Sweep interval. Information about secondary files (if any).

The –data Switch

This line

```
gstat -data db_path_and_name
```

retrieves a table-by-table database summary displaying information about data pages. To include the system tables (RDB$XXX) in the report, add the –system switch. Figure 18-6 shows an example of the output.

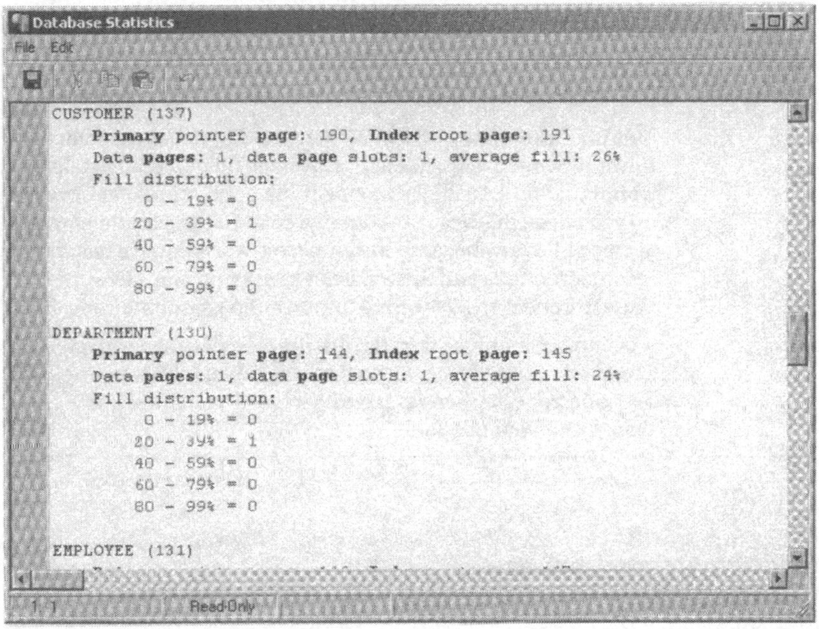

*Figure 18-6. Example of **gstat** data page summary output*

The command-line output is similar:

```
COUNTRY (31)
Primary pointer page: 190, Index root page: 19
Data pages: 1, data page slots: 1, average fill: 26%
Fill distribution:
 0 - 19% = 0
20 - 39% = 1
40 - 59% = 0
60 - 79% = 0
80 - 99% = 0
```

For each table in the database, the figures outlined in Table 18-4 are displayed.

Table 18-4. **gstat** *–d[ata] Output*

ITEM	DESCRIPTION
Primary pointer page	The page number of the first page of indirection pointers to pages storing data from the table.
Index root page	The page number that is the first pointer page for the table's indexes.
Data pages	The total number of data pages on which the tables data are stored. The count includes pages storing uncommitted record versions and garbage, since this program cannot distinguish the difference.
Data page slots	The number of pointers to database pages kept on pointer pages. Should be the same as the number of data pages.
Average fill	This is a histogram with five 20-percent "bands," each showing the number of data pages whose average fill percentage falls within that range. Fill percentage is the proportion of the space on each page that actually contains data. In the sample here, the average fill is low because the employee.fdb database has small record structures and there are not many of them. The sum of these numbers gives the total number of pages containing data.
Fill distribution	A histogram summarizing the distribution of usage capacity across all of the pages allocated for the table. In this example, only one page happens to have been used so far and it is less than 40-percent filled.

Restricting the Output from gstat –data

If you do not want a data report for every table, the –t switch allows you to specify a list of tables in which you are interested.

The syntax is

```
gstat -data db_path_and_name -t TABLENAME1 [TABLENAME2 [TABLENAME3 ..]]
```

NOTE Table names must be typed in uppercase. Unfortunately, **gstat** does not support the –t[able-list] switch on databases that use quoted, case-sensitive table identifiers.

The -r[ecords] Switch

This line

```
gstat -r db_path_and_name
```

retrieves and displays record size and version statistics.

- **For rows**: Average row length (bytes) and total rows in the table

- **For back versions**: Average version length (bytes), total versions in the table, and maximum version chain for a record

The total number of rows reported in a table could include both active and dead transactions. Record and version length are applicable to the actual user data—they do not take into account the header that prefixes every record version.

Example

The three tables CAULDRON, CAULDRON1, and CAULDRON2 have identical metadata and cardinality of 100,000 records. The nominal, uncompressed record length is ~900 bytes.

CAULDRON is a clean table of rows with no back versions. The average stored row length is ~121 bytes—about an 87-percent compression efficiency.

CAULDRON1 has an active transaction that just executed:

```
DELETE FROM CAULDRON1;
```

Every row has a zero (0.00) length because the primary record is a *delete stub* that contains only a row header. The committed records were all restored as back versions and compressed to the same size they had when they were the primary records. The table still has the same number of pages (4,000) as before the DELETE operation. The average fill factor rose from 85 to 95 percent to house all the delete stubs.

CAULDRON2 has an active transaction that just executed:

```
UPDATE CAULDRON2 SET F2OFFSET = 5.0
```

The updated records have each grown by 2 bytes (121 to 123), attributable to lower compression.

The value 5.0 replaced many missing and zero values, which made the field value different from its neighboring fields. There are now 100,000 back versions averaging 10 bytes each. The average fill factor has risen to 99 percent and the table grew 138 pages to 4,138.

```
> gstat proj.gdb -r -t CAULDRON CAULDRON1 CAULDRON2
...
Analyzing database pages ...
CAULDRON (147)
Primary pointer page: 259, Index root page: 260
Average record length: 120.97, total records: 100000
Average version length: 0.00, total versions: 0, max versions: 0
Data pages: 4000, data page slots: 4000, average fill: 85%
Fill distribution:
0 -19%=0
20 -39%=0
40 -59%=0
60 -79%=0
80 -99%=4000
CAULDRON1 (148)
Primary pointer page: 265, Index root page: 266
Average record length: 0.00, total records: 100000
Average version length: 120.97, total versions: 100000,
max versions: 1
Data pages: 4000, data page slots: 4000, average fill: 95%
Fill distribution:
0 -19%=0
20 -39%=0
40 -59%=0
60 -79%=0
80 -99%=4000
CAULDRON2 (149)
Primary pointer page: 271, Index root page: 272
Average record length: 122.97, total records: 100000
Average version length: 10.00, total versions: 100000, max
versions: 1
Data pages: 4138, data page slots: 4138, average fill: 99%
Fill distribution:
0 -19%=0
20 -39%=0
40 -59%=0
60 -79%=0
80 -99%=4138
```

 TIP For API programmers, the Firebird API function isc_database_info() and the Services API provide items that enable you to retrieve performance timings and database operation statistics into your application programs. For Delphi, C++Builder, and Kylix programmers, several suites of components are available with support for capturing database statistics.

Up Next

Here we end the discussions about database objects and change focus to the language for creating and changing data. Our examination begins with a broad look at SQL in terms of the standards and how Firebird's implementation breaks down into a number of overlapping subsets. Following that, in Chapter 20, we begin a more intensive look at data as sets and at the data manipulation language (DML) statements for defining and operating on them.

Part Five

Firebird SQL

CHAPTER 19

Firebird's SQL Language

SQL (PRONOUNCED "ESS CUE ELL") is a data sub-language for accessing relational database management systems. Its elements, syntax, and behavior became standardized under ANSI and ISO in 1986.

Since its introduction, the SQL standard has undergone three major reviews: SQL-89 (published in 1989), SQL-92 (1992 or thereabouts) and, more recently, SQL 3, an ongoing work published in part as SQL-99.

The standard SQL query language is non-procedural; that is, it is oriented toward the results of operations rather than toward the means of getting the results. It is intended to be a generic sub-language, to be used alongside a host language. The purpose of standards is to prescribe a surface-level mechanism whereby a specified query request returns a predictable result, regardless of how database engines manipulate input internally.

So, while the standard prescribes in great detail how the elements of the language shall be expressed and how the logic of operations is to be interpreted, it makes no rules about how a vendor should implement it. A "conforming" implementation is expected to provide the basic set of features and may include other features, grouped and standardized at levels above "entry level."

Firebird and the Standards

Conformance with the standard is a matter of degree, rather than an absolute. Vendors may freely implement language features that the standard does not prescribe. Conformance is about the ways that features recognized and described by the standards are implemented, if they are present. Conformance varies inversely with the number of standard features that are implemented in an idiosyncratic fashion.

Firebird's SQL language adheres closely to the SQL-92 standards (ISO/IEC 9075:1992) at entry level. Firebird 1.5 introduced a number of features in accordance with the more recently released SQL-99 standard. Although Firebird SQL follows standards closely, there are small differences.

SQL Statements

An SQL statement is used to submit a *query* to the database. The language of the query is expressed in statements that specify purpose: what is to be done (an operation), the objects to which it is to be done, and the details of how it is to be done. In theory, every possible interaction between the outside world and a database is surfaced through a statement syntax.

Statement syntaxes are grouped according to two broad purposes:

- Those that CREATE, ALTER, or DROP metadata objects (also known as schema objects or schema elements). Such queries are referred to as *data definition language*, or DDL.

- Those that operate on data. They provide language for defining sets of data in columns and rows and specifying operations to

    - Retrieve and transform (SELECT) images of those sets from storage for reading by applications.

    - Change the state of the database by adding, modifying, or deleting the specified sets (INSERT, UPDATE, and DELETE operations).

    These statements that operate on data are referred to as *data manipulation language*, or DML.

The Firebird implementation of the SQL language falls into a number of overlapping subsets, each used for a specific purpose and incorporating its own language *extensions*:

- Embedded SQL (ESQL): This is the "base" SQL implementation, consisting of DDL and DML syntax that the other subsets incorporate, where possible. It was the original implementation of SQL in the InterBase predecessors, designed to be embedded in client applications and pre-compiled.

- Dynamic SQL (DSQL): This is the subset in most common use today. It is used by all database interface layers that communicate with the server through the application programming interface (API). Some DDL commands available to ESQL that cannot be implemented in DSQL are replaced by API function call structures.

- Interactive (ISQL): This is the language implemented for the command-line **isql** utility. It is based on DSQL with extensions for viewing metadata and some system statistics and for controlling **isql** sessions.

- Procedural SQL (PSQL): This is the language for writing stored procedures and triggers. This consists of all DML statements, with the addition of a number of procedural extensions.

Data Definition Language (DDL)

When defining metadata for use in a Firebird database, we use a lexicon of standard SQL statements and parameters that provide for the creation of an object by its type and name—or *identifier*—and for specifying and modifying its attributes. Also in this lexicon are statements for removing objects.

Queries using DDL are reserved for the purpose of metadata definition, so

- Control them carefully if you are implementing them in end-user applications.

- Expect compiler exceptions if you attempt to use them in stored procedures.

Firebird's DDL is described in Parts Three and Four. View definitions and the granting and revoking of SQL permissions are also DDL. Views, which incorporate both DDL and DML, are discussed in Chapter 24. Defining and manipulating SQL permissions is described in Chapter 35.

Data Manipulation Language (DML)

The DML statements, syntaxes, and expressions for retrieving and manipulating sets of data form the content of this part of the book.

- Chapter 20 introduces the concept of sets, and the structure and syntax of DML queries. It includes an "Optimization Topic" section that covers working with the query optimizer.

- Chapter 21 describes functions, operations, and expressions, and how to use them.

- Chapter 22 looks at queries that operate on multiple tables using joins, subqueries, and unions.

- Chapter 23 examines the syntax and issues for specifying sets that require sorting or grouping and those that retrieve rows from multiple tables without joining.

- Chapter 24 covers the definition and use of views and other derived, table-like objects.

Embedded Language Features (ESQL)

Some SQL database management systems, including Firebird, provide the capability to embed SQL statements directly inside 3GL host programming language modules. The standard provides conceptual algorithms by which embedded application programming is to be accomplished, but it does not make any implementation rules.

Firebird's embedded application programming capabilities include a subset of SQL-like statements and constructs that can be incorporated into the source code of a program for pre-processing before the code goes to the compiler. The embedded SQL language constructs are known as *embedded SQL* (ESQL). ESQL statements cannot be generated dynamically.

ESQL is not valid in stored procedures and triggers, and procedure language (PSQL) is not valid in embedded SQL. ESQL can execute stored procedures. ESQL is used in programs written in traditional languages such as C and COBOL, prefaced by the EXEC SQL statement. The pre-processor, **gpre**, converts ESQL statements into host language data structures and calls to the Firebird server.

For more information, see the *Embedded SQL Guide* in the Borland InterBase 6.*x* Media Kit or EmbedSQL.pdf in the corresponding electronic document set.

Dynamic vs. Static SQL

SQL statements embedded and pre-compiled in code are sometimes referred to as *static SQL*. By contrast, statements that are generated by a client program and submitted to the server for execution during runtime are known as *dynamic SQL* (DSQL).

Unless you are writing code for ESQL applications, you are using DSQL. Statements executed by the interactive SQL utility (**isql**) or other interactive desktop utility programs are DSQL, as are those processed through client applications that use the API directly or indirectly (through database access drivers such as ODBC, JDBC, and the BDE).

In embedded applications, static SQL allows queries to bypass the Firebird API, instead being pre-compiled to use macro calls to the API structures. Because the whole query process is pre-compiled, it can execute faster than dynamic statements, which are submitted, parsed, and prepared at runtime.

Language Subset Variations

By design, or by accident of history, some minor variations exist between the subsets of Firebird's SQL language:

- The formats of certain regular SQL statements may vary slightly between the static and dynamic SQL variants.

- Statement terminators can vary according to the language subset:

  - ESQL and PSQL statements are terminated with semicolons.

  - The terminator is omitted in DSQL statements passed through the API structures.

  - DSQL passed through the **isql** interactive query utility requires terminators, which can be set, using SET TERM, to any printable character from the first 127-character ASCII subset.

Interactive SQL (ISQL)

The interactive query tool **isql** uses DSQL statements, along with two subsets of extension commands (the SET XXX and SHOW XXX groups), which allow certain settings and schema queries, respectively, to be performed interactively. Certain SET commands can also be included in *data definition scripts* (DDL scripts for batch execution in **isql**) and in embedded SQL.

For more information about the **isql** language subset, see Chapter 37.

Procedural Language (PSQL)

The standard does not prescribe procedural language features since, in principle, it assumes that general programming tasks will be accomplished using the host language. There is no specification for language constructs to manipulate, calculate, or create data programmatically inside the database management system.

Those RDBMS engines that support server-based programming usually provide SQL-like statement formats and syntaxes to extend SQL. Each vendor's implementation freely provides its own variants of these constructs. Typically, such code modules in the database are called *stored procedures*.

Firebird provides them as *procedure language* (sometimes referred to as PSQL), a set of SQL extensions that programmers use, along with a variant of the ESQL language set, to write the source code for stored procedures and triggers. PSQL is extended to include flow control, conditional expressions, and error handling. It has the unique ability to generate multi-row output sets that can be directly accessed using SELECT statements.

Certain SQL constructs, including all DDL statements, are excluded. However, from Firebird 1.5 onward, the EXECUTE STATEMENT syntax is supported in PSQL to enable the execution of DSQL commands, including some DDL.

PSQL for stored procedures and triggers is described in detail in Part Seven.

SQL Dialects

In Firebird, each client and database has a *SQL dialect*, an attribute that indicates to a Firebird server how to interpret features and elements that are implemented differently in legacy Borland InterBase databases earlier than version 6.

Dialect is a transition feature allowing the Firebird engine to recognize, accept, and correctly process the older features and elements of legacy databases (dialect 1); to access these older data for conversion to the new features and elements (dialect 2); or to apply the full Firebird set of features, elements, and rules to converted or newly created databases (dialect 3).

It is possible to create a new database in Firebird as dialect 1 or dialect 3. It is not recommended to create new databases in dialect 1, since it will be deprecated eventually. It is not possible to create a dialect 2 database, since dialect 2 is intended for converting dialect 1 databases to dialect 3. The dialect 2 attribute can be applied only to a client connection.

SQL Resources

Appendix I is an alphabetically listed external function reference.

Use the alphabetical glossary near the end of the guide to look up any unfamiliar terms.

Books

If your previous contact with SQL has been minimal, a good book on SQL-92 basics is invaluable. The following list (which is not exhaustive) may be helpful.

Joe Celko writes SQL books aimed at problem solving. These are some of his titles: *Joe Celko's SQL For Smarties: Advanced SQL Programming, Joe Celko's Data and Databases: Concepts in Practice*, and *Joe Celko's SQL Puzzles and Answers*. The SQL is mostly standard, with perhaps a bias toward Oracle.

The Essence of SQL by David Rozenshtein and Tom Bondur is very concise and very much a beginner book.

The Practical SQL Handbook by Judith S. Bowman, Sandra Emerson, and Marcy Darnovsky is a how-to and desktop reference for standard SQL that has been well reviewed.

A Guide to the SQL Standard by Hugh Darwen and Chris Date contains all the things you wanted to know—and much that you didn't know you didn't know—about SQL-92, by the RDBMS "gods."

Understanding the New SQL: A Complete Guide by Jim Melton and Alan Simon covers SQL-89 and SQL-92. It is a comprehensive, good lookup reference for the beginner, and it includes some basic modeling theory.

Mastering SQL by Martin Gruber is the updated and expanded new version of the author's *Understanding SQL*, which makes standard SQL reachable, even for the beginner, and helps solid skills to develop quickly.

Free SQL Support

For all Firebird SQL-related questions, join the firebird-support forum at http://www.yahoogroups.com/community/firebird-support. This is a volunteer e-mail list where longtime and new Firebird users share experience. If you prefer a newsgroup interface, the list is mirrored at news://news.atkin.com/egroups.ib-support. You can post list messages through the newsgroup mirror if you subscribe to the mail list and use the same sender address.

Up Next

Data manipulation language (DML) is the SQL language subset that we use to define the sets that we want applications to read or operate on. In the next chapter, we look at the base syntax of the "big four" SQL statements: SELECT, INSERT, UPDATE, and DELETE.

DML Queries

USER APPLICATIONS CAN ACCESS THE DATA in Firebird tables only one way: by querying them. A query is, in its essence, an SQL statement that has been submitted to the server. An SQL statement is a sentence consisting of keywords, phrases, and clauses in a formalized, English-like language. It has a limited vocabulary that is understood by both the client library and the Firebird server—and, desirably, by the human who composes the sentence! All metadata and data creation, modification, and management tasks, without exception, are done with queries.

Strictly speaking, a statement does not become a query until it is submitted to the server. However, most developers use the terms *statement* and *query* interchangeably.

All DML queries target data that is persistently stored in databases as columns in tables. A query specifies a *set of data* and one or more *operations* to be performed upon the set. It can use *expressions* to transform data for retrieval or storage or to provide special search conditions for sets of data.

Sets of Data

A DML query defines a logical collection of data items arranged in order from left to right in one or more columns, known as a *set*. A query may confine a set's specification to being a single row or it may consist of multiple rows. In a multi-row set, the column arrangement of one row is identical to all others in the set.

People often casually refer to sets as "queries." They are not synonymous.

A Table Is a Set

A table is a set whose complete specification can be accessed in the system tables by the database server when the table is referred to by a query from a client. The Firebird server performs its own internal queries on the system tables to extract the metadata it needs in order to execute client queries.

Output Sets

A common use of a query statement beginning with the keyword SELECT is to output a set to the client application, for the purpose of displaying data to users. The terms *dataset* and *recordset* are synonymous with *output set*. The output set may be in no particular row order, or it can be delivered as a *sorted set*, as specified in an ORDER BY clause.

NOTE "No particular row order" means just that. Rows for tables are stored with no attributes whatsoever and the order of unordered sets is not predictable from one query to another.

For example, the following query will output a set of three columns from TABLEA, containing every row that matches the conditions specified in the WHERE clause. The rows will be sorted so that the row with the lowest value in COL1 will appear first:

```
SELECT COL1, COL2, COL3 FROM TABLEA
WHERE COL3 = 'Mozart'
ORDER BY COL1;
```

If no WHERE clause is provided, the set will contain every row from TABLEA, not just those that have the value 'Mozart' in COL3.

If all columns of TABLEA are wanted, then the symbol * can optionally be used instead of itemizing the columns of the set, for example:

```
SELECT * FROM TABLEA;
```

defines an output set consisting of all columns and all rows from TABLEA.

Cardinality and Degree

A term you will sometimes encounter with respect to sets—including tables—is *cardinality*. Cardinality describes the number of rows in a set, which might be a table or an output set. More loosely, you may encounter *cardinality of a row* or *cardinality of a key value*, referring to the *position* of a row in an ordered output set.

The term used to refer to the number of columns in a set is *degree*. By extension, you may encounter a phrase like *the degree of a column*, meaning its position in the left-to-right order of the columns in the set.

Input Sets

Just as the SELECT … FROM part of a retrieval query specifies a set for an output or cursor operation, so the other DML statements (INSERT, UPDATE, and DELETE) specify input sets identifying the data upon which the operation is to be performed.

An INSERT query's input set is specified by identifying a single table and a left-to-right ordered list of identifiers for columns that are to receive input values in the subsequent VALUES() clause. The VALUES() clause must supply a list of values that corresponds exactly to the input set's order and the data types of its members.

The following example defines an input set consisting of three columns from TABLEB. The constants in the VALUES() clause will be checked to ensure that there are exactly three values and that they are of the correct data types:

```
INSERT INTO TABLEB(COLA, COLB, COLC)
VALUES(99, 'Christmas 2004', '2004-12-25');
```

INSERT has an alternative syntax where the VALUES() clause is replaced by selecting a set from one or more other tables, real or virtual. INSERT statements are discussed in more detail in the section "The INSERT Statement."

An UPDATE query defines its input set by identifying a single table and listing one or more input columns, together with their new values, in a SET clause. It identifies the target rows using a WHERE clause:

```
UPDATE TABLEB
SET COLB ='Labor Thanksgiving Day (Japan)',
    COLC = '2002-23-11'
WHERE ...;
```

UPDATE statements are discussed in more detail in the section "The UPDATE Statement."

A DELETE query cannot specify columns in its input set—it is implicitly always * (all columns). It identifies the target rows using a WHERE clause. For example, the following query will delete every row where COLC (a DATE type) is earlier than December 13, 1999:

```
DELETE FROM TABLEB
WHERE COLC < '1999-12-13';
```

DELETE statements are discussed in more detail in the section "The DELETE Statement."

Output Sets As Input Sets

Grouped or Aggregated Queries

SQL has an important feature that uses an input set formed from an output set generated within the same SELECT query: the GROUP BY clause. Instead of the output set from the column list being passed to the client, it is passed instead to a further stage of processing, where the GROUP BY clause causes the data to be partitioned into one or more nested groups. Each partition typically extracts summaries by way of expressions that aggregate numeric values at one or more levels.

For more information about aggregated queries, see Chapter 23.

Streams and Rivers for JOINs

When columns in one table are linked to columns in another table to form joined sets, the input column sets from each table are known as *streams*. The output of two joined streams is referred to as a *river*. When joins involve more than two tables, streams and rivers become the input for further joining of streams and rivers until the final river becomes the output of the query.

A group of Firebird engine routines known as the *optimizer* subjects a join query specification and the indexes available to a cost-evaluation process referred to as *optimization*. The optimizer generates a plan, which is a "best-cost" map of the course the engine will take when generating that final "output river" on subsequent executions of the statement.

JOIN syntax is discussed in Chapter 22. Refer to the "Optimization Topic" section at the end of that chapter for a discussion of the optimizer and query plans.

Cursor Sets

A SELECT statement can define a set that is not output to the client at all, but remains on the server to be operated on by a *server-side cursor*. The cursor itself is a pointer that the application instructs to fetch rows one by one, on demand, by progressing forward through a prepared SELECT statement.

A *named cursor* declaration, which must be compiled in advance in ESQL or specified through an API structure in DSQL, includes a client-side statement variable that points to the statement. The client application is responsible for ensuring that the prepared statement is available for assignment at the appropriate point in execution of the program.

PSQL has a commonly used language extension that takes the following form:

```
FOR SELECT <any valid select specification>
INTO <list of pre-declared local variables> DO
  BEGIN
    < optionally operate on variables >;
    SUSPEND;
  END
```

This is an *unnamed cursor* syntax.[1]

The objective of a cursor operation is to use data from the cursor set and "do something" consistently for each cursor set row processed. It can be an efficient way

---

[1]. Actually, named cursor syntax is available as a "hidden feature" in PSQL as well, although it is incompletely implemented at Firebird v.1.5. It has been extended in post-1.5 development and should appear in a sub-release.

to batch-process sets, where the process performs one or more tasks on the current cursor row, inside a single iteration of a loop through the cursor set. For example, at each iteration, data items could be taken from the current cursor set row and used for inserting new rows into a specified input set.

Another statement can optionally link to an opened cursor, using WHERE CUR-RENT OF *<cursor-name>* instead of a search condition, to perform positioned updates or deletes on the rows "bookmarked" by the cursor set.

Implementing Cursors

Firebird provides several methods for implementing cursors:

- Embedded SQL (ESQL) provides the DECLARE CURSOR statement[2] for implementing the pre-compiled named cursor declaration.

- To use a cursor, a dynamic application must pre-declare it using the function *isc_dsql_set_cursor_name*.[3] While some data access components realize this interface, many do not.

- The PSQL language provides syntax to operate on both named and unnamed cursors locally inside a stored procedure or trigger. For more information, refer to Chapter 29.

NOTE   Except for techniques available in PSQL, cursors are beyond the scope of this guide. For more information, refer to Chapter 30.

Nested Sets

Nested sets are formed using a special kind of SQL expression syntax known as a *subquery*. This kind of expression takes the form of a bracketed SELECT statement that can be embedded into the column specification list of the main query to output a single, runtime output value per row or, in a WHERE clause, as part of a search condition. The allowed SELECT syntaxes vary according to the context in which the subquery is used.

---

2. For more information, consult the *Embedded SQL Guide* (EmbedSQL.pdf) of the InterBase 6.0 documentation set published by Borland.

3. Direct-to-API programmers and interface component developers can get more information from the *InterBase API Guide* (APIGuide.pdf) of the InterBase 6.0 documentation set published by Borland.

In the following simple example, a query on TABLEA uses a nested subquery to include a runtime output column named DESCRIPTION derived from COLX in TABLEB:

```
SELECT COL1, COL2, COL3,
(SELECT COLA FROM TABLEB WHERE COLX='Espagnol')
  AS DESCRIPTION
FROM TABLEA
WHERE ... ;
```

Notice the use of the keyword AS to mark the identifier (DESCRIPTION) of the derived column. It is optional, but recommended for code clarity.

It is very common for an embedded query to be *correlated* to the main query. A correlated subquery is one whose WHERE clause is linked to one or more values in the outer query's output list or other values in the underlying tables of the outer query. A correlated subquery is similar in effect to an inner join and can sometimes be used to good effect in place of a join.

The topic of subqueries is discussed in detail in the following two chapters, but especially in Chapter 22.

Privileges

Reading and writing to tables are database privileges, controlled by declarations made with GRANT and REVOKE. For information, refer to Chapter 35.

The SELECT Statement

The SELECT statement is the fundamental method for clients to retrieve sets of data from the database. It has the following general form:

```
SELECT
 [FIRST (m)] [SKIP (n)] [[ALL] | DISTINCT]
  <list of columns> [, [column-name] | expression |constant ] AS alias-name]
FROM <table-or-procedure-or-view>
[{[[INNER] | [{LEFT | RIGHT | FULL} [OUTER]] JOIN}] <table-or-procedure-or-view>
  ON <join-conditions [{JOIN..]]
[WHERE <search-conditions>]
[GROUP BY <grouped-column-list>]
[HAVING <search-condition>]
[UNION <select-expression> [ALL]]
[PLAN <plan-expression>]
[ORDER BY <column-list>]
[FOR UPDATE [OF col1 [,col2..]] [WITH LOCK]]
```

Clauses in a SELECT Statement

In the following topics, we take an introductory look at each allowable clause of the SELECT statement. Most clauses are optional, but it is important to present those you do use in the correct order.

Optional Set Quantifiers

Following the SELECT keyword, a set quantifier can be included to govern the inclusion or suppression of rows in the output set once they have met all other conditions.

ALL

This is the default quantifier for output lists and is usually omitted. It returns all rows that meet the conditions of the specification.

DISTINCT

This row quantifier suppresses all duplicate rows in the sets that are output. For example, the table EMPLOYEE_PROJECT stores an intersection record for each employee (EMP_NO) and project (PROJ_ID) combination, resolving a many-to-many relationship. EMP_NO + PROJ_ID forms the primary key.

```
SELECT DISTINCT EMP_NO, PROJ_ID FROM EMPLOYEE_PROJECT;
```

returns 28 rows—that is, all of them, which is the same as SELECT [ALL], because every occurrence of (EMP_NO + PROJ_ID) is, by nature, distinct.

```
SELECT DISTINCT EMP_NO FROM EMPLOYEE_PROJECT;
```

and

```
SELECT DISTINCT PROJ_ID FROM EMPLOYEE_PROJECT;
```

return 22 and 5 rows, respectively.

Evaluation of distinctness is applied to all of the output columns, making it useful in some queries that use joins to produce a denormalized set. Test it well to ensure that it produces the result you expect.[4]

---

4. Because the output of a DISTINCT set implies the existence of duplicates, its fields cannot be relied on to provide a unique search stream for a positioned update. Some development interfaces explicitly treat the output sets from DISTINCT queries as non-updateable.

FIRST (m) SKIP (n)

The optional keywords FIRST (*m*) and/or SKIP (*n*), if used, precede all other specifications. They provide the option to select the first *m* rows from the output of an ordered set and to ignore the first *n* rows of an ordered set, respectively. It does not make sense to use this construct with an unordered set. The ORDER BY clause obviously needs to use an ordering condition that actually makes sense with regard to the selection of the candidate rows.

The two keywords can be used together or individually. The arguments *m* and *n* are integers, or expressions that resolve to integers. The brackets around the *m* and *n* values are required for expression arguments and optional for simple integer arguments.

Since FIRST and SKIP operate on the set that is output by the rest of the specification, they cannot be expected to make the query execute faster than the full specification would otherwise do. Any performance benefit comes from the reduction of traffic across the wire.

The following example will return five rows, starting at row 101 in the ordered set:

```
SELECT FIRST 5 SKIP 100 MEMBER_ID, MEMBERSHIP_TYPE, JOIN_DATE
FROM MEMBERS
ORDER BY JOIN_DATE;
```

TIP To return the n highest-order rows according to the ordering conditions, order the set in DESC[ENDING] order.

SELECT <List of Columns>

The SELECT clause defines the list of columns that are to be returned in the output set. It must contain at least one column, which does not have to be a column that exists in a table. That statement is not as strange as it sounds. The column list is really an output specification and this is data manipulation language (DML). The output specifications can include any of the following:

- The identifier of a column that is stored in a table, specified in a view, or declared as an output argument to a stored procedure. Under some conditions, the column identifier must be qualified with the name or alias of the table it belongs to.

- A simple or complex expression, accompanied by a runtime identifier.

- A constant value, accompanied by a runtime identifier.

- A server context variable, accompanied by a runtime identifier.

- The * symbol, popularly known as "select star," which specifies every column. Although SELECT * does not preclude selecting one or more columns from the same table individually, it does not make sense to do so in general. To include a duplicated column for a special purpose, apply the AS keyword and an alias to it and return it as a computed (read-only) field.

The following SELECT specifications are all valid.
Simple list of columns:

```
SELECT COLUMN1, COLUMN2 ...
```

Qualified column names, required in multi-table specifications:

```
SELECT
  TABLEA.ID,
  TABLEA.BOOK_TITLE,
  TABLEB.CHAPTER_TITLE,
  CURRENT_TIMESTAMP AS RETRIEVE_DATE ...
```

Expression (aggregating):

```
SELECT MAX(COST * QUANTITY) AS BEST_SALE ...
```

Expression (transforming):

```
SELECT 'EASTER'||CAST(EXTRACT(YEAR FROM CURRENT_DATE) AS CHAR(4)) AS SEASON ...
```

Variables and constants:

```
SELECT
  ACOLUMN,
  BCOLUMN,
  CURRENT_USER, /* context variable */
  'Jaybird' AS NICKNAME ... /* run-time constant */
```

All columns in a table:

```
SELECT * ...
```

Quantifiers:

```
SELECT FIRST 5 SKIP 100 ACOLUMN, BCOLUMN ...
/* this has no sense in absence of a later ORDER BY */
```

Expressions and Constants As Output Fields

A constant or an expression—which may or may not include a column name—can be returned as a read-only, runtime output field. The field should be given a column name of its own, unique in all sets involved. Names for runtime columns are known as *column aliases*. For clarity, the column alias can be marked optionally with the keyword AS.

Taking the previous example

```
SELECT 'EASTER'||CAST(EXTRACT(YEAR FROM CURRENT_DATE) AS CHAR(4)) AS SEASON ...
```

In 2004, this column alias will be returned in every row of the set as

```
...    SEASON        ...
===== ============ ====
        EASTER2004
```

Constants, many different kinds of expressions involving functions and calculations, and scalar subqueries (including correlated subqueries) can be massaged into read-only output fields.

 NOTE   Constants of types BLOB and ARRAY cannot be output as runtime fields.

For details about expressions and functions, refer to the next chapter.

FROM <Table-or-Procedure-or-View>

The FROM clause specifies the *source of data*, which may be a table, a view, or a stored procedure that has output arguments. If the statement involves joining two or more structures, the FROM clause specifies the leftmost structure. Other tables are added to the specification by way of succeeding ON clauses (see the upcoming section "JOIN <Specification>").

In the following examples, some FROM clauses are added to the SELECT specifications in the previous set of examples:

```
SELECT COLUMN1, COLUMN2 FROM ATABLE ...
SELECT
  TABLEA.ID,
  TABLEA.BOOK_TITLE,
  TABLEB.CHAPTER_TITLE,
  CURRENT_TIMESTAMP AS RETRIEVE_DATE
  FROM TABLEA ...
SELECT MAX(COST * QUANTITY) AS BEST_SALE
  FROM SALES ...
```

```
SELECT 'EASTER'||CAST(EXTRACT(YEAR FROM CURRENT_DATE) AS CHAR(2)) AS SEASON
  FROM RDB$DATABASE ;
SELECT ACOLUMN, BCOLUMN, CURRENT_USER, 'Jaybird' AS NICKNAME
  FROM MYTABLE ...
```

SQL-89 Inner Join Syntax

Firebird provides backward support for the deprecated SQL-89 implicit inner join syntax, for example:

```
SELECT
  TABLEA.ID,
  TABLEA.BOOK_TITLE,
  TABLEB.CHAPTER_TITLE,
  CURRENT_TIMESTAMP AS RETRIEVE_DATE
FROM TABLEA, TABLEB ...
```

For several reasons, you should avoid this syntax in new applications. For more information about it, see Chapter 22.

....

What Is This Table RDB$DATABASE?

RDB$DATABASE is a system table that stores one and only one row that consists of bits of header information about the database. What's stored in it is immaterial to the widespread use Firebird developers make of it. The fact that it always has one row—no more, no less—makes it handy when we want to retrieve a value from the server that is not stored in a table, view, or stored procedure.

For example, to get a new generator value into an application, which is something we may need for creating rows on the detail side of a new master-detail structure, we create a function in our application that calls this query:

```
SELECT GEN_ID(MyGenerator, 1) FROM RDB$DATABASE;
```

If you have had anything to do with Oracle databases, you will recognize it as Firebird's answer to *DUAL*.

....

JOIN <Specification>

Use this clause to add the names and joining conditions of the second and each subsequent data stream (table, view, or selectable stored procedure) that contributes to a multi-table SELECT statement—one JOIN ... ON clause for each source set. JOIN syntax and issues are discussed in detail in Chapter 22. The following statement illustrates a simple inner join between the two tables from the previous example:

```
SELECT
  TABLEA.ID,
  TABLEA.BOOK_TITLE,
  TABLEB.CHAPTER_TITLE,
  CURRENT_TIMESTAMP AS RETRIEVE_DATE
  FROM TABLEA
  JOIN TABLEB
  ON TABLEA.ID = TABLEB.ID_B ...
```

Table Aliases

In the same statement fragment, table identifiers can be optionally substituted with table aliases, for example:

```
SELECT
  T1.ID,
  T1.BOOK_TITLE,
  T2.CHAPTER_TITLE,
  CURRENT_TIMESTAMP AS RETRIEVE_DATE
  FROM TABLEA T1
  JOIN TABLEB T2
  ON T1.ID = T2.ID_B ...
```

The use of table aliases in multi-table queries is explored in more depth in Chapter 22.

WHERE <Search-Conditions>

Search conditions limiting the *rows* for output are located in the WHERE clause. Search conditions can vary from a simple match condition for a single column to complex conditions involving expressions; AND, OR, and NOT predicates; type casting; character set and collation conditions; and more.

The WHERE clause is the *filtering* clause that determines which rows are candidates for inclusion in the output set. Those rows that are not eliminated by the search conditions of the WHERE clause may be ready for output to the requestor or they may "go forward" for further processing, ordering by an ORDER BY clause, with or without consolidation by a GROUP BY clause.

The following simple examples illustrate some WHERE clauses using a sampling of conditions to limit the rows selected:

```
SELECT COLUMN1, COLUMN2 FROM ATABLE
WHERE ADATE BETWEEN '2002-12-25' AND '2004-12-24'...
```

```
/**/
SELECT T1.ID, T2.TITLE, CURRENT_TIMESTAMP AS RETRIEVE_DATE
FROM TABLEA
  JOIN TABLEB
  ON TABLEA.ID = TABLEB.ID_B
  WHERE TABLEA.ID = 99 ;
/**/
SELECT MAX(COST * QUANTITY) AS BEST_SALE
  FROM SALES
  WHERE SALES_DATE > '31.12.2003'...
```

The next chapter is devoted to the topic of expressions and predicates for defining search conditions.

Parameters in WHERE Clauses

Data access interfaces that implement the Firebird API have the capability to process the constants in search conditions as *replaceable parameters*. Thus, an application can set up a statement with dynamic search conditions in the WHERE clause, for which values do not need to be assigned until just before execution. This capability is sometimes referred to as *late binding*.

For more details, see the upcoming section "Using Parameters."

GROUP BY <Grouped-Column-List>

The output from the SELECT statement can optionally be partitioned into one or more nested groups that aggregate (summarize) the sets of data returned at each nesting level. These groupings often include *aggregating expressions*, expressions containing functions that work on multiple values, such as totals, averages, row counts, and minimum/maximum values.

The following simple example illustrates a grouping query. The SQL aggregating function SUM() is used to calculate the total items sold for each product type:

```
SELECT PRODUCT_TYPE, SUM(NUMBER_SOLD) AS SUM_SALES
FROM TABLEA
WHERE SERIAL_NO BETWEEN 'A' AND 'K'
GROUP BY PRODUCT_TYPE;
```

The output might be similar to the following:

```
PRODUCT_TYPE SUM_SALES
------------ ---------
Gadgets            174
Whatsits            25
Widgets            117
```

Firebird provides an extensive range of grouping capability, with very strict rules governing the logic.

 CAUTION If you are converting a database from InterBase to Firebird, this is one area where you need to be aware of differences. Firebird is less tolerant of illogical grouping specifications than its ancestor.

Aggregating expressions are discussed in the next chapter. For detailed information about GROUP BY and its issues, refer to Chapter 23.

HAVING <Grouping-Column Predicate>

The optional HAVING clause may be used in conjunction with a grouping specification to include or exclude rows or groups, similar to the way the WHERE clause limits row sets. Often, in a grouping query, a HAVING clause can replace the WHERE clause. However, because HAVING operates on the intermediate set created as input to the GROUP BY specification, it may be more economical to prefer a WHERE condition to limit rows and a HAVING condition to limit groups.

The previous example is modified by a HAVING clause, to return just the PRODUCT_TYPE that has been sold in quantities greater than 100:

```
SELECT PRODUCT_TYPE, SUM(NUMBER_SOLD) AS SUM_SALES
FROM TABLEA
WHERE SERIAL_NO BETWEEN 'A' AND 'K'
AND PRODUCT_TYPE = 'WIDGETS'
GROUP BY PRODUCT_TYPE
HAVING SUM(NUMBER_SOLD) > 100;
```

This is the output:

```
PRODUCT_TYPE SUM_SALES
------------ ---------
Widgets           117
```

UNION <Select-Specification>

UNION sets are formed by combining two or more separate query specifications, which may involve different tables, into one output set. The only restriction is that the output columns in each separate output specification must match by degree, type, and size. That means they must each output the same number of columns in the same left-to-right order and that each column must be consistent throughout in data type and size.

By default, a UNION set suppresses duplicates in the final output set. To retain all duplicates, include the keyword ALL.

UNION sets are discussed in more detail in Chapter 23.

PLAN <Plan-Expression>

The PLAN clause allows a query plan to be optionally included in the query specification. It is an instruction to the optimizer to use particular indexes, join order, and access methods for the query. The optimizer creates its own plan when it prepares a query statement. You can view the plan in **isql** and many of the available GUI utilities. Usually, "the optimizer knows best," but sometimes it can be worthwhile to experiment with variations to the optimizer's plan when a query is slow.

Query plans and the syntax of plan expressions are discussed at the end of Chapter 22, in the "Optimization Topic" section.

ORDER BY <Column-List>

Use this clause when your output set needs to be sorted. For example, the following gets a list of names in alphabetical order by last name and first name:

```
SELECT EMP_NO, LAST_NAME, FIRST_NAME FROM EMPLOYEE
ORDER BY LAST_NAME, FIRST_NAME;
```

Unlike GROUP BY columns, ORDER BY columns do not have to be present in the output specification (SELECT clause). The identifier of any ordering column that also appears in the output specification can be replaced by its position number in the output spec, counting from left to right:

```
SELECT EMP_NO, LAST_NAME, FIRST_NAME FROM EMPLOYEE
ORDER BY 2, 3;
```

Pay close attention to the indexes on columns that are going to be used for sorting. Refer to Chapter 18 for guidance. For more about syntaxes and issues, see Chapter 23.

The FOR UPDATE Clause

This is the syntax:

```
[FOR UPDATE [OF col1 [,col2..]] [WITH LOCK]]
```

Broadly, the FOR UPDATE clause is meaningless except in the context of a SELECT statement that is used to specify a named cursor. It instructs the engine to wait for a FETCH call, fetch one row into the cursor for a "current row" operation, and then wait for the next FETCH call. As each row is fetched, it becomes earmarked for an update operation.

The optional sub-clause OF *<column-list>* can be used to provide a list of fields present in the cursor that are allowed to be updated.

- In ESQL applications, a DECLARE CURSOR statement is used to set up the named cursor. For more information, refer to the InterBase 6.0 Embedded SQL documentation.

- Applications providing DSQL interfaces must use the *isc_dsql_set_cursor_name* function to obtain a named cursor and use FOR UPDATE meaningfully. For more information, refer to the *InterBase API Guide*.

Dynamic Applications

Because DSQL does not surface FETCH as a language element, application interfaces implement it using an API function call named *isc_dsql_fetch*.

The API "knows" the order and format of the output fields because of the descriptive structures—named Extended SQL Descriptor Areas, or XSQLDAs—that dynamic SQL applications are required to pass to it. One XSQLDA contains an array of complex variable descriptors named SQLVARs, one for each output field.

Client application interfaces use isc_dsql_fetch to request a row of output, which is a freshly populated XSQLDA. The typical behavior for many modern client application interfaces is to provide looping calls to isc_dsql_fetch, in order to receive output rows in batches and buffer them into client-side structures that are variously known as *recordsets*, *datasets*, or *result sets*.

Some API application interfaces implement a named cursor and surface FOR UPDATE behavior, but most do not.

The WITH LOCK Sub-clause

Firebird 1.5 introduced an optional WITH LOCK extension, for use with or without the FOR UPDATE clause syntax, to support a restricted level of explicit, row-level pessimistic locking. Pessimistic locking is antithetical to the transaction architecture of Firebird and introduces complexity. Its use is recommended only by developers with an advanced understanding of how multi-user concurrency is implemented in Firebird. Pessimistic locking is discussed in Chapter 27.

Queries that Count Rows

An entrenched practice exists among some programmers of designing applications that need to perform a row count on output sets. Firebird does not have a quick or reliable way to return the number of rows that will be returned in an output set. Because of its multi-generational architecture, Firebird has no mechanism to "know" the cardinality of rows in persistent tables. If an application must have a row count, it can get an approximation using a SELECT COUNT(*) query.

SELECT COUNT (*) Queries

A SELECT statement with the COUNT() function call replacing a column identifier will return the approximate cardinality of a set defined by a WHERE clause. COUNT() takes practically anything as an input argument: a column identifier, a column list, the keyword symbol * representing "all columns," or even a constant.

For example, all of the following statements are equivalent, or nearly so. However, SELECT COUNT (*some-column-name*) does *not* include in the count any rows where *some-column-name* is NULL:

```
SELECT COUNT (*) FROM ATABLE WHERE COL1 BETWEEN 40 AND 75;
SELECT COUNT (COL1) FROM ATABLE WHERE COL1 BETWEEN 40 AND 75;
SELECT COUNT (COL1, COL2, COL3) FROM ATABLE WHERE COL1 BETWEEN 40 AND 75;
SELECT COUNT 1 FROM ATABLE WHERE COL1 BETWEEN 40 AND 75;
SELECT COUNT ('Sticky toffee') FROM ATABLE WHERE COL1 BETWEEN 40 AND 75;
```

COUNT(*) is a very costly operation, since it can work only by walking the entire dataset and literally counting each row that is visible to the current transaction as committed. It should be treated as a "rough count," since it will become out of date as soon as any other transaction commits work.

Although it is possible to include COUNT(*) as a member of an output set that includes other columns, it is neither sensible nor advisable. It will cause the entire dataset to be walked each time a row is selected for output.

The exception is when COUNT(*) is included in an output set being aggregated by a GROUP BY clause. Under those conditions, the count is cheap—it will be performed on the aggregated group in the course of the aggregation process, for example:

```
SELECT COL1, SUM(COL2), COUNT(*) FROM TABLEA
GROUP BY COL1;
```

For more details about using COUNT with aggregations, refer to Chapter 23.

Existence Checking

Do not use SELECT COUNT(*) as a way to check for the existence of rows meeting some criteria. This technique frequently shows up in applications that have had their "back-end" upgraded to Firebird from file-based, table-locking databases such as Paradox or MySQL, and it needs to be abandoned. Instead, use the EXISTS() function predicate, which is designed for the purpose and is very fast. Refer to the next chapter for details of EXISTS() and other function predicates.

"Next Value" Calculations

Another technique that must be abandoned in Firebird is using COUNT(*) and adding 1 to "generate" the next value for a primary key. It is unsafe in any multi-user DBMS that isolates concurrent tasks. In Firebird, it is also extremely slow, because the table management system has no "file of records" that can be counted by the computer's file management methods.

Use generators for anything that needs a unique numbering sequence. For details about generators, refer to the "Generators" section in Chapter 9.

Variations with COUNT()

The result of COUNT() will never be NULL, because it counts rows. If count has been predicated over an empty set, it returns zero. It can never be negative.

COUNT(*) in a table counts all rows with no conditions on the existence of data in columns. It can use an index if the query contains a WHERE condition that the optimizer can match to it. For example, the statement

```
SELECT COUNT(*) FROM EMPLOYEE
WHERE LAST_NAME BETWEEN 'A%' AND 'M%';
```

may be a little less costly if there is an index on LAST_NAME.

COUNT(*column_name*) counts only rows where *column_name* is not NULL.
COUNT(DISTINCT *column_name*) counts only the distribution of distinctly different values in that column. That is, all repetitions of the same value are accounted for in one counted item.

With COUNT(DISTINCT..), if the column allows NULL, then all rows holding NULL in the column are excluded from the count. If you must count them, it can be done with a "hack":

```
SELECT COUNT (DISTINCT TABLE.COLX) +
(SELECT COUNT(*) FROM RDB$DATABASE
   WHERE EXISTS(SELECT * FROM TABLE T
    WHERE T.COLX IS NULL))
FROM TABLE
```

The INSERT Statement

The INSERT statement is used for adding new rows to a single table. SQL does not permit rows to be inserted to more than one table in a single INSERT statement.

INSERT statements can operate on views, under some conditions. Refer to Chapter 24 for a discussion of views that can accept inserts on behalf of an underlying table.

The INSERT statement has two general forms for passing the values for the input column list.

Use this form for inserting a list of constants:

```
INSERT INTO table-name | view-name (<list of columns>)
VALUES (<matching list of values>)
```

Use this form for inserting from an inline query:

```
INSERT INTO <table> (<list of columns>)
SELECT [[FIRST m] [SKIP n]] <matching list of values from another set>
[ORDER BY <in-line column[s]> [DESC]]
```

In the following example, an INSERT INTO clause defines an input set for TABLEB and a SELECT clause defines a corresponding inline query from TABLEA to supply values to the input set:

```
INSERT INTO TABLEB(COLA, COLB, COLC)
SELECT COL1, COL2, COL3 FROM TABLEA;
```

NOTE   It is not possible to insert into an inline query.

Inserting into BLOB Columns

The INSERT INTO … SELECT technique passes BLOBs to BLOBs directly. As a rule, if you need to insert BLOBs as part of a VALUES( ) list, they must be constructed in the client application using API functions and structures. In DSQL applications, they are usually passed as streams. The segment size can simply be disregarded except in ESQL applications.

However, if you are passing a VALUES( ) entry to a BLOB as text, Firebird will accept character strings as input, for example:

```
INSERT INTO ATABLE (BLOBMEMO)
  VALUES ('Now is the time for all good men to come to the aid of the party');
```

This capability will suit conditions where the text to be stored will never exceed 32,767 bytes (or 32,765, if you are reading a VARCHAR field into a BLOB). For many programming interfaces, the problem may seem a non-issue, because they cannot handle such large strings anyway. However, since Firebird will accept concatenated SQL string expressions, such as MYVARCHAR1 || MYVARCHAR2, it will be necessary to protect string inputs from overflows.

Inserting into ARRAY Columns

In embedded applications (ESQL), it is possible to construct a pre-compiled SQL statement to insert entire arrays into an array column. Errors can occur if the data does not exactly fill the array.

In DSQL, it is not possible to insert data into ARRAY columns at all. It is necessary to implement a custom method in application or component code that calls the API function *isc_array_put_slice*.

Using INSERT with Automatic Fields

Table definitions may have defined columns whose field values are populated with data automatically when a new row is inserted. This may happen in several ways:

- A column is defined by a COMPUTED BY clause.

- A column, or a domain under which it was defined, includes a DEFAULT clause.

- A BEFORE INSERT trigger has been added to the table to populate the column automatically.

Automatic fields may affect the way you formulate INSERT statements for the table.

COMPUTED BY Columns

Including a computed column in the input column list is not valid and will cause an exception, as illustrated by the following example:

```
CREATE TABLE EMPLOYEE (
  EMP_NO INTEGER NOT NULL PRIMARY KEY,
  FIRST_NAME VARCHAR(15),
  LAST_NAME VARCHAR(20),
  BIRTH_COUNTRY VARCHAR(30) DEFAULT 'TAIWAN',
  FULL_NAME COMPUTED BY FIRST_NAME || ' ' || LAST_NAME);
COMMIT;
INSERT INTO EMPLOYEE (EMP_NO, FIRST_NAME, LAST_NAME, FULL_NAME)
VALUES (99, 'Jiminy', 'Cricket', 'Jiminy Cricket');
```

Columns with Defaults

If a column has a default defined for it, the default will work only on inserts and only if the defaulted column is omitted from the input column list. If the statement in the previous example is corrected, it will cause 'TAIWAN' to be written to the BIRTH_COUNTRY column:

```
INSERT INTO EMPLOYEE (EMP_NO, FIRST_NAME, LAST_NAME)
VALUES (99, 'Jiminy', 'Cricket');
COMMIT;
```

```
SELECT * FROM EMPLOYEE WHERE EMP_NO = 99;

EMP_NO  FIRST_NAME  LAST_NAME  BIRTH_COUNTRY  FULL_NAME
======= =========== ========== ============== ===============
99      Jiminy      Cricket    Taiwan         Jiminy Cricket
```

Defaults do not kick in to replace NULLs:

```
INSERT INTO EMPLOYEE (EMP_NO, FIRST_NAME, LAST_NAME, BIRTH_COUNTRY)
VALUES (100, 'Maria', 'Callas', NULL);
COMMIT;
SELECT * FROM EMPLOYEE WHERE EMP_NO = 100;

EMP_NO  FIRST_NAME  LAST_NAME  BIRTH_COUNTRY  FULL_NAME
======= =========== ========== ============== ===============
100     Maria       Callas                    Maria Callas
```

If you are developing applications using components that generate INSERT statements from the column specifications of the datasets' SELECT statements—for example, Delphi and JBuilder—be especially aware of this behavior. If your component does not support a method to get the server defaults, it may be necessary to customize the update statement that it uses to perform an insert from a dataset.

BEFORE INSERT Triggers

When inserting into a table that uses triggers to populate certain columns automatically, make sure you omit those columns from your input list if you want to ensure that the trigger will do its work.

This is not to say that you must always omit triggered fields from input lists. A trigger that is designed to provide a value in case no value is supplied by INSERT statements is highly recommended, to bombproof data integrity—especially where multiple applications and tools are used to access your databases. The trigger should test the input for certain conditions (NULL, for example) and do its stuff according to the conditions.

In the following example, the primary key, OID, is populated by a trigger:

```
CREATE TABLE AIRCRAFT (
  OID INTEGER NOT NULL,
  REGISTRATION VARCHAR(8) NOT NULL,
  CONSTRAINT PK_AIRCRAFT
    PRIMARY KEY (OID));
COMMIT;
/**/
SET TERM ^;
CREATE TRIGGER BI_AIRCRAFT FOR AIRCRAFT
ACTIVE BEFORE INSERT POSITION 0
AS
BEGIN
```

```
    IF (NEW.OID IS NULL) THEN
       NEW.OID = GEN_ID(ANYGEN, 1);
END ^
SET TERM ;^
COMMIT;
/**/
INSERT INTO AIRCRAFT (REGISTRATION)
SELECT FIRST 3 SKIP 2 REGISTRATION FROM AIRCRAFT_OLD
ORDER BY REGISTRATION;
COMMIT;
```

In this case, the trigger fetches the generator value for the primary key, because no value was passed in the input list for it. However, because the trigger was set up to do this only when it detects NULL, the following INSERT statement will work just fine, too—provided, of course, that the value supplied for OID does not violate the unique constraint on the PK:

```
INSERT IN AIRCRAFT (OID, REGISTRATION)
VALUES(1033, 'ECHIDNA');
```

When would you do this? Surprisingly often, in Firebird. When implementing master-detail structures, you can secure the primary key of the master row from its generator *before* that row is posted to the database, by a simple DSQL call:

```
SELECT GEN_ID(YOURGENERATOR, 1) FROM RDB$DATABASE;
```

Generators operate outside transaction control and, once you have that number, it is yours. You can apply it to the foreign key column of the detail rows in client buffers, as you create them, without posting a master record to the database. If the user decides to cancel the work, there is nothing to "undo" on the server. If you have ever struggled to achieve this kind of capability with a DBMS that uses an autoincrement or "identity" type, you will learn to love this feature.

For more angles on this technique, see Chapter 31.

The UPDATE Statement

The UPDATE statement is used for changing the values in columns in existing rows of tables. It can also operate on tables through cursor sets and updatable views. SQL does not allow a single UPDATE statement to target rows in multiple tables.

Refer to Chapter 24 for a discussion of views that can accept updates on behalf of an underlying table. An UPDATE query that modifies only the current row of a cursor is known as a *positioned* update. One that may update multiple rows is known as a *searched* update.

Positioned vs. Searched Operations

UPDATE and DELETE statements may be *positioned* (targeted at one and only one row) or *searched* (targeted at zero or more rows). Strictly speaking, a positioned update can occur only in the context of the current row of a cursor operation, while a searched update, optionally limited by the search conditions in a WHERE clause, occurs in all other contexts.

Most dataset component interfaces *emulate* the positioned update or delete by using a searched update with a uniquely targeted WHERE clause. These unidirectional or scrolling dataset classes maintain a "current row buffer" that stores or links to the column and key values for the row that the user task has selected for an operation. When the user is ready to post an UPDATE or DELETE request, the component constructs a searched UPDATE or DELETE statement that targets one database row uniquely by using the primary key (or some other unique column list) in the WHERE clause.

 CAUTION   Not all component interfaces have the "smarts" to detect duplicate rows in supposedly "live" buffers. In these products, it is up to the developer to ensure uniqueness or to find some other way to prevent the application from unexpectedly updating multiple rows.

Using the UPDATE Statement

The UPDATE statement has the following general form:

```
UPDATE table-name | view-name
SET column-name = value [,column-name = value ...]
[WHERE <search conditions> | WHERE CURRENT OF cursor-name]
```

For searched updates, if a WHERE clause is not specified, the update will be performed on every row in the table.

The SET Clause

The syntax pattern for the SET clause is

```
SET column-name = value [,column-name = value ...]
```

The SET clause is a comma-separated list that identifies each column for modification, along with the new value to be assigned to it. The new value must be of the correct type and size for the column's definition. If a column is nullable, it can also be set to NULL instead of a value.

A value can be

- A constant value of the correct type (e.g., SET COLUMNB = '99'). If the column is a character type of a specified character set that is different from the character set of the connection, an update value can be forced to that special character set by including the appropriate *character set introducer* to the left of the constant string. A character set introducer is the character set name prefixed with an underscore symbol, for example:

```
SET COLUMNY = _ISO8859_1 'fricassée'
```

- The identifier of another column in the same table, provided it is of the correct type. For example, SET COLUMNB = COLUMNX will replace the current value of COLUMNB with the current value of COLUMNX. A character set introducer (see the previous item) can be used if appropriate.

- An expression. For example, SET REVIEW_DATE = REVIEW_DATE + 14 updates a date column to 2 weeks later than its current value. For details about expressions, refer to the next chapter.

- A server context variable (e.g., SET DATE_CHANGED = CURRENT_DATE). Context variables are discussed and listed in Chapter 8.

- A parameter placeholder symbol appropriate to the syntax implemented in the application code (e.g., from Delphi, SET LAST_NAME = :LAST_NAME, or from another application interface, SET LAST_NAME = ?).

- An SQL or user-defined function (UDF) call. For example, SET BCOLUMN = UPPER(ACOLUMN) uses the internal SQL function UPPER to transform the value of ACOLUMN to uppercase and store the result in BCOLUMN. For information about using functions, refer to the next chapter.

A COLLATE clause can be included when modifying character (but not BLOB) columns, if appropriate. For most character sets, it would be necessary to use one in the previous example, since the default (binary) collation sequence does not usually support the UPPER() function. For example, if ACOLUMN and BCOLUMN are in character set ISO8859_1, and the language is Spanish, the SET clause should be

```
SET BCOLUMN = UPPER(ACOLUMN) COLLATION ES_ES
```

For details about character sets and collations, refer to Chapter 11.

Value Switching

Take care when "switching" values between columns. A clause like

```
...
SET COLUMNA = COLUMNB
```

will cause the current value in COLUMNA to be overwritten by the current value in COLUMNB immediately. If you then do

```
SET COLUMNB = COLUMNA
```

the old value of COLUMNA is gone and the value of COLUMNB and COLUMNA will stay the same as they were after the first switch.

To switch the values, you would need a third column in which to "park" the value of COLUMNA until you were ready to assign it to COLUMNB:

```
...
SET
  COLUMNC = COLUMNA,
  COLUMNA = COLUMNB,
  COLUMNB = COLUMNC
...
```

You can use expressions with SET so, if switching two integer values, it is possible to "work" the switch by performing arithmetic on the two values. For example, suppose COLUMNA is 10 and COLUMNB is 9:

```
...
SET
  COLUMNB = COLUMNB + COLUMNA, /* COLUMNB is now 19 */
  COLUMNA = COLUMNB - COLUMNA, /* COLUMNA is now 9 */
  COLUMNB = COLUMNB - COLUMNA  /* COLUMNB is now 10 */
...
```

Always test your assumptions when performing switch assignments!

Updating BLOB Columns

Updating a BLOB column actually replaces the old BLOB with a completely new one. The old BLOB_ID does not survive the update. Also

- It is not possible to update a BLOB by concatenating another BLOB or a string to the existing BLOB.

- A text BLOB can be set using a string as input. For example, MEMO in the next example is a text BLOB:

```
UPDATE ATABLE
  SET MEMO = 'Friends, Romans, countrymen, lend me your ears:
  I come not to bury Caesar, but to praise him.';
```

CAUTION Remember that, although BLOBs are unlimited in size, string types are limited to 32,765 bytes (VARCHAR) or 32,767 bytes (CHAR)—that is bytes, not characters. Take care with concatenations and multi-byte character sets.

Updating ARRAY Columns

In embedded applications (ESQL), it is possible to construct a pre-compiled SQL statement to pass slices of arrays to update (replace) corresponding slices in stored arrays.

It is not possible to update ARRAY columns in DSQL at all. To update arrays, it is necessary to implement a custom method in application or component code that calls the API function *isc_array_put_slice*.

Column Defaults

Column DEFAULT constraints are *never* considered when UPDATE statements are processed.

The DELETE Statement

The DELETE query is used for deleting whole rows from a table. SQL does not allow a single DELETE statement to erase rows in more than one table. A DELETE query that modifies only the current row of a cursor is known as a *positioned* delete. One that may delete multiple rows is known as a *searched* delete. The DELETE statement has the following general form:

```
DELETE FROM table-name
[WHERE <search predicates> | WHERE CURRENT OF cursor-name]
```

If a WHERE clause is not specified, every row in the table will be deleted.

The EXECUTE Statement

The EXECUTE statement is available only in ESQL. It is used in embedded applications to execute a previously prepared dynamic SQL statement. This is in contrast with regular DML statements in ESQL, which are pre-compiled and hence are not prepared at runtime.

 NOTE Don't confuse the EXECUTE statement with the EXECUTE STATEMENT statement syntax that is provided in PSQL extensions from Firebird 1.5 onward and the EXECUTE PROCEDURE statement in DSQL (introduced next in the section "Executable Procedures").

Queries That Call Stored Procedures

Firebird supports two styles of stored procedures: *executable* and *selectable*. For details about the differences in technique for writing and using these procedure styles, refer to Chapters 28, 29, and 30.

Executable Procedures

In DSQL, EXECUTE PROCEDURE executes (calls) an *executable stored procedure*—that is, a stored procedure designed to perform some operations on the server, optionally returning a single line of one or more return values. The statement for executing such a procedure has the following general format:

```
EXECUTE PROCEDURE procedure-name [(<list of input values>)]
```

The following simple example illustrates calling an executable procedure that accepts two input arguments, performs some operations on the server, and exits:

```
EXECUTE PROCEDURE DO_IT(49, '25-DEC-2004');
```

In applications, it is more powerful to use parameters (see the section "Using Parameters") in query statements that execute stored procedures, for example:

```
EXECUTE PROCEDURE DO_IT(:IKEY, :REPORT DATE);
```

or

```
EXECUTE PROCEDURE DO_IT(?, ?);
```

Selectable Procedures

A selectable stored procedure is capable of returning a multi-row set of data in response to a specialized SELECT statement form, as follows:

```
SELECT <list of output columns>
FROM procedure-name [(<list of input values>)]
[WHERE <search predicates>]
[ORDER BY <list drawn from output columns>]
```

In the following PSQL fragment, a stored procedure is defined to accept a single key as an input argument and return a set of rows. The RETURNS clause defines the output set:

```
CREATE PROCEDURE GET_COFFEE_TABLE (IKEY INTEGER)
RETURNS (
```

```
      BRAND_ID INTEGER,
      VARIETY_NAME VARCHAR(40),
      COUNTRY_OF_ORIGIN VARCHAR(30))
AS ..........
```

The application selects the output set from the stored procedure as follows:

```
SELECT BRAND_ID, VARIETY_NAME, COUNTRY_OF_ORIGIN
FROM GET_COFFEE_TABLE(5002);
```

This is the same example, with the input argument parameterized:

```
SELECT BRAND_ID, VARIETY_NAME, COUNTRY_OF_ORIGIN
FROM GET_COFFEE_TABLE(:IKEY);/* Delphi */
```

or

```
SELECT BRAND_ID, VARIETY_NAME, COUNTRY_OF_ORIGIN
FROM GET_COFFEE_TABLE(?);
```

Using Parameters

A "non-parameterized" query uses constants in expressions for search conditions. For example, in this query

```
SELECT MAX(COST * QUANTITY) AS BEST_SALE
  FROM SALES
  WHERE SALES_DATE > '31.12.2003' ;
```

the query is asked to operate on all of the rows in SALES that have a SALES_DATE later than the last day of 2003.

Data access interfaces that implement the Firebird API have the capability to process the constants in search conditions as *replaceable parameters*. The API allows a statement to be submitted to the server as a kind of template that represents these parameters as placeholders. The client request asks for the statement to be *prepared*— by obtaining syntax and metadata validation—without actually executing it.

A DSQL application can set up a statement with dynamic search conditions in the WHERE clause, have it prepared once, and then assign values to the parameters one or many times, just before each execution. This capability is sometimes referred to as *late binding*. Application interfaces vary in the way they surface late parameter binding to the host language. Depending on the interface you use for application development, a parameterized version of the last example may look something like the following:

```
SELECT MAX(COST * QUANTITY) AS BEST_SALE
  FROM SALES
  WHERE SALES_DATE > ? ;
```

The replaceable parameter in this example allows the application to prepare the statement and capture from the user (or some other part of the application) the actual date on which the query is to be filtered. The same query can be run repeatedly, within the same transaction or in successive transactions, with a variety of dates, without needing to be prepared again.

The API "knows" the order and format of multiple parameters because the application interface passes descriptive structures, XSQLDAs, that contain an array of SQLVARs, the variable descriptors that describe each parameter, and other data describing the array as a whole.

Delphi and some other object-oriented API implementations use the methods and properties of classes to hide the machinery used for creating and managing the raw statement and the descriptors internally. Other interfaces code the structures closer to the surface. The statement is passed to the server with a format like the following:

```
INSERT INTO DATATABLE(DATA1, DATA2, DATA3, DATA4, DATA5,....more columns)
VALUES (?, '?', '?', ?, ?, ....more values);
```

If parameters are implemented in your application programming language, or can be, then it is highly recommended to make use of them.

Note for Delphi Users

Delphi, having been "made in Borland" like Firebird's InterBase ancestors, implements a format that mimics that used in PSQL to refer to the values of local variables in SQL statements and in ESQL to pass host variables. It requires all parameters to be explicitly named and prefixed with the colon symbol. In Delphi, the preceding simple example would be expressed in the SQL property of a data access object as follows:

```
SELECT MAX(COST * QUANTITY) AS BEST_SALE
  FROM SALES
  WHERE SALES_DATE > :SALES_DATE ;
```

Once the Prepare call has validated the statement and passed the metadata description back to the client application, the data access object then lets the latest value be assigned to the parameter using a local method that converts the value to the format required by Firebird:

```
aQuery.ParamByName ('SALES_DATE').AsDate := ALocalDateVariable;
```

Batch Operations

It is a very common requirement to perform a task that inserts, updates, or deletes many rows in a single operation. For example, an application reads a data file from a device and massages it into INSERT statements for posting to a database table, or a replication service processes batches of changes between satellite and parent databases. Many similar statements are posted within a single transaction, usually by means of a prepared statement and replaceable runtime parameters.

Batch Inserts

A statement for a batch insert may look something like this:

```
INSERT INTO DATATABLE(DATA1, DATA2, DATA3, DATA4, DATA5,....more columns)
VALUES ('x', 'y', 'z', 99, '2004-12-25', ....more values);
```

Using parameters, it looks like this:

```
INSERT INTO DATATABLE(DATA1, DATA2, DATA3, DATA4, DATA5,....more columns)
VALUES (?, '?', '?', ?, ?, ....more values);
```

Often, a stored procedure will be the most elegant way to set up a repeatable batch operation, especially if there is a requirement to transform data en route to the database table or to insert rows into multiple tables.

Preventing Slowdown on Batches

Two behaviors can cause huge batches to get progressively slower during execution.

- The maintenance of indexes, which adds work to the task and also tends to distort the geometry of the index trees.

- The accumulation of *back versions*, the deltas of the old rows that are marked for obsolescence once the update or delete operations are committed. Back versions do not become available for garbage collection until the transaction completes. In transactions involving back versions numbering in the tens to hundreds of thousands (or more), garbage collection may never win its battle to clean out obsolete versions. Under these conditions, only a backup and restore will sanitize the database completely.

Deactivating Indexes

A strategy for mitigating batch slowdown when other users are not accessing the input table is to deactivate the secondary indexes. This is simple to do:

```
ALTER INDEX index-name INACTIVE;
```

When the large batch operation is finished, reactivate and rebuild the indexes:

```
ALTER INDEX index-name ACTIVE;
```

Partitioning Large Batches

Unfortunately, you cannot disable the indexes that enforce primary and foreign keys without dropping the actual constraints. Often, it will be impracticable to drop constraints because of chained dependencies. For this reason and others, judicious partitioning of the task is recommended to help offset both the deterioration of index balance and the generation of an unnecessarily large number of new database pages.

When posting large numbers of inserts in batch, it is preferable to partition them into groups and commit work about every 5,000–10,000 rows. The actual size of an optimal partition will vary according to the size of the row and the database page size. Optimal groups may be smaller or larger than this range.

TIP   When you need to partition huge batches, a stored procedure is often the way to go. You can make use of local counter variables, event messages, and return values to keep completing procedure calls in sync with the calling client.

DML Operations and State-Changing Events

Firebird incorporates some features that can be implemented in database design to respond to DML operations that change the state of data, namely the posting of INSERT, UPDATE, and DELETE statements.

Referential Integrity Action Clauses

Referential integrity triggers are modules of compiled code created by the engine when you define referential integrity constraints for your tables. By including ON UPDATE and ON DELETE *action clauses* in FOREIGN KEY constraint declarations, you can specify one of a selection of pre-defined response actions that will occur when these DML events execute. For details, refer to Chapter 17.

Custom Triggers

With custom triggers (those you write yourself using the PSQL language), you have the capability to specify exactly what is to happen when the server receives a request to insert, change, or delete rows in tables. Custom triggers can be applied not just to the update and delete events, but also to inserts. Triggers can include exception handling, feedback, and (in Firebird 1.5) custom query plans.

DML Event Phases

Trigger syntax splits the custom DML actions into two phases: the first phase occurs *before* the event, and the second occurs *after* the event.

- The BEFORE phase makes it possible to manipulate and transform the values that are input by the DML statement and to define defaults with much more flexibility than is permitted by the standard SQL DEFAULT constraint. The BEFORE phase completes before any column, table, or integrity constraints are tested.

- In the AFTER phase, response actions can be performed on other tables. Usually, such actions involve inserting to, updating, or deleting from these other tables, using the NEW and OLD variables to provide the *context* of the current row and operation. The AFTER phase begins after all of the owning table's constraints have been applied. AFTER triggers cannot change values in the current row of the owning table.

Table 20-1 describes the six phases/events of custom triggers.

Table 20-1. The Six Phases/Events of Custom Triggers

INSERTING	UPDATING	DELETING
BEFORE INSERT	BEFORE UPDATE	BEFORE DELETE
AFTER INSERT	AFTER UPDATE	AFTER DELETE

NEW and OLD Context Variables

The server makes two sets of context variables available to triggers. One consists of all the field values of the current row, as they were in the current row just before the row was last posted. The identifiers for this set consist of the word "OLD." prefixed to each column identifier. In the same manner, all of the new values have "NEW." prefixed to each column identifier. Of course, "OLD." is meaningless in an insert trigger and "NEW." is meaningless in a delete trigger.

Multi-action Triggers

From Firebird 1.5 onward, you can optionally write triggers with conditioned logic to roll all of the events (insert, update, and delete) for one phase—BEFORE or AFTER—into one trigger module. This is a long-awaited enhancement that can save up to two-thirds of the coding of triggers.

Multiple Triggers per Event

Another useful option is the ability to have multiple triggers for each phase/event combination. CREATE TRIGGER syntax includes the keyword POSITION, taking an integer argument that can be used to set the zero-based firing order of multiple triggers within a phase.

For detailed instructions, syntax, and language extensions for creating triggers, refer to Chapter 31.

Up Next

DML draws its real power from its ability to use expressions to search stored data and to transform abstract data into output that is meaningful to end users as *information*. The next chapter explores the logic of expression usage in SQL, along with the internal and external functions you can use to build simple or complex algorithms to effect the transformations you need.

CHAPTER 21

Expressions and Predicates

IN ALGEBRA, AN EXPRESSION SUCH AS $a + b = c$ can be resolved as "true" or "false" by substituting constant values into a, b, and c. Alternatively, given values for any two of a, b, or c, we can calculate the missing value. So it is with SQL expressions because, simply, they are substitution formulae.

SQL expressions provide formal shorthand methods for calculating, transforming, and comparing values. In this chapter we take a close look at the ways and means of expressions in Firebird SQL.

The latter part of this chapter is a comprehensive reference to the internal SQL functions available in Firebird for building expressions, along with the most common external functions.

Expressions

Storing data in its plainest, most abstract state is what databases do. The retrieval language—in Firebird's case, this is usually SQL—combines with the database engine to provide an armory of ready-made formulae into which actual data can be substituted at runtime to transform these pieces of abstract data into information that is meaningful to humans.

To take a simple example, a table, Membership, has the columns FIRST_NAME, LAST_NAME, and DATE_OF_BIRTH. To get a list of members' full names and birthdays, we can use a statement containing expressions to transform the stored data:

```
SELECT
  FIRST_NAME ||' '||LAST_NAME AS FULL_NAME,
  EXTRACT(MONTH FROM DATE_OF_BIRTH)||'/'||EXTRACT (DAY FROM DATE_OF_BIRTH)
    AS BIRTHDAY
FROM MEMBERSHIP
WHERE FIRST_NAME IS NOT NULL AND LAST_NAME IS NOT NULL
ORDER BY 2;
```

At the time we send this request to the server, we do not know what the stored values are. However, we know what they should be like (their semantic values and data types), and that is sufficient for us to construct expressions to retrieve a list that is meaningful in the ways we want it to be.

In this single statement we make use of three different kinds of SQL expressions:

- For the first field, FULL_NAME, the *concatenation operator* (in SQL, the double-pipe || symbol) is used to construct an expression that joins two database fields into one, separated by a space.

- For the second field, BIRTHDAY, a *function* is used to extract first the month and then the day of the month from the date field. In the same expression, the concatenation operator is again used, to tie the extracted numbers together as a birthday, the day and month separated by a slash.

- For the search condition, the WHERE clause uses another kind of expression, *a logical predicate*, to test for eligible rows in the table. Rows that failed this test would not be returned in the output.

In the example, expressions were used

- To transform data for retrieval as an output column.

- To set search conditions in a WHERE clause for a SELECT statement. The same approach can be used also for searched UPDATE and DELETE statements.

Other contexts in which expressions can be used include

- To set validation conditions in CHECK constraints

- To define COMPUTED BY columns in CREATE TABLE and ALTER TABLE definitions

- To transform or create input data in the process of storing them in a table using INSERT or UPDATE statements

- To decide the ordering or grouping of output sets

- To set runtime conditions to determine output

- To condition the flow of control in PSQL modules

Predicates

A *predicate* is simply an expression that asserts a fact about a value. SQL statements generally test predicates in WHERE clauses and CASE expressions. ON is the test for JOIN predicates; HAVING tests attributes in grouped output. In PSQL, flow-of-control statements test predicates in IF, WHILE, and WHEN clauses. Decisions are made according to whether the predicates are evaluated as true or false.

Strictly speaking, a predicate can be true, false, or not proven. For SQL purposes, false and not proven results are rolled together and treated as if all were false. In effect, "If it is not true, then it is false."

The standard SQL language has formal specifications for a number of *expression operators* that are recognized as necessary for constructing search predicates. A predicate consists of three basic elements: two comparable values and an operator that *predicates* the assertion to be tested on the pair of values.

All of the operators included in Table 21-1 (which appears later in the chapter) can be predicate operators. The values involved with the predicate can be simple or they can be extremely complex, nested expressions. As long as it is possible for the expressions being compared to melt down to constant values for the test, they will be valid, no matter how complex.

Take this simple statement where the equivalence operator = is used to test for exact matches:

```
SELECT * FROM EMPLOYEE
WHERE LAST_NAME = 'Smith';
```

The predicate is "that the value in the column LAST_NAME is 'Smith'." Two constants (the current column value and a string literal) are compared to test the assertion that they are equal. Taking each row in the Employee table, the engine will discard any where the predicate is either false (the value is something other than 'Smith') or not proven (the column has NULL, so it cannot be determined whether it is 'Smith' or a value that is not 'Smith').

The Truth Testers

The syntax elements that test the truth or non-truth of an assertion form a no-name paradigm of "truth testers" or "condition testers." They all test predicates. They are

- **In DDL**: CHECK, for testing validation conditions

- **In SQL**: WHERE (for search conditions), HAVING and NOT HAVING (for group selection conditions), ON (for join conditions), and the multi-conditional case testers CASE, COALESCE, and NULLIF

- **In PSQL**: IF (the universal true/false tester), WHILE (for testing loop conditions), and WHEN (for testing exception codes)

Assertions

Often, the condition being tested by WHERE, IF, and so on is not a single predicate, but a cluster of several predicates, each of which, when resolved, contributes to the truth or otherwise the ultimate assertion. The assertion might be a single predicate, or it might contain multiple predicates logically associated by AND or OR within it, which themselves might nest predicates. Resolution of an assertion to the ultimate true or false result is a process that works from the inner predicates outward. Each "level" must be resolved in precedence order, until it becomes possible to test the overall assertion.

In the next set of search conditions, the assertion tested encloses two conditions. The keyword AND ties the two predicates to each other, causing the ultimate assertion to be that both predicates must be true in order for the whole assertion to be true:

```
SELECT * FROM EMPLOYEE
WHERE (
  (HIRE_DATE > CURRENT_DATE - 366)
  AND (SALARY BETWEEN 25000.00 AND 39999.99));
```

Rows where one assertion is true but the other is false will be discarded.

The first predicate, (HIRE_DATE > CURRENT_DATE - 366), uses an expression consisting of a variable and a calculation to establish the value that is to be tested against the column value. In this case, the assertion uses a different *operator*—the comparison is not that the column value and the resolved value of the expression be equal, but that the column value be *greater than* that value.

The second predicate uses a different operator again. The BETWEEN symbol implements the test "greater than or equal to the value on the left AND less than or equal to the value on the right."

The parentheses here are not obligatory, although, in many complex expressions, parentheses must be used to specify the order of precedence for evaluation of both expressions and the predicates. In situations where a series of predicates is to be tested, choosing to parenthesize predicates even where it is optional can be helpful for documentation and debugging.

Deciding What Is True

Figure 21-1 depicts the possible results of the two predicates in the previous example.

In our example, (HIRE_DATE > CURRENT_DATE - 366) is tested first, because it is the leftmost predicate. If it nested any predicates, those would be evaluated first. There is no test for NULL in either of the predicates, but it is included here to illustrate that a null ("not known") encountered in the test data will cause a result of *false* because it cannot return *true*. Predicates must be provably true in order to be true.

If NULL occurs in HIRE_DATE, testing will stop immediately and return *false*.[1] The AND association causes that: Logically, two predicates conjoined by AND cannot be true if one is false, so there is nothing to gain by continuing on to test the second predicate.

---

1. This is a "shortcut" Boolean evaluation, as implemented in Firebird 1.5 onward. Firebird 1.0.*x* uses full Boolean evaluation. For those who love inventing abstruse assertions, the old method can be resurrected using the configuration parameter *FullBooleanEvaluation*.

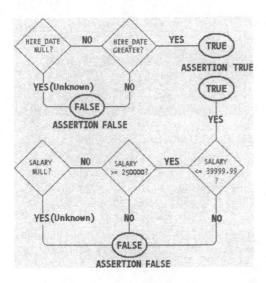

Figure 21-1. Truth evaluation

If the data being tested is not null, the next test is whether it is true that the value is greater than the test condition. If not, testing finishes here. In other words, NULL and *false* have the same effect because neither is true.

If the first predicate is true, a similar process of elimination occurs with the second predicate. Only when that is all done can the ultimate assertion be evaluated.

Symbols Used in Expressions

Table 21-1 describes the symbols that can appear in SQL expressions.

Table 21-1. Elements of SQL Expressions

ELEMENT	DESCRIPTION
Column names	Identifiers of columns from specified tables representing a field value to be used in a calculation or comparison, or as a search condition. Any database column can be referred to in an expression except columns of ARRAY types. (Exception: An array column can be tested for IS [NOT] NULL.)
Array elements	Array elements can be referred to in an expression.
Output-only column names	Identifiers provided for runtime computed columns or as aliases for database columns.
The keyword AS	Used (optionally) as a marker for the name of an output-only column in SELECT column lists.
Arithmetic operators	The symbols +, –, *, and /, used to calculate and evaluate values.

continued

Table 21-1. Elements of SQL Expressions (continued)

ELEMENT	DESCRIPTION
Logical operators	The reserved words NOT, AND, and OR, used in simple search conditions or to combine simple search conditions to form complex predicates.
Comparison operators	<, >, <=, >=, =, and <>, used for predicating assertions about pairs of values.
Other comparison operators	LIKE, STARTING WITH, CONTAINING, BETWEEN, and IS [NOT] NULL.
Existential operators	Predicators used for determining the existence of a value in a set. IN can be used with sets of constants or with scalar subqueries. EXISTS, SINGULAR, ALL, ANY, and SOME can be used only with subqueries.
Concatenation operator	The pair of pipe symbols (ASCII 124) ||, used to combine character strings. Note that + and & are not valid string concatenators in standard SQL.
Constants	Hard-coded numbers or single-quoted literals, such as 507 or 'Tokyo' that can be involved in calculations and comparisons or output as runtime fields.
Date literals	Stringlike quoted expressions that will be interpreted as date, time, or date-time values in EXTRACT, SELECT, INSERT, and UPDATE operations. Date literals can be the pre-defined literals ('TODAY', 'NOW', 'YESTERDAY', 'TOMORROW') or acceptable date and time strings, as described in Chapter 10. In dialect 3, date literals usually need to be CAST as a valid date/time type when used in EXTRACT and SELECT expressions.
Internal context variables	Variables retrievable from the server that return context-dependent values such as the server clock time or the ID of the current transaction.
Subqueries	Inline SELECT statements that return single (scalar) values for runtime output or for a comparison in a predicate.
Local variables	Named stored procedure, trigger, or (in ESQL) application program variables containing values that will vary during execution.
Function identifiers	Identifiers of internal or external functions, in function expressions.
CAST(value AS type)	Function expressions explicitly casting a value of one data type to another data type.
Conditional expressions	Functions predicating two or more mutually exclusive conditions for a single column, beginning with the keyword CASE, COALESCE, or NULLIF.
Parentheses	Used to group expressions into hierarchies. Operations inside parentheses are performed before operations outside them. When parentheses are nested, the contents of the innermost set are evaluated first and evaluation proceeds outward.
COLLATE clause	Can be used with CHAR and VARCHAR values to force string comparisons to use a specific collation sequence.

SQL Operators

Firebird SQL syntax includes operators for comparing and evaluating columns, constants, variables, and embedded expressions to produce distinct assertions.

Precedence of Operators

Precedence determines the order in which operators and the values they affect are evaluated in an expression.

When an expression contains several operators of the same type, those operators are evaluated from left to right unless there is a conflict where two operators of the same type affect the same values. When there is a conflict, operator precedence within the type determines the order of evaluation. Table 21-2 lists the precedence of Firebird operator types, from highest to lowest.

Table 21-2. Operator Type Precedence

OPERATOR TYPE	PRECEDENCE	EXPLANATION
Concatenation	1	Strings are concatenated before all other operations take place.
Arithmetic	2	Arithmetic is performed after string concatenation, but before comparison and logical operations.
Comparison	3	Comparison operations are evaluated after string concatenation and arithmetic, but before logical operations.
Logical	4	Logical operations are evaluated after all other operations. **Precedence:** When search conditions are combined, the order of evaluation is determined by precedence of the operators that connect them. A NOT condition is evaluated before AND, and AND is evaluated before OR. Parentheses can be used to change the order of evaluation.

Concatenation Operator

The concatenation operator || combines two character strings to produce a single string. Character strings can be constants or values retrieved from a column:

```
SELECT Last_name ||', ' || First_Name AS Full_Name FROM Membership;
```

NOTE   Firebird is more particular about string overflow than its forebears. It will check the lengths of input columns and block concatenation if the aggregate width would potentially exceed the limit for a VARCHAR (32,765 bytes).

Arithmetic Operators

Arithmetic expressions are evaluated from left to right, except when ambiguities arise. In these cases, arithmetic operations are evaluated according to the precedence specified in Table 21-3. For example, multiplications are performed before divisions, and divisions are performed before subtractions.

Arithmetic operations are always performed before comparison and logical operations. To change or force the order of evaluation, group operations in parentheses.

Table 21-3. Arithmetic Operator Precedence

OPERATOR	PURPOSE	PRECEDENCE
*	Multiplication	1
/	Division	2
+	Addition	3
–	Subtraction	4

The following example illustrates how a complex calculation would be nested to ensure that the expression would be computed in the correct, unambiguous order:

```
...
SET COLUMN_A = 1/((COLUMN_B * COLUMN_C/4) - ((COLUMN_D / 10) + 28))
```

The engine will detect syntax errors—such as unbalanced parentheses and embedded expressions that do not produce a result—but it cannot detect logic errors or ambiguities that are correct syntactically. Very complicated nested calculations should be worked out on paper. To simplify the process of composing these predicates, always start by isolating the innermost operation and working "toward the outside," testing predicates with a calculator at each step.

Comparison Operators

Comparison operators test a specific relationship between a value to the left of the operator, and a value or range of values to the right of the operator. Every test predicates a result that can be either true or false. Rules of precedence apply to evaluation, as indicated in Table 21-4.

Comparisons that encounter NULL on either the left or right side of the operator *always* follow SQL rules of logic and evaluate the result of the comparison as NULL and return false, for example:

```
IF (YEAR_OF_BIRTH < 1950)
```

This returns false if YEAR_OF_BIRTH is 1950 or later or is NULL.

For more discussion of NULL, refer to the upcoming section "Considering NULL."

Value pairs compared can be columns, constants, or calculated expressions,[2] and they must resolve to the same data type. The CAST( ) function can be used to translate a value to a compatible data type for comparison.

Table 21-4. Comparison Operator Precedence

OPERATOR	PURPOSE	PRECEDENCE
=	Is equal to, identical to	1
<>, !=, ~=, ^=	Is not equal to	2
>	Is greater than	3
<	Is less than	4
>=	Is greater than or equal to	5
<=	Is less than or equal to	6
!>, ~>, ^>	Is not greater than	7
!<, ~<, ^<	Is not less than	8

Arithmetical predicates using these symbols need no explanation. However, string tests can use them as well. Tests using the = and <> comparisons are clear enough. The following statement uses the >= operator to return all rows where LAST_NAME is equal to the test string and also where LAST_NAME evaluates as alphanumerically "greater":

```
SELECT * FROM EMPLOYEE
WHERE LAST_NAME >= 'Smith';
```

There is no 'Smith' in Employee, but the query returns 'Stansbury', 'Steadman', and so on, right through to 'Young'. The Employee database in the example uses default character set NONE, in which lowercase characters take precedence over uppercase characters. In our example, 'SMITH' would not be selected because the search string 'SM' (83 + 77) evaluates as less than 'Sm' (83 + 109).

Character Sets and Collations

Alphanumeric sequence is determined at two levels: character set and collation sequence. Each character set has its own, unique rules of precedence and, when an alternative collation sequence is in use, the rules of the collation sequence override those of the character set.

The default collation sequence for any character set—that is, the one whose name matches that of the character set—is binary. The binary collation sequence is determined to ascend according to the numeric code of the character in the system in which it is encoded (ASCII, ANSI, Unicode, etc.). Alternative collation sequences typically override the default order to comply with the rules of the locale or with special rules, such as case insensitivity or dictionary orderings.

---

2. The Firebird comparison operators support comparing the left-side value with the result of a scalar subquery (inline query) on the right side of the operator. For more details on this subject, see the section "Existential Queries" later in this chapter and the discussion of subqueries in the next chapter.

Other Comparison Predicators

The predicators BETWEEN, CONTAINING, LIKE, and STARTING WITH, summarized in Table 21-5, have equal precedence in evaluations, behind the comparison operators listed in Table 21-4. When they conflict with one another they are evaluated strictly from left to right.

Table 21-5. Other Comparison Predicators

PREDICATOR	PURPOSE
BETWEEN...AND...	Value falls within an inclusive range of values.
CONTAINING	String value contains specified string. The comparison is case insensitive.
IN	Value is present in the given set.[†]
LIKE	Equals a specified string, with wildcard substitution.
STARTING WITH	String value begins with a specified string.

[†] This is most efficient when the set is a small group of constants. The set cannot exceed 1,500 members. See also the upcoming section "Existential Predicates."

BETWEEN takes two arguments of compatible data types separated by the keyword AND. The lower value must be the first argument. If not, the query will find no rows matching the predicate. The search is inclusive—that is, values matching both arguments will be included in the returned set, for example:

```
SELECT * FROM EMPLOYEE
  WHERE HIRE_DATE BETWEEN '01.01.1992' AND CURRENT_TIMESTAMP;
```

BETWEEN will use an ascending index on the searched column if there is one available.

CONTAINING searches a string or string-like type looking for a sequence of characters that matches its argument. By some internal magic, it can be used for an alphanumeric (string-like) search on numbers and dates. A CONTAINING search is case insensitive.

The following example

```
SELECT * FROM PROJECT
  WHERE PROJ_NAME CONTAINING 'Map';
```

returns two rows for the projects 'AutoMap' and 'MapBrowser port'. This example

```
SELECT * FROM SALARY_HISTORY
  WHERE CHANGE_DATE CONTAINING 93;
```

returns all rows where the date is in the year 1993.

CAUTION   In some releases, CONTAINING is unpredictable when used with BLOBs of more than 1024 bytes. It was recognized as a bug and fixed soon after the v.1.5 release.

IN takes a list of values as an argument and returns all rows where the column value on the left side matches *any value* in the set, for example:

```
SELECT * FROM EMPLOYEE
  WHERE FIRST_NAME IN('Pete', 'Ann', 'Roger');
```

NULL cannot be included in the search set.

IN( ) can be made to form its own argument list from a subquery that returns single-column rows. For details, see the section "Existential Predicates" later in this chapter.

CAUTION   It is a common "newbie" mistake to treat the predicate "IN(<value>)" as if it were equivalent to "= <value>" because the two are logically equivalent, insofar as both return the same result. However, IN( ) does not use an index. Since equality searches are usually better optimized by an index, usage of IN( ) as a substitute is a poor choice from the perspective of performance.

LIKE is a case-sensitive pattern search operator. It is quite a blunt instrument compared to pattern searches in regular expression engines. It recognizes two "wild-card" symbols, % and _ (the underscore character), that work as follows:

- **%** can be substituted into a search string to represent any number of unknown characters, including none, for example:

  ```
  LIKE '%mit%'
  ```

  will be true with strings such as 'black**smith**', '**mit**genommen', 'com**mit**', as well as '**mit**'.

- An underscore character (_) can be substituted into a search string to represent a single, unknown character. For example, the following searches for records where the surname might be 'Smith', 'Smyth', or a similar pattern:

  ```
  LIKE 'Sm_th'
  ```

If you need to search for a string that contains one or both of the wildcard characters in the literal part of the pattern, you can "escape" the literal character—that is, mark it as a literal character by prepending a special escape character. To make this work, you need to tell the engine to recognize your escape character.

For example, say you want to use the LIKE operator to select all of the names of the system tables. Assume that all system table identifiers have at least one underscore character—well, it is almost true! You decide to use '#' as your escape character. Here is how you would do it:

```
SELECT RDB$RELATION_NAME FROM RDB$RELATIONS
  WHERE RDB$RELATION_NAME LIKE '%#_%' ESCAPE '#';
```

LIKE searches, per se, do not use an index. However, a predicate using LIKE 'Your string%' will be resolved to a STARTING WITH predicate, which does use an index, if one is available.

STARTING WITH predicates a case-sensitive search for a string that starts with the supplied string. It follows the byte-matching rules of the prevailing character set and collation. If necessary, it can take a COLLATION argument to force the search to use a specific collation sequence.

The following example:

```
SELECT LAST_NAME, FIRST_NAME FROM EMPLOYEE
  WHERE LAST_NAME STARTING WITH 'Jo';
```

would return rows where the last name was 'Johnson', 'Jones', 'Joabim', etc.

In a database storing character columns in German, where the default character set was ISO8859_1, you might want to force the collation sequence, as follows:

```
SELECT FAM_NAME, ERSTE_NAME FROM ARBEITNEHMER
  WHERE COLLATE DE_DE FAM_NAME STARTING WITH 'Schmi';
```

STARTING WITH will use an index if one is available.

Logical Operators

Firebird provides three logical operators that can operate on or with other predicates in distinct ways:

- NOT predicates the negative of the search condition to which it is applied. It has the highest precedence.

- AND forms a complex predicate by combining two or more predicates, all of which must be true for the entire predicate to be true. It is next in precedence.

- OR forms a complex predicate by combining two or more predicates, of which one must be true for the entire predicate to be true. OR is last in precedence. By default, Firebird 1.5 uses "shortcut" Boolean logic to determine the outcome of an ORed predicate. As soon as one embedded predicate returns as true, evaluation stops and the entire predicate returns as true.[3]

This is an example of a logical predicate:

```
COLUMN_1 = COLUMN_2
OR ((COLUMN_1 > COLUMN_2 AND COLUMN_3 < COLUMN_1)
    AND NOT (COLUMN_4 = CURRENT_DATE))
```

The effect of this predicate will be as follows:

If COLUMN_1 and COLUMN_2 are equal, evaluation stops and the predicate returns true.

Otherwise, the next predicate—with two embedded predicates—is tested to see whether it could be true. The first embedded predicate itself has two predicates embedded, both of which must be true to make it true as a whole. If COLUMN_1 is less than COLUMN_2, evaluation stops and the predicate as a whole returns false.

If COLUMN_1 is greater, then the COLUMN_3 is evaluated against COLUMN_1. If COLUMN_3 is equal to or greater than COLUMN_1, evaluations stops and the predicate as a whole returns false.

Otherwise, evaluation proceeds to the final embedded predicate. If COLUMN_4 is equal to the current date, the predicate as a whole returns false; if not, it returns true.

Inclusive vs. Exclusive OR

Firebird's OR is the *inclusive OR* (any single condition or all conditions can be true). The *exclusive OR* (which evaluates to true if any single condition is true but false if all conditions are true) is not supported.

The IS [NOT] NULL Predicate

IS NULL and its alter ego IS NOT NULL are a pair of predicators that defy grouping. Because NULL is not a value, they are not comparison operators. They test the assertion that the value to the left has a value (IS NOT NULL) or has no value (IS NULL).

---

3. Firebird 1.0.*x* has full Boolean evaluation. Shortcut Boolean evaluation in later versions can be disabled at the server level by setting the configuration parameter *CompleteBooleanEvaluation*. For details, refer to Chapter 3.

If there is a value, IS NOT NULL returns true, regardless of the content, size, or data type of the value.

Newcomers to SQL sometimes confuse the NOT NULL constraint with the IS [NOT] NULL predicates. It is a common mistake to presume that IS NULL and IS NOT NULL test whether a column has been defined with the NOT NULL constraint. It is not true. They test the current contents of a column to determine the presence or absence of a value.

An IS [NOT] NULL predicate can be used to test input data destined for posting to database columns that are constrained as NOT NULL. It is very common to use this predicate in Before Insert triggers.

For more information about NULL, see the upcoming section "Considering NULL."

Existential Predicates

The last group of predicates comprises those that use *subqueries* to supply values for assertions of various kinds in search conditions. The predicating keywords are ALL, ANY, EXISTS, IN, SINGULAR, and SOME. They came to be referred to as *existential* because all play roles in search predicates that test in some way for the *existence* of the left-side value in the output of embedded queries on other tables.

All of these predicators—summarized in Table 21-6—are involved in some way with subqueries. The topic of subqueries gets detailed treatment in the next chapter.

Table 21-6. Existential Predicators

PREDICATOR	PURPOSE
ALL	Tests whether the comparison is true for ALL values returned by the subquery.
[NOT] EXISTS	Exists (or not) in *at least one* value returned by the subquery.
[NOT] IN	Exists (or not) in *at least one* value returned by the subquery.
[NOT] SINGULAR	Tests whether *exactly one* value is returned by the subquery. If NULL is returned, or more than one value, then SINGULAR is false (and NOT SINGULAR is true).
SOME	Tests whether the comparison is true for at least one value returned by the subquery.
ANY	Tests whether the comparison is true for at least one value returned by the subquery. SOME and ANY are equivalent.

The EXISTS( ) Predicate

By far the most useful of all of the existential predicators, EXISTS provides the fastest possible method to test for the existence of a value in another table.

Often, in stored procedures or queries, you want to know whether there are any rows in a table meeting a certain set of criteria. You are not interested in how many such rows exist—you only want to determine whether there is at least one. The strategy of performing a COUNT(*) on the set and evaluating any returned value greater than 0 as "true" is costly in Firebird.

 CAUTION A row count performed in the context of one transaction to establish a condition for proceeding with work in another—for example, to calculate the value for a "next" key—is completely unreliable.

The standard SQL predicate EXISTS(*subqueried value*) and its negative counterpart NOT EXISTS provide a way to perform the set-existence test very cheaply, from the point of view of resources used. It does not generate an output set but merely courses through the table until it meets a row complying with the conditions predicated in the subquery. At that point, it exits and returns true. If it finds no match in any row, it returns false.

In the first example, the EXISTS( ) test predicates the conditions for performing an update using a dynamic SQL statement:

```
UPDATE TABLEA
SET COL6 ='SOLD'
WHERE COL1 = 99
AND EXISTS(SELECT COLB FROM TABLEB WHERE COLB = 99);
```

A statement like the example would typically take replaceable parameters on the right side of the predicate expressions in the WHERE clause.

In reality, many subqueries in EXISTS( ) predicates are *correlated*—that is, the search conditions for the subquery are relationally linked to one or more columns in the main query. Taking the preceding example and replacing the hard-coded constant in the search condition with a column reference, a more likely query would be

```
UPDATE TABLEA
SET TABLEA.COL6 ='SOLD'
WHERE EXISTS(SELECT TABLEB.COLB FROM TABLEB
             WHERE TABLEB.COLB = TABLEA.COL1);
```

The effect of the existential expression is to set the condition "If there is at least one matching row in TABLEB, then perform the update."

The IN( ) Predicate

The IN( ) predicate, when used with a subquery, is similar to EXISTS( ) insofar as it can predicate on the output of a subquery, for example:

```
UPDATE TABLEA
SET COL6 ='SOLD'
WHERE COL1 IN (SELECT COLB FROM TABLEB
               WHERE COLJ > 0);
```

In this case, the subquery returns a set of all values for COLB in the second table that comply with its own WHERE clause. The IN( ) predicate causes COL1 to be compared with each returned value in the set, until a match is found. It will perform the update on every row of TABLEA whose COL1 value matches any value in the set.

NOTE In Firebird, an IN( ) predicate that specifies a subqueried set is actually resolved to an EXISTS( ) predicate for the comparison operation.

Limitations

From a performance point of view, IN( ) is not useful where the subquery is likely to produce more than a few values. It is of most use in forming a set of comparison values from a small lookup table or from a fixed set of *constants*, for example:

```
UPDATE TABLEA
SET COL6 ='SOLD'
WHERE COL1 IN ('A', 'B', 'C', 'D');
```

The number of constant values that can be supplied for a set is limited to a maximum of 1,500 values—possibly less, if the values are large and the size of the query string would exceed its 64K limit.

The ALL( ) Predicate

Usage is best illustrated by starting with an example:

```
SELECT * FROM MEMBERSHIP
WHERE
  (EXTRACT (YEAR FROM CURRENT_DATE) - EXTRACT(YEAR FROM DATE_OF_BIRTH))
  < ALL (SELECT MINIMUM_AGE FROM AGE_GROUP);
```

The left-side expression calculates the age in years of each member in the Membership table and outputs only those members who are younger than the minimum age in the Age_Group table. ALL( ) is of limited use, since it is really only appropriate for predicating this sort of greater-than or less-than search to test for exclusion.

The SINGULAR( ) Predicate

SINGULAR is similar to ALL( ), except that it predicates that one and only one matching value be found in the embedded set. For example, this query is looking for all orders that have only a single order-detail line:

```
SELECT OH.ORDER_ID FROM ORDER_HEADER OH
WHERE OH.ORDER_ID = SINGULAR (SELECT OD.ORDER_ID FROM ORDER_DETAIL OD);
```

ANY( ) and SOME( ) Predicates

These two predicators are identical in behavior. Apparently, both are present in the SQL standard for interchangeable use to improve the readability of statements. For equality comparisons, they are logically equivalent to the EXISTS( ) predicate. However, because they can predicate on other comparisons, such as >, <, >=, <=, STARTING WITH, LIKE, and CONTAINING, they are especially useful for existential tests that EXISTS( ) cannot perform.

The following statement will retrieve a list of all employees who had at least one salary review within a year of being hired:

```
SELECT E.EMP_NO, E.FULL_NAME, E.HIRE_DATE
  FROM EMPLOYEE E
  WHERE E.HIRE_DATE + 365 > SOME (
    SELECT SH.CHANGE_DATE FROM SALARY_HISTORY SH
      WHERE SH.EMP_NO = E.EMP_NO);
```

Table Aliases

Notice the use of *table aliases* in the last two examples to eliminate ambiguity between matching column names in two tables. Firebird is very particular about aliasing tables in multi-table queries. Table aliases are discussed in Chapter 22.

Considering NULL

NULL can be quite a sticking point for folks who have previously worked with desktop databases that conveniently swallow NULLs by storing them as "zero values": empty strings, 0 for numerics, false for logicals, and so on. In SQL, any data item in a *nullable* column (that is, a column that does not have the NOT NULL constraint) will be stored with a NULL token if no value is ever provided for it in a DML statement or through a column default.

All column definitions in Firebird default to being nullable. Unless your database has been consciously designed to prevent NULLs from being stored, your expressions need to be prepared to encounter them.

NULL in Expressions

NULL is not a value, so it cannot be "equal to" any value. For example, a predicate such as

```
WHERE (COL1 = NULL)
```

will return an error because the equivalence operator is not valid for NULLs. NULL is a state and the correct predicator for a NULL test is IS NULL. The corrected predicate for the preceding failed test would be

```
WHERE (COL1 IS NULL)
```

You can also test for NOT NULL:

```
WHERE (COL1 IS NOT NULL)
```

Two NULLs are not equal to each other, either. When constructing expressions, be mindful of the cases when a predicate might resolve to

```
WHERE <NULL result> = <NULL result>
```

because false is *always* the result when two NULLs are compared.

An expression like

```
WHERE COL1 > NULL
```

will fail because an arithmetic operator is not valid for NULL.

NULL in Calculations

In an expression where a column identifier "stands in" for the current value of a data item, a NULL operand in a calculation will produce NULL as the result of the calculation. For example, the following:

```
UPDATE TABLEA
SET COL4 = COL4 + COL5;
```

will set COL4 to NULL if COL5 is NULL.

In aggregate expressions using operators like SUM( ) and AVG( ) and COUNT (*<specific_column_name>*), rows containing NULL in the targeted column are ignored for the aggregation. AVG( ) forms the numerator by aggregating the non-null values and the denominator by counting the rows containing non-null values.

Gotchas with True and False

Semantically, if a predicate returns "unknown," it is neither false nor true. However, in SQL, assertions resolve as either "true" or "false"—an assertion that does not evaluate as "true" shakes out as "false."

The "IF" condition implicit in search predicates can trip you up when the NOT predicator is used on an embedded assertion:

NOT *<condition evaluating to false>* evaluates to TRUE

whereas

NOT *<condition evaluating to null>* evaluates to NULL

To take an example of where our assumptions can bite, consider this:

```
WHERE
  NOT (COLUMNA = COLUMNB)
```

If both COLUMNA and COLUMNB have values and they are not equal, the inner predicate evaluates to false. The assertion NOT(FALSE) returns true, the flip side of false.

However, if either of the columns is NULL, the inner predicate evaluates to NULL, standing for the semantic meaning "unknown" ("not proven," "unknowable"). The assertion that is finally tested is NOT(NULL) and the result returns NULL. Take note also that NOT(NULL) is not the same as IS NOT NULL—a pure binary predicate that never returns "unknown."

 CAUTION   The lesson in this is to be careful with SQL logic and always to test your expressions hard. Cover the null conditions and, if you can do so, avoid NOT assertions altogether in nested predicates.

NULL and External Functions (UDFs)

NULL cannot be passed as either input to or output from functions in many external function libraries, because they follow the InterBase convention of passing arguments by reference or by value. Most of the UDF libraries available use the InterBase convention.

The Firebird engine is capable of passing arguments to UDFs *by descriptor*, a mechanism that standardizes arguments on Firebird data types, making it possible to pass NULL as an argument to host code, although not to receive NULL as a return value. The functions in the library fbudf (in the /UDF directory of your server installation) use descriptors.

Setting a Value to NULL

A data item can be made NULL only in a column that is not subject to the NOT NULL constraint. Refer to the section "The NOT NULL Constraint" in Chapter 16.

In an UPDATE statement the assignment symbol is "=":

```
UPDATE FOO SET COL3 = NULL
 WHERE COL2 = 4;
```

In an INSERT statement, pass the keyword NULL in place of a value:

```
INSERT INTO FOO (COL1, COL2, COL3)
VALUES (1, 2, NULL);
```

NOTE   In this case, NULL overrides any default set for the column.

Another way to cause NULL to be stored by an INSERT statement is to omit the nullable column from the input list. For example, the following statement has the same effect as the previous one, as long as no default is defined for the column COL3:

```
INSERT INTO FOO (COL1, COL2)
VALUES (1, 2);
```

In PSQL (stored procedure language), use the "=" symbol as the assignment operator when assigning NULL to a variable and use IS [NOT] NULL in the predicate of an IF test:

```
...
DECLARE VARIABLE foobar integer;
...
IF (COL1 IS NOT NULL) THEN
FOOBAR = NULL;
...
```

Using Expressions

Computed Columns

A useful feature of SQL is its ability to generate runtime output fields using expressions. Firebird supports two kinds of computed output: fields that are created in DML statements and columns that are pre-defined by DDL in tables using the COMPUTED BY keywords and a contextual expression. Usually, such fields are *derived* from stored data, although they need not be. They can be constants or, more commonly, context variables or values derived from context variables.

Fields Created in Statements

When an output column is created using an expression, it is known as a *computed* output column. The output value is always read-only, because it is not a stored value. Any expression that performs a comparison, computation, or evaluation and returns a single value as a result can be involved in specifying such a column.

It often happens that an expression uses more than one "formula" to get the result. In our earlier example, both a function (EXTRACT( )) and an operation (concatenation) were used to derive the BIRTHDAY string that was output in the list. Such complex expressions are not unusual at all.

Derived Fields and Column Aliasing

Expressions, subquery output, and constants can be used in Firebird to return derived or "made up" fields in output sets. To enable you to provide runtime names for such fields, Firebird supports the SQL column-aliasing standard, which allows any column to be output using an alias of one or more characters.

For example, the following:

```
SELECT COL_ID, COLA||','||COLB AS comput_col
FROM TABLEA;
```

returns a column concatenating two column values separated by a comma.

 CAUTION   When two columns are concatenated in this fashion in any expression, the output field will be NULL if either of the columns is NULL. This, too, is standard SQL behavior.

In the next example, a *scalar subquery* on another table is used to create a runtime output field:

```
SELECT COL_ID,
       COLA,
       COLB,
       (SELECT SOMECOL FROM TABLEB
           WHERE UNIQUE_ID = '99') AS B_SOMECOL
FROM TABLEA
```

A scalar (sub)query is one that returns the value of a single column from a single row. Subqueries are discussed Chapter 22.

Firebird permits the standard to be relaxed slightly in respect to the AS keyword—it is optional. Omitting it is not recommended, since it can make aliased column names harder to find in source code.

Another part of the standard requires columns that are computed or subqueried in the statement to be explicitly named with an alias. Current versions of the Firebird engine let you omit the alias name of computed or subqueried columns altogether. For example, the following query:

```
SELECT CAST(CURRENT_DATE as VARCHAR(10))||'-'||REGISTRATION
FROM AIRCRAFT;
```

generates the following output:

```
<blank title line>
==================
2003-01-01-GORILLA
2004-02-28-KANGAROO
...
```

Some regard this as a bug, others as a feature. It is convenient for a DBA to make a quick query without bothering with the detail. It is definitely not recommended as a "feature" to exploit in applications. Output columns with no name too often cause bugs and ambiguities in client interfaces. The same difficulties can arise with application interfaces if you use the same alias more than once in a single output.

Constants and Variables As Runtime Output

It is possible to "create" an output column in a SELECT statement using an expression that involves no columns but is just a constant or a context variable and an alias. In this trivial example, the query adds a column to every row, carrying the constant value 'This is just a demo':

```
SELECT
  LAST_NAME,
  FIRST_NAME,
```

```
'This is just a demo' AS DEMO_STRING
FROM MEMBERSHIP;
```

Trivial as it appears in this example, it can be a handy way to customize output, especially if used with a CASE expression.

Using Context Variables

Firebird provides a range of variables supplying server snapshot values. As we have already seen, many of these values can be used in expressions that perform calculations. They can also be used in expressions that store them into database columns, either as "hard" values or in COMPUTED BY specifications (see the section "COMPUTED BY Column Definitions").

Context variables can also be used in an output column expression to return a server value directly to the client or to a PSQL module. To illustrate

```
SELECT
  LOG_ID,
  LOG_DATE,
  ...,
  CURRENT_DATE AS BASE_DATE,
  CURRENT_TRANSACTION AS BASE_TRANSACTION,
  ...
FROM LOG
WHERE ...
```

Refer to the section "Context Variables" in Chapter 8 for a detailed list of available variables and more examples of use.

Expressions Using CASE( ) and Friends

Firebird provides the SQL-99 standard CASE expression syntax and its two "shorthand" derivative functions, COALESCE( ) and NULLIF( ). A CASE( ) expression can be used to output a constant value that is determined conditionally at runtime according to the value of a specified column in the current row of the queried table.

CASE( )

The CASE( ) function allows the output for a column to be determined by the outcome of evaluating a group of mutually exclusive conditions.

Availability

DSQL, PSQL, ISQL, ESQL, Firebird 1.5 and higher versions. Any platform.

Syntax
```
CASE {value 1 | <empty-clause}
  WHEN {{NULL |<value 2} | <search-predicate> } THEN {result 1 | NULL }
  WHEN...THEN {result 2 | NULL}
  [WHEN...THEN {result n | NULL}]
  [ELSE {result (n + 1) | NULL} ]
END [,]
```

Additional Keywords

WHEN … THEN are keywords in each condition/result clause. At least one condition/result clause is required.

ELSE precedes an optional "last resort" result, to be returned if none of the conditions in the preceding clauses is met.

Arguments

value 1 is the identifier of the column value that is to be evaluated. It can be omitted, in which case each WHEN clause must be a search predicate containing this column identifier.

value 2 is the match part for the search condition: a simple constant or an expression that evaluates to data type that is compatible with the column's data type.

- If the column identifier (*value 1*) is named in the CASE clause, *value 2* stands alone in each WHEN clause and will be compared with *value 1*.

- If the column identifier is not named in the CASE clause, both *value 1* and *value 2* are included in each WHEN clause as a search predicate of the form (*value1* = *value 2*).

result 1 is the result that will be returned in the event that value 1 matches value 2.

result 2 is the result that will be returned in the event that value 1 matches value 3 and so on.

Return Value

The CASE clause returns a single result. If no condition is met and no ELSE clause is specified, the result returned will be NULL.

Notes

You should use one form of the syntax or the other. Mixed syntax is not valid.

Using a single condition/result clause makes sense only if there is an ELSE clause. However, it is less elegant than the related functions COALESCE( ) and NULLIF( ).

Examples

The following two examples demonstrate how each of the two syntaxes could be used to operate on the same set of predicates.

This is the simple syntax:

```
SELECT
    o.ID,
    o.Description,
    CASE o.Status
      WHEN 1 THEN 'confirmed'
      WHEN 2 THEN 'in production'
      WHEN 3 THEN 'ready'
      WHEN 4 THEN 'shipped'
      ELSE 'unknown status ''' || o.Status || ''''
    END
FROM Orders o;
```

This syntax uses search predicates in the WHEN clause:

```
  SELECT
    o.ID,
    o.Description,
    CASE
      WHEN (o.Status IS NULL) THEN 'new'
      WHEN (o.Status = 1) THEN 'confirmed'
      WHEN (o.Status = 3) THEN 'in production'
      WHEN (o.Status = 4) THEN 'ready'
      WHEN (o.Status = 5) THEN 'shipped'
      ELSE 'unknown status ''' || o.Status || ''''
    END
  FROM Orders o;
```

Related or Similar Functions
Firebird 1.0.x users, see the external functions INULLIF( ) and NVL( ).

COALESCE( )
The COALESCE( ) function allows a column value to be calculated from a series of expressions, from which the first expression to return a non-null value is returned as the output value.

Availability
DSQL, PSQL, ISQL, ESQL, Firebird 1.5 and higher versions. Any platform.

Syntax
```
COALESCE (value 1> { , value 2 [, ...value n })
```

Arguments

value 1 is the primary column value or expression that is evaluated. If it is not NULL, it is the value returned.

value 2 is the column value or expression that is evaluated if value 1 resolves to NULL.

value n is the final value or expression that is evaluated if the preceding value in the list resolves to NULL.

Return Value

It returns the first non-null result from the list.

Notes

COALESCE( ) can be used to evaluate a pair of conditions, or a list of three or more conditions.

In the first (simple, binary) syntax COALESCE(value1, value2), the evaluation logic is equivalent to

```
CASE WHEN V1 IS NOT NULL THEN V1 ELSE V2 END
```

When there are three or more arguments—COALESCE(value1, value2, ...valuen)—the evaluation logic is equivalent to

```
CASE
  WHEN V1 IS NOT NULL THEN V1
    ELSE COALESCE (V2,...,Vn)
END
```

The last value in the list should be specified so as to ensure that *something* is returned.

Example

In the first query, if the join fails to find a match in the Employee table for the TEAM_LEADER in the Project table, the query will return the string "[Not assigned]" in place of the NULL that the outer join would otherwise return as the value for FULL_NAME:

```
SELECT
  PROJ_NAME AS Projectname,
  COALESCE(e.FULL_NAME,'[Not assigned]') AS Employeename
FROM PROJECT p
  LEFT JOIN EMPLOYEE e ON (e.EMP_NO = p.TEAM_LEADER);
```

In the next query, evaluation starts at the leftmost position in the list. If no PHONE value is present, the query looks to see whether a MOBILEPHONE value is present. If so, it returns this in PHONENUMBER; otherwise, as a last resort, it returns the string "Unknown":

```
SELECT
  COALESCE(Phone,MobilePhone,'Unknown') AS Phonenumber
FROM Relations
```

Related or Similar Functions
Firebird 1.0.*x* users, see the external functions INVL( ) and SNVL( ).

NULLIF( )
NULLIF( ) substitutes NULL for a value if the value resolves to a supplied non-null value; otherwise, it returns the value of the sub-expression.

Availability
DSQL, PSQL, ISQL, ESQL, Firebird 1.5 and higher versions. Any platform.

Syntax
```
NULLIF (value 1, value 2)
```

Arguments
value 1 is the column or expression that is to be evaluated.

value 2 is a constant or expression with which value 1 is to be compared. If there is a match, the NULLIF expression will return NULL.

Return Value
The return value will be NULL if *value 1* and *value 2* resolve to a match. If there is no match, then *value 1* is returned.

Notes
NULLIF( ) is a shorthand for the CASE expression

```
CASE WHEN (value_1 = value_2) THEN NULL ELSE value_1 END
```

Example
This statement will cause the STOCK value in the PRODUCTS table to be set to NULL on all rows where it is currently stored as 0:

```
UPDATE PRODUCTS
    SET STOCK = NULLIF(STOCK, 0)
```

Related or Similar Functions
Firebird 1.0.*x* users, see INULLIF( ) and SNULLIF( ).

COMPUTED BY Column Definitions

In table specifications, you can create columns, known as *computed columns*, that store no "hard" values, but instead store an expression that computes a value whenever the column is referred to by a query. The expression defining the column usually involves the values of one or more other columns in the current row or a server context variable. The following is a simple illustration:

```
ALTER TABLE MEMBERSHIP
  ADD FULL_NAME COMPUTED BY FIRST_NAME ||' ' || LAST_NAME;
```

It is also possible to use a subquery expression to obtain the runtime value of such a column, a feature that needs to be designed with care to avoid undesirable dependencies. For more information about computed columns, see Chapter 16.

Search Conditions

The ability to construct "formulae" to specify search conditions for selecting sets, locating rows for updates and deletes, and applying rules to input is a fundamental characteristic of a query language. Expressions pervade SQL because they provide the algebra for inserting context into abstract stored data and delivering it as information. Expressions also play an important role in stripping context from input data.

WHERE Clauses

A WHERE clause in a statement sets the conditions for choosing rows for an output set or for targeting rows for searched operations (UPDATE, DELETE). Almost any column in a table can be targeted for a search expression in a WHERE clause. If a data item can be operated on by SQL, it can be tested. Recall that a search predicate is an assertion. Simple or complex assertions are the formulae we construct to specify the conditions that must be true for every row in the set that the main clause of our query is to operate on.

Reversal of Operands

The simplified syntax of predicates for the WHERE clause specifies only that it take the form

```
WHERE value operator value
```

In other words, according to syntax, both of these assertions are valid:

```
WHERE ACOL = value
```

and

```
WHERE value = ACOL
```

For predicate types involving the equivalence symbol operators (= and <>) and for a few others, such as LIKE, the SQL parser understands both ways and treats them as equivalent. Other operators will throw exceptions or undetected errors if the left and right sides of a predicate are reversed.

In the case of the "reversible" types, the placement of the operands in predicates is a question of style. However, in the author's experience, the *readability* of complex SQL predicates in client code and PSQL sources is inversely proportional to the number of predicates presented with the tested value placed to the *right* of the operator, as in the second example.

For example, a nest of predicates of the form

```
<expression-or-constant> = COLUMNX
```

makes hard labor out of troubleshooting and code review, compared with

```
COLUMNX = <expression-or-constant>
```

It is worth any perceived extra "effort" to make the structures of all expressions consistent.

Arrays, BLOBs, and Strings

An ARRAY type cannot be used in a search predicate at all, because SQL has no way to access the data stored in arrays. Expressions targeting BLOB columns are quite limited. A BLOB cannot be compared for equivalence with another BLOB, nor with any other data type. A text BLOB can be targeted using STARTING WITH and, with limitations, the LIKE and CONTAINING predicators. Several external functions are available for BLOB types—refer to the BLOB functions in Appendix I.

Strings can be tested with any comparison operator, although some, such as >, <, >=, and <=, are not often useful.

Ordering and Grouping Conditions

When an output field is created from an expression, it can be used for setting the conditions for ordering or grouping the set. However, the syntax rules for expressions in ORDER BY and GROUP BY are different, and there are differences between versions 1.0.*x* and 1.5.

ORDER BY with Expressions

A field created using an expression at runtime cannot be referred to as a condition in an ORDER BY clause by its alias. It can be used by referring to its *degree* in the set—that is, its position across the row, counting 1 as the position of the leftmost output field. For example, the following:

```
SELECT
  MEMBER_ID,
  LAST_NAME || ', ' || FIRST_NAME AS FULL_NAME,
  JOIN_DATE
FROM MEMBERSHIP
ORDER BY 2;
```

produces a list that is ordered by the concatenated field.

In v.1.5 and later, in sets other than UNIONs, the ordering condition can be an expression that returns a value that can be meaningfully ordered. For example, the ORDER BY clause in the following statement calls a function that returns the length of a description column and uses it to order the output from longest to shortest:

```
SELECT DOCUMENT_ID, TITLE, DESCRIPTION FROM DOCUMENT
  ORDER BY STRLEN(DESCRIPTION) DESC;
```

GROUP BY with Expressions

In SQL, a GROUP BY statement is used to collect sets of data and organize or summarize them hierarchically.

In all versions of Firebird, you can form a hierarchical grouping based on a call to an external function (UDF), but in v.1.0.*x* you cannot use the degree number of an output column as a grouping condition. Firebird 1.5 added the capability to GROUP BY degree and also by certain other types of expressions, including subquery expressions.

Other changes in Firebird 1.5 tightened some grouping rules, removing support for certain illegal grouping syntaxes that are permitted in Firebird 1.0.*x*.

The rules and interactions of grouping and ordering by expression are sometimes complicated to implement. The topics are covered in detail in Chapter 23.

The following v.1.5 example queries the Membership table and outputs a statistic showing how many members joined in each month, by month:

```
SELECT
  MEMBER_TYPE,
  EXTRACT(MONTH FROM JOIN_DATE) AS MONTH_NUMBER, /* 1, 2, etc. */
  F_CMONTHLONG(JOIN_DATE) AS SMONTH, /* UDF that returns month as a string */
  COUNT (*) AS MEMBERS_JOINED
FROM MEMBERSHIP
GROUP BY
  MEMBER_TYPE, EXTRACT(MONTH FROM JOIN_DATE);
```

CHECK Expressions in DDL

The use of expressions is not restricted to DML, as we have already seen from their use in table definitions for computed columns. Any time you define a CHECK constraint for a table, column, or domain, you will use expressions. By nature, a CHECK constraint performs a *check* on one or more values; that is, it tests a predicate. Here is an example where the member's cell phone number is checked to make sure that, if it is present, it begins with a zero:

```
ALTER TABLE MEMBERSHIP
  ADD CONSTRAINT CHECK_CELLPHONE _NO
  CHECK (CELLPHONE_NO IS NULL OR CELLPHONE_NO STARTING WITH '0');
```

Expressions in PSQL

PSQL, the procedure language for triggers and stored procedures, makes extensive use of expressions for flow control. PSQL provides IF (*<predicate>*) THEN and WHILE (*<predicate>*) DO structures. Any predicate that can be tested as a search condition can also be a predicate for program flow condition.

An important function of triggers is to test incoming new values, using expressions, and to use other expressions to transform or create values in the current row or in rows in related tables. For example, this common trigger checks whether a value is null and, if so, calls a function to create a value for it:

```
CREATE TRIGGER BI_MEMBERSHIP FOR MEMBERSHIP
ACTIVE BEFORE INSERT POSITION 0
AS
BEGIN
  IF (NEW.MEMBER_ID IS NULL) THEN
    NEW.MEMBER_ID = GEN_ID(GEN_MEMBER_ID, 1);
END
```

For detailed information about writing triggers and procedures, refer to Part Seven.

Function Calls

Out of the box, Firebird comes with a minimal set of internally implemented SQL functions. Although new functions get implemented from time to time, the broad view of the user community is to retain one of Firebird's main benefits: the small footprint of the server.

The server's functional capabilities can be extended simply, by its ability to access functions in externally implemented libraries. Traditionally, such functions were called user-defined functions (UDFs). Correctly, they are *external function libraries*. In reality, most DBAs use well-tested libraries that are in common use and freely distributed.

Internal SQL Functions

Table 21-7 lists the SQL internal functions available in Firebird.

Table 21-7. Internally Implemented SQL Functions

FUNCTION	TYPE	PURPOSE
CAST( )	Conversion	Converts a column from one data type to another
EXTRACT( )	Conversion	Extracts date and time parts (year, month, day, etc.) from DATE, TIME, and TIMESTAMP values
SUBSTRING( )	String	Retrieves any sequence of characters from a string
UPPER( )	String	Converts a string to all uppercase
GEN_ID( )	General	Returns a value from a generator
AVG( )	Aggregating	Calculates the average of a set of values
COUNT( )	Aggregating	Returns the number of rows that satisfy a query's search condition
MAX( )	Aggregating	Retrieves the maximum value from a set of values
MIN( )	Aggregating	Retrieves the minimum value from a set of values
SUM( )	Aggregating	Totals the values in a set of numeric values

Conversion Functions

Conversion functions transform data types, for example, by converting them from one type to another compatible type, changing the scale or precision of numeric values, or by distilling some inherent attribute from a data item. Many string functions can be said to be conversion functions, too, because they transform the way stored string values are represented in output.

CAST( )

CAST( ) is a wide-ranging function that allows a data item of one type to be converted to or treated as another type.

Availability
DSQL, PSQL, ISQL, ESQL. Any platform.

Syntax
```
CAST(value AS <data-type>)
```

Additional Keywords
AS <data-type> within the argument phrase is mandatory.

Arguments

value is a column or expression that evaluates to a data type that can validly be converted to the data type named by the AS keyword.

<data-type> must be a native Firebird data type. A domain is not valid. Figure 8-1 in Chapter 8 shows all allowed type-to-type castings.

Return Value

The function returns a computed field of the designated data type.

Example

In the following PSQL snippet, a TIMESTAMP field, LOG_DATE, is cast to a DATE type because a calculation needs to be performed on whole days:

```
...
IF (CURRENT_DATE - CAST(LOG_DATE AS DATE) = 30) THEN
  STATUS = '30 DAYS';
```

The following statement takes the value of an integer column, casts it as a string, and concatenates it to a CHAR(3) column to form the value for another column:

```
UPDATE MEMBERSHIP
SET MEMBER_CODE = MEMBER_GROUP || CAST(MEMBER_ID AS CHAR(8))
WHERE MEMBER_CODE IS NULL;
```

Related Material

Refer to Chapter 8 for a more detailed discussion of CAST( ) and to the succeeding chapters that deal with each data type individually.

EXTRACT( )

This function extracts a part of a DATE, TIME, or TIMESTAMP field as a number.

Availability

DSQL, PSQL, ISQL, ESQL. Any platform.

Syntax

```
EXTRACT(part FROM field)
```

Optional Keywords

```
YEAR | MONTH | DAY | HOUR | MINUTE | SECOND | WEEKDAY | YEARDAY
```

Arguments

part is one member of the preceding optional keywords set. WEEKDAY extracts the day of the week (having Sunday = 1, Monday = 2, and so on), and YEARDAY extracts the day of the year (from January 1 = 1, to 366).

field is a valid DATE, TIME, or TIMESTAMP field (column, variable, or expression).

Return Value

All parts return SMALLINT except SECOND, which is DECIMAL(6,4).

Notes

EXTRACT will work only with values that evaluate as date-time fields.

Example

This statement returns names and birthdays, in BIRTHDAY order, of all members who have their birthdays in the current month:

```
SELECT
  FIRST_NAME,
  LAST_NAME,
  EXTRACT(DAY FROM DATE_OF_BIRTH) AS BIRTHDAY
FROM MEMBERSHIP
WHERE DATE_OF_BIRTH IS NOT NULL
AND EXTRACT(MONTH FROM DATE_OF_BIRTH) = EXTRACT(MONTH FROM CURRENT_DATE)
ORDER BY 3;
```

String Functions

Firebird has only two internal string functions. A large variety of string functions is available in external functions (see the next section in this chapter).

SUBSTRING( )

SUBSTRING( ) is an internal function implementing the ANSI SQL SUBSTRING() function. It will return a stream consisting of the byte at *startpos* and all subsequent bytes up to the end of the *value* string. If the optional FOR *length* clause is specified, it will return the lesser of *length* bytes or the number of bytes up to the end of the input stream.

Availability

DSQL, PSQL, ISQL, ESQL. Any platform.

Syntax
```
SUBSTRING(value FROM startpos [FOR length])
```

Optional Keywords
FOR precedes an optional clause specifying the length of the substring to return.

Arguments
value can be any expression, constant, or column identifier that evaluates to a string.

pos must evaluate to an integer >= 1. It cannot be a replaceable parameter.

length must evaluate to an integer >= 1. It cannot be a replaceable parameter.

Return Value
The return value is a string.

Notes
The values *pos* and *length* are byte positions, which matters for multi-byte character sets.

For a string argument, the function will handle any character set. The calling statement is responsible for handling any issues arising with multi-byte character sets.

For BLOB column arguments, the column named can be a binary BLOB (SUB_TYPE 0) or a text BLOB (SUB_TYPE 1) with an underlying 1-byte-per-character character set. The function currently does not handle text BLOBs with Chinese (2-byte-per-character maximum) or Unicode (3-byte-per-character maximum) character sets.

Example
The following statement will update the value in COLUMNB to be a string of up to 99 characters, starting at the fourth position of the original string:

```
UPDATE ATABLE
SET COLUMNB = SUBSTRING(COLUMNB FROM 4 FOR 99)
WHERE ...
```

Related or Similar Functions
See also the external functions SUBSTR( ), SUBSTRLEN( ), and RTRIM( ).

UPPER( )
Converts a string to all uppercase characters.

Availability
DSQL, PSQL, ISQL, ESQL, provided the string is of a character set or collation sequence that supports a lowercase-to-uppercase conversion. Any platform.

Syntax
```
UPPER(value)
```

Arguments
value is a column, variable, or expression that evaluates to a character type.

Return Value
If the character set or collation sequence supports uppercasing, it returns a string of converted, all-uppercase characters of the same length as the input *value*. For unsupported character sets, it returns the input *value* unchanged.

Notes
The input *value* cannot be a BLOB type.

Example
The following CHECK constraint validates a string input by testing whether it consists of all uppercase characters:

```
ALTER TABLE MEMBERSHIP
  ADD CONSTRAINT CHECK_LOCALITY_CASE
  CHECK(LOCALITY = UPPER(LOCALITY));
```

Related or Similar Functions
See also the external functions LOWER( ) and F_PROPERCASE( ).

Function for Getting a Generator Value

The GEN_ID( ) function is the mechanism by which PSQL modules and applications draw numbers from generators. Generators are discussed in detail in Chapter 9. See also "Implementing Auto-incrementing Keys" in Chapter 31.

GEN_ID( )
GEN_ID( ) calculates and returns a value from a generator.

Availability
DSQL, PSQL, ISQL, ESQL. Any platform.

Syntax
```
GEN_ID(value1, value2)
```

Arguments

value1 is the identifier of an existing generator.

value2 is the stepping value, an integer type, or an expression that evaluates to an integer type.

Return Value

It returns a BIGINT.

Notes

Normally, the stepping value is 1. A stepping value of 0 will return the last value generated. Larger steps as well as negative ones are possible. However, you should avoid negative stepping unless you really mean to break the forward sequence.

GEN_ID( ) always executes outside of all transactions. It is the only user-accessible operation in Firebird that can do so. Once a number has been acquired from a generator, it can never be generated again from the same generator, unless a user intervenes and breaks the sequence using a negative step or a SET GENERATOR statement.

Example

The following statement returns a new value from a generator named GEN_SERIAL:

```
SELECT GEN_ID(GEN_SERIAL, 1) FROM RDB$DATABASE;
```

In the next example, a generator is used in a BEFORE INSERT trigger to populate a primary key:

```
CREATE TRIGGER BI_AUTHORS FOR AUTHORS
ACTIVE BEFORE INSERT POSITION 0
AS
BEGIN
  IF (NEW.AUTHOR_ID IS NULL) THEN
    NEW.AUTHOR_ID = GEN_ID(GEN_AUTHOR_ID, 1);
END ^
```

Aggregating Functions

Aggregating functions perform calculations over a column of values, such as the values selected in a numeric column from a queried set. Firebird has a group of aggregating functions that are most typically used in combination with *grouping conditions* to calculate group-level totals and statistics. The aggregating functions are SUM( ), which calculates totals; MAX( ) and MIN( ), which return the highest and lowest values, respectively; and AVG( ), which calculates averages. The COUNT( ) function also behaves as an aggregating function in grouped queries.

Chapter 23 looks more closely at the participation of aggregating functions in grouped queries.

"Non-grouped" Aggregations

In a few situations, aggregating functions can operate on sets that are not subject to GROUP BY, returning at most a single row. Logically, the result of such a query cannot output any database column values or values derived from non-aggregating functions. To illustrate, the following query aggregates the budgets for one project for one fiscal year. The table has one budget record for each of five departments:

```
SELECT
 'MKTPR-1994' AS PROJECT,
 SUM(PROJECTED_BUDGET) AS TOTAL_BUDGET
FROM PROJ_DEPT_BUDGET
WHERE PROJ_ID = 'MKTPR' AND FISCAL_YEAR = 1994;
```

The output is a single line: the runtime string field and the calculated total.

External Functions (UDFs)

External functions are code routines written in a host language such as C, C++, or Pascal and compiled as shared binary libraries—DLLs on Windows and shared objects on other platforms that support dynamic loading. Like the standard, built-in SQL functions, external functions can be designed to do conversions or calculations that are either too complex or impossible to do with the SQL language.

You can access external functions by using them in expressions, just as you use a built-in SQL function. Like the internal functions, they can also return values to variables or SQL expressions in stored procedure and trigger bodies.

The "user-defined" part comes in because you can write your own functions. The possibilities for creating custom functions for your Firebird server are limited only by your imagination and skill as a host-language programmer. Possibilities include statistical, string, date, and mathematical functions; data-formatting routines; or even a custom engine for processing regular expressions (regexes).

External functions should *not* be designed to make their own connections to databases. Like the internal functions, they must operate on data, in expressions, in the context of the current server process and transaction and a single statement. Because external functions can take only arguments that are (or can be resolved as) native Firebird data types, they cannot take a query set specifier as an argument. Thus, for example, it is not possible to write aggregate functions that do not operate on constant arguments.

Existing Libraries

Firebird ships with two pre-built libraries of external functions (UDFs). The default installations place these shared object libraries in the ./UDF directory beneath the Firebird root directory. File extensions are .dll on Windows and .so on other supported platforms.

- **ib_udf**: Firebird inherited this library of useful, basic functions with its InterBase ancestry. This library needs to call some memory utilities that are located in a companion shared object name ib_util, located in the ./bin directory. This library passes parameters either *by value* or *by reference*, in the conventional InterBase style. Several routines have been bug-fixed in Firebird, so do make certain you avoid versions that ship with Borland products.

- **fbudf**: Created by Claudio Valderrama, this library passes parameters *by Firebird descriptor*, which is considered a more robust way to ensure that internal errors do not occur as a result of memory allocation and type conversion errors.

Also freely available are several public domain UDF libraries,[4] including *FreeUDFLib*, originally written in Borland Delphi by Gregory Deatz. FreeUDFLib contains a vast number of string, math, BLOB, and date functions. This library has been maintained, corrected, and augmented by several people over the years. Care should be taken to obtain a version of this library that works properly with dialect 3 date and time types. Such a version for Windows is available from http://www.cvalde.net. C source code for a POSIX version is available as FreeUDFLibC but, at the time of this writing, no trusted binary was available for download.

Configuration and Security Issues

External code modules are inherently vulnerable to malicious intruders and careless administrators. They are, after all, just files in the filesystem.

In Firebird 1.0.*x*, you can—and should—configure the location(s) of external function libraries for the server explicitly, using the *external_function_directory* parameter in the configuration file (isc_config on POSIX servers and ibconfig on Windows). It behooves the DBA to ensure that libraries cannot be overwritten by accident or by unauthorized visitors.

From Firebird 1.5 onward, access to external files of any sort can be restricted to various levels of access. By default, if you decide to place external function libraries in non-default locations, they will be inaccessible to the server. Study the notes in Chapter 36 about configuring the UDFAccess parameter in firebird.conf to resolve such problems.

---

4. A library of links to free UDF libraries is maintained at http://www.ibphoenix.com.

Stability

A bad UDF will crash the server and is capable of corrupting data. It is important to test your home-built external function routines with utter thoroughness, both outside and from within the server, before deciding to deploy them into production databases.

Declaring a Function to a Database

Once a UDF has been written, compiled, *tested thoroughly*, and installed into the appropriate directory on the server, it must be declared to the database in order to be used as an SQL function. To do this, use the DDL statement DECLARE EXTERNAL FUNCTION. You can declare functions using **isql**, another interactive SQL tool, or a script.

After the function has been declared in any database on the server, the library that contains it will be loaded dynamically at runtime the first time an application calls any function included in it. It is necessary to declare *each function* you want to use to *each database* in which it will be used.

Declaring a function to a database informs the database regarding

- The function name as it will be used in SQL statements. You can use your own custom name in the declaration—see the following syntax notes.

- The number and data types of its arguments.

- The data type of the return value.

- The name (ENTRY_POINT) of the function as it exists in the library.

- The name of the library (MODULE_NAME) that contains the function.

This is the declaration syntax:

```
DECLARE EXTERNAL FUNCTION name [data-type | CSTRING (int)
[, data-type | CSTRING (int) ...]]
RETURNS {data-type [BY VALUE] | CSTRING (int)} [FREE_IT]
[RETURNS PARAMETER n]
ENTRY_POINT 'entry-name'
MODULE_NAME 'module-name';
```

Table 21-8 describes the arguments in detail.

Table 21-8. Arguments for DECLARE EXTERNAL FUNCTION

ARGUMENT	DESCRIPTION
name	Name of the UDF to use in SQL statements. It can be different from the name of the function specified after the ENTRY_POINT keyword. If you are using an existing library, it is fine to change the supplied name—just avoid making it too confusing by declaring the same function with different names in different databases!
data-type	Data type of an input or return parameter. Unless arguments are being passed by descriptor, this is a data type of the host language. All input parameters are passed to a UDF by reference or by descriptor. Return parameters can be passed by reference, by value, or by descriptor. The data type cannot be an array or an array element.
RETURNS	Specification for the return value of a function.
BY VALUE	Specifies that a return value should be passed by value rather than by reference.
CSTRING *(int)*	Specifies a UDF that returns a null-terminated string up to a maximum of *int* bytes in length.
FREE_IT	Frees memory of the return value after the UDF finishes running. Use this only if the memory is allocated dynamically in the UDF using the ib_util_malloc function defined in the ib_util library. The ib_util library must be present in the /bin directory for FREE_IT to work.
RETURNS PARAMETER *n*	Specifies that the function returns the *n*th input parameter. This is required for returning BLOBs.
entry-name	Quoted string specifying the name of the UDF in the source code and as stored in the UDF library.
module-name	Quoted file specification identifying the library that contains the UDF. The library must reside on the server. See note below regarding path names.

External Function Library Scripts

Most external function libraries are distributed with their own DDL scripts, containing a declaration for each function and, usually, some brief documentation. The convention is to name the script after the library, using the file extension .SQL or .sql. Not all public domain libraries adhere to that convention, however.

The *ib_udf.sql* and *fbudf.sql* scripts are in the /UDF directory of your server installation. The FreeUDFLib kit comes with a script named *ext_funcs.sql*. You can freely copy and paste declarations to assemble your own library of favorite declarations.

This declaration is an example from the ib_udf.sql script:

```
DECLARE EXTERNAL FUNCTION lpad
  CSTRING(80), INTEGER, CSTRING(1)
  RETURNS CSTRING(80) FREE_IT
  ENTRY_POINT 'IB_UDF_lpad' MODULE_NAME 'ib_udf';
```

The next comes from fbudf, which passes arguments by descriptor in some functions:

```
DECLARE EXTERNAL FUNCTION sright
VARCHAR(100) BY DESCRIPTOR, SMALLINT,
VARCHAR(100) RETURNS PARAMETER 3
ENTRY_POINT 'right' MODULE_NAME 'fbudf';
```

The Function Identifier (Name)

When declaring an external function to a database, you are not restricted to using the name that appears in the script. A function name must be unique among all function declarations in the database. The libraries in general circulation usually conform to a convention of supplying declarations that do not "step on" identifiers that are commonly in use in another library, hence the strangeness of some names that you see in the scripts.

Sometimes, you want to declare the same function more than once in your database. As long as you use different names for the EXTERNAL FUNCTION, you can declare a function having the same ENTRY_POINT and MODULE_NAME as many times as you need to.

 CAUTION   Never alter the ENTRY_POINT argument. The MODULE_NAME argument should not be altered except where it is necessary to use the library's full path—see "Path Names in Function Declarations."

String Argument Sizes

The scripts contain default size declarations for external functions that take variable string arguments. For security reasons, the default sizes are kept small, to avoid the risk of accidental or malicious overflows. If string functions receive input or return results that are larger than the declared size, exceptions are thrown.

If you need an argument for a string function that is larger than the default, declare the argument according to your requirement, ensuring that the inputs and outputs are consistent with one another and no argument exceeds the maximum VARCHAR size of 32,765 bytes—note *bytes*, not characters.

In the following example, the function that is scripted in fbudf.sql as *sright* is declared with the name *sright200*, and the parameters are resized to permit 200 bytes:

```
DECLARE EXTERNAL FUNCTION sright200
VARCHAR(200) BY DESCRIPTOR, SMALLINT,
VARCHAR(200) RETURNS PARAMETER 3
ENTRY_POINT 'right' MODULE_NAME 'fbudf';
```

Path Names in Function Declarations

On any platform, the module can be referenced with no path name or file extension. This is desirable if you want to be able to transport a database containing function declarations to multiple operating systems. The default configuration of Firebird 1.5 enables this.

On v.1.0.*x*, it will be necessary to configure the *external_function_directory* parameter in isc_config/ibconfig on each platform where the functions will be used, since that version has no generalized "default path" for function modules. The /UDF directory should work as a default, but experience has shown it is unreliable unless specifically configured.

For Firebird 1.5 and onward, there are other configuration (UDFAccess) options for function library locations (refer to Chapter 36), including RESTRICT, which lets you specify one or more directory locations for them. If you use RESTRICT, it is necessary to include the module's full path specification, including file extension, in the declaration. In this case, the database will not be portable to another operating system unless you drop the functions and their dependencies from the database first.

This example shows a function declaration with a full path specification:

```
DECLARE EXTERNAL FUNCTION lpad
  CSTRING(80), INTEGER, CSTRING(1)
  RETURNS CSTRING(80) FREE_IT
  ENTRY_POINT 'IB_UDF_lpad' MODULE_NAME '/opt/extlibs/ib_udf.so';
```

External Function Reference

Appendix I is a detailed reference, with examples, for the external functions in the ib_udf and fbudf libraries in the /UDF directory of your Firebird installation, along with many of those in FreeUDFLib.

Up Next

The importance of expression logic in transforming abstract data into meaningful information is paralleled by the importance of SQL's capability to merge data from multiple tables into single sets of correlated data. In the next chapter, we examine the ways that DML offers to perform these multi-table extractions. The chapter ends with a special topic about Firebird's query optimizer and the syntax and use of query plans (the PLAN clause) with SELECT queries.

Querying Multiple Tables

FIREBIRD DYNAMIC SQL SUPPORTS THREE WAYS to query multiple tables with a single SQL statement: joins, subqueries, and unions. The output from joins, subqueried columns, and unions is read-only by nature.

Firebird does not support a multi-table query that spans multiple databases. However, it can query tables from multiple databases simultaneously inside a single transaction, with a full two-phase commit (2PC). Client applications can correlate data and perform atomic DML operations across database boundaries. Multi-database transactions are discussed in Part Six.

In this chapter, we explore the three methods for dynamically retrieving sets from multiple tables[1] in the context of a single statement and a single database: by joining, by subqueries, and by unions.

This chapter ends with an "Optimization Topic" discussing query plans and how the Firebird optimizer chooses and uses indexes to build them. An understanding of how the optimizer "thinks" can be helpful in the design of well-performing indexes and query statements.

Multi-table Query Kinds

The three methods of retrieving data from multiple tables are quite distinct from one another and, as a rule, perform different kinds of retrieval tasks. Because joining and subquerying both involve *merging* streams of data from rows in different tables, their roles overlap under some conditions. A *correlated subquery*, which can form a relational linkage with columns in the main table, can sometimes enable a set specification to produce the same output as a join, without the use of a join. Union queries, on the other hand, do not merge streams; rather, they "stack" rows. Their role never overlaps with those of joining queries or subqueries.

Joins, subqueries, and unions are not mutually exclusive, although union sets cannot be joined to one another or to other sets. Joined and union set specifications can include subqueries, and some subqueries can contain joins.

---

1. Program logic, in combination with the DSQL techniques described in this chapter, can be employed in PSQL modules that return virtual tables to clients and to other PSQL modules. Refer to Part Seven. Views, discussed in Chapter 24, provide other options for extracting multiple-table sets.

Joining

Joining is one of the most powerful features of a relational database because of its capacity to retrieve abstract, normalized data from storage and deliver denormalized sets to applications in context. In JOIN operations, two or more related tables are combined by linking related columns in each table. Through these linkages, a virtual table is generated that contains columns from all of the tables.

Join operations produce read-only sets that cannot be targeted for INSERT, UPDATE, or DELETE operations. Some application interface layers implement ways to make joined sets behave as if they were updatable.

Subqueries

A subquery is a SELECT statement that is embedded within another query. *Embedded query*, *in-line query*, *nested query*, and *sub-select* are all synonyms for *subquery*. They are used under a variety of conditions for reading data from other tables into the enclosing query. The rules for subqueries vary according to purpose. The data they retrieve is always read-only.

UNION Queries

Union queries provide the ability to extract rows with matching formats from different sets into a unified set that applications can use as if it were a single, read-only table. The subsets retrieved from the tables do not need to be related to one another—they simply have to match one another structurally.

Joining

Joining is used in SELECT statements to generate denormalized sets containing columns from multiple tables that store related data. The sets of columns extracted from each table are known as *streams*. The joining process merges the selected columns into a single output set. The simplest case is a two-table join, where two tables are linked by matching elements of a key that occurs in both tables.

The key columns for making the linkage are chosen on the basis that they implement the relationship unambiguously—that is, a key in the left-side table of the join will find *only* the rows in the right-side table that belong to the relationship, and it will find *all* of them. Typically, the linkage is made between a unique key in the left-side table (primary key or another unique key) and a formal or implied foreign key in the right-side table.

However, join conditions are not restricted to primary and foreign key columns, and the engine does not refuse to output duplicate rows. Duplicate rows may cause undesirable results. Please refer to the note on this subject in the "Optimization Topic" section.

The Inner Join

The following statement joins two tables that are related by a foreign key, FK, on the right-side table (Table2) that links to the primary key (PK) of Table1:

```
SELECT
  Table1.PK,
  Table1.COL1,
  Table2.PKX,
  Table2.COLX
FROM Table1 INNER JOIN Table2
  ON Table1.PK = Table2.FK
WHERE... <search-conditions>
```

This is a specification for an *inner* join. We will examine the *outer* join presently. Figure 22-1 shows the two streams as they exist in the tables and the set that is generated.

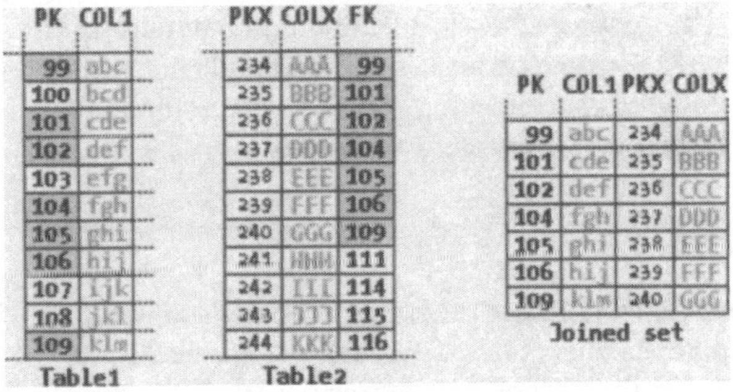

PK	COL1
99	abc
100	bcd
101	cde
102	def
103	efg
104	fgh
105	ghi
106	hij
107	ijk
108	jkl
109	klm

Table1

PKX	COLX	FK
234	AAA	99
235	BBB	101
236	CCC	102
237	DDD	104
238	EEE	105
239	FFF	106
240	GGG	109
241	HHH	111
242	III	114
243	JJJ	115
244	KKK	116

Table2

PK	COL1	PKX	COLX
99	abc	234	AAA
101	cde	235	BBB
102	def	236	CCC
104	fgh	237	DDD
105	ghi	238	EEE
106	hij	239	FFF
109	klm	240	GGG

Joined set

Figure 22-1. Inner join

As the diagram indicates, the inner join merges the two streams so that any non-matching rows in either stream are discarded. Another name for the inner join is *exclusive join*, because its rules stipulate that non-matching pairs in both streams be excluded from the output.

The SQL standards describe two syntaxes for the inner join. The preceding example uses the more modern SQL-92 syntax, distinguished from the older, more limited SQL-89 as *explicit join*, because it uses an explicit JOIN clause to specify the join conditions.

SQL-89 Implicit INNER JOIN Syntax

Under SQL-89, the tables participating in the join are listed as a comma-separated list in the FROM clause of a SELECT query. The conditions for linking tables are specified among the search conditions in the WHERE clause. There is no special syntax to indicate which conditions are for searching and which are for joining. The join conditions are assumed to be self-evident. In hindsight, with the introduction of the JOIN clause, the old syntax came to be called the *implicit join* syntax.

The implicit join syntax can implement *only* the inner join—SQL implementations that do not support a JOIN clause cannot do outer joins.

Here is the previous example rewritten as an implicit join:

```
SELECT
  Table1.PK,
  Table1.COL1,
  Table2.PKX,
  Table2.COLX
FROM Table1, Table2
WHERE Table1.PK = Table2.FK
AND <search-conditions>
```

The implicit join is supported in Firebird for compatibility with legacy application code. It is not recommended for new work because it is inconsistent with the syntaxes for other styles of joins, making maintenance and self-documentation unnecessarily awkward. Some data access software, including drivers, may not handle the SQL-89 syntax well because of parsing problems distinguishing join and search conditions. It can be anticipated that it will be dropped from future standards.

SQL-92 Explicit INNER JOIN Syntax

The explicit inner join is preferred for Firebird and other RDBMSs that support it. If the optimizer is allowed to compute the query plan, there is no reason the SQL-92 syntax would perform better or worse than the older syntax, since the DSQL interpreter translates either statement into an identical binary language form for analysis by the optimizer.

Explicit joining makes statement code more readable and consistent with other styles of joins supported by SQL-92 and subsequent standards. It is sometimes referred to as a *conditional join syntax* because the JOIN ... ON clause structure enables the join conditions to be distinguished from search conditions. Not surprisingly, this usage of the term "conditional" can be confusing!

The keyword INNER is entirely optional and is usually omitted. Alone, JOIN has exactly the same meaning as INNER JOIN. (If JOIN is preceded by LEFT, RIGHT, or FULL, then it is not an inner join.)

Three or More Streams

If there are more than two streams (tables), just continue to add JOIN ... ON clauses for each relationship. The following example adds a third stream to the previous example, joining it to the second stream through another foreign key relationship:

```
SELECT
  Table1.PK,
  Table1.COL1,
  Table2.PK,
  Table2.COLX,
  Table3.COLY
FROM Table1 JOIN Table2
ON Table1.PK = Table2.FK
JOIN Table3 ON TABLE2.PKX = Table3.FK
WHERE Table3.STATUS = 'SOLD'
AND <more-search-conditions>
```

Multi-column Key Linkages

If a single relationship is linked by more than one column, use the keyword AND to separate each join condition, just as you would do in a WHERE clause with multiple conditions. Take, for example, a table called TableA with a primary key (PK1, PK2) being linked to by TableB through a foreign key (FK1, FK2):

```
SELECT
  TableA.COL1,
  TableA.COL2,
  TableB.COLX,
  TableB.COLY
FROM TableA JOIN TableB
ON TableA.PK1 = TableB.FK1
AND TableA.PK1 = TableB.FK2
WHERE...
```

Mixing Implicit and Explicit Syntaxes

Writing statements that include a mixture of implicit and explicit syntaxes is illegal in Firebird 1.5 and allowable (but discouraged) in Firebird 1.0.*x*. The following is an example of how *not* to write a join statement:

```
SELECT
  Table1.PK,
  Table1.COL1,
  Table2.PK,
  Table2.COLX,
  Table3.COLY
FROM Table1, Table2
JOIN Table3 ON TABLE1.PK = Table3.FK
AND Table3.STATUS = 'SOLD' /* this is a search condition !! */
WHERE Table1.PK = Table2.FK
AND <more-search-conditions>
```

Outer Joins

In contrast to the inner join, an outer join operation outputs rows from participating tables, even if no match is found in some cases. Wherever a complete matching row cannot be formed from the join, the "missing" data items are output as NULL. Another term for an outer join is *inclusive join*.

Each outer join has a left and right side, the left side being the stream that appears to the left of the JOIN clause, and the right side being the stream that is named as the argument of the JOIN clause. In a statement that has multiple joins, "leftness" and "rightness" may be relative—the right stream of one join clause may be the left stream of another, typically where the join specifications are "flattening" a hierarchical structure.

"Leftness" and "rightness" are significant to the logic of outer join specifications. Outer joins can be left, right, or full. Each type of outer join produces a different output set from the same input streams. The keywords LEFT, RIGHT, and FULL are sufficient to establish that the joins are "outer" and the keyword OUTER is an optional part of the syntax.

LEFT OUTER JOIN

A LEFT OUTER JOIN causes the query to output a set consisting of fully populated columns where matching rows are found (as in the inner join) and also partly populated rows for each instance where a right-side match is not found for the left-side key. The unmatchable columns are "filled" with NULL. Here is a statement using the same input streams as our INNER JOIN example:

```
SELECT
  Table1.PK,
  Table1.COL1,
  Table2.PKX,
  Table2.COLX
FROM Table1 LEFT OUTER JOIN Table2
  ON Table1.PK = Table2.FK
WHERE... <search-conditions>
```

Figure 22-2 depicts how the streams are merged in a left join.

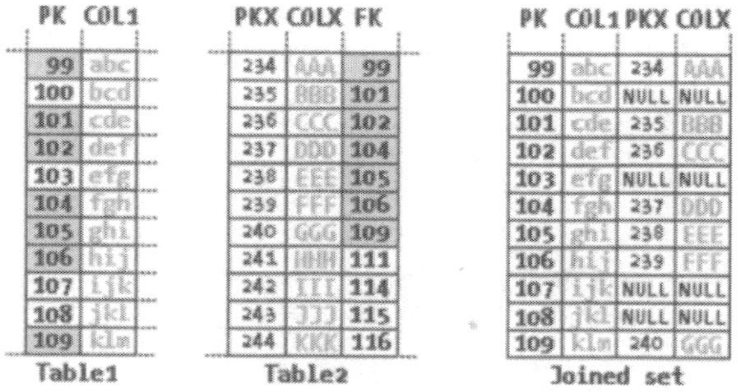

Figure 22-2. Left join

This time, instead of discarding the left stream rows for which there is no match in the right stream, the query creates a row containing the data from the left stream and NULL in each of the specified right-stream columns.

RIGHT OUTER JOIN

A RIGHT OUTER JOIN causes the query to output a set consisting of fully populated columns where matching rows were found (as in the inner join) and also partly populated rows for each instance where a right-side row exists with no corresponding set in the left-side stream. The unmatchable columns are "filled" with NULL. Here is a statement using the same input streams as our INNER JOIN example. The optional keyword OUTER is omitted here.

```
SELECT
  Table1.PK,
  Table1.COL1,
  Table2.PKX,
  Table2.COLX
FROM Table1 RIGHT JOIN Table2
  ON Table1.PK = Table2.FK
WHERE... <search-conditions>
```

Figure 22-3 depicts how the streams are merged in a right join.

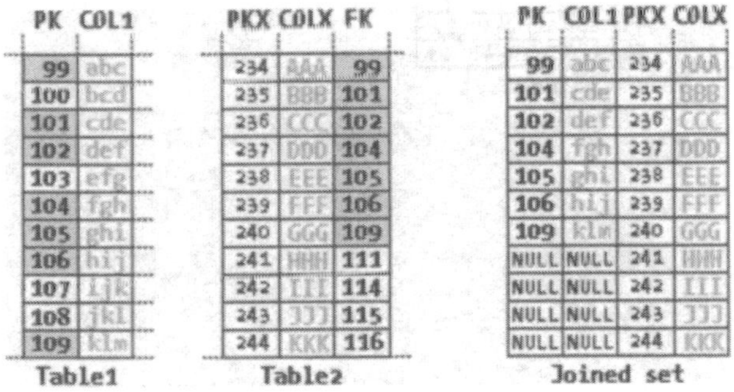

Figure 22-3. Right join

FULL OUTER JOIN

The FULL OUTER JOIN is fully inclusive. It returns one row for each pair of matching streams and one partly populated row for each row in each stream where matches are not found. It combines the behaviors of the right and left joins. Here is the statement, using the same input streams as our INNER JOIN example:

```
SELECT
  Table1.PK,
  Table1.COL1,
  Table2.PKX,
  Table2.COLX
FROM Table1 FULL JOIN Table2
  ON Table1.PK = Table2.FK
WHERE... <search-conditions>
```

Figure 22-4 depicts how the streams are merged in a full join.

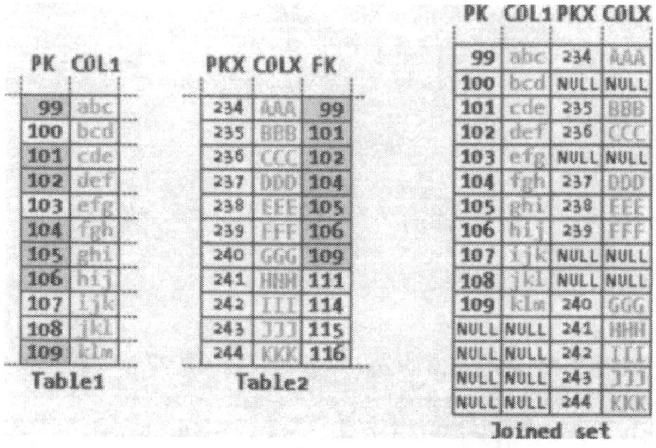

Figure 22-4. Full join

Cross Joins

Firebird does not provide language token support for the CROSS JOIN syntax, which produces an output set that is the Cartesian product of two tables. That is, for each row in the left stream, an output stream will be generated for each row in the right stream. In the unlikely event that you need a Cartesian product, you can use the SQL-89 syntax without any joining criteria in the WHERE clause, for example:

```
SELECT T1.*, T2.* FROM T1 TABLE1, T2 TABLE2;
```

The Firebird query engine sometimes forms cross joins internally, when constructing "rivers" during joining operations (see the "Optimization Topic" section near the end of this chapter).

Natural Joins

Firebird does not support the NATURAL JOIN (also known as EQUIJOIN), which forms sets by linking two streams on the basis of matching columns that share common column identifiers that have equal values. In Firebird, you always need to cite the join conditions.

Ambiguity in JOIN Queries

Various database theory texts will tell you that ambiguity can exist only where the same column names occur in multiple streams. The practitioner may have a different story to tell. The question of sorting out ambiguities gets down to the way database engines implement the parsing, streaming, and sorting that goes on during a join operation.

InterBase was lenient about the use of disambiguating syntax in joins, with sometimes unfortunate results. If you are migrating your existing application code from an InterBase heritage, do not feel too bad about the SQL exceptions that Firebird throws up during the first test run through queries with joins. It is showing you places in your code where, in the past, you have been allowed to submit queries that could produce wrong output.

Firebird will not accept JOIN queries containing column references that do not have full, consistent table qualification. Table qualification can be by *table identifier* or by *table aliasing*. From version 1.5 onward, it cannot be a mixture of each. If you are using version 1.0.*x*, take care to be consistent if you wish to avoid recoding when upgrading.

The preceding examples used the table identifier. Table aliasing is more elegant, more compact and, for certain queries (see the section "Re-entrant Joins") it is mandatory.

Table Aliases

When the name of the table is long or complicated, or there are many tables, table aliases are useful (and, in some cases, essential) to clarify statements. The query engine treats a table alias as a synonym of the table it represents. Table aliases are mandatory in queries that form multiple streams from within the same table.

 TIP In a dialect 3 database that was created using delimited identifiers combined with lowercase or mixed case object names and/or "illegal characters," typing queries could get quite exhausting and error-prone if table aliasing were not available.

An alias can be used wherever it is valid to use the table's name as a qualifier and all table identifiers must be substituted. Mixing table identifiers with aliases in the same query will cause exceptions from Firebird 1.5 onward.

The following example uses table identifiers:

```
SELECT
  TABLEA.COL1,
  TABLEA.COL2,
  TABLEB.COLB,
  TABLEB.COLC,
  TABLEC.ACOL
FROM TABLEA
  JOIN TABLEB ON TABLEA.COL1 = TABLEB.COLA
  JOIN TABLEC ON TABLEB.COLX = TABLEC.BCOL
WHERE TABLEA.STATUS = 'SOLD'
  AND TABLEC.SALESMAN_ID = '44'
ORDER BY TABLEA.COL1;
```

This is the same example using aliases:

```
SELECT
  A.COL1,
  A.COL2,
  B.COLB,
  B.COLC,
  C.ACOL
FROM TABLEA A  /* identifies the alias */
  JOIN TABLEB B ON A.COL1 = B.COLA
  JOIN TABLEC C ON B.COLX = C.BCOL
WHERE A.STATUS = 'SOLD'
  AND C.SALESMAN_ID = '44'
ORDER BY A.COL1;
```

Legal Table Alias Names

Use any useful string composed of up to 31 of the characters that are valid for metadata qualifiers (i.e., alphanumeric characters with ASCII codes in the ranges 35–38, 48–57, 64–90, and 97–122). Spaces, diacritics, double-quoted alias names, and alias names that begin with a numeral are not legal.

The Internal Cursor

When reading through a stream, the database engine implements a pointer, whose address changes as the read advances from top to bottom. This pointer is known as a *cursor*—not to be confused with the cursor set that is implemented in SQL with DECLARE CURSOR. Internal cursors are not accessible to clients except through the medium of join and subquery syntax.

The current address of an internal cursor is an absolute offset from the address of the first stream in the set, which means it can only advance forward. Internally, the optimizer utilizes indexes and organizes input streams into a *plan*, to ensure that a query begins returning output in the shortest possible time. The optimization process and plans are discussed in detail in the "Optimization Topic" section at the end of this chapter.

In any multi-table operation, the Firebird engine maintains one internal cursor for each stream. In the preceding JOIN examples, both TableA and TableB have their own cursors. When a match occurs, the engine creates a merged image for the output stream by copying the streams from the current addresses of the two cursors, as shown in Figure 22-5.

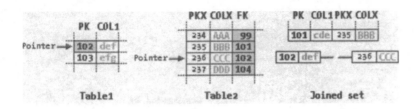

Figure 22-5. Internal cursors for a two-table join

Re-Entrant Joins

Design conditions sometimes require forming a joined set from two or more streams that come from the same table. Commonly, a table has been designed with a hierarchical or tree structure, where each row in the table is logically the "child" of a "parent" in the same table. The table's primary key identifies the child-level node of the tree, while a foreign key column stores a "parent" key referring to the primary key value of a different row.

A query to "flatten" the parent-child relationship requires a join that draws one stream for "parents" and another for "children" from the same table. The popular term for this is *self-referencing join*. The term *re-entrant join* is morphologically more appropriate, since there are other types of re-entrant query that do not involve joins. The "Subqueries" section later in this chapter discusses these other types of re-entrant queries.

Cursors for Re-Entrant Joins

To perform the re-entrant join, the engine maintains one internal cursor for each stream, within the same table image. Conceptually, it treats the two cursor contexts as though they were separate tables. In this situation, the syntax of the table references uses mandatory aliasing to distinguish the cursors for the two streams.

In the following example, each department in an organization is stored with a parent identifier that points to the primary key of its supervising department. The query treats the departments and the parent departments as if they were two tables:

```
SELECT
  D1.ID,
  D1.PARENTID,
  D1.DESCRIPTION AS DEPARTMENT,
  D2.DESCRIPTION AS PARENT_DEPT
FROM DEPARTMENT D1
LEFT JOIN DEPARTMENT D2 /* left join catches the root of the tree, ID 100 */
  ON D1.PARENTID = D2.ID;
```

Figure 22-6 illustrates how the child records are selected on the re-entrant visit to the DEPARTMENT table.

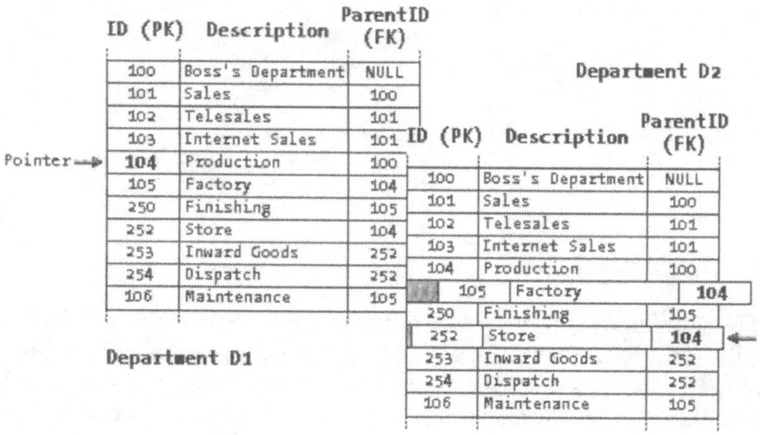

Figure 22-6. Internal cursors for a simple re-entrant join

The simple, two-layered output looks like Figure 22-7.

The output from this query is very simple: a one-level denormalization. Tree output operations on tables with this kind of structure are often recursive, using stored procedures to implement and control the recursions.[2]

---

2. In *Joe Celko's SQL for Smarties*, Joe Celko offers some interesting solutions for storing and maintaining tree structures in relational databases (Morgan Kaufmann, 1999).

ID	ParentID	Department	Parent_Dept
100	NULL	Boss's Department	NULL
101	100	Sales	Boss's Department
102	101	Telesales	Sales
103	101	Internet Sales	Sales
104	100	Production	Boss's Department
105	104	Factory	Production
250	105	Finishing	Factory
252	104	Store	Production
253	252	Inward Goods	Store
254	252	Dispatch	Store
106	105	Maintenance	Factory

Figure 22-7. Output from the simple re-entrant join

Subqueries

A subquery is a special form of expression that is actually a SELECT query on another table, embedded within the main query specification. The embedded query expression is referred to variously as a subquery, a nested query, an inline query, and sometimes (erroneously) a sub-select.

In Firebird, up to and including version 1.5, subquery expressions are used in three ways:

- To provide a single or multi-row input set for an INSERT query. The syntax is described in the section "The INSERT Statement" in Chapter 20.

- To specify a runtime, read-only output column for a SELECT query.

- To provide values or conditions for search predicates.

In versions later than Firebird 1.5, a fourth implementation of subqueries appears: the "virtual table." It is discussed briefly in Chapter 24.

Specifying a Column Using a Subquery

A runtime output column can be specified by querying a single column in another table. The output column should be given a new identifier that, for completeness, can optionally be marked by the AS keyword. See the section "Derived Fields and Column Aliasing" in Chapter 21.

The nested query must always have a WHERE condition to restrict output to a single column from a single row (known as a *scalar query*); otherwise, you will see some variant of the error message "Multiple rows in singleton select."

This query uses a subquery to derive an output column:

```
SELECT
  LAST_NAME,
  FIRST_NAME,
  ADDRESS1,
  ADDRESS2,
  POSTCODE,
  (SELECT START_TIME FROM ROUTES
   WHERE POSTCODE = '2261' AND DOW = 'MONDAY') AS START_TIME
FROM MEMBERSHIP
WHERE POSTCODE = '2261';
```

The subquery targets a single postcode in order to return the start time of a transport route. The postcode columns in both the main query and the subquery could be substituted with replaceable parameters. To make the query more general and more useful, we can use a correlated subquery.

Correlated Subqueries

When the data item extracted in the nested subquery needs to be selected in the context of a linking value in the current row of the main query, a *correlated subquery* is possible. Firebird requires fully qualified identifiers in correlated subqueries.

In the next example, the linking columns in the main query and the subquery are correlated, and table aliasing is enforced to eliminate any ambiguity:

```
SELECT
  M.LAST_NAME,
  M.FIRST_NAME,
  M.ADDRESS1,
  M.ADDRESS2,
  M.POSTCODE,
  (SELECT R.START_TIME FROM ROUTES R
   WHERE R.POSTCODE = M.POSTCODE AND M.DOW = 'MONDAY') AS START_TIME
FROM MEMBERSHIP M
WHERE...;
```

The query returns one row for each selected member, whether or not a transport route exists that matches the member's postcode. START_TIME will be NULL for non-matches.

Subquery or Join?

The query in the previous example could have been framed using a left join instead of the subquery:

```
SELECT
  M.LAST_NAME,
  M.FIRST_NAME,
  M.ADDRESS1,
  M.ADDRESS2,
  M.POSTCODE,
  R.START_TIME
FROM FROM MEMBERSHIP M
LEFT JOIN ROUTES R
   ON R.POSTCODE = M.POSTCODE
WHERE M.DOW = 'MONDAY';
```

The relative cost of this query and the preceding one, using the subquery, is similar. Although each may arrive at the result by a different route, both require a full scan of the searched stream with evaluation from the searching stream.

Cost differences can become significant when the same correlated subquery is used in place of an *inner* join:

```
SELECT
  M.LAST_NAME,
  M.FIRST_NAME,
  M.ADDRESS1,
  M.ADDRESS2,
  M.POSTCODE,
  R.START_TIME
FROM FROM MEMBERSHIP M
JOIN ROUTES R
   ON R.POSTCODE - M.POSTCODE
WHERE M.DOW = 'MONDAY';
```

The inner join does not have to traverse every row of the searched stream, since it discards any row in the searched stream (ROUTES) that does not match the search condition. In contrast, the context of the correlated subquery changes with each row, with no condition to exclude any having a non-matching POSTCODE from being scanned. Thus, the correlated subquery must be run once for each row in the set.

If the output set is potentially large, consider how important the need is to do an inclusive search. A well-judged correlated subquery is useful for small sets. There is no absolute threshold of numbers for choosing one over another. As always, testing under real-life load conditions is the only reliable way to decide what works best for your own particular requirements.

When Not to Consider a Subquery

The subquery approach becomes outlandish when you need to fetch more than a single field from the same table. A subquery can return one and only one field. To fetch multiple fields, a separate correlated subquery and alias is required for each field fetched. If a left join is possible to meet these conditions, it should always be chosen.

Searching Using a Subquery

The use of existential predicators with subqueries—especially the EXISTS( ) predicator—was discussed in the previous chapter. Subqueries can also be used in other ways to predicate search conditions for WHERE clauses and groupings.

Re-entrant Subqueries

A query can use a re-entrant subquery to set a search condition derived from the same table. Table aliasing is mandatory. In the following example, the statement subqueries the main table to find the date of the latest transaction, in order to set the search condition for the main query:

```
SELECT
  A1.COL1,
  A1.COL2,
  A1.TRANSACTION_DATE
FROM ATABLE A1
WHERE A1.TRANSACTION_DATE =
  (SELECT MAX(A2.TRANSACTION_DATE) FROM ATABLE A2);
```

Inserting Using a Subquery with Joins

In Chapter 20, we examined the inline select method of feeding data into an INSERT statement, for example:

```
INSERT INTO ATABLE (
  COLUMN2, COLUMN3, COLUMN4)
SELECT BCOLUMN, CCOLUMN, DCOLUMN
  FROM BTABLE
  WHERE...;
```

The method is not limited to a single-stream query. Your input subquery can be joined. This capability can be very useful when you need to export denormalized data to an external table for use in another application, such as a spreadsheet, desktop database, or off-the-shelf accounting application, for example:

```
INSERT INTO EXTABLE (
  TRANDATE, INVOICE_NUMBER, EXT_CUST_CODE, VALUE)
SELECT
  INV.TRANSACTION_DATE,
  INV.INVOICE_NUMBER,
```

```
  CUS.EXT_CUS_CODE,
  SUM(INVD.PRICE * INVD.NO_ITEMS)
FROM INVOICE INV
JOIN CUSTOMER CUS
  ON INV.CUST_ID = CUS.CUST_ID
JOIN INVOICE_DETAIL INVD
  ON INVD.INVOICE_ID = INV.INVOICE_ID
WHERE...
GROUP BY...;
```

The UNION Operator

The set operator UNION can be used to combine the output of two or more SELECT statements and produce a single, read-only set comprising rows derived from different tables or from different sets queried from the same table. Multiple queries are "stacked," with each subset specification being linked to the next by the UNION keyword. Data must be chosen and the query constructed in such a way as to ensure the contributing input sets are all *union compatible*.

Union-Compatible Sets

For each SELECT operation contributing a stream as input to a UNION set, the specification must be a column list that exactly matches those of all the others by degree (number and order of columns) and respective data type. For example, suppose we have these two table specifications:

```
CREATE TABLE CURRENT_TITLES (
   ID INTEGER NOT NULL,
   TITLE VARCHAR(60) NOT NULL,
   AUTHOR_LAST_NAME VARCHAR(40),
   AUTHOR_FIRST_NAMES VARCHAR(60),
   EDITION VARCHAR(10),
   PUBLICATION_DATE DATE,
   PUBLISHER_ID INTEGER,
   ISBN VARCHAR(15),
   LIST_PRICE DECIMAL(9,2));
/**/
CREATE TABLE PERIODICALS (
   PID INTEGER NOT NULL,
   PTITLE VARCHAR(60) NOT NULL,
   EDITOR_LAST_NAME VARCHAR(40),
   EDITOR_FIRST_NAMES VARCHAR(60),
   ISSUE_NUMBER VARCHAR(10),
   PUBLICATION_DATE DATE,
   PUBLISHER_ID INTEGER,
   LIST_PRICE DECIMAL(9,2));
```

The tables are union compatible because we can query both to obtain sets with matching "geometry":

```
SELECT
  ID,
  TITLE,
  AUTHOR_LAST_NAME,
  AUTHOR_FIRST_NAMES,
  EDITION VARCHAR(10),
  LIST_PRICE
FROM CURRENT_TITLES
UNION SELECT
  ID,
  TITLE,

EDITOR_LAST_NAME,
  EDITOR_FIRST_NAMES,
  ISSUE_NUMBER,
  LIST_PRICE
FROM PERIODICALS;
```

A UNION having SELECT * FROM either table would not work because the table structures are different—the second table has no ISBN column.

Using Runtime Columns in Unions

The column identifiers of the output set are those specified in the first SELECT specification. If you would like to use alternative column names, column aliasing can be used in the output list of the first SELECT specification. Additionally, if needed, runtime fields derived from constants or variables can be included in the SELECT clause of each contributing stream. The next query provides a much more satisfactory listing of publications from these two tables:

```
SELECT
  ID,
  TITLE as PUBLICATION,
  'BOOK      ' AS PUBLICATION_TYPE,

  CAST (AUTHOR_LAST_NAME || ', ' || AUTHOR_FIRST_NAMES AS VARCHAR(50))
    AS AUTHOR_EDITOR,
  EDITION AS EDITION_OR_ISSUE,
  PUBLICATION_DATE DATE,
  PUBLISHER_ID,
  CAST(ISBN AS VARCHAR(14)) AS ISBN,
  LIST_PRICE
FROM CURRENT_TITLES
WHERE ...
```

```
UNION SELECT
  ID,
  TITLE,
  'PERIODICAL',
  EDITOR_LAST_NAME || ', '|| EDITOR_FIRST_NAMES AS AUTHOR_EDITOR,
  CAST (AUTHOR_LAST_NAME || ', ' || AUTHOR_FIRST_NAMES AS VARCHAR(50)),
  ISSUE_NUMBER,
  PUBLICATION_DATE,
  PUBLISHER_ID,
  'Not applicable',
  LIST_PRICE
FROM PERIODICALS
WHERE ...
ORDER BY 2;
```

Search and Ordering Conditions

Notice in the preceding example that search conditions are possible in each contributing SELECT specification. They are normal search expressions, which must be confined to the contributing set controlled by the current SELECT expression. There is no way to correlate search conditions across the boundaries of the subsets.

Only one ordering clause is allowed, and it must follow all subsets. The ORDER BY *degree* syntax (i.e., ordering by column position number) is required for ordering union sets.

Re-Entrant UNION Queries

It is possible to apply a re-entrant technique to produce a union query that draws multiple subsets from a single table. Table aliases are required in the FROM clauses, but column references need not be fully qualified. Returning to our CURRENT_TITLES table, suppose we want a list that splits out the book titles according to price range. The re-entrant query could be something like this:

```
SELECT
  ID,
  TITLE,
  CAST('UNDER $20' AS VARCHAR(10)) AS RANGE,

  CAST (AUTHOR_LAST_NAME || ', ' || AUTHOR_FIRST_NAMES AS VARCHAR(50))
    AS AUTHOR,
  EDITION,
  LIST_PRICE
FROM CURRENT_TITLES CT1
WHERE LIST_PRICE < 20.00
UNION SELECT
```

```
   ID,
   TITLE,
   CAST('UNDER $40' AS VARCHAR(10),

   CAST (AUTHOR_LAST_NAME || ', ' || AUTHOR_FIRST_NAMES AS VARCHAR(50)),
   EDITION,
   LIST_PRICE
FROM CURRENT_TITLES CT2
WHERE LIST_PRICE >= 20.00 AND LIST_PRICE < 40.00
UNION SELECT
   ID,
   TITLE,
   CAST('$40 PLUS' AS VARCHAR(10)),

   CAST (AUTHOR_LAST_NAME || ', ' || AUTHOR_FIRST_NAMES AS VARCHAR(50)),
   EDITION,
   LIST_PRICE
FROM CURRENT_TITLES CT3
WHERE LIST_PRICE >= 40.00;
```

UNION ALL

If duplicate rows are formed during the creation of the union set, the default behavior
is to exclude the duplicate rows from the set. To include the duplicates, use UNION
ALL instead of UNION on its own.

OPTIMIZATION TOPIC: Query Plans and the Optimizer

This section looks at the Firebird optimizer subsystem and the strategies it uses to
devise the query plans that the engine will use for SELECTs and subqueries at execution time. We take a look at query plan syntax and some possibilities for presenting
your own custom plan to the engine.

Plans and the Firebird Query Optimizer

To process a SELECT statement or a search condition, the Firebird engine subjects the
statement to a set of internal algorithms known as the *query optimizer*. Each time
the statement is prepared for execution, the optimizer computes a *retrieval plan*.

The Plan

The query plan provides a kind of road map that tells the engine the least costly route
through the required process of searching, sorting, and matching to arrive at the

requested output. The more efficient a plan the optimizer can construct, the faster the statement will begin returning results.

A plan is built according to the indexes available, the way indexes or streams are joined or merged, and a method for searching (*access method*).

When calculating a plan, the optimizer will consider every index available, choosing or rejecting indexes according to their cost. It takes other factors into account besides the existence of an index, including the size of the table and, to a degree, the distribution of distinct values throughout the index. If the optimizer can determine that an index would incur more overhead than stepping row by row through a stream, it may choose to ignore the index in favor of forming an intermediate sorted stream itself or processing the stream in natural order.

Plan Expressions

Firebird provides the same plan expression syntax elements for setting plans in SQL as it provides to the engine. Understanding the plans generated by the optimizer can be very useful, both for anticipating how the optimizer will resolve the task to be done and for using as a basis for custom plans.

Plan Expression Syntax

The syntax pattern for the PLAN clause is

```
<query-specification>
PLAN <plan_expression>
```

This syntax allows specification of a single relation or a join of two or more relations in one pass. Nested parentheses can be used to specify any combination of joins. The operations pass their results from left to right through the expression.

Symbols

In the notation used here, the round brackets and commas are elements of the syntax. Curly braces, square brackets, and pipe symbols are not part of the syntax—as with earlier syntax layouts, they indicate, respectively, mandatory and optional phrases and mutually exclusive variations.

```
plan-expression := [join-type] (plan-item-list)
   join-type := JOIN | MERGE
   plan-item-list := plan-item | plan-item, plan-item-list
     plan-item := table-identifier access-type | plan_expression
     table-identifier := { table-identifier | alias-name } [ table-identifier ]
     access-type := { NATURAL | INDEX (index-list) | ORDER index-name }
       index-list := index-name | index-name, index-list
```

The Elements

join-type can be JOIN or MERGE:

- The default join type is JOIN (i.e., to join two streams using an index on the right-side stream to search for matching keys in the left-side stream).

- MERGE is chosen if there is no useable index. It causes the two streams to be sorted into matching orders and then merged. In custom plans, it will improve retrieval speed to specify this join type for joins where no indexes are available.

table-identifier identifies a stream. It must be the name of a table in the database or an alias. If the same table will be used more than once, it must be aliased for *each* usage and followed by the name of the table being aliased. To enable the base tables of a *view* to be specified, the syntax allows multiple table identifiers. Plans for views are discussed in Chapter 24.

access-type must be one of the following:

- NATURAL order, which means rows are accessed sequentially in no particular order. It is the default access type and can be omitted, although, again, it is wise to include it in custom plans to aid documentation.

- INDEX allows one or more indexes to be specified for testing predicates and satisfying join conditions in the query.

- ORDER specifies that the result of the query is to be sorted (ordered) on the *leftmost stream*, using the index.

A *plan_item* comprises an access type and the table identifier or alias.

Understanding the Optimizer

If you are unfamiliar with query plans, you are probably quite confused about how all of this syntax translates to a plan. A little later, the syntax will make more sense when we take a look at some plans generated by the optimizer. However, at this point, it will be helpful to examine how the optimizer evaluates the "materials" for its operations: the join and search conditions requested in the statement, the streams underlying the query specification, and the indexes that are available.

Factors in Cost Evaluation

The objective of the optimizer is to establish a plan that reflects the strategy that, according to several factors, is likely to start returning the output stream fastest. The evaluation may be quite imprecise, using several variables that are no more than rough estimates. Factors considered include

- Availability of an index and the selectivity of that index. The selectivity factor used in estimates is that read from the system tables when the database was opened. Even at startup, it may not be accurate and it may have been altered due to distribution changes in operations since the last selectivity was computed.

- The cardinality (number of rows) in the table streams.

- Whether there are selection criteria and, if so, whether an index is available or is suitable.

- The need to perform sorts, both intermediate (for merges) and final (for ordering and grouping).

Streams

The term "stream" that crops up in discussions about the optimizer is merely a generic way to refer to a set of rows. The set might be all of the rows and columns in a table, or it might be a set from a table that is restricted in some way by column specifications and search conditions. During the evolution of a query, the engine may create new streams from contributing stream, such as an internal, sorted set or a set of subqueried values for an IN( ) comparison. See also the upcoming "Rivers" section.

Use of Indexes

In queries, the Firebird engine can use an index for three kinds of tasks:

- **Equality comparisons**: These perform an equality, greater than, less than, or STARTING WITH comparison between the value in a column and a constant. If the column is indexed, the index key is used to eliminate ineligible rows, making it unnecessary to fetch and scan unwanted rows of table data just to eliminate them.

- **Matching streams for joins**: If an index is available for the columns named as the join condition for the stream on one side of the join, the stream on the other side is retrieved first and its join columns are matched with the index.

- **Sorting and grouping**: If an ORDER BY or GROUP BY condition specifies a column that has an index, the index is used to retrieve the rows in order and a sort operation is not required.

Bitmapping of Streams

When join criteria can be matched to an indexed column, the Firebird engine generates a bitmap of each stream selected. Subsequently, using AND and OR logic in accordance with the search criteria, the individual bitmapped row streams are combined into a single bitmap that describes all of the eligible rows. When the query needs to scan the same stream in multiple passes, scanning the bitmap is much faster than revisiting the indexes.

Binary Language Representation

Underlying Firebird's SQL engine is its native binary language representation (BLR) language and a bare-bones interpreter consisting of a lexer, a parser, a symbol table, and code generator. The DSQL engine and embedded applications pass BLR to the optimizer, and it is BLR—not strings—that the optimizer analyzes. It can happen that two different SQL statements are interpreted into identical BLR.

 TIP If you are curious about what BLR looks like, you can use the **qli** tool (in your Firebird bin directory) to inspect statements. Start **qli** and submit the command SET BLR to toggle on BLR display. A PDF manual for **qli** can be downloaded from some Firebird resource websites, including http://www.ibphoenix.com.

If you have any SELECT statements in a stored procedure or trigger, you can view them in **isql** by submitting a SET BLOB 2 command and then querying the column RDB$PROCEDURE_BLR in the system table RDB$PROCEDURES.

Joins Without Indexes

If no index is available for a join term, the optimizer specifies a *sort merge* between the two streams. A sort merge involves sorting both streams and then scanning one time through both to merge the matching streams into a river. Sorting both streams avoids the need to scan the right stream repeatedly to find matches for the left stream's keys.

Rivers

A *river* is a stream that is formed when two streams are merged by a join. When joins are nested, a river can become a stream in a subsequent operation. Various strategies for merging streams into rivers are compared for cost. The resulting plan captures the best strategy that the optimizer can determine for joining pairs of streams in order from left to right.

In calculating the cost of a joining strategy, the optimizer gives a weighting to the *order* in which streams are joined. Alternative ordering evaluations are more likely with inner joins than with outer. Full joins require special processing and extra weighting.

The length of a particular river comes into account after the longest path is determined in the course of join order evaluation. The optimizer initially favors the longest join path—the maximum number of stream pairs that can be joined directly. The favored access method is to scan through the longest stream (ideally, the leftmost stream) and loop through shorter streams.

However, more important than the length of the join path is how rows from the right stream are read. The access type is evaluated according to the indexes available and their attributes (selectivity) compared with natural order and any sorting specifications that are in the picture.

If a better index is available for a shorter stream, choosing the longest stream as the controlling stream may be less important than the cost saving from choosing a shorter stream with a highly selective (ideally, unique) index. In this case, the eligible rows in the searched stream are retrieved in a single visit and ineligible rows are ignored.

Examples of Plans

Many graphical database admin and SQL monitor tools provide the capability to inspect the optimizer's plan when a statement is prepared. Firebird's own **isql** utility provides two interactive commands for viewing plans.

Inspecting Plans with isql

SET PLAN

In an interactive **isql** session, you can use SET PLAN, with the optional keywords ON or OFF, to toggle the option to display the plan at the head of the console output:

```
SQL>SET PLAN;
SQL>SELECT FIRST_NAMES, SURNAME FROM PERSON
CON>ORDER BY SURNAME;

PLAN (PERSON ORDER XA_SURNAME)

FIRST_NAMES                   SURNAME
============================= =========
George                        Abraham
Stephanie                     Allen
```

SET STATS

With another toggle command, you can have **isql** display some statistics about queries at the end of the data output, which can be very useful for testing alternative query structures and plans:

```
SQL>SET STATS ON;
SQL> < run your query >

PLAN..
< output >
Current memory = 728316
Delta memory = 61928
Max memory = 773416
Elapsed time = 0.17 sec
Buffers = 2048
Reads = 15
Writes = 0
Fetches = 539
```

SET PLANONLY

An alternative toggle command, SET PLANONLY [ON | OFF], prepares the statement and displays the plan, without executing the query:

```
SQL>SET PLAN OFF;
SQL>SET PLANONLY ON;
SQL>SELECT FIRST_NAMES, SURNAME FROM PERSON
CON>ORDER BY SURNAME;

PLAN (PERSON ORDER XA_SURNAME)
```

If you intend to use the optimizer's plan as a starting point for constructing a custom PLAN clause, the expression syntax that is output is identical to that required in the statement's plan expression.[3] Inconveniently, there is no provision in **isql** to capture the optimizer's plan into a text file.

 TIP Graphical tools that display plans usually provide a copy/paste facility.

---

3. Many aspects of the plan that is constructed internally by the optimizer are neither visible in the plan shown by **isql** nor accessible via the PLAN clause syntax for custom plans. The syntax surfaces only a subset of the real plan that the query engine will follow.

The following examples use queries that you can test yourself using the employee.fdb test database that is installed in your Firebird samples directory.[4]

Simplest Query

This query merely retrieves every row from a lookup table, in no specific order. The optimizer determines that, although an index is available (the primary key index), it has no use for it:

```
SQL>SET PLANONLY ON;
SQL> SELECT * FROM COUNTRY;

PLAN (COUNTRY NATURAL)
```

Ordered Query

This is still a simple query, without joins:

```
SQL>SELECT * FROM COUNTRY ORDER BY COUNTRY;

PLAN (COUNTRY ORDER RDB$PRIMARY1)
```

However, the optimizer chooses the primary key index because it provides the requested ordering without the need to form an intermediate stream for sorting.

Now, let's see what happens when we decide to order the same plain query on a non-indexed column:

```
SELECT * FROM COUNTRY ORDER BY CURRENCY;

PLAN SORT ((COUNTRY NATURAL))
```

The optimizer chooses to perform the sort by walking through COUNTRY in natural order.

Cross Join

The cross join, which produces a generally useless set, does not use join criteria at all:

```
SQL> SELECT E.*, P.* FROM EMPLOYEE E, PROJECT P;
PLAN JOIN (P NATURAL,E NATURAL)
```

---

4. Because the sample database has no tables without indexes, some of the examples in this topic use specially scripted non-indexed versions of the Employee, Project, and Department tables, named Employee1, Project1, and Department1, respectively. A script for creating these tables, named NO_INDEXES.SQL, can be downloaded from http://www.apress.com.

It simply merges each stream on the left with each stream on the right. The optimizer has no use for an index. However, this example is useful for introducing the connection between table aliases in the join specification and those in the plan.

The aliases specified in the query are used in the plan printed by the optimizer. When specifying a custom plan, it is a good idea to use the same mode of table identification as is used in the query, for consistency. However, whereas the SQL parser disallows mixing table identifiers and aliases in queries, the PLAN clause accepts any mixture.[5] For example, the following is accepted. Note that the optimizer keeps the table identifiers consistent with those used in the query specification.

```
SQL> SELECT E.*, P.* FROM EMPLOYEE E, PROJECT P
CON> PLAN JOIN (PROJECT NATURAL,EMPLOYEE NATURAL);

PLAN JOIN (P NATURAL,E NATURAL)
```

Join with Indexed Equality Keys

This join denormalizes a one-to-many relationship—each employee has one or more salary history records:

```
SELECT E.*, S.OLD_SALARY, S.NEW_SALARY
FROM EMPLOYEE E
JOIN SALARY_HISTORY S
ON S.EMP_NO = E.EMP_NO;

PLAN JOIN (S NATURAL, E INDEX (RDB$PRIMARY7))
```

The optimizer chooses to loop over the (potentially) longer detail stream in order to search for relevant rows by the unique primary key index of the EMPLOYEE table. In this instance, either the number of rows in each table is roughly equal, or the number of rows in SALARY_HISTORY does not exceed the number of rows in EMPLOYEE sufficiently to outweigh the benefit of using the unique index as the lookup key. This is an inner join and the optimizer reasonably guesses that the right stream will determine the length of the river.

Let's look at the optimizer's treatment of the same streams, when the join is *left outer*:

```
SELECT E.*, S.OLD_SALARY, S.NEW_SALARY
FROM EMPLOYEE E
```

---

5. Another reason it would be a good idea to keep aliasing in the query specification and the plan consistent is that consistency is likely to be enforced in a future version of Firebird.

```
LEFT JOIN SALARY_HISTORY S
ON S.EMP_NO = E.EMP_NO;

PLAN JOIN (E NATURAL, S INDEX (RDB$FOREIGN21))
```

This time, one row will be returned for each row in the right stream, regardless of whether there is a matching key in the controlling stream. The length of the river has no relevance here, since outer joins are unequivocal about which table must be on the left side, to be looped over. It is the algorithm for the outer join that determines the access method, not the sizes of the streams. With EMPLOYEE on the left side, it would be impossible to form the outer join by looping over the SALARY_HISTORY table to look up in EMPLOYEE.

Because optimizer does not have any choice about the order in which the streams could be joined, it simply picks the most usable index on SALARY_HISTORY.

When Size Matters

In the next example, table size comes into account and is not overlooked by using the unique primary key index. DEPARTMENT has 21 rows, PROJECT has 6 rows, and the optimizer chooses the smaller table's foreign key index to optimize the lookup on the larger table:

```
SELECT * FROM DEPARTMENT D
JOIN PROJECT P
ON D.MNGR_NO = P.TEAM_LEADER ;

PLAN JOIN (D NATURAL,P INDEX (RDB$FOREIGN13))
```

Join with an Indexed ORDER BY Clause

The involvement of an indexed ordering specification can influence how the optimizer chooses to navigate the streams. Take the following example:

```
SQL> SELECT P.*, E.FULL_NAME FROM PROJECT P
JOIN EMPLOYEE E
ON E.EMP_NO = P.TEAM_LEADER
ORDER BY P.PROJ_NAME ;

PLAN JOIN (P ORDER RDB$11, E INDEX (RDB$PRIMARY7))
```

The unique index on EMPLOYEE is chosen because of the filter condition implicit in the join criteria. The query will eliminate employees who are not team leaders, and the unique index permits that to happen without needing to search the EMPLOYEE table. The choice of the filter index may also be influenced by the need to use the navigational index on PROJ_NAME for the sort.[6]

The optimizer chooses the index on the right side because the right stream will be as long as the left or (potentially) longer. Again, the optimizer cannot tell that the relationship is, in fact, one to one. The Proj_Name column specified to order the set has a unique index, created for a UNIQUE constraint, to use for the sort and the optimizer chooses it. The sort index appears first, instructing the engine to sort the left stream before it begins matching the join key from the right stream.

Equality Join with no Available Indexes

The tables in the following query are non-indexed copies of the Project and Employee tables (see footnote 4 earlier in the chapter):

```
SQL> SELECT P1.*,    E1.FULL_NAME FROM PROJECT1 P1
JOIN EMPLOYEE1 E1
ON E1.EMP_NO = P1.TEAM_LEADER
ORDER BY P1.PROJ_NAME;

PLAN SORT (MERGE (SORT (E1 NATURAL),SORT (P1 NATURAL)))
```

The streams from both sides will be sorted and then merged by a single pass through both sorted streams and, finally, the river is sorted again because neither of the contributing streams has the requested sort order.

Three-Way Join with Indexed Equalities

Consider the triple equijoin in this example:

```
SQL> SELECT P.PROJ_NAME, D.DEPARTMENT, PDB.PROJECTED_BUDGET
FROM PROJECT P
JOIN PROJ_DEPT_BUDGET PDB ON P.PROJ_ID = PDB.PROJ_ID
JOIN DEPARTMENT D ON PDB.DEPT_NO = D.DEPT_NO;

PLAN JOIN (D NATURAL, PDB INDEX (RDB$FOREIGN18), P INDEX (RDB$PRIMARY12))
```

Because plenty of usable indexes are available, the optimizer chooses the JOIN access method. The index linking the PDB stream with Department is used to select

---

6. "Sorting by index" represents a misconception. ORDER in the plan instructs the engine to read the stream in out-of-storage order (i.e., to use the navigational index to retrieve the rows). The method can only operate on the looping control stream and produces a pre-ordered result. Because ORDER can be used only on the leftmost stream in the join path, any rule that forced or influenced the join order—an outer join that precluded the stream from being the leftmost, for example—would take precedence and the navigational index could not be used.

the Department stream. When forming between the resulting river and the Project stream, the equijoin between the primary key of Project and the (potentially) longer river is able to be formed by using Project's primary key index to select from the river.

Three-Way Join with Only One Indexed Equality

For this example, we use the non-indexed copies of Project and Department to demonstrate how the optimizer will use an available index where it can and will do its best to short-circuit the non-indexed equijoin conditions:

```
SQL> SELECT P1.PROJ_NAME, D1.DEPARTMENT, PDB.PROJECTED_BUDGET
FROM PROJECT1 P1
JOIN PROJ_DEPT_BUDGET PDB ON P1.PROJ_ID = PDB.PROJ_ID
JOIN DEPARTMENT1 D1 ON PDB.DEPT_NO = D1.DEPT_NO;

PLAN MERGE (SORT
 (P1 NATURAL), SORT (JOIN (D1 NATURAL, PDB INDEX (RDB$FOREIGN18))))
```

In the innermost loop, the foreign key index for the equijoin between the PDB stream is chosen to select the eligible rows from the Department stream. Notice that its selection of this index has nothing to do with the foreign key that the index was constructed to support, since the referenced table is not even present in the statement.

Next, the resulting river and the Project stream are both sorted. Finally (in the outermost loop), the two sorted streams are merged by a single read through the two streams.

Queries with Multiple Plans

When subqueries and unions are specified in a query, multiple SELECT statements are involved. The optimizer constructs an independent plan for each SELECT statement. Take the following example:

```
SELECT
  P.PROJ_NAME,
  (SELECT E.FULL_NAME FROM EMPLOYEE E
    WHERE P.TEAM_LEADER = E.EMP_NO) AS LEADER_NAME
  FROM PROJECT P
  WHERE P.PRODUCT = 'software';

PLAN (E INDEX (RDB$PRIMARY7))
PLAN (P INDEX (PRODTYPEX))
```

The first plan selects the primary key index of EMPLOYEE to look up the TEAM_LEADER code in the primary table for the subquery. The second uses the index PRODTYPEX on the PROJECT table for the PRODUCT filter, because the first key of the index is the PRODUCT column.

Interestingly, if the same query is modified to include an ordering clause, the optimizer overrules its choice to use an index for the filter and chooses instead to use a unique index on PROJ_NAME to navigate the ordering column:

```
SELECT
  P.PROJ_NAME,
  (SELECT E.FULL_NAME FROM EMPLOYEE E
    WHERE P.TEAM_LEADER = E.EMP_NO) AS LEADER_NAME
  FROM PROJECT P
  WHERE P.PRODUCT = 'software'
  ORDER BY 1;

PLAN (E INDEX (RDB$PRIMARY7))
PLAN (P ORDER RDB$11)
```

Specifying Your Own Plan

The expression syntax that the optimizer provides in the plan it passes to the Firebird engine is available in SQL, via the PLAN clause. It enables you to define your own plan and restrict the optimizer to your choices.

A PLAN clause can be specified for almost any SELECT statement, including those used in creating views, in stored procedures, and in subqueries. Firebird versions 1.5 and above also accept PLAN clauses in triggers. Multiple plans can be specified independently for the query and any subqueries. However, there is no "all or none" requirement—any plan clause is optional.

A PLAN clause is generated for a SELECT from a selectable stored procedure. Since the output of a selectable stored procedure is a virtual set, any conditions will be based on NATURAL access. However, any SELECT statements within the stored procedure itself will be optimized and can be subjected to a custom plan.

NOTE Constructing a custom plan for a SELECT on a view presents its own special problems for the developer. For more information, refer to the section "Using Query Plans for Views" in Chapter 24.

You must specify the names and usages of all indexes that are to be used.

The optimizer always creates a plan, even if a custom plan is specified. While the optimizer does not interfere with a user-supplied plan, it does check that the indexes are valid for the context. Alternative paths are discarded, but otherwise it is business as usual. A custom plan does not cause the optimizer to short-circuit the aspects of plan evaluation and generation that are not surfaced in the PLAN clause syntax.

An invalid index will cause the query request to fail. If any predicates or join conditions are left after all of the indexes named in the plan expression have been used, the optimizer simply evaluates the streams according to natural order and default collation.

By providing your own plan expression, you may gain a little performance speed through bypassing the optimization sequences. However, devising a plan of your own based on the structural rules governing your data may not have the satisfactory outcome you expect, especially if your plan is inherited from another DBMS that uses structural rules to optimize queries.

The Firebird optimizer is primarily cost-based and generally will produce the best plan if your database is well kept through good housekeeping practices. Since the geometry of both indexes and data can change during execution of a statement—particularly if large numbers of rows are updated or deleted by the statement—no optimizer-generated plan can be counted on to remain static from one prepare to another. If you provide a static PLAN expression, the degradation in efficiency may result in performance losses that exceed any advantage gained through avoiding the optimizer.

The message here is that setting your own plan can be a two-edged sword. At design time, you may perceive a gain from forcing a plan that you believe is better than what the optimizer can calculate. In so doing, you switch off the benefit of a dynamic optimizer that can respond to and compensate for successive changes in data or index distributions.

Improving the Query Plan

Badly performing queries in Firebird are most often caused by poor indexes and suboptimal query specifications. In the "Optimization Topic" section in Chapter 18, we explored the effect of indexes with poor selectivity. In this section, we take a further look at indexes and some of the misadventures that can befall the optimizer and the designer when indexing interferes with the efficiency of retrieval.

Careful Indexing

It is not a "given" that using an index on a join or a search will make the query faster. There are actually aspects of metadata structure and indexing that cause selection of some indexes to kill performance in comparison with a natural scan.

Duplicated or overlapping indexes may interfere with the optimizer's ability to use other indexes. Drop any indexes that duplicate the index created automatically for a primary or foreign key or for a unique constraint. Composite primary and foreign key pairs, especially those that are long or carry semantic content, can make queries vulnerable to poor performance, wrong index choices and, not least, human error. When designing tables, consider using surrogate keys to separate the "meaningfulness" of columns for searching and ordering from the functional purpose of the formal key for joins.

Compound Indexes

Compound (composite, complex) indexes are those that comprise more than one key column. A well-considered compound index may help speed queries and searches on complex ANDed conditions, especially when the table is large or a searched column on its own has low selectivity.

With compound indexes, *degree* (the number of elements and their relative left-to-right positions) is important. The optimizer can make use of an individual column of a compound index or a subgroup of columns in search, join, or ordering operations, provided other columns not involved in the operation do not "obscure" it to the left or interrupt the left-to-right sequence. Figure 22-8 illustrates the possibilities available to the optimizer when evaluating a compound index on (COL1, COL2, COL3).

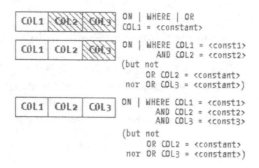

Figure 22-8. Availability of partial index keys

If a compound index can be used to advantage in place of one or more single column indexes, it makes sense to create and test it. There is no benefit in creating compound indexes for groups of OR conditions—they will not be used. Do not be tempted to create a compound index with the expectation that "one index will fit all cases." Create indexes for identified needs and be prepared to drop any that do not work well.

In practice, it is essential to consider the usefulness of any compound indexes in terms of the most likely output requirements, on a case-by-case basis. The more you allow redundant compound indexes to proliferate, the higher the likelihood that you will defeat the optimizer and get sub-optimal plans. The key elements of compound indexes often overlap with those of other indexes, forcing the optimizer to choose one from a range of two or more competing indexes. The optimizer cannot be guaranteed to choose the best one in every case, and it may even decide to use no index in cases where it cannot determine a winner.

Confirm any assumptions you make about the effect of adding a compound index by testing not just the query in question but all regular or large query tasks that involve one or more of the same columns.

TIP   It is not a bad idea to keep a log of the index structures you have tested, along with a record of their effects. This helps to keep the temperature down in the test lab!

Single-Column Indexes

Single-column indexes are much more flexible than compound indexes, because they can be used in combination. They are preferred for any conditions that have no special need for a compound index, and they are needed for each searched column that is part of an ORed condition.

Natural Ordering

Don't be upset to see NATURAL in a query plan and don't be afraid to use it when testing custom plans. Natural order specifies a top-to-bottom scan through the table, page by page. It is frequently faster for some data, especially matches and searches on columns for which an index would be very unselective, and on tables where the number of rows is small and fairly static.

Deciding on a Join Order

When two or more streams have to be joined, the order in which the streams are retrieved is often more important than all of the other factors combined. Streams are retrieved in left-to-right order, with the leftmost stream of a particular join pair being the "prime controller" determining the search logic for the remaining joins and merges that are connected to it.

Ideally, this controlling stream is searched once. Streams that it joins *to* are searched iteratively until all matching rows are found. It follows, therefore, that the stream that is costlier to retrieve should be placed to the left of the "cheaper" stream, in the controlling position. The last stream in the join list will be fetched the most times, so make sure it will be the cheapest to retrieve.

Fooling the Optimizer

In situations where the optimizer chooses an index that you want it to ignore, you can trick it into ignoring the index by adding a dummy OR condition. For a simple example, suppose you have a WHERE clause specifying a column that has a poorly selective index that you really want to keep, perhaps to enforce a referential integrity constraint:

```
SELECT ...
WHERE PARENT_COUNTRY = 'AU'
...
```

If this database is deployed in Australia (country code 'AU'), the selectivity of PARENT_COUNTRY in this database may be so low as to kill performance, but you are stuck with a mandatory index. To have the optimizer ignore the index, change the search predicate to

```
SELECT ...
WHERE PARENT_COUNTRY = 'AU' OR 1=1
...
```

Getting the Instinct

Getting the "shape" of a join specification right isn't rocket science and, with experience, you will develop an instinct for it. However, it is a technique that some people struggle with. With all query specifications, but especially with multi-table queries, the secret is to design them *conscientiously*. If you are inexperienced with SQL, do not rely on a CASE tool or query builder utility to teach you. It is a classic catch-22 situation: Until you acquire the experience, you cannot judge how mindless these tools are. If you always rely on the dumb tool, you will never develop the instinct.

Get acquainted with the performance characteristics inherent in both the structures and content of your data. Understand the normalizations in your database and recognize the shortest routes between your tables and your output specifications. Use pencil and paper to map and mold join lists and search conditions to fit output specifications with precision and without waste.

Up Next

Output sets are often not as useful to end users as they would be if they were ordered or grouped in meaningful ways. The next chapter examines SQL's capabilities for ordering sets and for aggregating intermediate output sets into summary or statistical groups.

CHAPTER 23

Ordered and Aggregated Sets

IN THIS CHAPTER WE TAKE A LOOK AT THE SYNTAX and rules for specifying queries that output ordered and grouped sets.

Sets specified with SELECT are, by default, fetched in no particular order. Often, especially when displaying data to a user or printing a report, you need some form of sorting. A phone list is clearly more useful if surnames are in alphabetical order. Groups of sales figures or test results are more meaningful if they are collated, grouped, and summarized. SQL provides two clauses for specifying the organization of output sets.

An ORDER BY clause can be included to sort sets lowest first (ascending order) or highest first (descending order), according to one or more of the set's columns. A GROUP BY clause can partition a set into nested groups, or levels, according to columns in the SELECT list and, optionally, perform *aggregating calculations* on sets of numeric columns in the bounds of a group.

Considerations for Sorting

Although ordering and aggregation are two operations with distinctly different outcomes, they interact to some degree when both are used in a query, and placement of their specifying clauses is important. Under the hood they share some characteristics with respect to forming intermediate sets and using indexes.

Presentation Order of Sorting Clauses

The following abridged SELECT syntax skeleton shows the position of ORDER BY and GROUP BY clauses in an ordered or grouped specification. Both clauses are optional and both may be present:

```
SELECT [FIRST m] [SKIP N] | [DISTINCT | ALL ]
{<column-list}
FROM <table-specification>
[WHERE <search-condition>]
[GROUP BY <grouping-item> [COLLATE collation ]
  [,<grouping-item> [COLLATE collation ]...]
[HAVING <search-condition>]
[UNION [ALL ]<select-expression>]
[PLAN <plan-expression>]
[ORDER BY <list of sorting items>]
[FOR UPDATE [OF col [,col ...]] [WITH LOCK]];
```

Temporary Sort Space

Queries with ORDER BY or GROUP BY clauses "park" the intermediate sets for sorting operations in temporary storage space. It is recommended that you have storage available that is approximately 2.5 times the size of the largest table you will sort. Firebird 1.5 and higher versions can configure sort space in RAM; all versions need to have temporary disk space to use for these operations.

Sort Memory

Version 1.5 and higher set the default block size of sort memory at 1MB. This is the size of each chunk of RAM that the server will allocate, up to a default maximum of 64MB on Superserver and 8MB on Classic server. Both of these values can be reconfigured by means of the configuration parameters *SortMemBlockSize* and *SortMemUpperLimit*, respectively, in firebird.conf.

 CAUTION Don't overstretch the memory resources of sort cache on a Classic host machine. Since Classic spawns a separate server process for each connection, a too-high upper limit will cause huge amounts of RAM to be consumed in a busy system.

Sort Space on Disk

If sort space on disk is not allocated, the engine will store the sort files in the /tmp filesystem on POSIX or the directory pointed to by the environment variables TMP and/or TEMP on Windows.

You can explicitly configure sort space in two ways. The first is to set up a directory location using the environment variable FIREBIRD_TMP (INTERBASE_TMP for v.1.0.*x*). The second is to configure the directories using the configuration parameter TempDirectories in firebird.conf for v.1.5 and higher, or to add one or more temp_directory entries in isc_config (POSIX) or ibconfig (Windows) for v.1.0.*x*.

The default installation does not configure any explicit sort space on disk. For details and syntax of these settings, refer to "Parameters for Configuring Sort Space" in Chapter 36.

Indexing

Ordered sets are costly to server resources and to performance in general. When evaluating a query and determining a plan, the optimizer has to choose between three methods of accessing the sets of data (known as *streams*) that are contributed by the specified tables: NATURAL (search in no particular order), INDEX (use an index to control the search), and MERGE (form bitmap images of the two streams and merge them on a one-to-one basis).

When a set is read in index order, the read order is contrived (i.e., it is in out-of-storage order). The likelihood that indexed reads will involve processing multiple pages is very high, and the cost grows with the size of the table. In the worst case, I/O operations will increase.

With the MERGE (also referred to as SORT) method, each row (and thus each page) is read only once and the reads are in storage order. In Firebird 1.5, which is more likely to use memory for sorts, the MERGE method is quicker in many cases.

The importance of good indexing to speed up and rationalize the sorting process in ordered queries is rightly emphasized. In ordered sets, if conditions are right, the INDEX method with a good index will speed the output of the first rows. However, the index can also slow down fetching considerably. The cost may be that the whole set is retrieved more slowly than when the alternative MERGE access method is used. With MERGE, the first row is found more slowly but the whole set is retrieved faster.

The same trade-off does not necessarily apply to grouped queries, since they require the full set to be fetched at the server before any row can be output. With grouping conditions, it may transpire that an index worsens, rather than improves, performance.

The ORDER BY Clause

The ORDER BY clause is used for sorting the output of a SELECT query and is valid for any SELECT statement that is capable of retrieving multiple rows for output. It is placed after all other clauses except a FOR UPDATE clause (if any) or an INTO clause (in a stored procedure).

The general form of the ORDER BY clause syntax is

```
...
ORDER BY <list of sorting items>
   <sorting item> = <column> | <expression> | <degree number>
                    ASC | DESC
                    [NULLS LAST | NULLS FIRST]
```

Sorting Items

The comma-separated *<list of sorting items>* determines the vertical sort order of the rows. Sorting for each sorting item can be in ascending (ASC) or descending (DESC) order. Ascending order is the default and need not be specified.

Firebird 1.5 supports placement of NULLs, if present in the sorting item. The default, NULLS LAST, causes nulls to be sorted to the end and need not be specified. Specify NULLS FIRST to have nulls placed before all values.

When there are multiple sorting items, the horizontal position of items in the clause is significant—the sorting precedence is from left to right.

Columns

Sorting items are commonly columns. Indexed columns are sorted much faster than non-indexed columns. If a sort involves multiple columns in an unbroken left-to-right sequence, a compound index made up of the sorting items in the same left-to-right sequence and the appropriate sort direction (ASC/DESC) could speed up the sort dramatically.

In UNION and GROUP BY queries, the column used for sorting has to be present in the output list. In other queries, non-output columns and (in v.1.5) expressions on non-output columns are valid ordering criteria.

The statement in Example 23-1 shows sorting by columns in its simplest form.

Example 23-1. Simple Sorting by Columns

```
SELECT COLA, COLB, COLC, COLD
FROM TABLEA
ORDER BY COLA, COLD;
```

Using Table Aliases

When specifying an ordered set that specifies joining or a correlated subquery, you must provide fully qualified identifiers for all sorting items that are database columns or refer to database columns, using the table identifiers or aliases that were initialized in the FROM and JOIN clauses, as shown in Example 23-2.

Example 23-2. Table Aliasing in the Ordering Clause

```
SELECT A.COLA, A.COLB, B.COL2, B.COL3
FROM TABLEA A
JOIN TABLEB B ON A.COLA = B.COL1
WHERE A.COLX = 'Sold'
ORDER BY A.COLA, B.COL3;
```

Expressions

From Firebird 1.5 onward, valid expressions are allowed as sort items, even if the expression is not output as a runtime column. You can sort sets on internal or external function expressions or correlated subqueried scalars (see Example 23-3). If the expression column you want to sort on is present in the output list, you cannot use its alias name as the ordering item. Either repeat the expression in the ORDER BY clause or use the column's degree number (see the section "Degree Number").

Example 23-3. Ordering by an Expression Field

```
SELECT EMP_NO || '-' || SUBSTRING(LAST_NAME FROM 1 FOR 3) AS NAMECODE
FROM EMPLOYEE
ORDER BY EMP_NO || '-' || SUBSTRING(LAST_NAME FROM 1 FOR 3);
```

Alternatively, substituting the expression in the ordering clause with the degree number of the expression field:

```
SELECT EMP_NO || '-' || SUBSTRING(LAST_NAME FROM 1 FOR 3) AS NAMECODE
FROM EMPLOYEE
ORDER BY 1;
```

If you need to sort by an expression in version 1.0.*x*, it is necessary to include the expression in the output list and use its degree number in the ORDER BY clause.

Sorting on Procedure or Function Expressions

A sort on values returned from a regular or external function or a stored procedure is just like any other sort: It will follow the regular ordinal rules for the data type of the returned field. It is your responsibility to specify sorting only on values that accord to some logical sequence. For an example of an inappropriate sequence, consider this:

```
...
ORDER BY CAST(SALES_DATE AS VARCHAR(24))
```

Rows would be ordered in the alphabetical collation sequence of the characters, with no relationship to the dates on which the expression operated.

 CAUTION   When using expressions as ordering criteria, bear in mind the considerable extra load placed on server resources by the doubling of the expression calculation for each row retrieved. The impact is, at best, unpredictable. Be conservative about the cardinality of the sets that you expose to this kind of operation.

Degree Number

A special kind of expression that can be specified a sorting criterion is the *degree number* of the output column list. Degree number is the position of the column in the output, counting from left to right, starting at 1. Example 23-4 respecifies the simple query in Example 23-1, using degree numbers instead of column identifiers.

Example 23-4. Substituting Degree Numbers for Column Names

```
SELECT COLA, COLB, COLC, COLD
FROM TABLEA
ORDER BY 1,4;
```

An ordering clause for sorting the output of a union query can use *only* degree numbers to refer to the ordering columns, as shown in Example 23-5.

Example 23-5. Ordering UNION Sets

```
SELECT
  T.FIRST_NAME, T.LAST_NAME, 'YES' AS "TEAM LEADER?"
FROM EMPLOYEE T
  WHERE EXISTS(SELECT 1 FROM PROJECT P1
    WHERE P1.TEAM_LEADER = T.EMP_NO)
UNION
SELECT
  E.FIRST_NAME, E.LAST_NAME, 'NO ' AS "TEAM LEADER?"
FROM EMPLOYEE E
  WHERE NOT EXISTS(SELECT 1 FROM PROJECT P2
    WHERE P2.TEAM_LEADER = E.EMP_NO)
ORDER BY 2, 1;
```

In v.1.0.*x*, ordering by degree number is the only way to use expressions as sort criteria, and the expression-derived column must be present in the output specification (see Example 23-6). In v.1.5, you have the option of using an expression as a sort item without including the expression item in the output set, as shown in Example 23-7.

Example 23-6. Any Version

```
SELECT
  FULL_NAME,
  STRLEN(FULL_NAME)
FROM EMPLOYEE
ORDER BY 2 DESC;
```

Example 23-7. Firebird 1.5 and Higher

```
SELECT FULL_NAME FROM EMPLOYEE
ORDER BY STRLEN(FULL_NAME) DESC;
```

Using the degree number is considered useful for saving typing and avoiding clutter when the output set involves joins, since all database columns named as ordering criteria must have fully qualified identifiers.

Sorting by degree number does not speed up the query; the engine recalculates expressions for the sorting operation.

Sort Direction

By default, sorts are performed in ascending order. To have the sort performed in descending order, include the keyword DESC, as shown in Example 23-8. If you need a descending sort, create a descending index for it. Firebird cannot "invert" an ascending index and use it for a descending sort, nor can it use a descending index for an ascending sort.

Example 23-8. Descending Order

```
SELECT FIRST 10 * FROM DOCUMENT
  ORDER BY STRLEN(DESCRIPTION) DESC
```

Nulls Placement

By default, Firebird positions sort columns having null in the sort column at the bottom of the output set. From v.1.5 onward, you can use the NULLS FIRST keyword to specify that nulls be placed first, at the top of the set, as shown in Example 23-9.

NOTE   An index cannot be used on any sorting item if NULLS FIRST is specified.

Example 23-9. Nulls Placement

```
SELECT * FROM EMPLOYEE
ORDER BY PHONE_EXT NULLS FIRST
```

The GROUP BY Clause

When a query includes a GROUP BY clause, the output of the column and table specification, namely

```
SELECT {<column-list}
FROM <table-specification>
[WHERE <search-condition>]
```

gets passed to a further stage of processing, where the rows are partitioned into one or more nested groups.

Each partition typically extracts summaries by way of expressions that perform some operation on groups of numeric values. This type of query is known as a *grouped query* and its output is often referred to as a *grouped set*.

This is the syntax:

```
SELECT <groupable-field-list> FROM <table-specification>
  [WHERE...]
  GROUP BY <grouping-item> [COLLATE collation-sequence] [, <grouping-item [..]]

    HAVING <grouping-column predicate>
  [ORDER BY ...];
```

The Groupable Field List

A group is formed by collecting together (aggregating) all of the rows where a column named in both the column list and the GROUP BY clause share a common value. The logic of aggregation means that the field list specified by SELECT for a grouped query is tightly restricted by the fields named as arguments in the GROUP BY clause. Fields having specifications that meet these requirements are often referred to as *groupable*. If you specify a column or field expression that is not groupable, the query will be rejected.

- A database column or non-aggregating expression cannot be specified in the column list if it is not also specified in the GROUP BY clause.

- An *aggregating expression* operating on a database column that is not in the GROUP BY clause can be included in the column list. The use of an alias for the result of the expression is strongly recommended.

 CAUTION In Firebird 1.0.*x* and InterBase, the enforcement of the groupability requirement is less restrictive. Grouped queries in client SQL calls and stored procedures may cause exceptions that did not occur previously. It is a long-standing bug that you should be aware of when migrating your application's back-end to Firebird 1.5 or higher.

Aggregating Expressions

Firebird has a group of aggregating functions that are typically used in combination with grouping conditions to calculate group-level totals and statistics.

The aggregating functions are SUM( ), which calculates totals; MAX( ) and MIN( ), which return the highest and lowest values, respectively; and AVG( ), which calculates averages. The COUNT( ) function also behaves as an aggregating function in grouped queries, providing a row count for all row members of the lowest level group.

Unlike other groupable items, an aggregating expression from the SELECT list cannot be used as a *grouping item* (see "The Grouping Item" section), since it outputs a value that is calculated from values beneath the context of the group.

The table PROJ_DEPT_BUDGET contains rows intersecting projects and departments. We are interested in retrieving a summary of the budgets allocated to each project, regardless of department. The following item list, which will be explored later in this section, specifies a field list of the two items we want:

```
SELECT
  PROJ_ID,
  SUM(PROJECTED_BUDGET) AS TOTAL_BUDGET
FROM PROJ_DEPT_BUDGET
  WHERE FISCAL_YEAR = 1994
GROUP BY PROJ_ID;
```

The two field specifications are going to be fine as groupable items. The department ID (DEPT_NO) is not in the list, because it is the project totals that we want. To get them, we make PROJ_ID the argument of the GROUP BY clause.

On the other hand, if we wanted to list the department budgets, regardless of project, the field list would be set up for DEPT_NO to be the argument of the GROUP BY clause:

```
SELECT
  DEPT_NO,
  SUM(PROJECTED_BUDGET) AS TOTAL_BUDGET
FROM PROJ_DEPT_BUDGET
  WHERE FISCAL_YEAR = 1994
GROUP BY DEPT_NO;
```

Effects of NULL in Aggregations

In aggregate expressions using operators like SUM( ) and AVG( ) and COUNT (<*specific_column_name*>), rows containing NULL in the targeted column are ignored for the aggregation. AVG( ) forms the numerator by aggregating the non-null values and the denominator by counting the rows containing non-null values.

NOTE If you have columns on which you want to calculate averages, it will be important at design time to consider whether you want average calculations to treat "empty" instances as null (and be excluded from the calculation) or as zero. You can implement a rule by means of a default or, better, by a Before Insert trigger.

The Grouping Item

The GROUP BY clause takes one or a list of *grouping items*:

- In Firebird 1.0, a grouping item can be only a *column name* or an appropriate *external function (UDF) expression*.

- Firebird 1.5 extended the range of options for grouping items to allow grouping also by *degree*, an ordinal number representing the left-to-right position of the corresponding item in the SELECT field list, parallel to the existing option for ORDER BY arguments.

- Firebird 1.5 and later versions also have the capability to group by most *function expressions*, such as CAST( ), EXTRACT( ), SUBSTRING( ), UPPER( ), CASE( ), and COALESCE( ).

The following statement completes the query begun by the previous example:

```
SELECT
  PROJ_ID,
  SUM(PROJECTED_BUDGET) AS TOTAL_BUDGET
FROM PROJ_DEPT_BUDGET
  WHERE FISCAL_YEAR = 1994
  GROUP BY PROJ_ID;
```

PROJ_ID	TOTAL_BUDGET
========	============
GUIDE	650000.00
HWRII	520000.00
MAPDB	111000.00
MKTPR	1480000.00
VBASE	2600000.00

Restriction

A grouping item cannot be any expression involving an aggregating function, such as AVG( ), SUM( ), MAX( ), MIN( ), or COUNT( )—that would aggregate in the same grouping context (level) as any grouping item. This restriction includes any aggregate expressions that are embedded inside another expression. For example, the DSQL parser will complain if you attempt this:

```
SELECT
  PROJ_ID,
  SUM(PROJECTED_BUDGET) AS TOTAL_BUDGET
FROM PROJ_DEPT_BUDGET
  WHERE FISCAL_YEAR = 1994
  GROUP BY 2;


ISC ERROR CODE:335544569
Cannot use an aggregate function in a GROUP BY clause
```

Using COUNT( ) As an Aggregating Function

The much-maligned COUNT( ) function has its legitimate uses when employed in a grouped query to output summary counts for groups. Consider the following modification to our example. The column DEPT_NO is not an eligible contender as either a groupable item or a grouping item for our requirements, but we can extract information about it in the grouping context of PROJ_ID:

```
SELECT
  PROJ_ID,
  SUM(PROJECTED_BUDGET) AS TOTAL_BUDGET,
  COUNT(DEPT_NO) AS NUM_DEPARTMENTS
FROM PROJ_DEPT_BUDGET
  WHERE FISCAL_YEAR = 1994
  GROUP BY PROJ_ID;
```

PROJ_ID	TOTAL_BUDGET	NUM_DEPARTMENTS
GUIDE	650000.00	2
HWRII	520000.00	3
MAPDB	111000.00	3
MKTPR	1480000.00	5
VBASE	2600000.00	3

Non-Aggregating Expressions

The ability to use internal and external function expressions for grouping opens up a wide range of possibilities for "massaging" stored attributes to generate output sets that would not be possible otherwise.

For example, the internal function EXTRACT( ) operates on date and time types, to return *date-parts*—numbers that isolate the year, month, day, hour, etc. parts of temporal types. The following v.1.5 example queries a Membership table and outputs a statistic showing how many members joined in each month, by month, regardless of the year or day of their join dates:

```
SELECT
  MEMBER_TYPE,
  EXTRACT(MONTH FROM JOIN_DATE) AS MONTH_NUMBER, /* 1, 2, etc. */
  COUNT (JOIN_DATE) AS MEMBERS_JOINED
FROM MEMBERSHIP
GROUP BY
  MEMBER_TYPE, EXTRACT(MONTH FROM JOIN_DATE);
```

A plethora of useful functions is available in the external function libraries for transforming dates, strings, and numbers into items for grouping. The following example illustrates grouping by some external functions found in the distributed ib_udf library:

```
SELECT STRLEN(RTRIM(RDB$RELATION_NAME)),
  COUNT(*)
FROM RDB$RELATIONS
  GROUP BY STRLEN(RTRIM(RDB$RELATION_NAME))
  ORDER BY 2;
```

It will work in any version of Firebird.

Some expressions are currently disallowed inside the GROUP BY list. For example, the parser rejects a grouping item that contains the concatenation symbol ||. So, for example, the query

```
SELECT
  PROJ_ID || '-1994' AS PROJECT,
  SUM(PROJECTED_BUDGET) AS TOTAL_BUDGET
FROM PROJ_DEPT_BUDGET
  WHERE FISCAL_YEAR = 1994
  GROUP BY  PROJ_ID || '-1994';
```

returns this exception in Firebird 1.5:

```
ISC ERROR CODE:335544569
Token unknown - line 6, char 21
||
```

Using the degree number of the expression field will work around the problem:

```
SELECT
  PROJ_ID || '-1994' AS PROJECT,
  SUM(PROJECTED_BUDGET) AS TOTAL_BUDGET
FROM PROJ_DEPT_BUDGET
  WHERE FISCAL_YEAR = 1994
  GROUP BY 1;
```

Grouping by Degree (Ordinal Number)

Using the degree number of the output column in the GROUP BY clause "copies" the expression from the select list (as does the ORDER BY clause). This means that, when a degree number refers to a subquery, the subquery is executed at least twice.

The HAVING Sub-Clause

The HAVING clause is a filter for the *grouped output*, corresponding to the way a WHERE clause filters the incoming, ungrouped set.

A HAVING condition uses exactly the same predicating syntax as a WHERE condition, but it should not be confused with the WHERE clause. The HAVING filter is applied to the groups *after* the set has been partitioned. You may still need a WHERE clause to filter the incoming set.

In Firebird 1.0.*x*, you can specify a HAVING condition using columns that are not included in the groupable items—"a lazy WHERE clause" and a "bug" in terms of standards conformance. From v.1.5, only groupable items can be used with HAVING.

It is important to recognize the impact of the HAVING condition on performance. It is processed *after* grouping is done. If it is used instead of WHERE conditions, to filter out unwanted members returned in groups named in the GROUP BY list, rows are wastefully double-processed, only to be eliminated when it is nearly all done.

For best performance, use WHERE conditions to *pre-filter* named groups, and use HAVING for filtering on the basis of results returned by aggregating expressions. For example, a group total calculated using a SUM(*x*) expression would be filtered by HAVING SUM(*x*) > *<minimum-value>*. A HAVING clause thus typically takes an aggregate expression as its argument.

Taking the previous query, we can use a WHERE clause to filter the project groups that are to appear in the output and a HAVING clause to set the starting range of the totals that we want to view:

```
SELECT
  PROJ_ID
  SUM(PROJECTED_BUDGET) AS TOTAL_BUDGET
FROM PROJ_DEPT_BUDGET
  WHERE FISCAL_YEAR = 1994
    AND PROJ_ID STARTING WITH 'M'
  GROUP BY PROJ_ID
  HAVING SUM(PROJECTED_BUDGET) >= 100000;

PROJ_ID  TOTAL_BUDGET
=======  ============
MAPDB       111000.00
MKTPR      1480000.00
```

The HAVING clause can take complex ANDed and ORed arguments, using the same precedence logic as the WHERE clause.

The COLLATE Sub-Clause

If you want a text grouping column to use a different collation sequence from the one defined as default for it, you can include a COLLATE clause. For more information about COLLATE, see the section "Collation Sequence" in Chapter 11.

Using ORDER BY in a Grouped Query

From v.1.5, items listed in the ORDER BY clause of a grouped query must be either aggregate functions that are valid for the grouping context or items that are present in the GROUP BY list.

Firebird 1.0.*x* is less restrictive—it will permit ordering on items or expressions that are out of the grouping context.

Advanced Grouping Conditions

Firebird 1.5 and later versions support some advanced grouping conditions that are not available in v.1.0.*x*.

Subqueries with Embedded Aggregations

A groupable field that is a correlated subquery expression can contain an aggregate expression that refers to an aggregate expression item in the GROUP BY list.

In the following example, a re-entrant subquery on the system table RDB$RELATION_FIELDS contains an aggregate expression (MAX(r.RDB$FIELD_POSITION) whose result is used to locate the name (RDB$FIELD_NAME) of the column having the highest field position number for each table (RDB$RELATION_NAME) in the database:

```
SELECT
  r.RDB$RELATION_NAME,
  MAX(r.RDB$FIELD_POSITION) AS MAXFIELDPOS,
  (SELECT
    r2.RDB$FIELD_NAME FROM RDB$RELATION_FIELDS r2
    WHERE
      r2.RDB$RELATION_NAME = r.RDB$RELATION_NAME
      and r2.RDB$FIELD_POSITION = MAX(r.RDB$FIELD_POSITION)) AS FIELDNAME
FROM RDB$RELATION_FIELDS r
/* we use a WHERE clause to filter out the system tables */
  WHERE r.RDB$RELATION_NAME NOT STARTING WITH 'RDB$'
  GROUP BY 1;

RDB$RELATION_NAME    MAXFIELDPOS  FIELDNAME
==================   ===========  ================
COUNTRY                        1  CURRENCY
CROSS_RATE                     3  UPDATE_DATE
CUSTOMER                      11  ON_HOLD
```

DEPARTMENT	6	PHONE_NO	
EMPLOYEE	10	FULL_NAME	
EMPLOYEE_PROJECT	1	PROJ_ID	
JOB	7	LANGUAGE_REQ	
PHONE_LIST	5	PHONE_NO	
PROJECT	4	PRODUCT	
PROJ_DEPT_BUDGET	4	PROJECTED_BUDGET	
SALARY_HISTORY	5	NEW_SALARY	
SALES	12	AGED	

Along the same lines, this time we use COUNT( ) to aggregate the number of columns stored in each table:

```
SELECT
  rf.RDB$RELATION_NAME AS "Table Name",
  (SELECT
    r.RDB$RELATION_ID
    FROM RDB$RELATIONS r
    WHERE r.RDB$RELATION_NAME = rf.RDB$RELATION_NAME) AS ID,
    COUNT(*) AS "Field Count"
  FROM RDB$RELATION_FIELDS rf
    WHERE rf.RDB$RELATION_NAME NOT STARTING WITH 'RDB$'
  GROUP BY
    rf.RDB$RELATION_NAME;
```

Table Name	ID	Field Count
COUNTRY	128	2
CROSS_RATE	139	4
CUSTOMER	137	12
DEPARTMENT	130	7
... and so on		

Aggregations with Embedded Subqueries

An aggregating function expression—COUNT, AVG, etc.—can take an argument that is a subquery expression returning a scalar result. For example, the following query passes the result of a SELECT COUNT(*) query to a higher level SUM( ) expression that outputs for each table (RDB$RELATION_NAME) the product of the field count and the number of indexes on that table:

```
SELECT
  r.RDB$RELATION_NAME,
  SUM((SELECT COUNT(*) FROM RDB$RELATION_FIELDS rf
    WHERE rf.RDB$RELATION_NAME = r.RDB$RELATION_NAME))
    AS "Fields * Indexes"
```

```
FROM RDB$RELATIONS r
  JOIN RDB$INDICES i
    ON (i.RDB$RELATION_NAME = r.RDB$RELATION_NAME)
  WHERE r.RDB$RELATION_NAME NOT STARTING WITH 'RDB$'
  GROUP BY r.RDB$RELATION_NAME;
```

```
RDB$RELATION_NAME    Fields * Indexes
==================   ================
COUNTRY                            2
CROSS_RATE                         4
CUSTOMER                          48
DEPARTMENT                        35
... and so on
```

Aggregations at Mixed Grouping Levels

Aggregate functions from *different* grouping levels can be mixed in the same grouped query.

In the following example, an expression result based on a subquery that does a COUNT( ) on a column in a lower level group (RDB$INDICES) is passed as output to the grouping level. The HAVING clause performs filtering predicated on two further aggregations on the lower level group.

```
SELECT
  r.RDB$RELATION_NAME,
  MAX(i.RDB$STATISTICS) AS "Max1",
  /* one aggregating expression nested within another */
  (SELECT COUNT(*) || ' - ' || MAX(i.RDB$STATISTICS)
    FROM RDB$RELATION_FIELDS rf
      WHERE rf.RDB$RELATION_NAME = r.RDB$RELATION_NAME) AS "Max2"
FROM
  RDB$RELATIONS r
  JOIN RDB$INDICES i
    ON (i.RDB$RELATION_NAME = r.RDB$RELATION_NAME)
  WHERE r.RDB$RELATION_NAME NOT STARTING WITH 'RDB$'
  GROUP BY
    r.RDB$RELATION_NAME
    HAVING
      MIN(i.RDB$STATISTICS) <> MAX(i.RDB$STATISTICS);
```

```
RDB$RELATION_NAME    Max1              Max2
==================   ===============   ========================
MTRANSACTION         000000000000001   18 - 1.000000000000000
MEMBER               0.0135135138407   12 - 0.01351351384073496
```

CAUTION You can get results from running this query in Firebird 1.0.*x*, but they will be incorrect.

Nesting Aggregate Functions

An aggregating expression can be nested inside another aggregate expression if the inner aggregate function is from a lower context, as illustrated in the previous query.

Up Next

In these DML chapters we have explored the power of SQL to transform the abstract data stored in tables into information that end users can read in meaningful contexts. Under some conditions, it makes good sense to store persistent definitions of useful output sets (virtual tables) to avoid reinventing the wheel each time a similar set is wanted. The next chapter examines ways to do that, especially with *views*.

CHAPTER 24

Views

In **SQL-89** and **SQL-92** terms, a *view* is a standard table type, also referred to as a *viewed* or *virtual table*. It is characterized as *virtual* because, instead of storing a table object and allocating pages for storing data, the Firebird engine stores a metadata object description. It comprises a unique identifier, a list of column specifications, and a compiled SELECT statement for retrieving the described data into those columns at runtime.

What Is a View?

At its simplest, a view is a table specification that stores no data. It acts as a filter on both the columns and the rows of the underlying tables referenced in the view—a "window" through which actual data is exposed. The query that defines the view can be from one or more tables or other views in the current database. It behaves in many ways like a persistent table and encapsulates some special extensions to link it with the underlying tables.

You query a view as if it were an ordinary table and perform joins, order and group output, specify search conditions, subquery it, derive runtime columns from its virtual data, process a named or unnamed cursor selected from it, and so on.

Many views can be "updated," thereby modifying the state of the underlying persistent tables, or they can be made updatable through triggers. When changes to the tables' data are committed, the data content of the view changes with them. When a view's data changes are committed, underlying tables' data changes accordingly.

Keys and Indexes

Views cannot have keys or indexes. The underlying tables, known as *base tables*, will be used as the sources of indexes when the optimizer constructs query plans. The topic of query plans for queries involving views is quite complicated. It is discussed later in this chapter, in the section "Using Query Plans for Views."

Row Ordering and Grouping

A view definition cannot be ordered. An exception is thrown if an ORDER BY clause is included. Consequently, it does not make sense to use the FIRST and/or SKIP quantifiers for SELECT, since they operate on ordered sets.

A grouped query specification (using a legal GROUP BY clause) is fine.

Some Simple View Specifications

A view can be created from virtually any SELECT query specification. Examples are presented in the following sections.

A Vertical Subset of Columns from a Single Table

The JOB table in the employee.fdb database has eight columns: JOB_CODE, JOB_GRADE, JOB_COUNTRY, JOB_TITLE, MIN_SALARY, MAX_SALARY, JOB_REQUIREMENT, and LANGUAGE_REQ.

The following view returns a list of salary ranges (subset of columns) for all jobs (all rows) in the JOB table:

```
CREATE VIEW JOB_SALARY_RANGES AS
SELECT JOB_CODE, MIN_SALARY, MAX_SALARY FROM JOB;
```

A Horizontal Subset of Rows from a Single Table

The next view returns all of the columns in the JOB table, but only the subset of rows where the MAX_SALARY is less than $15,000:

```
CREATE VIEW LOW_PAYING_JOBS AS
SELECT * FROM JOB
WHERE MAX_SALARY < 15000;
```

A Combined Vertical and Horizontal Subset

This view returns only the JOB_CODE and JOB_TITLE columns and only those jobs where MAX_SALARY is less than $15,000:

```
CREATE VIEW ENTRY_LEVEL_JOBS AS
SELECT JOB_CODE, JOB_TITLE FROM JOB
WHERE MAX_SALARY < 15000;
```

A Subset of Rows and Columns from Multiple Tables

The next example shows a view that joins the JOB and EMPLOYEE tables. EMPLOYEE contains 11 columns: EMP_NO, FIRST_NAME, LAST_NAME, PHONE_EXT, HIRE_DATE, DEPT_NO, JOB_CODE, JOB_GRADE, JOB_COUNTRY, SALARY, and FULL_NAME. It returns two columns from the JOB table and two columns from EMPLOYEE, filtering so that records for workers whose salary is $15,000 or more are suppressed:

```
CREATE VIEW ENTRY_LEVEL_WORKERS AS SELECT
  E.JOB_CODE,
  J.JOB_TITLE,
  E.FIRST_NAME,
  E.LAST_NAME
FROM JOB J
JOIN EMPLOYEE E
  ON J.JOB_CODE = E.JOB_CODE
  WHERE E.SALARY < 15000;
```

Why Views Can Be Useful

The data requirements of an individual user or user group are often quite consistent. Views provide the means to create custom versions of the underlying tables to target clusters of data that are pertinent to specific users and their tasks. The following list summarizes the benefits of views:

- **Simplified, reuseable data access paths**: Views enable you to encapsulate a subset of data from one or more tables to use as a foundation for future queries.

- **Customized access to the data**: Views provide a way to tailor the database output so that it is task oriented, suits the specific skills and requirements of users, and reduces the volume of data moving across networks.

- **Data independence**: Views can shield user applications from the effects of changes to database structure. For example, if the DBA decides to split one table into two, a view can be created that joins the two new tables. Applications can continue to query the view as if it were still a single, persistent table.

- **Data security**: Views enable access to sensitive or irrelevant portions of tables to be restricted. For example, a user might be able to look up job information through a view over an Employee table, without seeing associated salary information.

Privileges

Because a view is a database object, it requires specific user privileges in order to be accessed. Through granting privileges to a view, it is possible to provide users with very fine-grained access to certain columns and rows from tables, while denying them access to other, more sensitive data stored in the underlying tables. In that case, the view is granted privileges to the tables and the users are granted privileges to the view.

Owner Privileges

The user that creates a view will be its owner. In order to create the view, the user must have the appropriate privileges on the base tables:

- Some views are read-only by nature (see the section "Read-Only and Updatable Views"). To create a read-only view, the creator needs SELECT privileges for any underlying tables.

- For views that are updatable, the creator needs ALL privileges to the underlying tables.

Additionally, the owners of the base tables and other views accessed by the view must grant all required privileges for accessing those objects and for modifying them through the view if required, *to the view itself.* That is, privileges *on* those base objects must be granted *to* the view.

The owner of the view has all privileges for it, including the ability to grant privileges on it to other users, to triggers, and to stored procedures.

User Privileges

The creator of the view must grant the appropriate privileges to users, stored procedures, and other views that need to access the view. A user can be granted privileges to a view without having access to its base tables.

In the case of updatable views, INSERT, UPDATE, and DELETE privileges must be assigned to any users who need to perform DML on underlying tables through the view. Conversely, grant the users only SELECT privileges if your intention is to provide a read-only view.

If a user already has the required rights on the view's base objects, it will automatically have the same rights on the view.

 CAUTION   The less direct a user's privileges are, the more secure the base objects. However, the potential multiplicity of the hierarchies of privileges can cause problems if the chain gets broken by revoking privileges from the view's owner. Considering the attraction of views as a mechanism for protecting data from being seen by the wrong eyes, it behooves the system administrator to maintain reliable documentation of all privileges granted.

For a detailed description of SQL privileges, refer to Chapter 35.

Creating Views

The DDL statement for defining the query specification that will be transformed into a view object is CREATE VIEW. Although it defines a table (albeit a virtual one) and optionally allows custom names to be declared for columns, the syntax does not include any data definitions for the columns. Its structure is formed around the column list of a SELECT statement and the tables specified in the FROM and, optionally, JOIN clauses of the statement.

All styles of joined and union sets that are supported in queries are supported for view definitions. However, it is not possible to define a view that is derived from the output set of a stored procedure and it is not legal to include an ORDER BY clause.

The CREATE VIEW Statement

The syntax pattern for CREATE VIEW is

```
CREATE VIEW view-name
  [(view-column-name [, view-column-name [,...]])]
AS
  <select-specification> [WITH CHECK OPTION];
```

View Name

The view name uniquely identifies the view as an object in the database. The name cannot be the same as the name of any other view, table, or stored procedure.

Specifying View Column Names

Specifying the list of column names for the view is optional if there are no duplicate names in the column list. The names of the underlying columns will be used by default.

In the case where a join would result in duplicates, it becomes mandatory to use a list and rename one of the columns.

This rather ugly example demonstrates how duplication of column names could occur:

```
CREATE VIEW VJOB_LISTING
AS
  SELECT E.*,
  J.JOB_CODE,
  J.JOB_TITLE
FROM EMPLOYEE E
JOIN JOB J
  ON E.JOB_CODE = J.JOB_CODE ;
```

```
ISC ERROR CODE:335544351
unsuccessful metadata update
STORE RDB$RELATION_FIELDS failed
attempt to store duplicate value (visible to active transactions)
in unique index "RDB$INDEX_15"
```

Index RDB$INDEX_15 is a unique index on the relation name and the field name. The JOB_CODE column from the EMPLOYEE table was already stored for VJOB_LISTING, hence the exception.

It is necessary to name all of the columns in this view:

```
CREATE VIEW VJOB_LISTING (
 EMP_NO, FIRST_NAME, LAST_NAME,
 PHONE_EXT, HIRE_DATE, DEPT_NO,
 EMP_JOB_CODE, /* alternative name */
 JOB_GRADE, JOB_COUNTRY, SALARY, FULL_NAME,
 JOB_JOB_CODE, /* alternative name */
 JOB_TITLE)
AS
  SELECT
    E.*,
    J.JOB_CODE,
    J.JOB_TITLE
FROM EMPLOYEE E
JOIN JOB J
  ON E.JOB_CODE = J.JOB_CODE ;
```

A list is mandatory also if the column list contains any fields created from expressions. For example, this fails:

```
CREATE VIEW VJOB_ALTNAMES
AS
  SELECT JOB_CODE || 'for ' || JOB_TITLE AS ALTNAME
  FROM JOB;
```

```
ISC ERROR CODE:335544569
Invalid command
must specify column name for view select expression
```

This succeeds:

```
CREATE VIEW VJOB_ALTNAMES
 (ALTNAME)
AS
  SELECT JOB_CODE || ' for ' || JOB_TITLE
  FROM JOB;
```

The view's column name list specification must correspond in order and number to the columns listed in the SELECT statement.

The SELECT Specification

The SELECT specification is an ordinary SELECT statement that can incorporate joins, expression fields, grouping specifications, and search conditions—but not ordering conditions.

The output list in the SELECT clause defines the types, degree, and, unless explicitly specified, the names of the view's columns.

A SELECT DISTINCT query is valid, if required.

The FROM clause, along with any JOIN clauses or subqueries, defines the base tables of the view.

NOTE   SELECT * FROM <relation> is valid, although not recommended for views if effective self-documentation is in your landscape. When it is used, the column order will follow that of the base table. It is important to remember that if you need to use the column-naming clause (see the "Specifying View Column Names" section).

A WHERE clause can be included if you want to specify search conditions. A valid GROUP BY clause with an optional HAVING clause can also be included.

Defining Computed Columns

The same rules that apply to any expression used for defining a runtime field for a query apply to runtime columns for the view specification. The output is almost parallel to a computed column in a table. However, a computed column has its own, distinct effects in a view:

- It forces the view column-list to become mandatory.

- It makes the query non-updatable.

Suppose you want to create a view that assigns a hypothetical 10-percent salary increase to all employees in the company. The next example creates a read-only view that displays all of the employees and their possible new salaries:

```
CREATE VIEW RAISE_BY_10
  (EMPLOYEE, NEW_SALARY)
AS
SELECT EMP_NO, SALARY * 1.1 FROM EMPLOYEE;
```

WITH CHECK OPTION

WITH CHECK OPTION is an optional syntax item used only in view specifications. It affects updatable views that have been defined with a WHERE clause. Its effect is to block any update operation that would result in a violation of a search condition in the WHERE clause.

Suppose you create a view that allows access to information about all departments with budgets between $10,000 and $500,000. The view, V_SUB_DEPT, could be defined as follows:

```
CREATE VIEW V_SUB_DEPT (
  DEPT_NAME,
  DEPT_NO,
  SUB_DEPT_NO,
  LOW_BUDGET)
AS SELECT
  DEPARTMENT,
  DEPT_NO,
  HEAD_DEPT,
  BUDGET
FROM DEPARTMENT
WHERE BUDGET BETWEEN 10000 AND 500000
WITH CHECK OPTION;
```

A user with INSERT privileges on the view can insert new data into the DEPARTMENT, DEPT_NO, HEAD_DEPT, and BUDGET columns of the base table though this view. WITH CHECK OPTION ensures that all budget values entered through the view fall within the range prescribed by the view.

The following statement inserts a new row for the Publications department through the V_SUB_DEPT view:

```
INSERT INTO V_SUB_DEPT (
  DEPT_NAME,
  DEPT_NO,
  SUB_DEPT_NO,
  LOW_BUDGET)
VALUES ('Publications', '999', '670', 250000);
```

But this statement will fail, because the value of LOW_BUDGET is outside the range prescribed for the target column, BUDGET:

```
INSERT INTO V_SUB_DEPT (
  DEPT_NAME,
  DEPT_NO,
  SUB_DEPT_NO,
  LOW_BUDGET)
VALUES ('Publications', '999', '670', 750000);

ISC ERROR CODE:335544558
Operation violates CHECK constraint  on view or table V_SUB_DEPT
```

A view WITH CHECK OPTION clause can be useful when you want to provide users with an updatable view, but you want to prevent them from updating certain columns. Just include a search condition for each column you want to protect. The clause's usefulness is limited somewhat by the fact that a view cannot be defined with replaceable parameters.

Read-Only and Updatable Views

When a DML operation is performed on a view, the changes can be passed through to the underlying tables from which the view was created only if certain conditions are met. If a view meets these conditions, it is *updatable*. If it does not meet these conditions, it is *read-only*, and writes to the view cannot be passed through to the underlying tables.

Values can only be inserted through a view for those columns named in the view. Firebird stores NULL into any unreferenced columns. A view will not be updatable if there are any columns not in the view that are non-nullable.

A read-only view can be made updatable by means of triggers.

Read-Only Views

A view will be read-only if its SELECT statement has any of the following characteristics:

- Specifies a row quantifier other than ALL (i.e., DISTINCT, FIRST, SKIP)

- Contains fields defined by subqueries or other expressions

- Contains fields defined by aggregating functions and/or a GROUP BY clause

- Includes UNION specifications

- Joins multiple tables

- Does not include all NOT NULL columns from the base table

- Selects from an existing view that is not updatable

Making Read-Only Views Updatable

You can write triggers that will perform the correct writes to the base tables when a DELETE, UPDATE, or INSERT operation is requested for a view. This Firebird feature can turn many non-updatable views into updatable views.

The following script creates two tables, creates a view that is a join of the two tables, and then creates three triggers (one each for DELETE, UPDATE, and INSERT) that will pass all updates on the view through to the base tables:

```
CREATE TABLE Table1 (
ColA INTEGER NOT NULL,
ColB VARCHAR(20),
CONSTRAINT pk_table PRIMARY KEY(ColA)
);
COMMIT;
CREATE TABLE Table2 (
ColA INTEGER NOT NULL,
ColC VARCHAR(20),
CONSTRAINT fk_table2 FOREIGN KEY REFERENCES Table1(ColA)
);
COMMIT;
CREATE VIEW TableView AS
SELECT Table1.ColA, Table1.ColB, Table2.ColC
FROM Table1, Table2
WHERE Table1.ColA = Table2.ColA;
COMMIT;
SET TERM ^;
CREATE TRIGGER TableView_Delete FOR TableView
ACTIVE BEFORE DELETE AS
BEGIN
DELETE FROM Table1
WHERE ColA = OLD.ColA;
DELETE FROM Table2
WHERE ColA = OLD.ColA;
END ^
CREATE TRIGGER TableView_Update FOR TableView
ACTIVE BEFORE UPDATE AS
BEGIN
UPDATE Table1
SET ColB = NEW.ColB
WHERE ColA = OLD.ColA;
UPDATE Table2
SET ColC = NEW.ColC
WHERE ColA = OLD.ColA;
END ^
CREATE TRIGGER TableView_Insert FOR TableView
ACTIVE BEFORE INSERT AS
BEGIN
INSERT INTO Table1 values (NEW.ColA,NEW.ColB);
INSERT INTO Table2 values (NEW.ColA,NEW.ColC);
END ^
COMMIT ^
SET TERM ;^
```

When defining triggers for views, take care to ensure that any triggers on the view do not create a conflict or an unexpected condition with regard to triggers defined for the base tables. The trigger event for the view precedes that for the table, respective of phase (BEFORE/AFTER).

For example, suppose you have a Before Insert trigger on the base table that fetches a fresh generator value for the primary key if its *new.value* is null. If the view trigger includes an INSERT statement for the base table, omit the primary key column from the view's statement. This causes NULL to be passed to the *new.value* of the primary key column, allowing the table trigger to do its work.

For more information about triggers and the *new.** context variables, refer to Chapter 31.

Hopeless Cases

Not all views can be made updatable by defining triggers for them. For example, this handy little read-only view reads a context variable from the server, but regardless of the triggers you define for it, all operations except SELECT will fail:

```
CREATE VIEW SYSTRANS
  (CURR_TRANSACTION) AS
  SELECT CURRENT_TRANSACTION FROM RDB$DATABASE;
```

Naturally Updatable Views

A view is *naturally updatable* if both of the following conditions are met:

- The view specification is a subset of a single table or another updatable view.

- All base table columns excluded from the view definition are nullable.

The following statement creates a naturally updatable view:

```
CREATE VIEW EMP_MNGRS (FIRST, LAST, SALARY) AS
SELECT FIRST_NAME, LAST_NAME, SALARY
FROM EMPLOYEE
WHERE JOB_CODE = 'Mngr'
WITH CHECK OPTION;
```

Because the WITH CHECK OPTION clause was included in this specification, applications will be prevented from changing the JOB_CODE, even if there is no violation of the foreign key constraint on this column in the base table.

Changing the Behavior of Updatable Views

Alternative behavior for naturally updatable views can be specified using triggers. For a particular phase (BEFORE/AFTER) of an operation, the view triggers fire before the base table's triggers. With care and skill, it is thus possible to use views to pre-empt the normal trigger behavior of the base table under planned circumstances.

It is also possible to create havoc with badly planned view triggers. Test, test, test!

Modify a View Definition?

The terms *updatable* and *read-only* refer to how the data in the base tables can be accessed, not to whether the *view definition* can be modified. Firebird does not provide an ALTER VIEW syntax.

To modify a view definition, you must drop the view and then re-create it.

Dropping a View

The DROP VIEW statement enables a view's owner to remove its definition from the database. It does not affect the base tables associated with the view.

This is the syntax:

```
DROP VIEW view-name;
```

The DROP VIEW operation will fail if you are not logged in as the owner of the view or if the view is used by another object, such as a view, a stored procedure, a trigger on another view, or a table or a CHECK constraint definition.

The following statement removes a view definition:

```
DROP VIEW SUB_DEPT;
```

Using Views in SQL

In SQL a view behaves in many ways just like a regular table. You can select from it, with or without ORDER BY, GROUP BY, and WHERE clauses.

If it is naturally updatable, or it has been made updatable by triggers, and the appropriate SQL privileges exist, you can perform both positioned and searched update, insert, and delete operations on it, which will operate on the underlying table. You can also do the following:

- You can create views of views.

- You can process the output of a selection from a view in PSQL modules.

- You can perform a JOIN between a view and other views and tables. In some cases, you can join views with selectable stored procedures.

For a simple illustration, we will create a view and a stored procedure on the Employee table and join them. This is the view:

```
CREATE VIEW V_EMP_NAMES
  AS
  SELECT EMP_NO, LAST_NAME, FIRST_NAME
  FROM EMPLOYEE ^
COMMIT ^
```

This is the stored procedure:

```
CREATE PROCEDURE P_EMP_NAMES
RETURNS (
  EMP_NO SMALLINT;
  EMP_NAME VARCHAR(35))
AS
BEGIN
  FOR SELECT EMP_NO, FIRST_NAME || ' ' || LAST_NAME
  FROM EMPLOYEE
  INTO :EMP_NO, :EMP_NAME
  DO
    SUSPEND;
END ^
COMMIT ^
```

This is a query that joins them:

```
SELECT
    V.EMP_NO,
    V.LAST_NAME,
    V.FIRST_NAME,
    P.EMP_NAME
  FROM V_EMP_NAMES V
  JOIN P_EMPNAMES P
  ON V.EMP_NO = P.EMPNO ^
```

Using Query Plans for Views

Views may present some difficulty for users of the PLAN feature. Ordinarily, users may treat a view the same as a table. However, if you want to define a custom plan, you need to be aware of the indexes and structures of the base table(s) participating in the view.

The optimizer treats a view reference as if the base tables used in creating the view were inserted into the FROM list of the query.

Suppose a view is created as follows:

```
CREATE VIEW V_PROJ_LEADERS (
  PROJ_ID,
  PROJ_TITLE,
```

```
    LEADER_ID,
    LEADER_NAME)
AS
  SELECT
    P.PROJ_ID,
    P.PROJ_NAME,
    P.TEAM_LEADER,
    E.FULL_NAME,
  FROM PROJECT P
    JOIN EMPLOYEE E
    ON P.TEAM_LEADER = E.EMPNO;
```

A simple query on the view

```
SELECT * FROM V_PROJ_LEADERS;
```

outputs this plan:

```
PLAN JOIN (V_PROJ_LEADERS P NATURAL,V_PROJ_LEADERS E INDEX (RDB$PRIMARY7))
```

Notice that the optimizer accesses the indexes of the base tables (through the aliases P and E) to evaluate the best way to retrieve the view. It is the SELECT specification of the CREATE VIEW declaration that determines the logic for executing the join.

The next query is a little more complex. This time, the view is joined to the table EMPLOYEE_PROJECT, an intersection of the primary keys of the EMPLOYEE and PROJECT tables. From there, it is joined back into the EMPLOYEE table, to provide a denormalized listing that includes the names of the members of all of the projects commanded by the view:

```
SELECT
  PL.*,
  EMP.LAST_NAME
FROM V_PROJ_LEADERS PL
JOIN EMPLOYEE_PROJECT EP
  ON PL.PROJ_ID = EP.PROJ_ID
JOIN EMPLOYEE EMP
  ON EP.EMP_NO = EMP.EMP_NO;

PLAN JOIN (EMP NATURAL,EP INDEX (RDB$FOREIGN15),PL P INDEX (RDB$PRIMARY12),
PL E INDEX (RDB$PRIMARY7))
```

This time, the foreign key index on the EMPLOYEE_PROJECT (aliased as EP) column EMP_NO is used to select the project members' names from the second "hit" on EMPLOYEE. As before, the join inside the view uses the primary key of EMPLOYEE to search for TEAM_LEADER matches.

If you decide to write a custom plan for a query that works on a view, you need to be familiar with the view definition in your own estimations of indexes and access methods.

A Known Bug with Views in Firebird 1.0.*x*

If you define a view that is a UNION of two or more sets, the view will misbehave badly if used in a subquery in Firebird 1.0.*x*. For example, the following query will crash the server:

```
SELECT 1 FROM Table1
WHERE EXISTS (
  SELECT FIELD1 FROM UNION_VIEW
    WHERE <search-conditions> )
```

The bug was fixed before the v.1.5 release.

Other Derived Tables

Firebird currently supports two other forms of derived table: the *selectable stored procedure* and the *external virtual table* (EVT).

Selectable Stored Procedures

Firebird's PSQL extensions provide syntax for defining a stored procedure that outputs a derived set of data from virtually anywhere: from the database, from context variables (even from input variables alone), from external tables, or from any combination. PSQL and DSQL SELECT syntax provides for these virtual tables to be retrieved just as though they were real tables.

The output set for a selectable stored procedure is defined as a set of output variables, using the RETURNS clause of a CREATE PROCEDURE statement. The output data is created by looping through a cursor set, defined by a SELECT statement, and reading the values of the specified columns into these output variables or into declared local variables. Within the loop, almost anything can be done to manipulate the data, including processing embedded loops. A selectable stored procedure can be called from (embedded in) another stored procedure. Anything that can be selected, calculated, or derived can be transformed to output.

As a simple illustration, the following stored procedure declaration sets up a loop and proceeds to pass processed rows, one at a time, to the output buffer:

```
CREATE PROCEDURE SHOW_JOBS_FOR_COUNTRY (
  COUNTRY VARCHAR(15))
RETURNS ( /* the virtual table */
  CODE VARCHAR(11),
  TITLE VARCHAR(25),
  GRADE SMALLINT)
```

```
AS
BEGIN
  FOR SELECT job_code, job_title, job_grade FROM job
        WHERE JOB_COUNTRY = :COUNTRY
        INTO :CODE, :TITLE, :GRADE
  DO
    BEGIN /* begin the loop */
      CODE = 'CODE: ' || CODE; /* mess about with the value a little */
      SUSPEND; /* this outputs one row per loop */
    END
END
```

When the stored procedure is compiled, it is ready for action. Retrieval of the set is by way of a slightly specialized SELECT statement that can, if required, take constant arguments as input parameters:

```
SELECT * FROM SHOW_JOBS_FOR_COUNTRY ('England');
```

```
CODE            TITLE                      GRADE
===========     =========================  =====
CODE: Admin     Administrative Assistant       5
CODE: Eng       Engineer                       4
CODE: Sales     Sales Co-ordinator             3
CODE: SRep      Sales Representative           4
```

For details about creating and using stored procedures, refer to Part Seven. Selectable stored procedures are discussed in detail in Chapter 30.

External Virtual Tables

An external virtual table (EVT) is a table that gets its data from some external data source rather than from the database. The results of a query on an EVT are treated in exactly the same way as the results of any other query, and they look exactly as if they came from a database table. This allows the integration of external data such as real-time data feeds, formatted data in operating system files, other databases (even non-SQL databases), and any other tabular data sources.

Firebird implements EVTs by means of the EXTERNAL FILE clause of the CREATE TABLE statement. External data is read from fixed-format text records into regular Firebird data columns.

Firebird external tables can also insert records into EVTs.

For more information, refer to the section "Using External Files As Tables" in Chapter 16.

Up Next

The next part of the book deals with the essential and underdocumented topic of transactions. The emphasis on the under-the-hood technical detail in the upcoming three chapters is deliberate: The better you understand what is happening during the interactions between multiple clients and the server, the more effective, intuitive, and productive your application designs can be.

Part Six

Transactions

CHAPTER 25

Overview of Firebird Transactions

IN A CLIENT/SERVER DATABASE SUCH AS FIREBIRD, client applications never touch the data that is physically stored in the pages of the database. Instead, the client applications conduct conversations with the database management system—"the server"—by packaging requests and responses inside transactions. This part of the book visits some of the key concepts and issues of transaction management in Firebird.

A data management system that is being updated by multiple users concurrently is vulnerable to a number of data integrity problems if work is allowed to overlap without any control. In summary, these problems are

- **Lost updates**: These occur when two users have the same view of a set and one user performs changes, closely followed by the other user, who overwrites the first user's work.

- **Dirty reads**: These permit one user to see the changes that another user is in the process of doing, with no guarantee that the other user's changes are final.

- **Non-reproducible reads**: These allow one user to select rows continually while other users are updating and deleting. Whether this is a problem depends on the circumstances. For example, a month-end financials process or a snapshot inventory audit will be skewed under these conditions, whereas a ticketing application needs to keep all users' views synchronized to avoid double booking.

- **Phantom rows**: These arise when one user can select some but not all new rows written by another user. Again, this may be acceptable in some situations, but it will skew the outcomes of some processes.

- **Interleaved transactions**: These can arise when changes in one row by one user affect the data in other rows in the same table or in other tables being accessed by other users. They are usually related to timing, occurring when there is no way to control or predict the sequence in which users will perform the changes.

To solve these problems, Firebird applies a management model that isolates every task inside a unique *context* that prescribes the outcome if work within that task would be at risk of overlapping work being performed by other tasks. The state of the database cannot change if there is any conflict.

NOTE   Firebird does not permit dirty reads. In certain conditions, by design, it allows non-reproducible reads.

The ACID Properties

It is now more than 20 years since two researchers, Theo Haërder and Andreas Reuter, published a review paper describing requirements for maintaining the integrity of a database in a parallel updating environment. They distilled the requirements into four precepts defined as *atomicity, consistency, isolation,* and *durability*—abbreviated as ACID.[1] Over the succeeding years, the ACID concept evolved as a benchmark for the implementation of transactions in database systems.

Atomicity

A transaction (also known as a *unit of work*) is described as consisting of a collection of data-transforming actions. To be "atomic," the transaction must be implemented in such a way that it provides the "all-or-nothing illusion that either all of these operations are performed or none of them is performed."[2] The transaction either completes as a whole (commits) or aborts (rolls back).

Consistency

Transactions are assumed to perform correct transformations of the abstract system state—that is, the database must be left in a consistent state after a transaction completes, regardless of whether it commits or rolls back. The transaction concept assumes that programmers have mechanisms available to them for declaring points of consistency and validating them. In SQL, the standards provide for triggers, referential integrity constraints, and check constraints to implement those mechanisms at the server.

Isolation

While a transaction is updating shared data, the system must give each transaction the illusion that it is running in isolation; it should appear that all other transactions ran

---

1. Theo Haërder and Andreas Reuter, "Principles of Transaction-Oriented Database Recovery," *ACM Computing Surveys* 15(4) (1983): 287–317.

2. Andreas Reuter and Jim Gray, *Transaction Processing Concepts and Techniques* (San Francisco, CA: Morgan Kaufmann, 1993).

either before it began or after it committed. While data is in transition from a starting consistent state to a final consistent state, it may be inconsistent with database state, but no data may be exposed to other transactions until the changes are committed.

Chapter 26 explores the three levels of isolation for transactions that Firebird implements, along with the options available to respond to conflicts and prevent the work of one transaction from interfering with the work of another.

Durability

Once a transaction commits, its updates must be *durable*—that is, the new state of all objects made visible to other transactions by the commit will be preserved and irreversible, regardless of events such as hardware failure or software crashing.

Context of a Transaction

A complete conversation between a client and the server is known as a *transaction*. Each transaction has a unique *context* that causes it to be isolated from all other transactions in a specific way. The rules for the transaction's context are specified by the client application program, by passing *transaction parameters*. A transaction starts when a client signals the beginning of the transaction and receives a *transaction handle* back from the server. It remains *active* until the client either *commits* the work (if it can) or *rolls it back*.

One Transaction, Many Requests

In Firebird, every operation requested by a client must occur in the context of an active transaction. One transaction can entail one or many client requests and server responses within its bounds. A single transaction can span more than a single database, encompassing reads from and writes to multiple databases in the course of a task. Tasks that create databases or change their physical structure (single or batched DDL statements) entail transactions, too. Client and server each has its role:

- **Client role**: Clients initiate all transactions. Once a transaction is under way, a client is responsible for submitting requests to read and write and also for completing (committing or rolling back) every transaction it starts.

  A single client connection can have multiple transactions active.

- **Server role**: It is the job of the server to account for each transaction uniquely and keep each transaction's view of database state consistent with its context. It has to manage all requests to change the database so that conflicts are handled appropriately and any risk of breaking the consistency of database state is pre-empted.

Figure 25-1 broadly illustrates a typical read-write transaction context from start to finish. It shows how the server manages many concurrent transactions independently of all others, even if the other transactions are active in the same client application.

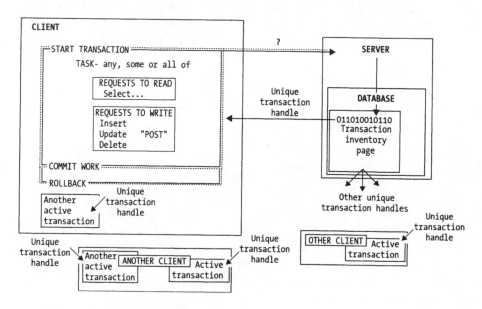

Figure 25-1. Transaction context and independence

In this illustration, the application may use the transaction to select (read) sets of rows, any of which may be chosen by the user for updating or deleting. In the same transaction, new rows might be inserted. Update, insert, or delete requests are "posted" to the server, one by one, as the user performs her task.

Atomicity of the Model

The capability for a client application to issue multiple, reversible requests inside a single Firebird transaction has obvious advantages for tasks that need to execute a single statement many times with a variety of input parameters. It inherently provides *atomicity* for tasks where a group of statements must be executed and, finally, either committed as a single job or rolled back entirely if an exception occurs.

Transactions and MGA

MGA, an acronym for *multi-generational architecture*, refers to the architectural model underlying Firebird's database state management.

In the MGA model, each row stored in the database holds the unique transaction ID of the transaction that writes it. If another transaction posts a change to the row, the server writes a new version of the row to disk, with the new transaction ID, and converts an image of the older version into a reference (known as the *delta*) to this new version. The server now holds two "generations" of the same row.

Post vs. COMMIT

The term "post" has probably been borrowed from older desktop accounting software as an analogy to the posting of journals in accounting systems. The analogy is useful for distinguishing the two separate operations of *writing a reversible change* to the database (by executing a statement) and *committing all of the changes* executed by one or several statements. Posted changes are invisible beyond the boundaries of their transaction context and can be rolled back. Committed changes are permanent and become visible to transactions that are subsequently started or updated.

If any conflict occurs upon posting, the server returns an exception message to the client and the commit fails. The application must then deal with the conflict according to its kind. The solution to an update conflict is often to roll back the transaction, causing all of the work to be "undone" as an atomic unit. If there is no conflict, the application can proceed to commit the work when it is ready.

NOTE　Calls from the client to COMMIT or to ROLLBACK are the only possible ways to end a transaction. A failure to commit does not cause the server to roll back the transaction.

Rollback

Rollback never fails. It will undo any changes that were requested during the transaction—the change that caused the exception as well as any that would have succeeded had the exception not occurred.

Some rolled-back transactions do not leave row images on the disk. For example, any rollbacks instigated by the server to undo work performed by triggers simply vanish, and the record images created by inserts are normally expunged during rollback, with reference to an auto-undo log that is maintained for inserts. If a single transaction inserts a huge number of records, the auto-undo log is abandoned, with the result that a rollback will leave the images on disk. Other conditions that may cause inserted record images to remain on disk include server crashes during the operation or use of a transaction setting that explicitly requests "no auto-undo."[3]

---

3. API programmers, look for the TPB constant *isc_tpb_no_auto_undo*.

Row Locking

Under MGA, the existence of a pending new version of a row has the effect of locking it. In most conditions, the existence of a *committed* newer version blocks a request to update or delete the row as well—a *locking conflict*.

On receiving a request to update or delete, the server inspects the states of any transactions that "own" newer versions of the row. If the newest of those owner transactions is active or has been committed, the server responds to the requesting transaction according to the context (isolation level and lock resolution parameters) of the requesting transaction.

If the newest version's transaction is *active*, the requesting transaction will, by default, wait for it to be completed (committed or rolled back), and then the server will allow it to proceed. However, if NOWAIT was specified, it returns a conflict exception to the requesting transaction.

If the newest version's transaction is *committed* and the requesting transaction is in SNAPSHOT (i.e., concurrency) isolation, the server refuses the request and reports a lock *conflict*. If the transaction is in READ COMMITTED isolation, with the default RECORD_VERSION setting, the server allows the request and writes a new record version on behalf of the transaction.

NOTE   Other conditions are possible when the requesting transaction is in READ COMMITTED. The outcome of any transaction request may also be affected by unusual, pre-emptive conditions in the context of the transaction that owns the *pending* change. For more information about these variations, refer to the next chapter, where the transaction parameters are explored in detail.

Firebird does not use conventional two-phase locking at all for the most usual transaction contexts. Hence, all normal locking is at the row level and is said to be *optimistic*—each row is available to all read-write transactions until a writer creates a newer version of it.

Upon a successful commit, the old record version referenced by the delta image becomes an obsolete record.

- If the operation was an update, the new image becomes the latest committed version and the original image of the record, with the ID of the transaction that last updated it, is made available for garbage collection.

- If the operation was a deletion, a "stump" replaces the obsolete record. A *sweep* or a backup clears this stump and releases the physical space on disk that was occupied by the deleted row.

For information about sweeping and garbage collection, refer to the section "Database 'Hygiene'" in Chapter 15. Manual sweeping is described in Chapter 39. In summary, under *normal* conditions:

- Any transaction can read any row that was committed before it started.

- Any read-write transaction can request to update or delete a row.

- A request (post) will usually succeed if no other read-write transaction has already posted or committed a change to a newer version of the record. Read-committed transactions are usually allowed to post changes overwriting versions committed by newer transactions.

- If a post succeeds, the transaction has a "lock" on the row. Other readers can still read the latest committed version, but none will succeed in posting an update or delete statement for that row.

Table-Level Locks

A transaction can be configured to lock whole tables. There are two acceptable ways to do this in DSQL: by isolating the transaction in SNAPSHOT TABLE STABILITY (aka consistency mode, forced repeatable read) or by *table reservation*. It should be emphasized that these configurations are for when unusually pre-emptive conditions are required. They are not recommended in Firebird for everyday use.

An *unacceptable* way to impose a table-level lock (Firebird 1.5 and later) is to apply a statement-level pessimistic lock that affects the whole table. A statement such as the following can do that:

```
SELECT * FROM ATABLE
FOR UPDATE WITH LOCK;
```

It is not, strictly speaking, an issue of transaction configuration. However, the configuration of the transaction that owns sets retrieved with this explicit pessimistic lock is important. The issue of pessimistic locking is discussed in Chapter 27.

Inserts

There are no deltas or locks for inserts. If another transaction has not pre-empted inserts by a table-level lock, an insert will always succeed if it does not violate any constraints or validation checks.

Transaction "Aging" and Statistics

When a client process secures a transaction handle, it acquires a unique internal identifier for the transaction and stores it on a transaction inventory page (TIP).

Transaction ID and Age

Transaction IDs (TIDs) are 32-bit integers that are generated in a single-stepping series. A new or freshly restored database begins the series at 1. Transaction age is determined from the TID: lowest is oldest.

TIDs and their associated state data are stored on TIPs. On the database header page, system accounting maintains a set of fields containing TIDs that are of interest to it, namely the oldest interesting transaction (OIT), the oldest active transaction (OAT), and the number to be used for the next transaction. A "snapshot" TID is also written each time the OAT increases—usually the same TID as the OAT or close to it.

Getting the Transaction ID

Firebird 1.5 and later provide the context variable CURRENT_TRANSACTION that returns the TID of the transaction that requests it. It can be used in SQL wherever it is appropriate to use an expression. For example, to store the TID into a log table, you could use it like this:

```
INSERT INTO BOOK_OF_LIFE
  (TID, COMMENT, SIGNATURE)
VALUES
  (CURRENT_TRANSACTION,
   'This has been a great day for transactions',
   CURRENT_USER);
```

It is important to remember that TIDs are cyclic. Because the numbering series will be reset after each restore, they should not be used for primary keys or unique constraints.

Transaction ID Overflow

As previously mentioned, the TID is a 32-bit integer. If a series hit its 4GB limit and rolls over, bad things will happen. When the last transaction ends, the system transaction will not work and metadata updates will be impossible. Garbage collection will stop. User transactions will not start.

At 100 transactions per second, it takes 1 year, 4 months, 11 days, 2 hours, and roughly 30 minutes to roll over the TID.[4]

---

4. Thanks, Ann Harrison!

Backing up and restoring into a fresh database resets the TID. Until recently, a neglected database would have had other trauma before the TID series exhausted itself. Now, with larger page sizes, larger disks, and a reduced need to watch the size of database files, the risk of blowing a TID series is more apparent.

"Interesting Transactions"

Server and client transaction accounting routines use TIDs to track the states of transactions. "Housekeeping" routines take the age of transactions into account when deciding which old record versions are "interesting" and which are not. Uninteresting transactions can be flagged for removal. The server remains "interested in" every transaction that has not been hard-committed by a COMMIT statement.

Active, limbo, rolled back, and "dead" transactions are all interesting. Transactions that have been committed using COMMIT WITH RETAIN (aka *soft commit* or *CommitRetaining*) remain active until they are hard-committed and are thus interesting. Conditions can develop in which interesting transactions become "stuck" and inhibit performance.

If neglected, stuck transactions will become the source of serious performance degradation. A stuck OIT will cause the number of transaction inventory pages to grow. The server maintains a bitmapped working table of the transactions stored in the TIPs. The table is copied and written to the database at the start of each transaction. As it becomes bloated by stuck transactions, it uses progressively more memory resources and memory becomes fragmented from constant reallocation of the resources.

Oldest Interesting Transaction

The OIT is the lowest numbered transaction in the TIPs that is in a non-committed state.

Oldest Active Transaction

The OAT is the lowest numbered transaction in the TIPs that is active. A transaction is active as long as it is not hard-committed, not rolled back, and not in limbo.

Read-Only Transactions

A read-only transaction remains active (and interesting in some ways) until it is committed. However, an active read-only transaction that is in the recommended READ COMMITTED isolation level (see Chapter 26) never gets stuck and will not interfere with system housekeeping.

CAUTION Don't confuse a read-only transaction with a read-write transaction that is in the process of passing output to a user interface from a SELECT statement. Even if the application makes the output set read-only, the underlying SELECT statement inside a read-write transaction can be—and often is—the cause of system slowdown.

Background Garbage Collection

Record versions from rolled-back transactions are purged from the database when they are found in the course of normal data processing. As a rule, if a row is accessed by a statement, any uninteresting old record versions that are eligible for removal will be tagged for collection by the garbage collection thread.

Some "corners" of the database might not be visited for a long time by any statements, so there is no guarantee that all of the record versions created by a rolled-back transaction will be tagged and, eventually, removed. As long as the record versions remain, the interesting transaction must remain "interesting" to preserve the state of the database.

TIP A full database scan (by a backup, typically) will perform garbage collection, but it cannot change the state of transactions. That is the job of the "full" garbage collection performed by a sweep.

Rolled-Back Transactions

Transactions in the rolled-back state are not garbage collected. They remain interesting until a database sweep tags them as "committed" and releases them for garbage collection. In systems with low contention, a periodic manual sweep may be all that is needed to deal with them.

Some systems that are not well designed to deal with conflicts demonstrate high levels of rollback and tend to accumulate interesting transactions faster than the automatic database housekeeping procedures can cope with. Such systems should be subjected to scheduled manual sweeps often if automatic sweeping seems not to manage well.

"Dead" Transactions

Transactions are said to be "dead" if they are in an active state, but there is no connection context associated with them. Transactions typically "die" in client applications that do not take care to end them before disconnecting users. Dead transactions are also part of the flotsam left behind when client applications crash or network connections are broken abnormally.

The server cannot tell the difference between a genuinely active transaction and a dead one. As long as the cleanup following connection timeout is able to proceed and the regular garbage collection kicks in in a timely fashion, dead transactions need not be a problem. The timeout cleanup will roll them back and their garbage will eventually be dealt with normally.

Frequent, large accumulations of dead transactions can be a problem. Because they are rolled back, too many of them remain interesting for too long. In a system where user behavior, frequent crashes, power cuts, or network faults generate huge numbers of dead transactions, dead-transaction garbage will become a big problem for performance.

Limbo Transactions

Limbo transactions, which are discussed in more detail in Chapter 26, happen in the course of a failed two-phase COMMIT operation across multiple databases. The system recognizes them as a special case for human intervention, since the server itself cannot determine whether it is safe to either commit them or roll them back without causing inconsistency in a different database.

The only way to resolve a limbo transaction is to run the **gfix** tool over the database with the appropriate switches to achieve the desired outcome. Resolution changes the state of a limbo transaction to either "committed" or "rolled back." From that point, it is managed just like any other committed or rolled-back transaction.

Keeping the OIT and OAT Moving

The admonition to "Keep the OIT and OAT moving" is a catchphrase around all support solutions where performance is the problem. Time spent understanding the life cycle of transactions in Firebird's multi-generational architecture will be one of your best investments for future work with Firebird and other open source databases.[5]

To begin understanding the interaction between the client processes that "own" transactions, on the one hand, and the transaction inventory accounting maintained in the database, on the other, it is useful to be acquainted with the way the server and transactions interact in the mechanism.

The Transaction State Bitmap

The internal *transaction state bitmap* (TSB) is a table of TIDs and their states, maintained by the server, that is initialized when an initial attachment is made to a database. In logical terms, the TSB tabulates each transaction found in the TIPs that is newer than

---

5. Understanding the transaction life cycle in Firebird is also a good investment if you are working with other RDBM systems, such as PostgreSQL, that have imitated Firebird's multi-generational architecture.

the OIT. While there are attachments to the database, the server process maintains the TSB *dynamically*, adding newer TIDs, updating states, and sloughing off the TIDs that become uninteresting (i.e., get committed). It writes updates to the TIPs without reading them again from disk.

Figure 25-2 illustrates the steps. Each time the server processes a request for a transaction handle, it reads the database header page to acquire the TID for the next transaction. The TSB is updated and updates are written to the transaction inventory pages in the database.

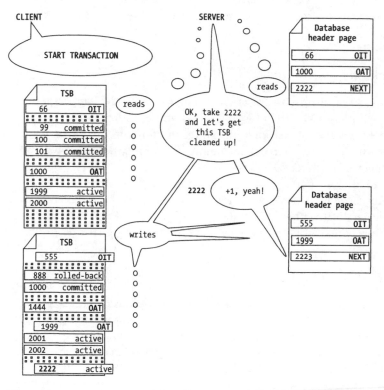

Figure 25-2. Interaction of the client/server process and the TSB

"Moving the OIT (and/or the OAT) forward" is Firebird-speak for the evolving increase in the values of the OIT and OAT in the bitmap and in the database header page as older transactions get committed and are eliminated from the TSB and newer transactions become identified as "oldest." Updating the database header page with the latest OIT, OAT, and Next Transaction values is part of this dynamic ecology.

If the new transaction is a SNAPSHOT transaction, it will have its own copy of the TSB to maintain a consistent view of database state as it was when it began. A READ COMMITTED transaction always refers to the latest "global" TSB to get access to versions committed after it began.

Conditions for Updating the OIT and OAT

Each time the server starts another transaction, it tests the state of the TIDs it is holding in the TSB, eliminates those whose state has changed to "committed," and re-evaluates the OIT and OAT values. It compares them with those stored in the database page and, if necessary, includes them in the data accompanying the write of the new "Next Transaction" ID it sends to the database header.

The OAT will keep moving forward if transactions are kept short enough to prevent active transactions and garbage from committed newer transactions from piling up. The OIT will keep moving forward as long as client processes are committing substantially more work than they are rolling back or losing as the result of crashes. Under these conditions, database performance will be in good shape.

A stuck OAT is worse than a stuck OIT. In a well-performing system, the difference between the OAT and the newest transaction should be a reasonably steady approximation of the number of client processes running times the average number of transactions running per process. Sweep in off-work hours or keep automatic sweeping in force, or do both.

In Chapter 27 you will find some client application strategies for optimizing the progress of the OIT and OAT.

The "Gap"

The "gap" is another piece of Firebird-speak. It refers to the difference between the OIT and the OAT. The gap will be small in comparison with overall transaction throughput or, ideally, zero. In these conditions, it can be a reasonable assumption that there are no transactions hanging around that are causing the TSB to bloat and the TIPs to proliferate outlandishly.

It is not the gap itself that impedes performance. The gap is an indicator of the volume of overhead that sub-optimal transaction management is adding to database activity—overuse and fragmentation of memory, excessive numbers of page-reads during searches, and new page-allocations during updates and inserts. Solving and avoiding problems of degrading performance is all about controlling and reducing the gap.

Sweeping vs. Garbage Collection

Garbage collection (GC) is a continual background process that is a function of the normal course of record retrieval and record-version checking that is performed for each transaction. When obsolete record versions are found with TIDs lower than the OAT, one of two things will happen:

- On Classic server, obsolete record versions are removed immediately. This is referred to as *cooperative* garbage collection, because each transaction and each server instance participates in clearing garbage left behind by others.

- On Superserver, obsolete record versions are "tagged" in an internal list of items for removal by the GC thread. When a GC thread is "woken up," it will deal with the items in this list and update it.

Sweeping performs this task too, but, unlike GC, it can deal with one category of interesting transactions: those that are in "rolled-back" state. It can also remove the "stumps" of deleted records and release the space for reuse.

The gap is important for *automatic sweeping* because the *sweep interval* setting of the database governs the maximum size the gap is allowed to be, before a sweep is triggered off. Automatic sweeping is a backstop that is rarely or never triggered in some databases because the gap never reaches the threshold number.

By default, each database is created with a sweep interval (maximum gap size) of 20,000. It can be varied up or down, if necessary, or disabled altogether by setting the interval to 0.

It should be stressed that a gap that is consistently smaller than the sweep interval is not an indication that the database never needs sweeping. All databases must be swept—it is a question of human management whether they are swept automatically, or manually with **gfix**, or both. Think of automatic sweeping as a safety net, not as a substitute for sensible database management.

Transaction Statistics

Firebird has some useful utilities for querying how well your database is managing the gap between the OIT and the OAT. You can use either to inspect the values on the database header page.

gstat

The command-line tool **gstat**, used with the –header switch, reveals a number of database statistics, including the current TIDs of the OIT, the OAT, and the next new transaction. To use **gstat**, log in as SYSDBA on the host machine in a command shell and go to your Firebird bin directory. Type the following in Windows:

```
gstat -h <path-to-database> -user sysdba -password masterkey
```

Type this in POSIX:

```
./gstat -h <path-to-database> -user sysdba -password masterkey
```

This is an extract from near the top of the output:

```
Oldest transaction 10075
Oldest active 100152
Oldest snapshot 100152
Next transaction 100153
```

The terms in the report can be confusing. When looking at the **gstat** output, note that

- The oldest transaction is the OIT.

- The oldest active is obviously the OAT.

- The oldest snapshot is usually the same as the OAT—it gets written when the OAT moves forward. It is the actual TID that the garbage collector reads as a signal that there is some garbage that it can handle.

isql

You can get a similar view of the database header statistics in an **isql** session, using the SHOW DATABASE command.

Many of the third-party Firebird admin tools provide equivalent reports.

What the Statistics Can Tell You

It is a "given" that no GC will ever be performed on obsolete record versions left behind by *interesting* transactions. However, the oldest snapshot marks the boundary where the garbage collector stops looking for *committed* transactions. Any garbage from that transaction number upward will be unattended.

If the gap between the OAT and the Next Transaction indicates a much higher number of transactions than you can account for by an enumeration of logged-in users and their tasks, you can be certain that a lot of garbage is missing the garbage collector. As that gap keeps growing, database performance becomes more and more sluggish. Servers have been known to throw an "Out of memory" error or just crash because the TSB exhausted memory or caused too much fragmentation for the system's memory management services to handle. Low-end servers—especially those being used to deliver other services—may not even have enough resources to record the evidence in the log.

If gaps, either between the OIT and the OAT or between the OAT and the Next Transaction, seem to be a problem in your system, you can learn a lot about the effects of sweeping the database and improving your client applications if you keep logs of the statistics.

 TIP To obtain a text file of the simple statistics, simply pipe the output of gstat –h to a text file according to the rules of your command shell. In the **isql** shell, use the output *<filename>* command to begin piping the output from the SHOW DATABASE command.

Up Next

Drivers that hide explicit transaction management from the application developer and flatten out the differences between different vendors' SQL implementations are rarely conducive to well-performing user applications or to good database health and hygiene. The next chapter examines the various parameter combinations available for configuring transactions and strategies you can use to tailor transactions for each task.

Configuring Transactions

A TRANSACTION IS A "BUBBLE" AROUND any piece of work affecting the state of a database or, indeed, of more than one database. A user process starts a transaction and the same user process finishes it. Because user processes come in many shapes and sizes, every transaction is configurable. The mandatory and optional properties of a transaction are important parts of any transaction context.

Concurrency

The term *concurrency* broadly refers to the state in which two or more tasks are running inside the same database at the same time. In these conditions, the database is sometimes said to be supporting *parallel tasks*. Inside a transaction's own "bubble," the owning process will be allowed to perform any operation that

- Is consistent with its own current view of the database

- Would not, if committed, interfere with the consistency of any other active transaction's current view of the database

Each transaction is configured by means of a constellation of parameters that enable the client process to predict, with absolute assurance, how the database engine will respond if it detects a potential inconsistency. The engine's interpretation of "consistency" is governed by the transaction's configuration. That, in turn, is governed by the client application.

Factors Affecting Concurrency

The four configurable parameters that affect concurrency are

- Isolation level

- Lock resolution mode (aka blocking mode)

- Access mode

- Table reservation

For one level of isolation (READ COMMITTED), the current states of the *record versions* are also considered.

Isolation Level

Firebird provides three outright levels of transaction isolation to define the "depth" of consistency the transaction requires. At one extreme, a transaction can get exclusive write access to an entire table, while at the other extreme, the uncommitted transaction becomes current with every external change of database state. No Firebird transaction will ever see any *uncommitted* changes pending for other transactions.

In Firebird, isolation level can be READ COMMITTED, SNAPSHOT, or SNAPSHOT TABLE STABILITY. Within READ COMMITTED, two sub-levels are available: RECORD_VERSION and NO_RECORD_VERSION.

Standard Levels of Isolation

The SQL standard for transaction isolation is "sympathetic" to the two-phase locking mechanism that most RDBMSs use to implement isolation. It is quite idiosyncratic in comparison with many of the other standards. It defines isolation not so much in terms of ideals as in terms of the *phenomena* each level allows (or denies). The phenomena with which the standard is concerned are

- **Dirty read**: Occurs if the transaction is able to read the uncommitted (pending) changes of others.

- **Non-repeatable read**: Occurs if subsequent reads of the same set of rows during the course of the transaction could be different from what was read in those rows when the transaction began.

- **Phantom rows**: Occur if a subsequent set of rows read during the transaction differs from the set that was read when the transaction began. The phantom phenomenon happens if the subsequent read includes new rows inserted and/or excludes rows deleted that were committed since the first read.

Table 26-1 shows the four standard isolation levels recognized by the standard, with the phenomena that govern their definitions.

Table 26-1. SQL Standard Isolation Levels and Governing Phenomena

ISOLATION LEVEL	DIRTY READ	NON-REPEATABLE READ	PHANTOMS
READ UNCOMMITTED	Allowed	Allowed	Allowed
READ COMMITTED	Disallowed	Allowed	Allowed
REPEATABLE READ	Disallowed	Disallowed	Allowed
SERIALIZABLE	Disallowed	Disallowed	Disallowed

READ UNCOMMITTED is not supported in Firebird at all. READ COMMITTED conforms to the standard. At the two deeper levels, the nature of MGA prevails over the two-phase locking limitations implied by the standard. Mapping to the standard governance of REPEATABLE READ and SERIALIZABLE is not possible.

READ COMMITTED

The shallowest level of isolation is READ COMMITTED. It is the only level whose view of database state changes during the course of the transaction since, every time the latest committed version of a record it is accessing changes, the newly committed record version replaces the version the transaction began with. Inserts committed since this transaction began are made visible to it.

By design, READ COMMITTED isolation allows non-repeatable reads and does not prevent the phenomenon of phantom rows. It is the most useful level for high-volume, real-time data entry operations because it reduces data contention, but it is unsuitable for tasks that need a reproducible view.

Because of the transient nature of READ COMMITTED isolation, the transaction (*ThisTransaction*) can be configured to respond more conservatively to external commits and other pending transactions:

- With RECORD_VERSION (the default flag), the engine lets ThisTransaction read the latest committed version. If ThisTransaction is in READ WRITE mode, it will be allowed to overwrite the latest committed version if its own TID is newer than the TID on the latest committed version.

- With NO_RECORD_VERSION, the engine effectively mimics the behavior of systems that use two-phase locking to control concurrency. It blocks ThisTransaction from reading the row if there is a pending update on it. Resolution depends on the *lock resolution* setting:

  - With WAIT, ThisTransaction waits until the other transaction either commits or rolls back its change. Its change will then be allowed if the other transaction is rolled back or if its own TID is newer than the other transaction's TID. It will fail with a lock conflict if the other transaction's TID is newer.

  - With NOWAIT, ThisTransaction immediately receives a lock conflict notification.

NOTE The Read Committed transaction can "see" all of the latest committed versions that its settings allow it to read, which is fine for insert, update, delete, and execute operations. However, any output sets SELECTed in the transaction must be requeried to get the updated view.

SNAPSHOT (Concurrency)

The "middle" level of isolation is SNAPSHOT, alternatively termed *Repeatable Read* or *Concurrency*. However, Firebird's SNAPSHOT isolation does not accord exactly with Repeatable Read as defined by the standard. It isolates the transaction's view from row-level changes to *existing* rows. However, because the MGA architecture, by nature, completely isolates SNAPSHOT transactions from new rows committed by other transactions, by denying SNAPSHOT transactions access to the global transaction state bitmap (TSB, see Chapter 25), there is no possibility of SNAPSHOT transactions seeing phantom rows. Hence, a Firebird SNAPSHOT transaction provides a deeper level of isolation than the SQL REPEATABLE READ.

Yet SNAPSHOT is not identical to SERIALIZABLE, because other transactions can update and delete rows that are in the purview of the SNAPSHOT transaction, provided they post first.

The transaction is guaranteed a non-volatile view of the database that will be unaffected by any changes committed by other transactions before it completes. It is a useful level for "historical" tasks like reporting and data export, which would be inaccurate if not performed over a reproducible view of the data.

SNAPSHOT is the default isolation level for the **isql** query tool and for many component and driver interfaces.

SNAPSHOT TABLE STABILITY (Consistency)

The "deepest" level of isolation is SNAPSHOT TABLE STABILITY, alternatively termed *Consistency* because it is guaranteed to fetch data in a non-volatile state that will remain externally consistent throughout the database as long as the transaction lasts. Read-write transactions cannot even read tables that are locked by a transaction with this isolation level.

The table-level locking imposed by this isolation comprises all tables accessed by the transaction, including those with referential constraint dependencies.

This level constitutes an aggressive extension that guarantees serialization in the strict sense that no other transaction can insert or delete—or indeed, change—rows in the tables involved if *any* transaction succeeds in acquiring a handle with this isolation. Conversely, the TABLE STABILITY transaction will not be able to acquire a handle if any read-write transaction is currently reading any table that is in its purview. In terms of the standard, it is unnecessary, since SNAPSHOT isolation already protects transactions from all three of the phenomena governed by the SQL standard SERIALIZABLE level.

A consistency transaction is also referred to as a *blocking* transaction because it blocks access by any other read-write transaction to any of the records that it accesses and to any records that depend on those records.

 CAUTION   Because of its potential to lock up portions of the database to other users needing to perform updates, SNAPSHOT TABLE STABILITY must be used with caution. Attend carefully to the size of the affected sets, the effects of joins and table dependencies, and the likely duration of the transaction.

Access Mode

Access mode can be READ WRITE or READ ONLY. A READ WRITE transaction can select, insert, update, and delete data. A READ ONLY transaction can only select data. The default access mode is READ WRITE.

 TIP   One of the benefits of a READ ONLY transaction is its ability to provide selection data for the user interface without tying up excessive resources on the server. Make sure your read-only transactions are configured with READ COMMITTED isolation, to ensure that garbage collection on the server can proceed past this transaction.

Lock Resolution Mode ("Blocking Mode")

Lock resolution mode determines behavior in the event the transaction (ThisTransaction) tries to post a change that conflicts with a change already posted by another transaction. The options are WAIT and NOWAIT.

WAIT

WAIT (the default) causes the transaction to wait until rows locked by a pending transaction are released, before determining whether it can update them. At that point, if the other transaction has posted a higher record version, the waiting transaction will notify that a lock conflict has occurred.

WAIT is often not the preferred blocking mode in high-volume, interactive environments because of its potential to slow down the busiest users and, in some conditions, to cause "livelocks" (see the section "What Is a Deadlock?").

WAIT is virtually pointless in SNAPSHOT isolation. Unless the blocking transaction eventually rolls back—the least likely scenario—the outcome of waiting is certain to be a lock conflict, anyway. In a READ COMMITTED transaction, the likelihood that the outcome of waiting would be a lock conflict is much reduced.

That is not to deny the usefulness of WAIT for some conditions. If the client application's exception handler handles conflicts by continually retrying without pausing, the bottlenecking caused by repeated retries and failures is likely to be worse than if WAIT is specified, especially if the blocking transaction takes a long time to complete. By contrast, WAIT is potentially going to cause one exception, eventually handled by one rollback.

Where the likelihood of transactions colliding is high but transactions are short, WAIT is to be preferred because it guarantees that waiting requests will proceed in a FIFO sequence, rather than be required to take their chances with each repeated request. However, in user environments where a quick turnover cannot be guaranteed, WAIT transactions are contraindicated because of their potential to hold back garbage collection.

NO WAIT

In a NO WAIT transaction, the server will notify the client immediately if it detects a new, uncommitted version of a row the transaction tries to change. In a reasonably busy multi-user environment, NO WAIT is sometimes preferable to the risk of creating bottlenecks of waiting transactions.

As a rule of thumb for SNAPSHOT transactions, throughput will be faster and interfaces more responsive if the client application chooses NO WAIT and handles lock conflicts through the use of rollback, timed retries, or other appropriate techniques.

Table Reservation

Firebird supports a *table locking* mode to force full locks on one or more tables for the duration of a transaction. The optional RESERVING *<list of tables>* clause requests immediate full locks on all committed rows in the listed tables, enabling a transaction to guarantee itself exclusive access at the expense of any transactions that become concurrent with it.

Unlike the normal locking tactic, reservation locks all rows *pessimistically*—it takes effect at the start of the transaction, instead of waiting until the point at which an individual row lock is required.

Table reservation has three main purposes:

- To ensure that the tables are locked when the transaction *begins*, rather than when they are first accessed by a statement, as is the case when TABLE STABILITY isolation is used for table-level locking. The lock resolution mode (WAIT/NOWAIT) is applied during the transaction request and any conflict with other transactions having pending updates will result in a WAIT for the handle or a denial of the handle in the NOWAIT case. This feature of table reservation is important because it greatly reduces the possibility of deadlocks.

- To provide *dependency locking* (i.e., the locking of tables that might be affected by triggers and integrity constraints). Dependency locking is not normal in Firebird. However, it will ensure that update conflicts arising from indirect dependency conflicts will be avoided.

- To strengthen the transaction's precedence with regard to one or more specific tables with which it will be involved. For example, a SNAPSHOT transaction that needs sole write access to all rows in a particular table could reserve it, while assuming normal precedence with regard to rows in other tables. This is a less aggressive way to apply table-level locking than the alternative, to use TABLE STABILITY isolation.

You can reserve more than one table in a transaction.

Uses of Table Reservation

Using table reservation with SNAPSHOT or READ COMMITTED isolation is recommended *in preference to* using SNAPSHOT TABLE STABILITY when table-level locking is required. Table reservation is the less aggressive and more flexible way to lock tables pre-emptively. It is available for use with any isolation level. However, using it in combination with SNAPSHOT TABLE STABILITY is not recommended, because it has no effect in mitigating access restrictions on tables that the transaction might access that are outside the scope of the RESERVING clause.

Pre-emptive table locking is not for everyday use, but it can be usefully employed for a task such as a pre-audit valuation or a "stock freeze" report prior to a stocktake.

Parameters for Table Reservation

Each table reservation can be configured with distinct attributes to specify how multiple transactions should be treated when they request access to a reserved table.

NOTE A SNAPSHOT TABLE STABILITY transaction cannot get any access to ANY table that is reserved by table reservation.

The choices are

```
[PROTECTED | SHARED] {READ | WRITE}
```

The PROTECTED attribute gives ThisTransaction an exclusive lock on the table it is reading and allows any other transaction that is in SNAPSHOT or READ COMMITTED isolation to read rows. Writes are restricted by one of the two modifiers:

- PROTECTED WRITE allows ThisTransaction to write to the table and blocks all other writes.

- PROTECTED READ disallows writing to the table by *any* transaction, including ThisTransaction itself.

The SHARED attribute lets any SNAPSHOT or READ COMMITTED transaction read the table and provides two options for concurrent updating by other transactions:

- SHARED WRITE allows any SNAPSHOT read-write or READ COMMITTED read-write transaction to update rows in the set as long as no transaction has or requests exclusive write.

- SHARED READ is the most liberal reserving condition. It allows any other read-write transaction to update the table.

Summary

Any other transaction can *read* a table reserved by ThisTransaction, provided there is no aspect of the other transaction's configuration that gives it an exclusive WRITE right on the table (i.e., all can read if they are configured only to read and not to have any pre-emptive right to write). The following conditions will always block the other transaction from reading a table reserved by ThisTransaction:

- The other transaction is in SNAPSHOT TABLE STABILITY isolation.

- The other transaction is configured to reserve the table PROTECTED WRITE (although it can read the table if ThisTransaction is reserving it with SHARED READ).

- The other transaction wants to reserve the table SHARED WRITE and ThisTransaction is reserving it with PROTECTED READ or PROTECTED WRITE.

In case this is all too confusing still, in Figure 26-1, some configured transactions speak for themselves.

Figure 26-1. Configuring table reservation

Record Versions

When an update request is successfully posted to the server, Firebird creates and writes to disk a reference linking the original row image as seen by the transaction—sometimes called a *delta*—and a new version of the row, incorporating the requested changes. The original and new row images are referred to as *record versions*. When a new record version is created by a newer transaction than the one that created the "live" version, other transactions will not be able to update or delete the original unless the owner-transaction of the new version rolls back. The versioning process is described in detail in the previous chapter.

Until the transaction is eventually committed, it does not touch the "live" version again until the commit occurs. Within its own context, it treats the posted version as if

529

it were the latest committed version. Meanwhile, other transactions continue to "see" the latest committed version. In the case of "snapshot" transactions that started before our transaction, the latest committed version that they see may be older than the one seen by our transaction and by other transactions that either started later or are in READ COMMITTED isolation.

Dependent Rows

If the table that has an update posted to it has foreign keys linked to it, the server creates deltas of the rows from those tables that "belong to" the updated row. Those dependent rows, and any that are dependent on them through foreign keys, are thus made inaccessible for update by other transactions too, for the duration of the transaction.

Locking and Lock Conflicts

With Firebird, locking is governed by the relative ages of transactions and the records managed by Firebird's versioning engine. All locking applies at the row level, except when a transaction is operating in SNAPSHOT TABLE STABILITY isolation or with a table reservation restriction that blocks write access.

Timing

The timing of the lock on the row in normal read-write activity is *optimistic*—no locking is in force on any row until the moment it is actually required. Until an update of the row is posted to the server, the row is free to be "won" by any read-write transaction.

Pessimistic Locking

Pessimistic, or pre-emptive, locking can be applied to sets of rows or to entire tables. The table-locking options have already been introduced (see the sections "Table Reservation" and "SNAPSHOT TABLE STABILITY (Consistency)").

Row-level and set-level pessimistic locking are options where there is an application requirement to reserve a row or a small set in advance of actually posting an update or deletion.

Explicit Locking

The capability to do explicit pessimistic row locking was added to Firebird's SQL SELECT statement syntax at version 1.5. It is restricted to "outer-level" SELECT statements that return output sets or define cursors. In cannot be applied to subqueries.

The abbreviated syntax for acquiring explicit pessimistic row locks is

```
SELECT <output-list>
FROM <table-or-procedure-or-view>
    [WHERE <search-conditions>]
```

```
    [GROUP BY <grouping-specification>]
    [UNION <select-expression> [ALL]]
    [PLAN <plan-expression>]
    [ORDER BY <column-list>]
 [FOR UPDATE [OF col1 [,col2..]] [WITH LOCK]]
```

FOR UPDATE, which is not a locking instruction, requests that the output set be delivered to the client one row at a time, rather than as a batch. The optional phrase WITH LOCK is the element that forces the pre-emptive lock on a row as soon as the server outputs it from the server. Rows waiting to be output are not locked.

Dummy Updates

The traditional way of achieving a pessimistic row lock with Firebird is the *dummy update*. It is a hack that takes advantage of record versioning. Simply put, the client posts an update statement for the row that does not update anything—it just sets a column to its current value, causing the server to create a new record version, and thus blocks other transactions from acquiring the row for updating or deletion.

The conditions where pessimistic locking might help and the recommended techniques are discussed in Chapter 27.

Lock Conflicts

A lock conflict is triggered when concurrent transactions try to update or delete the same row during a time when their views of database state overlap. Lock conflicts are the planned outcome of Firebird's transaction isolation and record versioning strategy, protecting volatile data from uncontrolled overwriting by parallel operations on the same data.

The strategy works so well that there are really only two conditions that can cause lock conflicts:

- **Condition 1**: One transaction (ThisTransaction) has posted an update or deletion for a row that another transaction, which started *before* ThisTransaction locked that row, attempts to update or delete. The other transaction encounters a lock conflict and has two choices:

  - It can roll back its attempt and try again later against the newest committed version.

  - It can *wait* until ThisTransaction either commits or rolls back.

- **Condition 2**: ThisTransaction is blocking the whole table against writes, because it has the table isolated in SNAPSHOT TABLE STABILITY or by a PROTECTED table reservation, and another transaction tries to update or delete a row or to insert a new row.

Suppose ThisTransaction posts a change to a row. Another transaction comes along and requests to change or delete the same row. In SNAPSHOT isolation with WAIT, the other transaction will keep waiting until ThisTransaction completes with either commit or rollback.

If ThisTransaction commits, then the other transaction will fail with an update conflict. The client that started the other transaction should have an exception handler that either rolls the transaction back and starts a new one to resubmit the request, or simply commits the transaction and exits.

Calling COMMIT in a lock conflict exception handler is not recommended, since it breaks the atomicity of the transaction—some work will complete, some will not, and it will be impossible to predict database state afterward. Rollback is almost always the right response to a lock conflict.

Unfortunately, Firebird tends to generalize all locking exceptions and report them as "deadlocks." The normal case just described is not a deadlock.

What Is a Deadlock?

Deadlock is just a nickname, borrowed from the sport of wrestling, for the condition where two transactions are contending to update rows in overlapping sets and one transaction does not take any precedence over the other.

For example, ThisTransaction has an update pending on Row X and wants to update Row Y, while the other transaction has an update pending on Row Y and wants to update Row X, and both transactions are in WAIT mode. As in wrestling, the deadlock can be resolved only if one contender withdraws its hold. One transaction must roll back and let the other commit its changes.

Firebird provides for the application to resolve the deadlock, by scanning for deadlocks every few seconds. It will arbitrarily pick one transaction from the deadlock and deliver a deadlock exception.

Developers should not dread deadlock messages. On the contrary, they are the essence of isolating the work of multiple users in transaction contexts. You should anticipate them and handle them effectively in your client application.

When ThisTransaction is selected to resolve the deadlock, the application's exception handler should roll it back to allow the other transaction to resume and complete its work. The alternative—committing ThisTransaction in the exception handler—is not recommended, since ThisTransaction becomes non-atomic and the other transaction will fail with a lock conflict.

Deadly Embrace

In rare cases, more than two transactions could be deadlocked in contention for the same overlapping sets. It is sometimes called the *deadly embrace*. The deadlock scan will fail one transaction (ThisTransaction), handing it over to the client for exception resolution, as before. However, this time, even if the client rolls back ThisTransaction, those other transactions are still deadlocked out there.

Livelock

The client might start a new transaction and retry, but the other contenders are still deadlocked, waiting for the next deadlock scan to extricate another of the contenders with a deadlock exception. As long as the retrying application keeps retrying with a WAIT transaction, it is just going to wait for some indefinite time for the other transactions to resolve the deadly embrace. For those futile retries, the transaction is said to be in a *livelock*.

In short, it is important in the first place to avoid transaction contexts that make it possible for a deadly embrace to occur. As added protection, exception handlers should be made capable of quickly dealing with deadlocks and ensuring that problem transactions finish cleanly and without delay.

Up Next

Next, we examine transactions from your perspective as a designer of client applications. Topics in the chapter are necessarily neutral with respect to host languages. However, given that all modern application environments and drivers for Firebird use the same API, in one form or another, what is good for one is good for another.

CHAPTER 27

Programming with Transactions

THE TRANSACTION IS THE STARTING POINT for anything a client application does in its dealings with the server. In this chapter we take a client's-eye view of the various interfaces for starting, managing, and ending transactions.

Many language and development environments can interface with Firebird. It is outside the scope of this manual to describe in detail how to manage Firebird transactions from each one.

The Language of Transactions

It is important to address the features Firebird implements for transactions, yet several transaction-related features are not implemented in dynamic SQL at all, but only through the API. Of the few transaction-related SQL statements available in the DSQL subset, only COMMIT and ROLLBACK are available to every interface. In a book that is deliberately scoped to be neutral about language environments and emphasize the dynamic SQL used for most current-day client application development, this chapter presents some problems for author and reader alike.

So, although this is not a chapter about ESQL[1] or the API,[2] the following topics will, in places, allude to both in a more or less general way to give some appreciation of what passes across the interface when clients talk to servers about transactions.

ESQL

The superset of SQL and SQL-like statements used widely in former times, even before the publication of the API and the introduction of the DSQL subset, offers a fairly standard SET TRANSACTION syntax for configuring and starting transactions. In some forms, it is available in DSQL and it can be used inside the **isql** utility. It will be a convenient stepping-off point for a general examination of how the API transports the equivalent information.

---

1. For the enthusiast, Borland publishes the *Embedded SQL Guide* as part of its InterBase media kit. Versions of this volume are also available in PDF format from some websites—just Google "EmbedSQL.pdf".

2. Ditto, the *API Guide* (APIGuide.pdf).

The API

The API presents a flexible, if exacting, interface environment of complex functions for C and C++ programmers to build client applications with the thinnest possible communication and connectivity layer. A group of API functions implements the equivalent SQL statements relating to transactions, for example, *isc_start_transaction()* for SET TRANSACTION and *isc_commit_transaction()* for COMMIT.

The API header file, ibase.h, declares the function prototypes, type definitions for each structure, parameter definitions, and macros that are used by functions. It is deployed with Firebird in the /include directory.

For several object-oriented development environments, such as Object Pascal, Borland C++Builder, Java, PHP, Python, and DBI::Perl, classes and components are available that encapsulate the Firebird API calls relating to transactions comprehensively. Custom drivers for standard SQL database connectivity interfaces—notably ODBC, JDBC, and .NET—similarly surface the API.[3]

Starting a Transaction

SQL

The SQL statement for starting a transaction has the following syntax:

```
SET TRANSACTION [NAME <transaction-name>]
[READ WRITE | READ ONLY] /* access mode */
[WAIT | NO WAIT] /* lock resolution (or blocking) mode */
[ISOLATION LEVEL] /* isolation level */
  {SNAPSHOT [TABLE STABILITY] | READ COMMITTED [[NO] RECORD VERSION]]}
[RESERVING <reserving-clause> | USING <db-handle> [, db-handle ...]];
```

The final clause RESERVING implements the optional table reservation, discussed in the previous chapter. Its syntax further breaks down to

```
<reserving-clause> ::= <table> [, <table> ...]
  [FOR [SHARED | PROTECTED] {READ | WRITE}]
    [, <reserving-clause> [, <reserving-clause>..]]
```

---

3. For most of these implementations, someone has done the job of translating Firebird's C header file into the appropriate high-level language, in order to provide the Firebird (or InterBase) API to that language. If you are planning to try your hand at direct-to-API programming, it is well worth your while to search the Web for an existing header translation.

NOTE The optional named transaction—declared in the application and referred to in the SET TRANSACTION clause—is not available anywhere except in ESQL.

You can try out this statement in **isql**. Open the employee.fdb database and start a new transaction as follows:

```
SQL> COMMIT;
SQL> SET TRANSACTION READ WRITE ISOLATION LEVEL SNAPSHOT TABLE STABILITY;
SQL> SELECT EMP_NO, FIRST_NAME, LAST_NAME
CON> FROM EMPLOYEE WHERE FIRST_NAME = 'Robert';
EMP_NO  FIRST_NAME  LAST_NAME
======  ==========  ===============
     2  Robert      Nelson
SQL>
```

TIP The keywords ISOLATION LEVEL are optional. READ WRITE and WAIT are default settings and can be omitted if non-default settings are not needed.

Next, open another **isql** shell, or another utility tool that lets you configure transactions, and start another read-write transaction on the same database:

```
SQL> COMMIT;
SQL> SET TRANSACTION READ WRITE NOWAIT SNAPSHOT;
```

Now, from this interface, try to update any row in employee.fdb:

```
SQL> UPDATE EMPLOYEE SET FIRST_NAME = 'Dodger'
SQL> WHERE FIRST_NAME = 'Roger';
ISC ERROR CODE:335544345
lock conflict on no wait transaction
```

As expected, this transaction was blocked from updating any row in EMPLOYEE because, in SELECTing from the same table, the first transaction had acquired a table-level lock. The second transaction had NO WAIT as its lock resolution setting and immediately excepted because it could not perform the update.

The Default Transaction

The following statement is also valid:

```
SQL> COMMIT;
SQL> SET TRANSACTION;
```

It starts a transaction, just as the more configured statements did, with a default configuration equivalent to

```
SQL> COMMIT;
SQL> SET TRANSACTION READ WRITE WAIT SNAPSHOT;
```

NOTE   There is another "default transaction," which is used by ESQL clients to start a ready configured, single transaction identified on server and client with the constant gds__trans. An ESQL client starts this transaction automatically if it passes a statement request and no transaction was explicitly started.

The API

The API function that does the equivalent job is called *isc_start_transaction()*.[4]
Starting each transaction has three parts:

1.   Creating (if necessary) and initializing the transaction handle.

2.   Creating (if necessary) and populating a *transaction parameter buffer* (TPB) to carry the configuration data. This is optional.

3.   Calling *isc_start_transaction()*.

Without the optional TPB, the client starts a transaction exactly like the default transaction that a bare SET TRANSACTION statement starts.

---

4. In fact, there are two different functions for starting transactions: *isc_start_transaction()* is used with languages that support passing a variable number of arguments to a function call; *isc_start_multiple()* is used with languages requiring a static argument list. isc_start_transaction limits a single, multi-database transaction to 16 databases, whereas isc_start_multiple can start transactions spanning more databases or where the number of databases spanned may vary and exceed 16.

The Transaction Handle

Each time you want to call this function, you must have a long pointer variable—called a *transaction handle*—already declared in your application and initialized to zero.[5] An application needs to provide one transaction handle for each concurrent transaction, and you can "recycle" used handles by reinitializing them.

A transaction handle must be set to zero in order to initialize it before starting a transaction. A transaction will fail to start up if it is passed a non-zero handle.

The Transaction Parameter Buffer

A TPB is a byte array (or vector) of constants, each representing a transaction parameter and starting with the prefix *isc_tpb_*. The first parameter is always the constant *isc_tpb_version3*, which defines the version of TPB structure.[6] The subsequent array members are all constants that map to an equivalent SQL transaction attribute. Table 27-1 shows each SQL transaction parameter and its equivalent TPB constant.

A typical TPB declaration in C looks like this:

```
static char isc_tpb[] =
  {
    isc_tpb_version3,
    isc_tpb_write,
    isc_tpb_wait,
    isc_read_committed,
    isc_tpb_no_rec_version
  };
```

This TPB is identical in its effect to

```
SET TRANSACTION READ WRITE WAIT READ COMMITTED NO RECORD_VERSION;
```

You can use the same TPB for all transactions that need the same characteristics. It is also fine to define a distinct TPB for each transaction. Transaction classes typically create a TPB instance whenever they need one and surface the settings to the design or runtime interface as read-write properties (aka data members).

In many cases, you can recognize the TPB constant in the property name. For standard DBC driver layers, the names of classes and members are more likely to be

---

5. The type *isc_tr_handle* is a void pointer defined in the header file *ibase.h*, which is in the /include directory of your Firebird installation.

6. If the TPB structure changes in the future, this constant will also change so that the server can handle clients compiled against a different version seamlessly.

dictated by the standard and mapped to the attributes most nearly matching the prescribed functionality.

Table 27-1. SQL Transaction Attributes and Equivalent TPB Constants

ATTRIBUTE TYPE	SQL ATTRIBUTE	TPB CONSTANT
Access mode	READ ONLY	isc_tpb_read
	READ WRITE	isc_tpb_write
Isolation level	READ COMMITTED	isc_tpb_read_committed
	SNAPSHOT	isc_tpb_concurrency
	SNAPSHOT TABLE STABILITY	isc_tpb_consistency
Lock resolution mode	WAIT	isc_tpb_wait
	NO WAIT	isc_tpb_nowait
Record version	RECORD_VERSION	isc_rec_version
	NO RECORD_VERSION	isc_no_rec_version
Table reservation	SHARED	isc_tpb_shared
	PROTECTED	isc_tpb_protected
	READ	isc_tpb_lock_read
	WRITE	isc_tpb_lock_write
No SQL equivalent	Disable the auto-undo log	isc_tpb_no_auto_undo

The Auto-Undo Log

By default, the server maintains an in-memory *internal savepoint log* of inserted and changed rows. In the normal course of events, log entries are erased as each transaction commits or rolls back. However, under certain conditions, the system will abandon the log and refer directly to the global transaction state bitmap (TSB) instead. The transition is likely to happen when a huge insert is rolled back or a transaction using many repeated *user savepoints* (see the section "Nested Transactions") has exhausted the capacity of the log.

An application can disable the use of this auto-undo log in a transaction by passing the *isc_no_auto_undo* constant in the TPB.

Accessing the Transaction ID

From Firebird 1.5 forward, the transaction ID (TID) of the current transaction (as deduced from the stored transaction state data) is available as a context variable. It is available in DSQL, **isql**, triggers, and stored procedures. The variable is CURRENT_TRANSACTION.

For example, to get it in a query, you could request this:

```
SELECT CURRENT_TRANSACTION AS TRAN_ID FROM RDB$DATABASE;
```

To store it in a table:

```
INSERT INTO TASK_LOG (USER_NAME, TRAN_ID, START_TIMESTAMP)
VALUES (CURRENT_USER, CURRENT_TRANSACTION, CURRENT_TIMESTAMP);
```

 CAUTION TIDs are not stable enough to use as keys. The numbering series for TIDs gets reset to 1 when a database is restored.

Firebird 1.0.*x* does not provide a mechanism for tracking transactions.

Using the TID in Applications

The TID from the server is not the same as the transaction handle that the Firebird client fetches back into your application. It is quite valid to associate a TID with a transaction handle, provided you remember to remap the relationship between TID and handle each time you reuse a handle. Every use of a handle should be atomic in your application.

The TID can be a useful asset for tracking down applications and users responsible for long-running transactions in a system that continually exhibits degrading performance. A completely cyclic tracking routine could record the server timestamps when transactions both start and finish (commit or roll back). In particular, missing finish times will help to find users who habitually use the "reset" button to terminate tasks or application workflows that are failing to commit work in a timely fashion.

Progress of a Transaction

At this point, you should be getting a sense of confidence about the *point* of operating a multi-user system as a series of atomic tasks, isolated in transactions. It is established that clients start transactions and clients end them. Beyond configuring a transaction to wrap a task for a specific set of access, isolation, and lock resolution conditions, the client has other opportunities to interact with the transaction during the course of its activity. Figure 27-1 illustrates these points of interaction and the remaining topics in this chapter expand on the techniques and implications surrounding them.

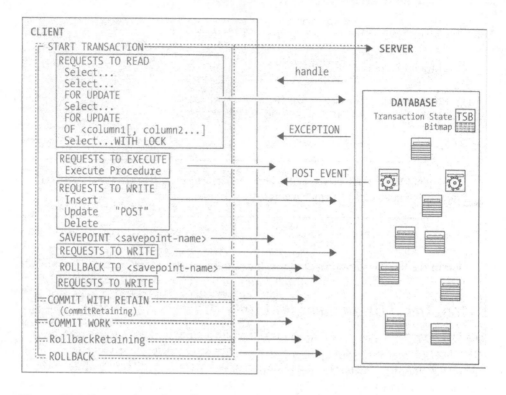

Figure 27-1. Interaction of application and transaction

Nested Transactions

In Firebird, transactions are always started and finished by a client. Some other DBMSs can start and commit transactions from within stored procedures because two-phase locks and transaction logging are used to control transactions. Instead, Firebird provides other mechanisms that can operate on the flow of work within a transaction without breaking atomicity. Two of these mechanisms, *exception handler blocks* and *executable strings*, are restricted for use within PSQL modules and are discussed in Part Seven. The other, not available in PSQL, is *user savepoints*.

NOTE   Executable strings and user savepoints were new features added to the language in Firebird 1.5.

User Savepoints

User savepoint statements, also known as *nested transactions*, enable you to "batch" groups of operations inside a transaction and signpost them when they post successfully. Should an exception occur later in the task sequence, the transaction can be rolled back to the last savepoint. Operations that were posted between the savepoint and the exception are rolled back and the application can correct, branch, commit, perform a full rollback, resume, or whatever is required.

Setting a Savepoint

User savepoints are a client-side operation, available only as DSQL statements.

The statement for setting a savepoint is

```
SAVEPOINT <identifier>;
```

The identifier can be any valid Firebird SQL identifier (31 characters maximum, U.S. ASCII alphanumeric characters, and distinct within the transaction). You can reuse the same identifier in the same transaction and it will overwrite any existing savepoint associated with the name.

Rolling Back to a Savepoint

A rollback to a savepoint begins by rolling back all the work posted after the savepoint was set. The named savepoint and any that *preceded* it are retained. Any savepoints that were set *after* the named savepoint are lost.

Any locks (explicit or implicit) that were acquired since the named savepoint was set are released. However, transactions that have been locked out, waiting for access to the released rows, still do not get access to them until the transaction completes. This ensures that currently waiting contenders will not interfere with the established workflow if it resumes. It does not block a transaction that was not waiting at the time of the nested rollback.

This is the syntax pattern for rolling back to a savepoint:

```
ROLLBACK [WORK] TO [SAVEPOINT] <identifier>;
```

If the transaction is allowed to resume after rolling back to a savepoint, the workflow can roll back to the same savepoint again, as many times as necessary. Record versions that get rolled back will not be eligible for garbage collection, because the transaction is still active.

Releasing Savepoints

On the server, the savepoint mechanism—a memory-based log—can have a significant impact on resources, especially if the same rows receive updates many times during the course of retracking through the task. The resources from unwanted savepoints can be released using a RELEASE SAVEPOINT statement:

```
RELEASE SAVEPOINT <identifier> [ONLY];
```

Without the keyword ONLY, the named savepoint and *all savepoints that were set after it* will be released and lost. Use ONLY to release just the named savepoint.

The following example illustrates how savepoints work:

```
CREATE TABLE SAVEPOINT_TEST (ID INTEGER);
COMMIT;
INSERT INTO SAVEPOINT_TEST
  VALUES(99);
COMMIT;
INSERT INTO SAVEPOINT_TEST
  VALUES(100);
/**/
SAVEPOINT SP1;
/**/
DELETE FROM SAVEPOINT_TEST;
SELECT * FROM SAVEPOINT_TEST; /* returns nothing */
/**/
ROLLBACK TO SP1;
/**/
SELECT * FROM SAVEPOINT_TEST; /* returns 2 rows */
ROLLBACK;
/**/
SELECT * FROM SAVEPOINT_TEST; /* returns the one committed row */
```

Internal Savepoints

When the server engine executes rollbacks, its default point of reference for backing out a transaction is to internal savepoints stored in the memory-based auto-undo log. At the end of the rollback, it commits the transaction. The purpose of this strategy is to reduce the amount of garbage generated by rollbacks.

When the volume of changes performed under a transaction-level savepoint is getting large—into the range of 10,000 to 1 million rows affected—the engine abandons the auto-undo log and takes its references directly from the global TSB. If you have a transaction that you expect to command a large number of changes, disabling auto-undo logging will forestall the wastage of resource consumption that would occur if the server decided to abandon the logging. For more information, see "The Auto-Undo Log" earlier in this chapter.

PSQL

Exception Handling Extensions

The equivalent of savepoints in PSQL modules is exception handling. Each PSQL exception-handling block is also bounded by automatic system savepoints. The PSQL extensions provide language wrappers implementing the same kind of nesting that user savepoints provide in DSQL. For more information, see Chapter 32.

The Logical Context

The simple way to look at a transaction between START TRANSACTION and COMMIT or ROLLBACK is to view it as a series of client operations and client/server interactions that map exactly to a task. It is a very useful model for understanding how a transaction wraps a unit of work. It does not necessarily reflect the reality of how users perform the actual task.

From the user's point of view, the "task" is not bounded by START TRANSACTION and COMMIT. Her task has a beginning, a middle, and an end that may involve multiple transactions to reach completion. For example, a failure to post or to commit a statement will entail a rollback to end the physical transaction. Some form of intervention follows that may cause the logical task to end or, in the normal case, will require another physical transaction in order to complete it.

A single physical transaction may involve a number of discrete user tasks forming a logical "whole" that requires the atomicity of a single physical transaction. Another variant—the typical "batch data entry" task—encompasses many repetitions of a similar task stacked up inside a single physical transaction to reduce keystrokes and comply with the user's workflow requirements.

In summary, the logical task—the one we as developers must address and design for—almost always extends beyond the boundaries of START TRANSACTION and COMMIT. The physical transaction is but one facet of the logical context in which it is conducted.

Two key factors of concern in the logical context of transaction workflow are

- How to retain the physical context of the initial transaction after ROLLBACK so that users' work does not disappear when the server refuses to accept it

- What to do if the flow is interrupted by an exception—how to diagnose the exception and how to correct it

To address these problems, we look at the COMMIT and ROLLBACK operations and the pros and cons of options available to preserve logical context between transactions. Following on from there, we examine the issue of diagnosing the exceptions that give rise to the need to "rerun" transactions.

Ending Transactions

A transaction ends when the client application commits it or rolls it back. Unless the COMMIT statement, or the call to the equivalent API function *isc_commit_transaction*, succeeds, the transaction is not committed. If a transaction that cannot be committed is not rolled back by an explicit client call to ROLLBACK (or the API function *isc_rollback_transaction*) the transaction is not rolled back. These statements are not the syllogism that they appear to be. Failure to terminate transactions is an all-too-common feature of problem scenarios in the support lists!

The COMMIT Statement

The syntax of the COMMIT statement is simple:

```
COMMIT [WORK] [RETAIN [SNAPSHOT]];
```

A simple COMMIT—sometimes referred to as a *hard commit*, for reasons that will become evident—makes changes posted to the database permanent and frees up all of the physical resources associated with the transaction. If COMMIT fails for some reason and returns an exception to the client, the transaction remains in an uncommitted state. The client application must handle the failure to commit by explicitly rolling back the transaction or, where possible, by fixing the problems and resubmitting the statement.

COMMIT with the RETAIN Option

The optional RETAIN [SNAPSHOT] extension to the COMMIT statement causes the server to retain a "snapshot" of the physical transaction's context at the time the statement is executed and start a new transaction as a clone of the committed one. If this so-called soft commit is used on a SNAPSHOT or SNAPSHOT TABLE STABILITY transaction, the cloned transaction preserves the same snapshot of the data as the original transaction had when it started.

Although it does commit the work permanently and thus change the state of the database, COMMIT RETAIN (CommitRetaining) does not release resources. In the lifespan of a logical task that comprises many repetitions of a similar operation, cloning the context reduces some of the overhead that would be incurred by clearing resources each time with COMMIT, only to allocate the identical resources all over again when a new transaction is started. In particular, it preserves the cursors on sets selected and currently "open."

The same TID remains active in the TSB and never appears there as "committed." For this reason, it is often referred to as *soft commit*, in contrast with the "hard" commit performed by an unmodified COMMIT statement.

Each soft commit is like a savepoint with no return. Any subsequent ROLLBACK reverses only the changes that have been posted since the last soft commit.

The benefit of the soft commit is that it makes life easy for programmers, especially those using components that implement "scrolling dataset" behavior. It was introduced to support the data grid user interface favored by many users of the Borland Delphi development environment. By retaining the transaction context, the application can display a seamless before-to-after transition that reduces the effort the programmer would otherwise need to invest in starting new transactions, opening new cursors, and resynchronizing them with row sets buffered on the client.

Data access implementations frequently combine posting a single update, insert or delete statement with an immediate COMMIT RETAIN in a mechanism that is dubbed "Autocommit." It is common for interface layers that implement Autocommit capability to "dumb out" explicit control of transactions by starting one invisibly in situations where the programmer-written code attempts to pass a statement without first starting a transaction itself.

Explicit transaction control is worth the extra effort, especially if you are using a connectivity product that exploits the flexible options provided by Firebird. In a busy environment, the COMMIT RETAIN option *can* save time and resources, but it has some serious disadvantages:

- A snapshot transaction continues to hold the original snapshot in its view, meaning the user does not see the effects of committed changes from other transactions that were pending at the start of the transaction.

- As long as the same transaction continues being committed with RETAIN, resource "housekeeping" on the server is inhibited, resulting in excessive growth of memory resources consumed by the TSB. This growth progressively slows down performance, eventually "freezing" the server and, under adverse operating system conditions, even causing it to crash.

- No old record versions made obsolete by operations committed by a COMMIT RETAIN transaction can be garbage collected as long as the original transaction is never "hard committed."

The ROLLBACK Statement

Like COMMIT, ROLLBACK frees resources on the server and ends the physical context of the transaction. However, the application's view of database state reverts to the way it would be if the transaction had never started. Unlike COMMIT, it never fails.

In the logical context of "the task" on the client, after rollback your application will provide the user with the means to resolve the problem that caused the exception and to try again in a new transaction.

RollbackRetaining

Firebird SQL does not implement a RETAIN syntax for ROLLBACK as it does for COMMIT. However, a similar cloning mechanism is implemented at the API with the function *isc_rollback_retaining()*. It restores the application's database view to the state it was in when the transaction handle was acquired or, in a ReadCommitted transaction, to the state it was in the last time *isc_rollback_retaining* was called. System resources allocated to the transaction are not released and cursors are retained.

RollbackRetaining has the same traps as COMMIT RETAIN—and one more. Since any rollback call is done in response to an exception of some sort, retaining the context of the transaction will also retain the cause of the exception. RollbackRetaining should not be used if there is any chance that your subsequent exception-handling code will not find and fix the inherent exception. Any failure subsequent to RollbackRetaining should be handled with a full rollback, to release the resources and clear the problem.

Diagnosing Exceptions

Common causes for failure to post or commit work include

- Lock conflicts

- "Bad data" that slipped through the user interface: arithmetic overflows, expressions that divide by zero, nulls in non-nullable fields, mismatched character sets, and so on

- "Good data" that fails a CHECK constraint or other validation

- Primary and foreign key violations

and others!

Firebird recognizes a comprehensive (nay, mind-boggling!) range of exceptions and provides error codes to identify them at two levels.

- At the higher-level is the SQLCODE, defined (more or less, with emphasis on "less") by the SQL standards.

- At the more detailed level is the GDSCODE, a larger and more precisely targeted, vendor-specific range of exception types that are grouped beneath the SQLCODE types.

SQLCODE

Table 27-2 shows the values that the SQL-89 and SQL-92 standards define for SQLCODE.

Table 27-2. SQLCODE Values and Definitions

SQLCODE	MESSAGE	INTERPRETATION
0	SUCCESS	The operation completed successfully.
1–99	SQLWARNING	Warning or information message from the server.
100	NOT FOUND	An operation was requested for which no rows were found. This is not an error—it often just means that an end-of-file or end-of-cursor condition was detected or simply that no matching value was found.
< 0	SQLERROR	Indicates the SQL statement did not complete. The numbers fall into broken ranges between –1 and –999.

The mapping of negative SQLCODEs to actual errors is not defined by the standards. Firebird's negative SQLCODEs are quite generalized and provide groupings that are largely coincidental and often bemusing. For example, while it is possible to guess that an SQLCODE of –204 means "something unknown," the code on its own tells nothing about what is unknown.

GDSCODE

The second-level GDSCODEs provide much better targeting of the actual exception. Each GDSCODE is a signed integer that is mapped to a constant in *iberror.h* (in your /include subdirectory) and also to a message text string in *firebird.msg* (or *interbase.msg* if you are using v.1.0.*x*).[7] As a rule, the GDSCODE message is quite precise about what occurred.[8] Firebird 1.5 delivered significant improvements in the information returned by messages. Nevertheless, the GDSCODE provides a highly useful diagnostic mechanism for applications, and you can map the constants to custom messages in your own host-code module, for use by exception handlers.

---

7. Non-English versions of the message file were not available when this guide went to press. Ongoing translation projects do exist. If you are interested in obtaining a localized message file, ask on the Firebird community lists. Do indicate if you are interested in participating in localization projects!

8. There are some notorious exceptions to this rule. For example, ISC ERROR CODE:335544321 "Arithmetic exception, numeric overflow, or string truncation" generalizes such a wide range of possibilities that its effect is usually to bemuse even the programmer who allowed the exception to occur.

Receiving Exceptions

In the following example, an application makes an attempt to insert a row into a table that does not exist:

```
INSERT INTO NON_EXISTENT (TEST)
  VALUES ('ABCDEF');
```

The following set of error information is returned to the application (the IB_SQL admin utility, in this case):

```
ISC ERROR CODE:335544569 <- GDSCODE
Dynamic SQL Error <- corresponding text from firebird.msg
SQL error code = -204 <- SQLCODE
Table unknown <- corresponding text from firebird.msg
NON_EXISTENT
```

Where does the application get the error codes and messages from? The answer is found in the *error status vector*, an array that is passed as a parameter in most of the API functions. These functions return status and error codes to the client, along with the corresponding strings from the Firebird message file.[9] The API also provides client applications with utility functions to read the contents of the error status vectors into local buffers. Exception handlers can then parse the contents of these buffers and use the information to decide what to do about the exception and to deliver a friendly message to the user.

iberror.h

The header file iberror.h, in your /include directory, contains the declarations that associate each SQLCODE and GDSCODE with a symbolic constant. For example, here are the constant declarations for the two error codes from the preceding example:

```
...
#define isc_dsql_error          335544569L
...
#define isc_dsql_relation_err   335544580L <- an SQLCODE -204 error
```

Most of the established high-level language and scripting host interfaces already have translations of the constant declarations, although some pre-date Firebird and

---

9. With Firebird 1.5, if a remote client's client library finds a copy of the message file locally in the recognized "root" location, it will use this and override the one in the server's RootDirectory. Because it hasn't yet been decided whether this is actually a desirable feature, it may be wise to avoid depending on it, in the interests of future proofing. In any case, workstation filesystems are famously vulnerable to user misbehavior.

may not be open source. If you need a translation, it is recommended that you inquire in the support lists. The full list of SQLCODE and GDSCODE codes and the standard English messages can be found in Appendix X. The use of these error codes and language extensions for exploiting them in PSQL is the subject of Chapter 32.

Multi-Database Transactions

Firebird supports operations across multiple databases under the control of a single transaction. It implements two-phase commit (2PC) automatically, to ensure that the transaction will not commit the work in one database unless it is possible to commit it in the others. Data is never left partly updated.

In the first phase of a two-phase commit or rollback, Firebird prepares to commit (or roll back) the work for each database by splitting the transaction into *sub-transactions*, one for each database, and posting the changes to each. At this point, the sub-transactions are all in a "transient" state. If the first phase completes, then the second phase flags each sub-transaction for committing or rolling back, as the case may be, in the order in which the parts were prepared.

- If it is a commit and any sub-transaction cannot be committed, an exception occurs. Any sub-transactions so far flagged for commit revert to "transient" and database state is unchanged in all cases.

- If the commit succeeds throughout, then all sub-transactions go into "committed" state and changes become permanent.

- If it is a rollback, the sub-transactions go into rolled-back state.

Limbo Transactions

If network interruption or a disk crash makes one or more databases unavailable, causing the two-phase commit to fail during the second phase, sub-transactions left behind will be in a transient state, flagged as neither committed nor rolled back. Within each individual database, these sub-transactions that never completed the second phase (became committed or rolled back) are recognized as being in a "limbo" state.

Because rows in a database sometimes become inaccessible because of their association with a transaction that is "in limbo," it is important to resolve these transactions.

Recovery

Until a limbo transaction is finished (by being committed or rolled back) it remains "interesting" to Firebird, which keeps statistics on unfinished transactions. *Recovering* a limbo transaction means committing it or rolling it back. The **gfix** tool can recover limbo transactions and let you deal with them interactively. For more information, refer to Chapter 39.

NOTE   Databases maintained by driver layers that do not support two-phase commit, such as the Borland Database Engine (BDE), never exhibit limbo transactions.

Restricting Databases

Cross-database transactions can use a lot of server resources. In Embedded SQL (ESQL), Firebird provides language support in the form of the USING clause, for optionally limiting the databases a transaction is permitted to access. DSQL does not provide language support. DSQL interfaces can use special API structures in the *transaction parameter block* for limiting multi-database transactions in various ways. Some data access component classes provide access to these options through properties.

Pessimistic Locking

In a pessimistic locking DBMS, rows that have been requested by one user or transaction for an operation that could potentially change data state become immediately inaccessible for reading or writing by other users or transactions. In some systems, the entire table becomes unavailable. Many developers moving databases and applications to Firebird from such systems are disconcerted by optimistic locking and search desperately for ways to mimic the old.

In Firebird, all updates are at row level—there is no mechanism to lock an individual column. At almost all levels of transaction isolation, the engine employs an optimistic locking principle: All transactions not constrained by some form of pessimistic locking begin with a view of the currently committed state of all rows in all tables—subject to privileges, of course. When a transaction submits a request to update a row, the old version of that row remains visible to all transactions. Writers do not block readers.

Internally, upon a successful update request, the engine creates a new version of the row that implicitly locks the original version. Depending on the settings of that user's transaction and others, some level of lock conflict will occur if another transaction attempts to update or delete the locked row. For more information about Firebird's locking conditions, refer to the previous chapter.

Firebird is designed for interactive use by many concurrent users and there are seldom any genuine reasons to use a pessimistic lock. It is not a magic bullet to be used to emulate the locking behavior of a desktop DBMS. Pessimistic locks by one transaction will cause conflicts for other transactions. There is no escape from the responsibility to work in sympathy with the multi-user transaction model and write handlers to anticipate locking conflicts.

Table-Level Locking

The transaction isolation level TABLE STABILITY (aka *consistency isolation*) provides full, table write-locking that flows on to dependent tables. It is too aggressive for interactive applications.

It is preferable to use a RESERVING clause with READ COMMITTED or SNAPSHOT isolation because it offers more flexibility and control for targeting tables that you want to lock for the duration of a transaction. It has parameters that determine how much protection is requested for each table:

```
RESERVING <reserving_clause>;
<reserving_clause> = table [, table ...]
[FOR [SHARED | PROTECTED] {READ | WRITE}] [, <reserving_clause>]
```

The *<reserving-clause>* can comprise multiple sets of reservation specifications, enabling different tables or groups of tables to be reserved with different rights. A specific table should appear only once in the entire reserving clause. Refer to the previous chapter for information about table reservation.

Statement-Level Locking

Pessimistic locking at statement level—affecting individual rows or sets—is not directly an issue of transaction configuration. However, the effects of these lock types *are* directly governed by the transaction settings of both the transaction in which the locking is defined and other transactions that try to access the locked row or set. It is essential to consider these techniques in terms of transaction settings.

Pessimistic locking of a row or a set is antithetical to the way Firebird was designed to work. In short, if you have lived with and depended on pessimistic locking until you discovered Firebird, then the time has come for you to get into the MGA groove and enjoy the benefits of optimistic row locking.

However, it cannot be denied that design requirements do occasionally call for a pessimistic lock, though the need in Firebird is much rarer than your experiences with other DBMSs may have taught you. The likely scenario involves an absolute requirement for exclusive access to rows that, notwithstanding, does not justify a table-level lock. Typically, a row, once read, must be secured by that reader exclusively for an update or deletion. This requirement is sometimes referred to as *strict task serialization*.

For conditions where a row-level pessimistic lock is necessary, a pessimistic locking mechanism and supporting SQL syntax were introduced in version 1.5. Before then, the Firebird engine did not support it, per se. In this section, we look first at the standard "hack" that client applications do—when language support for it is absent—to achieve a pessimistic lock. Next we examine the syntax and conditions for the explicit SELECT ... WITH LOCK that brought pessimistic locking support to Firebird SQL at release 1.5.

The "Dummy Update" Hack

"Editing" is not a server-side activity, hence, when the user clicks the Edit button (or whatever device your program uses to give her an editing interface) it changes nothing on the server. As far as the server is concerned, the transaction is merely reading. No new record version is created. There is no lock. Nothing changes until the user is finished editing the row and the application actually *posts* the user's work.

Developers who regard this behavior as a problem get around it by having their applications post a "dummy update" to a row as soon as the user asks to edit it. The "hack" is to post an update statement that sets a stable column to its current value. Usually, the primary key column is used, for example:

```
UPDATE ATABLE
  SET PKEY = PKEY
    WHERE PKEY = PKEY;
```

Thus, the server creates a new record version, in which nothing is actually different from the latest committed version, and applies a lock to the row. Once the user signals that she has finished editing the row, the application posts the real update, for example:

```
UPDATE ATABLE
  SET COLUMN2 = 'Some new value',
      COLUMN3 = 99,
      ...
WHERE PKEY = <the value of the primary key>;
```

On the server, a second new record version is posted, overwriting the first.

If you really need a pessimistic lock and there is no combination of transaction attributes that suits your special need, this technique is effective. It works on a single row only and lasts until the transaction is committed, even if the user decides not to perform any actual change to the row.

 CAUTION If you use this technique, make certain that you condition any BEFORE UPDATE and BEFORE DELETE triggers on the tables you subject to the dummy update, to preclude any possibility that they will fire.

 TIP It may be necessary to create a special, hidden FLAG column in your table for use specifically to flag dummy updates. For example, a hidden integer column could be incremented by your dummy update statement. Triggers would then be set up to perform "real" updates only IF (NEW.FLAG <> OLD.FLAG).

About "Double-Dipped" Updates

It's not recommended to update the same row more than once in a single transaction, because it will interfere with the integrity of both automatic (referential integrity) and custom triggers. Where savepoints are involved, it causes record versions to proliferate. This "double-dipping" generally reflects careless application design logic. However, a "two-update update" is exactly the intent of the "dummy update" technique. As long as the use of savepoints is avoided in these transactions and triggers are carefully conditioned to test for actual changes, it can be rendered harmless.

Explicit Locking in v.1.5 and Later

The syntax pattern for explicit locks is

```
SELECT output-specification FROM table-name
  [WHERE search-condition]
  [FOR UPDATE [OF col1 [, col2 [,...]]]]
  WITH LOCK;
```

How It Works

As the engine considers, in turn, each record falling under an explicit lock statement, it returns either the record version that is the most currently committed, regardless of database state when the statement was submitted, or an exception.

Wait behavior and conflict reporting depend on the transaction parameters specified in the TPB block.

The engine guarantees that all records returned by an explicit lock statement are actually locked and meet the search conditions specified in WHERE clause, as long as no search condition depends on any other tables, for example, through a join or subquery. It also guarantees to lock only rows that meet the search conditions.

However, the potential set is subject to the settings of its transaction: isolation level, lock resolution, and record version. A row does not get its lock until it is actually output to the server's row buffer. There is no guarantee that the potential set will or will not be affected by parallel transactions that commit during the course of the locking statement's execution, making further rows eligible for selection by your transaction.

Refer to Table 27-3 for a summary of interactions between transaction settings and explicit locks. ThisTransaction is the transaction that has, or is trying to get, an explicit lock on a row or set.

Table 27-3. Interaction of Transaction Settings and Explicit Locks

ISOLATION	LOCK RESOLUTION	BEHAVIOR
isc_tpb_consistency (SNAPSHOT TABLE STABILITY)	--	Ignored. Table-level locks override explicit locks.
isc_tpb_concurrency (SNAPSHOT)	isc_tpb_nowait (NO WAIT)	If a row gets modified by any transaction that was committed since ThisTransaction started, or an already active transaction modified the row before it was output to the row cache, an update conflict exception is raised immediately.
isc_tpb_concurrency (SNAPSHOT)	isc_tpb_wait (WAIT)	If a row gets modified by any transaction that was committed since ThisTransaction started, or an already active transaction modified the row before it was output to the row cache, an update conflict exception is raised immediately. If an active transaction is holding the row with an explicit lock or a normal write lock, ThisTransaction waits for the outcome of the blocking transaction. If the blocking transaction then commits a modified version of this record, an update conflict exception will be raised.
isc_tpb_read_committed (READ COMMITTED)	isc_tpb_nowait (NO WAIT)	If an active transaction is holding the row with an explicit lock or a normal write lock, ThisTransaction gets an update conflict exception immediately.
isc_tpb_read_committed (READ COMMITTED)	isc_tpb_wait (WAIT)	If an active transaction is holding the row with an explicit lock or a normal write lock, ThisTransaction waits for the outcome of blocking transaction. When the blocking transaction completes, ThisTransaction attempts to get the lock on the row again. Update conflict exceptions can never be raised by an explicit lock statement with this configuration.

If a SELECT ... WITH LOCK clause succeeds and the optional FOR UPDATE sub-clause is omitted, all of the rows in the set are pre-emptively locked, whether you actually update them or not. With careful transaction configuration and client-side control of buffering, the lock will prevent any other transaction from obtaining write access to any of those rows, or their dependants, until your transaction ends. Pre-emptively locking a multi-row set will cause deadlocks to escalate and your application code must be ready to manage them.

The number of rows in the specified output set has important consequences if you use an access method that requests "datasets" or "recordsets" in packets of a few hundred rows at a time ("buffered fetches") and buffers them in the client, typically to implement a scrolling interface. If the lock fails upon fetching a certain row and causes an exception, none of the rows currently in waiting in the server's buffer will be sent and those already passed to the client buffer become invalid. Your application will have to roll back the transaction.

With this style of access, it is essential to provide your applications with a way to handle exceptions as they occur. Use a very strict WHERE clause to limit the range of the lock to one or a very small set of rows and avoid having partly fetched sets made invalid. If your data access interface supports it, set the data access component's fetch buffer to one row, for example:

```
SELECT * FROM DOCUMENT
  WHERE ID = ? WITH LOCK /* ID is the primary key */
```

The optional FOR UPDATE clause provides a way to define a multi-row set and fetch and process rows one at a time.

The FOR UPDATE Clause

If the FOR UPDATE clause is included, buffered fetching will be disabled and the lock will be applied to each row, one by one, as it is fetched into the server-side row cache. If a named cursor[10] is controlling the position of the update, the clause can take an optional OF *<column-list>* to target updates at specific cursor columns.

Because the normal isolation rules apply to the transaction, it is possible for a lock that was available at the start of the request to fail subsequently. Unfetched rows remain "clear" and available for other transactions to obtain for update, leaving a "moving window" in which any unfetched row may become locked by another transaction, even if the lock appeared to succeed when the set was requested.

Example Using WITH LOCK

This statement defines an unrestricted multi-row output set and causes each row to be fetched into the server-side buffer individually. It will not fetch the next row until he

---

10. For reasons of scope, the subject of named cursors is barely touched in this guide. The API provides a group of isc_dsql_* functions for operating them. The DECLARE CURSOR statement syntax, fully implemented in ESQL, is available in some DSQL programming environments. See Chapters 29 and 30 for topics regarding the use of named cursors in PSQL modules.

client signals that it is ready. WITH LOCK causes the pessimistic lock to be attempted upon each row request. It will return either the next row in the set or an exception.

```
SELECT * FROM DOCUMENT
  WHERE PARENT_ID=? FOR UPDATE WITH LOCK
```

Restrictions on Explicit Locking

The SELECT … WITH LOCK construct is available in DSQL and PSQL. It can succeed only in a top-level, single-table SELECT statement.

- It is not available in a subquery or a joined set.

- It cannot be specified with set quantifier (the DISTINCT operator, FIRST, or SKIP), a GROUP BY clause, or any other aggregating operation.

- It cannot be used in or with a view, an external table, or the output set of a selectable stored procedure.

Stored Procedures, Triggers, and Transactions

For information about writing and using stored procedures and triggers, read on to Part Seven.

Stored Procedures

Stored procedures execute in the context of the transaction that calls them. Work done, including any tasks fulfilled in embedded and recursive calls, will only take effect if everything completes without error, with exceptions handled, and is committed. If the resolution to an exception condition in a single operation is to roll back the transaction, then all work in the transaction is rolled back.

Triggers

Triggers fire inside the context of the DML statement that prompts them. Work done, including any tasks fulfilled in embedded procedure calls, updates, inserts, or deletes to other tables or through internal referential integrity or other triggers belonging to any of the tables, will be committed in its entirety or returned to the client in an unresolved state. Unhandled exceptions in one operation will abort the operation where the error occurred and leave the transaction in a state where the application can decide to roll back or to attempt to fix the error and resubmit the request. Rollback will undo all of the operations executed in the transaction up to the point where the exception occurred.

"Savepoints" in PSQL

The introduction of user savepoints in Firebird 1.5 allows the scope of rollbacks to be controlled from the application. PSQL has always had this capability: exceptions. For details, refer to Chapter 32.

Tips for Optimizing Transaction Behavior

Choose an Appropriate Transaction Model

The single-transaction model tempts the inexperienced developer to ignore multi-user issues in favor of "easy programming." The result is application architectures that perform poorly at all levels: slow queries and refresh responses, glutted networks, user-unfriendly workflows, and high levels of conflict.

Don't Go "Generic" Unless You Need To

Generic application-to-database interfaces, such as ODBC or Borland's BDE layers, merge a single database connection and a single transaction. Because their purpose is to hide the differences between low-end, file-based data repositories and sophisticated, transaction-capable database management systems, they do not support the capability to have multiple transactions concurrently active in a database session or to have a transaction that spans connections to multiple databases.

At best, these generic interfaces provide an easy route for scaling up low-end databases or flattening out the differences between different vendors' DBMS implementations. If you don't need the lowest common denominator, don't choose it.

Exploit Multiple Transaction Capabilities

A Firebird client can run multiple concurrent transactions. A user working on multiple tasks in a single application can perform a variety of activities over the same (or overlapping) sets of target data. Firebird's transaction model provides great benefits for designs that need to cater for a modular, multiple-tasking environment in a highly responsive manner. It is an important responsibility for the software engineer to develop techniques to keep commits flowing and user views synchronized with database state.

Keep the OAT Moving!

A slow-moving OAT almost always indicates long-running transactions. Avoiding them is one of the best skills you can acquire when learning to write client applications for Firebird.

It is easy to blame long transactions on user behavior. You can help them to help themselves by teaching them to complete tasks within a reasonable time: not to go for coffee breaks, leaving tasks unfinished; not to submit "wild queries" at peak times; and so on. However, good client application design avoids depending on users to behave well.

- Mechanisms that "time out" neglected transactions are effective.

- As a general rule, avoid browsing interfaces and favor the drill-down kind.

- If a browsing interface is unavoidable, isolate the statements that select the browsed data in READ-ONLY READ COMMITTED transactions.

- Ensure that READ-WRITE transactions are committed regularly—even if users are using them only to view data.

- Restrict applications that permit random querying by enforcing the inclusion of WHERE clauses and timeout limits.

- Make certain that your applications provide the means to perform periodic "hard commits" on any transactions that employ COMMIT RETAIN.

- Make it a rule to use RollbackRetaining not more than once in an exception handler. Don't put RollbackRetaining inside a loop!

- Understand what's going on inside transactions! Use **gstat** –h or equivalent tools to monitor the OIT and the OAT, and pay attention to the "gaps."

- Don't allow housecleaning to be neglected. Sweeps must be allowed to happen at timely intervals, and regular backups, even without restoring, will help to keep the transaction inventory in good shape.

Up Next

Now that you are on top of the complicated matter of transaction management, it is time to turn your talents to server-side programming. In Part Seven, you get to try your hand with the powerful features available through PSQL: stored procedures and triggers with custom exception handling and Firebird's events mechanism. In Chapter 28, we begin by taking a look at the advantages of using server-side processing to centralize business rules and reduce network traffic, before moving on to syntax and technique in the succeeding chapters.

Part Seven

Server Programming

Introduction to Firebird Programming

ONE OF THE GREAT BENEFITS OF A FULL-BLOODED SQL relational database implementation is its capability to compile and execute internal code modules (stored procedures and triggers) supplied as source code by the developer. The language that provides this capability on a Firebird server is PSQL, a simple but powerful set of SQL extensions that combines with regular data manipulation language (DML) statements to become compilable source modules.

Overview of Server Code Modules

The high-level language for Firebird server-side programming is SQL. Source code is presented to the engine in the form of SQL programming language extensions—PSQL statements and constructs—and DML statements. These statements are, themselves, wrapped inside single DDL statements of the form

```
{CREATE | RECREATE | ALTER} {TRIGGER | PROCEDURE} <name> ...
...
AS
...
BEGIN
  <one or more blocks of statements>
END
```

The syntax for writing PSQL modules is explored in depth in the next chapters.

The objective of each of these "DDL super-statements" is to create and store one executable code module (stored procedure or trigger) or to redefine (RECREATE or ALTER) an existing object. A DDL statement is also used to destroy (DROP) executable code objects.

PSQL supports the three data manipulation statements, INSERT, UPDATE, and DELETE, and the ability to SELECT single-row or multiple-row sets of data items into local variables. The PSQL extensions provide the following language and logic support:

- Local variables and assignment statements.

- Conditional control-flow statements.

- Special context variables (for triggers only) for accessing the old and new values of each column of all DML input sets.

- Posting of user-defined database events to a listening client.

- Exceptions, including user-defined ones declared as database objects, and (in v.1.5) context-specific exception messages, and supporting structure and syntax for error handling.

- Input and output arguments (for stored procedures only).

- Encapsulation of cursor behavior in FOR SELECT … INTO … DO looping syntax.

- The SUSPEND statement (for stored procedures only), providing the capability to write stored procedures that output a virtual table in direct response to a SELECT statement—*selectable stored procedures*.

- Embedding of stored procedure calls in both stored procedures and triggers.

- Capability to define multiple triggers for the BEFORE and AFTER phases of triggers for each DML event and to position them in a predefined execution order. v.1.5 introduced the ability to write conditional BEFORE and AFTER triggers encompassing any or all possible DML events.

Except for the specific elements mentioned, the entire PSQL language set is available to both stored procedures and triggers.

About Stored Procedures

Stored procedures can be used in applications in a variety of ways.

- Selectable procedures are used in place of a table or view in a SELECT statement.

- Executable procedures are used with an EXECUTE PROCEDURE statement to perform a single operation or start a set of operations on the server side.

- A stored procedure can be invoked by another stored procedure or by a trigger. It can call itself recursively.

All stored procedures are defined with the complex DDL statement CREATE PROCEDURE. Executable and selectable stored procedure declarations follow the same syntax rules. Optional language elements distinguish a selectable one from an executable one. One procedure can be nested within another, each performing a part of an atomic sequence of work that will be committed by the client application as a whole or rolled back as a whole.

Benefits of Using Stored Procedures

The benefits of using procedural code modules that run inside the database include

- **Modular design**: All applications that access the same database share stored procedures, thus centralizing business rules, reusing code, and reducing the size of the applications.

- **Streamlined maintenance**: When a procedure is modified, changes propagate automatically to all applications without the need for further recompiling on the application side, unless changes affect input or output argument sets.

- **Improved performance**: Execution of complex processing is delegated to the server, reducing network traffic and the overhead of operating on external sets.

- **Architectural economy**: Client applications can focus on capturing user input and managing interactive tasks while delegating complex data refinement and dependency management to a dedicated data management engine.

- **Extra functionality**: Tricky accessing and massaging of data that cannot be achieved with regular SQL usually can be managed with one or a suite of stored procedures.

About Triggers

A *trigger* is a self-contained routine associated with a table or view that automatically performs an action when a row in the table or view is inserted, updated, or deleted.

A trigger is never called directly. Instead, when an application or user attempts to INSERT, UPDATE, or DELETE a row in a table, any triggers associated with that table and operation are automatically executed, or *fired*. Triggers can make use of exceptions and can trigger events. They can also call stored procedures.

Triggers are a powerful feature with a variety of uses. Among the ways that triggers can be used are

- To make correlated updates when DML is performed on the table. For example, a trigger could insert records to an internal or external change log. An AFTER DELETE trigger could insert a row to a history table.

- To validate input data.

- To transform data, for example, to automatically convert text input to uppercase or to fetch an auto-incrementing key value from a generator.

- To notify applications of changes in the database using event alerters.

- To perform custom cascading referential integrity updates.

- To make a read-only view updatable. For details, see the section "Making Read-Only Views Updatable" in Chapter 24.

Triggers are stored as objects in a database, like stored procedures and exceptions. Once defined to be ACTIVE, they remain active until deactivated with ALTER TRIGGER or removed from the database with DROP TRIGGER.

A trigger is never explicitly called—an active trigger fires automatically when the specified DML operation occurs on the owning table.

Benefits of Using Triggers

The benefits of using triggers include

- **Automatic enforcement of data restrictions**, to make sure users enter only valid values into columns.

- **Reduced application maintenance**, since changes to a trigger are automatically reflected in all applications that use the associated table without the need to recompile and relink.

- **Automatic logging of changes to tables**. An application can keep a running log of changes with a trigger that fires whenever a table is modified.

- **Automatic notification of changes to the database with event alerters in triggers**.

Triggers As an Auto-increment Mechanism

Triggers can be used in combination with generators to implement an auto-incrementing key. Detailed instructions can be found in Chapter 31.

Triggers and Transactions

Triggers always operate within the context of a specific DML operation, as part of that operation and inside the transaction that makes the DML statement request. They are in no sense separated from the transaction or from the operation that causes them to fire. If the transaction is rolled back, then any actions performed by triggers are also rolled back.

PSQL Language Extensions

The PSQL language extensions include the following language elements:

- BEGIN and END statements for defining code blocks, which can be nested.

- DECLARE VARIABLE statements for declaring local variables.

- FOR SELECT *<select-specification>* INTO *<variable-list>* DO encapsulating an SQL cursor, for looping through sets. Loops can be nested.

- WHILE loops.

- SUSPEND statement for sending a row of output to the row cache.

- IF … THEN and ELSE for branching logic.

- The EXCEPTION *<declared exception name>* statement for raising custom exceptions.

- Optional WHEN *<exception condition>* DO blocks for catching and handling exceptions.

- POST_EVENT *<string>* to pass notifications to the client.

Firebird 1.5 and later also support

- EXECUTE STATEMENT statement for executing ad hoc DML and DDL statements from within the module (v.1.5 and later)

- Boolean context variables UPDATING, INSERTING, and DELETING

- Context variable ROW_COUNT to read the number of rows affected by a completed DML statement within the same block

- Optional syntaxes for EXCEPTION, with no argument for reraising exceptions and with an optional text argument for passing runtime information back to the client

Restrictions on PSQL

Certain language restrictions apply to the code in PSQL modules:

- Statements using the data definition language (DDL) subset of Firebird SQL are not permissible in PSQL.[1]

- Transaction control statements are not valid in PSQL, because stored procedures and triggers always execute within an existing client transaction context and Firebird does not support embedded transactions.

- Some other statement types are reserved for use in different environments (e.g., **isql**, scripts, or embedded SQL—see the next section). All dynamic DML statements are allowed.

- Metadata object identifiers, such as the names of tables, columns, views, or stored procedures, cannot be passed to or returned from stored procedures in arguments.

- Trigger procedures cannot accept or return arguments.

Statement Types Not Supported in PSQL

The following statement types are not supported in triggers or stored procedures:

- Data definition language statements (i.e., any beginning with any of the keywords CREATE, RECREATE, ALTER, or DROP; SET GENERATOR; DECLARE EXTERNAL FUNCTION; and DECLARE FILTER)

- Transaction control statements: SET TRANSACTION, COMMIT, COMMIT RETAIN, ROLLBACK, SAVEPOINT, RELEASE SAVEPOINT, ROLLBACK TO SAVEPOINT

- ESQL statements: PREPARE, DESCRIBE, EXECUTE

- CONNECT/DISCONNECT, and sending SQL statements to another database

- GRANT/REVOKE

- EVENT INIT/EVENT WAIT

---

1. In v.1.5, it is possible to pass a DDL statement in an EXECUTE STATEMENT string. Do it only with extreme caution.

- BEGIN DECLARE SECTION/END DECLARE SECTION

- BASED ON

- WHENEVER

- DECLARE CURSOR

- OPEN

- FETCH

- Any statement beginning with the keywords SET or SHOW

Exceptions

Exception handlers can be written to "swallow" an error by dealing with it in some way. For example, an input row in an iterative routine that causes an exception does not need to cause the entire process to stop. The exception handling inside the trigger or procedure can allow the problem input to be skipped—perhaps logging the error in a text file or error table—and let further processing continue.

The code module can handle an error itself with an optional piece of code, known as an *exception block*, which is a sequence of statements bounded by BEGIN and END, preceded by a directive beginning with the keyword WHEN.

An unhandled exception stops processing, undoes any work done thus far, and returns an error message to the application. You can also have your code raise a custom exception itself and stop processing. You can handle the error in your code—or stop the processing and return a custom message to the client application. If the code module is a trigger, the DML operation in which the error occurred will be undone also. You can create as many custom exceptions as you need in a database. From v.1.5 on, you can use runtime data and construct extensions to your exception messages "on the fly."

Exceptions and error handling are discussed in detail in Chapter 32.

Events

Firebird events are optional "signals" that PSQL modules can accumulate during execution, to be passed to client applications once the work has been committed. Client applications anywhere on the network can optionally listen—by way of "event alerters"—for specific events that they are interested in, without needing to poll for changes specifically.

Programming for events and setting up applications to listen for them are topics covered in Chapter 32.

Security

Procedures and triggers can be granted privileges for specific actions (SELECT, INSERT, DELETE, and so on) on tables, just as users or roles can be granted privileges. There is no special syntax: An ordinary GRANT statement is used, but the recipient named in the TO clause is a trigger or procedure, instead of a user or a role. Similarly, privileges can be revoked from procedures and triggers.

It is not always necessary to grant privileges to trigger and procedure modules. It is enough for *either* the user or the module to have the privileges for the actions the module has to perform.

For example, if a user performs an UPDATE of table A, which fires a trigger, and the trigger performs an INSERT on table B, the action is allowed if the user has INSERT privileges on the table or the trigger has INSERT privileges on the table.

If there are not sufficient privileges for a trigger or procedure to perform its actions, Firebird fires an SQL error and sets the appropriate error code number. You can intercept this error code with an exception handler, just as with other exceptions. For more information about GRANT and REVOKE, see Chapter 35.

Internals of the Technology

When any *request* invokes a stored procedure, the current definition for that stored procedure is copied at that moment to a *metadata cache*. On Classic server, this copy persists for the lifetime of the user's connection. On Superserver, it stays "live" until the last connection is logged out.

A request comes from one of the following:

- A client application that executes the stored procedure directly.

- A trigger that executes the stored procedure. This includes system triggers that are part of referential integrity or check constraints.

- Another stored procedure that executes the stored procedure.

Effects of Changes

Once invoked, a trigger or stored procedure request persists in the metadata cache while there are clients connected to the database, regardless of whether any connected client makes use of the trigger or stored procedure. There is no mechanism to force these outstanding requests to update their metadata cache. For this reason, changes to PSQL modules are "deferred" to a greater or lesser extent in most cases. The ability of clients to see changes is different for Superserver than for Classic server.

Superserver

Because existing requests are emptied from the metadata cache only when the last client disconnects from the database, they simply may never update on a 24/7 system. The only way to guarantee that all copies of stored procedures and triggers are purged from the metadata cache is for all connections to the database to terminate. When users log in again, they will all see the newest version of the stored procedure.

Classic Server

Altering or dropping a stored procedure takes effect immediately for new connections made after the change is committed. New connections that invoke the stored procedure will see the latest version. However, other connections continue to see the version of the stored procedure that they first saw. In practical terms, it makes sense to disconnect clients before you commit your changed module.

Up Next

Next, we look at the structure of PSQL modules: broadly, what triggers and procedures have in common and how they differ.

Developing PSQL Modules

STORED PROCEDURES AND TRIGGERS ARE DEFINED with the CREATE PROCEDURE and CREATE TRIGGER statements, respectively. Each of these complex statements is composed of a *header* and a *body*.

Elements of Procedures and Triggers

PSQL module definitions are really a single SQL statement that begins with a CREATE clause and ends with a terminator. Within the module definition are a number of elements: clauses, keywords, blocks of multiple statements, branches, loops, and others. Some elements are mandatory; others are optional.

Although the complex definition of a PSQL module is a DDL statement, the SQL extensions within it are elements of a structured, high-level language that has certain distinctive rules. An important one to know about before you begin is the *statement terminator*.

The CREATE Statement

Source code for procedures and triggers is constructed inside a "super-statement" that begins with the keyword CREATE PROCEDURE or CREATE TRIGGER and ends with a terminator symbol following the final END statement, for example:

```
CREATE PROCEDURE Name...
...
AS
...
BEGIN
...
END ^
```

With both stored procedures and triggers, all statements following the keyword AS comprise the local variables (if any) and the logic of the program module. The main difference between triggers and stored procedures is in the header portion of the CREATE statement (see Figure 29-1 later in this chapter).

Statement Terminator

Each statement inside a stored procedure or trigger body—other than BEGIN and END—must be terminated by a semicolon. No other symbol is valid for terminating statements in PSQL. In DSQL, for both DML and DDL, the semicolon also happens to be the default statement terminator in Firebird and it is also the SQL standard for terminating statements.

This situation is going to present a logical problem for the parser that pre-compiles our PSQL modules: Which semicolons terminate statements inside the module and which one terminates the CREATE definition?

To get around this problem, Firebird has a switching SET TERM syntax that allows you to set a different external terminator, to be in effect for external statements while PSQL definitions are being parsed. In scripts, experienced developers often use a single SET TERM statement at the beginning of all scripts, to have their favorite alternative terminator in effect at all times during scripting. Some database admin tools support configuring their editors and metadata extraction programs with an alternative terminator.

SET TERM statements are used in **isql** and in scripts.

isql pre-parses every statement and sends any terminated statement directly to the server as a single command. SET TERM is one of its own ISQL statements that it responds to not by sending a request to the server but by preparing its parser to interpret terminators differently. (Other ISQL SET statements also invoke special activity in the **isql** program that is not meaningful outside **isql**.)

The DSQL layer does not recognize terminators for statements at all. Most of the other utilities that process scripts actually dispatch the DDL statements off to the server one by one without terminators. They provide parsing of their own to recognize the beginning and end of CREATE PROCEDURE statements and pass the internal semicolon terminators simply as regular symbols within the compound statement syntax.

When you use such a utility for creating PSQL modules interactively, it will usually throw exceptions at SET TERM since, as an SQL statement, it has no meaning outside **isql**. However, in scripts, these utilities usually parse for and expect a SET TERM statement and use the alternative terminator internally, in a manner equivalent to the way **isql** handles it.

So, use SET TERM in **isql** if you are using that tool to process your CREATE PROCEDURE statements interactively, and use it in scripts.

The alternative terminator can be any string symbol you like, except a semicolon, a space character, or a single-quote character. If you use an ordinary character, it will be case sensitive. It can be multiple characters if you prefer, including embedded spaces, and it must not be a reserved keyword. Both of the following statements are valid:

```
SET TERM ^;
SET TERM boing! ;
```

 TIP   Don't get too creative with your terminator strings or you'll end up with a lot of awkward extra typing!

In PSQL definitions, use semicolons for all internal statements except BEGIN and END, and use the alternative terminator for the final END statement:

```
...
END ^
```

To return to "normal" statement termination, issue a second SET TERM statement that is the reverse of the first:

```
...
END ^
COMMIT ^
SET TERM ;^
```

In Figure 29-1, the main elements of a PSQL module definition are split to illustrate the required elements of the module's *header* and *body* sections. The mandatory parts are shaded.

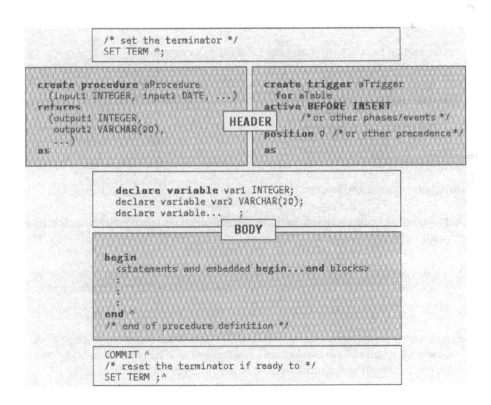

Figure 29-1. Required elements of a PSQL module definition

Header Elements

The *name of the procedure or trigger* must be unique in the database.

For a trigger:

- The keyword FOR and a *table name*, identifying the table that causes the trigger to fire

- A mode (ACTIVE or INACTIVE)

- A *phase parameter* (BEFORE or AFTER) that determines *when* the trigger fires

- An event parameter (INSERT, UPDATE, DELETE)[1]

- Optionally, the keyword POSITION followed by an integer, indicating *firing sequence*

For a stored procedure:

- An optional list of *input parameters* and their data types

- If the procedure returns values to the calling program, a list of *output parameters* and their data types

Body Elements

For stored procedures and triggers:

- The module body can begin with a list of one or more *local variable declarations* (name and SQL data type—no domains).

- A *block* of statements in Firebird procedure and trigger language, bracketed by BEGIN and END. A block can itself include other blocks, so that there may be many levels of nesting.

- Some embedded blocks can be *handlers for exceptions* occurring in preceding blocks. Such blocks are conditioned by a preceding WHEN predicate. Module-global exception handlers should follow all other embedded blocks.

---

1. From v.1.5 onward, it is possible to combine events in one trigger. For more details, refer to Chapter 31.

Language Elements

Table 29-1 shows the PSQL language elements available in Firebird.

Table 29-1. PSQL Extensions for Stored Procedures and Triggers

STATEMENT	DESCRIPTION	V.1.5	V.1.0.X
BEGIN ... END	Defines a block of statements that executes as one. The BEGIN reserved word starts the block; the END reserved word terminates it. Neither should be followed by a semicolon. In v.1.0.*x*, it is not valid to submit a CREATE PROCEDURE statement without at least one statement between BEGIN and END. "Empty" definitions are fine in v.1.5 and later.	Y	Y
variable = expression	Assigns the value of *expression* to *variable*, a local variable, input parameter, or output parameter.	Y	Y
/* comment-text * /	Programmer's comment, where *comment-text* can be any number of lines of text between a "/* */" pair. Can also be used for inline comments.	Y	Y
-- comment-text	Programmer's single-line comment, where *comment-text* can be inline (v.1.5 only) or occupy a single line in which the double-hyphen (--) marker is the first item in the line.	Y	Y
EXCEPTION *exception-name*	Raises the named exception for optional handling by a WHEN block. Exception is pre-defined by the DBA using CREATE EXCEPTION.	Y	Y
EXCEPTION	Reraises the exception	Y	N
EXCEPTION *exception-name* *runtime-message*	Raises the named exception and attaches *runtime-message*, a local VARCHAR variable that can be assigned a runtime message during the course of execution. For details about defining and using exceptions, refer to Chapter 32.	Y	N
EXECUTE PROCEDURE *proc-name [var [, var ...]]* [RETURNING_VALUES *var [, var ...]]*	Executes stored procedure *proc-name*. Input arguments follow the procedure name; return values are listed following the keyword RETURNING_VALUES. Enables procedure nesting and recursion. Input and output parameters must be variables defined within the procedure.	Y	Y

continued

Table 29-1. PSQL Extensions for Stored Procedures and Triggers (continued)

STATEMENT	DESCRIPTION	V.1.5	V.1.0.X
EXECUTE STATEMENT *<string>*	Executes a dynamic SQL statement contained by *<string>*.	Y	N
EXIT	Jumps to the final END statement in the procedure. Optional.	Y	Y
FOR ... SELECT ... INTO ... DO ...	Compound looping block syntax for processing an implicit cursor and optionally generating a virtual table for direct output to a SELECT request from a client. For more details, see the section "Multiple-Row SELECTs."	Y	Y
IF ... THEN ... [ELSE] ...	Compound branching syntax. For more details, see the section "Conditional Blocks" later in this chapter.	Y	Y
LEAVE[2]	Statement taking no parameters, for breaking out of loops. Causes execution to jump to the first statement following the end of the block that encloses the loop in which the LEAVE statement is executed.	Y	N
NEW.*column-name*	*Triggers only.* Context variables available to INSERT and UPDATE triggers. There is one NEW variable for each column of the owning table, indicating the new value submitted by the client request. Also available in some CHECK constraints. Note: In v.1.5 multi-action trigger code, reference to NEW.variables is not invalid, although it returns NULL if used in a deleting context.	Y	Y
OLD.*column-name*	*Triggers only.* Context variables available to UPDATE and DELETE triggers. There is one OLD variable for each column of the owning table, indicating the value as it was before the client request was submitted. Also available in some CHECK constraints. Note, in v.1.5 multi-action triggers, reference to OLD.variables is valid, even though the trigger includes inserting action. It returns NULL if used in an inserting context.	Y	Y

---

2. In v.1.5, LEAVE deprecates an undocumented BREAK statement that was partly implemented in v.1.0.x. Do not use BREAK.

Table 29-1. PSQL Extensions for Stored Procedures and Triggers (continued)

STATEMENT	DESCRIPTION	V.1.5	V.1.0.X
POST_EVENT *event_name*	Causes the event *event_name* to be "posted" to a stack. *Event_name* can be any string up to 78 characters and is not pre-defined on the server. Stacked events will be broadcast to clients "listening" via event alerter host routines. For details, refer to the section "Events" in Chapter 32.	Y	Y
SELECT ... INTO ...	Passes output from an ordinary singleton SELECT specification into a list of pre-declared variables. It will throw an exception if the statement returns multiple rows.	Y	Y
SUSPEND	*Not valid in triggers!* Statement used in procedures designed to output multiple-row sets as virtual tables—"selectable" stored procedures. It suspends execution of the procedure until the row is fetched from the row cache by the client application. It does not have this effect in an "executable" stored procedure, where it is equivalent to EXIT.	Y	Y
WHILE *<condition>* DO	Conditional looping syntax that causes the succeeding block to be executed repeatedly until *<condition>* is false. For more details, see the section "Conditional Blocks" later in this chapter.	Y	Y
WHEN *{error* [*, error ...*] *| ANY}*	Provides syntax for handling exceptions. Arguments can be one or more user-defined EXCEPTIONs or internally defined GDSCODE or SQLCODE exceptions. For details, refer to Chapter 32.	Y	Y

Programming Constructs

The following sections examine the general programming constructs that are recognized in PSQL.

BEGIN ... END Blocks

PSQL is a structured language. Once variables are declared, the procedural statements are bounded by the keywords BEGIN and END. In the course of developing the logic of the procedure, other blocks can be embedded, and any block can embed another block bounded by a BEGIN ... END pair.

No terminator symbol is used for the BEGIN or END keywords, except for the final END keyword that closes the procedure block and terminates the CREATE PROCEDURE or CREATE TRIGGER statement. This final END keyword takes the special terminator that was defined with the SET TERM statement before the definition began.

Conditional Blocks

PSQL recognizes two types of conditional structures:

- Branching, controlled by IF ... THEN and, optionally, ELSE blocks

- Looping through and executing a block repeatedly until a WHILE condition becomes false

From v.1.5 on, the Boolean INSERTING, UPDATING, and DELETING, and integer ROW_COUNT context variables are available for predicates within a block that performs a data state-changing operation. Refer to Chapter 31 for details of using the Boolean context variables in multi-event triggers.

The IF ... THEN ... ELSE Construct

The IF ... THEN ... ELSE construct branches to alternative courses of action by testing a specified condition. The syntax is

```
IF (<condition>)
THEN <compound_statement>
[ELSE <compound_statement>]
<compound_statement> = {<block>|<statement>;}
```

The *condition* clause is a predicate that must evaluate to true in order to execute the statement or block following THEN. The optional ELSE clause specifies an alternative statement or block to be executed if *condition* is false. *Condition* can be any valid predicate.

NOTE   The predicate being tested by IF must be enclosed in brackets.

When you code conditional branching with SQL, use of the ELSE clause is sometimes a necessary "fallback" for situations where the predicate tested by IF might not evaluate to either true or false. This could occur where runtime data conditions caused the IF predicate to compare two nulls and a logical result of true or false was impossible. An ELSE branch is the means for your code to guarantee that the block produces an outcome whenever the IF clause fails to do so.

The following code snippet illustrates the use of IF ... THEN, assuming FIRST_NAME, LAST_NAME, and LINE2 have been previously declared as variables or arguments:

```
...
IF (FIRST_NAME IS NOT NULL) THEN
  LINE2 = FIRST_NAME || ' ' || LAST_NAME;
ELSE
  BEGIN
    IF (LAST_NAME IS NOT NULL) THEN
      LINE2 = LASTNAME;
    ELSE
      LINE2 = 'NO NAME SUPPLIED';
  END
...
```

> **TIP** Pascal programmers, observe that the IF ... THEN branch is terminated!

About CASE

PSQL does not yet support CASE logic as a programming construct. The CASE *expression* logic is, of course, available in PSQL. For more information, refer to Chapter 21.

The WHILE ... DO Construct

WHILE ... DO is a looping construct that repeats a statement or block of statements as long as the predicating condition is true. The condition is tested at the start of each loop. WHILE ... DO uses the following syntax:

```
...
WHILE (<condition>) DO
  BEGIN
    <execute one or more statements> ;
    <change the value of an operand of the predicating condition> ;
  END
/* Continue execution here */
...
```

In the following simple procedure, WHILE tests the value of a variable, *i*, that is initialized as an input argument. The looping block decrements *i* on each iteration and, as long as i remains greater than zero, the value of the output argument, *r*, is raised by 1. When the procedure exits, the value of *r* is returned.

```
SET TERM ^;
CREATE PROCEDURE MORPH_ME (i INTEGER) RETURNS (r INTEGER)
AS
BEGIN
  r = 0;
  WHILE (i > 0) DO
  BEGIN
    r = r +i;
    i = i - 1;
  END
END^
```

Calling the procedure from **isql**

```
SQL> EXECUTE PROCEDURE MORPH_ME(16);
```

we get

```
          R
==========
        136
```

Variables

Five types of variables can be used in the body of a code module, with some restrictions according to whether the module is a stored procedure or a trigger:

- Local variables, used to hold values used only within the trigger or procedure.

- The NEW.ColumnName and OLD.ColumnName context variables, restricted to use in triggers, which store the new and old values of each column of the table when a DML operation is pending.

- Other context variables—those specific to PSQL as well as those available to **isql** and DSQL.

- Input arguments, used to pass constant values to a stored procedure from a client application, another stored procedure, or a trigger. *Not available for triggers.*

- Output arguments, used to return values from a stored procedure back to the requester. *Not available for triggers.*

Any of these types of variables can be used in the body of a stored procedure where an expression can appear. They can be assigned a *literal* value or assigned a value derived from queries or expression evaluations.

Use of Domains

Because domain definitions have the potential to be changed, they cannot be used in place of native SQL data types for declaring variables and stored procedure arguments. PSQL modules are compiled into a binary form at creation time and changes to domains would break them if domain use were allowed.

The Colon (:) Marker for Variables

In SQL statements, prefix the variable's name with a colon character (:) whenever

- The variable is used in an SQL statement.

- The variable is receiving a value from a [FOR] SELECT ... INTO construct.

Omit the colon in all other situations.

NOTE   Never prefix context variables with a colon.

Assignment Statements

A procedure assigns values to variables with the syntax

```
variable = expression;
```

The *expression* can be any valid combination of variables, operators, and expressions, and can include calls to external functions (UDFs) and SQL functions, including the GEN_ID() function for stepping and returning a generator value.

The following code snippet performs several assignments:

```
...
WHILE (SI < 9) DO
  BEGIN
    SI = SI + 1; /* arithmetic expression */
    IF (SUBSTRING(SMONTH FROM 1 FOR 1) = 'R') THEN
    BEGIN
      RESPONSE = 'YES'; /* simple constant */
```

```
       LEAVE;
    END
    SMONTH = SUBSTRING(SMONTH FROM 2); /* function expression */
  END
...
```

Variables and arguments should be assigned values of the data type that they are declared to be. Numeric variables should be assigned numeric values, and character variables assigned character values. Although Firebird provides automatic type conversion in some cases, it is advisable to use explicit casting to avoid unanticipated type mismatches.

More information about explicit casting and data type conversion can be found in Chapters 8 and 21.

Local Variables

Local variables are declared, one line per variable, preceding the first BEGIN statement. They have no effect outside the procedure or trigger, and their scope does not extend to any procedures they call. They must be declared before they can be used.

You should always ensure that your variables are initialized as early as possible in your procedure. From Firebird 1.5 you can declare and initialize in a single statement. For example, each of the following statements is valid to declare a counter variable and initialize it to 0:

```
...
DECLARE VARIABLE COUNTER1 INTEGER DEFAULT 0;
DECLARE VARIABLE COUNTER2 INTEGER = 0;
```

Example Using Local Variables

The following procedure is a piece of superstitious fun, assuming there is truth in the proverb "Never eat pork when there is an 'R' in the month," it returns an opinion about a given date. For the sake of illustration, it declares one local variable that is used to get a starting condition for a WHILE loop and another to control the number of times the loop will execute:

```
CREATE PROCEDURE IS_PORK_SAFE(CHECK_MONTH DATE)
RETURNS (RESPONSE CHAR(3))
AS
DECLARE VARIABLE SMONTH VARCHAR(9);
DECLARE VARIABLE SI SMALLINT;
BEGIN
  SI = 0;
  RESPONSE = 'NO ';
```

```
SELECT CASE (EXTRACT (MONTH FROM :CHECK_MONTH))
   WHEN 1 THEN 'JANUARY'
   WHEN 2 THEN 'FEBRUARY'
   WHEN 3 THEN 'MARCH'
   WHEN 4 THEN 'APRIL'
   WHEN 5 THEN 'MAY'
   WHEN 6 THEN 'JUNE'
   WHEN 7 THEN 'JULY'
   WHEN 8 THEN 'AUGUST'
   WHEN 9 THEN 'SEPTEMBER'
   WHEN 10 THEN 'OCTOBER'
   WHEN 11 THEN 'NOVEMBER'
   WHEN 12 THEN 'DECEMBER' END
FROM RDB$DATABASE
INTO :SMONTH;
WHILE (SI < 9) DO
BEGIN
  SI = SI + 1;
  IF (SUBSTRING(SMONTH FROM 1 FOR 1) = 'R') THEN
  BEGIN
    RESPONSE = 'YES';
    LEAVE;
  END
  SMONTH = SUBSTRING(SMONTH FROM 2);
END
END ^
COMMIT ^
SET TERM ;^
```

Is it safe for the author to eat pork on her birthday?

```
EXECUTE PROCEDURE IS_PORK_SAFE ('2004-05-16');
RESPONSE
========
NO
```

TIP   If this were a serious procedure, SQL has faster ways to get this result. For example, instead of the WHILE loop, you could simply test the variable SMONTH:

```
IF (SMONTH CONTAINING 'R') THEN RESPONSE = 'YES' ELSE RESPONSE = 'NO ';
```

You would probably want to use an external function to get the name of the month and, in v.1.5, you can initialize variables in the declaration.

Input Arguments

Input arguments (also known as *parameters*) are used to pass values from an application to a procedure or from one PSQL module to another. They are declared in a comma-separated list in parentheses following the procedure name. Once declared, they can be used in the procedure body anywhere an expression can appear.

For example, the following procedure snippet specifies one input argument, to tell the procedure which country the caller wants to be used in a search.

```
CREATE PROCEDURE SHOW_JOBS_FOR_COUNTRY (
  COUNTRY VARCHAR(15))
...
```

Input parameters are passed *by value* from the calling program to a stored procedure. This means that if the procedure changes the value of an input parameter, the change has effect only within the procedure. When control returns to the calling program, the input parameter still has its original value.

Input arguments are not valid in triggers.

Output Arguments

An output argument (parameter) is used to specify a value that is to be returned from a procedure to the calling application or PSQL module. If there are to be multiple return values, declare the arguments in a comma-separated list in parentheses, following the keyword RETURNS in the procedure header. Once declared, they can be used in the procedure body anywhere an expression can appear.

The following code completes the procedure definition shown in the previous snippet. It defines three items of data to be returned to the caller as a virtual table:

```
CREATE PROCEDURE SHOW_JOBS_FOR_COUNTRY (
  COUNTRY VARCHAR(15))
RETURNS (
  CODE VARCHAR(11),
  TITLE VARCHAR(25),
  GRADE SMALLINT)
AS
BEGIN
  FOR SELECT JOB_CODE, JOB_TITLE, JOB_GRADE FROM job
      WHERE JOB_COUNTRY = :COUNTRY
      INTO :CODE, :TITLE, :GRADE
  DO
    BEGIN /* begin the loop */
      CODE = 'CODE: ' || CODE; /* mess about with the value a little */
      SUSPEND; /* this outputs one row per loop */
    END
END ^
```

If you declare output parameters in the procedure header, the procedure must assign values to them to return to the calling application. Values can be derived from any valid expression in the procedure.

TIP   Always initialize output parameters before beginning to process the data that will be sent to them.

NEW and OLD Context Variables

Triggers can use two complete sets of context variables representing the "old" and "new" values of each column in the owning table. OLD.*column-name* refers to the current or previous values of the named column in a row being updated or deleted. It has no meaning for inserts. NEW.*column-name* refers to the values submitted by the request to update, insert, or delete. It has no meaning for deletes. If an update does not change some columns, the NEW variable will have the same value as the OLD for each of those columns. Context variables are often used to compare the values of a column before and after it is modified.

Context variables can be used anywhere a regular variable can be used. NEW values for a row can be altered only by *before* actions. OLD values are read-only. For details and examples of usage, refer to Chapter 31.

TIP   Since Firebird creates triggers to implement CHECK constraints, the OLD and NEW context variables can be used directly in a CHECK constraint, for example:

```
ALTER TABLE EMPLOYEE
ADD CONSTRAINT EMPLOYEE_SALARY_RAISE_CK
CHECK ((OLD.SALARY IS NULL) OR (NEW.SALARY > OLD.SALARY));
```

SELECT ... INTO Statements

Use a SELECT statement with an INTO clause to retrieve column values from tables and store them into local variables or output arguments.

Singleton SELECTs

An ordinary SELECT statement in PSQL must return *at most* one row from the database—a standard *singleton* SELECT. An exception is thrown if the statement returns more than one row. An ORDER BY clause is not valid for a singleton select unless it is a quantified SELECT FIRST 1 statement. (For information about the set quantifier FIRST, refer to Chapter 20.)

Normal rules apply to the input list and the WHERE clause and to the GROUP BY clause, if used. The INTO clause is required and must be the last clause in the statement.

For example, the following is a singleton SELECT statement in a parameterized DSQL query in an application:

```
SELECT SUM(BUDGET), AVG(BUDGET)
FROM DEPARTMENT
WHERE HEAD_DEPT = :head_dept;
```

To use this statement in a procedure, declare local variables or output arguments and add the INTO clause at the end as follows:

```
...
DECLARE VARIABLE TOT_BUDGET NUMERIC(18,2);
DECLARE VARIABLE AVG_BUDGET NUMERIC(18,2);
...
SELECT SUM(BUDGET), AVG(BUDGET)
FROM DEPARTMENT
WHERE HEAD_DEPT = :head_dept
INTO :tot_budget, :avg_budget;
```

Multiple-Row SELECTs

Any PSQL module can operate on multiple rows of input, acquired through a SELECT statement, as long as it provides a looping structure that can "move" through the set and perform identical processing on each row. PSQL cannot handle multi-row sets otherwise and, in the absence of looping logic context, a multi-row select will cause an exception ("Multiple rows in singleton select").

FOR SELECT ... Loops

The main method for implementing a looping structure for handling multi-row input sets is the FOR SELECT ... INTO ... DO structure. The abridged syntax is as follows:

```
FOR SELECT <set-specification-list>
FROM table-name
[JOIN..]
[WHERE..]
```

```
[GROUP BY..]
[ORDER BY..]
INTO <list-of-variables> DO
  BEGIN
    <process-block>
    ...
    [SUSPEND];
  END
...
```

As an example, the following procedure defines and acquires a set using a SELECT statement that brings the rows, one at a time, in the procedure's cursor buffer. It courses through the set, massaging each set of variables to fit a table specification. At the end of the loop, it inserts a record into the external table:

```
CREATE PROCEDURE PROJECT_MEMBERS
AS
DECLARE VARIABLE PROJ_NAME CHAR(23);
DECLARE VARIABLE EMP_NO CHAR(6);
DECLARE VARIABLE LAST_NAME CHAR(23);
DECLARE VARIABLE FIRST_NAME CHAR(18);
DECLARE VARIABLE HIRE_DATE CHAR(12);
DECLARE VARIABLE JOB_TITLE CHAR(27);
DECLARE VARIABLE CRLF CHAR(2);
BEGIN
  CRLF = ASCII_CHAR(13)||ASCII_CHAR(10); /* Windows EOL */
FOR SELECT DISTINCT
  P.PROJ_NAME,
  E.EMP_NO,
  E.LAST_NAME,
  E.FIRST_NAME,
  E.HIRE_DATE,
  J.JOB_TITLE
FROM EMPLOYEE E
  JOIN JOB J ON E.JOB_CODE = J.JOB_CODE
  JOIN EMPLOYEE_PROJECT EP ON E.EMP_NO = EP.EMP_NO
  JOIN PROJECT P ON P.PROJ_ID = EP.PROJ_ID
ORDER BY P.PROJ_NAME, E.LAST_NAME, E.FIRST_NAME
INTO /* column variables */
  :PROJ_NAME, :EMP_NO, :LAST_NAME, :FIRST_NAME,
  :HIRE_DATE, :JOB_TITLE
DO
  BEGIN /* starts the loop that massages the variable */
    PROJ_NAME = '"'||CAST(PROJ_NAME AS CHAR(20))||'"'||',';
    EMP_NO = CAST(EMP_NO AS CHAR(5))||',';
    LAST_NAME = '"'||CAST(LAST_NAME AS CHAR(20))||'"'||',';
    FIRST_NAME = '"'||CAST(FIRST_NAME AS CHAR(15))||'"'||',';
    HIRE_DATE = CAST(HIRE_DATE AS CHAR(11))||',';
    JOB_TITLE = '"'||CAST(JOB_TITLE AS CHAR(25))||'"';
```

```
    INSERT INTO EXT_FILE
      VALUES (:PROJ_NAME, :EMP_NO, :LAST_NAME,
              :FIRST_NAME,:HIRE_DATE, :JOB_TITLE,
              :CRLF);
  END /* completes the DO-loop */
END ^
```

> **CAUTION**   If an output parameter has not been assigned a value, its value is
> unpredictable, which can lead to errors. A procedure should ensure that all
> output parameters are initialized in advance of the processing that will assign
> values, to ensure that a SUSPEND will pass valid output.

SUSPEND

The SUSPEND statement has a specific use with the FOR ... SELECT ... INTO ... DO
construct just described. If SUSPEND is included in the DO loop, after the SELECT row
has been read into the row variables, it causes the loop to wait until that row has been
output to the server's row cache before fetching the next row from the SELECT cursor.
This is the operation that enables Firebird's *selectable stored procedures* feature.

In the next chapter, we take a closer look at using SELECT statements that return
multiple rows to a stored procedure, particularly the technique for writing selectable
stored procedures.

The SUSPEND statement is not valid in triggers. In executable stored procedures it
has the same effect as an EXIT statement—that is, it terminates the procedure immediately and any statements following it will never execute.

By contrast, if a select procedure has executable statements following the last
SUSPEND statement in the procedure, all of those statements are executed, even
though no more rows are returned to the calling program. This style of procedure
terminates with the final END statement.

Flow of Control Statements

PSQL provides a number of statements that affect the flow of control through code
modules. The SUSPEND statement just discussed effectively passes control back to the
calling procedure or client program, waiting for a just-processed row to be fetched
from the server's row cache.

EXIT

In both selectable and executable procedures, EXIT causes program control to jump
to the final END statement in the procedure. It is not meaningful in triggers.

The behaviors of SUSPEND, EXIT, and END statements are summarized in Table 29-2.

Table 29-2. SUSPEND, EXIT, and END

MODULE TYPE	SUSPEND	EXIT	END
Selectable procedure	Execution is suspended until the calling application or procedure fetches the preceding set of output variables.	Returns values (if any) and jumps to final END	Returns control to application and sets SQLCODE to 100
Executable procedure	Jumps to final END—not recommended.	Jumps to final END	Returns values and returns control to application
Triggers	Never used.	Jumps to final END	Causes execution of the next trigger in the same phase (BEFORE or AFTER) as the current one, if any; otherwise, terminates trigger processing for the phase

LEAVE

Firebird 1.5 introduced the LEAVE statement for breaking out of code blocks. It deprecates the BREAK statement that was partly implemented in v.1.0.*x*. An example of its use is in the WHILE loop of our IS_PORK_SAFE procedure:

```
...
WHILE (SI < 9) DO
  BEGIN
    SI = SI + 1; /* arithmetic expression */
    IF (SUBSTRING(SMONTH FROM 1 FOR 1) = 'R') THEN
    BEGIN
      RESPONSE = 'YES'; /* simple constant */
      LEAVE;
    END
    SMONTH = SUBSTRING(SMONTH FROM 2); /* function expression */
  END
...
```

LEAVE causes execution to leave the loop—in this case, to stop testing the letters of a word for the character "R." If the branching containing the LEAVE statement is not executed, execution continues to the end of the loop.

EXCEPTION

The EXCEPTION statement stops execution and passes control to the first exception handler block (a block starting with the keyword WHEN) that can handle the exception. If no handler is found for the exception, control passes to the final END statement and the procedure aborts. When this happens, one or more exception codes are passed back to the client via the *error status vector* (array).

The EXCEPTION statement is used in an IF … THEN … ELSE block to invoke custom exceptions that have been previously declared as database objects. The Firebird engine throws its own exceptions for SQL and context errors. Flow of control in these cases is the same as when a custom exception is called.

The syntax and techniques for calling and handling exceptions are addressed in Chapter 32.

Execute Statement

Firebird 1.5 introduced a PSQL extension supporting the *executable string*. An application or procedure can pass a DSQL statement (DML or DDL) as a string input argument, or the procedure definition can construct one as a local variable within its own boundaries, for execution using the EXECUTE STATEMENT command.

EXECUTE STATEMENT adds a degree of extra flexibility to stored procedures and triggers, along with a high risk of errors. Return values are strictly checked for data type in order to avoid unpredictable type-casting exceptions. For example, the string '1234' would convert to an integer, 1234, but 'abc' would give a conversion error. Beyond that, the string cannot be parsed or validated at compile time.

This is the syntax pattern:

```
[FOR] EXECUTE STATEMENT <string>
  [INTO :var1 [, var2 [, :varn]]] DO
    <compound-statement>];
<compound-statement> = {statement | block-of-statements}
```

The construction of the expression or string variable that is to form the DSQL statement string argument must be complete at the time EXECUTE STATEMENT is executed. The DSQL statement string argument to be executed cannot contain any replaceable parameters.

In its simplest form, EXECUTE STATEMENT executes an SQL statement requesting an operation that does not return any data rows, namely

- INSERT, UPDATE, DELETE

- EXECUTE PROCEDURE

- Any DDL statement except CREATE/DROP DATABASE

For example:

```
CREATE PROCEDURE EXEC_PROC (PROC_NAME VARCHAR(31))
AS
DECLARE VARIABLE SQL VARCHAR(1024);
DECLARE VARIABLE ...;
BEGIN
   ...
   SQL = 'EXECUTE PROCEDURE '||PROC_NAME;
   EXECUTE STATEMENT SQL;
END ^
```

calling it

```
EXECUTE PROCEDURE EXEC_PROC('PROJECT_MEMBERS');
```

Variable Values from a Singleton SELECT

The next snippet shows how to execute a SELECT statement string that returns a single row into a set of variables. As with any SELECT statement in a PSQL module, it will throw an exception if the statement returns multiple rows. Here, we are also able to do something that is not possible in regular PSQL: perform an operation involving a table or column whose name is not known at compile time.

```
CREATE PROCEDURE SOME_PROC
  (TABLE_NAME VARCHAR(31), COL_NAME VARCHAR(31))
AS
DECLARE VARIABLE PARAM DATE;
BEGIN
   EXECUTE STATEMENT 'SELECT MAX(' || COL_NAME || ') FROM '|| TABLE_NAME
   INTO :PARAM;
   ...
   FOR SELECT .... FROM ....
   WHERE END_DATE = :PARAM
   INTO ... DO
   ...
END ^
```

Variable Values from a Multi-Row SELECT

The EXECUTE STATEMENT syntax also supports executing a SELECT statement string inside a FOR loop, to return output a row at a time into a list of variables. There are no restrictions on the SELECT statement that is used, but remember that the compile-time parser cannot validate the contents of the string.

```
CREATE PROCEDURE DYNAMIC_SAMPLE (
   TEXT_COL VARCHAR(31),
   TABLE_NAME VARCHAR(31))
RETURNS (LINE VARCHAR(32000))
AS
DECLARE VARIABLE ONE_LINE VARCHAR(100);
DECLARE VARIABLE STOP_ME SMALLINT;
BEGIN
LINE = '';
STOP_ME = 1;
FOR EXECUTE STATEMENT
   'SELECT ' || TEXTCOL || ' FROM ' || TABLE_NAME
   INTO :ONE_LINE
   DO
   BEGIN
     IF (STOP_ME > 320) THEN
       EXIT;
     IF (ONE_LINE IS NOT NULL) THEN
       LINE = LINE || ONE_LINE || ' ';
     STOP_ME = STOP_ME + 1;
   END
   SUSPEND;
END ^
```

Caveats

The EXECUTE STATEMENT feature is intended only for very cautious use and should be used with all factors taken into account. Operations using it are slow and risky. Make a rule to use it only when it is impossible to achieve the objective by other means or in the unlikely event that it actually improves the performance of the statement. Be aware of the risks:

- There is no way to validate the syntax of the statement string argument.

- No dependency checks or protections exist to prevent tables or columns from being dropped or altered.

- Operations will be slow because the embedded statement has to be prepared every time it is executed.

- If the stored procedure has special privileges on some objects, the dynamic statement submitted in the EXECUTE STATEMENT string does not inherit them. Privileges are restricted to those granted to the user who is executing the procedure.

POST_EVENT

Firebird events provide a signaling mechanism that enables applications to listen for database changes made by concurrently running applications without the need for applications to incur CPU cost or consume bandwidth to poll one another directly.

The statement syntax is

```
POST_EVENT event_name;
```

It causes the event *event_name* to be "posted" to a stack. *Event_name* can be any string up to 78 characters and is not pre-defined on the server. Stacked events will be broadcast to clients "listening" via event alerter host routines.

When the transaction commits, any events that occurred during triggers or stored procedures can be delivered to listening client applications. An application can then respond to the event by, for example, refreshing its open datasets upon being alerted to changes.

For details, refer to the section "Events" in Chapter 32.

Developing Modules

Developing the PSQL modules that give the "grunt" to the data management system is a vital and precious part of the roles of both developer and database administrator. Because Firebird's administrative demands are light, it is usually practicable for the roles to merge. During development, it is not unusual for many members of a software team to be developing, testing, and modifying server-side program modules concurrently. Thus, the measures taken to protect and standardize application code are just as important for PSQL code.

Adding Comments

Stored procedure code should be commented to aid debugging and application development. Comments are especially important in stored procedures since they are global to the database and can be used by many different application developers.

Both multi-line and in-line comments can be included in the headers and bodies of PSQL modules. The syntax for comments is discussed in detail in Chapter 14 in the section "Schema Scripts."

Case Sensitivity and White Space

If double-quote delimiters were used when your database objects were defined, then all case-sensitivity and quoting rules that apply to your data in dynamic SQL must also be applied when you refer to those objects in procedure statements.

All other code is case insensitive. For example (assuming no delimited object identifiers are involved), these two statement fragments are equivalent:

```
CREATE PROCEDURE MYPROC...
create procedure myproc...
```

The compiler places no restrictions on white space or line feeds. It can be useful, for readability of your code, to adopt some form of standard convention in the layout of your procedure code. For example, you might write all keywords in uppercase, indent code blocks, list variable declarations in separate lines, place comma separators at the beginning of lines, and so on.

Managing Your Code

Considering that the high-level language for Firebird server-side programming is SQL and that source code is presented to the engine in the form of DDL "super-statements" for compilation into database objects, it is not surprising that all code maintenance is also performed using DDL statements. These statements are consistent with the conventions for maintenance of other objects in SQL databases:

- Redefinition of compiled objects (stored procedures and triggers) employs the ALTER PROCEDURE | TRIGGER syntax. For stored procedures, Firebird also provides RECREATE PROCEDURE and (from v.1.5 onward) CREATE OR REPLACE PROCEDURE syntaxes.

- DROP PROCEDURE | TRIGGER statements are used to remove modules.

There are two ways to manage procedures and triggers: entering the statements interactively through **isql** or another tool that can submit direct DSQL, or with one or more input files containing data definition statements, commonly known as scripts.

The interactive interface seems a quick and easy way to do things—until the first time you need to change, check, or recover something. Using scripts is the recommended way, because scripts not only provide retrievable documentation of the code you submitted, but also can include comments and can be modified easily.

Editing Tools

Any ASCII plain text editor can be used, as long as it does not save any non-printable characters other than carriage returns (ASCII 13), line feeds (ASCII 10), and tab characters (ASCII 9). Some editors are available that provide syntax highlighting for SQL: the IDE editors of Borland Delphi and Kylix, along with several of the tools listed in Appendix V.

TIP   The **isql** command shell utility can be used as an editor, using the EDIT command. EDIT will use your choice of text editor if the appropriate environment variables are set up on your system. On POSIX, set the environment variable VISUAL or EDITOR. On Window, set EDITOR.

It is a useful practice to add the extension .sql to Firebird script files. Apart from its usefulness in identifying scripts in your filesystem, the .sql extension is recognized as an SQL batch file by many editing tools that support SQL syntax highlighting.

Compiling Stored Procedures and Triggers

To complete any script file, you must include at least one "empty line" past the last statement or comment in the file. To do this, press the Return (Enter) key at least once in your text editor. When you have completed your procedure, save it to a file of any name you prefer.

To compile your stored procedure, simply run your script using the INPUT command in **isql** or through the scripting interface of your database management tool.

Script Errors

Firebird generates errors during parsing if there is incorrect syntax in a CREATE PROCEDURE | TRIGGER statement. Error messages look similar to this:

```
Dynamic SQL Error
-SQL error code = -104
-Token unknown - line 4, char 9
-tmp
```

The line numbers are counted from the beginning of the CREATE statement, not from the beginning of the script file. Characters are counted from the left, and the unknown token indicated is either the source of the error or immediately to the right of the source of the error. When in doubt, examine the entire line to determine the source of the syntax error.

TIP   If you are using a version of **isql** later than Firebird 1.0, you will notice an improvement in its capability to describe script errors and to pinpoint their locations. Although Firebird does not provide a debugging feature for stored procedures, several third-party tools do provide this capability.

Object Dependencies

The Firebird engine is meticulous about maintaining information about the interdependencies of the database objects under its management. Special considerations are necessary when making changes to stored procedures that are currently in use by other requests. A procedure is "in use" when it is currently executing or if it has been compiled internally to the metadata cache by a user request. Furthermore, the engine will defer or disallow compilation of ALTER or DROP statements if the existing compiled version is found in the metadata cache.

Changes to procedures are not visible to client applications until they disconnect from and reconnect to the database.

 NOTE   Triggers and procedures that invoke procedures that have been altered or re-created do not have access to the new version until the database is in a state in which all clients are disconnected.

Ideally, submit CREATE, RECREATE, and ALTER statements for PSQL modules when there are no client applications running.

Altering and Dropping Modules

When you alter a procedure or trigger, the new procedure definition replaces the old one. To alter a procedure or trigger definition, follow these steps:

1. Copy the original data definition file used to create the procedure. Alternatively, use *isql -extract* to extract the source of a procedure or trigger from the database to a file.

2. Edit the file, changing CREATE to RECREATE or ALTER and modifying the definition as desired.

3. Run the modified script in "clean" conditions, as outlined previously.

To drop a module:

```
DROP {PROCEDURE | TRIGGER} module-name;
```

Privileges

Only SYSDBA and the owner of a procedure or trigger can alter or drop it.

"Object Is in Use" Error

This error tends to frustrate developers more than any other. You are logged in, typically, as SYSDBA or owner of the database. You have exclusive access, which is desirable when changing metadata, and yet here is this phantom user, somewhere, using the object whose metadata you want to modify or delete.

The source of this mystery will be one or more of the following:

- In shutting down the database, preparing to get exclusive access, you (or another human) were already logged in as SYSDBA, owner, or (on Linux/UNIX) a suitably privileged operating system user. In testing the conditions for shutdown, Firebird ignores these users and any transactions they may have current or that begin after shutdown has begun. Any uncommitted transaction whatsoever—even a SELECT—that involves the object or any objects that depend on it, or upon which the object itself depends, will raise this error.

- An "interesting transaction" that remains in the database through an abnormal termination by some user at some point, that involves dependencies related to this object, will raise this error.

- You, or another suitably privileged user, previously attempted to redefine or delete this object, or another dependent object, and the operation was deferred because that object was in use.

 CAUTION This situation can provoke a chain of inconsistencies in your database. For example, if a **gbak** is performed while the database has objects in this state, the backup file may fail to restore.

Whenever you see this error and believe that you have eliminated all possible reasons for it, take it as a sign that your database needs a validation before you proceed with any further metadata changes (see Chapter 39).

To see a list of procedures or triggers and their dependencies in **isql**, use the SHOW PROCEDURES or SHOW TRIGGERS command, respectively.

Deleting Source from Modules

Developers often want to "hide" the source code of their PSQL modules when they deploy databases. You can delete the stored source code without affecting the capability of the module. Just be sure that you have up-to-date scripts before you do it!

The sources for all modules are stored in the system tables RDB$PROCEDURES and RDB$TRIGGERS.

To delete the source for a procedure:

```
UPDATE RDB$PROCEDURES
  SET RDB$PROCEDURE_SOURCE = NULL
  WHERE RDB$PROCEDURE_NAME = 'MYPROC';
```

To delete the source for a trigger:

```
UPDATE RDB$TRIGGERS
  SET RDB$TRIGGER_SOURCE = NULL
  WHERE RDB$TRIGGER_NAME = 'MYTRIGGER';
```

 CAUTION Be aware that deleting the source won't stop someone who is determined to steal your code. The executable code is stored in a language-like binary format that is very simple to reverse-engineer back into PSQL. So, consider whether the gain from obscuring the PSQL is worth the cost of you and others who maintain the system losing the ability to review and extract the source.

Up Next

Next, we take a closer look at the PSQL language features and techniques you can use to develop stored procedures and structure your source code. A special topic at the end of the chapter introduces the RDB$DB_KEY, an internal, unique attribute of every row in every set that can be of particular help in optimizing the performance of some PSQL operations.

CHAPTER 30

Stored Procedures

A *STORED PROCEDURE* IS A SELF-CONTAINED program written in Firebird PSQL, compiled by the Firebird's internal binary language interpreter and stored as executable code within the metadata of a database. Once compiled, the stored procedure can be invoked directly from an application or another PSQL module, using an EXECUTE PROCEDURE or SELECT statement, according to the style of procedure that has been specified.

Stored procedures can accept *input parameters* from client applications as arguments to the invoking query. They can return a set of values to applications as *output parameters*.

Firebird procedure and trigger language includes SQL data manipulation statements and some powerful extensions, including IF … THEN … ELSE, WHILE … DO, FOR SELECT … DO, system-defined exceptions, error handling, and events.

Stored procedures can be called from applications using dynamic SQL statements. They can also be invoked interactively in **isql** or many of the database desktop tools recommended for use with Firebird. Executable modules, including nested procedures, can be used in scripts, with the limitation that all input parameters be constants and that there be no outputs. It is not possible to pass variable parameters around in scripts.

Executable Stored Procedures

Procedures that are invoked with an EXECUTE PROCEDURE statement can optionally return a single row of one or more output values. They are often used to perform insert, update, or delete operations, or to launch a suite of operations such as a batch import of external data.

Selectable Stored Procedures

"Selectable" stored procedures are so-named because they are written with some special language extensions to produce a multiple-row output set that is returned to the caller using a SELECT query—a "virtual table."

The engine does not differentiate between an executable and a selectable stored procedure. If requested, it will try to form a set from an executable procedure or to execute something in a selectable procedure—and throw exceptions when the logic of the request fails, of course! It is up to you to make sure that your server code does what you intend it to do and that your client code submits appropriate requests.

Creating Stored Procedures

In your script or in **isql**, begin by setting the terminator symbol that will be used to mark the end of the CREATE PROCEDURE syntax. The following example will set the terminator symbol to &:

```
...
SET TERM &;
```

The syntax pattern is

```
CREATE PROCEDURE procedure-name
  [(argument data-type [, argument data-type [...]])]
[RETURNS (argument data-type [, argument data-type [...]])
AS
<procedure-body>
<procedure-body> =
[DECLARE [VARIABLE] var data-type;

[...]]]
BEGIN
  <compound-statement>;
END <terminator>
```

Header Elements

In the header, declare

- The name of the procedure, which is required and must be unique in the database, for example:

```
CREATE PROCEDURE MyProc
```

- Any optional input arguments (parameters) required by the procedure, and their data types, as a comma-separated list enclosed by brackets, for example:

```
CREATE PROCEDURE MyProc
(invar1 integer, invar2 date)
```

  - The name of each argument must be unique within the procedure. The data type can be any standard SQL data type, except arrays of data types. The name of an input argument need not match the name of any parameter in the calling program.

- Any optional output arguments (parameters) required, and their data types, as a comma-separated list enclosed in brackets following the keyword RETURNS, for example:

```
CREATE PROCEDURE MyProc
(invar1 INTEGER, invar2 DATE)
RETURNS (outvar1 INTEGER, outvar2 VARCHAR(20), outvar3 DOUBLE PRECISION)
```

- The name of each argument must be unique within the procedure. The data type can be any standard SQL data type except arrays of data types.

- The keyword AS, which is required:

```
CREATE PROCEDURE MyProc
(invar1INTEGER, invar2 DATE)
RETURNS(outvar1 INTEGER, outvar2 VARCHAR(20), outvar3 DOUBLE PRECISION)
AS
```

Body Elements

The syntax outline is

```
<procedure_body>=[<variable-declaration-list>]
<compound-statement>
```

Local Variables

If you have *local variables* to declare, their declarations come next. Each declaration is terminated with a semicolon. In v.1.5, local variables can be optionally initialized in the declaration. The syntax pattern is

```
<variable_declaration_list>=
DECLARE [VARIABLE] var datatype [{'=' | DEFAULT} value];
[DECLARE [VARIABLE] var datatype; ...]
```

For example:

```
CREATE PROCEDURE MyProc (
  invar 1 INTEGER,
  invar2 DATE)
```

```
RETURNS (
  outvar1 INTEGER,
  outvar2 VARCHAR(20),
  outvar3 DOUBLE PRECISION)
AS
DECLARE VARIABLE localvar integer DEFAULT 0;
DECLARE VARIABLE anothervar DOUBLE PRECISION = 0.00;
```

 NOTE The keyword VARIABLE is optional from v.1.5 onward.

Main Code Block

Next comes the *main code block*, designated in the higher-level syntax diagram as
<compound-statement>. It starts with the keyword BEGIN and ends with the keyword END.
The syntax outline is

```
<compound-statement> =
BEGIN
  <compound_-statement>
  [<compound-statement>...]
END <terminator>
```

All <compound-statement> structures consist of single statements and/or other
<compound-statement> structures that can nest others, for example:

```
CREATE PROCEDURE MyProc (
  invar 1 INTEGER,
  invar2 DATE)
RETURNS (
  outvar1 INTEGER,
  outvar2 VARCHAR(20),
  outvar3 DOUBLE PRECISION)
AS
DECLARE VARIABLE localvar integer DEFAULT 0;
DECLARE VARIABLE anothervar DOUBLE PRECISION = 0.00;
BEGIN
  <compound-statement>
END &
```

The <compound-statement> element can be any or all of a single statement, a block of statements, and embedded blocks of statements bounded by BEGIN … END pairs. Blocks can include

- Assignment statements, to set values of local variables and input/output parameters.

- SELECT statements, to retrieve column values into variables. SELECT statements must have an INTO clause as the last clause and corresponding local variable or output argument declarations for each column selected.

- Looping structures, such as FOR SELECT … DO and WHILE … DO, to perform conditional or looping tasks.

- Branching structures using IF … THEN … [ELSE].

- EXECUTE PROCEDURE statements, to invoke other procedures, with optional RETURNING_VALUES clauses to return values into variables. Recursion is allowed.

- SUSPEND and EXIT statements that return control and, optionally, return values to the calling application or PSQL module.

- Comments to annotate procedure code.

- EXCEPTION statements, to return custom error messages to applications or to signal conditions for exception handlers.

- WHEN statements to handle specific or general error conditions.

- POST_EVENT statements to add an event notification to the stack.

For example:

```
...
BEGIN
  FOR SELECT COL1, COL2, COL3, COL4
  FROM TABLEA INTO :COL1, :COL2, :COL3 DO
  BEGIN
    <statements>
  END
  <statements>
END &
SET TERM ; &
COMMIT;
```

Notice the termination of the entire procedure declaration with the terminator character previously defined by the SET TERM statement. After the procedure body is complete, the terminator character is set back to the default semicolon. It need not always be the case. In a DDL script, where you may be declaring several PSQL modules, you can keep the alternative terminator current. Some people make it a practice to use an alternative terminator throughout *all* of their scripts, thus reserving the semicolon only for PSQL statement terminators. It is a matter of personal preference.

Executable Procedures

When you work with Firebird's stored procedure language and program module structures, it is necessary to make the distinction between procedures that are *executed*, with the aim of altering data, and those that are intended to return a virtual table to the caller by way of a SELECT statement. The first is the form most familiar to those used to working with other database management systems: the *executable* procedure.

Complex Processing

One of the more obvious and common uses of executable procedures is to perform complex calculations on input data and perform updates on one or many tables. Complex business rules and routines are centralized on the server. Any client application with the appropriate permissions can invoke the same routines and get the same results, regardless of the host language environment. Apart from the savings in programmer and testing hours, server-side execution eliminates the integrity risks inherent in repeating and maintaining the same complex operations in multiple client language environments.

Support for "Live" Client Sets

Many client interface layers implement dataset or recordset classes that fetch output sets via SELECT statements. These client classes typically provide DML methods that target a single row from a buffer that stores and manages output from a server-side cursor. The row is selected by the user, and the class instance (object) uses the row's unique key to simulate a positioned update or delete in the underlying database table. For inserts, the object "opens an empty row," an input list of columns of the same types as those in the buffer, and accepts key and other values as input for the columns.

A single UPDATE, DELETE, or INSERT statement in SQL can operate on only one table. When the dataset (recordset) is selected from a natural table and contains the table's unique key, it can be considered "live," since its methods can pass an ordinary UPDATE, DELETE, or INSERT statement. The usual term for this type of set is *naturally updatable*. A set that joins multiple tables is not naturally updatable. Executable stored procedures can be designed with input arguments that accept keys and values for multiple tables and execute the required operations on each table. The technique allows the client applications to treat joined sets as though they were "live."

Operations in Executable Procedures

Virtually every data manipulation in SQL is available to the executable stored procedure. All activity is executed within the transaction context of the caller and is committed when the transaction commits. Rows that are changed by an operation in the procedure are versioned in exactly the same way as those posted by a DML request from the client.

Procedures can call other procedures, passing variables to input arguments and accepting return values into variables by way of a RETURNING_VALUES clause. They can insert one or many rows, change single rows, form cursors to target rows serially for positioned updates and deletes, and perform searched updates and deletes.

Once the procedure begins executing, values brought in as input arguments become local variables. Output arguments are read-write variables that can change value (though not data type) many thousands of times during the course of execution. Figure 30-1 illustrates typical activities in an executable procedure.

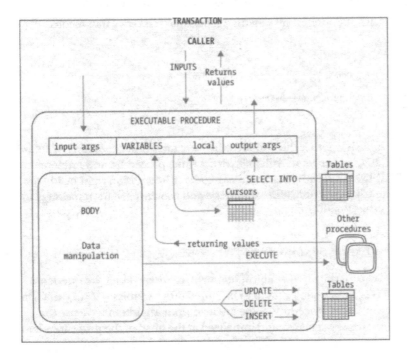

Figure 30-1. Operations in an executable procedure

A Multi-Table Procedure

The executable procedure DELETE_EMPLOYEE is a version of one that you can find in the EMPLOYEE database in your Firebird /examples directory. It implements some business rules regarding employees who are leaving the company.

Declaring an Exception

Because we are going to use an exception in this procedure, it needs to be created before the procedure:

```
CREATE EXCEPTION REASSIGN_SALES
  'Reassign the sales records before deleting this employee.' ^
COMMIT ^
```

The Procedure

Now, the procedure itself. The input argument, EMP_NUM, corresponds to the primary key of the EMPLOYEE table, EMP_NO. It allows the procedure to select and operate on a single employee record and foreign keys in other tables that reference that record.

```
CREATE PROCEDURE DELETE_EMPLOYEE (
  EMP_NUM INTEGER )
AS
  DECLARE VARIABLE any_sales INTEGER DEFAULT 0;
BEGIN
```

We want to establish whether the employee has any sales orders pending. If so, we raise an exception. In Chapter 32, we will pick up the same procedure and implement some extra processing to trap the exception and handle the condition right inside the procedure. For now, we let the procedure terminate and use the exception message to inform the caller of the situation.

The SELECT ... INTO Construct

The SELECT ... INTO construct is very common in PSQL. When values are queried from tables, the INTO clause enables them to be stored into variables—local variables or output arguments. In this procedure, there are no output arguments. We use the variable ANY_SALES that we declared and initialized at the head of the procedure body to store a count of some sales records. Notice the colon (:) prefix on the variable ANY_SALES. We will look at that when the procedure is done.

```
SELECT count(po_number) FROM sales
  WHERE sales_rep = :emp_num
```

```
INTO :any_sales;
IF (any_sales > 0) THEN
  EXCEPTION reassign_sales;
```

In the case that order records are found, the procedure ends tidily with the EXCEPTION statement that, in the absence of an exception handler, takes execution directly to the last END statement in the whole procedure. Under these conditions, the procedure has completed and the exception message is transmitted back to the caller.[1]

If there is no exception, execution continues. Next, the procedure has some little jobs to do, to update some positions as vacant (NULL) if they are currently held by our employee, remove the employee from projects, and delete his or her salary history. Finally, the employee record itself is deleted.

```
UPDATE department
  SET mngr_no = NULL
  WHERE mngr_no = :emp_num;
UPDATE project
  SET team_leader = NULL
  WHERE team_leader = :emp_num;
DELETE FROM employee_project
  WHERE emp_no = :emp_num;

DELETE FROM salary_history
  WHERE emp_no = :emp_num;
DELETE FROM employee
  WHERE emp_no = :emp_num;
```

Job done, employee gone. An optional EXIT statement can be included for documentation purposes. It can help a lot when you are navigating scripts where there are many procedure definitions and those procedures have many nested BEGIN ... END blocks:

```
  EXIT;
END ^
COMMIT^
```

---

1. This procedure, from the example database, is a very poor piece of PSQL programming. SQL has a better way to test for the existence of rows than counting them. When we look at this procedure again in Chapter 32, we do some recoding to clean it up. If you inspect the source for this procedure in the database, you will also notice that SUSPENDs and EXITs are splashed liberally in places where they are not needed. At this point in the original, SUSPEND was used (redundantly) to terminate execution. SUSPEND and EXIT have identical usage in executable procedures. However, in selectable procedures, SUSPEND has a particularly special, other use. For clarity and effective self-documentation, it is preferable to avoid using SUSPEND as a synonym for EXIT.

The Colon (:) Prefix for Variables

In this procedure, we noted two different ways in which the colon prefix was used on variables:

- Earlier, it was applied to the local variable :ANY_SALES when it was being used in an INTO clause as the destination for a data item returned from a SELECT.

- In the latter statements, it was used for a slightly different reason. PSQL syntax requires the colon prefix to be on *any variable or argument* when it is used in a DSQL statement.

These two usages of the colon prefix are consistent throughout PSQL. If you forget them when they should be used, or use them when PSQL does not require them, your procedures will not compile and the parser will throw an exception. Worse, if a variable of the same name as a column in the table is used in an SQL statement, without the colon, the engine thinks it is the column that is being referred to, processes it on that assumption, and throws no exception. Needless to say, the result of the operation will be quite unpredictable.

Using (Calling) Executable Procedures

An executable procedure is invoked with EXECUTE PROCEDURE. It can return, at most, one row of output. To execute a stored procedure in **isql**, use the following syntax:

```
EXECUTE PROCEDURE name [(] [argument [, argument ...]] [)];
```

The procedure *name* must be specified.

Calling Rules About Input Argument Values

The calling rules pertaining to arguments can be summarized as follows:

- Values must be supplied for all input arguments.

- If there are multiple input arguments, they are passed as a comma-separated list.

- Each *argument* is a constant, an expression that evaluates to a constant or a replaceable parameter.

- Variables can be passed as input arguments only inside a PSQL module.

- Replaceable parameters can be passed only by external DSQL statements

- Constants and expressions that resolve to constants are valid for any call.

- Expressions that operate on variables or replaceable parameters are not allowed.

- Brackets enclosing the argument list are optional.

Because our procedure DELETE_EMPLOYEE has no return arguments, the syntax for calling it from a client application or from another procedure is the same:

```
EXECUTE PROCEDURE DELETE_EMPLOYEE (29);
```

However, when executing a procedure from within another procedure, input arguments can be (and usually are) furnished as variables. Because EXECUTE PROCEDURE is a DSQL statement, the syntax requires that the variable name be prefixed by a colon:

```
EXECUTE PROCEDURE DELETE_EMPLOYEE (:EMP_NUMBER);
```

Another procedure ADD_EMP_PROJ takes two input arguments, keys for an employee and a project, respectively. An instance might be called like this:

```
EXECUTE PROCEDURE ADD_EMP_PROJ (32, 'MKTPR');
```

Replaceable parameters are used for input arguments when calling this procedure from a client application:

```
EXECUTE PROCEDURE ADD_EMP_PROJ (?, ?);
```

Outputs and Exits

If an output parameter has not been assigned a value, its value is unpredictable and this can lead to errors, sometimes subtle enough to compromise data integrity. A procedure should ensure that all output parameters are initialized to a default final value, in advance of the processing that will assign values, to ensure that valid output is available when SUSPEND or EXIT is executed.

EXIT and SUSPEND

In both select and executable procedures, EXIT causes execution to jump immediately to the final END statement in the procedure, without executing anything.

What happens when a procedure reaches the final END statement depends on the type of procedure:

- In a SELECT procedure, the SQLCODE 100 is set to indicate that there are no more rows to retrieve, and control returns to the caller.

- In an executable procedure, control returns to the caller, passing the final output values, if any. Calling triggers or procedures receive the output into variables, as RETURNING_VALUES. Applications receive them in a record structure.

In executable procedures, SUSPEND has exactly the same effect as EXIT.

Recursive Procedures

If a procedure calls itself, it is *recursive*. Recursive procedures are useful for tasks that involve repetitive steps.

Each invocation of a procedure is referred to as an *instance*, since each procedure call is a separate entity that performs as if called from an application, reserving memory and stack space as required to perform its tasks.

Stored procedures can be nested up to 1,000 levels deep. This limitation helps to prevent infinite loops that can occur when a recursive procedure provides no absolute terminating condition. However, memory and stack limitations of the server can restrict nesting to fewer than 1,000 levels.

The procedure DEPT_BUDGET, in the example employee database, illustrates how a recursive procedure might work. It accepts as input a code DNO, equivalent to DEPT_NO, the key of the DEPARTMENT table. DEPARTMENT has a multiple-level tree structure: Each department that is not a head department has a foreign key HEAD_DEPT pointing to the DEPT_NO of its immediate "parent."

The procedure queries for the targeted DEPARTMENT by the input key. It saves the BUDGET value for this row into the output variable TOT. It also performs a count of the number of departments immediately below this one in the departmental structure. If there are no sub-departments, the EXIT statement causes execution to jump right through to the final END ^ statement. The current value of TOT is output and the procedure ends.

```
SET TERM ^ ;
CREATE PROCEDURE DEPT_BUDGET (
  DNO CHAR(3) )
RETURNS (
  TOT DECIMAL(12,2) )
AS
  DECLARE VARIABLE sumb DECIMAL(12, 2);
  DECLARE VARIABLE rdno CHAR(3);
  DECLARE VARIABLE cnt INTEGER;
```

```
BEGIN
  tot = 0;
  SELECT budget FROM department WHERE dept_no = :dno INTO :tot;
  SELECT count(budget) FROM department WHERE head_dept = :dno INTO :cnt;
  IF (cnt = 0) THEN
EXIT;
```

If there are sub-departments, execution continues. The input code DNO is used in the WHERE clause of a FOR ... SELECT cursor (see the section "Cursors in PSQL") to target each DEPARTMENT row, in turn, that has this DNO as its HEAD_DEPT code and place its DEPT_NO into local variable, RDNO:

```
FOR SELECT dept_no FROM department
  WHERE head_dept = :dno
  INTO :rdno DO
  BEGIN
```

This local variable now becomes the input code for a recursive procedure call. At each recursion, the output value TOT is incremented by the returned budget value, until all of the eligible rows have been processed:

```
  EXECUTE PROCEDURE dept_budget :rdno RETURNING_VALUES :sumb;
tot = tot + sumb;
END
```

Finally, the return value accumulated by the recursions is passed to the caller and the procedure is done:

```
  EXIT;  /* the EXIT statement is optional */
END^
COMMIT^
```

Calling the Procedure

This time, our procedure has input parameters. Our simple DSQL call might look like this:

```
EXECUTE PROCEDURE DEPT_BUDGET ('600');
```

Or, we can use a replaceable parameter:

```
EXECUTE PROCEDURE DEPT_BUDGET (?);
```

Cursors in PSQL

Cursors consist of three main elements:

- A set of rows defined by a SELECT expression

- A pointer that passes through the set from the first row to the last, isolating that row for some kind of activity

- A set of variables—defined as local variables, output arguments, or both—to receive the columns returned in each row as it is touched by the pointer

The passage of the pointer through the set can be considered a "looping" operation. The operations that occur during the "loop" when a row has the pointer can be simple or complex.

PSQL has two cursor implementations, one well known, the other not previously documented:

- The better-known implementation is surfaced in the FOR ... SELECT construct, which fully implements looping syntax and is widely used for selectable procedures. It is discussed in detail in the next section. It is, however, a perfectly valid and common usage to run FOR ... SELECT cursor loops inside an executable procedure, as we saw in the preceding example.

- The lesser-known implementation is an earlier implementation, sometimes known as an *updatable* or *named cursor,* that was inherited from ESQL and has long been considered as deprecated. It surfaces a cursor object and allows positioned updates and deletes. Its syntax will be more familiar to those who have used cursors in the procedure languages of other DBMSs. We take a brief look at it now.

NOTE The syntax and machinery for the named cursor have been undergoing a reimplementation during the ongoing development for Firebird 2. This brief description is the swan song of the old cursor, since the new syntax is unlikely to be compatible with the old.

The "Old" Updatable Cursor

The syntax pattern looks like this:

```
...
FOR SELECT <column-list>
```

```
  FROM <named-table>
  FOR UPDATE
  INTO <variables>
AS CURSOR <cursor-name>
DO
/* either UPDATE ... */
  BEGIN
    UPDATE <named-table>
      SET ... WHERE CURRENT OF <cursor-name>;
      ...
  END
/* or DELETE */
  BEGIN
    DELETE FROM <named-table>
    WHERE CURRENT OF <cursor-name>
  END
...
```

Use it for now, but expect enhancements in a later version of Firebird. It is a very fast way to do bulk operations in a stored procedure, since it uses the RDB$DB_KEY to locate its targets. RDB$DB_KEY (or just "the DBKEY") is an internal feature that can be used with care in a number of situations. See the section "Optimization Topic: Using the Internal RDB$DB_KEY" at the end of this chapter.

TIP   Watch the release notes of ongoing sub-releases for the new PSQL cursor syntax. At the time of this writing, it was not far away.

The latter implementation of cursors, discussed next, is much more flexible.

Selectable Stored Procedures

Selectable stored procedures are so-called because they are designed to be executed using a SELECT statement. To readers accustomed to the server programming techniques available to other DBMSs, the concept of a stored procedure that outputs rows directly to the calling application or procedure, without any form of intermediate "temporary" table, will be much less familiar than the executable procedure.

Uses for Selectable Procedures

Selectable procedures can be used to specify virtually any set, but they are especially useful when you need a set that cannot be extracted, or is slow or difficult to extract, in a single DSQL statement.

615

Esoteric Sets

The selectable stored procedure technique offers enormous flexibility for extracting sets that defeat the logic available through regular SELECT statement specifications. It literally makes it possible to form a reproducible set from any combination of data you store. You can use calculations and transformations across a number of columns or rows in the set to condition what appears in the output. For example, output sets with running totals are difficult or impossible to achieve from a dynamic query but can be generated and managed speedily and efficiently with a selectable stored procedure.

Selectable procedures can come in handy for generating sets of data that are not stored in the database at all. It is a technique for which we all find a use sometime. In the following trivial example, a comma-separated list of strings, each of 20 or fewer characters, is fed in as input. The procedure returns each string to the application as a numbered row:

```
CREATE PROCEDURE BREAKAPART(
  INPUTLIST VARCHAR(1024))
RETURNS (
  NUMERO SMALLINT,
  ITEM VARCHAR(20)
        )
AS
  DECLARE CHARAC CHAR;
  DECLARE ISDONE SMALLINT = 0;
BEGIN
  NUMERO = 0;
  ITEM = '';
  WHILE (ISDONE = 0) DO
  BEGIN
    CHARAC = SUBSTRING(INPUTLIST FROM 1 FOR 1);
    IF (CHARAC = '') THEN
      ISDONE = 1;
    IF (CHARAC = ',' OR CHARAC = '') THEN
    BEGIN
      NUMERO = NUMERO + 1;
      SUSPEND;  /* Sends a row to the row buffer */
      ITEM = '';
    END
    ELSE
      ITEM = ITEM || CHARAC;
    INPUTLIST = SUBSTRING(INPUTLIST FROM 2);
  END
END ^
COMMIT;
/*  */
SELECT * FROM BREAKAPART('ALPHA,BETA,GAMMA,DELTA');
```

```
NUMERO  ITEM
------  --------------------
     1  ALPHA
     2  BETA
     3  GAMMA
     4  DELTA
```

Performance Gain for Complex Sets

Often, complex queries involving many joins or subqueries are too slow to be satis-factory for interactive applications. Some queries can be slow because of unpropitious indexes on foreign keys. Because of its ability to operate on sets in nested loops, a stored procedure is capable of producing the required sets much more quickly and, especially, to begin returning rows much sooner than the conventional SQL sequences permit.

The Technique

The technique for extracting and manipulating the data for the output set uses a cursor to read each row in turn from a SELECT statement into a pre-declared set of variables. Often, it may be the output arguments that the column values are read into, but it can be local variables. Inside the loop, the variables are operated on in whatever manner is required: transformed by calculations, if need be, or used as search arguments for nested loops to pick up values from further queries. At the end of the loop, when all output arguments have their final values, a SUSPEND statement causes execution to pause while the set is passed to the row cache. Execution resumes when the next fetch is called.

As we saw in the previous BREAKAPART example, the SUSPEND statement is the element that causes the procedure to deliver a row.

The FOR SELECT ... DO Construct

To retrieve multiple rows in a procedure, we use the FOR SELECT ... DO construct. The syntax is

```
FOR
<select-expression>
INTO <:variable [, :variable [, ...]]
DO
<compound_statement>;
```

The *select-expression* can be any select query, using joins, unions, views, other select procedures, expressions, function calls, and so on, in any valid combination.

A FOR SELECT differs from a standard SELECT statement in that it requires variables into which to receive the columns and fields specified.

The *<compound-statement>* can be a single SUSPEND statement or a block of two or more statements. The *<compound-statement>* can nest other compound statements.

FOR SELECT … DO is a loop construct that retrieves the row specified in the *select-expression* and performs the statement or block following DO for each row in turn.

The INTO *<variables>* clause is required and must come last.[2]

Processing in the Loop

Figure 30-2 illustrates some typical activities that can be performed inside loops to generate output for a selectable stored procedure.

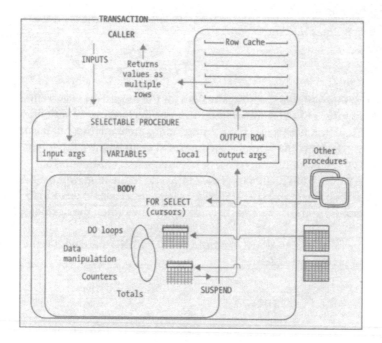

Figure 30-2. Operations in a selectable procedure

In the following examples, we will take a look at how combinations of the operations available in PSQL can meet your less ordinary SQL challenges.

---

2. ESQL, the "super-set" of DSQL, has a slightly different syntax for INTO clauses. It places INTO immediately after the SELECT keyword and the row quantifier (if any). The relegation of the INTO clause to last in PSQL enables UNION sets to be used as inputs to PSQL cursors.

A Simple Procedure with Nested SELECTs

The selectable procedure ORG_CHART, which is in the example *employee* database, takes no input arguments. It uses a FOR ... SELECT loop to line up a set from a self-referencing join on the DEPARTMENT table and pass column values, one row at a time, to a set of variables—some local, some declared as output arguments.

```
CREATE PROCEDURE ORG_CHART
RETURNS (
  HEAD_DEPT CHAR(25),
  DEPARTMENT CHAR(25),
  MNGR_NAME CHAR(20),
  TITLE CHAR(5),
  EMP_CNT INTEGER )
AS
  DECLARE VARIABLE mngr_no INTEGER;
  DECLARE VARIABLE dno CHAR(3);
BEGIN
  FOR SELECT h.department, d.department, d.mngr_no, d.dept_no
    FROM department d
    LEFT OUTER JOIN department h ON d.head_dept = h.dept_no
    ORDER BY d.dept_no
  INTO :head_dept, :department, :mngr_no, :dno
  DO
```

Each time the loop processes a row, it picks up a key value (MNGR_NO) into the local variable mngr_no. If the variable is null, the procedure fabricates values for the output arguments MNGR_NAME and TITLE. If the variable has a value, it is passed as a search argument to a *nested query* on the EMPLOYEE table, uniquely targeting a row and extracting the name and job code of a department manager. These values are passed to the remaining output arguments.

```
BEGIN
  IF (:mngr_no IS NULL) THEN
  BEGIN
    mngr_name = '--TBH--';
    title = '';
  END
  ELSE
    SELECT full_name, job_code
      FROM employee
      WHERE emp_no = :mngr_no
    INTO :mngr_name, :title;
  SELECT COUNT(emp_no)
    FROM employee
    WHERE dept_no = :dno
  INTO :emp_cnt;
```

When all of the outputs for one row are assigned, a SUSPEND statement passes the row to the cache. Execution resumes back at the start of the loop when the next fetch request is made.

```
  SUSPEND;
 END
END^
COMMIT^
```

Notice how the nested query neatly bypasses the problem we have in DSQL with subqueries—we can return one and only one value to a subquery. If we want multiple values and left join logic will not work, we have to use multiple subqueries with multiple sets of aliases to extract each value from its own cursor.

Calling a Selectable Procedure

The syntax pattern for calling a selectable procedure is very similar to that for a table or view. The one difference is that a procedure may have input arguments:

```
SELECT <column-list> from name ([argument [, argument ...]])
WHERE <search-conditions>
ORDER BY <order-list>;
```

The procedure *name* must be specified.

Input argument rules are identical to those for executable procedures—see the earlier section titled "Calling Rules About Input Argument Values."

The *column-list* is a comma-separated list of one or more of the output parameters returned by the procedure, or * to select all columns.

The output set can be limited by a *search-condition* in a WHERE clause and sorted by an ORDER BY clause.

Calling the ORG_CHART Procedure

This procedure has no input parameters, so the SELECT call looks like a simple select on a table, namely

```
SELECT * FROM ORG_CHART;
```

Selecting Aggregates from Procedures

In addition to selecting values from a procedure, you can use aggregate functions. For example, to use our procedure to display a count of the number of departments, use the following statement:

```
SELECT COUNT(DEPARTMENT) FROM ORG_CHART;
```

Similarly, to use ORG_CHART to display the maximum and average number of employees in each department, use the following statement:

```
SELECT
  MAX(EMP_CNT),
  AVG(EMP_CNT)
FROM ORG_CHART;
```

 TIP   If a procedure encounters an error or exception, the aggregate functions do not return the correct values, since the procedure terminates before all rows are processed.

Nested Procedures

A stored procedure can itself execute a stored procedure. Each time a stored procedure calls another procedure, the call is said to be *nested* because it occurs in the context of a previous and still active call to the first procedure. A stored procedure called by another stored procedure is known as a *nested procedure*.

The following procedure returns a listing of users, roles, and privileged objects in a database, with their SQL privileges. Inside the procedure, two calls to another procedure are nested. It is necessary to begin by defining and committing the nested procedure—otherwise, the outer procedure will fail to commit. You should always start at the bottom of the "chain" when creating procedures that nest other procedures.

As it happens, this nested procedure performs no SQL.[3] It simply takes an obscure constant from a set used internally by Firebird to represent object types, and returns a string that is more meaningful to humans:

```
SET TERM ^ ;
CREATE PROCEDURE SP_GET_TYPE (
  IN_TYPE SMALLINT )
RETURNS (
  STRING VARCHAR(7) )
AS
BEGIN
  STRING = 'Unknown';
  IF (IN_TYPE = 0) THEN STRING = 'Table';
  IF (IN_TYPE = 1) THEN STRING = 'View';
  IF (IN_TYPE = 2) THEN STRING = 'Trigger';
```

---

3. In Firebird 1.5, the work performed by the nested procedure could be done with a CASE expression. For details, refer to Chapter 21.

```
    IF (IN_TYPE = 5) THEN STRING = 'Proc';
    IF (IN_TYPE = 8) THEN STRING = 'User';
    IF (IN_TYPE = 0) THEN STRING = 'Table';
    IF (IN_TYPE = 9) THEN STRING = 'Field';
    IF (IN_TYPE = 13) THEN STRING = 'Role';
END^
COMMIT^
```

Now for the outer procedure. The table it queries for its data is the system table RDB$USER_PRIVILEGES. It uses a number of manipulation techniques, including calls to the internal SQL function CAST( ) and to an external function RTRIM( ), from the standard external function library *ib_udf*, to massage CHAR(31) items into VARCHAR(31). We do this because we want to concatenate some of these strings and we do not want the trailing blanks.

```
SET TERM ^ ;
CREATE PROCEDURE SP_PRIVILEGES
RETURNS (
  Q_ROLE_NAME VARCHAR(31),
  ROLE_OWNER VARCHAR(31),
  USER_NAME VARCHAR(31),
  Q_USER_TYPE VARCHAR(7),
  W_GRANT_OPTION CHAR(1),
  PRIVILEGE CHAR(6),
  GRANTOR VARCHAR(31),
  QUALIFIED_OBJECT VARCHAR(63),
  Q_OBJECT_TYPE VARCHAR(7) )
AS
  DECLARE VARIABLE RELATION_NAME VARCHAR(31);
  DECLARE VARIABLE FIELD_NAME VARCHAR(31);
  DECLARE VARIABLE OWNER_NAME VARCHAR(31);
  DECLARE VARIABLE ROLE_NAME VARCHAR(31);
  DECLARE VARIABLE OBJECT_TYPE SMALLINT;
  DECLARE VARIABLE USER_TYPE SMALLINT;
  DECLARE VARIABLE GRANT_OPTION SMALLINT;
  DECLARE VARIABLE IS_ROLE SMALLINT;
  DECLARE VARIABLE IS_VIEW SMALLINT;
BEGIN
```

First we loop through the table RDB$USER_PRIVILEGES, extracting and massaging some values directly into output arguments and others into local variables:

```
FOR SELECT
  RTRIM(CAST(RDB$USER AS VARCHAR(31))),
  RDB$USER_TYPE,
  RTRIM(CAST(RDB$GRANTOR AS VARCHAR(31))),
  RTRIM(CAST(RDB$RELATION_NAME AS VARCHAR(31))),
  RTRIM(CAST(RDB$FIELD_NAME AS VARCHAR(31))),
```

```
  RDB$OBJECT_TYPE,
  RTRIM(CAST(RDB$PRIVILEGE AS VARCHAR(31))),
  RDB$GRANT_OPTION
FROM RDB$USER_PRIVILEGES
INTO :USER_NAME, :USER_TYPE, :GRANTOR, :RELATION_NAME,
:FIELD_NAME, :OBJECT_TYPE, :PRIVILEGE, :GRANT_OPTION
```

Taking the current value of the output variable USER_NAME, we query RDB$ROLES to get the matching role owner and name, in case the "user" in the current row is actually a role. If it is not a role, these fields will be represented in the output by dashes:

```
DO BEGIN
  SELECT
    RTRIM(CAST(RDB$OWNER_NAME AS VARCHAR(31))),
    RTRIM(CAST(RDB$ROLE_NAME AS VARCHAR(31)))
  FROM RDB$ROLES
  WHERE RDB$ROLE_NAME = :USER_NAME
  INTO :ROLE_OWNER, :ROLE_NAME;
  IF (ROLE_NAME IS NOT NULL) THEN
    Q_ROLE_NAME = ROLE_NAME;
  ELSE
  BEGIN
    Q_ROLE_NAME = '-';
    ROLE_OWNER = '-';
  END
```

WITH GRANT OPTION is a special privilege that we want to know about in our output so, next, we convert this attribute to 'Y' if it is positive (1) or a blank if it is not:

```
IF (GRANT_OPTION = 1) THEN
  W_GRANT_OPTION = 'Y';
ELSE
  W_GRANT_OPTION = '';
```

Now another query into RDB$ROLES, this time to find out whether the object that the privilege applies to is a role. If it is, we add a helpful prefix to its object name. If it is not a role, we go on to test whether our object is a column in a table and give it a qualified name if it is.

```
IS_ROLE = NULL;
SELECT 1 FROM RDB$ROLES
  WHERE RDB$ROLE_NAME = :RELATION_NAME
INTO :IS_ROLE;
IF (IS_ROLE = 1) THEN
  QUALIFIED_OBJECT = '(Role) '||RELATION_NAME;
ELSE
```

```
BEGIN
  IF (
    (FIELD_NAME IS NULL)
    OR (RTRIM(FIELD_NAME) = '')) THEN
    FIELD_NAME = '';
  ELSE
    FIELD_NAME = '.'||FIELD_NAME;
  QUALIFIED_OBJECT = RELATION_NAME||FIELD_NAME;
END
```

In RDB$USER_PRIVILEGES, tables and views are both object type 0. That is not good enough for us, so the next query checks the table RDB$RELATIONS to discover whether this particular object is a view:

```
IF (OBJECT_TYPE = 0) THEN
BEGIN
  IS_VIEW = 0;
  SELECT 1 FROM RDB$RELATIONS
    WHERE RDB$RELATION_NAME = :RELATION_NAME
    AND RDB$VIEW_SOURCE IS NOT NULL
  INTO :IS_VIEW;
  IF (IS_VIEW = 1) THEN
    OBJECT_TYPE = 1;
END
```

At this point in our loop, we have almost everything we need. But our object still has its internal number and we still do not know what sort of "user" we have. Users can be other things besides people. Here is where we make the nested calls to get the internal numbers translated to meaningful strings. When that is done, the record is ready to output to the row cache and we call SUSPEND to complete the loop.

Return Values

Nested procedure calls in triggers or stored procedures are almost identical to the calls we make from DSQL to execute them. Where the syntax differs is in the handling of the return values. In DSQL, the engine transports the return values back to the client in a record structure. In stored procedures, we use the PSQL keyword RETURNING_VALUES and provide variables to receive the values.

```
EXECUTE PROCEDURE SP_GET_TYPE(:OBJECT_TYPE)
  RETURNING_VALUES (:Q_OBJECT_TYPE);
EXECUTE PROCEDURE SP_GET_TYPE (:USER_TYPE)
  RETURNING_VALUES (:Q_USER_TYPE);
SUSPEND;
  END
END^
```

Calling the Procedure

This is another simple call:

```
SELECT * FROM SP_PRIVILEGES;
```

If we do not want all of the columns, or we want them in a special order, we can do that. For example, suppose we just want to look at the privileges for all humanoid users other than SYSDBA:

```
SELECT
  USER_NAME,
  QUALIFIED_OBJECT,
  PRIVILEGE
FROM SP_PRIVILEGES
  WHERE Q_USER_TYPE = 'User'
  AND USER_NAME <> 'SYSDBA'
ORDER BY USER_NAME, QUALIFIED_OBJECT;
```

Replaceable search parameters can be used:

```
SELECT
  USER_NAME,
  QUALIFIED_OBJECT,
  PRIVILEGE
FROM SP_PRIVILEGES
  WHERE Q_USER_TYPE = ?
ORDER BY USER_NAME, QUALIFIED_OBJECT;
```

 TIP You might find this procedure useful for checking out the SQL privileges in your database. For information on setting up privileges, refer to Chapter 35.

A Procedure with Running Totals

In this procedure, we process records from the SALES table in the EMPLOYEE database. We keep two running totals: one for each sales representative and one for overall sales. As inputs we have just a start and end date for the group of sales records we want.

```
SET TERM ^;
CREATE PROCEDURE LOG_SALES (
  START_DATE DATE,
  END_DATE DATE)
```

```
RETURNS (REP_NAME VARCHAR(37),
         CUST VARCHAR(25),
         ORDDATE TIMESTAMP,
         ITEMTYP VARCHAR(12),
         ORDTOTAL NUMERIC(9,2),
         REPTOTAL NUMERIC(9,2),
         RUNNINGTOTAL NUMERIC(9,2))
AS
  DECLARE VARIABLE CUSTNO INTEGER;
  DECLARE VARIABLE REP SMALLINT;
  DECLARE VARIABLE LASTREP SMALLINT DEFAULT -99;
  DECLARE VARIABLE LASTCUSTNO INTEGER DEFAULT -99;
BEGIN
  RUNNINGTOTAL = 0.00;
  FOR SELECT
    CUST_NO,
    SALES_REP,
    ORDER_DATE,
    TOTAL_VALUE,
    ITEM_TYPE
  FROM SALES
    WHERE ORDER_DATE BETWEEN :START_DATE AND :END_DATE + 1
    ORDER BY 2, 3
  INTO :CUSTNO, :REP, :ORDDATE, :ORDTOTAL, :ITEMTYP
```

Notice that we are using an ordered set. If you are making a virtual table from a selectable stored procedure and you want an ordered set, it can be valuable to do the ordering set inside the procedure code. The optimizer can help performance here if it has useful indexes to work with, whereas ordering applied to the output set has, by its nature, no indexes to work with.

Once inside the loop, we begin massaging the data for our row and for the two running totals. We do a little magic to avoid repeating the rep's name—it looks neater on a read-only display—although you would not do this if your application needed to target a row at random and use that column as a search key! We control the customer name in a similar way, to avoid an unnecessary search when the same customer occurs in consecutive records.

```
  DO
  BEGIN
    IF(REP = LASTREP) THEN
    BEGIN
      REPTOTAL = REPTOTAL + ORDTOTAL;
      REP_NAME = '"';
    END
    ELSE
    BEGIN
      REPTOTAL = ORDTOTAL;
      LASTREP = REP;
      SELECT FULL_NAME FROM EMPLOYEE
        WHERE EMP_NO = :REP
```

```
    INTO :REP_NAME;
  END
  IF (CUSTNO <> LASTCUSTNO) THEN
  BEGIN
    SELECT CUSTOMER FROM CUSTOMER
      WHERE CUST_NO = :CUSTNO
    INTO :CUST;
    LASTCUSTNO = CUSTNO;
  END
  RUNNINGTOTAL = RUNNINGTOTAL + ORDTOTAL;
  SUSPEND;
```

Our row is now complete and it goes to the row cache with the two running totals updated.

```
  END
END^
SET TERM ;^
```

Calling the Procedure

Our input arguments are of DATE type, a start date and an end date. The procedure is searching a TIMESTAMP to select the rows for the cursor. It adds a day to the input end date, to ensure that we get every record up to the end of that day. That keeps things simple: When we call the procedure, we need only provide the first and last dates, without having to worry about any records with timestamps later than midnight of the final day.

This call is certain to return the whole table:

```
SELECT * FROM LOG_SALES ('16.05.1970', CURRENT_DATE);
```

We might want a procedure like this to be parameterized:

```
SELECT * FROM LOG_SALES (?, ?);
```

Viewing an Array Through a Stored Procedure

If a table contains columns defined as arrays, you cannot view the data in the column with a simple SELECT statement, since only the array ID is stored in the table. A stored procedure can be used to display array values, as long as the dimensions and data type of the array column are known in advance.

The JOB table in the sample database has a column named LANGUAGE_REQ containing the languages required for the position. The column is defined as an array of five VARCHAR(15) elements.

The following example uses a stored procedure to view the contents of the column. The procedure uses a FOR ... SELECT loop to retrieve each row from JOB for which LANGUAGE_REQ is not null. Then a WHILE loop retrieves each element of the array and returns the value to the calling application.

```
SET TERM ^;
CREATE PROCEDURE VIEW_LANGS
RETURNS (
  code VARCHAR(5),
  grade SMALLINT,
  cty VARCHAR(15),
  lang VARCHAR(15))
AS
  DECLARE VARIABLE i INTEGER;
BEGIN
  FOR SELECT
    JOB_CODE,
    JOB_GRADE,
    JOB_COUNTRY
  FROM JOB
    WHERE LANGUAGE_REQ IS NOT NULL
  DO
  BEGIN
    i = 1;
    WHILE (i <= 5) DO
    BEGIN
      SELECT LANGUAGE_REQ[:i] FROM JOB
        WHERE ((JOB_CODE = :code)
        AND (JOB_GRADE = :grade)
        AND (JOB_COUNTRY = :cty))
      INTO :lang;
      i =i + 1;
      SUSPEND;
    END
  END
END ^
SET TERM ; ^
```

Invoking it:

```
SELECT * FROM VIEW_LANGS;
```

CODE	GRADE	CTY	LANG
Eng	3	Japan	Japanese
Eng	3	Japan	Mandarin
Eng	3	Japan	English
Eng	3	Japan	
Eng	3	Japan	
Eng	4	England	English
Eng	4	England	German
Eng	4	England	French

...

The procedure could be modified to take input arguments and return a different combination of data as output.

Testing Procedures

It should be unnecessary to remind developers of the need to test PSQL modules with rigor and skepticism before launching them into production environments where, on a bad day, they could really do some harm. The parser will spank you for PSQL coding errors but, as programs, your modules are at least as vulnerable to logic and runtime errors as any application code you write.

For example, our procedure LOG_SALES works fine as long as every sales record has a non-null SALES_REP value. However, this is a nullable column. The procedure happens to be one that generates a result set in which each output row depends on values in the preceding rows. If we do not address the potential effects of null occurring in that key, our procedure is vulnerable to inconsistent results. In the section "Changing Stored Procedures," later in this chapter, we add a safeguard to the logic to deal with this particular problem.

Procedures for Combined Use

Although it is possible to write a selectable procedure that executes a data-changing operation in the course of constructing an output set, it is not recommended. A selectable stored procedure is designed to output a set of data to the client, in the transaction context that invokes it. Until the client application has finished using that output set, the transaction remains uncommitted. If DML operations are included in the code that generates the output set, those DML requests remain uncommitted until the transaction is completed by the client.

In particular, data has the potential to be stored inconsistently if values from the stored procedure output are passed as parameters to operations in other transactions.

Changing Stored Procedures

Firebird 1.0.*x* offers two ways to change stored procedures using DDL statements, and Firebird 1.5 adds a third one. They are

- ALTER PROCEDURE, which changes the definition of an existing stored procedure while preserving its dependencies on other objects.

- RECREATE PROCEDURE, which works even if the named procedure does not exist. If it does exist, the existing version is dropped and then recreated. Existing dependencies do not survive.

- CREATE OR ALTER PROCEDURE (available from v.1.5 onward), which gives the best of both. If the procedure exists, ALTER rules apply and dependencies are preserved. If not, it will work exactly as CREATE PROCEDURE does.

Any of these operations will fail with an exception if any change is attempted that would break a dependency.

Effect on Applications

Changes made internally to a procedure are transparent to all client applications that use the procedure. You do not have to rebuild the applications unless the changes affect the *interface* between the caller and the procedure—type, number, or order of input and output arguments.

Syntax for Changing Procedures

Except for the keyword you choose to effect a change to a stored procedure, the syntax of the statements for each is the same as for CREATE PROCEDURE. Just as with any compiled or interpreted module, there is no way to direct a change at an element without recreating the whole module. Every "alteration," regardless of the keyword you choose to specify the operation, is a matter of creating a new source version and a new binary-coded object.

The syntax pattern is

```
{CREATE | ALTER | RECREATE | CREATE OR ALTER}  PROCEDURE name
[(var datatype [, var datatype ...])]
[RETURNS (var datatype [, var datatype ...])]
AS
procedure_body;
```

ALTER PROCEDURE

For ALTER PROCEDURE, the procedure *name* must be the name of an existing procedure.

This is the low-impact way to change procedure code because, if it has dependencies that are not logically affected by the changes, there will be no structural side effects.

In general, dependencies involving other objects that depend on the changed procedure are not affected, either. However, if the changes to the stored procedure alter the definitions of its input or output arguments, it will be necessary to perform a RECREATE PROCEDURE on any other stored procedure that gets called during the execution.

CAUTION Some versions of Firebird 1.0.*x* exhibit a bug, whereby dependent objects will throw an exception when the depended-on object is recompiled, even if the interface between the objects is not affected by the change.

RECREATE PROCEDURE

RECREATE PROCEDURE is identical to CREATE PROCEDURE, except that it causes any existing procedure of the same name to be subjected internally to a full DROP PROCEDURE operation before the new binary object is created. The procedure name does not have to exist.

You can use it like ALTER PROCEDURE, but it will not preserve existing dependencies. The operation will be blocked if there are dependent objects (views or other procedures that refer to the procedure).

The procedure *name* need not exist, but take care with case sensitivity of object names if quoted identifiers were used when creating the procedure. For example, suppose you created this procedure:

```
CREATE PROCEDURE "Try_Me"
RETURNS (AWORD VARCHAR(10))
AS
BEGIN
  AWORD = "turtle';
END ^
```

Now you decide to change it using RECREATE PROCEDURE:

```
RECREATE PROCEDURE Try_Me
RETURNS (AWORD VARCHAR(10))
AS
BEGIN
  AWORD = "Venezuela";
END ^
```

The original procedure, with its case-sensitive name Try_Me remains, unchanged. The "re-created" procedure is a new and quite separate object with the case-insensitive name TRY_ME.

CREATE OR ALTER PROCEDURE

New in v.1.5, this tolerant syntax creates a new procedure if there is none of the supplied name, or alters an existing procedure of that name.

Fixing the LOG_SALES Procedure

As an example, we are going to fix that procedure, LOG_SALES, that promises to bite us because we overlooked a nullable key. Here is the block that could cause the problems:

```
CREATE PROCEDURE LOG_SALES (...
...
  DO
  BEGIN
```

```
                    IF(REP = LASTREP) THEN /* will be false if both values are null */
                    BEGIN
                      REPTOTAL = REPTOTAL + ORDTOTAL;
                      REP_NAME = '"';
                    END
                    ELSE
                    BEGIN
                      REPTOTAL = ORDTOTAL;
                      LASTREP = REP;
                      SELECT FULL_NAME FROM EMPLOYEE
                        WHERE EMP_NO = :REP
                        INTO :REP_NAME; /* will return null if variable REP is null */
                    END
                  ...
              END ^
```

We fix the logic to handle nulls (grouped together at the end of the cursor, because the set is ordered by this column) and use CREATE OR ALTER to update the code:

```
CREATE OR ALTER PROCEDURE LOG_SALES (...
...
  DO
  BEGIN
    /* ************* */
    IF((REP = LASTREP) OR (LASTREP IS NULL)) THEN
    /* ************* */
    BEGIN
      REPTOTAL = REPTOTAL + ORDTOTAL;
      REP_NAME = '"';
    END
    ELSE
    BEGIN
      REPTOTAL = ORDTOTAL;
      LASTREP = REP;
      /* ************* */
      IF (REP IS NOT NULL) THEN
        SELECT FULL_NAME FROM EMPLOYEE
          WHERE EMP_NO = :REP
        INTO :REP_NAME;
      ELSE
        REP_NAME = 'Unassigned';
      /* ************* */
    END
  ...
  END ^
COMMIT ^
```

"Object Is in Use" Error

Committing the change will throw the notorious error (discussed in the previous chapter) if any user is currently using the procedure or another object that depends on it. Even if we clear that hurdle, the new version of the procedure will not be immediately available on Superserver if the old version is still in the cache. All users must log out and, when they log in again, they will see the new version.

On Classic server, the new version will be available to the next client that logs in.

Dropping Stored Procedures

The DROP PROCEDURE statement deletes an existing stored procedure from the database. You can use this statement anywhere it is possible to use DDL statements.

> **NOTE** DDL statements cannot be executed as PSQL statements, per se. However, in Firebird 1.5, a DDL statement can be passed via an EXECUTE STATEMENT construct. Is it necessary to caution the reader against using EXECUTE STATEMENT to have a procedure drop itself?

The syntax is

```
DROP PROCEDURE name;
```

The procedure *name* must be the name of an existing procedure. Take care with case sensitivity of object names if quoted identifiers were used when creating the procedure.

The following statement deletes the LOG_SALES procedure:

```
DROP PROCEDURE LOG_SALES;
```

Restrictions

The following restrictions apply to dropping a procedure:

- Only SYSDBA or the owner of a procedure can drop it.

- A procedure that is in use by any transaction cannot be dropped. This will be a special issue in systems where procedures are being called from transactions that are committed using CommitRetaining.

- If any other objects in the database refer to or call the procedure, it will be necessary to alter the dependent objects to remove the references and commit that work, before the procedure can be dropped.

- A recursive procedure cannot be dropped without first removing the recursive calls and committing that change. Similar complications apply to a procedure that calls other procedures that, in turn, call the procedure you want to drop. All such dependencies must be removed and committed before the procedure is free to be dropped.

OPTIMIZATION TOPIC: Using the Internal RDB$DB_KEY

Firebird inherited an undocumented feature that can speed up query performance in some conditions. This is RDB$DB_KEY (usually referred to simply as the *db_key*), an internal cardinality key maintained by the database engine for internal use in query optimization and record version management. Inside the transaction context in which it is captured, it represents a row's position in the table.[4]

About RDB$DB_KEY

The first lesson to learn is that RDB$DB_KEY is a *raw position*, related to the database itself and not to a physical address on disk. The second is that the numbers do not progress in a predictable sequence. Don't consider performing calculations involving their relative positions! The third lesson is that they are volatile—they change after a backup and subsequent restore and, sometimes, after the transaction is committed. It is essential to understand the transience of the db_key and to make no assumptions about its existence once an operation that refers to it is committed or rolled back.

Size of RDB$DB_KEY

For tables, RDB$DB_KEY uses 8 bytes. For a view, it uses as many multiples of 8 bytes as there are underlying tables. For example, if a view joins three tables, its RDB$DB_KEY uses 24 bytes. This is important if you are working with stored procedures and want to store RDB$DB_KEY in a variable. You must use a CHAR(n) data type of the correct length.

---

4. The man who did the research on the RDB$DB_KEY and was the source of many of the examples in this piece is Claudio Valderrama C., who lives in Chile. Claudio, alias "robocop," is the official code scrutineer for the Firebird Project. He maintains an eclectic collection of articles and code about Firebird and InterBase at his website, http://www.cvalde.net.

By default, db_keys are returned as hex values—2 hex digits represent each byte, causing 16 hex digits to be returned for 8 bytes. Try it on one of your sample tables in **isql**:

```
SQL> SELECT RDB$DB_KEY FROM MYTABLE;
RDB$DB_KEY
================
000000B600000002
000000B600000004
000000B600000006
000000B600000008
000000B60000000A
```

Benefits

Because an RDB$DB_KEY marks the raw position of a row, it is faster for a search than even a primary key. If for some special reason a table has no primary key or active unique index, or it is primed on a unique index that is allowed to contain nulls, it is possible for exact duplicate rows to exist. Under such conditions, an RDB$DB_KEY is the only way to identify each row unequivocally.

Several kinds of statements run faster when moved into a stored procedure using an RDB$DB_KEY—typically, updates and deletions with complex conditions. For inserts (even huge batches) the RDB$DB_KEY is of no avail, since there is no way to ascertain what the values will be.

However, if the database pages being searched for update or delete are already in main memory, the difference in access speed is likely to be negligible. The same is true if the searched set is quite small and all of the searched rows are close to one another.

Optimization of Queries

Performance problems are likely if you try to run a DSQL update like the following example against a huge table:

```
UPDATE TABLEA A
SET A.TOTAL = (SELECT SUM (B.VALUEFIELD)
               FROM TABLEB B
               WHERE B.FK= A.PK)
where <conditions..>
```

If you run the same operation often and it affects a lot of rows, it would be worth the effort to write a stored procedure that handles the correlated total on each row without needing to perform a subquery:

```
CREATE PROCEDURE ...
..
AS
```

```
BEGIN
  FOR SELECT B.FK, SUM(B.VALUEFIELD) FROM TABLEB B
  GROUP BY B.FK
  INTO:B_FK, :TOTAL DO
    UPDATE TABLEA A SET A.TOTAL = :TOTAL
    WHERE A.PK= :B_FK


  AND ...
END
```

Although speedier, it still has the problem that records in A have to be located by primary key each time a new pass of the FOR ... DO loop happens.

Some people claim better results with this alien syntax:

```
...
DECLARE VARIABLE DBK CHAR(8); /* 8 CHARS FOR A TABLE'S DBKEY */
...
FOR SELECT B.FK,
SUM(B.VALUEFIELD),
A.RDB$DB_KEY
FROM TABLEB B
JOIN TABLEA A ON A.PK = B.FK
WHERE <conditions>
GROUP BY B.FK, A.RDB$DB_KEY
INTO :B_FK, :TOTAL, :DBK DO
  UPDATE TABLEA SET A.TOTAL = :TOTAL
  WHERE A.RDB$DB_KEY = :DBK;
```

NOTE Firebird does not need the key column to form the join, but it does need to be present in the SELECT list in order for the GROUP BY clause to be valid.

The benefits of this approach are

- Filtering of the common records for A and B is efficient where the optimizer can make a good filter from the explicit join.

- If the join can apply its own search clause, there is a gain in getting the extra filtering *before* the update checks its own condition.

- Rows from the right-side table (A) are located by raw db_key values, extracted at the time of the join, making the search faster than looking through the primary key or its index.

Inserting

Since inserting does not involve a search, the simplest insert operations—for example, reading constant values from an import set in an external table—are not affected by the need to locate keys.

Not every INSERT statement's VALUES input set is obtained so simply, however. It can be a very complicated set of values derived from expressions, joins, or aggregations. In a stored procedure, an INSERT operation may well be branched into the ELSE sub-clause of an IF (EXISTS(...)) predicate, for example:

```
IF EXISTS(SELECT...) THEN
...
ELSE
BEGIN
  INSERT INTO TABLEA
  SELECT
    C.PKEY,
    SUM(B.AVALUE),
    AVG(B.BVALUE),
    COUNT(DISTINCT C.XYZ)
  FROM TABLEB B JOIN TABLEC C
    ON B.X = C.Y
    WHERE C.Z = 'value'
    AND C.PKEY NOT IN(SELECT PKEY FROM TABLEA)
  GROUP BY C.PKEY;
END
...
```

Implementing this in a stored procedure:

```
FOR SELECT
    C.PKEY,
    SUM(B.AVALUE),
    AVG(B.BVALUE),
    COUNT(DISTINCT C.XYZ)
  FROM TABLEB B JOIN TABLEC C
    ON B.X = C.Y
    WHERE C.Z = 'value'
    AND C.PKEY NOT IN(SELECT PKEY FROM TABLEA)
  GROUP BY C.PKEY
INTO :C_KEY, :TOTAL, :B_AVG, :C_COUNT DO
BEGIN
  SELECT A.RDB$DBKEY FROM TABLEA A
    WHERE A.PKEY = :C_KEY
    INTO :DBK;
  IF (DBK IS NULL) THEN /* the row doesn't exist */
    INSERT INTO TABLEA(PKEY, TOTAL, AVERAGE_B, COUNT_C)
    VALUES(:C_KEY, :TOTAL, :B_AVG, :C_COUNT);
```

```
    ELSE
      UPDATE TABLEA SET
        TOTAL = TOTAL + :TOTAL,
        AVERAGE_B = AVERAGE_B + :B_AVG,
        COUNT_C = COUNT_C + :C_COUNT
      WHERE A.RDB$DB_KEY = :DBK;
END
...
```

Duration of Validity

By default, the scope of a db_key is the current transactions. You can count on it to remain valid for the duration of the current transaction. A commit or rollback will cause the RDB$DB_KEY values you had to become unpredictable. If you are using CommitRetaining, the transaction context is retained, blocking garbage collection and thus preventing the old db_key from being "recycled." Under these conditions, the RDB$DB_KEY values of any rows affected by your transaction remain valid until a "hard" commit or rollback occurs.

After the hard commit or rollback, another transaction might delete a row that was isolated inside your transaction's context and was thus considered "existent" by your application. Any RDB$DB_KEY value might now point to a non-existent row. If there is a long interval between the moment when your transaction began and when your work completes, you should check that the row has not been changed or locked by another transaction in the meantime.

Some application interfaces, for example, IB Objects, are super-smart about inserts and can prepare a "slot" for a newly inserted row in the client buffers to short-circuit the refresh following the commit. Such features are important for performance across the network. However, "smarts" like this are based on exact, real keys. Since the db_key is merely a proxy key for a set that has been derived from *previously* committed data, it has no meaning for a new row—it is not available for spot updates of the client buffers.

Changing the Scope of Duration

The default duration of RDB$DB_KEY values can be changed at connection time, by using the API parameter *isc_dpb_dbkey_scope*. Some development—for example, the IB Objects components in Borland ObjectPascal environments tools—surface it in a connectivity class. However, it is not recommended to extend the scope of db_keys in a highly interactive environment, since it will disable garbage collection, with the unwanted side effect of causing your database file to grow at an alarming rate and slowing down performance until the system hangs or crashes. Do not pool connections having non-default db_key scope.

RDB$DB_KEY with Multi-Table Sets

All tables maintain their own distinct, 8-byte RDB$DB_KEY columns. Views and joins generate runtime db_keys by concatenating those of the rows in the source tables. If you use RDB$DB_KEY in multi-table sets, be very careful to qualify each one accurately.

RDB$DB_KEY cannot be used *across* tables. There is no possibility of establishing a dependency relationship between the RDB$DB_KEY of one table and another, except in re-entrant (self-referencing) joins.

Up Next

Many of the techniques described in this chapter are applicable to any PSQL modules you write. Next, the focus is on the special PSQL techniques and language features you can use when writing triggers to respond automatically to changes in the state of a row's data changes or to the insertion of a new row.

CHAPTER 31

Triggers

TRIGGERS ARE A KEY ELEMENT AMONG the capabilities provided by Firebird for implementing business rules centrally inside the database management system. A trigger is a self-contained module that executes automatically when a request is executed that will change the state of data in a table.

Triggers are stored procedures and the PSQL techniques for writing and executing code for them are no different from those for callable procedures. However, triggers cannot be invoked by applications or other procedures. Accordingly, they cannot take inputs or pass outputs as other procedures do. In addition, PSQL includes certain contextual language extensions applicable only to trigger modules.

All triggers in Firebird execute at row level, once each time the row image changes. Firebird supports a high degree of granularity for defining the timing, sequence, and conditions under which a particular trigger module will fire. Multiple modules can be defined for each *phase* and *event*.

Triggers are part of the work of the transaction in which a DML event changes the state of a row. If the transaction commits successfully, all of the trigger actions will "take." If the transaction is rolled back, the trigger actions are all undone.

Phase, Event, and Sequence

A trigger can execute in one of two phases relative to the execution of the requested change of data state: *before* the write or *after* it. It can apply to one of three DML events: inserting, updating, or deleting. From Firebird 1.5, it is possible to combine the trigger actions for two or three DML events into one before or after trigger module.

Phase and Event

Table 31-1 summarizes the eight kinds of trigger module.

Table 31-1. Phase/Event Combinations for Trigger Modules

TRIGGER KIND	DESCRIPTION	VERSION
BEFORE INSERT	Fires before a new row is created. Allows input values to be changed.	All
AFTER INSERT	Fires after a new record version is created. Does not allow input values to be changed. Usually used to modify other tables.	All

continued

Table 31-1. Phase/Event Combinations for Trigger Modules (continued)

TRIGGER KIND	DESCRIPTION	VERSION
BEFORE UPDATE	Fires before a new record version is created. Allows input values to be changed.	All
AFTER UPDATE	Fires after a new record version is created. Does not allow input values to be changed. Usually used to modify other tables.	All
BEFORE DELETE	Fires before an existing row is deleted. Does not accept changes to any columns in the row.	All
AFTER DELETE	Fires after the row has been deleted. Does not accept changes to any columns in the row. Usually used to modify other tables.	All
BEFORE *<event>* OR *<event>* [OR *<event>*]	Fires before any requested data state change is executed. DML event actions must be coded conditionally. "Deleting" action cannot change any columns in the row.	V.1.5+
AFTER *<event>* OR *<event>* [OR *<event>*]	Fires after any requested data state change is executed. DML event actions must be coded conditionally. Actions cannot change any columns in the row. Usually used to modify other tables.	V.1.5+

Sequence

Firebird allows multiple trigger modules for any phase/event combination. There is probably some practical limit, but it is safe to say you can create as many as you need, using whole numbers between 0 and 32,767. The default is sequence number ("POSITION") zero. It is good science to set an order of execution by numbering the triggers, but explicit sequencing is optional. If sequence numbers are present, the triggers will be executed in ascending order. Numbers don't have to be unique and the sequence can have gaps.

Suites of triggers for a phase/event with the default POSITION 0 will be executed in the alphabetical order of their names. The same can be expected if you have groupings of triggers sharing the same non-zero sequence number.

The following example demonstrates how four update triggers for the ACCOUNT table would be fired:

```
CREATE TRIGGER BU_ACCOUNT5 FOR ACCOUNT
  ACTIVE BEFORE UPDATE POSITION 5 AS ...
CREATE TRIGGER BU_ACCOUNT0 FOR ACCOUNT
  ACTIVE BEFORE UPDATE POSITION 0 AS ...
CREATE TRIGGER AU_ACCOUNT5 FOR ACCOUNT
  ACTIVE AFTER UPDATE POSITION 5 AS ...
CREATE TRIGGER AU_ACCOUNT3 FOR ACCOUNT
ACTIVE AFTER UPDATE POSITION 3 AS ...
```

Someone updates some rows in ACCOUNTS:

```
UPDATE ACCOUNT
  SET C ='CANCELED'
  WHEREC2 = 5;
```

This is the sequence of events on each affected row:

1. Trigger BU_ACCOUNT0 fires.

2. Trigger BU_ACCOUNT5 fires.

3. The new record version is written to disk.

4. Trigger AU_ACCOUNT3 fires.

5. Trigger AU_ACCOUNT5 fires.

Status

A trigger can be *active* or *inactive*. Only active triggers fire. Refer to the notes on ALTER TRIGGER for details about deactivating a trigger.

Creating Triggers

A trigger is defined with the CREATE TRIGGER statement, which is composed of a *header* and a *body*. The trigger header, which is quite different from a stored procedure header, contains

- A trigger name that is unique within the database

- A table name that identifies the table with which to associate the trigger

- Attributes that determine state, phase, DML event, and, optionally, sequence

The trigger body, like a stored procedure body, contains

- An optional list of local variables and their data types.

- A block of statements in Firebird procedure and trigger language, bracketed by BEGIN and END. These statements are performed when the trigger fires. A block can itself include other blocks, so that there may be many levels of nesting.

Syntax

For all versions of Firebird, the syntax pattern for CREATE TRIGGER is

```
CREATE TRIGGER name FOR {table | view}
[ACTIVE | INACTIVE]
{BEFORE | AFTER} {DELETE | INSERT | UPDATE}
[POSITION number]
AS <trigger_body> ^
<trigger_body>=[<variable_declaration_list>] <block>
<variable_declaration_list> =DECLARE VARIABLE variable datatype;
[DECLARE [VARIABLE] variable datatype;...]
<block>=
BEGIN
<compound_statement>[<compound_statement>...]
END
<compound_statement>=<block>|statement;
```

In v.1.5, it is possible to merge all events into a single phase-trigger:

```
CREATE TRIGGER name FOR {table | view}
[ACTIVE | INACTIVE]
{BEFORE | AFTER}
  {DELETE OR {[INSERT [OR UPDATE]} | {INSERT OR [..]} | {UPDATE OR [..]}}
[POSITION number]
AS <trigger_body> ^
```

Header Elements

Everything preceding the AS clause forms the trigger header. The header must specify the unique name of the trigger and the name of an existing, committed table or view that it is to belong to.

Naming Triggers

The syntax requires that the trigger name be unique among all trigger names in the database. It is good practice to adopt some convention for naming triggers that is meaningful to you and obvious to others who will work with your database. The author uses a "formula" identifying phase and event (BI | AI | BU | AU | BD | AD | BA | AA, the latter two representing "Before All" and "After All"), table name, and sequence number, if relevant. For example, a Before Insert trigger for the Customer table might be named BI_Customer1.

```
CREATE TRIGGER BI_CUSTOMER FOR CUSTOMER...
```

Trigger Attributes

The remaining attributes in the trigger header are

- The *trigger status*, ACTIVE or INACTIVE, determines whether the trigger will be "up and running" when it is created. ACTIVE is the default. Deactivating a trigger is useful during development and testing.

- The *phase indicator*, BEFORE or AFTER, determines the timing of the trigger relative to the write action being executed by the DML event.

- The *DML event indicator* specifies the type of SQL operation that shall trigger execution of the module: INSERT, UPDATE, or DELETE.

- In Firebird 1.0.*x*, exactly one event indicator must be specified. From v.1.5 onward, the optional *<event>* OR *<event>*... extension allows two or three events to be coded conditionally into a single module. For example, ...BEFORE INSERT OR UPDATE OR DELETE... allows you to provide actions for all three events. The Boolean context variables INSERTING, UPDATING, and DELETING support the branching logic.

- The optional *sequence indicato*r, POSITION *number*, specifies when the trigger is to fire in relation to other trigger modules for the same phase and event.

The Trigger Body

In all Firebird code modules, the body consists of an optional list of local variable declarations followed by a block of statements. Programming a trigger body is exactly the same as programming a stored procedure body—refer to the preceding chapter. Of interest to us in this chapter are some special extensions PSQL provides to support the trigger context and some special roles for triggers in implementing and enforcing business rules.

Triggers can invoke stored procedures. The calling rules are exactly the same for trigger modules as for stored procedures. Exception-handling techniques are discussed in the next chapter.

Triggers can process cursors, perform operations on other tables, and post events. They can throw and handle exceptions, including those raised from nested procedures.

Triggers are never called by procedures, other triggers, or applications. They do not support input or output arguments at all.

Special PSQL for Triggers

Two special PSQL elements are available for triggers: the Boolean event context variables INSERTING, UPDATING, and DELETING, and the NEW and OLD context variables.

Event Variables

Firebird 1.5 introduced the Boolean context variables INSERTING, UPDATING, and DELETING to support the conditional branching for the multi-event trigger feature. Possible syntax patterns would be

```
IF ({INSERTING | UPDATING | DELETING}
   OR {UPDATING | DELETING | INSERTING}
   [OR {DELETING | INSERTING | UPDATING}]) THEN ...
```

Follow through the examples in the rest of this chapter to see these useful predicates at work.

NEW and OLD Variables

The NEW and OLD context variables are a trigger-specific extension to PSQL[1] that enables your code to refer to the existing ("old") and requested ("new") values of each column. The NEW.* variables have values in INSERT and UPDATE events; OLD.* variables have values in UPDATE and DELETE events. NEW.* in delete events and OLD.* in insert events are null. The applicable old and new counterparts are available for all columns in a table or view, even if the columns themselves are not referred to in the DML statement.

The OLD.* values (if available) can be manipulated as variables within the trigger, but changes of value do not affect the stored old values. The NEW.* values (if available) are read-write during the BEFORE phase and read-only during the AFTER phase. If you want to manipulate them as variable values in an After trigger, move the values into local variables and refer to those.

Uses for NEW and OLD

For harnessing the power of Firebird triggers to develop databases that take care of data integrity independently of humans and external programming, NEW and OLD variables are the essential tool. They can be used to

- Provide valid default values under any conditions.

- Validate and, if required, transform user input.

- Supply keys and values for performing automatic updates to other tables.

- Implement auto-incrementing keys by means of generators.

---

1. NEW.* and OLD.* are also valid in DDL for table-level CHECK constraints—for example, CREATE TABLE BLAH (ID INTEGER, DATA INTEGER, CONSTRAINT CHECK_INCR CHECK(NEW.DATA > OLD.DATA)).

New values for a row can only be altered by *before* actions. A trigger that fires in the AFTER phase and tries to assign a value to NEW.*column* will have no effect.

NEW values are writeable all through the BEFORE phase and take up a reassignment of their value immediately. The new record version will receive any reassignments only when all BEFORE triggers have completed. At this point, the NEW values become read-only. Hence, if you have multiple triggers adjusting the same NEW values, it is important to ensure that they all have different POSITION numbers, correctly ordered.

Implementing Auto-Incrementing Keys

A recommended usage of BEFORE INSERT triggers in Firebird is for implementing @IDENTITY-style auto-incrementing primary keys. The technique is simple and most Firebird developers can write these triggers in their sleep. It involves two steps:

1. Create a generator to be used to generate the unique numbers for the key.

2. Write a BEFORE INSERT trigger for the table.

To illustrate the technique, we'll implement an auto-incrementing primary key for a table named CUSTOMER that has the primary key CUSTOMER_ID, an integer type or BigInt (v.1.5) or NUMERIC(18,0) (v.1.0.*x*). For a dialect 1 database, CUSTOMER_ID would be an integer.

First, create the generator:

```
CREATE GENERATOR GEN_PK_CUSTOMER;
```

Now, create the trigger:

```
CREATE TRIGGER BI_CUSTOMER FOR CUSTOMER
ACTIVE BEFORE INSERT POSITION 0
AS
BEGIN
  IF (NEW.CUSTOMER_ID IS NULL) THEN
    NEW.CUSTOMER_ID = GEN_ID(GEN_PK_CUSTOMER, 1);
END ^
COMMIT ^
```

When an insert is performed, CUSTOMER_ID is deliberately omitted from the input list of the INSERT statement:

```
INSERT INTO CUSTOMER (
  LAST_NAME,
  FIRST_NAME,
  ...)
VALUES (?, ?, ...);
```

Without the trigger, this statement would cause an exception because primary keys are not nullable. However, the BEFORE INSERT trigger executes before the constraint validation, detects that CUSTOMER_ID is null, and does its stuff.

Why NEW.value Is Tested for Null

If the trigger can do that for me, you might ask, why should it need to test for null?

It can be of benefit for an application to know what the primary key of a new row will be without having to wait until its transaction commits. For example, it is a very common requirement to create a "master" record and link new "detail" records to it, usually by way of a foreign key, in a single transaction. It is clumsy—even risky sometimes—to break the atomicity of the master-detail creation task by committing the master in order to acquire the foreign key value for the detail records, as you need to do when relying solely on the trigger.

Applications written for Firebird take advantage of one peculiar characteristic of generators: They are not subject to any user transaction. Once generated, a value cannot be taken by another transaction, and it cannot be rolled back.

A quick query in its own transaction[2] returns the value

```
SELECT GEN_ID(GEN_PK_CUSTOMER, 1) AS RESULT
  FROM RDB$DATABASE;
```

If our trigger omitted the null test and just did this

```
...
AS
  NEW.CUSTOMER_ID = GEN_ID (GEN_PK_CUSTOMER, 1);
END ^
```

then the value posted by the application would get overwritten by the second "pull" off the generator and break the link to the detail records.

This situation is not an argument for dispensing with the triggered key. On the contrary, the trigger with the null test ensures that the business rule will be enforced under any conditions.

 CAUTION In an environment where there is not good integration of the application work of different developers, or where users are allowed free access to the database using query tools, it will be necessary for your triggers to include more protection for the integrity of keys, such as range-checking or another appropriate form of validation.

---

2. Some component interfaces provide methods or members to perform this little task automatically.

Transformations

A NEW variable can be used to transform a value into something else. A common trick is to use a trigger (or a pair of triggers, in the case of v.1.0.*x*) to maintain a "proxy" column for doing case-insensitive searches on another column that may be any mixture of case. The trigger reads the NEW value of the mixed-case column, converts it to uppercase, and writes it to the NEW value of the search column. The column being "proxied" should have a NOT NULL constraint to ensure that there will always be a value to find:

```
CREATE TABLE MEMBER (
  MEMBER_ID INTEGER NOT NULL PRIMARY KEY,
  LAST_NAME VARCHAR(40) NOT NULL,
  FIRST_NAME VARCHAR(35),
  PROXY_LAST_NAME VARCHAR(40),
  MEMBER_TYPE CHAR(3) NOT NULL,
  MEMBERSHIP_NUM VARCHAR(13),
  ....);
COMMIT;
/* */
SET TERM ^;
CREATE TRIGGER BA_MEMBER1 FOR MEMBER
  ACTIVE BEFORE INSERT OR UPDATE
  POSITION 0
AS
BEGIN
  ...
NEW.PROXY_LAST_NAME = UPPER(NEW.LAST_NAME);
  ...
END ^
```

All kinds of transformations are possible. Suppose we want to issue membership numbers (MEMBERSHIP_NUM) made up of the MEMBER_TYPE followed by a string of ten digits, left-padded with zeros, based on the generated primary key of the MEMBER table. We can have them automatically generated in a BEFORE INSERT trigger:[3]

```
CREATE TRIGGER BI_MEMBER2 FOR MEMBER
  ACTIVE BEFORE INSERT
  POSITION 2
AS
  DECLARE VARIABLE ID_AS_STRING VARCHAR(10);
BEGIN
```

---

3. This manipulation would be much more straightforward using an external function to calculate the length of the cast integer. I chose—perhaps a little contrarily—to demonstrate that it is possible to do some string manipulations without external functions.

```
      ID_AS_STRING = CAST(NEW.ID AS VARCHAR(10));
      WHILE (NOT (ID_AS_STRING LIKE '_____%')) /* 10-character mask */
      DO
        ID_AS_STRING = '0'||ID_AS_STRING;
      NEW.MEMBERSHIP_NUM = NEW.MEMBER_TYPE||ID_AS_STRING;
    END ^
```

Validation and Defaults

Triggers can improve on standard SQL constraints when it comes to the issues validating input and applying default values.

Validation

SQL provides for CHECK constraints to ensure that only "good" data is stored. For example, columns created under this domain are restricted to uppercase characters and digits:

```
CREATE DOMAIN TYPECODE CHAR(3)
  CHECK (VALUE IS NULL OR VALUE = UPPER(VALUE));
```

This is fine—we want this rule to be enforced. On its own, the constraint will throw an exception if any client application tries to submit lowercase characters. With a trigger, we can avoid the exception altogether by fixing any attempted violations *in situ*:

```
CREATE TRIGGER BA_ATABLE FOR ATABLE
ACTIVE BEFORE INSERT OR UPDATE
AS
BEGIN
  NEW.ATYPECODE = UPPER(NEW.ATYPECODE);
END ^
```

 NOTE   Currently, Firebird supports triggers only for tables and views. It is not possible to supply triggers for domains, but it would be an elegant enhancement.

Default Values

In domains and column definitions, you can specify a DEFAULT value. While it seems a good idea to be able to default a non-nullable column to some zero-impact value, the SQL DEFAULT attribute is a toothless beast. It works if and only if two conditions are met:

- The operation is an INSERT.

- The column has not been included in the statement's input list.

Since many modern application interfaces automatically compose an INSERT statement using the output columns of a SELECT statement as the basis of the input list, it follows that "something" is always passed for each column. If the application itself does not apply a default, the usual behavior is for the application to pass NULL. When the server receives NULL for a defaulted column, it stores NULL. Other column constraints may kick in and cause an exception to be thrown—especially a NOT NULL constraint—but a column default never overrides or corrects any value passed from the client interface.

The second problem, of course, is that column defaults are never applied when the operation is an update.

In short, triggers do a far more effective job at managing defaults than do default column attributes. Take, for example, a column defined under this domain:

```
CREATE DOMAIN MONEY NUMERIC(18,0)
NOT NULL DEFAULT 0.00;
```

A BEFORE INSERT OR UPDATE trigger on any column using the MONEY domain will take care of the default, no matter what comes through:

```
CREATE TRIGGER BI_ACCOUNT FOR ACCOUNT
ACTIVE BEFORE INSERT OR UPDATE
AS
BEGIN
  IF (NEW.BALANCE IS NULL) THEN
    NEW.BALANCE = 0.00;
END ^
```

TIP   You can take care of all of the defaults for a table in a single trigger module (v.1.5 and up) or two parallel modules, one for BEFORE INSERT and one for BEFORE UPDATE (v.1.0.*x*).

Auto-Stamping

Triggers are useful for "auto-stamping" contextual information into columns defined for the purpose. Firebird provides a number of context variables that you can use for this sort of operation. You can also provide "flags" of your own that you calculate or simply supply as constants during the course of the trigger's execution.

In this example, we use an "after" multi-event trigger to auto-stamp the user name, a timestamp, and the transaction ID onto a log file, along with some information about the data event. Since process logging (if we do it) is likely to be the last thing we want to do in a DML event, the trigger has a high sequence number:

```
CREATE TRIGGER AA_MEMBER FOR MEMBER
  ACTIVE AFTER INSERT OR UPDATE OR DELETE
  POSITION 99
AS
  DECLARE VARIABLE MEM_ID INTEGER;
  DECLARE VARIABLE DML_EVENT CHAR(4);
BEGIN
  IF (DELETING) THEN
  BEGIN
    MEM_ID = OLD.MEMBER_ID;
    DML_EVENT = 'DEL ';
  END
  ELSE
  BEGIN
    MEM_ID = NEW.MEMBER_ID;
    IF (UPDATING) THEN
      DML_EVENT = 'EDIT';
    ELSE
      DML_EVENT = 'NEW ';
  END
  INSERT INTO PROCESS_LOG (
    TRANS_ID,
    USER_ID,
    MEMBER_ID,
    DML_EVENT,
    TIME_STAMP)
  VALUES (
    CURRENT_TRANSACTION,
    CURRENT_USER,
    :MEM_ID,
    :DML_EVENT,
    CURRENT_TIMESTAMP);
END ^
```

Of course, you can auto-stamp your new or edited rows directly as well, in the course of a "before" trigger.

Updating Other Tables

We just saw in the previous example how "after" triggers can perform updates on other tables to automate management tasks such as logging. The capability to extend the reach of a DML event beyond the immediate context of the table and row that "own" the data has some important applications for managing difficult relationships.

Enforcing a Mandatory Relationship

A mandatory relationship exists when two tables are linked by a foreign key dependency and there must be at least one dependent row for each primary row. Since SQL does not provide a "mandatoriness" constraint, trigger logic is needed to enforce the "minimum of one child" rule, not only at creation time but also when dependent rows are deleted.

The following example outlines one way to use triggers to enforce this mandatory master-detail relationship. It assumes that the primary key of the master table is known by the application before the new row is posted.

First, we create the two tables:

```
CREATE TABLE MASTER (
  ID INTEGER NOT NULL PRIMARY KEY,
  DATA VARCHAR(10));
COMMIT;
CREATE TABLE DETAIL (
  ID INTEGER NOT NULL PRIMARY KEY,
  MASTER_ID INTEGER, /* The foreign key column is deliberately nullable */
  DATA VARCHAR(10),
  TEMP_FK INTEGER,
  CONSTRAINT FK_MASTER FOREIGN KEY(MASTER_ID)
  REFERENCES MASTER
  ON DELETE CASCADE);
COMMIT;
```

When the application posts the rows for the master and detail tables, it will pass the detail rows first, with NULL in the foreign key column and the primary key value of the master in the column TEMP_FK.

Next, we need an exception that can be raised if an attempt is made to violate the mandatory rule and delete the last detail row. We also create a generator for the detail row.

```
CREATE EXCEPTION CANNOT_DEL_DETAIL
  'This is the only detail record: it can not be deleted.';
CREATE GENERATOR GEN_DETAIL;
COMMIT;
```

This trigger tests the detail table after the new master record version has been written. It can "see" the details rows previously posted in the same transaction that have its primary key value (NEW.ID) in the TEMP_FK column. In the case of an update, rather than an insert, it can also identify any rows that it already "owns." Any that meet the TEMP_FK condition get their foreign key filled and TEMP_FK is set to null.

If it finds no rows meeting these conditions, it inserts an "empty" detail row itself.

```
SET TERM ^;
CREATE TRIGGER AI_MASTER FOR MASTER
ACTIVE AFTER INSERT OR UPDATE POSITION 1
AS
BEGIN
  IF (NOT (EXISTS (
    SELECT 1 FROM DETAIL WHERE MASTER_ID = NEW.ID
            OR TEMP_FK = NEW.ID))) THEN
    INSERT INTO DETAIL (MASTER_ID)
    VALUES (NEW.ID);
  ELSE
  IF (NOT (EXISTS (
    SELECT 1 FROM DETAIL WHERE MASTER_ID = NEW.ID))) THEN
    UPDATE DETAIL SET
      MASTER_ID = NEW.ID,
      TEMP_FK = NULL
    WHERE TEMP_FK = NEW.ID;
END ^
```

The detail table gets an automatically generated key:

```
CREATE TRIGGER BI_DETAIL FOR DETAIL
ACTIVE BEFORE INSERT AS
BEGIN
  IF (NEW.ID IS NULL) THEN
    NEW.ID = GEN_ID(GEN_DETAIL, 1);
END ^
```

This BEFORE DELETE trigger for the detail table will ensure that the row cannot be deleted if it is the only one.

```
CREATE TRIGGER BD_DETAIL FOR DETAIL
ACTIVE BEFORE DELETE POSITION 0
AS
BEGIN
  IF (NOT (EXISTS (
    SELECT 1 FROM DETAIL
    WHERE MASTER_ID = OLD.MASTER_ID
    AND ID <> OLD.ID)))
  THEN
    EXCEPTION CANNOT_DEL_DETAIL;
END ^
```

Currently, we have the situation where the mandatory relationship is protected so well that, if an attempt is made to delete the master row, this trigger will cause the cascading delete to fail. We need two more triggers for the master, extending the automatic triggers created by the system for the cascading delete. In the master's BEFORE DELETE, we "null out" the last detail row's foreign key and "stamp" the TEMP_FK column. After the master row's deletion has been written, we go back and delete the detail row.

```
CREATE TRIGGER BD_MASTER FOR MASTER
ACTIVE BEFORE DELETE
AS
BEGIN
  UPDATE DETAIL
    SET MASTER_ID = NULL,
    TEMP_FK = OLD.ID
    WHERE MASTER_ID = OLD.ID;
END ^
/* */
CREATE TRIGGER AD_MASTER FOR MASTER
ACTIVE AFTER DELETE AS
BEGIN
  DELETE FROM DETAIL
  WHERE TEMP_FK = OLD.ID;
END ^
COMMIT ^
SET TERM ;^
```

Let it be stressed that this example is unlikely to fit every requirement for mandatory relationships. There are usually several other factors to consider, in terms of both the business rules requirements and the programming interface. It is rare for trigger logic not to rise to the occasion.

Referential Integrity Support

Formal—or declarative—referential integrity (RI) constraints should be used wherever it is practicable to do so. The checking that occurs when formal referential integrity constraints are in force is all done with triggers, internally. If you want to extend the activity of the RI actions you have defined for a relationship, triggers are the way to do it.

The internal triggers in each phase fire after the custom ones you define yourself. Take care not to write triggers that conflict with what the declarative triggers have been assigned to do. If you find that your desired custom trigger action conflicts with the internal actions, a rethink will be needed of both your declarative RI definition and your custom trigger action.

Implementing RI Without Constraints

Some diehards who have been developing with Firebird and its InterBase cousins for years eschew declarative RI with a passion and use triggers to "roll their own." There is no technical reason, with any Firebird version, to avoid declarative RI if you need RI—it works very well and it doesn't eat much.

However, declarative RI requires a foreign key that, in turn, requires a mandatory index. Firebird does not yet have a way to enforce foreign keys without the mandatory index. There is a situation, common enough to warrant special attention, where the index on a foreign key may be so bad for the performance of queries involving the tables concerned that a formal referential relationship must be avoided. The phenomenon occurs when the design incorporates tables of the sort known as the "lookup" or "system" or "control" table.

The Lookup Table

A lookup or control table is typically a static table with a small row count, which may be used in a similar way in several different contexts. It consists of a small primary key and a description field, calculation factor, or some rule that processes need to refer to. Examples are tax tables, account types, transaction types, reason codes, and so on. It has been distilled out of the normalization process as a system table that is linked to by other tables, often many different ones, by storing the lookup key in the user table. Because *one row* in a lookup table supplies information to *many rows*, a slavish adherence to relational analysis rules often results in foreign keys being bestowed on the lookup key columns of the user tables.

It is a perfectly valid and standard way to use relations—what would we do without it? However, it tends to distribute a small range of possible lookup key values across a large, dynamic user table. Such large tables often carry a number of these lookup keys as foreign keys and with them a number of very unhealthy automatic indexes that cannot be dropped. The phenomenon of few values in a large index can give rise to indexes that become less and less selective as the table grows. Because of the nature of indexing in Firebird, these lookup indexes can kill query performance. For a discussion of the problem, refer to the "Optimization Topic" section at the end of Chapter 18.

The indexes that support foreign keys are mandatory and can be dropped only by dropping the constraint. Yet, by dropping the constraint, you lose the protection of the automatic referential integrity triggers. The way out of this dilemma is to write your own referential integrity triggers.

Special Relationship: Custom RI Handling

This section addresses a particular kind of relationship, system lookups, that is not usually supported by declarative RI. The terms used here reflect the requirements of this case, since a fully customized RI setup is pointless for regular master-detail relationships. Figure 31-1 illustrates the situation. A requestor, which can be any table, has a lookup key that points to a single, uniquely keyed row in a lookup table. The value in the row is provided by the lookup table on request.

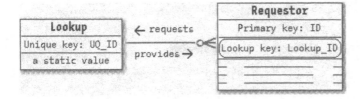

Figure 31-1. Lookup-Requestor relationship

To preserve referential integrity, we want triggers that will provide an eclectic set of safeguards for the users of the lookup table (the requestors), just as declarative RI provides safeguards to protect master-detail dependencies:

- The lookup row must not be deleted if a requestor is using it. For this, we need a BEFORE DELETE trigger on Lookup to check this and, if necessary, raise an exception and stop the action.

- We should make and enforce a rule that requires the Requestor's lookup key to be one that matches a key in Lookup. Our rule may or may not permit the lookup key to be null.

- We may want to make a rule that the static value should never be changed. In a tax table, for example, the same (external) tax code may be associated with different rates and formulas from year to year. Perhaps the chief accountant may be permitted to change a lookup row.

- A BEFORE UPDATE trigger on the Requestor would be required to handle a complex rule such as the one described in the previous point to check dates and possibly other criteria, in order to enforce the rule and pick the correct key.

Implementing the Custom RI

Suppose we have these two tables:

```
CREATE TABLE LOOKUP (
  UQ_ID SMALLINT NOT NULL UNIQUE,
  VALUE1 VARCHAR(30) NOT NULL,
  VALUE2 CHAR(2) NOT NULL,
  START_DATE DATE,
  END_DATE DATE);
COMMIT;
```

```
/* */
CREATE TABLE REQUESTOR (
  ID INTEGER NOT NULL PRIMARY KEY,
  LOOKUP_ID SMALLINT,
  DATA VARCHAR(20)
  TRANSAC_DATE TIMESTAMP NOT NULL);
COMMIT;
```

We'll proceed to set up the existence rules for the two tables. We plan to use exceptions to stop DML events that would violate integrity, so we create them first:

```
CREATE EXCEPTION NO_DELETE
  'Can not delete row required by another table';
CREATE EXCEPTION NOT_VALID_LOOKUP
  'Not a valid lookup key';
CREATE EXCEPTION NO_AUTHORITY
  'You are not authorized to change this data';
COMMIT;
```

The first trigger does the existence check when an attempt is made to delete a lookup row:

```
SET TERM ^;
CREATE TRIGGER BD_LOOKUP FOR LOOKUP
ACTIVE BEFORE DELETE
AS
BEGIN
  IF (EXISTS(
    SELECT LOOKUP_ID FROM REQUESTOR
    WHERE LOOKUP_ID = OLD.UQ_ID)) THEN
    EXCEPTION NO_DELETE;
END ^
```

This one is the other side of the existence enforcement: a lookup key cannot be assigned if it does not exist in the lookup table:

```
CREATE TRIGGER BA_REQUESTOR FOR REQUESTOR
ACTIVE BEFORE INSERT OR UPDATE
AS
BEGIN
  IF (NEW.LOOKUP_ID IS NOT NULL
  AND NOT EXISTS (
    SELECT UQ_ID FROM LOOKUP
    WHERE UQ_ID = NEW.LOOKUP_ID)) THEN
    EXCEPTION NOT_VALID_LOOKUP;
END ^
```

We might now add further triggers to enforce other integrity rules we need. For example, this trigger will restrict any update or delete of the Lookup table to a specific user:

```
CREATE TRIGGER BA_LOOKUP FOR LOOKUP
ACTIVE BEFORE UPDATE OR DELETE
AS
BEGIN
  IF (CURRENT_USER <> 'CHIEFACCT') THEN
    EXCEPTION NO_AUTHORITY;
END ^
```

This trigger will check the input lookup code to make sure that it is the right one for the period of the transaction and correct it if necessary:

```
CREATE TRIGGER BA_REQUESTOR1 FOR REQUESTOR
ACTIVE BEFORE INSERT OR UPDATE POSITION 1
AS
DECLARE VARIABLE LOOKUP_NUM SMALLINT;
DECLARE VARIABLE NEED_CHECK SMALLINT = 0;
BEGIN
  IF (INSERTING AND NEW.LOOKUP_ID IS NOT NULL) THEN
    NEED_CHECK = 1;
  IF (UPDATING) THEN
    IF (
        (OLD.LOOKUP_ID IS NULL
          AND NEW.LOOKUP_ID IS NOT NULL)
        OR (OLD.LOOKUP_ID IS NOT NULL
              AND NEW.LOOKUP_ID <> OLD.LOOKUP_ID)) THEN
      NEED_CHECK = 1;
  IF (NEED_CHECK = 1) THEN
  BEGIN
    SELECT L1.UQ_ID FROM LOOKUP L1
      WHERE L1.START_DATE <= CAST(NEW.TRANSAC_DATE AS DATE)
      AND L1.END_DATE >= CAST(NEW.TRANSAC_DATE AS DATE)
      AND L1.VALUE2 = (SELECT L2.VALUE2 FROM LOOKUP L2
                        WHERE L2.UQ_ID = NEW.LOOKUP_ID)
    INTO :LOOKUP_NUM;
    NEW.LOOKUP_ID = LOOKUP_NUM;
  END
END ^
COMMIT ^
SET TERM ;^
```

Updating Rows in the Same Table

Before considering using a trigger to update other rows in the same table, look carefully at the effect of setting off a cycle of nested activity. If a trigger performs an action that causes it to fire again, or it fires another trigger that performs an action that causes it to fire, an infinite loop results. For this reason, it is important to ensure that a trigger's actions never cause the trigger to launch itself, even indirectly.

If you arrive at a point in your database design at which it is necessary to write a trigger to implement a data dependency between rows in the same table, it is likely to be a sign of poor normalization unless the dependency pertains to a tree structure. If a segment of the row structure affects, or is affected by, a change of state in another row, that segment should be normalized out to a separate table, with foreign keys to enforce the dependency rule.

Self-Referencing Tables and Trees

Self-referencing tables that implement tree structures[4] are a special case. Each row in such a table is a node in a tree and inter-row dependencies are inherent. Any node potentially has two "lives": one as a parent to nodes beneath it, the other as a child to a higher node. Triggers are likely to be required for all DML events, both to modify the behavior of referential integrity constraints and to maintain the metatables (graphs) used by some tree algorithms to make the state of the tree's geometry available to queries. Triggers for trees should always be designed with conditions and branches that protect the structure from infinite loops.

Updating the Same Row

Never try to use an SQL statement to update or delete the same row that the trigger is operating on. The following, for example, is not advisable:

```
CREATE TRIGGER O_SO_SILLY FOR ATABLE
BEFORE UPDATE
AS
BEGIN
  UPDATE ATABLE SET ACQLUMN = NEW.ACOLUMN
  WHERE ID = NEW.ID;
END ^
```

Always use the NEW variables for same-row modifications and never resolve an exception by attempting to delete the row from within the trigger.

---

4. Designing tree structures in a relational database is a science unto itself. While fascinating, it is beyond the scope of this guide. Search the Web for the writings of Joe Celko. He has written a book on the subject: *Joe Celko's Trees and Hierarchies in SQL for Smarties* (Morgan Kaufmann, 2004).

Changing Triggers

Firebird 1.0.*x* offers just one way to change triggers using DDL statements and Firebird 1.5 adds another:

- ALTER TRIGGER changes the definition of an existing trigger module while preserving its dependencies on other objects. It can be used with minimal disturbance to deactivate a trigger.

- CREATE OR ALTER TRIGGER (available from v.1.5 onward) creates the trigger module if it does not exist and works exactly as CREATE TRIGGER does. Otherwise, ALTER rules apply and dependencies are preserved.

Either operation will fail with an exception if any change is attempted that would break a dependency.

Syntax for Changing Triggers

The syntax pattern is

```
{ALTER TRIGGER name} | {CREATE OR ALTER TRIGGER name FOR {table | view}
[ACTIVE | INACTIVE]
[{BEFORE | AFTER} {DELETE | INSERT | UPDATE}]
[POSITION number]
AS <trigger_body>;
```

ALTER TRIGGER

The FOR *name* clause that is used in CREATE TRIGGER is omitted. ALTER TRIGGER cannot be used to change the table with which the trigger is associated.

Changing Only the Header

When you use it to change only a trigger header, ALTER TRIGGER requires at least one altered attribute after the trigger name. Any header attribute omitted from the statement remains unchanged.

The following statement deactivates the trigger SAVE_SALARY_CHANGE:

```
ALTER TRIGGER SAVE_SALARY_CHANGE INACTIVE;
```

If the *phase indicator* (BEFORE or AFTER) is altered, then the *event* (UPDATE, INSERT, or DELETE) must also be specified. For example, the following statement reactivates the trigger VERIFY_FUNDS and specifies that it fire before an update instead of after:

```
ALTER TRIGGER SAVE_SALARY_CHANGE
ACTIVE BEFORE UPDATE;
```

Changing the Body

Any change to the trigger body causes the new body definition to replace the old definition. ALTER TRIGGER need not contain any header information other than the trigger's name.

For example, the following statement modifies the trigger SET_CUST_NO that was created with this definition:

```
CREATE TRIGGER SET_CUST_NO FOR CUSTOMER
  BEFORE INSERT
AS
BEGIN
  IF (NEW.CUST_NO IS NULL) THEN
    NEW.CUST_NO = GEN_ID(CUST_NO_GEN, 1);
END^
```

We will alter the trigger to have it insert a row into a new table, NEW_CUSTOMERS, each time a new row is inserted into the CUSTOMER table:

```
SET TERM ^;
ALTER TRIGGER SET_CUST_NO
BEFORE INSERT AS
BEGIN
  IF (NEW.CUST_NO IS NULL) THEN
    NEW.CUST_NO = GEN_ID(CUST_NO_GEN, 1);
  INSERT INTO NEW_CUSTOMERS(NEW.CUST_NO, CURRENT_DATE)
END ^
SET TERM ;^
```

CREATE OR ALTER TRIGGER

New in v.1.5, this tolerant syntax creates a new trigger if one with the supplied name is not found, or alters an existing trigger of that name. Simply edit the original CREATE definition as required, inserting the keywords OR ALTER.

"Object Is in Use" Error

As with stored procedures, committing the change will throw the notorious error if any user is currently using the procedure or another object that depends on it. In any event, the new version of the trigger will not be immediately available on Superserver if the old version is still in the cache. All users must log out and, when they log in again, they will see the new version.

On Classic server, the new version will be available to the next client that logs in.

Inactive/Active

In v.1.5 and later, performing ALTER TRIGGER … INACTIVE | ACTIVE does not usually invoke the "Object in use" error unless an existing transaction has a table lock. The change will not affect transactions that already have the table in their purview. However, it should be visible to the next transaction that requests a state change on the table.

Dropping Triggers

During database design and application development, a trigger may cease to be useful. To remove a trigger permanently, log in as the owner or SYSDBA and use DROP TRIGGER.

The syntax pattern is

```
DROP TRIGGER name;
```

The trigger *name* must be the name of an existing trigger. The following example drops the trigger SET_CUST_NO:

```
DROP TRIGGER SET_CUST_NO;
```

NOTE   To disable a trigger temporarily, use ALTER TRIGGER *<name>* INACTIVE.

Up Next

The last chapter in this part puts the icing on the cake for the database developer. Firebird has two PSQL features that put it into a class of its own with regard to server-side programming: custom exception handling and events. With exceptions, you have fine-grained control over the trapping and handling of hundreds of internally defined error conditions and any number of your own, custom exceptions. With events, you can implement a callback mechanism to make remote client application nodes aware of one another's committed changes.

Error Handling
and Events

IN THIS CHAPTER, WE EXAMINE HOW THE execution of PSQL modules—both triggers and procedures—can be enhanced to trap errors and handle them within the executing code.

The standard behavior of PSQL modules when an exception occurs is to stop executing, undo all work done since the initial BEGIN statement, jump to the final END statement, and return control to the client, passing one or more error messages. If the module is a trigger, the exception will undo any previously executed triggers and prevent the requested DML changes from being posted.

Types of Exceptions

Three types of exceptions can occur:

- **SQL errors**—that is, SQL messages having a negative SQLCODE.

- **Internal Firebird errors** that have to do with concurrency, data, metadata, and environmental conditions. They have a nine-digit error code, usually beginning with 3355, that uniquely identifies the GDSCODE. Most GDSCODEs fall into generic groups beneath SQLCODEs, and you will usually get both a SQLCODE and a GDSCODE when an exception occurs.

- **Custom exceptions** that you declare as persistent objects in the database and "invoke" in code when a specified condition is detected.

What Is an Exception?

An *exception* is simply a message that is generated when an error occurs.

All of the predefined exceptions—SQLCODE and GDSCODE—have text messages associated with them. The default messages are in English, but they don't have to be. Versions of the messages are available in a few other languages (including pig Latin!), while others are either "works in progress" or "jobs waiting for volunteers."

Firebird has DDL syntax for creating custom exceptions with text messages up to 78 bytes long. In Firebird 1.5, you can extend your custom exceptions at runtime and replace the text, including context-specific details, to the message that goes back across the wire.

Creating an Exception

Creating an exception is one of the simplest pieces of DDL in the lexicon. The syntax is

```
CREATE EXCEPTION exception-name <message>;
```

exception-name is a regular Firebird identifier of 31 characters or less. It must be unique among identifiers for exceptions and, in dialect 3, it can be double quoted and case sensitive.

<message> is a single-quoted string of text in character set NONE. The text is necessarily terse because of the length limit. For example:

```
CREATE EXCEPTION NO_DOGS 'No dogs allowed!';
COMMIT;
```

A CREATE EXCEPTION statement needs to be committed, just as any other DDL statement does.

Altering or Dropping an Exception

As SYSDBA or the owner of an exception that is used in stored procedures, you can alter or drop it at any time. If it is used in a trigger, it can only be altered and then only to change the text message. No dependencies are stored for exceptions used by stored procedures. This makes it a problem if you drop one and forget to replace it—it is embarrassing to have an exception occur because of a missing exception!

To drop our NO_DOGS exception:

```
DROP EXCEPTION NO_DOGS;
```

To alter it:

```
ALTER EXCEPTION NO_DOGS 'No dogs allowed except Irish Wolfhounds!';
```

TIP When constructing schema scripts, group your CREATE EXCEPTION statements together in some position that is easy to find during development for modification and self-documentation. Developers often use short prefixes or a systematic naming scheme to accord various sorts of categories to custom exceptions.

Exceptions in Action

The internally defined exceptions are thrown by the engine in response to corresponding errors that require execution to stop. They cover a very large range of conditions,
including every kind of constraint violation, arithmetic and string overflows, references to missing objects, data corruption, and so on. The SQLCODE and GDSCODE
exceptions are the same ones that are used when errors occur during dynamic SQL
operations. They are listed in Appendix X.

Custom exceptions, which are available only in PSQL modules, do not need to
duplicate the work of the internally defined ones. Define *your* exceptions for use when
you want your code to detect error conditions that break *your* business rules. The three
exception types are depicted in Figure 32-1.

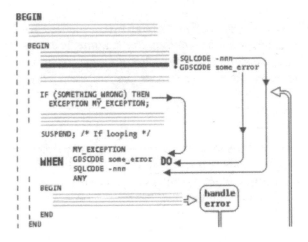

Figure 32-1. Standard PSQL response to exceptions

We encountered an example in Chapter 30 in which a custom exception was used
in a trigger for the purpose of stopping an event, where letting it continue would break
a business rule. In this case, a stored procedure was taking care of tidying up dependencies left in the organizational structure by the departure of an employee. It was
declared like this:

```
CREATE EXCEPTION REASSIGN_SALES
  'Reassign the sales records before deleting this employee.' ^
COMMIT ^
```

At the point where the exception is to be used, the procedure checks whether the
employee appears as the sales rep on any outstanding sales orders. If so, the custom
exception is used to end the procedure. Of course, the exception, if it occurs, causes all
of the other tasks performed by the procedure to be undone.

```
...
BEGIN
  IF (EXISTS(SELECT PO_NUMBER FROM SALES
        WHERE SALES_REP = :emp_num)) THEN
    EXCEPTION reassign_sales;
```

> **NOTE**   In selectable stored procedures, output rows that have already been
> fetched by the client in previous loops through FOR SELECT ... DO ... SUSPEND
> are unaffected and remain available to the client. For the mechanism at work
> here, refer to the upcoming section "The WHEN Statement."

There are cases where it is possible to use the custom exception as a way to intervene,
deal with a problem condition, and let the procedure continue. We can *trap* the exception and write code to *handle* it, right there in the procedure. The next section examines
how this trap-and-fix technique can be used to deal with our *reassign_sales* exception.

Handling Exceptions

PSQL code can trap errors when they occur and hand them on to exception handler
routines. If an exception is handled in your code—you provide a fix or a workaround
for the error and allow execution to continue—then no exception message is returned
to the client. Figure 32-2 illustrates the logic of trapping and handling errors.

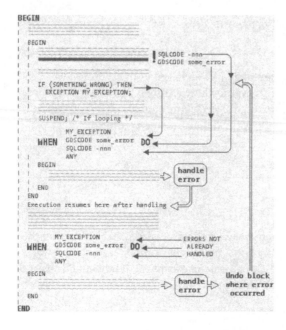

Figure 32-2. Error trapping and handling logic

As before, the exception causes execution in the block to stop. Instead of letting execution pass to the final END statement, now the procedure searches through the layers of nested blocks, starting in the block where the error was detected and backing through the outer blocks, looking for some handler code that "knows" about this exception. It is looking for the first WHEN statement that can handle the error.

The WHEN Statement

A WHEN statement takes the form

```
WHEN <exception> DO <compound-statement>
```

where *<exception>* can be any one of the following:

```
<exception-name> | GDSCODE code | SQLCODE code | ANY
```

<compound-statement> is one statement or a number of ordinary PSQL statements in a BEGIN … END block.

Scope of Exception Types

The paradigm of exception types shown in the syntax pattern represents a scale of scope and granularity.

The custom exception can target any condition you choose, including rules that you may not be able to or choose not to express in constraints. WHEN statements and handler code that target custom exceptions are best placed within the same block where the error would occur.

Next in granularity is the GDSCODE. In v.1.0.*x*, it is a context variable of sorts, insofar as the procedure can read the code returned and compare it with the code specified in the WHEN predicate:

```
WHEN GDSCODE foreign_key DO
BEGIN
  ...
END
```

From v.1.5 on, GDSCODE is a full-blown context variable. As long as you read it inside the block where the exception is raised, you can capture its number code and store it in a log record.

 TIP All GDSCODEs have symbolic constants that are more or less meaningful in English. It is these symbolic constants that you must use in WHEN GDSCODE statements, not the numeric codes. If you look in the header file iberror.h in your /include directory, you will see that the symbolic constant definitions there have the prefix isc_. The prefix must be omitted in WHENGDSCODE statements.

Some errors detected by GDSCODE can be fixed inside the scope of the block where they occur. If so, the WHEN statement for handling the error can be included here; otherwise, it should go into an outer loop and be handled there.

SQLCODE is quite generic and it does not always reflect an error. SQL operations pass SQLCODE 0 for successful completion and SQLCODE 100 for end-of-file. A range of unused "slots" exists between 1 and 99 for warnings and information messages. The SQLERROR range is all sub-zero numbers greater than –1000. These SQLERROR SQLCODEs tend to be high-level groupings of several GDSCODEs.

Like a GDSCODE, a SQLCODE is only program readable in v.1.0.*x* but becomes a context variable in v.1.5 and later. You can capture and log it.

NOTE   You can capture *either* the GDSCODE or the SQLCODE. You will get the code for one and null for the other.

SQLCODEs are less granular and, in many cases, are the least likely to yield a condition that can be fixed inside the module. Look up the codes in Appendix X and notice that a single SQLCODE often groups many GDSCODEs. Usually, they are most useful in the outermost block of the module.

ANY is like "an exception of last resort." It provides a hook for any internally defined exception that has not otherwise been handled. In v.1.5, with the ability to read the GDSCODE or the SQLCODE (provided they are in scope), ANY has better potential to provide a default handler than it does in lower versions.

Placement of WHEN Blocks

Always place your WHEN blocks immediately preceding the END statement that will close the block where you want the exception handled. Do not place any other statements—not even SUSPEND or EXIT—between the end of your handlers and the closing END statement. Refer back to Figure 32-2 for a depiction of this flow.

TIP   If you want to use an EXIT statement immediately before the final END statement of your module, for documentation purposes, that's fine. At that point, EXIT cannot affect execution flow.

When a procedure encounters an error in the cursor loop of a *selectable procedure*, the statements since the last are undone back to the previous SUSPEND. Any rows already output from previous calls to SUSPEND are unaffected and remain available to the client.

SUSPEND should *not* be used in executable procedures. Let your execution logic determine when blocks end and when errors should be thrown back as exceptions.

Nested Exceptions As Savepoints

The nested architecture of PSQL module execution blocks means, of course, that PSQL supports "nested" transactions. Every PSQL module's activity is under the control of the transaction context from which it was invoked. The standard execution flow ensures that the work either completes as a whole or fails as a whole. In the case of stored procedures, an exception causes the entire invocation instance to fail. In the case of triggers, an exception causes the DML and all related events already performed to fail.

Handling exceptions provides the means to partition the execution into stages that can be undone back to specified points without necessarily discarding the entire task of the module. The level of "undoing" is determined by the point at which the error occurs and the proximity of the WHEN handler clause to the error point. The "savepoint"— equivalent to a named savepoint in a client-controlled transaction—is the start of the code block in which the WHEN handler code executes.

Handling the reassign_sales Exception

Now, back to our DELETE_EMPLOYEE procedure. In Chapter 30, when the procedure bumped into a case where the departing employee had orders on file, it threw the custom exception *reassign_sales* and simply stopped, undid its work, and sent the exception message back for a human to deal with.

However, we can have the procedure handle it and allow the procedure to complete. For example, the handler could null out the SALES_REP key and send a message to another procedure that creates a log table record of each affected sales record.

We begin by creating the log table:

```
SET  TERM ^;
CREATE TABLE EMPLOYEE_LOG (
  EMP_NO SMALLINT,
  TABLE_AFFECTED CHAR(31),
  FIELD_AFFECTED CHAR(31),
  FIELD_VALUE VARCHAR(20),
  USER_NAME VARCHAR(31),
  DATESTAMP TIMESTAMP) ^
COMMIT ^
```

Next, we need to create the procedure that will take care of the logging. It is quite generic, since we'll assume that the same logging procedure might be wanted for other tasks in this system:

```
CREATE PROCEDURE LOG_ACTION (
  EMP_NO SMALLINT,
  TABLE_AFFECTED CHAR(31),
```

```
  FIELD_AFFECTED CHAR(31),
  FIELD_VALUE VARCHAR(20))
AS
BEGIN
  INSERT INTO EMPLOYEE_LOG
  VALUES (:EMP_NO, :TABLE_AFFECTED, :FIELD_AFFECTED,
          :FIELD_VALUE, CURRENT_USER, CURRENT_TIMESTAMP);
END ^
```

The last thing left to do is to add the exception-handling code to our DELETE_EMPLOYEE procedure:

```
RECREATE PROCEDURE DELETE_EMPLOYEE (
  :emp_num INTEGER)
AS
  DECLARE VARIABLE PO_NUMBER CHAR(8);
BEGIN
  IF (EXISTS(SELECT PO_NUMBER FROM SALES
      WHERE SALES_REP = :emp_num)) THEN
    EXCEPTION reassign_sales;
```

At this point, if the exception occurs, the following statements are bypassed and execution jumps to the first WHEN statement that can handle the exception.

```
  UPDATE department ...
    SET ...
  ...
  ...
DELETE FROM employee
    WHERE emp_no = :emp_num;
```

Here is the handler block. First, it loops through the SALES table and sets the SALES_REP to null on all records in which our departed employee's code appears. On each iteration of the loop, it calls the logging procedure, passing the employee's code along with the details of the affected Sales record:

```
WHEN EXCEPTION REASSIGN_SALES DO
BEGIN
  FOR SELECT PO_NUMBER FROM SALES
    WHERE SALES_REP = :emp_num
    INTO :PO_NUMBER
    AS CURSOR C
  DO
  BEGIN
    UPDATE SALES SET SALES_REP = NULL
      WHERE CURRENT OF C;
    EXECUTE PROCEDURE LOG_ACTION (
        :emp_num, 'SALES', 'PO_NUMBER', :PO_NUMBER);
  END
```

After the loop is finished, the main procedure calls itself once more, to complete the processing that was skipped previously because of the exception:

```
    EXECUTE PROCEDURE DELETE_EMPLOYEE1 (:emp_num);
  END
END^
COMMIT ^
```

Error Logs

If it is important to keep an error log, keep in mind that exceptions eventually raised to the client cause all of the work done in the module to be undone. If you are logging to a database table, the log records disappear along with the other undone work. For conditions where handlers fix or "swallow" every error, an internal log table will work just fine.

If you need a log that will survive an unhandled exception, use an external table. For details, refer to the section "Using External Files As Tables" in Chapter 16.

TIP There is a technique in a procedure at the end of this chapter that inserts rows to an external table, although it is not an error log table.

SQLCODE and GDSCODE

In v.1.5 and higher, you can trap the numeric error code that is passed to an internally defined exception in the context variable SQLCODE or GDSCODE. This provides a very compact way to log the current exception as part of your exception-handling routine.

Internally defined exceptions have both a SQLCODE and a GDSCODE. Your code can access one; the other will be unavailable.

NOTE Anytime you try to access either of these codes outside the handler block, it will return zero.

The following code block framework ends with a series of exception handlers. The first two handle SQLCODE errors by handing them on to custom exceptions. These custom exceptions may be handled in an outer block, or their purpose may be to abort the procedure and return a useful message to the client.

If neither of the targeted exceptions occurs but some other, unpredicted exception does, the WHEN ANY statement picks it up. Its handler calls a stored procedure to write a log record, passing the SQLCODE, along with others taken from the context of the block, as input:

```
BEGIN
...
  WHEN SQLCODE -802 DO
    EXCEPTION E_EXCEPTION_1;
  WHEN SQLCODE -803 DO
    EXCEPTION E_EXCEPTION_2;
  WHEN ANY DO
    EXECUTE PROCEDURE P_ANY_EXCEPTION(SQLCODE, other inputs...);
END
```

Re-raising an Exception

Suppose you want to trap and log an unpredicted error to an external log table before allowing the exception to take its course and terminate the procedure or trigger. From v.1.5, you can *re-raise* an exception, meaning you can provide some handling for an exception and finish the handler with a bare EXCEPTION statement to raise it to the final END statement. Execution stops and control passes back to the client, with the exception code or name and the applicable message in the error status array.

In your handler, you pick up the GDSCODE or SQLCODE and some other context variables, write the log record, and then re-raise the exception:

```
BEGIN
...
  WHEN ANY DO
  BEGIN
    EXECUTE PROCEDURE P_ANY_EXCEPTION(SQLCODE, other inputs...);
    EXCEPTION;
  END
END ^
```

Exceptions in Triggers

Custom exceptions in triggers have the power to enforce business rules. The example Employee database has a rule that customers who have had their credit stopped are flagged by column ON_HOLD, which is constrained to be either NULL or '*'. When a SALES record is inserted or an existing, unshipped one is updated for such a customer, the order is to be refused if the ON_HOLD flag is not null. Another rule says that an order that has already been shipped cannot be changed.

When inserting or updating sales order records, we can write BEFORE triggers that raise exceptions if the rules are violated and block the operation.

For either Firebird version, we can write two triggers to enforce these rules: a BEFORE INSERT and a BEFORE UPDATE.

We create exceptions for two conditions:

```
CREATE EXECPTION E_CANT_ACCEPT
  'Operation refused. REASON: Customer is on hold.' ^
CREATE EXCEPTION E_CANT_EXTEND
  'Operation refused. REASON: Order already shipped.' ^
COMMIT ^
```

These are the v.1.0.*x* triggers:

```
CREATE TRIGGER BI_SALES0 FOR SALES
ACTIVE BEFORE INSERT POSITION 0 AS
BEGIN
  IF (EXISTS (SELECT 1 FROM CUSTOMER
          WHERE CUST_NO = NEW.CUST_NO
          AND ON_HOLD IS NOT NULL)) THEN
    EXCEPTION E_CANT_ACCEPT;
END ^
/* */
CREATE TRIGGER BU_SALES0 FOR SALES
ACTIVE BEFORE UPDATE POSITION 0 AS
BEGIN
  IF (OLD.ORDER_STATUS = 'shipped') THEN
    EXCEPTION E_CANT_EXTEND;
  ELSE
    IF (EXISTS (SELECT 1 FROM CUSTOMER
          WHERE CUST_NO = NEW.CUST_NO
          AND ON_HOLD IS NOT NULL)) THEN
      EXCEPTION E_CANT_ACCEPT;
END ^
```

Runtime Exception Messaging

Some v.1.5 enhancements to exception message handling provide more options for writing exception handlers. The static exception message, defined by CREATE EXCEPTION, can be replaced with a runtime string to provide a much better context for the user to identify problem data.

In the next example, we use the v.1.5 capabilities to enforce the same rules as the two triggers in the previous example. This time, we roll the rules into a single trigger and use runtime message extensions.

This is the exception:

```
CREATE EXCEPTION E_REFUSE_ORDER 'Operation refused. ' ^
```

This is the trigger:

```
CREATE TRIGGER BA_SALESO FOR SALES
ACTIVE BEFORE INSERT OR UPDATE POSITION O AS
  DECLARE VARIABLE ORDER_STATE SMALLINT = 0;
BEGIN
  IF (UPDATING AND OLD.ORDER_STATUS = 'shipped') THEN
    ORDER_STATE = 1;
  IF (
       (EXISTS (SELECT ON_HOLD FROM CUSTOMER
           WHERE CUST_NO = NEW.CUST_NO
           AND ON_HOLD IS NOT NULL)
         AND (INSERTING OR ORDER_STATE = 0)) THEN
    ORDER_STATE = 2;
  IF (ORDER_STATE = 1) THEN
    EXCEPTION E_REFUSE_ORDER 'Order ' || NEW.PO_NUMBER || ' already shipped.';
  ELSE
  IF (ORDER_STATE = 2) THEN
    EXCEPTION E_REFUSE_ORDER
    'Order '|| NEW.PO_NUMBER ||'. Customer ' || NEW.CUST_NO || ' is on hold.';
END ^
```

In the error status array, the client will receive the name of the exception, along with the runtime message.

Error Codes Listing

Appendix X lists the internally defined exceptions, including SQLCODEs, GDSCODEs, the symbols for the GDSCODEs, and the English-language messages current at the release of Firebird 1.5.0.

When a Firebird binary is built, the English-language messages are extracted from an internal database. The SQLCODEs are stored, but the GDSCODEs are calculated on the fly. The file firebird.msg, in your Firebird root directory, is built as a binary tree that the client and the server refer to when the server is running.

Rolling Your Own Error Code List

For the curious, a **gbak** version of the database (named msg.gbak) can be easily downloaded from the Firebird CVS browser. Go to http://sourceforge.net/projects/firebird and follow the "CVS Browser" links until you get to the branch named ./firebird/firebird2/src/msgs/. At the bottom of the display, click the drop-down list box to find the branch you are interested in. You can download the file from there.

The following stored procedure generated the list in Appendix X. It outputs the list to an external table, but you can modify the procedure to suit yourself.

```
SET TERM ^;
/* The output file */
CREATE TABLE ERRORCODES
  EXTERNAL FILE
  'C:\Program Files\Firebird\Firebird_1_5\MyData\2794app10.txt'
  (ListItem CHAR(169))^
COMMIT ^
/* If needed, uncomment the section below and declare the ASCII_CHAR() function
   to get us a carriage return and line feed */
/* DECLARE EXTERNAL FUNCTION ascii_char
   INTEGER
   RETURNS CSTRING(1) FREE_IT
   ENTRY_POINT 'IB_UDF_ascii_char' MODULE_NAME 'ib_udf'^
COMMIT ^
*/
/* Finally, the SP that created the textfile that became Appendix X */
CREATE PROCEDURE OUTPUT_ERRCODES
AS
DECLARE VARIABLE SQC SMALLINT;
DECLARE VARIABLE NUM SMALLINT;
DECLARE VARIABLE FAC SMALLINT;
DECLARE VARIABLE SYM VARCHAR(32);
DECLARE VARIABLE TXT VARCHAR(118);
DECLARE VARIABLE GDC CHAR(9) CHARACTER SET OCTETS;
DECLARE VARIABLE BASEO INTEGER = 335544320;
DECLARE VARIABLE CALCNUM INTEGER;
DECLARE VARIABLE EOL CHAR(2);
BEGIN
  EOL = ASCII_CHAR(13)||ASCII_CHAR(10); /* end-of-line sequence */
  FOR SELECT
    S.SQL_CODE,
    S.NUMBER,
    S.FAC_CODE,
    S.GDS_SYMBOL,
    M.TEXT
    FROM SYSTEM_ERRORS S
      JOIN MESSAGES M
      ON
        M.FAC_CODE = S.FAC_CODE
        AND M.NUMBER = S.NUMBER
        AND M.SYMBOL = S.GDS_SYMBOL
    /* Eliminate some unwanted/unused codes */
      WHERE M.TEXT NOT CONTAINING 'journal'
        AND M.TEXT NOT CONTAINING 'dump'
        AND s.GDS_SYMBOL NOT CONTAINING 'license'
        AND S.GDS_SYMBOL NOT CONTAINING 'wal_'
        AND S.GDS_SYMBOL IS NOT NULL
        AND S.SQL_CODE < 102
      ORDER BY 1 DESC, 2
```

677

```
    INTO :SQC, :NUM, :FAC, :SYM, :TXT
DO
BEGIN
/* The message texts are all in lower case, so we do a little
   jiggery-pokery to uppercase the first letter. */
  IF (TXT IS NULL) THEN
    TXT = '{Message unknown}';
  ELSE
    TXT = UPPER(SUBSTRING(TXT FROM 1 FOR 1))||
      SUBSTRING(TXT FROM 2);

/* Having worked out how the facility code (FAC_CODE) and NUMBER values are
   used to generate the GDSCODE numbers, it's very straightforward to serve
   them freshly-cooked from the latest SYSTEM_ERRORS and MESSAGES tables */
  IF (FAC IS NOT NULL AND NUM IS NOT NULL) THEN
  /*  We don't want any half-cooked errcodes! */
  BEGIN
    CALCNUM = BASE0 + (FAC * 65535);
    CALCNUM = CALCNUM + NUM + FAC;
    GDC = CAST(CALCNUM AS CHAR(9));
    INSERT INTO ERRORCODES
    VALUES(
    /* all vars go into a single string */
    :SQC||'|'||:GDC||'|'||:SYM||'|'||:TXT||:EOL) ;
  END
 END
END ^
COMMIT ^
EXECUTE PROCEDURE OUTPUT_ERRCODES ^
COMMIT ^
SET TERM ;^
/* The text file is now ready to go to the word processor for a little tidying,
   to get rid of all the white space created by the right-padding on the output
   string.  A quick search and replace replaced all the '|' separators with
   ASCII 9 (tab) because that was the formatting required by the pre-press
   people for the tabulating.
   ASCII_CHAR(9) could have been called in the SP but it seemed more useful to
   avoid confusing tabs with all the unwanted white space at editing time.
*/
```

Events

Firebird events provide a signaling mechanism by which stored procedures and triggers can pass an alert to client applications when other applications commit changes to data. The client applications are set up to "listen" for specific events through a server-to-client interface, avoiding the system cost of polling for changes.

Client subsystems that poll the server for news of database state changes are not rare in the world of relational database subsystems. However, Firebird's event notification model does not expend network or CPU resources on polling or timers. It is a subsystem of the server that is maintained on and by the server. A client "registers interest" in an event and, when it is ready, it signals that it is waiting for notification.

When a transaction commits, notifications of any events that occurred are posted to those listening client applications that are waiting. The client application can then respond to the event in some manner.

Uses for Events Notification

The Firebird events notification provisions can meet numerous application requirements that call for the means to respond rapidly to changes in database state performed by others using the system. The techniques can be used in combination with external telecoms, process control, scheduling, and messaging technologies to automate time-critical and state-critical response flows.

The possibilities are limitless in terms of scope and application. Some examples are

- Background data replication services are prompted to expect a new item.

- A ticketing application uses the scheme as a signal to refresh open datasets in other booking offices whenever a seat allocation or a timetable change happens.

- An inventory application flashes a "stock out" message to the purchasing department when an inventory item goes under its minimum stocking level.

- Retail chains are notified when a new price list is loaded.

- A monitoring device on processing machinery signals the store when the levels of materials are running low.

Elements of the Mechanism

The originators of events are database state-changing operations—successful INSERTs, UPDATEs, and DELETEs. Event signaling happens in triggers and stored procedures through the medium of the PSQL statement POST_EVENT.

POST_EVENT is but one piece of the mechanism—in isolation, it does nothing. It is merely a call sign that applications listen for. It transports no information about the database event it signals; it is up to the application to provide its own context for each event on the basis of its call sign.

The event mechanism itself consists of several interacting server-side and application pieces.

Server-Side Elements

The server-side elements are

- One or more triggers or stored procedures that invoke POST_EVENT statements

- An internal event table—the destination of the POST_EVENT calls—that maintains a list of events posted to it by procedures and triggers, for the duration of the transactions in which the events occur

- An internal event manager subsystem that maintains a list of listeners and waiters, and acts as "traffic cop" to marshal and match up events with listeners

Application Elements

On the application side, the mechanism needs

- An application that is capable of registering an interest in events

- Other applications that actually perform the DML operations that the listening application is interested in

Of course, the listening application also needs its own mechanism for responding to events.

Interface Elements

Events transport from server to client uses a different pair of ports than that used for the main client/server channel (usually port 3050). The server and the client library find a random pair of ports to use for event traffic.

The software element is a routine in the client layer known as an *event callback function*. It is client-based code that is called by the server to inform the client of events as soon as the transaction that posted an awaited event has committed. For embedded applications, the pre-compiler, **gpre**, generates the code for this callback function. For dynamic applications that want to listen *synchronously* (refer to the next section), as ESQL applications do, the callback function lives in the client library. Dynamic applications can—and usually do—listen *asynchronously* (see the sections "Asynchronous Signaling" and "Asynchronous Listening"). For this, they need to supply a custom callback function known as an *asynchronous trap* (AST).

TIP   If your firewall strategy disallows random port selection by applications, Firebird versions 1.5 onward allow this *auxiliary port* to be specifically configured—use the firebird.conf parameter RemoteAuxPort.

Synchronous Listening

Figure 32-3 illustrates the bare-bones event model that is implemented in the ESQL language for embedded applications with the EVENT INIT and EVENT WAIT statements. Dynamic SQL has no equivalent SQL statements. For dynamic SQL applications, the same synchronous event model is implemented in the API through the *isc_wait_for_event( )* function.

An ESQL application uses EVENT INIT to signal that it is listening for an event and EVENT WAIT to await the notification. It listens for notifications through an auxiliary port-to-port channel on the network, using the main connection channel's database handle. Once EVENT WAIT is called, execution of the client application is suspended until the event notification arrives.

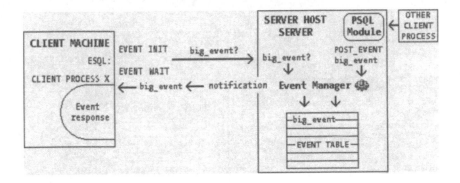

Figure 32-3. Synchronous signaling

A client out in the network posts an update to a row in MYTABLE. It is received by the server and executed. During the AFTER UPDATE phase, a trigger posts an event named *big_event*, to notify the event manager that it has completed the update

The event manager adds the event to its list of events. At this point, the update is uncommitted and the event manager does nothing further. In its list of listeners, it sees that process X is listening for that event. Process X will now wait until one or more events named *big_event* are committed.

On the COMMIT, the event manager sends process X, and any other listeners waiting for *big_event*, a notification that *big_event* happened. Even if the transaction caused *big_event* to be posted many times, the waiting client gets a single notification.

If no processes have registered an interest in *big_event*, the event manager simply ignores the POST_EVENT call. Any processes currently signaling EVENT WAIT for *big_event* receive the notification immediately. If any processes have registered an interest in *big_event*, but are not waiting, the event manager retains the event until they either signal wait or cancel their interest. Once the interested applications have lost interest, *big_event* will be erased from the table.

An application can wait on up to 15 events per EVENT INIT request. It can spread events over multiple EVENT INIT requests, but, with synchronous events, it can wait on the handle of only one EVENT INIT request at a time.

Asynchronous Signaling

Synchronous signaling has its limitations. In particular, it requires the application to wait an indefinite time to get notification. This limiting model was extended to support *asynchronous signaling.*

Under this model, an application process still registers interest and waits and listens, but it is able to continue its own execution and make database requests while awaiting the notifications. The application has its own, client-side event queue to manage. Figure 32-4 depicts the elements of the setup for asynchronous listening.

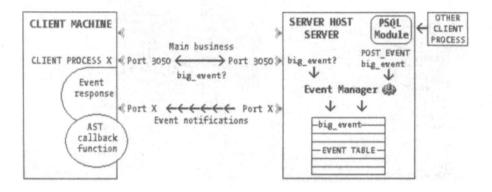

Figure 32-4. Asynchronous events mechanism

A stock-brokering application, for example, requires constant access to the Stocks database to provide brokers with real-time information as prices fluctuate, but it also needs to watch particular stocks continuously and trigger off the appropriate Buy or Sell procedure when certain events occur.

DSQL applications use API calls to implement events listening, both synchronous and asynchronous. There is no language equivalent in DSQL, and setting up the application interface from raw ingredients is rather complex.

An application registers interest in events by way of an *events parameter buffer* (EPB) that is populated by a call to the *isc_event_block( )* function. One EPB can register up to 15 events, specifying different EPBs and *event_ list buffers* for each call. The named events need to match (case sensitively) the events that will be posted. Applications that need to respond to more than 15 events can make multiple calls to *isc_event_block( )*.

Synchronous Listening via the API

Setting up synchronous listening through the API is similar to what is needed for asynchronous signaling, except that it calls the *isc_wait_for_event( )* function rather than *isc_que_events( )*. As with the ESQL equivalent, EVENT WAIT, program execution is suspended during the wait. The *isc_wait_for_event( )* function listens for the wake-up notification that will occur when the server "pings" the callback function.

Asynchronous Listening

Before you can use the API continuous-signaling function *isc_que_events( )*, you need a callback function at the client, for the server to call when an event is posted. The term for this kind of function is an *asynchronous trap*, or AST.

The AST Function

The AST function has to provide some form of global flag to notify the application when the server has called it. It has to process the server's event list into buffers that the application can access for its own management of the event queue. It must take three arguments:

- A copy of the list of posted events

- The length of the *events_list* buffer

- A pointer to the *events_list* buffer

The *InterBase API Guide*[1] has guidelines for writing an AST function.

The *isc_event_block( )* function accepts into its *isc_callback* parameter a pointer to the AST function and, into its *event_function_arg* parameter, a pointer to the first argument of the AST. This argument generally accepts event counts as they change.

When the application calls the function *isc_que_events( )* to signal events that it wants to wait for, it passes a pointer to the AST callback function, along with a list. A single call to *isc_que_events( )* can manage up to 15 events. The application calls the *isc_event_counts( )* function to determine which event occurred.

Multiple *isc_que_events( )* calls can be operating simultaneously in a single client/server process. Applications switch off waiting with calls to *isc_cancel_events( )*.

 NOTE   The event block setup details for synchronous listening via *isc_event_wait( )* are similar. Events are not continuous, as they are with the asynchronous *isc_que_events( )* technique. Synchronous signaling does not require an external AST function.

---

1. See APIGuide.pdf, from the InterBase 6 documentation set published by Borland Software Inc.

Component Interfaces

Fortunately for nearly all of us, the pieces for implementing events in client applications have been encapsulated in classes and components for most of the application development tools that support Firebird. Comprising the AST, the encapsulated API *isc_event** function calls and event parameter blocks and the client-side management of the event buffers, they are usually referred to as *event alerters*. The term is somewhat confusing in list forums and literature, since the triggers and stored procedures that post the POST_EVENT calls are also often referred to generically as "event alerters."

Using POST_EVENT

To use an event alerter in a stored procedure or trigger, use the following syntax pattern:

```
POST_EVENT <event-name>;
```

The parameter, *event_name*, can be either a quoted literal or a string variable. It is case sensitive and it can begin with a numeral. Event names are restricted to 64 characters.

When the procedure is executed, this statement notifies the event manager, which stores the alert in the event table. On commit, the event manager alerts applications waiting for the named event. For example, the following statement posts an event named new_order:

```
POST_EVENT 'new_order';
```

Alternatively, using a *variable* for the event name allows a statement to post different events, according to the current value of the string variable (e.g., *event_name*).

```
POST_EVENT event_name;
```

NOTE Although POST_EVENT is an SQL statement, the event name argument should not be prefixed by a colon.

A trigger or stored procedure that posts an event is sometimes called an event alerter.[2] The following script creates a trigger that posts an event to the event manager whenever any application inserts data in a table:

---

2. Not to be confused with *event alerter components*, which are encapsulations of the client side of the event mechanism.

```
SET TERM ^;
CREATE TRIGGER POST_NEW_ORDER FOR SALES
ACTIVE AFTER INSERT POSITION 0
AS
BEGIN
  POST_EVENT 'new_order';
END ^
SET TERM ; ^
```

Trigger or Procedure?

POST_EVENT is available to both triggers and stored procedures, so how do you decide which is the better place to post events?

The rule of thumb is to use *triggers* when applications need know about row-level events—either single row or multiple row, depending on the scope of the transactions— and *procedures* to signal those events whose impact on applications is broader.

This is only a guideline—often, procedures have row-level scope and yet the interested client wants to know about a particular operation when it happens to be performed by that procedure. A POST_EVENT from a trigger in this case would be unable to tell the listener anything about the context of the event, and the designer might wish to use the procedure-based event call-sign to ascertain which kind of caller was responsible for the work. Alternatively, the designer might wish to place the event in a trigger to ensure that a particular DML action is consistently signaled, regardless of the context in which it is executed.

Up Next

Next, we move focus to security in your networked database management environment. In this part, we look at the risks and safeguards associated with running your Firebird database servers. To begin, the next chapter discusses some of the vulnerabilities in the operating environment and measures you can take to address them.

Part Eight

Security

CHAPTER 33

Security in the Operating Environment

FIREBIRD HAS NO FACILITY TO ENCRYPT AND decrypt data (other than user passwords) that pass through its client interface. It does provide certain restrictions on the use of Firebird tools that access databases but, ultimately, at the software level alone, no system is safe from a raider who is determined to access your databases without authority.

This chapter highlights some areas where you need to take precautions with your Firebird server and client environments. It is in no sense a blueprint for solving all of the environmental security issues that might affect your server and your network. In short, if security is a serious concern for your deployments, then treat it seriously. Research it, recognize potential risk areas, and be prepared to consult specialists.

Chapters 34 and 35 examine Firebird's provisions for maintaining access control at the levels of the Firebird server and databases, respectively. Chapter 36 includes details for configuring Firebird servers to reduce exposure to some environmental security risks.

Physical Security

Keep servers and sensitive or critical client machines behind well-locked doors. If you have FAT32 partitions on servers or workstations, anyone logging into the machine locally can access anything on them. If possible, lock resources such as CD-ROM, floppy, and Zip drives, and disable ports that can accept bootable devices or set boot options in the BIOS to prevent boot-ups from removable media. Password-protect the BIOS to prevent unauthorized changes to boot options. Password-protect all servers and workstations.

The overriding factor in physical security is to protect these security-sensitive machines from any physical contact by unauthorized hands. All else is to no avail if someone can get to the machine and steal it, or if someone can open the door of the rack room and steal the hard drives attached to the server.

Use Securable Filesystems

Remote database users (client applications) do not need filesystem permissions on databases. However, they do need the appropriate permissions for using external applications to write to and read from external data files that are linked to tables.

You can combine operating system permissions and the server's ExternalFileAccess configuration to limit the risk exposure.

Users of embedded applications, including a local (Classic) connection on POSIX, do need rights to paths, the database file, and other files, such as lock files, logs, external tables, and so on. The same applies to any user account that runs a Firebird server as an application.

Protect the Firebird tree and other directories that are accessed by Firebird using the maximum possible restrictions supported by your operating system and your chosen filesystem.

Don't store Firebird software files, databases, scripts, backups, or externally accessed data files on FAT32 partitions. On Windows, don't allow shares to these partitions to ordinary users. Share permissions to NTFS partitions housing Firebird-related files and executables should be as limited as possible. Additionally, the most restrictive possible object permissions should be in force.

Use group accounts in preference to individual accounts. Avoid multi-group membership where possible.

Protect Backups

Back up regularly, and compress backups to transportable media and store them securely off-site.

Don't leave backup files and database archives lying around the network where network cruisers can find them. A stolen copy of a **gbak** file can be restored with full visibility on any other Firebird server. That means that if you let me steal a copy of your database or you let me get your **gbak** file, I can restore it on my server. Because I am SYSDBA, I can open it and see everything.

Some False Assumptions

A couple of false assumptions have been known to gull DBAs into being careless about protecting database or backup files:

- **A file copy is bound to be corrupt, so it is no use to an intruder**. Do not assume that a file copy of a running database will be corrupt and unusable. An illicit copy may well prove to be usable, especially if update activity on the database is relatively infrequent, or if the attacker can try copying repeatedly.

- **gbak files are not databases so they are no use to an intruder**. Anybody can re-create your database from a copy of your **gbak** file.

Platform-Based Protection

The degree of platform-based protection you are able to apply to your database server installation depends on two general factors: how well the operating system platform and its filesystem can protect your system (software as well as data) and how secure your system has to be. The second may well be prescriptive for choosing the first.

Unless you have overpowering reasons to do otherwise, you should run the Firebird server as a service.

If possible, use a special user account to start the Firebird service. In Firebird 1.5, this is implemented by default on Linux and some other POSIX builds. On Windows, and for Firebird 1.0.*x*, it will be necessary to set it up yourself.

Restrict Operating System Logins

Require passwords for all logins and disable login caching on Windows servers and workstations. On networks, disable the ability for users and groups to change their own login settings. Require strong passwords. Enforce account lockout on all servers and workstations that connect to databases.

Enforce the use of ordinary accounts for normal work. Restrict root or Administrator logins to administrative sessions. Eliminate "guest," "world," and "everyone" accounts.

Monitor failed logins, failures to log out, failed file and program object accesses, failed user privileges, unusual shutdowns, and boot-ups.

POSIX

Linux, UNIX, and other POSIX-compliant platforms are preferable to Windows when security is a major concern. The technologies for securing these platforms are mature and widely understood by implementers. Filesystem security and trusted access are inherent in design requirements that are determined by public standards. That is not to imply that merely installing a database server on a POSIX-conformant platform is a guarantee of security. It says that the elements needed for setting up secure systems that are reliably secure are present and capable of being implemented.

Microsoft Windows Platforms

Windows server installations are so infamously hard to secure that intense security requirements may simply rule out Windows altogether as a deployment platform for database servers where on-site security expertise and monitoring are not available.

In a lab presentation entitled "Hardening Windows 2000,"[1] network security guru Philip Cox of SystemExperts Corporation begins by outlining "Four Steps to Practical Win2K Security" as follows:

1.   Locate Windows system.

2.   Insert *nix CD.

---

1.   See http://security.ucdavis.edu/HardenWin2Klab.pdf.

3. Reboot.

4. Follow installation prompts.

Yes, they were words spoken in jest, accompanied by the obligatory "smiley." Cox's paper provides a seriously useful outline for system administrators for whom running Windows servers is the only option. He is the primary author of an authoritative and engagingly frank book about Windows server security titled *Windows 2000 Security Handbook*.[2] Microsoft itself publishes a number of free white papers with detailed, practical instructions for implementing security on its server platforms and keeping abreast of its frequent security patches. The website http://activewin.com is a useful source for coherent descriptions of the many security patches that have been released and continue to be released for various Windows versions.

Windows NT/2000 and XP

On Windows NT/2000 or XP systems, services are available to remote clients even when no user is logged in at the server—the correct condition in which to leave an unattended server.

When running as a service, Firebird, like most Windows services, runs under the *localsystem* account. *Localsystem* is a built-in account that, on NT 4 and lower server versions, had few powers. On later Windows server platforms, *localsystem* was vested with an extraordinary level of access privileges for local system resources, including privileges that cannot be granted even to members of the Administrators group.

By contrast, applications are run from regular user accounts and require the user to be logged into the server host. Any standard Windows user can start the Firebird server as an application.

File Protection

On Windows, restricting the directory (folder) locations where database files and server artifacts live and protecting access to them are strongly recommended. Implement both object and share permissions on every file that network users can potentially reach. To be capable of protection, the directories and files must be on NTFS partitions, in trees dedicated to the purpose, and made readable only by a suitably privileged account or group.

When read access is thus restricted, remote clients must connect to the server through the TCP/IP protocol, not through Windows Networking (often referred to as *NetBEUI*).

Additionally, from Firebird 1.5 onward, you can (and should) restrict the locations from which the *server* may read database files, by configuring the *DatabaseAccess* parameter in firebird.conf.

---

2. *Windows 2000 Security Handbook* (Osborne-McGraw Hill, 2000) was written by Philip Cox and Tom Sheldon. For Philip Cox's bio, see http://www.systemexperts.com/bios.html.

Windows 95/98 and ME

When security is an issue, Windows 95/98 and ME systems should not be considered for use as Firebird hosts. They lack support for either services or file-level security. Anyone with access to the filesystem can readily make a duplicate copy of the database with a file-copying or archiving command, or simply use the GUI features (drag and drop, copy and paste, etc.) to steal a Firebird database.

The Firebird 1.5 feature to configure the *DatabaseAccess* restriction in firebird.conf (see Chapter 36) is available to these "non-server" platforms. At least it will restrict the directory locations from which the server is allowed to read database files. However, the FAT32 filesystem is open to the world and offers no protection from accidental or malicious overwriting of databases, external function code, or other Firebird-related files.

Execution of Arbitrary Code

On a poorly protected system, all current Firebird versions provide the opportunity for arbitrary code to be executed, through the medium of external function libraries, BLOB filters, and custom character set implementations. These external code modules run in the same address space as the server process and with the same privileges.

Accordingly, it is important to protect the server from the possibility of accessing external files and modules that have been written by unauthorized users.

Firebird 1.0.x

In Firebird 1.0.*x*, you can configure specific directories to store external code modules and externally mapped data files and apply operating system–level restrictions to prevent unauthorized access. It is strongly recommended that you make use of this capability on filesystems that are capable of supporting it with filesystem access permissions.

However, a Firebird 1.0.*x* server can access external code and data anywhere on the filesystem that is under the host machine's control.

Firebird 1.5

From v.1.5 onward, the locations of external executables and other external objects can be tightly configured to ensure that the server will throw exceptions if it gets a request to access external objects in the wrong places. For details about these configurations, refer to the notes about external objects at the end of Chapter 36.

Special Risks with Windows Services

Services running under the *localsystem* profile are considered to be part of the *trusted code base* (TCB)—they have the same level of implied trust as Windows itself. Running the Firebird service on Windows 2000 and higher carries a recognized risk with regard to malicious exploits designed to execute arbitrary code. The importance of assuring the programmatic integrity of Firebird's external executables, even under very secure conditions, is crucial. In a Windows environment that is left open to exploits, the fire danger rises to "extreme."

In short, Windows operating system software on its own provides no credible guarantee of security for database servers, either within a local network or beyond. Potential exploiters must be stopped by tightly configured user access control within the LAN and dependable, third-party firewall products to detect and block attacks.

Windows Embedded Server

The Windows Embedded Server library is, of course, designed to run on machines that do not run a full server. If you have a copy of fbembed.dll housed anywhere on a full server machine, the server security is at risk. Here's why.

Embedded Server does not use server authentication to verify that a user logging into a database has a right to be doing so. Most application interfaces require a user name and password. Any user name and any password will do—nothing is verified. The internal security of a database designed for embedded server use has to be protected with SQL permissions (see Chapter 35) that limit access to a specific user name. That in itself is a can of worms on a stand-alone machine that is physically available to passers-by.

However, on a machine that is running a Firebird 1.5 server and also has the Embedded Server software on board, a malicious program could be set to run under an Embedded Server when databases are shut down, connect to security.fdb as SYSDBA, steal or damage the user records, read encrypted passwords, and generally please itself by visiting other databases as SYSDBA. When an application connects to each database through fbembed.dll, it locks each database exclusively. A malicious application could hold its connections on databases—including security.fdb—indefinitely.

Embedded Server applications and clients run in the address space of the operating system user. To avoid the risk of a malicious Embedded Server program being dropped into the system, restrict user and group access in the filesystem spaces where databases and Firebird system files live.

Wire Security

Much of the communication between the client and the server carries sensitive information that can be quite easily "sniffed" by someone eavesdropping on network communications. For example, the encrypted password could be sniffed and used to gain unauthorized access to the server.

It is vital, therefore, to ensure that all pieces of the network path between any client and the server are trusted.

Add-on products can be purchased to provide encrypted network tunneling solutions to block potentially insecure pathways.

Web and Other n-Tier Server Applications

Relying on default user names can have unforeseen effects, such as unintentionally bestowing the privileges of the database owner, or even the server process owner, on ordinary users. It is strongly recommended that you have your server application enforce input of a user name and password before any calls are made to the Firebird server process.

Use Dedicated Servers

Avoid sharing the host machine with other services, especially vulnerable ones such as web and FTP servers that potentially invite anonymous logins. Shut down all services not required to run Firebird. On Windows, restrict network access to the Registry on database servers.

Use a Firewall

Placing your server machines behind a firewall is recommended, for obvious reasons. It may be less obvious that providing *firewall protection to client processes* is also a good idea. It is possible for a rogue user running on a trusted client machine to feed incorrect information to the server and gain privileged access to its databases. Windows clients are notoriously insecure.

A Linux/UNIX server can be configured to recognize trusted clients explicitly. From there, the server implicitly trusts a process running on a trusted client.

Denial-of-Service Attacks

The Firebird 1.0.*x* code has a large number of string copy commands that do not check the length of the data they are requested to copy. Certain of these overruns may be able to be manipulated externally by passing large strings of binary data into SQL statements or pushing random garbage into the server port (currently 3050). Use of these functions is a common technique for malicious buffer overrun attacks intended to bring down servers.

These vulnerabilities are more easily exploited if the server and client processes are not running on trusted networks and/or are not adequately firewalled.

Defensive programming can help to pre-empt denial-of-service (DoS) attacks on your system. Validating the lengths of strings from web input, for example, may be extremely useful.

Up Next

In the next chapter, the protection afforded (or not afforded) by Firebird's server security database is discussed, along with use of the **gsec** tool for managing the server's user access list. The chapter ends with a special topic about customizing the security database to enhance some aspects of this built-in protection.

CHAPTER 34

Server Protection

THE SERVER INSTALLATION INCLUDES A user authentication database for storing defini-tions of all users that have access to the Firebird server. A case-sensitive password must be defined for each user and used to gain access to the server. The command-line tool for maintaining the user database is **gsec**.

The name of the database on Firebird 1.5 and higher servers is *security.fdb*. On v.1.0.*x*, it is *isc4.gdb*. It must be located in the Firebird root directory of all server installations except Windows Embedded Server.[1]

User authentication is required whenever a remote or local client connects to a Firebird database. The solitary exception is when the client connects through an Embedded Server application on Windows. In this situation, it is the database that will require a user name corresponding to SQL permissions defined on its objects. No user name/password authentication is performed during the embedded client/server con-nection process.

Entering User Credentials

It is essential to use **gsec**—or an interface to **gsec**—to enter user credentials. The **gsec** interface encrypts passwords before it stores them. Do not connect a user application or admin tool directly to the security database or run a script in order to "batch-enter" users, because the passwords will be stored in clear text.

> **TIP** Firebird has a Services API that interfaces with **gsec**, among several other command-line tools. Several third-party admin tools provide access to **gsec** through the Services API, providing a friendlier interface than the shell and the command line for maintaining user credentials.

The required entries are a *user name* and a *password*. International character sets are currently not supported for user names or passwords.

---

1. For security reasons, systems should not be deployed with the Embedded Server library avail-able on an active Firebird server, unless the Firebird root directory is tightly locked against unauthorized visitors. For more details, refer back to Chapter 33.

Only the SYSDBA user can maintain the security database. That means Firebird, out of the box, does not support users changing their own passwords. Refer to the "Special Topic" at the end of this chapter for a technique to customize user authentication on your server and implement this feature.

User names are case insensitive and unique. Currently, to be usable, they should include only characters allowed for object identifiers: A–Z (or a–z), numerals, and the symbols !, #, $, &, and @. A user name can theoretically be up to 128 characters, but you should consider it restricted to 31 characters, since a longer name will not be valid for use with SQL permissions.

 CAUTION **gsec** will let you define silly user names, such as a string of asterisks or IRC-style "smiley" faces, like this :-), but don't be tempted! Such strings are not accepted in the places where user names are employed—in connection parameters and permissions statements.

Passwords can be up to 32 characters, but only the first eight characters are significant. Hence, for example, the passwords *masterkey* and *masterkeeper* are seen by the server as identical. Passwords are case sensitive. The characters allowed are the same as for user names, but uppercase characters are distinct from lowercase. Passwords need not be unique, although it is desirable from a security perspective to make them so.

 NOTE Some admin interfaces actually impose an eight-character limit and refuse user names or passwords that begin with numerals. Although it is not a limitation in the security database, it reflects a practice that makes good sense to follow.

Password Encryption

The **gsec** interface encrypts passwords using a weak method based on a DES hash algorithm. Because of the current eight-character limit, Firebird user authentication should not be regarded as a "centurion at the gate for the modern age."

Nevertheless, avoid obvious passwords like *password* or *sesame*. Mix case, include numerals, and ensure that passwords are changed regularly.

TIP Because it is impossible to retrieve lost passwords by querying the system, you should have a bombproof system for recording user passwords whenever they are changed. Yellow sticky notes on users' monitors are not the system of choice for security-conscious organizations! Lost passwords can be reset by the SYSDBA. If the SYSDBA password gets lost, the entire security database can be replaced by restoring security.fbk, which you will find in the Firebird root directory (isc4.gbk for Firebird 1.0.*x*) and starting over with the password *masterkey*.

User Credentials in SQL

Because Firebird users are maintained at server level, no SQL language statements are implemented for maintaining them. However, user names do crop up in SQL, as the argument for the GRANT ... TO and REVOKE ... FROM statements. For more information, refer to the next chapter.

The user name is also widely available in many SQL expression contexts through the context variable CURRENT_USER and the server literal USER.

The SYSDBA User

All new installations of Firebird on Windows install the SYSDBA user into the security database, with the password *masterkey*. Obviously, this is widely known and is not intended to be secure. It should be changed at the first opportunity.

On Linux, some installers may generate a random password for SYSDBA. If so, you will find it in the text file SYSDBA.password, located in the Firebird /bin directory.

SYSDBA is the owner of the security database. Keep in mind that Firebird databases have "one SYSDBA to rule them all." The SYSDBA user has full destructive rights over all databases on the server. The SYSDBA password should not be distributed to ordinary users.

The POSIX Hole

Firebird can admit client connections to servers on POSIX platforms that bypass Firebird user authentication and use the operating system user and permissions scheme instead. It is a long-time feature that was inherited from InterBase virtually undocumented. Not knowing about it leaves a big security hole on POSIX platforms if the POSIX user access path is left wide open and the system admin mistakenly assumes that the security database is the ultimate gatekeeper.

It is not. When POSIX users log in without passing a Firebird user name and password, the authentication routine substitutes the current operating system identity for the Firebird user identity. If the operating system user has root privileges, be afraid—be very afraid.

In order for POSIX users to be allowed access to Firebird databases via their operating system user credentials, it is essential to define a trusted host relationship between the server and each client workstation. This translates to entries in */etc/host.equiv*, or by other means, such as an *.rhost* file in the user's home directory on the server.

 TIP The reader might also like to experiment with a */etc/gds_host.equiv* file—see the white paper entitled "Installing InterBase to start automatically and run as a service under Linux" by Richard Combs, at `http://community.borland.com/article/0,1410,27761,00.html`.

The environment variables ISC_USER and ISC_PASSWORD must be eliminated from the system.

 CAUTION The author is not aware of any way to define a trusted host relationship between a Windows workstation and a UNIX server, but that is in no sense a statement that it cannot be done.

The gsec Utility

Firebird provides the **gsec** utility as a command-line interface for maintaining the security database. It has its own shell for interactive use, or **gsec** commands can be run directly from an operating system command shell or an executable script (shell script or batch file).

Any authentic user can run **gsec**, but only the SYSDBA user can modify the user data stored in it. The user name and password will be required unless the environment variables ISC_USER and ISC_PASSWORD are visible to the command shell in which you are running. On POSIX, if you are logged in as *root*, you can invoke **gsec** without entering –user and –password parameters.

Starting a gsec Interactive Session

At the command line, at Firebird's /bin directory prompt, type the following.
For POSIX:

```
./gsec -user sysdba -password masterkey
```

For Windows:

```
gsec -user sysdba -password masterkey
```

The prompt changes to GSEC>, indicating that you are running **gsec** in interactive mode.

To end an interactive session, type QUIT at the prompt.

Running gsec As a Remote Client

SYSDBA can use **gsec** on a client machine to administer user authentication on a remote server. The invocation syntax is different: It needs the –database switch followed by the full network path to the security database. For example (single command), this example shows a POSIX client to Windows server v.1.5:

```
./gsec -database hotchicken:c:\Program Files\Firebird\Firebird_1_5\security.fdb
    -user sysdba -password masterkey
```

This example shows a Windows client to POSIX server v.1.0.*x*:

```
gsec -database coolduck:/opt/firebird/isc4.gdb
    -user sysdba -password masterkey
```

Interactive Commands

The **gsec** interactive commands are display, add, modify, delete, help, and quit. They are not case sensitive.

- *add*, *modify*, and *delete* are used for adding and deleting users and for changing passwords. They require the *username* as a parameter, along with the relevant option switches and arguments.

- *display* without the username argument lists all users. Passwords are not shown. *display* can optionally take a *username* and display the details of that user.

- *help* or its alias *?* displays some help text for the commands.

- *quit* ends **gsec** and closes the shell.

The USERS Table and gsec Options

Table 34-1 shows the columns in the USERS table, together with their corresponding **gsec** option switches. Only USER_NAME and PASSWD are required fields when using **gsec**.

Table 34-1. Columns in the USERS Table and **gsec** *Options*

COLUMN	DESCRIPTION	GSEC OPTION	ARGUMENT
USER_NAME	User name, as recognized by the server's user authentication. **gsec** requires it as a parameter for the interactive add, modify, and delete commands, and for the corresponding command-line switches –a[dd], –mo[dify], and –d[elete].		*username* parameter
SYS_USER_NAME	Not used.		
GROUP_NAME	Not used.		
UID	On some POSIX platforms, the UNIX userid. Not required.	–uid	integer
GID	On some POSIX platforms, the UNIX groupid. Not required.	–gid	integer
PASSWD	The current password for this user. Required.	–pw	string(10)
PRIVILEGE	Not used.		
COMMENT	Not used.		
FIRST_NAME	The user's first name. Not required.	–fname	string(31)
MIDDLE_NAME	User's middle name. Not required.	–mname	string(31)
LAST_NAME	User's last name. Not required.	–lname	string(31)
FULL_NAME	Computed; not updateable.		N/A
	Also, when running **gsec** from a remote workstation:		
	Server and file path of the security database	–database	*filespec*

gsec Examples

display

This displays the main columns of the USERS table in the security database. Passwords are never displayed.

```
user_name   uid   gid full name
--------------------------------------------
SYSDBA
MICKEY      123   345 Mickey Mouse
D_DUCK      124   345 Donald Duck
JULIUS      125   345 J. Caesar
```

. . .

To display the same information for a single row from the USERS table:

```
GSEC> display username
```

For example:

```
GSEC> display julius
user_name   uid   gid full name
-------------------------------------------------
JULIUS      125   345 J. Caesar
```

a[dd]

This adds a user to the USERS table:

```
a[dd] user_name -pw password [other switches]
```

where *username* is a unique, new user name and *password* is the password associated with that user.

> **NOTE** The switch for the new password when adding a user or changing a password is –pw. Don't confuse it with the abbreviated form of the SYSDBA login password switch, which is –pa.

For example:

```
GSEC> add mmouse -pw veritas
```

To add authorization for a user named Harry Potter with the user name *hpotter* and the password *noMuggle*, enter

```
GSEC> add hpotter -fname Harry -lname Potter -pw noMuggle
```

To verify the new entry:

```
GSEC> display hpotter
user_name   uid   gid full name
-------------------------------------------------
HPOTTER               Harry Potter
```

NOTE   If you try to use illegal characters in a password string, **gsec** will simply terminate with no message.

mo[dify]

This is for changing (editing) a column value on an existing USERS record. Supply the user name of the user to change, followed by one or more switches indicating the items to change and the new value for each.

For example, to set the user ID of user *mickey* to 25, change the first name to Michael and change the password to *icecream*, enter the following switches:

```
GSEC> modify mickey -uid 25 -fname Michael -pw icecream
```

You can't change a user name. Delete the old user and add a new one.

de[lete]

This deletes the user username from the USERS table. Delete takes no other arguments or switches.

```
de[lete] username
```

For example:

```
GSEC> delete mickey
```

You can use the *display* command to confirm that the entry has been deleted.

h[elp] or ?

Either of these switches displays a summary of the **gsec** commands, switches, and syntax.

q[uit]

This ends the interactive session.

Using gsec from a Command Prompt

To use **gsec** from a command prompt, convert each **gsec** interactive command to a command switch by prefixing it with a hyphen (–). The option switches are the same.

For example, to add the user *claudio* and assign the password *dbkeycop*, you would enter the following on the command line.

On Windows:

```
..\BIN> gsec -add claudio -pw dbkeycop -user SYSDBA -password masterkey
```

On POSIX:

```
bin]$ ./gsec -add claudio -pw dbkeycop -user SYSDBA -password masterkey
```

To display the contents of the USERS table, enter

```
> gsec -display
```

and so on.

gsec Error Messages

Table 34-2 summarizes the **gsec** error messages.

*Table 34-2. **gsec** Error Messages*

ERROR MESSAGE	CAUSES AND SUGGESTED ACTIONS TO TAKE
Add record error	Invalid syntax, or you tried to add a user that already exists, or you are not the SYSDBA. Use modify if the user already exists.
<string> already specified	You included a switch more than once in an add or modify command. Re-enter the command.
Error in switch specifications	This message accompanies other error messages and indicates that invalid syntax was used. Check other error messages for the cause.
Find/delete record error	The delete command could not find the named user, or you are not the SYSDBA.
Find/display record error	The display command could not find the named user, or you are not the SYSDBA.
Find/modify record error	The modified command could not find the named user, or you are not the SYSDBA.
Incompatible switches specified	For example, you entered multiple switches for the delete command, which requires only the mandatory *username* argument. Correct the syntax and try again.
Invalid parameter, no switch defined	You specified a value without a preceding argument.
Invalid switch specified	You specified an unrecognized option. Fix it and try again.

continued

*Table 34-2. **gsec** Error Messages (continued)*

ERROR MESSAGE	CAUSES AND SUGGESTED ACTIONS TO TAKE
No user name specified	Specify a user name after any add, modify, or delete command or switch.
Record not found for user: *<string>*	An entry for the specified user could not be found. List the users with display, and try again.
Unable to open database	The security database does not exist or cannot be located by the server. Are you running **gsec** from outside of the Firebird tree? Are you remotely trying to access a server that is not installed?

SPECIAL TOPIC: Customizing User Security

This section written and printed here with permission by Ivan Prenosil.

Firebird user authentication is—well—problematic. The good news is that it's all going to change for the better in Firebird 2. The bad news is that we have to live with it for some time yet. Ivan Prenosil, a long-time, well-practiced expert in developing with Firebird and its ancestors, developed some techniques for customizing the security database. Ivan agreed to share his tips and scripts with you in this special topic.

The Security Database

When a user logs into a Firebird database, its password is verified against an encrypted password in the security database. On v.1.0.*x*, the name of the database is isc4.gdb. It is security.fdb on v.1.5. It is an ordinary Firebird database, and the table that's used for user authentication is USERS. Its (simplified) structure looks like this:

```
CREATE TABLE USERS (
  USER_NAME VARCHAR(128),
  PASSWD VARCHAR(32) );
/* */
GRANT SELECT ON USERS TO PUBLIC;
```

On examining the permissions for this table, two major drawbacks are obvious. One is that any user can read the full list of users and encrypted passwords. The other is that only SYSDBA can modify the table—so users cannot change their own passwords.

However, if you are SYSDBA, you can connect to the security database, just as you can to any other database, and modify its structure. That means you can *improve* it.

 CAUTION   Be certain you make a backup of the security database before you start playing!

Version Differences

In Firebird 1.0.x, when authenticating users, the server connects to the security database, retrieves the necessary information, and then disconnects. Between connections, you can "mess around" with isc4.gdb.

In Firebird 1.5, however, once a connection has been established to the security database, it is retained until the server is shut down. With v.1.5, therefore, you'll need make all changes to a *copy* of the security database and install it afterward. Here are the steps:

1. Make a backup of *security.fdb* using **gbak**.

2. Restore it under a different name.

3. Run the script(s) on that copy.

4. Shut down the server.

5. Swap the old and new versions of security.fdb and rename.

6. Restart the server.

Allowing Users to Change Their Own Passwords

The easiest and best-known modification is to grant update permissions to give non-SYSDBA users access, GRANT UPDATE ON USERS TO PUBLIC, and add a trigger to prevent any user except SYSDBA from modifying somebody else's password.

Here is my script:

```
/* Copyright Ivan Prenosil 2002-2004 */
CONNECT 'C:\Program Files\Firebird\Firebird_1_5\security.fdb'
  USER 'SYSDBA' PASSWORD 'masterkey';
CREATE EXCEPTION E_NO_RIGHT 'You have no rights to modify this user.';
SET TERM !!;
CREATE TRIGGER user_name_bu FOR USERS BEFORE UPDATE
AS
BEGIN
  IF (NOT (USER='SYSDBA' OR USER=OLD.USER_NAME)) THEN
    EXCEPTION E_NO_RIGHT;
END !!
SET TERM ;!!
/** Grants. **/
GRANT UPDATE(PASSWD, GROUP_NAME, UID, GID, FIRST_NAME, MIDDLE_NAME, LAST_NAME)
  ON USERS TO PUBLIC;
```

It's awkward having to grant permissions on all of the columns when PASSWD is the only one you really want to make accessible. Unfortunately, it is needed if your password application is going to use **gsec** or the Services API.

This modification doesn't get around the problem that the full list of users and their encrypted passwords is visible to PUBLIC. It makes it very easy for a user to download a list of the other users' passwords and try to break them locally by brute force.

How to Hide the Users/Passwords List

If you rename the USERS table and re-create USERS as a view of the renamed table, you can have the best of both worlds. Users will be able to modify their own passwords, and the full list of users and passwords can be hidden from PUBLIC. Each non-SYSDBA user will see only one record in security.fdb (or isc4.gdb, if your server is v.1.0.*x*). The new structures in security.fdb will be more like the following schema:

```
/* Copyright Ivan Prenosil 2002-2004 */
CONNECT 'C:\Program Files\Firebird\Firebird_1_5\security.fdb'
  USER 'SYSDBA' PASSWORD 'masterkey';
/** Rename existing USERS table to USERS2. **/
CREATE TABLE USERS2 (
  USER_NAME       USER_NAME,
  SYS_USER_NAME   USER_NAME,
  GROUP_NAME      USER_NAME,
  UID             UID,
  GID             GID,
  PASSWD          PASSWD,
  PRIVILEGE       PRIVILEGE,
  COMMENT         COMMENT,
  FIRST_NAME      NAME_PART,
  MIDDLE_NAME     NAME_PART,
  LAST_NAME       NAME_PART,
  FULL_NAME COMPUTED BY (first_name || _UNICODE_FSS ' ' || middle_name ||
    _UNICODE_FSS ' ' || last_name ));
COMMIT;
INSERT INTO USERS2
  (USER_NAME, SYS_USER_NAME, GROUP_NAME,
  UID, GID, PASSWD, PRIVILEGE, COMMENT,
  FIRST_NAME, MIDDLE_NAME, LAST_NAME)
SELECT
  USER_NAME, SYS_USER_NAME, GROUP_NAME,
  UID, GID, PASSWD, PRIVILEGE, COMMENT,
  FIRST_NAME, MIDDLE_NAME, LAST_NAME
FROM USERS;
COMMIT;
/* */
DROP TABLE USERS;
/* */
CREATE UNIQUE INDEX USER_NAME_INDEX2 ON USERS2(USER_NAME);
/** Create the view that will be used instead of original USERS table. **/
CREATE VIEW USERS AS
```

```
SELECT *
  FROM USERS2
 WHERE USER = ''
    OR USER = 'SYSDBA'
    OR USER = USER_NAME;
/** Permissions **/
GRANT SELECT ON USERS TO PUBLIC;
GRANT UPDATE(PASSWD, GROUP_NAME, UID, GID, FIRST_NAME, MIDDLE_NAME, LAST_NAME)
  ON USERS
  TO PUBLIC;
```

The real table USERS2 is visible only to SYSDBA. The condition

```
USER = USER_NAME
```

ensures that each user sees its own record. The condition

```
USER = 'SYSDBA'
```

ensures that SYSDBA can see all records. The condition

```
USER = ''
```

is important because the USER and CURRENT_USER variables contain empty strings during password verification.

NOTE   Unfortunately, the next two techniques can't be implemented on a Firebird 1.5 server. They involve writing to log files. Security enhancements made to v.1.5 mean that the user authentication routine is now done in a read-only transaction, so no writes to logs! A similar scheme could be implemented by delegating the logging function to external functions.

How to Log Login Attempts

Replacing the USERS table in the security database with a USERS view has one great benefit: It allows us to call a stored procedure whenever a user tries to log in. When the Firebird server executes the statement

```
SELECT PASSWD
  FROM USERS
 WHERE USER_NAME =?;
```

we can execute a procedure that acts like a select trigger or a login trigger. The procedure could be written so that it could, for example, refuse login during some parts of the day, or log a timestamp when users try to log in.

We can log only the names of known users—that is, names already stored in the USERS table—and it is *not* possible to report whether login was successful. Still, even the limited information we can log can be useful. It will inform us of login attempts at unusual times, and it will reveal suspicious numbers of logins over short periods.

To implement this, we need a table to log into and a stored procedure to do the work.

The Log Table

The log table has to be an external table, because the transaction used by the server to do its authentication is not committed, but rolled back. External tables don't get "unwritten" by rollback as inserts to a regular table would.

```
CREATE TABLE log_table

    EXTERNAL FILE 'C:\Program Files\Firebird\Firebird_1_5\security.log'
    ( tstamp TIMESTAMP,
      uname  CHAR(31) );
```

If you want the log table to be readable as a text file, you can use CHAR(20) instead of TIMESTAMP and cast it, and add two more columns: a single CHAR to separate the *tstamp* and *uname* columns and a CHAR(2) to be filled with carriage return and line-feed codes.

The Logging Procedure

The stored procedure is a selectable type, able to be called from the view. When a login succeeds, SUSPEND gets called and a row is written to the log. When the login fails, because the row requested from the view is forbidden, the procedure just terminates without writing anything. The output parameter is just formal; its value is ignored.

```
CREATE PROCEDURE log_proc
    (un VARCHAR(31))
RETURNS
    (x CHAR(1))
AS
BEGIN
  IF (USER = '') THEN
    INSERT INTO log_table (TSTAMP, UNAME)
      VALUES ( CURRENT_TIMESTAMP, :un);
/* and don't forget to change the fields written
   if you modify log_table to make it a text file! */
  IF (USER = '' OR USER = 'SYSDBA' OR USER = :un) THEN
    SUSPEND;
END
```

We test (USER = '') because, when Firebird verifies the password, the USER variable is empty. It helps distinguish whether the password is being verified by the server or the user is directly connected to the security database.

Implementing the New Setup

We need to drop the view that is being used in our restructured security database and create a new version that calls the stored procedure:

```
CREATE VIEW USERS (USER_NAME) AS
  SELECT * FROM users2
    WHERE EXISTS (SELECT * FROM log_proc(users2.user_name));
```

Remember to reinstate the permissions that were lost when the view was dropped:

```
GRANT SELECT ON USERS TO PUBLIC;
/* */
GRANT UPDATE(PASSWD, GROUP_NAME, UID, GID, FIRST_NAME, MIDDLE_NAME, LAST_NAME)
  ON USERS
  TO PUBLIC;
```

There are some more permissions to add, relating to the stored procedure:

```
GRANT INSERT
  ON log_table
  TO PROCEDURE log_proc;
GRANT EXECUTE
  ON PROCEDURE log_proc
  TO PUBLIC;
```

Because log entries are constantly appended to log_table, it will be necessary to delete or rename the external file from time to time. The security database and, thus, the external file, are released after the user authentication is finished, so renaming the file should not be a problem.

How to Slow Down Intruders

Once we are able to log the user names that tried to log into the database, and the times they tried, we can use this information to further restrict access.

For example, it would be possible to count the number of login attempts by a given user name during the last minute and, if the number reached some ceiling, to block connection by that user name. It would allow us some protection from brute-force attacks, where someone tries to break into the database by repeatedly scanning possible passwords. We can put a temporary block on any user name that displays attackerlike behavior.

The time interval and the login count limit need to be chosen carefully, so as to slow down the intruder but not impose penalties on bona fide users who just type badly. OpenVMS uses a similar approach.

The relevant piece of code in the stored procedure is as simple as this:

```
...
DECLARE VARIABLE cnt INTEGER;
...
  SELECT COUNT(*)
    FROM log_table
   WHERE uname=:un
     AND tstamp>CURRENT_TIMESTAMP-0.0007
    INTO :cnt;
  IF (cnt>=3) THEN EXIT;
```

You can change the constants, namely 3 (the allowed number of mistakes) and 0.0007 (the interval, approximately 1 minute). This procedure will affect all users.

One possible modification would be to choose one non-SYSDBA user (not SYSDBA, because it is the user name most likely to be targeted) and exclude it from the blocking procedure. Make it the user that owns all the databases, thus endowing it with the rights to perform database shutdowns.

Up Next

Server-level security in Firebird clearly has its deficiencies. The next chapter discusses Firebird's support for SQL permissions that can be implemented within all databases. SQL permissions are notoriously complicated to manage, but, when implemented cleanly, they do provide that essential inner level of data security for databases on systems that are adequately protected from outright theft.

CHAPTER 35

Database-Level Security

DATABASE-LEVEL SECURITY IN FIREBIRD enables two security objectives: first, to prevent authorized users of the *server* from accessing the data in *your* database and, second, to enable access for users who do have business with your database. The means to implement this database-level security is by SQL privileges.

The first objective, to lock out unwanted server-authenticated users, has its uses in environments where databases owned by multiple entities are being run on the same server—typically, at a site providing shared co-location services for multiple customers. In such arrangements, customers of the provider do not normally have SYSDBA access.

The second objective has more to do with an organization's requirements to restrict the purview of confidential or sensitive data. SQL privileges can support any level of granularity for access to any item of data, down to the column level.

Unlike users (as discussed in the previous chapter), privileges apply at database level and are stored right in the database, in the system table REDB$USER_PRIVILEGES.

Default Security and Access

A database and all its objects (tables, views, and stored procedures) are secured against unauthorized access when they are created. That is, access is "opt-in." No user can access any object in the database unless granted permission to do so. Except for especially privileged users—owner, SYSDBA, and (on POSIX) the Superuser—users must be granted SQL privileges for any operation, even a SELECT.

And Now the Bad News

There is a big catch with this, so don't be lulled into a false sense of security. Non-existent objects are not protected. Any user with access to a database may create any valid database object—including declarations for external functions and tables linked to external tables—that could potentially be used in combination to install and run malicious code on the server.

With the ability to limit the places a server is allowed to access external artifacts in Firebird 1.5 installations, the situation is less risky. However, it has not gone away—you must take explicit steps to implement the feature and the supporting operating system filesystem restrictions. Default access to external files is set to NONE by the installers, and the external function directories are restricted to the UDF tree. It is up to you to take care of the system restrictions.

The system tables, where Firebird stores all metadata, including the SQL privileges themselves, are not protected by SQL privileges at all.

A Trick to Beat Idiot Users and Bad Guys

My esteemed colleague Pavel Cisar offered to share his workaround for the lack of SQL privilege protection for Firebird metadata, which tempts idiot users to avoid DDL and change metadata by messing with the system tables. It also beats malicious attempts to break your metadata with a script. Here it is.

Although it appears that PUBLIC has ALL access to the system tables, it's just a weird backdoor to SQL rights management that could be easily fixed. You can restrict access to the system tables, just as to any other table in the database, by granting and revoking permissions. However, rights have to be granted in order to be revoked.

What is needed is just to set access management for the system tables to the standard routine by executing a series of GRANT ALL ON *<system-table>* TO PUBLIC statements. After that, we can revoke rights at will.

I don't know the exact technical explanation for why it works the way it does, but here's my guess. The GRANT statement creates an access control list (ACL) for the system table, which is checked by the code. Some branch in the code assumes "Grant all to public if no ACL is found for a system table, else use the ACL."

Keep in mind that

- This setup doesn't survive a restore from backup, so write a script that you can use each time you kick in a freshly restored database.

- You need to be careful about removing SELECT rights from PUBLIC on certain system tables, as the API functions *isc_blob_lookup_desc( )* and *isc_array_lookup_bounds( )* depend on its being available. Some tools and libraries may depend on it as well.

- Removing write rights to system tables doesn't restrict the ability to update them the *right and proper way*, through DDL commands. Only fiddling directly with the system tables is prevented.

A privilege enables a user to have some kind of access to an object in the database. It is enabled using a GRANT statement and taken away using a REVOKE statement.

The syntax pattern for enabling access is

```
GRANT <privilege>
  ON <object>
    TO <user>;
```

A *<privilege>* granted to a *<user>* on an *<object>* constitutes a *permission*.

For removing a permission:

```
REVOKE <privilege>
  ON <object>
    FROM <user>;
```

Several variants to the "core" syntax are available. We'll explore them a little later.

Privileges

A privilege represents permission to perform a DML operation. Table 35-1 lists the SQL privileges that can be granted and revoked.

Table 35-1. SQL Privileges

PRIVILEGE	ACCESS
SELECT	Read data.
INSERT	Create new rows.
UPDATE	Modify existing data.
DELETE	Delete rows.
REFERENCES	Refer to a primary key from a foreign key. It is always a necessary accompaniment to granting privileges on tables containing foreign keys.
ALL	Select, insert, update, delete, and refer to a primary key from a foreign key.
EXECUTE	Execute a stored procedure or call it using SELECT. This privilege is never granted as part of the ALL privilege (see the section "The ALL Keyword").
ROLE	Acquire all privileges assigned to the role. Once a role exists and has privileges assigned to it, it becomes a privilege that can be granted explicitly to users. A role is never granted as part of the ALL privilege.

Packaging Privileges

Firebird SQL implements features for packaging multiple privileges for assignment to individual recipients, lists, or special groupings of users. One is the *ALL* package, another is comma-separated lists, and yet another is SQL *roles*.

The ALL Keyword

The ALL keyword packages the SELECT, INSERT, UPDATE, DELETE, and REFERENCES privileges in a single assignment. Roles and the EXECUTE privilege are not included in the ALL package.

Lists of Privileges

SELECT, INSERT, UPDATE, DELETE, and REFERENCES privileges can also be granted or revoked singly or in comma-separated lists. However, statements that grant or revoke either the EXECUTE privilege or a role cannot grant or revoke other privileges.

Roles

A role is created in a database and is available only to that database. Think of a role as a container for a bundle of privileges. Once the container is "filled" by having some privileges granted to it, it becomes available to be assigned—as a privilege—to some types of users.

Multiple roles can be created, the idea being to package and control discrete sets of privileges that can be granted and revoked as a whole, rather than as numerous collections of individual privileges being granted and revoked repetitively and in an ad hoc fashion.

A role can never be granted as part of the ALL package, although a role can be granted ALL privileges.

Roles Are Not Groups

Roles are not like operating system user groups. A Firebird user can be assigned more than one role, but can log in under only one role in a session.

UNIX Groups

Firebird supports UNIX groups on POSIX platforms. If system-level authentication is implemented, you can grant privileges to UNIX groups. Refer to the TO GROUP *<UNIX-group>* option for GRANT and REVOKE.

Objects

The "other half" of a permission is the object on which the privilege is to be applied or from which it is to be removed. An object can be a table, a view, a stored procedure, or a role, although not all privileges are necessarily applicable to all types of objects. An UPDATE privilege, for example, is not applicable to a procedure, and an EXECUTE privilege is not applicable to a table or a view.

There is no "packaged object" that encompasses all, or groups of, objects. There will be at least one GRANT statement for each database object.

Privilege Restrictions

The privileges SELECT, INSERT, UPDATE, and DELETE are applied only to objects that are tables or views. REFERENCES applies only to tables—specifically, those that are referenced by foreign keys.

For views, the user of the view must have privileges for the view itself, but permissions on the base tables must somehow be granted as well. The rule is that either the view's owner, the view itself, or the view's user must have the appropriate privileges to the base tables. It doesn't matter how the privileges are acquired, but one of the three must have it.

Naturally updateable views also need SELECT, INSERT, UPDATE, and DELETE permissions on the base tables. When read-only views are made updateable by means of triggers, the *triggers* need permissions on the underlying tables, according to the operations defined by the trigger events.

NOTE To be able to *create* a view, it is necessary to have SELECT permissions for the base tables. In the rare case that any of those SELECT privileges is revoked after the view is created, it must be added to the view itself or to users of the view.

EXECUTE can be applied only to stored procedures. A role is never granted "on" any object.

Users

Users are the recipients of permissions and the losers when permissions are revoked. A user can be a user that is defined in the security database, a UNIX account or group, a special user, or a database object.

- **Roles as users**: When a role is being awarded privileges, it is a user. Once a role has been granted the required privileges to objects, it "changes hats" and becomes a privilege that can be granted to some other types of users. When the login to the database is done under that role, those users assume the privileges that were awarded to the role.

- **Views as users**: Views need permissions to access tables, other views, and stored procedures.

- **Procedures and triggers as users**: A stored procedure that accesses tables and views and executes other procedures needs permissions on those objects. A trigger that executes procedures needs permissions on those and also on any tables or views it accesses other than the table that it belongs to.

Special Users

The SYSDBA user has special rights to all databases and the objects within them, regardless of which user owns them. Furthermore, on operating systems that implement the concept of a Superuser—a user with *root* or *locksmith* privileges—such a user also has full access and destructive rights access to all databases and their objects if it logs in under the root ID. For more details, refer to the section "The POSIX Hole" in the previous chapter.

Initially, an object's creator, its *owner*, is the only user other than SYSDBA or the Superuser that has access to an object (table, view, stored procedure, or role) or can permit other users to access it. Either user can then start off "chains" of permissions by granting other users the right to grant privileges. This right is optionally passed on by appending the WITH GRANT OPTION qualifier to the permission.

In a similar manner, SYSDBA or the owner of a role can optionally qualify a role privilege that it grants to a user as WITH ADMIN OPTION. However, a privilege assumed by a user that logs in under a role does not inherit WITH GRANT OPTION authority from the role. More on this later.

The PUBLIC User

PUBLIC is a user that stands for all users in the security database. It does not refer to or comprise stored procedures, triggers, views, or roles.

If multiple databases are running on the server, granting large packages of privileges to PUBLIC might save a lot of typing, but it is fairly easy to grant privileges by mistake to users that should not have them.

Embedded Servers

It is strongly recommended that databases intended for use in the embedded server be tightly protected with permissions. The user of an embedded server on Windows is not authenticated, by design, since there is no security database! As no user verification is performed on GRANT statements, permissions statements can be accepted for a "mock user" (i.e., a made-up name that your application uses for connection to the database via the embedded client).

Granting Privileges

Access privileges can be granted on an entire table or view. It is also possible to restrict UPDATE and REFERENCES privileges to specific columns.

A GRANT statement is used to give a user, role, or stored procedure a specific privilege for an object. The general syntax pattern for granting privileges on objects is

```
GRANT <privileges>
  ON [TABLE] <table> | <view>  | <object> | <omit ON clause>
  TO <generic-user>
  [{WITH GRANT OPTION} | {WITH ADMIN OPTION}];
```

```
<privileges> = <privilege> | <privilege-list> | <role-name> | ALL
<privilege> = INSERT | DELETE | UPDATE [(column [, column [,..]] ) ]
| REFERENCES [(column [, column [,..]] ) ] | EXECUTE
<privilege-list = [, privilege [, <privilege-list [,...]]]
```

Notice that the *<privilege>* syntax includes the provisions for restricting UPDATE or REFERENCES to certain columns, as discussed in the next section.

```
<object = <stored-proc> | <role-with-privileges>

<generic-user> = <user> | PUBLIC | <user-list> | <UNIX-user>
               | GROUP <UNIX-group> | <user-object>
<user-list> = <user>, {<user> | <user-list>}
<user-object> = <role> | <trigger> | <stored-proc>
```

The *<user>* is generally a user that is defined in the USERS table of the Firebird security database. On all-POSIX client/server networks, it can also be a user account that is in */etc/password* on both the server and client machines, or a UNIX group that both have in */etc/group*. For databases used with the Windows Embedded Server, a "mock user" user name (known to the application) is allowed.

The following statement grants some privileges for the DEPARTMENTS table to a user, CHALKY:

```
GRANT SELECT, UPDATE, INSERT, DELETE ON DEPARTMENTS TO CHALKY;
```

UPDATE Rights on Columns

The UPDATE privilege, unmodified, lets the user update any column in the table. However, if you specify a comma-separated list of columns, the user will be restricted to updating only the specified columns.

In the following statement, all users will have update permissions for the CUSTOMER table, but they will only be able to update CONTACT_FIRST, CONTACT_LAST, and PHONE_NO:

```
GRANT UPDATE (CONTACT_FIRST, CONTACT_LAST, PHONE_NO) ON CUSTOMER TO PUBLIC;
```

- When the option to grant UPDATE on a list of columns is used, multiple permissions are stored in the system table RDB$USER_PRIVILEGES, one for each column. Rights can be granted or revoked on each column individually.

- When the column-level permission is not used, only one permission is created. There is no way to remove rights on some columns and keep others. It would be necessary to revoke the permissions that contain the rights you want to remove and add a new one with the amended rights.

Thanks to the rules for SQL privileges—"The funniest thing since the Marx Brothers," according to a colleague—it is possible to grant both column-level permissions and the unqualified table-level UPDATE and REFERENCES privileges to the same user. It can cause complications if a user's column-level UPDATE or REFERENCES right is revoked, since the same user's table-level permission is unaffected.

Views offer an elegant way to restrict access to tables, by restricting the columns and/or the rows that are visible to the user in highly customized ways. This topic is discussed in Chapter 24.

REFERENCES Rights on Columns

The REFERENCES privilege is a necessary accompaniment to granting permissions on a table that has a foreign key. It is needed if a user creating a foreign key in a table does not own the table referenced by the key.

REFERENCES grants permissions on columns. All of the columns referenced by the grantee table's foreign key must be involved. If the GRANT REFERENCES statement refers to the table, without specifying columns, then the permissions are granted on every column. The columns that are not involved in the link between the foreign key and the referenced table's primary key are not affected.

If you prefer, you can specify just the key columns and, perhaps, save a little overhead if the referenced table has a lot of columns. If you do so, you must specify *all* of the linking key columns. The simplified syntax pattern is

```
GRANT REFERENCES
  ON <primary-table> [ ( key-column [, <key-column> [, ...]] ) ]
    TO <needful-user>
[WITH GRANT OPTION] ;
```

The next example grants REFERENCES privileges on DEPARTMENTS to CHALKY, permitting CHALKY to write a foreign key that references the primary key of the DEPARTMENTS table, even though he doesn't own that table:

```
GRANT REFERENCES ON DEPARTMENTS(DEPT_NO) TO CHALKY;
```

 TIP If the visibility of the keys is not an issue, grant the REFERENCES privileges to PUBLIC.

Privileges on Objects

When a trigger, stored procedure, or view needs to access a table or view, it is sufficient for either the owner of the accessing object, the accessing object, or the user who is executing it to have the necessary permissions.

On the other hand, privileges on tables can be granted to a procedure instead of to individual users, as a security measure. The user needs only the EXECUTE privilege on a procedure that accesses a table.

A stored procedure, view, or trigger sometimes needs privileges to access a table or view that has a different owner. To grant privileges to a trigger or stored procedure, include the keywords TRIGGER or PROCEDURE, as appropriate, before the name of the module.

Here, the procedure COUNT_CHICKENS is granted INSERT permission for the PROJ_DEPT_BUDGET table:

```
GRANT INSERT ON PROJ_DEPT_BUDGET TO PROCEDURE COUNT_CHICKENS;
```

Granting the EXECUTE Privilege

To use a stored procedure, users, triggers, or other stored procedures need the EXECUTE privilege on it. If a view selects output fields from a selectable stored procedure, the view must have the EXECUTE privilege, not the SELECT privilege.

The simplified syntax pattern is

```
GRANT EXECUTE
  ON PROCEDURE <procedure-name>
    TO <grantee>;
<grantee> = [ PROCEDURE <procedure-name> [, <procedure-name> [, ..]]]
            [ TRIGGER <trigger-name> [, <trigger-name [, ...]]]
            [ VIEW <view-name> [, <view-name> [, ...]]]
            | <role-name | <user-or-list> | PUBLIC
[WITH GRANT OPTION];
```

A stored procedure or trigger needs the EXECUTE privilege on a stored procedure whose owner is not the same as its own. Note that a trigger is owned by the owner of the table that owns the trigger.

If your GRANT EXECUTE statement is granting privileges to PUBLIC, no other types of grantees can be listed as TO arguments.

Here, the GRANT EXECUTE statement grants the privilege on the procedure CALCULATE_BEANS to two ordinary users, FLATFOOT and KILROY, and to two stored procedures whose owners are not the owner of CALCULATE_BEANS:

```
GRANT EXECUTE ON PROCEDURE CALCULATE_BEANS
  TO FLATFOOT,
    KILROY,
    PROCEDURE DO_STUFF, ABANDON_OLD;
```

Privileges on Views

Privileges on views are somewhat complicated. The owner of the view needs to grant the SELECT privilege to users, just as a table owner would. The complications start if the view is updateable—either naturally or through view triggers—or the view involves other views or selectable stored procedures. Data changes on an updateable view are actually made to the base tables. Unless the owners of the base objects have already granted the user the applicable rights (INSERT, UPDATE, DELETE, EXECUTE) on the base tables and objects, and any selectable stored procedures or views, the user will need to acquire them from the view's owner.

REFERENCES privileges are not applicable to views, except under one (usually avoidable) situation. If a view uses a table that has foreign keys to other tables, the view needs REFERENCES privileges to those other tables if the tables themselves are not used in the view.

For more on the subject, refer to the section "Privileges" in Chapter 24.

Multiple Privileges and Multiple Grantees

It is possible to grant several privileges in one statement and to grant one or more privileges to multiple grantee users or objects.

Multiple Privileges

To give a grantee several privileges on a table, name the granted privileges in a comma-separated list. The following statement assigns INSERT and UPDATE permissions on the DEPARTMENT table to user CHALKY:

```
GRANT INSERT, UPDATE ON DEPARTMENT TO CHALKY;
```

A list of privileges can be any combination, in any order, of SELECT, INSERT, UPDATE, DELETE, and REFERENCES. EXECUTE has to be assigned in a separate statement, on its own.

The REFERENCES privilege cannot be assigned to a view.

The ALL Privilege

The ALL privilege combines SELECT, INSERT, UPDATE, DELETE, and REFERENCES all in one package. For example, the following statement grants CHALKY the whole package of permissions for the DEPARTMENT table:

```
GRANT ALL ON DEPARTMENT TO CHALKY;
```

You can also assign the ALL package to triggers and procedures. In this statement, the procedure COUNT_CHICKENS gets full rights to the PROJ_DEPT_BUDGET table:

```
GRANT ALL ON PROJ_DEPT_BUDGET TO PROCEDURE COUNT_CHICKENS;
```

Privileges for Multiple Users

Several syntaxes enable you to grant privileges to multiple users in a single statement. You can assign privileges to

- A list of named users or procedures

- A UNIX group

- All users (PUBLIC)

- A role (then assign that role to a user list, to PUBLIC, or to a UNIX group)

To a List of Named Users

To assign the same access privileges to a number of users in a single statement, provide a comma-separated list of users in place of the single user name.

The following statement gives INSERT and UPDATE permissions on the DEPARTMENT table to MICKEY, DONALD, and HPOTTER:

```
GRANT INSERT, UPDATE ON DEPARTMENTS TO MICKEY, DONALD, HPOTTER;
```

To a List of Procedures

To assign privileges to several procedures in a single statement, provide a comma-separated list of procedures. Here, two procedures get privileges in one statement:

```
GRANT INSERT, UPDATE
  ON PROJ_DEPT_BUDGET
    TO PROCEDURE CALCULATE_ODDS, COUNT_BEANS;
```

To a UNIX Group

Operating system *account names* on Linux/UNIX are accessible to Firebird security through a feature of Firebird privileges that is not standard SQL. A client running as a UNIX user adopts that user identity in the database, even if the account is not defined in the Firebird security database.

The machine accessing the server must be listed as a trusted host on the server (files */etc/host.equiv* or */etc/gds_host.equiv*, or in *.rhost* in the user's home directory on the server). On connecting, the user gets logged in under its group identity, as long as it does not supply its Firebird user name and password as a connection parameter—Firebird credentials overrule UNIX credentials.

Linux/UNIX *groups* share this behavior: SYSDBA or a Superuser can assign SQL privileges to UNIX groups. Any operating system–level account that is a member of the group inherits the privileges granted to the group, for example:

```
GRANT ALL ON CUSTOMER TO GROUP sales;
```

To All Users (PUBLIC)

To assign the same access privileges on a table to all users, grant the privileges to PUBLIC. PUBLIC encompasses only users—not triggers, procedures, views, or roles.

```
GRANT SELECT, INSERT, UPDATE ON DEPARTMENT TO PUBLIC;
```

Privileges granted to users by way of PUBLIC can be revoked only by revoking them from PUBLIC. You can't, for example, revoke a privilege from CHALKY that CHALKY acquired as a member of PUBLIC.

Privileges Through Roles

Implementing roles is a four-step process:

1. Create a role using the CREATE ROLE statement.

2. Assign privileges to the role using GRANT *privilege* TO *rolename.*

3. Grant the role to users using GRANT *rolename* TO *user.*

4. Specify the role, along with the user name, when attaching to a database.

Creating a Role

The syntax pattern for creating a role is simple:

```
CREATE ROLE <role-name>;
```

SYSDBA or the database owner can create roles, grant privileges to them and, initially, grant these "loaded" roles to users. If a role is granted WITH ADMIN OPTION, the recipient of the role can grant it on to other users, WITH ADMIN OPTION or without.

Assigning Role Privileges

To "load" a role with privileges, just grant the required privileges as if the role were a user:

```
GRANT <privileges> TO <role-name>;
```

Granting a Role to Users

The GRANT statement for granting a role to users omits the ON clause—it's implicit in the permissions "loaded" into the role.

```
GRANT <role-name> [, <role-name> [, ...]]]
  TO [USER] <user-name> [, [USER] <user-name> [, ...]]]
    [WITH ADMIN OPTION];
```

The optional WITH ADMIN OPTION allows grantees to grant the role to other users and to revoke it. It works in a similar way to WITH GRANT OPTION for regular permissions—see the section "Granting the Right to Grant Privileges."

The following example creates the MAITRE_D role, grants ALL privileges on the DEPARTMENT table to this role, and then grants the role to HORTENSE. This gives HORTENSE the privileges SELECT, INSERT, UPDATE, DELETE, and REFERENCES on DEPARTMENT.

```
CREATE ROLE MAITRE_D;
COMMIT;
GRANT ALL
  ON DEPARTMENT
    TO MAITRE_D;
GRANT MAITRE_D TO HORTENSE;
```

Attaching to the Database Under a Role

When connecting, include ROLE in the connection parameters and specify the role whose privileges you want to acquire for that connection. It will only work if your user name has been granted the role:

```
CONNECT <database-path>
  USER <your-user-name>
    ROLE <role-name>
      PASSWORD <your-password>;
```

Dropping a Role

If you drop a role, all privileges that were conferred by that role are revoked. To drop the role MAITRE_D:

```
DROP ROLE MAITRE_D;
```

> **NOTE**   If you only want to remove the privileges granted to a user through a role, or to remove privileges from a role, use a REVOKE statement (see the section "Revoking Permissions").

Granting the Right to Grant Privileges

Initially, only the owner of a table or view, or SYSDBA, can grant permission on the object to other users. Add WITH GRANT OPTION to the end of the GRANT statement to transfer the right to grant privileges on to the user, along with the privilege itself.

The following statement assigns a SELECT permission to user HPOTTER and allows HPOTTER to grant the SELECT permission to others:

```
GRANT SELECT ON DEPARTMENT TO HPOTTER WITH GRANT OPTION;
```

WITH GRANT OPTION cannot be assigned to a trigger or procedure.

WITH GRANT OPTION rights are cumulative, even if issued by different users. For example, HPOTTER can get the grant authority for SELECT on DEPARTMENT from one user and for INSERT on DEPARTMENT from another.

In the example, HPOTTER was granted SELECT access to the DEPARTMENT table with grant authority. HPOTTER can grant this SELECT permission to other users. Suppose HPOTTER is now granted INSERT permission on the table as well, but *without* the grant authority:

```
GRANT INSERT ON DEPARTMENT TO HPOTTER;
```

HPOTTER can select from and insert to DEPARTMENT. He can grant SELECT permissions on DEPARTMENT to other users, but he cannot assign INSERT permissions because he does not have grant authority for that privilege.

The user's existing privileges can be extended to include grant authority, by issuing a second GRANT statement for the same privilege that includes WITH GRANT OPTION.

To give HPOTTER authority to grant INSERT permission on DEPARTMENT, just issue a new statement:

```
GRANT INSERT ON DEPARTMENT TO HPOTTER WITH GRANT OPTION;
```

In summary, a user can grant an access privilege (SELECT, INSERT, UPDATE, DELETE, and REFERENCES) on an object to other users or objects, if the user either

- Owns the object

- Has been granted that privilege on that object WITH GRANT OPTION

- Has acquired the privilege by being granted a role containing that privilege WITH ADMIN OPTION

SQL does not reject GRANT statements that cause a user's permissions to be duplicated.

Unintended Effects

SQL allows the same grantee to get the same permissions from different grantors, even if it would duplicate a permission the grantee already has. Every time one user extends grant authority to another user, it opens one more source through which any user could receive permissions. The permissions structure has the potential to become the proverbial bird's nest, from which it is very difficult to extricate the actual state of permissions for an individual user or object.

Suppose two users to whom the appropriate privileges and grant authority have been extended, SERENA and HPOTTER, both issue the following statement:

```
GRANT INSERT
  ON DEPARTMENT
    TO BRUNHILDE
      WITH GRANT OPTION;
```

Later, SERENA revokes the privilege and grant authority for BRUNHILDE:

```
REVOKE INSERT
  ON DEPARTMENT
    FROM BRUNHILDE;
```

SERENA thinks BRUNHILDE no longer has INSERT permission or grant authority for the DEPARTMENT table. However, the REVOKE appears to have no effect, since BRUNHILDE still has the INSERT permission and grant authority assigned by HPOTTER.

As the number of users with privileges and grant authority for a table proliferates, the likelihood that different users can grant the same privileges and grant authority to any single user also expands. Quite simply, like nuclear fission, it can go out of control. It can become a big job just to revoke a specific permission. Revoking all (or many) permissions for a particular user can become an astronomical challenge.

If it is possible that the user might have received rights from several grantors, there are two possible solutions, both messy:

- Find each and every permission granted to that user, along with the grantor in each case, and have each grantor revoke each permission it granted. This gets complicated when ALL and PUBLIC are involved, since revoking a more targeted permission doesn't revoke rights acquired through ALL, PUBLIC, roles, or groups.

- The owner of each table or object (or SYSDBA) issues REVOKE statements affecting all users of the table, and then issues GRANT statements to re-establish access privileges for the users who need to keep their rights.

The server gives no feedback about any REVOKE command, regardless of whether it succeeds or fails. It's around about this point in your first misadventure with SQL permissions that you roll your eyes to the heavens and ponder the real mission of standards committees on Earth. A well-designed graphic rights manager utility can save your sanity. Fortunately, many of the desktop admin programs do provide this support and a number of custom grant manager tools are available. Refer to Appendix XII for links to the offerings.

For more information about revoking permissions, see the next section.

 TIP Although defining users and roles and applying privileges are often deferred until a system is ready to deploy, designing the privileges scheme and coordinating it with the user list needs to be a planned part of overall system design. Maintaining a tree diagram of the scheme is very useful, both for designing and testing the scheme and for documenting it.

Revoking Permissions

A REVOKE statement is required for removing permissions assigned by GRANT statements. According to the standard, the REVOKE should cascade down through all grantees that acquired the same privilege as a result of a WITH GRANT OPTION grant from this user. However, you should not rely on this in Firebird, since conflicting rules in the standard could cause implementation logic to prevail over the standard under some conditions.

REVOKE statements can remove any privilege that GRANT can assign. Only SYSDBA or the user that granted a privilege can revoke it—the same or other privileges that were granted by other users are not affected.

Permissions acquired "in bulk" can't be revoked individually. That means

- A privilege that a user acquired by being granted ALL or a role can be removed only by the original grantor revoking ALL or the role, respectively.

- Revoking a privilege for a user that got the privilege by way of a grant to PUBLIC or to a UNIX group can be achieved only by the original grantor revoking the privilege on PUBLIC or the group, respectively.

- Privileges granted to PUBLIC can only be revoked FROM PUBLIC.

Using REVOKE

The simplified syntax pattern for REVOKE is the other face of the GRANT syntax. The TO *<grantee>* clause is replaced by FROM *<grantee>*:

```
REVOKE <privileges>
  ON <object>
    FROM <grantee> ;
```

The following statement removes the SELECT privilege for the user KILROY on the DEPARTMENT table if it was granted with GRANT SELECT:

```
REVOKE SELECT ON DEPARTMENT FROM KILROY;
```

The following statement removes the UPDATE privilege for the procedure COUNT_BEANS on the CUSTOMER table:

```
REVOKE UPDATE ON CUSTOMER FROM PROCEDURE COUNT_BEANS;
```

The next statement removes the EXECUTE privilege that was granted to the procedure COUNT_BEANS on the ABANDON_OLD procedure:

```
REVOKE EXECUTE ON PROCEDURE ABANDON_OLD FROM PROCEDURE COUNT_BEANS;
```

Revoking Multiple Privileges

To remove some, but not all, of the access privileges assigned to a user or procedure, list the privileges to remove, separating them with commas. For example, the following statement removes the INSERT and UPDATE privileges on DEPARTMENT from a user, SERENA:

```
REVOKE INSERT, UPDATE ON DEPARTMENT FROM SERENA;
```

The next statement removes two privileges on the CUSTOMER table from a stored procedure, COUNT_BEANS:

```
REVOKE INSERT, DELETE
  ON CUSTOMER
    FROM PROCEDURE COUNT_BEANS;
```

Any combination of previously assigned SELECT, INSERT, UPDATE, DELETE, or REFERENCES privileges can be revoked from a grantee, whether they were granted individually, in a list, or using ALL.

As with GRANT, the REVOKE ALL privilege combines the SELECT, INSERT, UPDATE, DELETE, and REFERENCES privileges into a single expression. It will revoke any of these permissions from a grantee that had the privilege assigned to its own name.

For example, the following statement revokes all access privileges on DEPARTMENT from a user named MAGPIE:

```
REVOKE ALL ON DEPARTMENTS FROM MAGPIE;
```

If the grantee does not have all of the privileges that ALL encompasses, it will not cause an exception. That can make REVOKE ALL quite useful if you do not know what privileges a grantee has. It will not necessarily solve the problem of eliminating all of the permissions available to the user, because REVOKE ALL has limits on what it is capable of revoking.

What REVOKE ALL Does Not Revoke

REVOKE ALL does not revoke

- The grantee's role membership or privileges the grantee inherits with role membership

- Any privileges the grantee has by way of PUBLIC

- The grantee's EXECUTE privileges

Revoking the EXECUTE Privilege

The syntax for revoking a grantee's EXECUTE privilege on a stored procedure has this syntax pattern:

```
REVOKE EXECUTE
  ON PROCEDURE <procedure-name>
    FROM <grantee> [, <grantee> [, ...]]]
    | [TRIGGER <trigger-name> [, <trigger-name> [,...]]]
```

```
[PROCEDURE <procedure-name> [, <procedure-name [, ...]]]
[VIEW <view-name> [, VIEW <view-name> [, ...]]];
```

The following statement removes the EXECUTE privilege from user HPOTTER on the procedure COUNT_CHICKENS:

```
REVOKE EXECUTE ON PROCEDURE COUNT_CHICKENS FROM HPOTTER;
```

Revoking from Grantees

Now, we take a look at how grantees—the objective of the FROM clause in the REVOKE statement—can be bundled for bulk denial of privileges.

From a List of Grantees

Use a comma-separated list of grantees to bulk-remove privileges from a number of users in a single statement. The following statement revokes INSERT and UPDATE permissions on DEPARTMENT from three grantees in one hit:

```
REVOKE INSERT, UPDATE
  ON DEPARTMENTS
    FROM MAGPIE, BRUNHILDE, KILROY;
```

From a Role

Revoking privileges granted to a role denies those privileges to any grantees having that role as a privilege:

```
REVOKE UPDATE
  ON DEPARTMENT
    FROM CARTEBLANCHE;
```

Now, users who were granted the CARTEBLANCHE role no longer have the UPDATE privilege on DEPARTMENT, but they retain other privileges (SELECT, INSERT, DELETE, REFERENCES, EXECUTE) that they might have inherited from their membership of CARTEBLANCHE.

You can use a single statement to revoke the same privileges from one or more roles:

```
REVOKE DELETE, INSERT
  ON DEPARTMENT
    FROM CARTEBLANCHE, MAITRE_D;
```

From a Role User

Revoking membership from a role that has been assigned to a grantee denies the grantee all of the permissions that it acquired through the role. Use REVOKE to remove a role that you assigned to users. The following statement revokes the CARTEBLANCHE role from KILROY:

```
REVOKE CARTEBLANCHE FROM KILROY;
```

KILROY no longer has any of the access privileges acquired as a result of membership in the role. However, other grantees who acquired the same privileges through membership of the role are unaffected.

From Objects

To revoke privileges from one or more procedures, triggers, or views, include the appropriate keyword (PROCEDURE, TRIGGER, VIEW) before the name of the grantee object.

You can revoke the same privilege from different types of grantee objects by making a separate comma-separated list for each object type. In that case, just start each list with the object type keyword.

The following statement revokes INSERT and UPDATE privileges on the CUSTOMER table from two procedures and a trigger:

```
REVOKE INSERT, UPDATE
  ON CUSTOMER
    FROM PROCEDURE COUNT_CHICKENS, ABANDON_OLD
       TRIGGER AI_SALES ;
```

From User PUBLIC

To revoke privileges that all users are granted as user PUBLIC, just treat PUBLIC as any other grantee. For example, the following statement revokes INSERT and DELETE permissions on DEPARTMENT from all users:

```
REVOKE SELECT, INSERT, UPDATE
  ON DEPARTMENT
    FROM PUBLIC;
```

Executing this statement leaves the table's owner and SYSDBA, as well as any stored procedures, views, or triggers that already had them, retaining INSERT and DELETE privileges on DEPARTMENT. Also, revoking privileges from PUBLIC does not strip privileges from users that had them in their own right.

Revoking Grant Authority

To revoke a user's grant authority for a given privilege, but keep the associated privilege, use REVOKE GRANT OPTION:

```
REVOKE GRANT OPTION
  FOR <privilege> [, <privilege> [,...]]
    ON <table> | <object>
      FROM <user> ;
```

For example, the following statement revokes grant authority for the SELECT privilege on DEPARTMENT from a user, HPOTTER, and he keeps his SELECT privilege:

```
REVOKE GRANT OPTION
  FOR SELECT
    ON DEPARTMENT
      FROM HPOTTER;
```

The execution of the statement will cascade down to any others users that have been granted grant authority by HPOTTER.

Security Scripts

If you have stayed with this chapter so far, no doubt you have reached the conclusion that implementing SQL privileges is one helluva lot of typing. Well, you'd be right. In reality, we don't use interactive methods to do this job. We write scripts—or, rather, we write stored procedures that write the scripts for us.

Generally, if we have a good privileges scheme worked out, we can generate a couple of scripts that load up our roles and general permissions. Usually, a manually written script is wanted for EXECUTE permissions, since it is fairly difficult to work up a formula for those.

With the advent of the EXECUTE STATEMENT statement in Firebird 1.5, which enables us to get past Firebird's inability to execute DDL statements in PSQL, we can bulk-load permissions directly to the database, through a stored procedure. An example of such a procedure is in Listing 35-2 later in this section.

For those who love a tool with a graphical interface, there are plenty of them around. Most provide a utility that automates the creation of security scripts; some carry through and install the permissions directly for you.

Creating a Script

The author prefers to generate a security script. It can be tested and annotated, and it provides most of the documentation needed for QA and as a basis for custom deployments. An example of such a script is Listing 35-1.

For the script, we might use an external file into which to output the script—for instructions and examples, refer to Chapter 16 and to the samples in Chapter 30. However, the *permscript* procedure listed here is designed to run in **isql** and to pass its output to a text file from there.

Listing 35-1. Procedure to Generate Permissions Script

```
/* (c) Helen Borrie 2004, free for use and modification
       under the Initial Developer's Public License */
SET TERM ^;
CREATE PROCEDURE PERMSCRIPT (
    CMD VARCHAR(6),                             /* enter 'G' or 'R' */
    PRIV CHAR(10),                 /* a privilege, or 'ALL' or 'ANY' */
    USR VARCHAR(31),                            /* a username */
    ROLENAME VARCHAR(31),               /* a role, existing or not */
    GRANTOPT SMALLINT,            /* 1 for 'WITH GRANT [ADMIN] OPTION' */
    CREATE_ROLE SMALLINT)             /* 1 to create new role ROLENAME */
RETURNS (PERM VARCHAR(80)) /* a permission statement, theoretically */
AS
  DECLARE VARIABLE RELNAME VARCHAR(31); /* for a table or view name */
  DECLARE VARIABLE STRING VARCHAR(80) = '';         /* used in proc */
  DECLARE VARIABLE STUB VARCHAR(60) = '';           /* used in proc */
  DECLARE VARIABLE VUSR VARCHAR(31); /* username for 'TO' or 'FROM' */
  DECLARE VARIABLE COMMENTS CHAR(20) = '/*                     */';
BEGIN
    /* Necessary for some UI editors */
    IF (ROLENAME = '') THEN ROLENAME = NULL;
    IF (USR = '') THEN USR = NULL;
    IF (PRIV = '') THEN PRIV = NULL;
    /* Not enough data to do anything with */
    IF ((PRIV IS NULL AND ROLENAME IS NULL) OR USR IS NULL) THEN EXIT;

    /* If there's a rolename, we'll do stuff with it */
    IF (ROLENAME IS NOT NULL) THEN
    BEGIN
      /* If a role name is supplied, create the role if requested */
      IF (CREATE_ROLE = 1) THEN
      BEGIN
        PERM = 'CREATE ROLE '||ROLENAME||';';
        SUSPEND;
        PERM = 'COMMIT;';
        SUSPEND;
        PERM = COMMENTS;
        SUSPEND;
      END
      VUSR = ROLENAME;
    END
```

```
/* If there's a rolename, we'll apply the permissions to the role
   and grant the role to the supplied user */
ELSE
  /* We are not interested in the role: permissions are just for user */
  VUSR = USR;
/* Decide whether it's a GRANT or a REVOKE script */
IF (CMD STARTING WITH 'G') THEN
  STUB = 'GRANT ';
ELSE
  STUB = 'REVOKE ';
IF (ROLENAME IS NOT NULL) THEN
BEGIN
  IF (STUB = 'GRANT') THEN
  BEGIN
    /* Grant the role to the user */
    STRING = STUB||ROLENAME||' TO '||USR;
    IF (GRANTOPT = 1) THEN
      STRING = STRING||'  WITH ADMIN OPTION ;';
  END
  ELSE
    STRING = STUB||ROLENAME||' FROM '||USR||';';
  PERM = STRING;
  SUSPEND;
  PERM = COMMENTS;
  SUSPEND;
END
/* If ANY was passed in as privilege, create all perms separately */
IF (PRIV = 'ANY') THEN
  STUB = STUB||'SELECT,DELETE,INSERT,UPDATE,REFERENCES ON ';
ELSE
  STUB = STUB||PRIV||' ON ';
/* Cycle through the table and view names and create a statement for each */
FOR SELECT RDB$RELATION_NAME FROM RDB$RELATIONS
WHERE RDB$RELATION_NAME NOT STARTING WITH 'RDB$'
INTO :RELNAME DO
BEGIN
  STRING = STUB||:RELNAME||' ';
  IF (CMD STARTING WITH 'G') THEN
    STRING = STRING||'TO ';
  ELSE
    STRING = STRING||'FROM ';
  STRING = STRING||VUSR;
  IF (CMD STARTING WITH 'G'
      AND GRANTOPT = 1 AND ROLENAME IS NULL) THEN
    STRING = STRING||'  WITH GRANT OPTION ;';
  ELSE
    STRING = STRING||' ;';
  PERM = STRING;
```

```
        SUSPEND;
      END
      PERM = COMMENTS;
      SUSPEND;
    END ^
SET TERM ;^
```

Creating and Running the Script

Go to the Firebird /bin directory and start **isql** under the SYSDBA login, connecting to the database. We will use the procedure to make a script that adds a role 'MANDRAKE', grants the role to user USER1, and then sets up the permissions for the role. Then it will do the same thing again with an existing role 'PURPLE' for user USER2:

```
SQL> OUTPUT L:\DATA\EXAMPLES\PERMSCRIPT.SQL;
SQL> SELECT * FROM PERMSCRIPT ('G', 'ALL', 'USER1', 'MANDRAKE', 1, 1);
SQL> COMMIT;
SQL> SELECT * FROM PERMSCRIPT ('G', 'ALL', 'USER2', 'PURPLE', 1, 0);
SQL> COMMIT;
SQL> OUTPUT;
SQL> INPUT L:\DATA\EXAMPLES\PERMSCRIPT.SQL;
SQL> COMMIT;
SQL> SHOW GRANT;
```

That's all there is to it. You will get an error message when the INPUT utility encounters the non-SQL "window dressing" printed by OUTPUT, but it will not interfere with writing the permissions.

Installing Perms Directly from a Procedure

The procedure grant_perms, shown in Listing 35-2, is basically the same procedure. Instead of producing a set of output lines for **isql** to run as a script, it actually installs the permissions directly, via EXECUTE STATEMENT. This technique isn't available for Firebird 1.0.*x*.

Listing 35-2. Permissions Procedure

```
/* (c) Helen Borrie 2004, free for use and modification
      under the Initial Developer's Public License */
SET TERM ^;
CREATE PROCEDURE GRANT_PERMS
  (CMD VARCHAR(6),
   PRIV CHAR(10),
   USR VARCHAR(31),
   ROLENAME VARCHAR(31),
   GRANTOPT SMALLINT)
```

```
AS
  DECLARE VARIABLE RELNAME VARCHAR(31);
  DECLARE VARIABLE EXESTRING VARCHAR(1024) = '';
  DECLARE VARIABLE EXESTUB VARCHAR(1024) = '';
BEGIN
    IF (ROLENAME = '') THEN ROLENAME = NULL;
    IF (USR = '') THEN USR = NULL;
    IF (PRIV = '') THEN PRIV = NULL;
    IF ((PRIV IS NULL AND ROLENAME IS NULL) OR USR IS NULL) THEN EXIT;
    IF (CMD STARTING WITH 'G') THEN
      EXESTUB = 'GRANT ';
    ELSE
      EXESTUB = 'REVOKE ';
    IF (ROLENAME IS NOT NULL) THEN
    BEGIN
      IF (EXESTUB = 'GRANT') THEN
      BEGIN
        EXESTUB = EXESTUB||ROLENAME||' TO '||USR;
        IF (GRANTOPT = 1) THEN
          EXESTUB = EXESTUB||' WITH ADMIN OPTION';
      END
      ELSE
        EXESTUB = EXESTUB||ROLENAME||' FROM '||USR;
      EXECUTE STATEMENT EXESTUB;
    END
    ELSE
    BEGIN
      IF (PRIV = 'ANY') THEN
        EXESTUB = EXESTUB||'SELECT,DELETE,INSERT,UPDATE,REFERENCES ON ';
      ELSE
        EXESTUB = EXESTUB||PRIV||' ON ';
      FOR SELECT RDB$RELATION_NAME FROM RDB$RELATIONS
      WHERE RDB$RELATION_NAME NOT STARTING WITH 'RDB$'
      INTO :RELNAME DO
      BEGIN
        EXESTRING = EXESTUB||:RELNAME||' ';
        IF (CMD STARTING WITH 'G') THEN
          EXESTRING = EXESTRING||'TO ';
        ELSE
          EXESTRING = EXESTRING||'FROM ';
        EXESTRING = EXESTRING||USR;
        IF (GRANTOPT = 1) THEN
          EXESTRING = EXESTRING||' WITH GRANT OPTION';
        EXECUTE STATEMENT EXESTRING;
      END
    END
END ^
SET TERM ;^
```

If you want to experiment with these scripts yourself and modify them to suit your needs, you can find the sources in the Downloads section of `http://www.apress.com`, in the file *permscripts.sql*.

Up Next

The next (and final) chapter in this part contains a number of topics to do with architectural variants of the server, including a section about installing and using the embedded Superserver on Windows. Configuration file settings in firebird.conf or isc_config/ibconfig can be found in this chapter, along with topics and security configuration parameters relating to Firebird's use of external executables and other files.

CHAPTER 36

Configuration and Special Features

THIS CHAPTER IS A POTPOURRI OF TOPICS that will be of interest to developers who have become familiar with the practical issues of running Firebird.

- First is a summary of the architectural differences between the Firebird Classic server and the Superserver models.

- Next, a miscellany of server configuration parameters is discussed.

- Some guidelines follow for developing with the Windows embedded server.

- Finally, we take an overview of the custom external code modules that you can write, for use by the server engine, to perform specialized calculations and transformations (external functions), convert BLOBs from one format to another (BLOB filters), and implement international character sets. At the end of this topic are details about configuring the server's filesystem access to these and other external objects.

Comparing Superserver and Classic Server Architecture

While Superserver and Classic server share many common characteristics—indeed, they are built from the same codebase—they present quite distinct models of operation under the hood.

Executable and Processes

Classic server runs one server process per connection, on demand (see Figure 36-1). When a client attempts to connect to a Firebird database, an instance of the fb_inet_server executable is initiated and remains dedicated to that client connection for the duration of the connection. When the client detaches from the database, the server process instance ends.

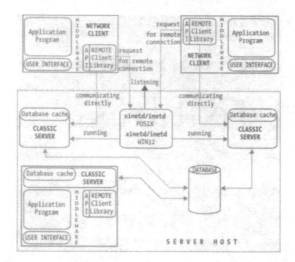

Figure 36-1. The Classic server network and process model

Superserver runs as a single invocation of the fbserver executable (see Figure 36-2). fbserver is started once, by a system boot script or by the system administrator, and stays running, waiting for connection requests. The process is terminated by an explicit shutdown.

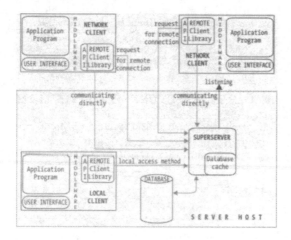

Figure 36-2. The Superserver network and process model

Lock Management

On Classic server, each client's server process has its own, dedicated database cache and multiple processes contend for access to the database. A lock manager subsystem, fb_lock_mgr, uses inter-process communication (IPC) methods to arbitrate and synchronize concurrent page access among the processes.

On Superserver, the lock manager is implemented as a thread within the fbserver process and uses inter-thread communication mechanisms instead of POSIX signaling.

For a detailed overview of lock manager internals, refer to Chapter 40.

Resource Use

On Classic server, each instance of fb_inet_server is allocated a static cache of database pages in its memory space. Resource growth per additional client connection is therefore linear. However, when the number of concurrent connections is relatively low, Classic server uses fewer overall resources.

Superserver employs a single cache space that is shared by client attachments, allowing more efficient use and management of cache memory when the number of simultaneous connections grows larger.

Local Access Method

Classic server permits application processes that are running on the same machine as the server and databases to perform I/O on database files directly.

Except for the Embedded Server, Superserver requires applications to use a network method for I/O requests and satisfies those requests by proxy. On Linux, Superserver does not support direct local access.

- On non-Windows platforms (and recommended for Windows too) local connections to Superserver are made through the localhost server (at IP address 127.0.0.1, by convention).

- A Windows server and local client can simulate a network connection in the shared IPC space. This mechanism, referred to as *the local access method*, cannot handle multiple connections safely. Beyond Firebird 1.5, it is superseded by a local access method using the XNET subsystem.

Embedded Server can use only the "Windows local" access method and supports *one and only one connection* to each local database. The embedded client can connect to multiple local databases exclusively and access them through the embedded server. The embedded client can also connect as a regular network client to databases on other servers.

The Firebird Configuration File

Firebird does not require the intense and constant reconfiguration that many other heavy-duty RDBMSs do. However, a range of configuration options is available for customizing a Firebird server and the host system on which it runs when special needs must be met.

The Firebird configuration file is named firebird.conf in all Firebird versions from 1.5 onward. In prior versions, its name depends on the operating system:

- On Linux/UNIX, the name is isc_config.

- On Windows, the name is ibconfig.

Several new parameters were added to version 1.5.

When the Firebird server startup process reads the configuration file, it adjusts its runtime flags to any non-default values contained in the configuration file. The file will not be read again until next time the server is restarted. The default configuration parameters and their values are listed in the configuration file, commented out by # comment markers. It is not necessary to uncomment the defaults in order to make them visible to the server's startup procedure.

The configuration file can be edited with any plain text editor, for example, vim (Linux) or Notepad (Windows). Do not copy the file from a Windows machine to a Linux one or vice versa, because the two systems store line breaks differently.

Parameters

Entries are in the form

```
parameter_name = value
```

- `parameter_name` is a string that contains no white space and names a property of the server being configured.

- `value` is a number, Boolean (1=True, 0=False), or string that specifies the value for the parameter.

To set any parameter to a non-default setting, delete the comment (#) marker and edit the value.

The Firebird 1.0.*x* ibconfig/isc_config parameter names and syntaxes are not interchangeable with those in firebird.conf. The format, size, and number of parameters are more restrictive.

The ibconfig/isc_config format is

```
parameter_name    value
```

where the white space between the name and the value can be tabs or spaces, as desired, to please the eye. Each line of the file is limited to 80 characters. Unused parameters and installation defaults are commented with '#'.

On Linux, you should assume that parameter names are case sensitive.

NOTE You can edit the configuration file while the server is running. To activate configuration changes, it is necessary to stop and restart the service.

"Missing" Parameters in Firebird 1.0.x

In pre–version 1.5 installations, some optional parameters, requiring settings that could not be configured as defaults, were omitted from the configuration file.

- If a missing parameter pertinent to ibconfig or isc_config is needed, it can be added.

- If you include a parameter that is not supported in the release version you are running, it will be ignored.

- The ibconfig/isc_config parameter names and syntaxes are not interchangeable with those in firebird.conf.

Lock Manager Settings

The advanced lock manager configuration settings are discussed toward the end of Chapter 40.

Filesystem-Related Parameters

RootDirectory

Version 1.5 forward

This value is a string, the absolute path to a directory root on the local filesystem. It should remain commented unless you want to force the startup procedure to override the path to the root directory of the Firebird server installation, that it would otherwise detect for itself. Firebird 1.5 and higher servers follow a predefined route to find the root directory. The logic of this route is explained in Chapter 3.

DatabaseAccess

```
Version 1.5 forward
```

In Firebird 1.0.*x*, the server can attach to any database in its local filesystem and is always accessed by applications passing the file's absolute filesystem path. This parameter was introduced in version 1.5 to provide tighter security controls on access to database files and to support the database-aliasing feature. This parameter provides options to restrict the server's access to only aliased databases or to only databases located in specific filesystem trees.

DatabaseAccess may be Full, None, or Restrict.

- **Full** (the default) permits database files to be accessed anywhere on the local filesystem.

- **None** permits the server to attach only databases that are listed in aliases.conf.

 CAUTION It is strongly recommended that you set this option and make use of the database-aliasing feature. Database aliasing is described, with examples, in Chapter 4.

- **Restrict** allows you to configure the locations of attachable database files to a specified list of filesystem tree roots. Supply a list of one or more tree roots, separated by semicolons, to define one or more permissible locations, for example:

```
POSIX: /db/databases;/userdir/data
Windows:  D:\data
```

Relative paths are treated as relative to the path that the running server recognizes as the root directory. For example, on Windows, if the root directory is C:\Program Files\Firebird, then the following value will restrict the server to accessing database files located under C:\Program Files\Firebird\userdata:

```
ExternalFileAccess = Restrict userdata
```

Parameters for Configuring Temporary Sort Space

When the size of the internal sort buffer is too small to accommodate the rows involved in a sort operation, Firebird needs to create temporary sort files on the server's filesystem. By default, it will look for the path specified in the environment variable INTERBASE_TMP. If that variable is not present, it will try to use the root of the /tmp filesystem on Linux/UNIX, or C:\Temp on Windows NT/2000/XP. None of these locations can be configured for size.

Firebird provides a parameter for configuring the disk space that will be used for storing these temporary files. It is prudent to use it, to ensure that sufficient sort space will be available under all conditions.

All CONNECT or CREATE DATABASE requests share the same list of temporary file directories and each creates its own temporary files. Sort files are released when the sort is finished or the request is released.

In release 1.5, the name of the parameter changed from tmp_directory to TempDirectories, and the syntax of the parameter value also changed.

TempDirectories

Version 1.5 forward

Supply a list of one or more directories, separated by semicolons (;), under which sort files may be stored. Each item may include an optional size argument, in bytes, to limit its storage. If the argument is omitted or is invalid, Firebird will use the space in that directory until it is exhausted, before moving on to the next listed directory, for example:

```
POSIX: /db/sortfiles1 100000000;/firebird/sortfiles2
Windows:  E:\sortfiles 500000000
```

Relative paths are treated as relative to the path that the running server recognizes as the root directory of the Firebird installation. For example, on Windows, if the root directory is C:\Program Files\Firebird, then the following value will tell the server to store temporary files in C:\Program Files\Firebird\userdata\sortfiles, up to a limit of about 477MB:

```
TempDirectories = userdata\sortfiles 500000000
```

tmp_directory

Versions prior to Firebird 1.5

The syntax for the older tmp_directory value is to include one tmp_directory line for each directory in which you want temporary sort files to be stored. Specify the number of bytes available in the directory and, within double quotes, the path to a directory that exists on a physical drive with sufficient spare capacity. There is no restriction on the name used for the directory. You can list multiple entries, one per line, and the spaces do not need to be contiguous or confined to a single storage device.

For example, the following entries constitute a list in a single configuration file:

```
tmp_directory 6000000 "d:\fbtemp"
tmp_directory 12000000 "f:\fbtemp"
tmp_directory 4000000 "w:\backwash"
```

pathname must be enclosed in double quotes, or the server will ignore this entry. Space will be used according to the order specified. If space runs out in a particular directory, Firebird creates a new temporary file in the next directory from the directory list. If there are no more entries in the directory list, Firebird displays an error message and stops processing the current request.

Resource-Related Parameters

CpuAffinityMask

```
Windows versions 1.5 forward
```

cpu_affinity

```
Windows versions prior to Firebird 1.5
```

With Firebird Superserver on Windows, there can be a problem with the operating system continually swapping the entire Superserver process back and forth between processors on SMP machines. In support lists, this is referred to as "the see-saw effect" and, on affected systems, it can have a severe effect on performance. This parameter must be used to set Firebird Superserver's processor affinity to one or more specific CPUs.

CpuAffinityMask and cpu_affinity take one integer: the CPU mask. For example:

```
CpuAffinityMask = 1
cpu_affinity = 1
```

only runs on the first CPU (CPU 0).

```
CpuAffinityMask = 2
cpu_affinity = 2
```

only runs on the second CPU (CPU 1).

```
CpuAffinityMask = 3
cpu_affinity = 3
```

runs on both first and second CPU.

CAUTION   This parameter has no effect in Windows9*x* or ME, as it uses an NT API call. Windows9*x* flavors do not utilize multiple processors.

Calculating the Affinity Mask Value

You can use this parameter to set Firebird's affinity to any single processor or (on Classic server) any combination of the CPUs installed in the system.

Consider the CPUs as an array numbered from 0 to *n*–1, where *n* is the number of processors installed and *i* is the array number of a CPU. *M* is another array, containing the MaskValue of each selected CPU. The value *A* is the sum of the values in *M*.

Use the following formula to arrive at *M* and calculate the MaskValue *A*:

```
Mᵢ = 2ᴵ
A = M₁ + M₂ + M₃. . .
```

$$M_i = 2^I$$
$$A = M_1 + M_2 + M_3 . . .$$

For example, to select the first and fourth processors (processor 0 and processor 3) calculate as follows:

$$A = 2^0 + 2^3 = 1 + 8 = 9$$

CAUTION   Firebird servers, up to and including release 1.5, may not support the hyperthreading feature of some later model motherboards. To avoid balancing problems, it may be necessary to disable hyperthreading at the system BIOS level.

The default CPU affinity mask is 1 (processor 0).

DefaultDbCachePages

```
Version 1.5 forward
```

database_cache_pages

```
Versions prior to Firebird 1.5
```

This sets the global server default (integer) number of database pages to allocate in memory for each database. The configured value can be overridden at database level.

The default value for Superserver is 2048 pages. For Classic server, it is 75.

Superserver and Classic server allocate and use cache memory differently. There is no "formula" that can be applied to set an optimal default cache size to suit all needs. However, the factors are discussed in greater detail in Chapter 15 in the section "The Database Cache."

EventMemSize

Version 1.5 forward

This is an integer representing the number of bytes of memory reserved for the event manager. The default is 65536 (64K).

SortMemBlockSize

Version 1.5 forward

This parameter allows you to configure, in bytes, the size of each memory block used by the in-memory sorting module. The installation default is 1MB, which you can reconfigure to any size up to the currently configured maximum value set by the SortMemUpperLimit parameter (see the next section).

SortMemUpperLimit

Version 1.5 forward

The maximum amount of memory, in bytes, to be allocated by the in-memory sorting module. The installation default is 67108864 bytes (64MB) for Superserver and 8388608 (8MB) for Classic server.

CAUTION For Classic server, the default is too large unless only a handful of clients are connected. Bear in mind that increasing either the block size or the maximum limit on Classic server affects each client connection/server instance and will ramp up the server's memory consumption in linear proportions.

Communications-Related Parameters

ConnectionTimeout

Version 1.5 forward

connection_timeout

```
Versions prior to Firebird 1.5
```

This is the number of seconds to wait before abandoning an attempt to connect. The default is 180.

DummyPacketInterval

```
Version 1.5 forward
```

dummy_packet_interval

```
Versions prior to Firebird 1.5
```

This is an old InterBase timeout parameter that sets the number of seconds (integer) the server should wait on a silent client connection before sending dummy packets to request acknowledgment. It is set by default to 0 on Firebird 1.5 (disabled) and to 60 on Firebird 1.0.*x*.

 CAUTION This parameter should not be enabled on Windows *at all* and it is not recommended on other operating systems.[1]

On Firebird 1.0.*x*, open ibconfig (Windows) or isc_config (other systems) and add the line:

```
dummy_packet_interval=0
```

Normally, Firebird keeps track of active connections using the SO_KEEPALIVE socket option, with a default timeout period of 2 hours. If you need to alter the timeout period, adjust server settings to suit:

- On POSIX servers, modify the contents of proc/sys/net/ipv4/tcp_keepalive_*.

- For Windows, obtain instructions from the article at
  `http://support.microsoft.com/default.aspx?kbid=140325`.

---

1. Due to a Windows bug, enabling DummyPacketInterval may hang or crash Windows on the client side. For an explanation, refer to this Microsoft Support article: `http://support.microsoft.com/default.aspx?kbid=296265`. It is not recommended to enable it for non-Windows systems, either, as it may actually interfere with the eventual disconnection of an inactive client.

RemoteServiceName

Version 1.5 forward

This is the name of the service as broadcast by the server. If the firebird.conf file is optionally included in a client-only installation (see Chapter 7), the client will use it to find the service name if necessary. See also RemoteServicePort (described in the next section). For more information, refer to the section "Configuring the Port Service" in Chapter 2.

Default = gds_db

RemoteServicePort

Version 1.5 forward

This parameter and RemoteServiceName provide the ability to override either the TCP/IP service name or the TCP/IP port number used to listen for client database connection requests, if one of them differs from the installed defaults (gds_db and port 3050).

Change one of the entries, not both. RemoteServiceName is checked first for a matching entry in the services file. If there is a match, the port number configured for RemoteServicePort is used. If there is not a match, then the installation default, port 3050, is used.

NOTE If a port number is provided in the TCP/IP connection string, it will always take precedence over RemoteServicePort.

RemoteAuxPort

Version 1.5 forward

The inherited InterBase behavior of passing event notification messages back to the network layer through randomly selected TCP/IP ports shows up in some types of installations as a persistent source of network errors and conflicts with firewalls, sometimes to the extent of causing the server to crash. This parameter allows you to configure a single TCP port for all event notification traffic.

The installation default (0) retains the traditional random port behavior. To dedicate one specific port for event notifications, use an integer that is an available port number.

RemoteBindAddress

```
Version 1.5 forward
```

By default, clients may connect from any network interface through which the host server accepts traffic. This parameter allows you to bind the Firebird service to incoming requests through a single IP address (e.g., network card) and to reject connection requests from any other network interfaces. This helps to solve problems in some networks when the server is hosting multiple subnets.

This is a string, in a valid dotted IP format. The default value (not bound) is an empty setting.

TcpRemoteBufferSize

```
Version 1.5 forward
```

The engine reads ahead of the client and can send several rows of data in a single packet. The larger the packet size, the more rows are sent per transfer. Use this parameter (with caution and complete comprehension of its effects on network performance) if you need to enlarge or reduce the TCP/IP packet size for send and receive buffers. It affects both the client and server.

The value is an integer (the size of the packet in bytes) in the range 1448 to 32768. The installation default is 8192.

POSIX-Specific Parameters

RemoteFileOpenAbility

```
Version 1.5 forward, POSIX only
```

 CAUTION Use RemoteFileOpenAbility only with *extreme* caution.

This is a Boolean parameter that, if set to True, allows the engine to open files that reside on a networked filesystem (NFS) mounted partition. It is intended to allow shadows on NFS drives that have high availability. It is not safe for database files—except possibly a read-only database—because the filesystem is beyond the control of the local system. It should not be enabled for the purpose of opening any read/write database whose survival matters to you.

The default is 0 (False, disabled) and you should leave it that way unless you are very clear about its effects.

TcpNoNagle

```
Version 1.5 forward, Linux only
```

tcp_no_nagle

```
Versions prior to Firebird 1.5, Linux only
```

On Linux, by default, the socket library will minimize physical writes by buffering writes before actually sending the data, using an internal algorithm (implemented as the TCP_NODELAY option of the socket connection) known as Nagle's algorithm. It was designed to avoid problems with small packets, called *tinygrams*, on slow networks.

By default, TCP_NODELAY is enabled (value 0) when Firebird Superserver is installed on Linux. On slow networks, disabling it can actually improve speed. Watch out for the double negative—set the parameter to True to disable TCP_NODELAY and False to enable it.

In releases up to and including v.1.5, this feature is active only for Superserver.

Windows-Specific Parameters

CreateInternalWindow

```
Version 1.5 forward, Windows only
```

The "Windows local" protocol uses a hidden window for IPC between the local client and the server. This IPC window is created at server startup when CreateInternalWindow is true (1, the default). Set it to 0 (off) to run the server without a window and thus to disable local protocol. With local protocol disabled, it is possible to run multiple instances of the server simultaneously.

DeadThreadsCollection

```
Version 1.5 forward, Windows only
```

A setting for the thread scheduler on Windows, this integer parameter establishes the number of priority switching cycles (see the section "PrioritySwitchDelay") that the scheduler is to execute before a thread is destroyed (or closed).

Immediate destruction (or closure) of worker threads would require a semaphore and blocking call, generating significant overhead. Instead, a thread scheduler maintains threads in a pool. When a thread has completed its task, it is marked as idle. The idle thread is destroyed (or closed) after n iterations of the scheduler loop, where n is the value of the DeadThreadsCollection parameter.

For a server handling a very large number of connections—in the high hundreds or more—the parameter value will need to be raised from its default setting of 50.

GuardianOption

`Version 1.5 forward, Windows only`

This is a Boolean parameter used on Windows servers to determine whether the Guardian should restart the server every time it terminates abnormally. The installation default is to do so (1=True). To disable the restart behavior, set this parameter off (0=False).

IpcMapSize

`Version 1.5 forward`

server_client_mapping

`Versions prior to Firebird 1.5`

This is the size in bytes of one client's portion of the memory-mapped file used for IPC in the connection model used for the "Windows local" connection. It has no equivalent on other platforms. It is an integer, from 1024 to 8192. The default is 4096.

Increasing the map size may improve performance when retrieving very wide or large data row sets, such as those returning graphics BLOBs.

NOTE If Firebird is running as an application, this setting can also be modified in the Guardian's system tray icon dialog. Stop and restart the server to have the new setting take effect.

IpcName

`Version 1.5 forward, applicable only on Windows platforms`

The default value is FirebirdIPI.

This is the name of the shared memory area used as a transport channel in local protocol.

The release 1.5 default value, FirebirdIPI, is not compatible with older releases of Firebird nor with InterBase. Use the value InterBaseIPI, if necessary, to retain compatibility with an existing application that refers to the shared memory (IPC space) by name.

MaxUnflushedWrites

```
Version 1.5 forward
Applicable on Windows servers only
```

This parameter was introduced in version 1.5 to handle a bug in the Windows server operating systems, whereby asynchronous writes were never flushed to disk except when the Firebird server underwent a controlled shutdown. (Asynchronous writes are not supported in Windows 9x or ME.) Hence, on 24/7 systems, asynchronous writes were never flushed at all.

This parameter determines how frequently the withheld pages are flushed to disk when Forced Writes are disabled (asynchronous writing is enabled). Its value is an integer that sets the number of pages to be withheld before a flush is flagged to be done the next time a transaction commits. The default is 100 in Windows installations and –1 (disabled) in installations for all other platforms.

If the end of the MaxUnflushedWriteTime cycle (see the next section) is reached before the count of withheld pages reaches the MaxUnflushedWrites count, the flush is flagged immediately and the count of withheld pages is reset to zero.

MaxUnflushedWriteTime

```
Version 1.5 forward
Applicable on Windows servers only
```

This parameter determines the maximum length of time that pages withheld for asynchronous writing are flushed to disk when Forced Writes are disabled (asynchronous writing is enabled). Its value is an integer that sets the interval, in seconds, between the last flush to disk and the setting of a flag to perform a flush the next time a transaction commits. The default is 5 seconds in Windows installations and –1 (disabled) in installations for all other platforms.

PrioritySwitchDelay

```
Version 1.5 forward, Windows only
```

A setting for the thread scheduler on Windows, this integer establishes the time, in milliseconds, to elapse before the priority of an inactive thread is reduced to LOW or the priority of an active thread is advanced to HIGH. One iteration of this switching sequence represents one thread-scheduler cycle.

The default value is 100 milliseconds, chosen on the basis of experiments on Intel PIII/P4 processors. For processors with lower clock speeds, a longer delay will be required.

PriorityBoost

Version 1.5 forward, Windows only

This integer sets the number of extra cycles given to a thread when its priority is switched to HIGH. The installation default is 5.

ProcessPriorityLevel

Version 1.5 forward, applicable only on Windows platforms

This is a parameter for setting a priority level/class for the server process, replacing the server_priority_class parameter of pre-1.5 releases with a new implementation.

The values are integer, as follows:

- 0: Normal priority

- Positive value: High priority (same as the –B[oostPriority] switch on instsvc.exe *configure* and *start* options)

- Negative value: Low priority

NOTE All changes to this value should be carefully tested to ensure that they actually cause the engine to be appropriately responsive to requests.

server_priority_class

Versions prior to Firebird 1.5

This setting assigns a priority class for the Firebird service on Windows NT or Windows 2000 only. The possible values are: 1 = low priority, 2 = high priority. The default is 1.

RemotePipeName

```
Version 1.5 forward, applicable only on Windows platforms for Named Pipes
connections
```

This string parameter is the name of the pipe used as a transport channel for Windows Named Pipes networking. The named pipe is equivalent to a port number for TCP/IP. The default value, *interbas*, is compatible with older releases of Firebird and with InterBase.

server_working_size_max and server_working_size_min

```
Versions prior to Firebird 1.5
```

These are two old, deprecated memory parameters that were inherited in ibconfig for older Firebird releases and were unsupported. They have been excluded from firebird.conf.

Compatibility Parameters

CompleteBooleanEvaluation

```
Version 1.5 forward
```

This establishes the Boolean evaluation method (complete or shortcut). The default (0=False) is to "shortcut" a Boolean evaluation expression involving the AND or OR predicates by returning as soon as a result of True or False is obtained that cannot be affected by the results of any further evaluation.

Under very rare (usually avoidable) conditions, it might happen that an operation inside an OR or an AND condition that remains unevaluated due to the shortcut behavior has the potential to affect the outcome of the original result. If you have the misfortune to inherit an application that has such characteristics in its SQL logic, you might wish to use this parameter to force complete evaluation until you have the opportunity to perform surgery on it. The parameter type is Boolean.

 CAUTION Don't overlook the fact that this flag affects all Boolean evaluations performed in any databases on the server.

OldParameterOrdering

```
Version 1.5 forward
```

Version 1.5 addressed an old InterBase bug that caused output parameters to be returned to the client with an idiosyncratic ordering in the XSQLDA structure. The bug was of such longevity that many existing applications, drivers, and interface components had built-in workarounds to correct the problem on the client side.

Releases 1.5 and later reflect the corrected condition in the API and are installed with OldParameterOrdering=0 (False). Set this Boolean parameter to True (1) if you need to revert to the old condition for compatibility with existing code.

Parameters Relating to External Objects

Locality and access parameter settings for external code modules and data files are discussed at the end of the section "Configuring External Locations."

Working with Embedded Server

Windows Embedded Server has the same features as Superserver, except multi-user support and password protection. The client library is embedded in the server and this conjoined pair does the work of both client and server, for one and only one attached application.

NOTE Windows Embedded Server is not supported in releases prior to 1.5.

When Embedded Server searches for the root directory of its installation, it ignores any Registry entries and the FIREBIRD environment variable. It treats as the root the folder where its binary file (*fbembed.dll*, renamed as *fbclient.dll* or *gds32.dll*) is located.

You should have a full set of the files required for Embedded Server under the home directory root of each embedded application. If external files are used (international language support, UDF libraries, BLOB filter libraries), Embedded Server needs to find firebird.conf under this root and, in firebird.conf, the RootDirectory parameter must point to the folder where the embedded server library file is located. For an example, see the section "Embedded Server" in Chapter 1.

Starting an Embedded Server

The only connection protocol allowed is "Windows local." Embedded Server does not support local loopback or any remote network protocol.

Provided the application is well configured and the server host is free of conflicts with other running Firebird servers or clients, the server process will start up as soon as the application connects successfully to a local database.

Applications

Any application that already works with a full server and a local or remote client will work with Embedded Server. Four details you need to address with your existing applications are

- Location and naming of the Embedded Server library

- Hard-coded database paths

- Utilities you have written that use the remote Services Manager

- Security or integrity implications arising from having an application interface that does not verify the user's right to access to the server

Location and Renaming of the Library

For Embedded Server—distributed as *fbembed.dll*—there is no problem with renaming the library to gds32.dll or fbclient.dll, or any other name that might be needed. For the Embedded Server package to be truly self-contained, the library should be in the same directory as the application executable, and the peripheral files and directories for the server functions arranged as recommended in Chapter 1.

If you have multiple Embedded Server applications on the same machine that need to use the library, there are choices:

- Place a copy of the library in the "application root" of each application and set up the peripheral files and directories as recommended in Chapter 1. This is the preferred option because it makes the "package" easy to deploy for hands-off installation independent of the surrounding filesystem structure. However, when you want to deploy multiple Embedded Server packages to the same workstation, redundancy will be a problem.

- Place a single copy of the library at some special location—with the peripheral files and directories correctly named and placed, relative to the library—and create a Registry key to be read by each application into its library-loading arguments. This may be less attractive from the perspective of portability, but it does simplify conflict and upgrade issues.

- Place the library—suitably named—in the system directory and use the FIRE-BIRD path variable to point to the root of a tree structure where the peripheral files and directories are located. This option will work only on a system that is not running a full Firebird 1.5 or higher server, and it heightens the vulnerability of the library to overwriting by other installers.

NOTE Do bear in mind that some Borland products are hard-coded to recognize only Borland's proprietary internal version strings. Even though the name and filesystem location are "correct" for the Borland elements, the version string limitation may make your application incompatible with Embedded Server. For example, applications compiled using the InterBaseXpress (IBX) connectivity components out of the box will not connect to fbembed.dll without modification.

Hard-Coded Database Paths

A connection string such as `WINSERVER:C:\Program Files\Firebird\Firebird_1_5\`
`employee.fdb` hard-coded into your application executable is clearly going to cause problems when you deploy your software to another machine. Your code will need to adapt its connection string handling to a database location that is unknown at design time and is also constrained to be a local (not localhost) connection. This is not a problem new to the case of Embedded Server. We frequently have the need to deploy our client/server application software with provision for users or system admins to configure network and filesystem locations for production databases.

Database aliasing allows you to compile applications with "soft" filesystem paths to databases. Everywhere in the application code that refers to the path segment of the connection string uses the alias instead and the specific filesystem location becomes a matter of a localized setting in aliases.conf.

For example, suppose you decide to use EMPDATA as your alias. In aliases.conf on your development machine, you point the alias to your path:

```
EMPDATA = C:\Program Files\Firebird\Firebird_1_5\employee.fdb
```

On another machine, it might be

```
EMPDATA = D:\databases\employee.fdb
```

That takes care of the path segment and removes one level of complexity. However, you may be still left with the problem of resolving the *connection protocol*. Some modification will be necessary if the application is hard-coded to expect a host name and a TCP/IP or Named Pipes connection string format.

Remote Service Utilities

Utility routines using the Services API or the older Services Manager switches for remote administration may need to be disabled or adapted to work with the local connection protocol. The exact measures required will depend on what is implemented for your client/server architecture and how it is being done currently. If your existing application provides capabilities that are restricted to protect server security and stability, you should also consider the implications of exposing the server to an application that inherently bypasses user authentication.

The Server Security Issue

Any embedded server library located on a machine that hosts databases is a potential Trojan horse. At the server level, security operates on the assumption that any user that managed to log in has been authenticated through the security database, security.fdb. However, when an embedded server attaches a client, user and password authentication are bypassed. Because any user is able to attach to any database, server security will be easily compromised if the host machine is not physically secure.

It is possible to write an embedded server application that "logs in as SYSDBA" using anything at all as the SYSDBA password. There is no way the server can tell that the SYSDBA user came in through the skylight without a valid password. If SYSDBA is active in any database, then SYSDBA is logged in and can do whatever it wants, without restriction. Anyone who has access to your network and is allowed filesystem privileges on the server could set up a malicious embedded server application that could read or write anything into any of your databases or delete them all.

Be mindful that the security database (security.fdb) is a database just like any other. SYSDBA has special SQL privileges in it—as in all databases—to create, modify, or destroy anything.

Provided the database host machine is safe from physical intrusion and unauthorized filesystem access, the "logged-in," non-SYSDBA user in a database will be subject to the normal SQL privilege restrictions. Data object SQL privileges in Firebird databases are applied on an "opt-in" basis—no user except the SYSDBA and the database owner has automatic rights to any object in any database.

It is still necessary, therefore, to provide a way for the user (or the application, silently) to pass a user name and, desirably, a role in a conventional-looking "login" procedure. It behooves the developer to provide both the privilege protection and the gatekeeping procedure.

Refer to the preceding two chapters for more information about server access security and database object SQL privileges.

Multiple Server Compatibility

Any number of embedded server applications can run simultaneously without any conflicts. However, it is not possible for multiple embedded servers to access a single database simultaneously, because of the exclusive lock that the Superserver architecture applies when the first database attachment succeeds.

Regular Firebird and InterBase servers can run simultaneously on a host machine that is running embedded servers, without conflict. For local client access, attention must be given to avoiding a namespace conflict between the regular client libraries (gds32.dll and fbclient.dll) and the name chosen for the embedded server library.

The "client" part of fbembed.dll can be a regular, remote client to other servers at the same time it is connecting internally to its embedded server.

Stopping an Embedded Server

A running embedded server cannot be stopped except by terminating the client application. Your application should terminate with the usual "housekeeping," completing all transactions and detaching cleanly from all databases.

External Code Modules

Firebird can extend its capabilities by accessing user-defined routines that are written in a host language and compiled in external shared libraries. This section provides an overview of some of the issues and techniques concerned with writing external functions (UDFs) and BLOB filters.

- **External functions**: Firebird "travels light" with respect to built-in functions. Instead of a vast library of esoteric functions to weigh down the server, Firebird provides for developers to select—and, if necessary, to define—their own libraries of external functions to suit the calculation and expression requirements in their databases. User-defined functions, known to all as UDFs, add great flexibility to your database environment. UDFs are server-side extensions to the Firebird server that are declared to databases and executed in the context of the server process.

  Like the standard, built-in SQL functions, UDFs can be designed to do conversions or calculations that are either complex or impossible to do with the SQL language. Possibilities include statistical, string, date, and mathematical functions.

  In Chapter 21 the section "External Functions (UDFs)" explains in detail how to locate, declare, and use external functions, and how to configure their file system location to avoid some of the security and integrity risks inherent in running external code from within the server engine. The filesystem configuration defaults and options are also discussed earlier in this chapter, under "UdfAccess" (v.1.5) and "external_file_directory" (v.1.0.x).

- **BLOB filters**: The Firebird engine uses several internally defined routines to convert byte streams from one format to another. These routines are known as BLOB filters. The SQL engine surfaces them as BLOB subtypes in DDL and metadata. It is also possible to write your own BLOB filters for converting BLOB data from one format to another, compatible format. For example, a BLOB filter could convert XML to rich text or a bitmap image to a JPEG.

Developing Your Own UDFs

UDF libraries are compiled as standard shared libraries to run on the server where the database resides. The libraries are dynamically loaded by the database at runtime when the library is referenced in an SQL expression. You can create UDF libraries on any platform that is supported by Firebird. To use the same set of UDFs with databases running on different platforms, create and compile separate libraries for each platform where the databases reside.

A *library*, in this context, is a shared object that typically has a .dll extension on Windows platforms, an .so extension on UNIX and Solaris, and an .sl extension on HP-UX. It can contain one or many *entry points* for user-defined functions.

TIP The Firebird /examples directory contains some old sample makefiles (makefile.bc and makefile.msc on Windows systems; makefile on UNIX) that build the ib_udf function library from ib_udf.c.

Creating and implementing a UDF is a four-step process:

1. Write the function in any programming language that can create a shared library. A function can take a limited number of entry parameters, but it must return one and only one result. *Functions written in Java are not supported.*

2. Compile the function and link it to a dynamically linked library or shared object library, as appropriate to the platform.

3. Place the library and any symbolic links required into the appropriate disk locations on the server machine so that the server can locate it—the default /UDF directory or an alternative location you have configured for external function libraries.

4. Use DECLARE EXTERNAL FUNCTION to declare each individual UDF to each database in which you need to use it.

NOTE It is always very good practice to create a script containing the declarations for your UDFs and some explanatory comments about usage.

Writing a Function Module

In the C language, a UDF is written like any standard function. The UDF can provide for up to ten input parameters, and must return one and only one C data value as its result.

A source code module can define one or more functions. If you include the Firebird *ibase.h* header file provided in your Firebird /include directory in the compilation, your C or C++ module can use the typedefs defined there. Translations exist for other languages, including several for Delphi. For example, the source kit for FreeUDFLib,[2] by Gregory Deatz, includes *ibase.pas.*

Specifying Parameters

Non-BLOB, non-array parameters are passed to and from the UDF either by reference,[3] using host language data types that are capable of being mapped to corresponding Firebird data types, or by descriptor, using a predefined structure that describes a Firebird data type to the host language. Up to ten parameters can be accepted, corresponding to any Firebird data type except an array type or element. If a UDF returns a BLOB, the number of input parameters is restricted to nine.

As an example of passing parameters *by reference*, the C function declaration for FN_ABS() accepts one parameter of the C type *double.* When FN_ABS() is called, it should be passed a parameter of the SQL data type DOUBLE PRECISION.

Passing parameters *by descriptor* is a capability surfaced in Firebird 1.0 that allows native Firebird data types to be passed. For some external functions, it simplifies the handling of NULL parameters and enables declaration overloading. The structure of a parameter descriptor can be found in *ibase.h*:

```
typedef struct paramdsc {
    unsigned char   dsc_dtype;
    signed char     dsc_scale;
    ISC_USHORT      dsc_length;
    short           dsc_sub_type;
    ISC_USHORT      dsc_flags;
    unsigned char   *dsc_address;
} PARAMDSC;
```

The most important field in the structure, of course, is *dsc_dtype*, because it is responsible for translating native Firebird data types to the host language types.

---

2. A public domain library of UDFs available from several download sites, including
   http://www.ibphoenix.com.

3. In C++ terms, "by pointer."

TIP Claudio Valderrama C., who implemented *by descriptor*, provides
a detailed description in an article entitled "Using descriptors with UDFs" at
http://www.cvalde.net/document/using_descriptors_with_udfs.htm.

BLOB Parameters

UDFs that accept BLOB parameters require special data structure for processing.
A BLOB is passed by reference to a BLOB control structure, described in the section
"Writing a BLOB Function."

Specifying a Return Value

The same data type restrictions apply to return values as to input parameters: Host
types must be able to correspond to a Firebird type. For example, the C function declaration for FN_ABS() returns a value of type *double*, which corresponds to the Firebird
data type DOUBLE PRECISION.

By default, return values are passed by reference. Numeric values can also be
returned by value, although it is a deprecated method and not highly recommended.
To return a numeric parameter by value, include the optional BY VALUE keyword after
the return value when declaring the UDF to a database.

A UDF that returns a BLOB does not actually define a return value. Instead, a
pointer to a structure describing the BLOB to return must be passed as the last input
parameter to the UDF.

Character Data Types

UDFs need to use host-language data types for both their input and return values.
Firebird must be able to translate between the declared type and the SQL data type.
In the case of strings, the input to a string UDF is a CSTRING type of a specified maximum length in bytes. CSTRING is used to translate an input of CHAR or VARCHAR type
into a null-terminated C string for processing, and to return a variable-length, null-
terminated C string to Firebird for automatic conversion to CHAR or VARCHAR. With
other host languages, ensure that your function returns null-terminated strings.

When declaring a UDF that returns a C string, CHAR or VARCHAR, the keyword
FREE_IT must be included in the declaration in order to free the memory used by the
return value if it was allocated with ib_util_malloc.

Calling Conventions

The calling convention determines how a function is called and how the parameters are passed. The function receiving the function call must be compatible with the *CDECL* calling convention used by Firebird. With C functions using the *CDECL* calling convention, the *__cdecl* reserved word must be added to the function declaration. With Pascal, use **cdecl**.

Here is an example in C that specifies *CDECL*:

```
ISC_TIMESTAMP* __cdecl addmonth(ISC_TIMESTAMP *preTime)
{
// body of function here
}
```

Threading Issues

In Superserver implementations of Firebird, the server runs as a single multi-threaded process. This means that you must take some care in the way you allocate and release memory when coding UDFs, and also in the way you declare UDFs. Several issues need to be considered when handling memory in the single-process, multi-thread architecture:

- UDFs must allocate memory using the *ib_util_malloc* function, in the ib_util library, rather than static arrays.

- Memory allocated dynamically is not automatically released, since the process does not end. You must use the reserved word FREE_IT when you declare the UDF to the database (DECLARE EXTERNAL FUNCTION).

- Static variables are not thread-safe. Users running the same UDFs concurrently will conflict when they step on the same static memory space. It would not be wise to use static variables unless you could guarantee that only one user at a time would be accessing the function.

  If you cannot avoid returning a pointer to static data, you must *not* use FREE_IT.

The ib_util Library

The *ib_util_malloc* function is in your Firebird /lib directory, in the shared library ib_util.so on POSIX, ib_util.dll on Windows, and ib_util.sl on HP-UX. The function prototype, for C and Pascal, is provided in the /include directory as *ib_util.h* and *ib_util.pas*, respectively.

Pointer Variables with Classic Server

For non-threaded use with Classic server, you can return a global pointer. In the following example for the UDF FN_LOWER(), the array must be global to avoid going out of context:

```
char buffer[256];
char *fn_lower(char *ups)
{
...
return (buffer);
}
```

Making UDFs Leakproof

The procedure for allocating and freeing memory for return values in a fashion that is both thread-safe and compiler independent is as follows:

Use the *ib_util_malloc( )* function in your host code to allocate memory for return values. If you use it, use the FREE_IT keyword in the RETURNS clause when declaring a function that returns dynamically allocated objects.

In the following example, the Firebird engine will free the buffer if the UDF is declared using the FREE_IT reserved word. Notice that this example uses Firebird's *ib_util_malloc( )* function to allocate memory:

```
char *fn_lower(char *ups)
{
char *buffer = (char *) ib_util_malloc(256);
...
return (buffer);
}
```

This is the declaration:

```
DECLARE EXTERNAL FUNCTION lowercase
VARCHAR(256)
RETURNS CSTRING(256) FREE_IT
ENTRY POINT 'fn_lower' MODULE_NAME 'ib_udf';
```

NOTE   Memory must be released by the same runtime library that allocated it.

Notes About Compiling and Linking

When a UDF module is ready, compile it in a normal fashion into object or library format.

Include ibase.h or its equivalent if you use typedefs defined in it.

If linking statically, link to the Firebird client library if you are calling any Firebird library functions. For Microsoft Visual C/C++ the typelibs fbclient_ms.lib and ib_util_ms.lib can be found in the Firebird /lib directory.

Modifying a Function Library

To add a UDF to an existing external function module, add the file containing the object code for the new UDF and recompile as usual. Some platforms allow you to add object files directly to existing libraries. For more information, consult the platform-specific compiler and linker documentation.

To remove a function, follow the linker's instructions for removing an object from a library. Deleting a function from a library does not remove its declaration from the database—use DROP EXTERNAL FUNCTION to do that.

Writing a BLOB Function

A BLOB function differs from other external functions, because pointers to *BLOB control structures* are passed to the function instead of references to actual data. The function cannot open or close a BLOB, but instead invokes API functions to perform BLOB access.

Creating a BLOB Control Structure

A BLOB control structure is a C struct, declared within a function module as a typedef. Programmers must provide the control structure definition that, in C, should be defined as follows:

```
typedef struct blob {
short (*blob_get_segment) ();
isc_blob_handle blob_handle;
long number_segments;
long max_seglen;
long total_size;
void (*blob_put_segment) ();
} *Blob;
```

Table 36-1 describes the fields in the BLOB control structure.

Table 36-1. Fields in the BLOB Control Structure[4]

FIELD	DESCRIPTION
blob_get_segment	NULL if the external function does not take a BLOB as an input argument. Otherwise, this field is a pointer to the function that is called to read a segment from a BLOB. The function takes four arguments: a BLOB handle, the address of a buffer for the BLOB segment, the size of the buffer, and the address of a variable to hold the *size* of the BLOB segment.
blob_handle	Required field. This is the BLOB handle that uniquely identifies a BLOB passed to or returned from the function.
number_segments	NULL if the external function does not take a BLOB as an input argument. Otherwise, it specifies the total number of segments in the BLOB.
max_seglen	NULL if the external function does not take a BLOB as an input argument. Otherwise, it specifies the size, in bytes, of the largest single segment passed.
total_size	NULL if the external function does not take a BLOB as an input argument. Otherwise, specifies the actual size, in bytes, of the BLOB as a single unit.
blob_put_segment	NULL if the external function does not take a BLOB as an input argument. Otherwise, this is a pointer to a function that is called to write a segment to a BLOB. It takes three arguments: a BLOB handle, the address of a buffer containing the data to write into the BLOB, and the size, in bytes, of the data to write.

Declaring a BLOB Function

A BLOB function is declared to the database using DECLARE EXTERNAL FUNCTION, with the difference that its type declaration is placed *before* the keyword RETURNS as the last argument of the parameter list, instead of following it as a return value. For the RETURNS argument, use the keyword PARAMETER and the ordinal number of the last parameter. For example, the following statement declares a BLOB function, blob_plus_blob, in an external function module named MyExtLib:

```
DECLARE EXTERNAL FUNCTION blob_plus_blob
Blob,
Blob,
Blob
RETURNS PARAMETER 3
ENTRY_POINT 'blob_concat' MODULE_NAME 'MyExtLib';
```

---

4. Defined in ibase.h as *blobcallback* (structure type) and BLOBCALLBACK (pointer to structure type). That declaration gives a full definition for the get/put function pointers, which makes it much easier to use with modern compilers. Refer also to notes above the declaration in ibase.h.

More Information

A number of tutorial papers about writing external functions are available from Firebird community websites. The knowledge bases and search engines will yield plenty of good, explanatory articles.

BLOB Filters

In Chapter 12, we touched on this special type of external function that could be used by Firebird to customize the conversion of BLOBs between two formats capable of representing compatible data. A *BLOB filter* is a server-based, user-defined utility routine—a specialized UDF, in fact—that is capable of taking a BLOB in one format, converting it, and returning it as a BLOB in a second format. Once compiled and declared to a database, the BLOB filter can be actioned using regular DML statements from client applications, stored procedures and triggers, and **isql**.

In Firebird SQL, a BLOB filter is recognized and referred to by its SUB_TYPE. You are already familiar with two subtypes: 0 (for BLOB of any format) and 1 (for unformatted or minimally formatted text). They are pre-defined internally, along with a number of others, all positive numbers, that Firebird uses internally for metadata and parsing. Other BLOB filters are user defined and can have any negative numbers as subtypes.

The Firebird engine has no "internal knowledge" of what is (or should be) stored in a BLOB of a given subtype numbered zero or less. It is up to the application to ensure that inputs and outputs are appropriate to the purpose of the subtype and any BLOB filters written to handle them.

Pairs of BLOB filters can be used to manage a useful range of regular conversions required by your applications, for example:

- Compressing and decompressing data. One subtype stores compressed data while the other handles it when it is decompressed. The BLOB filter might be designed to take a SUB_TYPE 0 (unknown format) BLOB and convert it to a compressed format (zip or rar, for example) and expand it for handling as SUB_TYPE 0.

- You might have one subtype to store generic application code and others to hold system-specific code, with a BLOB filter to add the necessary system-specific variations to the generic code when it is requested in a query.

- You might have a subtype to store XML-formatted text and BLOB filters to transform it into to specific output formats—HTML, rich text, Portable Document Format (PDF), UNIX 'man' files, word-processor formats—for output as another subtype.

Firebird's BLOB filter capability enables it to relegate the "bloat" associated with data converters to external processors. The transformation code in a filter routine can be as simple or complex as it needs to be. It can call other modules, if necessary, thus putting at your disposal the ability to incorporate existing converters into your server's operations. Since the engine itself is concerned only with the outputs and inputs, while the filter code is maintained externally, your filters can be kept in step with the latest innovations of the technology without impacting the server.

Writing BLOB Filters

Writing BLOB filters involves the same care with memory and threading and similar steps to those for other external functions, namely

1. Write the filters and compile them into object code.

2. Create a shared filter library (shared object or DLL).

3. Configure the Firebird server to know where to find the library at runtime.

4. Use DECLARE FILTER to declare the filters to the database.

5. Define columns in tables to store BLOBs of the subtypes "known" to the filter.

6. Write applications or PSQL modules that request the filtering.

Declaring BLOB Filters

A filter is recognized at database level by way of a metadata declaration using this syntax:

```
DECLARE FILTER <filter-name>
  INPUT_TYPE <sub-type> /* identifies subtype of object to be converted */
  OUTPUT_TYPE <sub-type> /* identifies subtype of object to be created */
  ENTRY_POINT '<entry-point-name>' /* name of exported function */
  MODULE_NAME '<external-library-name>'; /* name of BLOB filter library */
```

Invoking BLOB Filters

The conversion from INPUT_TYPE to OUTPUT_TYPE is invoked automatically when MODULE_NAME is called with parameters that have been defined with the correct subtype numbers.

Suppose, for example, you create a library named filters.so or filters.dll that is in a legal location for BLOB filter libraries on the server. In it, you have a function named xml_to_rtf that takes a BLOB consisting of XML marked-up text, passes it to a program that converts it to a rich text document, and finally passes the result back in a new BLOB. You store XML documents in a BLOB SUB_TYPE –10 and rich text in a BLOB SUB_TYPE –15.

First, you would declare the BLOB filter to the database:

```
DECLARE FILTER XML2RTF /* your choice of name */
  INPUT_TYPE -10  /* XML marked-up text */
  OUTPUT_TYPE -15 /* rich text, formatted to company rules */
  ENTRY_POINT 'xml_to_rtf' /* first stop for the conversion routine */
  MODULE_NAME 'filters'; /* name of BLOB filter library */
```

Now, in your SQL or PSQL, all you need to invoke the conversion automatically is a variable or database column, declared as BLOB SUB_TYPE –10, containing your good, valid XML document and a destination variable or column of SUB_TYPE –15 to receive the converted document.

TIP   Included in Firebird's set of special internal BLOB filters are converters for transforming SUB_TYPE 0 to SUB_TYPE 1 (TEXT), and SUB_TYPE 1 to SUB_TYPE 0. These filters can also convert BLOB data of any Firebird system SUB_TYPE—for example, BLR=2 to SUB_TYPE 1 (TEXT), which may be useful for returning the contents of a column in a system table to a database management application. In subtype 1, blocks are segmented from the start to the first newline character, from the next character to the following newline character, and so on.

Tools for Writing Filters

The Firebird API has a group of macro functions beginning with *isc_blob_filter_* that are the "programmer's toolbox" for writing BLOB filters. Both the *API Guide* and the *Embedded SQL Guide*, from the Borland InterBase v.6.0 beta manual set, have sections on writing BLOB filters. A number of how-to documents can be located at community websites with little searching.

The Firebird API also has structures—with headers for them in ibase.h—for passing and reading information about BLOBs. If your curiosity has been whetted, look for *BLOB descriptors* and the *BLOB parameter buffer (BPB)*. A group of related functions can be used in your BLOB filter code and also for requesting BLOB filters directly from your application code.

International Language Modules

Firebird is distributed with an ever-growing library of support for international languages and collation sequences. All but the four "basic" languages are distributed in the library *fbintl* (on POSIX) or *fbintl.dll* (on Windows). Firebird expects to find language libraries in the installation directory /intl.

It is possible to write your own character sets and collations, and have the Firebird engine load them from a shared library, which should be named *fbintl2* in order to be recognized and linked. David Brookestone Schnepper, developer of the *fbintl2* plug-in, makes a do-it-yourself language kit freely available at http://www.ibcollate.com.

From Firebird 1.5 onward, it is also possible to implement custom character sets or collations using external functions. Because the *fbintl2* kit includes lucid instructions for creating character sets, it is also a useful reference if you plan to use the external function approach to implement a custom character set.

Configuring External Locations

Having external code and data that are accessed by the server can present a security vulnerability if the server's filesystem is inadequately protected from intruders or is exposed through holes in the network. These external pieces can be made less vulnerable by configuring restrictions on where the Firebird engine may access them. The capability to deny access to unrecognized locations helps in the overall task of securing the filesystem and the network.

> **TIP**   Configure few locations, rather than many, to reduce the scope of the engine's search and the degree of access control maintenance required.

Settings in the Configuration File

The Firebird configuration file, as discussed earlier in this chapter, provides settings for restricting access to external function libraries, BLOB filter modules, and data files linked to tables defined using CREATE TABLE.*<table-name>* EXTERNAL (external tables or EVTs). The settings for Firebird 1.5, in firebird.conf, are different from those for Firebird 1.0.*x*, in *isc_config* (POSIX) or *ibconfig* (Windows).

The v.1.5 configuration applies to any model of the v.1.5 server. The v.1.0.*x* configuration applies only to Superserver.

UdfAccess

Version 1.5 forward, in firebird.conf

This parameter is used to restrict access to external function libraries and BLOB filter modules, perceived as a potential target for malicious intruder attacks. You can elect one of three levels of access to all such modules, to be applied serverwide. Before v.1.5, it was regarded as a benefit to be able to store external modules in multiple filesystem locations. It is now recommended that they be limited to a single tree or, in very exposed situations, disallowed altogether.

UdfAccess may be None, Restrict, or Full.

- **None** disallows all use of user-defined external libraries. It is the installation default on most distributions.

- **Restrict** (the default setting) restricts the location of callable external libraries to specific filesystem locations. By default, the search will begin in the /UDF directory beneath your Firebird root. To locate external function libraries or BLOB filter modules elsewhere in the local filesystem, supply a list of one or more directory tree-roots, separated by semicolons (;), within and beneath which these modules may be stored, for example:

```
POSIX: /db/extern;/mnt/extern
Windows:  C:\ExternalModules
```

Relative paths are treated as relative to the path that the running server recognizes as the root directory of the Firebird installation. For example, on Windows, if the root of the Firebird installation is C:\Program Files\Firebird\Firebird_1_5, then the following value will restrict the server to accessing external files only if they are located in C:\Program Files\Firebird\Firebird_1_5\userdata\extern:

```
UDFAccess = Restrict userdata\ExternalModules
```

- **Full** permits external libraries to be accessed anywhere on the system. When Full access is enabled, the full file path and name must be included in the MODULE_NAME clause of the DECLARE EXTERNAL FUNCTION statement that declares the function to the database. For more information, refer to the section "External Functions (UDFs)" in Chapter 21.

external_function_directory

```
Firebird 1.0.x, in isc_config/ibconfig
```

This parameter can be used in v.1.0.*x* to specify an arbitrary number of locations for external function libraries, BLOB filters, and/or character set modules. If this configuration parameter does not exist, Firebird checks the subdirectories ..\udf or ..\intl beneath the path that the running server recognizes as the root directory of the Firebird installation. These are some examples:

```
external_function_directory <double-quoted directory path>
external_function_directory "/opt/firebird/my_functions"
external_function_directory "/opt/extlibs/lang"
external_function_directory "d:\udfdir"
```

ExternalFileAccess

Version 1.5 forward, in firebird.conf

This parameter provides three levels of security regarding external files accessed from within the database through tables. The value is a string, which may be None, Full, or Restrict.

- **None** (the default value) disables any use of external files on your server.

- **Restrict** provides the ability to restrict the location of external files for database access to specific path-trees. Supply a list of one or more directory tree-roots, separated by semicolons (;), within and beneath which external files may be stored, for example:

  Unix: /db/extern;/mnt/extern
  Windows: C:\ExternalTables

  Relative paths are treated as relative to the path that the running server recognizes as the root directory of the Firebird installation.

  For example, on Windows, if the root that the running server recognizes as the root directory of the Firebird installation is C:\Program Files\Firebird, then the following value will restrict the server to accessing external files only if they are located in C:\Program Files\Firebird\userdata\ExternalTables:

  ExternalFileAccess = Restrict userdata\ExternalTables

  The following entry on POSIX will restrict access to only files located in or beneath /exportdata or /importdata:

  ExternalFileAccess = Restrict /exportdata;/importdata

- **Full** permits external files to be accessed anywhere on the system.

For more information about external files, refer to the section "Using External Files As Tables" in Chapter 16.

external_file_directory

```
Firebird 1.0.x, in ibconfig
```

On Windows only, this is for concentrating external files into one or more restricted locations. There is no limit to the number of directories that can be in the search list. Make a one-line entry per directory as follows:

```
external_file_directory <double-quoted directory path>
external_file_directory "d:\x-files"
```

Up Next

The final chapters describe usage of the remaining command-line tools that are distributed with Firebird. The statistics tool **gstat** was described earlier, in Chapter 18, and you met the user access management tool **gsec** in Chapter 35. Next to receive the treatment is the interactive SQL utility, **isql**.

Part Nine

Tools

CHAPTER 37

Interactive SQL Utility (isql)

THE ISQL UTILITY, INSTALLED IN THE /BIN directory beneath your Firebird root, provides a non-graphical interface to Firebird databases that is consistent on all server and client platforms.

isql accepts both DDL and DML statements, as well as a subset of SQL-like console commands not available in DSQL. It can be used both for creating and maintaining metadata and for querying and changing data. It includes several admin tools and the option to perform some database operations directly from a command shell or through a shell script or batch file.

CAUTION   Several other DBMSs have adopted the "isql" name for their interactive query programs. Always run Firebird's **isql** program from its own directory or provide the absolute file path if this is a problem on your server.

Interactive Mode

Interactive **isql** can be run locally or from a remote client.

- From a remote client, a valid user name and password are always required to run **isql**.

- If you are connecting locally, you can set the operating system variables ISC_USER and ISC_PASSWORD and avoid the need to enter them on commands. For more information about these variables, refer to Chapter 3.

NOTE   Some additional command-line switches can be used when invoking the interactive shell. They are noted in Table 37-1 toward the end of this chapter.

Default Text Editor

Some **isql** commands access your system's default text editor.

- On UNIX, Linux, and some other POSIX platforms, the default editor is defined by one or the other of the two environment variables EDITOR and VISUAL. The installation default is usually vi, vim, or emacs, but you can set it to another preferred console (not X) text editor.

- On Windows, the story is similar. The default editor is defined by the environment variable EDITOR. On current versions of Windows, it is Notepad.exe, but you can set it to be any text editor you prefer. On very old Windows versions, the default editor was probably mep.exe or edit.exe.

Starting isql

To start **isql**, open a command shell and *cd* to the Firebird /bin directory of your Firebird server or client installation. Key in the following command at the shell prompt and press the Enter key:

```
isql [database_name] [-u[ser] <user-name> -pas[sword] <password>]
```

database_name is optional. If you include it, **isql** will open a connection to the database and start its shell already connected. It must be either the full path to the database from where you are or, in version 1.5 and later, a valid alias.

The switches *–user <user-name>* and *–password <password>* are *optional* when you are starting **isql** without a connection to the database and *required* when you are starting **isql** remotely. If the ISC_USER and ISC_PASSWORD environment variables are not set, they will also be required when you start **isql** locally.

On POSIX:

```
./isql
```

On Windows:

```
isql
```

starts the program.

```
./isql -user TEMPDBA -password osoweary [on POSIX]
isql -user TEMPDBA -password osoweary [on Windows]
```

starts the program and stores the supplied user name and password without authenticating them.

```
isql hotchicken:/data/mydatabase.fdb -user TEMPDBA -password osoweary
```

starts the program on a Windows client and connects to the database on a POSIX server, provided the user name and password are valid on the server.

```
./isql /data/mydatabase.fdb
```

starts the program locally on a Linux server and connects to the database, provided the environment variables ISC_USER and ISC_PASSWORD are set and are available to your Linux user profile.

If you are logged into the database when **isql** starts up, you will see a console display similar to Figure 37-1. The appearance of the surrounding shell depends on the operating system. The **isql** shell is the same on all platforms.

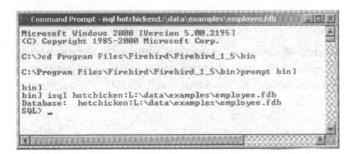

*Figure 37-1. Console display when **isql** starts logged-in*

If you did not enter a database path or you used a user name and password that are not defined on the server, you will see something similar to Figure 37-2.

*Figure 37-2. Console display when **isql** starts not logged-in*

If there were errors in the command string, or authentication problems, you might also see some error messages. If you can see the SQL> prompt, you are in the **isql** shell and you can connect to your database from there.

Connecting to a Database

To connect to a database from the SQL> prompt in the **isql** shell, use the following examples as syntax patterns. Notice that the syntax inside the **isql** shell is different from that used when passing the connection parameters from the system shell.

```
CONNECT 'HOTCHICKEN:L:\DATA\EXAMPLES\EMPLOYEE.FDB'
USER 'SYSDBA' PASSWORD 'masterkey';
```

connects to a remote or local server named HOTCHICKEN.

```
CONNECT 'L:\DATA\EXAMPLES\EMPLOYEE.FDB';
```

connects to a local server where **isql** already knows your Firebird user name and password—either because you entered them correctly when you started **isql** or because **isql** is executing in a shell that can see the environment variables ISC_USER and ISC_PASSWORD.

```
CONNECT 'HOTCHICKEN:EMP3' USER 'SYSDBA' PASSWORD 'masterkey';
```

is equivalent to the first example, in Firebird 1.5 and later, using an alias stored in aliases.conf on the server, that points to the path.

```
CONNECT 'L:/DATA/EXAMPLES/EMPLOYEE.FDB';
```

is equivalent to the second example—slashes may be forward or backward in **isql**.

Server and Path Names

On Windows, do not confuse server names and shared disk resource names. The client/server network layer does not recognize mapped drives or shares. A drive identifier must always point to the actual drive letter of a hard drive or partition on the server host machine.

User Authentication

Regardless of whether you log in from the command line or do so when connecting inside the **isql** shell, authentication will fail if the server does not recognize the user name or the password. For example, Figure 37-3 displays what you will see if your CONNECT statement fails.

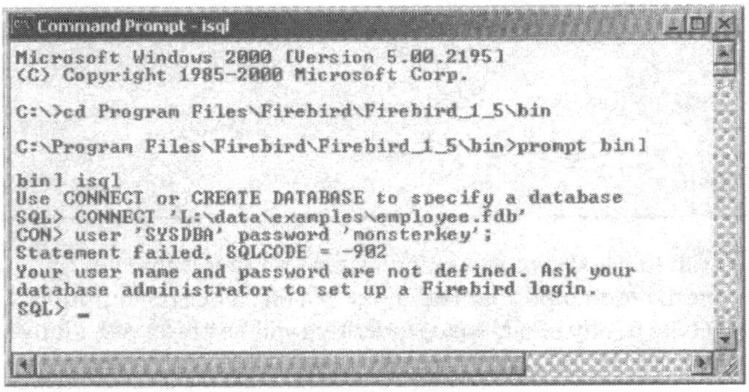

Figure 37-3. Failed authentication

If this happens to you, double-check that you have spelled the username and password correctly, and that the password is correct for case. Passwords are case sensitive; user names are not.

The Terminator Character

The default statement terminator is the semicolon (;), which is used for all of the examples in this chapter. You can change the terminator to any character or group of characters with the SET TERM[INATOR] command. For example, to change it to "!!", use this statement:

```
SQL> SET TERM !!;
SQL>
```

The Continuation Prompt

If you press Enter without remembering to finish a statement with a terminator, you will see the continuation prompt CON> instead of the **isql** prompt SQL>:

```
SQL> SHOW DATABASE
CON>
```

If it was a mistake, simply type the terminator character and press Enter again. However, you can use this feature to make your typing easier to read, for example:

```
SQL> CREATE TABLE ATABLE (
CON>    ID INTEGER NOT NULL,
CON>    DATA VARCHAR(20),
CON>    DATE_ENTERED DATE
```

```
CON>     DEFAULT CURRENT_DATE
CON> );
SQL>
```

> **TIP**   One good reason to use the continuation feature at times is that you can use the OUTPUT command to pipe your **isql** input to a file. Since the output is saved exactly as you type it, any blank-space indenting will be preserved. Many Firebird users use **isql** as their only script editor!

Transactions in isql

Transaction management in **isql** differs according to whether you issue a DDL statement, a SHOW command, or other kinds of statements.

When **isql** starts, it starts a transaction in SNAPSHOT (concurrency) isolation with a lock resolution setting of WAIT. Unless you run DDL statements or SHOW commands, the transaction stays current until you issue a COMMIT or ROLLBACK statement.

You can start an explicit transaction by committing the current transaction and using a SET TRANSACTION statement to start a new one. For example, to start a READ COMMITTED NO WAIT transaction:

```
SQL> COMMIT;
SQL> SET TRANSACTION
CON> NO WAIT READ COMMITTED;
```

When you have finished your task, just issue a COMMIT statement as usual. The next statement will revert to the default configuration.

DDL Statements

Each time you issue a DDL statement, **isql** starts a special transaction for it and commits it immediately after you press Enter. A new transaction is started immediately afterward. You can change this automatic behavior by issuing the SET AUTODDL OFF command from the SQL prompt before you begin issuing your DDL statements:

```
SQL> SET AUTODDL OFF;
```

To switch back to autocommit mode for DDL statements:

```
SQL> SET AUTODDL ON;
```

For switching back and forth between autoddl on and off, a short version is available that simply sets autoddl off if it is on, and vice versa:

```
SQL> SET AUTO;
```

SHOW Commands

The **isql** SHOW commands query the system tables. Whenever you invoke a SHOW command, **isql** commits the existing transaction and starts a new one in READ COMMITTED isolation. This ensures that you always have an up-to-date view of metadata changes as soon as they occur.

Retrieving the Line Buffer

From v.1.5 onward, **isql** allows you to retrieve the line buffer, in a similar fashion to the way the *readline* feature works on POSIX platforms. Use the up and down arrow keys to "scroll through" the **isql** buffer, a line at a time, to retrieve copies of lines you typed previously.

Using Warnings

By default, **isql** issues warnings for certain conditions, for example:

- Statements with no effect

- Ambiguous join specifications in Firebird 1.0.*x* (in v.1.5 and higher, they will cause exceptions)

- Expressions that produce different results in different versions of Firebird

- API calls that will be replaced in future versions

- When a database shutdown is pending

For toggling the display off and on during an interactive **isql** session, use SET WARNINGS or its shorthand counterpart, SET WNG.

Exception Handling

Errors in **isql** are handled and delivered in the same way as they are in a DSQL application. **isql** displays an error message consisting of the SQLCODE variable and the text message from the Firebird status array, as shown in Figure 37-4.

Figure 37-4. Example of an error message in **isql**

SQL errors with sub-zero SQLCODEs mean the statement has failed to execute. They are all listed in Appendix X. You may also see one of the SQL warning or information messages, namely

0: SUCCESS (successful execution)

+1–99: SQLWARNING (system warning or information message)

+100: NOT FOUND (indicates that no qualifying rows were found, or "end of file"; that is, the end of the current active set of rows was detected)

Setting Dialect in isql

If you start **isql** and attach to a database without specifying a dialect, **isql** takes on the dialect of the database.

You can set the **isql** dialect in the following ways:

- When starting **isql**:

  ```
  bin] isql -s n
  ```

  where *n* is 1, 2, or 3. If you specify the dialect this way, **isql** retains that dialect after connection unless you explicitly change it.

- Within an **isql** session or in an SQL script:

  ```
  SET SQL DIALECT n;
  ```

  isql continues to operate in that dialect unless it is explicitly changed.

The dialect cannot be set as a parameter of a CREATE DATABASE statement.

 CAUTION   When you create a database interactively using **isql**, the database will be in the dialect that is current in **isql** at the time the CREATE DATABASE statement is issued. You need to watch this if you had a dialect 1 database open previously, because **isql** stays in dialect 1 after it disconnects from the dialect 1 database.

Dialect Effects

The effects of commands may show some variations according to dialect:

- A dialect 1 client processes all commands according to the expectations of InterBase 5 language and syntax, with certain variations. For example, if you create a table that specifies a column of type DATE, you will see an information message telling you that "DATE data type is now called TIMESTAMP."

- In a dialect 2 client, elements that have different interpretations in dialect 1 and 3 are all flagged with warnings or errors, to assist in migrating databases to dialect 3.

- A dialect 3 client parses all statements according to native Firebird SQL semantics: double quotes are delimited identifiers and are not recognized as string delimiters, the DATE data type is date-only, and exact numerics with precision greater than 9 are stored as BIGINT (NUMERIC(18,0) in Firebird 1.0.*x*).

Interactive Commands

You can enter three kinds of commands or statements interactively at the SQL> prompt:

- **SQL data definition** (DDL) statements, such as CREATE, ALTER, DROP, GRANT, and REVOKE. These statements create, modify, or remove metadata and objects or control user access permission (privileges) to the database.

- **SQL data manipulation** (DML) statements such as SELECT, INSERT, UPDATE, and DELETE. The output of SELECT statements can be displayed or directed to a file (see the OUTPUT command).

- **isql** commands, which fall into three main categories:

  - General commands (for example, commands to read an input file, write to an output file, or end an **isql** session)

  - SHOW commands (to display metadata or other database information)

  - SET commands (to modify the **isql** environment)

Creating and Altering Database Objects

In an **isql** session you can submit DDL statements one by one to CREATE or DROP databases, domains, generators, tables, indexes, triggers, and stored procedures. With the exception of generators, you can also issue ALTER statements for any of these objects.

While it is possible to build a database by submitting and committing a series of DDL statements during an interactive **isql** session, this approach is ad hoc. It leaves you with no documentation of the process and potential holes in your QA review process.

Scripts

It is very good practice to use a *script* to create your database and its objects. A script for creating and altering database objects is sometimes known as a schema script, a data definition file, or just a *DDL script*. The topic of schema scripting is covered in detail in Chapter 14.

Scripting ongoing changes in a DDL script gives you a permanent record of the evolution of your database and the ability to review and reverse any imprudent changes. **isql** can create a script during an interactive session by passing your keyboard input to a named file. To find out how to do this, read the notes on the OUTPUT command in the next section.

You can run scripts—whether created in **isql** or by another text editor—using the INPUT command. INPUT can be used inside scripts, too, to build nested scripts.

General isql Commands

The general **isql** commands perform a variety of useful tasks, including reading, recording, and processing schema scripts, and executing shell commands. The commands are BLOBDUMP, BLOBVIEW, EDIT, EXIT, HELP, INPUT, OUTPUT, QUIT, and SHELL.

BLOBDUMP stores BLOB data into a named file:

```
BLOBDUMP blob_id filename ;
```

blob_id	Identifier consisting of two hex numbers separated by a colon (:). The first number is the ID of the table containing the BLOB column; the second is a sequenced instance number. To get the blob_id, issue any SELECT statement that selects a column of BLOB data. The output will show the hex blob_id above or in place of the BLOB column data, depending on whether SET BLOB[DISPLAY] is ON or OFF.
filename	Fully qualified filesystem name of the file that is to receive the data.

Example:

```
SQL> BLOBDUMP 32:d48 IMAGE.JPG ;
```

BLOBVIEW displays BLOB data in the default text editor.

```
BLOBVIEW blob_id ;
```

blob_id	Identifier consisting of two hex numbers separated by a colon (:). See BLOBDUMP for instructions on how to determine the blob_id you are looking for. In current versions, BLOBVIEW does not support online editing of the BLOB. It may be introduced in a future release.

Example:

```
SQL> BLOBVIEW 85:7 ;
```

Bug note: BLOBVIEW may return an "Invalid transaction handle" error after you close the editor. To correct the situation, start a transaction manually, with

```
SQL> SET TRANSACTION;
```

EDIT allows editing and re-execution of the previous **isql** command or of a batch of commands in a source file.

```
SQL> EDIT [filename];
```

filename	Optional, fully qualified filesystem name of the file to edit

Example:

```
SQL> EDIT /usr/mystuff/batch.sql
```

EDIT can also be used to open the previous statements in the editor:

```
SQL> SELECT EMP_CODE, EMP_NAME FROM EMPLOYEE ;
SQL> EDIT ;
```

Press Enter to display the "scroll" from your **isql** session in the default ASCII text editor in your system. Edit it, save it if you wish, and exit. The edited batch of commands will be re-executed in your **isql** shell when you exit the editor.

EXIT commits the current transaction without prompting, closes the database, and ends the **isql** session. If you need to roll back the transaction instead of committing it, use QUIT instead.

```
SQL> EXIT ;
```

EXIT takes no arguments.

HELP displays a list of **isql** commands with descriptions. You can combine it with OUTPUT to print the list to a file.

```
SQL> HELP ;
```

Example:

```
SQL> OUTPUT HELPLIST.TXT ;
SQL> HELP ;
SQL> OUTPUT ; /* toggles output back to the monitor */
```

HELP takes no arguments.

INPUT reads and executes a block of commands from a named text file (SQL script). Input files can embed other INPUT commands, thus providing the capability to design chained or structured suites of DDL scripts. To create scripts, use a text editor or build them interactively, using the OUTPUT or EDIT commands.

```
SQL> INPUT filename ;
```

filename	Fully qualified filesystem path to a file containing SQL statements and commands

Example:

```
SQL> INPUT /data/schemascripts/myscript.sql ;
```

In a script:

```
...
CREATE EXCEPTION E010 'This is an exception.';
COMMIT;
-- TABLE DEFINITIONS
INPUT '/data/schemascripts/tabledefs.sql';
-- CONSTRAINT DEFINITIONS
INPUT 'data/schemascripts/constraintdefs.sql';
...
```

OUTPUT redirects output to a disk file or (back) to the standard output device (monitor). Use SET ECHO commands to include or exclude commands:

- SET ECHO ON to output both commands and data

- SET ECHO OFF to output data only

```
SQL> OUTPUT [filename];
```

filename	Fully qualified filesystem path to a file containing SQL statements and commands. If no file name is given, results appear on the standard monitor output (i.e., output-to-file is switched off).

Example:

```
SQL> OUTPUT d:\data\employees.dta ;
SQL> SELECT EMP_NO, EMP_NAME FROM EMPLOYEE ; /* output goes to file */
SQL> OUTPUT ; /* toggles output back to the monitor */
```

> **TIP**   If you are using OUTPUT to build scripts, it will be necessary to edit them to remove any stray interactive **isql** commands. However, when you "replay" output in **isql** using INPUT, **isql** usually just ignores the echoed interactive commands.

QUIT rolls back the current transaction and closes the **isql** shell.

```
SQL> QUIT ;
```

QUIT takes no arguments. If you need to commit the transaction instead of rolling it back, use EXIT instead.

SHELL gives temporary access to a command-line shell without committing or rolling back any transaction.

```
SQL> SHELL [operating system command];
```

operating system command	Optional. A command or call that is valid in command shell from which **isql** was launched. The command will be executed and control returned to **isql**. If no command is specified, **isql** opens an interactive session in the command shell. Typing exit returns control to **isql**.

Example:

```
SQL> SHELL dir /mydir | more ;
```

The example will display the contents of the directory /mydir and return control to **isql** when the display completes or the *more* utility is terminated by Ctrl+C.

SHOW Commands

SHOW commands are used to display metadata, including tables, indexes, procedures, triggers, and privileges. They can list the names of all objects of the specified type or supply detailed information about a particular object named in the command.

The SHOW commands are (approximately) the interactive equivalent of the command-line *–extract*, *–x*, or *–a* option (see "Extracting Metadata"). However, although you can use the OUTPUT command to send the output of the SHOW commands to a file, the saved text is not ready to use as a schema script without editing. Use the command-line options if obtaining a schema script is your goal.

Each SHOW command runs in its own READ COMMITTED statement, ensuring that each call returns the most up-to-date view of the state of the database.

SHOW CHECK displays the names and sources for all user-defined CHECK constraints defined for a specified table.

```
SQL> SHOW CHECK tablename ;
```

tablename	Name of a table that exists in the attached database

Example:

```
...
SQL> SHOW CHECK JOB ;
CONSTRAINT INTEG_12
  CHECK (min_salary < max_salary)
```

SHOW DATABASE displays information about the attached database (file name, page size and allocation, sweep interval, transaction numbers, Forced Writes status, default character set). SHOW DB is a shorthand version of the command.

```
SQL> SHOW DATABASE | DB ;
```

SHOW DATABASE takes no arguments. Figure 37-5 shows the output you can expect from SHOW DATABASE.

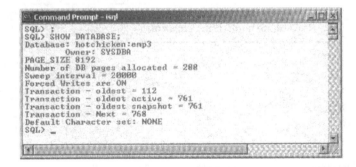

Figure 37-5. SHOW DATABASE output

TIP   For version and on-disk structure information, use SHOW VERSION.

SHOW DOMAIN[S] displays domain information.

```
SQL> SHOW { DOMAINS | DOMAIN name };
```

DOMAINS	Lists the names of all the domains declared in the database
DOMAIN *name*	Displays definition of the named single domain

Examples:

```
SQL> SHOW DOMAINS ;
D_CURRENCY D_NOTES
D_BOOLEAN D_PHONEFAX
... ...
SQL> SHOW DOMAIN D_BOOLEAN ;
D_BOOLEAN SMALLINT NOT NULL
DEFAULT O
CHECK (VALUE IN (0,1)
```

SHOW EXCEPTION[S] displays exception information.

```
SQL> SHOW { EXCEPTIONS | EXCEPTION name };
```

EXCEPTIONS	Lists the names and texts of all exceptions declared in the database
EXCEPTION *name*	Displays text of the named single exception

Examples:

```
...
SQL> SHOW EXCEPTIONS ;
Exception Name Used by, Type
=============== ============================
BAD_WIZ_TYPE UPD_FAVEFOOD, Stored procedure
Invalid Wiz type, check CAPS LOCK
...
SQL> SHOW EXCEPTION BAD_WIZ_TYPE ;
Exception Name Used by, Type
=============== ============================
BAD_WIZ_TYPE UPD_FAVEFOOD, Stored procedure
Invalid Wiz type, check CAPS LOCK
```

SHOW FUNCTION[S] displays information about external functions declared in the attached database.

```
SQL> SHOW { FUNCTIONS | FUNCTION name };
```

FUNCTIONS	Lists the names of all external functions declared in the database
FUNCTION *name*	Displays the declaration of the named external function

Examples:

```
...
SQL> SHOW FUNCTIONS ;
ABS MAXNUM
LOWER SUBSTRLEN
... ...
SQL> SHOW FUNCTION maxnum ;
Function MAXNUM:
Function library is /usr/firebird/udf/ib_udf.so
Entry point is FN_MAX
Returns BY VALUE DOUBLE PRECISION
Argument 1: DOUBLE PRECISION
Argument 2: DOUBLE PRECISION
```

SHOW GENERATOR[S] displays information about generators declared in the attached database.

```
SQL> SHOW { GENERATORS | GENERATOR name };
```

GENERATORS	Lists the names of all generators declared in the database, along with their current values
GENERATOR *name*	Displays the declaration of the named generator, along with its current value

Examples:

```
...
SQL> SHOW GENERATORS ;
Generator GEN_EMPNO, Next value: 1234
Generator GEN_JOBNO, Next value: 56789
Generator GEN_ORDNO, Next value: 98765
... ...
SQL> SHOW GENERATOR gen_ordno ;
Generator GEN_ORDNO, Next value: 98765
```

SHOW GRANT displays privileges and role ownership information about a named object in the attached database or displays user membership within roles.

```
SQL> SHOW GRANT { object | rolename };
```

object	Name of an existing table, view, or procedure in the current database.
rolename	Name of an existing role in the current database. Use SHOW ROLES to list all the roles defined for this database.

Examples:

```
...
SQL> SHOW GRANT JOB ;
GRANT SELECT ON JOB TO ALL
GRANT DELETE, INSERT, SELECT, UPDATE ON JOB TO MANAGER
SQL> SHOW GRANT DO_THIS ;
GRANT DO_THIS TO MAGICIAN
```

SHOW INDEX (SHOW INDICES) displays information about a named index, about indices for a specified table, or about indices for all tables in the attached database. The command can be abbreviated to SHOW IND.

```
SQL> SHOW {INDICES | INDEX { index | table }};
```

index	Name of an existing index in the current database
table	Name of an existing table in the current database

Examples:

```
...
SQL> SHOW INDEX ;
RDB$PRIMARY1 UNIQUE INDEX ON COUNTRY(COUNTRY)
CUSTNAMEX INDEX ON CUSTOMER(CUSTOMER)
CUSTREGION INDEX ON CUSTOMER(COUNTRY, CITY)
RDB$FOREIGN23 INDEX ON CUSTOMER(COUNTRY)
...
SQL> SHOW IND COUNTRY ;
RDB$PRIMARY20 UNIQUE INDEX ON CUSTOMER(CUSTNO)
CUSTNAMEX INDEX ON CUSTOMER(CUSTOMER)
```

NOTE For information about the current states of indexes in the database, use *gstat –i*. Use of the **gstat** utility is discussed at the end of Chapter 18.

SHOW PROCEDURE[S] lists all procedures in the attached database, with their dependencies, or displays the text of the named procedure with the declarations and types (input/output) of any arguments. The command can be abbreviated to SHOW PROC.

```
SQL> SHOW {PROCEDURES | PROCEDURE name } ;
```

PROCEDURES	Lists out all procedures by name, together with their dependencies
PROCEDURE *name*	For the named procedure, lists the source, dependencies, and arguments

Examples:

```
SQL> SHOW PROCEDURES ;
Procedure Name Dependency Type
================ ======================== =======
ADD_EMP_PROJ EMPLOYEE_PROJECT Table
UNKNOWN_EMP_ID Exception
DELETE_EMPLOYEE DEPARTMENT Table
EMPLOYEE Table
EMPLOYEE_PROJECT Table
...
SQL> SHOW PROC ADD_EMP_PROJ ;
Procedure text:
================================================================
BEGIN
BEGIN
INSERT INTO EMPLOYEE_PROJECT (
EMP_NO, PROJ_ID)
VALUES (
:emp_no, :proj_id) ;
WHEN SQLCODE -530 DO
EXCEPTION UNKNOWN_EMP_ID;
END
RETURN ;
END
================================================================
Parameters:
EMP_NO INPUT SMALLINT
PROJ_ID INPUT CHAR(5)
```

SHOW ROLE[S] displays the names of SQL roles for the attached database.

```
SQL> SHOW ROLES ;
```

SHOW ROLES takes no arguments.
Examples:

```
...
SQL> SHOW ROLES ;
MAGICIAN MANAGER
PARIAH SLEEPER
...
```

To show user membership within roles, use SHOW GRANT *rolename*.

SHOW SQL DIALECT displays the SQL dialects of the client and of the attached database, if there is one.

```
SQL> SHOW SQL DIALECT;
```

Example:

```
...
SQL> SHOW SQL DIALECT;
Client SQL dialect is set: 3 and database SQL dialect is: 3
```

SHOW SYSTEM displays the names of system tables and system views for the attached database. It can be abbreviated to SHOW SYS.

```
SQL> SHOW SYS [ TABLES ] ;
```

The command takes no arguments. TABLES is an optional keyword that does not affect the behavior of the command.
Examples:

```
...
SQL> SHOW SYS ;
RDB$CHARACTER_SETS RDB$CHECK_CONSTRAINTS
RDB$COLLATIONS RDB$DATABASE
...
```

For more detailed information about the system tables, see Appendix IX.

SHOW TABLE[S] lists all tables or views, or displays information about the named table or view.

```
SQL> SHOW { TABLES | TABLE name };
```

SHOW TABLES	Lists out names of all tables and views in alphabetical order.
SHOW TABLE *name*	Shows details about the named table or view. If the object is a table, the output contains column names and definitions; PRIMARY KEY, FOREIGN KEY, and CHECK constraints; and triggers. If the object is a view, the output contains column names and the SELECT statement that the view is based on.

Examples:

```
...
SQL> SHOW TABLES ;
COUNTRY CUSTOMER
DEPARTMENT EMPLOYEE
EMPLOYEE_PROJECT JOB
...
SQL> SHOW TABLE COUNTRY ;
COUNTRY COUNTRYNAME VARCHAR(15) NOT NULL
CURRENCY VARCHAR(10) NOT NULL
PRIMARY KEY (COUNTRY)
```

See also SHOW VIEWS (later in the chapter).

SHOW TRIGGER[S] displays all triggers defined in the database, along with the table they depend on or, for the named trigger, displays its sequence, type, activity status (active/inactive), and PSQL definition. It can be abbreviated to SHOW TRIG.

```
SQL> SHOW {TRIGGERS | TRIGGER name } ;
```

SHOW TRIGGERS	Lists out all table names with their trigger names alphabetically
SHOW TRIGGER *name*	For the named trigger, identifies the table it belongs to, displays the header parameters, activity status, and PSQL source of the body

Examples:

```
SQL> SHOW TRIGGERS ;
Table name Trigger name
================ ========================
```

```
EMPLOYEE SET_EMP_NO
EMPLOYEE SAVE_SALARY_CHANGE
CUSTOMER SET_CUST_NO
SALES POST_NEW_ORDER
SQL> SHOW TRIG SET_CUST_NO ;
Trigger:
SET_CUST_NO, Sequence: 0, Type: BEFORE INSERT, Active
AS
BEGIN
    new.custno = gen_id(cust_no_gen, 1);
END
```

SHOW VERSION displays information about the software versions of **isql** and the Firebird server program, and the on-disk structure of the attached database. It can be abbreviated to SHOW VER.

```
SQL> SHOW VERSION ;
```

The command takes no arguments.
Example, from a server named "dev" running Firebird 1.5 on Windows 2000:

```
. . .
SQL> SHOW VER ;
ISQL Version: WI-V1.5.0.4306 Firebird 1.5
Firebird/x86/Windows NT (access method),
    version "WI-V1.5.0.4306 Firebird 1.5"
Firebird/x86/Windows NT (remote server),
    version "WI-V1.5.0.4306 Firebird 1.5/tcp (dev)/P10"
Firebird/x86/Windows NT (remote interface),
    version "WI-V1.5.0.4306 Firebird 1.5/tcp (dev)/P10"
on disk structure version 10.1
```

SHOW VIEW[S] lists all views, or displays information about the named view. (See also SHOW TABLES.)

```
SQL> SHOW { VIEWS | VIEW name } ;
```

SHOW VIEWS	Lists out the names of all views in alphabetical order.
SHOW VIEW *name*	The output displays column names and the SELECT statement that the view is based on.

Example:

```
SQL> SHOW VIEWS ;
PHONE_LIST CUSTOMER
. . .
```

```
SQL> SHOW VIEW PHONE_LIST;
EMP_NO                          (EMPNO) SMALLINT Not Null
FIRST_NAME                      (FIRSTNAME) VARCHAR(15) Not Null
LAST_NAME                       (LASTNAME) VARCHAR(20) Not Null
PHONE_EXT                       VARCHAR(4) Nullable
LOCATION                        VARCHAR(15) Nullable
PHONE_NO                        (PHONENUMBER) VARCHAR(20) Nullable
View Source:
==== ======
 SELECT
    emp_no, first_name, last_name, phone_ext, location, phone_no
    FROM employee, department
    WHERE employee.dept_no = department.dept_no
```

SET Commands

The SET commands enable you to view and change things about the **isql** environment. Some are available in scripts.

SET AUTODDL specifies whether DDL statements are committed automatically after being executed or committed only after an explicit COMMIT. It is available in scripts.

```
SQL> SET AUTODDL [ON | OFF] ; /* default is ON */
```

ON	Toggles automatic commit on
OFF	Toggles automatic commit off

SET AUTO (with no argument) simply toggles AUTODDL on and off. Example:

```
...
SQL> SET AUTODDL OFF ;
SQL> CREATE TABLE WIZZO (x integer, y integer) ;
SQL> ROLLBACK; /* Table WIZZO is not created */
...
SQL>SET AUTO ON ;
SQL> CREATE TABLE WIZZO (x integer, y integer) ;
SQL> /* table WIZZO is created */
```

SET BLOBDISPLAY specifies both the subtype of BLOB to display and whether BLOB data should be displayed.

```
SQL> SET BLOBDISPLAY [ n |ALL |OFF ];
```

SET BLOB is a shortened version of the same command.

n	BLOB SUB_TYPE to display. Default: *n= 1* (text). Positive numbers are system defined; negative numbers are user-defined.
ALL	Display BLOB data of any subtype.
OFF	Toggles display of BLOB data off. The output shows only the BLOBID (two hex numbers separated by a colon). The first number is the ID of the table containing the BLOB column. The second is a sequenced instance number.

Example:

```
...
SQL> SET BLOBDISPLAY OFF ;
SQL> SELECT PROJ_NAME, PROJ_DESC FROM PROJECT ;
SQL> /* rows show values for PROJ_NAME and Blob ID */
...
SQL>SET BLOB 1 ;
SQL> SELECT PROJ_NAME, PROJ_DESC FROM PROJECT ;
SQL> /* rows show values for PROJ_NAME and Blob ID */
SQL> /* and the blob text appears beneath each row */
```

SET COUNT toggles off/on whether to display the number of rows retrieved by queries.

```
SQL> SET COUNT [ON | OFF] ;
```

ON	Toggles on display of "rows returned" message
OFF	Toggles off display of "rows returned" message (default)

Example:

```
...
SQL> SET COUNT ON ;
SQL> SELECT * FROM WIZZO WHERE FAVEFOOD = 'Pizza' ;
SQL> /* displays the data, followed by */
...
40 rows returned
```

SET ECHO toggles off/on whether commands are displayed before being executed. The default is ON but you might want to toggle it to OFF if sending your output to a script file.

```
SQL> SET ECHO [ON | OFF] ; /* default is ON */
```

ON	Toggles on command echoing (default)
OFF	Toggles off command echoing

Example script wizzo.sql:

```
...
SET ECHO OFF;
SELECT * FROM WIZZO WHERE FAVEFOOD = 'Pizza' ;
SET ECHO ON ;
SELECT * FROM WIZZO WHERE FAVEFOOD = 'Sardines' ;
EXIT;
...
SQL > INPUT wizzo.sql ;
WIZTYPE FAVEFOOD
=============== ===================
alpha Pizza
epsilon Pizza
SELECT * FROM WIZZO WHERE FAVEFOOD = 'Sardines' ;
WIZTYPE FAVEFOOD
=============== ===================
gamma Sardines
lamda Sardines
```

SET NAMES specifies the character set that is to be active in database transactions. This is very important if your database's default character set is not NONE. If the client and database character sets are mismatched, you risk transliteration errors and storing wrong data if you use **isql** for performing updates or inserts or for searches (including searched updates and deletes).

SET NAMES is available in scripts.

```
SQL> SET NAMES charset ;
```

charset	Name of the character set to activate. Default: NONE.

Example in script:

```
...
SET NAMES ISO8859_1 ;
CONNECT 'HOTCHICKEN:/usr/firebird/examples/employee.gdb' ;
```

SET PLAN specifies whether to display the optimizer's query plan.

```
SQL> SET PLAN [ON|OFF ];
```

ON	Turns on display of the query plan. This is the default.
OFF	Turns off display of the query plan.

As a shortcut, you can omit ON|OFF and just use SET PLAN as a toggle. Example in a script:

```
...
SET PLAN ON ;
SELECT JOB_COUNTRY, MIN_SALARY
FROM JOB
WHERE MIN_SALARY > 50000
AND JOB_COUNTRY = 'Sweden';
...
SQL> INPUT iscript.sql
PLAN (JOB INDEX (RDB$FOREIGN3,MINSALX,MAXSALX)
JOB_COUNTRY MIN_SALARY
================ =====================
Sweden 120550.00
```

SET PLANONLY specifies to prepare SELECT queries and display just the plan, without executing the actual query.

```
SQL> SET PLANONLY ON | OFF;
```

The command works as a toggle switch. The argument is optional.

SET SQL DIALECT sets the Firebird SQL dialect to which the client session is to be changed. If the session is currently attached to a database of a different dialect from the one specified in the command, a warning is displayed and you are asked whether you want to commit existing work (if any).

```
SQL> SET SQL DIALECT n ;
```

n	Dialect number. *n* = 1 for dialect 1, 2 for dialect 2, and 3 for dialect 3.

Example:

```
SQL> SET SQL DIALECT 3 ;
```

SET STATS specifies whether to display performance statistics following the output of a query.

```
SQL> SET STATS [ON |OFF];
```

ON	Turns on display of performance statistics.
OFF	Turns off display of performance statistics. This is the default.

You can omit ON|OFF and use just SET STATS as a toggle. Figure 37-6 shows a typical statistics summary being displayed after the output of a query.

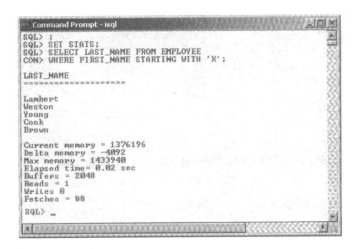

Figure 37-6. SET STATS example

SET STATISTICS

SET STATISTICS is an SQL (not **isql**) command that you can use in **isql**—as well as in other programs—to recompute the selectivity of an index. It is mentioned here because, not surprisingly, people often get it confused with SET STATS. To find out why selectivity can be important in very dynamic tables, refer to the "Optimization Topic" at the end of Chapter 18.

The syntax is SET STATISTICS *index-name*. The statement can be run only by the user that owns the index.

SET TERM specifies the character that will be used as the command or statement *terminator*, from the next statement forward. It is available in scripts. See the notes about this command earlier in this chapter.

```
SQL> SET TERM string ;
```

string	Character or characters that will be used as the statement terminator. The default is ";".

Example:

```
...
SET TERM ^^;
CREATE PROCEDURE ADD_WIZTYPE (WIZTYPE VARCHAR(16), FAVEFOOD VARCHAR(20))
AS
BEGIN
  INSERT INTO WIZZO(WIZTYPE, FAVEFOOD)
  VALUES ( :WIZTYPE, :FAVEFOOD) ;
END ^^
SET TERM ;^^
...
```

SET TIME specifies whether to display the time portion of a DATE value (dialect 1 only).

```
SQL> SET TIME [ON|OFF ];
```

ON	Toggles on time portion display in dialect 1 DATE value.
OFF	Toggles on time portion display in dialect 1 DATE value. This is the default.

Example:

```
SQL> SELECT HIRE_DATE FROM EMPLOYEE WHERE EMP_NO = 145;
HIRE_DATE
------------------
16-MAY-2004
...
SQL>SET TIME ON ;
SQL> SELECT HIRE_DATE FROM EMPLOYEE WHERE EMP_NO = 145;
HIRE_DATE
------------------
16-MAY-2004 18:20:00
```

SET WARNINGS specifies whether warnings are to be output. SET WNG, used as a simple toggle, can be substituted.

```
SQL> SET WARNINGS [ON |OFF ];
```

ON	Toggles on display of warnings if it was toggled off, or if the session was started with the –nowarnings option
OFF	Toggles off display of warnings if it is currently toggled on

Exiting an Interactive isql Session

To exit the **isql** utility and *roll back* all uncommitted work, enter

```
SQL> QUIT;
```

To exit the **isql** utility and *commit* all work, enter

```
SQL> EXIT;
```

Command Mode

Although **isql** has some handy interactive features, it is not restricted to being run in its shell. Many of the interactive commands are available as command-line switches. Some **isql** utilities, such as metadata extraction, are available only from the command shell. Operations on input and output files need not be interactive—in fact, calling **isql** with the –i[nput] and –o[utput] switches will not invoke the interactive shell.

Commands execute and, upon completion, return control automatically to the command shell. Calls to **isql** can also be batched inside shell scripts or batch files.

Certain switches can be used when invoking the interactive **isql** shell; they are noted in Table 37-1.

Operating isql in Command Mode

Open a command shell and *cd* to the Firebird /bin directory of your Firebird server or client installation. Use the following syntax pattern for **isql** calls:

```
isql [options] [database_name] [-u[ser] <user-name> -pas[sword] <password>]
```

For SYSDBA operations, you can set the operating system variables ISC_USER and ISC_PASSWORD and avoid the need to enter them on commands. For non-SYSDBA activities, you will always need the owner credentials for operations on the database and/or objects.

The default terminator is the semicolon (;). You can change it to any character or group of characters with a command-line option.

> **NOTE** If your command is connecting to a database for the purpose of running a script, and its default character set is not NONE, you need to include the SET NAMES command in your script.

You can set the **isql** dialect from the command line when invoking **isql**:

```
isql -s n ;
```

where *n* is 1, 2, or 3.

Command-Line Switches

Only the initial characters in an option are required. You can also type any portion of the text shown in Table 37-1 in square brackets, including the full option name. For example, specifying –n, –no, or –noauto has the same effect.

*Table 37-1. Switches for **isql** Command-Line Options*

OPTION	DESCRIPTION
–a	Extracts all DDL for the named database, including non-DDL statements.
–d[atabase] *name*	Used with the –x (extract) switch. Changes the CREATE DATABASE statement that is extracted to a file. It should be a fully qualified file path. Without the –d switch, CREATE DATABASE appears as a C-style comment, using the database name specified in the command line.
–c[ache]	Sets the number of cache pages used for this connection to the database. You can use this switch to override the cache size that is currently set for the database, for the duration.
–e[cho]	Displays (echoes) each statement before executing it.
–ex[tract]	Extracts DDL for the named database, and displays DDL to the screen unless output is redirected to a file.
–i[nput] *file*	Reads commands from an input file instead of from keyboard input. The *file* argument must be a fully qualified file path. Input files can contain –input commands that call other files, enabling execution to branch and then return. **isql** commits work in the current file before opening the next.

*Table 37-1. Switches for **isql** Command-Line Options (continued)*

OPTION	DESCRIPTION
–m[erge_stderr]	Merges stderr output with stdout. Useful for capturing output and errors to a single file when running **isql** in a shell script or batch file.
–n[oauto]	Turns off automatic committing of DDL statements. By default, DDL statements are committed automatically in a separate transaction.
–nowarnings	Displays warning messages if and only if an error occurs (by default, **isql** displays any message returned in a status vector, even if no error occurred).
–o[utput] *file*	Writes results to an output file instead of to standard output. The *file* argument must be a fully qualified file path.
–pas[sword] *password*	Used with –user to specify a password when connecting to a remote server or when required for a local operation. For access, both *password* and *user* must represent valid entries in the security database *on the server*.
–page[length] *n*	In query output, prints column headers every *n* lines instead of the default 20.
–q[uiet]	Suppresses the "Use CONNECT or CREATE DATABASE . . ." message when the database path is not supplied on the command line.
–r[ole] *rolename*	Passes role *rolename* along with user credentials on connection to the database.
–s[ql_dialect] *n*	Interprets subsequent commands as dialect *n* until end of session or until dialect is changed by a SET SQL DIALECT statement. Refer to the section "Setting Dialect in isql" earlier in this chapter.
–t[erminator] *x*	Changes the end-of-statement symbol from the default semicolon (;) to *x*, where *x* is a single character or any sequence of characters.
–u[ser] *user*	Used with –password. Specifies a user name when connecting to a remote server. For access, both *password* and *user* must represent a valid entry in the security database.
–x	Same as –extract.
–z	Displays the software version of **isql**.

Extracting Metadata

From the command line, you can use the –extract option to output the DDL statements that define the metadata for a database.

All reserved words and objects are extracted into the file in uppercase unless the local language uses a character set that has no uppercase. The output script is created with commit following each set of commands, so that tables can be referenced in subsequent definitions. The output file includes the name of the object and the owner, if one is defined.

The optional –output flag reroutes output to a named file.

Use this syntax:

```
isql [[-extract | -x][-a] [[-output | -o] outputfile]] database
```

The –x option can be used as an abbreviation for –extract. The –a flag directs **isql** to extract all database objects. Note that the output file specification, *outputfile*, must be a fully qualified path and follow the –output flag. The path and name of the database being extracted can be at the end of the command.

You can use the resulting text file to

- Examine the current state of a database's system tables before planning alterations. This is especially useful when the database has changed significantly since its creation.

- Create a database with schema definitions that are identical to the extracted database.

- Open in your text editor to make changes to the database definition or create a new database source file.

NOTE   The –extract function is not always as smart as it should be about dependencies. It is sometimes necessary to edit the output file to rectify creation order.

Using isql -extract

The following statement extracts the SQL schema from the database *employee.fdb* to a schema script file called *employee.sql*:

```
isql -extract -output /data/scripts/employee.sql /data/employee.fdb
```

This command is equivalent:

```
isql -x -output /data/scripts/employee.sql /data/employee.fdb
```

These objects and items are not extracted:

- System tables and views, system triggers

- External function and BLOB filter code (it's not part of the database)

- Object ownership attributes

Using isql -a

The –(e)x(tract) option extracts metadata for SQL objects only. If you wish to extract a schema script that includes declarations, such as DECLARE EXTERNAL FUNCTION and DECLARE FILTER, use the –a option.

For example, to extract DDL statements from database *employee.fdb* and store in the file *employee.sql*, enter

```
isql -a -output /data/scripts/employee.sql /data/employee.fdb
```

Up Next

Next, we explore **gbak**, the command-line backup and housecleaning utility.

Database Backup and Restore (gbak)

A PROPER FIREBIRD DATABASE BACKUP saves the metadata and data of a database compactly to a file on a hard disk or other storage medium. It is strongly recommended that backup files be transferred to a portable storage medium and stored at a secure physical location remote from the server.

Regular backup is essential for good housekeeping, data integrity, security, and disaster fallback. Firebird's command-line backup and restore utility, **gbak**, creates and restores backups of your databases. It creates a platform-independent, stable snapshot archive of the database that can be written to a disk file and compressed, if desired, using a third-party utility.

Firebird's backup is a "hot" backup—normal database activity can continue while **gbak** is analyzing the metadata and writing the backup file. The operation runs in a snapshot transaction and captures database state as it stands when the transaction begins. Data changes that clients commit to the database after the backup begins are not recorded in the backup file.

CAUTION   Operating systems usually include facilities to archive database files. Do not rely on backups of your Firebird databases made by these utilities or filesystem copy utilities, or compression utilities such as gzip or WinZip, *unless the database is completely shut down.* Such database copies are not "hygienic"—uncleared garbage will be restored along with the rest of the file. Because these filesystem utilities usually place low-level locks on blocks of disk, their use is a recognized cause of corruption if they are allowed to run while there are live connections.

About gbak Files

The **gbak** utility analyzes and decomposes Firebird database files, storing cleaned metadata and data separately, in a compact format. A backup made with **gbak** is not a database file and will not be recognized by the server. In order to become useable, it must be restored to a Firebird format that is readable by the server, using the version of **gbak** that corresponds to the version of Firebird server that is running.

When restoring its files back to database format, **gbak** performs validation of both metadata and data before using query-language commands internally to reconstruct the database and repopulate it with its data.

If corrupt structures or data are detected, **gbak** stops restoring and reports the condition. Its ability to analyze problems makes it an invaluable helper when recovery of broken databases is being attempted. If you are in this unfortunate situation, refer to Appendix IV.

CAUTION   Making backups is but one part of a data protection scheme. If you have blind faith in the integrity of backups then, regardless of the backup system you use, you will be tempting fate. The fact that a backup completes is no guarantee that it will restore. Always make test restores as essential and regular a part of your backup and data assurance regime as the backups themselves.

gbak's Other Talents

gbak also performs an important sequence of other utility tasks in the course of analyzing, storing, and restoring your database. Some are automatic; others can be requested by means of switches in the command-line call when you invoke the program.

- **gbak** performs garbage collection on outdated records during backup—an optional switch, enabled by default. If enabled, this housekeeping occurs even if you don't restore the backup and begin working with a fresh file. Note, however, that running **gbak** doesn't pack the database that it is backing up—run a full sweep to do that.

Restore tasks can include

- Balancing indexes, to refresh the performance capability of your database.

- Reclaiming space occupied by deleted records and packing the remaining data. This often reduces database size and improves performance by "packing" data.

- Optionally changing the database page size on restore.

- Changing the database owner. This is optional—but watch out! It can happen by accident if you are not careful.

- Upgrading an InterBase database to Firebird or a lower version Firebird database to a higher version (i.e., upgrading the on-disk structure [ODS]).

- Splitting the database into multiple files or resizing existing multiple files. This is optional.

- Distributing a multi-file database across multiple disks. This is optional.

Backup and restore also have important roles to play in the unfortunate event that databases become corrupt. For a detailed walk-through of a database recovery strategy, refer to Appendix IV.

Upgrading the On-Disk Structure

New major releases of the Firebird server are likely to feature changes that alter the *on-disk structure* (ODS). If the ODS has changed and you want to take advantage of any new Firebird features, upgrade your databases to the new ODS. A new server version can access databases created with some previous versions, but it will not be able to share any of its new features with an older database with a lower ODS.

You can use most Firebird 1.0.*x* databases directly with Firebird 1.5, even though the ODS of v.1.5 (10.1) is a point higher than that of v.1.0.*x* (10.0). All the same, it is recommended that you do follow the upgrade procedure on your databases when you do the transition from 10.0 to 10.1, to take advantage of the performance increase made possible by the v.1.5 indexing of system tables.

To upgrade existing databases to a new ODS, perform the following steps:

1. Before installing the new ODS version of Firebird, back up databases using the *old* version of **gbak.**

2. Install the new version of the Firebird server as described in Chapter 1.

3. Once the new version is installed, restore the databases using the **gbak** that is installed along with it, in the \bin directory beneath the Firebird root.

Dialect 1 Databases

A dialect 1 database remains dialect 1 when it is restored. The database remains limited to the language features of InterBase 5, although some restrictions apply to a dialect 1 database under the new ODS that do not apply to InterBase 5. For example, Firebird has a number of new reserved words that will be "illegal" in a dialect 1 database. Refer to Appendix XI for a complete list of reserved words.

To diverge from the topic slightly, it is possible to change the dialect of a restored dialect 1 database to dialect 3, using the **gfix** tools discussed in the next chapter. However, migration is not as simple as that. Language is not the only thing about the two dialects that has differences. Data type differences are at least as important, if not more so.

For example, fixed numeric domains and columns retain their old attributes when the database is changed to dialect 3. NUMERIC and DECIMAL types with precision higher than 10 are stored as DOUBLE PRECISION in dialect 1. Conversion to true, 64-bit fixed numeric types is not done when you change the dialect to 3—you must create new columns of the required type and cast the old values into the new columns.

Firebird inherited some features to assist with migrating from dialect 1 to Firebird's native SQL dialect (known as dialect 3). It's widely acknowledged that there are much easier and safer ways to do this migration. Best results are achieved by extracting a metadata script, updating it, if necessary, and reconstituting an "empty" dialect 3 database. Excellent free and low-cost data-pumping tools are widely available for repopulating your new database with your old data. Refer to Appendix V for recommendations and links and to the special migration topic at the end of Chapter 8 for a summary of the language issues.

Database Backup and Restore Rights

Use of **gbak** is restricted to SYSDBA and the owner of the database named in the backup or restore request.

NOTE   Any user can restore a database using the –[c]reate switch (see the section "Running a Restore"), as long as the database being created will not overwrite an existing database.

Changing Ownership of a Database

A restored database file, or one created from a **gbak** file, is owned by the user that performed the restore. Backing up and restoring a database is thus a mechanism for changing the ownership of a database.

CAUTION   Anyone can steal a Firebird database by restoring a backup file to a machine where he knows the SYSDBA password. It is important to ensure that your backup files are secured from unauthorized access.[1]

---

1. Filesystem and other environmental security issues are discussed in Chapters 33 and 34.

User Name and Password

When Firebird checks authority to run **gbak**, it determines the user according to the following hierarchy:

1. The user name and password specified as switches in the **gbak** command.

2. For a local **gbak** only,[2] the user name and password specified in the ISC_USER and ISC_PASSWORD environment variables, provided they also exist in the security database (security.fdb in v.1.5; isc4.gdb in v.1.0.x). Keeping these environment variables set permanently is strongly *not* recommended, since it is extremely insecure.

3. For POSIX only, if no user credentials are supplied at either of the previous levels, Firebird allows the *root* user to run **gbak** from the server or from a trusted host.

Running a Backup

To invoke **gbak**, either *cd* to the Firebird /bin directory where **gbak** is located or use an absolute root path. The entire command must be on a single line. In the following syntax patterns and examples, the wrapped portions of lines are shown as indented.
   POSIX:

```
$] ./gbak -b[ackup] <options> source target [n]
```

   or

```
$] /opt/firebird/bin/gbak -b[ackup] <options> source target [n]
```

   Windows:

```
C:\Program Files\Firebird\Firebird_1_5\bin> gbak -b[ackup]
     <options> source target [n]
```

   or

```
C:\> C:\Program Files\Firebird_1_5\bin\gbak -b[ackup]
     <options> source target [n]
```

---

2. In fact, if you are really careless and leave the environment variables lying about on workstations, showing the SYSDBA password to the world, remote users can do backups without entering credentials, too. Needless to say, it is certainly a practice to avoid.

Arguments for gbak -b[ackup]

source is the full path and file name of a database to back up. In Firebird 1.5, it can be an alias. If backing up a multi-file database, use only the name of the *first* (primary) database file.

target is the full path and file name of a storage device or backup file to which the backed-up database is to be sent.

In the case that the backup is being output to multiple files, there will be multiple targets. The token *n* is an integer parameter, included with each output file except the last, to indicate the length of the file in (by default) bytes. A lowercase character can be appended to the number to specify that *size* is in kilobytes (*k*), megabytes (*m*), or gigabytes (*g*). Refer to the examples that follow.

On POSIX, target can also be *stdout*. In this case, **gbak** writes its output to the standard output (usually a pipe).

options can be a valid combination of switches from Table 38-1. The switches are case insensitive.

Backup Switches

Table 38-1 lists and describes the switches that can be used with **gbak** when running backups.

*Table 38-1. **gbak** Switches for Backups*

SWITCH	EFFECT
–b[ackup_database]	Causes **gbak** to run a backup of the named database to file or device.
–co[nvert]	Converts external files into internal tables. On restore, any external tables are converted to intra-database tables and the association with the external file will be gone.
–e[xpand]	Creates the backup without compression.
–fa[ctor] *n*	Uses a blocking factor *n* for a tape device.
–g[arbage_collect]	Suppresses garbage collection during backup. Use this switch if you are planning to restore the database from the backup into immediate use afterward. **gbak** does not store garbage, so it does not make sense to add the extra overhead if you are not going to use the old database afterward.
–i[gnore]	Causes checksums to be ignored during backup. You can use this switch on a rerun of a backup that failed from checksum errors.
–l[imbo]	(Lowercase letter "L") Causes limbo transactions to be ignored. Do not use this switch for regular backups. It is available for cleanup after a two-phase transaction has failed due to losing a server before commits have taken place.
–m[etadata]	Backs up just the metadata—no data is saved. It can be a quick way to get an "empty" database in preparation for deploying into production.

Table 38-1. **gbak** *Switches for Backups (continued)*

SWITCH	EFFECT
–nt	Creates the backup in non-transportable format. By default, the data stored in **gbak** files are in XDR format, a standard protocol for porting data across platforms.
–ol[d_descriptions]	A deprecated switch—it backs up metadata in an older InterBase format.
–pas[sword] *password*	Checks for password *password* before accessing the database. This is required (along with a user name) for remote backups and also locally, where ISC_USER and ISC_PASSWORD environment variables are not available. Note that the abbreviated form of the –password switch (–pa) for **gbak** is different from that for isql (–pas).
–role *name*	Connects under role *name*. Currently, this seems a pointless switch that you can simply ignore.
–se[rvice] *servicename*	Creates the backup files on the host where the original database files are located. The *servicename* argument invokes the Service Manager on the server host. For details of syntax, refer to the section "Using gbak with the Firebird Service Manager."
–t[ransportable]	Stores the **gbak** data in XDR transportable format. It is the default. To store data in a compressed native format, use the –nt switch.
–u[ser] *name*	Checks for user *name* before accessing the database. This is required (along with a password) for remote backups and also locally, where ISC_USER and ISC_PASSWORD environment variables are not available.
–v[erify]	Provides a detailed trail of what **gbak** does. You can optionally output the text to a file, using the –y switch.
–y {*filespec* | *suppress_output*}	Directs status messages to *filespec*, a fully qualified path to the file you want to have created. It will fail if the named file already exists. If the backup finishes normally and the –v[erify switch] is not used, the file will be empty. **suppress_output** can be used instead for a "silent" backup with no output messages at all.
–z	Shows the version numbers of both **gbak** and the Firebird engine.

Transportable Backups

Accept the default –*transportable* switch if you operate in a multi-platform environment. It writes data in the cross-platform standard eXternal Data Representation (XDR)[3] format, allowing the file to be read by the **gbak** program on a platform different from the one on which it was backed up.

---

3. For information about the XDR standard, see http://asg.web.cmu.edu/rfc/rfc1832.html.

Cross-version Backups

The **gbak** program on servers with lower ODS than the Firebird server that created a database will generally *not* be able to restore from the higher ODS backup. In practice, however, the InterBase 5.*x* version of **gbak** appears to be capable of restoring most dialect 1 databases created with Firebird 1.0.*x*.

 CAUTION   You should never attempt to back up databases with a version of **gbak** that does not match the server version on which the database runs.

Backing Up to a Single File

For a simple local backup of a single-file or multiple-file database, use

```
gbak -b d:\data\ourdata.fdb d:\data\backups\ourdata.fbk
```

The source name is the same whether the database you are backing up is a single or a multiple-file database. When you are backing up a multi-file database, specify *only the first file* in the backup command. The paths to the second and subsequent files will be found by **gbak** in the database and file headers during the course of the backup. If you name the subsequent database files, they will be interpreted as backup file names.

The target file can have any name you wish, as long as it is valid on the filesystem to which it is being written.

Backing Up a Multi-file Database to Multiple Files

When you back up a multi-file database to multiple **gbak** files, there is no requirement to match the database file for file with the backup. If there is to be more than one target file, the names and sizes of the target files need to be specified for all except the last file in the set. By default, the file size (an integer) is taken to be in bytes. To modify that, append a lowercase character to tell **gbak** you intend the size to be in kilobytes (k), megabytes (m), or gigabytes (g).

The following command backs up a database to three backup files on different filesystem partitions and writes a verbose log. It is all one command; the indented portions are wrapped here for easier reading.

POSIX:

```
./gbak -b /data/accounts.fdb /backups/accounts.fb1 2g
    /backups2/accounts.fb2 750m /backups3/accounts.fb3
        -user SYSDBA -password m1llp0nd
            -v -y /logs/backups/accounts.20040703.log
```

Windows:

```
gbak -b d:\data\accounts.fdb e:\backups\accounts.fb1 2g
    f:\backups2\accounts.fb2 750m g:\backups3\accounts.fb3
        -user SYSDBA -password m1llp0nd
            -v -y d:\data\backuplogs\accounts.20040703.log
```

Single-File Database to Multiple Targets

If you back up a single-file database to multiple targets, the syntax is identical. In fact, **gbak** is not interested in whether your source database is single- or multiple-file.

It is important to note the following points:

- The backup will fail if any designated target file is smaller than 2048 bytes. If you are logging, the reason will appear in the log.

- **gbak** fills the named target files in left-to-right order. It won't begin the next file until the previous one has reached its designated capacity. In the preceding example, accounts.fb3 will not be created if accounts.fb2 is not filled.

- File paths for targets need not be physically controlled by the host but, if you are using the *–service* switch (refer to the section "Using gbak with the Firebird Service Manager") on systems where file permissions are in force, your user profile must have the appropriate write permissions. In some v.1.5 installations, this may be the *firebird* user or group by default; in some v.1.0.*x* installations, it may be the *interbase* user by default.

Metadata-Only Backup

A metadata-only backup is typically needed for creating an "empty" database when you are ready to deploy a system into production, load QA data, or reconstitute a database for the purpose of migrating. The following command does a metadata-only backup of our *accounts* database:

```
gbak -b -m d:\data\accounts.fdb e:\QA\accounts.fbk
```

Remote Backups

If you run **gbak** from a remote client machine, it writes the backup files to the current directory or to a specified, fully qualified local path. If you specify a location for the backup file, it must be accessible by the machine where **gbak** is executing. The location can be any of the following:

- On a drive or partition that is local to the client machine

- On a drive that the local machine is mapping to (Windows)

- In a network filesystem (NFS) location (Linux/UNIX)

With the –se[rvice] switch, you can invoke the Firebird Service Manager on the remote server and have **gbak** delegate the execution of your command on the server itself. The database and backup file specifications must then refer to a location and file name local to the server machine. Locations local to where **gbak** is launched are not valid for a Service Manager backup. For more about Service Manager, see the upcoming section "Using gbak with the Firebird Service Manager."

Security Considerations

It is a good precaution to set the read-only property on your backup files at the filesystem level after creating them, to prevent them from being accidentally or maliciously overwritten.

You can protect your databases from being "kidnapped" on UNIX and on Windows NT/2000/XP systems by placing the backup files in directories with restricted access.

 CAUTION   Backup files that are kept on Windows 95/98/ME systems, or in unrestricted areas of other systems, are completely vulnerable.

Return Codes and Feedback

A backup run on Windows returns an error level of 0 on success and 1 on failure. If an error occurs, check the *firebird.log* file (*interbase.log* in v.1.0.x). For a full backup log file, use the –y and –v switches.

Running a Restore

The syntax pattern for the restore options is as follows.
POSIX:

```
$] ./gbak {-c[reate] | -r[eplace_database] }  <options> source target
```

or

```
$] /opt/firebird/bin/gbak {-c[reate] | -r[eplace_database] }
    <options> source target
```

Windows:

```
C:\Program Files\Firebird\Firebird_1_5\bin> {-c[reate] | -r[eplace_database] }
    <options> source target
```

or

```
C:\> C:\Program Files\Firebird_1_5\bin\gbak {-c[reate] | -r[eplace_database] }
    <options> source target
```

Arguments for gbak Restores

source is the full path and file name of an authentic **gbak** file. If the backup is a multiple-file set, name only the first (primary) **gbak** file. On POSIX, *source* can also be *stdin*, in which case **gbak** reads its input from the standard input (usually a pipe).

target is the full path and file name for the restored database. In Firebird 1.5, it can be an alias. The target can be a single file or multiple files. The possible syntax options for target databases are discussed in later sections of this chapter.

options can be a valid combination of switches from Table 38-2. The switches are case insensitive.

Restore Switches

Table 38-2 lists and describes the switches that can be used with **gbak** when running restores.

*Table 38-2. **gbak** Switches for Restores*

SWITCH	EFFECT
–c[reate_database]	Restores database to a new file.
–b[uffers]	Sets default cache size (in database pages) for the restored database.
–i[nactive]	Makes indexes inactive in the restored database. Useful when retrying a restore that failed because of an index error.
–k[ill]	Suppresses re-creation of any shadows that were previously defined.
–mo[de] {[read_write | read_only}	Specifies whether the restored database is to be read-only or read-write. Possible values are *read_write* (default) or *read_only*.

continued

Table 38-2. **gbak** *Switches for Restores (continued)*

SWITCH	EFFECT
–n[o_validity]	Deletes validity constraints from restored metadata. Use if you need to retry a restore that failed because of CHECK constraint violations.
–o[ne_at_a_time]	Restores one table at a time. Can be used for partial recovery if a database contains corrupt data.
–pa[ge_size] *n*	Resets page size to *n* bytes (1024, 2048, 4096, 8192, or 16384). Default is 4096. A page size of 16384 is not possible if the filesystem does not support 64-bit file I/O.
–pas[sword] *password*	Checks for password *password*, along with –u[ser], before attempting to (re)create the database
–r[eplace_database]	Restores database, replacing the existing file matching the named target, if it exists; if not, creates a new file with the target name.
–se[rvice] *servicename*	Creates the restored database on the host where the backup files are located. Use this switch if you are running **gbak** from a remote node and want to restore from a backup that resides on the same server as the database. It invokes the Firebird Service Manager on the server host and saves both time and network traffic. More details in the section "Using gbak with the Firebird Service Manager."
–u[ser] *name*	Checks for user *name*, along with –pa[ssword], before attempting to re-create the database.
–use_[all_space]	Restores database with 100-percent fill ratio on every data page, instead of the default 80-percent fill ratio. This is ideal for read-only databases, since they do not need to keep reserve space on database pages to allow for variations in data size as rows are inserted, updated, and deleted. To revert a restored database to normal fill ratio, use the **gfix** –use switch (i.e., gfix -use reserve).
–v[erify]	Provides a detailed trail of what **gbak** does. You can optionally output the text to a file, using the –y switch.
–y {*filespec* | **suppress_output**}	Directs status messages to *filespec*, a fully qualified path to the file you want to have created. It will fail if the named file already exists. If the backup finishes normally and the –v[erify switch] is not used, the file will be empty. **suppress_output** can be used instead for a "silent" backup with no output messages at all.
–z	Shows the version numbers of both **gbak** and the Firebird engine.

Restore or Create?

The notion of "restoring a database" by overwriting it was born in another age, when disk space was worth more than hiring an expert to reconstruct a broken database or taking on a team of data-entry staff to reconstruct the company's system from paper records.

In short, overwriting a database whose survival you care about is not recommended under any circumstances. Ponder these painful facts:

- If a restore fails to complete, the overwritten database is gone forever—and things can go wrong with any restore.

- Restoring over a database that is in use will cause corruption.

- Allowing users to log into a partly restored database will also cause corruption.

 TIP Hot backup is cool. Hot restore is a big chill.

If you decide to use –r[eplace_database] anyway, despite the risks, then you can only do so if you supply the login credentials of the database owner, or of SYSDBA. Any user authenticated on the server can restore using the –c[reate] option. Consider the implications of that fact and take the appropriate precautions to keep your backups out of the wrong hands.

User-Defined Objects

When restoring a backup file to a server other than the one on which it was backed up, you must ensure that any character sets and collations referenced in the backup file exist on the destination server. The backup will not be able to be restored if the language objects are missing.

External function and BLOB filter libraries referred to by declarations in the database, similarly, must be present for a restored database to work without errors.

Restoring to a Single File

The following command performs a simple restore from one backup file to one database file:

```
gbak -c d:\data\backups\ourdata.fbk d:\data\ourdata_trial.fdb
```

Multiple-File Restores

Single or multiple backup files can be restored to single- or multiple-volume database files. There is no requirement to have a one-to-one correspondence between a backup file volume and a database file volume.

When restoring from a multi-file backup, you must name all of the backup files, in the order in which they were backed up. **gbak** complains noisily if it gets the list in the wrong order or if a volume is missing.

For the target (database) files, you need to supply a *size* parameter for all files except the last. The minimum value is 200 database pages. The last file always expands as needed to fill all available space.

Single-Volume Backup to Multiple-Volume Database

POSIX:

```
./gbak -c /backups/stocks.fbk /data/stocks_trial.fdb
    -user SYSDBA -password m1llp0nd
        -v -y /logs/backups/stocks_r.20040703.log
```

Windows:

```
gbak -c e:\backups\stocks.fbk d:\data\stocks_trial.fdb
    -user SYSDBA -password m1llp0nd
      -v -y d:\data\backuplogs\stocks_r.20040703.log
```

If you specify several target database files but have only a small amount of data, the target files are initially quite small—around 800K for the first one and 4KB for subsequent files. They grow in sequence, to the specified sizes, as you populate the database.

Multiple-Volume Backup to Single-Volume Database

POSIX:

```
./gbak -c /backups/accounts.fb1 /backups2/accounts.fb2 /backups3/accounts.fb3
    /data/accounts_trial.fdb -user SYSDBA -password m1llp0nd
        -v -y /logs/backups/accounts.20040703.log
```

Windows:

```
gbak -c e:\backups\accounts.fb1 f:\backups2\accounts.fb2
    g:\backups3\accounts.fb3 d:\data\accounts_trial.fdb
        -user SYSDBA -password m1llp0nd
          -v -y d:\data\backuplogs\accounts.20040703.log
```

Restoring to Multiple Files from Multiple Files

POSIX:

```
./gbak -c /backups/accounts.fb1 /backups2/accounts.fb2 /backups3/accounts.fb3
    /data/accounts_trial.fd1 500000  /data/accounts_trial.fd2
        -user SYSDBA -password m1llp0nd
            -v -y /logs/backups/accounts.20040703.log
```

Windows:

```
gbak -c e:\backups\accounts.fb1 f:\backups2\accounts.fb2
    g:\backups3\accounts.fb3 d:\data\accounts_trial.fdb 500000
        d:\data\account_trial.fd2
            -user SYSDBA -password m1llp0nd
                -v -y d:\data\backuplogs\accounts.20040703.log
```

Return Codes and Feedback

A restore on Windows returns an error level of 0 on success and 1 on failure. If an error occurs, check the log file (firebird.log on v.1.5; interbase.log on v.1.0.*x*).

Page Size and Default Cache Size

You can optionally change the page size when restoring, by including a –p[age_size] parameter switch in the command, followed by an integer representing the size in bytes. Refer to Table 38-2 for valid page sizes.

This example tells **gbak** to restore the database with a page size of 8192 bytes:

```
gbak -c -p 8192 d:\data\backups\ourdata.fbk d:\data\ourdata_trial.fdb
```

Similarly, you can use a restore to change the default database cache size (in pages, or "buffers"):

```
gbak -c -b 10000 d:\data\backups\ourdata.fbk d:\data\ourdata_trial.fdb
```

Page Size and Performance

The size of a restored database is specified in database pages. The default size for database files is 200 pages. The default database page size is 4K, so if the page size has not been changed, the default database size is 800K. This is sufficient for only a very small database.

Changing the page size can improve performance in the following conditions:

- Firebird performs better if rows do not span pages. Consider increasing the page size if a database contains any frequently accessed tables with long rows of data.

- If a database contains any large indexes, a larger database page size reduces the number of levels in the index tree. The smaller the depth of indexes, the faster they can be traversed. Consider increasing the page size if index depth is greater than three on any frequently used index. Refer to Chapter 18, especially the "Optimization Topic" near the end of the chapter and the notes about using the **gstat** utility to work out how well your indexes are performing.

- Storing and retrieving BLOB data is most efficient when the entire BLOB fits on a single database page. If an application stores many BLOBs exceeding 4K, a larger page size reduces the time for accessing BLOB data.

- Reducing the page size may be appropriate if most transactions involve only a few rows of data, because the volume of data needing to be passed back and forth is lower and less memory is used by the disk cache.

Using gbak with the Firebird Service Manager

The –se[rvice_mgr] switch invokes the Service Manager on a (usually) remote server. It can save a significant amount of time and network traffic when you want the backup or the restored file to be created on the host on which the database resides.

On a Windows server, with a local connection, using the Service Manager offers no advantage.

On a POSIX server, it saves time and traffic—even on a localhost connection.

When you run **gbak** with the –service switch, it operates differently from the way it does otherwise. It causes **gbak** to invoke the backup and restore functions of Firebird's Service Manager *on the server where the database resides*.

You can back up to multiple files and restore from multiple files using Service Manager.

The –se switch takes an argument that consists of the host name of the server concatenated to the constant string *service_mgr* by a special symbol. The syntax of this argument varies according to the network protocol you are using:

- TCP/IP: *hostname*:service_mgr

- Named Pipes: *hostname*\service_mgr

Restoring on POSIX

The user that was current on the server when the Service Manager was invoked to perform the backup—either *root*, *firebird*, or *interbase*—is the owner the backup file at the filesystem level, causing it to be readable to only that user.

When you need to restore a database on a POSIX server that has been backed up using the Service Manager, you must either use the Service Manager for the restore or be logged into the system as that file owner.

When the –service option is not used, the filesystem ownership of the backup file is attributed to the login of the person who ran **gbak**.

These constraints don't apply on Windows platforms.

Backup

In this example, we back up a database residing on the remote server's D drive to a backup file on the F drive of the same remote machine. We pass the verbose output of the operation to a log file in another directory. As usual, the example is a single string:

```
gbak -b -se hotchicken:service_mgr
    d:\data\stocks.fdb
        f:\backups\stocks.20040715.fbk
            -v -y f:\backups\logs\stocks.20040715.log
```

> **NOTE**   Switch order matters when you use the –se switch. If you want to specify a log file, make sure that you place it after the host service has been identified, to avoid the command failing because the location for the log file could not be found.

Restore

The next example restores a multi-volume database from the */january* directory of the *hotchicken* server to the */currentdb* directory. It uses the –r[eplace_database] switch and will overwrite the database *magic.fdb* if it is found in */currentdb*. The first two files of the restored database are 500 pages long and the last file grows as needed.

```
gbak -r -user frodo -pas pipeweed -se hotchicken:service_mgr
    /january/magic1.fbk /january/magic2.fbk /january/magicLast.fbk
        /currentdb/magic.fdb 500 /currentdb/magic.fd2 500
            /currentdb/magic.fd3
```

The next example executes on server hotchicken and restores a backup that is on hotchicken to another server called icarus:

```
gbak -c -user frodo -pas pipeweed -se hotchicken:service_mgr
    /january/magic.fbk /currentdb/magic.fdb
```

gbak Error Messages

Table 38-3 describes error messages that might appear during backups and restores, together with some tips for dealing with the errors.

*Table 38-3. Error Messages from **gbak** Backup and Restore*

ERROR MESSAGE	CAUSES AND SUGGESTED ACTIONS TO TAKE
Array dimension for column <string> is invalid	Fix the array definition before backing up.
Bad attribute for RDB$CHARACTER_SETS	An incompatible character set is in use.
Bad attribute for RDB$COLLATIONS	Fix the attribute in the named system table.
Bad attribute for table constraint	Check integrity constraints; if restoring, consider using the –no_validity option to delete validity constraints.
Blocking factor parameter missing	Supply a numeric argument for "factor" option (e.g., on a tape backup device).
Cannot commit files	Database contains corruption or metadata violates integrity constraints. Try restoring tables using the –one_at_a_time option, or delete validity constraints using the –no_validity option.
Cannot commit index <string>	Data might conflict with defined indexes. Try restoring using "inactive" option to prevent rebuilding indexes.
Cannot find column for blob …	Try using –one_at_a_time to find the problem table.
Cannot find table <string> …	Ditto.
Cannot open backup file <string>	Correct the file name you supplied and try again.
Cannot open status and error output file <string>	Messages are being redirected to invalid file name or a file that already exists. Check the format of the file or access permissions on the directory of the output file, or delete the existing file, or choose another name for the log file.
Commit failed on table <string>	Data corruption or violation of integrity constraint in the specified table. Check metadata or restore "one table at a time."
Conflicting switches for backup/restore	A backup-only option and restore-only option were used in the same operation. Fix the command and execute again.

Table 38-3. Error Messages from **gbak** *Backup and Restore (continued)*

ERROR MESSAGE	CAUSES AND SUGGESTED ACTIONS TO TAKE
Could not open file name <string>	Fix the file name and re-execute command.
Could not read from file <string>	Fix the file name and re-execute command.
Could not write to file <string>	Fix the file name and re-execute command.
Datatype n not understood	An illegal data type is specified somewhere. Check the metadata and, if necessary, retry using –one_at_at_time.
Database format n is too old to restore to	The **gbak** version used is incompatible with the version of Firebird that created the database or the backup. Try backing up the database using the –expand or –old options and then restoring it.
Database <string> already exists	You used –create in restoring a backup file, but the target database already exists. If you actually want to replace the existing database, use the –R switch; otherwise, use another database file name.
Could not drop database <string> (database might be in use)	You used –replace in restoring a file to an existing database, but the database is in use. Either rename the target database or wait until it is not in use.
Do not recognize record type n ...	Check metadata and, if necessary, restore using –one_at_a_time.
Do not recognize <string> attribute n --continuing ...	A non-fatal data error.
Do not understand BLOB INFO item n ...	
Error accessing BLOB column <string> -- continuing ...	A non-fatal data error.
ERROR: Backup incomplete The backup cannot be written to the target device or file system	Cause could be insufficient space, a hardware write problem, or data corruption.
Error committing metadata for table <string>	The table could be corrupt. If restoring a database, try using –one_at_a_time to isolate the table.
Exiting before completion due to errors	This message accompanies other error messages and indicates that backup or restore could not execute. Check other error messages for the cause.
Expected array dimension n but instead found m	There is a problem with an array.
Expected array version number n but instead found m	There is a problem with an array.
Expected backup database <string>, found <string>	Check the names of the backup files being restored.
Expected backup description record ...	
Expected backup start time <string>, found <string> ...	

continued

*Table 38-3. Error Messages from **gbak** Backup and Restore (continued)*

ERROR MESSAGE	CAUSES AND SUGGESTED ACTIONS TO TAKE
Expected backup version 1, 2, or 3. Found n ...	
Expected blocking factor, encountered <string>	The –factor option requires a numeric argument.
Expected data attribute ...	
Expected database description record ...	
Expected number of bytes to be skipped, encountered <string> ...	
Expected page size, encountered <string>	The –page_size option requires a numeric argument.
Expected record length ...	
Expected volume number n, found volume n	When backing up or restoring with multiple tapes, be sure to specify the correct volume number.
Expected XDR record length ...	
Failed in put_blr_gen_id ...	
Failed in store_blr_gen_id ...	
Failed to create database <string>	The target database specified is invalid; it might already exist.
Column <string> used in index <string> seems to have vanished	An index references a non-existent column. Check either the index definition or column definition.
Found unknown switch	An unrecognized **gbak** option was specified.
Index <string> omitted because n of the expected m keys were found ...	
Input and output have the same name Disallowed.	A backup file and database must have distinct names. Correct the names and try again.
Length given for initial file (n) is less than minimum (m)	Insufficient space was allocated for restoring a database into multiple files. Firebird automatically increases the page length to the minimum value. No action necessary.
Missing parameter for the number of bytes to be skipped ...	
Multiple sources or destinations specified	Only one device name can be specified as a source or target.
No table name for data	The database contains data that is not assigned to any table. Use **gfix** to validate or mend the database.
Page size is allowed only on restore or create	The –page_size option was used during a backup instead of a restore.
Page size parameter missing	The –page_size option requires a numeric argument.

Table 38-3. Error Messages from **gbak** *Backup and Restore (continued)*

ERROR MESSAGE	CAUSES AND SUGGESTED ACTIONS TO TAKE
Page size specified (n bytes) rounded up to m bytes	Non-fatal error. Invalid page sizes are rounded up to 1024, 2048, 4096, 8192, or 16384— whichever is closest.
Page size specified (n) greater than limit (16384 bytes)	Specify a page size of 1024, 2048, 4096, 8192, or 16384.
Password parameter missing	The backup or restore is accessing a remote machine. Use the –password switch and specify a password.
Protection is not there yet	Unimplemented option –unprotected used.
Redirect location for output is not specified	You specified an option reserved for future use by Firebird.
REPLACE specified, but the first file <string> is a database	Check that the file name following the –replace option is a backup file rather than a database.
Requires both input and output file names	Specify both a source and target when backing up or restoring.
RESTORE: decompression length error	Possible incompatibility in the **gbak** version used for backing up and the **gbak** version used for restoring. Check whether –expand should be specified during backup.
Restore failed for record in table <string>	Possible data corruption in the named table.
Skipped n bytes after reading a bad attribute n ...	Non-fatal.
Skipped n bytes looking for next valid attribute, encountered attribute m ...	Non-fatal.
Trigger <string> is invalid ...	
Unexpected end of file on backup file	Restoration of the backup file failed; the backup procedure that created the backup file might have terminated abnormally. If possible, create a new backup file and use it to restore the database.
Unexpected I/O error while accessing <string> backup file	A disk error or other hardware error might have occurred during a backup or restore.
Unknown switch <string>	An unrecognized **gbak** option was specified.
User name parameter missing	The backup or restore is accessing a remote machine. Supply a user name with the –user switch.
Validation error on column in table <string>	The database cannot be restored because it contains data that violates integrity constraints. Try deleting constraints from the metadata by specifying –no_validity during restore.
Warning -- record could not be restored	Possible corruption of the named data.
Wrong length record, expected n encountered n ...	

Up Next

The **gbak** utility has its roles to play in database housekeeping and in cleanup after certain types of data corruption. The other tool that you can use to perform a variety of administrative, housekeeping, and recovery tasks is **gfix**, discussed next. The combined use of **gfix** and **gbak** to analyze and, sometimes, to repair a corrupted database is described in Appendix IV.

Housekeeping Tool (gfix)

As **SYSDBA** OR THE DATABASE OWNER you can use the command-line administrative tool **gfix** to attach to a database and perform a variety of housekeeping and recovery tasks. With **gfix** you can

- Perform a sweep

- Change the sweep interval

- Initiate a database shutdown to get exclusive access, and put the database back online

- Switch between synchronous (forced) and asynchronous writes

- Change a read-write database to read-only and vice versa

- Change the dialect

- Set the size of the database cache

- Find and commit or recover limbo transactions

- Mend corrupted databases and data in certain conditions

- Activate and drop shadow databases

Using gfix

The **gfix** utilities can be run only from the command line and you must be the database owner or SYSDBA to use the utilities. To run **gfix**, open a command shell and *cd* to the \bin directory beneath the Firebird root directory.

The syntax pattern for **gfix** commands is

```
gfix [options] db_name
```

db_name must be the full name of the *primary* file of the database on which you want the operations to be performed.

The primary file of a single-file database is the database file itself. For multiple-file databases, the primary file is *first* file in the set.

options are valid combinations of switches and, in some cases, arguments. They are listed later in Table 39-1. Abbreviations can be used for most option switches. Optional characters are shown in square brackets ([ ]).

 TIP   As with the other Firebird command-line tools, you may include any number of the optional characters in the switch names, up to and including the full identifier of the switch, as long as no characters are missing in left-to-right sequence.

Getting Database Access with gfix

If you are connecting to the server remotely, the user name and password of either the SYSDBA user or the database owner must be included among the switches you supply. The switches are

```
-pas[sword] <password> -u[ser] <name>
```

The following example of a **gfix** command sets Forced Writes.
POSIX:

```
bin]$ ./gfix -w sync customer.fdb -pas heureuse -user SYSDBA
```

Windows:

```
bin> gfix -w sync customer.fdb -pas heureuse -user SYSDBA
```

User and Password on a Local Connection

Before starting up the server in order to do extended work locally on a copy of a damaged database or on transaction recovery, you can add the two operating system variables ISC_USER and ISC_PASSWORD to avoid having to type the SYSDBA or owner user name and password in every command:

```
shell prompt> SET ISC_USER=SYSDBA
shell prompt> SET ISC_PASSWORD=heureuse
```

For security reasons, you should remove these environment variables as soon as you finish your task. It is not recommended that you configure these variables beyond the scope of your current shell or make them permanent on the system.

Sweeping

Firebird's multi-generational architecture creates the situation where multiple versions of data rows are stored directly on the data pages. Firebird keeps the old versions when a row is updated or deleted. In the normal course of events, obsolete record versions created by updates are cleaned up by background garbage collection. However, under some conditions, these old versions can get "stuck" and accumulate, causing the database file(s) to grow out of proportion to the size of accessible data. Sometimes, stuck transactions will impact performance.

Sweeping is a systematic way to remove outdated rows from the database and prevent it from growing too large. By default, Firebird databases are always set up to be swept automatically when certain conditions occur. However, because performance can be affected during a sweep, sweeping can be tuned to optimize its benefits while minimizing its impact on users.

It can be a positive tuning strategy to disable automatic sweeping and take charge of it yourself. You can monitor the database statistics and perform manual sweeps, either on an "as required" basis or at scheduled times. You can, for example, include a sweep command in a *cron* script or scheduled batch file.

For information about how database statistics reports can help in the analysis of the sweeping requirements in your database, refer to the section "Getting Index Statistics," near the end of Chapter 18.

Garbage Collection

Firebird performs *garbage collection* (GC) in the background to limit the database growth from obsolete record versions. GC frees up space allocated to outdated versions of a row as soon as possible after the row is freed from any transactions that it was involved in. Transactions kick off GC when they encounter back versions of rows discarded by other transactions. Deleted rows and abandoned versions left after rollbacks escape this garbage collection. Rows that are infrequently touched will cause back versions to accumulate, too.

GC also happens whenever the database is backed up using **gbak**, since **gbak**'s task touches every row in every table. However, **gbak** doesn't perform a full sweep. Like the regular GC, it leaves deleted and rolled-back versions alone. Sweeping is the only way to get rid of these, short of restoring the database from a backup.

Sweep Interval

Sweep interval is an integer setting in the database that specifies the threshold for a particular set of conditions that will trigger off an automatic sweep.

The Firebird server maintains an inventory of transactions. Any transaction that is in any state except committed is known as an *interesting transaction*. The oldest of these "interesting" transactions (oldest interesting transaction, or OIT) marks the starting point for a condition known as "the gap."

The opposite end of the gap is the oldest transaction that is still active: the oldest active transaction, or OAT. The gap is thus the difference between the OIT and the OAT. When the size of the gap reaches the number specified as the sweep interval, an automatic sweep will occur next time a new transaction starts.

Databases are created with a sweep interval of 20,000.

It is a subtle but important distinction that the automatic sweep does *not* occur every 20,000 transactions. It occurs when the *difference* between the OIT and the OAT—the gap—reaches the threshold. If database applications take good care of committing every transaction promptly, the OAT will keep increasing until the gap reaches the threshold of the sweep interval and automatic sweep will be kicked off.

Changing the Sweep Interval

Changing the sweep interval has little effect on database size unless the database has accumulated a lot of rolled-back transactions. However, if you are seeing an increase in transaction startup times as the time since the last sweep increases, then lowering the sweep interval might help to reduce the buildup of rollback artifacts.

If the sweep interval is too low, application performance might tend to go down because of too-frequent sweeping. Raising the sweep interval could help improve overall performance in this case.

The option switch for setting the sweep interval is –h[ousekeeping] *n*, where *n* represents the count (interval) that you want to change to.

```
gfix -h 10000 /data/accounts.fdb -user SYSDBA -pas masterkey
```

sets the new sweep interval for *accounts.fdb* to 10000.

Disabling Automatic Sweeping

You might consider disabling the automatic sweep if you need to avoid the occasional, unpredictable delays imposed by automatic sweeps. Disabling it is not recommended unless back-version housekeeping is being managed effectively by alternative means, such as monitoring statistics and running regular manual sweeps.

Automatic sweeping can be *disabled* by setting a sweep interval of 0.

```
./gfix -h 0 /data/accounts.fdb -user SYSDBA -pas masterkey
```

or (Windows)

```
gfix -h 0 d:\data\accounts.fdb -user SYSDBA -pas masterkey
```

sets the sweep interval to 0, thus disabling automatic sweeping.

Performing a Manual Sweep

A manual sweep can be done at any time to release space held by back versions, especially record versions left behind by rollbacks and deletions. It is common to schedule sweeps at times of low activity on the database server, to avoid competing with clients for resources.

You may wish to do your own sweeping if

- You are monitoring the gap and want to choose the appropriate time to housekeep the "sticky" back versions.

- You think occasional updates of infrequently visited records have built up a backlog of uncollected garbage.

- A large run of deletions has been done and you want to shift the garbage promptly.

To start an immediate sweep:

```
gfix -sweep C:\data\accounts.fdb -user SYSDBA -pas masterkey
```

or (POSIX)

```
./gfix -sweep /data/accounts.fdb -user SYSDBA -pas masterkey
```

Exclusive Access for Manual Sweeps

Sweeping a database does not strictly require it to be shut down—it can be done at any time—but it can impact system performance and should be avoided at busy times.

There is a benefit if a sweep is performed with exclusive access and with all clients' work committed. Under these conditions, not only is more memory available to the sweep operation, but also the sweep is able to do a thorough cleanup of the states of data records and transaction inventory. Unresolved transactions are finally rendered obsolete and the resources being used to track them are freed.

We look next at using **gfix** to shut down a database and gain exclusive access.

Shutting Down a Database

Database shutdown is not the same as shutting down the server. The server stays running when a database is shut down.

A database is implicitly "in a shutdown state" when no connections are active. An explicit shutdown condition can be imposed, using **gfix** with the –sh[ut] switch, to enable the SYSDBA or the database owner to get exclusive access. Once this explicit shutdown state is achieved, it remains until explicitly deactivated by **gfix** –o[nline]. The

The two operations are referred to as "shutting down a database" and "putting a database online."

Database Shutdown Before Server Shutdown

Whenever you need to shut down the server in a production environment, you will normally want to use **gfix** –shut to shut down individual databases in a controlled way first.

The gfix -shut Command

The syntax pattern for **gfix** –sh[ut] is as follows.
POSIX:

```
./gfix -sh[ut] {-at n |-t n |-f n } db_name
```

Windows:

```
gfix -sh[ut] {-at n |-t n |-f n } db_name
```

Qualifying Arguments

The **gfix** –shut switch comes with a choice of three qualifiers to qualify the strategy for the shutdown: –at[tach] *n*, –tr[an] *n*, and –f[orce] *n*. In each case, *n* sets a timeout period in seconds. You must use one argument.

–at[tach] *n* is used to prevent new database connections. It doesn't force existing connections off, but it blocks any new ones. If no processes are still connected when the timeout period of *n* seconds expires, the database will be in the shutdown state. If there are still processes connected, the shutdown is cancelled.

–tr[an] *n* is used to prevent new transactions from starting. It doesn't forcibly end existing transactions, but it disallows any new ones from being started. If no processes are connected when the timeout period of *n* seconds expires, the database will be in the shutdown state. If there are still transactions active, the shutdown is cancelled.

–f[orce] *n* will force the database into a shutdown state after *n* seconds, regardless of any connected processes or active transactions. This is a drastic operation that could cause users to lose their work. It should be used with caution.

 TIP If you need to resort to the –f[orce] switch to kill a rogue query, at least be kind to your well-behaved users and use –at[tach] or –tr[an] first to give them the opportunity to save work and exit gracefully from their applications.

Examples:

```
gfix -sh -at 300
```

initiates a shutdown that will take effect in 5 minutes, if all users detach from the database.

```
gfix -sh -f 600
```

will force all users off the system in 10 minutes. Any transactions still running will be rolled back and users will lose their uncommitted work.

Exclusive Access

When a database is in a shutdown state, SYSDBA or the owner can log in and have exclusive access. However, watch out for these "gotchas":

- If either the owner or SYSDBA was already logged in when the shutdown took effect, the server will not block the other from logging in once the shutdown is in effect.

- Once either SYSDBA or the owner logs in after the shutdown, the other will be blocked from logging in. That's good. If the same user wants to log in again, it will be permitted. That's not so good.

This puts the onus on the SYSDBA or owner user who needs exclusive access to ensure that either itself or the other is not logged in somewhere, using a visual admin tool, an SQL monitor, another command-line tool, or even another **gfix** option, for example. Once you get exclusive access, keep it exclusive—don't start up more than one application.

Terminating a Shutdown

Use **gfix** –o[nline] to cancel a shutdown and put the database back online for multiple-user access. You can also use it to cancel a scheduled shutdown (i.e. one that has not completed its timeout).

Server Shutdowns and Restarts

Be aware that shutting down or restarting *the server* does not have any effect on the shutdown state of any databases. If a database is in a shutdown state when the server is stopped, it will still be in a shutdown state when the server is next started. Shutting down the server does not put any database into a shutdown state.

> **NOTE**   If you file-copy a database that is in a shutdown state and then try to connect to the copy, the copy will be in a shutdown state.

Changing Database Settings

A number of **gfix** command options permit certain configuration settings to be set or changed for a database. To perform these commands, SYSDBA or owner privileges are required and exclusive access is required.

Setting the Default Cache Size

Using **gfix** is the preferred way to set the default cache size for the database. Some points important to remember are

- If you increase the page size, the cache size will rise accordingly. You should ensure that you take the amount of physical RAM on the machine into consideration when altering cache size. Once the cache reaches the point where it is too large to be kept in RAM, it will begin swapping out to disk, thereby quite defeating the benefit of having a cache at all.

- On a Classic server, every client gets its own cache. Even the default cache size of 75 pages will be too large if the database is using a big page_size.

This is the syntax:

```
gfix -b[uffers] n db_name
```

where *n* is the size of the cache (number of page-sized buffers) to be reserved.
  For example:

```
gfix -b 5000 d:\data\accounts.fdb
```

If the database page_size is 8192, a cache of 5,000 pages will allocate a cache of around 40MB.

Other Cache Options

The switch –c[ache] *n* is currently unused; it is reserved for future implementation.

Changing the Access Mode

Use the **gfix** –mo[de] option to switch the access mode, for any connections to the database, between read-only and read-write. A read-only database cannot be written to at all—not even by SYSDBA, its owner, or any server process.

This is the syntax pattern:

```
gfix -mo[de] {read_write | read_only} db_name
```

To switch a database from read-write to read-only:

```
./gfix -mo read_only /data/accounts.fdb
```

To switch from read-only to read-write:

```
./gfix -mo read_write /data/accounts.fdb
```


Changing the Database Dialect

With this switch, you can change a dialect 1 database to Firebird's native dialect 3 format. The database then stops being dialect 1 and obeys the full syntax rules of Firebird SQL and can accept all of Firebird's data types.

But (aren't there always some of those?) the database retains any existing data and definitions in accordance with dialect 1. Some traps lie here, especially with respect to fixed numeric types.

In short, changing the dialect with **gfix** is neither a quick-fix migration tactic nor the most bombproof way to migrate from dialect 1 to dialect 3. A quick change with **gfix** means a slow route to a fully migrated database. Experienced users recommend, instead, to extract a schema script from your dialect 1 database, modify the definitions to suit your needs, and then to use a datapump tool to move the old data across.

Still, if you want to do it this way anyway, here's how. This is the syntax:

```
gfix -sql[_dialect] n db_name
```

where *n* is either 1 or 3.

For example, to change the dialect of the database to 3:

```
./gfix -sql 3 /data/accounts.fdb
```

or, on Windows, you might do this:

```
gfix -sql_dialect 3 d:\data\accounts.fdb
```

Enabling and Disabling "Use All Space"

Firebird fills database pages so that the ratio of data stored per page does not exceed 80 percent. A certain amount of compaction can be achieved by switching the ratio to 100 percent. This may produce a performance benefit during huge bulk inserts, especially if row size is smaller than page size and row size multiples can be stored economically within a one-page space.

It also makes sense to fill pages to full capacity in a database that you plan to distribute as a read-only database, as a catalog or a demonstration, for example.

The command switch is –u[se] and it has two arguments:

```
gfix -u[se] {reserve | full}
```

reserve sets the page use to 80 percent, and *full* sets the page use to 100 percent.

To enable "use all space" use the command

```
./gfix -use full /demos/catalog.fdb
```

To disable "use all space" and return to the 80-percent fill ratio, use the command

```
./gfix -use reserve /demos/catalog.fdb
```

NOTE The database needs to be in read-write mode for this command to work.

Enabling and Disabling Forced Writes

Forced Writes is synonymous with *synchronous writes*. When the behavior is synchronous ("Forced Writes enabled"), new records, new record versions, and deletions are physically written to disk immediately upon posting. With *asynchronous writes* ("Forced Writes disabled"), new and changed data is retained in the system file cache, relying on the flushing behavior of the operating system to make it permanent on disk.

The term "disabling Forced Writes" means switching the write behavior from synchronous to asynchronous.

The command syntax pattern is

```
gfix -w[rite] {sync | async}
```

To enable Forced Writes:

```
gfix -w sync d:\data\accounts.fdb
```

To disable Forced Writes:

```
gfix -w async d:\data\accounts.fdb
```

Firebird is installed on Windows NT/2000/XP and Linux with Forced Writes enabled. In a very robust environment with highly reliable UPS support, a DBA may disable Forced Writes to reduce I/O and improve performance. When Forced Writes is disabled in less dependable environments, the database becomes susceptible to data loss and even corruption in the event of an uncontrolled shutdown.

Forced writes are not applicable to Windows 95. On Windows 98 and ME servers, you should never disable forced writes.

Disabling Forced Writes on Windows Servers

Windows is less dependable than other operating systems with regard to cache flushing. It appears that, if applications do not explicitly request the Windows system to flush the cache, it may defer all writes until the database file is closed.

- Firebird 1.0.*x*: If Forced Writes is disabled on a 24/7 Windows server, flushing may never occur.

- Firebird 1.5: New configuration settings were added for flushing the cache buffers on Windows. Refer to the parameters MaxUnflushedWrites and MaxUnflushedWriteTime (firebird.conf) in Chapter 36.

System Restore on Windows ME and XP

Windows ME, along with the XP Home and Professional editions, has a feature named *System Restore*, which causes the operating system to update its own filesystem backup of files with certain suffixes each time a file I/O operation occurs. System Restore is *not* a substitute for forced writes.[1]

Converted InterBase 6 Databases

Be aware that a Firebird database that started life in InterBase 6.*x* (commercial or Open Edition) will have been created with Forced Writes *disabled by default*.

---

1. The suffix .gdb is included in filelist.xml, the list of files so affected, which lives in the Windows/ System folder. Unfortunately, file types cannot be removed. Firebird databases with the file extension .gdb are affected—System Restore causes the initial connection to such databases to be slow and there has been anecdotal evidence that it caused data corruption.

Querying Firebird Server Version

The switch –z (with no parameters) shows the version of **gfix** and the Firebird engine installed on the server.

This is the syntax:

```
gfix -z
```

Data Validation and Repair

In day-to-day operation, a database is sometimes subjected to events that pose minor problems to database structures. These events include

- **Abnormal termination of the server**. The integrity of the database is not affected by an abnormal termination. However, if Firebird has already assigned a data page for uncommitted changes requested by clients, the page becomes an "orphan." While orphan pages are quite benign, they occupy unassigned disk space that should be returned to free space. Validation can find and release these spaces.

- **Write errors in the operating system or hardware**. Write errors usually create problems for database integrity. They can cause data structures such as database pages and indexes to become broken or lost. At worst, these corrupt data structures can make committed data irrecoverable. Sometimes, validation may be able to help find these broken pieces and eliminate them.

When to Validate a Database

You should validate a database

- Whenever a database backup is unsuccessful

- Whenever an application receives a "corrupt database" error

- Periodically, as a regular housekeeping routine, to monitor for corrupt data structures or misallocated space

- Any time you suspect data corruption

The command-line utility **gbak** can be used in conjunction with **gfix** to perform a sequence of validation and repair steps.

Performing a Database Validation

Database validation requires exclusive access to the database. Without exclusive access, you get the error message

```
OBJECT database_name IS IN USE
```

To validate a database, simply enter the command

```
gfix -v
```

Validation will silently locate and free any unassigned pages or misallocated structures it finds. It will report any corrupt structures but does not attempt to mend them. To have **gfix** report faults but not attempt to free the spaces, include the –n[o_update] switch:

```
gfix -v -n
```

You can have the validation ignore checksum errors by adding the –i[gnore] switch:

```
gfix -v -i
```

> **NOTE** Even if you can restore a mended database that reported checksum errors, the extent of data loss may be difficult to determine. If this is a concern, you may want to locate an earlier backup copy and restore the database from it.

Repairing a Corrupt Database

If you suspect you have a corrupt database, it is important to follow a proper sequence of recovery steps in order to avoid further corruption. For a detailed description of the recommended recovery procedure, see Appendix IV.

For a description of the **gfix** switches to use during this recovery procedure, refer to Table 39-1.

Transaction Recovery

gfix provides tools for recovering transactions left in limbo after a connection is lost during a multi-database transaction.

Two-Phase Commit

A transaction that spans multiple Firebird databases is committed in two steps, or *phases*. This two-phase commit guarantees that, if the transaction cannot complete the updates to all of the databases involved, it will not update any of them.

In the first phase of a two-phase commit, Firebird prepares a *sub-transaction* for each database involved in the transaction and writes the appropriate changes to each database.

In the second phase, following the same order in which it prepared and wrote them, Firebird marks each sub-transaction as committed.

Limbo Transactions

Limbo transactions are sub-transactions that remain unresolved if something traumatic happens to one or more database connections during the second phase of the two-phase commit, for example, a network fault or a power failure. The server cannot tell whether limbo transactions should be committed or rolled back.

Consequently, some records in a database may become inaccessible until explicit action is taken to resolve the limbo transactions with which they are associated.

Transaction Recovery

With **gfix**, you have a number of options for inquiring about and resolving limbo transactions after the traumatic failure of a two-phase commit. The process of identifying a limbo transaction and either committing it or rolling it back is known as *transaction recovery*.

You can attempt to recover all limbo transactions or you can perform the recovery, transaction by transaction, using the transaction ID of each individual transaction.

Finding Limbo Transactions

To list the IDs of all limbo transactions, along with an indication of what would happen to each if an automatic two-phase recovery were requested, use the –l[ist] switch (that's "l" as in "list"):

```
gfix -l db_name
```

Prompting for Recovery

Use the –p[rompt] switch together with –l[ist] to have **gfix** list the limbo transactions one by one and prompt you for COMMIT or ROLLBACK action:

```
gfix -l -p db_name
```

Automated Two-Phase Recovery

Since limbo transactions result from either failed commits or failed rollbacks, the server knows how each should end. Hence, automatic recovery is merely a way of confirming that you want **gfix** to proceed with the original intentions as they stood when the two-phase commit was interrupted.

The –t[wo_phase] {ID | all} switch initiates an automated two-phase recovery.

Use *all* to perform a two-phase recovery for all limbo transactions:

```
gfix -t all db_name
```

Use the *ID* option by entering the transaction ID of a single transaction for which you want a two-phase recovery performed:

```
gfix -t nnnnnn db_name
```

where *nnnnnn* is the ID of the targeted transaction.

Specifically Committing or Rolling Back

To attempt to resolve limbo transactions by committing them, use the –c[ommit] {ID | all} switch. To recover all limbo transactions in this manner, enter

```
gfix -c all db_name
```

To resolve a single limbo transaction by attempting to commit it, enter

```
gfix -c nnnnnn db_name
```

where *nnnnnn* is the ID of the targeted transaction.

To attempt to resolve limbo transactions by rolling them back, use the –r[ollback] {ID | all} switch. To recover all limbo transactions in this manner, enter

```
gfix -r all db_name
```

To resolve a single limbo transaction by attempting to roll it back, enter

```
gfix -r nnnnnn db_name
```

where *nnnnnn* is the ID of the targeted transaction.

Shadows

The concept, creation, and maintenance of database shadows are discussed in detail in Chapter 15. **gfix** has utilities for operating shadows.

Activating a Shadow

The switch for activating a shadow when a database dies is –ac[tivate]. The syntax is

```
gfix -ac <path-to-first-shadow-volume>
```

Suppose the shadow's first volume, *employee.sh1*, is in a directory /opt/dbshadows. You would activate it with this command:

```
./gfix -ac /opt/dbshadows/employee.sh1
```

Dropping Unavailable Shadows

The switch for dropping unavailable shadows is –k[ill]. The syntax is

```
gfix -k[ill] db_name
```

To kill unavailable shadows for employee.fdb:

```
./gfix -k /opt/firebird/examples/employee.fdb
```

Summary of gfix Switches

In summary, the possible switches for **gfix** are as described in Table 39-1. Often, multiple switches are applicable to a task. Switch order is not important, but review the preceding notes in this chapter to determine the appropriate combinations. Combinations that do not make sense logically will cause exceptions.

Table 39-1. Summary of **gfix** *Switches*

SWITCH	TASK	PURPOSE
–ac[tivate] *shadow-file*	Shadowing	Used with the primary shadow file path, to activate a shadow.
–at[tach]	Shutdown	Used with –shut to prevent new database connections during timeout period of *n* seconds. Shutdown will be cancelled if there are still active connections after *n* seconds.
–b[uffers] *n*	Cache buffers	Set default database cache buffers for the database to *n* pages. This is the recommended way to set the default database cache size.
–ca[che] *n*	Not used	

Table 39-1. Summary of **gfix** *Switches (continued)*

SWITCH	TASK	PURPOSE
–c[ommit] *{ID* | all}	Transaction recovery	Commit limbo transaction specified by *ID* or commit all limbo transactions.
–f[orce] *n*	Shutdown	Used with –shut to force shutdown of a database after *n* seconds—a drastic solution that should be used only as a last resort.
–full	Data repair	Used with –v[alidate] to check record and page structures, causing unassigned record fragments to be released.
–h[ousekeeping]	Sweeping	Change threshold for automatic sweeping to *n* transactions. Default is 20,000. Set *n* to 0 to disable automatic sweeping.
–i[gnore]	Data repair	Ignore checksum errors when validating or sweeping.
–k[ill] *db_name*	Shadowing	Used with the database file path to kill any unavailable shadows.
–l[ist]	Transaction recovery	Display IDs of each limbo transaction and indicate what would occur if –t[wo_phase] were used for automated two-phase recovery.
–m[end]	Data repair	Mark corrupt records as unavailable, so that they will be skipped during a subsequent validation or backup.
–n[o_update]	Data repair	Used with –v[alidate] to validate corrupt or misallocated structures, reporting them but not fixing them.
–o[nline]	Shutdown	Cancels a –shut operation that has been scheduled, or rescinds a shutdown that is currently in effect.
–pa[ssword] *password*	Remote access	Submits *password* for accessing database. For most **gfix** operations, this must be the password of the SYSDBA, the database owner, or (on POSIX) a user with *root* privileges.
–p[rompt]	Transaction recovery	Used with –l[ist] to prompt for action during transaction recovery.
–r[ollback] *{ID* | all}	Transaction recovery	Roll back limbo transaction specified by *ID* or roll back all limbo transactions.
–s[weep]	Sweeping	Force an immediate sweep of the database.

continued

*Table 39-1. Summary of **gfix** Switches (continued)*

SWITCH	TASK	PURPOSE
–sh[ut]	Shutdown	Shut down the database. Requires to be qualified by either –at[ach], –f[orce], or –tr[an] *n*.
–sql[_dialect] *n*	Migration	*n*=3. Changes SQL dialect of the database from 1 to 3. It does not change data or convert existing data types.
–t[wo_phase] *{ID*	all}	Transaction recovery	Perform automated two-phase recovery, either for a limbo transaction specified by *ID* or for all limbo transactions.
–tr[an] *n*	Shutdown	Used with –shut to prevent new transactions from starting during timeout period of *n* seconds. Shutdown will be cancelled if there are still active transactions after *n* seconds.
–use {reserve	full}	Use all space	Enable or disable full use of the space available on database pages. The default *reserve* fills pages using a fill ratio of 80 percent. Switching to *full* uses all space available.
–user *username*	Remote access	Submits *username* for accessing database. For most **gfix** operations, this must be SYSDBA, the database owner, or (on POSIX) a user with *root* privileges.
–v[alidate]	Data repair	Locates and releases pages that are allocated but unassigned to any data structures. Also reports corrupt structures.
–w[rite] {sync	async}	Forced writes	Enable or disable forced (synchronous, buffered) writes. *sync* enables; *async* disables.
–z	Information	Report version of **gfix** and Firebird server.

gfix Error Messages

Table 39-2 lists exceptions that might occur in **gfix** commands, together with tips to help with correcting your commands.

*Table 39-2. **gfix** Error Messages*

ERROR MESSAGE	CAUSES AND SUGGESTED ACTIONS TO TAKE
Database file name <string> already given	A command-line option was interpreted as a database file because the option was not preceded by a hyphen (-) or slash (/). Correct the syntax.
Invalid switch	A command-line option was not recognized.
Incompatible switch combinations	You specified at least two options that do not work together, or you specified an option that has no meaning without another option (for example, –full on its own).
More limbo transactions than fit. Try again.	The database contains more limbo transactions than **gfix** can print in a single session. Commit or roll back some of the limbo transactions, and then try again.
Numeric value required	The –housekeeping option requires a single, non-negative argument specifying the number of transactions per sweep.
Please retry, specifying <string>	Both a file name and at least one option must be specified.
Transaction number or "all" required	You specified –commit, –rollback, or –two_phase without supplying the required argument.
–mode read_only or read_write	The –mode option takes either read_only or read_write as a switch.
"read_only" or "read_write" required	The –mode option must be accompanied by one of these two arguments.

Up Next

To end the book, Chapter 40 presents a very technical examination of Firebird's least user-friendly utility, Lock Print, and the resource-locking subsystem that it reports on. It includes explanations of the lock-related settings in firebird.conf or isc_config/ibconfig, which might otherwise remain a total enigma to most of us!

CHAPTER 40

Understanding the Lock Manager

LOCKS ARE USED IN MULTI-USER ENVIRONMENTS to synchronize work and prevent processes from destroying the integrity of one another's work. Firebird uses both operating system locking and a proprietary lock manager to coordinate database access.

This topic will be heavy going for the reader who is new to Firebird. It gets into some seriously technical areas that cause gurus[1] to be met with glazed eyes at conferences. Yet the lock print utilities—raw as they are—are a revealing tool for troubleshooting deep problems in the approaches that some developers take to implementing their application interfaces. By all means, put this chapter on ice until some day when you'll be very glad it's here.

Why, you might well ask, should we be interested in locks in a system that doesn't lock things? The concurrency and consistency that are visible to clients are based on transactions and controlled through record versions. However, the answer is that Firebird *does use locks internally*. It maintains the consistency of the on-disk structure through locks and careful write. Coincidentally, it also uses the operating system locking services to control access to database files to prevent the Superserver from opening the same file twice under different names.

Transaction-based locking allows locks to be acquired at any point during the transaction. However, once acquired, they can be released only at the end. Even the statement-level explicit locking introduced in Firebird 1.5 does not allow an "unlock" statement. Statements execute in a normal transaction and commit or rollback releases the lock, as usual.

While Firebird eschews the standard two-phase locking for its primary concurrency control because it cannot provide adequate levels of concurrency and consistency, it does use locks for the duration of changes, to keep two transactions from writing to the same page at the same time. The internal locking is controlled by the system itself. Objects in the system—known as "lock owners," or simply "owners"—contend for locks on a number of resources. These, not surprisingly, comprise the pages containing rows that have been earmarked for update.

When a transaction gets a lock on a page, it holds the lock until the Lock Manager asks it to release the page, so a transaction can make many changes to a single page without releasing and re-reading it.

---

1. For the insights and much of the material in the Lock Print topic, thanks and gratitude go to Ann Harrison, who was the first to document this useful but obscure troubleshooting tool in detail, in a white paper she wrote for IBPhoenix. "Reading a Lock Print" can be found in the Documentation section at http://www.ibphoenix.com.

Firebird's Lock Manager

In Superserver, the Lock Manager can be thought of as a separate "control center" that transactions negotiate with to acquire the right to proceed with requests. The Lock Manager comprises a chunk of memory region and some request-handling routines. Its memory is tabulated into various blocks: lock blocks, which refer to resources; request blocks, which represent requests for a lock on a resource; owner blocks, which represent transactions and other objects that request locks; and history blocks. Its routines are responsible for accepting and managing requests by owners for locks on resources, for allocating the locks, and for releasing them. Superserver also manages "latches" for coordinating changes by concurrent transactions.

Classic is simpler: owners queue to get control of the lock table so that each process's lock management code can queue, grant, and release locks for its owners.

Lock States

Every operating system offers some kind of free/busy mechanism for synchronizing resource events. Because Firebird needs a multi-state control mechanism, it implements its own seven-state lock management system. Figure 40-1 illustrates how the locking levels are decided.

	0 no lock	1 null lock	2 shared read	3 protected read	4 shared write	5 protected write	6 exclusive
0 no lock	Y	Y	Y	Y	Y	Y	Y
1 null lock	Y	Y	Y	Y	Y	Y	Y
2 shared read	Y	Y	Y	Y	Y	Y	n
3 protected read	Y	Y	Y	Y	n	n	n
4 shared write	Y	Y	Y	n	Y	n	n
5 protected write	Y	Y	Y	n	n	n	n
6 exclusive	Y	Y	n	n	n	n	n

Figure 40-1. Firebird internal lock states

- 0 is *free*.

- 1 is a *null lock*, which indicates an interest in the object but no restrictions on others' use of it. Acquiring a null lock allows a transaction to read the lock data.

- 2 is a *shared read*, which allows writers. Shared read is the normal mode for table locking until the transaction changes some part of the table.

- 3 is a *protected read*, which allows other readers, but not writers. Protected read is the normal mode for locking a database page that is in cache and has not been modified.

- 4 is a *shared write*, the other normal table locking mode. Shared write is compatible with shared read and other shared writers, but not with either protected mode.

- 5 is a *protected write*, which allows shared readers and null locks, and nothing else. Protected write is used for consistency mode (table stability) and for locking a database so normal users cannot access it.

- 6 is *exclusive* and is used for internal structures when concurrent access could interfere with an update or cause the second transaction to read incomplete data.

The Lock Table

The Lock Manager maintains a *lock table* to coordinate resource sharing among the client threads. The information stored here can be useful when trying to correct deadlock situations, for example:

- All the locks currently in the system, with their states

- Global header statistics such as the size of the lock table, the number of free locks, the number of deadlocks, and so on

- Process flags, indicating such things as whether the lock has been granted or is waiting

Locks are stored in *series*, each series identified by a number, according to the type of resource locked. The series numbers are explained in Table 40-5.

Use of Null Locks

Transactions starting up use the lock table as a bulletin board. To avoid garbage collecting record versions that another transaction needs, each transaction needs to know the identity of the oldest action any other transaction has seen. Here is how it is done:

1. When it starts, a transaction stores the ID of the oldest transaction still running into the data portion of its transaction lock.

2. It then gets null locks on all concurrent transactions. When each lock is acquired, the contents of its data portion are returned.

The new transaction checks the lock of each existing transaction to discover the identifier of the oldest transaction that any active transaction knows about.

"Free . . ." Lists

Lists of owners, resources, and requests are chained forward and backward. An offset in each block contains the pointer to the next block. The lists of offsets are used when the Lock Manager needs to allocate a new block and tries to find blocks that are free to be reused. It will allocate a new block only if there are no free blocks of the right type and size.

The "free..." items indicate the forward and backward pointers to the offsets of the first and last free request blocks, respectively.

Deadlocks

A deadlock occurs when Owner A wants a lock on Resource 1, which is held in an incompatible mode by Owner B, and Owner B wants a lock on Resource 2, which is held in an incompatible mode by Process A. A deadlock can also occur with a single resource if both owners start with read locks and request conversions to write locks.

It is a standoff that the owners cannot resolve without intervention. Resolution comes once the deadlock is detected by the next scan and the lock manager returns a fatal error to one owner or the other. The default deadlock scan interval—DeadlockTimeout in the configuration file—is 10 seconds. They are not done under every condition where there is a WAIT. Waiting is normal in a system that manages parallel updates, and unnecessary scanning is costly.

"Deadlocks" That Are Not Deadlocks

The deadlocks reported may not help to pinpoint "deadlock problems" observed in your applications. Deadlocks always involve *two owners* (or two separate transactions), each being stymied by the other. Firebird tends to deliver "deadlock" messages to clients for most types of locking conflict, even though a true deadlock—such as would be reported in a lock print—is relatively rare.

- Errors that are returned as "lock conflict" from NO WAIT lock requests are not recorded in the lock table as deadlocks because only one owner is waiting.

- Errors returned as "deadlock" with the secondary message "Update conflicts with concurrent update" are not actual deadlocks either. What has happened in those cases is that one owner has modified (or deleted) a row and moved on. Another concurrent owner has attempted to modify (or delete) the same record, has waited for the first owner to release it, and now fails because the latest committed version has changed.

The lock table data can be reported in a more or less human-readable format, by way of the *Lock Print utility*.

The Lock Print Utility

The program that extracts the lock table statistics is an executable named *fb_lock_print*, which you will find in the /bin directory of your Firebird installation. (For v.1.0.*x*, look for *iblockpr.exe* on Windows, or *gds_lock_pr* on POSIX.) Two syntaxes are available: one for static reports, the other for capturing a sampling interactively at specified intervals.

This is the syntax for Firebird 1.5 and higher:

```
fb_lock_print <switches>
```

v.1.0.*x*, POSIX:

```
gds_lock_pr <switches>
```

v.1.0.*x*, Windows:

```
iblockpr <switches>
```

The fb_lock_print program accepts a number of switches, described in Table 40-1. When no switches are provided, fb_lock_print prints summary information describing the lock header and the owners communicating with the lock manager.

Table 40-1. Switches for Lock Print Reports

SWITCH	DESCRIPTION
(no switches)	Prints summary information describing the lock header and the owners communicating with the lock manager.
–a	Prints the contents of the lock table including the lock header, lock blocks, owner blocks, and request blocks. A lock block represents a resource that can be locked (database, transaction, relation, database page, etc.) and identifies owners that have or have requested a lock on the object. A request block describes a request by a process for a lock on a resource. A request block may represent either a granted lock or a pending request for a lock.
–c	Indicates that the lock table should be copied rather than used live. The copy is quick and produces a static snapshot of the lock table. It will, however, stop all database access on the computer while it runs.
–f	Specifies that analysis should be done on a named file rather than the live lock file. Unfortunately, this switch appears not to work in Firebird.
–h	Prints only the history.
–i <switches> <t> <n>	Begins interactive mode (see the section "Interactive Reports"). If –i is used alone, it prints everything.
–l	Prints only lock blocks.
–n	Indicates that there is "no bridge." A bridge is a transitional mechanism recognizing multiple servers with different major versions of Firebird on the same machine. It is not applicable to Firebird v.1.0.*x* or v.1.5 but is likely to be implemented when future major versions of Firebird are released.

continued

Table 40-1. Switches for Lock Print Reports (continued)

SWITCH	DESCRIPTION
–o	Prints owner blocks.
–p	Same as –o. (Owner blocks used to be called process blocks.)
–r	Prints request blocks.
–s <n>	Prints out the lock table header block, the owner blocks, and the locks in a particular series. The argument <n> is a number identifying the lock resource type that you want to report on. Refer to Table 40-5 for the numbers.
–t	Prints statistics for all series (interactive reporting only).
–w	Prints the "waiting on" graph—owner blocks with waiting requests, what they are waiting for, what those owners are waiting for, and so on. With this report you can work out which owner's request is blocking others' in the lock table. This is the easiest way to find a blockage, though a full lock print will tell you more about the interrelationships of the enqueued requests.

Static Reports

Static reports print a snapshot of the lock table. Any switches are valid except –i, and you can "stack" multiple switches into one. For example, to print the "waiting on" graph plus the history block:

```
fb_lock_print -wh
```

Interactive Reports

The second form collects a specified number of samples at fixed intervals and produces an interactive report monitoring current lock table activity. The syntax is

```
fb_lock_print [-i{a,o,w}] [t n]
```

t specifies the time in seconds between samplings. *n* specifies the number of samples to be taken. If you do not supply values for *n* and *t*, the default is *n = 1*.

Sampling occurs *n* times at intervals of *t* seconds. One line is printed for each sample. The average of the sample values is printed at the end of each column.

The following statement prints "acquire" statistics (access to lock table: acquire/s, acqwait/s, %acqwait, acqrtry/s, and rtrysuc/s) every 3 seconds until 10 samples have been taken:

```
fb_lock_print -ia 3 10
```

At the end of the chapter is a snapshot of an interactive report with explanations of the meanings of the columns.

 TIP   Buffer limits in the command shell may cause all but the last part of the output to "vanish." You can pipe the output to the **more** utility (or **less** on POSIX, if you prefer it).

```
fb_lock_print -wh | more
```

Once the shell display is full, press or hold down the Return (Enter) key to display more output, a row at a time. Ctrl+C terminates either **more** or **less**.

Reporting to a File

The results are usually quite long for viewing on the console. You can supply a pipe to an output file, for example in a directory named /data/server_reports/ (your choice!), like this: `fb_lock_print -a > /data/server_reports/lock.txt`. If you find a lock print running for more than a minute or two, or find that it is filling your disk, kill it with Ctrl+C or your platform equivalent.

The blocks are listed in the order of the internal lists. New blocks are put at the head of the list, so a newly minted lock table will be shown with blocks in reverse numeric order. As lock, request, and owner blocks are released and reused, the order becomes thoroughly scrambled. A text editor is very useful for chasing through the relationships.

A Simple Lock Print

We'll take a look at an example from a very simple static lock print with no switches.

- The lock header is always first.

- Next come the owner blocks—owner block followed by all the requests for that owner. Each owner in the chain is printed with its requests.

- After all owners and requests come the locks.

- The last items are the history records.

The Lock_Header Block

First, we'll consider only the lock header block that describes the general shape and condition of the lock table. In Figure 40-2, numbers have been added for reference to each item of explanation in Table 40-2.

Our lock print represents a database that has just been created and is being accessed by a single copy of **isql** on the v.1.0.*x* Windows Superserver version.

```
1)LOCK_HEADER BLOCK
  (2)Version: 114,(3)Active owner: 0, (4)Length: 32768, (5)Used: 12976
  (6) Semmask: 0x0,  (7) Flags: 0x0001
  (8)Enqs:  10, (9)Converts: 0, (10) Rejects:  0, (11) Blocks:      0
  (12)Deadlock scans: 0, (13)Deadlocks: 0,  (14) Scan interval:  10
  (15) Acquires:  36,  (16) Acquire blocks:  0,  (17) Spin count: 0
  (18)Mutex wait: 0.0%
  (19)Hash slots:  101, (20)Hash lengths (min/avg/max):    0/   0/   1
  (21)Remove node: 0, (22) Insert queue: 0, (23)Insert prior: 0
  (24)Owners (5):   forward:  12056, backward:  11628
  (25)Free owners (4):   forward:  11804, backward:  12232
  (26) Free locks(1):    forward:  11560, backward:  11560
  (27) Free requests (1): forward:  12116, backward:  12116
  (28)Lock Ordering: Enabled
```

Figure 40-2. The Lock Header block

Table 40-2. Lock Header Block Entries

TAG #	ITEM	EXPLANATION
1	LOCK_HEADER_BLOCK	First block on any lock print report. Each report outputs exactly one lock header block.
2	Version	The lock manager version number. For Firebird 1.5, the version is 115 for Superserver and 5 for Classic. For Firebird 1.0.*x* (like our sample), the versions are 114 and 4, respectively.
3	Active owner	The offset of the owner block representing the owner that currently has control of the lock table, if any. In this case, no process is writing to the lock table, so the Active Owner is 0.
4	Length	Total space allocated to the lock table in bytes.
5	Used	The highest offset in the lock table that is currently in use. There may be free blocks in the table between the beginning and the used point if owners have come and gone. Before new blocks are allocated between this point and the end of the lock table, any free blocks will be reused.

Table 40-2. Lock Header Block Entries (continued)

TAG #	ITEM	EXPLANATION
6	Semmask	On systems that use static semaphores (e.g., POSIX), this is the pointer to an SMB block containing the number of semaphores in use. When a semaphore is needed and none is available, the lock manager will loop through the owner blocks, looking for one that has a semaphore that it's not using. Failing that, the system returns the error "Semaphores are exhausted," meaning that all the semaphores compiled into the system are in use.
7	Flags	Two flag bits are defined: *LHB_shut_manager*, which, if set, indicates that the database is shutting down and the lock manager ought not to grant more requests; and *LHB_lock_ordering*. The Firebird default for *LHB_lock_ordering* is that locks are granted in the order requested (FIFO order). The alternative setting relates to an obsolete locking strategy and is not used.
8	Enqs	Enqueue requests—requests that have been received for locks. This number comprises requests that cannot yet be satisfied and requests that can be satisfied immediately, but not requests that have come and gone.
9	Converts	Requests to increase the level of a lock. A process that holds a lock on a resource will request a mode change if its access to the resource changes. Conversions move from a lower-level lock (e.g., shared read) to a more restrictive level (e.g., exclusive). For example, a transaction in concurrency mode that has been reading a table and decides to change data in the table will convert its lock from shared read to shared write. Conversions are very common on page locks because a page is usually read before being altered.
10	Rejects	Requests that cannot be satisfied. These may be locks requested in "no wait" mode, or they may be requests that were rejected because they caused deadlocks. Since the access method occasionally requests "no wait" locks for internal structures, you will sometimes see rejects even when all transactions run in "wait" mode and there is no conflict between their operations.
11	Blocks	Requests that could not be satisfied immediately because some other owner has an incompatible lock on the resource.
12	Deadlock scans	The number of times that the lock manager walked a chain of locks and owners looking for deadlocks. The lock manager initiates a deadlock scan when a process has been waiting 10 seconds for a lock.
13	Deadlocks	The number of actual deadlocks found. See the previous section "Deadlocks."
14	Scan interval	The number of seconds the Lock Manager waits, after a request starts waiting, before starting a deadlock scan. The default is 10 seconds.

continued

Table 40-2. Lock Header Block Entries (continued)

TAG #	ITEM	EXPLANATION
15	Acquires	The number of times an owner—or the server on behalf of a specific owner—acquired exclusive control of the lock table to make changes.
16	Acquire blocks	The number of times an owner—or the server on behalf of a specific owner—had to wait to acquire exclusive control of the lock table.
17	Spin count	There is an option to wait on a spin lock and retry acquiring the Firebird lock table. By default, it is set to zero (disabled), but it can be enabled with the configuration file.
18	Mutex wait	The percentage of attempts that were blocked when owner tried to acquire the lock table—that is, ((acquire blocks) / (acquires)) * 100.
19	Hash slots	Resources are located through a hash table. They are stored according to value. By default, the hash table is 101 slots wide. That value (which should be a prime number) can be increased using the configuration file. It should never be reduced to less than 101.
20	Hash lengths	Below each hash slot hang the resources (lock blocks) that hash to that slot. This item reports the minimum, average, and maximum length of the chain of lock blocks hanging from the hash slots. An average hash length > 15 indicates that there are not enough slots.
21	Remove node	To avoid the awkward problems caused when the active owner dies with the lock table acquired and potentially half-updated, the owner records the intention to remove a node from the table. When the operation succeeds, the owner removes the remove notation. If any owner finds a remove notation that it did not create, it cleans up.
22	Insert queue	The equivalent of the preceding remove node entry, except that this is the node being inserted.
23	Insert prior	To clean up a failed insert, it is necessary to know not just what was being inserted, but also *where* it was being put. This is *where*.
24	Owners	The number of owners that have connections to the lock table. Only one of those owners can update the table at any one time (the "active owner"). Other owners hold and wait for locks. In our example there are four owners, none active. Two owners are attachments from **isql**; one may be an attachment from DSQL and one is the database itself.
25	Free owners	The number of owner blocks that have been allocated for owners that have terminated their connections leaving the blocks unused. In this case, there are two, probably transactions involved in creating the database that have since committed.

Table 40-2. Lock Header Block Entries (continued)

TAG #	ITEM	EXPLANATION
26	Free locks	*Lock blocks* identify a resource (database, relation, transaction, etc.) that has been locked, not a lock on the resource. This item is the number of lock blocks that have been released and not yet reused. In this case, there is one free lock. When an owner requests a lock on a resource that is not currently locked, the lock manager looks first to the free lock list in the lock header. If there is a block there with the right key length, that lock block is reused. If not, a new lock block will be allocated out of free space.
27	Free requests	*Request blocks* identify a request for a lock on a resource, whether satisfied or not. This item is the number of request blocks that have been released and not reused.
28	Lock ordering	*Lock ordering* means taking lock requests in the order received, even if that blocks subsequent requests that could be served immediately. It is enabled when the *LHB_lock_ordering* flag (see item 7) is set. It is the default in Firebird, since it provides optimal throughput overall. The alternative (deprecated now) is to grant locks to all owners willing to share and "starve" non-sharing owners that have existing requests. This deprecated strategy would ensure that the sharers would be handled quickly, but at the risk of being a detriment to the others.

Owner Blocks

An owner block, depicted in Figure 40-3, describes a transaction or other user of the Lock Manager. Owners fall into one of several types, identified by one of five numbers:

- 1: Process.

- 2: Database.

- 3: Client attachment. In Classic server, client attachments are always processes.

- 4: Transaction.

- 255: Dummy process.

NOTE By some bizarre coding convention, transactions are never referred to by this identity number (4), but by 255 instead.

```
(1) OWNER BLOCK  11872
        (2) Owner id: 9909104, (3) type:  2, (4) flags:  0x202, (5) pending:  0,
(6) semid: 3
        (7) Process id:   1868, (8) UID:  0x0  (9) Alive
        (10) Flags:  0x02                          scan
        (11) Requests (3):   12300, backward:  12124
        (12) Blocks:  *empty*
```

Figure 40-3. An owner block

The offset of the particular owner block in the lock table (here it is 11872) is also the ID used in the lock header for the "active owner," if that owner is actively modifying the lock table. The first block printed will usually be the number printed in the Lock Header Block as the beginning of the Owner list. The value of the list pointers is actually a field in the block that contains the block's own forward and backward pointers. Table 40-3 describes the entries in an owner block.

 TIP If you inspect your lock print in an editor, you can search for requests belonging to this owner ID.

Table 40-3. Owner Block Entries

TAG #	ITEM	EXPLANATION
1	OWNER BLOCK	Identifies the particular owner. The number following the header (11872) is the offset of the owner block in the lock table and is used as this owner's ID throughout the table.
2	Owner ID	In Classic server, the owner is always a *process* and the Owner ID is always a process ID. In Superserver, the owner is either the database and the ID is that of the database block, or the owner is the attachment and the ID is that of the attachment block.
3	Owner type	The owner type is a number between 1 and 4, or 255 (dummy process).
4	Flags	Bits that indicate a specific state. A process can be in more than one state at once—refer to Table 40-4.
5	Pending	The offset of a lock request block describing a lock that this owner has requested but has not yet been granted. An owner can have at most one pending lock request at a time.
6	Semid	The ID of the semaphore assigned to this owner. If it could be used, the word "Available" would follow the ID.
7	Process_id	On Classic server, the process ID of the owning process. On Superserver, if the owner is an attachment, database, or transaction, it will be the process ID of the Superserver process.

Table 40-3. Owner Block Entries (continued)

TAG #	ITEM	EXPLANATION
8	UID	On POSIX, the user ID of the owner process. On Windows, it is always zero.
9	Alive | Dead	The lock printer invokes the routine ISC_check_process_existence and reports the results.
10	Flags	The flag mnemonics—correctly printing 2 as 0x02 (not 0x202, as in (4)).
11	Requests	Lock requests, either acquired or pending, that are associated with this process. The forward and backward numbers are the beginnings of the forward and backward self-relative queues of requests that belong to the process. The numbers are offsets.
12	Blocks	Transitory list of locks (request blocks) owned by this process that are blocking other lock requests. It is cleared when the process has been notified that it should release or downgrade its lock, assuming it is able to do so.

Table 40-4 describes the states represented by the various owner flags.

Table 40-4. Owner Flag States

SYMBOL	VALUE	STATE
OWN_blocking	1	Owner is blocking. If set, the process in question has at least one lock that another owner wants non-shared.
OWN_scanned	2	Owner has been checked in the current deadlock scan.
OWN_manager	4	Systems that disallow signals to cross groups have a privileged lock manager to transmit signals. This owner is that manager.
OWN_signal	8	Owner needs to signal and has failed to do so directly, so it is being called on by the manager.
OWN_wakeup	32	Owner has been poked to release a lock.
OWN_starved	128	This thread may be starved. Starvation happens in Solaris multi-threading and indicates that the Owner (process) has made more than 500 unsuccessful attempts to get the lock table to release a lock.
OWN_signaled	16	Signal is thought to be delivered. It applies to OWN_ast_flags, but is ORed into the reported flags. NB: The value printed here, hex 202, seems to be a print-parsing error.

Lock Blocks (Resource Blocks)

Lock blocks follow request blocks in the printout, but it makes request blocks easy if you understand lock blocks first. A lock block represents a *resource that has been locked.*

Lock Types: "Series"

Resource locks come in different types, or *series*, according to the type of resource that owners request to lock. Table 40-5 identifies and describes the various resource lock types and summarizes their purposes.

Table 40-5. Resource Types (Series)

SYMBOL	SERIES	TYPE
LCK_database	1	Root of lock tree. In Classic server, a database lock is taken by each process that attaches a database. The first process takes an exclusive lock. The next process notices a conflict and signals the first to downgrade its lock from exclusive to shared. Thereafter, all locks on the database itself are for shared read. In Superserver, the database takes out an exclusive lock on itself.
LCK_relation	2	Individual table lock. A table lock indicates that the process has read from or written to the specified table in its current transaction, or that it has used the RESERVING clause on the START TRANSACTION statement to declare its intention to read or write to the table. In this case, both owners are reading the table. The key field is the RDB$RELATION_ID value for the table. Note that both requests report their state as 2(2), indicating that they requested and received a shared read lock on the table.
LCK_bdb	3	Individual buffer block. A BDB lock is a lock on a database page. These locks are held when two or more owners have attached a database on Classic server. They are taken when the process wants to read or write a page, and released when the process runs out of buffers in cache and needs to free up space or when another owner needs the page.
LCK_tra	4	Individual transaction lock. Each action takes an exclusive lock on its own transaction ID when it starts. Other owners can acquire null locks on it to read its state.
LCK_rel_exist	5	Relation existence lock. Prevents tables from being dropped while any owner has a prepared request that uses that table.
LCK_idx_exist	6	Index existence lock. Prevents indexes from being dropped or inactivated while any owner has a prepared request that uses the resource.
LCK_attachment	7	Not used. Attachment lock to support dBase record locks, which can exist across transaction boundaries.
LCK_shadow	8	Lock to synchronize addition of shadows, mainly on Classic server.
LCK_sweep	9	Sweep lock for single sweeper. Sweep is a moderately expensive operation and works best if only one thread or attachment does it. The actual sweeper keeps an exclusive lock in this series to avoid conflicts. This series is used for interprocess communication in Classic server.
LCK_file_extend	10	Lock to synchronize file extension. Extending the database file is another operation that doesn't go as well if two transactions try to do it at once. This series is used for interprocess communication in Classic server.

Table 40-5. Resource Types (Series) (continued)

SYMBOL	SERIES	TYPE
LCK_retaining	11	Youngest commit retaining transaction. This is used only on VMS. It probably marks a place where Firebird has extended the locking semantics to fit its needs and so requires a special hack to work with the VMS lock manager.
LCK_expression	12	Expression index caching mechanism. Originally this series was intended to describe expression indexes—how to evaluate them, what the result of the evaluation was likely to look like, etc. For some reason, they're now used when deleting any index.
LCK_record_locking	13	Lock on the existence of record locking. This series indicates that record locking has been requested for a particular table. The first process to request record locking for a table also gets a protected lock on the table. Until that lock is challenged, record locks are kept in the attachment. When a second transaction arrives, the table lock is downgraded to shared and locks are expressed. This series is used only in the deprecated PC emulation code.
LCK_record	14	Record lock. This series is also used only in the deprecated PC emulation code and uses the record's RDB$DB_KEY as the lock name.
LCK_prc_exist	15	Procedure existence lock. Prevents procedures and triggers from being dropped while any owner has a prepared request that uses (or depends on) that resource.
LCK_range_relation	16	Relation refresh range lock. Again, this series is used only in the PC emulation code, which has a concept of update ranges.
LCK_update_shadow	17	Shadow update sync lock. This series is used to limit to one the number of processes that cause processing to roll over to a shadow or disable shadowing.

Syntax Variation for Lock Block Reports

To print the resource lock blocks for a specific series, you need to include the series number as an argument:

```
fb_lock_print -s 2
```

Series 1: Database

The lock block in Figure 40-4 represents the database itself. It is being held exclusively by one owner—itself. In Classic server, you would see several owners for the database.

```
(1) LOCK BLOCK  11988
    (2) Series: 1, (3) Parent: 0, (4) State: 6, (5) size: 12(6) length: 12
       (7) data: 0
    (8) Key: <61><172><21>x<0><0><13><0><145>k<0><0>, Flags: 0x00, Pending
       request count:     0
    (9) Hash que (1): forward:     768, backward:     768
    (10) Requests (1): forward: 12300, backward: 12300
    (11) Request 12300, Owner: 11872, State: 6 (6), Flags: 0x00
```

Figure 40-4. A lock block, Series 1 (database)

Table 40-6 explains what the report entries indicate.

Table 40-6. Lock (Resource) Block Entries

TAG #	VALUE	EXPLANATION
1	LOCK BLOCK	Identifies the block as the description of a resource that has been locked. The number is the offset of that block in the lock table. It identifies the block in the other blocks that refer to it.
2	Series	The type of resource this lock represents. This one is a Series 1 type—a database resource.
3	Parent	The parent of all locks associated with a database is the database lock itself. The only resource locks that should be 0 for the parent are the database locks and journal. The keys that identify locks within a series are meaningful only in the context of a database. NB: Discrepancies (aka bugs) will be noticed by the careful reader.
4	State	The highest current state of the lock. Locks have seven possible states—refer to Figure 40-1. Firebird internal lock states, right at the beginning of this topic. A null lock allows a process to acquire a lock on a resource regardless of whether (and how) someone else has locked it. Acquiring that lock allows the locker to read the data from the lock itself. Firebird keeps some important but volatile information in locks—see the preceding section "Use of Null Locks."
5	Size	The length, in bytes, of the portion of the lock block that holds the key. The size is rounded to the natural boundary (word, longword, quadword) for the machine.
6	Length	The actual length of the key, which, because of rounding, may be less than the size.
7	Data	Only journal locks and transaction locks carry data. The data portion is a 32-bit integer.
8	Key	The identifier of the resource being locked. The combination of the key, the series, and the parent uniquely identify the resource being locked. For the database, the key is the name of the database (or something equivalent). It may not print on systems that use an integer identifier. For relation and relation existence locks, the key is the relation ID. For index existence locks, the key is the relation ID * 1000 plus the index ID. For a shadow lock, the key is null because there is only one state of shadowing for a database. For a transaction, the key is the transaction ID. For an attachment, the key is the attachment ID.

Table 40-6. Lock (Resource) Block Entries (continued)

TAG #	VALUE	EXPLANATION
9	Hash queue	The beginning and end of the hash queue for the resource key. The lock manager keeps a hash table to facilitate lookup of resources by name. When a process requests a lock on a resource, it identifies the resource by series, parent, and key. The lock manager mashes the values together to create a hash key, and then searches the list associated with that hash key value for the desired lock block.
10	Requests	First the number of lock requests for this resource, then forward and backward pointers to the request blocks. Note that the backward pointer points to the end of the last block.
--	Request	The list of requests including the identifier of the request block, the process that made the request, the actual state of the lock with the requested state in parentheses. The state–6(6) in this case–indicates an actual state of 6 and a requested state 6.
--	Flags	The request flag contains bits that can be combined. They are

1. Blocking: A request is marked as blocking if someone else wants the resource and cannot share it because of its current lock level. The blocking bit is cleared when a blocking notice has been sent to the blocking owner.

2. Pending: This bit is the one most often seen. It indicates that the request is waiting for a blocking process to release its lock. You should not see the pending bit set for BDB locks.

4. Converting: A request is converting if the process already has a lock on the resource and wants a higher-level lock and the conversion cannot be done immediately.

8. Rejected: A lock request is rejected if the request is in "no wait" mode and cannot be satisfied immediately or if granting the request would cause a deadlock.

Series 2: Relation

Figure 40-5 shows a block for a relation resource (table, view).

```
LOCK BLOCK 2120
Series: 2, Parent: 1220, State: 2. size: 4 length: 4 data: 0
Key: 5
Hash que (4): forward: 148, backward: 9884
Requests (2): forward: 11432, backward: 5840
Request 11412, Process: 1124, State: 2 (2).  Flags: 0
Request 5820, Process: 1124, State: 2 (2), Flags: 0
```

Figure 40-5. A Series 2 (Relation resource) block

In this case, both owners are reading the relation. The key field is the RDB$RELATION_ID value for the relation. Note that both requests report their state as 2(2), indicating that they requested and received a shared read lock on the table.

Series 3: BDB Descriptor (Database Page)

Figure 40-6 shows a block for a database page (BDB Descriptor) lock.

```
LOCK BLOCK 5384
Series: 3, Parent: 1220.  State: 3. size: 4 length: 4 data: 0
Key: 14
Hash que (2): forward: 11468, backward: 220
Requests (2): forward: 7644. backward: 1712
Request 7624, Process: 2556, State: 3 (3), Flags: 0
Request 1692, Process: 1124, State: 3 (3), Flags: 0
```

Figure 40-6. A Series 3 (BDB Descriptor) block

A BDB lock is a lock on a database page. These locks are held when two or more owners have attached a database on Classic server. They are taken when the process wants to read or write a page, and they are released when the process runs out of buffers in cache and needs to free up space or when another owner needs the page. In this example, both owners are reading page 14 (key value). On Classic server there are a lot of Series 3 type locks—one for each page buffer in the cache of each independent attachment. On Superserver, most page locks are held within the server and not expressed in the lock table.

Series 4: Transaction

Figure 40-7 shows a transaction resource block.

```
LOCK BLOCK 10492
Series: 4, Parent: 1220, State: 6, size: 4 length: 4 data: 585
Key: 585
Hash que (1): forward: 748, backward: 748
Requests (2): forward: 11528, backward: 6416
Request 11508, Process: 1124, State:6 (6),  Flags: 0
Request 6396, Process: 2556.  State: 0 (3), Flags: 2
```

Figure 40-7. A Series 4 (Transaction resource) block

Each action takes an exclusive lock on its own transaction ID when it starts. This block describes the state of the locks on transaction 595. One transaction is waiting for the other to finish so it can decide whether the update it wants to do is legitimate. When the owner that holds the lock departs, its locks will be released and the waiting transaction can read the transaction inventory page to determine the fate of the vanished transaction.

Series 5, 6, and 15: Existence

Figure 40-8 shows an existence lock block for a relation.

```
SERIES 5 RELATION EXISTENCE LOCKS
     LOCK BLOCK 7176
     Series: 5, Parent: 1220, State: 2, size: 4 length: 4 data: 0
     Key: 22
     Hash que (2): forward: 284, backward: 1556
     Requests (1): forward: 2192, backward: 2192
     Request 2172.  Process: 2556, State: 2 (2), Flags: 0
SERIES 6 INDEX EXISTENCE LOCKS
     LOCK BLOCK 1832
     Series: 6. Parent: 1220, State: 2. size: 4 length: 4 data: 0
     Key:12000
     Hash que (2): forward: 2516, backward: 764
     Requests (2): forward: 7880. backward: 3536
     Request 7860, Process: 2556, State: 2 (2), Flags: 0
     Request 3516, Process: 1124, State: 2 (2), Flags: 0
  also
SERIES 15  PROCEDURE EXISTENCE LOCKS
```

Figure 40-8. Series 5, 6, and 15 Existence lock blocks

The *relation existence locks* (Series 5) prevent tables from being deleted while any process has a prepared request that uses that table. This lock is the source of "Object in use" errors that often occur when attempting to drop tables.

When a statement is prepared into a database "request," the compiling process takes out a shared read lock on the existence of the relations and indexes included in the statement. Those locks are held until the request is released or the database is detached.

When a process wants to drop a relation from the database, rather than just delete its content, it must get an exclusive lock on the existence of the relation. Because no one can get an exclusive lock on a resource that is locked for shared read by another process, the shared read locks prevent the relation from being destroyed, and so prevent online metadata operations from breaking prepared requests.

This particular relation existence lock is on a relation that has an RDB$RELATION_ID of 22.

The *index existence locks* prevent indexes from being dropped or deactivated while any process has saved a request that uses the index.

When a statement is prepared into a database "request," the compiling process also takes out a shared read lock on the existence of the indexes included in the statement. Those locks are held until the request is released or the database is detached.

When a process wants to delete or deactivate an index, it must get an exclusive lock on the existence of the index.

Because no one can get an exclusive lock on a resource that is locked for shared read by another process, the shared read locks prevent the relation or index from being destroyed, and so prevent online metadata operations from corrupting compiled requests.

The index existence lock ID is 12000, which is the relation ID times 1000 plus the index ID. This lock records an interest in the existence of index 0 for relation 12.

The *procedure existence locks* are exactly like relation and index existence locks, and serve a similar purpose. The key is the procedure ID from the system table RDB$PROCEDURES.

Series 8: Shadow

Figure 40-9 shows a block for locks on a shadow resource.

```
LOCK BLOCK 1352
     Series: 8, Parent: 1220, State: 2, size: 4 length: 4 data: 0
     Key: 0
     Hash que (3): forward: 1460. backward: 108
     Requests (2):  forward: 6844, backward: 7152
     Request 6824, Process: 2556, State:  2 (2), Flags: 0
     Request 7132, Process: 1124.  State: 2 (2), Flags: 0
```

Figure 40-9. A Series 8 (Shadow resource) block

Every process that attaches to a database takes out a shared read lock on the state of shadowing for the database. If a process wants to add a new shadow file, it converts its lock to exclusive, which notifies all other processes that a shadow file is about to appear and they should write changes to that file. This series is used for interprocess communication in Classic server. It is also used in Superserver, although not to any great effect, since IPC is not required.

Request Blocks

Figure 40-10 shows some request blocks. Table 40-7 explains the meanings of the request block entries.

```
(1) REQUEST BLOCK 7624
(2) Process: 2556,(3) Lock: 5384,(4) State: 3,(5) Mode: 3. (6) Flags:0
(7) AST:3afc4c30,  (8) argument: 3af776e0


REQUEST BLOCK 11508
Process: 1124, Lock: 10492, State: 6,  mode: 6,  Flags: 0
AS'I': 0, argument: 3af76a2c


REQUEST BLOCK 6396
Process:2556, Lock: 10492, State: 0. Mode. 3,Flags: 2 AST:0,  argument: 0
```

Figure 40-10. Some request blocks

Table 40-7. Request Block Entries

TAG #	ITEM	EXPLANATION
1	REQUEST BLOCK	The identifier of this particular request.
2	Process	The offset of the process block that describes the process that made this request.
3	Lock	The offset of the lock block that describes the resource being locked.
4	State	The state of the lock that has been granted on the resource.
5	Mode	The state in which the lock was requested. In the first two examples, the state is the same as the mode. These are locks that have been granted. The first was granted in protected read mode, the second in exclusive. In the third example, the lock is pending, so the state is 0 (no lock), but the mode is 3 (protected read).
6	Flags	The request flag contains bits, which can be combined. They are 1: Blocking 2: Pending 4: Converting 8: Rejected
7	AST	The address of a routine to call if someone wants a conflicting lock on the resource held by this request. Routines to downgrade or release locks are always supplied for locks on the database, the state of shadowing, and the buffer descriptor blocks that identify a database page in cache. The database lock will be downgraded from exclusive (for the first user) to shared read when the second user shows up in the classic architecture. In Superserver, the database holds an exclusive lock on itself. The shadow shared read lock is released when another process requests the lock in exclusive mode so it can create new shadow file(s). As soon as the files are created, everyone re-seizes shared read locks on the state of shadowing. When there is a conflict for a database page, the process that holds the page immediately releases it and downgrades its lock unless the page is actually in the process of being modified. If so, the page is marked as needing to be released as soon as the modification is done.

continued

Table 40-7. Request Block Entries (continued)

TAG #	ITEM	EXPLANATION
8	Argument	The address of something that the AST routine will want. In the case of a BDB, it is the address of the structure in the process that describes the buffer. In the case of the database and shadow locks, it is the address of the master block (DBB) that describes the database.

The History Block

The Lock Manager keeps track of the I/O actions it took on behalf of any owner. The most recent actions are output as the last two items in the printout, History and Events. Figure 40-11 is a snapshot of a sequence of History records.

```
GRANT:   owner =  11628, lock =  11744, request =  12516
ENQ:     owner =  12056, lock =      0, request =  11512
DENY:    owner =  12056, lock =  11744, request =  11512
ENQ:     owner =  12056, lock =      0, request =  12408
POST:    owner =  11628, lock =  11744, request =  12516
WAIT:    owner =  12056, lock =  11744, request =  12408
SCAN:    owner =  12056, lock =  11744, request =  12408
POST:    owner =  11628, lock =  11744, request =  12516
POST:    owner =  11628, lock =  11744, request =  12516
POST:    owner =  11628, lock =  11744, request =  12516
DEQ:     owner =  11628, lock =  11744, request =  12516
GRANT:   owner =  12056, lock =  11744, request =  12408
```

Figure 40-11. Snapshot of History printout

Owner 11628 is GRANTed a lock on resource 11744. Owner 12056 ENQueues a request for the same resource, asking to get it with no wait. The lock held by owner 11628 is in an incompatible mode, so that request is denied (DENY). Owner 12056 comes back with a different ENQueue request, asking for the lock again, but willing to wait. The Lock Manager POSTs pokes a notification to owner 11628 on the subject of resource 11744. Owner 12056 is told to WAIT. After 10 seconds, owner 12056 is still waiting, so the lock manager starts a deadlock SCAN. That yields nothing, so the lock manager goes back to poking owner 11628 (POST, POST, POST). Eventually the pokes get through, 11628 gives up (DEQueues) the lock, and it is GRANTed to 12056.

The Events printouts deliver the same history information in a different format. Figure 40-12 is a snapshot of a sequence of history records output in the Events part of the printout.

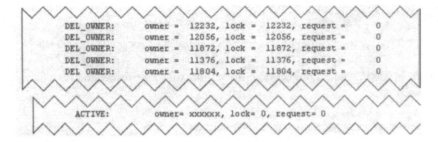

```
  DEL_OWNER:      owner =  12232, lock =  12232, request =    0
  DEL_OWNER:      owner =  12056, lock =  12056, request =    0
  DEL_OWNER:      owner =  11872, lock =  11872, request =    0
  DEL_OWNER:      owner =  11376, lock =  11376, request =    0
  DEL OWNER:      owner =  11804, lock =  11804, request =    0


  ACTIVE:         owner= xxxxxx, lock= 0, request= 0
```

Figure 40-12. Snapshot of Events printout

On Classic server, an Event record like the "Active" one shown in the figure might be cause for concern. It indicates that one Classic server process got a mutex for access to the resource, wrote its owner ID into the lock header block, and then got killed while it still held the lock table acquisition. However, the secondary lock header block should have enough information to enable a new process to undo any actions left partly completed by the killed process.

Interactive Sampling

The interactive time-series lock activity reports that fb_lock_print generates with the –i switch measure Lock Manager performance. The layout is modeled after the UNIX "sar" (System Activity Reporter) utility. The output shown in Figure 40-13 sampled every 4 seconds for ten intervals. The sampling depicted in Figure 40-13 was generated on a Classic version of Firebird running four local processes with a significant number of conflicts:

```
fb_lock_print -ia 4 10
```

	(1)	(2)	(3)	(4)	(5)
14:32:55	acquire/s	acqwait/s	%acqwait	acqrtry/s	rtrysuc/s
14:32:59	15654	110	0	0	0
14:33:03	16328	91	0	0	0
14:33:07	16639	106	0	0	0
14:33:11	15467	115	0	0	0
14:33:15	14864	87	0	0	0
14:33:19	15292	117	0	0	0
14:33:23	14939	85	0	0	0
14:33:27	14992	103	0	0	0
14:33:31	15660	124	0	0	0
14:33:35	14800	114	0	0	0
Average:	15463	105	0	0	0

Figure 40-13. Interactive sampling

fb_lock_print –ia "acquire" statistics:

1. acquire/s: Average number of attempts to acquire the lock table per second

2. acqwait/s: Average number of acquire attempts that were forced to wait each second

3. %acqwait: Percent of attempts that were forced to wait

4. acqrtry/s: Average number of retries following a spin wait for the lock table mutex per second (SMP machines only, in theory)

5. rtrysuc/s: Average number of successful retries per second

---

 TIP   For clues as to what the columns in the many varieties of interactive reports mean, read the white paper "Reading a Lock Print," by Ann Harrison, at http://www.ibphoenix.com.

Lock Configuration Settings

The Lock Manager's default settings should suit most environments initially. Under load, especially with the Classic server, there may be benefits in tuning the settings to improve throughput or to resolve deficiencies in the lock resources.

Configuration Files

Configuration files are located in the Firebird root directory. For Firebird 1.5 and later servers, the configuration file is named firebird.conf. For v.1.0.*x*, it is named ibconfig on Windows and isc_config on POSIX. Use a plain text editor to open and edit the file.

Changes made to the configuration file on a Classic server will affect the next attachment that is made after the modifications are saved. On Superserver, they will not take effect until all users have logged out and the first user logs back in.

LockAcquireSpins

Version 1.5 forward, firebird.conf

lock_acquire_spins

Versions prior to Firebird 1.5, isc_config/ibconfig

This setting is relevant only on SMP machines running Classic server.

In Classic server, only one client process may access the lock table at any time. A mutex governs access to the lock table. Client processes may request the mutex conditionally or unconditionally. If it is conditional, the request fails and must be retried. If it is unconditional, the request will wait until it is satisfied. LockAcquireSpins establishes the number of attempts that will be made if the mutex request is conditional.

An integer is required. The default is 0 (unconditional). There is no recommended minimum or maximum.

LockHashSlots

Version 1.5 forward, firebird.conf

lock_hash_slots

Versions prior to Firebird 1.5, isc_config/ibconfig

Use this parameter for tuning the lock hash list. Under heavy load, throughput might be improved by raising the number of hash slots to disperse the list in shorter hash chains. The value is integer; prime number values are recommended. The default is 101.

This parameter and the LockMemSize (see the next section) should be evaluated at the same time, using the Lock Print tool. If the lock hash chains are longer than 20 on average, the number of hash slots is too small. If you need to increase the number of hash slots, you should increase the lock table size by the same percentage.

LockMemSize

Version 1.5 forward, firebird.conf

any_lock_mem_size

Versions prior to Firebird 1.5, isc_config/ibconfig

This integer parameter represents the number of bytes of shared memory allocated to the memory table used by the lock manager. For a Classic server, the LockMemSize gives the initial allocation, which will grow dynamically until memory is exhausted (*"Lock manager is out of room"* does not mean somebody went for coffee!) This parameter's value is related to the size of the database cache, since each page will require a separate lock in table. When the number of pages of database cache is set to a high value, it often causes problems with the lock memory table.

In Superserver, the memory allocated for the lock manager does not grow.

The default size on Linux and Solaris is 98,304 bytes (96K). On Windows, it is 262,144 (256K).

LockGrantOrder

Version 1.5 forward, firebird.conf

lock_grant_order

Versions prior to Firebird 1.5, isc_config/ibconfig

When a connection wants to lock an object, it gets a lock request block, which specifies the object and the lock level requested. Each locked object has a lock block. Request blocks are connected to those lock blocks either as requests that have been granted or as pending requests.

The LockGrantOrder parameter is a Boolean. The default (1=True) indicates that locks are to be granted on a first-come, first-served basis.

The False setting (0), emulating InterBase v.3.3 behavior, grants the lock as soon as it becomes available. It can result in lock requests being "starved." Treat this as a deprecated setting and don't try to set it unless you need it for debugging some modification to the database engine.

LockSemCount

Version 1.5 forward, firebird.conf

any_lock_sem_count

Versions prior to Firebird 1.5, isc_config/ibconfig

This is an integer parameter, specifying the number of semaphores available for inter-process communication (IPC) between Classic server processes. The default is 32. Set this parameter on a Classic server to raise or lower the number of available semaphores.

External Function Summary

Conditional Logic Functions

FBUDF	INULLIF (VALUE1, VALUE2)
Linux, Win32	Returns NULL for a sub-expression if it resolves to a non-null value; otherwise, returns the value of the sub-expression. Applicable to fixed numeric types only and should be used only with Firebird 1.0.x. With Firebird 1.5 and higher, use internal function NULLIF( ).
Arguments	*value1*: The column or expression that is to be evaluated. *value2*: A constant or expression with which *value1* is to be compared. If there is a match, the iNullIf expression will return NULL.
Return value	Will be NULL if *value1* and *value2* resolve to a match; if there is no match, then value 1 is returned.
Notes	iNullIf( ) has an effect equivalent to using the internal SQL function NULLIF( ), implemented in Firebird 1.5 and higher, with fixed numeric types. The iNullIf( ) external function comes in three implementations: two for 32-bit and 16-bit types (inullif and dnullif), the other for 64-bit types (i64nullif). If you want to be able to use it with any fixed numeric type, declare *all implementations*. The declarations can be found in the script fbudf.sql, in the /UDF directory of your Firebird installation. Do not declare the i64nullif implementation in any database that does not support 64-bit numerics—in an unported InterBase 5 database, for example.

Example	This statement will cause the STOCK value in the PRODUCTS table to be set to NULL on all rows where it is currently stored as 0:
	 `UPDATE PRODUCTS`
	`    SET STOCK = iNULLIF(STOCK, 0)`

Related or similar functions	See also NULLIF( ), sNullIf( ).

FBUDF	**INVL(VALUE1, VALUE2)**
Linux, Win32	This function attempts to mimic the NVL( ) function of Oracle, for fixed numeric types only. It will cause a specified non-null value to be output if the column is actually storing a NULL.
Arguments	*value1*: A column or expression involving a column. Floating-point types are not supported. If necessary, use CAST( ) in your expression to transform the value to a numeric type.
	value2: An expression or constant that will resolve to the value which is to be output if *value 1* resolves to NULL.
Return value	A non-null value. If *value1* is not null, it is returned; otherwise, *value2* is returned. If both *value1* and *value2* resolve to NULL, then NULL is returned.
Notes	Logically, this function is equivalent to the simple form of the v.1.5 COALESCE( ) function when used with a column of a fixed numeric type, namely COALESCE(value1, value2).
	It should be regarded as deprecated for versions of Firebird from 1.5 onward.
	The iNVL( ) external function comes in three implementations: two for 32-bit and 16-bit types (invl and dnvl), the other for 64-bit types (i64nvl). If you want to be able to use it with any fixed numeric type, declare *all implementations*. The declarations can be found in the script fbudf.sql, in the /UDF directory of your Firebird installation. Do not declare the i64nvl implementation in any database that does not support 64-bit numerics—in an unported InterBase 5 database, for example.
Example	The following query outputs 0 if STOCK is NULL:
| | ```
SELECT
  PRODUCT_ID,    PRODUCT_NAME,
  INVL(STOCK, 0)
FROM PRODUCTS;
``` |
| Related or similar functions | See also sNVL( ), iNullIf( ), internal function COALESCE( ). |

FBUDF	**SNULLIF (VALUE1, VALUE2)**
Linux, Win32	Returns NULL for a sub-expression if it resolves to a non-null value; otherwise, returns the value of the sub-expression. Applicable to character types only and should be used only with Firebird 1.0.*x*. With Firebird 1.5 and higher, use NULLIF( ).
Arguments	*value1*: The column or expression that is to be evaluated.
	value2: A constant or expression with which *value1* is to be compared. If there is a match, the sNullIf expression will return NULL.
```

FBUDF	**SNULLIF (VALUE1, VALUE2)** *(continued)*
Return value	Will be NULL if *value1* and *value2* resolve to a match. If there is no match, then *value1* is returned.
Notes	sNullIf( ) has an effect equivalent to using the internal SQL function NULLIF( ), implemented in Firebird 1.5 and higher, with character types.

Example	This query will set the column IS_REGISTERED to NULL in all rows where its value is 'T' and REGISTRATION_DATE is NULL:
	```UPDATE ATABLE```
	``` SET IS_REGISTERED = SNULLIF(IS_REGISTERED, 'T')```
	``` WHERE REGISTRATION_DATE IS NULL;```

Related or similar functions	See also iNullIf( ). For Firebird 1.5 and higher, see internal function NULLIF( ).

FBUDF	**SNVL(VALUE1, VALUE2)**
Linux, Win32	This function attempts to mimic the NVL( ) function of Oracle, for character types only. It will cause a specified non-null value to be output if the column is actually storing a NULL.
Arguments	*value1*: A column or expression involving a column. *value2*: An expression or constant that will resolve to the value that is to be output if *value1* resolves to NULL.
Return value	A non-null value. If *value1* is not null, it is returned; otherwise, *value2* is returned. If both *value1* and *value2* resolve to NULL, then NULL is returned.
Notes	Logically, this function is equivalent to the simple form of the v.1.5 COALESCE( ) function when used with a column of a character type, namely COALESCE(value1, value2). sNVL( ) should be regarded as deprecated for versions of Firebird from 1.5 onward.

Example	The following query calculates and outputs a runtime column, BIRTH_YEAR, for each student. Where this value resolves to NULL, the string "Not known" is output instead:
	```SELECT```
	``` FIRST_NAME, LAST_NAME,```
	``` SNVL(CAST(EXTRACT(YEAR FROM BIRTH_DATE) AS VARCHAR(9)), 'Not known')```
	``` AS BIRTH_YEAR```
	```FROM STUDENT_REGISTER;```

Related or similar functions	See also iNVL( ), sNullIf( ), internal function COALESCE( ).

Mathematical Functions

IB_UDF	**ABS(VALUE)**
Linux, Win32	Returns the absolute value of a number.
Arguments	*value* is column or expression that is compatible with a signed or unsigned DOUBLE PRECISION NUMBER.
Return value	A DOUBLE PRECISION number.

Example	This statement will calculate a total of values that are negative and return it as a positive value:
	`SELECT ABS(SUM(ASSET_VALUE)) AS LIABILITY`
	`  FROM ASSET_REGISTER`
	`  WHERE ASSET_VALUE < 0;`

Similar function	See f_DoubleAbs( )—another external function that performs the same task.

IB_UDF	**BIN_AND(VALUE1, VALUE2)**
Linux, Win32	Returns the result of a bitwise AND operation performed on the two input values.
Arguments	*value1* and *value2* are columns or expressions that evaluate to SMALLINT or INTEGER type.
Return value	An INTEGER number.
Example	`SELECT BIN_AND(128,24) AS ANDED_RESULT` `  FROM RDB$DATABASE;`

IB_UDF	**BIN_OR(VALUE1, VALUE2)**
Linux, Win32	Returns the result of a binary (bitwise) OR operation performed on the two input values.
Arguments	*value1* and *value2* are columns or expressions that evaluate to SMALLINT or INTEGER type.
Return value	An INTEGER number.
Example	`SELECT BIN_OR(128,24) AS ORED_RESULT` `  FROM RDB$DATABASE;`

IB_UDF	**BIN_XOR(VALUE1, VALUE2)**
Linux, Win32	Returns the result of a binary (bitwise exclusive or) XOR operation performed on the two input values.
Arguments	*value1* and *value2* are columns or expressions that evaluate to SMALLINT or INTEGER type.

IB_UDF	**BIN_XOR(VALUE1, VALUE2)** *(continued)*
Return value	An INTEGER number.
Example	`SELECT BIN_XOR(128,24) AS EXORED_RESULT` `    FROM RDB$DATABASE;`

IB_UDF	**CEILING(VALUE)**
Linux, Win32	Returns a DOUBLE PRECISION value representing the smallest integer that is greater than or equal to the input value.
Arguments	*value* is a column or expression that evaluates to a number of DOUBLE PRECISION type.
Return value	A DOUBLE PRECISION number with a zero decimal part.
Example	`SELECT CEILING(LAST_TOTAL) AS ROUND_UP_NEAREST` `    FROM SALES_HISTORY;`

IB_UDF	**DIV(VALUE1, VALUE2)**
Linux, Win32	Divides the two integer inputs and returns the quotient, discarding the decimal part.
Arguments	*value1* and *value2* are columns or expressions that evaluate to numbers of SMALLINT or INTEGER type.
Return value	A DOUBLE PRECISION number with a zero decimal part.
Notes	The function behaves almost like integer-by-integer division in databases created in dialect 3— the distinction being that the division returns a double.

Example	`SELECT DIV(TERM, (CURRENT_DATE - START_DATE)/365) AS`
	`YEARS_REMAINING`
	`    FROM MORTGAGE_ACCOUNT`
	`    WHERE ACCOUNT_ID = 12345;`

FBUDF	**DPOWER(VALUE, EXPONENT)**
Linux, Win32	Takes a number and an exponent and returns to exponential value.
Arguments	*value*: A column or expression that evaluates to a number of type DOUBLE PRECISION. *exponent*: A column or expression that evaluates to a number of type DOUBLE PRECISION.
Return value	Returns the exponential value as a DOUBLE PRECISION number.
Example	`SELECT DPOWER(2.64575,2) AS NEARLY_7` `    FROM RDB$DATABASE;`
Related or similar functions	See also SQRT( ).

FREEUDFLIB	**F_DOUBLEABS(VALUE)**
Win32	Returns the absolute value of a floating-point number.
Arguments	*value* is a column or expression that evaluates to a number of type DOUBLE PRECISION or FLOAT.
Return value	A positive number of type DOUBLE PRECISION.

Example	`SELECT ABS(SUM(ASSET_VALUE)) AS LIABILITY`
	`  FROM ASSET_REGISTER`
	`  WHERE ASSET_VALUE < 0;`

Related or similar functions	See also ABS( ), another external function that performs the same task and is available on non-Windows platforms.

FREEUDFLIB	**F_ISDVISIBLEBY(VALUE1, VALUE2)**
Win32	Determines whether a value is evenly divisibly by another value. Returns 1 if *Numerator (value1)* is evenly divisible by *Denominator (value2)*; otherwise, returns 0.
Arguments	*value1*: A column or expression that evaluates to an integer type, the number that is be divided (the numerator). *value2*: Another integer, the number to use as the denominator.
Return value	Returns 1 if True, 0 if False.

Example	This function could be called in a CHECK constraint as follows:
	`ALTER TABLE ORDER_DETAIL`
	`  ADD CONSTRAINT CHECK_MULTIPLE`
	`  CHECK (ISDIVISIBLEBY(ORDER_QTY, PACK_QTY) = 1);`
	Such a check might be used for validation where multiple pre-packaged units are priced on a per-unit basis, rather than per-pack.

FREEUDFLIB	**F_MODULO(VALUE1, VALUE2)**
Win32	Modulo function—returns the remainder from a division between two integers.
Arguments	*value1* and *value2* are columns or expressions that evaluate to numbers of SMALLINT or INTEGER type.
Return value	A number of an integer type.
Notes	This version of the modulo( ) function might be more useful than MOD( ) in complex expressions where the return value is part of another expression that operates on an integer. (MOD( ) returns a floating-point number.)

Example	A snippet from a trigger:
	`...IF (MODULO(NEW.HOURS * 100, 775) > 0.25) THEN`
	`  NEW.OVERTIME_HOURS = MODULO(NEW.HOURS * 100, 775) / 100;`

Related or similar functions	See also MOD( ), which returns a floating-point result.

FREEUDFLIB	**F_ROUNDFLOAT(VALUE1, VALUE2)**
Win32	Attempt to round the passed value up or down to the nearest specified fraction.
Arguments	*value1*: A column or expression that evaluates to a floating-point type. This is the number to be rounded.
	value2: A column or expression that evaluates to a floating-point type. This must be a number less than 1 and greater than 0. For example, pass a *value2* of 0.25 to round to the nearest quarter.
Return value	A floating-point number, which will be *value1* rounded up or down to the nearest specified *value2* fraction.
Example	The following statement calculates PAID_HOURS by rounding HOURS_WORKED up or down to the nearest quarter-hour:

```
UPDATE TIMESHEET
  SET PAID_HOURS = F_ROUNDFLOAT(HOURS_WORKED, 0.25)
  WHERE DATE_TIMESTAMP > CURRENT_DATE - 7;
```

Related or similar functions	See also ROUND( ).

FREEUDFLIB	**F_TRUNCATE(VALUE)**
Win32	Truncates a floating-point value to an integer.
Arguments	*value* is a column or expression that evaluates to a floating-point type.
Return value	Strips the decimal part from *value* and returns the whole-number part as an integer type.
Example	This statement will return an integer:

```
SELECT F_TRUNCATE(SUM(AMT_OUTSTANDING)) AS ESTIMATED_DEBTORS
  FROM ACCOUNT
  WHERE AMT_OUTSTANDING > 0;
```

Related or similar functions	See also TRUNCATE( ), ROUND( ).

IB_UDF	**FLOOR(VALUE)**
Linux, Win32	Returns a floating-point value representing the largest integer that is less than or equal to *value*.
Arguments	*value* is a column or expression that evaluates to a number of DOUBLE PRECISION type.
Return value	A DOUBLE PRECISION number with a zero decimal part.
Example	

```
SELECT FLOOR(CURRENT_DATE - START_DATE) AS DAYS_ELAPSED
  FROM DVD_LOANS;
```

IB_UDF	**LN(VALUE)**
Linux, Win32	Returns the natural logarithm of a number.
Arguments	*value* is a column or expression that evaluates to a number of DOUBLE PRECISION type.
Return value	A DOUBLE PRECISION number.
Example	```SELECT LN((CURRENT_TIMESTAMP - LEASE_DATE)/7) AS NLOG_WEEKS FROM LEASE_ACCOUNT;```

IB_UDF	**LOG(VALUE1, VALUE2)**
Linux, Win32	Returns the logarithm base *x=value1* of number *y=value2*.
Arguments	*value1* (the logarithm base) and *value2* (the number to be operated on) are columns or expressions that evaluate to numbers of DOUBLE PRECISION type.
Return value	A DOUBLE PRECISION number.
Notes	The Firebird 1.0.*x* and InterBase versions of this function have a bug: LOG(x,y) erroneously inverts the arguments and returns the log base *y* of number *x*. It was corrected in v.1.5. Be aware that older stored procedures and application code may have workaround code for the bug.
Example	```SELECT LOG(8, (CURRENT_TIMESTAMP - LEASE_DATE)/7)) AS LOG_WEEKS FROM LEASE_ACCOUNT;```

IB_UDF	**LOG10(VALUE)**
Linux, Win32	Returns the logarithm base 10 of the input value.
Arguments	*value* is a column or expression that evaluates to a number of DOUBLE PRECISION type.
Return value	A DOUBLE PRECISION number.
Example	```SELECT LOG10((CURRENT_TIMESTAMP - LEASE_DATE)/7) AS LOG10_WEEKS FROM LEASE_ACCOUNT;```

IB_UDF	**MODULO(VALUE1, VALUE2)**
Linux, Win32	Modulo function—returns the remainder from a division between two integers.
Arguments	*value1* and *value2* are columns or expressions that evaluate to numbers of SMALLINT or INTEGER type.
Return value	A DOUBLE PRECISION number.
Example	A snippet from a trigger: ```...IF (MODULO(NEW.HOURS * 100, 775) > 25.0) THEN NEW.OVERTIME_HOURS = MODULO(NEW.HOURS * 100, 775) / 100;```
Related or similar functions	See also f_Modulo( ), which returns an integer.

IB_UDF	**PI()**
Linux, Win32	Returns the value of *?* = 3.14159 . . .
Arguments	No arguments, but parentheses are required.
Return value	The value of *?*, as a DOUBLE PRECISION number.
Example	`SELECT PI() AS PI_VALUE` `    FROM RDB$DATABASE;`

IB_UDF	**RAND()**
Linux, Win32	Returns a random number between 0 and 1. Note that this function does not work in Firebird 1.5.
Arguments	No arguments, but parentheses are required.
Return value	A DOUBLE PRECISION number.
Notes	The current time is used to seed the random number generator.
Example	`SELECT RAND() AS RANDOM_NUMBER` `    FROM RDB$DATABASE;`

FBUDF	**ROUND (VALUE)**
Linux, Win32	Rounds a fixed numeric number up or down to the nearest integer.
Arguments	*value* is a column or expression that evaluates to a fixed numeric type with a scale > 0.
Return value	A number of an integer type.
Notes	This is plain rounding—if the digit immediately to the right of the decimal is equal to or greater than 5, it adds 1 to the digit at the left of the decimal point, and then truncates any digits to the right. Otherwise, it truncates all digits to the right of decimal point.

Example	The following statement calculates an estimate based on the result of rounding the product of two NUMERIC(11,2) numbers up or down:
	`SELECT  JOB_NO,  ROUND(RATE * HOURS) + 1 AS ESTIMATE`
	`    FROM QUOTATION`
	`    WHERE RATE IS NOT NULL AND HOURS IS NOT NULL;`

Related or similar functions	See also TRUNCATE( ), F_ROUNDFLOAT( ).

IB_UDF	**SIGN(VALUE)**
Linux, Win32	Returns 1, 0, or -1 depending on whether the input value is positive, zero, or negative, respectively.
Arguments	*value* is a column or expression that evaluates to a number of DOUBLE PRECISION type.
Return value	A DOUBLE PRECISION number.
Example	A snippet from a trigger: `...IF (SIGN(NEW.CURRENT_VALUE) < 1) THEN ...;`

IB_UDF	SQRT(VALUE)
Linux, Win32	Returns the square root of a number.
Arguments	*value* is a column or expression that evaluates to a number of DOUBLE PRECISION type.
Return value	A DOUBLE PRECISION number.

Example	A snippet from a trigger:
	```...IF (SQRT(NEW.HYPOTENUSE) = SQRT(NEW.SIDE1) +```
	```SQRT(NEW.SIDE2)) THEN```
	``` NEW.RIGHT_ANGLED_TRIANGLE = 'T';```

FBUDF	TRUNCATE (VALUE)
Linux, Win32	Truncates a fixed numeric type to the next lowest integer.
Arguments	*value* is a column or expression that evaluates to a fixed numeric type with a scale > 0.
Return value	A number of an integer type.
Notes	As with some other functions in this library, you need to make two declarations to get "coverage" for both 32-bit and 64-bit inputs. Check the declarations in the script fdudf.sql for *truncate* and *i64truncate*.

Example	The following statement calculates an estimate based on the result of truncating the product of two NUMERIC(11,2) numbers:
	```SELECT JOB_NO,```
	``` TRUNCATE(RATE * HOURS) + 1 AS ESTIMATE```
	```FROM QUOTATION```
	``` WHERE RATE IS NOT NULL AND HOURS IS NOT NULL;```

Related or similar functions	See also ROUND( ), F_TRUNCATE( ).

Date and Time Functions

FBUDF	DOW(VALUE)
Linux, Win32	Takes a TIMESTAMP and returns the day of the week (in English) as a mixed-case string.
Arguments	*value* is a column or expression that evaluates to a TIMESTAMP type.
Return value	'Monday', 'Tuesday', 'Wednesday', 'Thursday', 'Friday', 'Saturday', or 'Sunday'.

Example	This statement adds four days and returns the day of the week for that adjusted date:
	```SELECT DOW(CURRENT_DATE + 4)```
	``` FROM RDB$DATABASE;```

Related or similar functions	See also SDOW( ), internal function EXTRACT( ).

FBUDF	**SDOW(VALUE)**
Linux Win32	Takes a TIMESTAMP and returns the day of the week (in English) as an abbreviated mixed-case string.
Arguments	*value* is a column or expression that evaluates to a TIMESTAMP type.
Return value	'Mon', 'Tue', 'Wed', 'Thu', 'Fri', 'Sat', or 'Sun'.

Example	This statement adds 4 days and returns the day of the week for that adjusted date:
	`SELECT DOW(CURRENT_DATE + 4)`
	`  FROM RDB$DATABASE;`

Related or similar functions	See also DOW( ), internal function EXTRACT( ).

FBUDF	**ADDDAY(VALUE1, VALUE2)**
Linux, Win32	Adds a whole number of days to a date or time type value and returns the adjusted date as a TIMESTAMP.
Arguments	*value1*: A column or expression that evaluates to a date or time type. *value2*: Number of days to add (integer) or an integer expression.
Return value	Adjusted TIMESTAMP (equivalent to *value1* + *value2*).
Notes	If the input is a TIME type, the days are added to that time of day on the *current date*. If it is a DATE type, the time of day will be midnight.

Example	This statement adds 4 days and returns the adjusted date and time as midnight, 4 days later:
	`SELECT ADDDAY(CURRENT_DATE, 4)`
	`FROM RDB$DATABASE;`

Related or similar functions	See also ADDHOUR( ), ADDMINUTE( ), etc.

FBUDF	**ADDHOUR(VALUE1, VALUE2)**
Linux, Win32	Adds a whole number of hours to a date or time type value and returns the adjusted date as a TIMESTAMP.
Arguments	*value1*: A column or expression that evaluates to a date or time type. *value2*: Number of hours to add (integer) or an integer expression.
Return value	Adjusted TIMESTAMP (equivalent to *value 1* + (*value 2*/12)).
Notes	If the input is a TIME type, the hours are added to that time of day on the *current date*. If it is a DATE type, they are added to midnight of the current date.

Example	This statement adds 10 hours and returns the adjusted date and time:
	`SELECT ADDHOUR(CURRENT_TIMESTAMP, 10)`
	`  FROM RDB$DATABASE;`

Related or similar functions	See also ADDDAY( ), ADDMINUTE( ), etc.

FBUDF	**ADDMILLISECOND(VALUE1, VALUE2)**
Linux, Win32	Adds a whole number of milliseconds to a date or time type value and returns the adjusted date as a TIMESTAMP.
Arguments	*value1*: A column or expression that evaluates to a date or time type. *value2*: Number of milliseconds to add (integer) or an integer expression.
Return value	TIMESTAMP.
Notes	If the input is a TIME type, the milliseconds are added to that time of day on the *current date*. If it is a DATE type, the input time of day will be midnight.
Example	This statement adds 61,234 milliseconds to the current system time. It effectively adds the milliseconds to the current system *timestamp*: `SELECT ADDMILLISECOND(CURRENT_TIME, 61234)` `FROM RDB$DATABASE;`
Related or similar functions	See also ADDDAY( ), ADDMINUTE( ), etc.

FBUDF	**ADDMINUTE(VALUE1, VALUE2)**
Linux, Win32	Adds a whole number of minutes to a date or time type value and returns the adjusted date as a TIMESTAMP.
Arguments	*value1*: A column or expression that evaluates to a date or time type. *value2*: Number of minutes to add (integer) or an integer expression.
Return value	TIMESTAMP.
Notes	If the input is a TIME type, the minutes are added to that time of day on the *current date*. If it is a DATE type, the input time of day will be midnight.
Example	This statement adds 45 minutes to the current system time. It effectively adds the minutes to the current system *timestamp*: `SELECT ADDMINUTE(CURRENT_TIME, 45)` `    FROM RDB$DATABASE;`
Related or similar functions	See also ADDDAY( ), ADDSECOND( ), etc.

FBUDF	**ADDMONTH(VALUE1, VALUE2)**
Linux, Win32	Adds a whole number of months to a date or time type value and returns the adjusted date as a TIMESTAMP.
Arguments	*value1*: A column or expression that evaluates to a TIMESTAMP type. *value2*: Number of months to add (integer) or an integer expression.
Return value	An adjusted TIMESTAMP that is (*value2*) calendar months later than *value1*.

FBUDF	**ADDMONTH(VALUE1, VALUE2)** *(continued)*
Notes	If the input is a TIME type, the months are added to that time of day on the *current date*. If it is a DATE type, the input time of day will be midnight.
Example	This statement uses ADDMONTH( ) to calculate the term for a contract:

```
UPDATE CONTRACT
  SET FINAL_DATE =
  CASE CONTRACT_TERM
     WHEN 'HALF-YEARLY' THEN ADDMONTH(START_DATE, 6)
     WHEN 'YEARLY' THEN ADDMONTH(START_DATE, 12)
  ELSE ADDWEEK(START_DATE, TRUNCATE(CONTRACT_AMT/WEEKLY_FEE))
  END
WHERE START_DATE IS NOT NULL
  AND AMT_PAID IS NOT NULL
  AND WEEKLY_FEE IS NOT NULL
  AND CONTRACT_ID = 12345;
```

Related or similar functions	See also ADDDAY( ), ADDYEAR( ), etc.

FBUDF	**ADDSECOND(VALUE1 , VALUE2)**
Linux, Win32	Adds a whole number of seconds to a date or time type value and returns the adjusted date as a TIMESTAMP.
Arguments	*value1*: A column or expression that evaluates to a date or time type. *value2*: Number of seconds to add (integer) or an integer expression.
Return value	TIMESTAMP.
Notes	If the input is a TIME type, the seconds are added to that time of day on the *current date*. If it is a DATE type, the input time of day will be midnight.
Example	This statement adds 120 seconds to the current system date. It effectively adds the seconds to midnight of the current system *date*:

```
SELECT ADDSECOND(CURRENT_DATE, 120)
   FROM RDB$DATABASE;
```

Related or similar functions	See also ADDMONTH( ), ADDMILLISECOND( ), etc.

FBUDF	**ADDWEEK(VALUE1, VALUE2)**
Linux, Win32	Adds a whole number of weeks to a date or time type value and returns the adjusted date as a TIMESTAMP.
Arguments	*value1*: A column or expression that evaluates to a date or time type. *value2*: Number of weeks to add (integer) or an integer expression.
Return value	Adjusted TIMESTAMP (equivalent to *value 1* + (7 * *value 2*).

continued

FBUDF	**ADDWEEK(VALUE1, VALUE2)**
Notes	If the input is a TIME type, the weeks are added to that time of day on the *current date*. If it is a DATE type, the input time of day will be midnight.

Example	This statement calculates how many weeks' fees were paid, and uses it with ADDWEEK( ) to calculate the final date of a contract:
	``
	UPDATE CONTRACT
	  SET FINAL_DATE = ADDWEEK(START_DATE,
	TRUNCATE(CONTRACT_AMT/WEEKLY_FEE))
	    WHERE START_DATE IS NOT NULL
	    AND AMT_PAID IS NOT NULL
	    AND WEEKLY_FEE IS NOT NULL
	    AND CONTRACT_ID = 12345;
	``

Related or similar functions	See also ADDDAY( ), ADDMONTH( ), etc.

FBUDF	**ADDYEAR(VALUE1, VALUE2)**
Linux, Win32	Adds a whole number of years to a date or time value and returns the adjusted date as a TIMESTAMP.
Arguments	*value1*: A column or expression that evaluates to a date or time type. *value2*: Number of years to add (integer) or an integer expression.
Return value	Adjusted TIMESTAMP.
Notes	If the input is a TIME type, the years are added to that time of day on the *current date*. If it is a DATE type, the input time of day will be midnight.

Example	This statement calculates the final date of a lease, given the starting date:
	``
	UPDATE LEASE
	  SET FINAL_DATE = ADDYEAR(START_DATE, 5)
	    WHERE START_DATE IS NOT NULL
	    AND LEASE_ID = 12345;
	``

Related or similar functions	See also ADDDAY( ), ADDMONTH( ), etc.

FBUDF	**GETEXACTTIMESTAMP( )**
Linux, Win32	Returns the system time as a TIMESTAMP, to the nearest millisecond.
Arguments	No arguments.
Return value	Returns a TIMESTAMP.
Notes	The date and time context variable CURRENT_TIMESTAMP and the predefined date literal 'NOW' return system time only to the nearest second. GETEXACTTIMESTAMP() is currently the only way to get the exact system time.
Example	This statement returns the exact timestamp: ``` SELECT GETEXACTTIMESTAMP() AS TSTAMP FROM RDB$DATABASE; ```

FREEUDFLIB	**F_AGEINDAYS(VALUE1, VALUE2)**
Win32	Computes the age in days of a date (*value1*) with reference to another date (*value2*). Typically, the reference date would be the current date, but it need not be. For example, you might want to find out the age of something as it stood on some other date.
Arguments	*value1*: A column or expression that evaluates to a number of type DATE or TIMESTAMP.
	value2: A column or expression that evaluates to a number of type DATE or TIMESTAMP.
Return value	A positive or negative number of type INTEGER.

Example	`SELECT FIRST_NAME, LAST_NAME,`
	`    F_AGEINDAYS(DATE_OF_BIRTH, CURRENT_DATE) AS CURRENT_AGE`
	`FROM MEMBERSHIP`
	`WHERE DATE_OF_BIRTH < CURRENT_DATE - (5 * 365);`

Related or similar functions	See also F_AgeInDaysThreshold( ).

FREEUDFLIB	**F_AGEINDAYSTHRESHOLD(VALUE 1, VALUE 2, MINVALUE, USEMIN, MAXVALUE, USEMAX)**
Win32	Computes the age in days of a date (*value1*) with reference to another date (*value2*) and, instead of returning that value, returns a specified minimum number that is lower than the calculated value, or a specified maximum number that is higher than the calculated value.
Arguments	*value1*: A column or expression that evaluates to a number of type DATE or TIMESTAMP.
	value2: A column or expression that evaluates to a number of type DATE or TIMESTAMP. It need not be an earlier date than *value1*.
	MinValue: An integer. The value to be returned if the calculated value is lower. Set to 0 if you want to use only a *MaxValue*.
	UseMin: Set to 1 if you want to use a *MinValue*. Set *UseMax* to 0 if you want to use only a *MinValue*.
	MaxValue: An integer. The value to be returned if the calculated value is higher. Set to 0 if you want to use only a *MinValue*.
	UseMax: Set to 1 if you want to use a *MaxValue*. Set *UseMin* to 0 if you want to use only a *MaxValue*.
Return value	A number of type INTEGER.
Notes	If the last four arguments are all 0, the function works exactly like F_AgeThreshold.

Example	This statement will return a list showing all accounts with due dates less than 30 days ago with an overdue age of 29 days and all with due dates more than 90 days ago with an overdue age of 90 days. All others will be shown with their actual age.
	`SELECT ACCOUNT_NAME,`
	`    F_AGEINDAYSTHRESHOLD(DUE_DATE, CURRENT_DATE, 29, 1, 90, 1) AS`
	`OVERDUE_AGE`
	`FROM ACCOUNT;`

Related or similar functions	See also AgeInDays( ).

FREEUDFLIB	**F_AGEINMONTHS(VALUE1, VALUE2)**
Win32	Computes the age in months of a date (*value1*) with reference to another date (*value2*). Typically, the reference date would be the current date, but it need not be. For example, you might want to find out the age of something as it stood on some other date.
Arguments	*value1*: A column or expression that evaluates to a number of type DATE or TIMESTAMP.
	value2: A column or expression that evaluates to a number of type DATE or TIMESTAMP. It need not be an earlier date than *value1*.
Return value	A positive or negative number of type INTEGER.

Example	`SELECT ACCOUNT_NAME,`
	`  F_AGEINMONTHS(DUE_DATE, CURRENT_DATE) AS OVERDUE_AGE`
	`FROM ACCOUNT`
	`  WHERE ACCT_BALANCE > 0`
	`  AND DUE_DATE < CURRENT_DATE - (6 * 7);`

Related or similar functions	See also F_AgeInMonthsThreshold( ).

FREEUDFLIB	**F_AGEINMONTHSTHRESHOLD(VALUE 1, VALUE 2, MINVALUE, USEMIN, MAXVALUE, USEMAX)**
Win32	Works for F_AgeInMonths just as F_AgeInDaysThreshold works for F_AgeInDays.

FREEUDFLIB	**F_AGEINWEEKS(VALUE1, VALUE2)**
Win32	Computes the age in weeks of a date (*value1*) with reference to another date (*value2*). Typically, the reference date would be the current date, but it need not be. For example, you might want to find out the age of something as it stood on some other date.
Arguments	*value1*: A column or expression that evaluates to a number of type DATE or TIMESTAMP.
	value2: A column or expression that evaluates to a number of type DATE or TIMESTAMP. It need not be an earlier date than *value1*.
Return value	A positive or negative number of type INTEGER.

Example	`SELECT ACCOUNT_NAME,`
	`  F_AGEINWEEKS(DUE_DATE, CURRENT_DATE) AS OVERDUE_AGE`
	`FROM ACCOUNT`
	`  WHERE ACCT_BALANCE > 0`
	`  AND DUE_DATE < CURRENT_DATE - (366/2);`

Related or similar functions	See also F_AgeInWeeksThreshold( ).

FREEUDFLIB	**F_AGEINWEEKSTHRESHOLD(VALUE 1, VALUE 2, MINVALUE, USEMIN, MAXVALUE, USEMAX)**
Win32	Works for AgeInWeeks just as F_AgeInDaysThreshold works for F_AgeInDays.

FREEUDFLIB	**F_CMONTHLONG(VALUE)**
Win32	Takes a TIMESTAMP or DATE and returns the name of the month (in English) fully spelled out as a mixed-case string.
Arguments	*value* is a column or expression that evaluates to a TIMESTAMP or DATE type.
Return value	'January', 'February', 'March', 'April', 'May', 'June', 'July', 'August', 'September', 'October', 'November', or 'December'.
Example	This statement adds 40 days to today's date and returns the month for that adjusted date as a string: SELECT F_CMONTHLONG(CURRENT_DATE + 40) FROM RDB$DATABASE;
Related or similar functions	See also F_CMONTHSHORT( ), SDOW( ), internal function EXTRACT( ).

FREEUDFLIB	**F_CMONTHSHORT(VALUE)**
Win32	Takes a TIMESTAMP or DATE and returns a three-character abbreviation of the month name (in English) as a mixed-case string.

FREEUDFLIB	**F_MAXDATE(VALUE1, VALUE2)**
Win32	Takes two date or time type values or expressions and returns the later of the two as a timestamp(TIMESTAMP in dialect 3; DATE in dialect 1).
Arguments	*value1*: A column or expression that evaluates to a TIMESTAMP or DATE type. *value2*: A column or expression that evaluates to a TIMESTAMP or DATE type.
Return value	The later date or date expression, resolved to TIMESTAMP.

FREEUDFLIB	**F_MINDATE(VALUE1, VALUE2)**
Win32	Takes two date or time type values or expressions and returns the earlier of the two as a timestamp.
Arguments	*value1*: A column or expression that evaluates to a TIMESTAMP or DATE type. *value2*: A column or expression that evaluates to a TIMESTAMP or DATE type.
Return value	The earlier date or date expression, resolved to TIMESTAMP.

FREEUDFLIB	**F_QUARTER(VALUE)**
Win32	Takes a date or time type value or expression and returns the quarter of the year.
Arguments	*value* is a column or expression that evaluates to a TIMESTAMP or DATE type.
Return value	Returns 1 for January to March, 2 for April to June, 3 for July to September, 4 for October to December.

FREEUDFLIB	**F_WOY(VALUE)**
Win32	Returns a string that concatenates the year of the date with the integer week of the year.
Arguments	*value* is a column or expression that evaluates to a TIMESTAMP or DATE type.
Return value	Returns an integer representing the digits of the year shifted left two places, followed by two digits representing the week of the year.

Example	The following example returns 200313:
	`SELECT WOY('26.03.2003')`
	`    FROM RDB$DATABASE;`

String and Character Functions

IB_UDF	**ASCII_CHAR(VALUE)**
Linux, Win32	Returns the ASCII character corresponding to the decimal value passed in.
Arguments	*value* is a column, constant, or expression of type SMALLINT or INTEGER.
Return value	A single-byte printable or non-printable character.

Example	This statement will insert a carriage return and a line feed into a column on every row of an external table:
	`UPDATE EXT_FILE`
	`    SET EOL= ASCII_CHAR(13) || ASCII_CHAR(10);`

IB_UDF	ASCII_VAL(VALUE)
Linux, Win32	Returns the ASCII value of the character passed in.
Arguments	*value* is a column, constant, or expression of type CHAR.
Return value	Integer—an ASCII decimal code.
Example	SELECT ASCII_VAL('&') AS ASC_NUM FROM RDB$DATABASE;

IB_UDF	LOWER(VALUE)
Linux, Win32	Returns the input string as lowercase characters. It works only with ASCII characters.
Arguments	*value* is a column or expression that evaluates to an ASCII string of 32,765 bytes or less.
Return value	A CHAR(n) or VARCHAR(n) of the same size as the input string.
Notes	This function can receive and return up to 32,767 characters, the limit for a Firebird character string.
Example	The following statement will return the string 'come and sit at my table': SELECT LOWER('Come and sit at MY TABLE') AS L_STRING FROM RDB$DATABASE;

IB_UDF	LPAD(VALUE, LENGTH, IN_CHAR)
Linux, Win32	Prepends the given character *in_char* to the beginning of the input string, *value*, until length of the result string becomes equal to the given number, *length*.
Arguments	*value*: A column or expression that evaluates to a string not longer than (32767 – *length*) bytes. *length*: An integer type or expression. *in_char*: A single character, to be used as the padding character.
Return value	A CHAR(n) OR VARCHAR(n), where *n* is the supplied *length* argument.
Notes	This function can return up to 32,765 bytes, the limit for a Firebird character string.
Example	The following statement will return the string '##########RHUBARB': SELECT LPAD('RHUBARB, 17, '#') AS LPADDED_STRING FROM RDB$DATABASE;
Related or similar functions	See also RPAD( ).

IB_UDF	**LTRIM(VALUE)**
Linux, Win32	Removes leading spaces from the input string.
Arguments	*value* is a column or expression that evaluates to a string not longer than 32,767 bytes.
Return value	A CHAR(n) OR VARCHAR(n) with no leading space characters.
Notes	This function can accept up to 32,765 bytes, including space characters, the limit for a Firebird character string.
Example	The following Before Insert trigger fragment will trim any leading spaces from the input: `NEW.CHARACTER_COLUMN = LTRIM(NEW.CHARACTER_COLUMN);`
Related or similar functions	See also RTRIM( ), F_RTRIM( ), F_LRTRIM( ).

FBUDF	**SRIGHT(VALUE, LENGTH)**
Linux, Win32	Returns a substring from the supplied *value*, being the rightmost *length* characters in *value*.
Arguments	*value*: A column or expression that evaluates to a string not longer than 32,767 bytes.~TSR*length*: An integer type or expression.
Return value	A CHAR(n) or VARCHAR(n).
Notes	This function can accept up to 32,765 bytes, the limit for a Firebird character string.

Example	The following statement will return the string 'fox jumps over the lazy dog.':
	`SELECT SRIGHT('The quick brown fox jumps over the lazy dog.',`
	`28) AS R_STRING`
	`FROM RDB$DATABASE;`

Related or similar functions	See also SUBSTR( ), SUBSTRLEN( ), internal function SUBSTRING( ).

IB_UDF	**RPAD(VALUE, LENGTH, IN_CHAR)**
Linux, Win32	Appends the given character *in_char* to the end of the input string, *value*, until the length of the result string becomes equal to the given number, *length*.
Arguments	*value*: A column or expression that evaluates to a string not longer than (32,765 – *length*) bytes. *length*: An integer type or expression. *in_char*: A single character, to be used as the padding character.
Return value	A CHAR(n) or VARCHAR(n), where *n* is the supplied *length* argument.
Notes	This function can return up to 32,765 bytes, the limit for a Firebird character string.

IB_UDF	**RPAD(VALUE, LENGTH, IN_CHAR)** *(continued)*
Example	The following statement will return the string 'Framboise***********':
| | ```
SELECT RPAD('Framboise, 20, '*') AS RPADDED_STRING
  FROM RDB$DATABASE;
``` |
| Related or similar functions | See also LPAD( ). |

IB_UDF	**RTRIM(VALUE)**
Linux, Win32	Removes trailing spaces from the input string.
Arguments	*value* is a column or expression that evaluates to a string not longer than 32,765 bytes.
Return value	A CHAR(n) or VARCHAR(n) with no leading space characters.
Notes	This function can accept up to 32,765 bytes, including space characters, the limit for a Firebird character string.
Example	The following Before Insert trigger fragment will trim any trailing spaces from the input:
| | ```
...
NEW.CHARACTER_COLUMN = RTRIM(NEW.CHARACTER_COLUMN);
``` |
| Related or similar functions | See also LTRIM( ), F_LRTRIM( ). |

IB_UDF	**STRLEN(VALUE)**
Linux, Win32	Returns the length of a string.
Arguments	*value* is a column or expression that evaluates to a string not longer than 32,765 bytes.
Return value	An integer, the length (count) of characters in the string.
Notes	This function can accept up to 32,765 bytes, including space characters, the limit for a Firebird character string.
Example	The following PSQL fragment returns the length of a column to a local variable:
| | ```
...
DECLARE VARIABLE LEN INTEGER;
...
SELECT COL1, COL2, COL3 FROM ATABLE
INTO :V1, :V2, :V3;
LEN = STRLEN(V3);
...;
``` |
| Related or similar functions | See also SUBSTRLEN( ). |
```

IB_UDF	**SUBSTR(VALUE, POS1, POS2)**
Linux, Win32	Returns a string consisting of the characters from *pos1* to *pos2* inclusively. If *pos2* is past the end of the string, the function will return all characters from *pos1* to the end of the string.
Arguments	*value*: A column or expression that evaluates to a string. *pos1*: A column or expression that evaluates to an integer type. *pos2*: A column or expression that evaluates to an integer type.
Return value	A string.
Notes	If you are porting a legacy application written for InterBase, be aware that this implementation of SUBSTR( ) differs from that of SUBSTR( ) in the Borland distributions of the ib_udf library, which returns NULL when *pos2* is past the end of the input string. This function can accept up to 32,765 bytes, including space characters, the limit for a Firebird character string.

Example	The following statement strips the first three characters from the string in COLUMNB and sets its value to be the string starting at position 4 and ending at position 100. If the string ends before position 100, the result will be all of the characters from position 4 to the end of the string:
	`UPDATE ATABLE`
	  `SET COLUMNB = SUBSTR(COLUMNB, 4, 100)`
	  `WHERE...`

Related or similar functions	See also SUBSTRLEN( ), RTRIM( ), internal function SUBSTRING( ).

IB_UDF	**SUBSTRLEN(VALUE, STARTPOS, LENGTH)**
Linux, Win32	Returns a string of size *length* starting at *startpos*. The length of the string will be the lesser of *length* or the number of characters from *startpos* to the end of the input *value*.
Arguments	*value*: A column or expression that evaluates to a string not longer than 32,765 bytes. *startpos*: An integer constant or expression. *length*: An integer constant or expression.
Return value	A string.
Notes	This function can accept up to 32,765 bytes, including space characters, the limit for a Firebird character string.

Example	The following statement takes the value of a column and updates it by removing the first three characters and, after that, removing any trailing characters if the remaining string is longer than 20 characters:
	`UPDATE ATABLE`
	  `SET COLUMNB = SUBSTRLEN(COLUMNB, 4, 20)`
	  `WHERE...`

Related or similar functions	See also SUBSTR( ), RTRIM( ), internal function SUBSTRING( ).

FREEUDFLIB	**F_CRLF()**
Win32	Returns the Windows carriage return/line feed string—ASCII(13) || ASCII(10).
Arguments	None.
Return value	A C-style (null-terminated) string.

Example	The following statement inserts a Windows end-of-line marker into a column in a table (e.g., an external table for export to another application):
	`INSERT INTO EXTABLE(COLUMN1, COLUMN2, EOL)`
	`    VALUES (99, 'An item of data', CRLF());`

FREEUDFLIB	**F_FINDWORD(VALUE, N)**
Win32	Given a starting position, *startpos*, return a word consisting of the character at that position and succeeding characters up to the next white space character.
Arguments	*value*: A column or expression that evaluates to a string type. *n*: An integer type, indicating the zero-based position in the string where the required word is to be located.
Return value	A string.
Notes	Consider strings passed to f_FindWord as arrays of characters starting at index 0.

Example	The following statement returns the word "pie":
	`SELECT F_FINDWORD('I never tasted pie like Mom used to make', 15)`
	`    FROM RDB$DATABASE;`

FREEUDFLIB	**F_LEFT(VALUE, N)**
Win32	Returns the first *num* characters from an input string, *value*.
Arguments	*value*: A column or expression that evaluates to a string type. *n*: An integer type, indicating the number of characters to return from the left side of *value*.
Return value	A string of *n* characters.

Example	The following statement returns the string "I never tasted pie":
	`SELECT F_LEFT('I never tasted pie like Mom used to make', 18)`
	`    FROM RDB$DATABASE;`

Related or similar functions	See also SUBSTRLEN( ), SUBSTR( ), internal function SUBSTRING( ).

FREEUDFLIB	**F_LINEWRAP(VALUE, STARTPOS, WIDTH)**
Win32	Given a starting position (*startpos*) in a string (*value*) and a column width (*width*), returns the portion of *value*, starting at *startpos*, that fits in *width* character spaces.
Arguments	*value*: A column or expression that evaluates to a string type. *startpos*: An integer type, indicating the zero-based position in the string where the return string is to begin. *width*: An integer type, indicating the width of the column (print/display) that the returned string must fit into.
Return value	A string of *width* (or fewer) characters.
Notes	Consider strings passed to f_LineWrap() as arrays of characters starting at index 0.

Example	The following statement returns the string 'which, taken at the flood':
	`SELECT F_WORDWRAP('There is a tide in the affairs of men which,`
	`taken at the flood, leads on to good fortune.', 38, 25)`
	`  FROM RDB$DATABASE;`

FREEUDFLIB	**F_LRTRIM(VALUE)**
Win32	Trims all leading and trailing white space from a string.
Arguments	*value* is a column or expression that evaluates to a string type.
Return value	A string with no leading or trailing white space characters.

Example	The following statement returns the string 'lean and mean':
	`SELECT F_LRTRIM('    lean and mean        ')`
	`  FROM RDB$DATABASE;`

Related or similar functions	See also LTRIM(), RTRIM().

FREEUDFLIB	**F_PROPERCASE(VALUE)**
Win32	Converts a string to "proper case" or "camel case"—that is, takes each word and replaces the first letter with its uppercase equivalent and replaces each remaining character with its lowercase equivalent.
Arguments	*value* is a column or expression that evaluates to a string type.
Return value	A string such as 'Now Is The Time For All Good Men To Come To The Aid Of The Party'.
Notes	Though convenient for a specific task, this function has limitations. It will not, for example, treat names like d'Oliveira, O'Halloran, or MacDonald correctly.

Example	The following statement returns the string 'Eric S. Raymond':
	`SELECT F_PROPERCASE('ERIC S. RAYMOND')`
	`  FROM RDB$DATABASE;`

Related or similar functions	See also LOWER(), UPPER().

BLOB Functions

FBUDF	**STRING2BLOB(VALUE)**
Linux, Win32	Takes a string field (column, variable, expression) and returns a text BLOB.
Arguments	*value* is a column or expression that evaluates to a VARCHAR type of 300 characters or less.
Return value	A text BLOB.
Notes	Under most conditions, it will not be necessary to call this function. Firebird will accept a string directly as input to a BLOB.
Example	This PSQL fragment concatenates two strings and converts the result to a text BLOB:

```
...
DECLARE VARIABLE V_COMMENT1 VARCHAR(250);
DECLARE VARIABLE V_COMMENT2 VARCHAR(45);
DECLARE VARIABLE V_MEMO VARCHAR(296) = '';

...
SELECT <..other fields...>, COMMENT1, COMMENT2
FROM APPLICATION
  WHERE APPLICATION_ID = :APP_ID
  INTO <..other variables..>, :V_COMMENT1, :V_COMMENT2;
IF (V_COMMENT1 IS NOT NULL) THEN
  V_MEMO = V_COMMENT1;
IF (V_COMMENT2 IS NOT NULL) THEN
BEGIN
  IF (V_MEMO = '') THEN
    V_MEMO = V_COMMENT2;
  ELSE
    V_MEMO = V_MEMO ||' '|| V_COMMENT2;
END
IF (V_MEMO <> '') THEN
  INSERT INTO MEMBERSHIP (
    FIRST_NAME, LAST_NAME, APP_ID, BLOB_MEMO)
  VALUES (
    :FIRST_NAME, :LAST_NAME, :APP_ID, STRING2BLOB(:V_MEMO));
...
```

Related or similar functions	See also F_BLOBASPCHAR( ).

FREEUDFLIB	**F_BLOBMAXSEGMENTLENGTH(VALUE)**
Win32	Given a column reference to a BLOB in storage, returns its maximum segment size.
Arguments	*value* is the identifier of a BLOB column in a table.
Return value	An integer representing the size of the largest stored segment in bytes.

continued

FREEUDFLIB	**F_BLOBMAXSEGMENTLENGTH(VALUE)** *(continued)*
| Example | ```
SELECT F_BLOBMAXSEGMENTSIZE(BLOB_MEMO) AS MEMO_SEGMENT_SIZE
  FROM MEMBERSHIP
WHERE MEMBER_ID = ....;
``` |
| Related or similar functions | See also F_BLOBSEGMENTLENGTH( ), F_BLOBSIZE( ). |

FREEUDFLIB	**F_BLOBSEGMENTCOUNT(VALUE)**
Win32	Given a column reference to a BLOB in storage, returns the number of segments used to store it.
Arguments	*value* is the identifier of a BLOB column in a table.
Return value	An integer representing the number of segments.
| Example | ```
SELECT F_BLOBSEGMENTCOUNT(BLOB_MEMO) AS SEGMENT_COUNT
  FROM MEMBERSHIP
WHERE MEMBER_ID = ....;
``` |
| Related or similar functions | See also F_MAXBLOBSEGMENTSIZE( ), F_BLOBSIZE( ). |

FREEUDFLIB	**F_BLOBSIZE(VALUE)**
Win32	Given a column reference to a BLOB in storage, returns its size in bytes.
Arguments	*value* is the identifier of a BLOB column in a table.
Return value	An integer representing the size of the BLOB in bytes.
| Example | ```
SELECT F_BLOBSIZE(BLOB_MEMO) AS SIZE_OF_MEMO
  FROM MEMBERSHIP
WHERE MEMBER_ID = ....;
``` |
| Related or similar functions | See also F_BLOBSEGMENTCOUNT( ), F_BLOBMAXSEGMENTSIZE( ). |

FREEUDFLIB	**F_BLOBASPCHAR(VALUE)**
Win32	Takes a reference to a BLOB field (column or variable) and returns its contents as a null-terminated string.
Arguments	*value* is the identifier of a BLOB column or variable.
Return value	A null-terminated string.
Notes	Use this function only on BLOBs that you are certain do not exceed the maximum length of a VARCHAR type (32,765 bytes). Beware of larger byte sizes in BLOBs storing multi-byte characters.
```

FREEUDFLIB	**F_BLOBASPCHAR(VALUE)** *(continued)*
Example	SELECT F_BLOBASPCHAR(BLOB_MEMO) AS MEMO_STRING FROM MEMBERSHIP WHERE MEMBER_ID = ...;
Related or similar functions	See also STRING2BLOB( ).

FREEUDFLIB	**F_BLOBLEFT(VALUE, N)**
Win32	Takes a reference to a BLOB field (column or variable) and returns the first *n* characters.
Arguments	*value*: The identifier of a BLOB column or variable. *n*: The maximum number of characters to return. It must not exceed the maximum length of a VARCHAR type (32,765 bytes).
Return value	A null-terminated string *n* or fewer characters in length.
Notes	Beware of larger byte sizes in BLOBs storing multi-byte characters.
Example	SELECT F_BLOBLEFT(BLOB_MEMO, 20) AS MEMO_START FROM MEMBERSHIP WHERE MEMBER_ID = ...;
Related or similar functions	See also F_BLOBMID( ), F_BLOBRIGHT( ).

FREEUDFLIB	**F_BLOBLLINE(VALUE, N)**
Win32	Takes a reference to a BLOB field (column or variable) and returns the *n*th line as a string.
Arguments	*value*: The identifier of a BLOB column or variable. *n*: The number of the line in the BLOB, counting the first line as line 1.
Return value	A null-terminated string *n* or fewer characters in length.
Notes	Use this function only on BLOBs that are arranged in CRLF-separated strings. Do not use it unless you are certain that lines do not exceed the maximum length of a VARCHAR type (32,765 bytes). Beware of larger byte sizes in BLOBs storing multi-byte characters.
Example	SELECT F_BLOBLINE(BLOB_MEMO, 20) AS MEMO_LINE20 FROM MEMBERSHIP WHERE MEMBER_ID = ...;
Related or similar functions	See also F_BLOBMID( ), F_BLOBRIGHT( ).

FREEUDFLIB	**F_BLOBMID(VALUE, STARTPOS, N)**
Win32	Takes a reference to a BLOB field (column or variable) and returns *n* characters, beginning at *startpos*.
Arguments	*value*: The identifier of a BLOB column or variable. *startpos*: The position of the first character in the returned string. *n*: The maximum number of characters to return. It must not exceed the maximum length of a VARCHAR type (32,765 bytes).
Return value	A null-terminated string *n* or fewer characters in length.
Notes	Beware of larger byte sizes in BLOBs storing multi-byte characters.

Example	`SELECT F_BLOBMID(BLOB_MEMO, 140, 20) AS MEMO_SUBSTRING`
	`  FROM MEMBERSHIP`
	`WHERE MEMBER_ID = ....;`

Related or similar functions	See also F_BLOBRIGHT( ), F_BLOBLEFT( ).

FREEUDFLIB	**F_BLOBRIGHT(VALUE, N)**
Win32	Takes a reference to a BLOB field (column or variable) and returns the last *n* characters.
Arguments	*value*: The identifier of a BLOB column or variable. *n*: The maximum number of characters to return. It must not exceed the maximum length of a VARCHAR type (32,765 bytes).
Return value	A null-terminated string *n* or fewer characters in length.
Notes	Beware of larger byte sizes in BLOBs storing multi-byte characters.

Example	`SELECT F_BLOBRIGHT(BLOB_MEMO, 20) AS MEMO_END`
	`  FROM MEMBERSHIP`
	`WHERE MEMBER_ID = ....;`

Related or similar functions	See also F_BLOBMID( ), F_BLOBLEFT( ).

FREEUDFLIB	**F_BLOBBINCMP(VALUE1, VALUE2)**
Win32	Performs a binary "diff" comparison on the contents of two BLOB fields (columns or variables) and returns a value indicating whether they are the same.
Arguments	*value1* and *value2* are the identifiers of two BLOB columns or variables that are to be compared.
Return value	1 (True) if the BLOBs are the same, 0 (False) if not.

FREEUDFLIB	**F_BLOBBINCMP(VALUE1, VALUE2)** *(continued)*
Example	This snippet from a Before Update trigger sets a flag if the supplied BLOB is not the same as the compared one:

```
...
DECLARE VARIABLE CMP_BLOB BLOB SUB_TYPE TEXT;
...
SELECT BLOB_MEMO FROM REPL_MEMBERSHIP
WHERE MEMBER_ID = NEW.MEMBER_ID
INTO :CMP_BLOB;
IF (F_BLOBBINCMP(NEW.BLOB_MEMO, CMP_BLOB) = 1) THEN
  NEW.UPDATE_MEMO = 'T';
ELSE
  NEW.UPDATE_MEMO = 'F';
...
```

Trigonometric Functions

IB_UDF	**ACOS(VALUE)**
Linux, Win32	Calculates the arccosine (inverse of cosine) of a number between –1 and 1. If the number is out of bounds, it returns NaN.
Arguments	*value* is a column or expression that is compatible with a signed or unsigned DOUBLE PRECISION number, evaluating to a valid cosine value.
Return value	A DOUBLE PRECISION number, in degrees.
Example	This snippet from a trigger converts a raw cosine value to degrees:

```
...
IF (NEW.RAW_VALUE IS NOT NULL) THEN
  NEW.READING1 = ACOS(NEW.RAW_VALUE);
```

Related or similar functions	See also COS( ), COSH( ), and other trigonometric functions.

IB_UDF	**ASIN(VALUE)**
Linux or Win32	Returns the arcsine (inverse of sine) of a number between –1 and 1. Returns NaN if the number is out of range.
Arguments	*value* is a column or expression that is compatible with a signed or unsigned DOUBLE PRECISION number, evaluating to a valid sine value.
Return value	A DOUBLE PRECISION number, in degrees.
Example	This snippet from a trigger converts a raw sine value to degrees:

```
...
IF (NEW.RAW_VALUE IS NOT NULL) THEN
  NEW.READING1 = ASIN(NEW.RAW_VALUE);
```

Related or similar functions	See also SIN( ), SINH( ), and other trigonometric functions.

IB_UDF	**ATAN(VALUE)**
Linux, Win32	Returns the arctangent (inverse of tangent) of the input value.
Arguments	*value* is a column or expression that is compatible with a signed or unsigned DOUBLE PRECISION number that is a valid tan(gent) value.
Return value	A DOUBLE PRECISION number, in degrees.
Example	This snippet from a trigger converts a raw tan(gent) value to an arc, in degrees:

```
...
IF (NEW.RAW_VALUE IS NOT NULL) THEN
  NEW.READING1 = ATAN(NEW.RAW_VALUE);
```

Related or similar functions	See also ATAN2( ), TAN( ), TANH( ), and other trigonometric functions.

IB_UDF	**ATAN2(VALUE1, VALUE2)**
Linux, Win32	Returns a value that is an arc, in degrees, calculated as the arctangent of the result of dividing one tangent by another.
Arguments	*value1* and *value2* are both numeric columns or expressions evaluating as DOUBLE PRECISION numbers that are valid tan(gent) values.
Return value	A DOUBLE PRECISION number, the result the arctangent of (*value1*/*value2*) in degrees.
Example	This PSQL snippet stores a value that is an arc, in degrees, calculated as the arctangent of the result of dividing one tangent by another:

```
...
UPDATE HEAVENLY_HAPPENINGS
  SET INCREASE_RATIO = ATAN2(INITIAL_TAN, FINAL_TAN)
  WHERE HAPPENING_ID = :happening_id;
```

Related or similar functions	See also ATAN( ), TAN( ), TANH( ).

IB_UDF	**COS(VALUE)**
Linux, Win32	Returns the cosine of *value*.
Arguments	*value* is a column or expression that is compatible with a signed or unsigned DOUBLE PRECISION number, evaluating to a value (in degrees) between –263 and 263.
Return value	A DOUBLE PRECISION number, or 0 if the input is out of range.
Notes	If *value* is greater than or equal to 263, or less than or equal to –263, there is a loss of significance in the result of the call, and the function generates a _TLOSS error and returns a 0.

IB_UDF	**COS(VALUE)** *(continued)*
Example	This snippet from a trigger calculates and stores the cosine of an angular measurement input in degrees:

```
...
IF (NEW.READING1 IS NOT NULL) THEN
  NEW.RDG_COSINE = COS(NEW.READING1);
```

Related or similar functions	See also SIN( ), COS( ), ACOS( ), COSH( ).

IB_UDF	**COSH(VALUE)**
Linux, Win32	Returns the hyperbolic cosine of *value*.
Arguments	*value* is a column or expression that is compatible with a signed or unsigned DOUBLE PRECISION number, evaluating to a value (in degrees) between –263 and 263.
Return value	A DOUBLE PRECISION number, or 0 if the input is out of range.
Notes	If *value* is greater than or equal to 263, or less than or equal to –263, there is a loss of significance in the result of the call, and the function generates a _TLOSS error and returns a 0.
Example	This snippet from a trigger calculates and stores the hyperbolic cosine of an angular measurement input in degrees:

```
...
IF (NEW.READING1 IS NOT NULL) THEN
  NEW.RDG_COS_HYP = COSH(NEW.READING1);
```

Related or similar functions	See also SINH( ), TANH( ), and other trigonometric functions.

IB_UDF	**COT(VALUE)**
Arguments	*value* is a column or expression that is compatible with a signed or unsigned DOUBLE PRECISION number, evaluating to a value (in degrees) between –263 and 263.
Return value	A DOUBLE PRECISION number, or 0 if the input is out of range.
Notes	If *value* is greater than or equal to 263, or less than or equal to –263, there is a loss of significance in the result of the call, and the function generates a _TLOSS error and returns a 0 ("a quiet NaN").
Example	This snippet from a trigger calculates and stores the cotangent of an angular measurement input in degrees:

```
...
IF (NEW.READING1 IS NOT NULL) THEN
  NEW.RDG_COTAN = COT(NEW.READING1);
```

Related or similar functions	See also TAN( ), ATAN( ), TANH( ).

IB_UDF	**SIN(VALUE)**
Linux, Win32	Returns the sine of *value*.
Arguments	*value* is a column or expression that is compatible with a signed or unsigned DOUBLE PRECISION number, evaluating to a value (in degrees) between –263 and 263.
Return value	A DOUBLE PRECISION number, or 0 if the input is out of range.
Notes	If *value* is greater than or equal to 263, or less than or equal to –263, there is a loss of significance in the result of the call, and the function generates a _TLOSS error and returns a 0.
Example	This snippet from a trigger calculates and stores the sine of an angular measurement input in degrees:

```
...
IF (NEW.READING1 IS NOT NULL) THEN
  NEW.RDG_SINE = SIN(NEW.READING1);
```

Related or similar functions	See also COS( ), ASIN( ), SINH( ).

IB_UDF	**SINH(VALUE)**
Linux, Win32	Returns the hyperbolic sine of *value*.
Arguments	*value* is a column or expression that is compatible with a signed or unsigned DOUBLE PRECISION number, evaluating to a value (in degrees) between –263 and 263.
Return value	A DOUBLE PRECISION number, or 0 if the input is out of range.
Notes	If *value* is greater than or equal to 263, or less than or equal to –263, there is a loss of significance in the result of the call, and the function generates a _TLOSS error and returns a 0.
Example	This snippet from a trigger calculates and stores the hyperbolic sine of an angular measurement input in degrees:

```
...
IF (NEW.READING1 IS NOT NULL) THEN
  NEW.RDG_SIN_HYP = SINH(NEW.READING1);
```

Related or similar functions	See also SIN( ), TANH( ), COSH( ).

IB_UDF	**TAN(VALUE)**
Linux, Win32	Returns the tangent of *value*.
Arguments	*value* is a column or expression that is compatible with a signed or unsigned DOUBLE PRECISION number, evaluating to a value (in degrees) between –263 and 263.
Return value	A DOUBLE PRECISION number, or 0 if the input is out of range.
Notes	If *value* is greater than or equal to 263, or less than or equal to –263, there is a loss of significance in the result of the call, and the function generates a _TLOSS error and returns a 0 ("quiet NaN").

IB_UDF	**TAN(VALUE)** *(continued)*
Example	This snippet from a trigger calculates and stores the tangent of an angular measurement input in degrees:

```
...
IF (NEW.READING1 IS NOT NULL) THEN
  NEW.RDG_TAN = TAN(NEW.READING1);
```

Related or similar functions	See also COT( ), ATAN( ), TANH( ).

IB_UDF	**TANH(VALUE)**
Linux, Win32	Returns the hyperbolic tangent of *value*.
Arguments	*value* is a column or expression that is compatible with a signed or unsigned DOUBLE PRECISION number, evaluating to a value (in degrees) between –263 and 263.
Return value	A DOUBLE PRECISION number, or 0 if the input is out of range.
Notes	If *value* is greater than or equal to 263, or less than or equal to –263, there is a loss of significance in the result of the call, and the function generates a _TLOSS error and returns a 0.
Example	This snippet from a trigger calculates and stores the hyperbolic tangent of an angular measurement input in degrees:

```
...
IF (NEW.READING1 IS NOT NULL) THEN
  NEW.RDG_TAN_HYP = TANH(NEW.READING1);
```

Related or similar functions	See also TAN( ), ATAN( ).

Data Formatting Routines

FREEUDFLIB	**F_DOLLARVAL(VALUE)**
Win32	Formats a floating-point number value into a string with a currency format, for example, "99,999,999.99", suitable for concatenating to currency symbols and other embellishments.
Arguments	*value* is a column or expression that evaluates to a number of type DOUBLE PRECISION or FLOAT.
Return value	A string of variable length.
Notes	Care will be needed with the likely precision of the input number, especially if it is to be derived from an expression. Wrong results can be expected if the result is passed to a CHAR or VARCHAR that is to small to accommodate it.

continued

913

FREEUDFLIB	**F_DOLLARVAL(VALUE)** *(continued)*
| Example | ```
SELECT '$' || F_DOLLARVAL(CAST(SUM(PURCHASE_AMT) AS DOUBLE
PRECISION)) ||' USD'
  AS TOTAL_SPEND
FROM MEMBER_ACCOUNT
WHERE MEMBER_ID = 440099;
``` |
| Related or similar functions | See also F_FixedPoint( ). |

FREEUDFLIB	**F_FIXEDPOINT(VALUE1, VALUE2)**
Win32	Formats the passed *value* as a fixed-point string with *DecimalPlaces* number decimal places.
Arguments	*value1*: A column or expression that evaluates to a number of a floating-point type: the number to be transformed. *value2*: A constant or expression that evaluates to an integer type: the number of decimal places to show in the output.
Return value	A string of variable length.
Notes	Care will be needed with the likely precision of the input number, especially if it is to be derived from an expression. Wrong results can be expected if the result is passed to a CHAR or VARCHAR that is to small to accommodate it.
| Example | ```
SELECT 'TOTAL YARDAGE: ' || F_FIXEDPOINT(SUM(YARDAGE), 3) || '
yds'
  AS TOTAL_YARDAGE
FROM PIECE_GOODS
 WHERE PRODUCT_ID = 100;
``` |
| Related or similar functions | See also F_DollarValue( ). |

FREEUDFLIB	**F_GENERATESNDXINDEX(VALUE)**
Win32	Given a string *value*, compute its *soundex* value.
Arguments	*value* is a column or expression that evaluates to a character type: a name for which a Soundex is to be generated.
Return value	A six-character Soundex index.
Notes	A simple Soundex algorithm is used to compute the Soundex index—it generates an algorithmic code that simplifies what the name "sounds like." You do not need to understand the algorithm to implement Soundex indexing.
| Example | The following Before Insert trigger snippet demonstrates how this function might be used to store a Soundex automatically as a search column in a membership register:<br>```
...
IF (NEW.LAST_NAME IS NOT NULL) THEN
  NEW.SOUNDEX_NAME = F_SNDXINDEX(NEW.LAST_NAME) ;
...
``` |
```

Solving Network
Problems

WHEN YOU HAVE PROBLEMS CONNECTING a client to the server, this collection of tests may help you to isolate the cause. If all else fails, never overlook the benefits of checking that network cables are actually plugged in and contacts are clean!

Checklist

The following checklist suggests some "basics" you can try.

Can You Connect to a Database at All?

If you are running Superserver on Windows or Classic server on POSIX, test whether you can make a local connection. (Superserver on POSIX and Classic server on Windows do not support local connections.)

1. Log into the console of the database server host, and run an application such as command-line **isql** or a Windows GUI management tool such as IB_SQL or IBAccess.

2. Attempt to connect to a database without specifying a host name—list just the path.

   POSIX (all in one command):

   ```
   ./isql /opt/firebird/examples/employee.fdb
        -user SYSDBA -password yourpwd
   ```

   Windows (all in one command):

   ```
   isql
    'c:\Program Files\Firebird\Firebird_1_5\examples\employee.fdb'
        -user SYSDBA -password yourpwd
   ```

   If it works, then the server is running and the database path is good. Otherwise, check passwords, and check that your application is actually finding the correct version of the client library.

Can You Connect to a Database on Local Loopback?

For any server version (other than Windows Embedded Server), you can simulate a client connecting to the server through the remote client interface by connecting in TCP/IP local loopback mode. This is actually the recommended mode for all local connections to full servers. If TCP/IP services are configured and running on the system, this should work, even if there is no network card installed.

First, open the *hosts* file in a text editor and make sure there is an entry like this:

```
127.0.0.1   localhost  # local loopback server
```

- On Windows, this file should be in the \drivers\etc directory beneath the %system% directory. On Windows 95/98, it is probably in the Windows directory itself.

- On POSIX, it should be in the /etc directory.

If the entry is missing, add it, save it, and close the file.

1. Log into the console of the database server host, and run an application such as command-line **isql** or a Windows GUI management tool such as IB_SQL or IBAccess.

2. Attempt to connect to a database without specifying a host name—list just the path.

   POSIX:

   ```
   ./isql localhost:/opt/firebird/examples/employee.fdb
       -user SYSDBA -password yourpwd
   ```

   Windows (all in one command):

   ```
   isql
   'localhost:c:\Program Files\Firebird\Firebird_1_5\examples\employee.fdb'
       -user SYSDBA -password yourpwd
   ```

If it works, then the server is running, TCP/IP is working, and the database path is good.

 NOTE POSIX systems do not use drive designators, but all server, path, and file names are case sensitive.

If local or local loopback connection fails and you are sure that the database name is spelled correctly, then something is wrong with the configuration of the server or the network. Read back through the chapters on server and network configuration and double-check your settings.

Is the Server Listening on the Firebird Port?

The *gds_db* service (port 3050) will not answer if the server process has not been started. See Table II-1 for instructions on starting the server.

Table II-1. Starting the Server

OS	INSTRUCTIONS
Superserver	
POSIX	In a command shell, *cd* to the Firebird /bin directory and enter the command *ibmgr –start*.
Windows: service	Use the Firebird Manager Control Panel applet and click Start or, at the command line, enter the command NET START FirebirdGuardianDefaultInstance. For v.1.0.*x*, enter the command NET START FirebirdGuardian. You may also try to start the service from the Services applet.
Windows: application	Start the Firebird Guardian or Firebird Server from the Start menu.
Classic Server	
POSIX	There is nothing to do. If the xinet daemon (or inet, on old systems) is running, it should start an instance of fb_inet_server (ib_inet_server for v.1.0.*x*) for you when you attempt to connect.
Windows: service	Go to a command window and type NET START FirebirdServerDefaultInstance. You may also try to start the service from the Services applet.
Windows: application	Start the Firebird Server from the Start menu. Note: Do not try to start Classic server from a Control Panel applet or by attempting to start the Guardian application.

Are You Getting Errors, Even Though the Service Is Running?

If the client reaches the server host and the gds_db service answers but still cannot attach to a database, you might see a "connection rejected" error. Possible causes to test are described in the following sections.

Is the Database on a Physically Local Drive?

A database file must not reside on an NFS filesystem, a mapped drive, or a share. When the ibserver process finds such a case, it denies the connection.

To correct this situation, move your database to a filesystem on a hard disk that is physically local to the database server and correct your connection string to reflect this.

Are the User Name and Password Valid?

The client application must use a user name and password combination that matches an entry in the security database *on the server*. This database must be located the Firebird installation root and it must be writable by the server process.

User names and passwords apply to the server, not to any specific database. If you transported the database from another server and there are roles and/or SQL privileges set up in it, you must set up the required users on the new server.

Does the Owner of the Server Process Have Sufficient Permissions to Open Files?

Filesystem permissions, including execute rights on directories, may be an issue on a POSIX platform. Directory permissions may be an issue on Windows NTFS partitions.

The server process may need more permissions to create files (e.g., firebird.log or interbase.log) in the Firebird root directory.

Trying to access databases in areas of the filesystem that are not configured for database access may be an issue in Firebird 1.5 and later—see the firebird.conf parameter *DatabaseAccess*.

NOTE   If you make a change to firebird.conf (v.1.5 +) or ibconfig/isc_config (v.1.0.*x*), you will need to stop and restart the server to have the changes take effect.

Can the Client Find the Host?

The error message "Unable to complete network request to host" appears when the Firebird client cannot establish a network connection to the server host. Some of the common causes are as follows:

The client cannot find the host in your network. The server you specify must be running on the network that you use. If the host name corresponds to a host that is inaccessible because of network interruption, or the host is not running, then the connection request cannot succeed.

Old drivers and/or client libraries are being used. You must use drivers (ODBC,

BDE, etc.) that are certified to work with your version of the Firebird server. For example, the SQL Explorer that ships with some Borland products probably won't work with Firebird because the BDE that it uses is too old.

The application is finding the wrong client library. All but the most recent builds of admin tools probably try to load libgds.so (POSIX clients) or gds32.dll (Windows clients) from the default system path. The Firebird 1.5 client is named libfbclient.so or fbclient.dll, and it is not located in the system path by default. Study the latest notes in the Firebird /doc directory and/or the root directory to find solutions.

An IP address is used in place of a server name. If you supplied an IP address instead of a host name (server name), the TCP/IP driver may be unable to resolve it or it may time out while trying to do so. This is usually a problem on Windows 95 and earlier versions of NT 4. See the previous notes about setting up an entry in the *hosts* file and apply it to all client machines.

The host's IP address is unstable. Systems that use dynamic IP addressing can cause the host's IP address to change without warning. Similar problems can occur if the host machine has more than one network interface card. Make hosts file entries on both the server and client machines to bind a server name to an IP address. Firebird 1.5 also provides the configuration option *RemoteBindAddress* to ensure that incoming connections can find the right channel to the Firebird Server.

There is a bad or missing gds_db entry in the services file. Firebird clients will look for the gds_db service by default at port 3050. If you reconfigured either the service symbol or the port number in the *services* file, you may have included insufficient information in the connection string for the linkage to be completed. Refer back to the section "Configuring the TCP/IP Port Service" in Chapter 2 if this could be an issue with your setup.

NOTE Problems with the port service are also likely if you have an InterBase server, or another Firebird server, running on the same host machine. Although it is possible to do this with v.1.5, it takes careful configuration and cannot be done straight out of the box.

The indicated network protocol is not available. The syntax of the Firebird connect string determines the network protocol the client uses to connect to the server host. If your server does not support the protocol indicated by your connect string, the connection attempt fails with the network error. For example, a Windows named pipes (NetBEUI) connection string will not work if the server is running on Windows 95/98, ME, or XP, nor if the server is running on Linux or another POSIX platform. Only TCP/IP will work with these platforms.

NOTE   The Firebird client library does not support the IPX/SPX network proto-col. Connection will fail if you attempt to use IPX/SPX by specifying the database connect string in the form server@volume:/path/database.fdb.

You are trying to connect to a share. It is not possible to connect to a database by way of a Windows, NFS, or SMB (Samba) shared device. The path must be an absolute native filesystem path as seen on the host.

The path string is inconsistent with an existing connection. A Firebird Superserver will block connection if the path string submitted is inconsistent with that used by an existing connection. Firebird added this mechanism to protect databases from a long-standing bug in the antecedent InterBase code, which is known to cause severe corruption to Windows-served databases.

CAUTION   Classic servers do not provide this protection. If you are using Classic server on Windows, make certain that different clients always connect using the exactly the same path string in their connection strings. The inconsistency arises because Windows will accept a drive designator without a following backslash, namely C:Databases\mydb.fdb instead of C:\Databases\mydb.fdb. It is not an issue on POSIX, which does not have the potential for this inconsistency.

Do You Need to Disable Automatic Internet Dialup on Windows?

Microsoft Windows operating systems provide by default a networking feature that is convenient for users who use a modem to connect to the Internet—any TCP/IP request that occurs on the system activates an automatic modem dialing program. It can be a problem on client systems that use TCP/IP to access a Firebird server on a local net-work. As soon as the client requests the TCP/IP service, the Windows automatic modem dialer fires up, interfering with network connections from client to server.

There are several ways to suppress the automatic modem dial feature. *No more than one* of these methods should be necessary to configure your system to work as you need it to.

Reorder Network Adapter Bindings

You probably have a dialup adapter and an Ethernet adapter for your local network. On Windows NT and Windows 98, you can reverse the bindings order of the two adapters to force the Ethernet adapter to service the TCP/IP request before the dialup adapter tries.

Access the Control Panel from the Start menu and choose Networking ➤ Bindings ➤ All Adapters ➤ Move Down to move the Ethernet adapter to the top of the list of bindings. The local Ethernet adapter satisfies any local TCP/IP requests and passes on any remaining requests—such as Internet requests—to the next adapter in the list, the dialup adapter.

Use Internet Explorer Configuration

If you have Microsoft Internet Explorer installed, you have an applet on the Control Panel that allows you to disable the autodial feature of the dialup network driver. Get to the Control Panel from the Start menu and choose Internet Options ➤ Connections.

There, you will find a series of check boxes giving autodial options. Actual wording varies from one Windows version to another. On Windows 2000, for example, you should select "Never dial a connection."

Disable Autodial in the Registry

To disable autodial, start the Registry editor (regedit.exe or regedt2.exe) and select the key

```
HKEY_CURRENT_USER\Software\Microsoft\Windows\CurrentVersion\Internet Settings
```

Find EnableAutoDial in the right panel and select Modify. Change its data value from 1 to 0.

Disable RAS AutoDial

On a services-capable Windows platform you can disable the RAS AutoDial service. To do so, start the Services Control Panel applet. On NT 4, it appears directly on the Control Panel. In later versions, the applet can be accessed through Administrative Tools, or its equivalent. Scroll down to Remote Access Auto Connection Manager (or Remote Access Dialup Manager on NT 4) and select it. Change the Startup option to Manual.

To stop the service right away, click Stop. To re-enable it, click Start.

Are You Still Stuck?

If you have a really sticky network problem, chances are that others have experienced something similar, too. The firebird-support list is a great place to go for solutions to those really elusive network problems. Refer to Appendix XII for subscribing details.

APPENDIX III

Application Interfaces

THE "NATIVE" INTERFACE TO FIREBIRD TO the client library is through the C functions and parameter structures exposed by the API. The C header file *ibase.h* is distributed with Firebird, in the /include directory. This header file can be used when writing C programs that use the client library, but it is also a useful reference when developing interfaces to the library from other languages.

The JayBird JDBC Drivers

The JayBird JDBC drivers for Firebird are a fully JDBC 2.0–compliant abstraction of the Firebird API that can be used in virtually any IDE that supports JDBC drivers; for example, Eclipse and Borland JBuilder.

The drivers run in Java 2 JRE 1.3.1 and Java 2 JRE 1.4.*x*, and can be used with all of the popular interface layers supporting JDBC 2.0, the JDBC 2.0 Standard Extensions, and JCA 1.0. Examples include JBoss 3.2.3, WebLogic 7.0, WebLogic 8.1, ColdFusion MX, Hibernate (transparent persistence layer), and TJDO.

The latest version, JayBird 1.5, was due for release in spring 2004.

Support for Firebird's two-phase commit accords with the standard contract for participating in distributed transactions in Java, supporting the JCA framework and XADataSource implementations. JayBird accords with the JDBC "one-transaction-per-connection" model. It does not surface multiple transactions per connection, although they are utilized invisibly within the JCA framework. JDBC does not support Firebird events or arrays.

Licensing: JayBird is open source, distributed free of charge under a modified BSD license.

Download: In your browser, go to http://sourceforge.net/projects/firebird/ and scroll down the page to find the row containing *firebird-jca-jdbc-driver*. Click the Download link at the right to go to the download page, where you can select the kit you want from the list under *firebird-jca-jdbc-driver*—for example, FirebirdSQL-1.*x*.zip.

Support: The developer and user support forum is at http://groups.yahoo.com/group/firebird-java. A large, actively maintained FAQ is distributed with the JayBird installations and is available at several community websites, including http://www.ibphoenix.com/main.nfs?a=ibphoenix&l=;FAQS;NAME='JayBird'.

ODBC

Firebird ODBC/JDBC Driver

This is a free, open source JDBC-compliant ODBC driver for Firebird and InterBase 6.*x*, sponsored originally by IBPhoenix and community donations and released free (in all senses) under the Initial Developer's Public License. Versions of the driver libraries are available for Windows, Linux (unixODBC and iODBC), FreeBSD, and Solaris. The latest version when this book went to press (v1.2.0060) complies with ODBC 3.0 specifications. It supports all versions and models of Firebird, including the v.1.5 Embedded Server for Windows.

Applications can be written to attach to Firebird databases optionally through a variety of DSN descriptors, each implementing a different client version. Attachments can be concurrent within a single application, if required. A two-phase commit transaction can support up to ten connections. Support for multiple transactions per connection was in development at the time this book went to press. Firebird events are not supported.

Makefiles are distributed for building the driver from C sources in gcc 2.96 Linux and later, gcc freeBSD, gcc for Windows (MinGW), cc Solaris, BCC55, and MsVC6. IDE projects with makefiles are available for DEV-C++ 4.8 and later and MsVC7.

The Firebird ODBC driver—said to be the fastest available for Firebird and InterBase—works well with Open Office 1.1.0, Microsoft (Excel, VC6, VC7, VB6, VFP6, MsQry32, Access, etc.), and any components supporting ADO. It supports encrypted passwords and scrollable cursors. Interface schemas include

- Universal components (Excel, VFP6, VB6, etc.), including support for Array columns, selectable and executable stored procedures with replaceable parameters (CALL MYPROC ?), {fn} capability, batches, and fully qualified column identifiers.

- ADO ➤ OLEDB ➤ ODBC Manager (odbc32.dll) ➤ OdbcJdbc

- OLEDB(MSDADC.DLL) ➤ ODBC Manager ➤ OdbcJdbc

- User program interfacing with ODBC Manager ➤ OdbcJdbc

The driver has AutoQuotedIdentifier support for full query compatibility with Microsoft query interfaces.

Download shared libraries:
http://www.ibphoenix.com/main.nfs?a=ibphoenix&page=ibp_60_odbc

Latest builds:
http://cvs.sourceforge.net/viewcvs.py/firebird/OdbcJdbc/Builds/

Latest snapshots: http://www.praktik.km.ua (Vladimir Tsvigun)

Support and development forum: Join the list at
https://lists.sourceforge.net/lists/listinfo/firebird-odbc-devel

Other ODBC Drivers

XTG ODBC Driver

This is a free, open source Firebird/InterBase 6.*x* ODBC driver for Windows, conforming to the ODBC 3 API CORE level and distributed under LGPL licensing. Version 1.0.0 (beta 15) may contain some bugs but is usable. The binary is distributed as a full Windows installer.

> **Download binary**: http://www.xtgsystems.com
>
> **Source**: http://ofbodbc.sourceforge.net/drvinfo.html

Gemini ODBC Driver

This is a commercial ODBC driver for Windows and Linux, conforming to the Call Level Interface (CLI) specification designed by SQL Access Group and then adopted by X/Open and ISO/IEC as an appendix to the current SQL language standard. Currently in version 2.2 beta, the driver conforms to the ODBC specification described in the *ODBC Programmer's Reference*, version 3.51. You can find more information and a free trial download at http://www.ibdatabase.com.

Easysoft ODBC Driver

This is a commercial InterBase ODBC driver for Windows and Linux. It supports UNICODE on some platforms. More information, a trial download, and a support forum subscription can be found at http://www.easysoft.com/products/interbase.

The Firebird .NET Provider

The open source Firebird .NET Provider is a data interface layer designed to work with applications developed in Microsoft .NET environments. The latest stable version (v.1.5.2) supports all versions of Firebird, both Classic server and Superserver for development in IDEs such as

- Microsoft Visual Studio 2002 and 2003

- SharpDevelop (http://www.icsharpcode.net/OpenSource/SD)

- Borland C#Builder

- Borland Delphi .NET (Delphi 8)

- MonoDevelop (http://www.monodevelop.com, in testing)

V.1.2, at the beta 2 stage when this book went to press, likely to be released in the summer of 2004, supports the Firebird 1.5 Embedded Server for Windows and Firebird events.

By design—a limitation of the ADO.NET architecture—the Provider does not support multiple transactions per connection or two-phase commit.

Language support includes C#, VB .NET, Microsoft Visual C++ .NET, Delphi .NET, and ASP.NET or any .NET language. It is known to be compatible with many other specialized .NET products, including Gentle.NET (`http://www.mertner.com/projects/gentle`), NHibernate (`http://nhibernate.sourceforge.net`), and aspxDelphi.net PORTAL & STORE (`http://www.aspxdelphi.net`). Firebird support is being added to the next version of the object-relational mapper framework LLBLGen Pro (`http://www.llblgen.com/defaultgeneric.aspx`).

Supported platforms are Microsoft .NET 1.0 and 1.1 (Windows only) and mono (`http://www.go-mono.com`), tested so far on Windows and Linux. Plans are for the Firebird .NET Provider to follow the course of mono as it becomes available for other platforms (Solaris, FreeBSD, HP-UX, and Mac OS X).

Downloads: Links to downloads and documentation are at `http://www.ibphoenix.com/main.nfs?a=ibphoenix&page=ibp_download_dotnet`.

Development and user support forum: Join at `http://lists.sourceforge.net/lists/listinfo/firebird-net-provider`. List archives are available to list subscribers at `http://sourceforge.net/mailarchive/forum.php?forum=firebird-net-provider`.

IBPP for C++ Development

This is a free, open source C++ client interface class library for Firebird Server versions 1.0, 1.5, and beyond that is free of any tool-specific dependencies. It is designed to enable Firebird access from any C++ application, whether developed as non-visual (CORBA/COM objects, other libraries of classes and functions, procedural "legacy" code) or in visual or RAD environments. IBPP provides a pure DSQL interface to Firebird through easy-to-use C++ classes for database administration and data manipulation.

The latest version at the time this book went to press was v.2.3, supporting all Firebird versions and client/server models (Superserver, Classic server, Embedded Server) with full support for multiple transactions, cross-database transactions, and Firebird events.

IBPP supports only pure, standard C++ code. The class library is distributed as source code that builds out of the box in the following compilers:

- Windows: Borland C++Builder 6, Borland free command-line compiler, MSVC 6, MSVC 7, Digital Mars C++, MingW, and CygWin.

- POSIX: gcc 3.2 or higher.

- BCCP should compile successfully on many other configurations, with a little tweaking, mostly in makefiles, to take issues such as "endianness" into account.

Licensing: Mozilla 1.1, derivative.

Downloads and support details: http://www.ibpp.org.

Support forum: Subscribe to http://lists.sourceforge.net/lists/listinfo/ ibpp-discuss.

Delphi, Kylix, and Borland C++Builder

IB Objects

This product encompasses two long-established systems of components for Firebird and InterBase that allow developers using the Borland IDE tools on Windows and Linux (Delphi, Kylix, and C++Builder) to exploit all of Firebird's features. One system is compatible with Borland's TDataset libraries and other third-party components that depend on the TDataset architecture. The other, known as "native IBO," is based on an original class hierarchy that has no dependency on TDataset architecture.

The current version is 4.3Xx, where the "Xx's" represent sub-releases and patch releases. It supports all Pascal versions of Delphi from v.3, all Kylix versions and C++Builder 3 and higher, and all versions and client/server models of Firebird.

The TDataset-compatible components are designed to emulate Borland's VCL data access components to the degree that a search-and-replace tool is sufficient to convert obsolete BDE application code directly to a working version under IBO in a few minutes.

The native IBO system includes its own datasource class and a range of "data-driven" data-aware controls. Unlike the TDataset-based components, native IBO can be used with low-end editions of the Borland tools. Several reporting tools provide support for the native components.

Both systems fully support live queries, multiple concurrent transactions and cross-database transactions within an application, Firebird events, unidirectional and scrollable cursors, and callbacks. The native system—which is compatible in the non-visual layer with the TDataset system—supports immediate execution, caching of DML events across application boundaries, and extra operational modes, including incremental search.

Support: Community oriented, with a support list, online FAQ querying a Firebird back-end database, community code repository, community update site for subscribers, and a large library of downloadable documentation. Join the list at http://groups.yahoo.com/community/ibobjects. The website is http://www.ibobjects.com; the subscribers' site is http://community.ibobjects.com.

Licensing: Trustware—full source (not open source) comes with commercial subscriptions or non-commercial free licensing to charities, open source projects, and students.

Evaluation: Fully functioning IB Objects with partial source, for unlimited trial, with nag screen in executables run outside the IDE, is always kept up to date. It can be downloaded from `http://www.ibobjects.com`.

FIBPlus

Another mature set of components for Delphi, Kylix, and C++Builder, FIBPlus was developed using FreeIBComponents as its basis, originally a set of freeware data access components. FIBPlus has now evolved into a fully commercial product, claiming maximum simplicity and flexibility of use.

Based on the Borland TDataset architecture, FIBPlus offers full compatibility with many commercial and open source controls. It offers an easy conversion route from the Borland InterBaseXpress components.

The latest version of FIBPlus is v.5.3. Trial versions are available for all supported IDEs: Delphi 5–7, C++Builder 5–6, and Kylix 3. Older FIBPlus versions are still available on request for lower versions of the Borland products.

FIBPlus supports all versions and client/server models of Firebird. It is compatible with all third-party tools and components that depend on the TDataset architectures. Some products provide custom FIBPlus support.

Support: The company runs both English and Russian newsgroups for user support and also has a "trouble ticket" system for one-on-one help. The newsgroup addresses are

- English language: `news://news-devrace.com/fibplus.en`

- Russian language: `news://news-devrace.com/fibplus.ru`

Website: `http://www.devrace.com`, for product details and trouble tickets.

Licensing: Not specified.

Others

Several other suites of components are available for interfacing with Firebird.

UIB Components

This is a set of open source, lightweight data access components and DBXpress drivers for Firebird, InterBase, and Yaffil.[1] It's free, under the Mozilla Public License. These components work not just with the Borland tools (Delphi, Kylix, C++Builder), but also with the open source Pascal development environments Lazarus and FreePascal.

---

1. Yaffil was a proprietary fork of Firebird for Windows. It was made open source near the end of 2003 and is being merged into the Firebird 2 codebase.

Platforms are Windows, Linux, and FreeBSD. Binaries and source can be found at `http://www.progdigy.com/UIB`.

Firebird DBXpress Drivers

Upscene Productions (`http://www.upscene.com`) produces low-cost DBXpress drivers for use with Delphi, Kylix, and C++Builder. Part of the proceeds of sales of these drivers goes toward fund-raising for Firebird Project developer grants.

Zeos Components

These are open source components for development and administration of database applications, including Firebird.

- Zeos Database Objects: Library of Delphi components for quick access to Firebird (and other RDBMSs).

- Zeos Controls: Delphi visual components library for use with Zeos Database Objects.

- Zeos Class Library: Library of classes for developing C++ applications on POSIX platforms. It includes interactive GUI utilities for querying, administration, and working with BLOBs.

Licensing is GPL, version currently 6.1.3. For more information, see `http://zcoslib.sourceforge.net`.

There are many more component packages available. See the listings at `http://www.ibphoenix.com/main.nfs?a=ibphoenix&page=ibp_dev_comps` and also search Google.

InterBaseXpress

InterBaseXpress (IBX) comprises open source connectivity and service components that are distributed by Borland with some of their Delphi, Kylix, and C++Builder products. Bug-fixed versions are available from the Code Central repository at `http://community.borland.com`. Do not use the versions that shipped with Delphi 5 and 6 and Kylix 2—they were very buggy beta versions that were capable of causing various kinds of data corruption. Later open source versions are free and can be used with Firebird 1.0.*x*. Some users have encountered problems using the database connectivity components with Firebird 1.5. IBX is not an ideal choice to use with Firebird in the long term because its developer has indicated that he will not include adaptations to recognize differences as Firebird and InterBase diverge.

IBOAdmin

This is a set of wrapper components for the Firebird Services API (backup, statistics, security, etc.) based on the code originally distributed as the IBX Service components. It is open source and requires IB Objects. IBOAdmin is available free from http://www.mengoni.it.

PHP

PHP has proved to be a very satisfying platform for developing web front-ends to Firebird databases, using the php-interbase extensions. PHP is currently stable at version 4.3.6 with PHP 5.0—a major rewrite—at a late beta stage. PHP 5.0 has added a number of new Firebird-compatible functions. Search on "ibase" at http://www.php.net/ChangeLog-5.php#5.0.0RC1 and subsequent update pages.

PHP (http://www.php.net) and Apache Web Server (http://httpd.apache.org) are an inseparable pair for developing Firebird applications for the Web. Platforms are Windows (CGI, ISAPI) and Linux (CGI). Firebird PHP Windows aficionados recommend using the CGI version on Windows Server 2003 and the ISAPI version on Windows 2000, for performance.

The php-interbase extensions run fine with all versions of Firebird on both Apache 1 and 2, with one implementation issue. PHP does not handle 64-bit integers (BIGINT type) natively, so you needs to convert BIGINT values to strings. It is probably not going to be addressed in PHP 5, either. A new function to fetch a Firebird generator value, ibase_gen_id(), returns an integer.

Like other generic data access interfaces, PHP appears to favor the one transaction/one connection model. However, it does support multiple transactions. PHP takes care of committing incomplete transactions. Firebird two-phase commit and events are coming in PHP 5.

On Windows, the php-interbase extensions are activated in the PHP.ini file after installation. On Linux, the extensions must be built from sources in order to run.

Many API functions are accessible, including user management. Lutz Bruckner built an admin interface (see http://ibwebadmin.sf.net), which suggests a full complement of access is possible.

Several abstraction layers are available for plugging pages into Firebird, including the ADODB classes (http://freshmeat.net/projects/adodb) and the more compact ezSQL (http://php.justinvincent.com). PEAR-DB is another abstraction layer, which forms part of the PHP project. A wide choice of PHP editors is available, too. See http://www.php-editors.com/review.

IDE: Eclipse (http://www.eclipse.org), with phpEclipse (http://www.phpeclipse.de/tiki-view_articles.php), provides debugging and a nice range of editing tools. Eclipse runs on both Linux and Windows, and includes a built-in CVS client, support for documentation, and plug-in capability (http://www.eclipse-plugins.info/eclipse/plugins.jsp). Eclipse 3 is due out in summer 2004.

Support: Firebird PHP developers run a small but busy peer support list. Subscribe at `http://www.yahoogroups.com/community/firebird-php`.

- For ADODB: `http://phplens.com/lens/lensforum/topics.php?id=4`

- For phpEclipse: `http://www.phpeclipse.de/tiki-forums.php`

Resources: The best starting point for PHP is the manual (`http://www.php.net/docs.php`). The site `http://www.hotscripts.com/PHP/index.html` is recommended as a source of myriad scripts and classes that Firebird can be plugged into.

Python

KInterbasDB is a Python extension package that implements Python Database API 2.0–compliant support for Firebird. In addition to the minimal feature set of the standard Python Database API, KInterbasDB exposes the entire native Firebird client API.

The newest version available is a late pre-release v.3.1, declared to be production ready. The package is distributed free under a permissive BSD-style license that both commercial and non-commercial users should find agreeable.

Support, downloads, online documentation, and information: `http://kinterbasdb.sourceforge.net/`

Perl

The DBI is a database interface module for Perl. It defines a set of methods, variables, and conventions that provide a consistent database interface independent of the actual database being used.

DBD::InterBase is an open source DBI driver for Firebird and InterBase, hosted at SourceForge (`http://sourceforge.net/projects/dbi-interbase`). The project welcomes both developers and users.

Support: Join the mailing list at `http://lists.sourceforge.net/mailman/listinfo/dbi-interbase-devel`.

Downloads: Go to `http://www.cpan.org/modules/by-module/DBD` for the latest stable release; visit `http://dbi.interbase.or.id` for both stable and development releases.

Database Repair How-to

YOU HAVE TO TRY VERY HARD TO CORRUPT a Firebird database—it's designed to survive the hard knocks that break databases in other systems. You will know a database has been corrupted if you cannot connect to it or back it up and a message in the firebird log, or from *gbak –b*, tells you that there is corruption, or some other message reports a checksum error.

If you want to understand how corruption might have occurred in your database, refer back to the section "How to Corrupt a Firebird Database," at the end of Chapter 15.[1]

Eight Steps to Recovery

This appendix describes the steps you need to take, using the command-line tools **gfix** and **gbak**, to try to recover undamaged data from some kinds of corruption. Be aware, however, that there are certain kinds of severe corruption that this procedure cannot fix. Refer to Appendix XII for resources available under those circumstances.

To use **gfix** and **gbak** for this procedure, *cd* to the Firebird /bin directory on the server machine.

Get Exclusive Access

The first thing to do when corruption is reported is to get all users off the system. Do not permit anyone to attempt any further work. Continuing to try to use the database might make the recoverable irrecoverable.

Database validation requires exclusive access to the database, otherwise you will see this message when you try to run **gfix**:

```
OBJECT database_name IS IN USE
```

The same message may appear if you are the only user but have another transaction in progress. The **isql** utility, for example, uses up to three concurrent transactions. Stop **isql** or any other admin applications you might have running.

---

1. At the time of this writing, the author heard of the first case of a new way to corrupt databases. The victim disregarded all advice and placed a database in an NFS directory. He then proceeded to connect clients to it via two Firebird 1.5 Classic servers on different host machines, neither of which owned the hard disk where the database was. He got corruption "in spades."

To get exclusive access, perform a database shutdown, under the SYSDBA account or the account of the database owner. Instructions are in Chapter 39. For example, this command will lock out all other login attempts and force a shutdown in 2 minutes:

```
gfix -sh -force 120 -user SYSDBA -password yourpword
```

Make a Working File Copy

At this point, **gbak** cannot back up a database containing corrupt data. Once you have exclusive access, make a *filesystem copy* (not a **gbak** file) of the database file. Use the **cp** command on POSIX or, on Windows, the **copy** command or an equivalent copy/paste action in the GUI interface. Make sure there are *no* users connected at this point—not even yourself!

For example, on Windows, in the database directory:

```
copy damaged.fdb repaircopy.fdb
```

CAUTION Even if you can restore a mended database that reported checksum errors, the extent of data loss may be difficult to determine. If this is a concern, you may want to locate an earlier backup from which you can retrieve missing data after validating and repairing corrupt structures in your current database.

Work with repaircopy.fdb.

Perform the Validation

The **gfix** switches –v[alidate] and –f[ull] are used first, to check record and page structures. This checking process reports corrupt structures and releases unassigned record fragments or "orphan pages" (i.e., pages that are allocated but unassigned to any data structures).

```
gfix -v -full {path}repaircopy.fdb -user SYSDBA -password yourpword
```

The switch –n[o update] can be used with –v, to validate and report on corrupt or misallocated structures without attempting to fix them:

```
gfix -v -n {path}repaircopy.fdb -user SYSDBA -password yourpword
```

If persistent checksum errors are getting in the way of validation, use the –i[gnore] switch to have the validation ignore them:

```
gfix -v -n -i {path}repaircopy.fdb -user SYSDBA -password yourpword
```

Mend Corrupted Pages

If **gfix** validation reports damage to data, the next step is to mend (or repair) the database by putting those structures out of the way.

The –m[end] switch marks corrupt records as unavailable, so they will be skipped during a subsequent backup. Include a –f[ull] switch to request *mend* for all corrupt structures and an –i[gnore] switch to bypass checksum errors during the mend.

```
gfix -mend -full -ignore {path}repaircopy.fdb -user SYSDBA -password yourpword
```

or, briefly

```
gfix -m -f -i {path}repaircopy.fdb -user SYSDBA -password yourpword
```

Validate After –mend

After the –mend command completes its work, again do

```
gfix -v -full {path}repaircopy.fdb -user SYSDBA -password yourpword
```

to check whether any corrupt structures remain.

Clean and Recover the Database

Next, do a full backup and restore using **gbak**, even if errors are still being reported. Include the –v[erbose] switch to watch progress. In its simplest form, the backup command would be (all in one command):

```
gbak -b -v -i {path}repaircopy.fdb {path}repaircopy.fbk -user SYSDBA
   -password yourpword
```

Dealing with gbak Complications During Backup

Garbage collection problems might cause **gbak** to fail. If this happens, try again, adding the –[g] switch to signify "no garbage collection":

```
gbak -b -v -i  -g {path}repaircopy.fdb {path}repaircopy.fbk -user SYSDBA
   -password yourpword
```

If there is corruption in record versions associated with a limbo transaction, you may need to include the –limbo switch:

```
gbak -b -v -i  -g -l {path}repaircopy.fdb {path}repaircopy.fbk -user SYSDBA
   -password yourpword
```

Restore the Cleaned Backup As a New Database

Now create a new database from the backup, using the –v[erbose] switch to watch what is being restored:

```
gbak -create -v {path}repaircopy.fbk{path} reborn.fdb -user SYSDBA
    -password yourpword
```

Validate the Restored Database

Verify that restoring the database fixed the problems by validating the restored database with the –n[o update] switch:

```
gfix -v -full {path}reborn.fdb -user SYSDBA -password yourpword
```

If there are problems on restore, you may need to consider further attempts using other **gbak** switches to eliminate the sources of these problems, for example:

- The –i[nactive] switch will eliminate problems with damaged indexes, by restoring without activating any indexes. Afterward, you can activate the indexes manually, one at a time, until the problem index is found.

- The –o[ne_at_a_time] switch will restore and commit each table, one by one, allowing you restore good tables and bypass the problem ones.

How to Proceed If Problems Remain

If the preceding steps do not work, but you are still able to access the corrupt database, you may still be able to transfer table structures and data from the damaged database to a new one, using the **qli** (Query Language Interpreter) tool. **qli** is in your Firebird /bin directory, and a syntax manual in Adobe PDF format can be downloaded from http://www.ibphoenix.com/downloads/qli_syntax.pdf. **qli** is an old tool, but it still works when you need it. Search the Web for how-tos on pumping data between databases using **qli**.

Look in Appendix V for links to do-it-yourself repair tools that might be able to get you further in your quest to recover damaged data.

There are companies that supply database recovery and repair services for severely damaged Firebird and InterBase databases—although, at the time of this writing, the author had yet to hear of a Firebird database that had been corrupted to the state of needing a magician!

Administration Tools

One of the "pleasant problems" a newbie user of Firebird has is to choose tools. Why? Because the Firebird community is loaded with a plethora of excellent tools, both commercial and free. Nearly all commercial vendors provide free trial versions, so your worst problem is to find the one that suits you best!

Graphical Admin Desktops

The following list is but a sampling of some of the more popular items. For full listings, see http://www.ibphoenix.com/main.nfs?a=ibphoenix&page=ibp_admin_tools.

Database Workbench

Database Workbench can connect to any Firebird server, on any platform. It features a consistent visual interface, a browser for metadata and dependencies, stored procedure debugging, data migration tools, import/export, a BLOB editor, user and permissions management, a test data generator, metadata search, a code snippet repository, metadata printout, automatic trigger generation for auto-incrementing keys and case-insensitive search columns, and more.

Environment: Windows.

Other information: Commercial software by Upscene Productions. Free trial available at http://www.upscene.com.

IBExpert

This feature-loaded administration tool has a hyperlinking feature and history replay in all editors. It also offers a SQL monitor, a visual query builder, selectable output options for queries, background query execution, direct CSV data import, code completion, debug, trace and tips for PSQL, customizable keyboard templates, BLOB editing and display (including images and hex), users and permissions editors, an "autogrant" option for automatic permissions creation on new objects, entity modeling, a database comparer with creation of update scripts, plan and performance profiling, scripting tools including scripted transfer of BLOB data, pre-defined and user-defined schema reports, a backup wizard, communications diagnosis, multiple-language support, and more.

Environment: Windows.

Other information: Commercial software by H-K Software GmbH. Free Personal Edition available. Educational version also available.

BlazeTop

BlazeTop features an unusual, modular interface to the basic tools that helps to solve "feature overload"—you install only the modules you want to use. It includes a smart text editor that creates statement templates and also includes schema management, a SQL Monitor, interactive data editing, a Delphi-style object inspector for database objects, and explicit transaction control. It can run multiple database sessions simultaneously.

Environment: Windows.

Other information: Commercial software by Devrace. Free trial available at http://www.devrace.com/en/blazetop.

IBAccess

This cross-platform database manager provides a graphical front-end for implementing all tasks that Firebird distros do with the command-line tools, making it compatible with Classic servers as well as Superservers. It offers online help, desktop configuration per user or per server, and the ability to run multiple instances to perform lengthy tasks in background. With it, you can also monitor SQL statements during execution; browse and manage data objects, permissions, and BLOBs; execute queries with replaceable parameters; and execute scripts step by step.

Environments: Linux, Windows.

Other information: Open source (Mozilla Public License), free software by Toni Martir. Sources available. See http://www.ibaccess.org.

IBAdmin

This is an online and offline database manager, featuring visual database design/CASE tools, a SQL debugger, Code-Insight, code completion, database compare with optional synchronized script update, macro capability, script runner tools, version control for PSQL modules, a database explorer tool, and a plug-in feature for adding your own tools (sample supplied).

Environments: Windows, Linux (cut-down version).

Other information: Commercial software by Sqlly Development. Products available in professional, standard, and "lite" versions. Trial downloads available at http://www.sqlly.com.

IB_SQL

A lighter weight multi-tool utility, this is a replacement for the old Borland WISQL, with a "live" browser for data and metadata, metadata extract, datapump, export, user management, SQL monitoring and profiling, scripting, interactive querying with replaceable parameters, and plan display. Features "layouts" that automatically save login details for different databases and a Query Forms tool for saving specific queries for future reuse.

IB_SQL can be downloaded as a binary or customized and compiled from Delphi sources distributed in the IB Objects evaluation kits (IB_SQL.dpr, in the root directory). If compiled this way, IB_SQL will display a modal nag screen when started outside the Delphi or C++Builder IDE.

Environment: Windows.

Other information: Free software. Sources are subject to Trustware licensing. See http://www.ibobjects.com for both the IB_SQL binary and latest IBO evaluation kit.

IBOConsole

This is the re-engineered version of the IBOConsole utility that shipped with the original InterBase 6 open source package, with enhancements, bug fixes, and support for Firebird developments. It implements the Services API (user management, backup, etc.) and interactive query and script features. The API abstraction layer is IB Objects instead of Borland's InterBaseXpress.

Environment: Windows.

Other information: Free, open source (InterBase Public License) software by Lorenzo Mengoni. Sources available. Downloads and details at http://www.mengoni.it.

Backup Tools

DBak

DBak is an alternative database backup utility that does not use **gbak** or the Services API. It backs up a database into a new one, using DDL scripts and data transfer. Its API abstraction layer is IB Objects.

Because DBak operates within a single snapshot transaction, it provides a reliable snapshot of database state at the start of the backup. As well as backup and restore, DBak can perform a direct rebuild, generating a working copy of a database without any intermediate stage.

Processing can be customized in many ways, making it particularly useful to assist with a controlled recovery from some kinds of corruption and for automating schema upgrades. The distribution includes both a graphical user interface and a console version for batch and scheduled operations.

Environment: Windows.

Other information: Executables and help file, by Telesis Computing Pty Ltd, are free. The full source version is available for a small fee under Trustware licensing. Information and download can be found at `http://www.telesiscomputing.com.au/dbk.htm`. Note that this is not **gbak** and it is important to read the documentation and understand the differences.

gbak BackupRunner

This is an elegant, small footprint, graphical front-end for the Firebird **gbak** utility. It does not use the Services API, providing instead direct flags to set **gbak** switches. The utility optionally generates the verbose output directly into a text window, which can be saved as a log. It requires gbak.exe to be present.

Environment: Windows.

Other information: Free binary by Marco Wobben. Information and download can be found at `http://www.bcp-software.nl/backuprunner`.

Time To Backup

This is a suite of programs for setting up scheduled Firebird backups as a Windows service or a Linux daemon on one or more host machines. It comes with a GUI configuration and control interface for local or remote use. A console-only configuration interface is also available for Linux.

Environments: Windows, Linux.

Other information: Open source software, under LGPL licensing, by Sqlly Development. The tools are distributed free with full Object Pascal sources. For information and downloads, see `http://www.sqlly.com/timetobackup.asp`.

Miscellaneous

IBSurgeon Database Repair Tools

The IBSurgeon company distributes a range of tools for diagnosing and repairing corrupted databases. Their diagnostic tools, IBFirstAid Diagnostician and IBSurgeon Viewer, can downloaded free. The tools that perform the actual repairs need to be purchased. Some kinds of damage are impossible to recover by an automatic tool, but the company claims that a damaged database can be brought back into production in 70 percent of cases.

To read about the tools and for advice about how to proceed when you have a corrupted database that **gfix** won't fix, see `http://www.ib-aid.com`.

Interbase DataPump

Interbase DataPump allows you to pump data and migrate from any ADO/BDE/ODBC sources (such as dBase, Paradox, Access, MSSQL, Sybase, Oracle, DB2, InterBase, etc.) and native Firebird databases into a new Firebird database simply and with full control of the process. It calculates important details like object creation order and dependencies.

The tool can generate a complete SQL script to create a Firebird database based on the metadata of an ADO/BDE/ODBC source, including full mapping of data types, indexes, keys, auto-incrementing fields, referential integrity, and validation checks. It can create the required generators and triggers for auto-inc columns and set the proper initial values.

Environment: Windows.

Other information: Free software from Clever Components. More information and downloads can be found at `http://www.clevercomponents.com/products/datapump/ibdatapump.asp`.

Advanced Data Generator for Firebird

Advanced Data Generator is a tool for generating test data that simulates real-life data. It features random address generation, referential integrity support, and BLOB support. It comes with a large data library of company, personal, and geographic names, and it can also use your own custom or legacy data. Multiple projects can be queued.

Data-generation environment: Windows.

Other information: Commercial software by Upscene Productions. Information and trial download can be found at `http://www.upscene.com`.

Permissions Managers

Try these tools for simplifying user management, roles administration, and SQL permissions:

- **Grant Manager**, by Eadsoft, at `http://www.eadsoft.com/english/products/grantmanager`. This Windows shareware program is available as a 30-day "try-and-buy" stand-alone utility or as a Delphi SDK.

- **Grant Master**, by Studio Plus Inc. More information on this Windows shareware program and a download of a 30-day trial are available at `http://www.studioplus.com.ua/GrantMaster/GrantMaster.phtml`.

Where to Look for More Tools and Information

The "master list" for third-party tools can be found in the Downloads ➤ Contributed section of http://www.ibphoenix.com.

Tools developers also post announcements to the mailing list firebird-tools@yahoogroups.com. You can subscribe to the list by going to http://groups.yahoo.com/group/firebird-tools or simply browse the mirror newsgroup (egroups.ib-tools) at news://news.atkin.com.

Don't overlook a Google search as a way to locate tools for specific tasks. Generally, entering the words "firebird," "interbase," and a keyword identifying the task will generate several good leads.

APPENDIX VI

The Sample Database

THE SAMPLE DATABASE IS INSTALLED with Firebird, in the directory /examples, beneath the Firebird root. In Firebird 1.0, it is a dialect 1 database and its name is *employee.gdb*. In v.1.5, it is dialect 3 and is named *employee.fdb*. Structurally, it is the same database.

This database was created many years ago, probably by trainee support staff. It is not a model of good design. Moreover, it does not have a default character set. However, it does, at least, provide a set of data to experiment with.

The sample database comes complete with a backup (employee.gbk and employee.fbk, respectively) so, no matter how you mess it up, you can always restore a fresh copy.

Building the Employee Database from Scripts

When a Firebird installer kit is made, the employee database is built and backed up each time from scripts. The scripts *empddl.sql* (which builds the metadata) and *empdml.sql* (which populates the database) are available from the Downloads area of http://www.apress.com, with a few amendments:

- A default character set has been included, set to ISO8859_1, which is compatible with the English-language data in empdml.sql.

- A SET SQL DIALECT 3 statement has been added since, without it, some tools will create it as dialect 1 and any experiments you try with Firebird's native SQL dialect will fail or have unexpected results.

- Full path strings for the CREATE DATABASE statement have been included to reflect properly how real people create databases. The "live" string will create the database on a POSIX server in a directory named /data/examples. The commented string will create the database in C:\data\examples. Uncomment, comment, and modify to suit your own needs.

- The quoting on the CREATE DATABASE path string has been corrected to single quotes.

- The empdml.sql script begins with a SET NAMES ISO8859_1 statement, to ensure that the incoming text data get stored in the correct character set.

In spite of these minor changes, the employee database remains substantially as it always was—an example of how not to design databases! A new sample database for Firebird is in the pipeline. It should be ready for release during the latter part of 2004, at `http://www.apress.com` and at other sites around the Firebird community. Eventually, it will find its way into the distribution kits.

Firebird Limits

MOST OF THE ACTUAL LIMITS ON A Firebird database are practical rather than defined by the software. For example, you can define up to 32,767 columns in a table, but why would you want to? Listed in Table VII-1 are a number of theoretical and practical limits applicable to Firebird 1.0.*x* and Firebird 1.5. Certain of these limits will rise in later versions, so make a point of studying release notes to track changes.

Table VII-1. Firebird 1.0.x and 1.5 Limits

OBJECT	ITEM	FIREBIRD 1.0.X	FIREBIRD 1.5	COMMENTS
Identifiers	Almost all objects	31 characters	31 characters	Cannot use characters outside the range of US ASCII (ASCIIZ).
	Constraint names	27 characters	27 characters	Same character restrictions as above.
Dates	Earliest and latest dates			January 1, 100 A.D.
	Latest			December 31, 9999 A.D. NB: It is believed that the engine is susceptible to crashing if the system date of the server is set higher than the year 2039.
Server	Maximum connected clients	1,024 (TCP/IP)	1,024 (TCP/IP)	The theoretical limit is lower for Windows named pipes (NetBEUI)—the server is likely to hang at more than 930 concurrent connections. As a practical guideline, work on a base maximum of about 150 concurrent Superserver clients for a normal interactive application on a server of low-to-medium specification, with low-to-moderate contention, before performance might make you consider upgrading. For Classic server, the numbers may be lower because each client consumes more resources.

continued

Table VII-1. Firebird 1.0.x and 1.5 Limits (continued)

OBJECT	ITEM	FIREBIRD 1.0.X	FIREBIRD 1.5	COMMENTS
	Maximum number of databases open in one transaction			The number of databases opened during a transaction started by isc_start_multiple() is limited only by available system resources. A transaction started by isc_start_transaction() limits concurrent database attachments to 16.
Database	Number of tables	32,767	32,767	
	Maximum size	7TB	7TB	Theoretical limit, approximate. There is no known record of a Firebird database as large as 7TB.
	Maximum file size			Depends on the file system. FAT32 and ext2 are 2GB. Older NTFS and some ext3 are usually 4GB. Many 64-bit file systems place no limit on the size of a shared-access file.
	Maximum number of files per database			Theoretically, 2^{16} (65,536), including shadow files. The limitation is more likely to be imposed by the operating system's limit on the number of files that can be opened simultaneously by one process. Some permit the limit to be raised.
	Maximum page_size	16,384 bytes	16,384 bytes	Other sizes are 1,024, 2,048, 4,096 (default), and 8192 bytes
	Maximum cache buffers	65,536 pages	65,536 pages	Practical limit depends on available RAM. The total size (cache pages * page_size on Superserver; cache pages * page_size * no. of concurrent users on Classic server) should never be more than half of the available RAM. Consider 10,000 pages as a practical limit and tweak backward or forward from there as performance dictates.

Table VII-1. Firebird 1.0.x and 1.5 Limits (continued)

OBJECT	ITEM	FIREBIRD 1.0.X	FIREBIRD 1.5	COMMENTS
Tables	Maximum versions per table	255	255	Firebird keeps account of up to 255 formats for each table. The format version steps up by 1 each time a metadata change is done. When any table reaches the limit, the whole database becomes unavailable—it must be backed up and then work resumed on the restored version.
	Maximum row size	64KB	64KB	Count bytes. BLOB and ARRAY columns each cost 8 bytes to store the ID; VARCHARs, byte length + 2; CHARs, byte-length; SMALLINT, 2; INTEGER, FLOAT, DATE and TIME, 4; BIGINT, DOUBLE PRECISION and TIMESTAMP, 8; NUMERIC and DECIMAL, 4 or 8, depending on precision. System tables have a row size limit of 128KB.
	Maximum number of rows	2^{32} rows	2^{32} rows	More or less. Rows are enumerated with a 32-bit unsigned integer per table and a 32-bit row slot index. A table with long rows—either a lot of fields or very long fields—will store fewer records than a table with very short rows. All rows—including deleted ones—use up numbers; BLOBs and BLOB fragments stored on table data pages use up numbers, too.
	Maximum number of columns			Depends on data types used (see Maximum row size).
	Maximum indexes per table	64	256	
	Maximum size of external file			4GB on Windows NTFS, 2GB on Windows FAT32, Linux ext2 and ext3, and Solaris.

continued

Table VII-1. Firebird 1.0.x and 1.5 Limits (continued)

OBJECT	ITEM	FIREBIRD 1.0.X	FIREBIRD 1.5	COMMENTS
Indexes	Maximum size	252 bytes	252 bytes	This theoretical maximum applies to a single-column index, where the character set is single-byte and uses the default (binary) collation sequence. *Count bytes, not characters.* The practical maximum is reduced by compound indexing, multi-byte character sets, and complex collation sequences. A single-column index using 3-byte UNICODE_FSS characters, for example, can have a maximum of (253 / 3) = 84 characters. Some ISO8859 collation sequences consume up to 4 bytes per character just for the sorting attributes.
	Maximum number of segments	16	16	
Queries	Maximum joined tables	256	256	Theoretical limit. Other factors come to bear, such as the number of Boolean evaluations required by the joins. From the point of view of resources and performance, the largest *practicable* number of table references is probably around 16. Always test with realistic volumes and kinds of data.
	Maximum nesting level			There is no theoretical limit, but deep nesting of subqueries is sub-optimal for performance. Performance and resource consumption will determine your practical limit, on a query-by-query basis.
	Maximum size of ORDER BY key-set data	32KB	32KB	

Table VII-1. Firebird 1.0.x and 1.5 Limits (continued)

OBJECT	ITEM	FIREBIRD 1.0.X	FIREBIRD 1.5	COMMENTS
PSQL modules	Maximum size of BLR	48KB	48KB	Stored procedure and trigger sources are compiled into BLR bytecode, which is more dense than the PSQL source. Still, if you hit this limit, try to break up your monumental procedure into a "master" procedure with callable chunks.
	Maximum number of events per module	No limit	No limit	Practical limit is related to the length limit for BLR byte code (above).
	Levels of embedded calls			750 on Windows, 1,000 for POSIX platforms.
BLOBs	Maximum BLOB size			Maximum depends on page_size. For a 2KB page size, the BLOB size maximum is 512MB. For a 4KB page size, the BLOB size maximum is 4GB. For a 8KB page size, it's 32GB, and for a 16KB page size, it's 256GB.
	Maximum segment size			BLOBs are stored in segments, the theoretical maximum size of which is 64KB. However, in DSQL, it is not essential to define a non-default segment size, since client settings cause BLOB data to be segmented for transport according to network packet size. Server economics determine the actual size of segments in storage.

Character Sets and Collations

TABLE VIII-1 LISTS THE CHARACTER SETS and collations available when Firebird 1.5.0 was released. Some of those items listed are not available in earlier Firebird versions. If you have installed a later version and the character set or collation sequence you want is not listed here, read the release notes of your version and any other versions since v.1.5 to see whether it has been added.

Table VIII-1. Character Sets and Collations, Firebird 1.5.0

ID	NAME	BYTES PER CHARACTER	COLLATION	LANGUAGE	ALIASES
2	ASCII	1	ASCII	English	ASCII7, USASCII
56	BIG_5	2	BIG_5	Chinese, Vietnamese, Korean	BIG5, DOS_950, WIN_950
50	CYRL	1	CYRL	Russian	
50			DB_RUS	dBase Russian	
50			PDOX_CYRL	Paradox Russian	
10	DOS437	1	DOS437	English—USA	DOS_437
10			DB_DEU437	dBase German	
10			DB_ESP437	dBase Spanish	
10			DB_FRA437	dBase French	
10			DB_FIN437	dBase Finnish	
10			DB_ITA437	dBase Italian	
10			DB_NLD437	dBase Dutch	
10			DB_SVE437	dBase Swedish	
10			DB_UK437	dBase English—UK	
10			DB_US437	dBase English— USA	
10			PDOX_ASCII	Paradox ASCII code page	

continued

Table VIII-1. Character Sets and Collations, Firebird 1.5.0 (continued)

ID	NAME	BYTES PER CHARACTER	COLLATION	LANGUAGE	ALIASES
10			PDOX_SWEDFIN	Paradox Swedish/ Finnish code pages	
10			PDOX_INTL	Paradox International English code page	
9	DOS737	1	DOS737	Greek	DOS_737
15	DOS775	1	DOS775	Baltic	DOS_775
11	DOS850	1	DOS850	Latin I (no Euro symbol)	DOS_850
11			DB_DEU850	German	
11			DB_ESP850	Spanish	
11			DB_FRA850	French	
11			DB_FRC850	French—Canada	
11			DB_ITA850	Italian	
11			DB_NLD850	Dutch	
11			DB_PTB850	Portuguese— Brazil	
11			DB_SVE850	Swedish	
11			DB_UK850	English—UK	
11			DB_US850	English—USA	
45	DOS852	1	DOS852	Latin II	DOS_852
45			DB_CSY	dBase Czech	
45			DB_PLK	dBase Polish	
45			DB_SLO	dBase Slovakian	
45			PDOX_PLK	Paradox Polish	
45			PDOX_HUN	Paradox Hungarian	
45			PDOX_SLO	Paradox Slovakian	
45			PDOX_CSY	Paradox Czech	
46	DOS857	1	DOS857	Turkish	DOS_857
46			DB_TRK	dBase Turkish	
16	DOS858	1	DOS858	Latin I + Euro symbol	DOS_858
13	DOS860	1	DOS860	Portuguese	DOS_860
13			DB_PTG860	dBase Portuguese	
47	DOS861	1	DOS861	Icelandic	DOS_861
47			PDOX_ISL	Paradox Icelandic	
17	DOS862	1	DOS862	Hebrew	DOS_862
14	DOS863	1	DOS863	French—Canada	DOS_863

Table VIII-1. Character Sets and Collations, Firebird 1.5.0 (continued)

ID	NAME	BYTES PER CHARACTER	COLLATION	LANGUAGE	ALIASES
14			DB_FRC863	dBase French—Canada	
18	DOS864	1	DOS864	Arabic	DOS_864
12	DOS865	1	DOS865	Nordic	DOS_865
12			DB_DAN865	dBase Danish	
12			DB_NOR865	dBase Norwegian	
12			PDOX_NORDAN4	Paradox Norwegian and Danish	
48	DOS866	1	DOS866	Russian	DOS_866
49	DOS869	1	DOS869	Modern Greek	DOS_869
6	EUCJ_0208	2	EUCJ_0208	EUC Japanese	EUCJ
57	GB_2312	2	GB_2312	Simplified Chinese (Hong Kong, PRC)	DOS_936, GB2312, WIN_936
21	ISO8859_1	1	ISO8859_1	Latin 1	ANSI, ISO88591, LATIN1
21			FR_CA	French—Canada	
21			DA_DA	Danish	
21			DE_DE	German	
21			ES_ES	Spanish	
21			FI_FI	Finnish	
21			FR_FR	French	
21			IS_IS	Icelandic	
21			IT_IT	Italian	
21			NO_NO	Norwegian	
21			DU_NL	Dutch	
21			PT_PT	Portuguese	
21			SV_SV	Swedish	
21			EN_UK	English—UK	
21			EN_US	English—USA	
22	ISO8859_2	1	ISO8859_2	Latin 2—Central European (Croatian, Czech, Hungarian, Polish, Romanian, Serbian, Slovakian, Slovenian)	ISO-8859-2, ISO88592, LATIN2
22			CS_CZ	Czech	

continued

Table VIII-1. Character Sets and Collations, Firebird 1.5.0 (continued)

ID	NAME	BYTES PER CHARACTER	COLLATION	LANGUAGE	ALIASES
22			ISO_HUN	Hungarian	
23	ISO8859_3	1	ISO8859_3	Latin3—Southern European (Maltese, Esperanto)	ISO-8859-3, ISO88593, LATIN3
34	ISO8859_4	1	ISO8859_4	Latin 4—Northern European (Estonian, Latvian, Lithuanian, Greenlandic, Lappish)	ISO-8859-4, ISO88594, LATIN4
35	ISO8859_5	1	ISO8859_5	Cyrillic (Russian)	ISO-8859-5, ISO88595
36	ISO8859_6	1	ISO8859_6	Arabic	ISO-8859-6, ISO88596
37	ISO8859_7	1	ISO8859_7	Greek	ISO-8859-7, ISO88597
38	ISO8859_8	1	ISO8859_8	Hebrew	ISO-8859-8, ISO88598
39	ISO8859_9	1	ISO8859_9	Latin 5	ISO-8859-9, ISO88599, LATIN5
40	ISO8859_13	1	ISO8859_13	Latin 7—Baltic Rim	ISO-8859-13, ISO885913, LATIN7
44	KSC_5601	2	KSC_5601	Korean (Unified Hangeul)	DOS_949, KSC5601, WIN_949
44			KSC_DICTIONARY	Korean—dictionary order collation	
19	NEXT	1	NEXT	NeXTSTEP encoding	
19			NXT_US	English—USA	
19			NXT_FRA	French	
19			NXT_ITA	Italian	
19			NXT_ESP	Spanish	
19			NXT_DEU	German	
0	NONE	1	NONE	Code-page neutral; uppercasing limited to ASCII codes 97–122	
1	OCTETS	1	OCTETS	Binary character	BINARY

Table VIII-1. Character Sets and Collations, Firebird 1.5.0 (continued)

ID	NAME	BYTES PER CHARACTER	COLLATION	LANGUAGE	ALIASES
5	SJIS_0208	2	SJIS_0208	Japanese	SJIS
3	UNICODE_FSS	3	3	UNICODE_FSS	UNICODE SQL_TEXT, UTF-8, UTF8, UTF_FSS
51	WIN1250	1	WIN1250	ANSI—Central European	WIN_1250
51			PXW_PLK	Polish	
51			PXW_HUN	Hungarian	
51			PXW_CSY	Czech	
51			PXW_HUNDC	Hungarian—dictionary sort	
51			PXW_SLOV	Slovakian	
52	WIN1251	1	WIN1251	ANSI—Cyrillic	WIN_1251
52			WIN1251_UA	Ukrainian	
52			PXW_CYRL	Paradox Cyrillic (Russian)	
53	WIN1252	1	WIN1252	ANSI—Latin I	WIN_1252
53			PXW_SWEDFIN	Swedish and Finnish	
53			PXW_NORDAN4	Norwegian and Danish	
53			PXW_INTL	English—International	
53			PXW_INTL850	Paradox Multi-lingual Latin I	
53			PXW_SPAN	Paradox Spanish	
54	WIN1253	1	WIN1253	ANSI Greek	WIN_1253
54			PXW_GREEK	Paradox Greek	
55	WIN1254	1	WIN1254	ANSI Turkish	WIN_1254
55			PXW_TURK	Paradox Turkish	
50	WIN1255	1	WIN1255	ANSI Hebrew	WIN_1255
59	WIN1256	1	WIN1256	ANSI Arabic	WIN_1256
60	WIN1257	1	WIN1257	ANSI Baltic	WIN_1257

System Tables and Views

WHEN YOU CREATE A DATABASE, Firebird begins by building its own tables in which to store the metadata for all database objects—not just your user-defined objects, but also its own internal objects. These tables are known as *system tables.* Following the metadata definitions for the system tables, you will find DDL listings for a number of views over the system that you might find useful.

System Tables

The descriptions in this section are intended to assist with designing queries to help you understand and administer your databases. *There are DDL statements for changing metadata.* It is not recommended at all to use SQL statements to update metadata tables. The risk of corruption from doing so is *extreme.*

The following abbreviations are used in the tables:

- **IDX**: Indexed

- **UQ**: Unique

Where there are compound indexes, numbers are given to indicate the precedence of the index segments.

RDB$CHARACTER_SETS stores keys for character sets available to the database.

COLUMN IDENTIFIER	TYPE	IDX	UQ	DESCRIPTION
RDB$CHARACTER_SET_NAME	CHAR(31)	Y	Y	Name of a character set known to Firebird.
RDB$FORM_OF_USE	CHAR(31)			Not used.
RDB$NUMBER_OF_CHARACTERS	INTEGER			Number of characters in the set (not used for the available character sets).
RDB$DEFAULT_COLLATE_NAME	CHAR(31)			Name of the binary collation sequence for the character set. It is always the same as the character set name.

continued

COLUMN IDENTIFIER	TYPE	IDX	UQ	DESCRIPTION
RDB$CHARACTER_SET_ID	SMALLINT	Y	Y	Unique identifier for this character set, wherever it is used.
RDB$SYSTEM_FLAG	SMALLINT			Will be 1 if the character set is defined by the system at database create; 0 for a user-defined character set.
RDB$DESCRIPTION	BLOB TEXT			For storing documentation.
RDB$FUNCTION_NAME	CHAR(31)			Not used, but may become available for user-defined character sets that are accessed via an external function.
RDB$BYTES_PER_CHARACTER	SMALLINT			Size of characters in the set, in bytes. For example, UNICODE_FSS uses 3 bytes per character.

RDB$CHECK_CONSTRAINTS cross-references names and triggers for CHECK and NOT NULL constraints.

COLUMN IDENTIFIER	TYPE	IDX	UQ	DESCRIPTION
RDB$CONSTRAINT_NAME	CHAR(31)	Y		Name of a constraint.
RDB$TRIGGER_NAME	CHAR(31)	Y		For a CHECK constraint, this is the name of the trigger that enforces the constraint. For a NOT NULL constraint, this is the name of the column to which the constraint applies—the table name can be found through the constraint name.

RDB$COLLATIONS stores definitions of collation sequences.

COLUMN IDENTIFIER	TYPE	IDX	UQ	DESCRIPTION
RDB$COLLATION_NAME	VARCHAR(31)	Y	Y	Name of the collation sequence
RDB$COLLATION_ID	SMALLINT	Y(1)	Y(1)	With the character set ID, unique collation identifier
RDB$CHARACTER_SET_ID	SMALLINT	Y(2)	Y(2)	With the collation ID, unique collation identifier
RDB$COLLATION_ATTRIBUTES	CHAR(31)			Not used externally
RDB$SYSTEM_FLAG	SMALLINT			User-defined=0; system-defined=1 or higher
RDB$DESCRIPTION	BLOB TEXT			For storing documentation
RDB$FUNCTION_NAME	CHAR(31)			Not currently used

RDB$DATABASE is a single-record file containing basic information about the database.

COLUMN IDENTIFIER	TYPE	IDX	UQ	DESCRIPTION
RDB$DESCRIPTION	BLOB TEXT			Comment text included with the CREATE DATABASE/CREATE SCHEMA statement is supposed to be written here. It doesn't happen. However, you can add any amount of text to it by way of documentation and it will survive a **gbak** and restore.
RDB$RELATION_ID	SMALLINT			A number that steps up by 1 each time a new table or view is added to the database.
RDB$SECURITY_CLASS	CHAR(31)			Can refer to a security class defined in RDB$SECURITY_CLASSES, to apply databasewide access control limits.
RDB$CHARACTER_SET_NAME	CHAR(31)			Default character set of the database. NULL if the character set is NONE.

RDB$DEPENDENCIES stores dependencies between database objects.

COLUMN IDENTIFIER	TYPE	IDX	UQ	DESCRIPTION
RDB$DEPENDENT_NAME	CHAR(31)	Y		Names the view, procedure, trigger, or computed column tracked by this record.
RDB$DEPENDED_ON_NAME	CHAR(31)	Y		The table that the view, procedure, trigger, or computed column refers to.
RDB$FIELD_NAME	VARCHAR(31)			Names one column in the depended-on table that the view, procedure, trigger, or computed column refers to.
RDB$DEPENDENT_TYPE	SMALLINT			Identifies the object type (view, procedure, trigger, computed column). The number comes from the table RDB$TYPES— objects are enumerated where RDB$FIELD_NAME = 'RDB$OBJECT_TYPE'.
RDB$DEPENDED_ON_TYPE	SMALLINT			Identifies the type of the object depended on (same object paradigm as for RDB$DEPENDENT_TYPE).

RDB$EXCEPTIONS stores custom exceptions.

COLUMN IDENTIFIER	TYPE	IDX	UQ	DESCRIPTION
RDB$EXCEPTION_NAME	CHAR(31)	Y	Y	Name of the custom exception
RDB$EXCEPTION_NUMBER	INTEGER	Y	Y	System-assigned unique exception number
RDB$MESSAGE	VARCHAR(78)			Custom message text
RDB$DESCRIPTION	BLOB TEXT			Can be used for documentation
RDB$SYSTEM_FLAG	SMALLINT			User-defined=0; system-defined=1 or higher

RDB$FIELD_DIMENSIONS stores information about dimensions of array columns.

COLUMN IDENTIFIER	TYPE	IDX	UQ	DESCRIPTION
RDB$FIELD_NAME	CHAR(31)	Y		Name of the array column. It must be a RDB$FIELD_NAME in the table RDB$FIELDS.
RDB$DIMENSION	SMALLINT			Identifies one dimension in the array column. The first has the identifier 0.
RDB$LOWER_BOUND	INTEGER			Lower bound of this dimension.
RDB$UPPER_BOUND	INTEGER			Upper bound of this dimension.

RDB$FIELDS stores definitions of domains and of column names for tables and views. Each row for a non-domain column has a corresponding row in RDB$RELATION_FIELDS. In reality, *every* instance of RDB$FIELDS is a domain. You can, for example, do this:

```
CREATE TABLE ATABLE (
  EXAMPLE VARCHAR(10) CHARACTER SET ISO8859_1);
COMMIT;
SELECT RDB$FIELD_SOURCE FROM RDB$RELATION_FIELDS
  WHERE RDB$RELATION_NAME = 'ATABLE'
  AND RDB$FIELD_NAME = 'EXAMPLE';
RDB$FIELD_SOURCE
==============================
SQL$99
/* */
ALTER TABLE ATABLE
  ADD EXAMPLE2 SQL$99;
COMMIT;
```

The new column is added, having the same attributes as the original.

COLUMN IDENTIFIER	TYPE	IDX	UQ	DESCRIPTION
RDB$FIELD_NAME	CHAR(31)	Y	Y	For domains, it is the domain name. For table and view columns, it is the internal, database-unique field name, linking to RDB$FIELD_SOURCE in RDB$RELATION_FIELDS. NB: Firebird creates a domain in this table for every column definition that is not derived from a user-defined domain.
RDB$QUERY_NAME	CHAR(31)			Not used in Firebird.
RDB$VALIDATION_BLR	BLOB BLR			Not used in Firebird.
RDB$VALIDATION_SOURCE	BLOB TEXT			Not used in Firebird.
RDB$COMPUTED_BLR	BLOB BLR			Binary language representation of the SQL expression that Firebird evaluates when a COMPUTED BY column is accessed.
RDB$COMPUTED_SOURCE	BLOB TEXT			Original source text of the expression that defines a COMPUTED BY column.
RDB$DEFAULT_VALUE	BLOB BLR			Default rule for the default value, in binary language representations.
RDB$DEFAULT_SOURCE	BLOB TEXT			Ditto; in original form.
RDB$FIELD_LENGTH	SMALLINT			Length of the column in bytes. Float, date, time, and integer are 4 bytes. Double precision, BigInt, timestamp, and blob_id are 8 bytes.
RDB$FIELD_SCALE	SMALLINT			Negative number representing the scale of a NUMERIC or DECIMAL column.
RDB$FIELD_TYPE	SMALLINT			Number code of the data type defined for the column: 7=smallint, 8=integer, 12=date, 13=time, 14=char, 16=bigint, 27=double precision, 35=timestamp, 37=varchar, 261=blob. Codes for numeric and decimal are the same as that of the integer-type that is used to store it.

COLUMN IDENTIFIER	TYPE	IDX	UQ	DESCRIPTION
RDB$FIELD_SUB_TYPE	SMALLINT			BLOB subtype, namely 0=untyped, 1=text, 2=BLR (binary language representation), 3=ACL (access control list), 5=encoded table metadata, 6=description of a cross-database transaction that didn't complete normally.
RDB$MISSING_VALUE	BLOB BLR			Not used in Firebird.
RDB$MISSING_SOURCE	BLOB TEXT			Not used in Firebird.
RDB$DESCRIPTION	BLOB TEXT			Available to use for documentation.
RDB$SYSTEM_FLAG	SMALLINT			1=system table; anything else, user-defined table.
RDB$QUERY_HEADER	BLOB TEXT			Not used in Firebird.
RDB$SEGMENT_LENGTH	SMALLINT			For BLOB columns, a suggested length for BLOB buffers. Not relevant in Firebird.
RDB$EDIT_STRING	VARCHAR(125)			Not used in Firebird.
RDB$EXTERNAL_LENGTH	SMALLINT			Length of the field as it is in an external table. Always 0 for regular tables.
RDB$EXTERNAL_SCALE	SMALLINT			Scale factor of an integer field in an external table; represents the power of 10 by which the integer is multiplied.
RDB$EXTERNAL_TYPE	SMALLINT			Data type of the field as it is in an external table. Data types are the same as for regular tables, but include 40=null-terminated text (CSTRING).
RDB$DIMENSIONS	SMALLINT			Number of dimensions defined, if column is an array type. Always 0 for non-array columns.
RDB$NULL_FLAG	SMALLINT			Indicates whether column is nullable (empty) or non-nullable (1).

continued

(continued)

COLUMN IDENTIFIER	TYPE	IDX	UQ	DESCRIPTION
RDB$CHARACTER_LENGTH	SMALLINT			Length of a CHAR or VARCHAR column, in characters (not bytes).
RDB$COLLATION_ID	SMALLINT			Number ID of the collation sequence (if defined) for a character column or domain.
RDB$CHARACTER_SET_ID	SMALLINT			Number ID of the character set for character columns, BLOB columns, or domains. Links to RDB$CHARACTER_SET_ID column in RDB$CHARACTER_SETS.
RDB$FIELD_PRECISION	SMALLINT			Indicates the number of digits of precision available to the data type of the column.

RDB$FILES stores volume details of database secondary files and shadow files.

COLUMN IDENTIFIER	TYPE	IDX	UQ	DESCRIPTION
RDB$FILE_NAME	VARCHAR(253)			Name of a database secondary file (volume) in a multi-volume database, or a shadow file.
RDB$FILE_SEQUENCE	SMALLINT			Sequence in the volume order of database secondary files, or sequence in the shadow file set.
RDB$FILE_START	INTEGER			Starting page number.
RDB$FILE_LENGTH	INTEGER			File length, in database pages.
RDB$FILE_FLAGS	SMALLINT			Internal use.
RDB$SHADOW_NUMBER	SMALLINT			Shadow set number. Required to identify the file as a member of a shadow set. If it is null or 0, Firebird assumes the file is a secondary database volume.

RDB$FILTERS stores and keeps track of information about BLOB filters.

COLUMN IDENTIFIER	TYPE	IDX	UQ	DESCRIPTION
RDB$FUNCTION_NAME	CHAR(31)			Unique name of the BLOB filter
RDB$DESCRIPTION	BLOB TEXT			User-written documentation about the BLOB filter and the two subtypes it is meant to operate on
RDB$MODULE_NAME	VARCHAR(253)			The name of the dynamic library/shared object where the BLOB filter code is located
RDB$ENTRYPOINT	CHAR(31)			The entry point in the filter library for this BLOB filter
RDB$INPUT_SUB_TYPE	SMALLINT	Y(1)	Y(1)	The BLOB subtype of the data to be transformed
RDB$OUTPUT_SUB_TYPE	SMALLINT	Y(2)	Y(2)	The BLOB subtype that the input data is to be transformed to
RDB$SYSTEM_FLAG	SMALLINT			Externally defined (i.e., user-defined=0, internally defined=1 or greater)

RDB$FORMATS keeps account of the number of metadata changes performed on tables. Each time a table or view gets a change, it gets a new format number. The purpose is to allow applications to access a changed table without the need to recompile. When the format number of any table reaches 255, the whole database becomes inaccessible for querying. It is then necessary to back up the database, restore it, and resume work in the newly built database.

COLUMN IDENTIFIER	TYPE	IDX	UQ	DESCRIPTION
RDB$RELATION_ID	SMALLINT	Y(1)	Y(1)	Number ID of a table or view in RDB$RELATIONS.
RDB$FORMAT	SMALLINT	Y(2)	Y(2)	Identifier of the table format. There can be up to 255 such rows for any particular table.
RDB$DESCRIPTOR	BLOB FORMAT			BLOB listing the columns and data attributes at the time the format record was created.

RDB$FUNCTION_ARGUMENTS stores the attributes of arguments (parameters) of external functions.

COLUMN IDENTIFIER	TYPE	IDX	UQ	DESCRIPTION
RDB$FUNCTION_NAME	CHAR(31)	Y		Unique name of the external function, matching a function name in RDB$FUNCTIONS.
RDB$ARGUMENT_POSITION	SMALLINT			Position of the argument in the argument list: 1=first, 2=second, etc.
RDB$MECHANISM	SMALLINT			Whether the argument is passed by value (0), by reference (1), by descriptor (2), or by BLOB descriptor (3).
RDB$FIELD_TYPE	SMALLINT			Number code of the data type defined for the column: 7=smallint, 8=integer, 12=date, 13=time, 14=char, 16=bigint, 27=double precision, 35=timestamp, 37=varchar, 40=cstring (null-terminated string), 261=blob.
RDB$FIELD_SCALE	SMALLINT			Scale of an integer or fixed numeric argument.
RDB$FIELD_LENGTH	SMALLINT			Length of the argument in bytes. For lengths of non-character types, refer to RDB$FIELDS.RDB$FIELD_LENGTH.
RDB$FIELD_SUB_TYPE	SMALLINT			For BLOB arguments, BLOB subtype.
RDB$CHARACTER_SET_ID	SMALLINT			Numeric ID for the character set, for a character argument, if applicable.
RDB$FIELD_PRECISION	SMALLINT			Digits of precision available to the data type of the argument.
RDB$CHARACTER_LENGTH	SMALLINT			Length of a CHAR or VARCHAR argument, in characters (not bytes).

RDB$FUNCTIONS stores information about external functions.

COLUMN IDENTIFIER	TYPE	IDX	UQ	DESCRIPTION
RDB$FUNCTION_NAME	CHAR(31)	Y	Y	Unique name of an external function.
RDB$FUNCTION_TYPE	SMALLINT			Not currently used.
RDB$QUERY_NAME	CHAR(31)			This is meant to be an alternative name for the function, for use in **isql** queries. It doesn't work.
RDB$DESCRIPTION	BLOB TEXT			Available for documentation.
RDB$MODULE_NAME	VARCHAR(253)			Name of the dynamic library/shared object where the code for the function is located.
RDB$ENTRYPOINT	CHAR(31)			Name of the entry point in the library where this function is to be found.
RDB$RETURN_ARGUMENT	SMALLINT			Ordinal position of the return argument in the parameter list, relative to the input arguments.
RDB$SYSTEM_FLAG	SMALLINT			Externally defined (user-defined)–1; system-defined=0.

RDB$GENERATORS stores names and IDs of generators.

COLUMN IDENTIFIER	TYPE	IDX	UQ	DESCRIPTION
RDB$GENERATOR_NAME	CHAR(31)	Y	Y	Name of generator.
RDB$GENERATOR_ID	RDB$GENERATOR_ID			System-assigned unique ID for the generator.
RDB$SYSTEM_FLAG	SMALLINT			0=user-defined; 1 or greater=system-defined. Firebird uses a number of generators internally.

RDB$INDEX_SEGMENTS stores the segments and positions of multi-segment indexes.

COLUMN IDENTIFIER	TYPE	IDX	UQ	DESCRIPTION
RDB$INDEX_NAME	CHAR(31)	Y		Name of the index. Must be kept consistent with the corresponding master record in RDB$INDICES.
RDB$FIELD_NAME	CHAR(31)			Name of a key column in the index. Matches the RDB$FIELD_NAME of the database column, in RDB$RELATION_FIELDS.
RDB$FIELD_POSITION	SMALLINT			Ordinal position of the column in the index (left to right).

RDB$INDICES stores definitions of all indexes.

COLUMN IDENTIFIER	TYPE	IDX	UQ	DESCRIPTION
RDB$INDEX_NAME	CHAR(31)	Y	Y	Unique name of the index.
RDB$RELATION_NAME	CHAR(31)	Y		Name of the table the index applies to. Matches a RDB$RELATION_NAME in a record in RDB$RELATIONS.
RDB$INDEX_ID	SMALLINT			Internal number ID of the index. Writing to this column from an application will break the index.
RDB$UNIQUE_FLAG	SMALLINT			Indicates whether the index is unique (1=unique, 0=not unique).
RDB$DESCRIPTION	BLOB TEXT			Available for documentation.
RDB$SEGMENT_COUNT	SMALLINT			Number of segments (columns) in the index.
RDB$INDEX_INACTIVE	SMALLINT			Indicates whether the index is currently inactive (1=inactive, 0=active).
RDB$INDEX_TYPE	SMALLINT			Not currently used; likely to distinguish regular indexes from expression indexes when the feature is implemented.

COLUMN IDENTIFIER	TYPE	IDX	UQ	DESCRIPTION
RDB$FOREIGN_KEY	VARCHAR(31)	Y		Name of the associated foreign key constraint, if any.
RDB$SYSTEM_FLAG	SMALLINT			Indicates whether the index is system-defined (1 or greater) or user-defined (0).
RDB$EXPRESSION_BLR	BLOB BLR			Binary language representation of an expression. Will be used for runtime evaluation when expression indexes are implemented.
RDB$EXPRESSION_SOURCE	BLOB TEXT			Source of an expression. Will be used when expression indexes are implemented.
RDB$STATISTICS	DOUBLE PRECISION			Stores the latest selectivity of the index, as calculated at start-up or by SET STATISTICS.

RDB$LOG_FILES is an obsolete system table.

RDB$PAGES stores information about database pages.

COLUMN IDENTIFIER	TYPE	IDX	UQ	DESCRIPTION
RDB$PAGE_NUMBER	INTEGER			Unique number of a database page that has been physically allocated
RDB$RELATION_ID	SMALLINT			ID of table whose data are stored on the page
RDB$PAGE_SEQUENCE	INTEGER			Sequence number of this page, relative to other pages allocated for this table
RDB$PAGE_TYPE	SMALLINT			Identifies the type of data stored on the page (table data, index, etc.)

RDB$PROCEDURE_PARAMETERS stores the parameters for stored procedures.

COLUMN IDENTIFIER	TYPE	IDX	UQ	DESCRIPTION
RDB$PARAMETER_NAME	CHAR(31)	Y(2)	Y(2)	Name of the parameter
RDB$PROCEDURE_NAME	CHAR(31)	Y(1)	Y(1)	Name of the procedure
RDB$PARAMETER_NUMBER	SMALLINT			Sequence number of parameter
RDB$PARAMETER_TYPE	SMALLINT			Indicates whether parameter is input (0) or output (1)
RDB$FIELD_SOURCE	CHAR(31)			System-generated unique column name
RDB$DESCRIPTION	BLOB TEXT			Available for documentation
RDB$SYSTEM_FLAG	SMALLINT			Indicates whether the parameter is system-defined (1 or greater) or user-defined (0)

RDB$PROCEDURES stores definitions of stored procedures.

COLUMN IDENTIFIER	TYPE	IDX	UQ	DESCRIPTION
RDB$PROCEDURE_NAME	CHAR(31)	Y	Y	Name of procedure
RDB$PROCEDURE_ID	SMALLINT	Y		System-defined unique ID of procedure
RDB$PROCEDURE_INPUTS	SMALLINT			Indicates whether there are input parameters (1) or not (0)
RDB$PROCEDURE_OUTPUTS	SMALLINT			Indicates whether there are output parameters (1) or not (0)
RDB$DESCRIPTION	BLOB TEXT			Available for documentation
RDB$PROCEDURE_SOURCE	BLOB TEXT			Source code of the procedure
RDB$PROCEDURE_BLR	BLOB BLR			Binary language representation (BLR) of the procedure code
RDB$SECURITY_CLASS	CHAR(31)			Can refer to a security class defined in RDB$SECURITY_CLASSES, to apply access control limits
RDB$OWNER_NAME	VARCHAR(31)			User name of the procedure's owner

(continued)

COLUMN IDENTIFIER	TYPE	IDX	UQ	DESCRIPTION
RDB$RUNTIME	BLOB SUMMARY			Description of metadata of procedure, internal use for optimization
RDB$SYSTEM_FLAG	SMALLINT			User-defined (0) or system-defined (1 or greater)

RDB$REF_CONSTRAINTS stores actions for referential constraints.

COLUMN IDENTIFIER	TYPE	IDX	UQ	DESCRIPTION
RDB$CONSTRAINT_NAME	CHAR(31)	Y	Y	Name of a referential constraint.
RDB$CONST_NAME_UQ	CHAR(31)			Name of the primary key or unique constraint referred to in the REFERENCES clause of this constraint.
RDB$MATCH_OPTION	CHAR(7)			Current value is FULL in all cases; reserved for future use.
RDB$UPDATE_RULE	CHAR(11)			Referential integrity action applicable to this foreign key when the primary key is updated: NO ACTION | CASCADE | SET NULL | SET DEFAULT.
RDB$DELETE_RULE	CHAR(11)			Referential integrity action applicable to this foreign key when the primary key is deleted. Rule options as defined in the column RDB$UPDATE_RULE.

RDB$RELATION_CONSTRAINTS stores information about table-level integrity constraints.

COLUMN IDENTIFIER	TYPE	IDX	UQ	DESCRIPTION
RDB$CONSTRAINT_NAME	CHAR(31)	Y	Y	Name of a table-level constraint
RDB$CONSTRAINT_TYPE	CHAR(11)	Y(2)		Primary key/unique/foreign key/pcheck/not null
RDB$RELATION_NAME	CHAR(31)	Y(1)		Name of the table this constraint applies to

continued

(continued)

COLUMN IDENTIFIER	TYPE	IDX	UQ	DESCRIPTION
RDB$DEFERRABLE	CHAR(3)			Currently NO in all cases; reserved for future implementation of deferred constraints
RDB$INITIALLY_DEFERRED	CHAR(3)			Ditto
RDB$INDEX_NAME	CHAR(31)	Y		Name of the index that enforces the constraint (applicable if constraint is PRIMARY KEY, UNIQUE, or FOREIGN KEY)

RDB$RELATION_FIELDS stores the definitions of columns.

COLUMN IDENTIFIER	TYPE	IDX	UQ	DESCRIPTION
RDB$FIELD_NAME	CHAR(31)	Y(1)	Y(1)	Name of the column, unique in table or view.
RDB$RELATION_NAME	CHAR(31)	Y(2)	Y(2)	Name of table or view.
		Y		(Another index.)
RDB$FIELD_SOURCE	CHAR(31)	Y		The system-generated name (SQL$nn) for this column, correlated in RDB$FIELDS. If the column is based on a domain, the two correlated RDB$FIELD_SOURCE columns store the domain name.
RDB$QUERY_NAME	CHAR(31)			Not used currently.
RDB$BASE_FIELD	CHAR(31)			For a query only, the column name from the base table. The base table is identified by an internal ID in the column RDB$VIEW_CONTEXT.
RDB$EDIT_STRING	VARCHAR(125)			Not used in Firebird.
RDB$FIELD_POSITION	SMALLINT			Position of column in table or view in relation to the other columns. Note that for tables, you can alter this using ALTER TABLE ALTER COLUMN POSITION *n*, where *n* is the new field_position.
RDB$QUERY_HEADER	BLOB TEXT			Not used in Firebird.
RDB$UPDATE_FLAG	SMALLINT			Not used in Firebird.

(continued)

COLUMN IDENTIFIER	TYPE	IDX	UQ	DESCRIPTION
RDB$FIELD_ID	SMALLINT			Transient number ID, used internally. It changes after backup and restore, so don't rely on it for queries in applications and don't change it.
RDB$VIEW_CONTEXT	SMALLINT			For a view column, internal number ID for the base table where the field comes from. Don't modify this column.
RDB$DESCRIPTION	BLOB TEXT			Can store documentation about the column.
RDB$DEFAULT_VALUE	BLOB BLR			Binary language representation of the DEFAULT clause, if any.
RDB$SYSTEM_FLAG	SMALLINT			User-defined (0) or system-defined (1 or greater).
RDB$SECURITY_CLASS	CHAR(31)			Can refer to a security class defined in RDB$SECURITY_CLASSES, to apply access control limits to all users of this column.
RDB$COMPLEX_NAME	CHARACTER(31)			Reserved for future implementation.
RDB$NULL_FLAG	SMALLINT			Indicates whether column is nullable (empty) or non-nullable (1).
RDB$DEFAULT_SOURCE	BLOB TEXT			Original source text of the DEFAULT clause, if any.
RDB$COLLATION_ID	SMALLINT			ID of non-default collation sequence (if any) for column.

RDB$RELATIONS stores tables and view definition header information.

COLUMN IDENTIFIER	TYPE	IDX	UQ	DESCRIPTION
RDB$VIEW_BLR	BLOB BLR			Binary language representation of the query specification for a view; null on tables.
RDB$VIEW_SOURCE	BLOB TEXT			The query specification for a view.

continued

(continued)

COLUMN IDENTIFIER	TYPE	IDX	UQ	DESCRIPTION
RDB$DESCRIPTION	BLOB TEXT			Optional documentation.
RDB$RELATION_ID	SMALLINT	Y		Internal number ID for the table. Don't modify this column.
RDB$SYSTEM_FLAG	SMALLINT			Indicates whether the table is user-created (0) or system-created (1 or greater). Don't modify this flag on user-defined or system tables.
RDB$DBKEY_LENGTH	SMALLINT			For views, aggregated length of the DB_KEY. It is 8 bytes for tables. For views, it is 8 * number of tables the view definition refers to. Don't modify this column. For more info about db_keys, refer to the "Optimization Topic" at the end of Chapter 30.
RDB$FORMAT	SMALLINT			Internal use—don't modify.
RDB$FIELD_ID	SMALLINT			Internal use—don't modify. It stores the number of columns in the table or view.
RDB$RELATION_NAME	CHAR(31)	Y	Y	Name of the table or view.
RDB$SECURITY_CLASS	CHAR(31)			Can refer to a security class defined in RDB$SECURITY_CLASSES, to apply access control limits to all users of this table.
RDB$EXTERNAL_FILE	VARCHAR(253)			Full path to the external data file, if any.
RDB$RUNTIME	BLOB SUMMARY			Description of table's metadata. Internal use for optimization.
RDB$EXTERNAL_DESCRIPTION	BLOB EFD			BLOB of sub_type external_file_description, a text BLOB type that can be used for documentation.
RDB$OWNER_NAME	VARCHAR(31)			User name of table's or view's owner (creator), for SQL security purposes.
RDB$DEFAULT_CLASS	CHAR(31)			Default security class, applied when new columns are added to a table.
RDB$FLAGS	SMALLINT			Internal flags.

RDB$ROLES stores role definitions.

COLUMN IDENTIFIER	TYPE	IDX	UQ	DESCRIPTION
RDB$ROLE_NAME	VARCHAR(31)	Y	Y	Role name
RDB$OWNER_NAME	VARCHAR(31)			User name of role owner

RDB$SECURITY_CLASSES stores and tracks access control lists.

COLUMN IDENTIFIER	TYPE	IDX	UQ	DESCRIPTION
RDB$SECURITY_CLASS	CHAR(31)	Y	Y	Name of security class. This name must stay consistent in all places where it is used (RDB$DATABASE, RDB$RELATIONS, RDB$RELATION_FIELDS).
RDB$ACL	BLOB ACL			Access control list associated with the security class. It enumerates users and their permissions.
RDB$DESCRIPTION	BLOB TEXT			Documentation of the security class here defined.

RDB$TRANSACTIONS tracks cross-database transactions.

COLUMN IDENTIFIER	TYPE	IDX	UQ	DESCRIPTION
RDB$TRANSACTION_ID	INTEGER	Y	Y	Unique ID of the transaction being tracked
RDB$TRANSACTION_STATE	SMALLINT			State of the transaction: limbo(0), committed(1), rolled back (2)
RDB$TIMESTAMP	TIMESTAMP			For future implementation
RDB$TRANSACTION_DESCRIPTION	BLOB T			BLOB of sub_type transaction_description, describing a prepared multi-database transaction, available in case a lost connection cannot be restored

RDB$TRIGGER_MESSAGES stores trigger message definitions (system use).

COLUMN IDENTIFIER	TYPE	IDX	UQ	DESCRIPTION
RDB$TRIGGER_NAME	CHAR(31)	Y		Name of the trigger the message is associated with
RDB$MESSAGE_NUMBER	SMALLINT			Message number (1 to a maximum of 32767)
RDB$MESSAGE	VARCHAR(78)			Trigger message text

RDB$TRIGGERS stores definitions of all triggers.

COLUMN IDENTIFIER	TYPE	IDX	UQ	DESCRIPTION
RDB$TRIGGER_NAME	CHAR(31)	Y	Y	Name of the trigger.
RDB$RELATION_NAME	CHAR(31)	Y		Name of the table or view that the trigger is for.
RDB$TRIGGER_SEQUENCE	SMALLINT			Sequence (position) of trigger. Zero usually means no sequence was defined.
RDB$TRIGGER_TYPE	SMALLINT			1=before insert, 2=after insert, 3=before update, 4=after update, 5=before delete, 6=after delete. Multi-event triggers (Firebird 1.5 and onward) have various trigger types using higher numbers. The actual type code depends on which events are covered and the order in which the events are presented. (NB: There is no apparent reason that the order of events should make a difference to the trigger_type code.)
RDB$TRIGGER_SOURCE	BLOB TEXT			Stores the PSQL source code for the trigger.
RDB$TRIGGER_BLR	BLOB BLR			Stores the binary language representation of the trigger.
RDB$DESCRIPTION	BLOB TEXT			Optional documentation.
RDB$TRIGGER_INACTIVE	SMALLINT			Whether the trigger is currently inactive (1=inactive, 0=active).
RDB$SYSTEM_FLAG	SMALLINT			User-defined (0) or system-defined (1 or greater).
RDB$FLAGS	SMALLINT			Internal use.

RDB$TYPES stores definitions of enumerated types used around Firebird.

COLUMN IDENTIFIER	TYPE	IDX	UQ	DESCRIPTION
RDB$FIELD_NAME	CHAR(31)			Column name for which this enumeration is defined. Note that the same column name appears consistently in multiple system tables.
RDB$TYPE	SMALLINT			Enumeration ID for type that RDB$TYPE_NAME identifies. The series of number is unique within a single enumerated type (e.g., 0=table, 1=view, 2=trigger, 3=computed column, 4=validation, 5=procedure are all types of RDB$OBJECT_TYPE).
RDB$TYPE_NAME	CHAR(31)	Y		The text representation of the type identified by the RDB$FIELD_NAME value and the RDB$TYPE value.
RDB$DESCRIPTION	BLOB TEXT			Optional documentation.
RDB$SYSTEM_FLAG	SMALLINT			User-defined (0) or system-defined (1 or greater).

RDB$USER_PRIVILEGES stores SQL permissions.

COLUMN IDENTIFIER	TYPE	IDX	UQ	DESCRIPTION
RDB$USER	CHAR(31)	Y		User who has been granted the permission
RDB$GRANTOR	CHAR(31)			Name of user who granted the permission
RDB$PRIVILEGE	CHAR(6)			The privilege that is granted by the permission
RDB$GRANT_OPTION	SMALLINT			Whether the permission carries WITH GRANT OPTION authority. 1=Yes, 0=No.
RDB$RELATION_NAME	CHAR(31)	Y		The object on which the permission has been granted

continued

(continued)

COLUMN IDENTIFIER	TYPE	IDX	UQ	DESCRIPTION
RDB$FIELD_NAME	CHAR(31)			Name of a column to which a column-level privilege applies (UPDATE or REFERENCES privileges only)
RDB$USER_TYPE	SMALLINT			Identifies the type of user that was granted the permission (e.g., a user, procedure, view, etc.)
RDB$OBJECT_TYPE	SMALLINT			Identifies the type of object on which the privilege was granted

RDB$VIEW_RELATIONS is an obsolete table.

System Views

The following system views are a subset of those defined in the SQL-92 standard. They can provide useful information about your data. You might like to copy the listings into a script and install the views in all your databases.

CHECK_CONSTRAINTS lists all of the CHECK constraints defined in the database, with the source of the constraint definition.

```
CREATE VIEW CHECK_CONSTRAINTS (
  CONSTRAINT_NAME,
  CHECK_CLAUSE )
AS
  SELECT RDB$CONSTRAINT_NAME,
  RDB$TRIGGER_SOURCE
  FROM RDB$CHECK_CONSTRAINTS RC, RDB$TRIGGERS RT
    WHERE RT.RDB$TRIGGER_NAME = RC.RDB$TRIGGER_NAME;
```

CONSTRAINTS_COLUMN_USAGE lists columns used by PRIMARY KEY and UNIQUE constraints and those defining FOREIGN KEY constraints.

```
CREATE VIEW CONSTRAINTS_COLUMN_USAGE (
  TABLE_NAME,
  COLUMN_NAME,
  CONSTRAINT_NAME )
AS
  SELECT RDB$RELATION_NAME, RDB$FIELD_NAME, RDB$CONSTRAINT_NAME
  FROM RDB$RELATION_CONSTRAINTS RC, RDB$INDEX_SEGMENTS RI
    WHERE RI.RDB$INDEX_NAME = RC.RDB$INDEX_NAME;
```

REFERENTIAL_CONSTRAINTS lists all the referential constraints defined in a database.

```
CREATE VIEW REFERENTIAL_CONSTRAINTS (
  CONSTRAINT_NAME,
  UNIQUE_CONSTRAINT_NAME,
  MATCH_OPTION,
  UPDATE_RULE,
  DELETE_RULE )
AS
  SELECT RDB$CONSTRAINT_NAME, RDB$CONST_NAME_UQ, RDB$MATCH_OPTION,
  RDB$UPDATE_RULE, RDB$DELETE_RULE
  FROM RDB$REF_CONSTRAINTS;
```

TABLE_CONSTRAINTS lists the table-level constraints.

```
CREATE VIEW TABLE_CONSTRAINTS (
  CONSTRAINT_NAME,
  TABLE_NAME,
  CONSTRAINT_TYPE,
  IS_DEFERRABLE,
  INITIALLY_DEFERRED )
AS
  SELECT RDB$CONSTRAINT_NAME, RDB$RELATION_NAME,
  RDB$CONSTRAINT_TYPE, RDB$DEFERRABLE, RDB$INITIALLY_DEFERRED
  FROM RDB$RELATION_CONSTRAINTS;
```

APPENDIX X

Error Codes

THE ERROR CODES RETURNED TO CLIENTS or PSQL modules by Firebird 1.5 .0 are listed in Table X-1. A few codes are unavailable to lower versions of Firebird. It is important to ensure that both server and client have the correct version of firebird.msg (interbase.msg for Firebird 1.0.*x*) stored in the Firebird root directory. It is not mandatory to install the *.msg file on clients but, if its present, it must be the correct one.

Table X-1. Firebird 1.5.0 Error Codes

SQLCODE	GDSCODE	SYMBOL	TEXT OF ERROR MESSAGE
101	335544366	segment	Segment buffer length shorter than expected
100	335544338	from_no_match	No match for first value expression
100	335544354	no_record	Invalid database key
100	335544367	segstr_eof	Attempted retrieval of more segments than exist
100	335544374	stream_eof	Attempt to fetch past the last record in a record stream
-84	335544554	nonsql_security_rel	Table/procedure has non-SQL security class defined
-84	335544555	nonsql_security_fld	Column has non-SQL security class defined
-84	335544668	dsql_procedure_use_err	Procedure <string> does not return any values
-85	335544747	usrname_too_long	The username entered is too long. Maximum length is 31 bytes.
-85	335544748	password_too_long	The password specified is too long. Maximum length is 8 bytes.
-85	335544749	usrname_required	A username is required for this operation.
-85	335544750	password_required	A password is required for this operation
-85	335544751	bad_protocol	The network protocol specified is invalid
-85	335544752	dup_usrname_found	A duplicate user name was found in the security database

continued

Table X-1. Firebird 1.5.0 Error Codes (continued)

SQLCODE	GDSCODE	SYMBOL	TEXT OF ERROR MESSAGE
-85	335544753	usrname_not_found	The user name specified was not found in the security database
-85	335544754	error_adding_sec_record	An error occurred while attempting to add the user.
-85	335544755	error_modifying_sec_record	An error occurred while attempting to modify the user record.
-85	335544756	error_deleting_sec_record	An error occurred while attempting to delete the user record.
-85	335544757	error_updating_sec_db	An error occurred while updating the security database.
-103	335544571	dsql_constant_err	Data type for constant unknown
-104	335544343	invalid_blr	Invalid request BLR at offset <number>
-104	335544390	syntaxerr	BLR syntax error: expected <string> at offset <number>, encountered <number>
-104	335544425	ctxinuse	Context already in use (BLR error)
-104	335544426	ctxnotdef	Context not defined (BLR error)
-104	335544429	badparnum	Bad parameter number
-104	335544440	bad_msg_vec	
-104	335544456	invalid_sdl	Invalid slice description language at offset <number>
-104	335544570	dsql_command_err	Invalid command
-104	335544579	dsql_internal_err	Internal error
-104	335544590	dsql_dup_option	Option specified more than once
-104	335544591	dsql_tran_err	Unknown transaction option
-104	335544592	dsql_invalid_array	Invalid array reference
-104	335544608	command_end_err	Unexpected end of command
-104	335544612	token_err	Token unknown
-104	335544634	dsql_token_unk_err	Token unknown—line <number>, char <number>
-104	335544709	dsql_agg_ref_err	Invalid aggregate reference
-104	335544714	invalid_array_id	Invalid blob id
-104	335544730	cse_not_supported	Client/Server Express not supported in this release
-104	335544743	token_too_long	Token size exceeds limit

Table X-1. Firebird 1.5.0 Error Codes (continued)

SQLCODE	GDSCODE	SYMBOL	TEXT OF ERROR MESSAGE
-104	335544763	invalid_string_constant	A string constant is delimited by double quotes
-104	335544764	transitional_date	DATE must be changed to TIMESTAMP
-104	335544796	sql_dialect_datatype_unsupport	Client SQL dialect <number> does not support reference to <string> datatype
-104	335544798	depend_on_uncommitted_rel	You created an indirect dependency on uncommitted metadata. You must roll back the current transaction.
-104	335544821	dsql_column_pos_err	Invalid column position used in the <string> clause
-104	335544822	dsql_agg_where_err	Cannot use an aggregate function in a WHERE clause, use HAVING instead
-104	335544823	dsql_agg_group_err	Cannot use an aggregate function in a GROUP BY clause
-104	335544824	dsql_agg_column_err	Invalid expression in the <string> (not contained in either an aggregate function or the GROUP BY clause)
-104	335544825	dsql_agg_having_err	Invalid expression in the <string> (neither an aggregate function nor a part of the GROUP BY clause)
-104	335544826	dsql_agg_nested_err	Nested aggregate functions are not allowed
-104	336003075	dsql_transitional_numeric	Precision 10 to 18 changed from DOUBLE PRECISION in SQL dialect 1 to 64-bit scaled integer in SQL dialect 3
-104	336003077	sql_db_dialect_dtype_unsupport	Database SQL dialect <number> does not support reference to <string> datatype
-104	336003087	dsql_invalid_label	Label <string> <string> in the current scope
-104	336003088	dsql_datatypes_not_comparable	Datatypes <string>are not comparable in expression <string>
-105	335544702	like_escape_invalid	Invalid ESCAPE sequence
-105	335544789	extract_input_mismatch	Specified EXTRACT part does not exist in input datatype

continued

Table X-1. Firebird 1.5.0 Error Codes (continued)

SQLCODE	GDSCODE	SYMBOL	TEXT OF ERROR MESSAGE
-150	335544360	read_only_rel	Attempted update of read-only table
-150	335544362	read_only_view	Cannot update read-only view <string>
-150	335544446	non_updatable	Not updatable
-150	335544546	constaint_on_view	Cannot define constraints on views
-151	335544359	read_only_field	Attempted update of read-only column
-155	335544658	dsql_base_table	<string> is not a valid base table of the specified view
-157	335544598	specify_field_err	Must specify column name for view select expression
-158	335544599	num_field_err	Number of columns does not match select list
-162	335544685	no_dbkey	Dbkey not available for multi-table views
-170	335544512	prcmismat	Parameter mismatch for procedure <string>
-170	335544619	extern_func_err	External functions cannot have more than 10 parameters
-171	335544439	funmismat	Function <string> could not be matched
-171	335544458	invalid_dimension	Column not array or invalid dimensions (expected <number>, encountered <number>)
-171	335544618	return_mode_err	Return mode by value not allowed for this data type
-172	335544438	funnotdef	Function <string> is not defined
-203	335544708	dyn_fld_ambiguous	Ambiguous column reference.
-204	335544463	gennotdef	Generator <string> is not defined
-204	335544502	stream_not_defined	Reference to invalid stream number
-204	335544509	charset_not_found	CHARACTER SET <string> is not defined
-204	335544511	prcnotdef	Procedure <string> is not defined
-204	335544515	codnotdef	Status code <string> unknown
-204	335544516	xcpnotdef	Exception <string> not defined

Table X-1. Firebird 1.5.0 Error Codes (continued)

SQLCODE	GDSCODE	SYMBOL	TEXT OF ERROR MESSAGE
-204	335544532	ref_cnstrnt_notfound	Name of Referential Constraint not defined in constraints table.
-204	335544551	grant_obj_notfound	Could not find table/procedure for GRANT
-204	335544568	text_subtype	Implementation of text subtype <number> not located.
-204	335544573	dsql_datatype_err	Data type unknown
-204	335544580	dsql_relation_err	Table unknown
-204	335544581	dsql_procedure_err	Procedure unknown
-204	335544588	collation_not_found	COLLATION <string> is not defined
-204	335544589	collation_not_for_charset	COLLATION <string> is not valid for specified CHARACTER SET
-204	335544595	dsql_trigger_err	Trigger unknown
-204	335544620	alias_conflict_err	Alias <string> conflicts with an alias in the same statement
-204	335544621	procedure_conflict_error	Alias <string> conflicts with a procedure in the same statement
-204	335544622	relation_conflict_err	Alias <string> conflicts with a table in the same statement
-204	335544635	dsql_no_relation_alias	There is no alias or table named <string> at this scope level
-204	335544636	indexname	There is no index <string> for table <string>
-204	335544640	collation_requires_text	Invalid use of CHARACTER SET or COLLATE
-204	335544662	dsql_blob_type_unknown	BLOB SUB_TYPE <string> is not defined
-204	335544759	bad_default_value	Can not define a not null column with NULL as default value
-204	335544760	invalid_clause	Invalid clause—'<string>'
-204	335544800	too_many_contexts	Too many Contexts of Relation/Procedure/Views. Maximum allowed is 127
-204	335544817	bad_limit_param	Invalid parameter to FIRST. Only integers >= 0 are allowed.

continued

Table X-1. Firebird 1.5.0 Error Codes (continued)

SQLCODE	GDSCODE	SYMBOL	TEXT OF ERROR MESSAGE
-204	335544818	bad_skip_param	Invalid parameter to SKIP. Only integers >= 0 are allowed.
-204	336003085	dsql_ambiguous_field_name	Ambiguous field name between <string> and <string>
-205	335544396	fldnotdef	Column <string> is not defined in table <string>
-205	335544552	grant_fld_notfound	Could not find column for GRANT
-206	335544578	dsql_field_err	Column unknown
-206	335544587	dsql_blob_err	Column is not a BLOB
-206	335544596	dsql_subselect_err	Subselect illegal in this context
-208	335544617	order_by_err	Invalid ORDER BY clause
-219	335544395	relnotdef	Table <string> is not defined
-239	335544691	cache_too_small	Insufficient memory to allocate page buffer cache
-260	335544690	cache_redef	Cache redefined
-281	335544637	no_stream_plan	Table <string> is not referenced in plan
-282	335544638	stream_twice	Table <string> is referenced more than once in plan; use aliases to distinguish
-282	335544643	dsql_self_join	The table <string> is referenced twice; use aliases to differentiate
-282	335544659	duplicate_base_table	Table <string> is referenced twice in view; use an alias to distinguish
-282	335544660	view_alias	View <string> has more than one base table; use aliases to distinguish
-282	335544710	complex_view	Navigational stream <number> references a view with more than one base table
-283	335544639	stream_not_found	Table <string> is referenced in the plan but not the from list
-284	335544642	index_unused	Index <string> cannot be used in the specified plan
-291	335544531	primary_key_notnull	Column used in a PRIMARY KEY constraint must be NOT NULL.

Table X-1. Firebird 1.5.0 Error Codes (continued)

SQLCODE	GDSCODE	SYMBOL	TEXT OF ERROR MESSAGE
-292	335544534	ref_cnstrnt_update	Cannot update constraints (RDB$REF_CONSTRAINTS).
-293	335544535	check_cnstrnt_update	Cannot update constraints (RDB$CHECK_CONSTRAINTS).
-294	335544536	check_cnstrnt_del	Cannot delete CHECK constraint entry (RDB$CHECK_CONSTRAINTS)
-295	335544545	rel_cnstrnt_update	Cannot update constraints (RDB$RELATION_CONSTRAINTS).
-296	335544547	invld_cnstrnt_type	Internal gds software consistency check (invalid RDB$CONSTRAINT_TYPE)
-297	335544558	check_constraint	Operation violates CHECK constraint <string> on view or table <string>
-313	335544669	dsql_count_mismatch	Count of column list and variable list do not match
-314	335544565	transliteration_failed	Cannot transliterate character between character sets
-315	336068815	dyn_dtype_invalid	Cannot change datatype for column <string>. Changing datatype is not supported for BLOB or ARRAY columns.
-383	336068814	dyn_dependency_exists	Column <string> from table <string> is referenced in <string>
-401	335544647	invalid_operator	Invalid comparison operator for find operation
-402	335544368	segstr_no_op	Attempted invalid operation on a BLOB
-402	335544414	blobnotsup	BLOB and array data types are not supported for <string> operation
-402	335544427	datnotsup	Data operation not supported
-406	335544457	out_of_bounds	Subscript out of bounds
-407	335544435	nullsegkey	Null segment of UNIQUE KEY
-413	335544334	convert_error	Conversion error from string "<string>"
-413	335544454	nofilter	Filter not found to convert type <number> to type <number>
-501	335544327	bad_req_handle	Invalid request handle
-501	335544577	dsql_cursor_close_err	Attempt to reclose a closed cursor

continued

Table X-1. Firebird 1.5.0 Error Codes (continued)

SQLCODE	GDSCODE	SYMBOL	TEXT OF ERROR MESSAGE
-502	335544574	dsql_decl_err	Declared cursor already exists
-502	335544576	dsql_cursor_open_err	Attempt to reopen an open cursor
-504	335544572	dsql_cursor_err	Cursor unknown
-508	335544348	no_cur_rec	No current record for fetch operation
-510	335544575	dsql_cursor_update_err	Cursor not updatable
-518	335544582	dsql_request_err	Request unknown
-519	335544688	dsql_open_cursor_request	The prepare statement identifies a prepare statement with an open cursor
-530	335544466	foreign_key	Violation of FOREIGN KEY constraint "<string>" on table "<string>"
-531	335544597	dsql_crdb_prepare_err	Cannot prepare a CREATE DATABASE/SCHEMA statement
-532	335544469	trans_invalid	Transaction marked invalid by I/O error
-551	335544352	no_priv	No permission for <string> access to <string> <string>
-551	335544790	insufficient_svc_privileges	Service <string> requires SYSDBA permissions. Reattach to the Service Manager using the SYSDBA account.
-552	335544550	not_rel_owner	Only the owner of a table may reassign ownership
-552	335544553	grant_nopriv	User does not have GRANT privileges for operation
-552	335544707	grant_nopriv_on_base	User does not have GRANT privileges on base table/view for operation
-553	335544529	existing_priv_mod	Cannot modify an existing user privilege
-595	335544645	stream_crack	The current position is on a crack
-596	335544644	stream_bof	Illegal operation when at beginning of stream
-597	335544632	dsql_file_length_err	Preceding file did not specify length, so <string> must include starting page number
-598	335544633	dsql_shadow_number_err	Shadow number must be a positive integer

Table X-1. Firebird 1.5.0 Error Codes (continued)

SQLCODE	GDSCODE	SYMBOL	TEXT OF ERROR MESSAGE
-599	335544607	node_err	Gen.c: node not supported
-599	335544625	node_name_err	A node name is not permitted in a secondary, shadow, cache or log file name
-600	335544680	crrp_data_err	Sort error: corruption in data structure
-601	335544646	db_or_file_exists	Database or file exists
-604	335544593	dsql_max_arr_dim_exceeded	Array declared with too many dimensions
-604	335544594	dsql_arr_range_error	Illegal array dimension range
-605	335544682	dsql_field_ref	Inappropriate self-reference of column
-607	335544351	no_meta_update	Unsuccessful metadata update
-607	335544549	systrig_update	Cannot modify or erase a system trigger
-607	335544657	dsql_no_blob_array	Array/BLOB/DATE data types not allowed in arithmetic
-607	335544746	reftable_requires_pk	"REFERENCES table" without "(column)" requires PRIMARY KEY on referenced table
-607	335544815	generator_name	GENERATOR <string>
-607	335544816	udf_name	UDF <string>
-607	336003074	dsql_dbkey_from_non_table	Cannot SELECT RDB$DB_KEY from a stored procedure.
-607	336003086	dsql_udf_return_pos_err	External function should have return position between 1 and <number>
-612	336068812	dyn_domain_name_exists	Cannot rename domain <string> to <string>. A domain with that name already exists.
-612	336068813	dyn_field_name_exists	Cannot rename column <string> to <string>. A column with that name already exists in table <string>.
-615	335544475	relation_lock	Lock on table <string> conflicts with existing lock
-615	335544476	record_lock	Requested record lock conflicts with existing lock
-615	335544507	range_in_use	Refresh range number <number> already in use
-616	335544530	primary_key_ref	Cannot delete PRIMARY KEY being used in FOREIGN KEY definition.

continued

Table X-1. Firebird 1.5.0 Error Codes (continued)

SQLCODE	GDSCODE	SYMBOL	TEXT OF ERROR MESSAGE
-616	335544539	integ_index_del	Cannot delete index used by an Integrity Constraint
-616	335544540	integ_index_mod	Cannot modify index used by an Integrity Constraint
-616	335544541	check_trig_del	Cannot delete trigger used by a CHECK Constraint
-616	335544543	cnstrnt_fld_del	Cannot delete column being used in an Integrity Constraint.
-616	335544630	dependency	There are <number> dependencies
-616	335544674	del_last_field	Last column in a table cannot be deleted
-616	335544728	integ_index_deactivate	Cannot deactivate index used by an Integrity Constraint
-616	335544729	integ_deactivate_primary	Cannot deactivate primary index
-617	335544542	check_trig_update	Cannot update trigger used by a CHECK Constraint
-617	335544544	cnstrnt_fld_rename	Cannot rename column being used in an Integrity Constraint.
-618	335544537	integ_index_seg_del	Cannot delete index segment used by an Integrity Constraint
-618	335544538	integ_index_seg_mod	Cannot update index segment used by an Integrity Constraint
-625	335544347	not_valid	Validation error for column <string>, value "<string>"
-637	335544664	dsql_duplicate_spec	Duplicate specification of <string>- not supported
-660	335544533	foreign_key_notfound	Non-existent PRIMARY or UNIQUE KEY specified for FOREIGN KEY.
-660	335544628	idx_create_err	Cannot create index <string>
-663	335544624	idx_seg_err	Segment count of 0 defined for index <string>
-663	335544631	idx_key_err	Too many keys defined for index <string>
-663	335544672	key_field_err	Too few key columns found for index <string> (incorrect column name?)
-664	335544434	keytoobig	Key size exceeds implementation restriction for index "<string>"
-677	335544445	ext_err	<string> extension error

Table X-1. Firebird 1.5.0 Error Codes (continued)

SQLCODE	GDSCODE	SYMBOL	TEXT OF ERROR MESSAGE
-685	335544465	bad_segstr_type	Invalid BLOB type for operation
-685	335544670	blob_idx_err	Attempt to index BLOB column in index <string>
-685	335544671	array_idx_err	Attempt to index array column in index <string>
-689	335544403	badpagtyp	Page <number> is of wrong type (expected <number>, found <number>)
-689	335544650	page_type_err	Wrong page type
-690	335544679	no_segments_err	Segments not allowed in expression index <string>
-691	335544681	rec_size_err	New record size of <number> bytes is too big
-692	335544477	max_idx	Maximum indexes per table (<number>) exceeded
-693	335544663	req_max_clones_exceeded	Too many concurrent executions of the same request
-694	335544684	no_field_access	Cannot access column <string> in view <string>
-802	335544321	arith_except	Arithmetic exception, numeric overflow, or string truncation
-803	335544349	no_dup	Attempt to store duplicate value (visible to active transactions) in unique index "<string>"
-803	335544665	unique_key_violation	Violation of PRIMARY or UNIQUE KEY constraint "<string>" on table "<string>"
-804	335544380	wronumarg	Wrong number of arguments on call
-804	335544583	dsql_sqlda_err	SQLDA missing or incorrect version, or incorrect number/type of variables
-804	335544586	dsql_function_err	Function unknown
-804	335544713	dsql_sqlda_value_err	Incorrect values within SQLDA structure
-806	335544600	col_name_err	Only simple column names permitted for VIEW WITH CHECK OPTION
-807	335544601	where_err	No WHERE clause for VIEW WITH CHECK OPTION

continued

Table X-1. Firebird 1.5.0 Error Codes (continued)

SQLCODE	GDSCODE	SYMBOL	TEXT OF ERROR MESSAGE
-808	335544602	table_view_err	Only one table allowed for VIEW WITH CHECK OPTION
-809	335544603	distinct_err	DISTINCT, GROUP or HAVING not permitted for VIEW WITH CHECK OPTION
-810	335544605	subquery_err	No subqueries permitted for VIEW WITH CHECK OPTION
-811	335544652	sing_select_err	Multiple rows in singleton select
-816	335544651	ext_readonly_err	Cannot insert because the file is readonly or is on a read only medium.
-816	335544715	extfile_uns_op	Operation not supported for EXTERNAL FILE table <string>
-817	335544361	read_only_trans	Attempted update during read-only transaction
-817	335544371	segstr_no_write	Attempted write to read-only BLOB
-817	335544444	read_only	Operation not supported
-817	335544765	read_only_database	Attempted update on read-only database
-817	335544766	must_be_dialect_2_and_up	SQL dialect <string> is not supported in this database
-817	335544793	ddl_not_allowed_by_db_sql_dial	Metadata update statement is not allowed by the current database SQL dialect <number>
-817	336003079	isc_sql_dialect_conflict_num	DB dialect <number> and client dialect <number> conflict with respect to numeric precision <number>.
-820	335544356	obsolete_metadata	Metadata is obsolete
-820	335544379	wrong_ods	Unsupported on-disk structure for file <string>; found <number>, support <number>
-820	335544437	wrodynver	Wrong DYN version
-820	335544467	high_minor	Minor version too high found <number> expected <number>
-823	335544473	invalid_bookmark	Invalid bookmark handle
-824	335544474	bad_lock_level	Invalid lock level <number>
-825	335544519	bad_lock_handle	Invalid lock handle
-826	335544585	dsql_stmt_handle	Invalid statement handle
-827	335544655	invalid_direction	Invalid direction for find operation

Table X-1. Firebird 1.5.0 Error Codes (continued)

SQLCODE	GDSCODE	SYMBOL	TEXT OF ERROR MESSAGE
-827	335544718	invalid_key	Invalid key for find operation
-828	335544678	inval_key_posn	Invalid key position
-829	335544616	field_ref_err	Invalid column reference
-829	336068816	dyn_char_fld_too_small	New size specified for column <string> must be at least <number> characters.
-829	336068817	dyn_invalid_dtype_conversion	Cannot change datatype for <string>. Conversion from base type <string> to <string> is not supported.
-829	336068818	dyn_dtype_conv_invalid	Cannot change datatype for column <string> from a character type to a non-character type.
-830	335544615	field_aggregate_err	Column used with aggregate
-831	335544548	primary_key_exists	Attempt to define a second PRIMARY KEY for the same table
-832	335544604	key_field_count_err	FOREIGN KEY column count does not match PRIMARY KEY
-833	335544606	expression_eval_err	Expression evaluation not supported
-833	335544810	date_range_exceeded	Value exceeds the range for valid dates
-834	335544508	range_not_found	Refresh range number <number> not found
-835	335544649	bad_checksum	Bad checksum
-836	335544517	except	Exception <number>
-837	335544518	cache_restart	Restart shared cache manager
-838	335544560	shutwarn	Database <string> shutdown in <number> seconds
-841	335544677	version_err	Too many versions
-842	335544697	precision_err	Precision must be from 1 to 18
-842	335544698	scale_nogt	Scale must be between zero and precision
-842	335544699	expec_short	Short integer expected
-842	335544700	expec_long	Long integer expected
-842	335544701	expec_ushort	Unsigned short integer expected
-842	335544712	expec_positive	Positive value expected
-901	335544322	bad_dbkey	Invalid database key

continued

Table X-1. Firebird 1.5.0 Error Codes (continued)

SQLCODE	GDSCODE	SYMBOL	TEXT OF ERROR MESSAGE
-901	335544326	bad_dpb_form	Unrecognized database parameter block
-901	335544328	bad_segstr_handle	Invalid BLOB handle
-901	335544329	bad_segstr_id	Invalid BLOB ID
-901	335544330	bad_tpb_content	Invalid parameter in transaction parameter block
-901	335544331	bad_tpb_form	Invalid format for transaction parameter block
-901	335544332	bad_trans_handle	Invalid transaction handle (expecting explicit transaction start)
-901	335544337	excess_trans	Attempt to start more than <number> transactions
-901	335544339	infinap	Information type inappropriate for object specified
-901	335544340	infona	No information of this type available for object specified
-901	335544341	infunk	Unknown information item
-901	335544342	integ_fail	Action cancelled by trigger (<number>) to preserve data integrity
-901	335544345	lock_conflict	Lock conflict on no wait transaction
-901	335544350	no_finish	Program attempted to exit without finishing database
-901	335544353	no_recon	Transaction is not in limbo
-901	335544355	no_segstr_close	BLOB was not closed
-901	335544357	open_trans	Cannot disconnect database with open transactions (<number> active)
-901	335544358	port_len	Message length error (encountered <number>, expected <number>)
-901	335544363	req_no_trans	No transaction for request
-901	335544364	req_sync	Request synchronization error
-901	335544365	req_wrong_db	Request referenced an unavailable database
-901	335544369	segstr_no_read	Attempted read of a new, open BLOB
-901	335544370	segstr_no_trans	Attempted action on blob outside transaction
-901	335544372	segstr_wrong_db	Attempted reference to BLOB in unavailable database

Table X-1. Firebird 1.5.0 Error Codes (continued)

SQLCODE	GDSCODE	SYMBOL	TEXT OF ERROR MESSAGE
-901	335544376	unres_rel	Table <string> was omitted from the transaction reserving list
-901	335544377	uns_ext	Request includes a DSRI extension not supported in this implementation
-901	335544378	wish_list	Feature is not supported
-901	335544382	random	<string>
-901	335544383	fatal_conflict	Unrecoverable conflict with limbo transaction <number>
-901	335544392	bdbincon	Internal error
-901	335544407	dbbnotzer	Database handle not zero
-901	335544408	tranotzer	Transaction handle not zero
-901	335544418	trainlim	Transaction in limbo
-901	335544419	notinlim	Transaction not in limbo
-901	335544420	traoutsta	Transaction outstanding
-901	335544428	badmsgnum	Undefined message number
-901	335544431	blocking_signal	Blocking signal has been received
-901	335544442	noargacc_read	Database system cannot read argument <number>
-901	335544443	noargacc_write	Database system cannot write argument <number>
-901	335544450	misc_interpreted	<string>
-901	335544468	tra_state	Transaction <number> is <string>
-901	335544485	bad_stmt_handle	Invalid statement handle
-901	335544510	lock_timeout	Lock time-out on wait transaction
-901	335544559	bad_svc_handle	Invalid service handle
-901	335544561	wrospbver	Wrong version of service parameter block
-901	335544562	bad_spb_form	Unrecognized service parameter block
-901	335544563	svcnotdef	Service <string> is not defined
-901	335544609	index_name	INDEX <string>
-901	335544610	exception_name	EXCEPTION <string>
-901	335544611	field_name	COLUMN <string>
-901	335544613	union_err	Union not supported
-901	335544614	dsql_construct_err	Unsupported DSQL construct
-901	335544623	dsql_domain_err	Illegal use of keyword VALUE

continued

Table X-1. Firebird 1.5.0 Error Codes (continued)

SQLCODE	GDSCODE	SYMBOL	TEXT OF ERROR MESSAGE
-901	335544626	table_name	TABLE <string>
-901	335544627	proc_name	PROCEDURE <string>
-901	335544641	dsql_domain_not_found	Specified domain or source column <string> does not exist
-901	335544656	dsql_var_conflict	Variable <string> conflicts with parameter in same procedure
-901	335544666	srvr_version_too_old	Server version too old to support all CREATE DATABASE options
-901	335544673	no_delete	Cannot delete
-901	335544675	sort_err	Sort error
-901	335544703	svcnoexe	Service <string> does not have an associated executable
-901	335544704	net_lookup_err	Failed to locate host machine.
-901	335544705	service_unknown	Undefined service <string>/<string>.
-901	335544706	host_unknown	The specified name was not found in the hosts file or Domain Name Services.
-901	335544711	unprepared_stmt	Attempt to execute an unprepared dynamic SQL statement.
-901	335544716	svc_in_use	Service is currently busy: <string>
-901	335544731	tra_must_sweep	
-901	335544740	udf_exception	A fatal exception occurred during the execution of a user defined function.
-901	335544741	lost_db_connection	Connection lost to database
-901	335544742	no_write_user_priv	User cannot write to RDB$USER_PRIVILEGES
-901	335544767	blob_filter_exception	A fatal exception occurred during the execution of a blob filter.
-901	335544768	exception_access_violation	Access violation. The code attempted to access a virtual address without privilege to do so.
-901	335544769	exception_datatype_ missalignment	Datatype misalignment. The attempted to read or write a value that was not stored on a memory boundary.

Table X-1. Firebird 1.5.0 Error Codes (continued)

SQLCODE	GDSCODE	SYMBOL	TEXT OF ERROR MESSAGE
-901	335544770	exception_array_bounds_exceeded	Array bounds exceeded. The code attempted to access an array element that is out of bounds.
-901	335544771	exception_float_denormal_operand	Float denormal operand. One of the floating-point operands is too small to represent a standard float value.
-901	335544772	exception_float_divide_by_zero	Floating-point divide by zero. The code attempted to divide a floating-point value by zero.
-901	335544773	exception_float_inexact_result	Floating-point inexact result. The result of a floating-point operation cannot be represented as a decimal fraction.
-901	335544774	exception_float_invalid_operand	Floating-point invalid operand. An indeterminant error occurred during a floating-point operation.
-901	335544775	exception_float_overflow	Floating-point overflow. The exponent of a floating-point operation is greater than the magnitude allowed.
-901	335544776	exception_float_stack_check	Floating-point stack check. The stack overflowed or underflowed as the result of a floating-point operation.
-901	335544777	exception_float_underflow	Floating-point underflow. The exponent of a floating-point operation is less than the magnitude allowed.
-901	335544778	exception_integer_divide_by_zero	Integer divide by zero. The code attempted to divide an integer value by an integer divisor of zero.
-901	335544779	exception_integer_overflow	Integer overflow. The result of an integer operation caused the most significant bit of the result to carry.
-901	335544780	exception_unknown	An exception occurred that does not have a description. Exception number %X.

continued

Table X-1. Firebird 1.5.0 Error Codes (continued)

SQLCODE	GDSCODE	SYMBOL	TEXT OF ERROR MESSAGE
-901	335544781	exception_stack_overflow	Stack overflow. The resource requirements of the runtime stack have exceeded the memory available to it.
-901	335544782	exception_sigsegv	Segmentation Fault. The code attempted to access memory without privileges.
-901	335544783	exception_sigill	Illegal Instruction. The Code attempted to perform an illegal operation.
-901	335544784	exception_sigbus	Bus Error. The Code caused a system bus error.
-901	335544785	exception_sigfpe	Floating Point Error. The Code caused an Arithmetic Exception or a floating point exception.
-901	335544786	ext_file_delete	Cannot delete rows from external files.
-901	335544787	ext_file_modify	Cannot update rows in external files.
-901	335544788	adm_task_denied	Unable to perform operation. You must be either SYSDBA or owner of the database
-901	335544794	cancelled	Operation was cancelled
-901	335544797	svcnouser	User name and password are required while attaching to the services manager
-901	335544801	datype_notsup	Data type not supported for arithmetic
-901	335544803	dialect_not_changed	Database dialect not changed.
-901	335544804	database_create_failed	Unable to create database <string>
-901	335544805	inv_dialect_specified	Database dialect <number> is not a valid dialect.
-901	335544806	valid_db_dialects	Valid database dialects are <string>.
-901	335544811	inv_client_dialect_specified	Passed client dialect <number> is not a valid dialect.
-901	335544812	valid_client_dialects	Valid client dialects are <string>.
-901	335544814	service_not_supported	Services functionality will be supported in a later version of the product
-901	335740929	gfix_db_name	Data base file name (<string>) already given

Table X-1. Firebird 1.5.0 Error Codes (continued)

SQLCODE	GDSCODE	SYMBOL	TEXT OF ERROR MESSAGE
-901	335740930	gfix_invalid_sw	Invalid switch <string>
-901	335740932	gfix_incmp_sw	Incompatible switch combination
-901	335740933	gfix_replay_req	Replay log pathname required
-901	335740934	gfix_pgbuf_req	Number of page buffers for cache required
-901	335740935	gfix_val_req	Numeric value required
-901	335740936	gfix_pval_req	Positive numeric value required
-901	335740937	gfix_trn_req	Number of transactions per sweep required
-901	335740940	gfix_full_req	"full" or "reserve" required
-901	335740941	gfix_usrname_req	User name required
-901	335740942	gfix_pass_req	Password required
-901	335740943	gfix_subs_name	Subsystem name
-901	335740945	gfix_sec_req	Number of seconds required
-901	335740946	gfix_nval_req	Numeric value between 0 and 32767 inclusive required
-901	335740947	gfix_type_shut	Must specify type of shutdown
-901	335740948	gfix_retry	Please retry, specifying an option
-901	335740951	gfix_retry_db	Please retry, giving a database name
-901	335740991	gfix_exceed_max	Internal block exceeds maximum size
-901	335740992	gfix_corrupt_pool	Corrupt pool
-901	335740993	gfix_mem_exhausted	Virtual memory exhausted
-901	335740994	gfix_bad_pool	Bad pool id
-901	335740995	gfix_trn_not_valid	Transaction state <number> not in valid range.
-901	335741012	gfix_unexp_eoi	Unexpected end of input
-901	335741018	gfix_recon_fail	Failed to reconnect to a transaction in database <string>
-901	335741036	gfix_trn_unknown	Transaction description item unknown
-901	335741038	gfix_mode_req	"read_only" or "read_write" required
-901	336068796	dyn_role_does_not_exist	SQL role <string> does not exist

continued

Table X-1. Firebird 1.5.0 Error Codes (continued)

SQLCODE	GDSCODE	SYMBOL	TEXT OF ERROR MESSAGE
-901	336068797	dyn_no_grant_admin_opt	User <string> has no grant admin option on SQL role <string>
-901	336068798	dyn_user_not_role_member	User <string> is not a member of SQL role <string>
-901	336068799	dyn_delete_role_failed	<string> is not the owner of SQL role <string>
-901	336068800	dyn_grant_role_to_user	<string> is a SQL role and not a user
-901	336068801	dyn_inv_sql_role_name	User name <string> could not be used for SQL role
-901	336068802	dyn_dup_sql_role	SQL role <string> already exists
-901	336068803	dyn_kywd_spec_for_role	Keyword <string> can not be used as a SQL role name
-901	336068804	dyn_roles_not_supported	SQL roles are not supported in on older versions of the database. A backup and restore of the database is required.
-901	336068820	dyn_zero_len_id	Zero length identifiers are not allowed
-901	336330753	gbak_unknown_switch	Found unknown switch
-901	336330754	gbak_page_size_missing	Page size parameter missing
-901	336330755	gbak_page_size_toobig	Page size specified (<number>) greater than limit (8192 bytes)
-901	336330756	gbak_redir_ouput_missing	Redirect location for output is not specified
-901	336330757	gbak_switches_conflict	Conflicting switches for backup/restore
-901	336330758	gbak_unknown_device	Device type <string> not known
-901	336330759	gbak_no_protection	Protection is not there yet
-901	336330760	gbak_page_size_not_allowed	Page size is allowed only on restore or create
-901	336330761	gbak_multi_source_dest	Multiple sources or destinations specified
-901	336330762	gbak_filename_missing	Requires both input and output filenames
-901	336330763	gbak_dup_inout_names	Input and output have the same name. Disallowed.
-901	336330764	gbak_inv_page_size	Expected page size, encountered "<string>"
-901	336330765	gbak_db_specified	REPLACE specified, but the first file <string> is a database

Table X-1. Firebird 1.5.0 Error Codes (continued)

SQLCODE	GDSCODE	SYMBOL	TEXT OF ERROR MESSAGE
-901	336330766	gbak_db_exists	Database <string> already exists. To replace it, use the-R switch
-901	336330767	gbak_unk_device	Device type not specified
-901	336330772	gbak_blob_info_failed	Gds_$blob_info failed
-901	336330773	gbak_unk_blob_item	Do not understand BLOB INFO item <number>
-901	336330774	gbak_get_seg_failed	Gds_$get_segment failed
-901	336330775	gbak_close_blob_failed	Gds_$close_blob failed
-901	336330776	gbak_open_blob_failed	Gds_$open_blob failed
-901	336330777	gbak_put_blr_gen_id_failed	Failed in put_blr_gen_id
-901	336330778	gbak_unk_type	Data type <number> not understood
-901	336330779	gbak_comp_req_failed	Gds_$compile_request failed
-901	336330780	gbak_start_req_failed	Gds_$start_request failed
-901	336330781	gbak_rec_failed	gds_$receive failed
-901	336330782	gbak_rel_req_failed	Gds_$release_request failed
-901	336330783	gbak_db_info_failed	gds_$database_info failed
-901	336330784	gbak_no_db_desc	Expected database description record
-901	336330785	gbak_db_create_failed	Failed to create database <string>
-901	336330786	gbak_decomp_len_error	RESTORE: decompression length error
-901	336330787	gbak_tbl_missing	Cannot find table <string>
-901	336330788	gbak_blob_col_missing	Cannot find column for BLOB
-901	336330789	gbak_create_blob_failed	Gds_$create_blob failed
-901	336330790	gbak_put_seg_failed	Gds_$put_segment failed
-901	336330791	gbak_rec_len_exp	Expected record length
-901	336330792	gbak_inv_rec_len	Wrong length record, expected <number> encountered <number>
-901	336330793	gbak_exp_data_type	Expected data attribute
-901	336330794	gbak_gen_id_failed	Failed in store_blr_gen_id
-901	336330795	gbak_unk_rec_type	Do not recognize record type <number>
-901	336330796	gbak_inv_bkup_ver	Expected backup version 1, 2, or 3. Found <number>
-901	336330797	gbak_missing_bkup_desc	Expected backup description record
-901	336330798	gbak_string_trunc	String truncated

continued

Table X-1. Firebird 1.5.0 Error Codes (continued)

SQLCODE	GDSCODE	SYMBOL	TEXT OF ERROR MESSAGE
-901	336330799	gbak_cant_rest_record	Warning—record could not be restored
-901	336330800	gbak_send_failed	Gds_$send failed
-901	336330801	gbak_no_tbl_name	No table name for data
-901	336330802	gbak_unexp_eof	Unexpected end of file on backup file
-901	336330803	gbak_db_format_too_old	Database format <number> is too old to restore to
-901	336330804	gbak_inv_array_dim	Array dimension for column <string> is invalid
-901	336330807	gbak_xdr_len_expected	Expected XDR record length
-901	336330817	gbak_open_bkup_error	Cannot open backup file <string>
-901	336330818	gbak_open_error	Cannot open status and error output file <string>
-901	336330934	gbak_missing_block_fac	Blocking factor parameter missing
-901	336330935	gbak_inv_block_fac	Expected blocking factor, encountered "<string>"
-901	336330936	gbak_block_fac_specified	A blocking factor may not be used in conjunction with device CT
-901	336330940	gbak_missing_username	User name parameter missing
-901	336330941	gbak_missing_password	Password parameter missing
-901	336330952	gbak_missing_skipped_bytes	Missing parameter for the number of bytes to be skipped
-901	336330953	gbak_inv_skipped_bytes	Expected number of bytes to be skipped, encountered "<string>"
-901	336330965	gbak_err_restore_charset	Bad attribute for RDB$CHARACTER_SETS
-901	336330967	gbak_err_restore_collation	Bad attribute for RDB$COLLATIONS
-901	336330972	gbak_read_error	Unexpected I/O error while reading from backup file
-901	336330973	gbak_write_error	Unexpected I/O error while writing to backup file
-901	336330985	gbak_db_in_use	Could not drop database <string> (database might be in use)
-901	336330990	gbak_sysmemex	System memory exhausted
-901	336331002	gbak_restore_role_failed	Bad attributes for restoring SQL role
-901	336331005	gbak_role_op_missing	SQL role parameter missing

Table X-1. Firebird 1.5.0 Error Codes (continued)

SQLCODE	GDSCODE	SYMBOL	TEXT OF ERROR MESSAGE
-901	336331010	gbak_page_buffers_missing	Page buffers parameter missing
-901	336331011	gbak_page_buffers_wrong_param	Expected page buffers, encountered "<string>"
-901	336331012	gbak_page_buffers_restore	Page buffers is allowed only on restore or create
-901	336331014	gbak_inv_size	Size specification either missing or incorrect for file <string>
-901	336331015	gbak_file_outof_sequence	File <string> out of sequence
-901	336331016	gbak_join_file_missing	Can't join—one of the files missing
-901	336331017	gbak_stdin_not_supptd	Standard input is not supported when using join operation
-901	336331018	gbak_stdout_not_supptd	Standard output is not supported when using split operation
-901	336331019	gbak_bkup_corrupt	Backup file <string> might be corrupt
-901	336331020	gbak_unk_db_file_spec	Database file specification missing
-901	336331021	gbak_hdr_write_failed	Can't write a header record to file <string>
-901	336331022	gbak_disk_space_ex	Free disk space exhausted
-901	336331023	gbak_size_lt_min	File size given (<number>) is less than minimum allowed (<number>)
-901	336331025	gbak_svc_name_missing	Service name parameter missing
-901	336331026	gbak_not_ownr	Cannot restore over current database, must be SYSDBA or owner of the existing database.
-901	336331031	gbak_mode_req	"read_only" or "read_write" required
-901	336331033	gbak_just_data	Just data ignore all constraints, etc.
-901	336331034	gbak_data_only	Restoring data only ignoring foreign key, unique, not null & other constraints
-901	336723983	gsec_cant_open_db	Unable to open database
-901	336723984	gsec_switches_error	Error in switch specifications
-901	336723985	gsec_no_op_spec	No operation specified

continued

Table X-1. Firebird 1.5.0 Error Codes (continued)

SQLCODE	GDSCODE	SYMBOL	TEXT OF ERROR MESSAGE
-901	336723986	gsec_no_usr_name	No user name specified
-901	336723987	gsec_err_add	Add record error
-901	336723988	gsec_err_modify	Modify record error
-901	336723989	gsec_err_find_mod	Find/modify record error
-901	336723990	gsec_err_rec_not_found	Record not found for user: <string>
-901	336723991	gsec_err_delete	Delete record error
-901	336723992	gsec_err_find_del	Find/delete record error
-901	336723996	gsec_err_find_disp	Find/display record error
-901	336723997	gsec_inv_param	Invalid parameter, no switch defined
-901	336723998	gsec_op_specified	Operation already specified
-901	336723999	gsec_pw_specified	Password already specified
-901	336724000	gsec_uid_specified	Uid already specified
-901	336724001	gsec_gid_specified	Gid already specified
-901	336724002	gsec_proj_specified	Project already specified
-901	336724003	gsec_org_specified	Organization already specified
-901	336724004	gsec_fname_specified	First name already specified
-901	336724005	gsec_mname_specified	Middle name already specified
-901	336724006	gsec_lname_specified	Last name already specified
-901	336724008	gsec_inv_switch	Invalid switch specified
-901	336724009	gsec_amb_switch	Ambiguous switch specified
-901	336724010	gsec_no_op_specified	No operation specified for parameters
-901	336724011	gsec_params_not_allowed	No parameters allowed for this operation
-901	336724012	gsec_incompat_switch	Incompatible switches specified
-901	336724044	gsec_inv_username	Invalid user name (maximum 31 bytes allowed)
-901	336724045	gsec_inv_pw_length	Warning—maximum 8 significant bytes of password used
-901	336724046	gsec_db_specified	Database already specified
-901	336724047	gsec_db_admin_specified	Database administrator name already specified
-901	336724048	gsec_db_admin_pw_specified	Database administrator password already specified
-901	336724049	gsec_sql_role_specified	SQL role name already specified
-901	336920577	gstat_unknown_switch	Found unknown switch

Table X-1. Firebird 1.5.0 Error Codes (continued)

SQLCODE	GDSCODE	SYMBOL	TEXT OF ERROR MESSAGE
-901	336920578	gstat_retry	Please retry, giving a database name
-901	336920579	gstat_wrong_ods	Wrong ODS version, expected \<number\>, encountered \<number\>
-901	336920580	gstat_unexpected_eof	Unexpected end of database file.
-901	336920605	gstat_open_err	Can't open database file \<string\>
-901	336920606	gstat_read_err	Can't read a database page
-901	336920607	gstat_sysmemex	System memory exhausted
-902	335544333	bug_check	Internal gds software consistency check (\<string\>)
-902	335544335	db_corrupt	Database file appears corrupt (\<string\>)
-902	335544344	io_error	I/O error for file %.0s"\<string\>"
-902	335544346	metadata_corrupt	Corrupt system table
-902	335544373	sys_request	Operating system directive \<string\> failed
-902	335544384	badblk	Internal error
-902	335544385	invpoolcl	Internal error
-902	335544387	relbadblk	Internal error
-902	335544388	blktoobig	Block size exceeds implementation restriction
-902	335544394	badodsver	Incompatible version of on-disk structure
-902	335544397	dirtypage	Internal error
-902	335544398	waifortra	Internal error
-902	335544399	doubleloc	Internal error
-902	335544400	nodnotfnd	Internal error
-902	335544401	dupnodfnd	Internal error
-902	335544402	locnotmar	Internal error
-902	335544404	corrupt	Database corrupted
-902	335544405	badpage	Checksum error on database page \<number\>
-902	335544406	badindex	Index is broken
-902	335544409	trareqmis	Transaction—request mismatch (synchronization error)
-902	335544410	badhndcnt	Bad handle count

continued

Table X-1. Firebird 1.5.0 Error Codes (continued)

SQLCODE	GDSCODE	SYMBOL	TEXT OF ERROR MESSAGE
-902	335544411	wrotpbver	Wrong version of transaction parameter block
-902	335544412	wroblrver	Unsupported BLR version (expected <number>, encountered <number>)
-902	335544413	wrodpbver	Wrong version of database parameter block
-902	335544415	badrelation	Database corrupted
-902	335544416	nodetach	Internal error
-902	335544417	notremote	Internal error
-902	335544422	dbfile	Internal error
-902	335544423	orphan	Internal error
-902	335544432	lockmanerr	Lock manager error
-902	335544436	sqlerr	SQL error code = <number>
-902	335544448	bad_sec_info	
-902	335544449	invalid_sec_info	
-902	335544470	buf_invalid	Cache buffer for page <number> invalid
-902	335544471	indexnotdefined	There is no index in table <string> with id <number>
-902	335544472	login	Your user name and password are not defined. Ask your database administrator to set up a Firebird login.
-902	335544506	shutinprog	Database <string> shutdown in progress
-902	335544528	shutdown	Database <string> shutdown
-902	335544557	shutfail	Database shutdown unsuccessful
-902	335544569	dsql_error	Dynamic SQL Error
-902	335544653	psw_attach	Cannot attach to password database
-902	335544654	psw_start_trans	Cannot start transaction for password database
-902	335544717	err_stack_limit	Stack size insufficient to execute current request
-902	335544721	network_error	Unable to complete network request to host "<string>".
-902	335544722	net_connect_err	Failed to establish a connection.
-902	335544723	net_connect_listen_err	Error while listening for an incoming connection.

Table X-1. Firebird 1.5.0 Error Codes (continued)

SQLCODE	GDSCODE	SYMBOL	TEXT OF ERROR MESSAGE
-902	335544724	net_event_connect_err	Failed to establish a secondary connection for event processing.
-902	335544725	net_event_listen_err	Error while listening for an incoming event connection request.
-902	335544726	net_read_err	Error reading data from the connection.
-902	335544727	net_write_err	Error writing data to the connection.
-902	335544732	unsupported_network_drive	Access to databases on file servers is not supported.
-902	335544733	io_create_err	Error while trying to create file
-902	335544734	io_open_err	Error while trying to open file
-902	335544735	io_close_err	Error while trying to close file
-902	335544736	io_read_err	Error while trying to read from file
-902	335544737	io_write_err	Error while trying to write to file
-902	335544738	io_delete_err	Error while trying to delete file
-902	335544739	io_access_err	Error while trying to access file
-902	335544745	login_same_as_role_name	Your login <string> is same as one of the SQL role name. Ask your database administrator to set up a valid Firebird login.
-902	335544791	file_in_use	The file <string> is currently in use by another process. Try again later.
-902	335544795	unexp_spb_form	Unexpected item in service parameter block, expected <string>
-902	335544809	extern_func_dir_error	Function <string> is in <string>, which is not in a permitted directory for external functions.
-902	335544819	io_32bit_exceeded_err	File exceeded maximum size of 2GB. Add another database file or use a 64 bit I/O version of Firebird.
-902	335544820	invalid_savepoint	Unable to find savepoint with name <string> in transaction context

continued

Table X-1. Firebird 1.5.0 Error Codes (continued)

SQLCODE	GDSCODE	SYMBOL	TEXT OF ERROR MESSAGE
-902	335544831	conf_access_denied	Access to <string> "<string>" is denied by server administrator
-904	335544324	bad_db_handle	Invalid database handle (no active connection)
-904	335544375	unavailable	Unavailable database
-904	335544381	imp_exc	Implementation limit exceeded
-904	335544386	nopoolids	Too many requests
-904	335544389	bufexh	Buffer exhausted
-904	335544391	bufinuse	Buffer in use
-904	335544393	reqinuse	Request in use
-904	335544424	no_lock_mgr	No lock manager available
-904	335544430	virmemexh	Unable to allocate memory from operating system
-904	335544451	update_conflict	Update conflicts with concurrent update
-904	335544453	obj_in_use	Object <string> is in use
-904	335544455	shadow_accessed	Cannot attach active shadow file
-904	335544460	shadow_missing	A file in manual shadow <number> is unavailable
-904	335544661	index_root_page_full	Cannot add index, index root page is full.
-904	335544676	sort_mem_err	Sort error: not enough memory
-904	335544683	req_depth_exceeded	Request depth exceeded. (Recursive definition?)
-904	335544758	sort_rec_size_err	Sort record size of <number> bytes is too big
-904	335544761	too_many_handles	Too many open handles to database
-904	335544792	service_att_err	Cannot attach to services manager
-904	335544799	svc_name_missing	The service name was not specified.
-904	335544813	optimizer_between_err	Unsupported field type specified in BETWEEN predicate.
-904	335544827	exec_sql_invalid_arg	Invalid argument in EXECUTE STATEMENT- cannot convert to string
-904	335544828	exec_sql_invalid_req	Wrong request type in EXECUTE STATEMENT '<string>'

Table X-1. Firebird 1.5.0 Error Codes (continued)

SQLCODE	GDSCODE	SYMBOL	TEXT OF ERROR MESSAGE
-904	335544829	exec_sql_invalid_var	Variable type (position <number>) in EXECUTE STATEMENT '<string>' INTO does not match returned column type
-904	335544830	exec_sql_max_call_exceeded	Too many recursion levels of EXECUTE STATEMENT
-906	335544744	max_att_exceeded	Maximum user count exceeded. Contact your database administrator.
-909	335544667	drdb_completed_with_errs	Drop database completed with errors
-911	335544459	rec_in_limbo	Record from transaction <number> is stuck in limbo
-913	335544336	deadlock	Deadlock
-922	335544323	bad_db_format	File <string> is not a valid database
-923	335544421	connect_reject	Connection rejected by remote interface
-923	335544461	cant_validate	Secondary server attachments cannot validate databases
-923	335544464	cant_start_logging	Secondary server attachments cannot start logging
-924	335544325	bad_dpb_content	Bad parameters on attach or create database
-924	335544441	bad_detach	Database detach completed with errors
-924	335544648	conn_lost	Connection lost to pipe server
-926	335544447	no_rollback	No rollback performed
-999	335544689	ib_error	Firebird error

Reserved Words

TABLE XI-1 CONTAINS KEYWORDS THAT are reserved in some way in Firebird. Some have special markings:

KEYWORD **(con.)** marks words that are reserved in their specific contexts. For example, the word UPDATING is a keyword in PSQL and will be disallowed as a variable or argument name.

[*KEYWORD*] marks words that are not currently reserved words but should be treated as such for planned future implementation or for compatibility with InterBase.

/* KEYWORD */ marks words that are reserved words in Firebird 1.0.*x* but were released in Firebird 1.5.

Table XI-1. Firebird Reserved Words

[ABS]	ACTION	ACTIVE
ADD	ADMIN	AFTER
ALL	ALTER	AND
ANY	ARE	AS
ASC	ASCENDING	AT
AUTO	AUTODDL	AVG
BASED	BASENAME	BASE_NAME
BEFORE	BEGIN	BETWEEN
BIGINT	BLOB	BLOBEDIT
[BOOLEAN]	[BOTH]	/* BREAK */
BUFFER	BY	CACHE
CASCADE	CASE	CAST
CHAR	CHARACTER	[CHAR_LENGTH]
[CHARACTER_LENGTH]	CHECK	CHECK_POINT_LEN
CHECK_POINT_LENGTH	CLOSE	COALESCE (con.)
COLLATE	COLLATION	COLUMN
COMMIT	COMMITTED	COMPILETIME
COMPUTED	CONDITIONAL	CONNECT
CONSTRAINT	CONTAINING	CONTINUE
COUNT	CREATE	CSTRING
CURRENT	CURRENT_CONNECTION	CURRENT_DATE
CURRENT_ROLE	CURRENT_TIME	CURRENT_TIMESTAMP

Table XI-1. Firebird Reserved Words (continued)

CURRENT_TRANSACTION	CURRENT_USER	DATABASE
DATE	DAY	DB_KEY
DEBUG	DEC	DECIMAL
DECLARE	DEFAULT	[DEFERRED]
DELETE	DELETING (con.)	DESC
DESCENDING	DESCRIBE	/* DESCRIPTOR */
DISCONNECT	DISPLAY	DISTINCT
DO	DOMAIN	DOUBLE
DROP	ECHO	EDIT
ELSE	END	ENTRY_POINT
ESCAPE	EVENT	EXCEPTION
EXECUTE	EXISTS	EXIT
EXTERN	EXTERNAL	EXTRACT
[FALSE]	FETCH	FILE
FILTER	/* FIRST */	FLOAT
FOR	FOREIGN	FOUND
FREE_IT	FROM	FULL
FUNCTION	GDSCODE	GENERATOR
GEN_ID	[GLOBAL]	GOTO
GRANT	GROUP	GROUP_COMMIT_WAIT
GROUP_COMMIT_WAIT_TIME	HAVING	HEADING
HELP	HOUR	IF
/* IIF */	IMMEDIATE	IN
INACTIVE	INDEX	INDICATOR
INIT	INNER	INPUT
INPUT_TYPE	INSERT	INSERTING (con.)
INT	INTEGER	INTO
IS	ISOLATION	ISQL
JOIN	KEY	LAST (con.)
LC_MESSAGES	LC_TYPE	[LEADING]
LEAVE (con.)	LEFT	LENGTH
LEV	LEVEL	LIKE
LOCK (con.)	LOGFILE	LOG_BUFFER_SIZE
LOG_BUF_SIZE	LONG	MANUAL
MAX	MAXIMUM	MAXIMUM_SEGMENT
MAX_SEGMENT	MERGE	MESSAGE
MIN	MINIMUM	MINUTE
MODULE_NAME	MONTH	NAMES
NATIONAL	NATURAL	NCHAR
NO	NOAUTO	NOT

Table XI-1. Firebird Reserved Words (continued)

NULL	NULLIF (con.)	NULLS (con.)
NUM_LOG_BUFS	NUM_LOG_BUFFERS	NUMERIC
[OCTET_LENGTH]	OF	ON
ONLY	OPEN	OPTION
OR	ORDER	OUTER
OUTPUT	OUTPUT_TYPE	OVERFLOW
PAGE	PAGELENGTH	PAGES
PAGE_SIZE	PARAMETER	PASSWORD
[PERCENT]	PLAN	POSITION
POST_EVENT	PRECISION	PREPARE
[PRESERVE]	PRIMARY	PRIVILEGES
PROCEDURE	PUBLIC	QUIT
RAW_PARTITIONS	RDB$DB_KEY	READ
REAL	RECORD_VERSION	RECREATE
REFERENCES	RELEASE	RESERV
RESERVING	RESTRICT	RETAIN
RETURN	RETURNING_VALUES	RETURNS
REVOKE	RIGHT	ROLE
ROLLBACK	ROW_COUNT	[ROWS]
RUNTIME	SAVEPOINT	SCHEMA
SECOND	SELECT	SET
SHADOW	SHARED	SHELL
SHOW	SINGULAR	SIZE
/* SKIP */	SMALLINT	SNAPSHOT
SOME	SORT	SQL
SQLCODE	SQLERROR	SQLWARNING
STABILITY	STARTING	STARTS
STATEMENT (con.)	STATIC	STATISTICS
SUB_TYPE	/* SUBSTRING */	SUM
SUSPEND	TABLE	[TEMPORARY]
TERM	TERMINATOR	THEN
[TIES]	TIME	TIMESTAMP
TO	[TRAILING]	TRANSACTION
TRANSLATE	TRANSLATION	TRIGGER
[TRIM]	[TRUE]	TYPE
UNCOMMITTED	UNION	UNIQUE
[UNKNOWN]	UPDATE	UPDATING (con.)
UPPER	USER	USING (con.)
VALUE	VALUES	VARCHAR

continued

Table XI-1. Firebird Reserved Words (continued)

VARIABLE	VARYING	VERSION
VIEW	WAIT	WEEKDAY
WHEN	WHENEVER	WHERE
WHILE	WITH	WORK
WRITE	YEAR	YEARDAY

Readings and Resources

FIREBIRD COMPRISES A HUGE COMMUNITY of helpers, experience, documentation, software, news and other resources to assist you as a Firebird developer or administrator. This list represents some of the best-known resources but it is not exhaustive—new resources come online daily!

Recommended Reading

API Guide (APIGuide.pdf) and *Embedded SQL Guide* (EmbedSQL.pdf) for InterBase 6 and 7, published by Borland. These guides are available in printed form in the media kit, from the Borland Shop at http://www.borland.com. The beta versions can be downloaded from numerous sites around the world—Google on the PDF document names. They are also available from the Downloads ➤ InterBase page at http://www.ibphoenix.com.

Data Modeling Essentials: Analysis, Design and Innovation, 2nd Edition (Coriolis Group, 2000) by Graeme Simsion, revised and updated by Graham Witt and Graeme Simsion. This is *the* book for learning from the ground up about data analysis, relationships, normalization, and creative ways to solve tough design problems. This edition includes sections on UML and an object-oriented approach, capturing patterns and a demo chapter on modeling for data warehousing. The appendix includes a walk-through example for presenting a large data model.

Joe Celko's SQL For Smarties: Advanced SQL Programming (Morgan Kaufmann, 1999), by Joe Celko. This is a classic book of magic spells for SQL programming, including one of the best discussions so far published on designing tree structures.

Joe Celko's Data and Databases: Concepts in Practice (Morgan Kaufmann, 1999), by Joe Celko. It is not a primer, but this book bridges the gap between theory and practice.

Joe Celko's SQL Puzzles and Answers (Morgan Kaufmann, 1997), by Joe Celko. This book offers a hands-on approach to solving those syntax challenges.

The Essence of SQL: Guide to Learning Most of SQL in the Least Amount of Time (Coriolis Group, 1997) by David Rozenshtein and Tom Bondur (editor). This very concise book cuts out the mystique of SQL for the newbie.

The Practical SQL Handbook: Using Structured Query Language, 3rd Edition (Addison-Wesley Professional, 1996) by Judith S. Bowman et al. This is a well-reviewed how-to and desktop reference for standard SQL.

A Guide to the SQL Standard, 4th Edition (Addison-Wesley Professional, 1997) by C.J. Date and Hugh Darwen. All the things you wanted to know—and much that you didn't know you didn't know—about SQL-92, by the RDBMS "gods."

Understanding the New SQL: A Complete Guide (Morgan Kaufmann, 1993) by Jim Melton and Alan Simon. This book covers SQL-89 and SQL-92, and is a comprehensive, good lookup reference for the beginner. Examples are consistent, although often impractical. The book includes some basic modeling theory.

Mastering SQL (Sybex, 2000) by Martin Gruber. This updated and expanded new version of the author's *Understanding SQL* makes standard SQL reachable, even for the beginner, and helps solid skills to develop quickly.

Reference Websites

Firebird Project Sites

`http://sourceforge.net/projects/firebird` is the development site where you can access the CVS tree, access source kits and binaries, and browse and record bugs.

`http://www.firebirdsql.org`, alias `http://firebird.sourceforge.net`, is where you can find information and news on the project. All Firebird binaries can be accessed through this site, along with how-tos, FAQs, subscription pages, and details of forums and newsgroups.

`http://www.firebirdsql.org/ff/foundation` offers information and news about the FirebirdSQL Foundation Inc., the non-profit group that raises funds for project grants.

Resource Websites

`http://www.ibphoenix.com` is an information and news center for users developing with Firebird or any version of InterBase. It has an online KnowledgeBase, dozens of authoritative articles, contacts for commercial support and consulting, links to tools and projects, and a CD subscription service.

`http://www.cvalde.net` is guru Claudio Valderrama's "Unofficial InterBase Site," home of the InterBase webring and links to many other sites where people are doing interesting things with Firebird and tools development. This site contains an eclectic collection of articles, mended software, news links, and more.

`http://www.volny.cz/iprenosil` is Ivan Prenosil's site. This site provides a repository of Ivan's insightful articles and online tools, written and maintained by a Firebird guru.

`http://www.interbase-world.com` is a site full of news, interviews, and practical articles in Russian and English, about Firebird and InterBase. It provides links to many other Firebird community sites in Russia and around the world.

`http://www.ibphoenix.cz` is a resource site for Czech users of Firebird and InterBase, maintained by Pavel Cisar, author of the first Czech book about Firebird and InterBase. The site offers links, downloads, and consultancy.

`http://firebird-fr.eu.org` is maintained by Philippe Makowski in French, and includes resources, articles, and news.

`http://www.comunidade-firebird.org` is an international Portuguese-language developer site, maintained for and by Portuguese-speaking developers and members of Communidade Firebird Língua Portuguesa. It offers downloads, links, services, articles, and jobs.

`http://www.firebase.com.br/fb` is a Brazilian site in Portuguese, maintained by Carlos Cantu. The site contains news, articles galore, courseware, and software downloads.

`http://tech.firebird.gr.jp` is the home of the Firebird Japanese Users Association. This site provides news, articles, links, and downloads.

`http://www.fingerbird.de` is a portal site containing links to Firebird sites, articles, downloads, resources, and more

Firebird Forums

Technical support: `firebird-support@yahoogroups.com`. This is the main support forum for database and application developers. It's the right place to take questions about SQL, installation, configuration, design, and quirks. It's the wrong place to go for questions about drivers and application development environments—these have their own forums. It's also the first place to raise a suspected bug for preliminary discussion. Join at `http://groups.yahoo.com/community/firebird-support`.

The core developers' lab: `firebird-devel@lists.sourceforge.net`. This list is for the engine workers and field testers. Members are usually happy to help with building from source code, but you are expected to search the list archive to discover the "basics" for yourself. Support questions and "noise" are off-topic there. Bug discussions are welcome, provided you have an excellent bug description available, provide exact details of the Firebird version, operating system, and hardware, and have already visited the Bug Tracker at the project site to establish that it not already known. Join at `https://lists.sourceforge.net/lists/listinfo/firebird-devel`.

QA testers' lab: `firebird-test@lists.sourceforge.net`. This is a field and unit testers' forum. Testers and test designers are welcome to join this group. It does not handle any support questions. Join at `https://lists.sourceforge.net/lists/listinfo/firebird-test`.

Java: firebird-java@yahoogroups.com. This is a developers' forum and user support for the JDBC/JCA drivers (see Appendix III). It's also the place to raise suspected bug issues for the Java drivers. Join up with this group at http://groups.yahoo.com/community/firebird-java.

 NOTE   Borland's InterClient and InterServer products are not maintained or developed in or for Firebird at all.

Firebird ODBC-JDBC driver project: firebird-odbc-devel@lists.sourceforge.net. This is a developer, tester, and users' forum for the Firebird ODBC-JDBC driver (see Appendix III). Note that third-party ODBC drivers are not supported in this list—see the proprietors' websites for support details. Join the Firebird ODBC list at https://lists.sourceforge.net/lists/listinfo/firebird-odbc-devel.

.NET Provider: firebird-net-provider@lists.sourceforge.net. This is a developer and users' forum for the Firebird .NET Provider interface project (see Appendix III). Join the forum at https://lists.sourceforge.net/lists/listinfo/firebird-net-provider.

PHP: firebird-PHP@yahoogroups.com. This is a peer support forum for developers building Firebird applications with PHP (see Appendix III). Join at http://groups.yahoo.com/community/firebird-php.

Visual Basic: firebird-vb@yahoogroups.com. This is a peer support forum for developers using Visual Basic to build front-ends. Join at http://groups.yahoo.com/community/firebird-vb.

Converting from other DBMSs: ib-conversions@yahoogroups.com. This is where you go for tips and advice about converting databases to Firebird. General support questions are not welcome—join firebird-support as well. Join at http://groups.yahoo.com/community/ib-conversions.

Architecture and design of the engine: firebird-architect@yahoogroups.com. Here's where the engine gurus hang out and discuss questions and proposals about enhancing the Firebird engine and its interfaces. Participants and lurkers are welcome but no support questions are permitted. Discussions are usually quite rarefied. Join at http://groups.yahoo.com/community/firebird-architect.

About tools: firebird-tools@yahoogroups.com. This is a forum for people developing tools and plug-ins for Firebird. Announcements occur regularly here and the tools developers are usually available to steer you to the right place for help. Join at http://groups.yahoo.com/community/firebird-tools. For a selection of tools available, see Appendix V.

General community discussions: firebird-general@yahoogroups.com. No support questions are allowed, but just about anything else goes as long as it is related to Firebird in some way. Topics range far and wide, from logos, to fluffy toys, to deployment discussions, to interesting mentions of Firebird in the online press.

Documentation: firebird-docs@lists.sourceforge.net. This is also a non-lurkers' list—a forum for people working on documentation or those who want to start. Again, support questions are unwelcome. If you are interested in getting involved with this XML project, join at https://lists.sourceforge.net/lists/listinfo/firebird-docs.

Website: firebird-website@lists.sourceforge.net. This isn't a support list for your web application projects. It's another non-lurkers' list—a forum for people working on the Firebird website or those who want to volunteer to help.

News group interface: All of these lists are mirrored to a news server at news://news.atkin.com. Anyone can read the list traffic through this interface, but you must be a subscribed member of the list community in order to post messages through your newsreader.

How to Become a Firebird Developer

The Firebird Project has a permanently open door to good C++ programmers who want to contribute to new design and development. People get membership of the project not by promises but by deeds. The first thing to do is get a SourceForge "nick" and then join the firebird-devel and firebird-architect lists (see the preceding section for details). Find an existing or new project that interests you, discuss it, and submit code.

The project is constantly interested to hear from serious test designers and testers, too.

The FirebirdSQL Foundation has funds that can be made available to assist serious contributors to commit to works on the project.

Glossary

TERM	DEFINITION
.fdb or .FDB	By convention, the suffix used for a Firebird primary database file. It is no more than a convention: Firebird works with any other file suffix, or none at all.
.gdb or .GDB	By convention, this is the file extension traditionally used for InterBase databases. However, a Firebird database file can have any extension, or none at all. Many Firebird developers use .fdb instead, to distinguish their Firebird databases from their InterBase databases, or as part of a solution to a performance-crippling "safety feature" introduced by Microsoft Corporation into their Windows ME and XP operating systems, targeted at files having the .gdb extension. Why "GDB"? It is an artifact of the name of the company that created the original InterBase, Groton Database Systems.
ADO	An abbreviation for *Active Data Objects*, a high-level application-to-data source interface introduced by Microsoft in 1996. Earlier versions could access only relational databases with fixed columns and data types, but later versions could interface also with other DBMS models, filesystems, data files, e-mail messages, tree structures, and heterogeneous data structures.
aggregate (function)	A function that returns a result derived from a calculation that aggregates (collects together) values from a set of rows that is grouped in some fashion by the syntax of the SQL statement. For example, the internal function SUM( ) operates on a non-null numerical column to return the result of adding all of the values in that column together for all of the rows cited by a WHERE or GROUP BY clause. Output that is aggregated by a WHERE clause returns one row of output, whereas that aggregated by a GROUP BY clause potentially returns multiple rows.
alerter (events)	A term coined to represent a client routine or class that is capable of "listening" for specific database EVENTs generated from triggers or stored procedures running on the server.
ALICE	The internal name for the source code for the **gfix** utilities—a corruption of the words "all else."

alternative key
(alternate key)

A term used for a unique key that is not the primary key. A unique key is created by applying the UNIQUE constraint to a column or group of columns. A foreign key in a formal referential integrity relationship can link its REFERENCES clause to an alternative key.

API

An abbreviation for *application programming interface*. An API provides a set of formal structures through which application programs can communicate with functions internal to another software. The Firebird API surfaces such an interface as a client library compiled specifically for each supported platform. The Firebird API structures are C structures, designed to be translatable to virtually any host application language. Translations can be found for Java, Pascal, Perl and, to some degree, PHP 4, Python, and others.

argument

A value of a prescribed data type and size that is passed to a function or stored procedure to be operated upon. Stored procedures can be designed to both accept *input* arguments and return *output* arguments. For the returned values of functions (both internal and user defined) the term *result* is more commonly used than *argument*.

The terms *parameter* and *argument* are often used interchangeably with regard to stored procedures, thanks to Borland's adoption of the term *parameter* in its Delphi data access classes to name the properties to which stored procedure arguments are assigned.

array slice

A contiguous range of elements from a Firebird array is known as a *slice*. A slice can consist of any contiguous block of data from an array, from a single element of one dimension to the maximum number of elements of all defined dimensions.

atomicity

In the context of transactions, *atomicity* refers to the character of the transaction mechanism that wraps a grouping of changes to rows in one or more tables to form a single unit of work that is either committed entirely or rolled back entirely. In the context of a key, a key is said to be atomic if its value has no meaning as data.

AutoCommit

When a change is posted to the database, it will not become permanent until the transaction in which it was posted is committed by the client application. If the client rolls back the transaction instead of committing it, the posted changes will be cancelled.

Some client development tools provide a mechanism by which posting any change to any table invokes a follow-up call to commit the transaction, without further action by the user. This mechanism is usually called *AutoCommit*, or some similar term. It is not a Firebird mechanism—Firebird never commits transactions started by clients.

backup/restore **(Firebird style)**	*Backup* is an external process initiated by a user—usually SYSDBA—to decompose a database into a collection of compressed disk structures comprising metadata and data, which are separated for storage. *Restore* is another external process—also user-initiated—which completely reconstructs the original database from these stored elements. The backup process also performs a number of housecleaning tasks on a database whilst reading it for backing up; and a restored database will be completely free of "garbage". See also **gbak**.
BDE	An abbreviation for *Borland Database Engine*. Originally designed as the database engine of Paradox, it was extended to provide a generic middleware connectivity layer between a variety of relational database engines and Borland application development tools for the Microsoft DOS and Windows platforms. The vendor-specific rules applicable to each RDBMS are encapsulated in a set of driver libraries known as *SQL Links*. The SQL Links drivers are version specific. By 2000, when Borland released the codebase from which Firebird 1.0 was developed, it had already deprecated the BDE in favor of more modern driver technologies. The last known version of the BDE (v.5.2) shipped with Borland Delphi 6. An InterBase driver in this distribution only partly supports Firebird.
binary tree	A logical tree structure in which a node can subtend a maximum of two branches. Firebird indexes are formed in binary tree structures.
BLOB	An acronym for *binary large object*. This is a data item of unlimited size, in any format, that is streamed into the database byte by byte and stored without any format modification. Firebird allows BLOBs of different types to be classed by means of *subtypes*. Firebird's ancestor, InterBase, was the first relational database to support storage of BLOBs. See also **CLOB**.
BLOB control structure	A C language structure, declared in a UDF module as a typedef, through which a BLOB UDF accesses a BLOB. A BLOB UDF cannot refer to actual BLOB data, but is a pointer to a BLOB control structure instead.
BLOB filter	A specialized UDF that transforms BLOB data from one subtype to another. Firebird includes a set of internal BLOB filters that it uses in the process of storing and retrieving metadata. One internal filter converts text data transparently between SUB_TYPE 0 (none) and SUB_TYPE 1 (text, sometimes referred to as "Memo").

BLR	An abbreviation for *binary language representation*, an internal relational language with a binary notation that is a super-set of the "human-readable" languages that can be used with Firebird, namely SQL and GDML. Firebird's DSQL interface to the server translates queries into BLR. The BLR versions of compiled triggers and stored procedures, check constraints, defaults, and views are stored in BLOBs. Some client tools—for example, IB_SQL and the command-line tool **isql**—have facilities to inspect this BLR code. In **isql**, execute the command SET BLOB ALL and perform SELECT statements to get the appropriate BLR fields from the system tables.
buffer	A block of memory for caching copies of pages read from the database. The term "buffer" is synonymous with "cache page."
BURP	Internal name for the **gbak** code—an acronym for *backup [and] restore program.*
cache	When a page is read from disk it is copied into a block of memory known as the *database cache* or, simply, the *cache*. The cache consists of *buffers*, each the size of a database page, determined by the page_size parameter declared when the database is created.
	The word "buffer" in this context means a block of memory exactly the same size as one database page. The cache size is configurable, as a number of pages (or buffers). Hence, to calculate the size of the cache, multiply page_size by the number of cache pages (buffers).
cardinality (of a set)	The number of rows in a physical or specified set. The *cardinality of a row* refers to its position in the top-to-bottom order of the set.
case-insensitive index	An index using a collation sequence in which lowercase characters are treated as though they were the same as their uppercase equivalents. Firebird 1.0 does not support case-insensitive indexes. A few case-insensitive collation sequences appeared from Firebird 1.5 onward.
cascading integrity constraints	Firebird provides the optional capability to prescribe specific behaviors and restrictions in response to requests to update or delete rows in tables that are pointed to by the REFERENCES sub-clause of a FOREIGN KEY constraint. The CASCADE keyword causes changes performed on the "parent" row to flow on to rows in tables having the FOREIGN KEY dependencies. ON DELETE CASCADE, for example, will cause dependent rows to be deleted when the parent is deleted.
casting	A mechanism for converting output or variable values of one data type into another data type by means of an expression. Firebird SQL provides the CAST( ) function for use in both dynamic SQL (DSQL) and procedural SQL (PSQL) expressions.

character set

Two super-sets of printable character images and control sequences are in general use today in software environments: ASCII and UNICODE. ASCII characters, represented by 1 byte, have 256 possible variants, whereas UNICODE characters, represented by 2, 3, or 4 bytes, can accommodate tens of thousands of possibilities. Because databases need to avoid the prohibitive overhead of making available every possible printable and control character used for programming anywhere in the world, the super-sets are divided up into *code pages*, also known as *code tables*. Each code page defines a subset of required characters for a specific language or family of languages, mapping each character image to a number. The images and control sequences within each code page are referred to collectively as a *character set*. A character image might be mapped to different numbers in different characters sets.

Firebird supports a default character set for a database and definition of an explicit character set for any character, character varying, or BLOB SUB_TYPE 1 (text BLOB) column. If no character set is defined for a database, its character set defaults to NONE, causing all character data to be stored exactly as presented, with no attempt to convert characters (transliterate) to any particular character set.

Classic architecture

The original InterBase model, where a separate server process is started for each client connection. This architecture predates the *Superserver* model, which threads all client processes from a single server process. Variants of both architectural models are available for many operating system platforms.

CLOB

An acronym for *character large object*. This term has crept into use recently, as other RDBMSs have mimicked Firebird's support for storing large objects in databases. A CLOB is equivalent to Firebird's BLOB SUB_TYPE 1 (TEXT). See also **BLOB**.

coercing data types

In the Firebird API's XSQLDA structures, converting a data item of one SQL type to another, compatible SQL type is known as *data type coercion.*

collation order

Defines how a sort operation orders character columns in output sets, the pairing of lowercase and uppercase characters for the UPPER( ) function, and how characters in character columns are compared in searches. A collation order applies to a specific character set. If multiple collation orders are available for a particular character set, one collation order will be treated as the default. By convention, the default collation order has the same name as the character set.

column	In SQL databases, data is stored in structures that can be retrieved as tables or, more correctly, *sets*. A set consists of one or more rows, each identical in the horizontal arrangement of distinctly defined items of data. One distinct item of data considered vertically for the length of the set is known as a *column*. Application developers often refer to columns as *fields*.
commit	When applications post changes affecting rows in database tables, new versions of those rows are created in temporary storage blocks. Although the work is visible to the transaction in which it occurred, it cannot be seen by other users of the database. The client program must instruct the server to *commit* the work in order for it to be made permanent. If a transaction is not committed, it must be rolled back in order to undo the work.
CommitRetaining	A transaction setting that implements the COMMIT WITH RETAIN attribute of a transaction. Also known as a *soft Commit*. With this attribute, a transaction's context is kept active on the server until the client application finally calls Commit (a *hard Commit*) and allows the transaction inventory management processes to pass it through for garbage collection. The widespread use of CommitRetaining in applications is a common cause of performance degradation. See also **oldest interesting transaction (OIT)**.
concurrency	Refers broadly to multiple users accessing the same data simultaneously. This term is also widely used in documentation and support lists to refer to the particular set of attributes that apply to a transaction: isolation level, locking policy, and others. For example, someone may ask you, "What are your concurrency settings?" Even more specifically, the word "concurrency" is sometimes used as a synonym for the SNAPSHOT isolation level.
constraint	Firebird makes many provisions for defining formal rules that are to be applied to data. Such formal rules are known as *constraints*. For example, a PRIMARY KEY is a constraint that marks a column or group of columns as a databasewide pointer to all of the other columns in the row defined by it. A CHECK constraint sets one or more rules to limit the values that a column can accept.
contention	When two transactions attempt to update the same row of a table simultaneously, they are said to be in *contention*; they are contending (or competing).
correlated subquery	A query specification can define output columns that are derived from expressions. A subquery is a special kind of expression that returns a single value that is itself the output of a SELECT statement. In a *correlated subquery*, the WHERE clause contains one or more search keys that are relationally linked to columns in the main query.

crash	A slang term for abnormal termination of the server or a client application.
crash recovery	Processes or procedures that are implemented to restore the server and/or client applications into running condition following an abnormal termination of either the server or the application, or both.
CVS	An abbreviation for *Concurrent Versions System*, an open source program that allows developers to keep track of different development versions of source code. CVS is widely used for open source projects, including the Firebird Project.
cyclic links	In a database context, an inter-table dependency where a foreign key in one table (TableA) refers to a unique key in another table (TableB) that contains a foreign key that points back, either directly or through a reference to another table, to a unique key in TableA.
database	In its broadest sense, the term "database" applies to any persistent file structure that stores data in some format that permits it to be retrieved and manipulated by applications.
DB_KEY	See **RDB$DB_KEY**.
DDL	An abbreviation for *Data Definition Language*, the subset of SQL that is used for defining and managing the structure of data objects. Any SQL statement starting with the keywords CREATE, ALTER, RECREATE, CREATE OR REPLACE, or DROP is a DDL statement. In Firebird, some DDL statements start with the keyword DECLARE, although not all DECLARE statements are DDL.
deadlock	When two transactions are in contention to update the same version of a row, the transactions are said to be in *deadlock* when one transaction (T1), having a lock on row A, requests to update row B, which is locked by another transaction (T2), and T2 wants to update row A. Normally, genuine deadlocks are rare, because the server can detect most deadlocks and resolves them itself without raising a deadlock exception. The Firebird server unfortunately generalizes all lock conflict exceptions into a single error code that reports a "deadlock," regardless of the actual source of the conflict. Client application code must resolve a lock conflict by having one transaction roll back in order to allow the other to commit its work.
degree (of a set)	The number of columns in a tabular set. The *degree of a column* refers to its position in the left-to-right sequence of columns, starting at 1.
deployment	The process of distributing and installing software components for production use.

dialect	A term that distinguishes Firebird's native language set from an older language set that was implemented in Firebird's predecessor, InterBase 5. The older language set remains available to Firebird for near compatibility with legacy databases, as dialect 1. The native Firebird set is dialect 3.
DML	An abbreviation for *data manipulation language*, the major subset of SQL statements, which perform operations on sets of data.
domain	A Firebird SQL feature whereby you can assign an identifying name to a set of data characteristics and constraints (CREATE DOMAIN), and then use this name in lieu of a data type when defining columns in tables.
DPB	An abbreviation for *database parameter buffer*, a character array defined by Firebird's API. It is used by applications to convey the parameters that specify the characteristics of a client connection request, along with their specific item values, across the API.
DSQL	An abbreviation for *dynamic SQL*, which refers to statements that an application submits in runtime, with or without parameters, as contrasted with "static SQL" statements, which are coded directly into special code blocks of a host language program and are subsequently preprocessed for compilation within embedded SQL applications. Applications that use Firebird API calls, either "raw" or through a class library that encapsulates the Firebird API, are using DSQL.
DTP	An abbreviation for *desktop publishing*, the activity of using computer methods to prepare documents for publication in print or on the Web.
DUDLEY	Internal name for the source code for the deprecated metadata utility **gdef**. The name derives from the abbreviation DDL.
dyn, also DYN	A byte-encoded language for describing data definition statements. Firebird's DSQL subsystem parses DDL statements and passes them to a component that outputs DYN for interpretation by the Y valve, another subsystem that is responsible for updating the system tables.
error	A condition in which a requested SQL operation cannot be performed because something is wrong with the data supplied to a statement or procedure, or with the syntax of the statement itself. When Firebird encounters an error, it does not proceed with the request but returns an exception message to the client application. See also **exception**.
error code	An integer constant returned to the client or to a calling procedure when Firebird encounters an error condition. See also **error**, **exception**.

ESQL   An abbreviation for *Embedded SQL*, the subset of SQL provided for embedding static SQL in special blocks within a host application.

event   Implements Firebird's capability to pass a notification to a "listening" client application if requested to do so by a POST_EVENT call in a trigger or stored procedure.

exception   The Firebird server's response to an error condition that occurs during a database operation. Several hundred exception conditions are realized as error codes, in a variety of categories, which are passed back to the client in the Error Status Vector (Array). Exceptions are also available to stored procedures and triggers, where they can be handled by a custom routine. Firebird supports user-defined exceptions as well.

external function   Firebird has but a few built-in, SQL-standard functions. To extend the range of functions available for use in expressions, the Firebird engine can access custom functions, written in a host language such as C/C++ or Delphi, as if they were built in. Several free libraries of ready-made external functions (also known as *user-defined functions*, or *UDFs*) exist among the Firebird community, including two that are included with the Firebird binary release distributions.

executable stored procedure   A stored procedure that is called using EXECUTE PROCEDURE and does not return a multi-row result set. See also **selectable stored procedure**.

execute   In a client application, *execute* is commonly used as a verb that means "perform my request" when a data manipulation statement or stored procedure call has been prepared by the client application.

In DSQL, the phrase EXECUTE PROCEDURE is used with a stored procedure identifier and its input arguments, to invoke executable stored procedures.

FIBPlus   The trade name of the extended, commercial version of the older FreeIBComponents of Greg Deatz, data access components encapsulating the Firebird and InterBase APIs, for use with Borland's Delphi, C++Builder, and Kylix products.

foreign key   A formal constraint on a column or group of columns in one table that links that table to another table's corresponding primary or unique key. If the foreign key is non-unique and the table itself has a primary key, the table is capable of being the "many" side of a one-to-many relationship.

Firebird supports the declaration of a formal *foreign key constraint*, which will enforce referential integrity automatically. When such a constraint is declared, Firebird automatically creates a non-unique index on the column or columns to which the constraint applies and also records the dependencies between the tables that are linked by the constraint.

garbage collection

A general term for the cleanup process that goes on in the database during normal use to remove obsolete back-versions of rows that have been updated. In Superserver, garbage collection runs as a background thread to the main server process. Garbage collection can also be performed by sweeping and by backing up the database.

gbak

The command-line utility (found in the /bin directory of your Firebird installation) that backs up and restores databases. It is not a file-copy program; its backup operation decomposes the metadata and data and stores them separately, in a compressed binary format, in a filesystem file. By convention, backup files are often given the filename suffix .gbk or .fbk. Restoring decompresses this file and reconstructs the database as a new database file, before feeding the data into the database objects and rebuilding the indexes.

Apart from normal data security tasks expected of a backup utility, **gbak** performs important roles in the regular maintenance of "database hygiene" and in the recovery of corrupted databases.

GDML

An abbreviation for *Groton Data Manipulation Language*, a high-level relational language similar to SQL. GDML was the original data manipulation language of InterBase, functionally equivalent to DML in Firebird SQL but with some data definition capabilities. It is still supported through the interactive query utility **qli**.

gdef

An older InterBase utility for creating and manipulating metadata. Since **isql** and the dynamic SQL interface can handle DDL, **gdef** is virtually redundant now. However, because it can output DYN language statements for several host programming languages, including C and C++, Pascal, COBOL, ANSI COBOL, Fortran, BASIC, PLI, and ADA, it still has its uses in the development of embedded SQL applications.

generator

A number-generating engine for producing unique numbers in series. The statement CREATE GENERATOR *generator_name* seeds a distinct series of signed 64-bit integer numbers. SET GENERATOR TO *n* sets the first number in the series. The function GEN_ID *(generator_name, m)* causes a new number to be generated that is *m* higher than the last generated number.

gfix

A collection of command-line utilities, including database repair tools of limited capability. It includes tools to activate database shadows, to put the database into single-user (exclusive access) mode (shutdown), and to restore the database to multi-user access (restart). It can resolve limbo transactions left behind by multiple-database transactions, set the database cache, enable or disable forced (synchronous) writes to disk, perform sweeping and set the sweep interval, switch a Firebird database from read/write to read-only or vice versa, and set the database dialect.

gpre
In embedded database development, the preprocessor for static SQL language blocks in host language source code that translates them to BLR format in preparation for compiling. It can preprocess C, C++, COBOL, and Pascal and ADA host code, on selected platforms.

grant/revoke
SQL commands GRANT and REVOKE, which are used for setting up user privileges for accessing the objects in a database.

Groton
Short for *Groton Data Systems*, the name of the original company that designed and developed the RDBMS that was named InterBase. From InterBase, eventually, evolved Firebird. Two of the original Groton directors, Jim Starkey and Ann Harrison, are actively involved in aspects of Firebird development.

gsec
Firebird's command-line security utility for managing the server-level user/password database (security.fdb for v.1.5; isc4.gdb for v.1.0), which applies to all users and all databases. This utility cannot be used to create or modify roles, since roles exist within a database.

gstat
The command-line utility with which to gather statistics about a Firebird database. It analyzes the internal layout, such as the fill factor, header page, index pages, log page, and system relations. Table-by-table information about record versions (usually lengthy) can be optionally obtained, using the –r and –t *tablename* switches together.

hierarchical database
An old design concept for implementing table-to-table relationships in databases by building up tree structures of inherited indexes.

host language
A general term referring to the language in which application code is written.

identity attribute
Some RDBMSs (MSSQL, for example) support a table attribute that automatically implements a surrogate primary key integer column for a table and causes a new value to be generated automatically for each new row inserted. Firebird does not support this attribute directly. A similar mechanism can be achieved by explicitly defining an integer field of adequate size, creating a generator to populate it, and defining a Before Insert trigger that calls the GEN_ID( ) function to get the next value of the generator.

IBO
An abbreviation for *IB Objects*, data access components and data-aware controls encapsulating the Firebird and InterBase APIs, for use with Borland Delphi, C++Builder, and Kylix products.

IBX	An abbreviation for *InterBaseXpress*, data access components encapsulating the InterBase API, distributed by Borland for use with their Delphi and C++Builder products.
index	A specialized data structure, maintained by the Firebird engine, that provides a compact system of data pointers to the rows of a table.
INET error	In the firebird.log, marks an error received by the Firebird network layer from a TCP/IP client/server connection.
installation	The procedure and process of copying software to a computer and configuring it for use.
InterBase	A RDBMS that is the ancestor of Firebird. Developed originally by a company named Groton Data Systems, it eventually passed into the ownership of the Borland Software Corporation. InterBase version 6 was released into open source in 2000 under the InterBase Public License. Firebird was developed by independent developers from this open source codebase and soon became a forked development.
InterClient	An obsolete JDBC Type 2 Java client for the original InterBase 6 open source server. In Firebird, it is superseded by JayBird, a family of open source JDBC/JCA-compliant Java drivers (Type 4 and Type 2).
InterServer	An obsolete, Java-driven server-based communication layer originally distributed with the InterBase 6 open source code release. Both InterServer and its companion InterClient have been superseded in Firebird by JayBird, a more modern and open Java interface.
ISC, isc, etc.	Error messages, some environment variables, and many identifiers in the Firebird API have the prefix "ISC" or "isc". As a matter of purely historical interest, these initials are derived from the initial letters of "InterBase Software Corporation," the name of a subsidiary company of Borland that existed during some periods of Borland's ownership of Firebird's ancestor, InterBase.
isolation level	This attribute of a transaction prescribes the way one transaction will interact with other transactions accessing the same database, in terms of visibility and locking behavior. Firebird supports three levels of isolation: Read Committed, Repeatable Read (also known as *Snapshot* or *Concurrency*), and Snapshot Table Stability (also known as *Consistency*). Although Read Committed is the default for most relational engines, Firebird's default level is Repeatable Read, thanks to optimistic, row-level locking. See also **transaction isolation**.

isql	The name of Firebird's console-mode interactive query utility, which can connect to one database at a time. It has a powerful set of commands, including its own subset of Firebird SQL, in addition to the regular dynamic SQL command set. It has a large set of embedded macros for obtaining metadata information. **isql** can output batches of commands, including embedded comments, to a file, and it can "run" such a file as a script—the recommended way to create and alter database objects.
JDBC	An abbreviation for *Java Database Connectivity*, a set of standards for constructing drivers for connecting Java applications to SQL databases.
join	JOIN is the SQL keyword for specifying to the engine that the output of the SELECT statement involves merging columns from multiple tables, linked by matching one or more pairs of keys.
jrd	The internal name of the Firebird database engine kernel. It is an abbreviation for *Jim's Relational Database*, an artifact of the original engine, invented by Jim Starkey, that became InterBase and, later, Firebird.
key	A constraint on a table that is applied to a column or group of columns in the table's row structure. A *primary key* or a *unique key* points to the unique row in which it exists, while a *foreign key* points to a unique row in another table by linking to its primary key or another unique key.
kill (shadows)	When a database shadow is created using the MANUAL keyword, and the shadow becomes unavailable, further attachments to the database are blocked. In order to re-enable attachments to the database, it is necessary to issue a –kill *database* command from the **gfix** utility to delete references to the shadow.
leaf bucket	In a binary index tree, the data item in the last index on a node of the tree. The leaf buckets figure reported in **gstat** index statistics provides an approximate count of the number of rows in the table.
limbo (transaction)	A limbo transaction can occur where a transaction spans more than one database. Multi-database transactions are protected by two-phase commit, which guarantees that, unless the portions of the transaction residing in each database get committed, all portions will be rolled back. If one or more of the databases involved in the transaction becomes unavailable before the completion of the two-phase commit, the transaction remains unresolved and is said to be in *limbo*.

locking conflict	Under Firebird's optimistic locking scheme, a row becomes locked against update from other transactions as soon as its transaction posts an update request for it. Where the isolation level of the transaction is SNAPSHOT TABLE STABILITY (also known as Consistency), the lock occurs as soon as the transaction reads the row. A locking conflict occurs when another transaction attempts to post its own update to that row. Locking conflicts have various causes, characteristics, and resolutions according to the specific settings of the transactions involved.
lock resolution	As a general term, refers to the measures taken in application code to resolve the conditions that occur when other trans-actions attempt to update a row that is locked by a transaction because of an update request. As a specific term, *lock resolution* refers to the WAIT/NO WAIT parameter setting of a transaction that specifies how a transaction should react if a locking conflict arises.
metadata	A generic quantity noun referring to the structure of all the objects that comprise a database. Because Firebird stores the definitions of its objects right inside the database, using its own native tables, data types, and triggers, the term "metadata" also refers to the data stored in these system tables.
multi-generational architecture (MGA)	The term used for the engine mechanism of Firebird that enables optimistic row locking and a high level of transaction isolation, which protects a transaction's dynamic view of the database and its changes to rows in that view, without blocking other readers. It is achieved by the engine's capability to store multiple versions of rows concurrently and to "age" these versions with respect to the original view. See also **versioning architecture**.
natural (scan)	Indicates that the associated table will be scanned in "natural order" (i.e., in no particular order and without reference to an index). This is seen sometimes in the query plans created by the optimizer.
non-standard SQL	A term often heard with reference to RDBMs that have a low degree of conformance with the ISO language and syntax standards for SQL. See also **standard SQL**.
non-unique key	A column or group of columns that can act as a pointer to a grouping of rows in a set. A foreign key constraint to implement a one-to-many relationship is typically formed by matching a non-unique column or group in a "child" or "detail" set to a unique key in a "parent" or "master" set.
normalization	A technique commonly used during the analysis of data preceding database design to abstract out repeating groups of data in multiple tables and eliminate the potential to duplicate the same "facts" in related tables.

null

Sometimes wrongly referred to as a "null value," the state of a data item that has no known value. Logically it is interpreted as *unknown* and is thus unable to be evaluated in expressions.

Null is never equivalent to zero, blank, or an empty (zero-length) string, and it does not represent either infinity or NaN. It represents the state of a data item that either has never been assigned a value or has been set NULL by an operation.

ODBC

An abbreviation for *Open Database Connectivity*. It is a call-level interface standard that allows applications to access data in any database that has a driver supporting this standard. Several ODBC drivers are available that support Firebird, including an open source one developed for Firebird that is internally consistent with the JDBC standard.

ODS

An abbreviation for *on-disk structure*. It is a number that refers to the version of the internal structure and layout of a Firebird or InterBase database. For IB4.0, it was 8; for IB4.2, it was 8.2; and for IB5.*x*, it was 9. Firebird 1 has ODS 10, and 1.5 has 10.1.

A database can be raised to a higher ODS by backing it up with the **gbak** –r[estore] –t[ransportable] option using the old version's **gbak** program, and restoring from that **gbak** file using the new version's **gbak**.

OLAP

An abbreviation for *Online Analytical Processing*, a technology that is applied to databases that have grown to such a volume that it is impracticable for them to be queried directly as the basis of business decisions. Typically, OLAP systems are designed to analyze and graph trends, identify and capture historical milestones or anomalies, manufacture projections and hypothetical scenarios, crunch large volumes of data for reports, and so on, in reasonable time.

OS

An abbreviation for *operating system*.

oldest active transaction (OAT)

A statistic maintained by the Firebird engine, global to a database, the oldest transaction still in the database that has not been either committed or rolled back.

oldest interesting transaction (OIT)

A statistic maintained by the Firebird engine, global to a database, the ID of the oldest transaction that has not been committed. It is sometimes the same transaction as the OAT but it may not be, since any transaction that is still active, has been rolled back, committed using COMMIT WITH RETAIN ("CommitRetaining"), or left in limbo by a failed two-phase commit remains "interesting." When the OIT gets "stuck" at a much lower transaction ID than the newest transactions, garbage collection (cleanup of old record versions) cannot proceed and database operations slow down and, eventually, hang completely. The OIT can be retrieved as "oldest transaction" using the –header switch of **gstat** command-line utility.

OLE DB	An abbreviation for *Object Linking and Embedding for Databases.* OLE is a Microsoft standard developed and promoted for incorporating binary objects of many diverse types (images, documents, etc.) into Windows applications, along with application-level linking to the software engines that create and modify them. OLE DB was added in an attempt to provide developers with the means to supply a more vendor-specific support for database connectivity—especially relational databases—than can be achieved with "open" standards such as ODBC. More recently, Microsoft layered the ADO technology on top of OLE DB.
OLTP	An abbreviation for *Online Transaction Processing*, recognized as one of the essential requirements for a database engine. Broadly speaking, OLTP refers to support for clients performing operations that read, alter, or create data in real time.
optimization	In general, refers to techniques for making the database and application software perform as responsively as possible. As a specific term, it is often applied to the techniques used by the Firebird engine to analyze SELECT statements and construct efficient plans for retrieving data. The routines in the Firebird engine that calculate these plans are known collectively as the Firebird *optimizer*.
page	A Firebird database is made up of fixed-sized blocks of disk space called *pages*. The Firebird engine allocates pages as it needs to. Once it stores data, a page could be any one of ten different types of pages, all of equal size—the size defined in the PAGE_SIZE attribute during database creation. The type of page the engine stores to disk depends on the type of data object being stored on the page: data, index, BLOB, etc.
page_size	The size of each fixed block is determined by the page_size specified for the database when the database is created or restored. Chunks of cache memory are also allocated in page_size units.
parameter	A widespread term in many Firebird contexts, it can refer to the values that are passed as arguments to and returned from stored procedures (input parameters, output parameters). The term can also refer to the data items that are passed to the function blocks of the Firebird API (database parameter block, transaction parameter block, service parameter block) or to the attributes, as seen from an application, of a connection instance (connection parameters) or a transaction (transaction parameters).

In client applications, placeholder tokens that are accepted for passing into WHERE clauses of SQL statements for substitution by constant values at runtime are often implemented as "parameters," hence the term "parameterized queries." |

PHP

An abbreviation for *PHP: Hypertext Preprocessor*, an open source embedded HTML scripting language used to create web applications, especially those with database back-ends. It has good support for a number of network protocols and web programming environments. Its strength lies in its compatibility with many types of databases. Also, PHP can talk across networks using IMAP, SNMP, NNTP, POP3, or HTTP. PHP's originator, in 1994, was Rasmus Lerdorf. Since 1997, it has been in the hands of a large open source community.

plan

See **query plan**.

platform

A term loosely used to refer to the combination of hardware and operating system software, or operating system software alone, for example, "the Windows 2000 platform," "the Linux platform," "UNIX platforms." *Cross-platform* usually means "applicable to multiple platforms" or "portable to other platforms."

prepare

An API function that is called before a query request is submitted for the first time, requesting validation of the statement, construction of a query plan, and several items of information about the data expected by the server.

primary key

A table-level constraint that marks one column or a group of columns as the key that must identify each row as unique within the table. Although a table may have more than one unique key, only one of those keys may be the primary key. When you apply the PRIMARY KEY constraint to columns in a Firebird table, uniqueness is enforced by the automatic creation of a unique index that is, by default, ascending and named according to a convention.

PSQL

An abbreviation for *Procedural SQL*, the subset of SQL extensions implemented for writing stored procedures and triggers. There are minor differences between the subsets of PSQL allowed for stored procedures and for triggers.

qli

The *Query Language Interpreter*, an interactive query client tool for Firebird. It can process DDL and DML statements in both SQL and GDML, the pre-SQL query language of Firebird's ancestor, InterBase 3. Although largely succeeded by **isql** and a number of third-party GUI tools, **qli** has some value for its capability to realize some engine features not so far implemented in Firebird SQL. Unlike its successor, **isql**, **qli** can connect to more than one database at the same time and can simulate multi-database joins.

query

A general term for any SQL request made to the server by a client application.

query plan	A strategy for the use of indexes and access methods for sorting and searching in queries. The Firebird optimizer always computes a plan for every SELECT query, including subqueries. It is possible to specify a custom plan using the PLAN clause syntax.
RDB$—	A prefix seen in the identifiers of many system-created objects in Firebird. It's a relic from *Relational DataBase*, the name of an early relational database developed by DEC. The design of RDB was the precursor to Firebird's ancestor, InterBase.
RDB$DB_KEY	The hidden, volatile, unique key that is calculated internally for every row in a table, from the physical address of the page on which the row starts and its offset from the beginning of the page. It is directly related to the cardinality of tables and sets and can change without trace or warning. It will always change when the database is restored from a backup. RDB$DB_KEY should never be treated as persistent. With care, it can be used dependably within an atomic operation to speed up certain operations in DSQL and PSQL dramatically.
RDBMS	An abbreviation for *relational database management system*. Generically, it is a concept for storing data according to an abstract model that uses matching keys to link a formal group of data to another formal group of data, thereby representing a relationship between the two groups.
Read Committed	The least restrictive isolation level for any Firebird transaction, Read Committed permits the transaction to update its view of the database to reflect work committed by other transactions since the transaction began. The isolation levels SNAPSHOT and SNAPSHOT TABLE STABILITY do not permit the original view to change.
redundancy	A condition in a database where the same "fact" is stored in two unrelated places. Ideally, redundancy should be avoided by attention to normalization during analysis. However, there are circumstances where a certain amount of redundancy is justified. For example, accounting transactions often contain data items that arguably could be derived by joining, looking up, or calculating from other structures. However, a legal requirement to store a permanent record that will not be altered if a database relationship's subsequently change would overrule the case for eliminating redundancy.
redundant indexes	Redundant indexes often arise when existing databases are imported to Firebird from another RDBMS. When a PRIMARY KEY, UNIQUE, or FOREIGN KEY constraint is applied to a column or columns, Firebird automatically creates an index to enforce the constraint. In so doing, Firebird ignores any existing indexes that duplicate its automatic index. Having duplicate indexes on keys or any other columns can defeat the query optimizer, causing it to create plans that are inherently slow.

referential integrity	Generally, refers to the way an RDBMS implements mechanisms that formally support and protect the dependencies between tables. *Referential integrity support* refers to the language and syntax elements available to provide these capabilities. Firebird provides formal mechanisms for supporting referential integrity, including cascading constraints for foreign key relationships. It is sometimes referred to as *declarative referential integrity*.
relation	In relational database theory, a self-contained body of data formally arranged in columns and rows. The term is almost interchangeable with "table," except that a relation cannot have duplicate rows, whereas a table can. In Firebird, the terminology persists in the names of some system tables (e.g., RDB$RELATIONS, which contains an entry for each table in the database).
relationship	An abstract term referring to the way relations (or tables) are linked to one another through matching keys. For example, an Order Detail table is said to be in a *dependency relationship* or a *foreign key relationship* with an Order Header table.
replication	A systematic process whereby data is copied from one database to another on a regular basis, according to predictable rules, in order to bring two or more databases into a synchronized state.
result table	The set of rows output from a SQL SELECT query. More correctly, it is termed a *result set*, synonymous with *output set*.
roles	A standard SQL mechanism for defining a set of permissions to use objects in a database. Once a role is created, permissions are assigned to it, using GRANT statements, as if it were a user. The role is then GRANTed to individual users as if it were itself a privilege, thus simplifying the maintenance of user permissions in a database.
rollback	In general, the act or process of undoing all of the work that has been posted during the course of a transaction. As long as a transaction has work pending that is posted but not committed, it remains unresolved and its effects are invisible to other transactions. If the client application calls for a ROLLBACK, all of the posted work is cancelled and the changes are lost. Once a transaction is committed, its work cannot be rolled back.
schema	The formal description of a database, usually realized as a script or set of scripts, containing the SQL statements defining each and every object in the database. The term "schema" is often interchangeable with the term "metadata."

schema cache
A mechanism whereby some descriptive elements of a database are stored on a client's local disk or in memory for quick reference at runtime, to avoid the need to constantly requery the database to obtain schema (metadata) attributes.

scrollable cursor
A *cursor* is a pointer to a row in a database table or output set. A cursor's position in the database is determined from the cardinality of the row to which it is currently pointing (i.e., its offset from the first row in the set). Repositioning the cursor requires returning the pointer to the first row in order to find the new position. A *scrollable cursor* is capable of locating itself at a specified new position (upward or downward) relative to its current position.

selectivity of an index
As a general term, refers to the spread of possible values for the index column throughout the table. The fewer the possible values, the lower the selectivity. Low selectivity can also occur where an index with a higher number of possible values is represented in actual data by a very high rate of duplication of a few values. Low selectivity is bad; high selectivity is good. A unique index has the highest possible selectivity.

selectable stored procedure
A stored procedure that is written using special PSQL syntax to output a multi-row result set to the caller. It is called using a SELECT statement. See also **executable stored procedure**.

Services API
An API to the functions of several of the Firebird command-line server utilities, providing a function-driven interface to backup, statistics, housekeeping, and other utilities. The Services API may be inapplicable to some Classic server versions.

sets
In relational database terms, collections of data are managed in *sets* consisting of one or more rows made up of one or more columns of data, with each column containing one data item of a specific size and type. For example, a SELECT query specification or a view defines a set for output to a client application or PSQL module, while an UPDATE query specification defines a set upon which the specified operation is to be performed.

shadowing/shadows
An optional process available on a Firebird server, whereby an exact copy of a database is maintained, warts and all, in real time, on a separate hard disk on the same server machine where the database resides. The copy is known as a *database shadow*. The purpose is to provide a way for a database to quickly resume operation after physical damage to the hard drive where the original database resides. A shadow is not a useful substitute for either replication or backup.

SMP	An abbreviation for *symmetric multiprocessing*, a computer architecture that makes multiple CPUs available to a single operating system, to execute individual processes simultaneously. In theory, any idle processor can be assigned any task and, the more CPUs on the system, the better performance and load capacity.
Snapshot	SNAPSHOT is one of the three transaction isolation levels supported by Firebird. It provides a stable view of the database that remains current to the user of the transaction throughout the life of that transaction. It is also known as *concurrency level isolation*. See also **Read Committed**, **Snapshot Table Stability**.
Snapshot Table Stability	SNAPSHOT TABLE STABILITY is the most protective of the three transaction isolation levels supported by Firebird. It enforces a consistent view of the database for the user of the transaction, by preventing any other transaction from updating any row it has selected, even if the transaction has not yet posted any change. It is also known as *consistency-level isolation*. See also **Read Committed**, **Snapshot**.
SQL	A query language designed to extract meaningful sets of data from a relational database. Its correct pronunciation is "ess-cue-ell," not "sequel," as some people believe. ("Sequel" was the name of another query language.) It is also not an abbreviation for Structured Query Language.
standard SQL, SQL standard	Refers to the syntax and implementation of SQL language elements as published by the International Organization for Standardization (ISO). This very complex standard prescribes definitions across an exhaustive range of syntax and functionality, at a number of levels.
stored procedure	A compiled module of code stored in the database for invocation by applications and by other server-based code modules (triggers, other procedures). It is defined to the database in a source language—procedural SQL, or PSQL—consisting of regular SQL statements as well as special SQL language extensions which supply structure, looping, conditional logic, local variables, input and output arguments, exception handling, and more.
subquery	A query specification can define output columns that are derived from expressions. A subquery is a special kind of expression that returns a result that is itself the output of a SELECT statement. Also known as a *sub-select* or *embedded query*.
sub-select, subselect	A *sub-selected column* is one that is specified or output from a subquery. Such columns are not updatable. See also **subquery**.

Superserver architecture   *Superserver* is the name given to the process-threading multi-user model, to distinguish it from the original InterBase model that instantiates one server process for each client connection. The original model is now referred to as *Classic server*.

surrogate key   In defining a unique key (e.g., a primary key), it may occur that no column or combination of columns can be guaranteed to provide a unique identifier for each and every row. In that case, a column can be added and populated by values that are certain to be unique. Such a key is known as a *surrogate key*.

In Firebird, surrogate keys are most commonly implemented using generators. Surrogate keys are also frequently used as a matter of good design principle, to conform with rules of atomicity. See also **atomicity**.

sweeping   The process that collects and frees obsolete versions of each record in a database when a threshold number is reached. This number, which defaults to 20,000 and is known as the *sweep interval*, is calculated on the difference between the OIT and the newest transaction. Automatic sweeping can be disabled by setting a sweep interval of zero. A manual sweep can be invoked ad hoc, using the **gfix** utility. Sweeping is not a feature of RDBMSs that do not store obsolete record versions.

SYSDBA   An abbreviation for *system database administrator*, a person with responsibility for administering databases.

system tables   Because relational database engines are self-contained, all of the metadata, or schema (data that describes the structure and attributes of database objects), is maintained within the database, in a suite of tables that is created by the CREATE DATABASE command. These tables, which store "data about data," are known as *system tables*. Firebird system tables all have identifiers that begin with the prefix RDB$ and actually include data about themselves, as well as every other object in the database.

table   A term borrowed from desktop database technology, depicting a logical structure that stores sets of data in a tabulated format, as records (rows) of fields, each record being, by definition, identical from left to right in the number and relative placement of fields and their data types and sizes. In reality, Firebird does not store data in a physically tabulated form at all, but in contiguous blocks of disk space known as *pages*.

transaction   A logical unit of work, which can involve one or many statements or executions of statements. A transaction begins when the client application starts it and ends when it either commits the transaction or rolls it back. A transaction is an atomic action—a commit must be able to commit every piece of pending work, otherwise all of its work is abandoned. A rollback, similarly, will cancel every piece of pending work that was posted since the start of the transaction.

transaction isolation A mechanism by which each transaction is provided with an environment that makes it appear (to itself) that it is running alone in the database. When multiple transactions are running concurrently, the effects of all of the other transactions are invisible to each transaction, from when it starts until it is committed. Firebird supports not just one but three levels of isolation, including one level that can see the effects of other transactions as they are committed. See **Read Committed**, **Snapshot, Snapshot Table Stability**.

transitively dependent A constraint or condition where one table (C) is dependent on another table (A), because table C is dependent on another table (B), which is dependent on A. Such a dependency would arise, for example, if table B had a foreign key referencing table A's primary key, and table C had a foreign key referencing table B's primary key. The term is also used in data modeling to refer to a condition where, during normalization, an attribute in one entity has a partial (but incomplete) dependency on a unique attribute set in another entity.

trigger A module of compiled code belonging to a table that performs an action when a DML event happens to a row in that table. Any number of event actions can be coded to occur in a prescribed sequence, before and/or after an insert, update, or delete operation on a table's row, with virtually the full range of procedural SQL (PSQL) being available.

tuple In relational database terminology, the "strictly correct" name for a row in a table, or a group of columns that is a subset of a row. Purists would say that *row* is the SQL name for a *tuple*.

UDF An abbreviation for *user-defined function*, more correctly named *external function*. See also **external function**.

unbalanced index Firebird indexes are maintained as binary tree structures. These structures are said to be unbalanced when new nodes are added continually in a manner that causes major branching on one "side" of the binary tree. Typically, this will occur when a process inserts hundreds of thousands of new rows inside a single transaction. For this reason, it is recommended that indexes be deactivated during massive inserts. Subsequent re-activation will rebuild fully balanced indexes.

uninstallation An ugly, back-formed word, confusing to non-English speakers, since it is not found in any self-respecting dictionary—yet! Its approximate meaning is "a process that is the reverse of installation" (i.e., removing a previously installed software product from a computer system).

union	A clause in a SELECT query specification that enables the output rows of two or more SELECT statements to be combined into one final output set, as long as each of the UNIONed sets matches all of the others by the degree, data type, and size of its output columns. The sets may be selected from different tables.
updatable view	A view is said to be updatable if it is constructed from a regular query on a single table and all of its columns exist in the underlying table. Some non-updatable views can be made updatable by the creation of triggers. See also **view**.
validation	A mechanism whereby new data applied to a column in a table is checked by some means to determine whether it fits a required format, value, or range of values. Two ways to implement validation in the database are CHECK constraints and triggers. A CHECK constraint will throw an exception if the input data fails to test true against the given expression or constant. With triggers, the new.value can be tested more thoroughly and, if it fails, can be passed to a custom exception.
versioning architecture	Also known as *multi-generational architecture* (MGA), the feature, until recently unique to Firebird and InterBase, of storing a new version of a changed row, or an inserted row on disk for the duration of a transaction, where it remains visible to that transaction even though it is not yet committed to the database. When the commit occurs, the new version becomes permanent in the database and the old version is flagged as obsolete. When considering contenders for a concurrent update in a conflict situation, the engine also uses attributes of the pending record versions concerned to determine precedence, if any.
view	A standard SQL object that is a stored query specification that can behave in many ways like a physical table. A view does not provide physical storage for user data—it acts as a predefined container for a set of output data that exist in one or more tables.
WNET error	In the firebird.log, marks an error received by the Firebird network layer from a Windows Named Pipes (Windows networking) client/server connection.
XSQLDA	An abbreviation for *eXtended SQL Descriptor Area*. It is a host-language data structure in the API that is used to transport data between a client application and the server's dynamic SQL parser module. XSQLDAs come in two types: input descriptors and output descriptors.
XSQLVAR	A structure for defining **sqlvar**, an important field in the XSQLDA structure that is used for passing and returning input and output parameters.

Y valve   The name given to the Firebird subsystem that determines which of Firebird's several "internal engines" should be used when attaching to a database. For example, one decision is whether to attach locally or as a remote client, and another is to determine whether the attachment is being attempted to a database with a compatible ODS.

Index

See the "Glossary" for a comprehensive list of terms used in this book.

Symbols

Numbers

A

E

forums.apress.com

Printed and bound by PG in the USA